AMERICA VOTES 16

A HANDBOOK OF CONTEMPORARY
AMERICAN ELECTION STATISTICS

COMPILED AND EDITED BY

RICHARD M. SCAMMON

and

ALICE V. McGILLIVRAY

1984

ELECTIONS   RESEARCH   CENTER

CONGRESSIONAL QUARTERLY   WASHINGTON   1985

Copies available from: Congressional Quarterly Inc., 1414 22nd St. N.W., Washington, D.C. 20037

Printed in the United States of America

Library of Congress Catalog Card Number: 56-10132
International Standard Book Number: 0-87187-218-8

CONTENTS

Chicago, Detroit, Los Angeles County, New York City and Philadelphia data will be found in the appropriate state sections.

INTRODUCTION

The sixteenth volume of AMERICA VOTES follows the general pattern used in the previous handbooks. The state chapter system is continued, with a profile sheet, map of the state by congressional districts, tables of the voting data by counties, time sequence vote for Congress where district boundaries have remained the same, note section with general election information and primary elections data. Also included within the appropriate state chapters are voting data for Chicago, Detroit, New York City, Philadelphia, and Los Angeles county, with voting division maps. In the chapters for the New England states, tables are included which list the voting by larger cities and towns except for Rhode Island which lists all cities and towns.

The implementation of the 1980 Census for redistricting purposes led to changes in the congressional district lines in most states for 1982 and ten states redistricted between 1982 and 1984. The congressional district maps for each state reflect these changes. Since voting data in each CD is carried back in time only to the point at which the district was set up in its present boundaries, most CD's will have only the results of the 1982 and 1984 balloting. For earlier election results (and earlier boundaries) previous volumes of AMERICA VOTES should be consulted.

Attention of AMERICA VOTES 16 users is directed particularly to the note sections at the close of each chapter. Many special situations develop in the politics and elections of the various states, and these are set out in detail in the individual state note sections. Distribution of the non-major party vote, recount tallies, withdrawal and substitution data, party nomenclature, boundary changes, discrepancies or corrections in the canvassed returns --these and similar special state situations are listed in the note sections.

This new volume of AMERICA VOTES carries tables of the state-by-state Presidential vote since 1920, extending the coverage of earlier volumes. In addition, data by state and summary tables are included for the Presidential preference primaries from 1972 through 1984.

AMERICA VOTES 16 seeks to draw from official state sources the raw material of American elections behavior. From that raw material is built a national reference volume on American politics. To make this reference volume of maximum efficiency in meeting the needs of its users, suggestions as to new materials, together with any corrections of data in this volume are solicited.

For AMERICA VOTES 16, as for its predecessors, it would be impossible to list all those to whom acknowledgement is due for aid in bringing this volume to the public. To all those who have helped in the preperation of this volume for publication must go the gratitude of the editors and of all those who will use this newest volume in the series AMERICA VOTES.

Richard M. Scammon
Alice V. McGillivray

Washington, D.C.
September, 1985

UNITED STATES

POST ELECTION CHANGES

Following the 1984 general election, and prior to September 1, 1985, there were two changes in the membership of the 99th Congress. There were no changes among the Governors and Senators and those in the House of Representatives are summarized below.

REPRESENTATIVES

8th Louisiana. Representative Gillis W. Long (D) died in January 1985; Cathy Long (D) was elected in March 1985 to succeed him.

1st Texas. Representative Sam B. Hall (D) resigned in May 1985 to accept a Judgeship; James L. Chapman (D) was elected in August 1985 to succeed him.

UNITED STATES

SPECIAL ELECTIONS TO THE 98TH CONGRESS

Between the General Elections of 1982 and 1984 ten special elections were held to fill vacancies in the 98th Congress. Details of these special elections are listed below.

SENATORS

WASHINGTON

Senator Henry M. Jackson (D) died in September 1983; Daniel J. Evans (R) was appointed to succeed him pending a special election to fill the remaining years of this term. A special primary election was held in October 1983 followed by a special election in November 1983. Details of these elections will be found in the Washington state chapter of this volume.

REPRESENTATIVES

CALIFORNIA 5TH CD

Representative Phillip Burton (D) died in April 1983; Sala Burton (D) was elected in June 1983 to succeed him.

June 21, 1983 Special All-Party Election

44,790 Sala Burton (D); 18,305 Duncan L. Howard (R); 6,582 Richard Doyle (D); 2,933 Tom Spinosa (R); 1,596 Gary R. Arnold (R); 1,117 Tibor Uskert (D); 1,043 Bill Dunlap (R); 880 Evelyn K. Lantz (D); 560 Michael O. Plunkett (D); 448 A. Paul Kangas (Peace and Freedom); 408 Eric Garris (Libertarian); 6 scattered. Mrs. Burton polled a clear majority of the total vote (56.9%) and was elected without further contest.

COLORADO 6TH CD

Representative Jack Swigert (R) died in December 1982; Daniel L. Schaefer (R) was elected in March 1983 to succeed him. Candidates were nominated by local party conventions.

March 29, 1983 Special Election

49,816 Daniel L. Schaefer (R); 27,779 Steve Hogan (D); 1,112 John Heckman (Concerns of People).

GEORGIA 7TH CD

Representative Larry McDonald (D) was killed in September 1983; George Darden (D) was elected in November 1983 to succeed him.

October 18, 1983 Special Non-Partisan Election

25,468 Kathryn McDonald; 22,951 George Darden; 21,181 Dave Sellers; 4,578 George Pullen; 4,283 Dan H. Fincher; 2,919 Lon L. Day; 791 Charles B. Sherrill; 359 Peggy Ann Childers; 131 M. G. Huntington; 116 Roy Rogers; 81 W. R. Holsomback; 81 Daniel C. Maltz; 62 Robert B. Brickell; 62 Raymond Fulton; 61 Sara Jean Johnston; 43 Fred C. Jones; 30 Marshall Uncapher; 27 James M. Livingston; 24 A. Craig Smith; 15 Benjamin S. Biggers.

November 8, 1983 Run-Off

56,267 George Darden; 38,949 Kathryn McDonald.

ILLINOIS 1ST CD

Representative Harold Washington (D) resigned in April 1983 following his election to be Mayor of Chicago; Charles A. Hayes (D) was elected in August 1983 to succeed him.

UNITED STATES

July 26, 1983 Republican Primary

385 Diane Preacely; 376 Betty H. Meyer; 189 Ralph Blakey; 118 William Murray; 7 scattered.

July 26, 1983 Democratic Primary

41,240 Charles A. Hayes; 29,571 Lu Palmer; 11,372 Al Raby; 4,388 Marian Humes; 1,790 Larry S. Bullock; 1,264 Charles Chew; 947 Ralph H. Metcalfe, Jr.; 351 Hiram Crawford; 148 Shelia Jones; 139 Allan G. Thomas; 118 James H. Sterdivant; 71 Donald W. Jones; 60 Lemuel E. Bentley; 19 Randell J. Hawthorne; 3 scattered.

August 23, 1983 Special Election

39,623 Charles A. Hayes (D); 2,272 Diane Preacely (R); 394 Ed Warren (Independent); 3 scattered.

KENTUCKY 7TH CD

Representative Carl D. Perkins (D) died in August 1984; Carl C. Perkins (D) was elected in November 1984 to fill out the remaining months of the term for the 98th Congress. Candidates were nominated by local party committees.

November 6, 1984 Special Election

75,047 Carl C. Perkins (D); 15,907 Aubrey Russell (R).

NEW JERSEY 13TH CD

Representative Edwin B. Forsythe (R) died in March 1984; H. James Saxton (R) was elected in November 1984 to fill out the remaining months of the term for the 98th Congress.

June 5,1984 Republican Primary

13,877 H. James Saxton; 12,178 M. Dean Haines; 4,107 John A. Rocco.

June 5, 1984 Democratic Primary

15,154 James B. Smith; 8,396 Herbert J. Buehler.

November 6, 1984 Special Election

143,080 H. James Saxton (R); 87,885 James B. Smith (D); 1,622 Don Smith (Constitutional Freedom).

NEW YORK 7TH CD

Representative Benjamin Rosenthal (D) died in January 1983; Gary L. Ackerman (D) was elected in March 1983 to succeed him. Candidates were nominated by local party committees.

March 1, 1983 Special Election

18,388 Gary L. Ackerman (D); 8,331 Albert Lemishow (R); 5,997 Douglas E. Schoen (Queens Independent); 4,318 Sheldon S. Leffler (Neighborhood Service). Mr. Ackerman received 1,401 of his total vote as the Liberal candidate; Mr. Lemishow received 1,738 of his total vote as the Right to Life candidate and 1,303 as the Conservative candidate.

TEXAS 6TH CD

Representative Phil Gramm (D) resigned in January 1983 on his change of party affiliation to Republican; he was re-elected as a Republican in February 1983.

UNITED STATES

February 12, 1983 Special All-Party Election

46,371 Phil Gramm (R); 33,201 Dan Kubiak (D); 3,070 John H. Faulk (D); 318 Bill Powers (D); 268 Rex Carey (D); 223 H. Martin Gibson (Libertarian); 153 George M. Chamberlain (D); 84 Louis C. Davis (D); 80 Joe R. English (D); 78 Carl Nigliazzo (D); 59 Joe Agris (D). Mr. Gramm polled a clear majority of the total vote (55.3%) and was elected without further contest.

WISCONSIN 4TH CD

Representative Clement J. Zablocki (D) died in December 1983; Gerald D. Kleczka (D) was elected in April 1984 to succeed him.

February 21, 1984 Republican Primary

7,742 Robert V. Nolan; 717 John F. Baumgartner; 598 Ray Derringer; 316 Joseph A. Ortiz.

February 21, 1984 Democratic Primary

33,384 Gerald D. Kleczka; 27,614 E. Michael McCann; 27,279 Lynn S. Adelman; 15,827 Gary J. Barczak; 1,149 James P. Buckley; 859 Roman R. Blenski.

April 3, 1984 Special Election

76,384 Gerald D. Kleczka (D); 41,007 Robert V. Nolan (R); 34 scattered.

PRESIDENT 1920

The Republican figure in South Carolina includes votes cast for two elector tickets; the figure in Florida is the vote cast for the one elector candidate who ran on both Republican tickets in that state. In Washington, the total vote for minor party candidates exceeded that for the Democratic candidates, but the Democratic total was greater than that for any one of the minor party nominees.

The full list of candidates for President and Vice-President was:

16,153,115	Warren G. Harding and Calvin Coolidge, Republican.
9,133,092	James M. Cox and Franklin D. Roosevelt, Democratic.
915,490	Eugene V. Debs and Seymour Stedman, Socialist.
265,229	Parley P. Christensen and Max S. Hayes, Farmer-Labor.
189,339	Aaron S. Watkins and D. Leigh Colvin, Prohibition.
48,098	James Ferguson and William J. Hough, American.
30,594	William W. Cox and August Gillhaus, Socialist Labor.
5,833	Robert C. Macauley and Richard C. Barnum, Single Tax.

In addition, 27,309 votes were cast in Texas for a Black-and-Tan Republican elector ticket and 514 scattered votes were reported from various states.

UNITED STATES

PRESIDENT 1920

State	Electoral Vote Rep.	Electoral Vote Dem.	Electoral Vote Other	Total Vote	Republican	Democratic	Other	Plurality	Percentage Total Vote Rep.	Percentage Total Vote Dem.	Percentage Major Vote Rep.	Percentage Major Vote Dem.
Alabama		12		233,951	74,719	156,064	3,168	81,345 D	31.9%	66.7%	32.4%	67.6%
Alaska												
Arizona	3			66,803	37,016	29,546	241	7,470 R	55.4%	44.2%	55.6%	44.4%
Arkansas		9		183,871	72,316	106,427	5,128	34,111 D	39.3%	57.9%	40.5%	59.5%
California	13			943,463	624,992	229,191	89,280	395,801 R	66.2%	24.3%	73.2%	26.8%
Colorado	6			292,053	173,248	104,936	13,869	68,312 R	59.3%	35.9%	62.3%	37.7%
Connecticut	7			365,518	229,238	120,721	15,559	108,517 R	62.7%	33.0%	65.5%	34.5%
Delaware	3			94,875	52,858	39,911	2,106	12,947 R	55.7%	42.1%	57.0%	43.0%
Florida		6		145,684	44,853	90,515	10,316	45,662 D	30.8%	62.1%	33.1%	66.9%
Georgia		14		149,558	42,981	106,112	465	63,131 D	28.7%	71.0%	28.8%	71.2%
Hawaii												
Idaho	4			138,281	91,351	46,930		44,421 R	66.1%	33.9%	66.1%	33.9%
Illinois	29			2,094,714	1,420,480	534,395	139,839	886,085 R	67.8%	25.5%	72.7%	27.3%
Indiana	15			1,262,974	696,370	511,364	55,240	185,006 R	55.1%	40.5%	57.7%	42.3%
Iowa	13			894,959	634,674	227,804	32,481	406,870 R	70.9%	25.5%	73.6%	26.4%
Kansas	10			570,243	369,268	185,464	15,511	183,804 R	64.8%	32.5%	66.6%	33.4%
Kentucky		13		918,636	452,480	456,497	9,659	4,017 D	49.3%	49.7%	49.8%	50.2%
Louisiana		10		126,397	38,539	87,519	339	48,980 D	30.5%	69.2%	30.6%	69.4%
Maine	6			197,840	136,355	58,961	2,524	77,394 R	68.9%	29.8%	69.8%	30.2%
Maryland	8			428,443	236,117	180,626	11,700	55,491 R	55.1%	42.2%	56.7%	43.3%
Massachusetts	18			993,718	681,153	276,691	35,874	404,462 R	68.5%	27.8%	71.1%	28.9%
Michigan	15			1,048,411	762,865	233,450	52,096	529,415 R	72.8%	22.3%	76.6%	23.4%
Minnesota	12			735,838	519,421	142,994	73,423	376,427 R	70.6%	19.4%	78.4%	21.6%
Mississippi		10		82,351	11,576	69,136	1,639	57,560 D	14.1%	84.0%	14.3%	85.7%
Missouri	18			1,332,140	727,252	574,699	30,189	152,553 R	54.6%	43.1%	55.9%	44.1%
Montana	4			179,006	109,430	57,372	12,204	52,058 R	61.1%	32.1%	65.6%	34.4%
Nebraska	8			382,743	247,498	119,608	15,637	127,890 R	64.7%	31.3%	67.4%	32.6%
Nevada	3			27,194	15,479	9,851	1,864	5,628 R	56.9%	36.2%	61.1%	38.9%
New Hampshire	4			159,092	95,196	62,662	1,234	32,534 R	59.8%	39.4%	60.3%	39.7%
New Jersey	14			910,251	615,333	258,761	36,157	356,572 R	67.6%	28.4%	70.4%	29.6%
New Mexico	3			105,412	57,634	46,668	1,110	10,966 R	54.7%	44.3%	55.3%	44.7%
New York	45			2,898,513	1,871,167	781,238	246,108	1,089,929 R	64.6%	27.0%	70.5%	29.5%
North Carolina		12		538,649	232,819	305,367	463	72,548 D	43.2%	56.7%	43.3%	56.7%
North Dakota	5			205,786	160,082	37,422	8,282	122,660 R	77.8%	18.2%	81.1%	18.9%
Ohio	24			2,021,653	1,182,022	780,037	59,594	401,985 R	58.5%	38.6%	60.2%	39.8%
Oklahoma	10			485,678	243,840	216,122	25,716	27,718 R	50.2%	44.5%	53.0%	47.0%
Oregon	5			238,522	143,592	80,019	14,911	63,573 R	60.2%	33.5%	64.2%	35.8%
Pennsylvania	38			1,851,248	1,218,215	503,202	129,831	715,013 R	65.8%	27.2%	70.8%	29.2%
Rhode Island	5			167,981	107,463	55,062	5,456	52,401 R	64.0%	32.8%	66.1%	33.9%
South Carolina		9		66,808	2,610	64,170	28	61,560 D	3.9%	96.1%	3.9%	96.1%
South Dakota	5			182,237	110,692	35,938	35,607	74,754 R	60.7%	19.7%	75.5%	24.5%
Tennessee	12			428,036	219,229	206,558	2,249	12,671 R	51.2%	48.3%	51.5%	48.5%
Texas		20		486,109	114,658	287,920	83,531	173,262 D	23.6%	59.2%	28.5%	71.5%
Utah	4			145,828	81,555	56,639	7,634	24,916 R	55.9%	38.8%	59.0%	41.0%
Vermont	4			89,961	68,212	20,919	830	47,293 R	75.8%	23.3%	76.5%	23.5%
Virginia		12		231,000	87,456	141,670	1,874	54,214 D	37.9%	61.3%	38.2%	61.8%
Washington	7			398,715	223,137	84,298	91,280	138,839 R	56.0%	21.1%	72.6%	27.4%
West Virginia	8			509,936	282,007	220,785	7,144	61,222 R	55.3%	43.3%	56.1%	43.9%
Wisconsin	13			701,281	498,576	113,422	89,283	385,154 R	71.1%	16.2%	81.5%	18.5%
Wyoming	3			56,253	35,091	17,429	3,733	17,662 R	62.4%	31.0%	66.8%	33.2%
United States	404	127	—	26,768,613	16,153,115	9,133,092	1,482,406	7,020,023 R	60.3%	34.1%	63.9%	36.1%

PRESIDENT 1924

Wisconsin's 13 electoral votes were cast for the Progressive nominees, and in eleven other states in the Midwest and West the Progressive candidates ran second. In several states the Progressive total includes votes cast for two or three elector tickets.

The full list of candidates for President and Vice-President was:

15,719,921	Calvin Coolidge and Charles G. Dawes, Republican.
8,386,704	John W. Davis and Charles W. Bryan, Democratic.
4,832,532	Robert M. LaFollette and Burton K. Wheeler, Progressive.
56,292	Herman P. Faris and Marie Caroline Brehm, Prohibition.
34,174	Frank T. Johns and Verne L. Reynolds, Socialist Labor.
33,360	William Z. Foster and Benjamin Gitlow, Communist.
24,340	Gilbert O. Nations and Leander L. Pickett, American.
2,948	William J. Wallace and John C. Lincoln, Commonwealth Land.

In addition, 4,752 scattered votes were reported from various states.

UNITED STATES

PRESIDENT 1924

State	Electoral Vote Rep.	Electoral Vote Dem.	Electoral Vote Other	Total Vote	Republican	Democratic	Progressive	Other	Plurality	Percentage Total Vote Rep.	Percentage Total Vote Dem.	Percentage Total Vote Prog.
Alabama		12		164,563	42,823	113,138	8,040	562	70,315 D	26.0%	68.8%	4.9%
Alaska												
Arizona	3			73,961	30,516	26,235	17,210		4,281 R	41.3%	35.5%	23.3%
Arkansas		9		138,540	40,583	84,790	13,167		44,207 D	29.3%	61.2%	9.5%
California	13			1,281,778	733,250	105,514	424,649	18,365	308,601 R	57.2%	8.2%	33.1%
Colorado	6			342,261	195,171	75,238	69,946	1,906	119,933 R	57.0%	22.0%	20.4%
Connecticut	7			400,396	246,322	110,184	42,416	1,474	136,138 R	61.5%	27.5%	10.6%
Delaware	3			90,885	52,441	33,445	4,979	20	18,996 R	57.7%	36.8%	5.5%
Florida		6		109,158	30,633	62,083	8,625	7,817	31,450 D	28.1%	56.9%	7.9%
Georgia		14		166,635	30,300	123,262	12,687	386	92,962 D	18.2%	74.0%	7.6%
Hawaii												
Idaho	4			147,690	69,791	23,951	53,948		15,843 R	47.3%	16.2%	36.5%
Illinois	29			2,470,067	1,453,321	576,975	432,027	7,744	876,346 R	58.8%	23.4%	17.5%
Indiana	15			1,272,390	703,042	492,245	71,700	5,403	210,797 R	55.3%	38.7%	5.6%
Iowa	13			976,770	537,458	160,382	274,448	4,482	263,010 R	55.0%	16.4%	28.1%
Kansas	10			662,456	407,671	156,320	98,461	4	251,351 R	61.5%	23.6%	14.9%
Kentucky	13			813,843	396,758	375,593	38,465	3,027	21,165 R	48.8%	46.2%	4.7%
Louisiana		10		121,951	24,670	93,218		4,063	68,548 D	20.2%	76.4%	
Maine	6			192,192	138,440	41,964	11,382	406	96,476 R	72.0%	21.8%	5.9%
Maryland	8			358,630	162,414	148,072	47,157	987	14,342 R	45.3%	41.3%	13.1%
Massachusetts	18			1,129,837	703,476	280,831	141,225	4,305	422,645 R	62.3%	24.9%	12.5%
Michigan	15			1,160,419	874,631	152,359	122,014	11,415	722,272 R	75.4%	13.1%	10.5%
Minnesota	12			822,146	420,759	55,913	339,192	6,282	81,567 R	51.2%	6.8%	41.3%
Mississippi		10		112,442	8,494	100,474	3,474		91,980 D	7.6%	89.4%	3.1%
Missouri	18			1,310,095	648,488	574,962	83,996	2,649	73,526 R	49.5%	43.9%	6.4%
Montana	4			174,425	74,138	33,805	66,124	358	8,014 R	42.5%	19.4%	37.9%
Nebraska	8			463,559	218,985	137,299	105,681	1,594	81,686 R	47.2%	29.6%	22.8%
Nevada	3			26,921	11,243	5,909	9,769		1,474 R	41.8%	21.9%	36.3%
New Hampshire	4			164,769	98,575	57,201	8,993		41,374 R	59.8%	34.7%	5.5%
New Jersey	14			1,088,054	676,277	298,043	109,028	4,706	378,234 R	62.2%	27.4%	10.0%
New Mexico	3			112,830	54,745	48,542	9,543		6,203 R	48.5%	43.0%	8.5%
New York	45			3,263,939	1,820,058	950,796	474,913	18,172	869,262 R	55.8%	29.1%	14.6%
North Carolina		12		481,608	190,754	284,190	6,651	13	93,436 D	39.6%	59.0%	1.4%
North Dakota	5			199,081	94,931	13,858	89,922	370	5,009 R	47.7%	7.0%	45.2%
Ohio	24			2,016,296	1,176,130	477,887	358,008	4,271	698,243 R	58.3%	23.7%	17.8%
Oklahoma		10		527,828	225,756	255,798	46,274		30,042 D	42.8%	48.5%	8.8%
Oregon	5			279,488	142,579	67,589	68,403	917	74,176 R	51.0%	24.2%	24.5%
Pennsylvania	38			2,144,850	1,401,481	409,192	307,567	26,610	992,289 R	65.3%	19.1%	14.3%
Rhode Island	5			210,115	125,286	76,606	7,628	595	48,680 R	59.6%	36.5%	3.6%
South Carolina		9		50,755	1,123	49,008	623	1	47,885 D	2.2%	96.6%	1.2%
South Dakota	5			203,868	101,299	27,214	75,355		25,944 R	49.7%	13.3%	37.0%
Tennessee		12		301,030	130,831	159,339	10,666	194	28,508 D	43.5%	52.9%	3.5%
Texas		20		657,054	130,794	483,381	42,879		352,587 D	19.9%	73.6%	6.5%
Utah	4			156,990	77,327	47,001	32,662		30,326 R	49.3%	29.9%	20.8%
Vermont	4			102,917	80,498	16,124	5,964	331	64,374 R	78.2%	15.7%	5.8%
Virginia		12		223,603	73,328	139,717	10,369	189	66,389 D	32.8%	62.5%	4.6%
Washington	7			421,549	220,224	42,842	150,727	7,756	69,497 R	52.2%	10.2%	35.8%
West Virginia	8			583,662	288,635	257,232	36,723	1,072	31,403 R	49.5%	44.1%	6.3%
Wisconsin			13	840,827	311,614	68,115	453,678	7,420	142,064 P	37.1%	8.1%	54.0%
Wyoming	3			79,900	41,858	12,868	25,174		16,684 R	52.4%	16.1%	31.5%
United States	382	136	13	29,095,023	15,719,921	8,386,704	4,832,532	155,866	7,333,217 R	54.0%	28.8%	16.6%

PRESIDENT 1928

The Republican figures in Georgia, Mississippi, and South Carolina include votes cast for two or three elector tickets; in Pennsylvania the Communist total includes votes cast for two elector tickets.

The full list of candidates for President and Vice-President was:

21,437,277	Herbert C. Hoover and Charles Curtis, <u>Republican</u>.
15,007,698	Alfred E. Smith and Joseph T. Robinson, <u>Democratic</u>.
265,583	Norman Thomas and James H. Maurer, <u>Socialist</u>.
46,896	William Z. Foster and Benjamin Gitlow, <u>Communist</u>.
21,586	Verne L. Reynolds and Jeremiah D. Crowley, <u>Socialist Labor</u>.
20,101	William F. Varney and James A. Edgerton, <u>Prohibition</u>.
6,390	Frank E. Webb and L. R. Tillman, <u>Farmer-Labor</u>.

In addition, 420 scattered votes were reported from various states.

UNITED STATES

PRESIDENT 1928

State	Electoral Vote Rep.	Dem.	Other	Total Vote	Republican	Democratic	Other	Plurality	Percentage Total Vote Rep.	Dem.	Major Vote Rep.	Dem.
Alabama		12		248,981	120,725	127,796	460	7,071 D	48.5%	51.3%	48.6%	51.4%
Alaska												
Arizona	3			91,254	52,533	38,537	184	13,996 R	57.6%	42.2%	57.7%	42.3%
Arkansas		9		197,726	77,784	119,196	746	41,412 D	39.3%	60.3%	39.5%	60.5%
California	13			1,796,656	1,162,323	614,365	19,968	547,958 R	64.7%	34.2%	65.4%	34.6%
Colorado	6			392,242	253,872	133,131	5,239	120,741 R	64.7%	33.9%	65.6%	34.4%
Connecticut	7			553,118	296,641	252,085	4,392	44,556 R	53.6%	45.6%	54.1%	45.9%
Delaware	3			104,602	68,860	35,354	388	33,506 R	65.8%	33.8%	66.1%	33.9%
Florida	6			252,068	145,860	101,764	4,444	44,096 R	57.9%	40.4%	58.9%	41.1%
Georgia		14		231,592	101,800	129,604	188	27,804 D	44.0%	56.0%	44.0%	56.0%
Hawaii												
Idaho	4			151,541	97,322	52,926	1,293	44,396 R	64.2%	34.9%	64.8%	35.2%
Illinois	29			3,107,489	1,769,141	1,313,817	24,531	455,324 R	56.9%	42.3%	57.4%	42.6%
Indiana	15			1,421,314	848,290	562,691	10,333	285,599 R	59.7%	39.6%	60.1%	39.9%
Iowa	13			1,009,189	623,570	379,011	6,608	244,559 R	61.8%	37.6%	62.2%	37.8%
Kansas	10			713,200	513,672	193,003	6,525	320,669 R	72.0%	27.1%	72.7%	27.3%
Kentucky	13			940,521	558,064	381,070	1,387	176,994 R	59.3%	40.5%	59.4%	40.6%
Louisiana		10		215,833	51,160	164,655	18	113,495 D	23.7%	76.3%	23.7%	76.3%
Maine	6			262,170	179,923	81,179	1,068	98,744 R	68.6%	31.0%	68.9%	31.1%
Maryland	8			528,348	301,479	223,626	3,243	77,853 R	57.1%	42.3%	57.4%	42.6%
Massachusetts		18		1,577,823	775,566	792,758	9,499	17,192 D	49.2%	50.2%	49.5%	50.5%
Michigan	15			1,372,082	965,396	396,762	9,924	568,634 R	70.4%	28.9%	70.9%	29.1%
Minnesota	12			970,976	560,977	396,451	13,548	164,526 R	57.8%	40.8%	58.6%	41.4%
Mississippi		10		151,568	27,030	124,538		97,508 D	17.8%	82.2%	17.8%	82.2%
Missouri	18			1,500,845	834,080	662,684	4,081	171,396 R	55.6%	44.2%	55.7%	44.3%
Montana	4			194,108	113,300	78,578	2,230	34,722 R	58.4%	40.5%	59.0%	41.0%
Nebraska	8			547,128	345,745	197,950	3,433	147,795 R	63.2%	36.2%	63.6%	36.4%
Nevada	3			32,417	18,327	14,090		4,237 R	56.5%	43.5%	56.5%	43.5%
New Hampshire	4			196,757	115,404	80,715	638	34,689 R	58.7%	41.0%	58.8%	41.2%
New Jersey	14			1,549,381	926,050	616,517	6,814	309,533 R	59.8%	39.8%	60.0%	40.0%
New Mexico	3			118,077	69,708	48,211	158	21,497 R	59.0%	40.8%	59.1%	40.9%
New York	45			4,405,626	2,193,344	2,089,863	122,419	103,481 R	49.8%	47.4%	51.2%	48.8%
North Carolina	12			635,150	348,923	286,227		62,696 R	54.9%	45.1%	54.9%	45.1%
North Dakota	5			239,845	131,419	106,648	1,778	24,771 R	54.8%	44.5%	55.2%	44.8%
Ohio	24			2,508,346	1,627,546	864,210	16,590	763,336 R	64.9%	34.5%	65.3%	34.7%
Oklahoma	10			618,427	394,046	219,174	5,207	174,872 R	63.7%	35.4%	64.3%	35.7%
Oregon	5			319,942	205,341	109,223	5,378	96,118 R	64.2%	34.1%	65.3%	34.7%
Pennsylvania	38			3,150,612	2,055,382	1,067,586	27,644	987,796 R	65.2%	33.9%	65.8%	34.2%
Rhode Island		5		237,194	117,522	118,973	699	1,451 D	49.5%	50.2%	49.7%	50.3%
South Carolina		9		68,605	5,858	62,700	47	56,842 D	8.5%	91.4%	8.5%	91.5%
South Dakota	5			261,857	157,603	102,660	1,594	54,943 R	60.2%	39.2%	60.6%	39.4%
Tennessee	12			353,192	195,388	157,143	661	38,245 R	55.3%	44.5%	55.4%	44.6%
Texas	20			717,733	372,324	344,542	867	27,782 R	51.9%	48.0%	51.9%	48.1%
Utah	4			176,603	94,618	80,985	1,000	13,633 R	53.6%	45.9%	53.9%	46.1%
Vermont	4			135,191	90,404	44,440	347	45,964 R	66.9%	32.9%	67.0%	33.0%
Virginia	12			305,364	164,609	140,146	609	24,463 R	53.9%	45.9%	54.0%	46.0%
Washington	7			500,840	335,844	156,772	8,224	179,072 R	67.1%	31.3%	68.2%	31.8%
West Virginia	8			642,752	375,551	263,784	3,417	111,767 R	58.4%	41.0%	58.7%	41.3%
Wisconsin	13			1,016,831	544,205	450,259	22,367	93,946 R	53.5%	44.3%	54.7%	45.3%
Wyoming	3			82,835	52,748	29,299	788	23,449 R	63.7%	35.4%	64.3%	35.7%
United States	444	87	—	36,805,951	21,437,277	15,007,698	360,976	6,429,579 R	58.2%	40.8%	58.8%	41.2%

PRESIDENT 1932

The Republican figure in Mississippi includes votes cast for two elector tickets.

The full list of candidates for President and Vice-President was:

22,829,501	Franklin D. Roosevelt and John N. Garner, <u>Democratic</u>.
15,760,684	Herbert C. Hoover and Charles Curtis, <u>Republican</u>.
884,649	Norman Thomas and James H. Maurer, <u>Socialist</u>.
103,253	William Z. Foster and James W. Ford, <u>Communist</u>.
81,872	William D. Upshaw and Frank S. Regan, <u>Prohibition</u>.
53,247	William H. Harvey and Frank Hemenway, <u>Liberty</u>.
34,043	Verne L. Reynolds and John W. Aiken, <u>Socialist Labor</u>.
7,431	Jacob S. Coxey and Julius J. Reiter, <u>Farmer-Labor</u>.
1,645	John Zahnd and Florence Garvin, <u>National</u>.
740	James R. Cox and Victor C. Tisdal, <u>Jobless</u>.

In addition, 157 votes were cast for a Jacksonian elector ticket in Texas and 9 in Arizona for an Arizona Progressive Democratic Ticket. There were 1,528 scattered votes reported from various states.

UNITED STATES

PRESIDENT 1932

State	Electoral Vote Rep.	Electoral Vote Dem.	Electoral Vote Other	Total Vote	Republican	Democratic	Other	Plurality	Percentage Total Vote Rep.	Percentage Total Vote Dem.	Percentage Major Vote Rep.	Percentage Major Vote Dem.
Alabama		11		245,303	34,675	207,910	2,718	173,235 D	14.1%	84.8%	14.3%	85.7%
Alaska												
Arizona		3		118,251	36,104	79,264	2,883	43,160 D	30.5%	67.0%	31.3%	68.7%
Arkansas		9		216,569	27,465	186,829	2,275	159,364 D	12.7%	86.3%	12.8%	87.2%
California		22		2,266,972	847,902	1,324,157	94,913	476,255 D	37.4%	58.4%	39.0%	61.0%
Colorado		6		457,696	189,617	250,877	17,202	61,260 D	41.4%	54.8%	43.0%	57.0%
Connecticut	8			594,183	288,420	281,632	24,131	6,788 R	48.5%	47.4%	50.6%	49.4%
Delaware	3			112,901	57,073	54,319	1,509	2,754 R	50.6%	48.1%	51.2%	48.8%
Florida		7		276,943	69,170	206,307	1,466	137,137 D	25.0%	74.5%	25.1%	74.9%
Georgia		12		255,590	19,863	234,118	1,609	214,255 D	7.8%	91.6%	7.8%	92.2%
Hawaii												
Idaho		4		186,520	71,312	109,479	5,729	38,167 D	38.2%	58.7%	39.4%	60.6%
Illinois		29		3,407,926	1,432,756	1,882,304	92,866	449,548 D	42.0%	55.2%	43.2%	56.8%
Indiana		14		1,576,927	677,184	862,054	37,689	184,870 D	42.9%	54.7%	44.0%	56.0%
Iowa		11		1,036,687	414,433	598,019	24,235	183,586 D	40.0%	57.7%	40.9%	59.1%
Kansas		9		791,978	349,498	424,204	18,276	74,706 D	44.1%	53.6%	45.2%	54.8%
Kentucky		11		983,059	394,716	580,574	7,769	185,858 D	40.2%	59.1%	40.5%	59.5%
Louisiana		10		268,804	18,853	249,418	533	230,565 D	7.0%	92.8%	7.0%	93.0%
Maine	5			298,444	166,631	128,907	2,906	37,724 R	55.8%	43.2%	56.4%	43.6%
Maryland		8		511,054	184,184	314,314	12,556	130,130 D	36.0%	61.5%	36.9%	63.1%
Massachusetts		17		1,580,114	736,959	800,148	43,007	63,189 D	46.6%	50.6%	47.9%	52.1%
Michigan		19		1,664,765	739,894	871,700	53,171	131,806 D	44.4%	52.4%	45.9%	54.1%
Minnesota		11		1,002,843	363,959	600,806	38,078	236,847 D	36.3%	59.9%	37.7%	62.3%
Mississippi		9		146,034	5,180	140,168	686	134,988 D	3.5%	96.0%	3.6%	96.4%
Missouri		15		1,609,894	564,713	1,025,406	19,775	460,693 D	35.1%	63.7%	35.5%	64.5%
Montana		4		216,479	78,078	127,286	11,115	49,208 D	36.1%	58.8%	38.0%	62.0%
Nebraska		7		570,135	201,177	359,082	9,876	157,905 D	35.3%	63.0%	35.9%	64.1%
Nevada		3		41,430	12,674	28,756		16,082 D	30.6%	69.4%	30.6%	69.4%
New Hampshire	4			205,520	103,629	100,680	1,211	2,949 R	50.4%	49.0%	50.7%	49.3%
New Jersey		16		1,630,063	775,684	806,630	47,749	30,946 D	47.6%	49.5%	49.0%	51.0%
New Mexico		3		151,606	54,217	95,089	2,300	40,872 D	35.8%	62.7%	36.3%	63.7%
New York		47		4,688,614	1,937,963	2,534,959	215,692	596,996 D	41.3%	54.1%	43.3%	56.7%
North Carolina		13		711,498	208,344	497,566	5,588	289,222 D	29.3%	69.9%	29.5%	70.5%
North Dakota		4		256,290	71,772	178,350	6,168	106,578 D	28.0%	69.6%	28.7%	71.3%
Ohio		26		2,609,728	1,227,319	1,301,695	80,714	74,376 D	47.0%	49.9%	48.5%	51.5%
Oklahoma		11		704,633	188,165	516,468		328,303 D	26.7%	73.3%	26.7%	73.3%
Oregon		5		368,751	136,019	213,871	18,861	77,852 D	36.9%	58.0%	38.9%	61.1%
Pennsylvania	36			2,859,021	1,453,540	1,295,948	109,533	157,592 R	50.8%	45.3%	52.9%	47.1%
Rhode Island		4		266,170	115,266	146,604	4,300	31,338 D	43.3%	55.1%	44.0%	56.0%
South Carolina		8		104,407	1,978	102,347	82	100,369 D	1.9%	98.0%	1.9%	98.1%
South Dakota		4		288,438	99,212	183,515	5,711	84,303 D	34.4%	63.6%	35.1%	64.9%
Tennessee		11		390,273	126,752	259,473	4,048	132,721 D	32.5%	66.5%	32.8%	67.2%
Texas		23		874,382	98,218	771,109	5,055	672,891 D	11.2%	88.2%	11.3%	88.7%
Utah		4		206,578	84,795	116,750	5,033	31,955 D	41.0%	56.5%	42.1%	57.9%
Vermont	3			136,980	78,984	56,266	1,730	22,718 R	57.7%	41.1%	58.4%	41.6%
Virginia		11		297,942	89,637	203,979	4,326	114,342 D	30.1%	68.5%	30.5%	69.5%
Washington		8		614,814	208,645	353,260	52,909	144,615 D	33.9%	57.5%	37.1%	62.9%
West Virginia		8		743,774	330,731	405,124	7,919	74,393 D	44.5%	54.5%	44.9%	55.1%
Wisconsin		12		1,114,814	347,741	707,410	59,663	359,669 D	31.2%	63.5%	33.0%	67.0%
Wyoming		3		96,962	39,583	54,370	3,009	14,787 D	40.8%	56.1%	42.1%	57.9%
United States	59	472	—	39,758,759	15,760,684	22,829,501	1,168,574	7,068,817 D	39.6%	57.4%	40.8%	59.2%

PRESIDENT 1936

The Republican figures in Delaware, Mississippi, and South Carolina include votes cast for two elector tickets. In New York the Democratic figure includes American Labor votes.

The full list of candidates for President and Vice-President was:

27,757,333	Franklin D. Roosevelt and John N. Garner, Democratic.
16,684,231	Alfred M. Landon and Frank Knox, Republican.
892,267	William Lemke and Thomas C. O'Brien, Union.
187,833	Norman Thomas and George A. Nelson, Socialist.
80,171	Earl Browder and James W. Ford, Communist.
37,677	D. Leigh Colvin and Claude A. Watson, Prohibition.
12,829	John W. Aiken and Emil F. Teichert, Socialist Labor.
1,598	William Dudley Pelley and Willard W. Kemp, Christian.

In addition, 824 scattered votes were reported from various states.

UNITED STATES

PRESIDENT 1936

State	Electoral Vote Rep.	Electoral Vote Dem.	Electoral Vote Other	Total Vote	Republican	Democratic	Other	Plurality	Total Vote Rep.	Total Vote Dem.	Major Vote Rep.	Major Vote Dem.
Alabama		11		275,744	35,358	238,196	2,190	202,838 D	12.8%	86.4%	12.9%	87.1%
Alaska												
Arizona		3		124,163	33,433	86,722	4,008	53,289 D	26.9%	69.8%	27.8%	72.2%
Arkansas		9		179,431	32,049	146,765	617	114,716 D	17.9%	81.8%	17.9%	82.1%
California		22		2,638,882	836,431	1,766,836	35,615	930,405 D	31.7%	67.0%	32.1%	67.9%
Colorado		6		488,685	181,267	295,021	12,397	113,754 D	37.1%	60.4%	38.1%	61.9%
Connecticut		8		690,723	278,685	382,129	29,909	103,444 D	40.3%	55.3%	42.2%	57.8%
Delaware		3		127,603	57,236	69,702	665	12,466 D	44.9%	54.6%	45.1%	54.9%
Florida		7		327,436	78,248	249,117	71	170,869 D	23.9%	76.1%	23.9%	76.1%
Georgia		12		293,170	36,943	255,363	864	218,420 D	12.6%	87.1%	12.6%	87.4%
Hawaii												
Idaho		4		199,617	66,256	125,683	7,678	59,427 D	33.2%	63.0%	34.5%	65.5%
Illinois		29		3,956,522	1,570,393	2,282,999	103,130	712,606 D	39.7%	57.7%	40.8%	59.2%
Indiana		14		1,650,897	691,570	934,974	24,353	243,404 D	41.9%	56.6%	42.5%	57.5%
Iowa		11		1,142,737	487,977	621,756	33,004	133,779 D	42.7%	54.4%	44.0%	56.0%
Kansas		9		865,507	397,727	464,520	3,260	66,793 D	46.0%	53.7%	46.1%	53.9%
Kentucky		11		926,214	369,702	541,944	14,568	172,242 D	39.9%	58.5%	40.6%	59.4%
Louisiana		10		329,778	36,791	292,894	93	256,103 D	11.2%	88.8%	11.2%	88.8%
Maine	5			304,240	168,823	126,333	9,084	42,490 R	55.5%	41.5%	57.2%	42.8%
Maryland		8		624,896	231,435	389,612	3,849	158,177 D	37.0%	62.3%	37.3%	62.7%
Massachusetts		17		1,840,357	768,613	942,716	129,028	174,103 D	41.8%	51.2%	44.9%	55.1%
Michigan		19		1,805,098	699,733	1,016,794	88,571	317,061 D	38.8%	56.3%	40.8%	59.2%
Minnesota		11		1,129,975	350,461	698,811	80,703	348,350 D	31.0%	61.8%	33.4%	66.6%
Mississippi		9		162,142	4,467	157,333	342	152,866 D	2.8%	97.0%	2.8%	97.2%
Missouri		15		1,828,635	697,891	1,111,043	19,701	413,152 D	38.2%	60.8%	38.6%	61.4%
Montana		4		230,502	63,598	159,690	7,214	96,092 D	27.6%	69.3%	28.5%	71.5%
Nebraska		7		608,023	247,731	347,445	12,847	99,714 D	40.7%	57.1%	41.6%	58.4%
Nevada		3		43,848	11,923	31,925		20,002 D	27.2%	72.8%	27.2%	72.8%
New Hampshire		4		218,114	104,642	108,460	5,012	3,818 D	48.0%	49.7%	49.1%	50.9%
New Jersey		16		1,820,437	720,322	1,083,850	16,265	363,528 D	39.6%	59.5%	39.9%	60.1%
New Mexico		3		169,135	61,727	106,037	1,371	44,310 D	36.5%	62.7%	36.8%	63.2%
New York		47		5,596,398	2,180,670	3,293,222	122,506	1,112,552 D	39.0%	58.8%	39.8%	60.2%
North Carolina		13		839,475	223,294	616,141	40	392,847 D	26.6%	73.4%	26.6%	73.4%
North Dakota		4		273,716	72,751	163,148	37,817	90,397 D	26.6%	59.6%	30.8%	69.2%
Ohio		26		3,012,660	1,127,855	1,747,140	137,665	619,285 D	37.4%	58.0%	39.2%	60.8%
Oklahoma		11		749,740	245,122	501,069	3,549	255,947 D	32.7%	66.8%	32.8%	67.2%
Oregon		5		414,021	122,706	266,733	24,582	144,027 D	29.6%	64.4%	31.5%	68.5%
Pennsylvania		36		4,138,105	1,690,300	2,353,788	94,017	663,488 D	40.8%	56.9%	41.8%	58.2%
Rhode Island		4		310,278	125,031	164,338	20,909	39,307 D	40.3%	53.0%	43.2%	56.8%
South Carolina		8		115,437	1,646	113,791		112,145 D	1.4%	98.6%	1.4%	98.6%
South Dakota		4		296,452	125,977	160,137	10,338	34,160 D	42.5%	54.0%	44.0%	56.0%
Tennessee		11		477,086	147,055	328,083	1,948	181,028 D	30.8%	68.8%	30.9%	69.1%
Texas		23		849,701	104,661	739,952	5,088	635,291 D	12.3%	87.1%	12.4%	87.6%
Utah		4		216,679	64,555	150,248	1,876	85,693 D	29.8%	69.3%	30.1%	69.9%
Vermont	3			143,689	81,023	62,124	542	18,899 R	56.4%	43.2%	56.6%	43.4%
Virginia		11		334,590	98,336	234,980	1,274	136,644 D	29.4%	70.2%	29.5%	70.5%
Washington		8		692,338	206,892	459,579	25,867	252,687 D	29.9%	66.4%	31.0%	69.0%
West Virginia		8		829,945	325,358	502,582	2,005	177,224 D	39.2%	60.6%	39.3%	60.7%
Wisconsin		12		1,258,560	380,828	802,984	74,748	422,156 D	30.3%	63.8%	32.2%	67.8%
Wyoming		3		103,382	38,739	62,624	2,019	23,885 D	37.5%	60.6%	38.2%	61.8%
United States	8	523	—	45,654,763	16,684,231	27,757,333	1,213,199	11,073,102 D	36.5%	60.8%	37.5%	62.5%

PRESIDENT 1940

The Republican figures in Connecticut, Georgia, Mississippi and South Carolina include votes cast for two or three elector tickets. In New York the Democratic figure includes American Labor votes.

The full list of candidates for President and Vice-President was:

27,313,041	Franklin D. Roosevelt and Henry A. Wallace, <u>Democratic</u>.
22,348,480	Wendell Willkie and Charles L. McNary, <u>Republican</u>.
116,410	Norman Thomas and Maynard C. Krueger, <u>Socialist</u>.
58,708	Roger Babson and Edgar V. Moorman, <u>Prohibition</u>.
46,259	Earl Browder and James W. Ford, <u>Communist</u>.
14,892	John W. Aiken and Aaron M. Orange, <u>Socialist Labor</u>.

In addition, 545 votes were cast in North Dakota for the individual candidacy of Alfred Knutson and 2,083 scattered votes were reported from various states.

UNITED STATES

PRESIDENT 1940

State	Electoral Vote Rep.	Dem.	Other	Total Vote	Republican	Democratic	Other	Plurality	Total Vote Rep.	Dem.	Major Vote Rep.	Dem.
Alabama		11		294,219	42,184	250,726	1,309	208,542 D	14.3%	85.2%	14.4%	85.6%
Alaska												
Arizona		3		150,039	54,030	95,267	742	41,237 D	36.0%	63.5%	36.2%	63.8%
Arkansas		9		200,429	42,122	157,213	1,094	115,091 D	21.0%	78.4%	21.1%	78.9%
California		22		3,268,791	1,351,419	1,877,618	39,754	526,199 D	41.3%	57.4%	41.9%	58.1%
Colorado	6			549,004	279,576	265,554	3,874	14,022 R	50.9%	48.4%	51.3%	48.7%
Connecticut		8		781,502	361,819	417,621	2,062	55,802 D	46.3%	53.4%	46.4%	53.6%
Delaware		3		136,374	61,440	74,599	335	13,159 D	45.1%	54.7%	45.2%	54.8%
Florida		7		485,640	126,158	359,334	148	233,176 D	26.0%	74.0%	26.0%	74.0%
Georgia		12		312,686	46,495	265,194	997	218,699 D	14.9%	84.8%	14.9%	85.1%
Hawaii												
Idaho		4		235,168	106,553	127,842	773	21,289 D	45.3%	54.4%	45.5%	54.5%
Illinois		29		4,217,935	2,047,240	2,149,934	20,761	102,694 D	48.5%	51.0%	48.8%	51.2%
Indiana	14			1,782,747	899,466	874,063	9,218	25,403 R	50.5%	49.0%	50.7%	49.3%
Iowa	11			1,215,432	632,370	578,802	4,260	53,568 R	52.0%	47.6%	52.2%	47.8%
Kansas	9			860,297	489,169	364,725	6,403	124,444 R	56.9%	42.4%	57.3%	42.7%
Kentucky		11		970,163	410,384	557,322	2,457	146,938 D	42.3%	57.4%	42.4%	57.6%
Louisiana		10		372,305	52,446	319,751	108	267,305 D	14.1%	85.9%	14.1%	85.9%
Maine	5			320,840	163,951	156,478	411	7,473 R	51.1%	48.8%	51.2%	48.8%
Maryland		8		660,104	269,534	384,546	6,024	115,012 D	40.8%	58.3%	41.2%	58.8%
Massachusetts		17		2,026,993	939,700	1,076,522	10,771	136,822 D	46.4%	53.1%	46.6%	53.4%
Michigan	19			2,085,929	1,039,917	1,032,991	13,021	6,926 R	49.9%	49.5%	50.2%	49.8%
Minnesota		11		1,251,188	596,274	644,196	10,718	47,922 D	47.7%	51.5%	48.1%	51.9%
Mississippi		9		175,824	7,364	168,267	193	160,903 D	4.2%	95.7%	4.2%	95.8%
Missouri		15		1,833,729	871,009	958,476	4,244	87,467 D	47.5%	52.3%	47.6%	52.4%
Montana		4		247,873	99,579	145,698	2,596	46,119 D	40.2%	58.8%	40.6%	59.4%
Nebraska	7			615,878	352,201	263,677		88,524 R	57.2%	42.8%	57.2%	42.8%
Nevada		3		53,174	21,229	31,945		10,716 D	39.9%	60.1%	39.9%	60.1%
New Hampshire		4		235,419	110,127	125,292		15,165 D	46.8%	53.2%	46.8%	53.2%
New Jersey		16		1,972,552	945,475	1,016,808	10,269	71,333 D	47.9%	51.5%	48.2%	51.8%
New Mexico		3		183,258	79,315	103,699	244	24,384 D	43.3%	56.6%	43.3%	56.7%
New York		47		6,301,596	3,027,478	3,251,918	22,200	224,440 D	48.0%	51.6%	48.2%	51.8%
North Carolina		13		822,648	213,633	609,015		395,382 D	26.0%	74.0%	26.0%	74.0%
North Dakota	4			280,775	154,590	124,036	2,149	30,554 R	55.1%	44.2%	55.5%	44.5%
Ohio		26		3,319,912	1,586,773	1,733,139		146,366 D	47.8%	52.2%	47.8%	52.2%
Oklahoma		11		826,212	348,872	474,313	3,027	125,441 D	42.2%	57.4%	42.4%	57.6%
Oregon		5		481,240	219,555	258,415	3,270	38,860 D	45.6%	53.7%	45.9%	54.1%
Pennsylvania		36		4,078,714	1,889,848	2,171,035	17,831	281,187 D	46.3%	53.2%	46.5%	53.5%
Rhode Island		4		321,152	138,654	182,181	317	43,527 D	43.2%	56.7%	43.2%	56.8%
South Carolina		8		99,830	4,360	95,470		91,110 D	4.4%	95.6%	4.4%	95.6%
South Dakota	4			308,427	177,065	131,362		45,703 R	57.4%	42.6%	57.4%	42.6%
Tennessee		11		522,823	169,153	351,601	2,069	182,448 D	32.4%	67.3%	32.5%	67.5%
Texas		23		1,124,437	212,692	909,974	1,771	697,282 D	18.9%	80.9%	18.9%	81.1%
Utah		4		247,819	93,151	154,277	391	61,126 D	37.6%	62.3%	37.6%	62.4%
Vermont	3			143,062	78,371	64,269	422	14,102 R	54.8%	44.9%	54.9%	45.1%
Virginia		11		346,608	109,363	235,961	1,284	126,598 D	31.6%	68.1%	31.7%	68.3%
Washington		8		793,833	322,123	462,145	9,565	140,022 D	40.6%	58.2%	41.1%	58.9%
West Virginia		8		868,076	372,414	495,662		123,248 D	42.9%	57.1%	42.9%	57.1%
Wisconsin		12		1,405,522	679,206	704,821	21,495	25,615 D	48.3%	50.1%	49.1%	50.9%
Wyoming		3		112,240	52,633	59,287	320	6,654 D	46.9%	52.8%	47.0%	53.0%
United States	82	449	—	49,900,418	22,348,480	27,313,041	238,897	4,964,561 D	44.8%	54.7%	45.0%	55.0%

PRESIDENT 1944

The Republican figures in Georgia, Mississippi and South Carolina include votes cast for two elector tickets. The Democratic figure in Mississippi includes votes cast for two elector tickets and in New York includes American Labor and Liberal votes.

In South Carolina an uncommitted Southern Democratic elector ticket ran in second place ahead of the Republican candidates.

The full list of candidates for President and Vice-President was:

25,612,610	Franklin D. Roosevelt and Harry S. Truman, Democratic.
22,017,617	Thomas E. Dewey and John W. Bricker, Republican.
79,003	Norman Thomas and Darlington Hoopes, Socialist.
74,799	Claude A. Watson and Andrew Johnson, Prohibition.
45,191	Edward A. Teichert and Arla A. Albaugh, Socialist Labor.
1,780	Gerald L. K. Smith and Harry Romer, American First.

In addition, 135,444 votes were cast in Texas for a Texas Regulars elector ticket and 7,799 in South Carolina for an uncommitted Southern Democratic elector ticket. There were 2,447 scattered votes reported from various states.

UNITED STATES

PRESIDENT 1944

State	Electoral Vote Rep.	Dem.	Other	Total Vote	Republican	Democratic	Other	Plurality	Total Vote Rep.	Dem.	Major Vote Rep.	Dem.
Alabama		11		244,743	44,540	198,918	1,285	154,378 D	18.2%	81.3%	18.3%	81.7%
Alaska												
Arizona		4		137,634	56,287	80,926	421	24,639 D	40.9%	58.8%	41.0%	59.0%
Arkansas		9		212,954	63,551	148,965	438	85,414 D	29.8%	70.0%	29.9%	70.1%
California		25		3,520,875	1,512,965	1,988,564	19,346	475,599 D	43.0%	56.5%	43.2%	56.8%
Colorado	6			505,039	268,731	234,331	1,977	34,400 R	53.2%	46.4%	53.4%	46.6%
Connecticut		8		831,990	390,527	435,146	6,317	44,619 D	46.9%	52.3%	47.3%	52.7%
Delaware		3		125,361	56,747	68,166	448	11,419 D	45.3%	54.4%	45.4%	54.6%
Florida		8		482,803	143,215	339,377	211	196,162 D	29.7%	70.3%	29.7%	70.3%
Georgia		12		328,129	59,900	268,187	42	208,287 D	18.3%	81.7%	18.3%	81.7%
Hawaii												
Idaho		4		208,321	100,137	107,399	785	7,262 D	48.1%	51.6%	48.3%	51.7%
Illinois		28		4,036,061	1,939,314	2,079,479	17,268	140,165 D	48.0%	51.5%	48.3%	51.7%
Indiana	13			1,672,091	875,891	781,403	14,797	94,488 R	52.4%	46.7%	52.9%	47.1%
Iowa	10			1,052,599	547,267	499,876	5,456	47,391 R	52.0%	47.5%	52.3%	47.7%
Kansas	8			733,776	442,096	287,458	4,222	154,638 R	60.2%	39.2%	60.6%	39.4%
Kentucky		11		867,924	392,448	472,589	2,887	80,141 D	45.2%	54.5%	45.4%	54.6%
Louisiana		10		349,383	67,750	281,564	69	213,814 D	19.4%	80.6%	19.4%	80.6%
Maine	5			296,400	155,434	140,631	335	14,803 R	52.4%	47.4%	52.5%	47.5%
Maryland		8		608,439	292,949	315,490		22,541 D	48.1%	51.9%	48.1%	51.9%
Massachusetts		16		1,960,665	921,350	1,035,296	4,019	113,946 D	47.0%	52.8%	47.1%	52.9%
Michigan		19		2,205,223	1,084,423	1,106,899	13,901	22,476 D	49.2%	50.2%	49.5%	50.5%
Minnesota		11		1,125,504	527,416	589,864	8,224	62,448 D	46.9%	52.4%	47.2%	52.8%
Mississippi		9		180,234	11,613	168,621		157,008 D	6.4%	93.6%	6.4%	93.6%
Missouri		15		1,571,697	761,175	807,356	3,166	46,181 D	48.4%	51.4%	48.5%	51.5%
Montana		4		207,355	93,163	112,556	1,636	19,393 D	44.9%	54.3%	45.3%	54.7%
Nebraska	6			563,126	329,880	233,246		96,634 R	58.6%	41.4%	58.6%	41.4%
Nevada		3		54,234	24,611	29,623		5,012 D	45.4%	54.6%	45.4%	54.6%
New Hampshire		4		229,625	109,916	119,663	46	9,747 D	47.9%	52.1%	47.9%	52.1%
New Jersey		16		1,963,761	961,335	987,874	14,552	26,539 D	49.0%	50.3%	49.3%	50.7%
New Mexico		4		152,225	70,688	81,389	148	10,701 D	46.4%	53.5%	46.5%	53.5%
New York		47		6,316,790	2,987,647	3,304,238	24,905	316,591 D	47.3%	52.3%	47.5%	52.5%
North Carolina		14		790,554	263,155	527,399		264,244 D	33.3%	66.7%	33.3%	66.7%
North Dakota	4			220,182	118,535	100,144	1,503	18,391 R	53.8%	45.5%	54.2%	45.8%
Ohio	25			3,153,056	1,582,293	1,570,763		11,530 R	50.2%	49.8%	50.2%	49.8%
Oklahoma		10		722,636	319,424	401,549	1,663	82,125 D	44.2%	55.6%	44.3%	55.7%
Oregon		6		480,147	225,365	248,635	6,147	23,270 D	46.9%	51.8%	47.5%	52.5%
Pennsylvania		35		3,794,793	1,835,054	1,940,479	19,260	105,425 D	48.4%	51.1%	48.6%	51.4%
Rhode Island		4		299,276	123,487	175,356	433	51,869 D	41.3%	58.6%	41.3%	58.7%
South Carolina		8		103,382	4,617	90,601	8,164	82,802 D	4.5%	87.6%	4.8%	95.2%
South Dakota	4			232,076	135,365	96,711		38,654 R	58.3%	41.7%	58.3%	41.7%
Tennessee		12		510,692	200,311	308,707	1,674	108,396 D	39.2%	60.4%	39.4%	60.6%
Texas		23		1,150,334	191,423	821,605	137,306	630,182 D	16.6%	71.4%	18.9%	81.1%
Utah		4		248,319	97,891	150,088	340	52,197 D	39.4%	60.4%	39.5%	60.5%
Vermont	3			125,361	71,527	53,820	14	17,707 R	57.1%	42.9%	57.1%	42.9%
Virginia		11		388,485	145,243	242,276	966	97,033 D	37.4%	62.4%	37.5%	62.5%
Washington		8		856,328	361,689	486,774	7,865	125,085 D	42.2%	56.8%	42.6%	57.4%
West Virginia		8		715,596	322,819	392,777		69,958 D	45.1%	54.9%	45.1%	54.9%
Wisconsin	12			1,339,152	674,532	650,413	14,207	24,119 R	50.4%	48.6%	50.9%	49.1%
Wyoming	3			101,340	51,921	49,419		2,502 R	51.2%	48.8%	51.2%	48.8%
United States	99	432	—	47,976,670	22,017,617	25,612,610	346,443	3,594,993 D	45.9%	53.4%	46.2%	53.8%

PRESIDENT 1948

The electoral votes of Alabama, Louisiana, Mississippi, and South Carolina were cast for the States Rights nominees. In addition, one of the 12 Democratic electors chosen in Tennessee cast his Electoral College vote for the States Rights nominees rather than for the national Democratic candidates.

In Alabama the Democratic electors were pledged to the States Rights candidates. There were no national Democratic electors on the ballot in that state.

The Republican figure in Mississippi includes votes cast for two elector tickets. In New York the Democratic figure includes Liberal votes.

The full list of candidates for President and Vice-President was:

24,179,345	Harry S. Truman and Alben W. Barkley, Democratic.
21,991,291	Thomas E. Dewey and Earl Warren, Republican.
1,176,125	Strom Thurmond and Fielding L. Wright, States Rights.
1,157,326	Henry A. Wallace and Glen H. Taylor, Progressive.
139,572	Norman Thomas and Tucker P. Smith, Socialist.
103,900	Claude A. Watson and Dale H. Learn, Prohibition.
29,241	Edward A. Teichert and Stephen Emery, Socialist Labor.
13,614	Farrell Dobbs and Grace Carlson, Socialist Workers.

In addition, 3,412 scattered votes were reported from various states.

UNITED STATES

PRESIDENT 1948

State	Electoral Vote Rep.	Dem.	Other	Total Vote	Republican	Democratic	Other	Plurality	Percentage Total Vote Rep.	Dem.	Major Vote Rep.	Dem.
Alabama			11	214,980	40,930		174,050	130,513 SR	19.0%		100.0%	
Alaska												
Arizona		4		177,065	77,597	95,251	4,217	17,654 D	43.8%	53.8%	44.9%	55.1%
Arkansas		9		242,475	50,959	149,659	41,857	98,700 D	21.0%	61.7%	25.4%	74.6%
California		25		4,021,538	1,895,269	1,913,134	213,135	17,865 D	47.1%	47.6%	49.8%	50.2%
Colorado		6		515,237	239,714	267,288	8,235	27,574 D	46.5%	51.9%	47.3%	52.7%
Connecticut	8			883,518	437,754	423,297	22,467	14,457 R	49.5%	47.9%	50.8%	49.2%
Delaware	3			139,073	69,588	67,813	1,672	1,775 R	50.0%	48.8%	50.6%	49.4%
Florida		8		577,643	194,280	281,988	101,375	87,708 D	33.6%	48.8%	40.8%	59.2%
Georgia		12		418,844	76,691	254,646	87,507	169,511 D	18.3%	60.8%	23.1%	76.9%
Hawaii												
Idaho		4		214,816	101,514	107,370	5,932	5,856 D	47.3%	50.0%	48.6%	51.4%
Illinois		28		3,984,046	1,961,103	1,994,715	28,228	33,612 D	49.2%	50.1%	49.6%	50.4%
Indiana	13			1,656,212	821,079	807,831	27,302	13,248 R	49.6%	48.8%	50.4%	49.6%
Iowa		10		1,038,264	494,018	522,380	21,866	28,362 D	47.6%	50.3%	48.6%	51.4%
Kansas	8			788,819	423,039	351,902	13,878	71,137 R	53.6%	44.6%	54.6%	45.4%
Kentucky		11		822,658	341,210	466,756	14,692	125,546 D	41.5%	56.7%	42.2%	57.8%
Louisiana			10	416,336	72,657	136,344	207,335	67,946 SR	17.5%	32.7%	34.8%	65.2%
Maine	5			264,787	150,234	111,916	2,637	38,318 R	56.7%	42.3%	57.3%	42.7%
Maryland	8			596,748	294,814	286,521	15,413	8,293 R	49.4%	48.0%	50.7%	49.3%
Massachusetts		16		2,107,146	909,370	1,151,788	45,988	242,418 D	43.2%	54.7%	44.1%	55.9%
Michigan	19			2,109,609	1,038,595	1,003,448	67,566	35,147 R	49.2%	47.6%	50.9%	49.1%
Minnesota		11		1,212,226	483,617	692,966	35,643	209,349 D	39.9%	57.2%	41.1%	58.9%
Mississippi			9	192,190	5,043	19,384	167,763	148,154 SR	2.6%	10.1%	20.6%	79.4%
Missouri		15		1,578,628	655,039	917,315	6,274	262,276 D	41.5%	58.1%	41.7%	58.3%
Montana		4		224,278	96,770	119,071	8,437	22,301 D	43.1%	53.1%	44.8%	55.2%
Nebraska	6			488,940	264,774	224,165	1	40,609 R	54.2%	45.8%	54.2%	45.8%
Nevada		3		62,117	29,357	31,291	1,469	1,934 D	47.3%	50.4%	48.4%	51.6%
New Hampshire	4			231,440	121,299	107,995	2,146	13,304 R	52.4%	46.7%	52.9%	47.1%
New Jersey	16			1,949,555	981,124	895,455	72,976	85,669 R	50.3%	45.9%	52.3%	47.7%
New Mexico		4		187,063	80,303	105,464	1,296	25,161 D	42.9%	56.4%	43.2%	56.8%
New York	47			6,177,337	2,841,163	2,780,204	555,970	60,959 R	46.0%	45.0%	50.5%	49.5%
North Carolina		14		791,209	258,572	459,070	73,567	200,498 D	32.7%	58.0%	36.0%	64.0%
North Dakota	4			220,716	115,139	95,812	9,765	19,327 R	52.2%	43.4%	54.6%	45.4%
Ohio		25		2,936,071	1,445,684	1,452,791	37,596	7,107 D	49.2%	49.5%	49.9%	50.1%
Oklahoma		10		721,599	268,817	452,782		183,965 D	37.3%	62.7%	37.3%	62.7%
Oregon	6			524,080	260,904	243,147	20,029	17,757 R	49.8%	46.4%	51.8%	48.2%
Pennsylvania	35			3,735,348	1,902,197	1,752,426	80,725	149,771 R	50.9%	46.9%	52.0%	48.0%
Rhode Island		4		327,702	135,787	188,736	3,179	52,949 D	41.4%	57.6%	41.8%	58.2%
South Carolina			8	142,571	5,386	34,423	102,762	68,184 SR	3.8%	24.1%	13.5%	86.5%
South Dakota	4			250,105	129,651	117,653	2,801	11,998 R	51.8%	47.0%	52.4%	47.6%
Tennessee		11	1	550,283	202,914	270,402	76,967	67,488 D	36.9%	49.1%	42.9%	57.1%
Texas		23		1,249,577	303,467	824,235	121,875	520,768 D	24.3%	66.0%	26.9%	73.1%
Utah		4		276,306	124,402	149,151	2,753	24,749 D	45.0%	54.0%	45.5%	54.5%
Vermont	3			123,382	75,926	45,557	1,899	30,369 R	61.5%	36.9%	62.5%	37.5%
Virginia		11		419,256	172,070	200,786	46,400	28,716 D	41.0%	47.9%	46.1%	53.9%
Washington		8		905,058	386,314	476,165	42,579	89,851 D	42.7%	52.6%	44.8%	55.2%
West Virginia		8		748,750	316,251	429,188	3,311	112,937 D	42.2%	57.3%	42.4%	57.6%
Wisconsin		12		1,276,800	590,959	647,310	38,531	56,351 D	46.3%	50.7%	47.7%	52.3%
Wyoming		3		101,425	47,947	52,354	1,124	4,407 D	47.3%	51.6%	47.8%	52.2%
United States	189	303	39	48,793,826	21,991,291	24,179,345	2,623,190	2,188,054 D	45.1%	49.6%	47.6%	52.4%

PRESIDENT 1952

The Republican figure in South Carolina includes votes cast for two elector tickets; in Mississippi the Republican total is the vote cast for an Independent elector ticket "pledged to vote for the nominees of the National Republican Party". In New York the Democratic figure includes Liberal votes.

The full list of candidates for President and Vice-President was:

33,936,234	Dwight D. Eisenhower and Richard M. Nixon, Republican.
27,314,992	Adlai E. Stevenson and John J. Sparkman, Democratic.
140,023	Vincent Hallinan and Charlotta Bass, Progressive.
72,949	Stuart Hamblen and Enoch A. Holtwick, Prohibition.
30,267	Eric Hass and Stephen Emery, Socialist Labor.
20,203	Darlington Hoopes and Samuel H. Friedman, Socialist.
10,312	Farrell Dobbs and Myra Tanner Weiss, Socialist Workers.
4,203	Henry B. Krajewski and Frank Jenkins, Poor Man's Party.

In addition, 17,205 votes were cast for various elector tickets filed on behalf of General Douglas MacArthur, including Christian Nationalist (with Jack B. Tenney as candidate for Vice-President), Constitution (with Vivien Kellems), and America First (with Senator Harry Flood Byrd). In California, Missouri, and Texas the MacArthur vote was cast for two elector tickets. 4,530 scattered votes were reported from various states.

UNITED STATES

PRESIDENT 1952

State	Electoral Vote Rep.	Electoral Vote Dem.	Electoral Vote Other	Total Vote	Republican	Democratic	Other	Plurality	Total Vote Rep.	Total Vote Dem.	Major Vote Rep.	Major Vote Dem.
Alabama		11		426,120	149,231	275,075	1,814	125,844 D	35.0%	64.6%	35.2%	64.8%
Alaska												
Arizona	4			260,570	152,042	108,528		43,514 R	58.3%	41.7%	58.3%	41.7%
Arkansas		8		404,800	177,155	226,300	1,345	49,145 D	43.8%	55.9%	43.9%	56.1%
California	32			5,141,849	2,897,310	2,197,548	46,991	699,762 R	56.3%	42.7%	56.9%	43.1%
Colorado	6			630,103	379,782	245,504	4,817	134,278 R	60.3%	39.0%	60.7%	39.3%
Connecticut	8			1,096,911	611,012	481,649	4,250	129,363 R	55.7%	43.9%	55.9%	44.1%
Delaware	3			174,025	90,059	83,315	651	6,744 R	51.8%	47.9%	51.9%	48.1%
Florida	10			989,337	544,036	444,950	351	99,086 R	55.0%	45.0%	55.0%	45.0%
Georgia		12		655,785	198,961	456,823	1	257,862 D	30.3%	69.7%	30.3%	69.7%
Hawaii												
Idaho	4			276,254	180,707	95,081	466	85,626 R	65.4%	34.4%	65.5%	34.5%
Illinois	27			4,481,058	2,457,327	2,013,920	9,811	443,407 R	54.8%	44.9%	55.0%	45.0%
Indiana	13			1,955,049	1,136,259	801,530	17,260	334,729 R	58.1%	41.0%	58.6%	41.4%
Iowa	10			1,268,773	808,906	451,513	8,354	357,393 R	63.8%	35.6%	64.2%	35.8%
Kansas	8			896,166	616,302	273,296	6,568	343,006 R	68.8%	30.5%	69.3%	30.7%
Kentucky		10		993,148	495,029	495,729	2,390	700 D	49.8%	49.9%	50.0%	50.0%
Louisiana		10		651,952	306,925	345,027		38,102 D	47.1%	52.9%	47.1%	52.9%
Maine	5			351,786	232,353	118,806	627	113,547 R	66.0%	33.8%	66.2%	33.8%
Maryland	9			902,074	499,424	395,337	7,313	104,087 R	55.4%	43.8%	55.8%	44.2%
Massachusetts	16			2,383,398	1,292,325	1,083,525	7,548	208,800 R	54.2%	45.5%	54.4%	45.6%
Michigan	20			2,798,592	1,551,529	1,230,657	16,406	320,872 R	55.4%	44.0%	55.8%	44.2%
Minnesota	11			1,379,483	763,211	608,458	7,814	154,753 R	55.3%	44.1%	55.6%	44.4%
Mississippi		8		285,532	112,966	172,566		59,600 D	39.6%	60.4%	39.6%	60.4%
Missouri	13			1,892,062	959,429	929,830	2,803	29,599 R	50.7%	49.1%	50.8%	49.2%
Montana	4			265,037	157,394	106,213	1,430	51,181 R	59.4%	40.1%	59.7%	40.3%
Nebraska	6			609,660	421,603	188,057		233,546 R	69.2%	30.8%	69.2%	30.8%
Nevada	3			82,190	50,502	31,688		18,814 R	61.4%	38.6%	61.4%	38.6%
New Hampshire	4			272,950	166,287	106,663		59,624 R	60.9%	39.1%	60.9%	39.1%
New Jersey	16			2,418,554	1,373,613	1,015,902	29,039	357,711 R	56.8%	42.0%	57.5%	42.5%
New Mexico	4			238,608	132,170	105,661	777	26,509 R	55.4%	44.3%	55.6%	44.4%
New York	45			7,128,239	3,952,813	3,104,601	70,825	848,212 R	55.5%	43.6%	56.0%	44.0%
North Carolina		14		1,210,910	558,107	652,803		94,696 D	46.1%	53.9%	46.1%	53.9%
North Dakota	4			270,127	191,712	76,694	1,721	115,018 R	71.0%	28.4%	71.4%	28.6%
Ohio	25			3,700,758	2,100,391	1,600,367		500,024 R	56.8%	43.2%	56.8%	43.2%
Oklahoma	8			948,984	518,045	430,939		87,106 R	54.6%	45.4%	54.6%	45.4%
Oregon	6			695,059	420,815	270,579	3,665	150,236 R	60.5%	38.9%	60.9%	39.1%
Pennsylvania	32			4,580,969	2,415,789	2,146,269	18,911	269,520 R	52.7%	46.9%	53.0%	47.0%
Rhode Island	4			414,498	210,935	203,293	270	7,642 R	50.9%	49.0%	50.9%	49.1%
South Carolina		8		341,087	168,082	173,004	1	4,922 D	49.3%	50.7%	49.3%	50.7%
South Dakota	4			294,283	203,857	90,426		113,431 R	69.3%	30.7%	69.3%	30.7%
Tennessee	11			892,553	446,147	443,710	2,696	2,437 R	50.0%	49.7%	50.1%	49.9%
Texas	24			2,075,946	1,102,878	969,228	3,840	133,650 R	53.1%	46.7%	53.2%	46.8%
Utah	4			329,554	194,190	135,364		58,826 R	58.9%	41.1%	58.9%	41.1%
Vermont	3			153,557	109,717	43,355	485	66,362 R	71.5%	28.2%	71.7%	28.3%
Virginia	12			619,689	349,037	268,677	1,975	80,360 R	56.3%	43.4%	56.5%	43.5%
Washington	9			1,102,708	599,107	492,845	10,756	106,262 R	54.3%	44.7%	54.9%	45.1%
West Virginia		8		873,548	419,970	453,578		33,608 D	48.1%	51.9%	48.1%	51.9%
Wisconsin	12			1,607,370	979,744	622,175	5,451	357,569 R	61.0%	38.7%	61.2%	38.8%
Wyoming	3			129,253	81,049	47,934	270	33,115 R	62.7%	37.1%	62.8%	37.2%
United States	442	89		61,550,918	33,936,234	27,314,992	299,692	6,621,242 R	55.1%	44.4%	55.4%	44.6%

PRESIDENT 1956

One of the 11 Democratic electors chosen in Alabama cast his Electoral College vote for Walter B. Jones and Herman Talmadge rather than for the national Democratic candidates.

The Republican figure in Mississippi includes votes cast for two elector tickets. In New York the Democratic figure includes Liberal votes.

The full list of candidates for President and Vice-President was:

35,590,472	Dwight D. Eisenhower and Richard M. Nixon, Republican.
26,022,752	Adlai E. Stevenson and Estes Kefauver, Democratic.
111,178	T. Coleman Andrews and Thomas H. Werdel, States Rights.
44,450	Eric Hass and Georgia Cozzini, Socialist Labor.
41,937	Enoch A. Holtwick and Edwin M. Cooper, Prohibition.
7,797	Farrell Dobbs and Myra Tanner Weiss, Socialist Workers.
2,657	Harry Flood Byrd and William E. Jenner, States Rights.
2,126	Darlington Hoopes and Samuel H. Friedman, Socialist.
1,829	Henry B. Krajewski and Anne Marie Yezo, American Third Party.
8	Gerald L. K. Smith and Charles F. Robertson, Christian Nationalist.

In addition, 196,318 votes were cast in Alabama, Louisiana, Mississippi, and South Carolina for Independent electors or for States Rights elector tickets not officially pledged to any candidate, and 5,384 scattered votes were reported from various states.

UNITED STATES

PRESIDENT 1956

State	Electoral Vote Rep.	Dem.	Other	Total Vote	Republican	Democratic	Other	Plurality	Total Vote Rep.	Dem.	Major Vote Rep.	Dem.
Alabama		10	1	496,861	195,694	280,844	20,323	85,150 D	39.4%	56.5%	41.1%	58.9%
Alaska												
Arizona	4			290,173	176,990	112,880	303	64,110 R	61.0%	38.9%	61.1%	38.9%
Arkansas		8		406,572	186,287	213,277	7,008	26,990 D	45.8%	52.5%	46.6%	53.4%
California	32			5,466,355	3,027,668	2,420,135	18,552	607,533 R	55.4%	44.3%	55.6%	44.4%
Colorado	6			657,074	394,479	257,997	4,598	136,482 R	60.0%	39.3%	60.5%	39.5%
Connecticut	8			1,117,121	711,837	405,079	205	306,758 R	63.7%	36.3%	63.7%	36.3%
Delaware	3			177,988	98,057	79,421	510	18,636 R	55.1%	44.6%	55.3%	44.7%
Florida	10			1,125,762	643,849	480,371	1,542	163,478 R	57.2%	42.7%	57.3%	42.7%
Georgia		12		669,655	222,778	444,688	2,189	221,910 D	33.3%	66.4%	33.4%	66.6%
Hawaii												
Idaho	4			272,989	166,979	105,868	142	61,111 R	61.2%	38.8%	61.2%	38.8%
Illinois	27			4,407,407	2,623,327	1,775,682	8,398	847,645 R	59.5%	40.3%	59.6%	40.4%
Indiana	13			1,974,607	1,182,811	783,908	7,888	398,903 R	59.9%	39.7%	60.1%	39.9%
Iowa	10			1,234,564	729,187	501,858	3,519	227,329 R	59.1%	40.7%	59.2%	40.8%
Kansas	8			866,243	566,878	296,317	3,048	270,561 R	65.4%	34.2%	65.7%	34.3%
Kentucky	10			1,053,805	572,192	476,453	5,160	95,739 R	54.3%	45.2%	54.6%	45.4%
Louisiana	10			617,544	329,047	243,977	44,520	85,070 R	53.3%	39.5%	57.4%	42.6%
Maine	5			351,706	249,238	102,468		146,770 R	70.9%	29.1%	70.9%	29.1%
Maryland	9			932,827	559,738	372,613	476	187,125 R	60.0%	39.9%	60.0%	40.0%
Massachusetts	16			2,348,506	1,393,197	948,190	7,119	445,007 R	59.3%	40.4%	59.5%	40.5%
Michigan	20			3,080,468	1,713,647	1,359,898	6,923	353,749 R	55.6%	44.1%	55.8%	44.2%
Minnesota	11			1,340,005	719,302	617,525	3,178	101,777 R	53.7%	46.1%	53.8%	46.2%
Mississippi		8		248,104	60,685	144,453	42,966	83,768 D	24.5%	58.2%	29.6%	70.4%
Missouri		13		1,832,562	914,289	918,273		3,984 D	49.9%	50.1%	49.9%	50.1%
Montana	4			271,171	154,933	116,238		38,695 R	57.1%	42.9%	57.1%	42.9%
Nebraska	6			577,137	378,108	199,029		179,079 R	65.5%	34.5%	65.5%	34.5%
Nevada	3			96,689	56,049	40,640		15,409 R	58.0%	42.0%	58.0%	42.0%
New Hampshire	4			266,994	176,519	90,364	111	86,155 R	66.1%	33.8%	66.1%	33.9%
New Jersey	16			2,484,312	1,606,942	850,337	27,033	756,605 R	64.7%	34.2%	65.4%	34.6%
New Mexico	4			253,926	146,788	106,098	1,040	40,690 R	57.8%	41.8%	58.0%	42.0%
New York	45			7,095,971	4,345,506	2,747,944	2,521	1,597,562 R	61.2%	38.4%	61.3%	38.7%
North Carolina		14		1,165,592	575,062	590,530		15,468 D	49.3%	50.7%	49.3%	50.7%
North Dakota	4			253,991	156,766	96,742	483	60,024 R	61.7%	38.1%	61.8%	38.2%
Ohio	25			3,702,265	2,262,610	1,439,655		822,955 R	61.1%	38.9%	61.1%	38.9%
Oklahoma	8			859,350	473,769	385,581		88,188 R	55.1%	44.9%	55.1%	44.9%
Oregon	6			736,132	406,393	329,204	535	77,189 R	55.2%	44.7%	55.2%	44.8%
Pennsylvania	32			4,576,503	2,585,252	1,981,769	9,482	603,483 R	56.5%	43.3%	56.6%	43.4%
Rhode Island	4			387,609	225,819	161,790		64,029 R	58.3%	41.7%	58.3%	41.7%
South Carolina		8		300,583	75,700	136,372	88,511	47,863 D	25.2%	45.4%	35.7%	64.3%
South Dakota	4			293,857	171,569	122,288		49,281 R	58.4%	41.6%	58.4%	41.6%
Tennessee	11			939,404	462,288	456,507	20,609	5,781 R	49.2%	48.6%	50.3%	49.7%
Texas	24			1,955,168	1,080,619	859,958	14,591	220,661 R	55.3%	44.0%	55.7%	44.3%
Utah	4			333,995	215,631	118,364		97,267 R	64.6%	35.4%	64.6%	35.4%
Vermont	3			152,978	110,390	42,549	39	67,841 R	72.2%	27.8%	72.2%	27.8%
Virginia	12			697,978	386,459	267,760	43,759	118,699 R	55.4%	38.4%	59.1%	40.9%
Washington	9			1,150,889	620,430	523,002	7,457	97,428 R	53.9%	45.4%	54.3%	45.7%
West Virginia	8			830,831	449,297	381,534		67,763 R	54.1%	45.9%	54.1%	45.9%
Wisconsin	12			1,550,558	954,844	586,768	8,946	368,076 R	61.6%	37.8%	61.9%	38.1%
Wyoming	3			124,127	74,573	49,554		25,019 R	60.1%	39.9%	60.1%	39.9%
United States	457	73	1	62,026,908	35,590,472	26,022,752	413,684	9,567,720 R	57.4%	42.0%	57.8%	42.2%

PRESIDENT 1960

Senator Harry Flood Byrd received 15 votes for President in the Electoral College; these were the votes of 6 of the 11 Democratic electors in Alabama, all 8 unpledged Democratic electors in Mississippi, and one of the 8 Republican electors in Oklahoma. The Alabama and Mississippi electors also cast 14 votes for Senator Strom Thurmond for Vice-President; the single Oklahoma elector voted for Senator Barry M. Goldwater for Vice-President.

In New York the Democratic figure includes Liberal votes.

The full list of candidates for President and Vice-President was:

34,226,731	John F. Kennedy and Lyndon B. Johnson, Democratic.
34,108,157	Richard M. Nixon and Henry Cabot Lodge, Republican.
47,522	Eric Hass and Georgia Cozzini, Socialist Labor.
46,203	Rutherford L. Decker and E. Harold Munn, Prohibition.
44,977	Orval E. Faubus and John G. Crommelin, National States Rights.
40,165	Farrell Dobbs and Myra Tanner Weiss, Socialist Workers.
18,162	Charles L. Sullivan and Merritt B. Curtis, Constitution.
8,708	J. Bracken Lee and Kent H. Courtney, Conservative.
4,204	C. Benton Coiner and Edward J. Silverman, Conservative.
1,767	Lar Daly and B. M. Miller, Tax Cut.
1,485	Clennon King and Reginald Carter, Independent Afro-American.
1,401	Merritt B. Curtis and B. M. Miller, Constitution.

In addition, 169,572 votes were cast in Louisiana for Independent electors and 116,248 in Mississippi for an unpledged Democratic elector ticket. 539 votes were cast in Michigan for an Independent American ticket and 2,378 scattered votes were reported from various states.

UNITED STATES

PRESIDENT 1960

State	Electoral Vote Rep.	Electoral Vote Dem.	Electoral Vote Other	Total Vote	Republican	Democratic	Other	Plurality	Percentage Total Vote Rep.	Percentage Total Vote Dem.	Percentage Major Vote Rep.	Percentage Major Vote Dem.
Alabama		5	6	570,225	237,981	324,050	8,194	86,069 D	41.7%	56.8%	42.3%	57.7%
Alaska	3			60,762	30,953	29,809		1,144 R	50.9%	49.1%	50.9%	49.1%
Arizona	4			398,491	221,241	176,781	469	44,460 R	55.5%	44.4%	55.6%	44.4%
Arkansas		8		428,509	184,508	215,049	28,952	30,541 D	43.1%	50.2%	46.2%	53.8%
California	32			6,506,578	3,259,722	3,224,099	22,757	35,623 R	50.1%	49.6%	50.3%	49.7%
Colorado	6			736,236	402,242	330,629	3,365	71,613 R	54.6%	44.9%	54.9%	45.1%
Connecticut		8		1,222,883	565,813	657,055	15	91,242 D	46.3%	53.7%	46.3%	53.7%
Delaware		3		196,683	96,373	99,590	720	3,217 D	49.0%	50.6%	49.2%	50.8%
Florida	10			1,544,176	795,476	748,700		46,776 R	51.5%	48.5%	51.5%	48.5%
Georgia		12		733,349	274,472	458,638	239	184,166 D	37.4%	62.5%	37.4%	62.6%
Hawaii		3		184,705	92,295	92,410		115 D	50.0%	50.0%	50.0%	50.0%
Idaho	4			300,450	161,597	138,853		22,744 R	53.8%	46.2%	53.8%	46.2%
Illinois		27		4,757,409	2,368,988	2,377,846	10,575	8,858 D	49.8%	50.0%	49.9%	50.1%
Indiana	13			2,135,360	1,175,120	952,358	7,882	222,762 R	55.0%	44.6%	55.2%	44.8%
Iowa	10			1,273,810	722,381	550,565	864	171,816 R	56.7%	43.2%	56.7%	43.3%
Kansas	8			928,825	561,474	363,213	4,138	198,261 R	60.4%	39.1%	60.7%	39.3%
Kentucky	10			1,124,462	602,607	521,855		80,752 R	53.6%	46.4%	53.6%	46.4%
Louisiana		10		807,891	230,980	407,339	169,572	176,359 D	28.6%	50.4%	36.2%	63.8%
Maine	5			421,767	240,608	181,159		59,449 R	57.0%	43.0%	57.0%	43.0%
Maryland		9		1,055,349	489,538	565,808	3	76,270 D	46.4%	53.6%	46.4%	53.6%
Massachusetts		16		2,469,480	976,750	1,487,174	5,556	510,424 D	39.6%	60.2%	39.6%	60.4%
Michigan		20		3,318,097	1,620,428	1,687,269	10,400	66,841 D	48.8%	50.9%	49.0%	51.0%
Minnesota		11		1,541,887	757,915	779,933	4,039	22,018 D	49.2%	50.6%	49.3%	50.7%
Mississippi			8	298,171	73,561	108,362	116,248	7,886 U	24.7%	36.3%	40.4%	59.6%
Missouri		13		1,934,422	962,221	972,201		9,980 D	49.7%	50.3%	49.7%	50.3%
Montana	4			277,579	141,841	134,891	847	6,950 R	51.1%	48.6%	51.3%	48.7%
Nebraska	6			613,095	380,553	232,542		148,011 R	62.1%	37.9%	62.1%	37.9%
Nevada		3		107,267	52,387	54,880		2,493 D	48.8%	51.2%	48.8%	51.2%
New Hampshire	4			295,761	157,989	137,772		20,217 R	53.4%	46.6%	53.4%	46.6%
New Jersey		16		2,773,111	1,363,324	1,385,415	24,372	22,091 D	49.2%	50.0%	49.6%	50.4%
New Mexico		4		311,107	153,733	156,027	1,347	2,294 D	49.4%	50.2%	49.6%	50.4%
New York		45		7,291,079	3,446,419	3,830,085	14,575	383,666 D	47.3%	52.5%	47.4%	52.6%
North Carolina		14		1,368,556	655,420	713,136		57,716 D	47.9%	52.1%	47.9%	52.1%
North Dakota	4			278,431	154,310	123,963	158	30,347 R	55.4%	44.5%	55.5%	44.5%
Ohio	25			4,161,859	2,217,611	1,944,248		273,363 R	53.3%	46.7%	53.3%	46.7%
Oklahoma	7		1	903,150	533,039	370,111		162,928 R	59.0%	41.0%	59.0%	41.0%
Oregon	6			776,421	408,060	367,402	959	40,658 R	52.6%	47.3%	52.6%	47.4%
Pennsylvania		32		5,006,541	2,439,956	2,556,282	10,303	116,326 D	48.7%	51.1%	48.8%	51.2%
Rhode Island		4		405,535	147,502	258,032	1	110,530 D	36.4%	63.6%	36.4%	63.6%
South Carolina		8		386,688	188,558	198,129	1	9,571 D	48.8%	51.2%	48.8%	51.2%
South Dakota	4			306,487	178,417	128,070		50,347 R	58.2%	41.8%	58.2%	41.8%
Tennessee	11			1,051,792	556,577	481,453	13,762	75,124 R	52.9%	45.8%	53.6%	46.4%
Texas		24		2,311,084	1,121,310	1,167,567	22,207	46,257 D	48.5%	50.5%	49.0%	51.0%
Utah	4			374,709	205,361	169,248	100	36,113 R	54.8%	45.2%	54.8%	45.2%
Vermont	3			167,324	98,131	69,186	7	28,945 R	58.6%	41.3%	58.6%	41.4%
Virginia	12			771,449	404,521	362,327	4,601	42,194 R	52.4%	47.0%	52.8%	47.2%
Washington	9			1,241,572	629,273	599,298	13,001	29,975 R	50.7%	48.3%	51.2%	48.8%
West Virginia		8		837,781	395,995	441,786		45,791 D	47.3%	52.7%	47.3%	52.7%
Wisconsin	12			1,729,082	895,175	830,805	3,102	64,370 R	51.8%	48.0%	51.9%	48.1%
Wyoming	3			140,782	77,451	63,331		14,120 R	55.0%	45.0%	55.0%	45.0%
United States	219	303	15	68,838,219	34,108,157	34,226,731	503,331	118,574 D	49.5%	49.7%	49.9%	50.1%

PRESIDENT 1964

In New York the Democratic figure includes Liberal votes.

The full list of candidates for President and Vice-President was:

43,129,566	Lyndon B. Johnson and Hubert H. Humphrey, Democratic.
27,178,188	Barry M. Goldwater and William E. Miller, Republican.
45,219	Eric Hass and Henning A. Blomen, Socialist Labor.
32,720	Clifton DeBerry and Edward Shaw, Socialist Workers.
23,267	E. Harold Munn and Mark R. Shaw, Prohibition.
6,953	John Kasper and J. B. Stoner, National States Rights.
5,060	Joseph B. Lightburn and T. C. Billings, Constitution.
19	James Hensley and John O. Hopkins, Universal.

In addition, 210,732 votes were cast in Alabama for an unpledged Democratic elector ticket and 12,868 scattered votes were reported from various states.

UNITED STATES

PRESIDENT 1964

State	Electoral Vote Rep.	Electoral Vote Dem.	Electoral Vote Other	Total Vote	Republican	Democratic	Other	Plurality	Total Vote Rep.	Total Vote Dem.	Major Vote Rep.	Major Vote Dem.
Alabama	10			689,818	479,085		210,733	268,353 R	69.5%		100.0%	
Alaska		3		67,259	22,930	44,329		21,399 D	34.1%	65.9%	34.1%	65.9%
Arizona	5			480,770	242,535	237,753	482	4,782 R	50.4%	49.5%	50.5%	49.5%
Arkansas		6		560,426	243,264	314,197	2,965	70,933 D	43.4%	56.1%	43.6%	56.4%
California		40		7,057,586	2,879,108	4,171,877	6,601	1,292,769 D	40.8%	59.1%	40.8%	59.2%
Colorado		6		776,986	296,767	476,024	4,195	179,257 D	38.2%	61.3%	38.4%	61.6%
Connecticut		8		1,218,578	390,996	826,269	1,313	435,273 D	32.1%	67.8%	32.1%	67.9%
Delaware		3		201,320	78,078	122,704	538	44,626 D	38.8%	60.9%	38.9%	61.1%
Florida		14		1,854,481	905,941	948,540		42,599 D	48.9%	51.1%	48.9%	51.1%
Georgia	12			1,139,335	616,584	522,556	195	94,028 R	54.1%	45.9%	54.1%	45.9%
Hawaii		4		207,271	44,022	163,249		119,227 D	21.2%	78.8%	21.2%	78.8%
Idaho		4		292,477	143,557	148,920		5,363 D	49.1%	50.9%	49.1%	50.9%
Illinois		26		4,702,841	1,905,946	2,796,833	62	890,887 D	40.5%	59.5%	40.5%	59.5%
Indiana		13		2,091,606	911,118	1,170,848	9,640	259,730 D	43.6%	56.0%	43.8%	56.2%
Iowa		9		1,184,539	449,148	733,030	2,361	283,822 D	37.9%	61.9%	38.0%	62.0%
Kansas		7		857,901	386,579	464,028	7,294	77,449 D	45.1%	54.1%	45.4%	54.6%
Kentucky		9		1,046,105	372,977	669,659	3,469	296,682 D	35.7%	64.0%	35.8%	64.2%
Louisiana	10			896,293	509,225	387,068		122,157 R	56.8%	43.2%	56.8%	43.2%
Maine		4		380,965	118,701	262,264		143,563 D	31.2%	68.8%	31.2%	68.8%
Maryland		10		1,116,457	385,495	730,912	50	345,417 D	34.5%	65.5%	34.5%	65.5%
Massachusetts		14		2,344,798	549,727	1,786,422	8,649	1,236,695 D	23.4%	76.2%	23.5%	76.5%
Michigan		21		3,203,102	1,060,152	2,136,615	6,335	1,076,463 D	33.1%	66.7%	33.2%	66.8%
Minnesota		10		1,554,462	559,624	991,117	3,721	431,493 D	36.0%	63.8%	36.1%	63.9%
Mississippi	7			409,146	356,528	52,618		303,910 R	87.1%	12.9%	87.1%	12.9%
Missouri		12		1,817,879	653,535	1,164,344		510,809 D	36.0%	64.0%	36.0%	64.0%
Montana		4		278,628	113,032	164,246	1,350	51,214 D	40.6%	58.9%	40.8%	59.2%
Nebraska		5		584,154	276,847	307,307		30,460 D	47.4%	52.6%	47.4%	52.6%
Nevada		3		135,433	56,094	79,339		23,245 D	41.4%	58.6%	41.4%	58.6%
New Hampshire		4		288,093	104,029	184,064		80,035 D	36.1%	63.9%	36.1%	63.9%
New Jersey		17		2,847,663	964,174	1,868,231	15,258	904,057 D	33.9%	65.6%	34.0%	66.0%
New Mexico		4		328,645	132,838	194,015	1,792	61,177 D	40.4%	59.0%	40.6%	59.4%
New York		43		7,166,275	2,243,559	4,913,102	9,614	2,669,543 D	31.3%	68.6%	31.3%	68.7%
North Carolina		13		1,424,983	624,844	800,139		175,295 D	43.8%	56.2%	43.8%	56.2%
North Dakota		4		258,389	108,207	149,784	398	41,577 D	41.9%	58.0%	41.9%	58.1%
Ohio		26		3,969,196	1,470,865	2,498,331		1,027,466 D	37.1%	62.9%	37.1%	62.9%
Oklahoma		8		932,499	412,665	519,834		107,169 D	44.3%	55.7%	44.3%	55.7%
Oregon		6		786,305	282,779	501,017	2,509	218,238 D	36.0%	63.7%	36.1%	63.9%
Pennsylvania		29		4,822,690	1,673,657	3,130,954	18,079	1,457,297 D	34.7%	64.9%	34.8%	65.2%
Rhode Island		4		390,091	74,615	315,463	13	240,848 D	19.1%	80.9%	19.1%	80.9%
South Carolina	8			524,779	309,048	215,723	8	93,325 R	58.9%	41.1%	58.9%	41.1%
South Dakota		4		293,118	130,108	163,010		32,902 D	44.4%	55.6%	44.4%	55.6%
Tennessee		11		1,143,946	508,965	634,947	34	125,982 D	44.5%	55.5%	44.5%	55.5%
Texas		25		2,626,811	958,566	1,663,185	5,060	704,619 D	36.5%	63.3%	36.6%	63.4%
Utah		4		401,413	181,785	219,628		37,843 D	45.3%	54.7%	45.3%	54.7%
Vermont		3		163,089	54,942	108,127	20	53,185 D	33.7%	66.3%	33.7%	66.3%
Virginia		12		1,042,267	481,334	558,038	2,895	76,704 D	46.2%	53.5%	46.3%	53.7%
Washington		9		1,258,556	470,366	779,881	8,309	309,515 D	37.4%	62.0%	37.6%	62.4%
West Virginia		7		792,040	253,953	538,087		284,134 D	32.1%	67.9%	32.1%	67.9%
Wisconsin		12		1,691,815	638,495	1,050,424	2,896	411,929 D	37.7%	62.1%	37.8%	62.2%
Wyoming		3		142,716	61,998	80,718		18,720 D	43.4%	56.6%	43.4%	56.6%
Dist. of Col.		3		198,597	28,801	169,796		140,995 D	14.5%	85.5%	14.5%	85.5%
United States	52	486	-	70,644,592	27,178,188	43,129,566	336,838	15,951,378 D	38.5%	61.1%	38.7%	61.3%

PRESIDENT 1968

In North Carolina one Republican elector voted in the Electoral College for the American Independent candidates for President and Vice-President.

In New York the Democratic figure includes Liberal votes and in Alabama the Democratic vote is the total of the Alabama Independent Democratic and National Democratic Party of Alabama vote. In certain states candidates appeared under variants of the party name used below and in most states the Vice-Presidential candidate of the American Independent party was listed as Marvin Griffin rather than Curtis E. LeMay.

The full list of candidates for President and Vice-President was:

31,785,480	Richard M. Nixon and Spiro T. Agnew, Republican.
31,275,166	Hubert H. Humphrey and Edmund S. Muskie, Democratic.
9,906,473	George C. Wallace and Curtis E. LeMay, American Independent.
52,588	Henning A. Blomen and George S. Taylor, Socialist Labor.
47,133	Dick Gregory, Peace and Freedom, with various Vice-Presidential candidates.
41,388	Fred Halstead and Paul Boutelle, Socialist Workers.
36,563	Eldridge Cleaver, Peace and Freedom, with various Vice-Presidential candidates.
25,552	Eugene J. McCarthy, under various titles and written-in, but without indication of Vice-Presidential candidates.
15,123	E. Harold Munn and Rolland E. Fisher, Prohibition.
1,519	Ventura Chavez and Adelicio Moya, People's Constitutional.
1,075	Charlene Mitchell and Michael Zagarell, Communist.
142	James Hensley and Roscoe B. MacKenna, Universal.
34	Richard K. Troxell and Merle Thayer, Constitution.
17	Kent M. Soeters and James P. Powers, Berkeley Defense Group.

In the vote listed above for Eldridge Cleaver, two states are included (California and Utah) in which only the party Vice-Presidential candidate appeared on the ballot.

In addition to these votes, 12,430 were cast for elector tickets for which there were no formal Presidential or Vice-Presidential candidates, and 11,192 scattered votes were reported from various states.

UNITED STATES

PRESIDENT 1968

State	Electoral Vote Rep.	Dem.	AIP	Total Vote	Republican	Democratic	AIP	Other	Plurality	Percentage Total Vote Rep.	Dem.	AIP
Alabama			10	1,049,922	146,923	196,579	691,425	14,995	494,846 A	14.0%	18.7%	65.9%
Alaska	3			83,035	37,600	35,411	10,024		2,189 R	45.3%	42.6%	12.1%
Arizona	5			486,936	266,721	170,514	46,573	3,128	96,207 R	54.8%	35.0%	9.6%
Arkansas			6	619,969	190,759	188,228	240,982		50,223 A	30.8%	30.4%	38.9%
California	40			7,251,587	3,467,664	3,244,318	487,270	52,335	223,346 R	47.8%	44.7%	6.7%
Colorado	6			811,199	409,345	335,174	60,813	5,867	74,171 R	50.5%	41.3%	7.5%
Connecticut		8		1,256,232	556,721	621,561	76,650	1,300	64,840 D	44.3%	49.5%	6.1%
Delaware	3			214,367	96,714	89,194	28,459		7,520 R	45.1%	41.6%	13.3%
Florida	14			2,187,805	886,804	676,794	624,207		210,010 R	40.5%	30.9%	28.5%
Georgia			12	1,250,266	380,111	334,440	535,550	165	155,439 A	30.4%	26.7%	42.8%
Hawaii		4		236,218	91,425	141,324	3,469		49,899 D	38.7%	59.8%	1.5%
Idaho	4			291,183	165,369	89,273	36,541		76,096 R	56.8%	30.7%	12.5%
Illinois	26			4,619,749	2,174,774	2,039,814	390,958	14,203	134,960 R	47.1%	44.2%	8.5%
Indiana	13			2,123,597	1,067,885	806,659	243,108	5,945	261,226 R	50.3%	38.0%	11.4%
Iowa	9			1,167,931	619,106	476,699	66,422	5,704	142,407 R	53.0%	40.8%	5.7%
Kansas	7			872,783	478,674	302,996	88,921	2,192	175,678 R	54.8%	34.7%	10.2%
Kentucky	9			1,055,893	462,411	397,541	193,098	2,843	64,870 R	43.8%	37.6%	18.3%
Louisiana			10	1,097,450	257,535	309,615	530,300		220,685 A	23.5%	28.2%	48.3%
Maine		4		392,936	169,254	217,312	6,370		48,058 D	43.1%	55.3%	1.6%
Maryland		10		1,235,039	517,995	538,310	178,734		20,315 D	41.9%	43.6%	14.5%
Massachusetts		14		2,331,752	766,844	1,469,218	87,088	8,602	702,374 D	32.9%	63.0%	3.7%
Michigan		21		3,306,250	1,370,665	1,593,082	331,968	10,535	222,417 D	41.5%	48.2%	10.0%
Minnesota		10		1,588,506	658,643	857,738	68,931	3,194	199,095 D	41.5%	54.0%	4.3%
Mississippi			7	654,509	88,516	150,644	415,349		264,705 A	13.5%	23.0%	63.5%
Missouri	12			1,809,502	811,932	791,444	206,126		20,488 R	44.9%	43.7%	11.4%
Montana	4			274,404	138,835	114,117	20,015	1,437	24,718 R	50.6%	41.6%	7.3%
Nebraska	5			536,851	321,163	170,784	44,904		150,379 R	59.8%	31.8%	8.4%
Nevada	3			154,218	73,188	60,598	20,432		12,590 R	47.5%	39.3%	13.2%
New Hampshire	4			297,298	154,903	130,589	11,173	633	24,314 R	52.1%	43.9%	3.8%
New Jersey	17			2,875,395	1,325,467	1,264,206	262,187	23,535	61,261 R	46.1%	44.0%	9.1%
New Mexico	4			327,350	169,692	130,081	25,737	1,840	39,611 R	51.8%	39.7%	7.9%
New York		43		6,791,688	3,007,932	3,378,470	358,864	46,422	370,538 D	44.3%	49.7%	5.3%
North Carolina	12		1	1,587,493	627,192	464,113	496,188		131,004 R	39.5%	29.2%	31.3%
North Dakota	4			247,882	138,669	94,769	14,244	200	43,900 R	55.9%	38.2%	5.7%
Ohio	26			3,959,698	1,791,014	1,700,586	467,495	603	90,428 R	45.2%	42.9%	11.8%
Oklahoma	8			943,086	449,697	301,658	191,731		148,039 R	47.7%	32.0%	20.3%
Oregon	6			819,622	408,433	358,866	49,683	2,640	49,567 R	49.8%	43.8%	6.1%
Pennsylvania		29		4,747,928	2,090,017	2,259,405	378,582	19,924	169,388 D	44.0%	47.6%	8.0%
Rhode Island		4		385,000	122,359	246,518	15,678	445	124,159 D	31.8%	64.0%	4.1%
South Carolina	8			666,978	254,062	197,486	215,430		38,632 R	38.1%	29.6%	32.3%
South Dakota	4			281,264	149,841	118,023	13,400		31,818 R	53.3%	42.0%	4.8%
Tennessee	11			1,248,617	472,592	351,233	424,792		47,800 R	37.8%	28.1%	34.0%
Texas		25		3,079,216	1,227,844	1,266,804	584,269	299	38,960 D	39.9%	41.1%	19.0%
Utah	4			422,568	238,728	156,665	26,906	269	82,063 R	56.5%	37.1%	6.4%
Vermont	3			161,404	85,142	70,255	5,104	903	14,887 R	52.8%	43.5%	3.2%
Virginia	12			1,361,491	590,319	442,387	321,833	6,952	147,932 R	43.4%	32.5%	23.6%
Washington		9		1,304,281	588,510	616,037	96,990	2,744	27,527 D	45.1%	47.2%	7.4%
West Virginia		7		754,206	307,555	374,091	72,560		66,536 D	40.8%	49.6%	9.6%
Wisconsin	12			1,691,538	809,997	748,804	127,835	4,902	61,193 R	47.9%	44.3%	7.6%
Wyoming	3			127,205	70,927	45,173	11,105		25,754 R	55.8%	35.5%	8.7%
Dist. of Col.		3		170,578	31,012	139,566			108,554 D	18.2%	81.8%	
United States	301	191	46	73,211,875	31,785,480	31,275,166	9,906,473	244,756	510,314 R	43.4%	42.7%	13.5%

PRESIDENT 1972

In Virginia one Republican elector voted in the Electoral College for the Libertarian candidates for President and Vice-President.

In New York the Republican figures include Conservative votes and the Democratic figures include Liberal votes. In Alabama the Democratic figures include votes cast on the National Democratic Party of Alabama ticket, and in South Carolina include United Citizens Party votes.

In certain states candidates appeared on the ballot under party names other than those used below; for the Socialist Workers party the votes listed for Jenness and Pulley were actually cast for substitute candidates (Reed and DeBerry) or without named candidates in several states.

The Democratic Vice-Presidential candidate originally was Senator Thomas F. Eagleton; on his withdrawal shortly after the party convention, R. Sargent Shriver was named by the Democratic National Committee as candidate.

The full list of candidates for President and Vice-President was:

47,169,911	Richard M. Nixon and Spiro T. Agnew, Republican.
29,170,383	George S. McGovern and R. Sargent Shriver, Democratic.
1,099,482	John G. Schmitz and Thomas J. Anderson, American.
78,756	Benjamin Spock and Julius Hobson, People's.
66,677	Linda Jenness and Andrew Pulley, Socialist Workers.
53,814	Louis Fisher and Genevieve Gunderson, Socialist Labor.
25,595	Gus Hall and Jarvis Tyner, Communist.
13,505	E. Harold Munn and Marshall E. Uncapher, Prohibition.
3,673	John Hospers and Theodora Nathan, Libertarian.
1,743	John V. Mahalchik and Irving Homer, America First.
220	Gabriel Green and Daniel Fry, Universal.

In addition to the above, 34,795 scattered votes were reported from various states.

Vice-President Agnew resigned in October 1973 and Representative Gerald R. Ford of Michigan was nominated by President Nixon to fill the vacancy. In November (Senate) and December (House of Representatives) this action was approved by Congress.

In August 1974 President Nixon resigned and was succeeded by Vice-President Ford. In the same month Nelson A. Rockefeller, former Governor of New York, was nominated to be Vice-President and was confirmed by Congress in December 1974.

UNITED STATES

PRESIDENT 1972

State	Electoral Vote Rep.	Dem.	Other	Total Vote	Republican	Democratic	Other	Plurality	Percentage Total Vote Rep.	Dem.	Major Vote Rep.	Dem.
Alabama	9			1,006,111	728,701	256,923	20,487	471,778 R	72.4%	25.5%	73.9%	26.1%
Alaska	3			95,219	55,349	32,967	6,903	22,382 R	58.1%	34.6%	62.7%	37.3%
Arizona	6			622,926	402,812	198,540	21,574	204,272 R	64.7%	31.9%	67.0%	33.0%
Arkansas	6			651,320	448,541	199,892	2,887	248,649 R	68.9%	30.7%	69.2%	30.8%
California	45			8,367,862	4,602,096	3,475,847	289,919	1,126,249 R	55.0%	41.5%	57.0%	43.0%
Colorado	7			953,884	597,189	329,980	26,715	267,209 R	62.6%	34.6%	64.4%	35.6%
Connecticut	8			1,384,277	810,763	555,498	18,016	255,265 R	58.6%	40.1%	59.3%	40.7%
Delaware	3			235,516	140,357	92,283	2,876	48,074 R	59.6%	39.2%	60.3%	39.7%
Florida	17			2,583,283	1,857,759	718,117	7,407	1,139,642 R	71.9%	27.8%	72.1%	27.9%
Georgia	12			1,174,772	881,496	289,529	3,747	591,967 R	75.0%	24.6%	75.3%	24.7%
Hawaii	4			270,274	168,865	101,409		67,456 R	62.5%	37.5%	62.5%	37.5%
Idaho	4			310,379	199,384	80,826	30,169	118,558 R	64.2%	26.0%	71.2%	28.8%
Illinois	26			4,723,236	2,788,179	1,913,472	21,585	874,707 R	59.0%	40.5%	59.3%	40.7%
Indiana	13			2,125,529	1,405,154	708,568	11,807	696,586 R	66.1%	33.3%	66.5%	33.5%
Iowa	8			1,225,944	706,207	496,206	23,531	210,001 R	57.6%	40.5%	58.7%	41.3%
Kansas	7			916,095	619,812	270,287	25,996	349,525 R	67.7%	29.5%	69.6%	30.4%
Kentucky	9			1,067,499	676,446	371,159	19,894	305,287 R	63.4%	34.8%	64.6%	35.4%
Louisiana	10			1,051,491	686,852	298,142	66,497	388,710 R	65.3%	28.4%	69.7%	30.3%
Maine	4			417,042	256,458	160,584		95,874 R	61.5%	38.5%	61.5%	38.5%
Maryland	10			1,353,812	829,305	505,781	18,726	323,524 R	61.3%	37.4%	62.1%	37.9%
Massachusetts		14		2,458,756	1,112,078	1,332,540	14,138	220,462 D	45.2%	54.2%	45.5%	54.5%
Michigan	21			3,489,727	1,961,721	1,459,435	68,571	502,286 R	56.2%	41.8%	57.3%	42.7%
Minnesota	10			1,741,652	898,269	802,346	41,037	95,923 R	51.6%	46.1%	52.8%	47.2%
Mississippi	7			645,963	505,125	126,782	14,056	378,343 R	78.2%	19.6%	79.9%	20.1%
Missouri	12			1,855,803	1,153,852	697,147	4,804	456,705 R	62.2%	37.6%	62.3%	37.7%
Montana	4			317,603	183,976	120,197	13,430	63,779 R	57.9%	37.8%	60.5%	39.5%
Nebraska	5			576,289	406,298	169,991		236,307 R	70.5%	29.5%	70.5%	29.5%
Nevada	3			181,766	115,750	66,016		49,734 R	63.7%	36.3%	63.7%	36.3%
New Hampshire	4			334,055	213,724	116,435	3,896	97,289 R	64.0%	34.9%	64.7%	35.3%
New Jersey	17			2,997,229	1,845,502	1,102,211	49,516	743,291 R	61.6%	36.8%	62.6%	37.4%
New Mexico	4			386,241	235,606	141,084	9,551	94,522 R	61.0%	36.5%	62.5%	37.5%
New York	41			7,165,919	4,192,778	2,951,084	22,057	1,241,694 R	58.5%	41.2%	58.7%	41.3%
North Carolina	13			1,518,612	1,054,889	438,705	25,018	616,184 R	69.5%	28.9%	70.6%	29.4%
North Dakota	3			280,514	174,109	100,384	6,021	73,725 R	62.1%	35.8%	63.4%	36.6%
Ohio	25			4,094,787	2,441,827	1,558,889	94,071	882,938 R	59.6%	38.1%	61.0%	39.0%
Oklahoma	8			1,029,900	759,025	247,147	23,728	511,878 R	73.7%	24.0%	75.4%	24.6%
Oregon	6			927,946	486,686	392,760	48,500	93,926 R	52.4%	42.3%	55.3%	44.7%
Pennsylvania	27			4,592,106	2,714,521	1,796,951	80,634	917,570 R	59.1%	39.1%	60.2%	39.8%
Rhode Island	4			415,808	220,383	194,645	780	25,738 R	53.0%	46.8%	53.1%	46.9%
South Carolina	8			673,960	477,044	186,824	10,092	290,220 R	70.8%	27.7%	71.9%	28.1%
South Dakota	4			307,415	166,476	139,945	994	26,531 R	54.2%	45.5%	54.3%	45.7%
Tennessee	10			1,201,182	813,147	357,293	30,742	455,854 R	67.7%	29.7%	69.5%	30.5%
Texas	26			3,471,281	2,298,896	1,154,289	18,096	1,144,607 R	66.2%	33.3%	66.6%	33.4%
Utah	4			478,476	323,643	126,284	28,549	197,359 R	67.6%	26.4%	71.9%	28.1%
Vermont	3			186,947	117,149	68,174	1,624	48,975 R	62.7%	36.5%	63.2%	36.8%
Virginia	11		1	1,457,019	988,493	438,887	29,639	549,606 R	67.8%	30.1%	69.3%	30.7%
Washington	9			1,470,847	837,135	568,334	65,378	268,801 R	56.9%	38.6%	59.6%	40.4%
West Virginia	6			762,399	484,964	277,435		207,529 R	63.6%	36.4%	63.6%	36.4%
Wisconsin	11			1,852,890	989,430	810,174	53,286	179,256 R	53.4%	43.7%	55.0%	45.0%
Wyoming	3			145,570	100,464	44,358	748	56,106 R	69.0%	30.5%	69.4%	30.6%
Dist. of Col.		3		163,421	35,226	127,627	568	92,401 D	21.6%	78.1%	21.6%	78.4%
United States	520	17	1	77,718,554	47,169,911	29,170,383	1,378,260	17,999,528 R	60.7%	37.5%	61.8%	38.2%

PRESIDENT 1976

In Washington, one Republican elector voted in the Electoral College for Ronald Reagan for President and Robert Dole for Vice-President.

In New York the Republican figures include Conservative votes and the Democratic figures include Liberal votes; in Vermont the Democratic figures include votes cast on the Independent Vermonters party ticket.

In a number of states candidates appeared on the ballot with variants of the party designations listed below and in several cases with entirely different party names.

The ballot designations for electors for Eugene J. McCarthy for President varied from state to state, as did the names of Vice-Presidential candidates running with him. In New Jersey, the Maddox Vice-Presidential candidate was Edmund O. Matzal.

The full list of candidates for President and Vice-President was:

40,830,763	Jimmy Carter and Walter F. Mondale, Democratic.
39,147,793	Gerald R. Ford and Robert Dole, Republican.
756,691	Eugene J. McCarthy with various Vice-Presidential candidates, Independent.
173,011	Roger L. MacBride and David D. Bergland, Libertarian.
170,531	Lester G. Maddox and William D. Dyke, American Independent.
160,773	Thomas J. Anderson and Rufus Shackelford, American.
91,314	Peter Camejo and Willie Mae Reid, Socialist Workers.
58,992	Gus Hall and Jarvis Tyner, Communist.
49,024	Margaret Wright and Benjamin Spock, People's.
40,043	Lyndon LaRouche and R. W. Evans, United States Labor.
15,934	Benjamin C. Bubar and Earl F. Dodge, Prohibition.
9,616	Julius Levin and Constance Blomen, Socialist Labor.
6,038	Frank P. Zeidler and J. Q. Brisben, Socialist.
361	Ernest L. Miller and Roy N. Eddy, Restoration.
36	Frank Taylor and Henry Swan, United American.

In addition to these votes, 39,861 scattered write-in votes were reported from various states and 5,108 votes were cast for "None of these Candidates" in Nevada.

UNITED STATES

PRESIDENT 1976

State	Electoral Vote Rep.	Dem.	Other	Total Vote	Republican	Democratic	Other	Plurality	Total Vote Rep.	Dem.	Major Vote Rep.	Dem.
Alabama		9		1,182,850	504,070	659,170	19,610	155,100 D	42.6%	55.7%	43.3%	56.7%
Alaska	3			123,574	71,555	44,058	7,961	27,497 R	57.9%	35.7%	61.9%	38.1%
Arizona	6			742,719	418,642	295,602	28,475	123,040 R	56.4%	39.8%	58.6%	41.4%
Arkansas		6		767,535	267,903	498,604	1,028	230,701 D	34.9%	65.0%	35.0%	65.0%
California	45			7,867,117	3,882,244	3,742,284	242,589	139,960 R	49.3%	47.6%	50.9%	49.1%
Colorado	7			1,081,554	584,367	460,353	36,834	124,014 R	54.0%	42.6%	55.9%	44.1%
Connecticut	8			1,381,526	719,261	647,895	14,370	71,366 R	52.1%	46.9%	52.6%	47.4%
Delaware		3		235,834	109,831	122,596	3,407	12,765 D	46.6%	52.0%	47.3%	52.7%
Florida		17		3,150,631	1,469,531	1,636,000	45,100	166,469 D	46.6%	51.9%	47.3%	52.7%
Georgia		12		1,467,458	483,743	979,409	4,306	495,666 D	33.0%	66.7%	33.1%	66.9%
Hawaii		4		291,301	140,003	147,375	3,923	7,372 D	48.1%	50.6%	48.7%	51.3%
Idaho	4			344,071	204,151	126,549	13,371	77,602 R	59.3%	36.8%	61.7%	38.3%
Illinois	26			4,718,914	2,364,269	2,271,295	83,350	92,974 R	50.1%	48.1%	51.0%	49.0%
Indiana	13			2,220,362	1,183,958	1,014,714	21,690	169,244 R	53.3%	45.7%	53.8%	46.2%
Iowa	8			1,279,306	632,863	619,931	26,512	12,932 R	49.5%	48.5%	50.5%	49.5%
Kansas	7			957,845	502,752	430,421	24,672	72,331 R	52.5%	44.9%	53.9%	46.1%
Kentucky		9		1,167,142	531,852	615,717	19,573	83,865 D	45.6%	52.8%	46.3%	53.7%
Louisiana		10		1,278,439	587,446	661,365	29,628	73,919 D	46.0%	51.7%	47.0%	53.0%
Maine	4			483,216	236,320	232,279	14,617	4,041 R	48.9%	48.1%	50.4%	49.6%
Maryland		10		1,439,897	672,661	759,612	7,624	86,951 D	46.7%	52.8%	47.0%	53.0%
Massachusetts		14		2,547,558	1,030,276	1,429,475	87,807	399,199 D	40.4%	56.1%	41.9%	58.1%
Michigan	21			3,653,749	1,893,742	1,696,714	63,293	197,028 R	51.8%	46.4%	52.7%	47.3%
Minnesota		10		1,949,931	819,395	1,070,440	60,096	251,045 D	42.0%	54.9%	43.4%	56.6%
Mississippi		7		769,361	366,846	381,309	21,206	14,463 D	47.7%	49.6%	49.0%	51.0%
Missouri		12		1,953,600	927,443	998,387	27,770	70,944 D	47.5%	51.1%	48.2%	51.8%
Montana	4			328,734	173,703	149,259	5,772	24,444 R	52.8%	45.4%	53.8%	46.2%
Nebraska	5			607,668	359,705	233,692	14,271	126,013 R	59.2%	38.5%	60.6%	39.4%
Nevada	3			201,876	101,273	92,479	8,124	8,794 R	50.2%	45.8%	52.3%	47.7%
New Hampshire	4			339,618	185,935	147,635	6,048	38,300 R	54.7%	43.5%	55.7%	44.3%
New Jersey	17			3,014,472	1,509,688	1,444,653	60,131	65,035 R	50.1%	47.9%	51.1%	48.9%
New Mexico	4			418,409	211,419	201,148	5,842	10,271 R	50.5%	48.1%	51.2%	48.8%
New York		41		6,534,170	3,100,791	3,389,558	43,821	288,767 D	47.5%	51.9%	47.8%	52.2%
North Carolina		13		1,678,914	741,960	927,365	9,589	185,405 D	44.2%	55.2%	44.4%	55.6%
North Dakota	3			297,188	153,470	136,078	7,640	17,392 R	51.6%	45.8%	53.0%	47.0%
Ohio		25		4,111,873	2,000,505	2,011,621	99,747	11,116 D	48.7%	48.9%	49.9%	50.1%
Oklahoma	8			1,092,251	545,708	532,442	14,101	13,266 R	50.0%	48.7%	50.6%	49.4%
Oregon	6			1,029,876	492,120	490,407	47,349	1,713 R	47.8%	47.6%	50.1%	49.9%
Pennsylvania		27		4,620,787	2,205,604	2,328,677	86,506	123,073 D	47.7%	50.4%	48.6%	51.4%
Rhode Island		4		411,170	181,249	227,636	2,285	46,387 D	44.1%	55.4%	44.3%	55.7%
South Carolina		8		802,583	346,149	450,807	5,627	104,658 D	43.1%	56.2%	43.4%	56.6%
South Dakota	4			300,678	151,505	147,068	2,105	4,437 R	50.4%	48.9%	50.7%	49.3%
Tennessee		10		1,476,345	633,969	825,879	16,497	191,910 D	42.9%	55.9%	43.4%	56.6%
Texas		26		4,071,884	1,953,300	2,082,319	36,265	129,019 D	48.0%	51.1%	48.4%	51.6%
Utah	4			541,198	337,908	182,110	21,180	155,798 R	62.4%	33.6%	65.0%	35.0%
Vermont	3			187,765	102,085	80,954	4,726	21,131 R	54.4%	43.1%	55.8%	44.2%
Virginia	12			1,697,094	836,554	813,896	46,644	22,658 R	49.3%	48.0%	50.7%	49.3%
Washington	8		1	1,555,534	777,732	717,323	60,479	60,409 R	50.0%	46.1%	52.0%	48.0%
West Virginia		6		750,964	314,760	435,914	290	121,154 D	41.9%	58.0%	41.9%	58.1%
Wisconsin		11		2,104,175	1,004,987	1,040,232	58,956	35,245 D	47.8%	49.4%	49.1%	50.9%
Wyoming	3			156,343	92,717	62,239	1,387	30,478 R	59.3%	39.8%	59.8%	40.2%
Dist. of Col.		3		168,830	27,873	137,818	3,139	109,945 D	16.5%	81.6%	16.8%	83.2%
United States	240	297	1	81,555,889	39,147,793	40,830,763	1,577,333	1,682,970 D	48.0%	50.1%	48.9%	51.1%

PRESIDENT 1980

In New York the Republican figures include Conservative votes and in a number of states candidates appeared on the ballot with variants of the party designations listed below, without any party designation, or with entirely different party names.

In several cases, Vice-Presidential nominees were different from those listed for most states and the Socialist Workers party nominee for President varied from state to state.

43,904,153	Ronald Reagan and George Bush, Republican.
35,483,883	Jimmy Carter and Walter F. Mondale, Democratic.
5,720,060	John B. Anderson and Patrick J. Lucey, Independent.
921,299	Edward E. Clark and David Koch, Libertarian.
234,294	Barry Commoner and LaDonna Harris, Citizens.
45,023	Gus Hall and Angela Davis, Communist.
41,268	John R. Rarick and Eileen M. Shearer, American Independent.
38,737	Clifton DeBerry and Matilde Zimmermann, Socialist Workers.
32,327	Ellen McCormack and Carroll Driscoll, Right to Life.
18,116	Maureen Smith and Elizabeth Barron, Peace and Freedom.
13,300	Deirdre Griswold and Larry Holmes, Workers World.
7,212	Benjamin C. Bubar and Earl F. Dodge, Statesman.
6,898	David McReynolds and Diane Drufenbrock, Socialist.
6,647	Percy L. Greaves and Frank L. Varnum, American.
6,272	Andrew Pulley and Matilde Zimmermann, Socialist Workers.
4,029	Richard Congress and Matilde Zimmermann, Socialist Workers.
3,694	Kurt Lynen and Harry Kieve, Middle Class.
1,718	Bill Gahres and J. F. Loughlin, Down With Lawyers.
1,555	Frank W. Shelton and George E. Jackson, American.
923	Martin E. Wendelken with no Vice-Presidential candidate, Independent.
296	Harley McLain and Jewelie Goeller, Natural Peoples.

In addition to these votes, 13,185 scattered write-in votes were reported from various states, 6,139 votes were cast in Minnesota for American party electors without designated national nominees, and 4,193 votes were cast for "None of these Candidates" in Nevada.

State-by-state vote details will be found in the individual state note sections and a supplementary state-by-state national table follows for all "other" candidates polling over 100,000 votes. An asterisk by the vote denotes write-in.

UNITED STATES

PRESIDENT 1980

State	Electoral Vote Rep.	Dem.	Other	Total Vote	Republican	Democratic	Other	Plurality	Percentage Total Vote Rep.	Dem.	Major Vote Rep.	Dem.
Alabama	9			1,341,929	654,192	636,730	51,007	17,462 R	48.8%	47.4%	50.7%	49.3%
Alaska	3			158,445	86,112	41,842	30,491	44,270 R	54.3%	26.4%	67.3%	32.7%
Arizona	6			873,945	529,688	246,843	97,414	282,845 R	60.6%	28.2%	68.2%	31.8%
Arkansas	6			837,582	403,164	398,041	36,377	5,123 R	48.1%	47.5%	50.3%	49.7%
California	45			8,587,063	4,524,858	3,083,661	978,544	1,441,197 R	52.7%	35.9%	59.5%	40.5%
Colorado	7			1,184,415	652,264	367,973	164,178	284,291 R	55.1%	31.1%	63.9%	36.1%
Connecticut	8			1,406,285	677,210	541,732	187,343	135,478 R	48.2%	38.5%	55.6%	44.4%
Delaware	3			235,900	111,252	105,754	18,894	5,498 R	47.2%	44.8%	51.3%	48.7%
Florida	17			3,686,930	2,046,951	1,419,475	220,504	627,476 R	55.5%	38.5%	59.1%	40.9%
Georgia		12		1,596,695	654,168	890,733	51,794	236,565 D	41.0%	55.8%	42.3%	57.7%
Hawaii		4		303,287	130,112	135,879	37,296	5,767 D	42.9%	44.8%	48.9%	51.1%
Idaho	4			437,431	290,699	110,192	36,540	180,507 R	66.5%	25.2%	72.5%	27.5%
Illinois	26			4,749,721	2,358,049	1,981,413	410,259	376,636 R	49.6%	41.7%	54.3%	45.7%
Indiana	13			2,242,033	1,255,656	844,197	142,180	411,459 R	56.0%	37.7%	59.8%	40.2%
Iowa	8			1,317,661	676,026	508,672	132,963	167,354 R	51.3%	38.6%	57.1%	42.9%
Kansas	7			979,795	566,812	326,150	86,833	240,662 R	57.9%	33.3%	63.5%	36.5%
Kentucky	9			1,294,627	635,274	616,417	42,936	18,857 R	49.1%	47.6%	50.8%	49.2%
Louisiana	10			1,548,591	792,853	708,453	47,285	84,400 R	51.2%	45.7%	52.8%	47.2%
Maine	4			523,011	238,522	220,974	63,515	17,548 R	45.6%	42.3%	51.9%	48.1%
Maryland		10		1,540,496	680,606	726,161	133,729	45,555 D	44.2%	47.1%	48.4%	51.6%
Massachusetts	14			2,524,298	1,057,631	1,053,802	412,865	3,829 R	41.9%	41.7%	50.1%	49.9%
Michigan	21			3,909,725	1,915,225	1,661,532	332,968	253,693 R	49.0%	42.5%	53.5%	46.5%
Minnesota		10		2,051,980	873,268	954,174	224,538	80,906 D	42.6%	46.5%	47.8%	52.2%
Mississippi	7			892,620	441,089	429,281	22,250	11,808 R	49.4%	48.1%	50.7%	49.3%
Missouri	12			2,099,824	1,074,181	931,182	94,461	142,999 R	51.2%	44.3%	53.6%	46.4%
Montana	4			363,952	206,814	118,032	39,106	88,782 R	56.8%	32.4%	63.7%	36.3%
Nebraska	5			640,854	419,937	166,851	54,066	253,086 R	65.5%	26.0%	71.6%	28.4%
Nevada	3			247,885	155,017	66,666	26,202	88,351 R	62.5%	26.9%	69.9%	30.1%
New Hampshire	4			383,990	221,705	108,864	53,421	112,841 R	57.7%	28.4%	67.1%	32.9%
New Jersey	17			2,975,684	1,546,557	1,147,364	281,763	399,193 R	52.0%	38.6%	57.4%	42.6%
New Mexico	4			456,971	250,779	167,826	38,366	82,953 R	54.9%	36.7%	59.9%	40.1%
New York	41			6,201,959	2,893,831	2,728,372	579,756	165,459 R	46.7%	44.0%	51.5%	48.5%
North Carolina	13			1,855,833	915,018	875,635	65,180	39,383 R	49.3%	47.2%	51.1%	48.9%
North Dakota	3			301,545	193,695	79,189	28,661	114,506 R	64.2%	26.3%	71.0%	29.0%
Ohio	25			4,283,603	2,206,545	1,752,414	324,644	454,131 R	51.5%	40.9%	55.7%	44.3%
Oklahoma	8			1,149,708	695,570	402,026	52,112	293,544 R	60.5%	35.0%	63.4%	36.6%
Oregon	6			1,181,516	571,044	456,890	153,582	114,154 R	48.3%	38.7%	55.6%	44.4%
Pennsylvania	27			4,561,501	2,261,872	1,937,540	362,089	324,332 R	49.6%	42.5%	53.9%	46.1%
Rhode Island		4		416,072	154,793	198,342	62,937	43,549 D	37.2%	47.7%	43.8%	56.2%
South Carolina	8			894,071	441,841	430,385	21,845	11,456 R	49.4%	48.1%	50.7%	49.3%
South Dakota	4			327,703	198,343	103,855	25,505	94,488 R	60.5%	31.7%	65.6%	34.4%
Tennessee	10			1,617,616	787,761	783,051	46,804	4,710 R	48.7%	48.4%	50.1%	49.9%
Texas	26			4,541,636	2,510,705	1,881,147	149,784	629,558 R	55.3%	41.4%	57.2%	42.8%
Utah	4			604,222	439,687	124,266	40,269	315,421 R	72.8%	20.6%	78.0%	22.0%
Vermont	3			213,299	94,628	81,952	36,719	12,676 R	44.4%	38.4%	53.6%	46.4%
Virginia	12			1,866,032	989,609	752,174	124,249	237,435 R	53.0%	40.3%	56.8%	43.2%
Washington	9			1,742,394	865,244	650,193	226,957	215,051 R	49.7%	37.3%	57.1%	42.9%
West Virginia		6		737,715	334,206	367,462	36,047	33,256 D	45.3%	49.8%	47.6%	52.4%
Wisconsin	11			2,273,221	1,088,845	981,584	202,792	107,261 R	47.9%	43.2%	52.6%	47.4%
Wyoming	3			176,713	110,700	49,427	16,586	61,273 R	62.6%	28.0%	69.1%	30.9%
Dist. of Col.		3		175,237	23,545	131,113	20,579	107,568 D	13.4%	74.8%	15.2%	84.8%
United States	489	49	—	86,515,221	43,904,153	35,483,883	7,127,185	8,420,270 R	50.7%	41.0%	55.3%	44.7%

UNITED STATES

OTHER VOTE 1980

State	Total Other Vote	Independent	Libertarian	Citizens	All Other
Alabama	51,007	16,481	13,318	517	20,691
Alaska	30,491	11,155	18,479		857
Arizona	97,414	76,952	18,784	551*	1,127
Arkansas	36,377	22,468	8,970	2,345	2,594
California	978,544	739,833	148,434	61,063	29,214
Colorado	164,178	130,633	25,744	5,614	2,187
Connecticut	187,343	171,807	8,570	6,130	836
Delaware	18,894	16,288	1,974	103*	529
Florida	220,504	189,692	30,524		288
Georgia	51,794	36,055	15,627	104*	8
Hawaii	37,296	32,021	3,269	1,548	458
Idaho	36,540	27,058	8,425		1,057
Illinois	410,259	346,754	38,939	10,692	13,874
Indiana	142,180	111,639	19,627	4,852	6,062
Iowa	132,963	115,633	13,123	2,273	1,934
Kansas	86,833	68,231	14,470		4,132
Kentucky	42,936	31,127	5,531	1,304	4,974
Louisiana	47,285	26,345	8,240	1,584	11,116
Maine	63,515	53,327	5,119	4,394	675
Maryland	133,729	119,537	14,192		
Massachusetts	412,865	382,539	22,038	2,056*	6,232
Michigan	332,968	275,223	41,597	11,930	4,218
Minnesota	224,538	174,990	31,592	8,407	9,549
Mississippi	22,250	12,036	5,465		4,749
Missouri	94,461	77,920	14,422	573*	1,546
Montana	39,106	29,281	9,825		
Nebraska	54,066	44,993	9,073		
Nevada	26,202	17,651	4,358		4,193
New Hampshire	53,421	49,693	2,064	1,320	344
New Jersey	281,763	234,632	20,652	8,203	18,276
New Mexico	38,366	29,459	4,365	2,202	2,340
New York	579,756	467,801	52,648	23,186	36,121
North Carolina	65,180	52,800	9,677	2,287	416
North Dakota	28,661	23,640	3,743	429	849
Ohio	324,644	254,472	49,033	8,564	12,575
Oklahoma	52,112	38,284	13,828		
Oregon	153,582	112,389	25,838	13,642	1,713
Pennsylvania	362,089	292,921	33,263	10,430	25,475
Rhode Island	62,937	59,819	2,458	67*	593
South Carolina	21,845	14,153	5,139		2,553
South Dakota	25,505	21,431	3,824		250
Tennessee	46,804	35,991	7,116	1,112	2,585
Texas	149,784	111,613	37,643	453*	75
Utah	40,269	30,284	7,226	1,009	1,750
Vermont	36,719	31,761	1,900	2,316	742
Virginia	124,249	95,418	12,821	14,024	1,986
Washington	226,957	185,073	29,213	9,403	3,268
West Virginia	36,047	31,691	4,356		
Wisconsin	202,792	160,657	29,135	7,767	5,233
Wyoming	16,586	12,072	4,514		
Dist. of Col.	20,579	16,337	1,114	1,840	1,288
United States	7,127,185	5,720,060	921,299	234,294	251,532

*Write-in

PRESIDENT 1984

In New York the Republican figures include Conservative votes and the Democratic figures include Liberal votes.

In Minnesota, the Republican candidates appear of the ballot as Independent-Republican, the Democratic as Democratic-Farmer-Labor. In many states various non-major party candidates appeared on the ballot with variations of the party designations given here, were listed as "Independent" or "Non-Party", or were carried with entirely different party lables.

The Workers World candidate for President was Gavrielle Holmes in Ohio and Rhode Island; in several states minor party Vice-Presidential candidates were different from those listed below.

The full list of candidates for President and Vice-President was:

54,455,075	Ronald Reagan and George Bush, <u>Republican</u>.
37,577,185	Walter F. Mondale and Geraldine A. Ferraro, <u>Democratic</u>.
228,314	David Bergland and James A. Lewis, <u>Libertarian</u>.
78,807	Lyndon H. LaRouche and Billy M. Davis, <u>Independent</u>.
72,200	Sonia Johnson and Richard Walton, <u>Citizens</u>.
66,336	Bob Richards and Maureen Salaman, <u>Populist</u>.
46,868	Dennis L. Serrette and Nancy Ross, <u>Alliance</u>.
36,386	Gus Hall and Angela Davis, <u>Communist</u>.
24,706	Mel Mason and Matilde Zimmermann, <u>Socialist Workers</u>.
17,985	Larry Holmes and Gloria LaRiva, <u>Workers World</u>.
13,161	Delmar Dennis and Traves Brownlee, <u>American</u>.
10,801	Ed Winn and Helen Halyard, <u>Workers League</u>.
4,242	Earl F. Dodge and Warren C. Martin, <u>Prohibition</u>.
1,486	John B. Anderson and Grace Pierce, <u>NationaNational Unity</u>.
892	Gerald Baker and Ferris Alger, <u>Big Deal</u>.
825	Arthur J. Lowery and Raymond L. Garland, <u>United Sovreign Citizens</u>.

The candidates listed above are those who appeared on the ballot in at least one state. Where identified by state authorities, write-in votes for minor party candidates are credited to their total above and listed in the individual state note sections. In addition to the votes listed, 13,623 scattered write-in votes were reported from various states and 3,950 votes were cast for "None of These Candidates" in Nevada.

UNITED STATES

PRESIDENT 1984

State	Electoral Vote Rep.	Electoral Vote Dem.	Electoral Vote Other	Total Vote	Republican	Democratic	Other	Plurality	Total Vote Rep.	Total Vote Dem.	Major Vote Rep.	Major Vote Dem.
Alabama	9			1,441,713	872,849	551,899	16,965	320,950 R	60.5%	38.3%	61.3%	38.7%
Alaska	3			207,605	138,377	62,007	7,221	76,370 R	66.7%	29.9%	69.1%	30.9%
Arizona	7			1,025,897	681,416	333,854	10,627	347,562 R	66.4%	32.5%	67.1%	32.9%
Arkansas	6			884,406	534,774	338,646	10,986	196,128 R	60.5%	38.3%	61.2%	38.8%
California	47			9,505,423	5,467,009	3,922,519	115,895	1,544,490 R	57.5%	41.3%	58.2%	41.8%
Colorado	8			1,295,380	821,817	454,975	18,588	366,842 R	63.4%	35.1%	64.4%	35.6%
Connecticut	8			1,466,900	890,877	569,597	6,426	321,280 R	60.7%	38.8%	61.0%	39.0%
Delaware	3			254,572	152,190	101,656	726	50,534 R	59.8%	39.9%	60.0%	40.0%
Florida	21			4,180,051	2,730,350	1,448,816	885	1,281,534 R	65.3%	34.7%	65.3%	34.7%
Georgia	12			1,776,120	1,068,722	706,628	770	362,094 R	60.2%	39.8%	60.2%	39.8%
Hawaii	4			335,846	185,050	147,154	3,642	37,896 R	55.1%	43.8%	55.7%	44.3%
Idaho	4			411,144	297,523	108,510	5,111	189,013 R	72.4%	26.4%	73.3%	26.7%
Illinois	24			4,819,088	2,707,103	2,086,499	25,486	620,604 R	56.2%	43.3%	56.5%	43.5%
Indiana	12			2,233,069	1,377,230	841,481	14,358	535,749 R	61.7%	37.7%	62.1%	37.9%
Iowa	8			1,319,805	703,088	605,620	11,097	97,468 R	53.3%	45.9%	53.7%	46.3%
Kansas	7			1,021,991	677,296	333,149	11,546	344,147 R	66.3%	32.6%	67.0%	33.0%
Kentucky	9			1,369,345	821,702	539,539	8,104	282,163 R	60.0%	39.4%	60.4%	39.6%
Louisiana	10			1,706,822	1,037,299	651,586	17,937	385,713 R	60.8%	38.2%	61.4%	38.6%
Maine	4			553,144	336,500	214,515	2,129	121,985 R	60.8%	38.8%	61.1%	38.9%
Maryland	10			1,675,873	879,918	787,935	8,020	91,983 R	52.5%	47.0%	52.8%	47.2%
Massachusetts	13			2,559,453	1,310,936	1,239,606	8,911	71,330 R	51.2%	48.4%	51.4%	48.6%
Michigan	20			3,801,658	2,251,571	1,529,638	20,449	721,933 R	59.2%	40.2%	59.5%	40.5%
Minnesota		10		2,084,449	1,032,603	1,036,364	15,482	3,761 D	49.5%	49.7%	49.9%	50.1%
Mississippi	7			941,104	582,377	352,192	6,535	230,185 R	61.9%	37.4%	62.3%	37.7%
Missouri	11			2,122,783	1,274,188	848,583	12	425,605 R	60.0%	40.0%	60.0%	40.0%
Montana	4			384,377	232,450	146,742	5,185	85,708 R	60.5%	38.2%	61.3%	38.7%
Nebraska	5			652,090	460,054	187,866	4,170	272,188 R	70.6%	28.8%	71.0%	29.0%
Nevada	4			286,667	188,770	91,655	6,242	97,115 R	65.8%	32.0%	67.3%	32.7%
New Hampshire	4			389,066	267,051	120,395	1,620	146,656 R	68.6%	30.9%	68.9%	31.1%
New Jersey	16			3,217,862	1,933,630	1,261,323	22,909	672,307 R	60.1%	39.2%	60.5%	39.5%
New Mexico	5			514,370	307,101	201,769	5,500	105,332 R	59.7%	39.2%	60.3%	39.7%
New York	36			6,806,810	3,664,763	3,119,609	22,438	545,154 R	53.8%	45.8%	54.0%	46.0%
North Carolina	13			2,175,361	1,346,481	824,287	4,593	522,194 R	61.9%	37.9%	62.0%	38.0%
North Dakota	3			308,971	200,336	104,429	4,206	95,907 R	64.8%	33.8%	65.7%	34.3%
Ohio	23			4,547,619	2,678,560	1,825,440	43,619	853,120 R	58.9%	40.1%	59.5%	40.5%
Oklahoma	8			1,255,676	861,530	385,080	9,066	476,450 R	68.6%	30.7%	69.1%	30.9%
Oregon	7			1,226,527	685,700	536,479	4,348	149,221 R	55.9%	43.7%	56.1%	43.9%
Pennsylvania	25			4,844,903	2,584,323	2,228,131	32,449	356,192 R	53.3%	46.0%	53.7%	46.3%
Rhode Island	4			410,492	212,080	197,106	1,306	14,974 R	51.7%	48.0%	51.8%	48.2%
South Carolina	8			968,529	615,539	344,459	8,531	271,080 R	63.6%	35.6%	64.1%	35.9%
South Dakota	3			317,867	200,267	116,113	1,487	84,154 R	63.0%	36.5%	63.3%	36.7%
Tennessee	11			1,711,994	990,212	711,714	10,068	278,498 R	57.8%	41.6%	58.2%	41.8%
Texas	29			5,397,571	3,433,428	1,949,276	14,867	1,484,152 R	63.6%	36.1%	63.8%	36.2%
Utah	5			629,656	469,105	155,369	5,182	313,736 R	74.5%	24.7%	75.1%	24.9%
Vermont	3			234,561	135,865	95,730	2,966	40,135 R	57.9%	40.8%	58.7%	41.3%
Virginia	12			2,146,635	1,337,078	796,250	13,307	540,828 R	62.3%	37.1%	62.7%	37.3%
Washington	10			1,883,910	1,051,670	807,352	24,888	244,318 R	55.8%	42.9%	56.6%	43.4%
West Virginia	6			735,742	405,483	328,125	2,134	77,358 R	55.1%	44.6%	55.3%	44.7%
Wisconsin	11			2,211,689	1,198,584	995,740	17,365	202,844 R	54.2%	45.0%	54.6%	45.4%
Wyoming	3			188,968	133,241	53,370	2,357	79,871 R	70.5%	28.2%	71.4%	28.6%
Dist. of Col.		3		211,288	29,009	180,408	1,871	151,399 D	13.7%	85.4%	13.9%	86.1%
United States	525	13	—	92,652,842	54,455,075	37,577,185	620,582	16,877,890 R	58.8%	40.6%	59.2%	40.8%

1972 PRESIDENTIAL PRIMARIES

In 1972 twenty states and the District of Columbia held preferential primaries. California, South Dakota and the District of Columbia held slate-type preferential primaries. In the other eighteen states the voter marked his ballot for his preference among the candidates listed and in some states could write in his choice if the candidate he preferred was not on the ballot. In a few states the voter had an additional option for uncommitted or for none of the listed candidates. In Alabama and New York, delegates to the national party conventions were elected in primaries, but neither state provided for a specific expression of Presidential preference by the voter, nor printed on the ballot any indication of the Presidential preference of the candidates for convention delegates.

In each state the vote used is the preferential vote if there was such a vote. In Ohio, where no specific preference vote was authorized, the major candidates ran state-wide at-large blocks of delegate candidates, and the vote given is that for the highest vote winner in each of these blocks. In several states there were both a preference and a delegate vote. In such cases the preference vote is indicated here, even though the delegate contest was controlling in terms of individuals chosen to go to the party national conventions in Miami Beach.

The tables included here give the vote in each state for those candidates on the ballot in ten or more states. Other votes, for ballot candidates or written-in, are included in the general "Other" category.

Republican candidates on the ballot in at least one state were John M. Ashbrook, Paul N. McCloskey, Richard M. Nixon, Patrick Paulsen.

Democratic candidates on the ballot in at least one state were Shirley Chisholm, Edward T. Coll, Walter E. Fauntroy, R. Vance Hartke, Hubert H. Humphrey, Henry M. Jackson, Edward M. Kennedy, John V. Lindsay, Eugene J. McCarthy, George S. McGovern, Wilbur D. Mills, Patsy Mink, Edmund S. Muskie, Terry Sanford, George C. Wallace, Samuel W. Yorty.

CALIFORNIA JUNE 6

Republican   2,058,825 Nixon slate; 224,922 Ashbrook slate; 175 scattered.

Democratic   1,550,652 McGovern slate; 1,375,064 Humphrey slate; 268,551 Wallace (write-in); 157,435 Chisholm slate; 72,701 Muskie slate; 50,745 Yorty slate; 34,203 McCarthy slate; 28,901 Jackson slate; 26,246 Lindsay slate; 20 scattered.

FLORIDA MARCH 14

Republican   360,278 Nixon; 36,617 Ashbrook; 17,312 McCloskey.

Democratic   526,651 Wallace; 234,658 Humphrey; 170,156 Jackson; 112,523 Muskie; 82,386 Lindsay; 78,232 McGovern; 43,989 Chisholm; 5,847 McCarthy; 4,539 Mills; 3,009 Hartke; 2,564 Yorty.

ILLINOIS MARCH 21

Republican   No Presidential candidates on the ballot. Write-in votes were 32,550 Nixon; 170 Ashbrook; 47 McCloskey; 802 scattered.

Democratic   766,914 Muskie; 444,260 McCarthy; 7,017 Wallace (write-in); 3,687 McGovern (write-in); 1,476 Humphrey (write-in); 777 Chisholm (write-in); 442 Jackson (write-in); 242 Kennedy (write-in); 118 Lindsay (write-in); 211 scattered.

INDIANA MAY 2

Republican   417,069 Nixon, unopposed.

Democratic   354,244 Humphrey; 309,495 Wallace; 87,719 Muskie.

1972 PRESIDENTIAL PRIMARIES

MARYLAND MAY 16

Republican   99,308 Nixon; 9,223 McCloskey; 6,718 Ashbrook.

Democratic   219,687 Wallace; 151,981 Humphrey; 126,978 McGovern; 17,728 Jackson; 13,584 Yorty; 13,363 Muskie; 12,602 Chisholm; 4,776 Mills; 4,691 McCarthy; 2,168 Lindsay; 573 Mink.

MASSACHUSETTS APRIL 25

Republican   99,150 Nixon; 16,435 McCloskey; 4,864 Ashbrook; 1,690 scattered.

Democratic   325,673 McGovern; 131,709 Muskie; 48,929 Humphrey; 45,807 Wallace; 22,398 Chisholm; 19,441 Mills; 8,736 McCarthy; 8,499 Jackson; 2,348 Kennedy (write-in); 2,107 Lindsay; 874 Hartke; 646 Yorty; 589 Coll; 760 scattered.

MICHIGAN MAY 16

Republican   321,652 Nixon; 9,691 McCloskey; 5,370 Uncommitted; 30 scattered.

Democratic   809,239 Wallace; 425,694 McGovern; 249,798 Humphrey; 44,090 Chisholm; 38,701 Muskie; 10,700 Uncommitted; 6,938 Jackson; 2,862 Hartke; 51 scattered.

NEBRASKA MAY 9

Republican   179,464 Nixon; 9,011 McCloskey; 4,996 Ashbrook; 801 scattered.

Democratic   79,309 McGovern; 65,968 Humphrey; 23,912 Wallace; 6,886 Muskie; 5,276 Jackson; 3,459 Yorty; 3,194 McCarthy; 1,763 Chisholm; 1,244 Lindsay; 377 Mills; 293 Kennedy (write-in); 249 Hartke; 207 scattered.

NEW HAMPSHIRE MARCH 7

Republican   79,239 Nixon; 23,190 McCloskey; 11,362 Ashbrook; 1,211 Paulsen; 2,206 scattered.

Democratic   41,235 Muskie; 33,007 McGovern; 5,401 Yorty; 3,563 Mills (write-in); 2,417 Hartke; 954 Kennedy (write-in); 348 Humphrey (write-in); 280 Coll; 197 Jackson (write-in); 175 Wallace (write-in); 1,277 scattered.

NEW JERSEY JUNE 6

Republican   No Presidential candidates on the ballot.

Democratic   51,433 Chisholm; 25,401 Sanford.

NEW MEXICO JUNE 6

Republican   49,067 Nixon; 3,367 McCloskey; 3,035 None of the Names Shown.

Democratic   51,011 McGovern; 44,843 Wallace; 39,768 Humphrey; 6,411 Muskie; 4,236 Jackson; 3,819 None of the Names Shown; 3,205 Chisholm.

1972 PRESIDENTIAL PRIMARIES

NORTH CAROLINA MAY 6

Republican   159,167 Nixon; 8,732 McCloskey.

Democratic   413,518 Wallace; 306,014 Sanford; 61,723 Chisholm; 30,739 Muskie; 9,416 Jackson.

OHIO MAY 2

Republican   692,828 Nixon, unopposed.

Democratic   499,680 Humphrey; 480,320 McGovern; 107,806 Muskie; 98,498 Jackson; 26,026 McCarthy.

OREGON MAY 23

Republican   231,151 Nixon; 29,365 McCloskey; 16,696 Ashbrook; 4,798 scattered.

Democratic   205,328 McGovern; 81,868 Wallace; 51,163 Humphrey; 22,042 Jackson; 12,673 Kennedy; 10,244 Muskie; 8,943 McCarthy; 6,500 Mink; 5,082 Lindsay; 2,975 Chisholm; 1,208 Mills; 618 scattered.

PENNSYLVANIA APRIL 25

Republican   No Presidential candidates on the ballot. Write-in votes were 153,886 Nixon; 30,915 scattered. Of the latter, most were for candidates for the Democratic nomination, including 20,472 Wallace.

Democratic   481,900 Humphrey; 292,437 Wallace; 280,861 McGovern; 279,983 Muskie; 38,767 Jackson; 306 Chisholm (write-in); 585 scattered.

RHODE ISLAND MAY 23

Republican   4,953 Nixon; 337 McCloskey; 175 Ashbrook; 146 Uncommitted.

Democratic   15,603 McGovern; 7,838 Muskie; 7,701 Humphrey; 5,802 Wallace; 490 Uncommitted; 245 McCarthy; 138 Jackson; 41 Mills; 6 Yorty.

SOUTH DAKOTA JUNE 6

Republican   52,820 Nixon slate, unopposed.

Democratic   28,017 McGovern slate, unopposed.

TENNESSEE MAY 4

Republican   109,696 Nixon; 2,419 Ashbrook; 2,370 McCloskey; 4 scattered.

Democratic   335,858 Wallace; 78,350 Humphrey; 35,551 McGovern; 18,809 Chisholm; 9,634 Muskie; 5,896 Jackson; 2,543 Mills; 2,267 McCarthy; 1,621 Hartke; 1,476 Lindsay; 692 Yorty; 24 scattered.

WEST VIRGINIA MAY 9

Republican   No Presidential candidates on the ballot.

Democratic   246,596 Humphrey; 121,888 Wallace.

1972 PRESIDENTIAL PRIMARIES

WISCONSIN APRIL 4

Republican   277,601 Nixon; 3,651 McCloskey; 2,604 Ashbrook; 2,315 None of the Names Shown; 273 scattered.

Democratic   333,528 McGovern; 248,676 Wallace; 233,748 Humphrey; 115,811 Muskie; 88,068 Jackson; 75,579 Lindsay; 15,543 McCarthy; 9,198 Chisholm; 2,450 None of the Names Shown; 2,349 Yorty; 1,213 Mink; 913 Mills; 766 Hartke; 183 Kennedy (write-in); 559 scattered.

DISTRICT OF COLUMBIA MAY 2

Republican   No slates entered.

Democratic   21,217 Fauntroy slate; 8,343 Uncommitted slate.

1972 REPUBLICAN PREFERENCE PRIMARIES

Date		State	Total Vote	Ashbrook	McCloskey	Nixon	Other
March	7	New Hampshire	117,208	11,362	23,190	79,239	3,417
	14	Florida	414,207	36,617	17,312	360,278	—
	21	Illinois	33,569	170	47	32,550	802
April	4	Wisconsin	286,444	2,604	3,651	277,601	2,588
	25	Massachusetts	122,139	4,864	16,435	99,150	1,690
	25	Pennsylvania	184,801	—	—	153,886	30,915
May	2	District of Columbia	No Slates Entered				
	2	Indiana	417,069	—	—	417,069	—
	2	Ohio	692,828	—	—	692,828	—
	4	Tennessee	114,489	2,419	2,370	109,696	4
	6	North Carolina	167,899	—	8,732	159,167	—
	9	Nebraska	194,272	4,996	9,011	179,464	801
	9	West Virginia	No Candidates Entered				
	16	Maryland	115,249	6,718	9,223	99,308	—
	16	Michigan	336,743	—	9,691	321,652	5,400
	23	Rhode Island	5,611	175	337	4,953	146
	23	Oregon	282,010	16,696	29,365	231,151	4,798
June	6	California	2,283,922	224,922	—	2,058,825	175
	6	New Jersey	No Candidates Entered				
	6	New Mexico	55,469	—	3,367	49,067	3,035
	6	South Dakota	52,820	—	—	52,820	—
			5,876,749	311,543	132,731	5,378,704	53,771

Other vote includes 1,211 Paulsen; 52,559 Uncommitted, None, and scattered.

1972 DEMOCRATIC PREFERENCE PRIMARIES

Date		State	Total Vote	Chisholm	Humphrey	Jackson	McCarthy	McGovern	Muskie	Wallace	Other
March	7	New Hampshire	88,854	—	348	197	—	33,007	41,235	175	13,892
	14	Florida	1,264,554	43,989	234,658	170,156	5,847	78,232	112,523	526,651	92,498
	21	Illinois	1,225,144	777	1,476	442	444,260	3,687	766,914	7,017	571
April	4	Wisconsin	1,128,584	9,198	233,748	88,068	15,543	333,528	115,811	248,676	84,012
	25	Massachusetts	618,516	22,398	48,929	8,499	8,736	325,673	131,709	45,807	26,765
	25	Pennsylvania	1,374,839	306	481,900	38,767	—	280,861	279,983	292,437	585
May	2	District of Columbia	29,560	—	—	—	—	—	—	—	29,560
	2	Indiana	751,458	—	354,244	—	—	—	87,719	309,495	—
	2	Ohio	1,212,330	—	499,680	98,498	26,026	480,320	107,806	—	—
	4	Tennessee	492,721	18,809	78,350	5,896	2,267	35,551	9,634	335,858	6,356
	6	North Carolina	821,410	61,723	—	9,416	—	—	30,739	413,518	306,014
	9	Nebraska	192,137	1,763	65,968	5,276	3,194	79,309	6,886	23,912	5,829
	9	West Virginia	368,484	—	246,596	—	—	—	—	121,888	—
	16	Maryland	568,131	12,602	151,981	17,728	4,691	126,978	13,363	219,687	21,101
	16	Michigan	1,588,073	44,090	249,798	6,938	—	425,694	38,701	809,239	13,613
	23	Rhode Island	37,864	—	7,701	138	245	15,603	7,838	5,802	537
	23	Oregon	408,644	2,975	51,163	22,042	8,943	205,328	10,244	81,868	26,081
June	6	California	3,564,518	157,435	1,375,064	28,901	34,203	1,550,652	72,701	268,551	77,011
	6	New Jersey	76,834	51,433	—	—	—	—	—	—	25,401
	6	New Mexico	153,293	3,205	39,768	4,236	—	51,011	6,411	44,843	3,819
	6	South Dakota	28,017	—	—	—	—	28,017	—	—	—
			15,993,965	430,703	4,121,372	505,198	553,955	4,053,451	1,840,217	3,755,424	733,645

Other vote includes 331,415 Sanford; 196,406 Lindsay; 79,446 Yorty; 37,401 Mills; 21,217 Fauntroy; 16,693 Kennedy; 11,798 Hartke; 8,286 Mink; 869 Coll; 30,114 Uncommitted, None, and scattered.

1976 PRESIDENTIAL PRIMARIES

In 1976 twenty-six states and the District of Columbia held preferential primaries. California and South Dakota held slate-type preferential primaries. In the District and the other twenty-four states the voter marked his ballot for his preference among the candidates listed and in some states could write in his choice if the candidate he preferred was not on the ballot. In a few states the voter had an additional option for uncommitted, no preference or none. In Alabama, New York and Texas delegates to the national party conventions were elected in primaries, but none of these states provided for a specific expression of Presidential preference by the voter save by an indication of the Presidential preference of the candidates for convention delegates.

In each state the vote used is the preferential vote if there was such a vote. In Ohio, the vote is for delegates at-large pledged to specific candidates and elected as a group. In several states there were both a preference and a delegate vote. In such cases the preference vote is indicated here, even though the delegate contest was controlling in terms of individuals chosen to go to the party national conventions in Kansas City and New York City.

The tables included here give the major party primary vote in each state for those candidates who were on the ballot in at least ten states or who polled a minimum of one percent of their party's total national Presidential preference vote.

Republican candidates on the ballot in at least one state were Lar Daly, Gerald R. Ford, Tommy Klein and Ronald Reagan.

Democratic candidates on the ballot in at least one state were Frank Ahern, Stanley N. Arnold, Birch Bayh, Lloyd Bentsen, Arthur O. Blessitt, Frank Bona, Edmund G. Brown, Jr., Robert C. Byrd, Jimmy Carter, Frank Church, Billy Joe Clegg, Gertrude W. Donahey, Abram Eisenman, John S. Gonas, Jesse Gray, Fred R. Harris, Hubert H. Humphrey, Henry M. Jackson, Robert L. Kelleher, Edward M. Kennedy, Rick Loewenherz, Frank Lomento, Floyd L. Lunger, Ellen McCormack, Fifi Rockefeller, George Roden, Ray Rollinson, Terry Sanford, Bernard B. Schechter, Milton Shapp, R. Sargent Shriver, Morris K. Udall and George C. Wallace.

ARKANSAS MAY 25

Republican   20,628 Reagan; 11,430 Ford; 483 Uncommitted.

Democratic   314,306 Carter; 83,005 Wallace; 57,152 Uncommitted; 37,783 Udall; 9,554 Jackson. Original uncorrected canvass gave the Uncommitted vote as 57,067.

CALIFORNIA JUNE 8

Republican   1,604,836 Reagan; 845,655 Ford; 20 scattered write-ins.

Democratic   2,013,210 Brown slate; 697,092 Carter slate; 250,581 Church slate; 171,501 Udall slate; 102,292 Wallace slate; 78,595 Uncommitted slate; 38,634 Jackson slate; 29,242 McCormack slate; 16,920 Harris slate; 11,419 Bayh slate; 215 scattered write-ins.

American Independent   3,447 Shea; 2,922 Rarick; 2,447 Watson; 1,719 Procell; 1,523 Goodloe; 7 scattered write-ins.

Peace & Freedom   4,351 Wright; 1,372 Zeidler; 12 scattered write-ins.

FLORIDA MARCH 9

Republican   321,982 Ford; 287,837 Reagan.

Democratic   448,844 Carter; 396,820 Wallace; 310,944 Jackson; 37,626 No Preference; 32,198 Shapp; 27,235 Udall; 8,750 Bayh; 7,889 Blessitt; 7,595 McCormack; 7,084 Shriver; 5,397 Harris; 5,042 Byrd; 4,906 Church.

1976 PRESIDENTIAL PRIMARIES

GEORGIA MAY 4

Republican   128,671 Reagan; 59,801 Ford.

Democratic   419,272 Carter; 57,594 Wallace; 9,755 Udall; 3,628 Byrd; 3,358 Jackson; 2,477 Church; 1,487 Ahern; 1,378 Shriver; 824 Bayh; 699 Harris; 635 McCormack; 351 Eisenman; 277 Bentsen; 263 Bona; 181 Shapp; 153 Roden; 139 Kelleher.

IDAHO MAY 25

Republican   66,743 Reagan; 22,323 Ford; 727 Uncommitted.

Democratic   58,570 Church; 8,818 Carter; 1,700 Humphrey; 1,453 Brown (write-in); 1,115 Wallace; 981 Udall; 964 Uncommitted; 485 Jackson; 319 Harris.

American   409 Rarick; 261 Anderson; 92 Uncommitted.

ILLINOIS MARCH 16

Republican   456,750 Ford; 311,295 Reagan; 7,582 Daly; 266 scattered write-ins.

Democratic   630,915 Carter; 361,798 Wallace; 214,024 Shriver; 98,862 Harris; 6,315 scattered write-ins.

INDIANA MAY 4

Republican   323,779 Reagan; 307,513 Ford.

Democratic   417,480 Carter; 93,121 Wallace; 72,080 Jackson; 31,708 McCormack.

KENTUCKY MAY 25

Republican   67,976 Ford; 62,683 Reagan; 1,781 Uncommitted; 1,088 Klein.

Democratic   181,690 Carter; 51,540 Wallace; 33,262 Udall; 17,061 McCormack; 11,962 Uncommitted; 8,186 Jackson; 2,305 Fifi Rockefeller.

MARYLAND MAY 18

Republican   96,291 Ford; 69,680 Reagan.

Democratic   286,672 Brown; 219,404 Carter; 32,790 Udall; 24,176 Wallace; 13,956 Jackson; 7,907 McCormack; 6,841 Harris.

MASSACHUSETTS MARCH 2

Republican   115,375 Ford; 63,555 Reagan; 6,000 No Preference; 3,519 scattered write-ins.

Democratic   164,393 Jackson; 130,440 Udall; 123,112 Wallace; 101,948 Carter; 55,701 Harris; 53,252 Shriver; 34,963 Bayh; 25,772 McCormack; 21,693 Shapp; 9,804 No Preference; 7,851 Humphrey (write-in); 1,623 Kennedy (write-in); 1,603 Kelleher; 364 Bentsen; 351 Sanford; 2,951 scattered write-ins.

American   No candidate names were printed on the ballot; there were 595 write-in votes including 86 for Wallace. In addition there were 98 No Preference votes.

1976 PRESIDENTIAL PRIMARIES

MICHIGAN MAY 18

Republican   690,180 Ford; 364,052 Reagan; 8,473 Uncommitted; 109 scattered write-ins.

Democratic   307,559 Carter; 305,134 Udall; 49,204 Wallace; 15,853 Uncommitted; 10,332 Jackson; 7,623 McCormack; 5,738 Shriver; 4,081 Harris; 3,142 scattered write-ins.

MONTANA JUNE 1

Republican   56,683 Reagan; 31,100 Ford; 1,996 No Preference.

Democratic   63,448 Church; 26,329 Carter; 6,708 Udall; 3,820 No Preference; 3,680 Wallace; 2,856 Jackson.

NEBRASKA MAY 11

Republican   113,493 Reagan; 94,542 Ford; 379 scattered write-ins.

Democratic   67,297 Church; 65,833 Carter; 12,685 Humphrey; 7,199 Kennedy; 6,033 McCormack; 5,567 Wallace; 4,688 Udall; 2,642 Jackson; 811 Harris; 407 Bayh; 384 Shriver; 1,467 scattered write-ins.

NEVADA MAY 25

Republican   31,637 Reagan; 13,747 Ford; 2,365 "None of these Candidates".

Democratic   39,671 Brown; 17,567 Carter; 6,778 Church; 4,603 "None of these Candidates"; 2,490 Wallace; 2,237 Udall; 1,896 Jackson.

NEW HAMPSHIRE FEBRUARY 24

Republican   55,156 Ford; 53,569 Reagan; 2,949 scattered write-ins.

Democratic   23,373 Carter; 18,710 Udall; 12,510 Bayh; 8,863 Harris; 6,743 Shriver; 4,596 Humphrey (write-in); 1,857 Jackson (write-in); 1,061 Wallace (write-in); 1,007 McCormack; 828 Blessitt; 371 Arnold; 174 Clegg; 173 Schechter; 135 Bona; 87 Kelleher; 53 Sanford; 49 Loewenherz; 1,791 scattered write-ins.

NEW JERSEY JUNE 8

Republican   242,122 Ford, unopposed.

Democratic   210,655 Carter; 49,034 Church; 31,820 Jackson; 31,183 Wallace; 21,774 McCormack; 3,935 Lunger; 3,574 Gray; 3,555 Lomento; 3,021 Rollinson; 2,288 Gonas.

NORTH CAROLINA MARCH 23

Republican   101,468 Reagan; 88,897 Ford; 3,362 No Preference.

Democratic   324,437 Carter; 210,166 Wallace; 25,749 Jackson; 22,850 No Preference; 14,032 Udall; 5,923 Harris; 1,675 Bentsen.

OHIO JUNE 8

Republican   516,111 Ford; 419,646 Reagan.

Democratic   593,130 Carter; 240,342 Udall; 157,884 Church; 63,953 Wallace; 43,661 Donahey; 35,404 Jackson.

1976 PRESIDENTIAL PRIMARIES

OREGON MAY 25

Republican   150,181 Ford; 136,691 Reagan; 11,663 scattered write-ins.

Democratic   145,394 Church; 115,310 Carter; 106,812 Brown (write-ins); 22,488 Humphrey; 11,747 Udall; 10,983 Kennedy; 5,797 Wallace; 5,298 Jackson; 3,753 McCormack; 1,344 Harris; 743 Bayh; 2,963 scattered write-ins.

PENNSYLVANIA APRIL 27

Republican   733,472 Ford; 40,510 Reagan (write-in); 22,678 scattered write-ins.

Democratic   511,905 Carter; 340,340 Jackson; 259,166 Udall; 155,902 Wallace; 38,800 McCormack; 32,947 Shapp; 15,320 Bayh; 13,067 Harris; 12,563 Humphrey (write-in); 5,032 scattered write-ins.

Constitutional 1,333 Cunningham; 87 scattered write-ins.

RHODE ISLAND JUNE 1

Republican   9,365 Ford; 4,480 Reagan; 507 Uncommitted.

Democratic   19,035 Uncommitted; 18,237 Carter; 16,423 Church; 2,543 Udall; 2,468 McCormack; 756 Jackson; 507 Wallace; 247 Bayh; 132 Shapp.

SOUTH DAKOTA JUNE 1

Republican   43,068 Reagan slate; 36,976 Ford slate; 4,033 No Preference slate.

Democratic   24,186 Carter slate; 19,510 Udall slate; 7,871 No Preference slate; 4,561 McCormack slate; 1,412 Wallace slate; 573 Harris slate; 558 Jackson slate.

TENNESSEE MAY 25

Republican   120,685 Ford; 118,997 Reagan; 2,756 Uncommitted; 97 scattered write-ins.

Democratic   259,243 Carter; 36,495 Wallace; 12,420 Udall; 8,026 Church; 6,148 Uncommitted; 5,672 Jackson; 1,782 McCormack; 1,628 Harris; 1,556 Brown (write-in); 507 Shapp; 109 Humphrey (write-in); 492 scattered write-ins, including all 424 write-ins in Shelby County.

VERMONT MARCH 2

Republican   27,014 Ford; 4,892 Reagan (write-in); 251 scattered.

Democratic   16,335 Carter; 10,699 Shriver; 4,893 Harris; 3,324 McCormack; 3,463 scattered.

Liberty Union   965 Wright; 150 scattered.

WEST VIRGINIA MAY 11

Republican   88,386 Ford; 67,306 Reagan.

Democratic   331,639 Byrd; 40,938 Wallace.

1976 PRESIDENTIAL PRIMARIES

WISCONSIN APRIL 6

Republican   326,869 Ford; 262,126 Reagan; 2,234 "None of the Names Shown"; 583 scattered write-ins.

Democratic   271,220 Carter; 263,771 Udall; 92,460 Wallace; 47,605 Jackson; 26,982 McCormack; 8,185 Harris; 7,154 "None of the Names Shown"; 5,097 Shriver; 1,730 Bentsen; 1,255 Bayh; 596 Shapp; 14,473 scattered write-ins.

American   No candidate names were printed on the ballot; there were 1,033 write-in votes.

DISTRICT OF COLUMBIA MAY 4

Republican   No Presidential candidates on the ballot.

Democratic   10,521 Carter; 10,149 Uncommitted (Fauntroy slate); 6,999 Udall; 5,161 Uncommitted (Washington slate); 461 Harris.

1976 REPUBLICAN PREFERENCE PRIMARIES

Date		State	Total Vote	Ford	Reagan	Other
February	24	New Hampshire	111,674	55,156	53,569	2,949
March	2	Massachusetts	188,449	115,375	63,555	9,519
	2	Vermont	32,157	27,014	4,892	251
	9	Florida	609,819	321,982	287,837	—
	16	Illinois	775,893	456,750	311,295	7,848
	23	North Carolina	193,727	88,897	101,468	3,362
April	6	Wisconsin	591,812	326,869	262,126	2,817
	27	Pennsylvania	796,660	733,472	40,510	22,678
May	4	District of Columbia	No Primary			
	4	Georgia	188,472	59,801	128,671	—
	4	Indiana	631,292	307,513	323,779	—
	11	Nebraska	208,414	94,542	113,493	379
	11	West Virginia	155,692	88,386	67,306	—
	18	Maryland	165,971	96,291	69,680	—
	18	Michigan	1,062,814	690,180	364,052	8,582
	25	Arkansas	32,541	11,430	20,628	483
	25	Idaho	89,793	22,323	66,743	727
	25	Kentucky	133,528	67,976	62,683	2,869
	25	Nevada	47,749	13,747	31,637	2,365
	25	Oregon	298,535	150,181	136,691	11,663
	25	Tennessee	242,535	120,685	118,997	2,853
June	1	Montana	89,779	31,100	56,683	1,996
	1	Rhode Island	14,352	9,365	4,480	507
	1	South Dakota	84,077	36,976	43,068	4,033
	8	California	2,450,511	845,655	1,604,836	20
	8	New Jersey	242,122	242,122	—	—
	8	Ohio	935,757	516,111	419,646	—
			10,374,125	5,529,899	4,758,325	85,901

Other vote includes 7,582 Daly; 1,088 Klein; 42,514 scattered write-ins; 15,391 No Preference; 14,727 Uncommitted; 2,365 "None of These Candidates"; 2,234 "None of the Names Shown".

1976 DEMOCRATIC PREFERENCE PRIMARIES

Date	State	Total Vote	Bayh	Brown	Byrd	Carter	Church	Harris	Jackson	McCormack	Shriver	Udall	Wallace	Other
February 24	New Hampshire	82,381	12,510	—	—	23,373	—	8,863	1,857	1,007	6,743	18,710	1,061	8,257
March 2	Massachusetts	735,821	34,963	—	—	101,948	—	55,701	164,393	25,772	53,252	130,440	123,112	46,240
2	Vermont	38,714	—	—	—	16,335	—	4,893	—	3,324	10,699	—	—	3,463
9	Florida	1,300,330	8,750	—	5,042	448,844	4,906	5,397	310,944	7,595	7,084	27,235	396,820	77,713
16	Illinois	1,311,914	—	—	—	630,915	—	98,862	—	—	214,024	—	361,798	6,315
23	North Carolina	604,832	—	—	—	324,437	—	5,923	25,749	—	—	14,032	210,166	24,525
April 6	Wisconsin	740,528	1,255	—	—	271,220	—	8,185	47,605	26,982	5,097	263,771	92,460	23,953
27	Pennsylvania	1,385,042	15,320	—	—	511,905	—	13,067	340,340	38,800	—	259,166	155,902	50,542
May 4	District of Columbia	33,291	—	—	—	10,521	—	461	—	—	—	6,999	—	15,310
4	Georgia	502,471	824	—	3,628	419,272	2,477	699	3,358	635	1,378	9,755	57,594	2,851
4	Indiana	614,389	—	—	—	417,480	—	—	72,080	31,708	—	—	93,121	—
11	Nebraska	175,013	407	—	—	65,833	67,297	811	2,642	6,033	384	4,688	5,567	21,351
11	West Virginia	372,577	—	—	331,639	—	—	—	—	—	—	—	40,938	—
18	Maryland	591,746	—	286,672	—	219,404	—	6,841	13,956	7,907	—	32,790	24,176	—
18	Michigan	708,666	—	—	—	307,559	—	4,081	10,332	7,623	5,738	305,134	49,204	18,995
25	Arkansas	501,800	—	—	—	314,306	—	—	9,554	—	—	37,783	83,005	57,152
25	Idaho	74,405	—	1,453	—	8,818	58,570	319	485	—	—	981	1,115	2,664
25	Kentucky	306,006	—	—	—	181,690	—	—	8,186	17,061	—	33,262	51,540	14,267
25	Nevada	75,242	—	39,671	—	17,567	6,778	—	1,896	—	—	2,237	2,490	4,603
25	Oregon	432,632	743	106,812	—	115,310	145,394	1,344	5,298	3,753	—	11,747	5,797	36,434
25	Tennessee	334,078	—	1,556	—	259,243	8,026	1,628	5,672	1,782	—	12,420	36,495	7,256
June 1	Montana	106,841	—	—	—	26,329	63,448	—	2,856	—	—	6,708	3,680	3,820
1	Rhode Island	60,348	247	—	—	18,237	16,423	—	756	2,468	—	2,543	507	19,167
1	South Dakota	58,671	—	—	—	24,186	—	573	558	4,561	—	19,510	1,412	7,871
8	California	3,409,701	11,419	2,013,210	—	697,092	250,581	16,920	38,634	29,242	—	171,501	102,292	78,810
8	New Jersey	360,839	—	—	—	210,655	49,034	—	31,820	21,774	—	—	31,183	16,373
8	Ohio	1,134,374	—	—	—	593,130	157,884	—	35,404	—	—	240,342	63,953	43,661
		16,052,652	86,438	2,449,374	340,309	6,235,609	830,818	234,568	1,134,375	238,027	304,399	1,611,754	1,995,388	591,593

Other vote includes 88,254 Shapp; 61,992 Humphrey; 43,661 Donahey; 19,805 Kennedy; 8,717 Blessitt; 4,046 Bentsen; 3,935 Lunger; 3,574 Gray; 3,555 Lomento; 3,021 Rollinson; 2,305 Fifi Rockefeller; 2,288 Gonas; 1,829 Kelleher; 1,487 Ahern; 404 Sanford; 398 Bona; 371 Arnold; 351 Eisenman; 174 Clegg; 173 Schechter; 153 Roden; 49 Loewenherz; 205,019 Uncommitted; 81,971 No Preference; 42,304 scattered write-ins; 7,154 "None of the Names Shown"; 4,603 "None of These Candidates".

1980 PRESIDENTIAL PRIMARIES

In 1980 thirty-five states and the District of Columbia held Presidential primaries. California Democrats and South Dakota Republicans and Democrats held slate-type preferential primaries. In New York, Democrats had a Presidential preference, but Republicans held primaries for the selection of delegates only, without indication of Presidential preference. In Mississippi, Republicans elected delegates by Congressional Districts pledged to candidates and the vote indicated is for the highest of each slate's candidates in each CD. In Arkansas, the Republicans did not hold a primary although Democrats did. In South Carolina, the Democrats did not hold a primary but Republicans did. The vote in Ohio is for delegates at-large pledged to specific candidates and elected as a group.

The tables included here give the major party primary vote in each state for those candidates who were on the ballot in at least ten states and polled at least 25,000 votes.

Republican candidates on the ballot in at least one state were John B. Anderson, Donald Badgley, Howard H. Baker, Jr., Nick Belluso, George Bush, William E. Carlson, Alvin G. Carris, John B. Connally, Philip M. Crane, Robert Dole, Benjamin Fernandez, Alvin J. Jacobson, V. A. Kelley, C. Leon Pickett, Ronald Reagan, Harold E. Stassen, R. W. Yeager.

Democratic candidates on the ballot in at least one state were Frank Ahern, Edmund G. Brown, Jr., Jimmy Carter, Cliff Finch, Richard B. Kay, Edward M. Kennedy, Lyndon H. LaRouche, Bob Maddox, William L. Nuckols, Don Reaux, Ray Rollinson.

ALABAMA MARCH 11

Republican   147,352 Reagan; 54,730 Bush; 5,099 Crane; 1,963 Baker; 1,077 Connally; 544 Stassen; 447 Dole; 141 Belluso.

Democratic   193,734 Carter; 31,382 Kennedy; 9,529 Brown; 1,670 Uncommitted; 609 Nuckols; 540 Maddox.

ARKANSAS MAY 27

Republican   No Presidential primary held.

Democratic   269,375 Carter; 80,904 Uncommitted; 78,542 Kennedy; 19,469 Finch.

CALIFORNIA JUNE 3

Republican   2,057,923 Reagan; 349,315 Anderson; 125,113 Bush; 21,465 Crane; 10,242 Fernandez; 14 scattered.

Democratic   1,507,142 Kennedy slate; 1,266,276 Carter slate; 382,759 Unpledged slate; 135,962 Brown slate; 71,779 LaRouche slate; 51 scattered.

American Independent   10,838 Downey; 10,358 Rarick; 9 scattered.

Peace & Freedom   4,071 Spock; 2,494 Hall; 1,596 McReynolds; 1,330 Griswold; 3 scattered.

CONNECTICUT MARCH 25

Republican   70,367 Bush; 61,735 Reagan; 40,354 Anderson; 4,256 Uncommitted; 2,446 Baker; 1,887 Crane; 598 Connally; 333 Dole; 308 Fernandez.

Democratic   98,662 Kennedy; 87,207 Carter; 13,403 Uncommitted; 5,617 LaRouche; 5,386 Brown.

FLORIDA MARCH 11

Republican   345,699 Reagan; 185,996 Bush; 56,636 Anderson; 12,000 Crane; 6,345 Baker; 4,958 Connally, 1,377 Stassen; 1,086 Dole; 898 Fernandez.

Democratic   666,321 Carter; 254,727 Kennedy; 104,321 No Preference; 53,474 Brown; 19,160 Kay.

1980 PRESIDENTIAL PRIMARIES

GEORGIA MARCH 11

Republican   146,500 Reagan; 25,293 Bush; 16,853 Anderson; 6,308 Crane; 2,388 Connally; 1,571 Baker; 809 Fernandez; 249 Dole; 200 Stassen.

Democratic   338,772 Carter; 32,315 Kennedy; 7,255 Brown; 3,707 Uncommitted; 1,378 Finch; 840 Kay; 513 LaRouche.

IDAHO MAY 27

Republican   111,868 Reagan; 13,130 Anderson; 5,416 Bush; 3,441 Uncommitted; 1,024 Crane.

Democratic   31,383 Carter; 11,087 Kennedy; 5,934 Uncommitted; 2,078 Brown.

American   97 Rarick; 63 Uncommitted.

Libertarian   88 Clark; 39 Uncommitted.

ILLINOIS MARCH 18

Republican   547,355 Reagan; 415,193 Anderson; 124,057 Bush; 24,865 Crane; 7,051 Baker; 4,548 Connally; 3,757 Kelley; 1,843 Dole; 1,412 scattered.

Democratic   780,787 Carter; 359,875 Kennedy; 39,168 Brown; 19,192 LaRouche; 2,045 scattered.

INDIANA MAY 6

Republican   419,016 Reagan; 92,955 Bush; 56,342 Anderson.

Democratic   398,949 Carter; 190,492 Kennedy.

KANSAS APRIL 1

Republican   179,739 Reagan; 51,924 Anderson; 35,838 Bush; 3,603 Baker; 2,067 Connally; 1,650 Fernandez; 1,367 Crane; 1,063 Yeager; 483 Carris; 383 Stassen; 311 Carlson; 244 Badgley; 6,726 "None of the Names Shown".

Democratic   109,807 Carter; 61,318 Kennedy; 9,434 Brown; 632 Maddox; 629 Finch; 571 Ahern; 364 Rollinson; 11,163 "None of the Names Shown".

KENTUCKY MAY 27

Republican   78,072 Reagan; 6,861 Bush; 4,791 Anderson; 3,084 Uncommitted; 1,223 Stassen; 764 Fernandez.

Democratic   160,819 Carter; 55,167 Kennedy; 19,219 Uncommitted; 2,609 Kay; 2,517 Finch.

LOUISIANA APRIL 5

Republican   31,212 Reagan; 7,818 Bush; 2,221 Uncommitted; 155 Belluso; 126 Stassen; 84 Fernandez; 67 Pickett.

Democratic   199,956 Carter; 80,797 Kennedy; 41,614 Uncommitted; 16,774 Brown; 11,153 Finch; 3,362 Kay; 2,830 Maddox; 2,255 Reaux.

MARYLAND MAY 13

Republican   80,557 Reagan; 68,389 Bush; 16,244 Anderson; 2,113 Crane.

Democratic   226,528 Carter; 181,091 Kennedy; 45,879 Uncommitted; 14,313 Brown; 4,891 Finch; 4,388 LaRouche.

1980 PRESIDENTIAL PRIMARIES

MASSACHUSETTS MARCH 4

Republican   124,365 Bush; 122,987 Anderson; 115,334 Reagan; 19,366 Baker; 4,714 Connally; 4,669 Crane; 2,243 No Preference; 577 Dole; 374 Fernandez; 218 Stassen; 5,979 scattered.

Democratic   590,393 Kennedy; 260,401 Carter; 31,498 Brown; 19,663 No Preference; 5,368 scattered.

MICHIGAN MAY 20

Republican   341,998 Bush; 189,184 Reagan; 48,947 Anderson; 10,265 Uncommitted; 2,248 Fernandez; 1,938 Stassen; 596 scattered.

Democratic   36,385 Uncommitted; 23,043 Brown; 8,948 LaRouche; 10,048 scattered.

MISSISSIPPI JUNE 3

Republican   23,028 Reagan slate; 2,105 Bush slate; 618 Unslated (CD's 3 and 4 only).

Democratic   No Presidential primary held.

MONTANA JUNE 3

Republican   68,744 Reagan; 7,665 Bush; 3,014 No Preference.

Democratic   66,922 Carter; 47,671 Kennedy; 15,466 No Preference.

NEBRASKA MAY 13

Republican   155,995 Reagan; 31,380 Bush; 11,879 Anderson; 1,420 Dole; 1,062 Crane; 799 Stassen; 400 Fernandez; 2,268 scattered.

Democratic   72,120 Carter; 57,826 Kennedy; 16,041 Uncommitted; 5,478 Brown; 1,169 LaRouche; 1,247 scattered.

NEVADA MAY 27

Republican   39,352 Reagan; 3,078 Bush; 4,965 "None of These Candidates".

Democratic   25,159 Carter; 19,296 Kennedy; 22,493 "None of These Candidates".

NEW HAMPSHIRE FEBRUARY 26

Republican   72,983 Reagan; 33,443 Bush; 18,943 Baker; 14,458 Anderson; 2,618 Crane; 2,239 Connally; 597 Dole; 1,876 scattered.

Democratic   52,692 Carter; 41,745 Kennedy; 10,743 Brown; 2,326 LaRouche; 566 Kay; 3,858 scattered.

NEW JERSEY JUNE 3

Republican   225,959 Reagan; 47,447 Bush; 4,571 Stassen.

Democratic   315,109 Kennedy; 212,387 Carter; 19,499 Uncommitted; 13,913 LaRouche.

1980 PRESIDENTIAL PRIMARIES

NEW MEXICO JUNE 3

Republican   37,982 Reagan; 7,171 Anderson; 5,892 Bush; 4,412 Crane, 1,795 Fernandez; 1,347 Uncommitted; 947 Stassen.

Democratic   73,721 Kennedy; 66,621 Carter; 9,734 Uncommitted; 4,798 LaRouche; 4,490 Finch.

NEW YORK MARCH 25

Republican   No Presidential primary was held. Delegates were elected, but without indication of Presidential preference.

Democratic   582,757 Kennedy; 406,305 Carter.

NORTH CAROLINA MAY 6

Republican   113,854 Reagan; 36,631 Bush; 8,542 Anderson; 4,538 No Preference; 2,543 Baker; 1,107 Connally; 629 Dole; 547 Crane.

Democratic   516,778 Carter; 130,684 Kennedy; 68,380 No Preference; 21,420 Brown.

OHIO JUNE 3

Republican   692,288 Reagan; 164,485 Bush.

Democratic   605,744 Carter; 523,874 Kennedy; 35,268 LaRouche; 21,524 Kay.

OREGON MAY 20

Republican   170,449 Reagan; 109,210 Bush; 32,118 Anderson; 2,324 Crane; 1,265 scattered.

Democratic   208,693 Carter; 114,651 Kennedy; 34,409 Brown; 10,569 scattered.

PENNSYLVANIA APRIL 22

Republican   626,759 Bush; 527,916 Reagan; 30,846 Baker; 26,890 Anderson (write-in); 10,656 Connally, 6,767 Stassen; 4,357 Jacobson; 2,521 Fernandez; 4,699 scattered.

Democratic   736,854 Kennedy; 732,332 Carter; 93,865 No Preference; 37,669 Brown; 12,831 scattered.

RHODE ISLAND JUNE 3

Republican   3,839 Reagan; 993 Bush; 348 Uncommitted; 107 Stassen; 48 Fernandez.

Democratic   26,179 Kennedy; 9,907 Carter; 1,160 LaRouche; 771 Uncommitted; 310 Brown.

SOUTH CAROLINA MARCH 8

Republican   79,549 Reagan; 43,113 Connally; 21,569 Bush; 773 Baker; 171 Fernandez; 150 Stassen; 117 Dole; 59 Belluso.

Democratic   No Presidential primary was held.

SOUTH DAKOTA JUNE 3

Republican   72,861 Reagan slate; 5,366 No Preference slate; 3,691 Bush slate; 987 Stassen slate.

Democratic   33,418 Kennedy slate; 31,251 Carter slate; 4,094 Uncommitted slate (in CD 1 only).

1980 PRESIDENTIAL PRIMARIES

TENNESSEE MAY 6

Republican   144,625 Reagan; 35,274 Bush; 8,722 Anderson; 4,976 Uncommitted; 1,574 Crane; 39 scattered.

Democratic   221,658 Carter; 53,258 Kennedy; 11,515 Uncommitted; 5,612 Brown; 1,663 Finch; 925 LaRouche; 49 scattered.

TEXAS MAY 3

Republican   268,798 Reagan; 249,819 Bush; 8,152 Uncommitted.

Democratic   770,390 Carter; 314,129 Kennedy; 257,250 Uncommitted; 35,585 Brown.

VERMONT MARCH 4

Republican   19,720 Reagan; 19,030 Anderson; 14,226 Bush; 8,055 Baker; 1,238 Crane; 884 Connally; 105 Stassen; 2,353 scattered.

Democratic   29,015 Carter; 10,135 Kennedy; 553 scattered.

Liberty Union 257 Gardner; 165 McReynolds; 76 Hall; 75 scattered.

WEST VIRGINIA JUNE 3

Republican   115,407 Reagan; 19,509 Bush; 3,100 Stassen.

Democratic   197,687 Carter; 120,247 Kennedy.

WISCONSIN APRIL 1

Republican   364,898 Reagan; 276,164 Bush; 248,623 Anderson; 3,298 Baker; 2,951 Crane; 2,312 Connally; 1,051 Fernandez; 1,010 Stassen; 2,595 "None of the Names Shown"; 4,951 scattered.

Democratic   353,662 Carter; 189,520 Kennedy; 74,496 Brown; 6,896 LaRouche; 1,842 Finch; 2,694 "None of the Names Shown"; 509 scattered.

DISTRICT OF COLUMBIA MAY 6

Republican   4,973 Bush; 2,025 Anderson; 270 Crane; 201 Stassen; 60 Fernandez.

Democratic   39,561 Kennedy; 23,697 Carter; 892 LaRouche.

1980 REPUBLICAN PREFERENCE PRIMARIES

Date		State	Total Vote	Anderson	Baker	Bush	Connally	Crane	Reagan	Other
Feb.	26	New Hampshire	147,157	14,458	18,943	33,443	2,239	2,618	72,983	2,473
Mar.	4	Massachusetts	400,826	122,987	19,366	124,365	4,714	4,669	115,334	9,391
	4	Vermont	65,611	19,030	8,055	14,226	884	1,238	19,720	2,458
	8	South Carolina	145,501	—	773	21,569	43,113	—	79,549	497
	11	Alabama	211,353	—	1,963	54,730	1,077	5,099	147,352	1,132
	11	Florida	614,995	56,636	6,345	185,996	4,958	12,000	345,699	3,361
	11	Georgia	200,171	16,853	1,571	25,293	2,388	6,308	146,500	1,258
	18	Illinois	1,130,081	415,193	7,051	124,057	4,548	24,865	547,355	7,012
	25	Connecticut	182,284	40,354	2,446	70,367	598	1,887	61,735	4,897
	25	New York	No Primary Held							
April	1	Kansas	285,398	51,924	3,603	35,838	2,067	1,367	179,739	10,860
	1	Wisconsin	907,853	248,623	3,298	276,164	2,312	2,951	364,898	9,607
	5	Louisiana	41,683	—	—	7,818	—	—	31,212	2,653
	22	Pennsylvania	1,241,411	26,890	30,846	626,759	10,656	—	527,916	18,344
May	3	Texas	526,769	—	—	249,819	—	—	268,798	8,152
	6	Indiana	568,313	56,342	—	92,955	—	—	419,016	—
	6	North Carolina	168,391	8,542	2,543	36,631	1,107	547	113,854	5,167
	6	Tennessee	195,210	8,722	—	35,274	—	1,574	144,625	5,015
	6	District of Columbia	7,529	2,025	—	4,973	—	270	—	261
	13	Maryland	167,303	16,244	—	68,389	—	2,113	80,557	—
	13	Nebraska	205,203	11,879	—	31,380	—	1,062	155,995	4,887
	20	Michigan	595,176	48,947	—	341,998	—	—	189,184	15,047
	20	Oregon	315,366	32,118	—	109,210	—	2,324	170,449	1,265
	27	Arkansas	No Primary Held							
	27	Idaho	134,879	13,130	5,416	—	—	1,024	111,868	3,441
	27	Kentucky	94,795	4,791	—	6,861	—	—	78,072	5,071
	27	Nevada	47,395	—	—	3,078	—	—	39,352	4,965
June	3	California	2,564,072	349,315	—	125,113	—	21,465	2,057,923	10,256
	3	Mississippi	25,751	—	—	2,105	—	—	23,028	618
	3	Montana	79,423	—	—	7,665	—	—	68,744	3,014
	3	New Jersey	277,977	—	—	47,447	—	—	225,959	4,571
	3	New Mexico	59,546	7,171	—	5,892	—	4,412	37,982	4,089
	3	Ohio	856,773	—	—	164,485	—	—	692,288	—
	3	Rhode Island	5,335	—	—	993	—	—	3,839	503
	3	South Dakota	82,905	—	—	3,691	—	—	72,861	6,353
	3	West Virginia	138,016	—	—	19,509	—	—	115,407	3,100
			12,690,451	1,572,174	112,219	2,958,093	80,661	97,793	7,709,793	159,718

Other vote includes 38,708 Uncommitted; 24,753 Stassen; 23,423 Fernandez; 15,161 No Preference; 9,321 "None of the Names Shown"; 7,298 Dole; 4,965 "None of These Candidates"; 4,357 Jacobson; 3,757 Kelley; 1,063 Yeager; 483 Carris; 355 Belluso; 311 Carlson; 244 Badgley; 67 Pickett; 25,452 scattered.

1980 DEMOCRATIC PREFERENCE PRIMARIES

Date		State	Total Vote	Brown	Carter	Kennedy	LaRouche	Other
Feb.	26	New Hampshire	111,930	10,743	52,692	41,745	2,326	4,424
Mar.	4	Massachusetts	907,323	31,498	260,401	590,393	—	25,031
	4	Vermont	39,703	—	29,015	10,135	—	553
	8	South Carolina	No Primary Held					
	11	Alabama	237,464	9,529	193,734	31,382	—	2,819
	11	Florida	1,098,003	53,474	666,321	254,727	—	123,481
	11	Georgia	384,780	7,255	338,772	32,315	513	5,925
	18	Illinois	1,201,067	39,168	780,787	359,875	19,192	2,045
	25	Connecticut	210,275	5,386	87,207	98,662	5,617	13,403
	25	New York	989,062	—	406,305	582,757	—	—
April	1	Kansas	193,918	9,434	109,807	61,318	—	13,359
	1	Wisconsin	629,619	74,496	353,662	189,520	6,896	5,045
	5	Louisiana	358,741	16,774	199,956	80,797	—	61,214
	22	Pennsylvania	1,613,551	37,669	732,332	736,854	—	106,696
May	3	Texas	1,377,354	35,585	770,390	314,129	—	257,250
	6	Indiana	589,441	—	398,949	190,492	—	—
	6	North Carolina	737,262	21,420	516,778	130,684	—	68,380
	6	Tennessee	294,680	5,612	221,658	53,258	925	13,227
	6	District of Columbia	64,150	—	23,697	39,561	892	—
	13	Maryland	477,090	14,313	226,528	181,091	4,388	50,770
	13	Nebraska	153,881	5,478	72,120	57,826	1,169	17,288
	20	Michigan	78,424	23,043	—	—	8,948	46,433
	20	Oregon	368,322	34,409	208,693	114,651	—	10,569
	27	Arkansas	448,290	—	269,375	78,542	—	100,373
	27	Idaho	50,482	2,078	31,383	11,087	—	5,934
	27	Kentucky	240,331	—	160,819	55,167	—	24,345
	27	Nevada	66,948	—	25,159	19,296	—	·22,493
June	3	California	3,363,969	135,962	1,266,276	1,507,142	71,779	382,810
	3	Mississippi	No Primary Held					
	3	Montana	130,059	—	66,922	47,671	—	15,466
	3	New Jersey	560,908	—	212,387	315,109	13,913	19,499
	3	New Mexico	159,364	—	66,621	73,721	4,798	14,224
	3	Ohio	1,186,410	—	605,744	523,874	35,268	21,524
	3	Rhode Island	38,327	310	9,907	26,179	1,160	771
	3	South Dakota	68,763	—	31,251	33,418	—	4,094
	3	West Virginia	317,934	—	197,687	120,247	—	—
			18,747,825	573,636	9,593,335	6,963,625	177,784	1,439,445

Other vote includes 950,378 Uncommitted; 301,695 No Preference; 48,061 Kay; 48,032 Finch; 22,493 "None of These Candidates"; 13,857 "None of the Names Shown"; 4,002 Maddox; 2,255 Reaux; 609 Nuckols; 571 Ahern; 364 Rollinson; 47,128 Scattered.

1984 PRESIDENTIAL PRIMARIES

In 1984 twenty-nine states and the District of Columbia held Presidential primaries though there was no Republican voting in Alabama, Connecticut, New York, North Carolina and South Dakota, and no Democratic voting in Texas.

In some jurisdictions balloting was for delegate groups linked to specific Presidential candidates, in others electors indicated only a personal preference as to their party's nominee. The votes listed in California for the Democratic primary are the sum of the highest delegate vote for each candidate in each of the state's forty-five Congressional Districts.

The tables included here give the major party primary vote in each state for those candidates who polled at least 100,000 votes. An asterisk in the table indicates votes written-in for a candidate not on the ballot.

Republican candidates on the ballot in at least one state were Gary R. Arnold, Benjamin Fernandez, David M. Kelley, Ronald Reagan, Harold E. Stassen.

Democratic candidates on the ballot in at least one state were Reubin Askew, Hugh G. Bagley, Martin J. Beckman, Bob Brewster, Walter R. Buchanan, Raymond J. Caplette, Roy J. Clendenan, Alan Cranston, John H. Glenn, Robert K. Griser, Gary W. Hart, Ernest F. Hollings, Jesse L. Jackson, Richard B. Kay, William King, Claude R. Kirk, Stephen A. Koczak, William P. Kreml, Lyndon H. LaRouche, George S. McGovern, Walter F. Mondale, Edward T. O'Donnell, Chester M. Rudnicki, Cyril E. Sagan, Alfred Timinski, Betty J. Williams, Gerald Willis.

ALABAMA MARCH 13

Republican   No Presidential primary held.

Democratic   148,165 Mondale; 89,286 Glenn; 88,465 Hart; 83,787 Jackson; 6,153 Willis; 4,759 Hollings; 4,464 Uncommitted; 1,827 Askew; 1,377 Cranston.

CALIFORNIA JUNE 5

Republican   1,874,897 Reagan; 78 scattered.

Democratic   1,155,499 Hart; 1,049,342 Mondale; 546,693 Jackson; 96,770 Glenn; 69,926 McGovern; 52,647 LaRouche; 26 scattered.

American Independent   7,374 Charles R. Glenn; 3,567 Lowery; 3,052 Mohr; 2,507 Willis; 4 scattered.

Peace & Freedom   3,171 Johnson; 1,160 Condit; 731 Serrette; 651 Holmes; 2 scattered.

Libertarian   34 scattered.

CONNECTICUT MARCH 27

Republican   No Presidential primary held.

Democratic   116,286 Hart; 64,230 Mondale; 26,395 Jackson; 6,098 Askew; 2,426 McGovern; 2,283 Hollings; 1,973 Uncommitted; 955 Glenn; 196 Cranston.

1984 PRESIDENTIAL PRIMARIES

FLORIDA MARCH 13

Republican 344,150 Reagan.

Democratic 463,799 Hart; 394,350 Mondale; 144,263 Jackson; 128,209 Glenn; 26,258 Askew; 17,614 McGovern; 3,115 Hollings; 2,097 Cranston; 1,328 Kay; 1,157 Koczak.

GEORGIA MARCH 13

Republican 50,793 Reagan.

Democratic 208,588 Mondale; 186,903 Hart; 143,730 Jackson; 122,744 Glenn; 11,321 McGovern; 3,800 Hollings; 3,068 Uncommitted; 1,804 Willis; 1,660 Askew; 923 Cranston.

IDAHO MAY 22

Republican 97,450 Reagan; 8,237 "None of the Names Shown".

Democratic 31,737 Hart; 16,460 Mondale; 3,104 Jackson; 2,225 "None of the Names Shown"; 1,196 LaRouche.

ILLINOIS MARCH 20

Republican 594,742 Reagan; 336 scattered.

Democratic 670,951 Mondale; 584,579 Hart; 348,843 Jackson; 25,336 McGovern; 19,800 Glenn; 4,797 Williams; 2,786 Cranston; 2,182 Askew; 151 scattered.

INDIANA MAY 8

Republican 428,559 Reagan.

Democratic 299,491 Hart; 293,413 Mondale; 98,190 Jackson; 16,046 Glenn; 9,815 Brewster.

LOUISIANA MAY 5

Republican 14,964 Reagan; 1,723 Uncommitted.

Democratic 136,707 Jackson; 79,593 Hart; 71,162 Mondale; 19,409 Uncommitted; 4,970 LaRouche; 3,158 McGovern; 1,924 Griser; 1,344 Kay; 543 Koczak.

MARYLAND MAY 8

Republican 73,663 Reagan.

Democratic 215,222 Mondale; 129,387 Jackson; 123,365 Hart; 15,807 Uncommitted; 7,836 LaRouche; 5,796 McGovern; 6,238 Glenn; 1,768 Cranston; 1,467 Hollings.

MASSACHUSETTS MARCH 13

Republican 58,996 Reagan; 5,005 No Preference; 1,936 scattered.

Democratic 245,943 Hart; 160,893 Mondale; 134,341 McGovern; 45,456 Glenn; 31,824 Jackson; 5,080 No Preference; 1,394 Askew; 1,203 Hollings; 853 Cranston; 3,975 scattered.

1984 PRESIDENTIAL PRIMARIES

MONTANA JUNE 5

Republican   66,432 Reagan; 5,378 No Preference; 77 scattered.

Democratic   28,385 No Preference; 3,080 Hart (write-in); 2,026 Mondale (write-in); 388 Jackson (write-in); 335 scattered.

NEBRASKA MAY 15

Republican   145,245 Reagan; 1,403 scattered.

Democratic   86,582 Hart; 39,635 Mondale; 13,495 Jackson; 4,631 Uncommitted; 1,561 McGovern; 1,227 LaRouche; 538 Cranston; 450 Hollings; 736 scattered.

NEW HAMPSHIRE FEBRUARY 28

Republican   65,033 Reagan; 1,543 Stassen; 360 Kelley; 252 Arnold; 202 Fernandez; 8,180 scattered.

Democratic   37,702 Hart; 28,173 Mondale; 12,088 Glenn; 5,311 Jackson; 5,217 McGovern; 3,583 Hollings; 2,136 Cranston; 1,025 Askew; 155 Koczak; 132 Buchanan; 127 Beckman; 74 O'Donnell; 50 Willis; 34 King; 27 Kay; 25 Kreml; 24 Bagley; 24 Kirk; 21 Rudnicki; 20 Clendenan; 20 Sagan; 19 Caplette; 5,144 scattered.

NEW JERSEY JUNE 5

Republican   240,054 Reagan.

Democratic   305,516 Mondale; 200,948 Hart; 159,788 Jackson; 10,309 LaRouche.

NEW MEXICO JUNE 5

Republican   40,805 Reagan; 2,189 Uncommitted.

Democratic   87,610 Hart; 67,675 Mondale; 22,168 Jackson; 5,143 McGovern; 3,330 LaRouche; 1,477 Uncommitted.

NEW YORK APRIL 3

Republican   No Presidential primary held.

Democratic   621,581 Mondale; 380,564 Hart; 355.541 Jackson; 15,941 Glenn; 6,815 Cranston; 4,547 McGovern; 2,877 Askew; 84scattered.

NORTH CAROLINA MAY 8

Republican   No Presidential primary held.

Democratic   342,324 Mondale; 289,877 Hart; 243,945 Jackson; 44,232 No Preference; 17,659 Glenn; 10,149 McGovern; 8,318 Hollings; 3,144 Askew; 1,209 Cranston.

1984 PRESIDENTIAL PRIMARIES

NORTH DAKOTA JUNE 12

Republican   44,109 Reagan.

Democratic   28,603 Hart; 4,018 LaRouche; 934 Mondale (write-in).

OHIO MAY 8

Republican   658,169 Reagan.

Democratic   608,528 Hart; 583,595 Mondale; 237,133 Jackson; 8,991 McGovern; 4,653 Cranston; 4,336 LaRouche.

OREGON MAY 15

Republican   238,594 Reagan; 4,752 scattered.

Democratic   233,638 Hart; 110,374 Mondale; 37,106 Jackson; 10,831 Glenn; 5,943 LaRouche; 1,787 scattered.

PENNSYLVANIA APRIL 10

Republican   616,916 Reagan; 4,290 scattered.

Democratic   747,267 Mondale; 551,335 Hart; 264,463 Jackson; 22,829 Cranston; 22,605 Glenn; 19,180 LaRouche; 13,139 McGovern; 6,090 Griser; 5,071 Askew; 2,972 Hollings; 1,343 scattered.

RHODE ISLAND MARCH 13

Republican   2,028 Reagan; 207 Uncommitted.

Democratic   20,011 Hart; 15,338 Mondale; 3,875 Jackson; 2,249 Glenn; 2,146 McGovern; 439 Uncommitted; 273 Cranston; 96 Askew; 84 Hollings.

SOUTH DAKOTA JUNE 5

Republican   No Presidential primary held.

Democratic   26,641 Hart; 20,495 Mondale; 2,738 Jackson; 1,383 LaRouche; 1,304 Uncommitted.

TENNESSEE MAY 1

Republican   75,367 Reagan; 7,546 Uncommitted; 8 scattered.

Democratic   132,201 Mondale; 93,710 Hart; 81,418 Jackson; 6,682 Uncommitted; 4,198 Glenn; 3,824 McGovern; 30 scattered.

TEXAS MAY 5

Republican   308,713 Reagan; 11,126 Uncommitted.

Democratic   No Presidential primary held.

1984 PRESIDENTIAL PRIMARIES

VERMONT MARCH 6

Republican   33,218 Reagan; 425 scattered.

Democratic   51,873 Hart; 14,834 Mondale; 5,761 Jackson; 444 Askew; 1,147 scattered.

Liberty   276 Serrette; 33 scattered.
Union

WEST VIRGINIA JUNE 5

Republican   125,790 Reagan; 11,206 Stassen.

Democratic   198,776 Mondale; 137,866 Hart; 24,697 Jackson; 7,274 LaRouche; 632 Timinski.

WISCONSIN APRIL 3

Republican   280,608 "Ronald Reagan Yes"; 14,047 "Ronald Reagan No"; 158 scattered.

Democratic   282,435 Hart; 261,374 Mondale; 62,524 Jackson; 10,166 McGovern; 7,036 "None of the Names Shown"; 6,398 Glenn; 2,984 Cranston; 1,650 Hollings; 683 Askew; 518 scattered.

Constitution   1,391 Uninstructed Delegation; 56 scattered.

Labor and   13,840 "William O. Hart Yes"; 1,769 "William O. Hart No"; 67 scattered.
Farm

Libertarian   3,513 "David P. Bergland Yes"; 857 "David P. Bergland No"; 15 scattered.

DISTRICT OF COLUMBIA MAY 1

Republican   5,692 Reagan.

Democratic   69,106 Jackson; 26,320 Mondale; 7,305 Hart.

1984 REPUBLICAN PREFERENCE PRIMARIES

Date		State	Total Vote	Reagan	Other
Feb.	28	New Hampshire	75,570	65,033	10,537
Mar.	6	Vermont	33,643	33,218	425
	13	Alabama	No Primary Held		
	13	Florida	344,150	344,150	—
	13	Georgia	50,793	50,793	—
	13	Massachusetts	65,937	58,996	6,941
	13	Rhode Island	2,235	2,028	207
	20	Illinois	595,078	594,742	336
	27	Connecticut	No Primary Held		
April	3	New York	No Primary Held		
	3	Wisconsin	294,813	280,608	14,205
	10	Pennsylvania	621,206	616,916	4,290
May	1	District of Columbia	5,692	5,692	—
	1	Tennessee	82,921	75,367	7,554
	5	Louisiana	16,687	14,964	1,723
	5	Texas	319,839	308,713	11,126
	8	Indiana	428,559	428,559	—
	8	Maryland	73,663	73,663	—
	8	North Carolina	No Primary Held		
	8	Ohio	658,169	658,169	—
	15	Nebraksa	146,648	145,245	1,403
	15	Oregon	243,346	238,594	4,752
	22	Idaho	105,687	97,450	8,237
June	5	California	1,874,975	1,874,897	78
	5	Montana	71,887	66,432	5,455
	5	New Jersey	240,054	240,054	—
	5	New Mexico	42,994	40,805	2,189
	5	South Dakota	No Primary Held		
	5	West Virginia	136,996	125,790	11,206
	12	North Dakota	44,109	44,109	
			6,575,651	6,484,987	90,664

Other vote includes 22,791 Uncommitted; 14,047 "Ronald Reagan No"; 12,749 Stassen; 10,383 No Preference; 8,237 "None of the Names Shown"; 360 Kelley; 252 Arnold; 202 Fernandez; 21,643 scattered.

1984 DEMOCRATIC PREFERENCE PRIMARIES

Date		State	Total Vote	Glenn	Hart	Jackson	LaRouche	McGovern	Mondale	Other
Feb.	28	New Hampshire	101,131	12,088	37,702	5,311	—	5,217	28,173	12,640
Mar.	6	Vermont	74,059	—	51,873	5,761	—	—	14,834	1,591
	13	Alabama	428,283	89,286	88,465	83,787	—	—	148,165	18,580
	13	Florida	1,182,190	128,209	463,799	144,263	—	17,614	394,350	33,955
	13	Georgia	684,541	122,744	186,903	143,730	—	11,321	208,588	11,255
	13	Massachusetts	630,962	45,456	245,943	31,824	—	134,341	160,893	12,505
	13	Rhode Island	44,511	2,249	20,011	3,875	—	2,146	15,338	892
	20	Illinois	1,659,425	19,800	584,579	348,843	—	25,336	670,951	9,916
	27	Connecticut	220,842	955	116,286	26,395	—	2,426	64,230	10,550
April	3	New York	1,387,950	15,941	380,564	355,541	—	4,547	621,581	9,776
	3	Wisconsin	635,768	6,398	282,435	62,524	—	10,166	261,374	12,871
	10	Pennsylvania	1,656,294	22,605	551,335	264,463	19,180	13,139	747,267	38,305
May	1	District of Columbia	102,731	—	7,305	69,106	—	—	26,320	—
	1	Tennessee	322,063	4,198	93,710	81,418	—	3,824	132,201	6,712
	5	Louisiana	318,810	—	79,593	136,707	4,970	3,158	71,162	23,220
	5	Texas	No Primary held							
	8	Indiana	716,955	16,046	299,491	98,190	—	—	293,413	9,815
	8	Maryland	506,886	6,238	123,365	129,387	7,836	5,796	215,222	19,042
	8	North Carolina	960,857	17,659	289,877	243,945	—	10,149	342,324	56,903
	8	Ohio	1,447,236	—	608,528	237,133	4,336	8,991	583,595	4,653
	15	Nebraska	148,855	—	86,582	13,495	1,227	1,561	39,635	6,355
	15	Oregon	399,679	10,831	233,638	37,106	5,943	—	110,374	1,787
	22	Idaho	54,722	—	31,737	3,104	1,196	—	16,460	2,225
June	5	California	2,970,903	96,770	1,155,499	546,693	52,647	69,926	1,049,342	26
	5	Montana	34,214	—	3,080*	388*	—	—	2,026*	28,720
	5	New Jersey	676,561	—	200,948	159,788	10,309	—	305,516	—
	5	New Mexico	187,403	—	87,610	22,168	3,330	5,143	67,675	1,477
	5	South Dakota	52,561	—	26,641	2,738	1,383	—	20,495	1,304
	5	West Virginia	369,245	—	137,866	24,697	7,274	—	198,776	632
	12	North Dakota	33,555	—	28,603	—	4,018	—	934	—
			18,009,192	617,473	6,503,968	3,282,380	123,649	334,801	6,811,214	335,707

Other vote includes 77,697 No Preference; 59,254 Uncommitted; 52,759 Askew; 51,437 Cranston; 33,684 Hollings; 9,815 Brewster; 9,261 "None of the Names Shown"; 8,014 Griser; 7,957 Willis; 4,847 Williams; 2,699 Kay; 1,855 Koczak; 632 Timinski; 132 Buchanan; 127 Beckman; 74 O'Donnell; 34 King; 25 Kreml; 24 Bagley; 24 Kirk; 21 Rudnicki; 20 Clendenan; 20 Sagan; 19 Caplette; 15,276 scattered.

ALABAMA

GOVERNOR
George C. Wallace (D). Elected 1982 to a four-year term. Previously elected 1974, 1970, 1962.

SENATORS
Jeremiah Denton (R). Elected 1980 to a six-year term.

Howell Heflin (D). Re-elected 1984 to a six-year term. Previously elected 1978.

REPRESENTATIVES
1. H. L. Callahan (R)
2. William Dickinson (R)
3. Bill Nichols (D)
4. Tom Bevill (D)
5. Ronnie G. Flippo (D)
6. Ben Erdreich (D)
7. Richard C. Shelby (D)

POSTWAR VOTE FOR GOVERNOR

Year	Total Vote	Republican Vote	Candidate	Democratic Vote	Candidate	Other Vote	Rep.-Dem. Plurality	Total Vote Rep.	Total Vote Dem.	Major Vote Rep.	Major Vote Dem.
1982	1,128,725	440,815	Folmar, Emory	650,538	Wallace, George C.	37,372	209,723 D	39.1%	57.6%	40.4%	59.6%
1978	760,474	196,963	Hunt, Guy	551,886	James, Forrest H.	11,625	354,923 D	25.9%	72.6%	26.3%	73.7%
1974	598,305	88,381	McCary, Elvin	497,574	Wallace, George C.	12,350	409,193 D	14.8%	83.2%	15.1%	84.9%
1970	854,952	—	—	637,046	Wallace, George C.	217,906	637,046 D	—	74.5%	—	100.0%
1966	848,101	262,943	Martin, James D.	537,505	Wallace, Mrs. George C.	47,653	274,562 D	31.0%	63.4%	32.8%	67.2%
1962	315,776	—	—	303,987	Wallace, George C.	11,789	303,987 D	—	96.3%	—	100.0%
1958	270,952	30,415	Longshore, W. L.	239,633	Patterson, John	904	209,218 D	11.2%	88.4%	11.3%	88.7%
1954	333,090	88,688	Amernethy, Tom	244,401	Folsom, James E.	1	155,713 D	26.6%	73.4%	26.6%	73.4%
1950	170,541	15,127	Crowder, John S.	155,414	Persons, Gordon	—	140,287 D	8.9%	91.1%	8.9%	91.1%
1946	197,324	22,362	Ward, Lyman	174,962	Folsom, James E.	—	152,600 D	11.3%	88.7%	11.3%	88.7%

POSTWAR VOTE FOR SENATOR

Year		Total Vote	Republican Vote	Candidate	Democratic Vote	Candidate	Other Vote	Rep.-Dem. Plurality	Total Vote Rep.	Total Vote Dem.	Major Vote Rep.	Major Vote Dem.
1984		1,371,238	498,508	Smith, Albert L.	860,535	Heflin, Howell	12,195	362,027 D	36.4%	62.8%	36.7%	63.3%
1980		1,296,757	650,362	Denton, Jeremiah	610,175	Folsom, James E., Jr.	36,220	40,187 R	50.2%	47.1%	51.6%	48.4%
1978		582,025	—	—	547,054	Heflin, Howell	34,971	547,054 D	—	94.0%	—	100.0%
1978	s	731,614	316,170	Martin, James D.	401,852	Stewart, Donald W.	13,592	85,682 D	43.2%	54.9%	44.0%	56.0%
1974		523,290	—	—	501,541	Allen, James B.	21,749	501,541 D	—	95.8%	—	100.0%
1972		1,051,099	347,523	Blount, Winston M.	654,491	Sparkman, John J.	49,085	306,968 D	33.1%	62.3%	34.7%	65.3%
1968		912,708	201,227	Hooper, Perry	638,774	Allen, James B.	72,707	437,547 D	22.0%	70.0%	24.0%	76.0%
1966		802,608	313,018	Grenier, John	482,138	Sparkman, John J.	7,452	169,120 D	39.0%	60.1%	39.4%	60.6%
1962		397,079	195,134	Martin, James D.	201,937	Hill, Lister	8	6,803 D	49.1%	50.9%	49.1%	50.9%
1960		554,081	164,868	Elgin, Julian	389,196	Sparkman, John J.	17	224,328 D	29.8%	70.2%	29.8%	70.2%
1956		330,191	—	—	330,182	Hill, Lister	9	330,182 D	—	100.0%	—	100.0%
1954		314,459	55,110	Guin, J. Foy	259,348	Sparkman, John J.	1	204,238 D	17.5%	82.5%	17.5%	82.5%
1950		164,011	—	—	125,534	Hill, Lister	38,477	125,534 D	—	76.5%	—	100.0%
1948		220,875	35,341	Parsons, Paul G.	185,534	Sparkman, John J.	—	150,193 D	16.0%	84.0%	16.0%	84.0%
1946	s	163,217	—	—	163,217	Sparkman, John J.	—	163,217 D	—	100.0%	—	100.0%

The 1946 election and one of the 1978 elections were for short terms to fill vacancies.

ALABAMA

Districts Established August 18, 1981

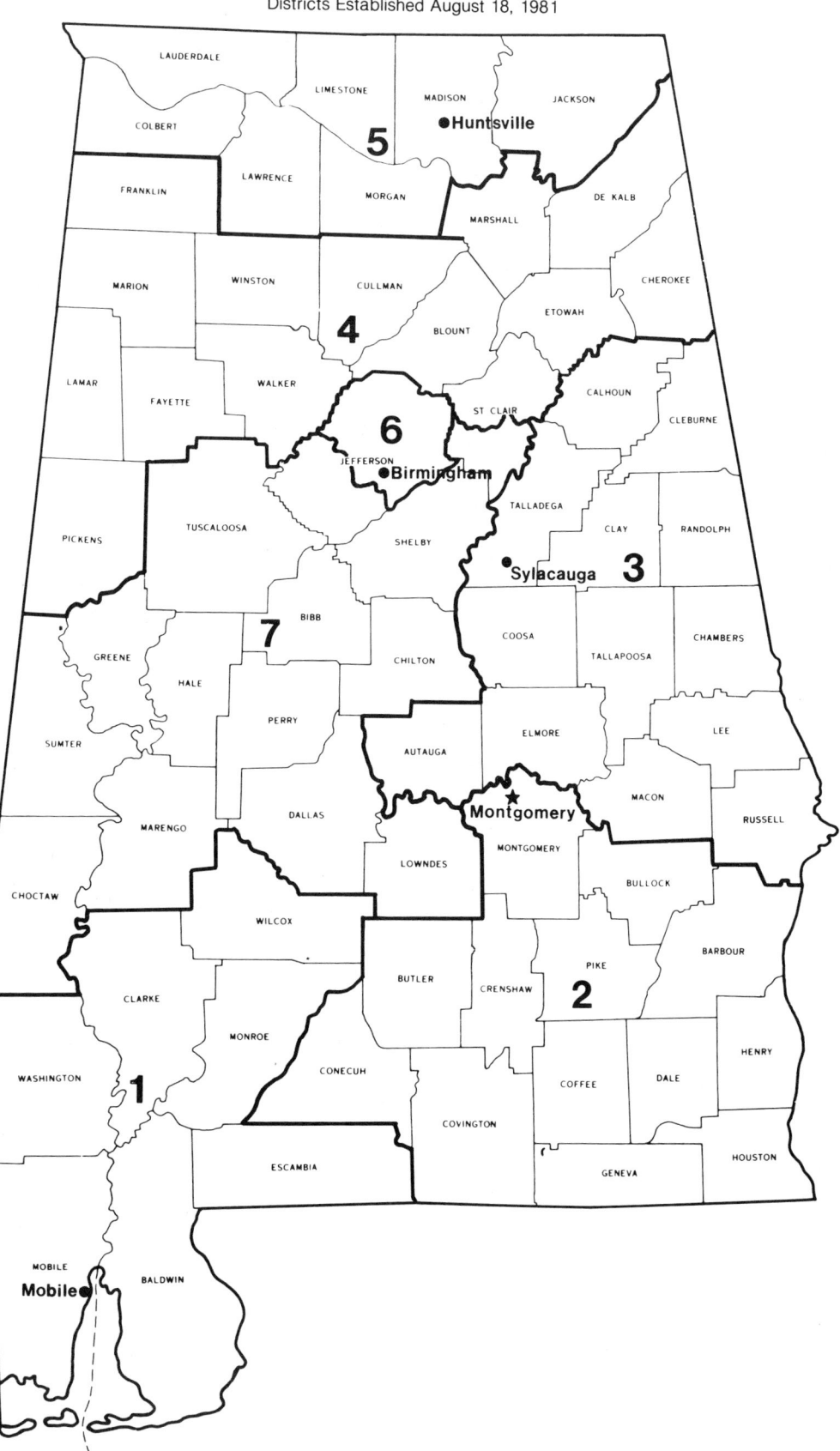

© ERC

ALABAMA

PRESIDENT 1984

1980 Census Population	County	Total Vote	Republican	Democratic	Other	Rep.-Dem. Plurality	Percentage Total Vote Rep.	Dem.	Major Vote Rep.	Dem.
32,259	AUTAUGA	11,917	8,350	3,366	201	4,984 R	70.1%	28.2%	71.3%	28.7%
78,556	BALDWIN	33,045	24,964	7,272	809	17,692 R	75.5%	22.0%	77.4%	22.6%
24,756	BARBOUR	10,161	5,459	4,591	111	868 R	53.7%	45.2%	54.3%	45.7%
15,723	BIBB	5,687	3,487	2,167	33	1,320 R	61.3%	38.1%	61.7%	38.3%
36,459	BLOUNT	12,482	8,508	3,738	236	4,770 R	68.2%	29.9%	69.5%	30.5%
10,596	BULLOCK	5,299	1,697	3,537	65	1,840 D	32.0%	66.7%	32.4%	67.6%
21,680	BUTLER	8,709	4,941	3,641	127	1,300 R	56.7%	41.8%	57.6%	42.4%
119,761	CALHOUN	38,082	23,291	12,752	2,039	10,539 R	61.2%	33.5%	64.6%	35.4%
39,191	CHAMBERS	13,463	8,024	5,302	137	2,722 R	59.6%	39.4%	60.2%	39.8%
18,760	CHEROKEE	6,319	3,225	3,029	65	196 R	51.0%	47.9%	51.6%	48.4%
30,612	CHILTON	12,678	8,243	3,924	511	4,319 R	65.0%	31.0%	67.7%	32.3%
16,839	CHOCTAW	7,349	3,960	3,373	16	587 R	53.9%	45.9%	54.0%	46.0%
27,702	CLARKE	10,811	6,282	4,452	77	1,830 R	58.1%	41.2%	58.5%	41.5%
13,703	CLAY	5,033	3,432	1,456	145	1,976 R	68.2%	28.9%	70.2%	29.8%
12,595	CLEBURNE	4,623	3,259	1,238	126	2,021 R	70.5%	26.8%	72.5%	27.5%
38,533	COFFEE	15,118	10,558	4,370	190	6,188 R	69.8%	28.9%	70.7%	29.3%
54,519	COLBERT	21,032	9,530	11,008	494	1,478 D	45.3%	52.3%	46.4%	53.6%
15,884	CONECUH	6,336	3,538	2,737	61	801 R	55.8%	43.2%	56.4%	43.6%
11,377	COOSA	4,379	2,585	1,781	13	804 R	59.0%	40.7%	59.2%	40.8%
36,850	COVINGTON	13,883	9,944	3,812	127	6,132 R	71.6%	27.5%	72.3%	27.7%
14,110	CRENSHAW	5,272	3,261	1,904	107	1,357 R	61.9%	36.1%	63.1%	36.9%
61,642	CULLMAN	23,126	14,782	7,989	355	6,793 R	63.9%	34.5%	64.9%	35.1%
47,821	DALE	13,692	10,319	3,215	158	7,104 R	75.4%	23.5%	76.2%	23.8%
53,981	DALLAS	20,718	9,585	10,955	178	1,370 D	46.3%	52.9%	46.7%	53.3%
53,658	DE KALB	19,349	12,098	7,212	39	4,886 R	62.5%	37.3%	62.7%	37.3%
43,390	ELMORE	16,077	11,694	4,198	185	7,496 R	72.7%	26.1%	73.6%	26.4%
38,440	ESCAMBIA	12,724	8,694	3,853	177	4,841 R	68.3%	30.3%	69.3%	30.7%
103,057	ETOWAH	38,781	19,243	19,074	464	169 R	49.6%	49.2%	50.2%	49.8%
18,809	FAYETTE	7,201	4,654	2,533	14	2,121 R	64.6%	35.2%	64.8%	35.2%
28,350	FRANKLIN	10,027	5,304	4,601	122	703 R	52.9%	45.9%	53.5%	46.5%
24,253	GENEVA	9,011	6,308	2,330	373	3,978 R	70.0%	25.9%	73.0%	27.0%
11,021	GREENE	5,209	1,361	3,675	173	2,314 D	26.1%	70.6%	27.0%	73.0%
15,604	HALE	6,056	2,691	3,289	76	598 D	44.4%	54.3%	45.0%	55.0%
15,302	HENRY	6,236	3,952	2,231	53	1,721 R	63.4%	35.8%	63.9%	36.1%
74,632	HOUSTON	27,485	20,834	6,488	163	14,346 R	75.8%	23.6%	76.3%	23.7%
51,407	JACKSON	14,572	6,730	7,635	207	905 D	46.2%	52.4%	46.8%	53.2%
671,324	JEFFERSON	266,547	158,362	107,506	679	50,856 R	59.4%	40.3%	59.6%	40.4%
16,453	LAMAR	5,867	3,943	1,910	14	2,033 R	67.2%	32.6%	67.4%	32.6%
80,546	LAUDERDALE	28,659	15,354	12,907	398	2,447 R	53.6%	45.0%	54.3%	45.7%
30,170	LAWRENCE	9,494	4,466	4,866	162	400 D	47.0%	51.3%	47.9%	52.1%
76,283	LEE	26,161	16,757	9,077	327	7,680 R	64.1%	34.7%	64.9%	35.1%
46,005	LIMESTONE	14,010	8,423	5,410	177	3,013 R	60.1%	38.6%	60.9%	39.1%
13,253	LOWNDES	5,252	1,629	3,567	56	1,938 D	31.0%	67.9%	31.4%	68.6%
26,829	MACON	9,499	1,543	7,857	99	6,314 D	16.2%	82.7%	16.4%	83.6%
196,966	MADISON	78,142	50,428	26,889	825	23,539 R	64.5%	34.4%	65.2%	34.8%
25,047	MARENGO	10,213	5,261	4,811	141	450 R	51.5%	47.1%	52.2%	47.8%
30,041	MARION	10,713	6,771	3,918	24	2,853 R	63.2%	36.6%	63.3%	36.7%
65,622	MARSHALL	20,391	12,330	7,704	357	4,626 R	60.5%	37.8%	61.5%	38.5%
364,980	MOBILE	130,959	81,923	47,252	1,784	34,671 R	62.6%	36.1%	63.4%	36.6%
22,651	MONROE	9,756	5,917	3,725	114	2,192 R	60.6%	38.2%	61.4%	38.6%
197,038	MONTGOMERY	75,005	43,328	31,206	471	12,122 R	57.8%	41.6%	58.1%	41.9%
90,231	MORGAN	35,543	24,103	11,324	116	12,779 R	67.8%	31.9%	68.0%	32.0%
15,012	PERRY	6,408	2,600	3,731	77	1,131 D	40.6%	58.2%	41.1%	58.9%
21,481	PICKENS	8,296	4,685	3,586	25	1,099 R	56.5%	43.2%	56.6%	43.4%
28,050	PIKE	9,953	6,231	3,541	181	2,690 R	62.6%	35.6%	63.8%	36.2%
20,075	RANDOLPH	7,515	4,940	2,439	136	2,501 R	65.7%	32.5%	66.9%	33.1%
47,356	RUSSELL	14,452	6,654	7,610	188	956 D	46.0%	52.7%	46.6%	53.4%
41,205	ST. CLAIR	14,654	10,408	4,000	246	6,408 R	71.0%	27.3%	72.2%	27.8%
66,298	SHELBY	28,068	21,858	5,884	326	15,974 R	77.9%	21.0%	78.8%	21.2%
16,908	SUMTER	6,993	2,493	4,478	22	1,985 D	35.6%	64.0%	35.8%	64.2%

ALABAMA

PRESIDENT 1984

1980 Census Population	County	Total Vote	Republican	Democratic	Other	Rep.-Dem. Plurality	Percentage Total Vote Rep.	Dem.	Major Vote Rep.	Dem.
73,826	TALLADEGA	23,020	14,067	8,490	463	5,577 R	61.1%	36.9%	62.4%	37.6%
38,676	TALLAPOOSA	13,666	9,045	4,458	163	4,587 R	66.2%	32.6%	67.0%	33.0%
137,541	TUSCALOOSA	44,739	28,075	16,066	598	12,009 R	62.8%	35.9%	63.6%	36.4%
68,660	WALKER	23,753	12,852	10,591	310	2,261 R	54.1%	44.6%	54.8%	45.2%
16,821	WASHINGTON	7,543	4,434	3,081	28	1,353 R	58.8%	40.8%	59.0%	41.0%
14,755	WILCOX	5,022	2,337	2,663	22	326 D	46.5%	53.0%	46.7%	53.3%
21,953	WINSTON	9,478	6,845	2,624	9	4,221 R	72.2%	27.7%	72.3%	27.7%
3,893,888	TOTAL	1,441,713	872,849	551,899	16,965	320,950 R	60.5%	38.3%	61.3%	38.7%

ALABAMA

SENATOR 1984

1980 Census Population	County	Total Vote	Republican	Democratic	Other	Rep.-Dem. Plurality	Percentage Total Vote Rep.	Dem.	Major Vote Rep.	Dem.
32,259	AUTAUGA	11,474	4,302	7,040	132	2,738 D	37.5%	61.4%	37.9%	62.1%
78,556	BALDWIN	31,469	14,702	16,459	308	1,757 D	46.7%	52.3%	47.2%	52.8%
24,756	BARBOUR	8,968	2,738	6,141	89	3,403 D	30.5%	68.5%	30.8%	69.2%
15,723	BIBB	5,293	1,871	3,411	11	1,540 D	35.3%	64.4%	35.4%	64.6%
36,459	BLOUNT	11,942	5,728	6,117	97	389 D	48.0%	51.2%	48.4%	51.6%
10,596	BULLOCK	4,910	866	4,000	44	3,134 D	17.6%	81.5%	17.8%	82.2%
21,680	BUTLER	8,012	2,641	5,274	97	2,633 D	33.0%	65.8%	33.4%	66.6%
119,761	CALHOUN	35,162	13,204	21,341	617	8,137 D	37.6%	60.7%	38.2%	61.8%
39,191	CHAMBERS	12,666	2,771	9,795	100	7,024 D	21.9%	77.3%	22.1%	77.9%
18,760	CHEROKEE	6,019	1,586	4,391	42	2,805 D	26.3%	73.0%	26.5%	73.5%
30,612	CHILTON	10,943	5,195	5,633	115	438 D	47.5%	51.5%	48.0%	52.0%
16,839	CHOCTAW	6,161	1,645	4,501	15	2,856 D	26.7%	73.1%	26.8%	73.2%
27,702	CLARKE	10,032	3483	6484	65	3,001 D	34.7%	64.6%	34.9%	65.1%
13,703	CLAY	4,538	1,930	2,545	63	615 D	42.5%	56.1%	43.1%	56.9%
12,595	CLEBURNE	4,056	1,650	2,376	30	726 D	40.7%	58.6%	41.0%	59.0%
38,533	COFFEE	14,495	5,650	8,709	136	3,059 D	39.0%	60.1%	39.3%	60.7%
54,519	COLBERT	20,509	3,480	16,889	140	13,409 D	17.0%	82.3%	17.1%	82.9%
15,884	CONECUH	5,811	1,992	3,683	136	1,691 D	34.3%	63.4%	35.1%	64.9%
11,377	COOSA	4,241	1,621	2,602	18	981 D	38.2%	61.4%	38.4%	61.6%
36,850	COVINGTON	12,557	4,880	7,543	134	2,663 D	38.9%	60.1%	39.3%	60.7%
14,110	CRENSHAW	4,735	1,581	3,089	65	1,508 D	33.4%	65.2%	33.9%	66.1%
61,642	CULLMAN	21,896	9,561	12,141	194	2,580 D	43.7%	55.4%	44.1%	55.9%
47,821	DALE	12,991	5,801	7,060	130	1,259 D	44.7%	54.3%	45.1%	54.9%
53,981	DALLAS	19,722	5,590	13,985	147	8,395 D	28.3%	70.9%	28.6%	71.4%
53,658	DE KALB	18,937	7,856	11,040	41	3,184 D	41.5%	58.3%	41.6%	58.4%
43,390	ELMORE	15,462	6,271	9,026	165	2,755 D	40.6%	58.4%	41.0%	59.0%
38,440	ESCAMBIA	11,035	4,424	6,450	161	2,026 D	40.1%	58.5%	40.7%	59.3%
103,057	ETOWAH	36,508	11,011	25,178	319	14,167 D	30.2%	69.0%	30.4%	69.6%
18,809	FAYETTE	7,076	2,797	4,257	22	1,460 D	39.5%	60.2%	39.7%	60.3%
28,350	FRANKLIN	9,493	2,792	6,598	103	3,806 D	29.4%	69.5%	29.7%	70.3%
24,253	GENEVA	7,857	2,757	4,941	159	2,184 D	35.1%	62.9%	35.8%	64.2%
11,021	GREENE	4,730	661	4,062	7	3,401 D	14.0%	85.9%	14.0%	86.0%
15,604	HALE	5,571	1,576	3,939	56	2,363 D	28.3%	70.7%	28.6%	71.4%
15,302	HENRY	5,795	1,632	4,126	37	2,494 D	28.2%	71.2%	28.3%	71.7%
74,632	HOUSTON	26,078	11,393	14,518	167	3,125 D	43.7%	55.7%	44.0%	56.0%
51,407	JACKSON	13,794	3,192	10,435	167	7,243 D	23.1%	75.6%	23.4%	76.6%
671,324	JEFFERSON	264,448	104,765	158,491	1,192	53,726 D	39.6%	59.9%	39.8%	60.2%
16,453	LAMAR	5,339	1,816	3,511	12	1,695 D	34.0%	65.8%	34.1%	65.9%
80,546	LAUDERDALE	27,885	6,325	21,315	245	14,990 D	22.7%	76.4%	22.9%	77.1%
30,170	LAWRENCE	8,769	1,821	6,811	137	4,990 D	20.8%	77.7%	21.1%	78.9%
76,283	LEE	24,660	9,890	14,382	388	4,492 D	40.1%	58.3%	40.7%	59.3%
46,005	LIMESTONE	13,391	3,831	9,452	108	5,621 D	28.6%	70.6%	28.8%	71.2%
13,253	LOWNDES	4,667	944	3,674	49	2,730 D	20.2%	78.7%	20.4%	79.6%
26,829	MACON	8,755	849	7,787	119	6,938 D	9.7%	88.9%	9.8%	90.2%
196,966	MADISON	71,103	22,090	48,287	726	26,197 D	31.1%	67.9%	31.4%	68.6%
25,047	MARENGO	9,536	3,074	6,389	73	3,315 D	32.2%	67.0%	32.5%	67.5%
30,041	MARION	10,325	3,921	6,367	37	2,446 D	38.0%	61.7%	38.1%	61.9%
65,622	MARSHALL	19,788	7,290	12,292	206	5,002 D	36.8%	62.1%	37.2%	62.8%
364,980	MOBILE	121,396	44,649	74,910	1,837	30,261 D	36.8%	61.7%	37.3%	62.7%
22,651	MONROE	8,595	3,129	5,368	98	2,239 D	36.4%	62.5%	36.8%	63.2%
197,038	MONTGOMERY	72,764	25,019	47,273	472	22,254 D	34.4%	65.0%	34.6%	65.4%
90,231	MORGAN	35,293	12,390	22,690	213	10,300 D	35.1%	64.3%	35.3%	64.7%
15,012	PERRY	6,182	1,591	4,553	38	2,962 D	25.7%	73.6%	25.9%	74.1%
21,481	PICKENS	7,663	2,635	5,001	27	2,366 D	34.4%	65.3%	34.5%	65.5%
28,050	PIKE	9,368	3,066	6,233	69	3,167 D	32.7%	66.5%	33.0%	67.0%
20,075	RANDOLPH	6,921	2,026	4,800	95	2,774 D	29.3%	69.4%	29.7%	70.3%
47,356	RUSSELL	13,018	2,731	10,105	182	7,374 D	21.0%	77.6%	21.3%	78.7%
41,205	ST. CLAIR	14,374	7,173	7,041	160	132 R	49.9%	49.0%	50.5%	49.5%
66,298	SHELBY	27,693	15,301	12,114	278	3,187 R	55.3%	43.7%	55.8%	44.2%
16,908	SUMTER	6,708	1,308	5,361	39	4,053 D	19.5%	79.9%	19.6%	80.4%

ALABAMA

SENATOR 1984

1980 Census Population	County	Total Vote	Republican	Democratic	Other	Rep.-Dem. Plurality	Percentage			
							Total Vote		Major Vote	
							Rep.	Dem.	Rep.	Dem.
73,826	TALLADEGA	21,042	9,610	11,145	287	1,535 D	45.7%	53.0%	46.3%	53.7%
38,676	TALLAPOOSA	13,191	4,965	8,109	117	3,144 D	37.6%	61.5%	38.0%	62.0%
137,541	TUSCALOOSA	43,507	19,446	23,603	458	4,157 D	44.7%	54.3%	45.2%	54.8%
68,660	WALKER	21,536	7,729	13,644	163	5,915 D	35.9%	63.4%	36.2%	63.8%
16,821	WASHINGTON	7,294	1,927	5,342	25	3,415 D	26.4%	73.2%	26.5%	73.5%
14,755	WILCOX	5,785	1,504	4,276	5	2,772 D	26.0%	73.9%	26.0%	74.0%
21,953	WINSTON	9,304	4,863	4,430	11	433 R	52.3%	47.6%	52.3%	47.7%
3,893,888	TOTAL	1,371,238	498,508	860,535	12,195	362,027 D	36.4%	62.8%	36.7%	63.3%

ALABAMA

CONGRESS

CD	Year	Total Vote	Republican		Democratic		Other Vote	Rep.-Dem. Plurality	Percentage			
			Vote	Candidate	Vote	Candidate			Total Vote Rep.	Dem.	Major Vote Rep.	Dem.
1	1984	200,934	102,479	CALLAHAN, H. L.	98,455	MCRIGHT, FRANK	4,024	4,024 R	51.0%	49.0%	51.0%	49.0%
1	1982	144,028	87,901	EDWARDS, JACK	54,315	GUDAC, STEVE	1,812	33,586 R	61.0%	37.7%	61.8%	38.2%
1	1980	117,221	111,089	EDWARDS, JACK			6,132	111,089 R	94.8%		100.0%	
1	1978	112,161	71,711	EDWARDS, JACK	40,450	NOONAN, L. W.		31,261 R	63.9%	36.1%	63.9%	36.1%
1	1976	157,170	98,257	EDWARDS, JACK	58,906	DAVENPORT, BILL	7	39,351 R	62.5%	37.5%	62.5%	37.5%
1	1974	102,066	60,710	EDWARDS, JACK	37,718	WILSON, AUGUSTA E.	3,638	22,992 R	59.5%	37.0%	61.7%	38.3%
1	1972	136,710	104,606	EDWARDS, JACK	24,357	MCCRORY, O. W.	7,747	80,249 R	76.5%	17.8%	81.1%	18.9%
2	1984	195,815	118,153	DICKINSON, WILLIAM	75,506	LEE, LARRY	2,156	42,647 R	60.3%	38.6%	61.0%	39.0%
2	1982	165,194	83,290	DICKINSON, WILLIAM	81,904	CAMP, BILLY JOE	1,386	1,386 R	50.4%	49.6%	50.4%	49.6%
2	1980	172,962	104,796	DICKINSON, WILLIAM	63,447	WYATT, CECIL	4,719	41,349 R	60.6%	36.7%	62.3%	37.7%
2	1978	107,265	57,924	DICKINSON, WILLIAM	49,341	MITCHELL, WENDELL		8,583 R	54.0%	46.0%	54.0%	46.0%
2	1976	156,362	90,069	DICKINSON, WILLIAM	66,288	KEAHEY, J. CAROLE	5	23,781 R	57.6%	42.4%	57.6%	42.4%
2	1974	81,818	54,089	DICKINSON, WILLIAM	27,729	CHISLER, CLAIR		26,360 R	66.1%	33.9%	66.1%	33.9%
2	1972	146,508	80,362	DICKINSON, WILLIAM	60,769	REEVES, BEN C.	5,377	19,593 R	54.9%	41.5%	56.9%	43.1%
3	1984	125,102			120,357	NICHOLS, BILL	4,745	120,357 D		96.2%		100.0%
3	1982	104,784			100,864	NICHOLS, BILL	3,920	100,864 D		96.3%		100.0%
4	1984	120,106			120,106	BEVILL, TOM		120,106 D		100.0%		100.0%
4	1982	118,607			118,595	BEVILL, TOM	12	118,595 D		100.0%		100.0%
5	1984	146,575			140,542	FLIPPO, RONNIE G.	6,033	140,542 D		95.9%		100.0%
5	1982	134,880	24,593	YAMBREK, LEOPOLD	108,807	FLIPPO, RONNIE G.	1,480	84,214 D	18.2%	80.7%	18.4%	81.6%
5	1980	124,967			117,626	FLIPPO, RONNIE G.	7,341	117,626 D		94.1%		100.0%
5	1978	71,236			68,985	FLIPPO, RONNIE G.	2,251	68,985 D		96.8%		100.0%
5	1976	113,560			113,553	FLIPPO, RONNIE G.	7	113,553 D		100.0%		100.0%
5	1974	56,381			56,375	JONES, ROBERT E.	6	56,375 D		100.0%		100.0%
5	1972	136,553	33,352	SCHRADER, DIETER J.	101,303	JONES, ROBERT E.	1,898	67,951 D	24.4%	74.2%	24.8%	75.2%
8	1970	90,058			76,413	JONES, ROBERT E.	13,645	76,413 D		84.8%		100.0%
8	1968	112,449			85,528	JONES, ROBERT E.	26,921	85,528 D		76.1%		100.0%
8	1966	91,386	25,404	MAYHALL, DONALD G.	65,982	JONES, ROBERT E.		40,578 D	27.8%	72.2%	27.8%	72.2%
8	1964	43,842			43,842	JONES, ROBERT E.		43,842 D		100.0%		100.0%
6	1984	219,710	87,550	WAGGONER, J. T.	130,973	ERDREICH, BEN	1,187	43,423 D	39.8%	59.6%	40.1%	59.9%
6	1982	165,387	76,726	SMITH, ALBERT L.	88,029	ERDREICH, BEN	632	11,303 D	46.4%	53.2%	46.6%	53.4%
7	1984	140,332			135,834	SHELBY, RICHARD C.	4,498	135,834 D		96.8%		100.0%
7	1982	128,139			124,070	SHELBY, RICHARD C.	4,069	124,070 D		96.8%		100.0%

ALABAMA

1984 GENERAL ELECTION

President   Other vote was 9,504 Bergland (Libertarian); 4,671 Hall (Independent); 1,401 Richards (Independent); 730 Mason (Independent); 659 Serrette (Independent).

Senator   Other vote was 12,191 Davis (Libertarian) and 4 scattered.

Congress   Other vote was Tipler (Libertarian) in CD 2; Thornton (Libertarian) in CD 3; Samsil (Libertarian) in CD 5; 1,043 Smith (Libertarian) and 144 Curtis (Socialist Workers) in CD 6; Ewing (Libertarian) in CD 7.

1984 PRIMARIES

SEPTEMBER 4 REPUBLICAN

Senator   27,304 Albert L. Smith; 8,067 Doug Carter; 5,171 Joseph Keith; 3,644 Clint Wilkes.

Congress   Unopposed in two CD's. No candidate in CD's 3, 4, 5, and 7. Contested as follows:

   CD   1   17,118 H. L. Callahan; 10,985 Billy Stoudenmire; 178 Tom Sawyer.

SEPTEMBER 4 DEMOCRATIC

Senator   399,817 Howell Heflin; 47,462 Charles W. Borden; 33,114 Mrs. Frank R. Stewart.

Congress   Unopposed in three CD's. Contested as follows:

   CD   1   37,806 Frank McRight; 31,551 Dan Alexander.
   CD   2   29,506 Larry Lee; 24,718 Jack Folsom; 5,676 Willie J. Fluker.
   CD   4   76,169 Tom Bevill; 10,054 Mike Sharp.
   CD   6   44,188 Ben Erdreich; 6,126 Steven T. Arnold.

SEPTEMBER 25 DEMOCRATIC RUN-OFF

Congress

   CD   2   27,195 Larry Lee; 16,352 Jack Folsom.

ALASKA

GOVERNOR
Bill Sheffield (D). Elected 1982 to a four-year term.

SENATORS
Frank H. Murkowski (R). Elected 1980 to a six-year term.

Ted Stevens (R). Re-elected 1984 to a six-year term. Previously elected 1978, 1972, and in 1970 to fill out term vacated by the death of Senator E. L. Bartlett; had been appointed December 1968 to fill this vacancy.

REPRESENTATIVE
At-Large. Don Young (R)

POSTWAR VOTE FOR GOVERNOR

Year	Total Vote	Republican Vote	Republican Candidate	Democratic Vote	Democratic Candidate	Other Vote	Rep.-Dem. Plurality	Total Vote Rep.	Total Vote Dem.	Major Vote Rep.	Major Vote Dem.
1982	194,885	72,291	Fink, Tom	89,918	Sheffield, Bill	32,676	17,627 D	37.1%	46.1%	44.6%	55.4%
1978	126,910	49,580	Hammond, Jay S.	25,656	Croft, Chancy	51,674	23,924 R	39.1%	20.2%	65.9%	34.1%
1974	96,163	45,840	Hammond, Jay S.	45,553	Egan, William A.	4,770	287 R	47.7%	47.4%	50.2%	49.8%
1970	80,779	37,264	Miller, Keith	42,309	Egan, William A.	1,206	5,045 D	46.1%	52.4%	46.8%	53.2%
1966	66,294	33,145	Hickel, Walter J.	32,065	Egan, William A.	1,084	1,080 R	50.0%	48.4%	50.8%	49.2%
1962	56,681	27,054	Stepovich, Mike	29,627	Egan, William A.	—	2,573 D	47.7%	52.3%	47.7%	52.3%
1958	48,968	19,299	Butrovich, John	29,189	Egan, William A.	480	9,890 D	39.4%	59.6%	39.8%	60.2%

POSTWAR VOTE FOR SENATOR

Year	Total Vote	Republican Vote	Republican Candidate	Democratic Vote	Democratic Candidate	Other Vote	Rep.-Dem. Plurality	Total Vote Rep.	Total Vote Dem.	Major Vote Rep.	Major Vote Dem.
1984	206,438	146,919	Stevens, Ted	58,804	Havelock, John E.	715	88,115 R	71.2%	28.5%	71.4%	28.6%
1980	156,762	84,159	Murkowski, Frank H.	72,007	Gruening, Clark S.	596	12,152 R	53.7%	45.9%	53.9%	46.1%
1978	122,741	92,783	Stevens, Ted	29,574	Hobbs, Donald W.	384	63,209 R	75.6%	24.1%	75.8%	24.2%
1974	93,275	38,914	Lewis, C. R.	54,361	Gravel, Mike	—	15,447 D	41.7%	58.3%	41.7%	58.3%
1972	96,007	74,216	Stevens, Ted	21,791	Guess, Gene	—	52,425 R	77.3%	22.7%	77.3%	22.7%
1970 s	80,364	47,908	Stevens, Ted	32,456	Kay, Wendell P.	—	15,452 R	59.6%	40.4%	59.6%	40.4%
1968	80,931	30,286	Rasmuson, Elmer	36,527	Gravel, Mike	14,118	6,241 D	37.4%	45.1%	45.3%	54.7%
1966	65,250	15,961	McKinley, Lee L.	49,289	Bartlett, E. L.	—	33,328 D	24.5%	75.5%	24.5%	75.5%
1962	58,181	24,354	Gruening, Ernest	33,827	Gruening, Ernest	—	9,473 D	41.9%	58.1%	41.9%	58.1%
1960	59,978	21,937	McKinley, Lee L.	38,041	Bartlett, E. L.	—	16,104 D	36.6%	63.4%	36.6%	63.4%
1958 s	49,525	23,462	Stepovich, Mike	26,063	Gruening, Ernest	—	2,601 D	47.4%	52.6%	47.4%	52.6%
1958 s	48,837	7,299	Robertson, R. E.	40,939	Bartlett, E. L.	599	33,640 D	14.9%	83.8%	15.1%	84.9%

The two 1958 elections were held to indeterminate terms and the Senate later determined by lot that Senator Gruening would serve four years, Senator Bartlett two. The 1970 election was for a short term to fill a vacancy.

ALASKA

(One At Large)
Election Districts Established June 10, 1981

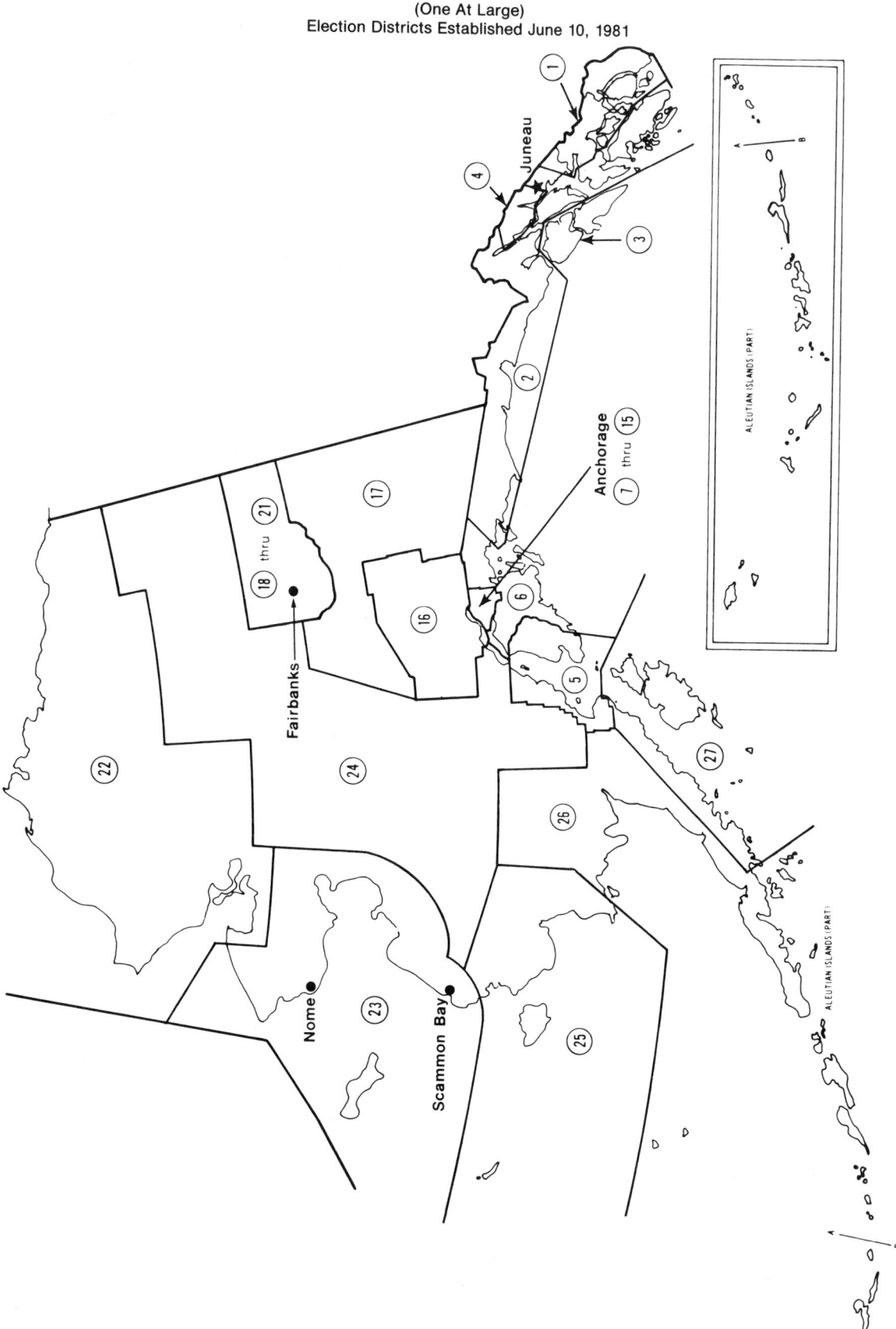

© ERC

ALASKA

PRESIDENT 1984

1980 Census Population	District	Total Vote	Republican	Democratic	Other	Rep.-Dem. Plurality	Percentage Total Vote Rep.	Dem.	Major Vote Rep.	Dem.
17,940	DISTRICT 1	8,406	5,256	2,937	213	2,319 R	62.5%	34.9%	64.2%	35.8%
9,301	DISTRICT 2	4,664	2,645	1,857	162	788 R	56.7%	39.8%	58.8%	41.2%
9,266	DISTRICT 3	4,236	2,540	1,561	135	979 R	60.0%	36.9%	61.9%	38.1%
19,528	DISTRICT 4	12,939	7,322	5,293	324	2,029 R	56.6%	40.9%	58.0%	42.0%
19,068	DISTRICT 5	11,627	8,188	2,896	543	5,292 R	70.4%	24.9%	73.9%	26.1%
9,267	DISTRICT 6	4,298	2,883	1,261	154	1,622 R	67.1%	29.3%	69.6%	30.4%
8,853	DISTRICT 7	6,154	4,363	1,539	252	2,824 R	70.9%	25.0%	73.9%	26.1%
18,202	DISTRICT 8	11,660	8,603	2,752	305	5,851 R	73.8%	23.6%	75.8%	24.2%
18,005	DISTRICT 9	11,818	8,361	3,186	271	5,175 R	70.7%	27.0%	72.4%	27.6%
17,686	DISTRICT 10	10,955	7,634	3,034	287	4,600 R	69.7%	27.7%	71.6%	28.4%
17,958	DISTRICT 11	8,121	5,176	2,621	324	2,555 R	63.7%	32.3%	66.4%	33.6%
18,170	DISTRICT 12	9,754	5,348	4,063	343	1,285 R	54.8%	41.7%	56.8%	43.2%
18,907	DISTRICT 13	9,004	6,106	2,616	282	3,490 R	67.8%	29.1%	70.0%	30.0%
19,031	DISTRICT 14	10,575	7,465	2,843	267	4,622 R	70.6%	26.9%	72.4%	27.6%
18,561	DISTRICT 15	12,113	8,993	2,749	371	6,244 R	74.2%	22.7%	76.6%	23.4%
17,725	DISTRICT 16	13,548	9,942	2,935	671	7,007 R	73.4%	21.7%	77.2%	22.8%
9,112	DISTRICT 17	5,012	3,793	1,014	205	2,779 R	75.7%	20.2%	78.9%	21.1%
9,300	DISTRICT 18	6,072	4,858	967	247	3,891 R	80.0%	15.9%	83.4%	16.6%
8,934	DISTRICT 19	6,141	3,880	1,905	356	1,975 R	63.2%	31.0%	67.1%	32.9%
18,320	DISTRICT 20	9,924	6,538	2,914	472	3,624 R	65.9%	29.4%	69.2%	30.8%
9,247	DISTRICT 21	6,347	3,629	2,433	285	1,196 R	57.2%	38.3%	59.9%	40.1%
9,030	DISTRICT 22	3,492	2,075	1,319	98	756 R	59.4%	37.8%	61.1%	38.9%
9,388	DISTRICT 23	3,816	2,165	1,546	105	619 R	56.7%	40.5%	58.3%	41.7%
9,549	DISTRICT 24	3,911	2,321	1,473	117	848 R	59.3%	37.7%	61.2%	38.8%
9,698	DISTRICT 25	3,964	2,004	1,825	135	179 R	50.6%	46.0%	52.3%	47.7%
9,479	DISTRICT 26	4,366	3,019	1,216	131	1,803 R	69.1%	27.9%	71.3%	28.7%
9,592	DISTRICT 27	4,688	3,270	1,252	166	2,018 R	69.8%	26.7%	72.3%	27.7%
369,117	TOTAL	207,605	138,377	62,007	7,221	76,370 R	66.7%	29.9%	69.1%	30.9%

ALASKA

SENATOR 1984

1980 Census Population	District	Total Vote	Republican	Democratic	Other	Rep.-Dem. Plurality	Percentage			
							Total Vote		Major Vote	
							Rep.	Dem.	Rep.	Dem.
17,940	DISTRICT 1	8,362	5,897	2,457	8	3,440 R	70.5%	29.4%	70.6%	29.4%
9,301	DISTRICT 2	4,517	2,934	1,578	5	1,356 R	65.0%	34.9%	65.0%	35.0%
9,266	DISTRICT 3	4,189	2,970	1,209	10	1,761 R	70.9%	28.9%	71.1%	28.9%
19,528	DISTRICT 4	12,885	8,318	4,517	50	3,801 R	64.6%	35.1%	64.8%	35.2%
19,068	DISTRICT 5	11,595	8,549	3,001	45	5,548 R	73.7%	25.9%	74.0%	26.0%
9,267	DISTRICT 6	4,267	3,072	1,175	20	1,897 R	72.0%	27.5%	72.3%	27.7%
8,853	DISTRICT 7	6,120	4,472	1,629	19	2,843 R	73.1%	26.6%	73.3%	26.7%
18,202	DISTRICT 8	11,583	8,646	2,886	51	5,760 R	74.6%	24.9%	75.0%	25.0%
18,005	DISTRICT 9	11,760	8,465	3,267	28	5,198 R	72.0%	27.8%	72.2%	27.8%
17,686	DISTRICT 10	10,857	7,652	3,143	62	4,509 R	70.5%	28.9%	70.9%	29.1%
17,958	DISTRICT 11	8,074	5,277	2,765	32	2,512 R	65.4%	34.2%	65.6%	34.4%
18,170	DISTRICT 12	9,718	5,867	3,810	41	2,057 R	60.4%	39.2%	60.6%	39.4%
18,907	DISTRICT 13	8,962	6,151	2,772	39	3,379 R	68.6%	30.9%	68.9%	31.1%
19,031	DISTRICT 14	10,530	7,609	2,883	38	4,726 R	72.3%	27.4%	72.5%	27.5%
18,561	DISTRICT 15	12,037	8,934	3,051	52	5,883 R	74.2%	25.3%	74.5%	25.5%
17,725	DISTRICT 16	13,480	10,121	3,302	57	6,819 R	75.1%	24.5%	75.4%	24.6%
9,112	DISTRICT 17	4,956	3,924	1,016	16	2,908 R	79.2%	20.5%	79.4%	20.6%
9,300	DISTRICT 18	6,073	4,858	1,194	21	3,664 R	80.0%	19.7%	80.3%	19.7%
8,934	DISTRICT 19	6,097	4,186	1,880	31	2,306 R	68.7%	30.8%	69.0%	31.0%
18,320	DISTRICT 20	9,896	6,999	2,868	29	4,131 R	70.7%	29.0%	70.9%	29.1%
9,247	DISTRICT 21	6,312	4,036	2,249	27	1,787 R	63.9%	35.6%	64.2%	35.8%
9,030	DISTRICT 22	3,469	2,501	963	5	1,538 R	72.1%	27.8%	72.2%	27.8%
9,388	DISTRICT 23	3,808	2,718	1,087	3	1,631 R	71.4%	28.5%	71.4%	28.6%
9,549	DISTRICT 24	3,894	2,896	992	6	1,904 R	74.4%	25.5%	74.5%	25.5%
9,698	DISTRICT 25	3,965	2,738	1,223	4	1,515 R	69.1%	30.8%	69.1%	30.9%
9,479	DISTRICT 26	4,352	3,485	862	5	2,623 R	80.1%	19.8%	80.2%	19.8%
9,592	DISTRICT 27	4,680	3,644	1,025	11	2,619 R	77.9%	21.9%	78.0%	22.0%
369,117	TOTAL	206,438	146,919	58,804	715	88,115 R	71.2%	28.5%	71.4%	28.6%

ALASKA

CONGRESS

CD	Year	Total Vote	Republican Vote	Candidate	Democratic Vote	Candidate	Other Vote	Rep.-Dem. Plurality	Percentage Total Vote Rep.	Total Vote Dem.	Major Vote Rep.	Major Vote Dem.
AL	1984	206,437	113,582	YOUNG, DON	86,052	BEGICH, PEGGE	6,803	27,530 R	55.0%	41.7%	56.9%	43.1%
AL	1982	181,084	128,274	YOUNG, DON	52,011	CARLSON, DAVE	799	76,263 R	70.8%	28.7%	71.2%	28.8%
AL	1980	154,618	114,089	YOUNG, DON	39,922	PARNELL, KEVIN	607	74,167 R	73.8%	25.8%	74.1%	25.9%
AL	1978	124,187	68,811	YOUNG, DON	55,176	RODEY, PATRICK	200	13,635 R	55.4%	44.4%	55.5%	44.5%
AL	1976	118,208	83,722	YOUNG, DON	34,194	HOPSON, EBEN	292	49,528 R	70.8%	28.9%	71.0%	29.0%
AL	1974	95,921	51,641	YOUNG, DON	44,280	HENSLEY, WILLIAM L.		7,361 R	53.8%	46.2%	53.8%	46.2%
AL	1972	95,401	41,750	YOUNG, DON	53,651	BEGICH, N. J.		11,901 D	43.8%	56.2%	43.8%	56.2%
AL	1970	80,084	35,947	MURKOWSKI, FRANK H.	44,137	BEGICH, N. J.		8,190 D	44.9%	55.1%	44.9%	55.1%
AL	1968	80,362	43,577	POLLOCK, HOWARD W.	36,785	BEGICH, N. J.		6,792 R	54.2%	45.8%	54.2%	45.8%
AL	1966	65,907	34,040	POLLOCK, HOWARD W.	31,867	RIVERS, RALPH J.		2,173 R	51.6%	48.4%	51.6%	48.4%
AL	1964	67,146	32,556	THOMAS, LOWELL	34,590	RIVERS, RALPH J.		2,034 D	48.5%	51.5%	48.5%	51.5%
AL	1962	58,591	26,638	THOMAS, LOWELL	31,953	RIVERS, RALPH J.		5,315 D	45.5%	54.5%	45.5%	54.5%
AL	1960	59,063	25,517	RETTIG, R. L.	33,546	RIVERS, RALPH J.		8,029 D	43.2%	56.8%	43.2%	56.8%
AL	1958	48,647	20,699	BENSON, HENRY A.	27,948	RIVERS, RALPH J.		7,249 D	42.5%	57.5%	42.5%	57.5%
AL	1956	28,266	9,332	GILLAM, BYRON A.	18,934	BARTLETT, E. L.		9,602 D	33.0%	67.0%	33.0%	67.0%
AL	1954	26,999	7,083	DIMOCK, BARBARA D.	19,916	BARTLETT, E. L.		12,833 D	26.2%	73.8%	26.2%	73.8%
AL	1952	25,112	10,893	REEVE, ROBERT C.	14,219	BARTLETT, E. L.		3,326 D	43.4%	56.6%	43.4%	56.6%
AL	1950	18,726	5,138	PETERSON, ALMER J.	13,588	BARTLETT, E. L.		8,450 D	27.4%	72.6%	27.4%	72.6%
AL	1948	22,309	4,789	STOCK, R. H.	17,520	BARTLETT, E. L.		12,731 D	21.5%	78.5%	21.5%	78.5%
AL	1946	16,384	4,868	PETERSON, ALMER J.	11,516	BARTLETT, E. L.		6,648 D	29.7%	70.3%	29.7%	70.3%

ALASKA

Population by districts excludes non-resident military and their dependents. The state-wide census population total is 401,851.

1984 GENERAL ELECTION

President   Other vote was 6,378 Bergland (Libertarian); 843 scattered.

Senator   Other vote was scattered.

Congress   Other vote was 6,508 Breck (Independent) and 295 scattered. The data for Congress on the previous page include the postwar voting for Delegate from 1946 to 1956 and for Representative at-large since statehood.

1984 PRIMARIES

Alaska's primaries are completely open, with all candidates for an office carried on the ballot together; thus a voter may vote for a Republican for Governor, a Democrat for Senator, and so on. Actual nominations go to the highest Republican and the highest Democrat, as determined in this so-called "jungle primary."

AUGUST 28 REPUBLICAN

Senator   65,522 Ted Stevens (only Republican candidate).

Congress

AL   52,175 Don Young (only Republican candidate).

AUGUST 28 DEMOCRATIC

Senator   19,074 John E. Havelock; 4,620 Dave Carlson; 2,443 Michael J. Beasley; 1,661 Joe Tracanna; 1,331 Phil Stoddard.

Congress

AL   26,519 Pegge Begich; 13,652 Thomas H. Dahl; 2,858 Ronald C. Mallott.

ARIZONA

GOVERNOR
Bruce Babbitt (D). Re-elected 1982 to a four-year term. Previously elected 1978; had succeeded to the Governorship in March 1978 on the death of Governor Wesley Bolin, who himself had succeeded Governor Raul H. Castro on the latter's October 1977 appointment to be an Ambassador.

SENATORS
Dennis DeConcini (D). Re-elected 1982 to a six-year term. Previously elected 1976.

Barry M. Goldwater (R). Re-elected 1980 to a six-year term. Previously elected 1974, 1968, 1958, 1952.

REPRESENTATIVES
1. John McCain (R)
2. Morris K. Udall (D)
3. Bob Stump (R)
4. Eldon Rudd (R)
5. Jim Kolbe (R)

POSTWAR VOTE FOR GOVERNOR

Year	Total Vote	Republican Vote	Candidate	Democratic Vote	Candidate	Other Vote	Rep.-Dem. Plurality	Total Vote Rep.	Total Vote Dem.	Major Vote Rep.	Major Vote Dem.
1982	726,364	235,877	Corbet, Leo	453,795	Babbitt, Bruce	36,692	217,918 D	32.5%	62.5%	34.2%	65.8%
1978	538,556	241,093	Mecham, Evan	282,605	Babbitt, Bruce	14,858	41,512 D	44.8%	52.5%	46.0%	54.0%
1974	552,202	273,674	Williams, Russell	278,375	Castro, Raul H.	153	4,701 D	49.6%	50.4%	49.6%	50.4%
1970*	411,409	209,522	Williams, John R.	201,887	Castro, Raul H.	—	7,635 R	50.9%	49.1%	50.9%	49.1%
1968	483,998	279,923	Williams, John R.	204,075	Goddard, Sam	—	75,848 R	57.8%	42.2%	57.8%	42.2%
1966	378,342	203,438	Williams, John R.	174,904	Goddard, Sam	—	28,534 R	53.8%	46.2%	53.8%	46.2%
1964	473,502	221,404	Kleindienst, Richard	252,098	Goddard, Sam	—	30,694 D	46.8%	53.2%	46.8%	53.2%
1962	365,841	200,578	Fannin, Paul	165,263	Goddard, Sam	—	35,315 R	54.8%	45.2%	54.8%	45.2%
1960	397,107	235,502	Fannin, Paul	161,605	Ackerman, Lee	—	73,897 R	59.3%	40.7%	59.3%	40.7%
1958	290,465	160,136	Fannin, Paul	130,329	Morrison, Robert	—	29,807 R	55.1%	44.9%	55.1%	44.9%
1956	288,592	116,744	Griffen, Horace B.	171,848	McFarland, Ernest W.	—	55,104 D	40.5%	59.5%	40.5%	59.5%
1954	243,970	115,866	Pyle, Howard	128,104	McFarland, Ernest W.	—	12,238 D	47.5%	52.5%	47.5%	52.5%
1952	260,285	156,592	Pyle, Howard	103,693	Haldiman, Joe C.	—	52,899 R	60.2%	39.8%	60.2%	39.8%
1950	195,227	99,109	Pyle, Howard	96,118	Frohmiller, Ana	—	2,991 R	50.8%	49.2%	50.8%	49.2%
1948	175,767	70,419	Brockett, Bruce	104,008	Garvey, Dan E.	1,340	33,589 D	40.1%	59.2%	40.4%	59.6%
1946	122,462	48,867	Brockett, Bruce	73,595	Osborn, Sidney P.	—	24,728 D	39.9%	60.1%	39.9%	60.1%

The term of office for Arizona's Governor was increased from two to four years effective with the 1970 election.

POSTWAR VOTE FOR SENATOR

Year	Total Vote	Republican Vote	Candidate	Democratic Vote	Candidate	Other Vote	Rep.-Dem. Plurality	Total Vote Rep.	Total Vote Dem.	Major Vote Rep.	Major Vote Dem.
1982	723,885	291,749	Dunn, Pete	411,970	DeConcini, Dennis	20,166	120,221 D	40.3%	56.9%	41.5%	58.5%
1980	874,238	432,371	Goldwater, Barry M.	422,972	Schulz, Bill	18,895	9,399 R	49.5%	48.4%	50.5%	49.5%
1976	741,210	321,236	Steiger, Sam	400,334	DeConcini, Dennis	19,640	79,098 D	43.3%	54.0%	44.5%	55.5%
1974	549,919	320,396	Goldwater, Barry M.	229,523	Marshall, Jonathan	—	90,873 R	58.3%	41.7%	58.3%	41.7%
1970	407,796	228,284	Fannin, Paul	179,512	Grossman, Sam	—	48,772 R	56.0%	44.0%	56.0%	44.0%
1968	479,945	274,607	Goldwater, Barry M.	205,338	Elson, Roy L.	—	69,269 R	57.2%	42.8%	57.2%	42.8%
1964	468,801	241,089	Fannin, Paul	227,712	Elson, Roy L.	—	13,377 R	51.4%	48.6%	51.4%	48.6%
1962	362,605	163,388	Mecham, Evan	199,217	Hayden, Carl	—	35,829 D	45.1%	54.9%	45.1%	54.9%
1958	293,623	164,593	Goldwater, Barry M.	129,030	McFarland, Ernest W.	—	35,563 R	56.1%	43.9%	56.1%	43.9%
1956	278,263	107,447	Jones, Ross F.	170,816	Hayden, Carl	—	63,369 D	38.6%	61.4%	38.6%	61.4%
1952	257,401	132,063	Goldwater, Barry M.	125,338	McFarland, Ernest W.	—	6,725 R	51.3%	48.7%	51.3%	48.7%
1950	185,092	68,846	Brockett, Bruce	116,246	Hayden, Carl	—	47,400 D	37.2%	62.8%	37.2%	62.8%
1946	116,239	35,022	Powers, Ward S.	80,415	McFarland, Ernest W.	802	45,393 D	30.1%	69.2%	30.3%	69.7%

ARIZONA

Districts Established April 2, 1982

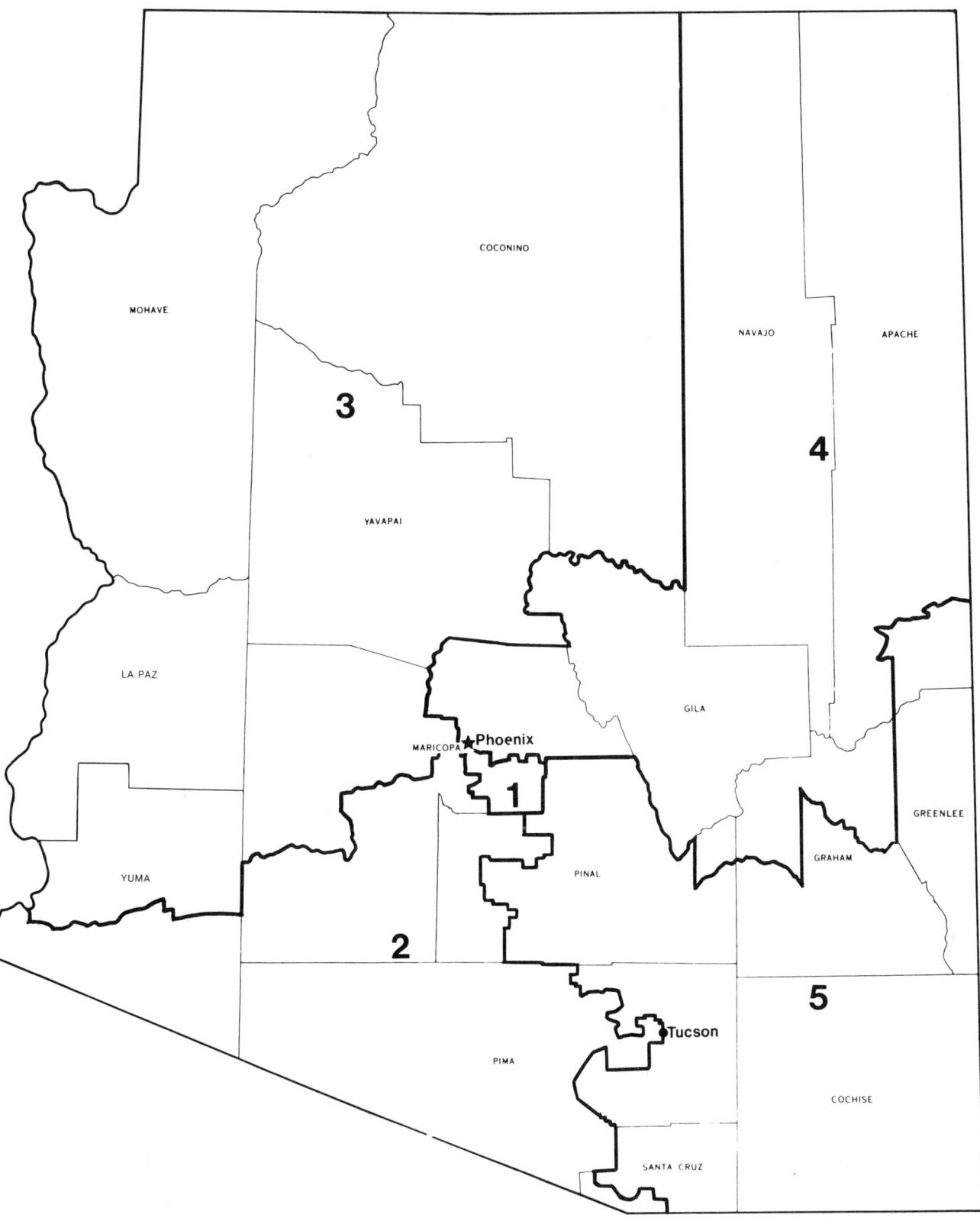

ARIZONA

PRESIDENT 1984

1980 Census Population	County	Total Vote	Republican	Democratic	Other	Rep.-Dem. Plurality	Percentage Total Vote Rep.	Dem.	Major Vote Rep.	Dem.
52,108	APACHE	13,032	5,638	7,277	117	1,639 D	43.3%	55.8%	43.7%	56.3%
85,686	COCHISE	26,355	16,405	9,671	279	6,734 R	62.2%	36.7%	62.9%	37.1%
75,008	COCONINO	29,735	17,581	11,528	626	6,053 R	59.1%	38.8%	60.4%	39.6%
37,080	GILA	15,249	8,543	6,509	197	2,034 R	56.0%	42.7%	56.8%	43.2%
22,862	GRAHAM	8,416	5,247	3,080	89	2,167 R	62.3%	36.6%	63.0%	37.0%
11,406	GREENLEE	3,785	1801	1963	21	162 D	47.6%	51.9%	47.8%	52.2%
12,557	LA PAZ	4,313	2,757	1,502	54	1,255 R	63.9%	34.8%	64.7%	35.3%
1,509,052	MARICOPA	572,273	411,902	154,833	5,538	257,069 R	72.0%	27.1%	72.7%	27.3%
55,865	MOHAVE	25,072	17,364	7,436	272	9,928 R	69.3%	29.7%	70.0%	30.0%
67,629	NAVAJO	19,578	11,379	8,017	182	3,362 R	58.1%	40.9%	58.7%	41.3%
531,443	PIMA	217,612	123,830	91,585	2,197	32,245 R	56.9%	42.1%	57.5%	42.5%
90,918	PINAL	28,619	16,464	11,923	232	4,541 R	57.5%	41.7%	58.0%	42.0%
20,459	SANTA CRUZ	6,389	3,855	2,463	71	1,392 R	60.3%	38.6%	61.0%	39.0%
68,145	YAVAPAI	34,988	24,802	9,609	577	15,193 R	70.9%	27.5%	72.1%	27.9%
77,997	YUMA	20,481	13,848	6,458	175	7,390 R	67.6%	31.5%	68.2%	31.8%
2,718,215	TOTAL	1,025,897	681,416	333,854	10,627	347,562 R	66.4%	32.5%	67.1%	32.9%

ARIZONA

CONGRESS

CD	Year	Total Vote	Republican Vote	Candidate	Democratic Vote	Candidate	Other Vote	Rep.-Dem. Plurality	Percentage Total Vote Rep.	Dem.	Major Vote Rep.	Dem.
1	1984	208,027	162,418	MCCAIN, JOHN	45,609	BRAUN, HARRY W.		116,809 R	78.1%	21.9%	78.1%	21.9%
1	1982	135,227	89,116	MCCAIN, JOHN	41,261	HEGARTY, WILLIAM E.	4,850	47,855 R	65.9%	30.5%	68.4%	31.6%
2	1984	121,215			106,332	UDALL, MORRIS K.	14,883	106,332 D		87.7%		100.0%
2	1982	103,674	28,407	LAOS, ROY B.	73,468	UDALL, MORRIS K.	1,799	45,061 D	27.4%	70.9%	27.9%	72.1%
3	1984	218,328	156,686	STUMP, BOB	57,748	SCHUSTER, BOB	3,894	98,938 R	71.8%	26.5%	73.1%	26.9%
3	1982	159,842	101,198	STUMP, BOB	58,644	BOSCH, PAT		42,554 R	63.3%	36.7%	63.3%	36.7%
4	1984	167,615	167,558	RUDD, ELDON			57	167,558 R	100.0%		100.0%	
4	1982	145,466	95,620	RUDD, ELDON	44,182	EARLEY, WAYNE O.	5,664	51,438 R	65.7%	30.4%	68.4%	31.6%
5	1984	227,938	116,075	KOLBE, JIM	109,871	MCNULTY, JIM	1,992	6,204 R	50.9%	48.2%	51.4%	48.6%
5	1982	166,802	80,531	KOLBE, JIM	82,938	MCNULTY, JIM	3,333	2,407 D	48.3%	49.7%	49.3%	50.7%

ARIZONA

The county of LaPaz was formed from the northern half of Yuma county after a vote on May 25, 1982 by the people of this region to form a new county. LaPaz became the fifteenth county in Arizona on January 1, 1983.

1984 GENERAL ELECTION

President   Other vote was 10,585 Bergland (Libertarian); 18 Johnson (write-in); 3 Winn (write-in); 21 scattered.

Congress   Other vote was 14,869 Torrez (People Before Profits) and 14 Raible (write-in Libertarian) in CD 2; Valencia (Libertarian) in CD 3; Rothe (write-in Libertarian) in CD 4; Johnson (Libertarian) in CD 5.

1984 PRIMARIES

SEPTEMBER 11 REPUBLICAN

Congress   Unopposed in four CD's. No candidate in CD 2.

SEPTEMBER 11 DEMOCRATIC

Congress   Unopposed in three CD's. No candidate in CD 4. Contested as follows:

   CD   2   30,587 Morris K. Udall; 5,109 Joseph D. Sweeney.

SEPTEMBER 11 LIBERTARIAN

Congress   Unopposed in two CD's. No candidate in CD's 1, 2, and 4.

ARKANSAS

GOVERNOR
Bill Clinton (D). Re-elected 1984 to a two-year term. Previously elected 1982, 1978.

SENATORS
Dale Bumpers (D). Re-elected 1980 to a six-year term. Previously elected 1974.

David H. Pryor (D). Re-elected 1984 to a six-year term. Previously elected 1978.

REPRESENTATIVES
1. William Alexander (D)
2. Tommy F. Robinson (D)
3. John Hammerschmidt (R)
4. Beryl F. Anthony (D)

POSTWAR VOTE FOR GOVERNOR

Year	Total Vote	Republican Vote	Republican Candidate	Democratic Vote	Democratic Candidate	Other Vote	Rep.-Dem. Plurality	Total Vote Rep.	Total Vote Dem.	Major Vote Rep.	Major Vote Dem.
1984	886,548	331,987	Freeman, Woody	554,561	Clinton, Bill	—	222,574 D	37.4%	62.6%	37.4%	62.6%
1982	789,351	357,496	White, Frank D.	431,855	Clinton, Bill	—	74,359 D	45.3%	54.7%	45.3%	54.7%
1980	838,925	435,684	White, Frank D.	403,241	Clinton, Bill	—	32,443 R	51.9%	48.1%	51.9%	48.1%
1978	528,912	193,746	Lowe, A. Lynn	335,101	Clinton, Bill	65	141,355 D	36.6%	63.4%	36.6%	63.4%
1976	726,949	121,716	Griffith, Leon	605,083	Pryor, David H.	150	483,367 D	16.7%	83.2%	16.7%	83.3%
1974	545,974	187,872	Coon, Ken	358,018	Pryor, David H.	84	170,146 D	34.4%	65.6%	34.4%	65.6%
1972	648,069	159,177	Blaylock, Len E.	488,892	Bumpers, Dale	—	329,715 D	24.6%	75.4%	24.6%	75.4%
1970	609,198	197,418	Rockefeller, Winthrop	375,648	Bumpers, Dale	36,132	178,230 D	32.4%	61.7%	34.4%	65.6%
1968	615,595	322,782	Rockefeller, Winthrop	292,813	Crank, Marion	—	29,969 R	52.4%	47.6%	52.4%	47.6%
1966	563,527	306,324	Rockefeller, Winthrop	257,203	Johnson, James D.	—	49,121 R	54.4%	45.6%	54.4%	45.6%
1964	592,113	254,561	Rockefeller, Winthrop	337,489	Faubus, Orval E.	63	82,928 D	43.0%	57.0%	43.0%	57.0%
1962	308,092	82,349	Ricketts, Willis	225,743	Faubus, Orval E.	—	143,394 D	26.7%	73.3%	26.7%	73.3%
1960	421,985	129,921	Britt, Henry M.	292,064	Faubus, Orval E.	—	162,143 D	30.8%	69.2%	30.8%	69.2%
1958	286,886	50,288	Johnson, George W.	236,598	Faubus, Orval E.	—	186,310 D	17.5%	82.5%	17.5%	82.5%
1956	399,012	77,215	Mitchell, Roy	321,797	Faubus, Orval E.	—	244,582 D	19.4%	80.6%	19.4%	80.6%
1954	335,176	127,004	Remmel, Pratt C.	208,121	Faubus, Orval E.	51	81,117 D	37.9%	62.1%	37.9%	62.1%
1952	391,592	49,292	Speck, Jefferson W.	342,292	Cherry, Francis	8	293,000 D	12.6%	87.4%	12.6%	87.4%
1950	317,087	50,309	Speck, Jefferson W.	266,778	McMath, Sidney S.	—	216,469 D	15.9%	84.1%	15.9%	84.1%
1948	249,301	26,500	Black, Charles R.	222,801	McMath, Sidney S.	—	196,301 D	10.6%	89.4%	10.6%	89.4%
1946	152,162	24,133	Mills, W. T.	128,029	Laney, Ben T.	—	103,896 D	15.9%	84.1%	15.9%	84.1%

POSTWAR VOTE FOR SENATOR

Year	Total Vote	Republican Vote	Republican Candidate	Democratic Vote	Democratic Candidate	Other Vote	Rep.-Dem. Plurality	Total Vote Rep.	Total Vote Dem.	Major Vote Rep.	Major Vote Dem.
1984	875,956	373,615	Bethune, Ed	502,341	Pryor, David H.	—	128,726 D	42.7%	57.3%	42.7%	57.3%
1980	808,812	330,576	Clark, Bill	477,905	Bumpers, Dale	331	147,329 D	40.9%	59.1%	40.9%	59.1%
1978	522,239	84,722	Kelly, Tom	399,916	Pryor, David H.	37,601	315,194 D	16.2%	76.6%	17.5%	82.5%
1974	543,082	82,026	Jones, John H.	461,056	Bumpers, Dale	—	379,030 D	15.1%	84.9%	15.1%	84.9%
1972	634,636	248,238	Babbitt, Wayne H.	386,398	McClellan, John L.	—	138,160 D	39.1%	60.9%	39.1%	60.9%
1968	591,704	241,739	Bernard, Charles T.	349,965	Fulbright, J. W.	—	108,226 D	40.9%	59.1%	40.9%	59.1%
1966 *	—	—	—	—	McClellan, John L.	—	—	—	—	—	—
1962	312,880	98,013	Jones, Kenneth	214,867	Fulbright, J. W.	—	116,854 D	31.3%	68.7%	31.3%	68.7%
1960 *	—	—	—	—	McClellan, John L.	—	—	—	—	—	—
1956	399,695	68,016	Henley, Ben C.	331,679	Fulbright, J. W.	—	263,663 D	17.0%	83.0%	17.0%	83.0%
1954	291,058	—	—	291,058	McClellan, John L.	—	291,058 D	—	100.0%	—	100.0%
1950	302,582	—	—	302,582	Fulbright, J. W.	—	302,582 D	—	100.0%	—	100.0%
1948	216,401	—	—	216,401	McClellan, John L.	—	216,401 D	—	100.0%	—	100.0%

Senator McClellan was re-elected in 1966 and in 1960, but his vote was not canvassed in many counties.

ARKANSAS

Districts Established February 25, 1981

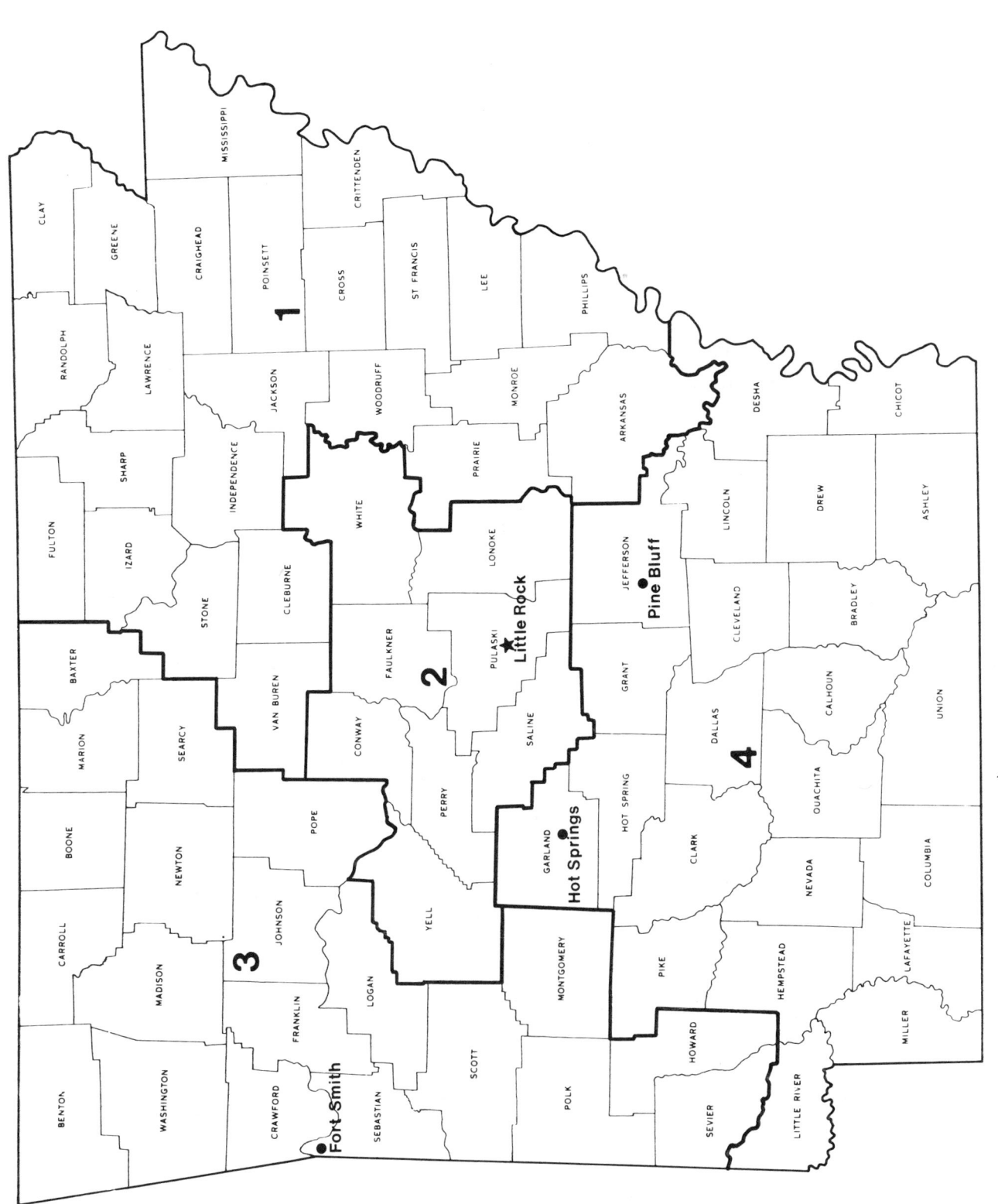

ARKANSAS

PRESIDENT 1984

1980 Census Population	County	Total Vote	Republican	Democratic	Other	Rep.-Dem. Plurality	Percentage Total Vote Rep.	Dem.	Major Vote Rep.	Dem.
24,175	ARKANSAS	8,008	4,804	3,153	51	1,651 R	60.0%	39.4%	60.4%	39.6%
26,538	ASHLEY	9,089	5,675	3,373	41	2,302 R	62.4%	37.1%	62.7%	37.3%
27,409	BAXTER	15,564	10,870	4,528	166	6,342 R	69.8%	29.1%	70.6%	29.4%
78,115	BENTON	32,010	24,296	7,306	408	16,990 R	75.9%	22.8%	76.9%	23.1%
26,067	BOONE	11,567	7,961	3,356	250	4,605 R	68.8%	29.0%	70.3%	29.7%
13,803	BRADLEY	5,017	2,690	2,313	14	377 R	53.6%	46.1%	53.8%	46.2%
6,079	CALHOUN	2,535	1,474	1,058	3	416 R	58.1%	41.7%	58.2%	41.8%
16,203	CARROLL	7,390	5,041	2,263	86	2,778 R	68.2%	30.6%	69.0%	31.0%
17,793	CHICOT	5,927	2,502	3,407	18	905 D	42.2%	57.5%	42.3%	57.7%
23,326	CLARK	8,853	4,185	4,638	30	453 D	47.3%	52.4%	47.4%	52.6%
20,616	CLAY	7,105	3,767	3,279	59	488 R	53.0%	46.2%	53.5%	46.5%
16,909	CLEBURNE	9,008	5,769	3,172	67	2,597 R	64.0%	35.2%	64.5%	35.5%
7,868	CLEVELAND	3,165	1,773	1,378	14	395 R	56.0%	43.5%	56.3%	43.7%
26,644	COLUMBIA	10,285	6,526	3,680	79	2,846 R	63.5%	35.8%	63.9%	36.1%
19,505	CONWAY	8,836	5,049	3,742	45	1,307 R	57.1%	42.3%	57.4%	42.6%
63,239	CRAIGHEAD	22,343	14,047	8,035	261	6,012 R	62.9%	36.0%	63.6%	36.4%
36,892	CRAWFORD	12,701	9,551	3,071	79	6,480 R	75.2%	24.2%	75.7%	24.3%
49,499	CRITTENDEN	13,934	6,663	6,520	751	143 R	47.8%	46.8%	50.5%	49.5%
20,434	CROSS	6,635	3,917	2,701	17	1,216 R	59.0%	40.7%	59.2%	40.8%
10,515	DALLAS	4,472	2,361	2,035	76	326 R	52.8%	45.5%	53.7%	46.3%
19,760	DESHA	5,878	2,696	2,918	264	222 D	45.9%	49.6%	48.0%	52.0%
17,910	DREW	6,073	3,407	2,638	28	769 R	56.1%	43.4%	56.4%	43.6%
46,192	FAULKNER	19,043	11,595	7,169	279	4,426 R	60.9%	37.6%	61.8%	38.2%
14,705	FRANKLIN	6,843	4,382	2,399	62	1,983 R	64.0%	35.1%	64.6%	35.4%
9,975	FULTON	4,223	2329	1864	30	465 R	55.2%	44.1%	55.5%	44.5%
70,531	GARLAND	33,958	21,213	11,484	1,261	9,729 R	62.5%	33.8%	64.9%	35.1%
13,008	GRANT	5,353	3,167	2,148	38	1,019 R	59.2%	40.1%	59.6%	40.4%
30,744	GREENE	11,000	6,179	4,730	91	1,449 R	56.2%	43.0%	56.6%	43.4%
23,635	HEMPSTEAD	8,268	4,904	3,327	37	1,577 R	59.3%	40.2%	59.6%	40.4%
26,819	HOT SPRING	11,546	5,629	5,836	81	207 D	48.8%	50.5%	49.1%	50.9%
13,459	HOWARD	4,832	3,079	1,746	7	1,333 R	63.7%	36.1%	63.8%	36.2%
30,147	INDEPENDENCE	11,911	7,428	4,415	68	3,013 R	62.4%	37.1%	62.7%	37.3%
10,768	IZARD	5,136	2,726	2,346	64	380 R	53.1%	45.7%	53.7%	46.3%
21,646	JACKSON	7,981	3,901	4,038	42	137 D	48.9%	50.6%	49.1%	50.9%
90,718	JEFFERSON	32,909	14,514	18,082	313	3,568 D	44.1%	54.9%	44.5%	55.5%
17,423	JOHNSON	7,827	4,720	3,056	51	1,664 R	60.3%	39.0%	60.7%	39.3%
10,213	LAFAYETTE	4,007	2,290	1,695	22	595 R	57.1%	42.3%	57.5%	42.5%
18,447	LAWRENCE	6,676	4,039	2,594	43	1,445 R	60.5%	38.9%	60.9%	39.1%
15,539	LEE	4,717	2,101	2,541	75	440 D	44.5%	53.9%	45.3%	54.7%
13,369	LINCOLN	4,272	1,860	2,406	6	546 D	43.5%	56.3%	43.6%	56.4%
13,952	LITTLE RIVER	5,295	3,155	2,090	50	1,065 R	59.6%	39.5%	60.2%	39.8%
20,144	LOGAN	8,969	5,663	3,206	100	2,457 R	63.1%	35.7%	63.9%	36.1%
34,518	LONOKE	13,142	8,425	4,636	81	3,789 R	64.1%	35.3%	64.5%	35.5%
11,373	MADISON	5,703	3,516	2,133	54	1,383 R	61.7%	37.4%	62.2%	37.8%
11,334	MARION	5,524	3,545	1,945	34	1,600 R	64.2%	35.2%	64.6%	35.4%
37,766	MILLER	13,088	8,302	4,686	100	3,616 R	63.4%	35.8%	63.9%	36.1%
59,517	MISSISSIPPI	17,766	10,180	7,548	38	2,632 R	57.3%	42.5%	57.4%	42.6%
14,052	MONROE	4,971	2,508	2,413	50	95 R	50.5%	48.5%	51.0%	49.0%
7,771	MONTGOMERY	3,757	2,221	1,497	39	724 R	59.1%	39.8%	59.7%	40.3%
11,097	NEVADA	4,152	2,352	1,783	17	569 R	56.6%	42.9%	56.9%	43.1%
7,756	NEWTON	4,173	2,749	1,414	10	1,335 R	65.9%	33.9%	66.0%	34.0%
30,541	OUACHITA	13,089	6,700	5,858	531	842 R	51.2%	44.8%	53.4%	46.6%
7,266	PERRY	3,480	2,047	1,404	29	643 R	58.8%	40.3%	59.3%	40.7%
34,772	PHILLIPS	10,723	4,686	5,946	91	1,260 D	43.7%	55.5%	44.1%	55.9%
10,373	PIKE	4,118	2,665	1,443	10	1,222 R	64.7%	35.0%	64.9%	35.1%
27,032	POINSETT	9,587	5,622	3,906	59	1,716 R	58.6%	40.7%	59.0%	41.0%
17,007	POLK	7,386	5,181	2,101	104	3,080 R	70.1%	28.4%	71.1%	28.9%
39,021	POPE	15,855	10,667	5,082	106	5,585 R	67.3%	32.1%	67.7%	32.3%
10,140	PRAIRIE	3,876	2,407	1,437	32	970 R	62.1%	37.1%	62.6%	37.4%
340,613	PULASKI	133,418	77,651	54,237	1,530	23,414 R	58.2%	40.7%	58.9%	41.1%

ARKANSAS

PRESIDENT 1984

1980 Census Population	County	Total Vote	Republican	Democratic	Other	Rep.-Dem. Plurality	Percentage Total Vote Rep.	Dem.	Major Vote Rep.	Dem.
16,834	RANDOLPH	5,733	3,188	2,507	38	681 R	55.6%	43.7%	56.0%	44.0%
30,858	ST. FRANCIS	10,322	5,378	4,866	78	512 R	52.1%	47.1%	52.5%	47.5%
53,161	SALINE	19,297	11,709	6,977	611	4,732 R	60.7%	36.2%	62.7%	37.3%
9,685	SCOTT	4,709	3,066	1,609	34	1,457 R	65.1%	34.2%	65.6%	34.4%
8,847	SEARCY	4,201	2,819	1,313	69	1,506 R	67.1%	31.3%	68.2%	31.8%
95,172	SEBASTIAN	36,817	27,595	8,688	534	18,907 R	75.0%	23.6%	76.1%	23.9%
14,060	SEVIER	5,271	3,302	1,942	27	1,360 R	62.6%	36.8%	63.0%	37.0%
14,607	SHARP	6,930	4,392	2,492	46	1,900 R	63.4%	36.0%	63.8%	36.2%
9,022	STONE	4,045	2,325	1,654	66	671 R	57.5%	40.9%	58.4%	41.6%
48,573	UNION	18,759	12,333	6,208	218	6,125 R	65.7%	33.1%	66.5%	33.5%
13,357	VAN BUREN	6,659	4,060	2,529	70	1,531 R	61.0%	38.0%	61.6%	38.4%
100,494	WASHINGTON	36,698	24,993	11,319	386	13,674 R	68.1%	30.8%	68.8%	31.2%
50,835	WHITE	19,435	12,566	6,603	266	5,963 R	64.7%	34.0%	65.6%	34.4%
11,222	WOODRUFF	3,759	1,675	2,055	29	380 D	44.6%	54.7%	44.9%	55.1%
17,026	YELL	6,802	4,051	2,679	72	1,372 R	59.6%	39.4%	60.2%	39.8%
2,286,435	TOTAL	884,406	534,774	338,646	10,986	196,128 R	60.5%	38.3%	61.2%	38.8%

ARKANSAS

GOVERNOR 1984

1980 Census Population	County	Total Vote	Republican	Democratic	Other	Rep.-Dem. Plurality	Percentage Total Vote Rep.	Dem.	Major Vote Rep.	Dem.
24,175	ARKANSAS	8,321	2,470	5,851		3,381 D	29.7%	70.3%	29.7%	70.3%
26,538	ASHLEY	8,953	2,536	6,417		3,881 D	28.3%	71.7%	28.3%	71.7%
27,409	BAXTER	15,608	7,682	7,926		244 D	49.2%	50.8%	49.2%	50.8%
78,115	BENTON	32,226	16,618	15,608		1,010 R	51.6%	48.4%	51.6%	48.4%
26,067	BOONE	10,908	5,175	5,733		558 D	47.4%	52.6%	47.4%	52.6%
13,803	BRADLEY	5,152	1,514	3,638		2,124 D	29.4%	70.6%	29.4%	70.6%
6,079	CALHOUN	2,558	912	1,646		734 D	35.7%	64.3%	35.7%	64.3%
16,203	CARROLL	7,053	3,307	3,746		439 D	46.9%	53.1%	46.9%	53.1%
17,793	CHICOT	5,754	1,209	4,545		3,336 D	21.0%	79.0%	21.0%	79.0%
23,326	CLARK	9,082	2,373	6,709		4,336 D	26.1%	73.9%	26.1%	73.9%
20,616	CLAY	7,340	2,803	4,537		1,734 D	38.2%	61.8%	38.2%	61.8%
16,909	CLEBURNE	9,201	4,110	5,091		981 D	44.7%	55.3%	44.7%	55.3%
7,868	CLEVELAND	3,427	1,408	2,019		611 D	41.1%	58.9%	41.1%	58.9%
26,644	COLUMBIA	9,813	4,380	5,433		1,053 D	44.6%	55.4%	44.6%	55.4%
19,505	CONWAY	9,231	2,987	6,244		3,257 D	32.4%	67.6%	32.4%	67.6%
63,239	CRAIGHEAD	22,149	10,410	11,739		1,329 D	47.0%	53.0%	47.0%	53.0%
36,892	CRAWFORD	13,262	7,335	5,927		1,408 R	55.3%	44.7%	55.3%	44.7%
49,499	CRITTENDEN	12,993	3,529	9,464		5,935 D	27.2%	72.8%	27.2%	72.8%
20,434	CROSS	6,682	2,065	4,617		2,552 D	30.9%	69.1%	30.9%	69.1%
10,515	DALLAS	4,904	1,499	3,405		1,906 D	30.6%	69.4%	30.6%	69.4%
19,760	DESHA	5,737	1,285	4,452		3,167 D	22.4%	77.6%	22.4%	77.6%
17,910	DREW	6,145	1,666	4,479		2,813 D	27.1%	72.9%	27.1%	72.9%
46,192	FAULKNER	18,287	6,201	12,086		5,885 D	33.9%	66.1%	33.9%	66.1%
14,705	FRANKLIN	6,969	3,596	3,373		223 R	51.6%	48.4%	51.6%	48.4%
9,975	FULTON	4,264	1,681	2,583		902 D	39.4%	60.6%	39.4%	60.6%
70,531	GARLAND	33,103	12,739	20,364		7,625 D	38.5%	61.5%	38.5%	61.5%
13,008	GRANT	5,485	2,127	3,358		1,231 D	38.8%	61.2%	38.8%	61.2%
30,744	GREENE	12,067	4,696	7,371		2,675 D	38.9%	61.1%	38.9%	61.1%
23,635	HEMPSTEAD	8,489	2,936	5,553		2,617 D	34.6%	65.4%	34.6%	65.4%
26,819	HOT SPRINGS	11,795	3,609	8,186		4,577 D	30.6%	69.4%	30.6%	69.4%
13,459	HOWARD	4,833	1,746	3,087		1,341 D	36.1%	63.9%	36.1%	63.9%
30,147	INDEPENDENCE	12,180	5,016	7,164		2,148 D	41.2%	58.8%	41.2%	58.8%
10,768	IZARD	5,182	1,965	3,217		1,252 D	37.9%	62.1%	37.9%	62.1%
21,646	JACKSON	8,007	2,907	5,100		2,193 D	36.3%	63.7%	36.3%	63.7%
90,718	JEFFERSON	31,688	7,089	24,599		17,510 D	22.4%	77.6%	22.4%	77.6%
17,423	JOHNSON	7,928	3,552	4,376		824 D	44.8%	55.2%	44.8%	55.2%
10,213	LAFAYETTE	4,028	1,451	2,577		1,126 D	36.0%	64.0%	36.0%	64.0%
18,447	LAWRENCE	6,802	2,776	4,026		1,250 D	40.8%	59.2%	40.8%	59.2%
15,539	LEE	5,287	1,020	4,267		3,247 D	19.3%	80.7%	19.3%	80.7%
13,369	LINCOLN	4,340	936	3,404		2,468 D	21.6%	78.4%	21.6%	78.4%
13,952	LITTLE RIVER	5,420	1,930	3,490		1,560 D	35.6%	64.4%	35.6%	64.4%
20,144	LOGAN	9,160	4,607	4,553		54 R	50.3%	49.7%	50.3%	49.7%
34,518	LONOKE	13,103	4,540	8,563		4,023 D	34.6%	65.4%	34.6%	65.4%
11,373	MADISON	5,788	2,841	2,947		106 D	49.1%	50.9%	49.1%	50.9%
11,334	MARION	5,639	2,335	3,304		969 D	41.4%	58.6%	41.4%	58.6%
37,766	MILLER	14,131	5,266	8,865		3,599 D	37.3%	62.7%	37.3%	62.7%
59,517	MISSISSIPPI	18,714	6,012	12,702		6,690 D	32.1%	67.9%	32.1%	67.9%
14,052	MONROE	5,144	1,348	3,796		2,448 D	26.2%	73.8%	26.2%	73.8%
7,771	MONTGOMERY	3,866	1,649	2,217		568 D	42.7%	57.3%	42.7%	57.3%
11,097	NEVADA	4,435	1,547	2,888		1,341 D	34.9%	65.1%	34.9%	65.1%
7,756	NEWTON	4,319	2,337	1,982		355 R	54.1%	45.9%	54.1%	45.9%
30,541	OUACHITA	12,271	3,564	8,707		5,143 D	29.0%	71.0%	29.0%	71.0%
7,266	PERRY	3,548	1,342	2,206		864 D	37.8%	62.2%	37.8%	62.2%
34,772	PHILLIPS	11,378	2,364	9,014		6,650 D	20.8%	79.2%	20.8%	79.2%
10,373	PIKE	4,167	1,752	2,415		663 D	42.0%	58.0%	42.0%	58.0%
27,032	POINSETT	10,093	3,679	6,414		2,735 D	36.5%	63.5%	36.5%	63.5%
17,007	POLK	7,447	3,314	4,133		819 D	44.5%	55.5%	44.5%	55.5%
39,021	POPE	16,030	7,441	8,589		1,148 D	46.4%	53.6%	46.4%	53.6%
10,140	PRAIRIE	3,936	1,363	2,573		1,210 D	34.6%	65.4%	34.6%	65.4%
340,613	PULASKI	128,665	37,789	90,876		53,087 D	29.4%	70.6%	29.4%	70.6%

ARKANSAS

GOVERNOR 1984

| 1980 Census Population | County | Total Vote | Republican | Democratic | Other | Rep.-Dem. Plurality | Percentage | | | |
| | | | | | | | Total Vote | | Major Vote | |
							Rep.	Dem.	Rep.	Dem.
16,834	RANDOLPH	5,848	2,252	3,596		1,344 D	38.5%	61.5%	38.5%	61.5%
30,858	ST. FRANCIS	10,682	2,958	7,724		4,766 D	27.7%	72.3%	27.7%	72.3%
53,161	SALINE	21,133	6,879	14,254		7,375 D	32.6%	67.4%	32.6%	67.4%
9,685	SCOTT	4,743	2,419	2,324		95 R	51.0%	49.0%	51.0%	49.0%
8,847	SEARCY	4,468	2,440	2,028		412 R	54.6%	45.4%	54.6%	45.4%
95,172	SEBASTIAN	36,163	19,665	16,498		3,167 R	54.4%	45.6%	54.4%	45.6%
14,060	SEVIER	5,427	1,839	3,588		1,749 D	33.9%	66.1%	33.9%	66.1%
14,607	SHARP	7,049	3,201	3,848		647 D	45.4%	54.6%	45.4%	54.6%
9,022	STONE	4,144	1,976	2,168		192 D	47.7%	52.3%	47.7%	52.3%
48,573	UNION	17,455	7,312	10,143		2,831 D	41.9%	58.1%	41.9%	58.1%
13,357	VAN BUREN	6,774	2,728	4,046		1,318 D	40.3%	59.7%	40.3%	59.7%
100,494	WASHINGTON	36,280	16,095	20,185		4,090 D	44.4%	55.6%	44.4%	55.6%
50,835	WHITE	20,549	7,722	12,827		5,105 D	37.6%	62.4%	37.6%	62.4%
11,222	WOODRUFF	3,777	803	2,974		2,171 D	21.3%	78.7%	21.3%	78.7%
17,026	YELL	7,569	3,362	4,207		845 D	44.4%	55.6%	44.4%	55.6%
2,286,435	TOTAL	886,548	331,987	554,561		222,574 D	37.4%	62.6%	37.4%	62.6%

ARKANSAS

SENATOR 1984

1980 Census Population	County	Total Vote	Republican	Democratic	Other	Rep.-Dem. Plurality	Percentage			
							Total Vote		Major Vote	
							Rep.	Dem.	Rep.	Dem.
24,175	ARKANSAS	8,319	2,772	5,547		2,775 D	33.3%	66.7%	33.3%	66.7%
26,538	ASHLEY	8,945	3,335	5,610		2,275 D	37.3%	62.7%	37.3%	62.7%
27,409	BAXTER	14,702	8,660	6,042		2,618 R	58.9%	41.1%	58.9%	41.1%
78,115	BENTON	30,878	18,923	11,955		6,968 R	61.3%	38.7%	61.3%	38.7%
26,067	BOONE	10,927	5,780	5,147		633 R	52.9%	47.1%	52.9%	47.1%
13,803	BRADLEY	5,138	1,413	3,725		2,312 D	27.5%	72.5%	27.5%	72.5%
6,079	CALHOUN	2,452	763	1,689		926 D	31.1%	68.9%	31.1%	68.9%
16,203	CARROLL	7,058	3,330	3,728		398 D	47.2%	52.8%	47.2%	52.8%
17,793	CHICOT	5,985	1,601	4,384		2,783 D	26.8%	73.2%	26.8%	73.2%
23,326	CLARK	9,152	2,425	6,727		4,302 D	26.5%	73.5%	26.5%	73.5%
20,616	CLAY	7,305	2,251	5,054		2,803 D	30.8%	69.2%	30.8%	69.2%
16,909	CLEBURNE	9,206	4,492	4,714		222 D	48.8%	51.2%	48.8%	51.2%
7,868	CLEVELAND	3,456	1,041	2,415		1,374 D	30.1%	69.9%	30.1%	69.9%
26,644	COLUMBIA	9,716	4,466	5,250		784 D	46.0%	54.0%	46.0%	54.0%
19,505	CONWAY	9,284	3,800	5,484		1,684 D	40.9%	59.1%	40.9%	59.1%
63,239	CRAIGHEAD	21,874	9,825	12,049		2,224 D	44.9%	55.1%	44.9%	55.1%
36,892	CRAWFORD	13,336	7,328	6,008		1,320 R	54.9%	45.1%	54.9%	45.1%
49,499	CRITTENDEN	12,403	4,406	7,997		3,591 D	35.5%	64.5%	35.5%	64.5%
20,434	CROSS	6,648	2,233	4,415		2,182 D	33.6%	66.4%	33.6%	66.4%
10,515	DALLAS	4,938	1,341	3,597		2,256 D	27.2%	72.8%	27.2%	72.8%
19,760	DESHA	5,571	1,377	4,194		2,817 D	24.7%	75.3%	24.7%	75.3%
17,910	DREW	6,112	2,054	4,058		2,004 D	33.6%	66.4%	33.6%	66.4%
46,192	FAULKNER	18,423	8,742	9,681		939 D	47.5%	52.5%	47.5%	52.5%
14,705	FRANKLIN	6,943	2,916	4,027		1,111 D	42.0%	58.0%	42.0%	58.0%
9,975	FULTON	4,330	1,510	2,820		1,310 D	34.9%	65.1%	34.9%	65.1%
70,531	GARLAND	28,517	14,000	14,517		517 D	49.1%	50.9%	49.1%	50.9%
13,008	GRANT	5,482	2,090	3,392		1,302 D	38.1%	61.9%	38.1%	61.9%
30,744	GREENE	12,047	4,389	7,658		3,269 D	36.4%	63.6%	36.4%	63.6%
23,635	HEMPSTEAD	8,461	3,127	5,334		2,207 D	37.0%	63.0%	37.0%	63.0%
26,819	HOT SPRINGS	11,805	3,739	8,066		4,327 D	31.7%	68.3%	31.7%	68.3%
13,459	HOWARD	4,907	1,844	3,063		1,219 D	37.6%	62.4%	37.6%	62.4%
30,147	INDEPENDENCE	12,316	4,933	7,383		2,450 D	40.1%	59.9%	40.1%	59.9%
10,768	IZARD	5,222	1,915	3,307		1,392 D	36.7%	63.3%	36.7%	63.3%
21,646	JACKSON	7,954	2,505	5,449		2,944 D	31.5%	68.5%	31.5%	68.5%
90,718	JEFFERSON	31,561	8,992	22,569		13,577 D	28.5%	71.5%	28.5%	71.5%
17,423	JOHNSON	7,909	3,443	4,466		1,023 D	43.5%	56.5%	43.5%	56.5%
10,213	LAFAYETTE	4,051	1,265	2,786		1,521 D	31.2%	68.8%	31.2%	68.8%
18,447	LAWRENCE	6,775	2,607	4,168		1,561 D	38.5%	61.5%	38.5%	61.5%
15,539	LEE	5,036	1,097	3,939		2,842 D	21.8%	78.2%	21.8%	78.2%
13,369	LINCOLN	4,305	922	3,383		2,461 D	21.4%	78.6%	21.4%	78.6%
13,952	LITTLE RIVER	5,323	2,210	3,113		903 D	41.5%	58.5%	41.5%	58.5%
20,144	LOGAN	9,301	3,887	5,414		1,527 D	41.8%	58.2%	41.8%	58.2%
34,518	LONOKE	13,117	5,798	7,319		1,521 D	44.2%	55.8%	44.2%	55.8%
11,373	MADISON	5,849	2,665	3,184		519 D	45.6%	54.4%	45.6%	54.4%
11,334	MARION	5,699	2,591	3,108		517 D	45.5%	54.5%	45.5%	54.5%
37,766	MILLER	14,077	6,152	7,925		1,773 D	43.7%	56.3%	43.7%	56.3%
59,517	MISSISSIPPI	18,659	5,915	12,744		6,829 D	31.7%	68.3%	31.7%	68.3%
14,052	MONROE	5,081	1,534	3,547		2,013 D	30.2%	69.8%	30.2%	69.8%
7,771	MONTGOMERY	3,878	1,644	2,234		590 D	42.4%	57.6%	42.4%	57.6%
11,097	NEVADA	4,502	1,496	3,006		1,510 D	33.2%	66.8%	33.2%	66.8%
7,756	NEWTON	4,311	2,191	2,120		71 R	50.8%	49.2%	50.8%	49.2%
30,541	OUACHITA	12,606	3,680	8,926		5,246 D	29.2%	70.8%	29.2%	70.8%
7,266	PERRY	3,537	1,430	2,107		677 D	40.4%	59.6%	40.4%	59.6%
34,772	PHILLIPS	11,168	3,112	8,056		4,944 D	27.9%	72.1%	27.9%	72.1%
10,373	PIKE	4,040	1,615	2,425		810 D	40.0%	60.0%	40.0%	60.0%
27,032	POINSETT	10,084	3,375	6,709		3,334 D	33.5%	66.5%	33.5%	66.5%
17,007	POLK	7,455	3,608	3,847		239 D	48.4%	51.6%	48.4%	51.6%
39,021	POPE	16,084	7,752	8,332		580 D	48.2%	51.8%	48.2%	51.8%
10,140	PRAIRIE	3,926	1,474	2,452		978 D	37.5%	62.5%	37.5%	62.5%
340,613	PULASKI	129,307	58,183	71,124		12,941 D	45.0%	55.0%	45.0%	55.0%

ARKANSAS

SENATOR 1984

1980 Census Population	County	Total Vote	Republican	Democratic	Other	Rep.-Dem. Plurality		Percentage			
---	---	---	---	---	---	---	---	Total Vote		Major Vote	
								Rep.	Dem.	Rep.	Dem.
16,834	RANDOLPH	5,843	2,447	3,396		949 D		41.9%	58.1%	41.9%	58.1%
30,858	ST. FRANCIS	10,147	3,118	7,029		3,911 D		30.7%	69.3%	30.7%	69.3%
53,161	SALINE	19,786	9,098	10,688		1,590 D		46.0%	54.0%	46.0%	54.0%
9,685	SCOTT	4,726	1,875	2,851		976 D		39.7%	60.3%	39.7%	60.3%
8,847	SEARCY	4,401	2,131	2,270		139 D		48.4%	51.6%	48.4%	51.6%
95,172	SEBASTIAN	35,410	19,434	15,976		3,458 R		54.9%	45.1%	54.9%	45.1%
14,060	SEVIER	5,420	2,265	3,155		890 D		41.8%	58.2%	41.8%	58.2%
14,607	SHARP	7,083	3,278	3,805		527 D		46.3%	53.7%	46.3%	53.7%
9,022	STONE	4,274	1,641	2,633		992 D		38.4%	61.6%	38.4%	61.6%
48,573	UNION	17,364	8,193	9,171		978 D		47.2%	52.8%	47.2%	52.8%
13,357	VAN BUREN	6,671	2,973	3,698		725 D		44.6%	55.4%	44.6%	55.4%
100,494	WASHINGTON	36,405	19,134	17,271		1,863 R		52.6%	47.4%	52.6%	47.4%
50,835	WHITE	19,611	10,060	9,551		509 R		51.3%	48.7%	51.3%	48.7%
11,222	WOODRUFF	3,834	925	2,909		1,984 D		24.1%	75.9%	24.1%	75.9%
17,026	YELL	7,528	3,079	4,449		1,370 D		40.9%	59.1%	40.9%	59.1%
2,286,435	TOTAL	875,956	373,615	502,341		128,726 D		42.7%	57.3%	42.7%	57.3%

ARKANSAS

CONGRESS

CD	Year	Total Vote	Republican		Democratic		Other Vote	Rep.-Dem. Plurality	Percentage			
			Vote	Candidate	Vote	Candidate			Total Vote Rep.	Dem.	Major Vote Rep.	Dem.
1	1984	124,528			121,047	ALEXANDER, WILLIAM	3,481	121,047 D		97.2%		100.0%
1	1982	191,635	67,427	BANKS, CHUCK	124,208	ALEXANDER, WILLIAM		56,781 D	35.2%	64.8%	35.2%	64.8%
2	1984	219,079	90,841	PETTY, JUDY	103,165	ROBINSON, TOMMY F.	25,073	12,324 D	41.5%	47.1%	46.8%	53.2%
2	1982	179,688	96,775	BETHUNE, ED	82,913	GEORGE, CHARLES L.		13,862 R	53.9%	46.1%	53.9%	46.1%
3	1984			HAMMERSCHMIDT, JOHN								
3	1982	202,998	133,909	HAMMERSCHMIDT, JOHN	69,089	MCDOUGAL, JIM		64,820 R	66.0%	34.0%	66.0%	34.0%
4	1984	119,639			117,123	ANTHONY, BERYL F.	2,516	117,123 D		97.9%		100.0%
4	1982	184,917	63,661	LESLIE, BOB	121,256	ANTHONY, BERYL F.		57,595 D	34.4%	65.6%	34.4%	65.6%

ARKANSAS

1984 GENERAL ELECTION

President   Other vote was 2,221 Bergland (Libertarian); 1,890 LaRouche (Independent); 1,499 Hall (People Before Profits); 1,461 Richards (Populist); 1,291 Serrette (Independent Alliance); 960 Johnson (Citizen's Group); 842 Dodge (Prohibition); 822 Lowery (United Sovereign Citizens).

Governor

Senator

Congress   Under present legislation, votes are not tallied in unopposed elections, so no total vote or candidate vote is available for unopposed Congressional districts except when there is an official write-in candidate. In 1984 there were official write-in candidates in CD's 1 and 4. Other vote was Cochran (write-in) in CD 1; Taylor (Independent) in CD 2; Rood (write-in) in CD 4.

1984 PRIMARIES

MAY 29 REPUBLICAN

Governor   13,030 Woody Freeman; 6,010 Erwin Davis.

Senator   Ed Bethune, unopposed.

Congress   Unopposed in two CD's. No candidate in CD's 1 and 4.

MAY 29 DEMOCRATIC

Governor   317,577 Bill Clinton; 119,266 Lonnie Turner; 31,727 Kermit Moss; 24,116 Monroe A. Schwarzlose.

Senator   David H. Pryor, unopposed.

Congress   Unopposed in one CD. No candidate in CD 3. Contested as follows:

   CD 1   100,490 William Alexander; 30,281 Steve Abernathy.
   CD 2   55,649 Tommy F. Robinson; 38,296 Paul Riviere; 20,289 Stanley Russ; 19,542 Thedford Collins; 5,098 Dale Alford.

JUNE 12 DEMOCRATIC RUN-OFF

Congress

   CD 2   67,052 Tommy F. Robinson; 58,666 Paul Riviere.

CALIFORNIA

GOVERNOR

George Deukmejian (R). Elected 1982 to a four-year term.

SENATORS

Alan Cranston (D). Re-elected 1980 to a six-year term. Previously elected 1974, 1968.

Pete Wilson (R). Elected 1982 to a six-year term.

REPRESENTATIVES

1. Douglas H. Bosco (D)
2. Eugene A. Chappie (R)
3. Robert T. Matsui (D)
4. Vic Fazio (D)
5. Sala Burton (D)
6. Barbara Boxer (D)
7. George Miller (D)
8. Ronald V. Dellums (D)
9. Fortney Stark (D)
10. Don Edwards (D)
11. Tom Lantos (D)
12. Ed Zschau (R)
13. Norman Y. Mineta (D)
14. Norman D. Shumway (R)
15. Tony Coelho (D)
16. Leon E. Panetta (D)
17. Charles Pashayan (R)
18. Richard Lehman (D)
19. Robert J. Lagomarsino (R)
20. William M. Thomas (R)
21. Bobbi Fiedler (R)
22. Carlos J. Moorhead (R)
23. Anthony C. Beilenson (D)
24. Henry A. Waxman (D)
25. Edward R. Roybal (D)
26. Howard L. Berman (D)
27. Mel Levine (D)
28. Julian C. Dixon (D)
29. Augustus Hawkins (D)
30. Matthew G. Martinez (D)
31. Mervyn M. Dymally (D)
32. Glenn M. Anderson (D)
33. David Dreier (R)
34. Esteban Torres (D)
35. Jerry Lewis (R)
36. George E. Brown (D)
37. Al McCandless (R)
38. Robert K. Dornan (R)
39. William E. Dannemeyer (R)
40. Robert E. Badham (R)
41. Bill Lowery (R)
42. Daniel E. Lungren (R)
43. Ron Packard (R)
44. Jim Bates (D)
45. Duncan L. Hunter (R)

POSTWAR VOTE FOR GOVERNOR

Year	Total Vote	Republican Vote	Candidate	Democratic Vote	Candidate	Other Vote	Rep.-Dem. Plurality	Total Vote Rep.	Total Vote Dem.	Major Vote Rep.	Major Vote Dem.
1982	7,876,698	3,881,014	Deukmejian, George	3,787,669	Bradley, Tom	208,015	93,345 R	49.3%	48.1%	50.6%	49.4%
1978	6,922,378	2,526,534	Younger, Evelle J.	3,878,812	Brown, Edmund G., Jr.	517,032	1,352,278 D	36.5%	56.0%	39.4%	60.6%
1974	6,248,070	2,952,954	Flournoy, Houston I.	3,131,648	Brown, Edmund G., Jr.	163,468	178,694 D	47.3%	50.1%	48.5%	51.5%
1970	6,510,072	3,439,664	Reagan, Ronald	2,938,607	Unruh, Jess	131,801	501,057 R	52.8%	45.1%	53.9%	46.1%
1966	6,503,445	3,742,913	Reagan, Ronald	2,749,174	Brown, Edmund G.	11,358	993,739 R	57.6%	42.3%	57.7%	42.3%
1962	5,853,270	2,740,351	Nixon, Richard M.	3,037,109	Brown, Edmund G.	75,810	296,758 D	46.8%	51.9%	47.4%	52.6%
1958	5,255,777	2,110,911	Knowland, William F.	3,140,076	Brown, Edmund G.	4,790	1,029,165 D	40.2%	59.7%	40.2%	59.8%
1954	4,030,368	2,290,519	Knight, Goodwin J.	1,739,368	Graves, Richard P.	481	551,151 R	56.8%	43.2%	56.8%	43.2%
1950	3,796,090	2,461,754	Warren, Earl	1,333,856	Roosevelt, James	480	1,127,898 R	64.8%	35.1%	64.9%	35.1%
1946 *	2,558,399	2,344,542	Warren, Earl	—	—	213,857	2,344,542 R	91.6%	—	100.0%	—

In 1946 the Republican candidate won both major party nominations.

POSTWAR VOTE FOR SENATOR

Year	Total Vote	Republican Vote	Candidate	Democratic Vote	Candidate	Other Vote	Rep.-Dem. Plurality	Total Vote Rep.	Total Vote Dem.	Major Vote Rep.	Major Vote Dem.
1982	7,805,538	4,022,565	Wilson, Pete	3,494,968	Brown, Edmund G., Jr.	288,005	527,597 R	51.5%	44.8%	53.5%	46.5%
1980	8,327,481	3,093,426	Gann, Paul	4,705,399	Cranston, Alan	528,656	1,611,973 D	37.1%	56.5%	39.7%	60.3%
1976	7,472,268	3,748,973	Hayakawa, S. I.	3,502,862	Tunney, John V.	220,433	246,111 R	50.2%	46.9%	51.7%	48.3%
1974	6,102,432	2,210,267	Richardson, H. L.	3,693,160	Cranston, Alan	199,005	1,482,893 D	36.2%	60.5%	37.4%	62.6%
1970	6,492,157	2,877,617	Murphy, George	3,496,558	Tunney, John V.	117,982	618,941 D	44.3%	53.9%	45.1%	54.9%
1968	7,102,465	3,329,148	Rafferty, Max	3,680,352	Cranston, Alan	92,965	351,204 D	46.9%	51.8%	47.5%	52.5%
1964	7,041,821	3,628,555	Murphy, George	3,411,912	Salinger, Pierre	1,354	216,643 R	51.5%	48.5%	51.5%	48.5%
1962	5,647,952	3,180,483	Kuchel, Thomas H.	2,452,839	Richards, Richard	14,630	727,644 R	56.3%	43.4%	56.5%	43.5%
1958	5,135,221	2,204,337	Knight, Goodwin J.	2,927,693	Engle, Clair	3,191	723,356 D	42.9%	57.0%	43.0%	57.0%
1956	5,361,467	2,892,918	Kuchel, Thomas H.	2,445,816	Richards, Richard	22,733	447,102 R	54.0%	45.6%	54.2%	45.8%
1954s	3,929,668	2,090,836	Kuchel, Thomas H.	1,788,071	Yorty, Samuel W.	50,761	302,765 R	53.2%	45.5%	53.9%	46.1%
1952*	4,542,548	3,982,448	Knowland, William F.	—	—	560,100	3,982,448 R	87.7%	—	100.0%	—
1950	3,686,315	2,183,454	Nixon, Richard M.	1,502,507	Douglas, Helen	354	680,947 R	59.2%	40.8%	59.2%	40.8%
1946	2,639,465	1,428,067	Knowland, William F.	1,167,161	Rogers, Will	44,237	260,906 R	54.1%	44.2%	55.0%	45.0%

The 1954 election was for a short term to fill a vacancy. In 1952 the Republican candidate won both major party nominations.

CALIFORNIA

Districts Established January 2, 1983

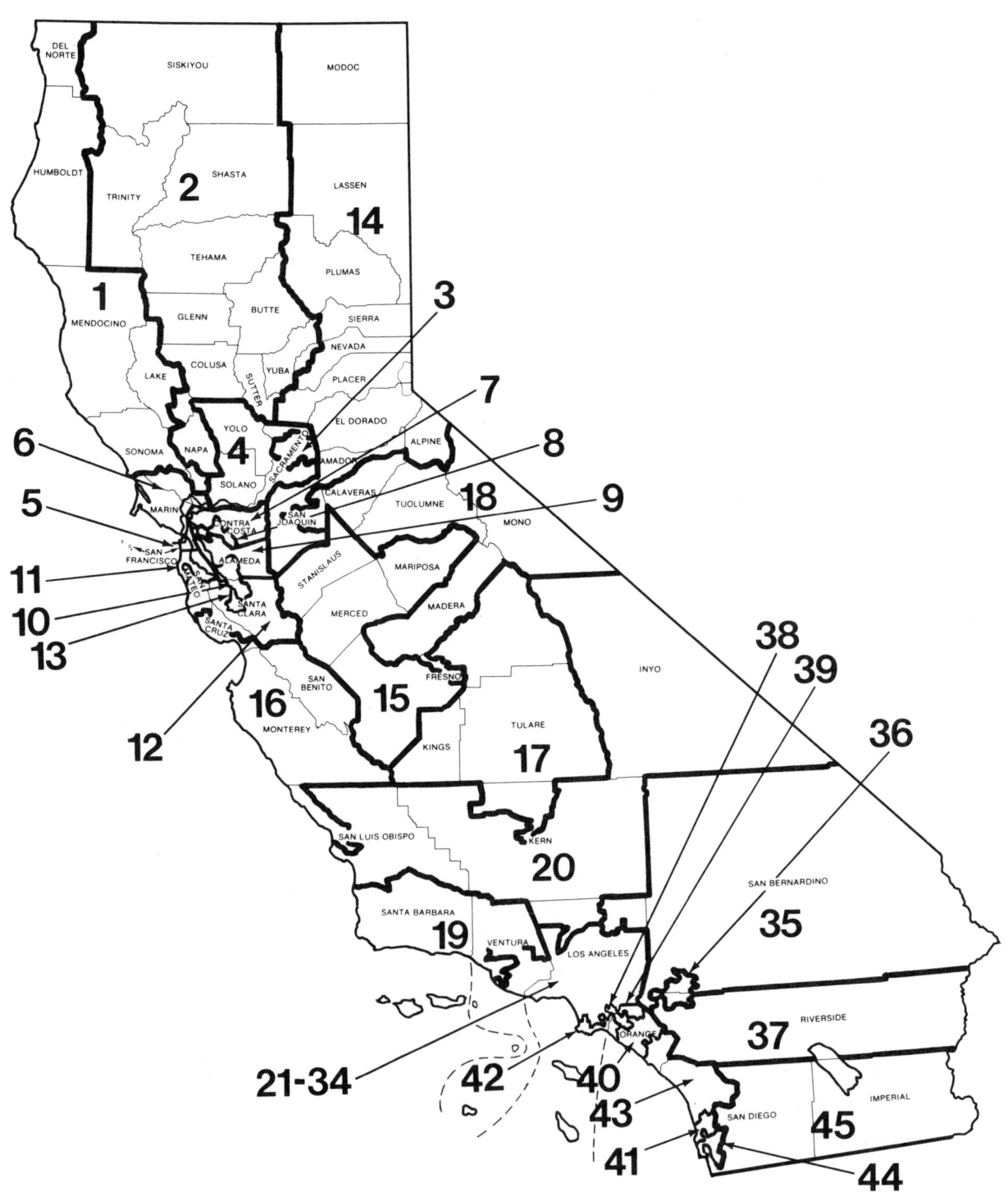

© ERC

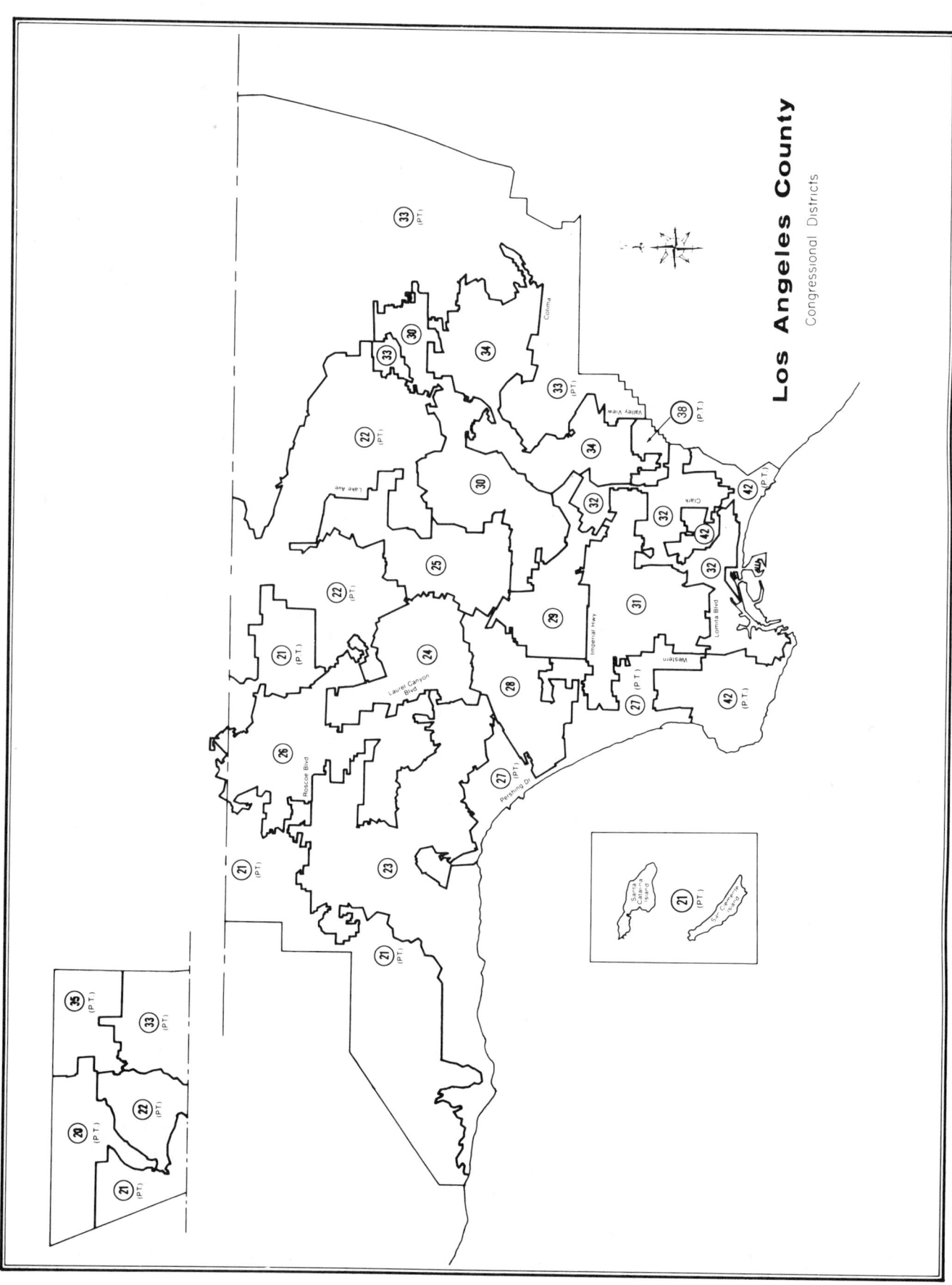

Los Angeles County
Congressional Districts

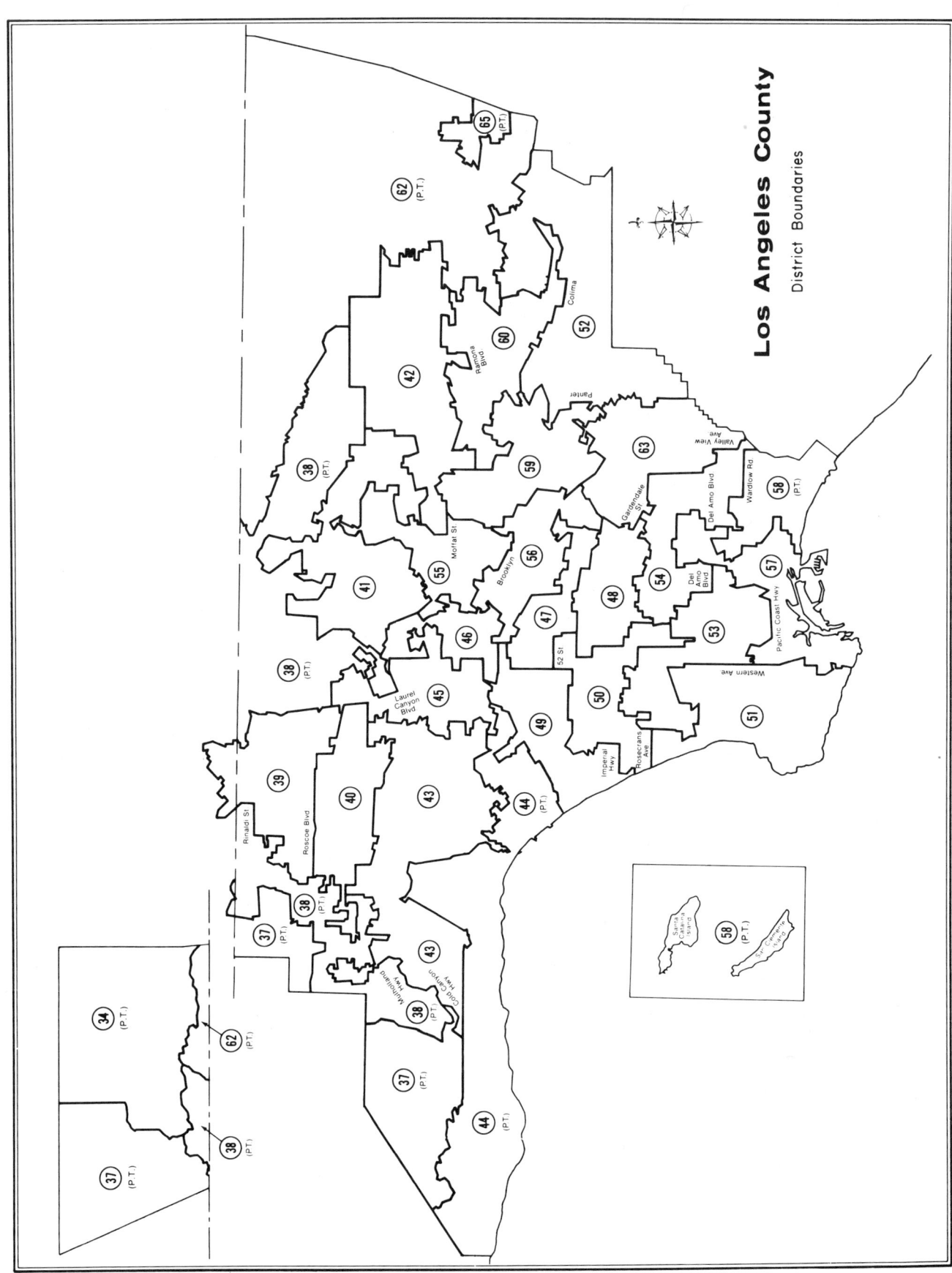

Los Angeles County

District Boundaries

© ERC

CALIFORNIA

PRESIDENT 1984

1980 Census Population	County	Total Vote	Republican	Democratic	Other	Rep.-Dem. Plurality	Percentage Total Vote Rep.	Dem.	Major Vote Rep.	Dem.
1,105,379	ALAMEDA	480,874	192,408	282,041	6,425	89,633 D	40.0%	58.7%	40.6%	59.4%
1,097	ALPINE	466	264	194	8	70 R	56.7%	41.6%	57.6%	42.4%
19,314	AMADOR	11,363	6,986	4,188	189	2,798 R	61.5%	36.9%	62.5%	37.5%
143,851	BUTTE	71,964	45,381	25,421	1,162	19,960 R	63.1%	35.3%	64.1%	35.9%
20,710	CALAVERAS	11,877	7,632	4,081	164	3,551 R	64.3%	34.4%	65.2%	34.8%
12,791	COLUSA	5,188	3,388	1,725	75	1,663 R	65.3%	33.2%	66.3%	33.7%
656,380	CONTRA COSTA	316,318	172,331	140,994	2,993	31,337 R	54.5%	44.6%	55.0%	45.0%
18,217	DEL NORTE	6,841	3,996	2,696	149	1,300 R	58.4%	39.4%	59.7%	40.3%
85,812	EL DORADO	42,478	27,583	14,312	583	13,271 R	64.9%	33.7%	65.8%	34.2%
514,621	FRESNO	192,936	104,757	86,315	1,864	18,442 R	54.3%	44.7%	54.8%	45.2%
21,350	GLENN	8,632	6,020	2,488	124	3,532 R	69.7%	28.8%	70.8%	29.2%
108,514	HUMBOLDT	53,891	27,832	25,217	842	2,615 R	51.6%	46.8%	52.5%	47.5%
92,110	IMPERIAL	22,301	13,829	8,237	235	5,592 R	62.0%	36.9%	62.7%	37.3%
17,895	INYO	8,338	5,863	2,360	115	3,503 R	70.3%	28.3%	71.3%	28.7%
403,089	KERN	145,744	94,776	49,567	1,401	45,209 R	65.0%	34.0%	65.7%	34.3%
73,738	KINGS	20,848	13,364	7,324	160	6,040 R	64.1%	35.1%	64.6%	35.4%
36,366	LAKE	19,831	10,874	8,648	309	2,226 R	54.8%	43.6%	55.7%	44.3%
21,661	LASSEN	8,761	5,352	3,254	155	2,098 R	61.1%	37.1%	62.2%	37.8%
7,477,503	LOS ANGELES	2,612,914	1,424,113	1,158,912	29,889	265,201 R	54.5%	44.4%	55.1%	44.9%
63,116	MADERA	23,241	13,954	8,994	293	4,960 R	60.0%	38.7%	60.8%	39.2%
222,568	MARIN	116,050	56,887	57,533	1,630	646 D	49.0%	49.6%	49.7%	50.3%
11,108	MARIPOSA	6,518	3,989	2,399	130	1,590 R	61.2%	36.8%	62.4%	37.6%
66,738	MENDOCINO	31,422	16,369	14,407	646	1,962 R	52.1%	45.9%	53.2%	46.8%
134,560	MERCED	42,477	24,997	17,012	468	7,985 R	58.8%	40.0%	59.5%	40.5%
8,610	MODOC	4,310	2,995	1,219	96	1,776 R	69.5%	28.3%	71.1%	28.9%
8,577	MONO	3,677	2,659	962	56	1,697 R	72.3%	26.2%	73.4%	26.6%
290,444	MONTEREY	97,470	55,710	40,733	1,027	14,977 R	57.2%	41.8%	57.8%	42.2%
99,199	NAPA	45,561	26,322	18,599	640	7,723 R	57.8%	40.8%	58.6%	41.4%
51,645	NEVADA	31,768	19,809	11,198	761	8,611 R	62.4%	35.2%	63.9%	36.1%
1,932,709	ORANGE	850,077	635,013	206,272	8,792	428,741 R	74.7%	24.3%	75.5%	24.5%
117,247	PLACER	60,427	38,035	21,294	1,098	16,741 R	62.9%	35.2%	64.1%	35.9%
17,340	PLUMAS	9,228	5,224	3,837	167	1,387 R	56.6%	41.6%	57.7%	42.3%
663,166	RIVERSIDE	287,202	182,324	102,043	2,835	80,281 R	63.5%	35.5%	64.1%	35.9%
783,381	SACRAMENTO	368,841	204,922	159,128	4,791	45,794 R	55.6%	43.1%	56.3%	43.7%
25,005	SAN BENITO	9,380	5,695	3,554	131	2,141 R	60.7%	37.9%	61.6%	38.4%
895,016	SAN BERNARDINO	342,705	222,071	116,454	4,180	105,617 R	64.8%	34.0%	65.6%	34.4%
1,861,846	SAN DIEGO	769,267	502,344	257,029	9,894	245,315 R	65.3%	33.4%	66.2%	33.8%
678,974	SAN FRANCISCO	286,972	90,219	193,278	3,475	103,059 D	31.4%	67.4%	31.8%	68.2%
347,342	SAN JOAQUIN	137,213	81,795	53,846	1,572	27,949 R	59.6%	39.2%	60.3%	39.7%
155,435	SAN LUIS OBISPO	76,950	49,035	26,946	969	22,089 R	63.7%	35.0%	64.5%	35.5%
587,329	SAN MATEO	260,631	135,185	122,268	3,178	12,917 R	51.9%	46.9%	52.5%	47.5%
298,694	SANTA BARBARA	142,320	89,314	51,243	1,763	38,071 R	62.8%	36.0%	63.5%	36.5%
1,295,071	SANTA CLARA	526,639	288,638	229,865	8,136	58,773 R	54.8%	43.6%	55.7%	44.3%
188,141	SNATA CRUZ	92,147	41,652	49,091	1,404	7,439 D	45.2%	53.3%	45.9%	54.1%
115,715	SHASTA	53,127	33,041	19,298	788	13,743 R	62.2%	36.3%	63.1%	36.9%
3,073	SIERRA	1,896	1,078	781	37	297 R	56.9%	41.2%	58.0%	42.0%
39,732	SISKIYOU	18,101	10,544	7,130	427	3,414 R	58.3%	39.4%	59.7%	40.3%
235,203	SOLANO	94,798	51,678	41,982	1,138	9,696 R	54.5%	44.3%	55.2%	44.8%
299,681	SONOMA	149,657	76,447	71,295	1,915	5,152 R	51.1%	47.6%	51.7%	48.3%
265,900	STANISLAUS	93,985	55,665	37,459	861	18,206 R	59.2%	39.9%	59.8%	40.2%
52,246	SUTTER	20,323	14,477	5,535	311	8,942 R	71.2%	27.2%	72.3%	27.7%
38,888	TEHAMA	18,455	11,586	6,527	342	5,059 R	62.8%	35.4%	64.0%	36.0%
11,858	TRINITY	5,935	3,544	2,218	173	1,326 R	59.7%	37.4%	61.5%	38.5%
245,738	TULARE	79,943	51,066	28,065	812	23,001 R	63.9%	35.1%	64.5%	35.5%
33,928	TUOLUMNE	18,051	10,485	7,283	283	3,202 R	58.1%	40.3%	59.0%	41.0%
529,174	VENTURA	220,462	151,383	66,550	2,529	84,833 R	68.7%	30.2%	69.5%	30.5%
113,374	YOLO	50,853	24,329	25,879	645	1,550 D	47.8%	50.9%	48.5%	51.5%
49,733	YUBA	15,397	9,780	5,339	278	4,441 R	63.5%	34.7%	64.7%	35.3%
23,667,902	TOTAL	9,505,423	5,467,009	3,922,519	115,895	1,544,490 R	57.5%	41.3%	58.2%	41.8%

LOS ANGELES COUNTY

PRESIDENT 1984

1980 Census Population	Assembly District	Total Vote	Republican	Democratic	Other	Rep.-Dem. Plurality	Percentage			
							Total Vote		Major Vote	
							Rep.	Dem.	Rep.	Dem.
105,028	DISTRICT 34 [PART]	51,177	41,114	9,481	582	31,633 R	80.3%	18.5%	81.3%	18.7%
147,812	DISTRICT 37 [PART]	71,527	53,128	17,596	803	35,532 R	74.3%	24.6%	75.1%	24.9%
301,250	DISTRICT 38	137,505	94,528	41,335	1,642	53,193 R	68.7%	30.1%	69.6%	30.4%
295,331	DISTRICT 39	94,827	54,424	39,363	1,040	15,061 R	57.4%	41.5%	58.0%	42.0%
291,137	DISTRICT 40	113,147	59,854	51,883	1,410	7,971 R	52.9%	45.9%	53.6%	46.4%
294,121	DISTRICT 41	125,764	82,220	41,798	1,746	40,422 R	65.4%	33.2%	66.3%	33.7%
293,648	DISTRICT 42	123,397	87,233	34,821	1,343	52,412 R	70.7%	28.2%	71.5%	28.5%
291,647	DISTRICT 43	149,316	75,084	72,537	1,695	2,547 R	50.3%	48.6%	50.9%	49.1%
292,765	DISTRICT 44	142,068	62,654	77,641	1,773	14,987 D	44.1%	54.7%	44.7%	55.3%
293,863	DISTRICT 45	119,214	52,051	65,588	1,575	13,537 D	43.7%	55.0%	44.2%	55.8%
299,036	DISTRICT 46	50,950	22,268	27,790	892	5,522 D	43.7%	54.5%	44.5%	55.5%
291,099	DISTRICT 47	56,861	10,652	45,720	489	35,068 D	18.7%	80.4%	18.9%	81.1%
300,319	DISTRICT 48	73,276	14,981	57,570	725	42,589 D	20.4%	78.6%	20.6%	79.4%
290,012	DISTRICT 49	116,917	36,620	79,386	911	42,766 D	31.3%	67.9%	31.6%	68.4%
290,112	DISTRICT 50	97,760	29,062	67,790	908	38,728 D	29.7%	69.3%	30.0%	70.0%
301,650	DISTRICT 51	144,870	104,082	38,697	2,091	65,385 R	71.8%	26.7%	72.9%	27.1%
289,931	DISTRICT 52	116,184	83,794	31,372	1,018	52,422 R	72.1%	27.0%	72.8%	27.2%
296,057	DISTRICT 53	92,075	51,326	39,645	1,104	11,681 R	55.7%	43.1%	56.4%	43.6%
291,565	DISTRICT 54	98,259	48,978	48,333	948	645 R	49.8%	49.2%	50.3%	49.7%
292,183	DISTRICT 55	67,904	27,412	39,601	891	12,189 D	40.4%	58.3%	40.9%	59.1%
293,880	DISTRICT 56	35,511	11,717	23,367	427	11,650 D	33.0%	65.8%	33.4%	66.6%
300,113	DISTRICT 57	80,201	40,209	38,953	1,039	1,256 R	50.1%	48.6%	50.8%	49.2%
151,539	DISTRICT 58 [PART]	75,111	47,627	26,482	1,002	21,145 R	63.4%	35.3%	64.3%	35.7%
296,546	DISTRICT 59	90,681	47,699	42,119	863	5,580 R	52.6%	46.4%	53.1%	46.9%
296,707	DISTRICT 60	70,596	40,479	29,324	793	11,155 R	57.3%	41.5%	58.0%	42.0%
249,390	DISTRICT 62 [PART]	102,692	70,521	31,138	1,033	39,383 R	68.7%	30.3%	69.4%	30.6%
297,416	DISTRICT 63	100,466	66,033	33,458	975	32,575 R	65.7%	33.3%	66.4%	33.6%
43,512	DISTRICT 65 [PART]	14,658	8,363	6,124	171	2,239 R	57.1%	41.8%	57.7%	42.3%
7,477,669	TOTAL	2,612,914	1,424,113	1,158,912	29,889	265,201 R	54.5%	44.4%	55.1%	44.9%

CALIFORNIA

CONGRESS

CD	Year	Total Vote	Republican		Democratic		Other Vote	Rep.-Dem. Plurality	Percentage Total Vote		Major Vote	
			Vote	Candidate	Vote	Candidate			Rep.	Dem.	Rep.	Dem.
1	1984	252,223	95,186	REDICK, DAVID	157,037	BOSCO, DOUGLAS H.		61,851 D	37.7%	62.3%	37.7%	62.3%
2	1984	228,472	158,679	CHAPPIE, EUGENE A.	69,793	COZAD, HARRY		88,886 R	69.5%	30.5%	69.5%	30.5%
3	1984	131,565			131,369	MATSUI, ROBERT T.	196	131,369 D		99.9%		100.0%
4	1984	211,921	77,773	CANFIELD, ROGER B.	130,109	FAZIO, VIC	4,039	52,336 D	36.7%	61.4%	37.4%	62.6%
5	1984	193,204	45,930	SPINOSA, TOM	139,692	BURTON, SALA	7,582	93,762 D	23.8%	72.3%	24.7%	75.3%
6	1984	239,096	71,011	BINDERUP, DOUGLAS	162,511	BOXER, BARBARA	5,574	91,500 D	29.7%	68.0%	30.4%	69.6%
7	1984	241,244	78,985	THAKAR, ROSEMARY	158,306	MILLER, GEORGE	3,953	79,321 D	32.7%	65.6%	33.3%	66.7%
8	1984	239,223	94,907	CONNOR, CHARLES	144,316	DELLUMS, RONALD V.		49,409 D	39.7%	60.3%	39.7%	60.3%
9	1984	195,308	51,399	BEAVER, J. T.	136,511	STARK, FORTNEY	7,398	85,112 D	26.3%	69.9%	27.4%	72.6%
10	1984	164,177	56,256	HERRIOTT, BOB	102,469	EDWARDS, DON	5,452	46,213 D	34.3%	62.4%	35.4%	64.6%
11	1984	211,115	59,625	HICKEY, JOHN J.	147,607	LANTOS, TOM	3,883	87,982 D	28.2%	69.9%	28.8%	71.2%
12	1984	252,693	155,795	ZSCHAU, ED	91,026	CARNOY, MARTIN	5,872	64,769 R	61.7%	36.0%	63.1%	36.9%
13	1984	214,353	70,666	WILLIAMS, JOHN D.	139,851	MINETA, NORMAN Y.	3,836	69,185 D	33.0%	65.2%	33.6%	66.4%
14	1984	244,476	179,238	SHUMWAY, NORMAN D.	58,384	CARLSON, RUTH	6,854	120,854 R	73.3%	23.9%	75.4%	24.6%
15	1984	167,406	54,730	HARNER, CAROL	109,590	COELHO, TONY	3,086	54,860 D	32.7%	65.5%	33.3%	66.7%
16	1984	216,687	60,065	RAMSEY, PATRICIA S.	153,377	PANETTA, LEON E.	3,245	93,312 D	27.7%	70.8%	28.1%	71.9%
17	1984	177,690	128,802	PASHAYAN, CHARLES	48,888	LAKRITZ, SIMON		79,914 R	72.5%	27.5%	72.5%	27.5%
18	1984	190,525	62,339	EWEN, DALE L.	128,186	LEHMAN, RICHARD		65,847 D	32.7%	67.3%	32.7%	67.3%
19	1984	227,626	153,187	LAGOMARSINO, ROBERT J.	70,278	CAREY, JAMES C.	4,161	82,909 R	67.3%	30.9%	68.6%	31.4%
20	1984	214,039	151,732	THOMAS, WILLIAM M.	62,307	LESAGE, MIKE		89,425 R	70.9%	29.1%	70.9%	29.1%
21	1984	239,968	173,504	FIEDLER, BOBBI	62,085	DAVIS, CHARLES	4,379	111,419 R	72.3%	25.9%	73.6%	26.4%
22	1984	217,176	184,981	MOORHEAD, CARLOS J.			32,195	184,981 R	85.2%		100.0%	
23	1984	228,134	84,093	PARRISH, CLAUDE	140,461	BEILENSON, ANTHONY C.	3,580	56,368 D	36.9%	61.6%	37.4%	62.6%
24	1984	153,607	51,010	ZERG, JERRY	97,340	WAXMAN, HENRY A.	5,257	46,330 D	33.2%	63.4%	34.4%	65.6%
25	1984	103,602	24,968	BLOXOM, ROY D.	74,261	ROYBAL, EDWARD R.	4,373	49,293 D	24.1%	71.7%	25.2%	74.8%
26	1984	186,452	69,372	OJEDA, MIRIAM	117,080	BERMAN, HOWARD L.		47,708 D	37.2%	62.8%	37.2%	62.8%
27	1984	212,781	88,896	SCRIBNER, ROBERT B.	116,933	LEVINE, MEL	6,952	28,037 D	41.8%	55.0%	43.2%	56.8%
28	1984	149,517	33,511	JETT, BEATRICE M.	113,076	DIXON, JULIAN C.	2,930	79,565 D	22.4%	75.6%	22.9%	77.1%
29	1984	125,559	16,781	GOTO, ECHO Y.	108,777	HAWKINS, AUGUSTUS	1	91,996 D	13.4%	86.6%	13.4%	86.6%
30	1984	124,333	53,900	GOMEZ, RICHARD	64,378	MARTINEZ, MATTHEW G.	6,055	10,478 D	43.4%	51.8%	45.6%	54.4%
31	1984	142,349	41,691	MINTURN, HENRY C.	100,658	DYMALLY, MERVYN M.		58,967 D	29.3%	70.7%	29.3%	70.7%
32	1984	169,716	62,176	FIOLA, ROGER E.	102,961	ANDERSON, GLENN M.	4,579	40,785 D	36.6%	60.7%	37.7%	62.3%
33	1984	208,619	147,363	DREIER, DAVID	54,147	MCDONALD, CLAIRE K.	7,109	93,216 R	70.6%	26.0%	73.1%	26.9%
34	1984	145,527	58,467	JACKSON, PAUL R.	87,060	TORRES, ESTEBAN		28,593 D	40.2%	59.8%	40.2%	59.8%
35	1984	206,467	176,477	LEWIS, JERRY			29,990	176,477 R	85.5%		100.0%	
36	1984	184,661	80,212	STARK, JOHN P.	104,438	BROWN, GEORGE E.	11	24,226 D	43.4%	56.6%	43.4%	56.6%

CALIFORNIA

CONGRESS

CD	Year	Total Vote	Republican Vote	Republican Candidate	Democratic Vote	Democratic Candidate	Other Vote	Rep.-Dem. Plurality	Percentage Total Vote Rep.	Dem.	Major Vote Rep.	Dem.
37	1984	235,863	149,955	MCCANDLESS, AL	85,908	SKINNER, DAVID E.		64,047 R	63.6%	36.4%	63.6%	36.4%
38	1984	162,797	86,545	DORNAN, ROBERT K.	73,231	PATTERSON, JERRY M.	3,021	13,314 R	53.2%	45.0%	54.2%	45.8%
39	1984	230,677	175,788	DANNEMEYER, WILLIAM E.	54,889	WARD, ROBERT E.		120,899 R	76.2%	23.8%	76.2%	23.8%
40	1984	254,974	164,257	BADHAM, ROBERT E.	86,748	BRADFORD, CAROL A.	3,969	77,509 R	64.4%	34.0%	65.4%	34.6%
41	1984	253,855	161,068	LOWERY, BILL	85,475	SIMMONS, BOB	7,312	75,593 R	63.4%	33.7%	65.3%	34.7%
42	1984	243,619	177,783	LUNGREN, DANIEL E.	60,025	BROPHY, MARY L.	5,811	117,758 R	73.0%	24.6%	74.8%	25.2%
43	1984	223,517	165,643	PACKARD, RON	50,996	HUMPHREYS, LOIS E.	6,878	114,647 R	74.1%	22.8%	76.5%	23.5%
44	1984	142,563	39,977	CAMPBELL, NEILL	99,378	BATES, JIM	3,208	59,401 D	28.0%	69.7%	28.7%	71.3%
45	1984	198,307	149,011	HUNTER, DUNCAN L.	45,325	GUTHRIE, DAVID W.	3,971	103,686 R	75.1%	22.9%	76.7%	23.3%

CALIFORNIA

1984 GENERAL ELECTION

President Other vote was 49,951 Bergland (Libertarian); 39,265 Richards (American Independent); 26,297 Johnson (Peace and Freedom); 16 Serrette (write-in); 366 scattered not reported by county.

Congress Other vote was Watkins (write-in) in CD 3; Pope (Libertarian) in CD 4; 4,008 Joseph Fuhrig (Libertarian) and 3,574 Clark (Peace and Freedom) in CD 5; Creighton (Libertarian) in CD 6; Last (write-in) in CD 7; Martha Fuhrig (Libertarian) in CD 9; 2,789 Cardestam (Libertarian) and 2,663 Kaiser (American Independent) in CD 10; Kudrovzeff (American Independent) in CD 11; White (Libertarian) in CD 12; Redding (Libertarian) in CD 13; 6,850 Colburn (Libertarian) and 4 Ramos (write-in) in CD 14; Harris (Libertarian) in CD 15; Anderson (Libertarian) in CD 16; Zekan (Peace and Freedom) in CD 19; Leet (Libertarian) in CD 21; 32,036 Yauch (Libertarian) and 159 Hereford (write-in) in CD 22; Leathers (Libertarian) in CD 23; 2,780 Green (Peace and Freedom) and 2,477 Custer (Libertarian) in CD 24; 4,370 Bajada (Libertarian) and 3 Zapata (write-in) in CD 25; 3,815 O'Connor (Peace and Freedom) and 3,137 Avrech (Libertarian) in CD 27; Federick (Libertarian) in CD 28; Evans (write-in) in CD 29; Myers (American Independent) in CD 30; 2,517 Denny (Libertarian), 2,051 McCoy (Peace and Freedom) and 11 Dennard (write-in) in CD 32; 4,738 Lightfoot (Libertarian) and 2,371 Noonan (Peace and Freedom) in CD 33; Akin (Peace and Freedom) in CD 35; Fowler (write-in) in CD 36; Bright (Peace and Freedom) in CD 38; Quirk (Peace and Freedom) in CD 40; 7,303 Baase (Libertarian) and 9 Vogel (write-in) in CD 41; Donohue (Peace and Freedom) in CD 42; Avery (Libertarian) in CD 43; 3,206 Conole (Libertarian) and 2 Hawkes (write-in) in CD 44; Wright (Libertarian) in CD 45.

LOS ANGELES COUNTY

President Other vote was 12,713 Bergland (Libertarian); 9,368 Richards (American Independent); 7,808 Johnson (Peace and Freedom).

1984 PRIMARIES

JUNE 5 REPUBLICAN

Congress Unopposed in twenty-four CD's. No candidate in CD 3. Contested as follows:

CD 1 28,722 David Redick; 21,115 Jim Fatland.
CD 2 53,870 Eugene A. Chappie; 6,378 Ed Brown.
CD 4 21,168 Roger B. Canfield; 16,098 Steve Waltrip.
CD 5 8,169 Tom Spinosa; 8,083 Anna M. Guth; 4,829 Mike Garza.
CD 6 19,778 Douglas Binderup; 15,976 Gregory Baka.
CD 7 19,153 Rosemary Thakar; 19,140 Jean D. Last.
CD 8 19,238 Charles Connor; 15,920 Roger Hefferan.
CD 10 10,492 Bob Herriott; 8,266 John P. Jarrett.
CD 13 28,154 John D. Williams; 5,803 Andrew G. Diaz.
CD 23 20,569 Claude Parrish; 16,553 Frank Mazzi.
CD 24 15,216 Jerry Zerg; 7,403 Roland Cayard.
CD 25 6,503 Roy D. Bloxom; 5,265 Howard Steninger.
CD 27 27,255 Robert B. Scribner; 9,659 Lionel Allen.
CD 31 8,426 Henry C. Minturn; 5,769 Mas Odoi.
CD 34 10,812 Paul R. Jackson; 8,049 John E. Dempsey; 1,681 Pablo O. Grabiel.
CD 36 16,440 John P. Stark; 8,202 Nina N. Pierce; 1,887 David Just; 1,655 Edward B. Vallen.
CD 37 47,651 Al McCandless; 10,737 Bud Mathewson.
CD 38 20,733 Robert K. Dornan; 7,775 Art Jacobson; 3,367 John G. Schmitz; 1,431 Jerry M. Patterson (write-in).
CD 43 53,590 Ron Packard; 15,626 Margaret Ferguson.
CD 44 8,801 Neill Campbell; 7,636 Richard Lahaye; 6 Cylvia L. Cole (write-in).

CALIFORNIA

JUNE 5 DEMOCRATIC

Congress Unopposed in eleven CD's. No candidate in CD's 22, 35. Contested as follows:

CD 2 24,434 Harry Cozad; 24,285 Harlan D. Lundberg; 12,512 Merton D. Short.
CD 3 79,799 Robert T. Matsui; 7,413 Bill Watkins.
CD 5 72,573 Sala Burton; 10,634 Evelyn K. Lantz.
CD 6 76,606 Barbara Boxer; 11,247 Brian Lantz.
CD 8 86,299 Ronald V. Dellums; 18,122 Andreas Vamis; 4,694 Fred B. Lehmkuhl.
CD 10 34,821 Don Edwards; 5,625 Lynn R. Fooks.
CD 11 60,170 Tom Lantos; 7,389 Lawrence K. Schenk.
CD 12 36,702 Martin Carnoy; 7,418 Richard Mattoon.
CD 14 26,297 Ruth Carlson; 18,730 Robert P. Lawrence; 18,197 Don Malberg.
CD 19 22,913 James C. Carey; 15,290 Wayne B. Norris; 12,465 Todd M. Doscher.
CD 20 20,646 Mike LeSage; 18,916 Bill Richardson; 10,722 Francis T. Serra.
CD 21 22,211 Charles Davis; 22,193 George H. Margolis.
CD 23 67,836 Anthony C. Beilenson; 9,265 Wanda Dastig.
CD 24 52,128 Henry A. Waxman; 7,652 Mary F. Platt.
CD 25 37,827 Edward R. Roybal; 6,022 Tim E. Pike.
CD 26 44,157 Howard L. Berman; 7,938 William J. Kurdi.
CD 27 66,181 Mel Levine; 8,522 Rodney Sabel.
CD 28 67,087 Julian C. Dixon; 6,470 Manuel D. Talley.
CD 29 65,179 Augustus Hawkins; 6,171 Mervin Evans.
CD 30 27,340 Matthew G. Martinez; 9,233 Gladys C. Danielson.
CD 31 50,844 Mervyn M. Dymally; 9,699 Ronald L. Smith.
CD 32 49,121 Glenn M. Anderson; 7,330 Dave Schweitzer; 37 Marva H. Dennard (write-in).
CD 33 31,451 Claire K. McDonald; 15,464 Paul Jeffrey; 5 Mike Noonan (write-in).
CD 34 28,045 Esteban Torres; 6,756 Frances J. Kelepecz.
CD 37 15,614 David E. Skinner; 14,098 Mel Gurtov; 12,485 Johnny Pearson; 7,207 Galen R. Walker; 2,045 Larry W. Wurth.
CD 38 35,959 Jerry M. Patterson; 8,754 Ruth Stephenson.
CD 39 26,343 Robert E. Ward; 14,528 Arthur Hoffmann.
CD 40 30,664 Carol A. Bradford; 12,567 Ken White.
CD 41 27,077 Bob Simmons; 10,872 Linda M. Carlston; 9,433 Daniel Hostetter; 4,688 Norman E. Mann.
CD 43 20,679 Lois E. Humphreys; 9,913 Kevin E. Schmidt; 6,519 Randall Toler.
CD 44 41,257 Jim Bates; 6,411 Peter K. Carlston.
CD 45 20,022 David W. Guthrie; 19,509 Georgia D. Irey.

JUNE 5 AMERICAN INDEPENDENT

Congress Unopposed in all CD's in which candidates were entered.

JUNE 5 PEACE AND FREEDOM

Congress Unopposed in all CD's in which candidates were entered except CD's 5 and 24 as follows:

CD 5 209 Henry Clark; 130 Theodore A. Zuur.
CD 24 153 James Green; 143 John Honigsfeld.

JUNE 5 LIBERTARIAN

Congress Unopposed in all CD's in which candidates were entered.

COLORADO

GOVERNOR

Richard D. Lamm (D). Re-elected 1982 to a four-year term. Previously elected 1978, 1974.

SENATORS

William L. Armstrong (R). Re-elected 1984 to a six-year term. Previously elected 1978.

Gary W. Hart (D). Re-elected 1980 to a six-year term. Previously elected 1974.

REPRESENTATIVES

1. Patricia Schroeder (D)
2. Timothy E. Wirth (D)
3. Michael L. Strang (R)
4. Hank Brown (R)
5. Ken Kramer (R)
6. Daniel L. Schaefer (R)

POSTWAR VOTE FOR GOVERNOR

| | | | | | | | | | Percentage | | | |
| | Total | Republican | | Democratic | | Other | Rep.-Dem. | Total Vote | | Major Vote | |
Year	Vote	Vote	Candidate	Vote	Candidate	Vote	Plurality	Rep.	Dem.	Rep.	Dem.
1982	956,021	302,740	Fuhr, John D.	627,960	Lamm, Richard D.	25,321	325,220 D	31.7%	65.7%	32.5%	67.5%
1978	823,807	317,292	Strickland, Ted	483,985	Lamm, Richard D.	22,530	166,693 D	38.5%	58.7%	39.6%	60.4%
1974	828,968	378,698	Vanderhoof, John D.	441,408	Lamm, Richard D.	8,862	62,710 D	45.7%	53.2%	46.2%	53.8%
1970	668,496	350,690	Love, John A.	302,432	Hogan, Mark	15,374	48,258 R	52.5%	45.2%	53.7%	46.3%
1966	660,063	356,730	Love, John A.	287,132	Knous, Robert L.	16,201	69,598 R	54.0%	43.5%	55.4%	44.6%
1962	616,481	349,342	Love, John A.	262,890	McNichols, Stephen	4,249	86,452 R	56.7%	42.6%	57.1%	42.9%
1958*	549,808	228,643	Burch, Palmer L.	321,165	McNichols, Stephen	—	92,522 D	41.6%	58.4%	41.6%	58.4%
1956	645,233	313,950	Brotzman, Donald G.	331,283	McNichols, Stephen	—	17,333 D	48.7%	51.3%	48.7%	51.3%
1954	489,540	227,335	Brotzman, Donald G.	262,205	Johnson, Ed C.	—	34,870 D	46.4%	53.6%	46.4%	53.6%
1952	613,034	349,924	Thornton, Dan	260,044	Metzger, John W.	3,066	89,880 R	57.1%	42.4%	57.4%	42.6%
1950	450,994	236,472	Thornton, Dan	212,976	Johnson, Walter	1,546	23,496 R	52.4%	47.2%	52.6%	47.4%
1948	501,680	168,928	Hamil, David A.	332,752	Knous, William Lee	—	163,824 D	33.7%	66.3%	33.7%	66.3%
1946	335,087	160,483	Lavington, Leon E.	174,604	Knous, William Lee	—	14,121 D	47.9%	52.1%	47.9%	52.1%

The term of office of Colorado's Governor was increased from two to four years effective with the 1958 election.

POSTWAR VOTE FOR SENATOR

| | | | | | | | | | Percentage | | | |
| | Total | Republican | | Democratic | | Other | Rep.-Dem. | Total Vote | | Major Vote | |
Year	Vote	Vote	Candidate	Vote	Candidate	Vote	Plurality	Rep.	Dem.	Rep.	Dem.
1984	1,297,809	833,821	Armstrong, William L.	449,327	Dick, Nancy	14,661	384,494 R	64.2%	34.6%	65.0%	35.0%
1980	1,173,646	571,295	Buchanan, Mary E.	590,501	Hart, Gary W.	11,850	19,206 D	48.7%	50.3%	49.2%	50.8%
1978	819,150	480,596	Armstrong, William L.	330,247	Haskell, Floyd K.	8,307	150,349 R	58.7%	40.3%	59.3%	40.7%
1974	824,166	325,508	Dominick, Peter H.	471,691	Hart, Gary W.	26,967	146,183 D	39.5%	57.2%	40.8%	59.2%
1972	926,093	447,957	Allott, Gordon	457,545	Haskell, Floyd K.	20,591	9,588 D	48.4%	49.4%	49.5%	50.5%
1968	785,536	459,952	Dominick, Peter H.	325,584	McNichols, Stephen	—	134,368 R	58.6%	41.4%	58.6%	41.4%
1966	634,898	368,307	Allott, Gordon	266,259	Romer, Roy	332	102,048 R	58.0%	41.9%	58.0%	42.0%
1962	613,444	328,655	Dominick, Peter H.	279,586	Carroll, John A.	5,203	49,069 R	53.6%	45.6%	54.0%	46.0%
1960	727,633	389,428	Allott, Gordon	334,854	Knous, Robert L.	3,351	54,574 R	53.5%	46.0%	53.8%	46.2%
1956	636,974	317,102	Thornton, Dan	319,872	Carroll, John A.	—	2,770 D	49.8%	50.2%	49.8%	50.2%
1954	484,188	248,502	Allott, Gordon	235,686	Carroll, John A.	—	12,816 R	51.3%	48.7%	51.3%	48.7%
1950	450,176	239,734	Millikin, Eugene D.	210,442	Carroll, John A.	—	29,292 R	53.3%	46.7%	53.3%	46.7%
1948	510,121	165,069	Nicholson, W. F.	340,719	Johnson, Ed C.	4,333	175,650 D	32.4%	66.8%	32.6%	67.4%

COLORADO

Districts Established June 3, 1982

COLORADO

PRESIDENT 1984

1980 Census Population	County	Total Vote	Republican	Democratic	Other	Rep.-Dem. Plurality	Percentage Total Vote Rep.	Dem.	Major Vote Rep.	Dem.
245,944	ADAMS	91,511	55,092	35,285	1,134	19,807 R	60.2%	38.6%	61.0%	39.0%
11,799	ALAMOSA	4,711	2,953	1,720	38	1,233 R	62.7%	36.5%	63.2%	36.8%
293,621	ARAPAHOE	149,555	107,556	39,891	2,108	67,665 R	71.9%	26.7%	72.9%	27.1%
3,664	ARCHULETA	2,163	1,557	584	22	973 R	72.0%	27.0%	72.7%	27.3%
5,419	BACA	2,509	1,903	580	26	1,323 R	75.8%	23.1%	76.6%	23.4%
5,945	BENT	2,199	1,314	859	26	455 R	59.8%	39.1%	60.5%	39.5%
189,625	BOULDER	97,238	53,535	42,195	1,508	11,340 R	55.1%	43.4%	55.9%	44.1%
13,227	CHAFFEE	5,550	3,680	1,779	91	1,901 R	66.3%	32.1%	67.4%	32.6%
2,153	CHEYENNE	1,218	892	307	19	585 R	73.2%	25.2%	74.4%	25.6%
7,308	CLEAR CREEK	3,292	2,151	1,089	52	1,062 R	65.3%	33.1%	66.4%	33.6%
7,794	CONEJOS	3,247	1,669	1,553	25	116 R	51.4%	47.8%	51.8%	48.2%
3,071	COSTILLA	1,631	621	997	13	376 D	38.1%	61.1%	38.4%	61.6%
2,988	CROWLEY	1,527	993	517	17	476 R	65.0%	33.9%	65.8%	34.2%
1,528	CUSTER	1,093	832	241	20	591 R	76.1%	22.0%	77.5%	22.5%
21,225	DELTA	9,639	6,678	2,835	126	3,843 R	69.3%	29.4%	70.2%	29.8%
492,365	DENVER	219,741	105,096	110,200	4,445	5,104 D	47.8%	50.1%	48.8%	51.2%
1,658	DOLORES	850	667	173	10	494 R	78.5%	20.4%	79.4%	20.6%
25,153	DOUGLAS	15,441	12,249	3,011	181	9,238 R	79.3%	19.5%	80.3%	19.7%
13,320	EAGLE	6,633	4,500	2,032	101	2,468 R	67.8%	30.6%	68.9%	31.1%
6,850	ELBERT	3,461	2,605	802	54	1,803 R	75.3%	23.2%	76.5%	23.5%
309,424	EL PASO	117,773	88,377	28,185	1,211	60,192 R	75.0%	23.9%	75.8%	24.2%
28,676	FREMONT	12,256	8,250	3,895	111	4,355 R	67.3%	31.8%	67.9%	32.1%
22,514	GARFIELD	10,285	7,111	3,076	98	4,035 R	69.1%	29.9%	69.8%	30.2%
2,441	GILPIN	1,571	896	634	41	262 R	57.0%	40.4%	58.6%	41.4%
7,475	GRAND	3,940	2,865	1,017	58	1,848 R	72.7%	25.8%	73.8%	26.2%
10,689	GUNNISON	4,606	3,100	1,424	82	1,676 R	67.3%	30.9%	68.5%	31.5%
408	HINSDALE	414	310	98	6	212 R	74.9%	23.7%	76.0%	24.0%
6,440	HUERFANO	3,224	1,581	1,602	41	21 D	49.0%	49.7%	49.7%	50.3%
1,863	JACKSON	923	722	191	10	531 R	78.2%	20.7%	79.1%	20.9%
371,753	JEFFERSON	180,628	124,496	53,700	2,432	70,796 R	68.9%	29.7%	69.9%	30.1%
1,936	KIOWA	1,130	850	265	15	585 R	75.2%	23.5%	76.2%	23.8%
7,599	KIT CARSON	3,584	2,762	778	44	1,984 R	77.1%	21.7%	78.0%	22.0%
8,830	LAKE	2,747	1,364	1,324	59	40 R	49.7%	48.2%	50.7%	49.3%
27,424	LA PLATA	12,918	8,719	4,040	159	4,679 R	67.5%	31.3%	68.3%	31.7%
149,184	LARIMER	74,849	49,883	23,896	1,070	25,987 R	66.6%	31.9%	67.6%	32.4%
14,897	LAS ANIMAS	6,742	2,992	3,670	80	678 D	44.4%	54.4%	44.9%	55.1%
4,663	LINCOLN	2,278	1,661	587	30	1,074 R	72.9%	25.8%	73.9%	26.1%
19,800	LOGAN	8,133	5,883	2,155	95	3,728 R	72.3%	26.5%	73.2%	26.8%
81,530	MESA	34,074	23,736	9,938	400	13,798 R	69.7%	29.2%	70.5%	29.5%
804	MINERAL	459	333	117	9	216 R	72.5%	25.5%	74.0%	26.0%
13,133	MOFFAT	4,981	3,630	1,228	123	2,402 R	72.9%	24.7%	74.7%	25.3%
16,510	MONTEZUMA	6,506	4,753	1,665	88	3,088 R	73.1%	25.6%	74.1%	25.9%
24,352	MONTROSE	10,173	7,162	2,864	147	4,298 R	70.4%	28.2%	71.4%	28.6%
22,513	MORGAN	8,556	6,097	2,331	128	3,766 R	71.3%	27.2%	72.3%	27.7%
22,567	OTERO	8,615	5,373	3,005	237	2,368 R	62.4%	34.9%	64.1%	35.9%
1,925	OURAY	1,290	914	366	10	548 R	70.9%	28.4%	71.4%	28.6%
5,333	PARK	2,902	2,041	782	79	1,259 R	70.3%	26.9%	72.3%	27.7%
4,542	PHILLIPS	2,367	1,689	651	27	1,038 R	71.4%	27.5%	72.2%	27.8%
10,338	PITKIN	5,528	3,117	2,293	118	824 R	56.4%	41.5%	57.6%	42.4%
13,070	PROWERS	5,095	3,501	1,467	127	2,034 R	68.7%	28.8%	70.5%	29.5%
125,972	PUEBLO	52,200	24,634	27,126	440	2,492 D	47.2%	52.0%	47.6%	52.4%
6,255	RIO BLANCO	2,637	2,131	484	22	1,647 R	80.8%	18.4%	81.5%	18.5%
10,511	RIO GRANDE	4,262	3,122	1,104	36	2,018 R	73.3%	25.9%	73.9%	26.1%
13,404	ROUTT	6,408	4,239	2,051	118	2,188 R	66.2%	32.0%	67.4%	32.6%
3,935	SAGUACHE	2,084	1,201	867	16	334 R	57.6%	41.6%	58.1%	41.9%
833	SAN JUAN	519	320	183	16	137 R	61.7%	35.3%	63.6%	36.4%
3,192	SAN MIGUEL	1,521	833	654	34	179 R	54.8%	43.0%	56.0%	44.0%
3,266	SEDGWICK	1,583	1,146	429	8	717 R	72.4%	27.1%	72.8%	27.2%
8,848	SUMMIT	4,918	3,253	1,588	77	1,665 R	66.1%	32.3%	67.2%	32.8%
8,034	TELLER	4,562	3,460	1,043	59	2,417 R	75.8%	22.9%	76.8%	23.2%

COLORADO

PRESIDENT 1984

1980 Census Population	County	Total Vote	Republican	Democratic	Other	Rep.-Dem. Plurality	Percentage			
							Total Vote		Major Vote	
							Rep.	Dem.	Rep.	Dem.
5,304	WASHINGTON	2,684	2,080	568	36	1,512 R	77.5%	21.2%	78.5%	21.5%
123,438	WELD	45,679	31,293	13,863	523	17,430 R	68.5%	30.3%	69.3%	30.7%
9,682	YUMA	4,567	3,394	1,121	52	2,273 R	74.3%	24.5%	75.2%	24.8%
2,889,964	TOTAL	1,295,380	821,817	454,975	18,588	366,842 R	63.4%	35.1%	64.4%	35.6%

COLORADO

SENATOR 1984

1980 Census Population	County	Total Vote	Republican	Democratic	Other	Rep.-Dem. Plurality	Percentage Total Vote Rep.	Dem.	Major Vote Rep.	Dem.
245,944	ADAMS	91,976	55,492	35,732	752	19,760 R	60.3%	38.8%	60.8%	39.2%
11,799	ALAMOSA	4,890	3,078	1,768	44	1,310 R	62.9%	36.2%	63.5%	36.5%
293,621	ARAPAHOE	147,678	106,179	39,856	1,643	66,323 R	71.9%	27.0%	72.7%	27.3%
3,664	ARCHULETA	2,162	1,559	584	19	975 R	72.1%	27.0%	72.7%	27.3%
5,419	BACA	2,555	1,882	661	12	1,221 R	73.7%	25.9%	74.0%	26.0%
5,945	BENT	2,129	1,283	822	24	461 R	60.3%	38.6%	61.0%	39.0%
189,625	BOULDER	101,201	56,288	43,588	1,325	12,700 R	55.6%	43.1%	56.4%	43.6%
13,227	CHAFFEE	5,452	3,668	1,714	70	1,954 R	67.3%	31.4%	68.2%	31.8%
2,153	CHEYENNE	1,221	909	300	12	609 R	74.4%	24.6%	75.2%	24.8%
7,308	CLEAR CREEK	3,330	2,163	1,127	40	1,036 R	65.0%	33.8%	65.7%	34.3%
7,794	CONEJOS	3,329	1,689	1,548	92	141 R	50.7%	46.5%	52.2%	47.8%
3,071	COSTILLA	1,662	619	1,017	26	398 D	37.2%	61.2%	37.8%	62.2%
2,988	CROWLEY	1,539	1,028	500	11	528 R	66.8%	32.5%	67.3%	32.7%
1,528	CUSTER	1,096	807	277	12	530 R	73.6%	25.3%	74.4%	25.6%
21,225	DELTA	9,811	7,074	2,679	58	4,395 R	72.1%	27.3%	72.5%	27.5%
492,365	DENVER	212,577	104,392	104,295	3,890	97 R	49.1%	49.1%	50.0%	50.0%
1,658	DOLORES	822	584	233	5	351 R	71.0%	28.3%	71.5%	28.5%
25,153	DOUGLAS	15,432	12,077	3,233	122	8,844 R	78.3%	20.9%	78.9%	21.1%
13,320	EAGLE	6,631	4,216	2,356	59	1,860 R	63.6%	35.5%	64.2%	35.8%
6,850	ELBERT	3,462	2,588	841	33	1,747 R	74.8%	24.3%	75.5%	24.5%
309,424	EL PASO	120,552	92,217	27,370	965	64,847 R	76.5%	22.7%	77.1%	22.9%
28,676	FREMONT	12,756	9,060	3,614	82	5,446 R	71.0%	28.3%	71.5%	28.5%
22,514	GARFIELD	10,495	7,298	3,126	71	4,172 R	69.5%	29.8%	70.0%	30.0%
2,441	GILPIN	1,516	829	658	29	171 R	54.7%	43.4%	55.7%	44.3%
7,475	GRAND	3,945	2,816	1,084	45	1,732 R	71.4%	27.5%	72.2%	27.8%
10,689	GUNNISON	4,537	2,930	1,549	58	1,381 R	64.6%	34.1%	65.4%	34.6%
408	HINSDALE	416	322	87	7	235 R	77.4%	20.9%	78.7%	21.3%
6,440	HUERFANO	3,281	1,735	1,522	24	213 R	52.9%	46.4%	53.3%	46.7%
1,863	JACKSON	933	727	200	6	527 R	77.9%	21.4%	78.4%	21.6%
371,753	JEFFERSON	180,007	124,278	53,903	1,826	70,375 R	69.0%	29.9%	69.7%	30.3%
1,936	KIOWA	1,124	828	287	9	541 R	73.7%	25.5%	74.3%	25.7%
7,599	KIT CARSON	3,630	2,789	823	18	1,966 R	76.8%	22.7%	77.2%	22.8%
8,830	LAKE	2,687	1,456	1,178	53	278 R	54.2%	43.8%	55.3%	44.7%
27,424	LA PLATA	12,867	8,765	3,995	107	4,770 R	68.1%	31.0%	68.7%	31.3%
149,184	LARIMER	75,102	50,450	23,936	716	26,514 R	67.2%	31.9%	67.8%	32.2%
14,897	LAS ANIMAS	6,832	3,020	3,727	85	707 D	44.2%	54.6%	44.8%	55.2%
4,663	LINCOLN	2,293	1,702	568	23	1,134 R	74.2%	24.8%	75.0%	25.0%
19,800	LOGAN	8,547	5,984	2,508	55	3,476 R	70.0%	29.3%	70.5%	29.5%
81,530	MESA	35,307	26,356	8,685	266	17,671 R	74.6%	24.6%	75.2%	24.8%
804	MINERAL	458	319	134	5	185 R	69.7%	29.3%	70.4%	29.6%
13,133	MOFFAT	4,820	3,466	1,243	111	2,223 R	71.9%	25.8%	73.6%	26.4%
16,510	MONTEZUMA	6,518	4,742	1,726	50	3,016 R	72.8%	26.5%	73.3%	26.7%
24,352	MONTROSE	10,251	7,510	2,680	61	4,830 R	73.3%	26.1%	73.7%	26.3%
22,513	MORGAN	8,340	5,938	2,307	95	3,631 R	71.2%	27.7%	72.0%	28.0%
22,567	OTERO	8,319	5,465	2,663	191	2,802 R	65.7%	32.0%	67.2%	32.8%
1,925	OURAY	1,295	943	348	4	595 R	72.8%	26.9%	73.0%	27.0%
5,333	PARK	2,827	1,907	858	62	1,049 R	67.5%	30.4%	69.0%	31.0%
4,542	PHILLIPS	2,385	1,678	685	22	993 R	70.4%	28.7%	71.0%	29.0%
10,338	PITKIN	5,568	2,495	3,003	70	508 D	44.8%	53.9%	45.4%	54.6%
13,070	PROWERS	4,935	3,172	1,645	118	1,527 R	64.3%	33.3%	65.9%	34.1%
125,972	PUEBLO	53,664	28,349	24,956	359	3,393 R	52.8%	46.5%	53.2%	46.8%
6,255	RIO BLANCO	2,492	1,921	559	12	1,362 R	77.1%	22.4%	77.5%	22.5%
10,511	RIO GRANDE	4,552	3,311	1,193	48	2,118 R	72.7%	26.2%	73.5%	26.5%
13,404	ROUTT	6,442	4,106	2,240	96	1,866 R	63.7%	34.8%	64.7%	35.3%
3,935	SAGUACHE	2,093	1,165	893	35	272 R	55.7%	42.7%	56.6%	43.4%
833	SAN JUAN	517	335	168	14	167 R	64.8%	32.5%	66.6%	33.4%
3,192	SAN MIGUEL	1,493	826	642	25	184 R	55.3%	43.0%	56.3%	43.7%
3,266	SEDGWICK	1,588	1,111	470	7	641 R	70.0%	29.6%	70.3%	29.7%
8,848	SUMMIT	4,903	3,081	1,774	48	1,307 R	62.8%	36.2%	63.5%	36.5%
8,034	TELLER	4,587	3,444	1,106	37	2,338 R	75.1%	24.1%	75.7%	24.3%

COLORADO

SENATOR 1984

1980 Census Population	County	Total Vote	Republican	Democratic	Other	Rep.-Dem. Plurality	Percentage Total Vote Rep.	Dem.	Major Vote Rep.	Dem.
5,304	WASHINGTON	2,715	2,093	605	17	1,488 R	77.1%	22.3%	77.6%	22.4%
123,438	WELD	46,661	31,861	14,335	465	17,526 R	68.3%	30.7%	69.0%	31.0%
9,682	YUMA	4,604	3,446	1,143	15	2,303 R	74.8%	24.8%	75.1%	24.9%
2,889,964	TOTAL	1,297,809	833,821	449,327	14,661	384,494 R	64.2%	34.6%	65.0%	35.0%

COLORADO

CONGRESS

CD	Year	Total Vote	Republican Vote	Republican Candidate	Democratic Vote	Democratic Candidate	Other Vote	Rep.-Dem. Plurality	Total Vote Rep.	Total Vote Dem.	Major Vote Rep.	Major Vote Dem.
1	1984	203,873	73,993	DOWNS, MARY	126,348	SCHROEDER, PATRICIA	3,532	52,355 D	36.3%	62.0%	36.9%	63.1%
1	1982	157,597	59,009	DECKER, ARCH	94,969	SCHROEDER, PATRICIA	3,619	35,960 D	37.4%	60.3%	38.3%	61.7%
2	1984	222,859	101,488	NORTON, MICHAEL J.	118,580	WIRTH, TIMOTHY E.	2,791	17,092 D	45.5%	53.2%	46.1%	53.9%
2	1982	163,654	59,590	BUECHNER, JOHN C.	101,202	WIRTH, TIMOTHY E.	2,862	41,612 D	36.4%	61.8%	37.1%	62.9%
3	1984	214,970	122,669	STRANG, MICHAEL L.	90,063	MITCHELL, W	2,238	32,606 R	57.1%	41.9%	57.7%	42.3%
3	1982	172,889	77,410	WIENS, TOM	92,384	KOGOVSEK, RAY	3,095	14,974 D	44.8%	53.4%	45.6%	54.4%
4	1984	205,930	146,469	BROWN, HANK	56,462	BATES, MARY F.	2,999	90,007 R	71.1%	27.4%	72.2%	27.8%
4	1982	151,300	105,550	BROWN, HANK	45,750	BISHOPP, CHARLES L.		59,800 R	69.8%	30.2%	69.8%	30.2%
5	1984	208,242	163,654	KRAMER, KEN	44,588	GEFFEN, WILLIAM		119,066 R	78.6%	21.4%	78.6%	21.4%
5	1982	141,871	84,479	KRAMER, KEN	57,392	CRONIN, TOM		27,087 R	59.5%	40.5%	59.5%	40.5%
6	1984	191,760	171,427	SCHAEFER, DANIEL L.			20,333	171,427 R	89.4%		100.0%	
6	1982	159,112	98,909	SWIGERT, JACK	56,598	HOGAN, STEVE	3,605	42,311 R	62.2%	35.6%	63.6%	36.4%

COLORADO

1984 GENERAL ELECTION

President   Other vote was 11,257 Bergland (Libertarian); 4,662 LaRouche (Independent); 978 Serrette (Independent Alliance); 810 Mason (Socialist Workers); 858 Dodge (Prohibition); 23 Johnson (write-in).

Senator   Other vote was 11,077 Green (Libertarian); 2,208 Martin (Socialist-Workers); 1,376 Higgerson (Prohibition).

Congress   Other vote was 1,846 Emminizer (Socialist Workers) and 1,686 Filley (Libertarian) in CD 1; VanSickle (Libertarian) in CD 2; 1,358 Jahelka (Libertarian) and 880 Olshaw (Independent) in CD 3; Fitzgerald (Libertarian) in CD 4; Heckman (Concerns of People) in CD 6.

1984 PRIMARIES

SEPTEMBER 11 REPUBLICAN

Senator   William L. Armstrong, unopposed.

Congress   Unopposed in five CD's. Contested as follows:

CD 3   24,036 Michael L. Strang; 11,133 Phil Klingsmith.

SEPTEMBER 11 DEMOCRATIC

Senator   78,248 Nancy Dick; 75,277 Carlos Lucero.

Congress   Unopposed in four CD's. No candidate in CD 6. Contested as follows:

CD 3   25,492 W Mitchell; 24,080 Dick Soash.

CONNECTICUT

GOVERNOR

William A. O'Neill (D). Elected 1982 to a four-year term. Elected Lieutenant-Governor in 1978 and became Governor in December 1980 on the resignation of Governor Ella T. Grasso.

SENATORS

Christopher J. Dodd (D). Elected 1980 to a six-year term.

Lowell P. Weicker (R). Re-elected 1982 to a six-year term. Previously elected 1976, 1970.

REPRESENTATIVES

1. Barbara B. Kennelly (D)
2. Samuel Gejdenson (D)
3. Bruce A. Morrison (D)
4. Stewart B. McKinney (R)
5. John G. Rowland (R)
6. Nancy L. Johnson (R)

POSTWAR VOTE FOR GOVERNOR

Year	Total Vote	Republican Vote	Candidate	Democratic Vote	Candidate	Other Vote	Rep.-Dem. Plurality	Total Vote Rep.	Total Vote Dem.	Major Vote Rep.	Major Vote Dem.
1982	1,084,156	497,773	Rome, Lewis B.	578,264	O'Neill, William A.	8,119	80,491 D	45.9%	53.3%	46.3%	53.7%
1978	1,036,608	422,316	Sarasin, Ronald A.	613,109	Grasso, Ella T.	1,183	190,793 D	40.7%	59.1%	40.8%	59.2%
1974	1,102,773	440,169	Steele, Robert H.	643,490	Grasso, Ella T.	19,114	203,321 D	39.9%	58.4%	40.6%	59.4%
1970	1,082,797	582,160	Meskill, Thomas J.	500,561	Daddario, Emilio	76	81,599 R	53.8%	46.2%	53.8%	46.2%
1966	1,008,557	446,536	Gengras, E. Clayton	561,599	Dempsey, John N.	422	115,063 D	44.3%	55.7%	44.3%	55.7%
1962	1,031,902	482,852	Alsop, John	549,027	Dempsey, John N.	23	66,175 D	46.8%	53.2%	46.8%	53.2%
1958	974,509	360,644	Zeller, Fred R.	607,012	Ribicoff, Abraham A.	6,853	246,368 D	37.0%	62.3%	37.3%	62.7%
1954	936,753	460,528	Lodge, John D.	463,643	Ribicoff, Abraham A.	12,582	3,115 D	49.2%	49.5%	49.8%	50.2%
1950*	878,735	436,418	Lodge, John D.	419,404	Bowles, Chester	22,913	17,014 R	49.7%	47.7%	51.0%	49.0%
1948	875,170	429,071	Shannon, James C.	431,296	Bowles, Chester	14,803	2,225 D	49.0%	49.3%	49.9%	50.1%
1946	683,831	371,852	McConaughy, J. L.	276,335	Snow, Wilbert	35,644	95,517 R	54.4%	40.4%	57.4%	42.6%

The term of office of Connecticut's Governor was increased from two to four years effective with the 1950 election.

POSTWAR VOTE FOR SENATOR

Year	Total Vote	Republican Vote	Candidate	Democratic Vote	Candidate	Other Vote	Rep.-Dem. Plurality	Total Vote Rep.	Total Vote Dem.	Major Vote Rep.	Major Vote Dem.
1982	1,083,613	545,987	Weicker, Lowell P.	499,146	Moffett, Anthony T.	38,480	46,841 R	50.4%	46.1%	52.2%	47.8%
1980	1,356,075	581,884	Buckley, James L.	763,969	Dodd, Christopher J.	10,222	182,085 D	42.9%	56.3%	43.2%	56.8%
1976	1,361,666	785,683	Weicker, Lowell P.	561,018	Schaffer, Gloria	14,965	224,665 R	57.7%	41.2%	58.3%	41.7%
1974	1,084,918	372,055	Brannen, James H.	690,820	Ribicoff, Abraham A.	22,043	318,765 D	34.3%	63.7%	35.0%	65.0%
1970	1,089,353	454,721	Weicker, Lowell P.	368,111	Duffey, Joseph D.	266,521	86,610 R	41.7%	33.8%	55.3%	44.7%
1968	1,206,537	551,455	May, Edwin H.	655,043	Ribicoff, Abraham A.	39	103,588 D	45.7%	54.3%	45.7%	54.3%
1964	1,208,163	426,939	Lodge, John D.	781,008	Dodd, Thomas J.	216	354,069 D	35.3%	64.6%	35.3%	64.7%
1962	1,029,301	501,694	Seely-Brown, Horace	527,522	Ribicoff, Abraham A.	85	25,828 D	48.7%	51.3%	48.7%	51.3%
1958	965,463	410,622	Purtell, William A.	554,841	Dodd, Thomas J.	—	144,219 D	42.5%	57.5%	42.5%	57.5%
1956	1,113,819	610,829	Bush, Prescott	479,460	Dodd, Thomas J.	23,530	131,369 R	54.8%	43.0%	56.0%	44.0%
1952	1,093,467	573,854	Purtell, William A.	485,066	Benton, William	34,547	88,788 R	52.5%	44.4%	54.2%	45.8%
1952s	1,093,268	559,465	Weicker, Lowell P.	530,505	Ribicoff, Abraham A.	3,298	28,960 R	51.2%	48.5%	51.3%	48.7%
1950	877,827	409,053	Talbot, Joseph E.	453,646	McMahon, Brien	15,128	44,593 D	46.6%	51.7%	47.4%	52.6%
1950s	877,135	430,311	Bush, Prescott	431,413	Benton, William	15,411	1,102 D	49.1%	49.2%	49.9%	50.1%
1946	682,921	381,328	Baldwin, Raymond	276,424	Tone, Joseph M.	25,169	104,904 R	55.8%	40.5%	58.0%	42.0%

One each of the 1952 and 1950 elections was for a short term to fill a vacancy.

CONNECTICUT

Districts Established October 29, 1981

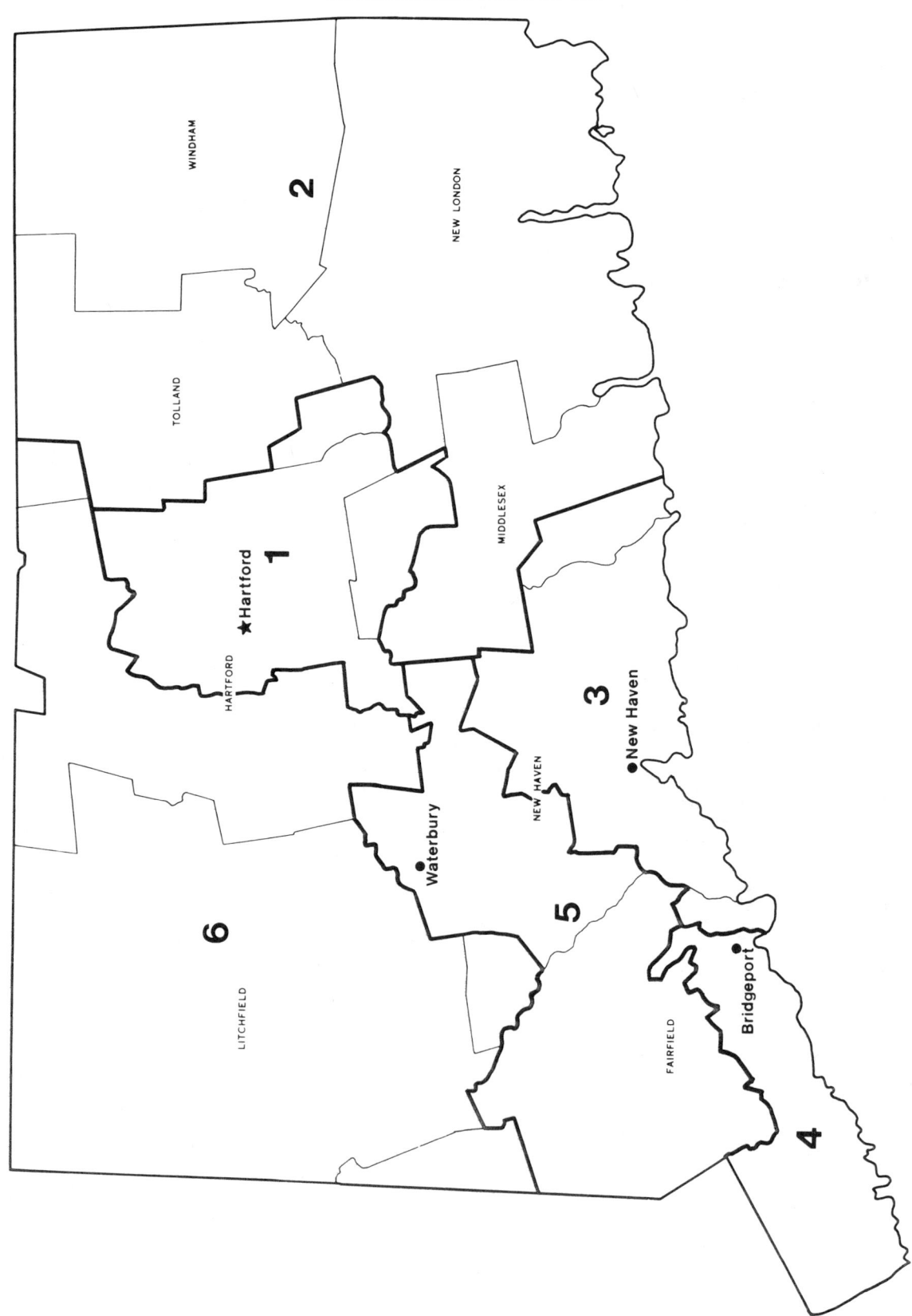

CONNECTICUT

PRESIDENT 1984

1980 Census Population	County		Total Vote	Republican	Democratic	Other	Rep.-Dem. Plurality	Percentage			
								Total Vote		Major Vote	
								Rep.	Dem.	Rep.	Dem.
807,143	FAIRFIELD		391,179	257,319	132,253	1,607	125,066 R	65.8%	33.8%	66.1%	33.9%
807,766	HARTFORD		378,405	208,210	168,609	1,586	39,601 R	55.0%	44.6%	55.3%	44.7%
156,769	LITCHFIELD		79,416	52,583	26,564	269	26,019 R	66.2%	33.4%	66.4%	33.6%
129,017	MIDDLESEX		66,722	39,580	26,915	227	12,665 R	59.3%	40.3%	59.5%	40.5%
761,337	NEW HAVEN		354,712	212,166	140,945	1,601	71,221 R	59.8%	39.7%	60.1%	39.9%
238,409	NEW LONDON		102,487	63,121	38,857	509	24,264 R	61.6%	37.9%	61.9%	38.1%
114,823	TOLLAND		53,298	32,981	20,103	214	12,878 R	61.9%	37.7%	62.1%	37.9%
92,312	WINDHAM		40,455	24,917	15,351	187	9,566 R	61.6%	37.9%	61.9%	38.1%
3,107,576	TOTAL		1,466,900	890,877	569,597	6,426	321,280 R	60.7%	38.8%	61.0%	39.0%

CONNECTICUT

PRESIDENT 1984

1980 Census Population	City/Town	Total Vote	Republican	Democratic	Other	Rep.-Dem. Plurality	Percentage Total Vote Rep.	Dem.	Major Vote Rep.	Dem.
19,039	ANSONIA	8,500	5,482	2,981	37	2,501 R	64.5%	35.1%	64.8%	35.2%
23,363	BRANFORD	12,848	8,118	4,679	51	3,439 R	63.2%	36.4%	63.4%	36.6%
142,546	BRIDGEPORT	48,909	24,256	24,332	321	76 D	49.6%	49.7%	49.9%	50.1%
57,370	BRISTOL	24,770	13,872	10,782	116	3,090 R	56.0%	43.5%	56.3%	43.7%
21,788	CHESHIRE	11,646	8,157	3,444	45	4,713 R	70.0%	29.6%	70.3%	29.7%
60,470	DANBURY	25,219	16,143	8,922	154	7,221 R	64.0%	35.4%	64.4%	35.6%
18,892	DARIEN	10,849	8,463	2,341	45	6,122 R	78.0%	21.6%	78.3%	21.7%
52,563	EAST HARTFORD	22,284	11,508	10,647	129	861 R	51.6%	47.8%	51.9%	48.1%
25,028	EAST HAVEN	11,232	7,075	4,124	33	2,951 R	63.0%	36.7%	63.2%	36.8%
42,695	ENFIELD	17,748	10,339	7,343	66	2,996 R	58.3%	41.4%	58.5%	41.5%
54,849	FAIRFIELD TOWN	31,079	21,396	9,573	110	11,823 R	68.8%	30.8%	69.1%	30.9%
24,327	GLASTONBURY	14,668	9,599	5,015	54	4,584 R	65.4%	34.2%	65.7%	34.3%
59,578	GREENWICH	33,076	23,361	9,620	95	13,741 R	70.6%	29.1%	70.8%	29.2%
41,062	GROTON	13,974	8,855	5,056	63	3,799 R	63.4%	36.2%	63.7%	36.3%
51,071	HAMDEN	27,096	15,965	11,029	102	4,936 R	58.9%	40.7%	59.1%	40.9%
136,392	HARTFORD CITY	41,208	11,621	29,327	260	17,706 D	28.2%	71.2%	28.4%	71.6%
49,761	MANCHESTER	25,015	14,878	10,023	114	4,855 R	59.5%	40.1%	59.7%	40.3%
20,634	MANSFIELD	6,870	3,103	3,727	40	624 D	45.2%	54.3%	45.4%	54.6%
57,118	MERIDEN	24,469	14,003	10,313	153	3,690 R	57.2%	42.1%	57.6%	42.4%
39,040	MIDDLETOWN	18,377	8,533	9,791	53	1,258 D	46.4%	53.3%	46.6%	53.4%
50,898	MILFORD	24,765	17,299	7,346	120	9,953 R	69.9%	29.7%	70.2%	29.8%
26,456	NAUGATUCK	11,650	7,865	3,732	53	4,133 R	67.5%	32.0%	67.8%	32.2%
73,840	NEW BRITAIN	28,508	13,723	14,608	177	885 D	48.1%	51.2%	48.4%	51.6%
126,109	NEW HAVEN CITY	49,285	16,483	32,518	284	16,035 D	33.4%	66.0%	33.6%	66.4%
28,841	NEWINGTON	15,553	8,960	6,523	70	2,437 R	57.6%	41.9%	57.9%	42.1%
28,842	NEW LONDON CITY	10,281	4,813	5,380	88	567 D	46.8%	52.3%	47.2%	52.8%
22,080	NORTH HAVEN	11,918	8,007	3,888	23	4,119 R	67.2%	32.6%	67.3%	32.7%
77,767	NORWALK	35,058	22,447	12,509	102	9,938 R	64.0%	35.7%	64.2%	35.8%
38,074	NORWICH	14,567	8,350	6,149	68	2,201 R	57.3%	42.2%	57.6%	42.4%
20,120	RIDGEFIELD	11,746	8,512	3,206	28	5,306 R	72.5%	27.3%	72.6%	27.4%
31,314	SHELTON	15,325	11,655	3,628	42	8,027 R	76.1%	23.7%	76.3%	23.7%
21,161	SIMSBURY	12,393	8,541	3,823	29	4,718 R	68.9%	30.8%	69.1%	30.9%
36,879	SOUTHINGTON	16,296	10,088	6,146	62	3,942 R	61.9%	37.7%	62.1%	37.9%
102,453	STAMFORD	48,855	29,167	19,432	256	9,735 R	59.7%	39.8%	60.0%	40.0%
50,541	STRATFORD	26,110	17,174	8,814	122	8,360 R	65.8%	33.8%	66.1%	33.9%
30,987	TORRINGTON	15,043	8,991	6,019	33	2,972 R	59.8%	40.0%	59.9%	40.1%
32,989	TRUMBULL	18,492	13,512	4,920	60	8,592 R	73.1%	26.6%	73.3%	26.7%
27,974	VERNON	12,850	8,075	4,736	39	3,339 R	62.8%	36.9%	63.0%	37.0%
37,274	WALLINGFORD	17,903	11,181	6,665	57	4,516 R	62.5%	37.2%	62.7%	37.3%
103,266	WATERBURY	43,209	24,764	18,217	228	6,547 R	57.3%	42.2%	57.6%	42.4%
61,301	WEST HARTFORD	37,496	20,517	16,882	97	3,635 R	54.7%	45.0%	54.9%	45.1%
53,184	WEST HAVEN	23,915	14,210	9,588	117	4,622 R	59.4%	40.1%	59.7%	40.3%
25,290	WESTPORT	14,967	9,162	5,774	31	3,388 R	61.2%	38.6%	61.3%	38.7%
26,013	WETHERSFIELD	15,805	9,661	6,098	46	3,563 R	61.1%	38.6%	61.3%	38.7%
21,062	WINDHAM TOWN	8,661	4,872	3,739	50	1,133 R	56.3%	43.2%	56.6%	43.4%
25,204	WINDSOR	12,956	7,417	5,490	49	1,927 R	57.2%	42.4%	57.5%	42.5%

CONNECTICUT

CONGRESS

CD	Year	Total Vote	Republican Vote	Republican Candidate	Democratic Vote	Democratic Candidate	Other Vote	Rep.-Dem. Plurality	Percentage Total Vote Rep.	Dem.	Major Vote Rep.	Dem.
1	1984	239,362	90,823	KLEIN, HERSCHEL A.	147,748	KENNELLY, BARBARA B.	791	56,925 D	37.9%	61.7%	38.1%	61.9%
1	1982	186,123	58,075	KLEIN, HERSCHEL A.	126,798	KENNELLY, BARBARA B.	1,250	68,723 D	31.2%	68.1%	31.4%	68.6%
2	1984	228,253	103,119	KOONTZ, ROBERTA F.	124,110	GEJDENSON, SAMUEL	1,024	20,991 D	45.2%	54.4%	45.4%	54.6%
2	1982	170,814	74,294	GUGLIELMO, TONY	95,254	GEJDENSON, SAMUEL	1,266	20,960 D	43.5%	55.8%	43.8%	56.2%
3	1984	245,795	115,939	DENARDIS, LAWRENCE J.	129,230	MORRISON, BRUCE A.	626	13,291 D	47.2%	52.6%	47.3%	52.7%
3	1982	181,458	88,951	DENARDIS, LAWRENCE J.	90,638	MORRISON, BRUCE A.	1,869	1,687 D	49.0%	49.9%	49.5%	50.5%
4	1984	235,310	165,644	MCKINNEY, STEWART B.	69,666	ORMAN, JOHN M.		95,978 R	70.4%	29.6%	70.4%	29.6%
4	1982	165,907	93,660	MCKINNEY, STEWART B.	71,110	PHILLIPS, JOHN A.	1,137	22,550 R	56.5%	42.9%	56.8%	43.2%
5	1984	240,657	130,700	ROWLAND, JOHN G.	109,425	RATCHFORD, WILLIAM	532	21,275 R	54.3%	45.5%	54.4%	45.6%
5	1982	173,376	70,808	HANLON, NEAL B.	101,362	RATCHFORD, WILLIAM	1,206	30,554 D	40.8%	58.5%	41.1%	58.9%
6	1984	242,911	155,422	JOHNSON, NANCY L.	87,489	HOUSE, ARTHUR H.		67,933 R	64.0%	36.0%	64.0%	36.0%
6	1982	192,997	99,703	JOHNSON, NANCY L.	92,178	CURRY, WILLIAM E.	1,116	7,525 R	51.7%	47.8%	52.0%	48.0%

CONNECTICUT

1984 GENERAL ELECTION

In addition to the county-by-county figures, data are presented for selected Connecticut communities. Since not all jurisdictions of the state are listed in this special tabulation, state-wide totals are shown only with the county-by-county statistics.

President   Other vote was 4,826 Hall (Communist); 1,374 Serrette (Connecticut Alliance); 204 Bergland (write-in); 14 Johnson (write-in); 8 scattered. State-wide total for other vote column includes these 226 write-in votes not published by county or city/town.

Congress   Other vote was Sundblade (Libertarian) in CD 1; Wood (Libertarian) in CD 2; 426 Cohen (Libertarian) and 200 Valenti (Independent) in CD 3; Peron (Libertarian) in CD 5.

1984 PRIMARIES

Party conventions nominate Connecticut candidates, subject to a system of "challenge" primaries. Any candidate who receives more than 20 percent of the convention vote is entitled to challenge the endorsed candidate in a primary. There were no challenge primary elections in either party in 1984.

DELAWARE

GOVERNOR
Michael N. Castle (R). Elected 1984 to a four-year term.

SENATORS
Joseph R. Biden (D). Re-elected 1984 to a six-year term. Previously elected 1978, 1972.

William V. Roth (R). Re-elected 1982 to a six-year term. Previously elected 1976, 1970.

REPRESENTATIVE
At-Large. Thomas R. Carper (D)

POSTWAR VOTE FOR GOVERNOR

| | Total | Republican | | Democratic | | Other | Rep.-Dem. | Percentage | | | |
| | | | | | | | | Total Vote | | Major Vote | |
Year	Vote	Vote	Candidate	Vote	Candidate	Vote	Plurality	Rep.	Dem.	Rep.	Dem.
1984	243,565	135,250	Castle, Michael N.	108,315	Quillen, William T.	—	26,935 R	55.5%	44.5%	55.5%	44.5%
1980	225,081	159,004	duPont, Pierre	64,217	Gordy, William J.	1,860	94,787 R	70.6%	28.5%	71.2%	28.8%
1976	229,563	130,531	duPont, Pierre	97,480	Tribbitt, Sherman W.	1,552	33,051 R	56.9%	42.5%	57.2%	42.8%
1972	228,722	109,583	Peterson, Russell W.	117,274	Tribbitt, Sherman W.	1,865	7,691 D	47.9%	51.3%	48.3%	51.7%
1968	206,834	104,474	Peterson, Russell W.	102,360	Terry, Charles L.	—	2,114 R	50.5%	49.5%	50.5%	49.5%
1964	200,171	97,374	Buckson, David P.	102,797	Terry, Charles L.	—	5,423 D	48.6%	51.4%	48.6%	51.4%
1960	194,835	94,043	Rollins, John W.	100,792	Carvel, Elbert N.	—	6,749 D	48.3%	51.7%	48.3%	51.7%
1956	177,012	91,965	Boggs, J. Caleb	85,047	McConnell, J. H. T.	—	6,918 R	52.0%	48.0%	52.0%	48.0%
1952	170,749	88,977	Boggs, J. Caleb	81,772	Carvel, Elbert N.	—	7,205 R	52.1%	47.9%	52.1%	47.9%
1948	140,335	64,996	George, Hyland P.	75,339	Carvel, Elbert N.	—	10,343 D	46.3%	53.7%	46.3%	53.7%

POSTWAR VOTE FOR SENATOR

| | Total | Republican | | Democratic | | Other | Rep.-Dem. | Percentage | | | |
| | | | | | | | | Total Vote | | Major Vote | |
Year	Vote	Vote	Candidate	Vote	Candidate	Vote	Plurality	Rep.	Dem.	Rep.	Dem.
1984	245,932	98,101	Burris, John M.	147,831	Biden, Joseph R.	—	49,730 D	39.9%	60.1%	39.9%	60.1%
1982	190,960	105,357	Roth, William V.	84,413	Levinson, David N.	1,190	20,944 R	55.2%	44.2%	55.5%	44.5%
1978	162,072	66,479	Baxter, James H.	93,930	Biden, Joseph R.	1,663	27,451 D	41.0%	58.0%	41.4%	58.6%
1976	224,859	125,502	Roth, William V.	98,055	Maloney, Thomas C.	1,302	27,447 R	55.8%	43.6%	56.1%	43.9%
1972	229,828	112,844	Boggs, J. Caleb	116,006	Biden, Joseph R.	978	3,162 D	49.1%	50.5%	49.3%	50.7%
1970	161,439	94,979	Roth, William V.	64,740	Zimmerman, Jacob	1,720	30,239 R	58.8%	40.1%	59.5%	40.5%
1966	164,549	97,268	Boggs, J. Caleb	67,281	Tunnell, James M., Jr.	—	29,987 R	59.1%	40.9%	59.1%	40.9%
1964	200,703	103,782	Williams, John J.	96,850	Carvel, Elbert N.	71	6,932 R	51.7%	48.3%	51.7%	48.3%
1960	194,964	98,874	Boggs, J. Caleb	96,090	Frear, J. Allen	—	2,784 R	50.7%	49.3%	50.7%	49.3%
1958	154,432	82,280	Williams, John J.	72,152	Carvel, Elbert N.	—	10,128 R	53.3%	46.7%	53.3%	46.7%
1954	144,900	62,389	Warburton, H. B.	82,511	Frear, J. Allen	—	20,122 D	43.1%	56.9%	43.1%	56.9%
1952	170,705	93,020	Williams, John J.	77,685	Bayard, A. I. duP.	—	15,335 R	54.5%	45.5%	54.5%	45.5%
1948	141,362	68,246	Buck, C. Douglas	71,888	Frear, J. Allen	1,228	3,642 D	48.3%	50.9%	48.7%	51.3%
1946	113,513	62,603	Williams, John J.	50,910	Tunnell, James M.	—	11,693 R	55.2%	44.8%	55.2%	44.8%

DELAWARE

One At Large

Wilmington●

NEW CASTLE

Dover★

KENT

SUSSEX

DELAWARE

PRESIDENT 1984

1980 Census Population	County	Total Vote	Republican	Democratic	Other	Rep.-Dem. Plurality	Percentage			
							Total Vote Rep.	Dem.	Major Vote Rep.	Dem.
98,219	KENT	33,403	21,531	11,789	83	9,742 R	64.5%	35.3%	64.6%	35.4%
398,115	NEW CASTLE	179,077	102,322	76,238	517	26,084 R	57.1%	42.6%	57.3%	42.7%
98,004	SUSSEX	42,092	28,337	13,629	126	14,708 R	67.3%	32.4%	67.5%	32.5%
594,338	TOTAL	254,572	152,190	101,656	726	50,534 R	59.8%	39.9%	60.0%	40.0%

DELAWARE

GOVERNOR 1984

1980 Census Population	County	Total Vote	Republican	Democratic	Other	Rep.-Dem. Plurality	Percentage			
							Total Vote Rep.	Dem.	Major Vote Rep.	Dem.
98,219	KENT	32,128	17,894	14,234		3,660 R	55.7%	44.3%	55.7%	44.3%
398,115	NEW CASTLE	171,259	93,393	77,866		15,527 R	54.5%	45.5%	54.5%	45.5%
98,004	SUSSEX	40,178	23,963	16,215		7,748 R	59.6%	40.4%	59.6%	40.4%
594,338	TOTAL	243,565	135,250	108,315		26,935 R	55.5%	44.5%	55.5%	44.5%

DELAWARE

SENATOR 1984

1980 Census Population	County	Total Vote	Republican	Democratic	Other	Rep.-Dem. Plurality	Percentage			
							Total Vote Rep.	Dem.	Major Vote Rep.	Dem.
98,219	KENT	32,335	13,424	18,911		5,487 D	41.5%	58.5%	41.5%	58.5%
398,115	NEW CASTLE	172,988	65,352	107,636		42,284 D	37.8%	62.2%	37.8%	62.2%
98,004	SUSSEX	40,609	19,325	21,284		1,959 D	47.6%	52.4%	47.6%	52.4%
594,338	TOTAL	245,932	98,101	147,831		49,730 D	39.9%	60.1%	39.9%	60.1%

DELAWARE

CONGRESS

CD	Year	Total Vote	Republican Vote	Republican Candidate	Democratic Vote	Democratic Candidate	Other Vote	Rep.-Dem. Plurality	Percentage Total Vote Rep.	Percentage Total Vote Dem.	Major Vote Rep.	Major Vote Dem.
AL	1984	243,014	100,650	DUPONT, ELISE	142,070	CARPER, THOMAS R.	294	41,420 D	41.4%	58.5%	41.5%	58.5%
AL	1982	188,064	87,153	EVANS, THOMAS B.	98,533	CARPER, THOMAS R.	2,378	11,380 D	46.3%	52.4%	46.9%	53.1%
AL	1980	216,629	133,842	EVANS, THOMAS B.	81,227	MAXWELL, ROBERT L.	1,560	52,615 R	61.8%	37.5%	62.2%	37.8%
AL	1978	157,566	91,689	EVANS, THOMAS B.	64,863	HINDES, GARY E.	1,014	26,826 R	58.2%	41.2%	58.6%	41.4%
AL	1976	214,799	110,677	EVANS, THOMAS B.	102,431	SHIPLEY, SAMUEL L.	1,691	8,246 R	51.5%	47.7%	51.9%	48.1%
AL	1974	160,328	93,826	DUPONT, PIERRE	63,490	SOLES, JAMES	3,012	30,336 R	58.5%	39.6%	59.6%	40.4%
AL	1972	225,851	141,237	DUPONT, PIERRE	83,230	HANDLOFF, NORMA	1,384	58,007 R	62.5%	36.9%	62.9%	37.1%
AL	1970	160,313	86,125	DUPONT, PIERRE	71,429	DANIELLO, JOHN D.	2,759	14,696 R	53.7%	44.6%	54.7%	45.3%
AL	1968	200,820	117,827	ROTH, WILLIAM V.	82,993	MCDOWELL, HARRIS B.		34,834 R	58.7%	41.3%	58.7%	41.3%
AL	1966	163,103	90,961	ROTH, WILLIAM V.	72,142	MCDOWELL, HARRIS B.		18,819 R	55.8%	44.2%	55.8%	44.2%
AL	1964	198,691	86,254	SNOWDEN, JAMES H.	112,361	MCDOWELL, HARRIS B.	76	26,107 D	43.4%	56.6%	43.4%	56.6%
AL	1962	153,356	71,934	WILLIAMS, WILMER F.	81,166	MCDOWELL, HARRIS B.	256	9,232 D	46.9%	52.9%	47.0%	53.0%
AL	1960	194,564	96,337	MCKINSTRY, JAMES T.	98,227	MCDOWELL, HARRIS B.		1,890 D	49.5%	50.5%	49.5%	50.5%
AL	1958	152,896	76,099	HASKELL, HARRY G.	76,797	MCDOWELL, HARRIS B.		698 D	49.8%	50.2%	49.8%	50.2%
AL	1956	176,182	91,538	HASKELL, HARRY G.	84,644	MCDOWELL, HARRIS B.		6,894 R	52.0%	48.0%	52.0%	48.0%
AL	1954	144,236	65,035	MARTIN, LILLIAN	79,201	MCDOWELL, HARRIS B.		14,166 D	45.1%	54.9%	45.1%	54.9%
AL	1952	170,015	88,285	WARBURTON, H. B.	81,730	SCANNELL, JOSEPH S.		6,555 R	51.9%	48.1%	51.9%	48.1%
AL	1950	129,404	73,313	BOGGS, J. CALEB	56,091	WINCHESTER, H. M.		17,222 R	56.7%	43.3%	56.7%	43.3%
AL	1948	140,535	71,127	BOGGS, J. CALEB	68,909	MCGUIGAN, J. CARL	499	2,218 R	50.6%	49.0%	50.8%	49.2%
AL	1946	112,621	63,516	BOGGS, J. CALEB	49,105	TRAYNOR, PHILIP A.		14,411 R	56.4%	43.6%	56.4%	43.6%

DELAWARE

1984 GENERAL ELECTION

President   Other vote was 269 Dennis (American); 268 Bergland (Libertarian); 121 Johnson (Citizens); 68 Serrette (Independent).

Governor

Senator

Congress   Other vote was Etzel (Libertarian).

1984 PRIMARIES

SEPTEMBER 8 REPUBLICAN

Governor   Michael N. Castle, Unopposed.

Senator   John M. Burris, unopposed.

Congress   Unopposed at-large.

SEPTEMBER 8 DEMOCRATIC

Governor   20,473 William T. Quillen; 14,185 Sherman W. Tribbitt.

Senator   Joseph R. Biden, unopposed.

Congress   Unopposed at-large.

FLORIDA

GOVERNOR
Robert Graham (D). Re-elected 1982 to a four-year term. Previously elected 1978.

SENATORS
Lawton Chiles (D). Re-elected 1982 to a six-year term. Previously elected 1976, 1970.

Paula Hawkins (R). Elected 1980 to a six-year term.

REPRESENTATIVES
1. Earl D. Hutto (D)
2. Don Fuqua (D)
3. Charles E. Bennett (D)
4. William V. Chappell (D)
5. Bill McCollum (R)
6. Buddy MacKay (D)
7. Sam M. Gibbons (D)
8. C. W. Young (R)
9. Michael Bilirakis (R)
10. Andrew P. Ireland (R)
11. Bill Nelson (D)
12. Tom Lewis (R)
13. Connie Mack (R)
14. Dan Mica (D)
15. Clay Shaw (R)
16. Larry Smith (D)
17. William Lehman (D)
18. Claude Pepper (D)
19. Dante B. Fascell (D)

POSTWAR VOTE FOR GOVERNOR

Year	Total Vote	Republican Vote	Republican Candidate	Democratic Vote	Democratic Candidate	Other Vote	Rep.-Dem. Plurality	Total Vote Rep.	Total Vote Dem.	Major Vote Rep.	Major Vote Dem.
1982	2,688,566	949,013	Bafalis, L. A.	1,739,553	Graham, Robert	—	790,540 D	35.3%	64.7%	35.3%	64.7%
1978	2,530,468	1,123,888	Eckerd, Jack M.	1,406,580	Graham, Robert	—	282,692 D	44.4%	55.6%	44.4%	55.6%
1974	1,828,392	709,438	Thomas, Jerry	1,118,954	Askew, Reubin	—	409,516 D	38.8%	61.2%	38.8%	61.2%
1970	1,730,813	746,243	Kirk, Claude R.	984,305	Askew, Reubin	265	238,062 D	43.1%	56.9%	43.1%	56.9%
1966	1,489,661	821,190	Kirk, Claude R.	668,233	High, Robert King	238	152,957 R	55.1%	44.9%	55.1%	44.9%
1964s	1,663,481	686,297	Holley, Charles R.	933,554	Burns, Haydon	43,630	247,257 D	41.3%	56.1%	42.4%	57.6%
1960	1,419,343	569,936	Petersen, George C.	849,407	Bryant, Farris	—	279,471 D	40.2%	59.8%	40.2%	59.8%
1956	1,014,733	266,980	Washburne, W. A.	747,753	Collins, LeRoy	—	480,773 D	26.3%	73.7%	26.3%	73.7%
1954s	357,783	69,852	Watson, J. Tom	287,769	Collins, LeRoy	162	217,917 D	19.5%	80.4%	19.5%	80.5%
1952	834,518	210,009	Swan, Harry S.	624,463	McCarty, Dan	46	414,454 D	25.2%	74.8%	25.2%	74.8%
1948	457,638	76,153	Acker, Bert Lee	381,459	Warren, Fuller	26	305,306 D	16.6%	83.4%	16.6%	83.4%

The 1954 election was for a short term to fill a vacancy. The 1964 vote was for a two-year term to permit shifting the vote for Governor to non-Presidential years.

POSTWAR VOTE FOR SENATOR

Year	Total Vote	Republican Vote	Republican Candidate	Democratic Vote	Democratic Candidate	Other Vote	Rep.-Dem. Plurality	Total Vote Rep.	Total Vote Dem.	Major Vote Rep.	Major Vote Dem.
1982	2,653,419	1,015,330	Poole, Van B.	1,637,667	Chiles, Lawton	422	622,337 D	38.3%	61.7%	38.3%	61.7%
1980	3,528,028	1,822,460	Hawkins, Paula	1,705,409	Gunter, Bill	159	117,051 R	51.7%	48.3%	51.7%	48.3%
1976	2,857,534	1,057,886	Grady, John	1,799,518	Chiles, Lawton	130	741,632 D	37.0%	63.0%	37.0%	63.0%
1974	1,800,539	736,674	Eckerd, Jack M.	781,031	Stone, Richard	282,834	44,357 D	40.9%	43.4%	48.5%	51.5%
1970	1,675,378	772,817	Cramer, William C.	902,438	Chiles, Lawton	123	129,621 D	46.1%	53.9%	46.1%	53.9%
1968	2,024,136	1,131,499	Gurney, Edward J.	892,637	Collins, LeRoy	—	238,862 R	55.9%	44.1%	55.9%	44.1%
1964	1,560,337	562,212	Kirk, Claude R.	997,585	Holland, Spessard L.	540	435,373 D	36.0%	63.9%	36.0%	64.0%
1962	939,207	281,381	Rupert, Emerson H.	657,633	Smathers, George A.	193	376,252 D	30.0%	70.0%	30.0%	70.0%
1958	542,069	155,956	Hyzer, Leland	386,113	Holland, Spessard L.	—	230,157 D	28.8%	71.2%	28.8%	71.2%
1956	655,418	—	—	655,418	Smathers, George A.	—	655,418 D	—	100.0%	—	100.0%
1952	617,800	—	—	616,665	Holland, Spessard L.	1,135	616,665 D	—	99.8%	—	100.0%
1950	313,487	74,228	Booth, John P.	238,987	Smathers, George A.	272	164,759 D	23.7%	76.2%	23.7%	76.3%
1946	198,640	42,408	Schad, J. Harry	156,232	Holland, Spessard L.	—	113,824 D	21.3%	78.7%	21.3%	78.7%

FLORIDA

Districts Established May 21, 1982

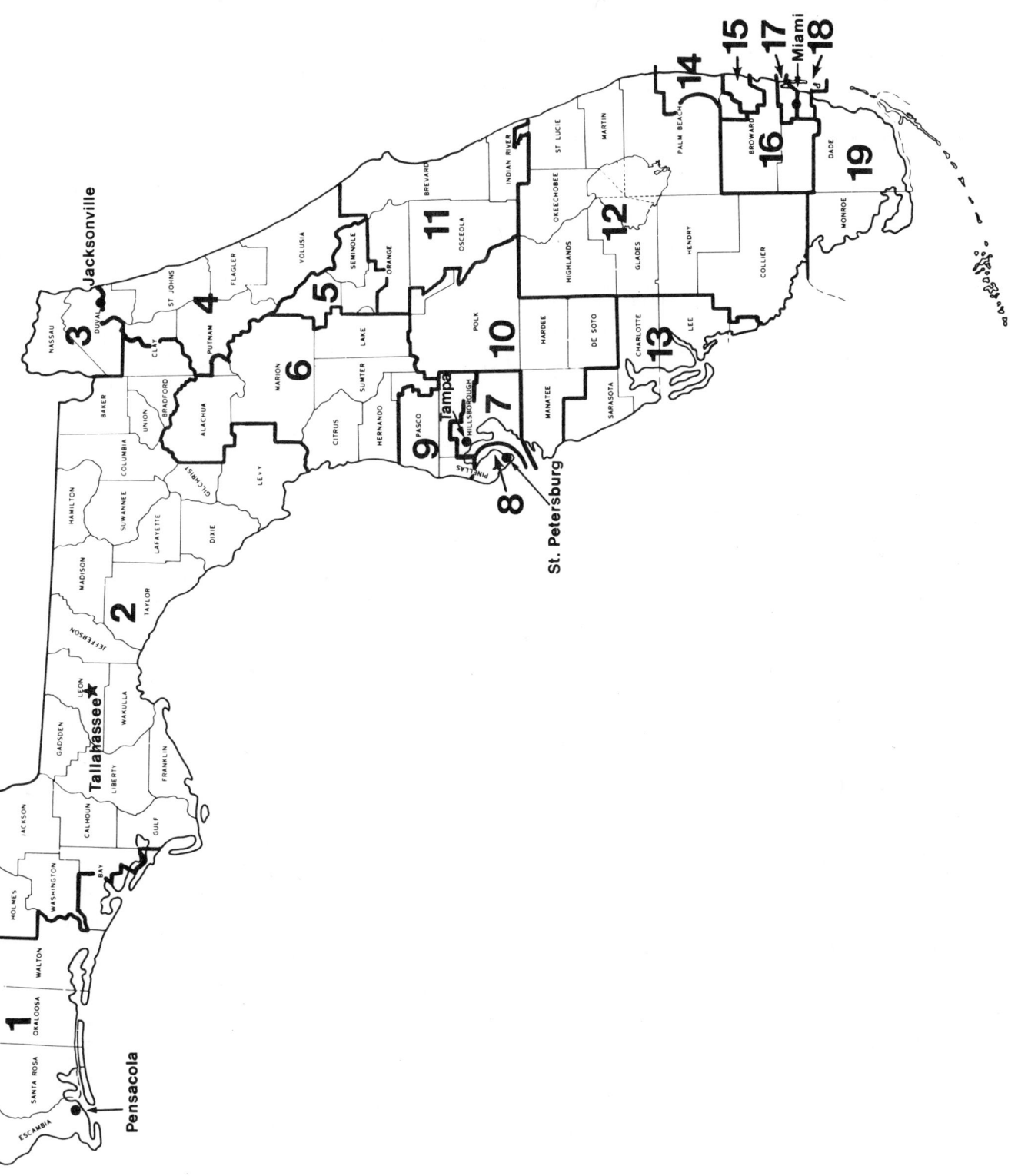

FLORIDA

PRESIDENT 1984

1980 Census Population	County	Total Vote	Republican	Democratic	Other	Rep.-Dem. Plurality	Percentage Total Vote Rep.	Dem.	Major Vote Rep.	Dem.
151,348	ALACHUA	57,193	30,582	26,551	60	4,031 R	53.5%	46.4%	53.5%	46.5%
15,289	BAKER	4,866	3,485	1,381		2,104 R	71.6%	28.4%	71.6%	28.4%
97,740	BAY	38,707	29,322	9,381	4	19,941 R	75.8%	24.2%	75.8%	24.2%
20,023	BRADFORD	6,469	4,128	2,341		1,787 R	63.8%	36.2%	63.8%	36.2%
272,959	BREVARD	139,349	102,339	36,963	47	65,376 R	73.4%	26.5%	73.5%	26.5%
1,018,200	BROWARD	449,077	254,501	194,542	34	59,959 R	56.7%	43.3%	56.7%	43.3%
9,294	CALHOUN	3,806	2,493	1,312	1	1,181 R	65.5%	34.5%	65.5%	34.5%
58,460	CHARLOTTE	38,769	27,464	11,303	2	16,161 R	70.8%	29.2%	70.8%	29.2%
54,703	CITRUS	31,221	20,754	10,463	4	10,291 R	66.5%	33.5%	66.5%	33.5%
67,052	CLAY	27,033	21,545	5,488		16,057 R	79.7%	20.3%	79.7%	20.3%
85,971	COLLIER	42,673	33,603	9,065	5	24,538 R	78.7%	21.2%	78.8%	21.2%
35,399	COLUMBIA	13,068	8,807	4,261		4,546 R	67.4%	32.6%	67.4%	32.6%
1,625,781	DADE	548,044	324,216	223,793	35	100,423 R	59.2%	40.8%	59.2%	40.8%
19,039	DESOTO	7,127	4,822	2,302	3	2,520 R	67.7%	32.3%	67.7%	32.3%
7,751	DIXIE	3,428	2,204	1,224		980 R	64.3%	35.7%	64.3%	35.7%
571,003	DUVAL	206,132	128,653	77,459	20	51,194 R	62.4%	37.6%	62.4%	37.6%
233,794	ESCAMBIA	93,458	66,638	26,798	22	39,840 R	71.3%	28.7%	71.3%	28.7%
10,913	FLAGLER	7,907	4,907	2,999	1	1,908 R	62.1%	37.9%	62.1%	37.9%
7,661	FRANKLIN	3,307	2,218	1,089		1,129 R	67.1%	32.9%	67.1%	32.9%
41,565	GADSDEN	13,206	5,805	7,399	2	1,594 D	44.0%	56.0%	44.0%	56.0%
5,767	GILCHRIST	3,108	2,056	1,051	1	1,005 R	66.2%	33.8%	66.2%	33.8%
5,992	GLADES	3,057	1,987	1,070		917 R	65.0%	35.0%	65.0%	35.0%
10,658	GULF	5,356	3,573	1,783		1,790 R	66.7%	33.3%	66.7%	33.3%
8,761	HAMILTON	3,322	1,921	1,401		520 R	57.8%	42.2%	57.8%	42.2%
19,379	HARDEE	5,493	3,957	1,536		2,421 R	72.0%	28.0%	72.0%	28.0%
18,599	HENDRY	6,542	4,524	2,018		2,506 R	69.2%	30.8%	69.2%	30.8%
44,469	HERNANDO	33,481	21,273	12,204	4	9,069 R	63.5%	36.5%	63.5%	36.5%
47,526	HIGHLANDS	23,685	16,465	7,217	3	9,248 R	69.5%	30.5%	69.5%	30.5%
646,960	HILLSBOROUGH	244,068	157,827	86,189	52	71,638 R	64.7%	35.3%	64.7%	35.3%
14,723	HOLMES	5,778	4,547	1,231		3,316 R	78.7%	21.3%	78.7%	21.3%
59,896	INDIAN RIVER	32,425	23,694	8,731		14,963 R	73.1%	26.9%	73.1%	26.9%
39,154	JACKSON	14,042	9,086	4,956		4,130 R	64.7%	35.3%	64.7%	35.3%
10,703	JEFFERSON	4,300	2,244	2,055	1	189 R	52.2%	47.8%	52.2%	47.8%
4,035	LAFAYETTE	2,375	1,513	862		651 R	63.7%	36.3%	63.7%	36.3%
104,870	LAKE	47,526	35,304	12,215	7	23,089 R	74.3%	25.7%	74.3%	25.7%
205,266	LEE	115,047	85,006	30,011	30	54,995 R	73.9%	26.1%	73.9%	26.1%
148,655	LEON	65,993	36,301	29,654	38	6,647 R	55.0%	44.9%	55.0%	45.0%
19,870	LEVY	8,664	5,561	3,103		2,458 R	64.2%	35.8%	64.2%	35.8%
4,260	LIBERTY	2,058	1,409	649		760 R	68.5%	31.5%	68.5%	31.5%
14,894	MADISON	4,917	2,816	2,101		715 R	57.3%	42.7%	57.3%	42.7%
148,442	MANATEE	76,668	55,775	20,887	6	34,888 R	72.7%	27.2%	72.8%	27.2%
122,488	MARION	54,023	37,796	16,221	6	21,575 R	70.0%	30.0%	70.0%	30.0%
64,014	MARTIN	37,882	28,897	8,976	9	19,921 R	76.3%	23.7%	76.3%	23.7%
63,188	MONROE	24,096	16,316	7,771	9	8,545 R	67.7%	32.3%	67.7%	32.3%
32,894	NASSAU	11,517	8,033	3,483	1	4,550 R	69.7%	30.2%	69.8%	30.2%
109,920	OKALOOSA	44,261	36,963	7,289	9	29,674 R	83.5%	16.5%	83.5%	16.5%
20,264	OKEECHOBEE	6,673	4,447	2,226		2,221 R	66.6%	33.4%	66.6%	33.4%
471,016	ORANGE	170,909	122,007	48,737	165	73,270 R	71.4%	28.5%	71.5%	28.5%
49,287	OSCEOLA	24,975	18,344	6,627	4	11,717 R	73.4%	26.5%	73.5%	26.5%
576,863	PALM BEACH	302,855	186,755	116,071	29	70,684 R	61.7%	38.3%	61.7%	38.3%
193,643	PASCO	107,578	66,609	40,961	8	25,648 R	61.9%	38.1%	61.9%	38.1%
728,531	PINELLAS	369,145	240,535	128,547	63	111,988 R	65.2%	34.8%	65.2%	34.8%
321,652	POLK	119,701	84,174	35,505	22	48,669 R	70.3%	29.7%	70.3%	29.7%
50,549	PUTNAM	19,249	11,424	7,821	4	3,603 R	59.3%	40.6%	59.4%	40.6%
51,303	ST. JOHNS	23,147	16,493	6,652	2	9,841 R	71.3%	28.7%	71.3%	28.7%
87,182	ST. LUCIE	41,235	28,189	13,039	7	15,150 R	68.4%	31.6%	68.4%	31.6%
55,988	SANTA ROSA	25,889	21,237	4,646	6	16,591 R	82.0%	17.9%	82.0%	18.0%
202,251	SARASOTA	118,294	87,713	30,512	69	57,201 R	74.1%	25.8%	74.2%	25.8%
179,752	SEMINOLE	74,071	56,229	17,789	53	38,440 R	75.9%	24.0%	76.0%	24.0%
24,272	SUMTER	9,713	6,252	3,460	1	2,792 R	64.4%	35.6%	64.4%	35.6%

FLORIDA

PRESIDENT 1984

1980 Census Population	County	Total Vote	Republican	Democratic	Other	Rep.-Dem. Plurality	Percentage Total Vote Rep.	Dem.	Major Vote Rep.	Dem.
22,287	SUWANNEE	8,867	6,079	2,788		3,291 R	68.6%	31.4%	68.6%	31.4%
16,532	TAYLOR	5,758	4,030	1,728		2,302 R	70.0%	30.0%	70.0%	30.0%
10,166	UNION	2,567	1,804	761	2	1,043 R	70.3%	29.6%	70.3%	29.7%
258,762	VOLUSIA	112,141	68,317	43,811	13	24,506 R	60.9%	39.1%	60.9%	39.1%
10,887	WAKULLA	4,556	3,087	1,469		1,618 R	67.8%	32.2%	67.8%	32.2%
21,300	WALTON	9,617	7,117	2,500		4,617 R	74.0%	26.0%	74.0%	26.0%
14,509	WASHINGTON	6,520	4,603	1,916	1	2,687 R	70.6%	29.4%	70.6%	29.4%
	SPECIAL ABSENTEE	2,067	1,575	472	20	1,103 R	76.2%	22.8%	76.9%	23.1%
9,746,324	TOTAL	4,180,051	2,730,350	1,448,816	885	1,281,534 R	65.3%	34.7%	65.3%	34.7%

FLORIDA

CONGRESS

CD	Year	Total Vote	Republican Vote	Republican Candidate	Democratic Vote	Democratic Candidate	Other Vote	Rep.-Dem. Plurality	Percentage Total Vote Rep.	Dem.	Major Vote Rep.	Dem.
1	1984					HUTTO, EARL D.						
1	1982	110,942	28,373	BECHTOL, J. TERRYL	82,569	HUTTO, EARL D.		54,196 D	25.6%	74.4%	25.6%	74.4%
2	1984					FUQUA, DON						
2	1982	128,244	49,101	MCNEIL, RON	79,143	FUQUA, DON		30,042 D	38.3%	61.7%	38.3%	61.7%
3	1984					BENNETT, CHARLES E.						
3	1982	87,774	13,972	GRIMSLEY, GEORGE	73,802	BENNETT, CHARLES E.		59,830 D	15.9%	84.1%	15.9%	84.1%
4	1984	207,912	73,218	STARLING, ALTON H.	134,694	CHAPPELL, WILLIAM V.		61,476 D	35.2%	64.8%	35.2%	64.8%
4	1982	125,352	41,457	GAUDET, LARRY	83,895	CHAPPELL, WILLIAM V.		42,438 D	33.1%	66.9%	33.1%	66.9%
5	1984			MCCOLLUM, BILL								
5	1982	119,063	69,993	MCCOLLUM, BILL	49,070	BATCHELOR, DICK		20,923 R	58.8%	41.2%	58.8%	41.2%
6	1984	168,583			167,409	MACKAY, BUDDY	1,174	167,409 D		99.3%		100.0%
6	1982	139,897	54,059	HAVILL, ED	85,825	MACKAY, BUDDY	13	31,766 D	38.6%	61.3%	38.6%	61.4%
7	1984	170,710	70,280	KAVOUKLIS, MICHAEL N.	100,430	GIBBONS, SAM M.		30,150 D	41.2%	58.8%	41.2%	58.8%
7	1982	114,963	29,632	AYERS, KEN	85,331	GIBBONS, SAM M.		55,699 D	25.8%	74.2%	25.8%	74.2%
8	1984	229,946	184,553	YOUNG, C. W.	45,393	KENT, ROBERT		139,160 R	80.3%	19.7%	80.3%	19.7%
8	1982			YOUNG, C. W.								
9	1984	243,493	191,343	BILIRAKIS, MICHAEL	52,150	WILSON, JACK		139,193 R	78.6%	21.4%	78.6%	21.4%
9	1982	185,742	95,009	BILIRAKIS, MICHAEL	90,697	SHELDON, GEORGE H.	36	4,312 R	51.2%	48.8%	51.2%	48.8%
10	1984	203,841	126,206	IRELAND, ANDREW P.	77,635	GLASS, PATRICIA M.		48,571 R	61.9%	38.1%	61.9%	38.1%
10	1982					IRELAND, ANDREW P.						
11	1984	240,890	95,115	QUARTEL, ROB	145,764	NELSON, BILL	11	50,649 D	39.5%	60.5%	39.5%	60.5%
11	1982	144,168	42,422	ROBINSON, JOEL	101,746	NELSON, BILL		59,324 D	29.4%	70.6%	29.4%	70.6%
12	1984			LEWIS, TOM								
12	1982	155,806	81,893	LEWIS, TOM	73,913	CULVERHOUSE, BRAD		7,980 R	52.6%	47.4%	52.6%	47.4%
13	1984			MACK, CONNIE								
13	1982	204,190	132,951	MACK, CONNIE	71,239	STEVENS, DANA N.		61,712 R	65.1%	34.9%	65.1%	34.9%
14	1984	277,861	123,926	ROSS, DON	153,935	MICA, DAN		30,009 D	44.6%	55.4%	44.6%	55.4%
14	1982	176,206	47,560	MITCHELL, STEVE	128,646	MICA, DAN		81,086 D	27.0%	73.0%	27.0%	73.0%
15	1984	194,930	128,097	SHAW, CLAY	66,833	HUMPHREY, BILL		61,264 R	65.7%	34.3%	65.7%	34.3%
15	1982	156,241	89,158	SHAW, CLAY	67,083	STACK, EDWARD J.		22,075 R	57.1%	42.9%	57.1%	42.9%
16	1984	192,313	83,903	BUSH, TOM	108,410	SMITH, LARRY		24,507 D	43.6%	56.4%	43.6%	56.4%
16	1982	135,346	43,458	BERKOWITZ, MAURICE	91,888	SMITH, LARRY		48,430 D	32.1%	67.9%	32.1%	67.9%
17	1984					LEHMAN, WILLIAM						
17	1982					LEHMAN, WILLIAM						
18	1984	126,222	49,818	NUNEZ, RICARDO	76,404	PEPPER, CLAUDE		26,586 D	39.5%	60.5%	39.5%	60.5%
18	1982	101,379	29,196	NUNEZ, RICARDO	72,183	PEPPER, CLAUDE		42,987 D	28.8%	71.2%	28.8%	71.2%
19	1984	179,951	64,317	FLANAGAN, BILL	115,631	FASCELL, DANTE B.	3	51,314 D	35.7%	64.3%	35.7%	64.3%
19	1982	126,281	51,969	RINKER, GLENN	74,312	FASCELL, DANTE B.		22,343 D	41.2%	58.8%	41.2%	58.8%

FLORIDA

1984 GENERAL ELECTION

President   Other vote was 754 Bergland (write-in); 58 Johnson (write-in); 34 Hall (write-in); 7 Mason (write-in); 32 scattered. Special absentee votes are ballots counted separately by court order.

Congress   Under present legislation, names of unopposed candidates are not printed on the ballot and no votes are tallied for them in such districts except when there is an official write-in candidate. Other vote was Tarnley (write-in) in CD 6; Lenhart (write-in) in CD 11; McArthur (write-in) in CD 19. In CD 10, Andrew P. Ireland was elected as a Democrat in 1982 and as a Republican in 1984. He had previously served as the Democratic member for three terms from the old 8th CD.

1984 PRIMARIES

SEPTEMBER 4 REPUBLICAN

Congress   Unopposed in eleven CD's. No candidate in CD's 1, 2, 3, 6 and 17.
Contested as follows:

CD 16   13,186 Tom Bush; 2,232 Doc Smith.
CD 18   13,245 Ricardo Nunez; 4,888 Evelio S. Estrella.
CD 19   11,163 Bill Flanagan; 5,469 Rudy Reinsprecht.

SEPTEMBER 4 DEMOCRATIC

Congress   Unopposed in ten CD's. No candidate in CD's 5, 12 and 13. Contested as follows:

CD 2   117,418 Don Fuqua; 14,278 Kim O'Connor; 10,972 Eugene A. Stinson.
CD 4   42,959 William V. Chappell; 25,568 Carol Granstrom.
CD 8   10,983 Claud Sutcliffe; 5,635 Robert Kent; 5,633 Mike Spuza. Mr. Sutcliffe withdrew after the primary and no run-off election was held; Mr. Kent became the nominee for the general election.
CD 10   30,873 Patricia M. Glass; 18,349 Jack Carter; 15,443 Gene Roberts.
CD 11   41,232 Bill Nelson; 6,935 Bill Roundtree.
CD 15   14,807 Bill Humphrey; 9,745 Tim Kolly.

OCTOBER 2 DEMOCRATIC RUN-OFF

Congress

CD 10   26,844 Patricia M. Glass; 22,548 Jack Carter.

GEORGIA

GOVERNOR
Joe Frank Harris (D). Elected 1982 to a four-year term.

SENATORS
Mack Mattingly (R). Elected 1980 to a six-year term.

Sam Nunn (D). Re-elected 1984 to a six-year term. Previously elected 1978, 1972.

REPRESENTATIVES
1. Lindsay Thomas (D)
2. Charles Hatcher (D)
3. Richard Ray (D)
4. Patrick L. Swindall (R)
5. Wyche Fowler (D)
6. Newt Gingrich (R)
7. George Darden (D)
8. J. Roy Rowland (D)
9. Ed Jenkins (D)
10. Doug Barnard (D)

POSTWAR VOTE FOR GOVERNOR

Year	Total Vote	Republican Vote	Candidate	Democratic Vote	Candidate	Other Vote	Rep.-Dem. Plurality	Total Vote Rep.	Total Vote Dem.	Major Vote Rep.	Major Vote Dem.
1982	1,169,041	434,496	Bell, Robert H.	734,090	Harris, Joe Frank	455	299,594 D	37.2%	62.8%	37.2%	62.8%
1978	662,862	128,139	Cook, Rodney M.	534,572	Busbee, George	151	406,433 D	19.3%	80.6%	19.3%	80.7%
1974	936,438	289,113	Thompson, Ronnie	646,777	Busbee, George	548	357,664 D	30.9%	69.1%	30.9%	69.1%
1970	1,046,663	424,983	Suit, Hal	620,419	Carter, Jimmy	1,261	195,436 D	40.6%	59.3%	40.7%	59.3%
1966*	975,019	453,665	Callaway, Howard H.	450,626	Maddox, Lester	70,728	3,039 R	46.5%	46.2%	50.2%	49.8%
1962	311,691	—	—	311,524	Sanders, Carl E.	167	311,524 D	—	99.9%	—	100.0%
1958	168,497	—	—	168,414	Vandiver, Ernest	83	168,414 D	—	100.0%	—	100.0%
1954	331,966	—	—	331,899	Griffin, Marvin	67	331,899 D	—	100.0%	—	100.0%
1950	234,430	—	—	230,771	Talmadge, Herman	3,659	230,771 D	—	98.4%	—	100.0%
1948s	363,763	—	—	354,711	Talmadge, Herman	9,052	354,711 D	—	97.5%	—	100.0%
1946	145,403	—	—	143,279	Talmadge, Herman	2,124	143,279 D	—	98.5%	—	100.0%

The 1948 election was for a short term to fill a vacancy. In 1966, in the absence of a majority for any candidate, the state legislature elected Lester Maddox to a four-year term.

POSTWAR VOTE FOR SENATOR

Year	Total Vote	Republican Vote	Candidate	Democratic Vote	Candidate	Other Vote	Rep.-Dem. Plurality	Total Vote Rep.	Total Vote Dem.	Major Vote Rep.	Major Vote Dem.
1984	1,681,344	337,196	Hicks, Jon Michael	1,344,104	Nunn, Sam	44	1,006,908 D	20.1%	79.9%	20.1%	79.9%
1980	1,580,340	803,686	Mattingly, Mack	776,143	Talmadge, Herman	511	27,543 R	50.9%	49.1%	50.9%	49.1%
1978	645,164	108,808	Stokes, John W.	536,320	Nunn, Sam	36	427,512 D	16.9%	83.1%	16.9%	83.1%
1974	874,555	246,866	Johnson, Jerry R.	627,376	Talmadge, Herman	313	380,510 D	28.2%	71.7%	28.2%	71.8%
1972	1,178,708	542,331	Thompson, Fletcher	635,970	Nunn, Sam	407	93,639 D	46.0%	54.0%	46.0%	54.0%
1968	1,141,889	256,796	Patton, E. Earl	885,093	Talmadge, Herman	—	628,297 D	22.5%	77.5%	22.5%	77.5%
1966	622,371	—	—	622,043	Russell, Richard B.	328	622,043 D	—	99.9%	—	100.0%
1962	306,250	—	—	306,250	Talmadge, Herman	—	306,250 D	—	100.0%	—	100.0%
1960	576,495	—	—	576,140	Russell, Richard B.	355	576,140 D	—	99.9%	—	100.0%
1956	541,267	—	—	541,094	Talmadge, Herman	173	541,094 D	—	100.0%	—	100.0%
1954	333,936	—	—	333,917	Russell, Richard B.	19	333,917 D	—	100.0%	—	100.0%
1950	261,293	—	—	261,290	George, Walter F.	3	261,290 D	—	100.0%	—	100.0%
1948	362,504	—	—	362,104	Russell, Richard B.	400	362,104 D	—	99.9%	—	100.0%

GEORGIA

Districts Established August 24, 1982

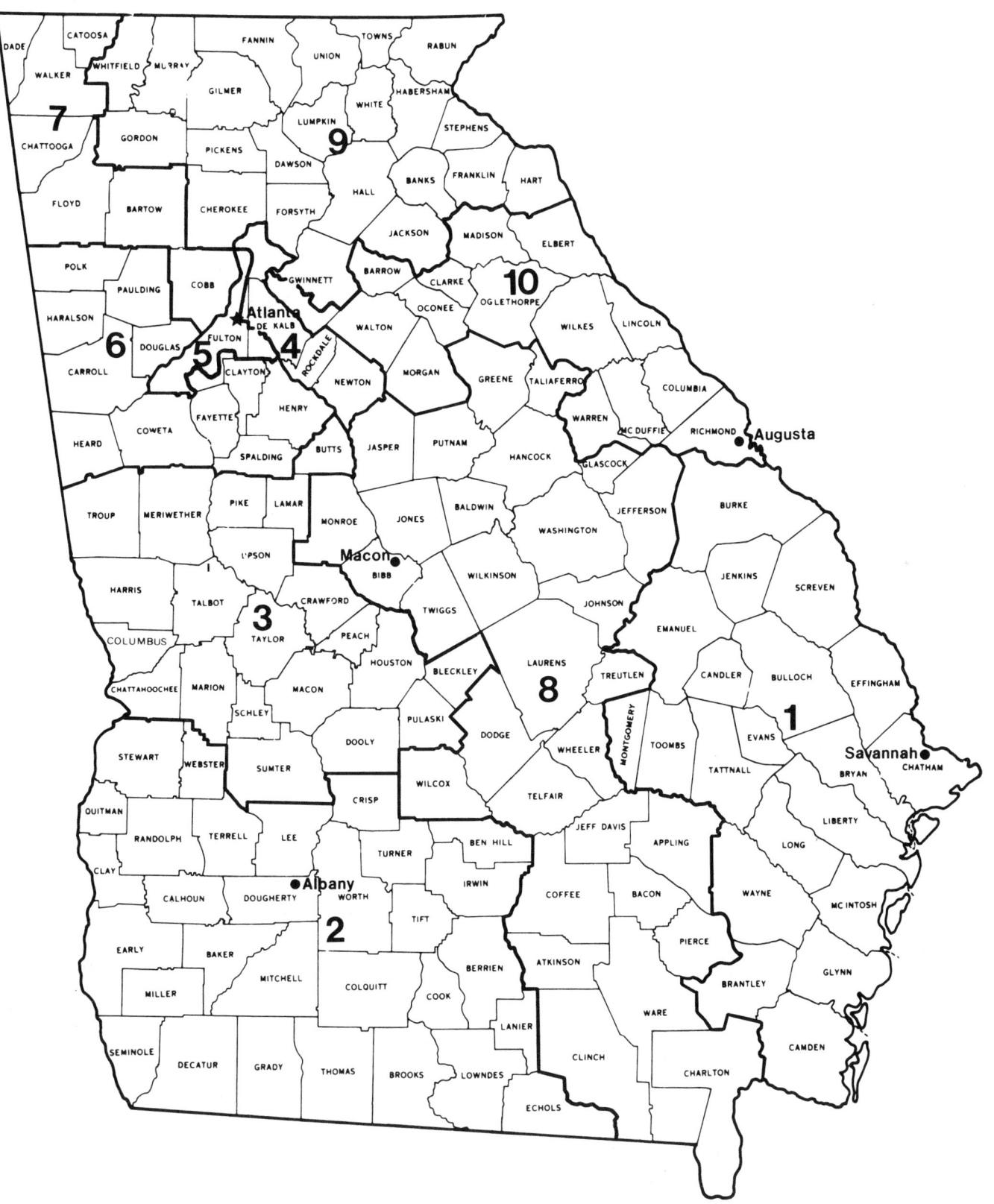

GEORGIA

PRESIDENT 1984

1980 Census Population	County	Total Vote	Republican	Democratic	Other	Rep.-Dem. Plurality		Percentage Total Vote Rep.	Dem.	Major Vote Rep.	Dem.
15,565	APPLING	4,887	2,929	1,958		971	R	59.9%	40.1%	59.9%	40.1%
6,141	ATKINSON	1,845	944	901		43	R	51.2%	48.8%	51.2%	48.8%
9,379	BACON	2,788	1,778	1,010		768	R	63.8%	36.2%	63.8%	36.2%
3,808	BAKER	1,366	675	691		16	D	49.4%	50.6%	49.4%	50.6%
34,686	BALDWIN	9,570	5,717	3,853		1,864	R	59.7%	40.3%	59.7%	40.3%
8,702	BANKS	2,612	1,549	1,063		486	R	59.3%	40.7%	59.3%	40.7%
21,354	BARROW	6,490	4,123	2,367		1,756	R	63.5%	36.5%	63.5%	36.5%
40,760	BARTOW	11,884	7,104	4,780		2,324	R	59.8%	40.2%	59.8%	40.2%
16,000	BEN HILL	4,172	2,313	1,859		454	R	55.4%	44.6%	55.4%	44.6%
13,525	BERRIEN	4,065	2,395	1,670		725	R	58.9%	41.1%	58.9%	41.1%
150,256	BIBB	50,597	24,170	26,427		2,257	D	47.8%	52.2%	47.8%	52.2%
10,767	BLECKLEY	3,377	1,912	1,465		447	R	56.6%	43.4%	56.6%	43.4%
8,701	BRANTLEY	3,196	1,679	1,517		162	R	52.5%	47.5%	52.5%	47.5%
15,255	BROOKS	3,890	2,229	1,661		568	R	57.3%	42.7%	57.3%	42.7%
10,175	BRYAN	3,663	2,265	1,398		867	R	61.8%	38.2%	61.8%	38.2%
35,785	BULLOCH	9,761	6,117	3,644		2,473	R	62.7%	37.3%	62.7%	37.3%
19,349	BURKE	6,264	3,137	3,127		10	R	50.1%	49.9%	50.1%	49.9%
13,665	BUTTS	3,961	2,141	1,820		321	R	54.1%	45.9%	54.1%	45.9%
5,717	CALHOUN	1,853	776	1,077		301	D	41.9%	58.1%	41.9%	58.1%
13,371	CAMDEN	5,005	2,841	2,164		677	R	56.8%	43.2%	56.8%	43.2%
7,518	CANDLER	2,511	1,497	1,014		483	R	59.6%	40.4%	59.6%	40.4%
56,346	CARROLL	17,026	11,436	5,590		5,846	R	67.2%	32.8%	67.2%	32.8%
36,991	CATOOSA	10,997	7,908	3,089		4,819	R	71.9%	28.1%	71.9%	28.1%
7,343	CHARLTON	2,479	1,368	1,111		257	R	55.2%	44.8%	55.2%	44.8%
202,226	CHATHAM	66,753	38,482	28,271		10,211	R	57.6%	42.4%	57.6%	42.4%
21,732	CHATTAHOOCHEE	887	459	428		31	R	51.7%	48.3%	51.7%	48.3%
21,856	CHATTOOGA	5,529	2,953	2,576		377	R	53.4%	46.6%	53.4%	46.6%
51,699	CHEROKEE	14,645	11,146	3,499		7,647	R	76.1%	23.9%	76.1%	23.9%
74,498	CLARKE	21,635	11,503	10,132		1,371	R	53.2%	46.8%	53.2%	46.8%
3,553	CLAY	1,169	419	750		331	D	35.8%	64.2%	35.8%	64.2%
150,357	CLAYTON	43,316	31,553	11,763		19,790	R	72.8%	27.2%	72.8%	27.2%
6,660	CLINCH	1,487	862	625		237	R	58.0%	42.0%	58.0%	42.0%
297,718	COBB	125,843	97,429	28,414		69,015	R	77.4%	22.6%	77.4%	22.6%
26,894	COFFEE	6,833	4,200	2,633		1,567	R	61.5%	38.5%	61.5%	38.5%
35,376	COLQUITT	9,023	5,815	3,208		2,607	R	64.4%	35.6%	64.4%	35.6%
40,118	COLUMBIA	16,021	12,294	3,727		8,567	R	76.7%	23.3%	76.7%	23.3%
13,490	COOK	3,370	1,860	1,510		350	R	55.2%	44.8%	55.2%	44.8%
39,268	COWETA	11,631	7,981	3,650		4,331	R	68.6%	31.4%	68.6%	31.4%
7,684	CRAWFORD	2,721	1,298	1,423		125	D	47.7%	52.3%	47.7%	52.3%
19,489	CRISP	5,023	2,895	2,128		767	R	57.6%	42.4%	57.6%	42.4%
12,318	DADE	3,900	2,750	1,150		1,600	R	70.5%	29.5%	70.5%	29.5%
4,774	DAWSON	1,965	1,322	643		679	R	67.3%	32.7%	67.3%	32.7%
25,495	DECATUR	6,790	4,134	2,656		1,478	R	60.9%	39.1%	60.9%	39.1%
483,024	DE KALB	182,026	104,697	77,329		27,368	R	57.5%	42.5%	57.5%	42.5%
16,955	DODGE	5,278	2,765	2,513		252	R	52.4%	47.6%	52.4%	47.6%
10,826	DOOLY	3,161	1,435	1,726		291	D	45.4%	54.6%	45.4%	54.6%
100,718	DOUGHERTY	29,824	16,920	12,904		4,016	R	56.7%	43.3%	56.7%	43.3%
54,573	DOUGLAS	16,799	12,428	4,371		8,057	R	74.0%	26.0%	74.0%	26.0%
13,158	EARLY	3,733	2,239	1,494		745	R	60.0%	40.0%	60.0%	40.0%
2,297	ECHOLS	680	453	227		226	R	66.6%	33.4%	66.6%	33.4%
18,327	EFFINGHAM	6,321	4,266	2,055		2,211	R	67.5%	32.5%	67.5%	32.5%
18,758	ELBERT	6,036	3,366	2,670		696	R	55.8%	44.2%	55.8%	44.2%
20,795	EMANUEL	6,378	3,920	2,458		1,462	R	61.5%	38.5%	61.5%	38.5%
8,428	EVANS	2,794	1,601	1,193		408	R	57.3%	42.7%	57.3%	42.7%
14,748	FANNIN	6,124	4,159	1,965		2,194	R	67.9%	32.1%	67.9%	32.1%
29043	FAYETTE	15,436	12,575	2,861		9,714	R	81.5%	18.5%	81.5%	18.5%
79,800	FLOYD	24,310	15,437	8,873		6,564	R	63.5%	36.5%	63.5%	36.5%
27,958	FORSYTH	9,116	6,841	2,275		4,566	R	75.0%	25.0%	75.0%	25.0%
15,185	FRANKLIN	4,387	2,549	1,838		711	R	58.1%	41.9%	58.1%	41.9%
589,904	FULTON	220,716	95,149	125,567		30,418	D	43.1%	56.9%	43.1%	56.9%

GEORGIA

PRESIDENT 1984

1980 Census Population	County	Total Vote	Republican	Democratic	Other	Rep.-Dem. Plurality	Percentage Total Vote Rep.	Dem.	Major Vote Rep.	Dem.
11,110	GILMER	4,206	2,972	1,234		1,738 R	70.7%	29.3%	70.7%	29.3%
2,382	GLASCOCK	1,144	827	317		510 R	72.3%	27.7%	72.3%	27.7%
54,981	GLYNN	18,298	11,724	6,574		5,150 R	64.1%	35.9%	64.1%	35.9%
30,070	GORDON	8,173	5,566	2,607		2,959 R	68.1%	31.9%	68.1%	31.9%
19,845	GRADY	6,147	3,886	2,261		1,625 R	63.2%	36.8%	63.2%	36.8%
11,391	GREENE	3,591	1,599	1,992		393 D	44.5%	55.5%	44.5%	55.5%
166,903	GWINNETT	68,888	54,749	14,139		40,610 R	79.5%	20.5%	79.5%	20.5%
25,020	HABERSHAM	6,772	4,647	2,125		2,522 R	68.6%	31.4%	68.6%	31.4%
75,649	HALL	22,497	15,076	7,421		7,655 R	67.0%	33.0%	67.0%	33.0%
9,466	HANCOCK	2,753	644	2,109		1,465 D	23.4%	76.6%	23.4%	76.6%
18,422	HARALSON	5,883	3,945	1,938		2,007 R	67.1%	32.9%	67.1%	32.9%
15,464	HARRIS	5,234	3,138	2,096		1,042 R	60.0%	40.0%	60.0%	40.0%
18,585	HART	5,338	2,842	2,496		346 R	53.2%	46.8%	53.2%	46.8%
6,520	HEARD	2,302	1,492	810		682 R	64.8%	35.2%	64.8%	35.2%
36,309	HENRY	13,238	9,142	4,096		5,046 R	69.1%	30.9%	69.1%	30.9%
77,605	HOUSTON	23,481	14,255	9,226		5,029 R	60.7%	39.3%	60.7%	39.3%
8,988	IRWIN	2,235	1,330	905		425 R	59.5%	40.5%	59.5%	40.5%
25,343	JACKSON	6,919	4,202	2,717		1,485 R	60.7%	39.3%	60.7%	39.3%
7,553	JASPER	2,553	1,431	1,122		309 R	56.1%	43.9%	56.1%	43.9%
11,473	JEFF DAVIS	3,613	2,233	1,380		853 R	61.8%	38.2%	61.8%	38.2%
18,403	JEFFERSON	5,815	2,999	2,816		183 R	51.6%	48.4%	51.6%	48.4%
8,841	JENKINS	2,507	1,399	1,108		291 R	55.8%	44.2%	55.8%	44.2%
8,660	JOHNSON	2,932	1,733	1,199		534 R	59.1%	40.9%	59.1%	40.9%
16,579	JONES	6,182	3,401	2,781		620 R	55.0%	45.0%	55.0%	45.0%
12,215	LAMAR	3,803	2,198	1,605		593 R	57.8%	42.2%	57.8%	42.2%
5,654	LANIER	1,593	852	741		111 R	53.5%	46.5%	53.5%	46.5%
36,990	LAURENS	12,652	7,181	5,471		1,710 R	56.8%	43.2%	56.8%	43.2%
11,684	LEE	4,256	2,972	1,284		1,688 R	69.8%	30.2%	69.8%	30.2%
37,583	LIBERTY	6,032	3,229	2,803		426 R	53.5%	46.5%	53.5%	46.5%
6,716	LINCOLN	2,472	1,357	1,115		242 R	54.9%	45.1%	54.9%	45.1%
4,524	LONG	1,915	1,099	816		283 R	57.4%	42.6%	57.4%	42.6%
67,972	LOWNDES	16,604	10,437	6,167		4,270 R	62.9%	37.1%	62.9%	37.1%
10,762	LUMPKIN	3,101	1,991	1,110		881 R	64.2%	35.8%	64.2%	35.8%
18,546	MCDUFFIE	5,290	3,284	2,006		1,278 R	62.1%	37.9%	62.1%	37.9%
8,046	MCINTOSH	3,308	1,512	1,796		284 D	45.7%	54.3%	45.7%	54.3%
14,003	MACON	4,036	1,515	2,521		1,006 D	37.5%	62.5%	37.5%	62.5%
17,747	MADISON	5,458	3,768	1,690		2,078 R	69.0%	31.0%	69.0%	31.0%
5,297	MARION	1,797	846	951		105 D	47.1%	52.9%	47.1%	52.9%
21,229	MERIWETHER	6,059	3,195	2,864		331 R	52.7%	47.3%	52.7%	47.3%
7,038	MILLER	1,874	1,348	526		822 R	71.9%	28.1%	71.9%	28.1%
21,114	MITCHELL	5,528	2,737	2,791		54 D	49.5%	50.5%	49.5%	50.5%
14,610	MONROE	4,609	2,420	2,189		231 R	52.5%	47.5%	52.5%	47.5%
7,011	MONTGOMERY	2,315	1,365	950		415 R	59.0%	41.0%	59.0%	41.0%
11,572	MORGAN	4,015	2,301	1,714		587 R	57.3%	42.7%	57.3%	42.7%
19,685	MURRAY	5,170	3,521	1,649		1,872 R	68.1%	31.9%	68.1%	31.9%
170,108	MOSCOGEE	44,651	23,816	20,835		2,981 R	53.3%	46.7%	53.3%	46.7%
34,489	NEWTON	9,199	5,810	3,389		2,421 R	63.2%	36.8%	63.2%	36.8%
12,427	OCONEE	4,938	3,471	1,467		2,004 R	70.3%	29.7%	70.3%	29.7%
8,929	OGLETHORPE	3,360	2,122	1,238		884 R	63.2%	36.8%	63.2%	36.8%
26,110	PAULDING	8,669	6,048	2,621		3,427 R	69.8%	30.2%	69.8%	30.2%
19,151	PEACH	6,021	2,652	3,369		717 D	44.0%	56.0%	44.0%	56.0%
11,652	PICKENS	4,130	2,801	1,329		1,472 R	67.8%	32.2%	67.8%	32.2%
11,897	PIERCE	3,479	1,978	1,501		477 R	56.9%	43.1%	56.9%	43.1%
8,937	PIKE	3,058	1,855	1,203		652 R	60.7%	39.3%	60.7%	39.3%
32,386	POLK	8,697	5,435	3,262		2,173 R	62.5%	37.5%	62.5%	37.5%
8,950	PULASKI	2,949	1,509	1,440		69 R	51.2%	48.8%	51.2%	48.8%
10,295	PUTNAM	3,166	1,830	1,336		494 R	57.8%	42.2%	57.8%	42.2%
2,357	QUITMAN	851	361	490		129 D	42.4%	57.6%	42.4%	57.6%
10,466	RABUN	3,458	2,191	1,267		924 R	63.4%	36.6%	63.4%	36.6%
9,599	RANDOLPH	3,032	1,578	1,454		124 R	52.0%	48.0%	52.0%	48.0%

GEORGIA

PRESIDENT 1984

1980 Census Population	County	Total Vote	Republican	Democratic	Other	Rep.-Dem. Plurality	Percentage Total Vote Rep.	Percentage Total Vote Dem.	Percentage Major Vote Rep.	Percentage Major Vote Dem.
181,629	RICHMOND	51,077	29,869	21,208		8,661 R	58.5%	41.5%	58.5%	41.5%
36,747	ROCKDALE	13,412	10,121	3,291		6,830 R	75.5%	24.5%	75.5%	24.5%
3,433	SCHLEY	1,017	614	403		211 R	60.4%	39.6%	60.4%	39.6%
14,043	SCREVEN	4,330	2,583	1,747		836 R	59.7%	40.3%	59.7%	40.3%
9,057	SEMINOLE	2,986	1,636	1,350		286 R	54.8%	45.2%	54.8%	45.2%
47,899	SPALDING	13,449	8,571	4,878		3,693 R	63.7%	36.3%	63.7%	36.3%
21,763	STEPHENS	6,329	4,057	2,272		1,785 R	64.1%	35.9%	64.1%	35.9%
5,896	STEWART	2,113	805	1,308		503 D	38.1%	61.9%	38.1%	61.9%
29,360	SUMTER	8,332	4,607	3,725		882 R	55.3%	44.7%	55.3%	44.7%
6,536	TALBOT	2,272	778	1,494		716 D	34.2%	65.8%	34.2%	65.8%
2,032	TALIAFERRO	868	318	550		232 D	36.6%	63.4%	36.6%	63.4%
18,134	TATTNALL	5,595	3,641	1,954		1,687 R	65.1%	34.9%	65.1%	34.9%
7,902	TAYLOR	2,632	1,292	1,340		48 D	49.1%	50.9%	49.1%	50.9%
11,445	TELFAIR	4,029	1,980	2,049		69 D	49.1%	50.9%	49.1%	50.9%
12,017	TERRELL	3,342	1,744	1,598		146 R	52.2%	47.8%	52.2%	47.8%
38,098	THOMAS	10,466	6,427	4,039		2,388 R	61.4%	38.6%	61.4%	38.6%
32,862	TIFT	7,165	4,429	2,736		1,693 R	61.8%	38.2%	61.8%	38.2%
22,592	TOOMBS	6,855	4,470	2,385		2,085 R	65.2%	34.8%	65.2%	34.8%
5,638	TOWNS	2,967	1,960	1,007		953 R	66.1%	33.9%	66.1%	33.9%
6,087	TREUTLEN	1,929	1,086	843		243 R	56.3%	43.7%	56.3%	43.7%
50,003	TROUP	14,612	9,340	5,272		4,068 R	63.9%	36.1%	63.9%	36.1%
9,510	TURNER	2,599	1,329	1,270		59 R	51.1%	48.9%	51.1%	48.9%
9,354	TWIGGS	2,898	1,143	1,755		612 D	39.4%	60.6%	39.4%	60.6%
9,390	UNION	3,026	1,914	1,112		802 R	63.3%	36.7%	63.3%	36.7%
25,998	UPSON	7,746	4,803	2,943		1,860 R	62.0%	38.0%	62.0%	38.0%
56,470	WALKER	15,734	10,734	5,000		5,734 R	68.2%	31.8%	68.2%	31.8%
31,211	WALTON	7,476	4,995	2,481		2,514 R	66.8%	33.2%	66.8%	33.2%
37,180	WARE	9,982	5,547	4,435		1,112 R	55.6%	44.4%	55.6%	44.4%
6,583	WARREN	2,345	1,087	1,258		171 D	46.4%	53.6%	46.4%	53.6%
18,842	WASHINGTON	5,921	2,887	3,034		147 D	48.8%	51.2%	48.8%	51.2%
20,750	WAYNE	6,132	3,698	2,434		1,264 R	60.3%	39.7%	60.3%	39.7%
2,341	WEBSTER	936	402	534		132 D	42.9%	57.1%	42.9%	57.1%
5,155	WHEELER	1,607	833	774		59 R	51.8%	48.2%	51.8%	48.2%
10,120	WHITE	3,459	2,369	1,090		1,279 R	68.5%	31.5%	68.5%	31.5%
65,789	WHITFIELD	17,241	11,957	5,284		6,673 R	69.4%	30.6%	69.4%	30.6%
7,682	WILCOX	2,430	1,218	1,212		6 R	50.1%	49.9%	50.1%	49.9%
10,951	WILKES	3,423	1,837	1,586		251 R	53.7%	46.3%	53.7%	46.3%
10,368	WILKINSON	3,858	1,756	2,102		346 D	45.5%	54.5%	45.5%	54.5%
18,064	WORTH	4,595	2,910	1,685		1,225 R	63.3%	36.7%	63.3%	36.7%
5,463,105	TOTAL	1,776,120	1,068,722	706,628	770	362,094 R	60.2%	39.8%	60.2%	39.8%

GEORGIA

SENATOR 1984

1980 Census Population	County	Total Vote	Republican	Democratic	Other	Rep.-Dem. Plurality	Percentage Total Vote Rep.	Dem.	Major Vote Rep.	Dem.
15,565	APPLING	3,593	477	3,116		2,639 D	13.3%	86.7%	13.3%	86.7%
6,141	ATKINSON	1,282	133	1,149		1,016 D	10.4%	89.6%	10.4%	89.6%
9,379	BACON	2,282	333	1,949		1,616 D	14.6%	85.4%	14.6%	85.4%
3,808	BAKER	947	107	840		733 D	11.3%	88.7%	11.3%	88.7%
34,686	BALDWIN	8,202	1,011	7,191		6,180 D	12.3%	87.7%	12.3%	87.7%
8,702	BANKS	2,556	357	2,199		1,842 D	14.0%	86.0%	14.0%	86.0%
21,354	BARROW	6,164	1,301	4,863		3,562 D	21.1%	78.9%	21.1%	78.9%
40,760	BARTOW	8,939	1,536	7,403		5,867 D	17.2%	82.8%	17.2%	82.8%
16,000	BEN HILL	3,896	657	3,239		2,582 D	16.9%	83.1%	16.9%	83.1%
13,525	BERRIEN	4,468	580	3,888		3,308 D	13.0%	87.0%	13.0%	87.0%
150,256	BIBB	39,936	4,575	35,361		30,786 D	11.5%	88.5%	11.5%	88.5%
10,767	BLECKLEY	2,873	293	2,580		2,287 D	10.2%	89.8%	10.2%	89.8%
8,701	BRANTLEY	2,706	254	2,452		2,198 D	9.4%	90.6%	9.4%	90.6%
15,255	BROOKS	3,170	354	2,816		2,462 D	11.2%	88.8%	11.2%	88.8%
10,175	BRYAN	3,365	425	2,940		2,515 D	12.6%	87.4%	12.6%	87.4%
35,785	BULLOCH	10,004	1,612	8,392		6,780 D	16.1%	83.9%	16.1%	83.9%
19,349	BURKE	5,353	556	4,797		4,241 D	10.4%	89.6%	10.4%	89.6%
13,665	BUTTS	3,998	536	3,462		2,926 D	13.4%	86.6%	13.4%	86.6%
5,717	CALHOUN	1,589	152	1,437		1,285 D	9.6%	90.4%	9.6%	90.4%
13,371	CAMDEN	3,742	824	2,918		2,094 D	22.0%	78.0%	22.0%	78.0%
7,518	CANDLER	2,009	222	1,787		1,565 D	11.1%	88.9%	11.1%	88.9%
56,346	CARROLL	17,082	3,092	13,990		10,898 D	18.1%	81.9%	18.1%	81.9%
36,991	CATOOSA	10,573	3,736	6,837		3,101 D	35.3%	64.7%	35.3%	64.7%
7,343	CHARLTON	1,542	255	1,287		1,032 D	16.5%	83.5%	16.5%	83.5%
202,226	CHATHAM	63,827	11,799	52,028		40,229 D	18.5%	81.5%	18.5%	81.5%
21,732	CHATTAHOOCHEE	669	90	579		489 D	13.5%	86.5%	13.5%	86.5%
21,856	CHATTOOGA	6,346	1,052	5,294		4,242 D	16.6%	83.4%	16.6%	83.4%
51,699	CHEROKEE	14,403	3,748	10,655		6,907 D	26.0%	74.0%	26.0%	74.0%
74,498	CLARKE	20,145	3,072	17,073		14,001 D	15.2%	84.8%	15.2%	84.8%
3,553	CLAY	1,024	91	933		842 D	8.9%	91.1%	8.9%	91.1%
150,357	CLAYTON	43,461	11,546	31,915		20,369 D	26.6%	73.4%	26.6%	73.4%
6,660	CLINCH	1,153	154	999		845 D	13.4%	86.6%	13.4%	86.6%
297,718	COBB	125,571	38,293	87,278		48,985 D	30.5%	69.5%	30.5%	69.5%
26,894	COFFEE	5,986	737	5,249		4,512 D	12.3%	87.7%	12.3%	87.7%
35,376	COLQUITT	7,606	1,199	6,407		5,208 D	15.8%	84.2%	15.8%	84.2%
40,118	COLUMBIA	16,454	4,506	11,948		7,442 D	27.4%	72.6%	27.4%	72.6%
13,490	COOK	3,427	355	3,072		2,717 D	10.4%	89.6%	10.4%	89.6%
39,268	COWETA	11,766	2,366	9,400		7,034 D	20.1%	79.9%	20.1%	79.9%
7,684	CRAWFORD	2,036	189	1,847		1,658 D	9.3%	90.7%	9.3%	90.7%
19,489	CRISP	4,144	449	3,695		3,246 D	10.8%	89.2%	10.8%	89.2%
12,318	DADE	2,811	798	2,013		1,215 D	28.4%	71.6%	28.4%	71.6%
4,774	DAWSON	1,757	458	1,299		841 D	26.1%	73.9%	26.1%	73.9%
25,495	DECATUR	5,157	840	4,317		3,477 D	16.3%	83.7%	16.3%	83.7%
483,024	DE KALB	180,599	42,679	137,920		95,241 D	23.6%	76.4%	23.6%	76.4%
16,955	DODGE	4,270	360	3,910		3,550 D	8.4%	91.6%	8.4%	91.6%
10,826	DOOLY	2,389	174	2,215		2,041 D	7.3%	92.7%	7.3%	92.7%
100,718	DOUGHERTY	29,455	4,955	24,500		19,545 D	16.8%	83.2%	16.8%	83.2%
54,573	DOUGLAS	16,382	3,937	12,445		8,508 D	24.0%	76.0%	24.0%	76.0%
13,158	EARLY	3,382	500	2,882		2,382 D	14.8%	85.2%	14.8%	85.2%
2,297	ECHOLS	539	64	475		411 D	11.9%	88.1%	11.9%	88.1%
18,327	EFFINGHAM	5,616	900	4,716		3,816 D	16.0%	84.0%	16.0%	84.0%
18,758	ELBERT	5,743	840	4,903		4,063 D	14.6%	85.4%	14.6%	85.4%
20,795	EMANUEL	5,696	435	5,261		4,826 D	7.6%	92.4%	7.6%	92.4%
8,428	EVANS	2,398	181	2,217		2,036 D	7.5%	92.5%	7.5%	92.5%
14,748	FANNIN	5,818	2,232	3,586		1,354 D	38.4%	61.6%	38.4%	61.6%
29043	FAYETTE	15,271	4,556	10,715		6,159 D	29.8%	70.2%	29.8%	70.2%
79,800	FLOYD	23,557	3,693	19,864		16,171 D	15.7%	84.3%	15.7%	84.3%
27,958	FORSYTH	9,210	2,078	7,132		5,054 D	22.6%	77.4%	22.6%	77.4%
15,185	FRANKLIN	4,313	823	3,490		2,667 D	19.1%	80.9%	19.1%	80.9%
589,904	FULTON	215,589	38,604	176,985		138,381 D	17.9%	82.1%	17.9%	82.1%

GEORGIA

SENATOR 1984

1980 Census Population	County	Total Vote	Republican	Democratic	Other	Rep.-Dem. Plurality	Percentage Total Vote Rep.	Dem.	Major Vote Rep.	Dem.
11,110	GILMER	4,226	1,001	3,225		2,224 D	23.7%	76.3%	23.7%	76.3%
2,382	GLASCOCK	957	137	820		683 D	14.3%	85.7%	14.3%	85.7%
54,981	GLYNN	19,055	3,566	15,489		11,923 D	18.7%	81.3%	18.7%	81.3%
30,070	GORDON	7,460	1,537	5,923		4,386 D	20.6%	79.4%	20.6%	79.4%
19,845	GRADY	5,074	520	4,554		4,034 D	10.2%	89.8%	10.2%	89.8%
11,391	GREENE	3,398	431	2,967		2,536 D	12.7%	87.3%	12.7%	87.3%
166,903	GWINNETT	68,408	24,690	43,718		19,028 D	36.1%	63.9%	36.1%	63.9%
25,020	HABERSHAM	6,232	904	5,328		4,424 D	14.5%	85.5%	14.5%	85.5%
75,649	HALL	22,398	3,402	18,996		15,594 D	15.2%	84.8%	15.2%	84.8%
9,466	HANCOCK	1,733	129	1,604		1,475 D	7.4%	92.6%	7.4%	92.6%
18,422	HARALSON	5,681	1,045	4,636		3,591 D	18.4%	81.6%	18.4%	81.6%
15,464	HARRIS	4,646	689	3,957		3,268 D	14.8%	85.2%	14.8%	85.2%
18,585	HART	4,476	686	3,790		3,104 D	15.3%	84.7%	15.3%	84.7%
6,520	HEARD	2,081	495	1,586		1,091 D	23.8%	76.2%	23.8%	76.2%
36,309	HENRY	13,147	2,736	10,411		7,675 D	20.8%	79.2%	20.8%	79.2%
77,605	HOUSTON	22,799	3,020	19,779		16,759 D	13.2%	86.8%	13.2%	86.8%
8,988	IRWIN	1,995	234	1,761		1,527 D	11.7%	88.3%	11.7%	88.3%
25,343	JACKSON	6,832	865	5,967		5,102 D	12.7%	87.3%	12.7%	87.3%
7,553	JASPER	2,319	341	1,978		1,637 D	14.7%	85.3%	14.7%	85.3%
11,473	JEFF DAVIS	2,624	273	2,351		2,078 D	10.4%	89.6%	10.4%	89.6%
18,403	JEFFERSON	4,472	467	4,005		3,538 D	10.4%	89.6%	10.4%	89.6%
8,841	JENKINS	2,287	208	2,079		1,871 D	9.1%	90.9%	9.1%	90.9%
8,660	JOHNSON	2,415	166	2,249		2,083 D	6.9%	93.1%	6.9%	93.1%
16,579	JONES	4,259	633	3,626		2,993 D	14.9%	85.1%	14.9%	85.1%
12,215	LAMAR	3,527	656	2,871		2,215 D	18.6%	81.4%	18.6%	81.4%
5,654	LANIER	1,215	93	1,122		1,029 D	7.7%	92.3%	7.7%	92.3%
36,990	LAURENS	9,398	1,270	8,128		6,858 D	13.5%	86.5%	13.5%	86.5%
11,684	LEE	3,930	913	3,017		2,104 D	23.2%	76.8%	23.2%	76.8%
37,583	LIBERTY	5,504	693	4,811		4,118 D	12.6%	87.4%	12.6%	87.4%
6,716	LINCOLN	2,458	290	2,168		1,878 D	11.8%	88.2%	11.8%	88.2%
4,524	LONG	1,608	216	1,392		1,176 D	13.4%	86.6%	13.4%	86.6%
67,972	LOWNDES	16,489	3,203	13,286		10,083 D	19.4%	80.6%	19.4%	80.6%
10,762	LUMPKIN	2,951	475	2,476		2,001 D	16.1%	83.9%	16.1%	83.9%
18,546	MCDUFFIE	4,469	601	3,868		3,267 D	13.4%	86.6%	13.4%	86.6%
8,046	MCINTOSH	2,721	300	2,421		2,121 D	11.0%	89.0%	11.0%	89.0%
14,003	MACON	3,321	231	3,090		2,859 D	7.0%	93.0%	7.0%	93.0%
17,747	MADISON	5,095	907	4,188		3,281 D	17.8%	82.2%	17.8%	82.2%
5,297	MARION	1,446	240	1,206		966 D	16.6%	83.4%	16.6%	83.4%
21,229	MERIWETHER	5,672	1,031	4,641		3,610 D	18.2%	81.8%	18.2%	81.8%
7,038	MILLER	1,467	220	1,247		1,027 D	15.0%	85.0%	15.0%	85.0%
21,114	MITCHELL	5,751	732	5,019		4,287 D	12.7%	87.3%	12.7%	87.3%
14,610	MONROE	4,601	666	3,935		3,269 D	14.5%	85.5%	14.5%	85.5%
7,011	MONTGOMERY	2,006	261	1,745		1,484 D	13.0%	87.0%	13.0%	87.0%
11,572	MORGAN	3,645	483	3,162		2,679 D	13.3%	86.7%	13.3%	86.7%
19,685	MURRAY	4,288	864	3,424		2,560 D	20.1%	79.9%	20.1%	79.9%
170,108	MOSCOGEE	45,100	6,810	38,290		31,480 D	15.1%	84.9%	15.1%	84.9%
34,489	NEWTON	8,995	1,966	7,029		5,063 D	21.9%	78.1%	21.9%	78.1%
12,427	OCONEE	4,762	1,010	3,752		2,742 D	21.2%	78.8%	21.2%	78.8%
8,929	OGLETHORPE	2,977	422	2,555		2,133 D	14.2%	85.8%	14.2%	85.8%
26,110	PAULDING	8,119	1,457	6,662		5,205 D	17.9%	82.1%	17.9%	82.1%
19,151	PEACH	5,653	513	5,140		4,627 D	9.1%	90.9%	9.1%	90.9%
11,652	PICKENS	3,543	538	3,005		2,467 D	15.2%	84.8%	15.2%	84.8%
11,897	PIERCE	2,892	242	2,650		2,408 D	8.4%	91.6%	8.4%	91.6%
8,937	PIKE	3,129	667	2,462		1,795 D	21.3%	78.7%	21.3%	78.7%
32,386	POLK	7,858	1,232	6,626		5,394 D	15.7%	84.3%	15.7%	84.3%
8,950	PULASKI	2,667	223	2,444		2,221 D	8.4%	91.6%	8.4%	91.6%
10,295	PUTNAM	2,736	367	2,369		2,002 D	13.4%	86.6%	13.4%	86.6%
2,357	QUITMAN	604	80	524		444 D	13.2%	86.8%	13.2%	86.8%
10,466	RABUN	3,050	516	2,534		2,018 D	16.9%	83.1%	16.9%	83.1%
9,599	RANDOLPH	2,791	306	2,485		2,179 D	11.0%	89.0%	11.0%	89.0%

GEORGIA

SENATOR 1984

1980 Census Population	County	Total Vote	Republican	Democratic	Other	Rep.-Dem. Plurality	Percentage Total Vote Rep.	Dem.	Major Vote Rep.	Dem.
181,629	RICHMOND	51,348	11,365	39,983		28,618 D	22.1%	77.9%	22.1%	77.9%
36,747	ROCKDALE	13,550	3,494	10,056		6,562 D	25.8%	74.2%	25.8%	74.2%
3,433	SCHLEY	891	108	783		675 D	12.1%	87.9%	12.1%	87.9%
14,043	SCREVEN	3,624	426	3,198		2,772 D	11.8%	88.2%	11.8%	88.2%
9,057	SEMINOLE	2,550	499	2,051		1,552 D	19.6%	80.4%	19.6%	80.4%
47,899	SPALDING	12,458	2,019	10,439		8,420 D	16.2%	83.8%	16.2%	83.8%
21,763	STEPHENS	5,249	1,174	4,075		2,901 D	22.4%	77.6%	22.4%	77.6%
5,896	STEWART	1,643	116	1,527		1,411 D	7.1%	92.9%	7.1%	92.9%
29,360	SUMTER	7,537	1,020	6,517		5,497 D	13.5%	86.5%	13.5%	86.5%
6,536	TALBOT	1,813	207	1,606		1,399 D	11.4%	88.6%	11.4%	88.6%
2,032	TALIAFERRO	777	47	730		683 D	6.0%	94.0%	6.0%	94.0%
18,134	TATTNALL	5,074	483	4,591		4,108 D	9.5%	90.5%	9.5%	90.5%
7,902	TAYLOR	2,603	308	2,295		1,987 D	11.8%	88.2%	11.8%	88.2%
11,445	TELFAIR	2,933	202	2,731		2,529 D	6.9%	93.1%	6.9%	93.1%
12,017	TERRELL	2,692	326	2,366		2,040 D	12.1%	87.9%	12.1%	87.9%
38,098	THOMAS	9,361	1,523	7,838		6,315 D	16.3%	83.7%	16.3%	83.7%
32,862	TIFT	6,144	675	5,469		4,794 D	11.0%	89.0%	11.0%	89.0%
22,592	TOOMBS	6,055	834	5,221		4,387 D	13.8%	86.2%	13.8%	86.2%
5,638	TOWNS	2,475	859	1,616		757 D	34.7%	65.3%	34.7%	65.3%
6,087	TREUTLEN	1,727	253	1,474		1,221 D	14.6%	85.4%	14.6%	85.4%
50,003	TROUP	13,840	2,891	10,949		8,058 D	20.9%	79.1%	20.9%	79.1%
9,510	TURNER	2,351	257	2,094		1,837 D	10.9%	89.1%	10.9%	89.1%
9,354	TWIGGS	3,172	370	2,802		2,432 D	11.7%	88.3%	11.7%	88.3%
9,390	UNION	3,138	887	2,251		1,364 D	28.3%	71.7%	28.3%	71.7%
25,998	UPSON	7,490	1,254	6,236		4,982 D	16.7%	83.3%	16.7%	83.3%
56,470	WALKER	14,984	4,603	10,381		5,778 D	30.7%	69.3%	30.7%	69.3%
31,211	WALTON	7,426	1,561	5,865		4,304 D	21.0%	79.0%	21.0%	79.0%
37,180	WARE	9,016	1,086	7,930		6,844 D	12.0%	88.0%	12.0%	88.0%
6,583	WARREN	1,685	166	1,519		1,353 D	9.9%	90.1%	9.9%	90.1%
18,842	WASHINGTON	4,503	557	3,946		3,389 D	12.4%	87.6%	12.4%	87.6%
20,750	WAYNE	4,752	619	4,133		3,514 D	13.0%	87.0%	13.0%	87.0%
2,341	WEBSTER	652	51	601		550 D	7.8%	92.2%	7.8%	92.2%
5,155	WHEELER	1,493	226	1,267		1,041 D	15.1%	84.9%	15.1%	84.9%
10,120	WHITE	3,249	695	2,554		1,859 D	21.4%	78.6%	21.4%	78.6%
65,789	WHITFIELD	16,714	3,261	13,453		10,192 D	19.5%	80.5%	19.5%	80.5%
7,682	WILCOX	2,284	299	1,985		1,686 D	13.1%	86.9%	13.1%	86.9%
10,951	WILKES	2,853	397	2,456		2,059 D	13.9%	86.1%	13.9%	86.1%
10,368	WILKINSON	2,875	343	2,532		2,189 D	11.9%	88.1%	11.9%	88.1%
18,064	WORTH	4,666	735	3,931		3,196 D	15.8%	84.2%	15.8%	84.2%
5,463,105	TOTAL	1,681,344	337,196	1,344,104	44	1,006,908 D	20.1%	79.9%	20.1%	79.9%

GEORGIA

CONGRESS

CD	Year	Total Vote	Republican Vote	Candidate	Democratic Vote	Candidate	Other Vote	Rep.-Dem. Plurality	Percentage Total Vote Rep.	Total Vote Dem.	Major Vote Rep.	Major Vote Dem.
1	1984	154,545	28,460	DOWNING, ERIE L.	126,082	THOMAS, LINDSAY	3	97,622 D	18.4%	81.6%	18.4%	81.6%
1	1982	102,425	36,799	JONES, HERB	65,625	THOMAS, LINDSAY	1	28,826 D	35.9%	64.1%	35.9%	64.1%
2	1984	110,566			110,561	HATCHER, CHARLES	5	110,561 D		100.0%		100.0%
2	1982	73,905			73,897	HATCHER, CHARLES	8	73,897 D		100.0%		100.0%
3	1984	136,473	25,410	CANTU, MITCHELL	111,061	RAY, RICHARD	2	85,651 D	18.6%	81.4%	18.6%	81.4%
3	1982	105,171	30,537	ELLIOTT, TYRON	74,626	RAY, RICHARD	8	44,089 D	29.0%	71.0%	29.0%	71.0%
4	1984	226,835	120,456	SWINDALL, PATRICK L.	106,376	LEVITAS, ELLIOTT H.	3	14,080 R	53.1%	46.9%	53.1%	46.9%
4	1982	59,185	20,418	WINDER, DICK	38,758	LEVITAS, ELLIOTT H.	9	18,340 D	34.5%	65.5%	34.5%	65.5%
5	1984	151,250			151,233	FOWLER, WYCHE	17	151,233 D		100.0%		100.0%
5	1982	65,955	3,633	JONES, PAUL	53,264	FOWLER, WYCHE	9,058	49,631 D	5.5%	80.8%	6.4%	93.6%
6	1984	168,717	116,655	GINGRICH, NEWT	52,061	JOHNSON, GERALD L.	1	64,594 R	69.1%	30.9%	69.1%	30.9%
6	1982	112,812	62,352	GINGRICH, NEWT	50,459	WOOD, JIM	1	11,893 R	55.3%	44.7%	55.3%	44.7%
7	1984	193,020	86,431	BRONSON, BILL	106,586	DARDEN, GEORGE	3	20,155 D	44.8%	55.2%	44.8%	55.2%
7	1982	117,224	45,569	SELLERS, DAVE	71,647	MCDONALD, LARRY	8	26,078 D	38.9%	61.1%	38.9%	61.1%
8	1984	100,940			100,936	ROWLAND, J. ROY	4	100,936 D		100.0%		100.0%
8	1982	75,035			75,009	ROWLAND, J. ROY	26	75,009 D		100.0%		100.0%
9	1984	162,156	52,731	COFER, FRANK	109,422	JENKINS, ED	3	56,691 D	32.5%	67.5%	32.5%	67.5%
9	1982	112,422	25,907	SHERWOOD, CHARLES	86,514	JENKINS, ED	1	60,607 D	23.0%	77.0%	23.0%	77.0%
10	1984	116,374			116,364	BARNARD, DOUG	10	116,364 D		100.0%		100.0%
10	1982	80,323			80,311	BARNARD, DOUG	12	80,311 D		100.0%		100.0%

GEORGIA

1984 GENERAL ELECTION

President   Other vote was all write-in as follows: 152 Bergland; 95 Richards; 34 LaRouche; 10 Mason; 4 Dennis; 4 Johnson; 3 Anderson; 3 Lowrey; 2 Holmes; 2 Serrette; 1 Hall; 460 scattered. These write-in votes were not reported by county.

Senator   Other vote was scattered and not reported by county.

Congress   Other vote was scattered in all CD's.

1984 PRIMARIES

AUGUST 14 REPUBLICAN

Senator   27,547 Jon Michael Hicks; 26,657 Kelly S. Brown; 12,849 J. W. Tibbs.

Congress   Unopposed in four CD's. No candidate in CD's 2, 5, 8 and 10. Contested as follows:

   CD 4   17,019 Patrick L. Swindall; 1,644 Howard Stopeck.
   CD 7   7,583 Bill Bronson; 6,494 Ben F. Clay; 5,929 David Downing.

AUGUST 14 DEMOCRATIC

Senator   801,412 Sam Nunn; 86,973 Jim Boyd.

Congress   Unopposed in six CD's. Contested as follows:

   CD 3   67,973 Richard Ray; 31,566 Tom Theus.
   CD 5   49,962 Wyche Fowler; 22,293 Hosea L. Williams; 3,091 Alveda K. Beal; 2,150 Henrietta M. Canty; 734 Robert Waymer.
   CD 6   28,772 Gerald L. Johnson; 16,761 Robert B. Watson; 13,154 Leonard Danley; 12,015 Gladys L. Pearson.
   CD 10   66,994 Doug Barnard; 11,725 Doug Teper.

SEPTEMBER 4 REPUBLICAN RUN-OFF

Senator   16,987 Jon Michael Hicks; 8,336 J. W. Tibbs. Although Mr. Tibbs finished third in the first primary, he successfully challenged Mr. Brown's filing status and won a place in the run-off.

Congress

   CD 7   7,083 Bill Bronson; 4,418 Ben F. Clay.

SEPTEMBER 4 DEMOCRATIC RUN-OFF

Congress

   CD 6   33,335 Gerald L. Johnson; 17,225 Robert B. Watson.

HAWAII

GOVERNOR
George R. Ariyoshi (D). Re-elected 1982 to a four-year term. Previously elected 1978, 1974.

SENATORS
Daniel K. Inouye (D). Re-elected 1980 to a six-year term. Previously elected 1974, 1968, 1962.

Spark M. Matsunaga (D). Re-elected 1982 to a six-year term. Previously elected 1976.

REPRESENTATIVES
1. Cecil Heftel (D)   2. Daniel K. Akaka (D)

POSTWAR VOTE FOR GOVERNOR

Year	Total Vote	Republican Vote	Candidate	Democratic Vote	Candidate	Other Vote	Rep.-Dem. Plurality	Total Vote Rep.	Total Vote Dem.	Major Vote Rep.	Major Vote Dem.
1982	311,853	81,507	Anderson, D. G.	141,043	Ariyoshi, George R.	89,303	59,536 D	26.1%	45.2%	36.6%	63.4%
1978	281,587	124,610	Leopold, John	153,394	Ariyoshi, George R.	3,583	28,784 D	44.3%	54.5%	44.8%	55.2%
1974	249,650	113,388	Crossley, Randolph	136,262	Ariyoshi, George R.	—	22,874 D	45.4%	54.6%	45.4%	54.6%
1970	239,061	101,249	King, Samuel P.	137,812	Burns, John A.	—	36,563 D	42.4%	57.6%	42.4%	57.6%
1966	213,164	104,324	Crossley, Randolph	108,840	Burns, John A.	—	4,516 D	48.9%	51.1%	48.9%	51.1%
1962	196,015	81,707	Quinn, William F.	114,308	Burns, John A.	—	32,601 D	41.7%	58.3%	41.7%	58.3%
1959s	168,662	86,213	Quinn, William F.	82,074	Burns, John A.	375	4,139 R	51.1%	48.7%	51.2%	48.8%

The 1959 election was for a short term pending the regular vote in 1962.

POSTWAR VOTE FOR SENATOR

Year	Total Vote	Republican Vote	Candidate	Democratic Vote	Candidate	Other Vote	Rep.-Dem. Plurality	Total Vote Rep.	Total Vote Dem.	Major Vote Rep.	Major Vote Dem.
1982	306,410	52,071	Brown, Clarence J.	245,386	Matsunaga, Spark M.	8,953	193,315 D	17.0%	80.1%	17.5%	82.5%
1980	288,006	53,068	Brown, Cooper	224,485	Inouye, Daniel K.	10,453	171,417 D	18.4%	77.9%	19.1%	80.9%
1976	302,092	122,724	Quinn, William F.	162,305	Matsunaga, Spark M.	17,063	39,581 D	40.6%	53.7%	43.1%	56.9%
1974	250,221	—		207,454	Inouye, Daniel K.	42,767	207,454 D	—	82.9%	—	100.0%
1970	240,760	124,163	Fong, Hiram L.	116,597	Heftel, Cecil	—	7,566 R	51.6%	48.4%	51.6%	48.4%
1968	226,927	34,008	Thiessen, Wayne C.	189,248	Inouye, Daniel K.	3,671	155,240 D	15.0%	83.4%	15.2%	84.8%
1964	208,814	110,747	Fong, Hiram L.	96,789	Gill, Thomas P.	1,278	13,958 R	53.0%	46.4%	53.4%	46.6%
1962	196,361	60,067	Dillingham, Ben F.	136,294	Inouye, Daniel K.	—	76,227 D	30.6%	69.4%	30.6%	69.4%
1959*	164,808	87,161	Fong, Hiram L.	77,647	Fasi, Frank F.	—	9,514 R	52.9%	47.1%	52.9%	47.1%
1959s	163,875	79,123	Tsukiyama, W. C.	83,700	Long, Oren E.	1,052	4,577 D	48.3%	51.1%	48.6%	51.4%

The two 1959 elections were held to indeterminate terms and the Senate later determined by lot that Senator Long would serve a short term, Senator Fong a long term.

HAWAII

Districts Established April 9, 1984

PRINCIPAL ISLANDS

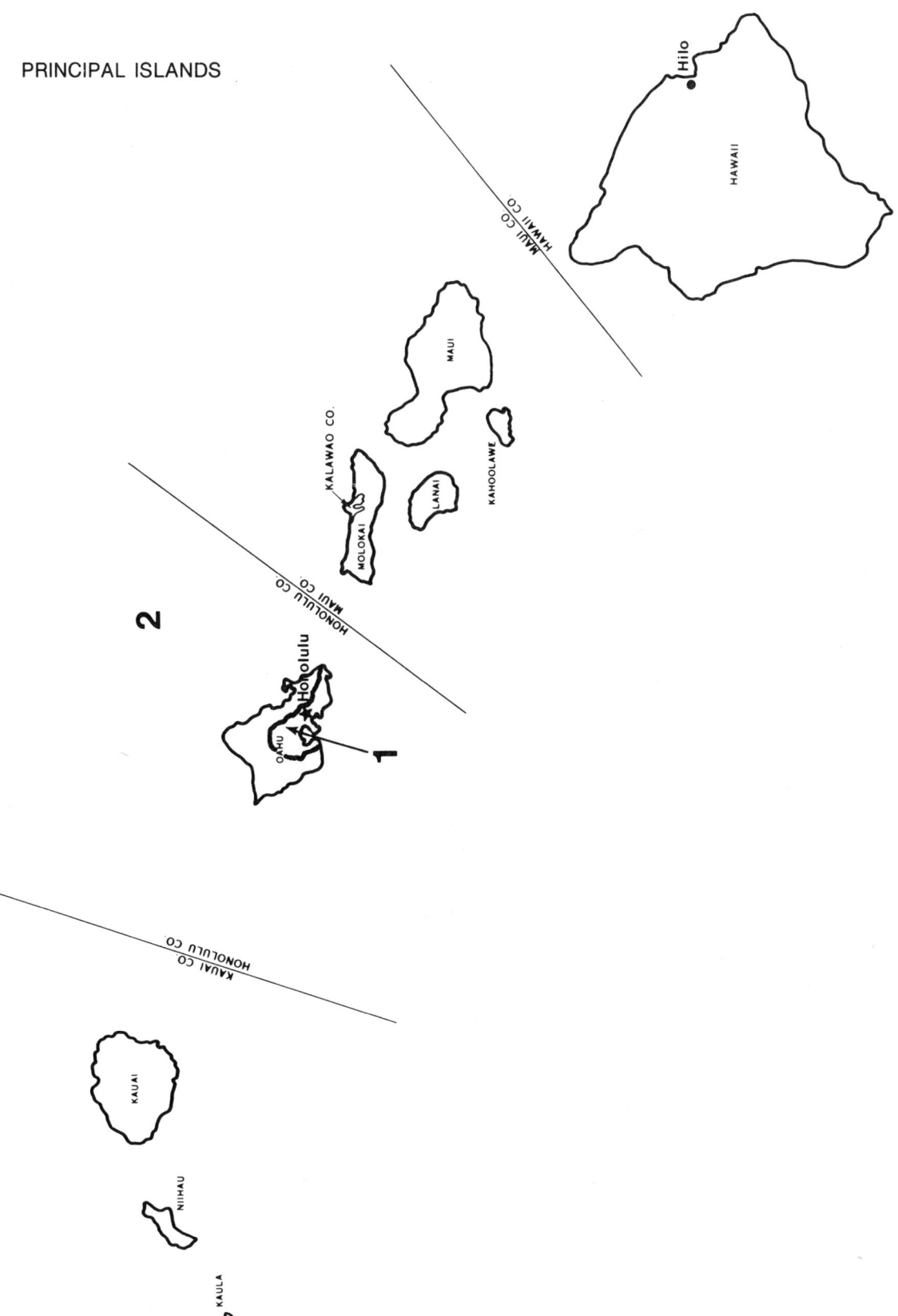

© ERC

HAWAII

PRESIDENT 1984

1980 Census Population	County	Total Vote	Republican	Democratic	Other	Rep.-Dem. Plurality	Percentage Total Vote Rep.	Dem.	Major Vote Rep.	Dem.
92,053	HAWAII	39,143	20,707	17,866	570	2,841 R	52.9%	45.6%	53.7%	46.3%
762,565	HONOLULU	250,132	140,258	107,404	2,470	32,854 R	56.1%	42.9%	56.6%	43.4%
39,082	KAUAI	18,332	9,249	8,862	221	387 R	50.5%	48.3%	51.1%	48.9%
70,991	MAUI	28,067	14,720	12,966	381	1,754 R	52.4%	46.2%	53.2%	46.8%
	SPECIAL BALLOTS	172	116	56		60 R	67.4%	32.6%	67.4%	32.6%
964,691	TOTAL	335,846	185,050	147,154	3,642	37,896 R	55.1%	43.8%	55.7%	44.3%

HAWAII

CONGRESS

CD	Year	Total Vote	Republican			Democratic			Other Vote	Rep.-Dem. Plurality	Percentage			
			Vote		Candidate	Vote		Candidate			Total Vote		Major Vote	
											Rep.	Dem.	Rep.	Dem.
1	1984	138,865	20,608		BEARD, WILLARD F.	114,884		HEFTEL, CECIL	3,373	94,276 D	14.8%	82.7%	15.2%	84.8%
2	1984	136,741	20,000		SHIPLEY, ARBIS D.	112,377		AKAKA, DANIEL K.	4,364	92,377 D	14.6%	82.2%	15.1%	84.9%

HAWAII

Kalawao county, an area of 14 square miles on Molokai Island with a population of 144, consists entirely of the Kalaupapa Hansen's disease settlement. The population and voting data for this settlement are included in the Maui county statistics.

1984 GENERAL ELECTION

President   Other vote was 2,167 Bergland (Libertarian); 821 Hall (People Before Profits); 654 LaRouche (Hawaiians for LaRouche). Special Ballots are votes cast by overseas electors.

Congress   Other vote was Winter (Libertarian) in CD 1; Fritts (Libertarian) in CD 2.

1984 PRIMARIES

SEPTEMBER 22 REPUBLICAN

Congress   Unopposed in both CD's.

SEPTEMBER 22 DEMOCRATIC

Congress   Unopposed in CD 1. Contested as follows:

   CD   2   80,859 Daniel K. Akaka; 11,070 Pamela S. Washburn.

SEPTEMBER 22 LIBERTARIAN

Congress   Unopposed in both CD's.

IDAHO

GOVERNOR
John V. Evans (D). Re-elected 1982 to a four-year term. Previously elected 1978; elected as Lieutenant-Governor in 1974 and succeeded upon the resignation of Governor Cecil D. Andrus in January 1977.

SENATORS
James A. McClure (R). Re-elected 1984 to a six-year term. Previously elected 1978, 1972.

Steven D. Symms (R). Elected 1980 to a six-year term.

REPRESENTATIVES
1. Larry Craig (R)   2. Richard Stallings (D)

POSTWAR VOTE FOR GOVERNOR

Year	Total Vote	Republican Vote	Candidate	Democratic Vote	Candidate	Other Vote	Rep.-Dem. Plurality	Percentage Total Vote Rep.	Dem.	Major Vote Rep.	Dem.
1982	326,522	161,157	Batt, Philip	165,365	Evans, John V.	—	4,208 D	49.4%	50.6%	49.4%	50.6%
1978	288,566	114,149	Larsen, Allan	169,540	Evans, John V.	4,877	55,391 D	39.6%	58.8%	40.2%	59.8%
1974	259,632	68,731	Murphy, Jack M.	184,142	Andrus, Cecil D.	6,759	115,411 D	26.5%	70.9%	27.2%	72.8%
1970	245,112	117,108	Samuelson, Don	128,004	Andrus, Cecil D.	—	10,896 D	47.8%	52.2%	47.8%	52.2%
1966	252,593	104,586	Samuelson, Don	93,744	Andrus, Cecil D.	54,263	10,842 R	41.4%	37.1%	52.7%	47.3%
1962	255,454	139,578	Smylie, Robert E.	115,876	Smith, Vernon K.	—	23,702 R	54.6%	45.4%	54.6%	45.4%
1958	239,046	121,810	Smylie, Robert E.	117,236	Derr, A. M.	—	4,574 R	51.0%	49.0%	51.0%	49.0%
1954	228,685	124,038	Smylie, Robert E.	104,647	Hamilton, Clark	—	19,391 R	54.2%	45.8%	54.2%	45.8%
1950	204,792	107,642	Jordan, Len B.	97,150	Wright, Calvin E.	—	10,492 R	52.6%	47.4%	52.6%	47.4%
1946	181,364	102,233	Robins, C. A.	79,131	Williams, Arnold	—	23,102 R	56.4%	43.6%	56.4%	43.6%

POSTWAR VOTE FOR SENATOR

Year	Total Vote	Republican Vote	Candidate	Democratic Vote	Candidate	Other Vote	Rep.-Dem. Plurality	Percentage Total Vote Rep.	Dem.	Major Vote Rep.	Dem.
1984	406,168	293,193	McClure, James A.	105,591	Busch, Peter M.	7,384	187,602 R	72.2%	26.0%	73.5%	26.5%
1980	439,647	218,701	Symms, Steven D.	214,439	Church, Frank	6,507	4,262 R	49.7%	48.8%	50.5%	49.5%
1978	284,047	194,412	McClure, James A.	89,635	Jensen, Dwight	—	104,777 R	68.4%	31.6%	68.4%	31.6%
1974	258,847	109,072	Smith, Robert L.	145,140	Church, Frank	4,635	36,068 D	42.1%	56.1%	42.9%	57.1%
1972	309,602	161,804	McClure, James A.	140,913	Davis, William E.	6,885	20,891 R	52.3%	45.5%	53.5%	46.5%
1968	287,876	114,394	Hansen, George V.	173,482	Church, Frank	—	59,088 D	39.7%	60.3%	39.7%	60.3%
1966	252,456	139,819	Jordan, Len B.	112,637	Harding, Ralph R.	—	27,182 R	55.4%	44.6%	55.4%	44.6%
1962	258,786	117,129	Hawley, Jack	141,657	Church, Frank	—	24,528 D	45.3%	54.7%	45.3%	54.7%
1962s	257,677	131,279	Jordan, Len B.	126,398	Pfost, Gracie	—	4,881 R	50.9%	49.1%	50.9%	49.1%
1960	292,096	152,648	Dworshak, Henry C.	139,448	McLaughlin, Bob	—	13,200 R	52.3%	47.7%	52.3%	47.7%
1956	265,292	102,781	Welker, Herman	149,096	Church, Frank	13,415	46,315 D	38.7%	56.2%	40.8%	59.2%
1954	226,408	142,269	Dworshak, Henry C.	84,139	Taylor, Glen H.	—	58,130 R	62.8%	37.2%	62.8%	37.2%
1950	201,417	124,237	Welker, Herman	77,180	Clark, D. Worth	—	47,057 R	61.7%	38.3%	61.7%	38.3%
1950s	201,970	104,068	Dworshak, Henry C.	97,902	Burtenshaw, Claude	—	6,166 R	51.5%	48.5%	51.5%	48.5%
1948	214,188	103,868	Dworshak, Henry C.	107,000	Miller, Bert H.	3,320	3,132 D	48.5%	50.0%	49.3%	50.7%
1946s	180,152	105,523	Dworshak, Henry C.	74,629	Donart, George E.	—	30,894 R	58.6%	41.4%	58.6%	41.4%

The 1946 election and one each of the 1962 and 1950 elections were for short terms to fill vacancies.

IDAHO

Districts Established July 30, 1981

IDAHO

PRESIDENT 1984

1980 Census Population	County	Total Vote	Republican	Democratic	Other	Rep.-Dem. Plurality	Percentage			
							Total Vote		Major Vote	
							Rep.	Dem.	Rep.	Dem.
173,036	ADA	82,924	60,036	21,760	1,128	38,276 R	72.4%	26.2%	73.4%	26.6%
3,347	ADAMS	1,956	1,381	540	35	841 R	70.6%	27.6%	71.9%	28.1%
65,421	BANNOCK	28,496	18,742	9,399	355	9,343 R	65.8%	33.0%	66.6%	33.4%
6,931	BEAR LAKE	3,267	2,760	481	26	2,279 R	84.5%	14.7%	85.2%	14.8%
8,292	BENEWAH	3,534	2,039	1,447	48	592 R	57.7%	40.9%	58.5%	41.5%
36,489	BINGHAM	15,116	11,900	3,064	152	8,836 R	78.7%	20.3%	79.5%	20.5%
9,841	BLAINE	5,657	3,603	1,971	83	1,632 R	63.7%	34.8%	64.6%	35.4%
2,999	BOISE	1,721	1,249	436	36	813 R	72.6%	25.3%	74.1%	25.9%
24,163	BONNER	11,699	6,889	4,628	182	2,261 R	58.9%	39.6%	59.8%	40.2%
65,980	BONNEVILLE	29,490	24,392	4,877	221	19,515 R	82.7%	16.5%	83.3%	16.7%
7,289	BOUNDARY	3,402	2,159	1,158	85	1,001 R	63.5%	34.0%	65.1%	34.9%
3,342	BUTTE	1,685	1,245	429	11	816 R	73.9%	25.5%	74.4%	25.6%
818	CAMAS	491	364	123	4	241 R	74.1%	25.1%	74.7%	25.3%
83,756	CANYON	32,587	24,613	7,527	447	17,086 R	75.5%	23.1%	76.6%	23.4%
8,695	CARIBOU	3,597	3,032	535	30	2,497 R	84.3%	14.9%	85.0%	15.0%
19,427	CASSIA	7,597	6,503	1,036	58	5,467 R	85.6%	13.6%	86.3%	13.7%
798	CLARK	415	353	59	3	294 R	85.1%	14.2%	85.7%	14.3%
10,390	CLEARWATER	3,848	2,176	1,608	64	568 R	56.5%	41.8%	57.5%	42.5%
3,385	CUSTER	2,144	1,653	461	30	1,192 R	77.1%	21.5%	78.2%	21.8%
21,565	ELMORE	6,105	4,595	1,458	52	3,137 R	75.3%	23.9%	75.9%	24.1%
8,895	FRANKLIN	3,742	3,261	439	42	2,822 R	87.1%	11.7%	88.1%	11.9%
10,813	FREMONT	4,853	4,006	818	29	3,188 R	82.5%	16.9%	83.0%	17.0%
11,972	GEM	5,350	3,644	1,607	99	2,037 R	68.1%	30.0%	69.4%	30.6%
11,874	GOODING	5,119	3,819	1,247	53	2,572 R	74.6%	24.4%	75.4%	24.6%
14,769	IDAHO	6,349	4,219	1,996	134	2,223 R	66.5%	31.4%	67.9%	32.1%
15,304	JEFFERSON	6,563	5,770	743	50	5,027 R	87.9%	11.3%	88.6%	11.4%
14,840	JEROME	6,259	4,913	1,284	62	3,629 R	78.5%	20.5%	79.3%	20.7%
59,770	KOOTENAI	26,689	17,330	9,004	355	8,326 R	64.9%	33.7%	65.8%	34.2%
28,749	LATAH	13,500	7,709	5,571	220	2,138 R	57.1%	41.3%	58.0%	42.0%
7,460	LEMHI	3,708	2,810	852	46	1,958 R	75.8%	23.0%	76.7%	23.3%
4,118	LEWIS	1,666	1,000	648	18	352 R	60.0%	38.9%	60.7%	39.3%
3,436	LINCOLN	1,615	1,211	386	18	825 R	75.0%	23.9%	75.8%	24.2%
19,480	MADISON	7,319	6,798	483	38	6,315 R	92.9%	6.6%	93.4%	6.6%
19,718	MINIDOKA	7,420	5,938	1,398	84	4,540 R	80.0%	18.8%	80.9%	19.1%
33,220	NEZ PERCE	14,330	8,153	5,981	196	2,172 R	56.9%	41.7%	57.7%	42.3%
3,258	ONEIDA	1,898	1,528	360	10	1,168 R	80.5%	19.0%	80.9%	19.1%
8,272	OWYHEE	2,755	2,141	574	40	1,567 R	77.7%	20.8%	78.9%	21.1%
15,722	PAYETTE	6,121	4,605	1,410	106	3,195 R	75.2%	23.0%	76.6%	23.4%
6,844	POWER	3,004	2,298	678	28	1,620 R	76.5%	22.6%	77.2%	22.8%
19,226	SHOSHONE	6,284	3,156	3,033	95	123 R	50.2%	48.3%	51.0%	49.0%
2,897	TETON	1,624	1,242	370	12	872 R	76.5%	22.8%	77.0%	23.0%
52,927	TWIN FALLS	21,771	16,974	4,567	230	12,407 R	78.0%	21.0%	78.8%	21.2%
5,604	VALLEY	3,286	2,299	945	42	1,354 R	70.0%	28.8%	70.9%	29.1%
8,803	WASHINGTON	4,188	3,015	1,119	54	1,896 R	72.0%	26.7%	72.9%	27.1%
943,935	TOTAL	411,144	297,523	108,510	5,111	189,013 R	72.4%	26.4%	73.3%	26.7%

IDAHO

SENATOR 1984

1980 Census Population	County	Total Vote	Republican	Democratic	Other	Rep.-Dem. Plurality	Percentage			
							Total Vote		Major Vote	
							Rep.	Dem.	Rep.	Dem.
173,036	ADA	82,825	59,259	20,989	2,577	38,270 R	71.5%	25.3%	73.8%	26.2%
3,347	ADAMS	1,894	1,423	459	12	964 R	75.1%	24.2%	75.6%	24.4%
65,421	BANNOCK	28,701	18,360	9,882	459	8,478 R	64.0%	34.4%	65.0%	35.0%
6,931	BEAR LAKE	3,066	2,623	438	5	2,185 R	85.6%	14.3%	85.7%	14.3%
8,292	BENEWAH	3,249	2,048	1,161	40	887 R	63.0%	35.7%	63.8%	36.2%
36,489	BINGHAM	15,263	11,789	3,245	229	8,544 R	77.2%	21.3%	78.4%	21.6%
9,841	BLAINE	5,629	3,058	2,464	107	594 R	54.3%	43.8%	55.4%	44.6%
2,999	BOISE	1,624	1,206	385	33	821 R	74.3%	23.7%	75.8%	24.2%
24,163	BONNER	10,728	6,654	3,971	103	2,683 R	62.0%	37.0%	62.6%	37.4%
65,980	BONNEVILLE	29,890	24,266	5,319	305	18,947 R	81.2%	17.8%	82.0%	18.0%
7,289	BOUNDARY	3,135	2,171	937	27	1,234 R	69.3%	29.9%	69.9%	30.1%
3,342	BUTTE	1,608	1,201	403	4	798 R	74.7%	25.1%	74.9%	25.1%
818	CAMAS	468	360	101	7	259 R	76.9%	21.6%	78.1%	21.9%
83,756	CANYON	32,786	24,256	7,619	911	16,637 R	74.0%	23.2%	76.1%	23.9%
8,695	CARIBOU	3,413	2,899	504	10	2,395 R	84.9%	14.8%	85.2%	14.8%
19,427	CASSIA	7,567	6,391	1,075	101	5,316 R	84.5%	14.2%	85.6%	14.4%
798	CLARK	398	328	65	5	263 R	82.4%	16.3%	83.5%	16.5%
10,390	CLEARWATER	3,903	2,290	1,560	53	730 R	58.7%	40.0%	59.5%	40.5%
3,385	CUSTER	2,024	1,609	398	17	1,211 R	79.5%	19.7%	80.2%	19.8%
21,565	ELMORE	5,776	4,394	1,334	48	3,060 R	76.1%	23.1%	76.7%	23.3%
8,895	FRANKLIN	3,776	3,267	466	43	2,801 R	86.5%	12.3%	87.5%	12.5%
10,813	FREMONT	4,640	3,864	753	23	3,111 R	83.3%	16.2%	83.7%	16.3%
11,972	GEM	5,428	3,665	1,614	149	2,051 R	67.5%	29.7%	69.4%	30.6%
11,874	GOODING	4,801	3,658	1,111	32	2,547 R	76.2%	23.1%	76.7%	23.3%
14,769	IDAHO	6,058	4,166	1,815	77	2,351 R	68.8%	30.0%	69.7%	30.3%
15,304	JEFFERSON	6,603	5,643	846	114	4,797 R	85.5%	12.8%	87.0%	13.0%
14,840	JEROME	5,855	4,704	1,113	38	3,591 R	80.3%	19.0%	80.9%	19.1%
59,770	KOOTENAI	26,733	17,909	8,423	401	9,486 R	67.0%	31.5%	68.0%	32.0%
28,749	LATAH	13,635	8,035	5,237	363	2,798 R	58.9%	38.4%	60.5%	39.5%
7,460	LEMHI	3,523	2,807	695	21	2,112 R	79.7%	19.7%	80.2%	19.8%
4,118	LEWIS	1,573	946	618	9	328 R	60.1%	39.3%	60.5%	39.5%
3,436	LINCOLN	1,538	1,149	379	10	770 R	74.7%	24.6%	75.2%	24.8%
19,480	MADISON	7,274	6,638	582	54	6,056 R	91.3%	8.0%	91.9%	8.1%
19,718	MINIDOKA	7,425	5,827	1,481	117	4,346 R	78.5%	19.9%	79.7%	20.3%
33,220	NEZ PERCE	14,392	7,640	6,513	239	1,127 R	53.1%	45.3%	54.0%	46.0%
3,258	ONEIDA	1,783	1,431	350	2	1,081 R	80.3%	19.6%	80.3%	19.7%
8,272	OWYHEE	2,649	2,084	518	47	1,566 R	78.7%	19.6%	80.1%	19.9%
15,722	PAYETTE	6,184	4,688	1,372	124	3,316 R	75.8%	22.2%	77.4%	22.6%
6,844	POWER	2,827	2,151	656	20	1,495 R	76.1%	23.2%	76.6%	23.4%
19,226	SHOSHONE	6,411	3,845	2,478	88	1,367 R	60.0%	38.7%	60.8%	39.2%
2,897	TETON	1,519	1,170	342	7	828 R	77.0%	22.5%	77.4%	22.6%
52,927	TWIN FALLS	20,434	16,062	4,090	282	11,972 R	78.6%	20.0%	79.7%	20.3%
5,604	VALLEY	3,168	2,288	839	41	1,449 R	72.2%	26.5%	73.2%	26.8%
8,803	WASHINGTON	3,992	2,971	991	30	1,980 R	74.4%	24.8%	75.0%	25.0%
943,935	TOTAL	406,168	293,193	105,591	7,384	187,602 R	72.2%	26.0%	73.5%	26.5%

IDAHO

CONGRESS

CD	Year	Total Vote	Republican Vote	Candidate	Democratic Vote	Candidate	Other Vote	Rep.-Dem. Plurality	Percentage Total Vote Rep.	Dem.	Major Vote Rep.	Dem.
1	1984	202,676	139,085	CRAIG, LARRY	63,591	HELLAR, BILL		75,494 R	68.6%	31.4%	68.6%	31.4%
1	1982	160,665	86,277	CRAIG, LARRY	74,388	LAROCCO, LARRY		11,889 R	53.7%	46.3%	53.7%	46.3%
2	1984	202,404	101,117	HANSEN, GEORGE V.	101,287	STALLINGS, RICHARD		170 D	50.0%	50.0%	50.0%	50.0%
2	1982	160,481	83,873	HANSEN, GEORGE V.	76,608	STALLINGS, RICHARD		7,265 R	52.3%	47.7%	52.3%	47.7%

IDAHO

1984 GENERAL ELECTION

President   Other vote was 2,823 Bergland (Libertarian); 2,288 Richards (Populist).

Senator   Other vote was Billings (Libertarian).

Congress

1984 PRIMARIES

MAY 22 REPUBLICAN

Senator   James A. McClure, unopposed.

Congress   Unopposed in CD 1. Contested as follows:

  CD 2   34,544 George V. Hansen; 33,134 Dan Adamson.

MAY 22 DEMOCRATIC

Senator   27,871 Peter M. Busch; 17,065 Louis A. Hatheway.

Congress   Unopposed in both CD's. Fred W. Craner, the unopposed candidate in CD 1, died after the primary and Bill Hellar was substituted by the local party committee.

ILLINOIS

GOVERNOR
James R. Thompson (R). Re-elected 1982 to a four-year term. Previously elected 1978 and in 1976 to a two-year term.

SENATORS
Alan J. Dixon (D). Elected 1980 to a six-year term.

Paul Simon (D). Elected 1984 to a six-year term.

REPRESENTATIVES
1. Charles A. Hayes (D)
2. Gus Savage (D)
3. Martin A. Russo (D)
4. George M. O'Brien (R)
5. William O. Lipinski (D)
6. Henry J. Hyde (R)
7. Cardiss Collins (D)
8. Daniel Rostenkowski (D)
9. Sidney R. Yates (D)
10. John E. Porter (R)
11. Frank Annunzio (D)
12. Philip M. Crane (R)
13. Harris W. Fawell (R)
14. John E. Grotberg (R)
15. Edward R. Madigan (R)
16. Lynn Martin (R)
17. Lane Evans (D)
18. Robert H. Michel (R)
19. Terry L. Bruce (D)
20. Richard J. Durbin (D)
21. Melvin Price (D)
22. Kenneth J. Gray (D)

POSTWAR VOTE FOR GOVERNOR

Year	Total Vote	Republican Vote	Candidate	Democratic Vote	Candidate	Other Vote	Rep.-Dem. Plurality	Total Vote Rep.	Dem.	Major Vote Rep.	Dem.
1982	3,673,681	1,816,101	Thompson, James R.	1,811,027	Stevenson, Adlai E., III	46,553	5,074 R	49.4%	49.3%	50.1%	49.9%
1978	3,150,095	1,859,684	Thompson, James R.	1,263,134	Bakalis, Michael	27,277	596,550 R	59.0%	40.1%	59.6%	40.4%
1976s	4,638,997	3,000,395	Thompson, James R.	1,610,258	Howlett, Michael J.	28,344	1,390,137 R	64.7%	34.7%	65.1%	34.9%
1972	4,678,804	2,293,809	Ogilvie, Richard B.	2,371,303	Walker, Daniel	13,692	77,494 D	49.0%	50.7%	49.2%	50.8%
1968	4,506,000	2,307,295	Ogilvie, Richard B.	2,179,501	Shapiro, Samuel H.	19,204	127,794 R	51.2%	48.4%	51.4%	48.6%
1964	4,657,500	2,239,095	Percy, Charles H.	2,418,394	Kerner, Otto	11	179,299 D	48.1%	51.9%	48.1%	51.9%
1960	4,674,187	2,070,479	Stratton, William G.	2,594,731	Kerner, Otto	8,977	524,252 D	44.3%	55.5%	44.4%	55.6%
1956	4,314,611	2,171,786	Stratton, William G.	2,134,909	Austin, Richard B.	7,916	36,877 R	50.3%	49.5%	50.4%	49.6%
1952	4,415,864	2,317,363	Stratton, William G.	2,089,721	Dixon, Sherwood	8,780	227,642 R	52.5%	47.3%	52.6%	47.4%
1948	3,940,257	1,678,007	Green, Dwight H.	2,250,074	Stevenson, Adlai E.	12,176	572,067 D	42.6%	57.1%	42.7%	57.3%

The 1976 vote was for a two-year term to permit shifting the vote for Governor to non-Presidential years.

POSTWAR VOTE FOR SENATOR

Year	Total Vote	Republican Vote	Candidate	Democratic Vote	Candidate	Other Vote	Rep.-Dem. Plurality	Total Vote Rep.	Dem.	Major Vote Rep.	Dem.
1984	4,787,473	2,308,039	Percy, Charles H.	2,397,303	Simon, Paul	82,131	89,264 D	48.2%	50.1%	49.1%	50.9%
1980	4,580,029	1,946,296	O'Neal, David C.	2,565,302	Dixon, Alan J.	68,431	619,006 D	42.5%	56.0%	43.1%	56.9%
1978	3,184,764	1,698,711	Percy, Charles H.	1,448,187	Seith, Alex	37,866	250,524 R	53.3%	45.5%	54.0%	46.0%
1974	2,914,666	1,084,884	Burditt, George M.	1,811,496	Stevenson, Adlai E., III	18,286	726,612 D	37.2%	62.2%	37.5%	62.5%
1972	4,608,380	2,867,078	Percy, Charles H.	1,721,031	Pucinski, Roman C.	20,271	1,146,047 R	62.2%	37.3%	62.5%	37.5%
1970s	3,599,272	1,519,718	Smith, Ralph T.	2,065,054	Stevenson, Adlai E., III	14,500	545,336 D	42.2%	57.4%	42.4%	57.6%
1968	4,449,757	2,358,947	Dirksen, Everett M.	2,073,242	Clark, William G.	17,568	285,705 R	53.0%	46.6%	53.2%	46.8%
1966	3,822,725	2,100,449	Percy, Charles H.	1,678,147	Douglas, Paul H.	44,129	422,302 R	54.9%	43.9%	55.6%	44.4%
1962	3,709,216	1,961,202	Dirksen, Everett M.	1,748,007	Yates, Sidney R.	7	213,195 R	52.9%	47.1%	52.9%	47.1%
1960	4,632,796	2,093,846	Witwer, Samuel W.	2,530,943	Douglas, Paul H.	8,007	437,097 D	45.2%	54.6%	45.3%	54.7%
1956	4,264,830	2,307,352	Dirksen, Everett M.	1,949,883	Stengel, Richard	7,595	357,469 R	54.1%	45.7%	54.2%	45.8%
1954	3,368,025	1,563,683	Meek, Joseph T.	1,804,338	Douglas, Paul H.	4	240,655 D	46.4%	53.6%	46.4%	53.6%
1950	3,622,673	1,951,984	Dirksen, Everett M.	1,657,630	Lucas, Scott W.	13,059	294,354 R	53.9%	45.8%	54.1%	45.9%
1948	3,900,285	1,740,026	Brooks, C. Wayland	2,147,754	Douglas, Paul H.	12,505	407,728 D	44.6%	55.1%	44.8%	55.2%

The 1970 election was for a short term to fill a vacancy.

154

ILLINOIS

Districts Established November 23, 1981

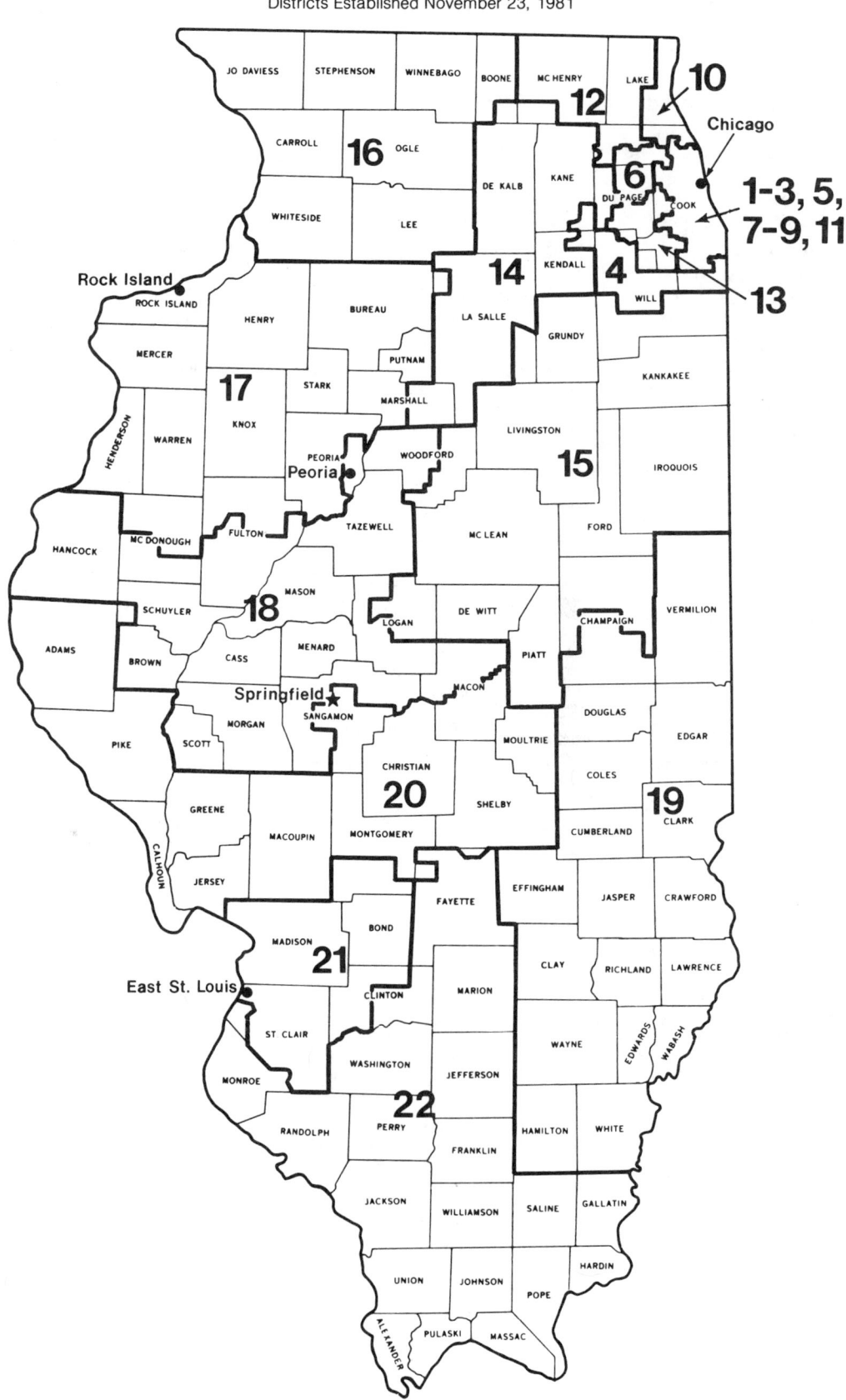

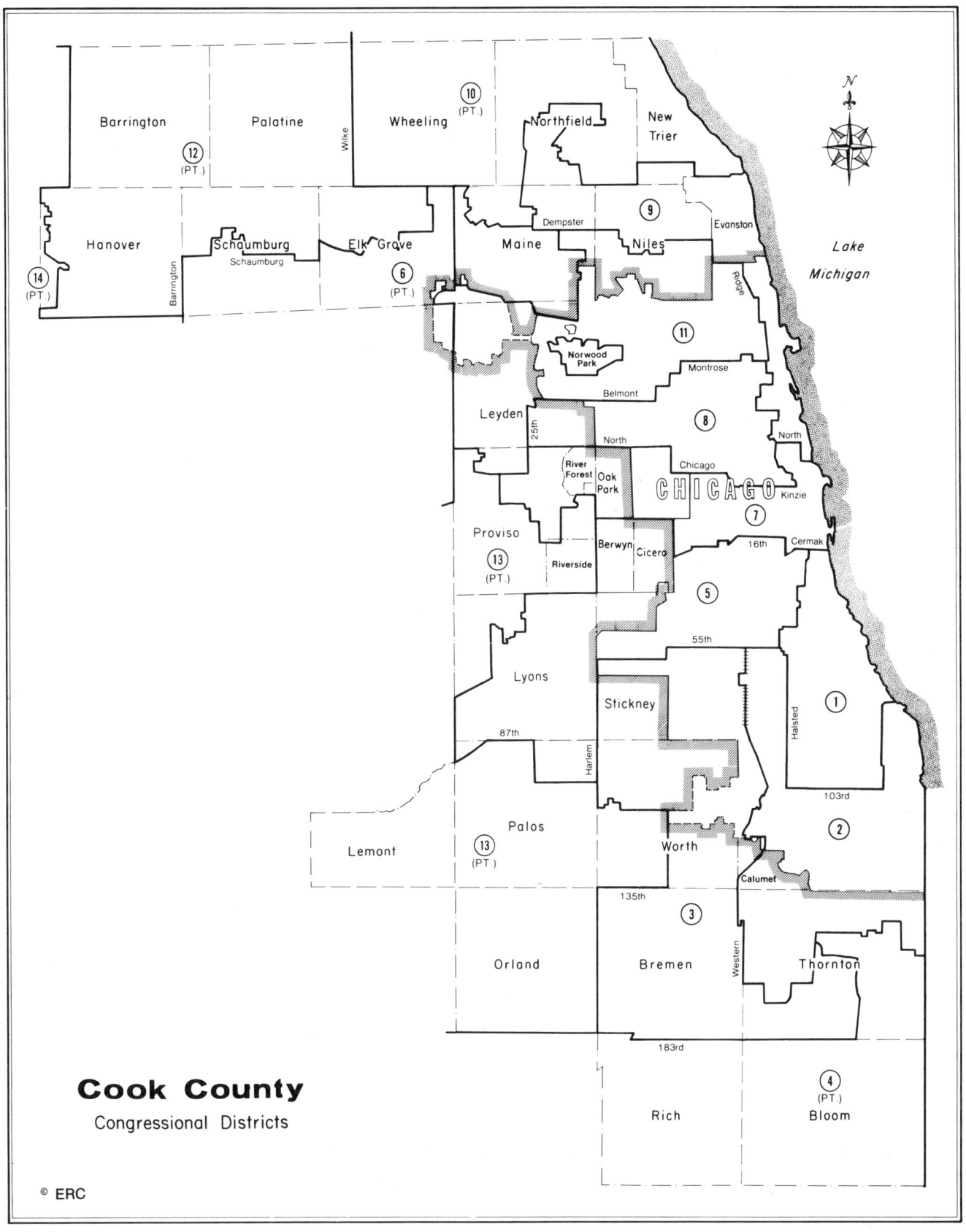

Cook County

Congressional Districts

© ERC

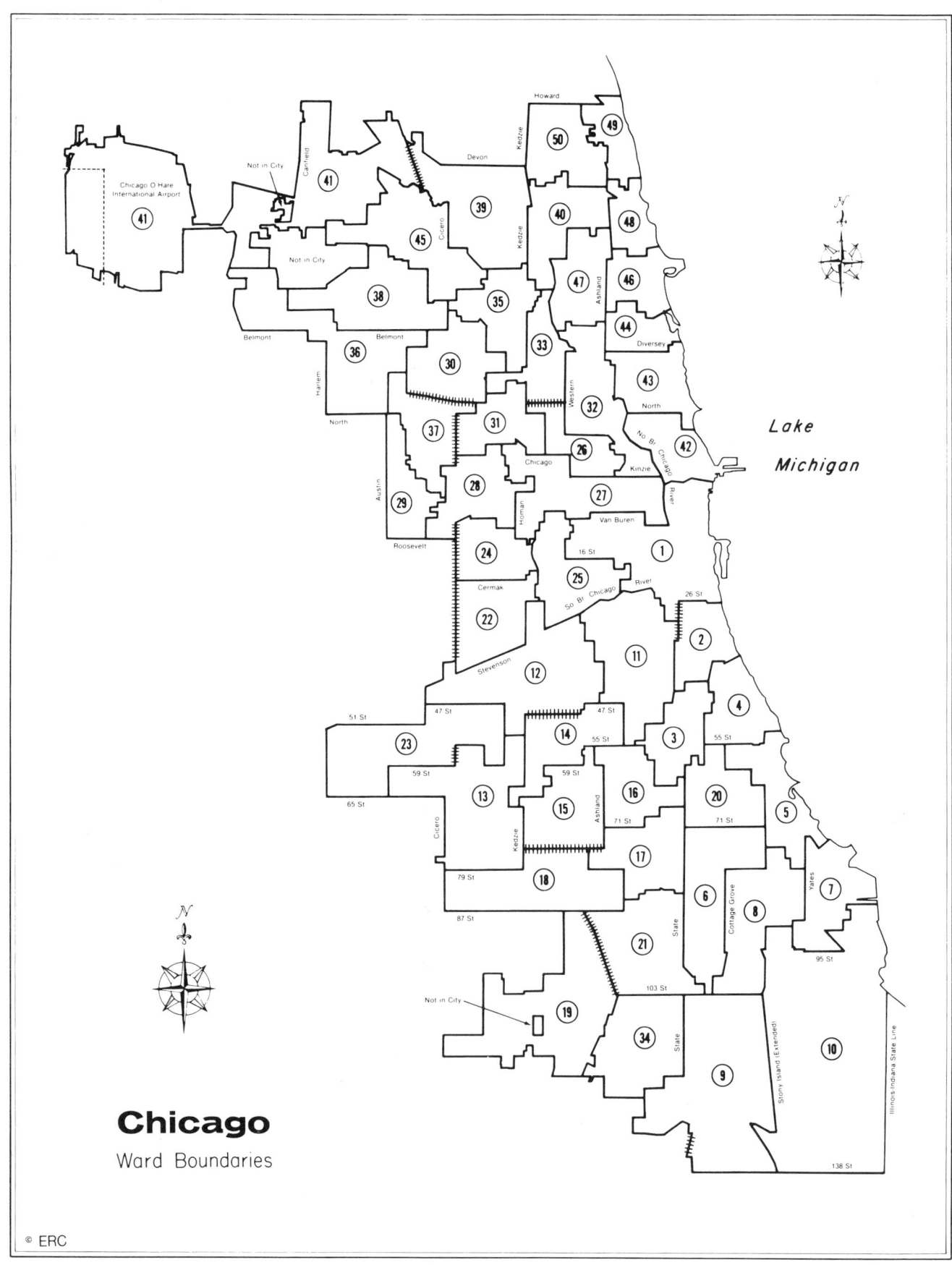

Chicago
Ward Boundaries

© ERC

ILLINOIS

PRESIDENT 1984

1980 Census Population	County	Total Vote	Republican	Democratic	Other	Rep.-Dem. Plurality	Percentage			
							Total Vote		Major Vote	
							Rep.	Dem.	Rep.	Dem.
71,622	ADAMS	30,649	20,225	10,336	88	9,889 R	66.0%	33.7%	66.2%	33.8%
12,264	ALEXANDER	5,467	2,574	2,872	21	298 D	47.1%	52.5%	47.3%	52.7%
16,224	BOND	7,131	4,240	2,870	21	1,370 R	59.5%	40.2%	59.6%	40.4%
28,630	BOONE	11,306	7,536	3,717	53	3,819 R	66.7%	32.9%	67.0%	33.0%
5,411	BROWN	2,446	1,478	959	9	519 R	60.4%	39.2%	60.6%	39.4%
39114	BUREAU	18,765	11,741	6,925	99	4,816 R	62.6%	36.9%	62.9%	37.1%
5,867	CALHOUN	3,107	1,648	1,443	16	205 R	53.0%	46.4%	53.3%	46.7%
18779	CARROLL	7,658	5,237	2,398	23	2,839 R	68.4%	31.3%	68.6%	31.4%
15,084	CASS	6,399	3,435	2,937	27	498 R	53.7%	45.9%	53.9%	46.1%
168,392	CHAMPAIGN	66,925	39,224	27,266	435	11,958 R	58.6%	40.7%	59.0%	41.0%
36,446	CHRISTIAN	16,152	8,534	7,541	77	993 R	52.8%	46.7%	53.1%	46.9%
16,913	CLARK	8,382	5,318	3,032	32	2,286 R	63.4%	36.2%	63.7%	36.3%
15,283	CLAY	7,104	4,562	2,524	18	2,038 R	64.2%	35.5%	64.4%	35.6%
32,617	CLINTON	13,899	9,233	4,628	38	4,605 R	66.4%	33.3%	66.6%	33.4%
52,260	COLES	21,295	14,044	7,156	95	6,888 R	65.9%	33.6%	66.2%	33.8%
5,253,655	COOK	2,180,735	1,055,558	1,112,641	12,536	57,083 D	48.4%	51.0%	48.7%	51.3%
20,818	CRAWFORD	9,424	6,261	3,130	33	3,131 R	66.4%	33.2%	66.7%	33.3%
11,062	CUMBERLAND	4,762	3,002	1,733	27	1,269 R	63.0%	36.4%	63.4%	36.6%
74,624	DE KALB	31,465	20,294	10,942	229	9,352 R	64.5%	34.8%	65.0%	35.0%
18,108	DE WITT	6,915	4,534	2,352	29	2,182 R	65.6%	34.0%	65.8%	34.2%
19,774	DOUGLAS	8,604	5,691	2,886	27	2,805 R	66.1%	33.5%	66.4%	33.6%
658,835	DU PAGE	300,215	227,141	71,430	1,644	155,711 R	75.7%	23.8%	76.1%	23.9%
21,725	EDGAR	10,099	6,821	3,241	37	3,580 R	67.5%	32.1%	67.8%	32.2%
7,961	EDWARDS	3,845	2,778	1,057	10	1,721 R	72.2%	27.5%	72.4%	27.6%
30,944	EFFINGHAM	13,504	9,617	3,841	46	5,776 R	71.2%	28.4%	71.5%	28.5%
22,167	FAYETTE	10,473	6,607	3,844	22	2,763 R	63.1%	36.7%	63.2%	36.8%
15,265	FORD	6,663	4,871	1,763	29	3,108 R	73.1%	26.5%	73.4%	26.6%
43,201	FRANKLIN	20,377	9,656	10,667	54	1,011 D	47.4%	52.3%	47.5%	52.5%
43,687	FULTON	18,377	9,147	9,131	99	16 R	49.8%	49.7%	50.0%	50.0%
7,590	GALLATIN	4,112	1,939	2,164	9	225 D	47.2%	52.6%	47.3%	52.7%
16,661	GREENE	6,655	4,057	2,563	35	1,494 R	61.0%	38.5%	61.3%	38.7%
30,582	GRUNDY	14,325	9,595	4,671	59	4,924 R	67.0%	32.6%	67.3%	32.7%
9,172	HAMILTON	5,346	3,074	2,251	21	823 R	57.5%	42.1%	57.7%	42.3%
23,877	HANCOCK	10,001	6,251	3,713	37	2,538 R	62.5%	37.1%	62.7%	37.3%
5,383	HARDIN	2,899	1,689	1,205	5	484 R	58.3%	41.6%	58.4%	41.6%
9,114	HENDERSON	4,278	2,289	1,969	20	320 R	53.5%	46.0%	53.8%	46.2%
57,968	HENRY	25,262	14,504	10,679	79	3,825 R	57.4%	42.3%	57.6%	42.4%
32,976	IROQUOIS	14,685	11,327	3,300	58	8,027 R	77.1%	22.5%	77.4%	22.6%
61,522	JACKSON	25,896	13,609	12,105	182	1,504 R	52.6%	46.7%	52.9%	47.1%
11,318	JASPER	5,454	3,673	1,750	31	1,923 R	67.3%	32.1%	67.7%	32.3%
36,552	JEFFERSON	16,885	9,642	7,200	43	2,442 R	57.1%	42.6%	57.2%	42.8%
20,538	JERSEY	8,934	5,146	3,762	26	1,384 R	57.6%	42.1%	57.8%	42.2%
23,520	JO DAVIESS	9,302	5,877	3,348	77	2,529 R	63.2%	36.0%	63.7%	36.3%
9,624	JOHNSON	5,083	3,424	1,647	12	1,777 R	67.4%	32.4%	67.5%	32.5%
278,405	KANE	105,159	72,655	31,875	629	40,780 R	69.1%	30.3%	69.5%	30.5%
102,926	KANKAKEE	39,665	23,807	15,246	612	8,561 R	60.0%	38.4%	61.0%	39.0%
37,202	KENDALL	14,730	10,872	3,789	69	7,083 R	73.8%	25.7%	74.2%	25.8%
61,607	KNOX	27,122	14,974	12,027	121	2,947 R	55.2%	44.3%	55.5%	44.5%
440,372	LAKE	173,224	118,401	53,947	876	64,454 R	68.4%	31.1%	68.7%	31.3%
112,033	LA SALLE	48,139	27,388	20,532	219	6,856 R	56.9%	42.7%	57.2%	42.8%
17,807	LAWRENCE	7,638	4,686	2,924	28	1,762 R	61.4%	38.3%	61.6%	38.4%
36,328	LEE	15,155	11,178	3,919	58	7,259 R	73.8%	25.9%	74.0%	26.0%
41,381	LIVINGSTON	16,919	12,291	4,567	61	7,724 R	72.6%	27.0%	72.9%	27.1%
31,802	LOGAN	14,046	9,932	4,052	62	5,880 R	70.7%	28.8%	71.0%	29.0%
37,467	MCDONOUGH	14,001	9,383	4,561	57	4,822 R	67.0%	32.6%	67.3%	32.7%
147,897	MCHENRY	62,042	47,282	14,420	340	32,862 R	76.2%	23.2%	76.6%	23.4%
119,149	MCLEAN	48,349	32,221	15,880	248	16,341 R	66.6%	32.8%	67.0%	33.0%
131,375	MACON	56,112	30,457	25,463	192	4,994 R	54.3%	45.4%	54.5%	45.5%
49,384	MACOUPIN	22,953	12,282	10,602	69	1,680 R	53.5%	46.2%	53.7%	46.3%
247,691	MADISON	105,713	57,021	48,352	340	8,669 R	53.9%	45.7%	54.1%	45.9%

ILLINOIS

PRESIDENT 1984

1980 Census Population	County	Total Vote	Republican	Democratic	Other	Rep.-Dem. Plurality	Percentage Total Vote		Major Vote	
							Rep.	Dem.	Rep.	Dem.
43,523	MARION	18,945	11,300	7,599	46	3,701 R	59.6%	40.1%	59.8%	40.2%
14,479	MARSHALL	6,493	4,060	2,386	47	1,674 R	62.5%	36.7%	63.0%	37.0%
19,492	MASON	7,486	4,109	3,354	23	755 R	54.9%	44.8%	55.1%	44.9%
14,990	MASSAC	7,049	3,827	3,194	28	633 R	54.3%	45.3%	54.5%	45.5%
11,700	MENARD	5,766	3,925	1,826	15	2,099 R	68.1%	31.7%	68.2%	31.8%
19,286	MERCER	8,927	4,907	3,982	38	925 R	55.0%	44.6%	55.2%	44.8%
20,117	MONROE	10,217	6,936	3,256	25	3,680 R	67.9%	31.9%	68.1%	31.9%
31,686	MONTGOMERY	14,605	8,191	6,360	54	1,831 R	56.1%	43.5%	56.3%	43.7%
37,502	MORGAN	16,097	10,683	5,361	53	5,322 R	66.4%	33.3%	66.6%	33.4%
14,546	MOULTRIE	6,072	3,593	2,458	21	1,135 R	59.2%	40.5%	59.4%	40.6%
46,338	OGLE	18,396	13,503	4,803	90	8,700 R	73.4%	26.1%	73.8%	26.2%
200,466	PEORIA	82,899	45,607	36,830	462	8,777 R	55.0%	44.4%	55.3%	44.7%
21,714	PERRY	10,472	5,852	4,584	36	1,268 R	55.9%	43.8%	56.1%	43.9%
16,581	PIATT	7,879	5,000	2,840	39	2,160 R	63.5%	36.0%	63.8%	36.2%
18,896	PIKE	9,285	5,295	3,965	25	1,330 R	57.0%	42.7%	57.2%	42.8%
4,404	POPE	2,492	1,545	940	7	605 R	62.0%	37.7%	62.2%	37.8%
8,840	PULASKI	3,664	1,923	1,724	17	199 R	52.5%	47.1%	52.7%	47.3%
6,085	PUTNAM	3,413	1,912	1,487	14	425 R	56.0%	43.6%	56.3%	43.7%
35,652	RANDOLPH	15,829	9,415	6,355	59	3,060 R	59.5%	40.1%	59.7%	40.3%
17,587	RICHLAND	7,874	5,665	2,182	27	3,483 R	71.9%	27.7%	72.2%	27.8%
165,968	ROCK ISLAND	75,672	35,121	40,208	343	5,087 D	46.4%	53.1%	46.6%	53.4%
267,531	ST. CLAIR	104,148	51,046	52,294	808	1,248 D	49.0%	50.2%	49.4%	50.6%
28,448	SALINE	13,251	7,176	6,038	37	1,138 R	54.2%	45.6%	54.3%	45.7%
176,089	SANGAMON	88,523	54,086	34,059	378	20,027 R	61.1%	38.5%	61.4%	38.6%
8,365	SCHUYLER	4,061	2,515	1,533	13	982 R	61.9%	37.7%	62.1%	37.9%
6,142	SCOTT	2,935	1,976	943	16	1,033 R	67.3%	32.1%	67.7%	32.3%
23,923	SHELBY	10,730	6,372	4,317	41	2,055 R	59.4%	40.2%	59.6%	40.4%
7,389	STARK	3,318	2,228	1,072	18	1,156 R	67.1%	32.3%	67.5%	32.5%
49,536	STEPHENSON	21,131	14,237	6,723	171	7,514 R	67.4%	31.8%	67.9%	32.1%
132,078	TAZEWELL	57,115	33,782	23,095	238	10,687 R	59.1%	40.4%	59.4%	40.6%
17,765	UNION	8,564	4,721	3,815	28	906 R	55.1%	44.5%	55.3%	44.7%
95,222	VERMILION	39,611	22,932	16,530	149	6,402 R	57.9%	41.7%	58.1%	41.9%
13,713	WABASH	5,453	3,639	1,795	19	1,844 R	66.7%	32.9%	67.0%	33.0%
21,943	WARREN	9,193	5,846	3,318	29	2,528 R	63.6%	36.1%	63.8%	36.2%
15,472	WASHINGTON	7,516	5,129	2,363	24	2,766 R	68.2%	31.4%	68.5%	31.5%
18,059	WAYNE	8,951	6,298	2,621	32	3,677 R	70.4%	29.3%	70.6%	29.4%
17,864	WHITE	8,983	5,500	3,457	26	2,043 R	61.2%	38.5%	61.4%	38.6%
65,970	WHITESIDE	28,096	16,743	11,226	127	5,517 R	59.6%	40.0%	59.9%	40.1%
324,460	WILL	124,397	78,684	45,193	520	33,491 R	63.3%	36.3%	63.5%	36.5%
56,538	WILLIAMSON	26,630	14,930	11,614	86	3,316 R	56.1%	43.6%	56.2%	43.8%
250,884	WINNEBAGO	109,451	64,203	44,629	619	19,574 R	58.7%	40.8%	59.0%	41.0%
33,320	WOODFORD	15,272	10,758	4,425	89	6,333 R	70.4%	29.0%	70.9%	29.1%
11,426,518	TOTAL	4,819,088	2,707,103	2,086,499	25,486	620,604 R	56.2%	43.3%	56.5%	43.5%

ILLINOIS

SENATOR 1984

1980 Census Population	County	Total Vote	Republican	Democratic	Other	Rep.-Dem. Plurality	Percentage Total Vote Rep.	Dem.	Major Vote Rep.	Dem.
71,622	ADAMS	30,596	17,119	13,152	325	3,967 R	56.0%	43.0%	56.6%	43.4%
12,264	ALEXANDER	5,462	1,871	3,559	32	1,688 D	34.3%	65.2%	34.5%	65.5%
16,224	BOND	7,065	3,192	3,807	66	615 D	45.2%	53.9%	45.6%	54.4%
28,630	BOONE	11,218	6,709	4,270	239	2,439 R	59.8%	38.1%	61.1%	38.9%
5,411	BROWN	2,440	1,260	1,155	25	105 R	51.6%	47.3%	52.2%	47.8%
39114	BUREAU	18,692	10,365	8,129	198	2,236 R	55.5%	43.5%	56.0%	44.0%
5,867	CALHOUN	3,109	1,260	1,838	11	578 D	40.5%	59.1%	40.7%	59.3%
18779	CARROLL	7,610	4,684	2,831	95	1,853 R	61.6%	37.2%	62.3%	37.7%
15,084	CASS	6,317	2,966	3,295	56	329 D	47.0%	52.2%	47.4%	52.6%
168,392	CHAMPAIGN	66,375	35,186	30,169	1,020	5,017 R	53.0%	45.5%	53.8%	46.2%
36,446	CHRISTIAN	16,152	7,031	8,904	217	1,873 D	43.5%	55.1%	44.1%	55.9%
16,913	CLARK	8,286	4,747	3,464	75	1,283 R	57.3%	41.8%	57.8%	42.2%
15,283	CLAY	7,010	4,076	2,860	74	1,216 R	58.1%	40.8%	58.8%	41.2%
32,617	CLINTON	13,758	6,473	7,128	157	655 D	47.0%	51.8%	47.6%	52.4%
52,260	COLES	21,281	12,238	8,824	219	3,414 R	57.5%	41.5%	58.1%	41.9%
5,253,655	COOK	2,164,460	904,806	1,222,716	36,938	317,910 D	41.8%	56.5%	42.5%	57.5%
20,818	CRAWFORD	9,273	5,711	3,482	80	2,229 R	61.6%	37.5%	62.1%	37.9%
11,062	CUMBERLAND	4,706	2,616	2,004	86	612 R	55.6%	42.6%	56.6%	43.4%
74,624	DE KALB	31,290	17,586	12,972	732	4,614 R	56.2%	41.5%	57.5%	42.5%
18,108	DE WITT	6,909	3,949	2,861	99	1,088 R	57.2%	41.4%	58.0%	42.0%
19,774	DOUGLAS	8,526	4,914	3,532	80	1,382 R	57.6%	41.4%	58.2%	41.8%
658,835	DU PAGE	298,477	198,901	92,044	7,532	106,857 R	66.6%	30.8%	68.4%	31.6%
21,725	EDGAR	9,962	6,170	3,676	116	2,494 R	61.9%	36.9%	62.7%	37.3%
7,961	EDWARDS	3,790	2,539	1,228	23	1,311 R	67.0%	32.4%	67.4%	32.6%
30,944	EFFINGHAM	13,338	7,380	5,665	293	1,715 R	55.3%	42.5%	56.6%	43.4%
22,167	FAYETTE	10,283	4,942	5,264	77	322 D	48.1%	51.2%	48.4%	51.6%
15,265	FORD	6,599	4,215	2,254	130	1,961 R	63.9%	34.2%	65.2%	34.8%
43,201	FRANKLIN	20,286	7,101	13,060	125	5,959 D	35.0%	64.4%	35.2%	64.8%
43,687	FULTON	18,408	8,335	9,872	201	1,537 D	45.3%	53.6%	45.8%	54.2%
7,590	GALLATIN	4,077	1,492	2,568	17	1,076 D	36.6%	63.0%	36.7%	63.3%
16,661	GREENE	6,762	3,072	3,629	61	557 D	45.4%	53.7%	45.8%	54.2%
30,582	GRUNDY	14,234	8,004	5,908	322	2,096 R	56.2%	41.5%	57.5%	42.5%
9,172	HAMILTON	5,291	2,229	3,042	20	813 D	42.1%	57.5%	42.3%	57.7%
23,877	HANCOCK	9,843	5,603	4,115	125	1,488 R	56.9%	41.8%	57.7%	42.3%
5,383	HARDIN	2,941	1,248	1,668	25	420 D	42.4%	56.7%	42.8%	57.2%
9,114	HENDERSON	4,287	2,330	1,906	51	424 R	54.4%	44.5%	55.0%	45.0%
57,968	HENRY	24,953	13,194	11,474	285	1,720 R	52.9%	46.0%	53.5%	46.5%
32,976	IROQUOIS	14,593	9,584	4,714	295	4,870 R	65.7%	32.3%	67.0%	33.0%
61,522	JACKSON	25,808	10,237	15,374	197	5,137 D	39.7%	59.6%	40.0%	60.0%
11,318	JASPER	5,416	3,071	2,223	122	848 R	56.7%	41.0%	58.0%	42.0%
36,552	JEFFERSON	16,848	7,610	9,135	103	1,525 D	45.2%	54.2%	45.4%	54.6%
20,538	JERSEY	8,906	4,010	4,830	66	820 D	45.0%	54.2%	45.4%	54.6%
23,520	JO DAVIESS	9,267	5,556	3,532	179	2,024 R	60.0%	38.1%	61.1%	38.9%
9,624	JOHNSON	5,089	2,691	2,367	31	324 R	52.9%	46.5%	53.2%	46.8%
278,405	KANE	104,913	62,684	39,220	3,009	23,464 R	59.7%	37.4%	61.5%	38.5%
102,926	KANKAKEE	38,998	20,490	17,678	830	2,812 R	52.5%	45.3%	53.7%	46.3%
37,202	KENDALL	14,652	9,221	4,957	474	4,264 R	62.9%	33.8%	65.0%	35.0%
61,607	KNOX	26,997	14,041	12,597	359	1,444 R	52.0%	46.7%	52.7%	47.3%
440,372	LAKE	172,070	101,250	66,369	4,451	34,881 R	58.8%	38.6%	60.4%	39.6%
112,033	LA SALLE	48,055	23,129	24,088	838	959 D	48.1%	50.1%	49.0%	51.0%
17,807	LAWRENCE	7,523	4,374	3,093	56	1,281 R	58.1%	41.1%	58.6%	41.4%
36,328	LEE	15,067	9,265	5,417	385	3,848 R	61.5%	36.0%	63.1%	36.9%
41,381	LIVINGSTON	16,836	10,909	5,694	233	5,215 R	64.8%	33.8%	65.7%	34.3%
31,802	LOGAN	14,029	8,584	5,251	194	3,333 R	61.2%	37.4%	62.0%	38.0%
37,467	MCDONOUGH	13,834	8,183	5,486	165	2,697 R	59.2%	39.7%	59.9%	40.1%
147,897	MCHENRY	61,620	40,846	18,968	1,806	21,878 R	66.3%	30.8%	68.3%	31.7%
119,149	MCLEAN	48,307	28,930	18,605	772	10,325 R	59.9%	38.5%	60.9%	39.1%
131,375	MACON	55,850	26,229	29,055	566	2,826 D	47.0%	52.0%	47.4%	52.6%
49,384	MACOUPIN	22,851	9,713	12,950	188	3,237 D	42.5%	56.7%	42.9%	57.1%
247,691	MADISON	105,056	41,837	62,247	972	20,410 D	39.8%	59.3%	40.2%	59.8%

ILLINOIS

SENATOR 1984

1980 Census Population	County	Total Vote	Republican	Democratic	Other	Rep.-Dem. Plurality	Percentage			
							Total Vote		Major Vote	
							Rep.	Dem.	Rep.	Dem.
43,523	MARION	18,888	8,392	10,357	139	1,965 D	44.4%	54.8%	44.8%	55.2%
14,479	MARSHALL	6,448	3,399	2,895	154	504 R	52.7%	44.9%	54.0%	46.0%
19,492	MASON	7,433	3,503	3,854	76	351 D	47.1%	51.8%	47.6%	52.4%
14,990	MASSAC	7,056	2,778	4,258	20	1,480 D	39.4%	60.3%	39.5%	60.5%
11,700	MENARD	5,749	3,284	2,355	110	929 R	57.1%	41.0%	58.2%	41.8%
19,286	MERCER	8,887	4,600	4,184	103	416 R	51.8%	47.1%	52.4%	47.6%
20,117	MONROE	10,196	4,715	5,395	86	680 D	46.2%	52.9%	46.6%	53.4%
31,686	MONTGOMERY	14,575	6,805	7,623	147	818 D	46.7%	52.3%	47.2%	52.8%
37,502	MORGAN	16,118	8,814	7,171	133	1,643 R	54.7%	44.5%	55.1%	44.9%
14,546	MOULTRIE	6,028	2,967	2,985	76	18 D	49.2%	49.5%	49.8%	50.2%
46,338	OGLE	18,187	11,418	6,296	473	5,122 R	62.8%	34.6%	64.5%	35.5%
200,466	PEORIA	82,933	39,822	41,698	1,413	1,876 D	48.0%	50.3%	48.8%	51.2%
21,714	PERRY	10,454	4,446	5,922	86	1,476 D	42.5%	56.6%	42.9%	57.1%
16,581	PIATT	7,829	4,290	3,415	124	875 R	54.8%	43.6%	55.7%	44.3%
18,896	PIKE	9,219	4,555	4,591	73	36 D	49.4%	49.8%	49.8%	50.2%
4,404	POPE	2,498	1,116	1,365	17	249 D	44.7%	54.6%	45.0%	55.0%
8,840	PULASKI	3,691	1,500	2,155	36	655 D	40.6%	58.4%	41.0%	59.0%
6,085	PUTNAM	3,398	1,689	1,663	46	26 R	49.7%	48.9%	50.4%	49.6%
35,652	RANDOLPH	15,914	6,549	9,241	124	2,692 D	41.2%	58.1%	41.5%	58.5%
17,587	RICHLAND	7,770	5,102	2,564	104	2,538 R	65.7%	33.0%	66.6%	33.4%
165,968	ROCK ISLAND	74,859	32,524	41,470	865	8,946 D	43.4%	55.4%	44.0%	56.0%
267,531	ST. CLAIR	102,459	39,426	61,688	1,345	22,262 D	38.5%	60.2%	39.0%	61.0%
28,448	SALINE	13,332	5,247	8,022	63	2,775 D	39.4%	60.2%	39.5%	60.5%
176,089	SANGAMON	88,843	44,877	42,730	1,236	2,147 R	50.5%	48.1%	51.2%	48.8%
8,365	SCHUYLER	4,019	2,222	1,757	40	465 R	55.3%	43.7%	55.8%	44.2%
6,142	SCOTT	2,932	1,672	1,239	21	433 R	57.0%	42.3%	57.4%	42.6%
23,923	SHELBY	10,638	5,127	5,337	174	210 D	48.2%	50.2%	49.0%	51.0%
7,389	STARK	3,276	1,913	1,280	83	633 R	58.4%	39.1%	59.9%	40.1%
49,536	STEPHENSON	20,978	12,613	7,912	453	4,701 R	60.1%	37.7%	61.5%	38.5%
132,078	TAZEWELL	56,643	28,448	27,165	1,030	1,283 R	50.2%	48.0%	51.2%	48.8%
17,765	UNION	8,657	3,581	5,025	51	1,444 D	41.4%	58.0%	41.6%	58.4%
95,222	VERMILION	39,393	21,176	17,781	436	3,395 R	53.8%	45.1%	54.4%	45.6%
13,713	WABASH	5,389	3,386	1,956	47	1,430 R	62.8%	36.3%	63.4%	36.6%
21,943	WARREN	9,141	5,613	3,418	110	2,195 R	61.4%	37.4%	62.2%	37.8%
15,472	WASHINGTON	7,396	4,019	3,292	85	727 R	54.3%	44.5%	55.0%	45.0%
18,059	WAYNE	8,772	5,580	3,104	88	2,476 R	63.6%	35.4%	64.3%	35.7%
17,864	WHITE	8,838	4,635	4,164	39	471 R	52.4%	47.1%	52.7%	47.3%
65,970	WHITESIDE	27,850	14,646	12,753	451	1,893 R	52.6%	45.8%	53.5%	46.5%
324,460	WILL	123,681	66,219	54,641	2,821	11,578 R	53.5%	44.2%	54.8%	45.2%
56,538	WILLIAMSON	26,606	10,954	15,501	151	4,547 D	41.2%	58.3%	41.4%	58.6%
250,884	WINNEBAGO	108,739	57,367	49,215	2,157	8,152 R	52.8%	45.3%	53.8%	46.2%
33,320	WOODFORD	15,110	9,092	5,691	327	3,401 R	60.2%	37.7%	61.5%	38.5%
11,426,518	TOTAL	4,787,473	2,308,039	2,397,303	82,131	89,264 D	48.2%	50.1%	49.1%	50.9%

CHICAGO

PRESIDENT 1984

1980 Census Population	Ward	Total Vote	Republican	Democratic	Other	Rep.-Dem. Plurality	Total Vote Rep.	Dem.	Major Vote Rep.	Dem.
59,725	WARD 1	19,985	5,557	14,250	178	8,693 D	27.8%	71.3%	28.1%	71.9%
60,141	WARD 2	19,258	867	18,221	170	17,354 D	4.5%	94.6%	4.5%	95.5%
60,267	WARD 3	19,280	566	18,504	210	17,938 D	2.9%	96.0%	3.0%	97.0%
60,051	WARD 4	23,062	1,870	20,980	212	19,110 D	8.1%	91.0%	8.2%	91.8%
60,215	WARD 5	24,564	2,464	21,910	190	19,446 D	10.0%	89.2%	10.1%	89.9%
60,576	WARD 6	31,110	1,101	29,826	183	28,725 D	3.5%	95.9%	3.6%	96.4%
59,906	WARD 7	18,362	1,925	16,313	124	14,388 D	10.5%	88.8%	10.6%	89.4%
59,928	WARD 8	28,192	1,040	26,991	161	25,951 D	3.7%	95.7%	3.7%	96.3%
60,477	WARD 9	21,925	1,385	20,396	144	19,011 D	6.3%	93.0%	6.4%	93.6%
60,133	WARD 10	28,780	9,663	18,991	126	9,328 D	33.6%	66.0%	33.7%	66.3%
60,060	WARD 11	24,847	9,726	14,991	130	5,265 D	39.1%	60.3%	39.3%	60.7%
59,989	WARD 12	22,243	11,908	10,218	117	1,690 R	53.5%	45.9%	53.8%	46.2%
60,420	WARD 13	34,189	22,084	11,991	114	10,093 R	64.6%	35.1%	64.8%	35.2%
59,825	WARD 14	21,608	10,987	10,505	116	482 R	50.8%	48.6%	51.1%	48.9%
60,407	WARD 15	23,250	6,858	16,194	198	9,336 D	29.5%	69.7%	29.8%	70.2%
59,937	WARD 16	21,374	653	20,488	233	19,835 D	3.1%	95.9%	3.1%	96.9%
60,144	WARD 17	25,274	755	24,335	184	23,580 D	3.0%	96.3%	3.0%	97.0%
59,662	WARD 18	30,902	13,185	17,591	126	4,406 D	42.7%	56.9%	42.8%	57.2%
59,786	WARD 19	33,825	19,480	14,210	135	5,270 R	57.6%	42.0%	57.8%	42.2%
59,981	WARD 20	21,652	685	20,800	167	20,115 D	3.2%	96.1%	3.2%	96.8%
60,168	WARD 21	29,396	904	28,291	201	27,387 D	3.1%	96.2%	3.1%	96.9%
59,598	WARD 22	8,693	2,718	5,894	81	3,176 D	31.3%	67.8%	31.6%	68.4%
58,596	WARD 23	31,955	20,418	11,440	97	8,978 R	63.9%	35.8%	64.1%	35.9%
60,003	WARD 24	20,136	489	19,430	217	18,941 D	2.4%	96.5%	2.5%	97.5%
59,936	WARD 25	10,869	3,119	7,653	97	4,534 D	28.7%	70.4%	29.0%	71.0%
60,911	WARD 26	15,152	5,706	9,339	107	3,633 D	37.7%	61.6%	37.9%	62.1%
60,110	WARD 27	17,024	1,309	15,506	209	14,197 D	7.7%	91.1%	7.8%	92.2%
61,055	WARD 28	18,395	610	17,580	205	16,970 D	3.3%	95.6%	3.4%	96.6%
60,273	WARD 29	17,848	1,341	16,334	173	14,993 D	7.5%	91.5%	7.6%	92.4%
59,498	WARD 30	22,026	12,792	9,121	113	3,671 R	58.1%	41.4%	58.4%	41.6%
60,879	WARD 31	14,875	4,635	10,125	115	5,490 D	31.2%	68.1%	31.4%	68.6%
61,212	WARD 32	17,599	6,395	11,048	156	4,653 D	36.3%	62.8%	36.7%	63.3%
59,228	WARD 33	17,629	7,512	9,951	166	2,439 D	42.6%	56.4%	43.0%	57.0%
60,091	WARD 34	25,752	875	24,684	193	23,809 D	3.4%	95.9%	3.4%	96.6%
59,110	WARD 35	20,572	11,981	8,463	128	3,518 R	58.2%	41.1%	58.6%	41.4%
59,830	WARD 36	31,264	20,446	10,686	132	9,760 R	65.4%	34.2%	65.7%	34.3%
60,032	WARD 37	19,593	3,078	16,337	178	13,259 D	15.7%	83.4%	15.9%	84.1%
60,618	WARD 38	31,036	20,776	10,146	114	10,630 R	66.9%	32.7%	67.2%	32.8%
60,669	WARD 39	24,674	14,319	10,224	131	4,095 R	58.0%	41.4%	58.3%	41.7%
59,680	WARD 40	20,865	11,298	9,466	101	1,832 R	54.1%	45.4%	54.4%	45.6%
60,579	WARD 41	33,998	23,936	9,941	121	13,995 R	70.4%	29.2%	70.7%	29.3%
60,173	WARD 42	29,730	14,032	15,537	161	1,505 D	47.2%	52.3%	47.5%	52.5%
60,156	WARD 43	33,903	16,354	17,293	256	939 D	48.2%	51.0%	48.6%	51.4%
60,163	WARD 44	28,549	11,010	17,303	236	6,293 D	38.6%	60.6%	38.9%	61.1%
60,740	WARD 45	32,604	21,641	10,833	130	10,808 R	66.4%	33.2%	66.6%	33.4%
59,848	WARD 46	21,948	7,735	14,056	157	6,321 D	35.2%	64.0%	35.5%	64.5%
60,005	WARD 47	23,743	12,127	11,466	150	661 R	51.1%	48.3%	51.4%	48.6%
60,134	WARD 48	21,951	8,524	13,257	170	4,733 D	38.8%	60.4%	39.1%	60.9%
60,231	WARD 49	22,821	8,073	14,568	180	6,495 D	35.4%	63.8%	35.7%	64.3%
59,916	WARD 50	28,100	11,710	16,234	156	4,524 D	41.7%	57.8%	41.9%	58.1%
	SPECIAL BALLOTS	1,196	492	701	3	209 D	41.1%	58.6%	41.2%	58.8%
3,005,072	TOTAL	1,187,578	409,114	770,612	7,852	361,498 D	34.4%	64.9%	34.7%	65.3%

CHICAGO

SENATOR 1980

1980 Census Population	Ward	Total Vote	Republican	Democratic	Other	Rep.-Dem. Plurality	Percentage			
							Total Vote		Major Vote	
							Rep.	Dem.	Rep.	Dem.
59,725	WARD 1	19,775	5,039	14,474	262	9,435 D	25.5%	73.2%	25.8%	74.2%
60,141	WARD 2	19,102	1,599	17,329	174	15,730 D	8.4%	90.7%	8.4%	91.6%
60,267	WARD 3	18,941	1,271	17,496	174	16,225 D	6.7%	92.4%	6.8%	93.2%
60,051	WARD 4	22,877	2,416	20,247	214	17,831 D	10.6%	88.5%	10.7%	89.3%
60,215	WARD 5	24,442	3,077	21,138	227	18,061 D	12.6%	86.5%	12.7%	87.3%
60,576	WARD 6	30,888	2,313	28,420	155	26,107 D	7.5%	92.0%	7.5%	92.5%
59,906	WARD 7	18,265	2,181	15,883	201	13,702 D	11.9%	87.0%	12.1%	87.9%
59,928	WARD 8	28,132	1,927	26,074	131	24,147 D	6.8%	92.7%	6.9%	93.1%
60,477	WARD 9	21,880	1,974	19,749	157	17,775 D	9.0%	90.3%	9.1%	90.9%
60,133	WARD 10	28,644	8,112	20,148	384	12,036 D	28.3%	70.3%	28.7%	71.3%
60,060	WARD 11	24,582	7,655	16,567	360	8,912 D	31.1%	67.4%	31.6%	68.4%
59,989	WARD 12	22,107	9,728	11,933	446	2,205 D	44.0%	54.0%	44.9%	55.1%
60,420	WARD 13	34,040	16,337	17,161	542	824 D	48.0%	50.4%	48.8%	51.2%
59,825	WARD 14	21,477	8,740	12,330	407	3,590 D	40.7%	57.4%	41.5%	58.5%
60,407	WARD 15	23,119	6,179	16,614	326	10,435 D	26.7%	71.9%	27.1%	72.9%
59,937	WARD 16	21,185	1,261	19,698	226	18,437 D	6.0%	93.0%	6.0%	94.0%
60,144	WARD 17	25,115	1,567	23,374	174	21,807 D	6.2%	93.1%	6.3%	93.7%
59,662	WARD 18	30,803	10,444	19,962	397	9,518 D	33.9%	64.8%	34.3%	65.7%
59,786	WARD 19	33,600	14,878	17,955	767	3,077 D	44.3%	53.4%	45.3%	54.7%
59,981	WARD 20	21,454	1,504	19,802	148	18,298 D	7.0%	92.3%	7.1%	92.9%
60,168	WARD 21	29,194	1,919	27,097	178	25,178 D	6.6%	92.8%	6.6%	93.4%
59,598	WARD 22	8,544	2,408	5,938	198	3,530 D	28.2%	69.5%	28.9%	71.1%
58,596	WARD 23	31,847	16,122	15,148	577	974 R	50.6%	47.6%	51.6%	48.4%
60,003	WARD 24	19,870	1,052	18,656	162	17,604 D	5.3%	93.9%	5.3%	94.7%
59,936	WARD 25	10,716	2,764	7,744	208	4,980 D	25.8%	72.3%	26.3%	73.7%
60,911	WARD 26	14,759	5,007	9,452	300	4,445 D	33.9%	64.0%	34.6%	65.4%
60,110	WARD 27	16,791	1,702	14,921	168	13,219 D	10.1%	88.9%	10.2%	89.8%
61,055	WARD 28	18,161	1,153	16,835	173	15,682 D	6.3%	92.7%	6.4%	93.6%
60,273	WARD 29	17,715	1,609	15,924	182	14,315 D	9.1%	89.9%	9.2%	90.8%
59,498	WARD 30	21,883	11,006	10,429	448	577 R	50.3%	47.7%	51.3%	48.7%
60,879	WARD 31	14,437	4,131	9,734	572	5,603 D	28.6%	67.4%	29.8%	70.2%
61,212	WARD 32	17,355	5,572	11,383	400	5,811 D	32.1%	65.6%	32.9%	67.1%
59,228	WARD 33	17,399	6,490	10,445	464	3,955 D	37.3%	60.0%	38.3%	61.7%
60,091	WARD 34	25,811	1,698	23,943	170	22,245 D	6.6%	92.8%	6.6%	93.4%
59,110	WARD 35	20,453	10,248	9,720	485	528 R	50.1%	47.5%	51.3%	48.7%
59,830	WARD 36	30,708	16,650	13,513	545	3,137 R	54.2%	44.0%	55.2%	44.8%
60,032	WARD 37	19,043	2,989	15,805	249	12,816 D	15.7%	83.0%	15.9%	84.1%
60,618	WARD 38	30,258	16,827	12,878	553	3,949 R	55.6%	42.6%	56.6%	43.4%
60,669	WARD 39	24,269	11,518	12,307	444	789 D	47.5%	50.7%	48.3%	51.7%
59,680	WARD 40	20,627	9,650	10,648	329	998 D	46.8%	51.6%	47.5%	52.5%
60,579	WARD 41	33,393	19,290	13,431	672	5,859 R	57.8%	40.2%	59.0%	41.0%
60,173	WARD 42	29,341	11,843	17,085	413	5,242 D	40.4%	58.2%	40.9%	59.1%
60,156	WARD 43	33,589	13,829	19,210	550	5,381 D	41.2%	57.2%	41.9%	58.1%
60,163	WARD 44	28,254	9,341	18,441	472	9,100 D	33.1%	65.3%	33.6%	66.4%
60,740	WARD 45	32,253	17,688	13,910	655	3,778 R	54.8%	43.1%	56.0%	44.0%
59,848	WARD 46	21,762	6,736	14,661	365	7,925 D	31.0%	67.4%	31.5%	68.5%
60,005	WARD 47	23,424	10,353	12,633	438	2,280 D	44.2%	53.9%	45.0%	55.0%
60,134	WARD 48	21,810	7,538	13,941	331	6,403 D	34.6%	63.9%	35.1%	64.9%
60,231	WARD 49	22,659	7,154	15,097	408	7,943 D	31.6%	66.6%	32.2%	67.8%
59,916	WARD 50	28,005	8,312	19,348	345	11,036 D	29.7%	69.1%	30.1%	69.9%
	SPECIAL BALLOTS	1,165	452	701	12	249 D	38.8%	60.2%	39.2%	60.8%
3,005,072	TOTAL	1,175,923	351,253	807,332	17,338	456,079 D	29.9%	68.7%	30.3%	69.7%

ILLINOIS

CONGRESS

CD	Year	Total Vote	Republican Vote	Republican Candidate	Democratic Vote	Democratic Candidate	Other Vote	Rep.-Dem. Plurality	Total Vote Rep.	Total Vote Dem.	Major Vote Rep.	Major Vote Dem.
1	1984	185,534			177,438	HAYES, CHARLES A.	8,096	177,438 D		95.6%		100.0%
1	1982	177,462	4,820	TALIAFERRO, CHARLES A.	172,641	WASHINGTON, HAROLD	1	167,821 D	2.7%	97.3%	2.7%	97.3%
2	1984	187,215	31,865	HARMAN, DALE F.	155,349	SAVAGE, GUS	1	123,484 D	17.0%	83.0%	17.0%	83.0%
2	1982	161,794	20,670	SPARKS, KEVIN W.	140,827	SAVAGE, GUS	297	120,157 D	12.8%	87.0%	12.8%	87.2%
3	1984	222,582	79,218	MURPHY, RICHARD D.	143,363	RUSSO, MARTIN A.	1	64,145 D	35.6%	64.4%	35.6%	64.4%
3	1982	185,659	48,268	MURPHY, RICHARD D.	137,391	RUSSO, MARTIN A.		89,123 D	26.0%	74.0%	26.0%	74.0%
4	1984	190,291	121,744	O'BRIEN, GEORGE M.	68,547	MARLOW, DENNIS E.		53,197 R	64.0%	36.0%	64.0%	36.0%
4	1982	146,172	79,842	O'BRIEN, GEORGE M.	66,323	MURER, MICHAEL A.	7	13,519 R	54.6%	45.4%	54.6%	45.4%
5	1984	167,708	61,109	PACZKOWSKI, JOHN M.	106,597	LIPINSKI, WILLIAM O.	2	45,488 D	36.4%	63.6%	36.4%	63.6%
5	1982	146,322	35,970	PARTYKA, DANIEL J.	110,351	LIPINSKI, WILLIAM O.	1	74,381 D	24.6%	75.4%	24.6%	75.4%
6	1984	209,562	157,370	HYDE, HENRY J.	52,189	RENSHAW, ROBERT H.	3	105,181 R	75.1%	24.9%	75.1%	24.9%
6	1982	143,168	97,918	HYDE, HENRY J.	45,237	KENNEL, LEROY E.	13	52,681 R	68.4%	31.6%	68.4%	31.6%
7	1984	172,908	37,411	BEVEL, JAMES L.	135,493	COLLINS, CARDISS	4	98,082 D	21.6%	78.4%	21.6%	78.4%
7	1982	154,974	20,994	CHEEKS, DANSBY	133,978	COLLINS, CARDISS	2	112,984 D	13.5%	86.5%	13.5%	86.5%
8	1984	160,417	46,030	GEORGESON, SPIRO F.	114,385	ROSTENKOWSKI, DANIEL	2	68,355 D	28.7%	71.3%	28.7%	71.3%
8	1982	148,985	24,666	HICKEY, BONNIE	124,318	ROSTENKOWSKI, DANIEL	1	99,652 D	16.6%	83.4%	16.6%	83.4%
9	1984	214,495	69,613	SOHN, HERBERT	144,879	YATES, SIDNEY R.	3	75,266 D	32.5%	67.5%	32.5%	67.5%
9	1982	171,529	54,851	BERTINI, CATHERINE	114,083	YATES, SIDNEY R.	2,595	59,232 D	32.0%	66.5%	32.5%	67.5%
10	1984	211,140	153,330	PORTER, JOHN E.	57,809	BRAVER, RUTH C.	1	95,521 R	72.6%	27.4%	72.6%	27.4%
10	1982	153,868	90,750	PORTER, JOHN E.	63,115	CHAPMAN, EUGENIA S.	3	27,635 R	59.0%	41.0%	59.0%	41.0%
11	1984	220,690	82,518	THEUSCH, CHARLES J.	138,171	ANNUNZIO, FRANK	1	55,653 D	37.4%	62.6%	37.4%	62.6%
11	1982	185,722	50,967	MOYNIHAN, JAMES F.	134,755	ANNUNZIO, FRANK		83,788 D	27.4%	72.6%	27.4%	72.6%
12	1984	205,119	159,582	CRANE, PHILIP M.	45,537	LA FLAMME, EDWARD J.		114,045 R	77.8%	22.2%	77.8%	22.2%
12	1982	130,701	86,487	CRANE, PHILIP M.	40,108	DEFOSSE, DANIEL G.	4,106	46,379 R	66.2%	30.7%	68.3%	31.7%
13	1984	235,234	157,603	FAWELL, HARRIS W.	77,623	DONOHUE, MICHAEL J.	8	79,980 R	67.0%	33.0%	67.0%	33.0%
13	1982	162,530	113,423	ERLENBORN, JOHN N.	49,105	BILY, ROBERT	2	64,318 R	69.8%	30.2%	69.8%	30.2%
14	1984	218,738	135,967	GROTBERG, JOHN E.	82,756	MCGRATH, DAN	15	53,211 R	62.2%	37.8%	62.2%	37.8%
14	1982	152,180	98,262	CORCORAN, TOM	53,914	MCGRATH, DAN	4	44,348 R	64.6%	35.4%	64.6%	35.4%
15	1984	203,613	149,096	MADIGAN, EDWARD R.	54,516	HOFFMANN, JOHN M.	1	94,580 R	73.2%	26.8%	73.2%	26.8%
15	1982	158,344	105,038	MADIGAN, EDWARD R.	53,303	HALL, TIM L.	3	51,735 R	66.3%	33.7%	66.3%	33.7%
16	1984	218,538	127,684	MARTIN, LYNN	90,850	SCHWERDTFEGER, CARL R.	4	36,834 R	58.4%	41.6%	58.4%	41.6%
16	1982	156,287	89,405	MARTIN, LYNN	66,877	SCHWERDTFEGER, CARL R.	5	22,528 R	57.2%	42.8%	57.2%	42.8%
17	1984	226,345	98,069	MCMILLAN, KENNETH G.	128,273	EVANS, LANE	3	30,204 D	43.3%	56.7%	43.3%	56.7%
17	1982	178,887	84,347	MCMILLAN, KENNETH G.	94,483	EVANS, LANE	57	10,136 D	47.2%	52.8%	47.2%	52.8%
18	1984	223,106	136,183	MICHEL, ROBERT H.	86,884	BRADLEY, GERALD A.	39	49,299 R	61.0%	38.9%	61.1%	38.9%
18	1982	188,694	97,406	MICHEL, ROBERT H.	91,281	STEPHENS, G. DOUGLAS	7	6,125 R	51.6%	48.4%	51.6%	48.4%
19	1984	225,103	107,463	CRANE, DANIEL B.	117,634	BRUCE, TERRY L.	6	10,171 D	47.7%	52.3%	47.7%	52.3%
19	1982	182,064	94,833	CRANE, DANIEL B.	87,231	GWINN, JOHN		7,602 R	52.1%	47.9%	52.1%	47.9%
20	1984	236,821	91,728	AUSTIN, RICHARD G.	145,092	DURBIN, RICHARD J.	1	53,364 D	38.7%	61.3%	38.7%	61.3%
20	1982	200,109	99,348	FINDLEY, PAUL	100,758	DURBIN, RICHARD J.	3	1,410 D	49.6%	50.4%	49.6%	50.4%
21	1984	211,194	84,148	GAFFNER, ROBERT H.	127,046	PRICE, MELVIN		42,898 D	39.8%	60.2%	39.8%	60.2%
21	1982	140,608	46,764	GAFFNER, ROBERT H.	89,500	PRICE, MELVIN	4,344	42,736 D	33.3%	63.7%	34.3%	65.7%
22	1984	232,728	115,775	PATCHETT, RANDY	116,952	GRAY, KENNETH J.	1	1,177 D	49.7%	50.3%	49.7%	50.3%
22	1982	186,972	63,279	PRINEAS, PETER G.	123,693	SIMON, PAUL		60,414 D	33.8%	66.2%	33.8%	66.2%

ILLINOIS

1984 GENERAL ELECTION

President   Other vote was 10,086 Bergland (Libertarian); 4,672 Hall (Communist); 2,716 Johnson (Citizens); 2,632 Winn (Independent); 2,386 Serrette (Independent); 2,132 Mason (Socialist Workers); 862 scattered.

Senator   Other vote was 59,777 Givot (Libertarian); 12,366 Pries (Citizens); 4,913 Gonzalez (Socialist Workers); 4,802 Flory (Communist); 273 scattered. Original uncorrected returns gave the Democratic vote in St. Clair county as 61,550 and the Democratic total vote as 2,397,165.

Congress   Other vote was 8,086 Warren (Socialist Workers) and 10 scattered in CD 1; scattered in all other CD's.

CHICAGO

President   Other vote was 2,101 Bergland (Libertarian); 1,961 Hall (Communist); 1,062 Mason (Socialist Workers); 1,041 Johnson (Citizens); 1,024 Serrette (Independent); 663 Winn (Independent). Special ballots are absentee votes counted centrally.

Senator   Other vote was 10,096 Givot (Libertarian); 2,849 Gonzalez; 2,427 Pries (Citizens); 1,966 Flory (Communist). Sepcial ballots are absentee votes counted centrally.

1984 PRIMARIES

MARCH 20 REPUBLICAN

Senator   387,865 Charles H. Percy; 239,847 Tom Corcoran; 13,533 John E. Roche; 9,236 V. A. Kelley; 3,607 Richard J. Castic; 45 scattered.

Congress   Unopposed in twelve CD's. No candidate in CD 1. Contested as follows:

CD 3   6,619 Richard D. Murphy; 4,965 Casimir G. Oksas; 2,025 Arthur J. Jones.
CD 7   3,871 James L. Bevel; 2,221 Larry Saska; 1 scattered.
CD 11   5,079 Charles J. Theusch; 4,031 Daniel Schmitt; 1,860 William J. Grutzmacher; 1 scattered.
CD 13   14,058 Harris W. Fawell; 10,731 George Hudson; 10,402 Diana Nelson; 5,582 Mark Q. Rhoads; 2,587 Donna N. Sumanas; 1,570 William M. Snyder; 1,101 Terrance M. Jordan; 717 Stanley S. Borys; 520 Kyle K. Kopitke.
CD 14   16,868 John E. Grotberg; 16,092 Tom Johnson; 12,449 Richard L. Verbic; 5,142 John A. Cunningham; 367 Carl C. Lodico; 1 scattered.
CD 16   39,010 Lynn Martin; 8,817 Kenneth F. Bohnsack.
CD 17   28,320 Kenneth G. McMillan; 5,694 Dan Lee; 5,076 Jack Michalski; 20 scattered.
CD 19   31,650 Daniel B. Crane; 16,068 Max E. Coffey; 5 scattered.
CD 21   6,268 Robert H. Gaffner; 5,220 George Farmer; 2,116 Charles S. —Russell; 863 Maurice Horton.

ILLINOIS

MARCH 20 DEMOCRATIC

Senator 556,757 Paul Simon; 360,182 Roland W. Burris; 327,125 Alex Seith; 303,397 Philip J. Rock; 17,985 Gerald M. Rose; 49 scattered.

Congress Unopposed in five CD's. Contested as follows:

CD 1 93,123 Charles A. Hayes; 18,685 Sheila Jones; 3 scattered.
CD 2 55,137 Gus Savage; 26,868 Glenn V. Dawson; 15,350 Leon Davis; 15,316 Robert Shaw; 9,727 James C. Taylor; 2 scattered.
CD 4 20,264 Dennis E. Marlow; 12,620 Gerald E. Berg; 1 scattered.
CD 5 64,816 William O. Lipinski; 13,693 Suzanne Rose.
CD 6 17,254 Robert H. Renshaw; 4,992 Warren L. Jewel; 3 scattered.
CD 7 46,047 Cardiss Collins; 36,776 Danny K. Davis; 7,242 Joseph N. Gomez; 2,838 E. Denardo Monroe; 2,049 Edward Florence.
CD 8 74,432 Daniel Rostenkowski; 9,877 Gerald Pechenuk.
CD 9 76,685 Sidney R. Yates; 10,042 Michael C. Markovitz; 9,079 James A. Wright.
CD 10 23,846 Ruth C. Braver; 10,421 Mark D. Adams; 2 scattered.
CD 11 94,872 Frank Annunzio; 12,330 Anthony K. Wikrent.
CD 13 22,432 Michael J. Donohue; 6,355 Robert J. Bily; 4,009 Carl N. Schoeppel; 1 scattered.
CD 14 20,256 Dan McGrath; 10,421 Greg Sparrow; 1,622 Eugene Mabeus; 1 scattered.
CD 18 24,242 Gerald A. Bradley; 10,639 Henry G. Jackson; 8,731 William D. Fogal; 11 scattered.
CD 19 19,928 Terry L. Bruce; 16,795 John Gwinn; 10,063 Tom Lindley; 6,949 Eric Jakobsson; 2 scattered.
CD 20 53,588 Richard J. Durbin; 4,363 Louis K Widmar.
CD 21 47,325 Melvin Price; 7,938 Sandra L. Climaco; 6,939 Floyd E. Fessler.
CD 22 43,156 Kenneth J. Gray; 34,095 Ken Buzbee.

INDIANA

GOVERNOR
Robert D. Orr (R). Re-elected 1984 to a four-year term. Previously elected 1980.

SENATORS
Richard G. Lugar (R). Re-elected 1982 to a six-year term. Previously elected 1976.

J. Danforth Quayle (R). Elected 1980 to a six-year term.

REPRESENTATIVES
1. Peter J. Visclosky (D)
2. Philip R. Sharp (D)
3. John P. Hiler (R)
4. Daniel R. Coats (R)
5. Elwood H. Hillis (R)
6. Dan Burton (R)
7. John T. Myers (R)
8. Francis McCloskey (D)
9. Lee H. Hamilton (D)
10. Andrew Jacobs, Jr. (D)

POSTWAR VOTE FOR GOVERNOR

| | | Republican | | Democratic | | Other | Rep.-Dem. | Percentage | | | |
| | | | | | | | | Total Vote | | Major Vote | |
Year	Total Vote	Vote	Candidate	Vote	Candidate	Vote	Plurality	Rep.	Dem.	Rep.	Dem.
1984	2,197,988	1,146,497	Orr, Robert D.	1,036,922	Townsend, W. Wayne	14,569	109,575 R	52.2%	47.2%	52.5%	47.5%
1980	2,178,403	1,257,383	Orr, Robert D.	913,116	Hillenbrand, John A.	7,904	344,267 R	57.7%	41.9%	57.9%	42.1%
1976	2,175,324	1,236,555	Bowen, Otis R.	927,243	Conrad, Larry A.	11,526	309,312 R	56.8%	42.6%	57.1%	42.9%
1972	2,120,847	1,203,903	Bowen, Otis R.	900,489	Welsh, Matthew E.	16,455	303,414 R	56.8%	42.5%	57.2%	42.8%
1968	2,049,072	1,080,271	Whitcomb, Edgar D.	965,816	Rock, Robert L.	2,985	114,455 R	52.7%	47.1%	52.8%	47.2%
1964	2,072,915	901,342	Ristine, Richard O.	1,164,620	Branigin, Roger D.	6,953	263,278 D	43.5%	56.2%	43.6%	56.4%
1960	2,128,965	1,049,540	Parker, Crawford F.	1,072,717	Welsh, Matthew E.	6,708	23,177 D	49.3%	50.4%	49.5%	50.5%
1956	1,954,290	1,086,868	Handley, Harold W.	859,393	Tucker, Ralph	8,029	227,475 R	55.6%	44.0%	55.8%	44.2%
1952	1,931,869	1,075,685	Craig, George N.	841,984	Watkins, John A.	14,200	233,701 R	55.7%	43.6%	56.1%	43.9%
1948	1,652,321	745,892	Creighton, Hobart	884,995	Schricker, Henry F.	21,434	139,103 D	45.1%	53.6%	45.7%	54.3%

POSTWAR VOTE FOR SENATOR

| | | Republican | | Democratic | | Other | Rep.-Dem. | Percentage | | | |
| | | | | | | | | Total Vote | | Major Vote | |
Year	Total Vote	Vote	Candidate	Vote	Candidate	Vote	Plurality	Rep.	Dem.	Rep.	Dem.
1982	1,817,287	978,301	Lugar, Richard G.	828,400	Fithian, Floyd	10,586	149,901 R	53.8%	45.6%	54.1%	45.9%
1980	2,198,376	1,182,414	Quayle, J. Danforth	1,015,962	Bayh, Birch	—	166,452 R	53.8%	46.2%	53.8%	46.2%
1976	2,171,187	1,275,833	Lugar, Richard G.	878,522	Hartke, R. Vance	16,832	397,311 R	58.8%	40.5%	59.2%	40.8%
1974	1,752,978	814,117	Lugar, Richard G.	889,269	Bayh, Birch	49,592	75,152 D	46.4%	50.7%	47.8%	52.2%
1970	1,737,697	866,707	Roudebush, Richard	870,990	Hartke, R. Vance	—	4,283 D	49.9%	50.1%	49.9%	50.1%
1968	2,053,118	988,571	Ruckelshaus, William	1,060,456	Bayh, Birch	4,091	71,885 D	48.1%	51.7%	48.2%	51.8%
1964	2,076,963	941,519	Bontrager, D. Russell	1,128,505	Hartke, R. Vance	6,939	186,986 D	45.3%	54.3%	45.5%	54.5%
1962	1,800,038	894,547	Capehart, Homer E.	905,491	Bayh, Birch	—	10,944 D	49.7%	50.3%	49.7%	50.3%
1958	1,724,598	731,635	Handley, Harold W.	973,636	Hartke, R. Vance	19,327	242,001 D	42.4%	56.5%	42.9%	57.1%
1956	1,963,986	1,084,262	Capehart, Homer E.	871,781	Wickard, Claude	7,943	212,481 R	55.2%	44.4%	55.4%	44.6%
1952	1,946,118	1,020,605	Jenner, William E.	911,169	Schricker, Henry F.	14,344	109,436 R	52.4%	46.8%	52.8%	47.2%
1950	1,598,724	844,303	Capehart, Homer E.	741,025	Campbell, Alex M.	13,396	103,278 R	52.8%	46.4%	53.3%	46.7%
1946	1,347,434	739,809	Jenner, William E.	584,288	Townsend, M. Clifford	23,337	155,521 R	54.9%	43.4%	55.9%	44.1%

INDIANA

Districts Established September 1, 1981

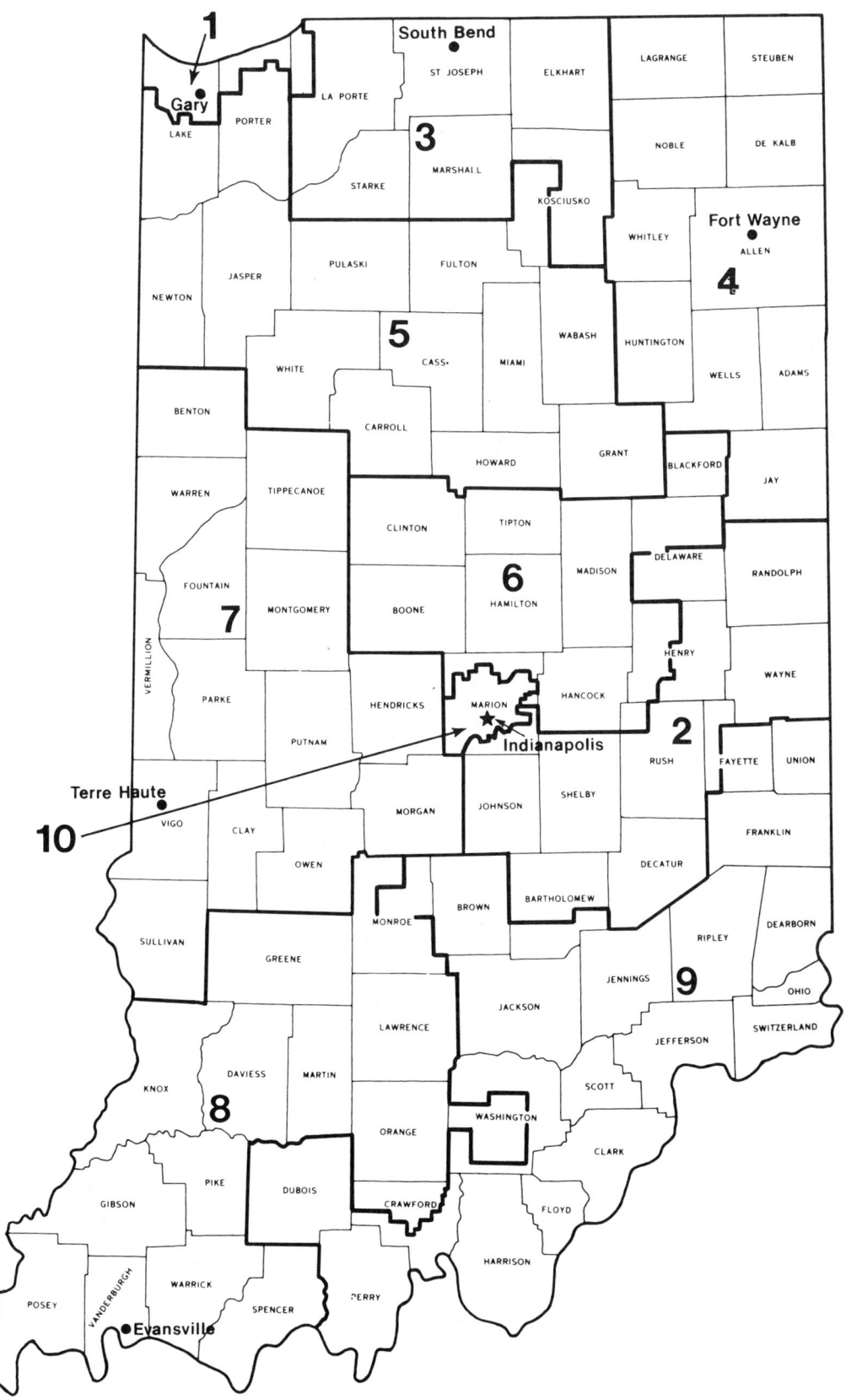

INDIANA

PRESIDENT 1984

1980 Census Population	County	Total Vote	Republican	Democratic	Other	Rep.-Dem. Plurality	Percentage Total Vote Rep.	Dem.	Major Vote Rep.	Dem.
29,619	ADAMS	11,952	7,958	3,923	71	4,035 R	66.6%	32.8%	67.0%	33.0%
294,335	ALLEN	114,975	75,505	38,462	1,008	37,043 R	65.7%	33.5%	66.3%	33.7%
65,088	BARTHOLOMEW	26,970	18,704	8,075	191	10,629 R	69.4%	29.9%	69.8%	30.2%
10,218	BENTON	4,662	3,281	1,357	24	1,924 R	70.4%	29.1%	70.7%	29.3%
15,570	BLACKFORD	6,230	3,787	2,395	48	1,392 R	60.8%	38.4%	61.3%	38.7%
36,446	BOONE	15,850	11,790	3,982	78	7,808 R	74.4%	25.1%	74.8%	25.2%
12,377	BROWN	6,198	3,517	2,657	24	860 R	56.7%	42.9%	57.0%	43.0%
19,722	CARROLL	8,364	5,528	2,774	62	2,754 R	66.1%	33.2%	66.6%	33.4%
40,936	CASS	17,971	12,355	5,521	95	6,834 R	68.7%	30.7%	69.1%	30.9%
88,838	CLARK	33,785	19,419	14,138	228	5,281 R	57.5%	41.8%	57.9%	42.1%
24,862	CLAY	10,725	6,957	3,707	61	3,250 R	64.9%	34.6%	65.2%	34.8%
31,545	CLINTON	13,363	8,969	4,329	65	4,640 R	67.1%	32.4%	67.4%	32.6%
9,820	CRAWFORD	4,910	2,633	2,256	21	377 R	53.6%	45.9%	53.9%	46.1%
27,836	DAVIESS	11,311	7,721	3,545	45	4,176 R	68.3%	31.3%	68.5%	31.5%
34,291	DEARBORN	14,132	9,149	4,920	63	4,229 R	64.7%	34.8%	65.0%	35.0%
23,841	DECATUR	9,363	6,551	2,766	46	3,785 R	70.0%	29.5%	70.3%	29.7%
33,606	DE KALB	13,528	8,769	4,617	142	4,152 R	64.8%	34.1%	65.5%	34.5%
128,587	DELAWARE	50,171	30,092	19,791	288	10,301 R	60.0%	39.4%	60.3%	39.7%
34,238	DUBOIS	14,962	9,391	5,423	148	3,968 R	62.8%	36.2%	63.4%	36.6%
137,330	ELKHART	48,097	34,621	13,240	236	21,381 R	72.0%	27.5%	72.3%	27.7%
28,272	FAYETTE	11,346	7,142	4,122	82	3,020 R	62.9%	36.3%	63.4%	36.6%
61,169	FLOYD	26,279	15,466	10,616	197	4,850 R	58.9%	40.4%	59.3%	40.7%
19,033	FOUNTAIN	8,397	5,450	2,897	50	2,553 R	64.9%	34.5%	65.3%	34.7%
19,612	FRANKLIN	7,472	5,202	2,225	45	2,977 R	69.6%	29.8%	70.0%	30.0%
19,335	FULTON	8,635	6,057	2,527	51	3,530 R	70.1%	29.3%	70.6%	29.4%
33,156	GIBSON	15,777	8,618	7,082	77	1,536 R	54.6%	44.9%	54.9%	45.1%
80,934	GRANT	30,673	20,482	9,986	205	10,496 R	66.8%	32.6%	67.2%	32.8%
30,416	GREENE	13,898	8,438	5,267	193	3,171 R	60.7%	37.9%	61.6%	38.4%
82,027	HAMILTON	36,761	30,254	6,364	143	23,890 R	82.3%	17.3%	82.6%	17.4%
43,939	HANCOCK	17,504	12,880	4,550	74	8,330 R	73.6%	26.0%	73.9%	26.1%
27,276	HARRISON	11,969	7,255	4,634	80	2,621 R	60.6%	38.7%	61.0%	39.0%
69,804	HENDRICKS	28,135	21,307	6,659	169	14,648 R	75.7%	23.7%	76.2%	23.8%
53,336	HENRY	19,062	11,926	7,064	72	4,862 R	62.6%	37.1%	62.8%	37.2%
86,896	HOWARD	33,046	22,386	10,458	202	11,928 R	67.7%	31.6%	68.2%	31.8%
35,596	HUNTINGTON	15,487	10,805	4,598	84	6,207 R	69.8%	29.7%	70.1%	29.9%
36,523	JACKSON	15,234	9,879	5,163	192	4,716 R	64.8%	33.9%	65.7%	34.3%
26,138	JASPER	9,444	6,537	2,821	86	3,716 R	69.2%	29.9%	69.9%	30.1%
23,239	JAY	9,207	5,975	3,174	58	2,801 R	64.9%	34.5%	65.3%	34.7%
30,419	JEFFERSON	12,639	7,482	4,952	205	2,530 R	59.2%	39.2%	60.2%	39.8%
22,854	JENNINGS	9,707	6,356	3,264	87	3,092 R	65.5%	33.6%	66.1%	33.9%
77,240	JOHNSON	31,368	23,482	7,715	171	15,767 R	74.9%	24.6%	75.3%	24.7%
41,838	KNOX	17,459	10,872	6,417	170	4,455 R	62.3%	36.8%	62.9%	37.1%
59,555	KOSCIUSKO	22,547	17,560	4,877	110	12,683 R	77.9%	21.6%	78.3%	21.7%
25,550	LAGRANGE	6,692	4,772	1,884	36	2,888 R	71.3%	28.2%	71.7%	28.3%
522,965	LAKE	214,143	94,870	117,984	1,289	23,114 D	44.3%	55.1%	44.6%	55.4%
108,632	LA PORTE	39,567	23,346	15,904	317	7,442 R	59.0%	40.2%	59.5%	40.5%
42,472	LAWRENCE	17,150	11,440	5,608	102	5,832 R	66.7%	32.7%	67.1%	32.9%
139,336	MADISON	59,014	36,510	22,254	250	14,256 R	61.9%	37.7%	62.1%	37.9%
765,233	MARION	317,148	184,880	130,185	2,083	54,695 R	58.3%	41.0%	58.7%	41.3%
39,155	MARSHALL	16,144	11,100	4,931	113	6,169 R	68.8%	30.5%	69.2%	30.8%
11,001	MARTIN	5,332	3,363	1,937	32	1,426 R	63.1%	36.3%	63.5%	36.5%
39,820	MIAMI	13,892	9,551	4,224	117	5,327 R	68.8%	30.4%	69.3%	30.7%
98,785	MONROE	36,826	21,772	14,719	335	7,053 R	59.1%	40.0%	59.7%	40.3%
35,501	MONTGOMERY	14,834	11,119	3,626	89	7,493 R	75.0%	24.4%	75.4%	24.6%
51,999	MORGAN	19,607	14,884	4,627	96	10,257 R	75.9%	23.6%	76.3%	23.7%
14,844	NEWTON	5,194	3,560	1,596	38	1,964 R	68.5%	30.7%	69.0%	31.0%
35,443	NOBLE	12,867	8,459	4,237	171	4,222 R	65.7%	32.9%	66.6%	33.4%
5,114	OHIO	2,577	1,503	1,068	6	435 R	58.3%	41.4%	58.5%	41.5%
18,677	ORANGE	8,515	5,909	2,571	35	3,338 R	69.4%	30.2%	69.7%	30.3%
15,841	OWEN	6,323	4,204	2,082	37	2,122 R	66.5%	32.9%	66.9%	33.1%

INDIANA

PRESIDENT 1984

1980 Census Population	County	Total Vote	Republican	Democratic	Other	Rep.-Dem. Plurality	Percentage Total Vote Rep.	Total Vote Dem.	Major Vote Rep.	Major Vote Dem.
16,372	PARKE	7,294	5,052	2,205	37	2,847 R	69.3%	30.2%	69.6%	30.4%
19,346	PERRY	9,588	4,785	4,760	43	25 R	49.9%	49.6%	50.1%	49.9%
13,465	PIKE	6,963	3,689	3,231	43	458 R	53.0%	46.4%	53.3%	46.7%
119,816	PORTER	50,682	32,505	17,862	315	14,643 R	64.1%	35.2%	64.5%	35.5%
26,414	POSEY	10,957	6,472	4,452	33	2,020 R	59.1%	40.6%	59.2%	40.8%
13,258	PULASKI	6,226	4,167	2,008	51	2,159 R	66.9%	32.3%	67.5%	32.5%
29,163	PUTNAM	11,272	7,820	3,392	60	4,428 R	69.4%	30.1%	69.7%	30.3%
29,997	RANDOLPH	11,671	7,793	3,805	73	3,988 R	66.8%	32.6%	67.2%	32.8%
24,398	RIPLEY	10,506	7,143	3,336	27	3,807 R	68.0%	31.8%	68.2%	31.8%
19,604	RUSH	7,771	5,429	2,307	35	3,122 R	69.9%	29.7%	70.2%	29.8%
241,617	ST. JOSEPH	102,493	54,404	47,513	576	6,891 R	53.1%	46.4%	53.4%	46.6%
20,422	SCOTT	7,588	4,110	3,460	18	650 R	54.2%	45.6%	54.3%	45.7%
39,887	SHELBY	16,522	11,056	5,357	109	5,699 R	66.9%	32.4%	67.4%	32.6%
19,361	SPENCER	9,846	5,816	4,005	25	1,811 R	59.1%	40.7%	59.2%	40.8%
21,997	STARKE	8,889	5,104	3,674	111	1,430 R	57.4%	41.3%	58.1%	41.9%
24,694	STEUBEN	8,921	6,424	2,441	56	3,983 R	72.0%	27.4%	72.5%	27.5%
21,107	SULLIVAN	8,813	4,771	4,006	36	765 R	54.1%	45.5%	54.4%	45.6%
7,153	SWITZERLAND	3,347	1,857	1,484	6	373 R	55.5%	44.3%	55.6%	44.4%
121,702	TIPPECANOE	45,876	29,706	15,789	381	13,917 R	64.8%	34.4%	65.3%	34.7%
16,819	TIPTON	8,069	5,687	2,328	54	3,359 R	70.5%	28.9%	71.0%	29.0%
6,860	UNION	2,800	1,970	816	14	1,154 R	70.4%	29.1%	70.7%	29.3%
167,515	VANDERBURGH	72,330	40,994	31,049	287	9,945 R	56.7%	42.9%	56.9%	43.1%
18,229	VERMILLION	8,154	4,428	3,666	60	762 R	54.3%	45.0%	54.7%	45.3%
112,385	VIGO	44,973	26,259	18,429	285	7,830 R	58.4%	41.0%	58.8%	41.2%
36,640	WABASH	14,028	9,862	4,077	89	5,785 R	70.3%	29.1%	70.8%	29.2%
8,976	WARREN	3,862	2,525	1,309	28	1,216 R	65.4%	33.9%	65.9%	34.1%
41,474	WARRICK	16,637	10,202	6,345	90	3,857 R	61.3%	38.1%	61.7%	38.3%
21,932	WASHINGTON	9,380	5,874	3,334	172	2,540 R	62.6%	35.5%	63.8%	36.2%
76,058	WAYNE	29,251	18,955	10,173	123	8,782 R	64.8%	34.8%	65.1%	34.9%
25,401	WELLS	10,920	7,579	3,274	67	4,305 R	69.4%	30.0%	69.8%	30.2%
23,867	WHITE	10,499	7,279	3,157	63	4,122 R	69.3%	30.1%	69.7%	30.3%
26,215	WHITLEY	11,551	7,763	3,690	98	4,073 R	67.2%	31.9%	67.8%	32.2%
5,490,224	TOTAL	2,233,069	1,377,230	841,481	14,358	535,749 R	61.7%	37.7%	62.1%	37.9%

INDIANA

GOVERNOR 1984

1980 Census Population	County	Total Vote	Republican	Democratic	Other	Rep.-Dem. Plurality		Percentage Total Vote Rep.	Dem.	Major Vote Rep.	Dem.
29,619	ADAMS	11,959	6,386	5,500	73	886	R	53.4%	46.0%	53.7%	46.3%
294,335	ALLEN	113,508	67,073	45,508	927	21,565	R	59.1%	40.1%	59.6%	40.4%
65,088	BARTHOLOMEW	26,783	15,506	11,086	191	4,420	R	57.9%	41.4%	58.3%	41.7%
10,218	BENTON	4,542	2,396	2,119	27	277	R	52.8%	46.7%	53.1%	46.9%
15,570	BLACKFORD	6,209	2,900	3,265	44	365	D	46.7%	52.6%	47.0%	53.0%
36,446	BOONE	15,715	9,681	5,942	92	3,739	R	61.6%	37.8%	62.0%	38.0%
12,377	BROWN	5,419	2,719	2,657	43	62	R	50.2%	49.0%	50.6%	49.4%
19,722	CARROLL	8,209	4,074	4,097	38	23	D	49.6%	49.9%	49.9%	50.1%
40,936	CASS	17,661	9,796	7,771	94	2,025	R	55.5%	44.0%	55.8%	44.2%
88,838	CLARK	32,574	17,282	15,077	215	2,205	R	53.1%	46.3%	53.4%	46.6%
24,862	CLAY	10,721	5,049	5,618	54	569	D	47.1%	52.4%	47.3%	52.7%
31,545	CLINTON	13,250	7,107	6,103	40	1,004	R	53.6%	46.1%	53.8%	46.2%
9,820	CRAWFORD	4,889	2,331	2,549	9	218	D	47.7%	52.1%	47.8%	52.2%
27,836	DAVIESS	11,195	6,312	4,844	39	1,468	R	56.4%	43.3%	56.6%	43.4%
34,291	DEARBORN	13,352	7,580	5,673	99	1,907	R	56.8%	42.5%	57.2%	42.8%
23,841	DECATUR	9,373	4,962	4,356	55	606	R	52.9%	46.5%	53.3%	46.7%
33,606	DE KALB	13,241	7,444	5,653	144	1,791	R	56.2%	42.7%	56.8%	43.2%
128,587	DELAWARE	49,431	24,789	24,375	267	414	R	50.1%	49.3%	50.4%	49.6%
34,238	DUBOIS	14,570	7,352	7,112	106	240	R	50.5%	48.8%	50.8%	49.2%
137,330	ELKHART	47,620	28,334	19,033	253	9,301	R	59.5%	40.0%	59.8%	40.2%
28,272	FAYETTE	11,034	5,858	5,093	83	765	R	53.1%	46.2%	53.5%	46.5%
61,169	FLOYD	25,804	14,151	11,525	128	2,626	R	54.8%	44.7%	55.1%	44.9%
19,033	FOUNTAIN	8,411	4,551	3,815	45	736	R	54.1%	45.4%	54.4%	45.6%
19,612	FRANKLIN	7,396	4,100	3,214	82	886	R	55.4%	43.5%	56.1%	43.9%
19,335	FULTON	8,581	4,493	4,028	60	465	R	52.4%	46.9%	52.7%	47.3%
33,156	GIBSON	15,726	7,051	8,627	48	1,576	D	44.8%	54.9%	45.0%	55.0%
80,934	GRANT	30,215	16,346	13,680	189	2,666	R	54.1%	45.3%	54.4%	45.6%
30,416	GREENE	13,736	6,751	6,876	109	125	D	49.1%	50.1%	49.5%	50.5%
82,027	HAMILTON	36,079	24,928	10,891	260	14,037	R	69.1%	30.2%	69.6%	30.4%
43,939	HANCOCK	17,224	9,894	7,212	118	2,682	R	57.4%	41.9%	57.8%	42.2%
27,276	HARRISON	11,978	6,708	5,177	93	1,531	R	56.0%	43.2%	56.4%	43.6%
69,804	HENDRICKS	27,842	17,139	10,430	273	6,709	R	61.6%	37.5%	62.2%	37.8%
53,336	HENRY	19,042	9,680	9,289	73	391	R	50.8%	48.8%	51.0%	49.0%
86,896	HOWARD	32,826	17,517	15,068	241	2,449	R	53.4%	45.9%	53.8%	46.2%
35,596	HUNTINGTON	15,318	8,942	6,282	94	2,660	R	58.4%	41.0%	58.7%	41.3%
36,523	JACKSON	14,957	8,123	6,691	143	1,432	R	54.3%	44.7%	54.8%	45.2%
26,138	JASPER	9,097	5,729	3,285	83	2,444	R	63.0%	36.1%	63.6%	36.4%
23,239	JAY	9,187	4,995	4,160	32	835	R	54.4%	45.3%	54.6%	45.4%
30,419	JEFFERSON	12,421	6,135	6,138	148	3	D	49.4%	49.4%	50.0%	50.0%
22,854	JENNINGS	9,421	4,841	4,526	54	315	R	51.4%	48.0%	51.7%	48.3%
77,240	JOHNSON	31,039	18,409	12,415	215	5,994	R	59.3%	40.0%	59.7%	40.3%
41,838	KNOX	16,982	8,591	8,301	90	290	R	50.6%	48.9%	50.9%	49.1%
59,555	KOSCIUSKO	22,361	14,443	7,766	152	6,677	R	64.6%	34.7%	65.0%	35.0%
25,550	LAGRANGE	6,655	3,751	2,870	34	881	R	56.4%	43.1%	56.7%	43.3%
522,965	LAKE	202,559	79,604	121,745	1,210	42,141	D	39.3%	60.1%	39.5%	60.5%
108,632	LA PORTE	39,843	18,327	21,052	464	2,725	D	46.0%	52.8%	46.5%	53.5%
42,472	LAWRENCE	16,853	9,788	6,952	113	2,836	R	58.1%	41.3%	58.5%	41.5%
139,336	MADISON	58,444	30,036	28,159	249	1,877	R	51.4%	48.2%	51.6%	48.4%
765,233	MARION	314,619	165,048	147,049	2,522	17,999	R	52.5%	46.7%	52.9%	47.1%
39,155	MARSHALL	16,012	8,825	7,093	94	1,732	R	55.1%	44.3%	55.4%	44.6%
11,001	MARTIN	5,380	2,560	2,809	11	249	D	47.6%	52.2%	47.7%	52.3%
39,820	MIAMI	13,699	7,548	6,030	121	1,518	R	55.1%	44.0%	55.6%	44.4%
98,785	MONROE	36,168	18,651	17,163	354	1,488	R	51.6%	47.5%	52.1%	47.9%
35,501	MONTGOMERY	14,579	8,749	5,737	93	3,012	R	60.0%	39.4%	60.4%	39.6%
51,999	MORGAN	19,378	11,743	7,484	151	4,259	R	60.6%	38.6%	61.1%	38.9%
14,844	NEWTON	5,131	3,008	2,079	44	929	R	58.6%	40.5%	59.1%	40.9%
35,443	NOBLE	12,623	6,815	5,671	137	1,144	R	54.0%	44.9%	54.6%	45.4%
5,114	OHIO	2,533	1,344	1,176	13	168	R	53.1%	46.4%	53.3%	46.7%
18,677	ORANGE	8,384	5,332	3,004	48	2,328	R	63.6%	35.8%	64.0%	36.0%
15,841	OWEN	6,300	3,192	3,077	31	115	R	50.7%	48.8%	50.9%	49.1%

INDIANA

GOVERNOR 1984

1980 Census Population	County	Total Vote	Republican	Democratic	Other	Rep.-Dem. Plurality	Percentage Total Vote Rep.	Dem.	Major Vote Rep.	Dem.
16,372	PARKE	7,300	3,794	3,474	32	320 R	52.0%	47.6%	52.2%	47.8%
19,346	PERRY	9,533	3,913	5,603	17	1,690 D	41.0%	58.8%	41.1%	58.9%
13,465	PIKE	6,942	2,984	3,922	36	938 D	43.0%	56.5%	43.2%	56.8%
119,816	PORTER	50,293	27,856	22,126	311	5,730 R	55.4%	44.0%	55.7%	44.3%
26,414	POSEY	10,913	5,327	5,543	43	216 D	48.8%	50.8%	49.0%	51.0%
13,258	PULASKI	6,132	3,213	2,861	58	352 R	52.4%	46.7%	52.9%	47.1%
29,163	PUTNAM	11,127	5,818	5,242	67	576 R	52.3%	47.1%	52.6%	47.4%
29,997	RANDOLPH	11,672	6,588	5,012	72	1,576 R	56.4%	42.9%	56.8%	43.2%
24,398	RIPLEY	10,323	5,908	4,387	28	1,521 R	57.2%	42.5%	57.4%	42.6%
19,604	RUSH	7,670	4,008	3,613	49	395 R	52.3%	47.1%	52.6%	47.4%
241,617	ST. JOSEPH	100,538	44,940	55,138	460	10,198 D	44.7%	54.8%	44.9%	55.1%
20,422	SCOTT	7,319	3,508	3,778	33	270 D	47.9%	51.6%	48.1%	51.9%
39,887	SHELBY	16,378	8,868	7,400	110	1,468 R	54.1%	45.2%	54.5%	45.5%
19,361	SPENCER	9,831	5,331	4,481	19	850 R	54.2%	45.6%	54.3%	45.7%
21,997	STARKE	8,714	3,803	4,833	78	1,030 D	43.6%	55.5%	44.0%	56.0%
24,694	STEUBEN	8,770	5,312	3,413	45	1,899 R	60.6%	38.9%	60.9%	39.1%
21,107	SULLIVAN	8,583	3,295	5,261	27	1,966 D	38.4%	61.3%	38.5%	61.5%
7,153	SWITZERLAND	3,217	1,493	1,716	8	223 D	46.4%	53.3%	46.5%	53.5%
121,702	TIPPECANOE	45,513	22,809	22,275	429	534 R	50.1%	48.9%	50.6%	49.4%
16,819	TIPTON	7,945	4,548	3,344	53	1,204 R	57.2%	42.1%	57.6%	42.4%
6,860	UNION	2,755	1,770	964	21	806 R	64.2%	35.0%	64.7%	35.3%
167,515	VANDERBURGH	71,709	36,654	34,758	297	1,896 R	51.1%	48.5%	51.3%	48.7%
18,229	VERMILLION	8,167	3,374	4,744	49	1,370 D	41.3%	58.1%	41.6%	58.4%
112,385	VIGO	44,932	19,505	25,222	205	5,717 D	43.4%	56.1%	43.6%	56.4%
36,640	WABASH	13,900	8,250	5,558	92	2,692 R	59.4%	40.0%	59.7%	40.3%
8,976	WARREN	3,839	2,020	1,797	22	223 R	52.6%	46.8%	52.9%	47.1%
41,474	WARRICK	17,033	8,562	8,393	78	169 R	50.3%	49.3%	50.5%	49.5%
21,932	WASHINGTON	9,079	5,206	3,740	133	1,466 R	57.3%	41.2%	58.2%	41.8%
76,058	WAYNE	28,774	16,717	11,902	155	4,815 R	58.1%	41.4%	58.4%	41.6%
25,401	WELLS	10,950	6,638	4,249	63	2,389 R	60.6%	38.8%	61.0%	39.0%
23,867	WHITE	10,482	5,269	5,158	55	111 R	50.3%	49.2%	50.5%	49.5%
26,215	WHITLEY	11,597	6,447	5,038	112	1,409 R	55.6%	43.4%	56.1%	43.9%
5,490,224	TOTAL	2,197,988	1,146,497	1,036,922	14,569	109,575 R	52.2%	47.2%	52.5%	47.5%

INDIANA

CONGRESS

CD	Year	Total Vote	Republican Vote	Republican Candidate	Democratic Vote	Democratic Candidate	Other Vote	Rep.-Dem. Plurality	Total Vote Rep.	Total Vote Dem.	Major Vote Rep.	Major Vote Dem.
1	1984	207,964	59,986	GRENCHIK, JOSEPH B.	147,035	VISCLOSKY, PETER J.	943	87,049 D	28.8%	70.7%	29.0%	71.0%
1	1982	155,096	66,921	KRIEGER, THOMAS	87,369	HALL, KATIE	806	20,448 D	43.1%	56.3%	43.4%	56.6%
2	1984	222,663	103,061	MACKENZIE, KEN	118,965	SHARP, PHILIP R.	637	15,904 D	46.3%	53.4%	46.4%	53.6%
2	1982	190,891	83,593	VAN NATTA, RALPH	107,298	SHARP, PHILIP R.		23,705 D	43.8%	56.2%	43.8%	56.2%
3	1984	219,752	115,139	HILER, JOHN P.	103,961	BARNES, MICHAEL P.	652	11,178 R	52.4%	47.3%	52.6%	47.4%
3	1982	170,004	86,958	HILER, JOHN P.	83,046	BODINE, RICHARD C.		3,912 R	51.2%	48.8%	51.2%	48.8%
4	1984	213,119	129,674	COATS, DANIEL R.	82,053	BARNARD, MICHAEL H.	1,392	47,621 R	60.8%	38.5%	61.2%	38.8%
4	1982	171,238	110,155	COATS, DANIEL R.	60,054	MILLER, ROGER M.	1,029	50,101 R	64.3%	35.1%	64.7%	35.3%
5	1984	211,355	143,560	HILLIS, ELWOOD H.	66,631	MAXWELL, ALLEN	1,164	76,929 R	67.9%	31.5%	68.3%	31.7%
5	1982	172,707	105,469	HILLIS, ELWOOD H.	67,238	MAXWELL, ALLEN		38,231 R	61.1%	38.9%	61.1%	38.9%
6	1984	245,864	178,814	BURTON, DAN	65,772	CAMPBELL, HOWARD O.	1,278	113,042 R	72.7%	26.8%	73.1%	26.9%
6	1982	201,864	131,100	BURTON, DAN	70,764	GRABIANOWSKI, GEORGE E.		60,336 R	64.9%	35.1%	64.9%	35.1%
7	1984	219,694	147,787	MYERS, JOHN T.	69,097	SMITH, ARTHUR E.	2,810	78,690 R	67.3%	31.5%	68.1%	31.9%
7	1982	186,133	115,884	MYERS, JOHN T.	70,249	BONNEY, STEPHEN S.		45,635 R	62.3%	37.7%	62.3%	37.7%
8	1984	234,092	116,641	MCINTYRE, RICHARD D.	116,645	MCCLOSKEY, FRANCIS	806	4 D	49.8%	49.8%	50.0%	50.0%
8	1982	195,725	94,127	DECKARD, H. JOEL	100,592	MCCLOSKEY, FRANCIS	1,006	6,465 D	48.1%	51.4%	48.3%	51.7%
9	1984	210,340	72,652	COATES, FLOYD E.	137,018	HAMILTON, LEE H.	670	64,366 D	34.5%	65.1%	34.7%	65.3%
9	1982	180,539	58,532	COATES, FLOYD E.	121,094	HAMILTON, LEE H.	913	62,562 D	32.4%	67.1%	32.6%	67.4%
10	1984	195,493	79,342	WATKINS, JOSEPH P.	115,274	JACOBS, ANDREW, JR.	877	35,932 D	40.6%	59.0%	40.8%	59.2%
10	1982	171,863	56,992	CARROLL, MICHAEL	114,674	JACOBS, ANDREW, JR.	197	57,682 D	33.2%	66.7%	33.2%	66.8%

INDIANA

1984 GENERAL ELECTION

President   Other vote was 7,617 Dennis (American); 6,741 Bergland (Libertarian).

Governor   Other vote was 7,455 Snyder (American); 7,114 Ridenour (Libertarian).

Congress   In CD 8 the vote given is the final re-count figure accepted by the U. S. House of Representatives. Other vote was Willis (Libertarian) in CD 1; Bohanan (Libertarian) in CD 2; Lutton (Libertarian) in CD 3; 858 Cameron (American) and 534 Laiacona (Libertarian) in CD 4; Osterfeld (Libertarian) in CD 5; Dilk (Libertarian) in CD 6; Bourland (Libertarian) in CD 7; Fallahay (Libertarian) in CD 8; Boggs (Libertarian) in CD 9; Warren (Libertarian) in CD 10.

1984 PRIMARIES

MAY 8 REPUBLICAN

Governor   319,889 Robert D. Orr; 126,778 John Snyder.

Congress   Unopposed in five CD's. Contested as follows:

CD 1   4,084 Joseph B. Grenchik; 3,299 A. F. Harrigan; 2,456 Owen W. Crumpacker; 2,090 Thomas H. Krieger; 1,168 William D. Cathey; 781 James K. Olson; 527 James E. Stone; 449 Daniel C. Langmesser; 449 Thaddeus Romanowski; 330 John F. Drac; 116 Damian J. Santay.
CD 2   31,106 Ken MacKenzie; 23,741 William G. Frazier.
CD 8   24,267 Richard D. McIntyre; 19,857 Jim Ludwyck; 4,366 Dave Waggoner.
CD 9   18,632 Floyd E. Coates; 6,591 James H. Logan.
CD 10   17,804 Joseph P. Watkins; 9,227 F. Perry Ray.

MAY 8 DEMOCRATIC

Governor   347,948 W. Wayne Townsend; 219,806 Virginia D. McCarty; 43,507 Donald W. Mantooth.

Congress   Contested as follows:

CD 1   44,713 Peter J. Visclosky; 42,345 Katie Hall; 40,776 Jack F. Crawford; 1,901 Sandra K. Smith.
CD 2   47,702 Philip R. Sharp; 2,792 Robert L. Murphy; 1,584 Milford Jones.
CD 3   33,392 Michael P. Barnes; 20,093 Steven Ross; 9,006 David M. Barrett; 2,822 Jerry Bolinger.
CD 4   33,352 Michael H. Barnard; 4,698 Michael E. Highlen; 3,915 Phillip D. Beachy.
CD 5   24,454 Allen Maxwell; 16,882 Donald L. Moseley; 3,808 Nikolaos A. Halkides.
CD 6   17,161 Howard O. Campbell; 9,492 Walter Pearson; 5,471 Virgil Hunt; 5,361 Robert R. Hunt; 4,634 Parker Lacy; 2,083 Henry G. Nunnery.
CD 7   34,112 Arthur E. Smith; 15,399 Carl Richard Greening; 5,668 Jamil J. Salfity.
CD 8   63,981 Francis McCloskey; 8,346 Vernon E. Hills.
CD 9   73,021 Lee H. Hamilton; 4,044 Phil S. Gillispie; 3,444 Raymond J. Finley.
CD 10   47,232 Andrew Jacobs, Jr.; 2,597 Benson D. Skelton.

IOWA

GOVERNOR
Terry E. Branstad (R). Elected 1982 to a four-year term.

SENATORS
Charles E. Grassley (R). Elected 1980 to a six-year term.

Tom Harkin (D). Elected 1984 to a six-year term.

REPRESENTATIVES

1. James A. Leach (R)	3. Cooper Evans (R)	5. Jim R. Lightfoot (R)
2. Tom Tauke (R)	4. Neal Smith (D)	6. Berkley Bedell (D)

POSTWAR VOTE FOR GOVERNOR

Year	Total Vote	Republican Vote	Candidate	Democratic Vote	Candidate	Other Vote	Rep.-Dem. Plurality	Percentage Total Vote Rep.	Dem.	Major Vote Rep.	Dem.
1982	1,038,229	548,313	Branstad, Terry E.	483,291	Conlin, Roxanne	6,625	65,022 R	52.8%	46.5%	53.2%	46.8%
1978	843,190	491,713	Ray, Robert	345,519	Fitzgerald, Jerome D.	5,958	146,194 R	58.3%	41.0%	58.7%	41.3%
1974*	920,458	534,518	Ray, Robert	377,553	Schaben, James. F.	8,387	156,965 R	58.1%	41.0%	58.6%	41.4%
1972	1,210,222	707,177	Ray, Robert	487,282	Franzenburg, Paul	15,763	219,895 R	58.4%	40.3%	59.2%	40.8%
1970	791,241	403,394	Ray, Robert	368,911	Fulton, Robert	18,936	34,483 R	51.0%	46.6%	52.2%	47.8%
1968	1,136,489	614,328	Ray, Robert	521,216	Franzenburg, Paul	945	93,112 R	54.1%	45.9%	54.1%	45.9%
1966	893,175	394,518	Murray, William G.	494,259	Hughes, Harold E.	4,398	99,741 D	44.2%	55.3%	44.4%	55.6%
1964	1,167,734	365,131	Hultman, Evan	794,610	Hughes, Harold E.	7,993	429,479 D	31.3%	68.0%	31.5%	68.5%
1962	819,854	388,955	Erbe, Norman A.	430,899	Hughes, Harold E.	—	41,944 D	47.4%	52.6%	47.4%	52.6%
1960	1,237,089	645,026	Erbe, Norman A.	592,063	McManus, E. J.	—	52,963 R	52.1%	47.9%	52.1%	47.9%
1958	859,095	394,071	Murray, William G.	465,024	Loveless, Herschel C.	—	70,953 D	45.9%	54.1%	45.9%	54.1%
1956	1,204,235	587,383	Hoegh, Leo A.	616,852	Loveless, Herschel C.	—	29,469 D	48.8%	51.2%	48.8%	51.2%
1954	848,592	435,944	Hoegh, Leo A.	410,255	Herring, Clyde E.	2,393	25,689 R	51.4%	48.3%	51.5%	48.5%
1952	1,230,045	638,388	Beardsley, William	587,671	Loveless, Herschel C.	3,986	50,717 R	51.9%	47.8%	52.1%	47.9%
1950	857,213	506,642	Beardsley, William	347,176	Gillette, Lester S.	3,395	159,466 R	59.1%	40.5%	59.3%	40.7%
1948	994,833	553,900	Beardsley, William	434,432	Switzer, Carroll O.	6,501	119,468 R	55.7%	43.7%	56.0%	44.0%
1946	631,681	362,592	Blue, Robert D.	266,190	Miles, Frank	2,899	96,402 R	57.4%	42.1%	57.7%	42.3%

The term of office of Iowa's Governor was increased from two to four years effective with the 1974 election.

POSTWAR VOTE FOR SENATOR

Year	Total Vote	Republican Vote	Candidate	Democratic Vote	Candidate	Other Vote	Rep.-Dem. Plurality	Percentage Total Vote Rep.	Dem.	Major Vote Rep.	Dem.
1984	1,292,700	564,381	Jepsen, Roger W.	716,883	Harkin, Tom	11,436	152,502 D	43.7%	55.5%	44.0%	56.0%
1980	1,277,034	683,014	Grassley, Charles E.	581,545	Culver, John C.	12,475	101,469 R	53.5%	45.5%	54.0%	46.0%
1978	824,654	421,598	Jepsen, Roger W.	395,066	Clark, Richard	7,990	26,532 R	51.1%	47.9%	51.6%	48.4%
1974	889,561	420,546	Stanley, David M.	462,947	Culver, John C.	6,068	42,401 D	47.3%	52.0%	47.6%	52.4%
1972	1,203,333	530,525	Miller, Jack	662,637	Clark, Richard	10,171	132,112 D	44.1%	55.1%	44.5%	55.5%
1968	1,144,086	568,469	Stanley, David M.	574,884	Hughes, Harold E.	733	6,415 D	49.7%	50.2%	49.7%	50.3%
1966	857,496	522,339	Miller, Jack	324,114	Smith, E. B.	11,043	198,225 R	60.9%	37.8%	61.7%	38.3%
1962	807,972	431,364	Hickenlooper, Bourke B.	376,602	Smith, E. B.	6	54,762 R	53.4%	46.6%	53.4%	46.6%
1960	1,237,582	642,463	Miller, Jack	595,119	Loveless, Herschel C.	--	47,344 R	51.9%	48.1%	51.9%	48.1%
1956	1,178,655	635,499	Hickenlooper, Bourke B.	543,156	Evans, R. M.	--	92,343 R	53.9%	46.1%	53.9%	46.1%
1954	847,355	442,409	Martin, Thomas E.	402,712	Gillette, Guy	2,234	39,697 R	52.2%	47.5%	52.3%	47.7%
1950	858,523	470,613	Hickenlooper, Bourke B.	383,766	Loveland, A. J.	4,144	86,847 R	54.8%	44.7%	55.1%	44.9%
1948	1,000,412	415,778	Wilson, George A.	578,226	Gillette, Guy	6,408	162,448 D	41.6%	57.8%	41.8%	58.2%

175

IOWA

Districts Established August 20, 1981

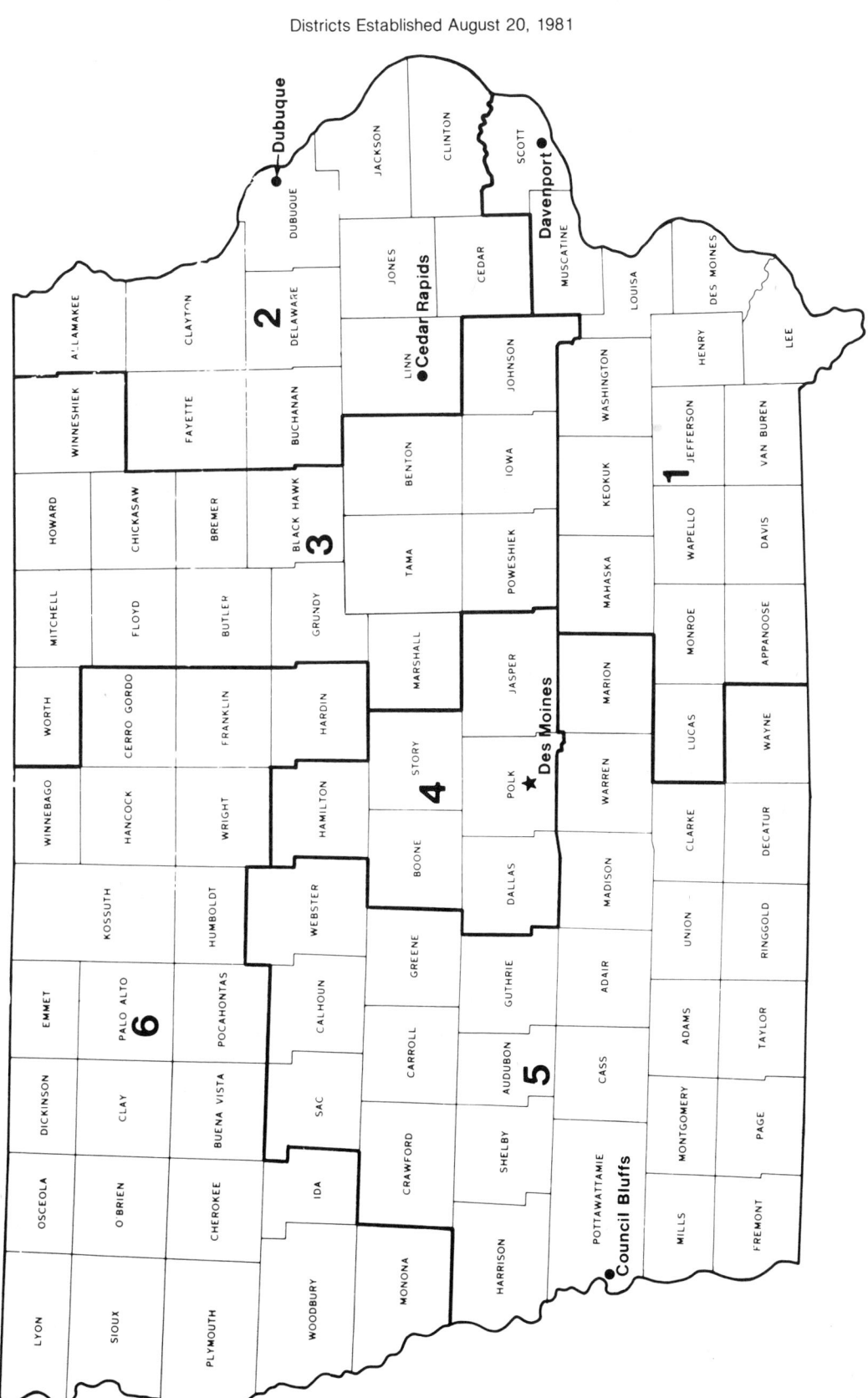

© ERC

IOWA

PRESIDENT 1984

1980 Census Population	County	Total Vote	Republican	Democratic	Other	Rep.-Dem. Plurality	Percentage Total Vote Rep.	Dem.	Major Vote Rep.	Dem.
9,509	ADAIR	4,619	2,615	1,979	25	636 R	56.6%	42.8%	56.9%	43.1%
5,731	ADAMS	2,960	1,706	1,221	33	485 R	57.6%	41.3%	58.3%	41.7%
15,108	ALLAMAKEE	6,354	3,997	2,282	75	1,715 R	62.9%	35.9%	63.7%	36.3%
15,511	APPANOOSE	6,759	3,412	3,289	58	123 R	50.5%	48.7%	50.9%	49.1%
8,559	AUDUBON	4,195	2,306	1,854	35	452 R	55.0%	44.2%	55.4%	44.6%
23,649	BENTON	10,678	5,566	4,993	119	573 R	52.1%	46.8%	52.7%	47.3%
137,961	BLACK HAWK	64,233	32,262	31,467	504	795 R	50.2%	49.0%	50.6%	49.4%
26,184	BOONE	12,277	5,746	6,485	46	739 D	46.8%	52.8%	47.0%	53.0%
24,820	BREMER	11,055	6,895	4,084	76	2,811 R	62.4%	36.9%	62.8%	37.2%
22,900	BUCHANAN	9,152	4,965	4,129	58	836 R	54.3%	45.1%	54.6%	45.4%
20,774	BUENA VISTA	9,405	5,193	4,109	103	1,084 R	55.2%	43.7%	55.8%	44.2%
17,668	BUTLER	6,924	4,570	2,323	31	2,247 R	66.0%	33.5%	66.3%	33.7%
13,542	CALHOUN	5,898	3,311	2,541	46	770 R	56.1%	43.1%	56.6%	43.4%
22,951	CARROLL	10,077	5,021	4,960	96	61 R	49.8%	49.2%	50.3%	49.7%
16,932	CASS	7,531	5,053	2,417	61	2,636 R	67.1%	32.1%	67.6%	32.4%
18,635	CEDAR	7,748	4,617	3,086	45	1,531 R	59.6%	39.8%	59.9%	40.1%
48,458	CERRO GORDO	22,950	11,214	11,570	166	356 D	48.9%	50.4%	49.2%	50.8%
16,238	CHEROKEE	7,470	4,046	3,349	75	697 R	54.2%	44.8%	54.7%	45.3%
15,437	CHICKASAW	6,917	3,661	3,186	70	475 R	52.9%	46.1%	53.5%	46.5%
8,612	CLARKE	4,321	2,262	2,030	29	232 R	52.3%	47.0%	52.7%	47.3%
19,576	CLAY	8,316	4,450	3,774	92	676 R	53.5%	45.4%	54.1%	45.9%
21,098	CLAYTON	8,553	5,029	3,446	78	1,583 R	58.8%	40.3%	59.3%	40.7%
57,122	CLINTON	25,404	13,914	11,240	250	2,674 R	54.8%	44.2%	55.3%	44.7%
18,935	CRAWFORD	8,053	4,552	3,396	105	1,156 R	56.5%	42.2%	57.3%	42.7%
29,513	DALLAS	12,707	6,080	6,564	63	484 D	47.8%	51.7%	48.1%	51.9%
9,104	DAVIS	4,182	1,956	2,187	39	231 D	46.8%	52.3%	47.2%	52.8%
9,794	DECATUR	4,242	2,104	2,098	40	6 R	49.6%	49.5%	50.1%	49.9%
18,933	DELAWARE	8,001	4,769	3,158	74	1,611 R	59.6%	39.5%	60.2%	39.8%
46,203	DES MOINES	20,850	9,559	11,173	118	1,614 D	45.8%	53.6%	46.1%	53.9%
15,629	DICKINSON	7,170	4,064	3,025	81	1,039 R	56.7%	42.2%	57.3%	42.7%
93,745	DUBUQUE	41,491	19,239	21,876	376	2,637 D	46.4%	52.7%	46.8%	53.2%
13,336	EMMET	5,725	2,946	2,746	33	200 R	51.5%	48.0%	51.8%	48.2%
25,488	FAYETTE	11,302	6,505	4,677	120	1,828 R	57.6%	41.4%	58.2%	41.8%
19,597	FLOYD	8,553	4,341	4,154	58	187 R	50.8%	48.6%	51.1%	48.9%
13,036	FRANKLIN	5,545	3,129	2,349	67	780 R	56.4%	42.4%	57.1%	42.9%
9,401	FREMONT	4,147	2,686	1,426	35	1,260 R	64.8%	34.4%	65.3%	34.7%
12,119	GREENE	5,554	2,579	2,831	144	252 D	46.4%	51.0%	47.7%	52.3%
14,366	GRUNDY	6,518	4,527	1,915	76	2,612 R	69.5%	29.4%	70.3%	29.7%
11,983	GUTHRIE	5,363	2,783	2,517	63	266 R	51.9%	46.9%	52.5%	47.5%
17,862	HAMILTON	7,695	4,279	3,330	86	949 R	55.6%	43.3%	56.2%	43.8%
13,833	HANCOCK	5,938	3,362	2,539	37	823 R	56.6%	42.8%	57.0%	43.0%
21,776	HARDIN	9,732	5,195	4,477	60	718 R	53.4%	46.0%	53.7%	46.3%
16,348	HARRISON	6,882	4,352	2,495	35	1,857 R	63.2%	36.3%	63.6%	36.4%
18,890	HENRY	7,955	4,516	3,377	62	1,139 R	56.8%	42.5%	57.2%	42.8%
11,114	HOWARD	4,898	2,718	2,135	45	583 R	55.5%	43.6%	56.0%	44.0%
12,246	HUMBOLDT	5,863	3,396	2,406	61	990 R	57.9%	41.0%	58.5%	41.5%
8,908	IDA	4,202	2,618	1,559	25	1,059 R	62.3%	37.1%	62.7%	37.3%
15,429	IOWA	7,251	4,352	2,815	84	1,537 R	60.0%	38.8%	60.7%	39.3%
22,503	JACKSON	9,340	4,811	4,400	129	411 R	51.5%	47.1%	52.2%	47.8%
36,425	JASPER	16,699	8,576	8,023	100	553 R	51.4%	48.0%	51.7%	48.3%
16,316	JEFFERSON	7,725	4,727	2,961	37	1,766 R	61.2%	38.3%	61.5%	38.5%
81,717	JOHNSON	45,044	18,677	26,000	367	7,323 D	41.5%	57.7%	41.8%	58.2%
20,401	JONES	8,791	4,907	3,825	59	1,082 R	55.8%	43.5%	56.2%	43.8%
12,921	KEOKUK	5,656	2,913	2,649	94	264 R	51.5%	46.8%	52.4%	47.6%
21,891	KOSSUTH	9,814	4,872	4,838	104	34 R	49.6%	49.3%	50.2%	49.8%
43,106	LEE	17,809	8,756	8,912	141	156 D	49.2%	50.0%	49.6%	50.4%
169,775	LINN	80,315	41,061	38,528	726	2,533 R	51.1%	48.0%	51.6%	48.4%
12,055	LOUISA	4,573	2,623	1,927	23	696 R	57.4%	42.1%	57.6%	42.4%
10,313	LUCAS	5,085	2,630	2,422	33	208 R	51.7%	47.6%	52.1%	47.9%
12,896	LYON	5,642	4,178	1,401	63	2,777 R	74.1%	24.8%	74.9%	25.1%

IOWA

PRESIDENT 1984

1980 Census Population	County	Total Vote	Republican	Democratic	Other	Rep.-Dem. Plurality	Percentage Total Vote Rep.	Dem.	Major Vote Rep.	Dem.
12,597	MADISON	6,261	3,168	3,067	26	101 R	50.6%	49.0%	50.8%	49.2%
22,867	MAHASKA	10,293	6,086	4,107	100	1,979 R	59.1%	39.9%	59.7%	40.3%
29,669	MARION	13,634	7,259	6,313	62	946 R	53.2%	46.3%	53.5%	46.5%
41,652	MARSHALL	19,840	10,839	8,809	192	2,030 R	54.6%	44.4%	55.2%	44.8%
13,406	MILLS	5,486	3,994	1,434	58	2,560 R	72.8%	26.1%	73.6%	26.4%
12,329	MITCHELL	5,743	3,144	2,531	68	613 R	54.7%	44.1%	55.4%	44.6%
11,692	MONONA	4,959	2,746	2,159	54	587 R	55.4%	43.5%	56.0%	44.0%
9,209	MONROE	4,291	1,927	2,342	22	415 D	44.9%	54.6%	45.1%	54.9%
13,413	MONTGOMERY	5,930	4,224	1,661	45	2,563 R	71.2%	28.0%	71.8%	28.2%
40,436	MUSCATINE	15,168	9,069	5,986	113	3,083 R	59.8%	39.5%	60.2%	39.8%
16,972	O'BRIEN	7,569	5,008	2,479	82	2,529 R	66.2%	32.8%	66.9%	33.1%
8,371	OSCEOLA	3,463	2,285	1,146	32	1,139 R	66.0%	33.1%	66.6%	33.4%
19,063	PAGE	7,828	5,876	1,914	38	3,962 R	75.1%	24.5%	75.4%	24.6%
12,721	PALO ALTO	5,810	2,715	3,018	77	303 D	46.7%	51.9%	47.4%	52.6%
24,743	PLYMOUTH	10,027	6,482	3,464	81	3,018 R	64.6%	34.5%	65.2%	34.8%
11,369	POCAHONTAS	5,188	2,627	2,481	80	146 R	50.6%	47.8%	51.4%	48.6%
303,170	POLK	147,848	71,413	75,413	1,022	4,000 D	48.3%	51.0%	48.6%	51.4%
86,561	POTTAWATTAMIE	34,112	21,527	12,329	256	9,198 R	63.1%	36.1%	63.6%	36.4%
19,306	POWESHIEK	8,889	4,715	4,103	71	612 R	53.0%	46.2%	53.5%	46.5%
6,112	RINGGOLD	3,117	1,512	1,593	12	81 D	48.5%	51.1%	48.7%	51.3%
14,118	SAC	5,729	3,298	2,363	68	935 R	57.6%	41.2%	58.3%	41.7%
160,022	SCOTT	71,212	38,034	32,550	628	5,484 R	53.4%	45.7%	53.9%	46.1%
15,043	SHEBLY	6,537	4,200	2,291	46	1,909 R	64.2%	35.0%	64.7%	35.3%
30,813	SIOUX	14,293	11,665	2,585	43	9,080 R	81.6%	18.1%	81.9%	18.1%
72,326	STORY	38,410	19,804	18,277	329	1,527 R	51.6%	47.6%	52.0%	48.0%
19,533	TAMA	8,990	4,882	4,061	47	821 R	54.3%	45.2%	54.6%	45.4%
8,353	TAYLOR	4,022	2,496	1,499	27	997 R	62.1%	37.3%	62.5%	37.5%
13,858	UNION	6,576	3,583	2,875	118	708 R	54.5%	43.7%	55.5%	44.5%
8,626	VAN BUREN	3,769	2,138	1,606	25	532 R	56.7%	42.6%	57.1%	42.9%
40,241	WAPELLO	17,800	7,098	10,545	157	3,447 D	39.9%	59.2%	40.2%	59.8%
34,878	WARREN	16,570	8,277	8,171	122	106 R	50.0%	49.3%	50.3%	49.7%
20,141	WASHINGTON	7,770	4,613	3,079	78	1,534 R	59.4%	39.6%	60.0%	40.0%
8,199	WAYNE	4,021	2,061	1,927	33	134 R	51.3%	47.9%	51.7%	48.3%
45,953	WEBSTER	19,802	9,619	9,930	253	311 D	48.6%	50.1%	49.2%	50.8%
13,010	WINNEBAGO	6,314	3,616	2,669	29	947 R	57.3%	42.3%	57.5%	42.5%
21,876	WINNESHIEK	9,105	5,277	3,724	104	1,553 R	58.0%	40.9%	58.6%	41.4%
100,884	WOODBURY	42,350	23,002	18,951	397	4,051 R	54.3%	44.7%	54.8%	45.2%
9,075	WORTH	4,266	1,985	2,263	18	278 D	46.5%	53.0%	46.7%	53.3%
16,319	WRIGHT	6,705	3,675	2,980	50	695 R	54.8%	44.4%	55.2%	44.8%
2,913,808	TOTAL	1,319,805	703,088	605,620	11,097	97,468 R	53.3%	45.9%	53.7%	46.3%

IOWA

SENATOR 1984

1980 Census Population	County	Total Vote	Republican	Democratic	Other	Rep.-Dem. Plurality	Percentage			
							Total Vote		Major Vote	
							Rep.	Dem.	Rep.	Dem.
9,509	ADAIR	4,545	1,777	2,745	23	968 D	39.1%	60.4%	39.3%	60.7%
5,731	ADAMS	2,873	1,283	1,577	13	294 D	44.7%	54.9%	44.9%	55.1%
15,108	ALLAMAKEE	6,130	3,611	2,460	59	1,151 R	58.9%	40.1%	59.5%	40.5%
15,511	APPANOOSE	6,592	2,884	3,651	57	767 D	43.8%	55.4%	44.1%	55.9%
8,559	AUDUBON	4,095	1,660	2,411	24	751 D	40.5%	58.9%	40.8%	59.2%
23,649	BENTON	10,373	4,595	5,603	175	1,008 D	44.3%	54.0%	45.1%	54.9%
137,961	BLACK HAWK	62,912	27,319	35,210	383	7,891 D	43.4%	56.0%	43.7%	56.3%
26,184	BOONE	12,203	4,239	7,917	47	3,678 D	34.7%	64.9%	34.9%	65.1%
24,820	BREMER	10,657	5,603	4,956	98	647 R	52.6%	46.5%	53.1%	46.9%
22,900	BUCHANAN	9,281	4,187	4,910	184	723 D	45.1%	52.9%	46.0%	54.0%
20,774	BUENA VISTA	9,042	3,960	4,999	83	1,039 D	43.8%	55.3%	44.2%	55.8%
17,668	BUTLER	6,795	4,019	2,740	36	1,279 R	59.1%	40.3%	59.5%	40.5%
13,542	CALHOUN	5,782	2,545	3,196	41	651 D	44.0%	55.3%	44.3%	55.7%
22,951	CARROLL	9,811	3,533	6,199	79	2,666 D	36.0%	63.2%	36.3%	63.7%
16,932	CASS	7,281	3,969	3,253	59	716 R	54.5%	44.7%	55.0%	45.0%
18,635	CEDAR	7,701	3,817	3,714	170	103 R	49.6%	48.2%	50.7%	49.3%
48,458	CERRO GORDO	22,398	9,909	12,330	159	2,421 D	44.2%	55.0%	44.6%	55.4%
16,238	CHEROKEE	7,204	2,984	4,137	83	1,153 D	41.4%	57.4%	41.9%	58.1%
15,437	CHICKASAW	6,723	2,993	3,692	38	699 D	44.5%	54.9%	44.8%	55.2%
8,612	CLARKE	4,263	1,584	2,669	10	1,085 D	37.2%	62.6%	37.2%	62.8%
19,576	CLAY	8,038	3,287	4,668	83	1,381 D	40.9%	58.1%	41.3%	58.7%
21,098	CLAYTON	8,313	4,294	3,943	76	351 R	51.7%	47.4%	52.1%	47.9%
57,122	CLINTON	24,904	11,420	13,352	132	1,932 D	45.9%	53.6%	46.1%	53.9%
18,935	CRAWFORD	7,777	3,221	4,429	127	1,208 D	41.4%	56.9%	42.1%	57.9%
29,513	DALLAS	12,890	4,558	8,115	217	3,557 D	35.4%	63.0%	36.0%	64.0%
9,104	DAVIS	4,039	1,622	2,394	23	772 D	40.2%	59.3%	40.4%	59.6%
9,794	DECATUR	4,184	1,473	2,697	14	1,224 D	35.2%	64.5%	35.3%	64.7%
18,933	DELAWARE	7,784	3,855	3,850	79	5 R	49.5%	49.5%	50.0%	50.0%
46,203	DES MOINES	20,438	8,058	12,255	125	4,197 D	39.4%	60.0%	39.7%	60.3%
15,629	DICKINSON	6,939	3,196	3,661	82	465 D	46.1%	52.8%	46.6%	53.4%
93,745	DUBUQUE	39,953	16,064	23,615	274	7,551 D	40.2%	59.1%	40.5%	59.5%
13,336	EMMET	5,470	2,515	2,923	32	408 D	46.0%	53.4%	46.2%	53.8%
25,488	FAYETTE	11,029	5,326	5,604	99	278 D	48.3%	50.8%	48.7%	51.3%
19,597	FLOYD	8,451	3,987	4,422	42	435 D	47.2%	52.3%	47.4%	52.6%
13,036	FRANKLIN	5,391	2,569	2,765	57	196 D	47.7%	51.3%	48.2%	51.8%
9,401	FREMONT	4,020	2,090	1,906	24	184 R	52.0%	47.4%	52.3%	47.7%
12,119	GREENE	5,753	2,020	3,673	60	1,653 D	35.1%	63.8%	35.5%	64.5%
14,366	GRUNDY	6,381	3,942	2,366	73	1,576 R	61.8%	37.1%	62.5%	37.5%
11,983	GUTHRIE	5,302	2,006	3,240	56	1,234 D	37.8%	61.1%	38.2%	61.8%
17,862	HAMILTON	7,648	3,385	4,190	73	805 D	44.3%	54.8%	44.7%	55.3%
13,833	HANCOCK	5,794	3,019	2,736	39	283 R	52.1%	47.2%	52.5%	47.5%
21,776	HARDIN	9,593	4,220	5,290	83	1,070 D	44.0%	55.1%	44.4%	55.6%
16,348	HARRISON	6,736	3,170	3,553	13	383 D	47.1%	52.7%	47.2%	52.8%
18,890	HENRY	7,688	3,740	3,924	24	184 D	48.6%	51.0%	48.8%	51.2%
11,114	HOWARD	5,048	2,504	2,479	65	25 R	49.6%	49.1%	50.3%	49.7%
12,246	HUMBOLDT	5,685	2,631	2,968	86	337 D	46.3%	52.2%	47.0%	53.0%
8,908	IDA	4,057	1,942	2,085	30	143 D	47.9%	51.4%	48.2%	51.8%
15,429	IOWA	7,110	3,669	3,317	124	352 R	51.6%	46.7%	52.5%	47.5%
22,503	JACKSON	8,968	3,898	4,971	99	1,073 D	43.5%	55.4%	44.0%	56.0%
36,425	JASPER	16,471	7,083	9,264	124	2,181 D	43.0%	56.2%	43.3%	56.7%
16,316	JEFFERSON	7,263	3,515	3,726	22	211 D	48.4%	51.3%	48.5%	51.5%
81,717	JOHNSON	44,977	13,576	30,549	852	16,973 D	30.2%	67.9%	30.8%	69.2%
20,401	JONES	8,598	4,154	4,390	54	236 D	48.3%	51.1%	48.6%	51.4%
12,921	KEOKUK	5,543	2,334	3,092	117	758 D	42.1%	55.8%	43.0%	57.0%
21,891	KOSSUTH	9,478	4,025	5,363	90	1,338 D	42.5%	56.6%	42.9%	57.1%
43,106	LEE	17,477	7,331	10,038	108	2,707 D	41.9%	57.4%	42.2%	57.8%
169,775	LINN	80,618	35,447	43,720	1,451	8,273 D	44.0%	54.2%	44.8%	55.2%
12,055	LOUISA	4,480	2,204	2,266	10	62 D	49.2%	50.6%	49.3%	50.7%
10,313	LUCAS	4,926	2,039	2,858	29	819 D	41.4%	58.0%	41.6%	58.4%
12,896	LYON	5,449	3,784	1,634	31	2,150 R	69.4%	30.0%	69.8%	30.2%

IOWA

SENATOR 1984

1980 Census Population	County	Total Vote	Republican	Democratic	Other	Rep.-Dem. Plurality	Percentage			
							Total Vote		Major Vote	
							Rep.	Dem.	Rep.	Dem.
12,597	MADISON	6,161	2,253	3,889	19	1,636 D	36.6%	63.1%	36.7%	63.3%
22,867	MAHASKA	10,157	5,006	4,993	158	13 R	49.3%	49.2%	50.1%	49.9%
29,669	MARION	13,325	5,755	7,475	95	1,720 D	43.2%	56.1%	43.5%	56.5%
41,652	MARSHALL	19,399	8,603	10,568	228	1,965 D	44.3%	54.5%	44.9%	55.1%
13,406	MILLS	5,262	3,162	2,066	34	1,096 R	60.1%	39.3%	60.5%	39.5%
12,329	MITCHELL	5,610	2,929	2,640	41	289 R	52.2%	47.1%	52.6%	47.4%
11,692	MONONA	4,805	2,057	2,709	39	652 D	42.8%	56.4%	43.2%	56.8%
9,209	MONROE	4,160	1,509	2,636	15	1,127 D	36.3%	63.4%	36.4%	63.6%
13,413	MONTGOMERY	5,707	3,350	2,316	41	1,034 R	58.7%	40.6%	59.1%	40.9%
40,436	MUSCATINE	14,921	7,509	7,302	110	207 R	50.3%	48.9%	50.7%	49.3%
16,972	O'BRIEN	7,305	3,962	3,304	39	658 R	54.2%	45.2%	54.5%	45.5%
8,371	OSCEOLA	3,269	1,837	1,412	20	425 R	56.2%	43.2%	56.5%	43.5%
19,063	PAGE	7,575	4,707	2,831	37	1,876 R	62.1%	37.4%	62.4%	37.6%
12,721	PALO ALTO	5,565	2,155	3,343	67	1,188 D	38.7%	60.1%	39.2%	60.8%
24,743	PLYMOUTH	9,643	4,905	4,667	71	238 R	50.9%	48.4%	51.2%	48.8%
11,369	POCAHONTAS	5,053	1,967	3,022	64	1,055 D	38.9%	59.8%	39.4%	60.6%
303,170	POLK	145,193	55,329	88,793	1,071	33,464 D	38.1%	61.2%	38.4%	61.6%
86,561	POTTAWATTAMIE	33,392	16,975	16,161	256	814 R	50.8%	48.4%	51.2%	48.8%
19,306	POWESHIEK	8,715	3,654	4,955	106	1,301 D	41.9%	56.9%	42.4%	57.6%
6,112	RINGGOLD	3,091	1,093	1,991	7	898 D	35.4%	64.4%	35.4%	64.6%
14,118	SAC	5,591	2,480	3,066	45	586 D	44.4%	54.8%	44.7%	55.3%
160,022	SCOTT	69,759	31,381	37,922	456	6,541 D	45.0%	54.4%	45.3%	54.7%
15,043	SHELBY	6,464	3,240	3,198	26	42 R	50.1%	49.5%	50.3%	49.7%
30,813	SIOUX	13,635	10,065	3,540	30	6,525 R	73.8%	26.0%	74.0%	26.0%
72,326	STORY	37,792	14,913	22,615	264	7,702 D	39.5%	59.8%	39.7%	60.3%
19,533	TAMA	8,754	3,885	4,838	31	953 D	44.4%	55.3%	44.5%	55.5%
8,353	TAYLOR	3,942	1,812	2,104	26	292 D	46.0%	53.4%	46.3%	53.7%
13,858	UNION	6,394	2,635	3,722	37	1,087 D	41.2%	58.2%	41.5%	58.5%
8,626	VAN BUREN	3,677	1,786	1,882	9	96 D	48.6%	51.2%	48.7%	51.3%
40,241	WAPELLO	17,439	5,669	11,628	142	5,959 D	32.5%	66.7%	32.8%	67.2%
34,878	WARREN	16,331	5,871	10,331	129	4,460 D	36.0%	63.3%	36.2%	63.8%
20,141	WASHINGTON	7,607	3,741	3,803	63	62 D	49.2%	50.0%	49.6%	50.4%
8,199	WAYNE	3,910	1,410	2,486	14	1,076 D	36.1%	63.6%	36.2%	63.8%
45,953	WEBSTER	19,156	7,100	11,850	206	4,750 D	37.1%	61.9%	37.5%	62.5%
13,010	WINNEBAGO	6,084	3,285	2,782	17	503 R	54.0%	45.7%	54.1%	45.9%
21,876	WINNESHIEK	8,887	4,244	4,541	102	297 D	47.8%	51.1%	48.3%	51.7%
100,884	WOODBURY	40,882	17,632	23,016	234	5,384 D	43.1%	56.3%	43.4%	56.6%
9,075	WORTH	4,150	1,881	2,261	8	380 D	45.3%	54.5%	45.4%	54.6%
16,319	WRIGHT	6,614	2,990	3,565	59	575 D	45.2%	53.9%	45.6%	54.4%
2,913,808	TOTAL	1,292,700	564,381	716,883	11,436	152,502 D	43.7%	55.5%	44.0%	56.0%

IOWA

CONGRESS

CD	Year	Total Vote	Republican Vote	Republican Candidate	Democratic Vote	Democratic Candidate	Other Vote	Rep.-Dem. Plurality	Total Vote Rep.	Total Vote Dem.	Major Vote Rep.	Major Vote Dem.
1	1984	196,489	131,182	LEACH, JAMES A.	65,293	READY, KEVIN	14	65,889 R	66.8%	33.2%	66.8%	33.2%
1	1982	151,332	89,585	LEACH, JAMES A.	61,734	GLUBA, WILLIAM E.	13	27,851 R	59.2%	40.8%	59.2%	40.8%
2	1984	214,255	136,893	TAUKE, TOM	77,335	WELSH, JOE	27	59,558 R	63.9%	36.1%	63.9%	36.1%
2	1982	169,037	99,478	TAUKE, TOM	69,539	APPEL, BRENT	20	29,939 R	58.8%	41.1%	58.9%	41.1%
3	1984	220,375	133,737	EVANS, COOPER	86,574	JOHNSTON, JOE	64	47,163 R	60.7%	39.3%	60.7%	39.3%
3	1982	187,675	104,072	EVANS, COOPER	83,581	CUTLER, LYNN G.	22	20,491 R	55.5%	44.5%	55.5%	44.5%
4	1984	225,674	88,717	LOCKARD, ROBERT R.	136,922	SMITH, NEAL	35	48,205 D	39.3%	60.7%	39.3%	60.7%
4	1982	179,972	60,534	READINGER, DAVE	118,849	SMITH, NEAL	589	58,315 D	33.6%	66.0%	33.7%	66.3%
5	1984	206,072	104,632	LIGHTFOOT, JIM R.	101,435	FITZGERALD, JERRY	5	3,197 R	50.8%	49.2%	50.8%	49.2%
5	1982	158,563	65,200	DANKER, ARLYN E.	93,333	HARKIN, TOM	30	28,133 D	41.1%	58.9%	41.1%	58.9%
6	1984	205,894	78,182	RENSINK, DARREL	127,706	BEDELL, BERKLEY	6	49,524 D	38.0%	62.0%	38.0%	62.0%
6	1982	158,184	56,487	BREMER, AL	101,690	BEDELL, BERKLEY	7	45,203 D	35.7%	64.3%	35.7%	64.3%

IOWA

1984 GENERAL ELECTION

President Other vote was 6,248 LaRouche (by petition); 1,844 Bergland (Libertarian); 892 Baker (Big Deal); 463 Serrette (by petition); 313 Mason (Socialist Workers); 286 Hall (Communist); 1,051 scattered.

Senator Other vote was 11,014 DeYoung (by petition); 422 scattered.

Congress Other vote was scattered in all CD's.

1984 PRIMARIES

JUNE 5 REPUBLICAN

Senator Roger W. Jepsen, unopposed.

Congress Unopposed in three CD's. Contested as follows:

CD 4 6,506 Robert R. Lockard; 3,293 Rich Eychaner; 2,977 Richard R. Vander Mey; 2,361 Scott Hayes; 3 scattered.
CD 5 19,456 Jim R. Lightfoot; 5,461 Dick Redman; 5,130 Arlyn E. Danker; 2,104 Dean Arbuckle; 1,301 Tom Hall; 4 scattered.
CD 6 16,454 Darrel Rensink; 6,974 Garry DeYoung.

JUNE 5 DEMOCRATIC

Senator Tom Harkin, unopposed.

Congress Unopposed in two CD's. Contested as follows:

CD 1 9,217 Kevin Ready; 5,179 John P. Masters; 26 scattered.
CD 2 14,464 Joe Welsh; 5,590 Merle L. Kopel; 13 scattered.
CD 5 15,571 Jerry Fitzgerald; 8,032 Phil Davitt; 3,293 Roger Blobaum.
CD 6 14,860 Berkley Bedell; 2,330 Michael F. Flannegan.

KANSAS

GOVERNOR
John Carlin (D). Re-elected 1982 to a four-year term. Previously elected 1978.

SENATORS
Robert Dole (R). Re-elected 1980 to a six-year term. Previously elected 1974, 1968.

Nancy Landon Kassebaum (R). Re-elected 1984 to a six-year term. Previously elected 1978.

REPRESENTATIVES
1. Pat Roberts (R)
2. Jim Slattery (D)
3. Jan Meyers (R)
4. Dan Glickman (D)
5. Robert Whittaker (R)

POSTWAR VOTE FOR GOVERNOR

Year	Total Vote	Republican Vote	Candidate	Democratic Vote	Candidate	Other Vote	Rep.-Dem. Plurality		Total Vote Rep.	Dem.	Major Vote Rep.	Dem.
1982	763,263	339,356	Hardage, Sam	405,772	Carlin, John	18,135	66,416	D	44.5%	53.2%	45.5%	54.5%
1978	736,246	348,015	Bennett, Robert F.	363,835	Carlin, John	24,396	15,820	D	47.3%	49.4%	48.9%	51.1%
1974*	783,875	387,792	Bennett, Robert F.	384,115	Miller, Vern	11,968	3,677	R	49.5%	49.0%	50.2%	49.8%
1972	921,552	341,440	Kay, Morris	571,256	Docking, Robert	8,856	229,816	D	37.1%	62.0%	37.4%	62.6%
1970	745,196	333,227	Frizzell, Kent	404,611	Docking, Robert	7,358	71,384	D	44.7%	54.3%	45.2%	54.8%
1968	862,473	410,673	Harman, Rick	447,269	Docking, Robert	4,531	36,596	D	47.6%	51.9%	47.9%	52.1%
1966	692,955	304,325	Avery, William H.	380,030	Docking, Robert	8,600	75,705	D	43.9%	54.8%	44.5%	55.5%
1964	850,414	432,667	Avery, William H.	400,264	Wiles, Harry G.	17,483	32,403	R	50.9%	47.1%	51.9%	48.1%
1962	638,798	341,257	Anderson, John	291,285	Saffels, Dale E.	6,256	49,972	R	53.4%	45.6%	54.0%	46.0%
1960	922,522	511,534	Anderson, John	402,261	Docking, George	8,727	109,273	R	55.4%	43.6%	56.0%	44.0%
1958	735,939	313,036	Reed, Clyde M.	415,506	Docking, George	7,397	102,470	D	42.5%	56.5%	43.0%	57.0%
1956	864,935	364,340	Shaw, Warren W.	479,701	Docking, George	20,894	115,361	D	42.1%	55.5%	43.2%	56.8%
1954	622,633	329,868	Hall, Fred	286,218	Docking, George	6,547	43,650	R	53.0%	46.0%	53.5%	46.5%
1952	872,139	491,338	Arn, Edward F.	363,482	Rooney, Charles	17,319	127,856	R	56.3%	41.7%	57.5%	42.5%
1950	619,310	333,001	Arn, Edward F.	275,494	Anderson, Kenneth	10,815	57,507	R	53.8%	44.5%	54.7%	45.3%
1948	760,407	433,396	Carlson, Frank	307,485	Carpenter, Randolph	19,526	125,911	R	57.0%	40.4%	58.5%	41.5%
1946	577,694	309,064	Carlson, Frank	254,283	Woodring, Harry H.	14,347	54,781	R	53.5%	44.0%	54.9%	45.1%

The term of office of Kansas' Governor was increased from two to four years effective with the 1974 election.

POSTWAR VOTE FOR SENATOR

Year	Total Vote	Republican Vote	Candidate	Democratic Vote	Candidate	Other Vote	Rep.-Dem. Plurality		Total Vote Rep.	Dem.	Major Vote Rep.	Dem.
1984	996,729	757,402	Kassebaum, Nancy Landon	211,664	Maher, James	27,663	545,738	R	76.0%	21.2%	78.2%	21.8%
1980	938,957	598,686	Dole, Robert	340,271	Simpson, John	—	258,415	R	63.8%	36.2%	63.8%	36.2%
1978	748,839	403,354	Kassebaum, Nancy Landon	317,602	Roy, William R.	27,883	85,752	R	53.9%	42.4%	55.9%	44.1%
1974	794,437	403,983	Dole, Robert	390,451	Roy, William R.	3	13,532	R	50.9%	49.1%	50.9%	49.1%
1972	871,722	622,591	Pearson, James B.	200,764	Tetzlaff, Arch O.	48,367	421,827	R	71.4%	23.0%	75.6%	24.4%
1968	817,096	490,911	Dole, Robert	315,911	Robinson, William I.	10,274	175,000	R	60.1%	38.7%	60.8%	39.2%
1966	671,345	350,077	Pearson, James B.	303,223	Breeding, J. Floyd	18,045	46,854	R	52.1%	45.2%	53.6%	46.4%
1962	622,232	388,500	Carlson, Frank	223,630	Smith, K. L.	10,102	164,870	R	62.4%	35.9%	63.5%	36.5%
1962s	613,250	344,689	Pearson, James B.	260,756	Aylward, Paul L.	7,805	83,933	R	56.2%	42.5%	56.9%	43.1%
1960	888,592	485,499	Schoeppel, Andrew F.	388,895	Theis, Frank	14,198	96,604	R	54.6%	43.8%	55.5%	44.5%
1956	825,280	477,822	Carlson, Frank	333,939	Hart, George	13,519	143,883	R	57.9%	40.5%	58.9%	41.1%
1954	618,063	348,144	Schoeppel, Andrew F.	258,575	McGill, George	11,344	89,569	R	56.3%	41.8%	57.4%	42.6%
1950	619,104	335,880	Carlson, Frank	271,365	Aiken, Paul	11,859	64,515	R	54.3%	43.8%	55.3%	44.7%
1948	716,342	393,412	Schoeppel, Andrew F.	305,987	McGill, George	16,943	87,425	R	54.9%	42.7%	56.3%	43.7%

One of the 1962 elections was for a short term to fill a vacancy.

KANSAS

Districts Established June 2, 1982

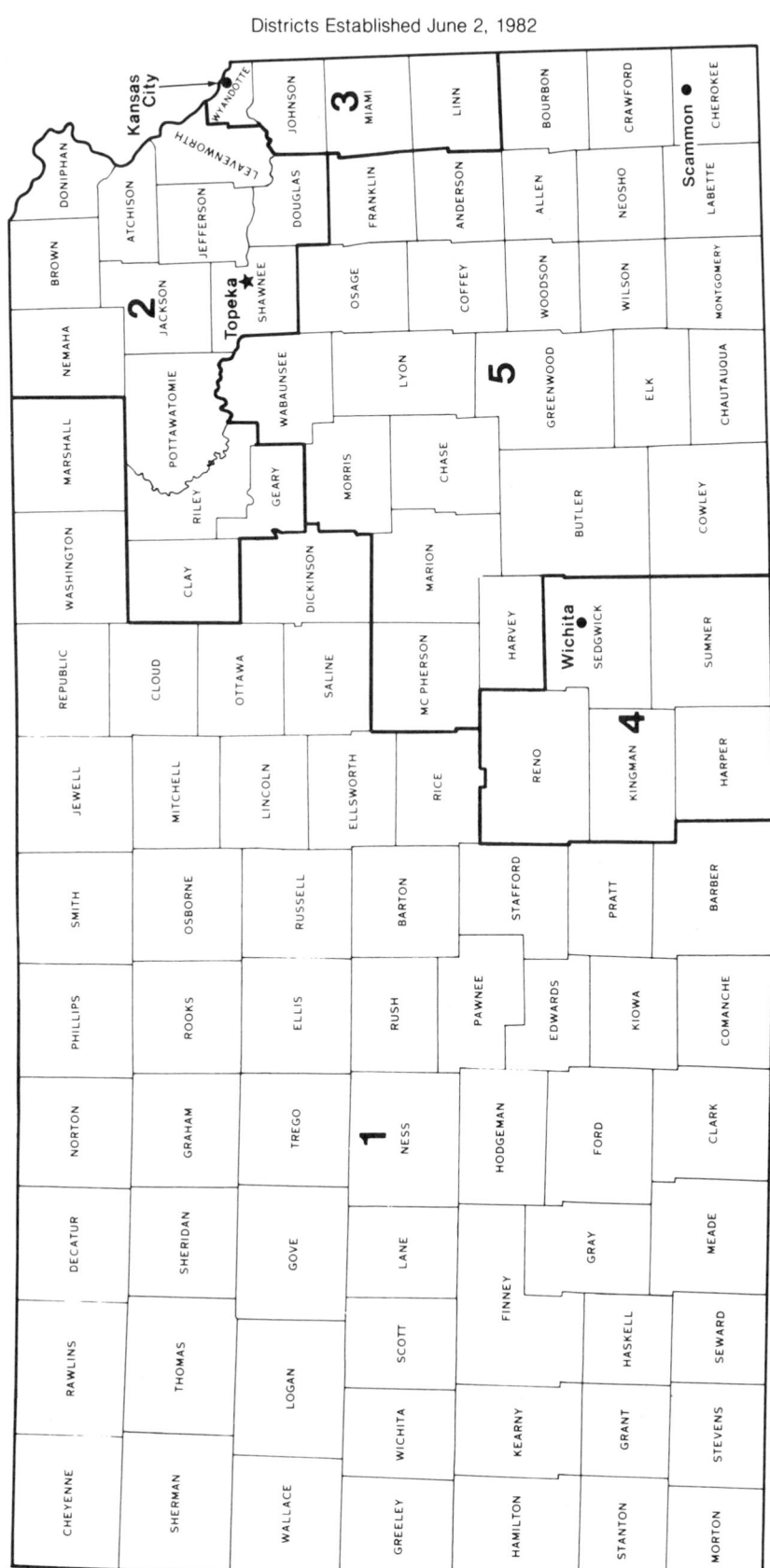

© ERC

KANSAS

PRESIDENT 1984

1980 Census Population	County	Total Vote	Republican	Democratic	Other	Rep.-Dem. Plurality	Percentage Total Vote Rep.	Dem.	Major Vote Rep.	Dem.
15,654	ALLEN	6,117	4,267	1,778	72	2,489 R	69.8%	29.1%	70.6%	29.4%
8,749	ANDERSON	3,667	2,462	1,155	50	1,307 R	67.1%	31.5%	68.1%	31.9%
18,397	ATCHISON	7,255	4,537	2,641	77	1,896 R	62.5%	36.4%	63.2%	36.8%
6,548	BARBER	2,940	2,112	806	22	1,306 R	71.8%	27.4%	72.4%	27.6%
31,343	BARTON	13,538	10,232	3,111	195	7,121 R	75.6%	23.0%	76.7%	23.3%
15,969	BOURBON	7,102	4,858	2,175	69	2,683 R	68.4%	30.6%	69.1%	30.9%
11,955	BROWN	5,264	3,894	1,303	67	2,591 R	74.0%	24.8%	74.9%	25.1%
44,782	BUTLER	19,564	12,976	6,371	217	6,605 R	66.3%	32.6%	67.1%	32.9%
3,309	CHASE	1,570	1,162	393	15	769 R	74.0%	25.0%	74.7%	25.3%
5,016	CHAUTAUQUA	2,205	1,688	497	20	1,191 R	76.6%	22.5%	77.3%	22.7%
22,304	CHEROKEE	9,553	5,801	3,663	89	2,138 R	60.7%	38.3%	61.3%	38.7%
3,678	CHEYENNE	1,824	1,442	356	26	1,086 R	79.1%	19.5%	80.2%	19.8%
2,599	CLARK	1,426	1,075	324	27	751 R	75.4%	22.7%	76.8%	23.2%
9,802	CLAY	4,519	3,559	919	41	2,640 R	78.8%	20.3%	79.5%	20.5%
12,494	CLOUD	5,811	3,860	1,880	71	1,980 R	66.4%	32.4%	67.2%	32.8%
9,370	COFFEY	4,139	3,063	1,037	39	2,026 R	74.0%	25.1%	74.7%	25.3%
2,554	COMANCHE	1,293	993	285	15	708 R	76.8%	22.0%	77.7%	22.3%
36,824	COWLEY	15,399	10,008	5,193	198	4,815 R	65.0%	33.7%	65.8%	34.2%
37,916	CRAWFORD	16,381	9,518	6,722	141	2,796 R	58.1%	41.0%	58.6%	41.4%
4,509	DECATUR	2,265	1,770	467	28	1,303 R	78.1%	20.6%	79.1%	20.9%
20,175	DICKINSON	8,771	6,487	2,168	116	4,319 R	74.0%	24.7%	75.0%	25.0%
9,268	DONIPHAN	3,820	2,818	962	40	1,856 R	73.8%	25.2%	74.6%	25.4%
67,640	DOUGLAS	32,233	18,975	12,880	378	6,095 R	58.9%	40.0%	59.6%	40.4%
4,271	EDWARDS	2,002	1,352	606	44	746 R	67.5%	30.3%	69.1%	30.9%
3,918	ELK	1,785	1,301	452	32	849 R	72.9%	25.3%	74.2%	25.8%
26,098	ELLIS	11,099	7,509	3,457	133	4,052 R	67.7%	31.1%	68.5%	31.5%
6,640	ELLSWORTH	3,298	2,353	905	40	1,448 R	71.3%	27.4%	72.2%	27.8%
23,825	FINNEY	9,494	6,938	2,458	98	4,480 R	73.1%	25.9%	73.8%	26.2%
24,315	FORD	9,947	6,935	2,914	98	4,021 R	69.7%	29.3%	70.4%	29.6%
22,062	FRANKLIN	8,899	6,284	2,523	92	3,761 R	70.6%	28.4%	71.4%	28.6%
29,852	GEARY	6,821	4,464	2,296	61	2,168 R	65.4%	33.7%	66.0%	34.0%
3,726	GOVE	1,784	1,310	426	48	884 R	73.4%	23.9%	75.5%	24.5%
3,995	GRAHAM	1,923	1,423	480	20	943 R	74.0%	25.0%	74.8%	25.2%
6,977	GRANT	2,679	2,043	615	21	1,428 R	76.3%	23.0%	76.9%	23.1%
5,138	GRAY	2,126	1,580	514	32	1,066 R	74.3%	24.2%	75.5%	24.5%
1,845	GREELEY	954	699	227	28	472 R	73.3%	23.8%	75.5%	24.5%
8,764	GREENWOOD	4,118	2,901	1,173	44	1,728 R	70.4%	28.5%	71.2%	28.8%
2,514	HAMILTON	1,468	1,037	408	23	629 R	70.6%	27.8%	71.8%	28.2%
7,778	HARPER	3,449	2,521	893	35	1,628 R	73.1%	25.9%	73.8%	26.2%
30,531	HARVEY	13,280	8,507	4,599	174	3,908 R	64.1%	34.6%	64.9%	35.1%
3,814	HASKELL	1,452	1,152	283	17	869 R	79.3%	19.5%	80.3%	19.7%
2,269	HODGEMAN	1,266	939	306	21	633 R	74.2%	24.2%	75.4%	24.6%
11,644	JACKSON	5,179	3,466	1,667	46	1,799 R	66.9%	32.2%	67.5%	32.5%
15,207	JEFFERSON	6,563	4,524	1,990	49	2,534 R	68.9%	30.3%	69.5%	30.5%
5,241	JEWELL	2,604	1,992	583	29	1,409 R	76.5%	22.4%	77.4%	22.6%
270,269	JOHNSON	140,882	101,987	38,019	876	63,968 R	72.4%	27.0%	72.8%	27.2%
3,435	KEARNY	1,548	1,214	321	13	893 R	78.4%	20.7%	79.1%	20.9%
8,960	KINGMAN	3,923	2,826	1,047	50	1,779 R	72.0%	26.7%	73.0%	27.0%
4,046	KIOWA	1,933	1,537	361	35	1,176 R	79.5%	18.7%	81.0%	19.0%
25,682	LABETTE	10,260	6,542	3,631	87	2,911 R	63.8%	35.4%	64.3%	35.7%
2,472	LANE	1,306	1,008	282	16	726 R	77.2%	21.6%	78.1%	21.9%
54,809	LEAVENWORTH	17,970	11,194	6,604	172	4,590 R	62.3%	36.8%	62.9%	37.1%
4,145	LINCOLN	2,293	1,723	551	19	1,172 R	75.1%	24.0%	75.8%	24.2%
8,234	LINN	3,974	2,795	1,152	27	1,643 R	70.3%	29.0%	70.8%	29.2%
3,478	LOGAN	1,603	1,235	331	37	904 R	77.0%	20.6%	78.9%	21.1%
35,108	LYON	14,121	9,796	4,188	137	5,608 R	69.4%	29.7%	70.1%	29.9%
26,855	MCPHERSON	12,004	8,630	3,185	189	5,445 R	71.9%	26.5%	73.0%	27.0%
13,522	MARION	6,116	4,407	1,632	77	2,775 R	72.1%	26.7%	73.0%	27.0%
12,787	MARSHALL	5,983	4,098	1,813	72	2,285 R	68.5%	30.3%	69.3%	30.7%
4,788	MEADE	2,338	1,804	491	43	1,313 R	77.2%	21.0%	78.6%	21.4%

KANSAS

PRESIDENT 1984

1980 Census Population	County	Total Vote	Republican	Democratic	Other	Rep.-Dem. Plurality	Percentage			
							Total Vote		Major Vote	
							Rep.	Dem.	Rep.	Dem.
21,618	MIAMI	9,036	5,877	3,076	83	2,801 R	65.0%	34.0%	65.6%	34.4%
8,117	MITCHELL	3,996	3,036	919	41	2,117 R	76.0%	23.0%	76.8%	23.2%
42,281	MONTGOMERY	17,127	12,023	4,933	171	7,090 R	70.2%	28.8%	70.9%	29.1%
6,419	MORRIS	3,103	2,240	820	43	1,420 R	72.2%	26.4%	73.2%	26.8%
3,454	MORTON	1,874	1,533	322	19	1,211 R	81.8%	17.2%	82.6%	17.4%
11,211	NEMAHA	5,485	3,653	1,761	71	1,892 R	66.6%	32.1%	67.5%	32.5%
18,967	NEOSHO	7,749	4,968	2,679	102	2,289 R	64.1%	34.6%	65.0%	35.0%
4,498	NESS	2,362	1,779	540	43	1,239 R	75.3%	22.9%	76.7%	23.3%
6,689	NORTON	3,176	2,515	611	50	1,904 R	79.2%	19.2%	80.5%	19.5%
15,319	OSAGE	6,443	4,288	2,072	83	2,216 R	66.6%	32.2%	67.4%	32.6%
5,959	OSBORNE	2,909	2,171	686	52	1,485 R	74.6%	23.6%	76.0%	24.0%
5,971	OTTAWA	3,096	2,345	699	52	1,646 R	75.7%	22.6%	77.0%	23.0%
8,065	PAWNEE	3,730	2,570	1,092	68	1,478 R	68.9%	29.3%	70.2%	29.8%
7,406	PHILLIPS	3,477	2,813	626	38	2,187 R	80.9%	18.0%	81.8%	18.2%
14,782	POTTAWATOMIE	6,468	4,598	1,798	72	2,800 R	71.1%	27.8%	71.9%	28.1%
10,275	PRATT	4,549	3,244	1,255	50	1,989 R	71.3%	27.6%	72.1%	27.9%
4,105	RAWLINS	2,082	1,625	412	45	1,213 R	78.0%	19.8%	79.8%	20.2%
64,983	RENO	26,159	16,568	9,229	362	7,339 R	63.3%	35.3%	64.2%	35.8%
7,569	REPUBLIC	3,934	3,009	887	38	2,122 R	76.5%	22.5%	77.2%	22.8%
11,900	RICE	5,239	3,598	1,559	82	2,039 R	68.7%	29.8%	69.8%	30.2%
63,505	RILEY	17,458	11,308	5,975	175	5,333 R	64.8%	34.2%	65.4%	34.6%
7,006	ROOKS	3,349	2,604	699	46	1,905 R	77.8%	20.9%	78.8%	21.2%
4,516	RUSH	2,530	1,758	718	54	1,040 R	69.5%	28.4%	71.0%	29.0%
8,868	RUSSELL	4,771	3,673	1,055	43	2,618 R	77.0%	22.1%	77.7%	22.3%
48,905	SALINE	21,961	15,244	6,526	191	8,718 R	69.4%	29.7%	70.0%	30.0%
5,782	SCOTT	2,486	2,017	427	42	1,590 R	81.1%	17.2%	82.5%	17.5%
366,531	SEDGWICK	153,315	95,874	55,263	2,178	40,611 R	62.5%	36.0%	63.4%	36.6%
17,071	SEWARD	6,484	5,222	1,198	64	4,024 R	80.5%	18.5%	81.3%	18.7%
154,916	SHAWNEE	70,589	43,465	26,338	786	17,127 R	61.6%	37.3%	62.3%	37.7%
3,544	SHERIDAN	1,725	1,274	419	32	855 R	73.9%	24.3%	75.3%	24.7%
7,759	SHERMAN	3,463	2,702	714	47	1,988 R	78.0%	20.6%	79.1%	20.9%
5,947	SMITH	3,079	2,332	684	63	1,648 R	75.7%	22.2%	77.3%	22.7%
5,694	STAFFORD	2,958	2,062	844	52	1,218 R	69.7%	28.5%	71.0%	29.0%
2,339	STANTON	1,022	783	205	34	578 R	76.6%	20.1%	79.3%	20.7%
4,736	STEVENS	2,271	1,863	386	22	1,477 R	82.0%	17.0%	82.8%	17.2%
24,928	SUMNER	10,793	6,942	3,708	143	3,234 R	64.3%	34.4%	65.2%	34.8%
8,451	THOMAS	4,051	3,107	887	57	2,220 R	76.7%	21.9%	77.8%	22.2%
4,165	TREGO	2,118	1,491	598	29	893 R	70.4%	28.2%	71.4%	28.6%
6,867	WABAUNSEE	3,130	2,276	805	49	1,471 R	72.7%	25.7%	73.9%	26.1%
2,045	WALLACE	1,010	838	152	20	686 R	83.0%	15.0%	84.6%	15.4%
8,543	WASHINGTON	3,936	2,979	889	68	2,090 R	75.7%	22.6%	77.0%	23.0%
3,041	WICHITA	1,161	916	232	13	684 R	78.9%	20.0%	79.8%	20.2%
12,128	WILSON	5,071	3,663	1,344	64	2,319 R	72.2%	26.5%	73.2%	26.8%
4,600	WOODSON	2,030	1,408	596	26	812 R	69.4%	29.4%	70.3%	29.7%
172,335	WYANDOTTE	64,136	27,459	36,042	635	8,583 D	42.8%	56.2%	43.2%	56.8%
2,363,679	TOTAL	1,021,991	677,296	333,149	11,546	344,147 R	66.3%	32.6%	67.0%	33.0%

KANSAS

SENATOR 1984

1980 Census Population	County	Total Vote	Republican	Democratic	Other	Rep.-Dem. Plurality	Percentage			
							Total Vote		Major Vote	
							Rep.	Dem.	Rep.	Dem.
31,308	ALLEN	6,104	4,856	1,166	82	3,690 R	79.6%	19.1%	80.6%	19.4%
17,498	ANDERSON	3,624	2,727	832	65	1,895 R	75.2%	23.0%	76.6%	23.4%
36,794	ATCHISON	7,062	4,985	1,503	574	3,482 R	70.6%	21.3%	76.8%	23.2%
13,096	BARBER	2,778	2,290	409	79	1,881 R	82.4%	14.7%	84.8%	15.2%
62,686	BARTON	13,516	11,095	1,924	497	9,171 R	82.1%	14.2%	85.2%	14.8%
31,938	BOURBON	7,010	5,189	1,701	120	3,488 R	74.0%	24.3%	75.3%	24.7%
23,910	BROWN	5,195	4,155	919	121	3,236 R	80.0%	17.7%	81.9%	18.1%
89,564	BUTLER	19,209	14,301	4,396	512	9,905 R	74.4%	22.9%	76.5%	23.5%
6,618	CHASE	1,520	1,211	264	45	947 R	79.7%	17.4%	82.1%	17.9%
10,032	CHAUTAUQUA	2,131	1,749	329	53	1,420 R	82.1%	15.4%	84.2%	15.8%
44,608	CHEROKEE	9,341	5,974	3,202	165	2,772 R	64.0%	34.3%	65.1%	34.9%
7,356	CHEYENNE	1,771	1,461	235	75	1,226 R	82.5%	13.3%	86.1%	13.9%
5,198	CLARK	1,421	1,200	195	26	1,005 R	84.4%	13.7%	86.0%	14.0%
19,604	CLAY	4,467	3,835	521	111	3,314 R	85.9%	11.7%	88.0%	12.0%
24,988	CLOUD	5,805	4,692	967	146	3,725 R	80.8%	16.7%	82.9%	17.1%
18,740	COFFEY	4,087	3,115	878	94	2,237 R	76.2%	21.5%	78.0%	22.0%
5,108	COMANCHE	1,261	1,068	162	31	906 R	84.7%	12.8%	86.8%	13.2%
73,648	COWLEY	15,264	11,848	3,069	347	8,779 R	77.6%	20.1%	79.4%	20.6%
75,832	CRAWFORD	16,117	11,305	4,587	225	6,718 R	70.1%	28.5%	71.1%	28.9%
9,018	DECATUR	2,224	1,892	256	76	1,636 R	85.1%	11.5%	88.1%	11.9%
40,350	DICKINSON	8,810	7,424	1,256	130	6,168 R	84.3%	14.3%	85.5%	14.5%
18,536	DONIPHAN	3,676	2,923	647	106	2,276 R	79.5%	17.6%	81.9%	18.1%
135,280	DOUGLAS	31,633	24,361	6,580	692	17,781 R	77.0%	20.8%	78.7%	21.3%
8,542	EDWARDS	1,991	1,547	358	86	1,189 R	77.7%	18.0%	81.2%	18.8%
7,836	ELK	1,737	1,389	285	63	1,104 R	80.0%	16.4%	83.0%	17.0%
52,196	ELLIS	10,895	7,777	2,452	666	5,325 R	71.4%	22.5%	76.0%	24.0%
13,280	ELLSWORTH	3,232	2,535	616	81	1,919 R	78.4%	19.1%	80.5%	19.5%
47,650	FINNEY	9,329	7,746	1,392	191	6,354 R	83.0%	14.9%	84.8%	15.2%
48,630	FORD	9,806	7,789	1,871	146	5,918 R	79.4%	19.1%	80.6%	19.4%
44,124	FRANKLIN	8,984	6,920	1,911	153	5,009 R	77.0%	21.3%	78.4%	21.6%
59,704	GEARY	6,762	5,294	1,364	104	3,930 R	78.3%	20.2%	79.5%	20.5%
7,452	GOVE	1,791	1,363	335	93	1,028 R	76.1%	18.7%	80.3%	19.7%
7,990	GRAHAM	1,914	1,556	322	36	1,234 R	81.3%	16.8%	82.9%	17.1%
13,954	GRANT	2,715	2,218	428	69	1,790 R	81.7%	15.8%	83.8%	16.2%
10,276	GRAY	2,146	1,821	298	27	1,523 R	84.9%	13.9%	85.9%	14.1%
3,690	GREELEY	949	767	141	41	626 R	80.8%	14.9%	84.5%	15.5%
17,528	GREENWOOD	4,184	3,156	583	445	2,573 R	75.4%	13.9%	84.4%	15.6%
5,028	HAMILTON	1,470	1,203	230	37	973 R	81.8%	15.6%	83.9%	16.1%
15,556	HARPER	3,434	2,924	463	47	2,461 R	85.1%	13.5%	86.3%	13.7%
61,062	HARVEY	13,157	10,338	2,563	256	7,775 R	78.6%	19.5%	80.1%	19.9%
7,628	HASKELL	1,445	1,198	205	42	993 R	82.9%	14.2%	85.4%	14.6%
4,538	HODGEMAN	1,267	1,054	174	39	880 R	83.2%	13.7%	85.8%	14.2%
23,288	JACKSON	5,197	4,156	984	57	3,172 R	80.0%	18.9%	80.9%	19.1%
30,414	JEFFERSON	6,550	5,119	1,242	189	3,877 R	78.2%	19.0%	80.5%	19.5%
10,482	JEWELL	2,576	2,152	373	51	1,779 R	83.5%	14.5%	85.2%	14.8%
540,538	JOHNSON	138,620	110,461	26,329	1,830	84,132 R	79.7%	19.0%	80.8%	19.2%
6,870	KEARNY	1,576	1,318	219	39	1,099 R	83.6%	13.9%	85.8%	14.2%
17,920	KINGMAN	3,887	3,121	706	60	2,415 R	80.3%	18.2%	81.6%	18.4%
8,092	KIOWA	1,903	1,589	258	56	1,331 R	83.5%	13.6%	86.0%	14.0%
51,364	LABETTE	10,388	7,931	2,349	108	5,582 R	76.3%	22.6%	77.1%	22.9%
4,944	LANE	1,265	1,101	135	29	966 R	87.0%	10.7%	89.1%	10.9%
109,618	LEAVENWORTH	17,517	11,631	5,414	472	6,217 R	66.4%	30.9%	68.2%	31.8%
8,290	LINCOLN	2,140	1,794	300	46	1,494 R	83.8%	14.0%	85.7%	14.3%
16,468	LINN	3,885	2,919	886	80	2,033 R	75.1%	22.8%	76.7%	23.3%
6,956	LOGAN	1,516	1,192	224	100	968 R	78.6%	14.8%	84.2%	15.8%
70,216	LYON	13,987	10,404	3,158	425	7,246 R	74.4%	22.6%	76.7%	23.3%
53,710	MCPHERSON	11,836	9,418	2,184	234	7,234 R	79.6%	18.5%	81.2%	18.8%
27,044	MARION	5,988	4,886	925	177	3,961 R	81.6%	15.4%	84.1%	15.9%
25,574	MARSHALL	5,843	4,474	1,253	116	3,221 R	76.6%	21.4%	78.1%	21.9%
9,576	MEADE	2,242	1,878	296	68	1,582 R	83.8%	13.2%	86.4%	13.6%

KANSAS

SENATOR 1984

1980 Census Population	County	Total Vote	Republican	Democratic	Other	Rep.-Dem. Plurality	Percentage			
							Total Vote		Major Vote	
							Rep.	Dem.	Rep.	Dem.
43,236	MIAMI	8,882	6,278	2,456	148	3,822 R	70.7%	27.7%	71.9%	28.1%
16,234	MITCHELL	3,878	3,108	673	97	2,435 R	80.1%	17.4%	82.2%	17.8%
84,562	MONTGOMERY	16,863	12,231	4,271	361	7,960 R	72.5%	25.3%	74.1%	25.9%
12,838	MORRIS	3,072	2,512	444	116	2,068 R	81.8%	14.5%	85.0%	15.0%
6,908	MORTON	1,666	1,346	273	47	1,073 R	80.8%	16.4%	83.1%	16.9%
22,422	NEMAHA	5,369	4,083	1,192	94	2,891 R	76.0%	22.2%	77.4%	22.6%
37,934	NEOSHO	7,615	5,648	1,829	138	3,819 R	74.2%	24.0%	75.5%	24.5%
8,996	NESS	2,324	1,890	365	69	1,525 R	81.3%	15.7%	83.8%	16.2%
13,378	NORTON	3,099	2,598	410	91	2,188 R	83.8%	13.2%	86.4%	13.6%
30,638	OSAGE	6,397	4,759	1,513	125	3,246 R	74.4%	23.7%	75.9%	24.1%
11,918	OSBORNE	2,813	2,222	482	109	1,740 R	79.0%	17.1%	82.2%	17.8%
11,942	OTTAWA	3,050	2,474	527	49	1,947 R	81.1%	17.3%	82.4%	17.6%
16,130	PAWNEE	3,670	2,900	670	100	2,230 R	79.0%	18.3%	81.2%	18.8%
14,812	PHILLIPS	3,351	2,863	401	87	2,462 R	85.4%	12.0%	87.7%	12.3%
29,564	POTTAWATOMIE	6,356	5,055	1,153	148	3,902 R	79.5%	18.1%	81.4%	18.6%
20,550	PRATT	4,494	3,539	849	106	2,690 R	78.7%	18.9%	80.7%	19.3%
8,210	RAWLINS	2,052	1,681	311	60	1,370 R	81.9%	15.2%	84.4%	15.6%
129,966	RENO	25,791	18,738	6,374	679	12,364 R	72.7%	24.7%	74.6%	25.4%
15,138	REPUBLIC	3,914	3,163	692	59	2,471 R	80.8%	17.7%	82.0%	18.0%
23,800	RICE	5,337	3,923	1,282	132	2,641 R	73.5%	24.0%	75.4%	24.6%
127,010	RILEY	17,321	14,216	2,741	364	11,475 R	82.1%	15.8%	83.8%	16.2%
14,012	ROOKS	3,234	2,361	680	193	1,681 R	73.0%	21.0%	77.6%	22.4%
9,032	RUSH	2,458	1,854	519	85	1,335 R	75.4%	21.1%	78.1%	21.9%
17,736	RUSSELL	4,742	3,681	614	447	3,067 R	77.6%	12.9%	85.7%	14.3%
97,810	SALINE	21,498	17,285	3,799	414	13,486 R	80.4%	17.7%	82.0%	18.0%
11,564	SCOTT	2,412	1,939	342	131	1,597 R	80.4%	14.2%	85.0%	15.0%
733,062	SEDGWICK	144,052	109,310	28,689	6,053	80,621 R	75.9%	19.9%	79.2%	20.8%
34,142	SEWARD	6,378	5,167	971	240	4,196 R	81.0%	15.2%	84.2%	15.8%
309,832	SHAWNEE	69,481	52,442	14,690	2,349	37,752 R	75.5%	21.1%	78.1%	21.9%
7,088	SHERIDAN	1,693	1,274	341	78	933 R	75.3%	20.1%	78.9%	21.1%
15,518	SHERMAN	3,413	2,913	381	119	2,532 R	85.4%	11.2%	88.4%	11.6%
11,894	SMITH	2,986	2,440	475	71	1,965 R	81.7%	15.9%	83.7%	16.3%
11,388	STAFFORD	2,951	2,301	560	90	1,741 R	78.0%	19.0%	80.4%	19.6%
4,678	STANTON	990	830	127	33	703 R	83.8%	12.8%	86.7%	13.3%
9,472	STEVENS	2,226	1,823	328	75	1,495 R	81.9%	14.7%	84.8%	15.2%
49,856	SUMNER	10,570	8,053	2,329	188	5,724 R	76.2%	22.0%	77.6%	22.4%
16,902	THOMAS	3,951	3,143	628	180	2,515 R	79.5%	15.9%	83.3%	16.7%
8,330	TREGO	2,084	1,628	378	78	1,250 R	78.1%	18.1%	81.2%	18.8%
13,734	WABAUNSEE	3,068	2,395	526	147	1,869 R	78.1%	17.1%	82.0%	18.0%
4,090	WALLACE	973	795	106	72	689 R	81.7%	10.9%	88.2%	11.8%
17,086	WASHINGTON	3,719	2,988	624	107	2,364 R	80.3%	16.8%	82.7%	17.3%
6,082	WICHITA	1,145	866	190	89	676 R	75.6%	16.6%	82.0%	18.0%
24,256	WILSON	4,993	3,938	889	166	3,049 R	78.9%	17.8%	81.6%	18.4%
9,200	WOODSON	2,009	1,572	390	47	1,182 R	78.2%	19.4%	80.1%	19.9%
344,670	WYANDOTTE	60,239	33,382	24,956	1,901	8,426 R	55.4%	41.4%	57.2%	42.8%
4,727,358	TOTAL	996,729	757,402	211,664	27,663	545,738 R	76.0%	21.2%	78.2%	21.8%

KANSAS

CONGRESS

CD	Year	Total Vote	Republican Vote	Republican Candidate	Democratic Vote	Democratic Candidate	Other Vote	Rep.-Dem. Plurality	Total Vote Rep.	Total Vote Dem.	Major Vote Rep.	Major Vote Dem.
1	1984	210,763	159,931	ROBERTS, PAT	49,015	RINGER, DARRELL T.	1,817	110,916 R	75.9%	23.3%	76.5%	23.5%
1	1982	169,133	115,749	ROBERTS, PAT	51,079	ROTH, KENT	2,305	64,670 R	68.4%	30.2%	69.4%	30.6%
2	1984	187,052	73,045	VAN SLYKE, JIM	112,263	SLATTERY, JIM	1,744	39,218 D	39.1%	60.0%	39.4%	60.6%
2	1982	150,228	63,942	KAY, MORRIS	86,286	SLATTERY, JIM		22,344 D	42.6%	57.4%	42.6%	57.4%
3	1984	213,902	117,159	MEYERS, JAN	85,441	REARDON, JOHN E.	11,302	31,718 R	54.8%	39.9%	57.8%	42.2%
3	1982	138,696	82,117	WINN, LARRY	53,140	KOSTAR, WILLIAM L.	3,439	28,977 R	59.2%	38.3%	60.7%	39.3%
4	1984	186,693	47,776	KRAUSE, WILLIAM V.	138,917	GLICKMAN, DAN		91,141 D	25.6%	74.4%	25.6%	74.4%
4	1982	145,167	35,478	CAYWOOD, GERALD	107,326	GLICKMAN, DAN	2,363	71,848 D	24.4%	73.9%	24.8%	75.2%
5	1984	195,915	144,075	WHITTAKER, ROBERT	49,435	BARNES, JOHN A.	2,405	94,640 R	73.5%	25.2%	74.5%	25.5%
5	1982	153,121	103,551	WHITTAKER, ROBERT	47,676	ROWE, LEE	1,894	55,875 R	67.6%	31.1%	68.5%	31.5%

KANSAS

1984 GENERAL ELECTION

President   Other vote was 3,564 Richards (Conservative); 3,329 Bergland (Libertarian); 2,544 Serrette (Independent); 2.109 Dodge (Prohibition).

Senator   Other vote was 9,380 Bieger (Conservative); 6,918 Jackson (American); 6,755 Merritt (Libertarian); 4,610 Steele (Prohibition).

Congress   Other vote was 1,816 Scoggin (Prohibition) and 1 scattered in CD 1; Peterson (Prohibition) in CD 2; Ralph (Independent) in CD 3; 2,382 Bacon (Prohibition) and 23 scattered in CD 5.

1984 PRIMARIES

AUGUST 7 REPUBLICAN

Senator   Nancy Landon Kassebaum, unopposed.

Congress   Unopposed in two CD's. Contested as follows:

CD   2   19.946 Jim Van Slyke; 12,236 Bob Laflin; 9,451 Stanley W. Eckert.
CD   3   16,884 Jan Meyers; 13,398 Russell C. Leffel; 7,636 John W. Uhlmann; 7,292 Marjorie P. Allen; 2,476 Jim Oyler.
CD   4   11,733 William V. Krause; 10,998 Robert N. Cowdrey.

AUGUST 7 DEMOCRATIC

Senator   James Maher, unopposed.

Congress   Unopposed in three CD's. Contested as follows:

CD   3   22,967 John E. Reardon; 6,105 C. Bertly Masterson.
CD   5   16,142 John A. Barnes; 15,469 Steven M. Dickson.

KENTUCKY

GOVERNOR

Martha Layne Collins (D). Elected 1983 to a four-year term.

SENATORS

Wendell H. Ford (D). Re-elected 1980 to a six-year term. Previously elected 1974.

Mitch McConnell (R). Elected 1984 to a six-year term.

REPRESENTATIVES

1. Carroll Hubbard (D)
2. William H. Natcher (D)
3. Romano L. Mazzoli (D)
4. M. G. Snyder (R)
5. Harold Rogers (R)
6. Larry J. Hopkins (R)
7. Carl C. Perkins (D)

POSTWAR VOTE FOR GOVERNOR

| | Total | Republican | | Democratic | | Other | Rep.-Dem. | Percentage | | | |
| | | | | | | | | Total Vote | | Major Vote | |
Year	Vote	Vote	Candidate	Vote	Candidate	Vote	Plurality	Rep.	Dem.	Rep.	Dem.
1983	1,030,671	454,650	Bunning, Jim	561,674	Collins, Martha Layne	14,347	107,024 D	44.1%	54.5%	44.7%	55.3%
1979	939,366	381,278	Nunn, Louie B.	558,088	Brown, J. Y., Jr.	—	176,810 D	40.6%	59.4%	40.6%	59.4%
1975	748,157	277,998	Gable, Robert E.	470,159	Carroll, Julian	—	192,161 D	37.2%	62.8%	37.2%	62.8%
1971	930,790	412,653	Emberton, Thomas	470,720	Ford, Wendell H.	47,417	58,067 D	44.3%	50.6%	46.7%	53.3%
1967	886,946	454,123	Nunn, Louie B.	425,674	Ward, Henry	7,149	28,449 R	51.2%	48.0%	51.6%	48.4%
1963	886,047	436,496	Nunn, Louie B.	449,551	Breathitt, Edward T.	—	13,055 D	49.3%	50.7%	49.3%	50.7%
1959	853,005	336,456	Robsion, John M.	516,549	Combs, Bert T.	—	180,093 D	39.4%	60.6%	39.4%	60.6%
1955	778,488	322,671	Denney, Edwin R.	451,647	Chandler, Albert B.	4,170	128,976 D	41.4%	58.0%	41.7%	58.3%
1951	634,359	288,014	Siler, Eugene	346,345	Wetherby, Lawrence	—	58,331 D	45.4%	54.6%	45.4%	54.6%
1947	672,372	287,130	Dummit, Eldon S.	385,242	Clements, Earle C.	—	98,112 D	42.7%	57.3%	42.7%	57.3%

POSTWAR VOTE FOR SENATOR

| | Total | Republican | | Democratic | | Other | Rep.-Dem. | Percentage | | | |
| | | | | | | | | Total Vote | | Major Vote | |
Year	Vote	Vote	Candidate	Vote	Candidate	Vote	Plurality	Rep.	Dem.	Rep.	Dem.
1984	1,292,407	644,990	McConnell, Mitch	639,721	Huddleston, Walter	7,696	5,269 R	49.9%	49.5%	50.2%	49.8%
1980	1,106,890	386,029	Foust, Mary Louise	720,861	Ford, Wendell H.	—	334,832 D	34.9%	65.1%	34.9%	65.1%
1978	476,783	175,766	Guenthner, Louie	290,730	Huddleston, Walter	10,287	114,964 D	36.9%	61.0%	37.7%	62.3%
1974	745,994	328,982	Cook, Marlow W.	399,406	Ford, Wendell H.	17,606	70,424 D	44.1%	53.5%	45.2%	54.8%
1972	1,037,861	494,337	Nunn, Louie B.	528,550	Huddleston, Walter	14,974	34,213 D	47.6%	50.9%	48.3%	51.7%
1968	942,865	484,260	Cook, Marlow W.	448,960	Peden, Katherine	9,645	35,300 R	51.4%	47.6%	51.9%	48.1%
1966	749,884	483,805	Cooper, John Sherman	266,079	Brown, J. Y.	—	217,726 R	64.5%	35.5%	64.5%	35.5%
1962	820,088	432,648	Morton, Thruston B.	387,440	Wyatt, Wilson W.	—	45,208 R	52.8%	47.2%	52.8%	47.2%
1960	1,088,377	644,087	Cooper, John Sherman	444,290	Johnson, Keen	—	199,797 R	59.2%	40.8%	59.2%	40.8%
1956	1,006,825	506,903	Morton, Thruston B.	499,922	Clements, Earle C.	—	6,981 R	50.3%	49.7%	50.3%	49.7%
1956s	1,011,645	538,505	Cooper, John Sherman	473,140	Wetherby, Lawrence	—	65,365 R	53.2%	46.8%	53.2%	46.8%
1954	797,057	362,948	Cooper, John Sherman	434,109	Barkley, Alben W.	—	71,161 D	45.5%	54.5%	45.5%	54.5%
1952s	960,228	494,576	Cooper, John Sherman	465,652	Underwood, Thomas R.	—	28,924 R	51.5%	48.5%	51.5%	48.5%
1950	617,121	278,368	Dawson, Charles L.	334,249	Clements, Earle C.	4,504	55,881 D	45.1%	54.2%	45.4%	54.6%
1948	794,469	383,776	Cooper, John Sherman	408,256	Chapman, Virgil	2,437	24,480 D	48.3%	51.4%	48.5%	51.5%
1946s	615,119	327,652	Cooper, John Sherman	285,829	Brown, J. Y.	1,638	41,823 R	53.3%	46.5%	53.4%	46.6%

One of the 1956 elections and those in 1952 and 1946 were for short terms to fill vacancies.

KENTUCKY

Districts Established March 10, 1982

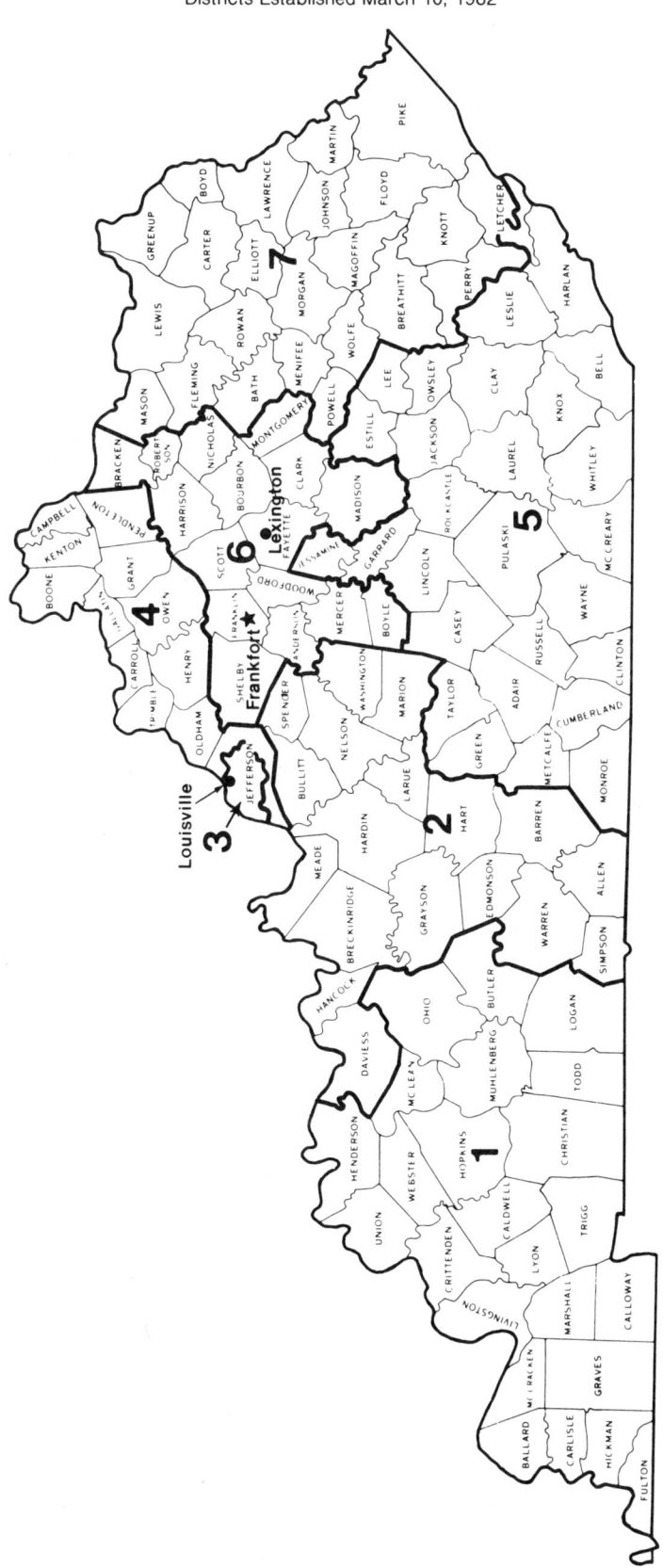

© ERC

KENTUCKY

PRESIDENT 1984

1980 Census Population	County	Total Vote	Republican	Democratic	Other	Rep.-Dem. Plurality	Percentage Total Vote Rep.	Dem.	Major Vote Rep.	Dem.
15,233	ADAIR	6,344	4,500	1,812	32	2,688 R	70.9%	28.6%	71.3%	28.7%
14,128	ALLEN	4,963	3,427	1,521	15	1,906 R	69.1%	30.6%	69.3%	30.7%
12,567	ANDERSON	5,185	3,425	1,717	43	1,708 R	66.1%	33.1%	66.6%	33.4%
8,798	BALLARD	3,685	1,663	2,002	20	339 D	45.1%	54.3%	45.4%	54.6%
34,009	BARREN	12,277	7,717	4,503	57	3,214 R	62.9%	36.7%	63.2%	36.8%
10,025	BATH	3,820	2,020	1,781	19	239 R	52.9%	46.6%	53.1%	46.9%
34,330	BELL	12,961	7,249	5,490	222	1,759 R	55.9%	42.4%	56.9%	43.1%
45,842	BOONE	17,649	12,690	4,853	106	7,837 R	71.9%	27.5%	72.3%	27.7%
19,405	BOURBON	6,553	3,836	2,649	68	1,187 R	58.5%	40.4%	59.2%	40.8%
55,513	BOYD	20,621	10,925	9,601	95	1,324 R	53.0%	46.6%	53.2%	46.8%
25,066	BOYLE	9,076	5,675	3,378	23	2,297 R	62.5%	37.2%	62.7%	37.3%
7,738	BRACKEN	2,976	1,812	1,136	28	676 R	60.9%	38.2%	61.5%	38.5%
17,004	BREATHITT	6,309	2,855	3,435	19	580 D	45.3%	54.4%	45.4%	54.6%
16,861	BRECKINRIDGE	7,132	4,432	2,669	31	1,763 R	62.1%	37.4%	62.4%	37.6%
43,346	BULLITT	14,676	9,556	5,005	115	4,551 R	65.1%	34.1%	65.6%	34.4%
11,064	BUTLER	4,191	3,121	1,055	15	2,066 R	74.5%	25.2%	74.7%	25.3%
13,473	CALDWELL	5,653	3,162	2,427	64	735 R	55.9%	42.9%	56.6%	43.4%
30,031	CALLOWAY	11,515	6,442	5,028	45	1,414 R	55.9%	43.7%	56.2%	43.8%
83,317	CAMPBELL	30,679	21,473	9,068	138	12,405 R	70.0%	29.6%	70.3%	29.7%
5,487	CARLISLE	2,608	1,308	1,277	23	31 R	50.2%	49.0%	50.6%	49.4%
9,270	CARROLL	3,400	1,824	1,564	12	260 R	53.6%	46.0%	53.8%	46.2%
25,060	CARTER	8,675	4,656	3,985	34	671 R	53.7%	45.9%	53.9%	46.1%
14,818	CASEY	5,513	4,356	1,122	35	3,234 R	79.0%	20.4%	79.5%	20.5%
66,878	CHRISTIAN	16,209	10,708	5,432	69	5,276 R	66.1%	33.5%	66.3%	33.7%
28,322	CLARK	9,757	6,130	3,595	32	2,535 R	62.8%	36.8%	63.0%	37.0%
22,752	CLAY	6,426	4,772	1,634	20	3,138 R	74.3%	25.4%	74.5%	25.5%
9,321	CLINTON	4,322	3,459	838	25	2,621 R	80.0%	19.4%	80.5%	19.5%
9,207	CRITTENDEN	3,663	2,167	1,483	13	684 R	59.2%	40.5%	59.4%	40.6%
7,289	CUMBERLAND	3,509	2,729	766	14	1,963 R	77.8%	21.8%	78.1%	21.9%
85,949	DAVIESS	33,086	19,495	13,347	244	6,148 R	58.9%	40.3%	59.4%	40.6%
9,962	EDMONSON	4,224	3,001	1,200	23	1,801 R	71.0%	28.4%	71.4%	28.6%
6,908	ELLIOTT	2,294	601	1,683	10	1,082 D	26.2%	73.4%	26.3%	73.7%
14,495	ESTILL	5,122	3,512	1,593	17	1,919 R	68.6%	31.1%	68.8%	31.2%
204,165	FAYETTE	81,746	51,993	28,961	792	23,032 R	63.6%	35.4%	64.2%	35.8%
12,323	FLEMING	4,459	2,824	1,616	19	1,208 R	63.3%	36.2%	63.6%	36.4%
48,764	FLOYD	15,543	5,218	10,259	66	5,041 D	33.6%	66.0%	33.7%	66.3%
41,830	FRANKLIN	19,024	11,057	7,790	177	3,267 R	58.1%	40.9%	58.7%	41.3%
8,971	FULTON	3,330	1,780	1,534	16	246 R	53.5%	46.1%	53.7%	46.3%
4,842	GALLATIN	2,093	1,042	1,042	9	0 D	49.8%	49.8%	50.0%	50.0%
10,853	GARRARD	4,885	3,284	1,566	35	1,718 R	67.2%	32.1%	67.7%	32.3%
13,308	GRANT	4,620	2,840	1,685	95	1,155 R	61.5%	36.5%	62.8%	37.2%
34,049	GRAVES	14,170	7,287	6,759	124	528 R	51.4%	47.7%	51.9%	48.1%
20,854	GRAYSON	7,777	5,524	2,200	53	3,324 R	71.0%	28.3%	71.5%	28.5%
11,043	GREEN	4,838	3,210	1,611	17	1,599 R	66.3%	33.3%	66.6%	33.4%
39,132	GREENUP	14,462	7,451	6,923	88	528 R	51.5%	47.9%	51.8%	48.2%
7,742	HANCOCK	3,301	1,967	1,287	47	680 R	59.6%	39.0%	60.4%	39.6%
88,917	HARDIN	20,771	14,293	6,329	149	7,964 R	68.8%	30.5%	69.3%	30.7%
41,889	HARLAN	14,762	6,959	7,663	140	704 D	47.1%	51.9%	47.6%	52.4%
15,166	HARRISON	5,890	3,467	2,405	18	1,062 R	58.9%	40.8%	59.0%	41.0%
15,402	HART	5,372	3,065	2,278	29	787 R	57.1%	42.4%	57.4%	42.6%
40,849	HENDERSON	14,242	7,389	6,795	58	594 R	51.9%	47.7%	52.1%	47.9%
12,740	HENRY	5,110	2,802	2,279	29	523 R	54.8%	44.6%	55.1%	44.9%
6,065	HICKMAN	2,437	1,380	1,049	8	331 R	56.6%	43.0%	56.8%	43.2%
46,174	HOPKINS	16,166	9,368	6,743	55	2,625 R	57.9%	41.7%	58.1%	41.9%
11,996	JACKSON	4,413	3,856	542	15	3,314 R	87.4%	12.3%	87.7%	12.3%
685,004	JEFFERSON	290,750	167,640	122,133	977	45,507 R	57.7%	42.0%	57.9%	42.1%
26,146	JESSAMINE	9,556	7,081	2,379	96	4,702 R	74.1%	24.9%	74.9%	25.1%
24,432	JOHNSON	8,349	5,225	3,078	46	2,147 R	62.6%	36.9%	62.9%	37.1%
137,058	KENTON	49,245	34,304	14,642	299	19,662 R	69.7%	29.7%	70.1%	29.9%
17,940	KNOTT	6,248	1,728	4,487	33	2,759 D	27.7%	71.8%	27.8%	72.2%

KENTUCKY

PRESIDENT 1984

1980 Census Population	County	Total Vote	Republican	Democratic	Other	Rep.-Dem. Plurality	Total Vote Rep.	Total Vote Dem.	Major Vote Rep.	Major Vote Dem.
30,239	KNOX	8,699	5,730	2,932	37	2,798 R	65.9%	33.7%	66.2%	33.8%
11,922	LARUE	4,400	2,873	1,514	13	1,359 R	65.3%	34.4%	65.5%	34.5%
38,982	LAUREL	12,929	9,621	3,267	41	6,354 R	74.4%	25.3%	74.7%	25.3%
14,121	LAWRENCE	4,959	2,713	2,223	23	490 R	54.7%	44.8%	55.0%	45.0%
7,754	LEE	2,640	1,862	768	10	1,094 R	70.5%	29.1%	70.8%	29.2%
14,882	LESLIE	4,475	3,385	1,075	15	2,310 R	75.6%	24.0%	75.9%	24.1%
30,687	LETCHER	8,830	4,073	4,707	50	634 D	46.1%	53.3%	46.4%	53.6%
14,545	LEWIS	4,947	3,445	1,484	18	1,961 R	69.6%	30.0%	69.9%	30.1%
19,053	LINCOLN	6,522	3,996	2,498	28	1,498 R	61.3%	38.3%	61.5%	38.5%
9,219	LIVINGSTON	3,891	1,866	2,007	18	141 D	48.0%	51.6%	48.2%	51.8%
24,138	LOGAN	8,310	4,889	3,347	74	1,542 R	58.8%	40.3%	59.4%	40.6%
6,490	LYON	2,255	969	1,272	14	303 D	43.0%	56.4%	43.2%	56.8%
61,310	MCCRACKEN	25,765	12,903	12,535	327	368 R	50.1%	48.7%	50.7%	49.3%
15,634	MCCREARY	5,707	4,028	1,609	70	2,419 R	70.6%	28.2%	71.5%	28.5%
10,090	MCLEAN	3,882	1,942	1,917	23	25 R	50.0%	49.4%	50.3%	49.7%
53,352	MADISON	17,926	11,309	6,509	108	4,800 R	63.1%	36.3%	63.5%	36.5%
13,515	MAGOFFIN	5,298	2,343	2,942	13	599 D	44.2%	55.5%	44.3%	55.7%
17,910	MARION	6,159	3,305	2,835	19	470 R	33.7%	46.0%	53.8%	46.2%
25,637	MARSHALL	10,917	5,152	5,725	40	573 D	47.2%	52.4%	47.4%	52.6%
13,925	MARTIN	4,770	3,248	1,471	51	1,777 R	68.1%	30.8%	68.8%	31.2%
17,765	MASON	5,446	2,751	2,663	32	88 R	50.5%	48.9%	50.8%	49.2%
22,854	MEADE	6,347	3,820	2,503	24	1,317 R	60.2%	39.4%	60.4%	39.6%
5,117	MENIFEE	1,770	785	956	29	171 D	44.4%	54.0%	45.1%	54.9%
19,011	MERCER	7,189	4,592	2,516	81	2,076 R	63.9%	35.0%	64.6%	35.4%
9,484	METCALFE	3,944	2,349	1,575	20	774 R	59.6%	39.9%	59.9%	40.1%
12,353	MONROE	5,753	4,670	1,052	31	3,618 R	81.2%	18.3%	81.6%	18.4%
20,046	MONTGOMERY	6,377	3,864	2,490	23	1,374 R	60.6%	39.0%	60.8%	39.2%
12,103	MORGAN	4,330	1,834	2,481	15	647 D	42.4%	57.3%	42.5%	57.5%
32,238	MUHLENBERG	12,277	6,094	6,157	26	63 D	49.6%	50.2%	49.7%	50.3%
27,584	NELSON	10,319	6,044	4,199	76	1,845 R	58.6%	40.7%	59.0%	41.0%
7,157	NICHOLAS	2,675	1,535	1,107	33	428 R	57.4%	41.4%	58.1%	41.9%
21,765	OHIO	8,417	5,119	3,253	45	1,866 R	60.8%	38.6%	61.1%	38.9%
27,795	OLDHAM	10,991	8,112	2,857	22	5,255 R	73.8%	26.0%	74.0%	26.0%
8,924	OWEN	3,408	1,778	1,612	18	166 R	52.2%	47.3%	52.4%	47.6%
5,709	OWSLEY	1,851	1,466	375	10	1,091 R	79.2%	20.3%	79.6%	20.4%
10,989	PENDLETON	4,340	2,767	1,529	44	1,238 R	63.8%	35.2%	64.4%	35.6%
33,763	PERRY	10,537	5,218	5,258	61	40 D	49.5%	49.9%	49.8%	50.2%
81,123	PIKE	27,812	11,869	15,817	126	3,948 D	42.7%	56.9%	42.9%	57.1%
11,101	POWELL	3,857	2,269	1,575	13	694 R	58.8%	40.8%	59.0%	41.0%
45,803	PULASKI	18,893	14,434	4,384	75	10,050 R	76.4%	23.2%	76.7%	23.3%
2,265	ROBERTSON	1,043	567	467	9	100 R	54.4%	44.8%	54.8%	45.2%
13,973	ROCKCASTLE	5,428	4,328	1,089	11	3,239 R	79.7%	20.1%	79.9%	20.1%
19,049	ROWAN	6,470	3,698	2,748	24	950 R	57.2%	42.5%	57.4%	42.6%
13,708	RUSSELL	5,954	4,476	1,448	30	3,028 R	75.2%	24.3%	75.6%	24.4%
21,813	SCOTT	7,144	4,461	2,606	77	1,855 R	62.4%	36.5%	63.1%	36.9%
23,328	SHELBY	8,739	5,390	3,326	23	2,064 R	61.7%	38.1%	61.8%	38.2%
14,673	SIMPSON	5,236	3,073	2,140	23	933 R	58.7%	40.9%	58.9%	41.1%
5,929	SPENCER	2,372	1,456	910	6	546 R	61.4%	38.4%	61.5%	38.5%
21,178	TAYLOR	9,245	5,932	3,286	27	2,646 R	64.2%	35.5%	64.4%	35.6%
11,874	TODD	4,280	2,364	1,505	411	859 R	55.2%	35.2%	61.1%	38.9%
9,384	TRIGG	4,436	2,512	1,905	19	607 R	56.6%	42.9%	56.9%	43.1%
6,253	TRIMBLE	2,490	1,389	1,088	13	301 R	55.8%	43.7%	56.1%	43.9%
17,821	UNION	5,637	2,524	3,090	23	566 D	44.8%	54.8%	45.0%	55.0%
71,828	WARREN	24,178	16,167	7,937	74	8,230 R	66.9%	32.8%	67.1%	32.9%
10,764	WASHINGTON	4,655	2,804	1,786	65	1,018 R	60.2%	38.4%	61.1%	38.9%
17,022	WAYNE	6,691	4,449	2,227	15	2,222 R	66.5%	33.3%	66.6%	33.4%
14,832	WEBSTER	5,580	2,504	3,042	34	538 D	44.9%	54.5%	45.1%	54.9%
33,396	WHITLEY	11,516	7,851	3,575	90	4,276 R	68.2%	31.0%	68.7%	31.3%
6,698	WOLFE	2,693	1,257	1,394	42	137 D	46.7%	51.8%	47.4%	52.6%
17,778	WOODFORD	7,112	4,746	2,290	76	2,456 R	66.7%	32.2%	67.5%	32.5%
3,660,777	TOTAL	1,369,345	821,702	539,539	8,104	282,163 R	60.0%	39.4%	60.4%	39.6%

KENTUCKY

GOVERNOR 1983

1980 Census Population	County	Total Vote	Republican	Democratic	Other	Rep.-Dem. Plurality	Total Vote Rep.	Total Vote Dem.	Major Vote Rep.	Major Vote Dem.
15,233	ADAIR	5,665	3,121	2,532	12	589 R	55.1%	44.7%	55.2%	44.8%
14,128	ALLEN	3,336	1,545	1,778	13	233 D	46.3%	53.3%	46.5%	53.5%
12,567	ANDERSON	4,239	1,528	2,652	59	1,124 D	36.0%	62.6%	36.6%	63.4%
8,798	BALLARD	2,575	660	1,865	50	1,205 D	25.6%	72.4%	26.1%	73.9%
34,009	BARREN	9,656	3,661	5,958	37	2,297 D	37.9%	61.7%	38.1%	61.9%
10,025	BATH	3,928	1,319	2,572	37	1,253 D	33.6%	65.5%	33.9%	66.1%
34,330	BELL	8,143	3,738	4,260	145	522 D	45.9%	52.3%	46.7%	53.3%
45,842	BOONE	12,858	6,453	6,338	67	115 R	50.2%	49.3%	50.4%	49.6%
19,405	BOURBON	4,905	1,690	3,079	136	1,389 D	34.5%	62.8%	35.4%	64.6%
55,513	BOYD	15,180	6,271	8,580	329	2,309 D	41.3%	56.5%	42.2%	57.8%
25,066	BOYLE	6,382	2,786	3,551	45	765 D	43.7%	55.6%	44.0%	56.0%
7,738	BRACKEN	2,623	1,121	1,492	10	371 D	42.7%	56.9%	42.9%	57.1%
17,004	BREATHITT	5,075	1,142	3,919	14	2,777 D	22.5%	77.2%	22.6%	77.4%
16,861	BRECKINRIDGE	5,189	2,339	2,832	18	493 D	45.1%	54.6%	45.2%	54.8%
43,346	BULLITT	9,882	4,337	5,387	158	1,050 D	43.9%	54.5%	44.6%	55.4%
11,064	BUTLER	3,261	2,113	1,132	16	981 R	64.8%	34.7%	65.1%	34.9%
13,473	CALDWELL	3,842	1,357	2,440	45	1,083 D	35.3%	63.5%	35.7%	64.3%
30,031	CALLOWAY	6,962	2,392	4,532	38	2,140 D	34.4%	65.1%	34.5%	65.5%
83,317	CAMPBELL	26,342	14,988	11,244	110	3,744 R	56.9%	42.7%	57.1%	42.9%
5,487	CARLISLE	1,819	542	1,257	20	715 D	29.8%	69.1%	30.1%	69.9%
9,270	CARROLL	2,974	968	1,999	7	1,031 D	32.5%	67.2%	32.6%	67.4%
25,060	CARTER	6,054	2,650	3,269	135	619 D	43.8%	54.0%	44.8%	55.2%
14,818	CASEY	4,723	3,358	1,324	41	2,034 R	71.1%	28.0%	71.7%	28.3%
66,878	CHRISTIAN	10,014	3,876	6,106	32	2,230 D	38.7%	61.0%	38.8%	61.2%
28,322	CLARK	6,789	2,523	4,161	105	1,638 D	37.2%	61.3%	37.7%	62.3%
22,752	CLAY	9,328	4,654	4,614	60	40 R	49.9%	49.5%	50.2%	49.8%
9,321	CLINTON	3,895	2,851	1,037	7	1,814 R	73.2%	26.6%	73.3%	26.7%
9,207	CRITTENDEN	2,639	1,248	1,379	12	131 D	47.3%	52.3%	47.5%	52.5%
7,289	CUMBERLAND	2,618	1,625	984	9	641 R	62.1%	37.6%	62.3%	37.7%
85,949	DAVIESS	23,053	10,487	12,229	337	1,742 D	45.5%	53.0%	46.2%	53.8%
9,962	EDMONSON	2,961	1,810	1,134	17	676 R	61.1%	38.3%	61.5%	38.5%
6,908	ELLIOTT	1,797	373	1,407	17	1,034 D	20.8%	78.3%	21.0%	79.0%
14,495	ESTILL	4,595	2,519	2,045	31	474 R	54.8%	44.5%	55.2%	44.8%
204,165	FAYETTE	53,562	25,170	26,966	1,426	1,796 D	47.0%	50.3%	48.3%	51.7%
12,323	FLEMING	3,838	1,554	2,268	16	714 D	40.5%	59.1%	40.7%	59.3%
48,764	FLOYD	13,441	3,997	9,365	79	5,368 D	29.7%	69.7%	29.9%	70.1%
41,830	FRANKLIN	17,856	4,612	12,888	356	8,276 D	25.8%	72.2%	26.4%	73.6%
8,971	FULTON	2,230	642	1,580	8	938 D	28.8%	70.9%	28.9%	71.1%
4,842	GALLATIN	1,882	535	1,342	5	807 D	28.4%	71.3%	28.5%	71.5%
10,853	GARRARD	3,749	2,073	1,633	43	440 R	55.3%	43.6%	55.9%	44.1%
13,308	GRANT	3,792	1,356	2,360	76	1,004 D	35.8%	62.2%	36.5%	63.5%
34,049	GRAVES	11,449	4,110	7,188	151	3,078 D	35.9%	62.8%	36.4%	63.6%
20,854	GRAYSON	6,110	3,316	2,712	82	604 R	54.3%	44.4%	55.0%	45.0%
11,043	GREEN	4,594	2,501	2,080	13	421 R	54.4%	45.3%	54.6%	45.4%
39,132	GREENUP	12,891	4,682	5,799	2,410	1,117 D	36.3%	45.0%	44.7%	55.3%
7,742	HANCOCK	2,088	834	1,215	39	381 D	39.9%	58.2%	40.7%	59.3%
88,917	HARDIN	14,640	6,438	8,012	190	1,574 D	44.0%	54.7%	44.6%	55.4%
41,889	HARLAN	9,198	3,261	5,845	92	2,584 D	35.5%	63.5%	35.8%	64.2%
15,166	HARRISON	4,727	1,567	3,114	46	1,547 D	33.1%	65.9%	33.5%	66.5%
15,402	HART	4,472	1,804	2,644	24	840 D	40.3%	59.1%	40.6%	59.4%
40,849	HENDERSON	9,030	3,218	5,765	47	2,547 D	35.6%	63.8%	35.8%	64.2%
12,740	HENRY	4,334	1,122	3,185	27	2,063 D	25.9%	73.5%	26.1%	73.9%
6,065	HICKMAN	1,882	488	1,352	42	864 D	25.9%	71.8%	26.5%	73.5%
46,174	HOPKINS	10,924	4,414	6,439	71	2,025 D	40.4%	58.9%	40.7%	59.3%
11,996	JACKSON	3,622	2,454	1,153	15	1,301 R	67.8%	31.8%	68.0%	32.0%
685,004	JEFFERSON	217,359	103,302	110,899	3,158	7,597 D	47.5%	51.0%	48.2%	51.8%
26,146	JESSAMINE	6,750	2,883	3,708	159	825 D	42.7%	54.9%	43.7%	56.3%
24,432	JOHNSON	5,076	2,426	2,587	63	161 D	47.8%	51.0%	48.4%	51.6%
137,058	KENTON	36,586	20,414	16,022	150	4,392 R	55.8%	43.8%	56.0%	44.0%
17,940	KNOTT	4,796	1,074	3,687	35	2,613 D	22.4%	76.9%	22.6%	77.4%

KENTUCKY

GOVERNOR 1983

1980 Census Population	County	Total Vote	Republican	Democratic	Other	Rep.-Dem. Plurality	Percentage Total Vote Rep.	Dem.	Major Vote Rep.	Dem.
30,239	KNOX	7,245	3,724	3,488	33	236 R	51.4%	48.1%	51.6%	48.4%
11,922	LARUE	3,732	1,430	2,277	25	847 D	38.3%	61.0%	38.6%	61.4%
38,982	LAUREL	9,388	5,346	3,985	57	1,361 R	56.9%	42.4%	57.3%	42.7%
14,121	LAWRENCE	3,150	1,357	1,771	22	414 D	43.1%	56.2%	43.4%	56.6%
7,754	LEE	2,527	1,414	1,094	19	320 R	56.0%	43.3%	56.4%	43.6%
14,882	LESLIE	5,451	3,213	2,213	25	1,000 R	58.9%	40.6%	59.2%	40.8%
30,687	LETCHER	7,923	2,980	4,868	75	1,888 D	37.6%	61.4%	38.0%	62.0%
14,545	LEWIS	3,438	1,993	1,434	11	559 R	58.0%	41.7%	58.2%	41.8%
19,053	LINCOLN	4,483	2,039	2,405	39	366 D	45.5%	53.6%	45.9%	54.1%
9,219	LIVINGSTON	2,499	774	1,719	6	945 D	31.0%	68.8%	31.0%	69.0%
24,138	LOGAN	5,461	1,406	3,965	90	2,559 D	25.7%	72.6%	26.2%	73.8%
6,490	LYON	1,888	514	1,365	9	851 D	27.2%	72.3%	27.4%	72.6%
61,310	MCCRACKEN	18,741	6,278	11,870	593	5,592 D	33.5%	63.3%	34.6%	65.4%
15,634	MCCREARY	3,492	2,195	1,250	47	945 R	62.9%	35.8%	63.7%	36.3%
10,090	MCLEAN	2,623	867	1,731	25	864 D	33.1%	66.0%	33.4%	66.6%
53,352	MADISON	12,950	5,842	6,802	306	960 D	45.1%	52.5%	46.2%	53.8%
13,515	MAGOFFIN	4,879	1,870	2,966	43	1,096 D	38.3%	60.8%	38.7%	61.3%
17,910	MARION	5,781	2,294	3,457	30	1,163 D	39.7%	59.8%	39.9%	60.1%
25,637	MARSHALL	7,148	2,469	4,660	19	2,191 D	34.5%	65.2%	34.6%	65.4%
13,925	MARTIN	2,347	1,054	1,281	12	227 D	44.9%	54.6%	45.1%	54.9%
17,765	MASON	5,457	2,211	3,234	12	1,023 D	40.5%	59.3%	40.6%	59.4%
22,854	MEADE	4,936	2,043	2,845	48	802 D	41.4%	57.6%	41.8%	58.2%
5,117	MENIFEE	1,433	398	985	50	587 D	27.8%	68.7%	28.8%	71.2%
19,011	MERCER	5,478	1,907	3,456	115	1,549 D	34.8%	63.1%	35.6%	64.4%
9,484	METCALFE	3,401	1,327	2,062	12	735 D	39.0%	60.6%	39.2%	60.8%
12,353	MONROE	4,764	2,832	1,911	21	921 R	59.4%	40.1%	59.7%	40.3%
20,046	MONTGOMERY	5,846	2,234	3,568	44	1,334 D	38.2%	61.0%	38.5%	61.5%
12,103	MORGAN	3,275	767	2,492	16	1,725 D	23.4%	76.1%	23.5%	76.5%
32,238	MUHLENBERG	7,426	2,919	4,463	44	1,544 D	39.3%	60.1%	39.5%	60.5%
27,584	NELSON	8,242	3,668	4,457	117	789 D	44.5%	54.1%	45.1%	54.9%
7,157	NICHOLAS	2,224	707	1,467	50	760 D	31.8%	66.0%	32.5%	67.5%
21,765	OHIO	5,861	3,003	2,829	29	174 R	51.2%	48.3%	51.5%	48.5%
27,795	OLDHAM	7,765	4,124	3,599	42	525 R	53.1%	46.3%	53.4%	46.6%
8,924	OWEN	2,989	672	2,304	13	1,632 D	22.5%	77.1%	22.6%	77.4%
5,709	OWSLEY	1,777	1,088	677	12	411 R	61.2%	38.1%	61.6%	38.4%
10,989	PENDLETON	3,327	1,427	1,885	15	458 D	42.9%	56.7%	43.1%	56.9%
33,763	PERRY	8,948	3,221	5,624	103	2,403 D	36.0%	62.9%	36.4%	63.6%
81,123	PIKE	20,204	7,692	12,391	121	4,699 D	38.1%	61.3%	38.3%	61.7%
11,101	POWELL	3,081	1,196	1,860	25	664 D	38.8%	60.4%	39.1%	60.9%
45,803	PULASKI	14,637	8,834	5,622	181	3,212 R	60.4%	38.4%	61.1%	38.9%
2,265	ROBERTSON	880	309	569	2	260 D	35.1%	64.7%	35.2%	64.8%
13,973	ROCKCASTLE	4,034	2,694	1,314	26	1,380 R	66.8%	32.6%	67.2%	32.8%
19,049	ROWAN	5,273	2,263	2,966	44	703 D	42.9%	56.2%	43.3%	56.7%
13,708	RUSSELL	5,233	3,195	2,029	9	1,166 R	61.1%	38.8%	61.2%	38.8%
21,813	SCOTT	5,507	1,809	3,567	131	1,758 D	32.8%	64.8%	33.6%	66.4%
23,328	SHELBY	7,206	1,810	5,373	23	3,563 D	25.1%	74.6%	25.2%	74.8%
14,673	SIMPSON	3,516	1,083	2,416	17	1,333 D	30.8%	68.7%	31.0%	69.0%
5,929	SPENCER	1,841	505	1,326	10	821 D	27.4%	72.0%	27.6%	72.4%
21,178	TAYLOR	7,244	3,360	3,863	21	503 D	46.4%	53.3%	46.5%	53.5%
11,874	TODD	2,192	596	1,543	53	947 D	27.2%	70.4%	27.9%	72.1%
9,384	TRIGG	3,022	958	2,053	11	1,095 D	31.7%	67.9%	31.8%	68.2%
6,253	TRIMBLE	2,167	666	1,487	14	821 D	30.7%	68.6%	30.9%	69.1%
17,821	UNION	4,374	1,510	2,844	20	1,334 D	34.5%	65.0%	34.7%	65.3%
71,828	WARREN	17,235	6,882	10,290	63	3,408 D	39.9%	59.7%	40.1%	59.9%
10,764	WASHINGTON	3,682	1,659	1,950	73	291 D	45.1%	53.0%	46.0%	54.0%
17,022	WAYNE	6,063	3,299	2,750	14	549 R	54.4%	45.4%	54.5%	45.5%
14,832	WEBSTER	4,544	1,512	2,998	34	1,486 D	33.3%	66.0%	33.5%	66.5%
33,396	WHITLEY	7,877	4,610	3,219	48	1,391 R	58.5%	40.9%	58.9%	41.1%
6,698	WOLFE	2,067	550	1,486	31	936 D	26.6%	71.9%	27.0%	73.0%
17,778	WOODFORD	6,317	1,759	4,403	155	2,644 D	27.8%	69.7%	28.5%	71.5%
3,660,777	TOTAL	1,030,671	454,650	561,674	14,347	107,024 D	44.1%	54.5%	44.7%	55.3%

KENTUCKY

SENATOR 1984

1980 Census Population	County	Total Vote	Republican	Democratic	Other	Rep.-Dem. Plurality	Total Vote Rep.	Total Vote Dem.	Major Vote Rep.	Major Vote Dem.
15,233	ADAIR	6,178	3,406	2,756	16	650 R	55.1%	44.6%	55.3%	44.7%
14,128	ALLEN	4,638	2,714	1,909	15	805 R	58.5%	41.2%	58.7%	41.3%
12,567	ANDERSON	4,844	2,438	2,371	35	67 R	50.3%	48.9%	50.7%	49.3%
8,798	BALLARD	3,654	1,157	2,492	5	1,335 D	31.7%	68.2%	31.7%	68.3%
34,009	BARREN	11,351	5,716	5,578	57	138 R	50.4%	49.1%	50.6%	49.4%
10,025	BATH	3,448	1,346	2,085	17	739 D	39.0%	60.5%	39.2%	60.8%
34,330	BELL	11,206	4,966	6,070	170	1,104 D	44.3%	54.2%	45.0%	55.0%
45,842	BOONE	16,382	10,059	6,203	120	3,856 R	61.4%	37.9%	61.9%	38.1%
19,405	BOURBON	5,685	2,465	3,172	48	707 D	43.4%	55.8%	43.7%	56.3%
55,513	BOYD	19,442	7,882	11,485	75	3,603 D	40.5%	59.1%	40.7%	59.3%
25,066	BOYLE	8,177	4,144	4,012	21	132 R	50.7%	49.1%	50.8%	49.2%
7,738	BRACKEN	2,654	1,125	1,507	22	382 D	42.4%	56.8%	42.7%	57.3%
17,004	BREATHITT	5,715	1,600	4,082	33	2,482 D	28.0%	71.4%	28.2%	71.8%
16,861	BRECKINRIDGE	6,998	3,233	3,745	20	512 D	46.2%	53.5%	46.3%	53.7%
43,346	BULLITT	14,146	7,572	6,451	123	1,121 R	53.5%	45.6%	54.0%	46.0%
11,064	BUTLER	4,101	2,799	1,294	8	1,505 R	68.3%	31.6%	68.4%	31.6%
13,473	CALDWELL	5,348	2,350	2,941	57	591 D	43.9%	55.0%	44.4%	55.6%
30,031	CALLOWAY	10,717	4,821	5,857	39	1,036 D	45.0%	54.7%	45.1%	54.9%
83,317	CAMPBELL	28,111	16,404	11,528	179	4,876 R	58.4%	41.0%	58.7%	41.3%
5,487	CARLISLE	2,371	856	1,479	36	623 D	36.1%	62.4%	36.7%	63.3%
9,270	CARROLL	3,150	1,249	1,875	26	626 D	39.7%	59.5%	40.0%	60.0%
25,060	CARTER	7,883	3,388	4,441	54	1,053 D	43.0%	56.3%	43.3%	56.7%
14,818	CASEY	5,185	3,532	1,618	35	1,914 R	68.1%	31.2%	68.6%	31.4%
66,878	CHRISTIAN	14,567	7,998	6,472	97	1,526 R	54.9%	44.4%	55.3%	44.7%
28,322	CLARK	8,776	4,329	4,397	50	68 D	49.3%	50.1%	49.6%	50.4%
22,752	CLAY	6,060	4,204	1,831	25	2,373 R	69.4%	30.2%	69.7%	30.3%
9,321	CLINTON	3,875	2,769	1,099	7	1,670 R	71.5%	28.4%	71.6%	28.4%
9,207	CRITTENDEN	3,531	1,872	1,649	10	223 R	53.0%	46.7%	53.2%	46.8%
7,289	CUMBERLAND	3,046	2,012	1,016	18	996 R	66.1%	33.4%	66.4%	33.6%
85,949	DAVIESS	31,847	16,096	15,546	205	550 R	50.5%	48.8%	50.9%	49.1%
9,962	EDMONSON	4,036	2,633	1,381	22	1,252 R	65.2%	34.2%	65.6%	34.4%
6,908	ELLIOTT	2,112	366	1,737	9	1,371 D	17.3%	82.2%	17.4%	82.6%
14,495	ESTILL	4,833	2,853	1,959	21	894 R	59.0%	40.5%	59.3%	40.7%
204,165	FAYETTE	75,854	40,676	34,504	674	6,172 R	53.6%	45.5%	54.1%	45.9%
12,323	FLEMING	4,193	2,107	2,071	15	36 R	50.3%	49.4%	50.4%	49.6%
48,764	FLOYD	13,882	3,476	10,289	117	6,813 D	25.0%	74.1%	25.3%	74.7%
41,830	FRANKLIN	17,493	7,405	9,912	176	2,507 D	42.3%	56.7%	42.8%	57.2%
8,971	FULTON	2,994	1,060	1,917	17	857 D	35.4%	64.0%	35.6%	64.4%
4,842	GALLATIN	1,840	526	1,303	11	777 D	28.6%	70.8%	28.8%	71.2%
10,853	GARRARD	4,670	2,842	1,801	27	1,041 R	60.9%	38.6%	61.2%	38.8%
13,308	GRANT	3,982	1,879	2,034	69	155 D	47.2%	51.1%	48.0%	52.0%
34,049	GRAVES	12,909	5,433	7,364	112	1,931 D	42.1%	57.0%	42.5%	57.5%
20,854	GRAYSON	7,380	4,324	3,017	39	1,307 R	58.6%	40.9%	58.9%	41.1%
11,043	GREEN	4,799	2,711	2,074	14	637 R	56.5%	43.2%	56.7%	43.3%
39,132	GREENUP	13,469	5,538	7,869	62	2,331 D	41.1%	58.4%	41.3%	58.7%
7,742	HANCOCK	3,092	1,492	1,564	36	72 D	48.3%	50.6%	48.8%	51.2%
88,917	HARDIN	20,064	9,721	10,186	157	465 D	48.4%	50.8%	48.8%	51.2%
41,889	HARLAN	12,452	5,009	7,328	115	2,319 D	40.2%	58.8%	40.6%	59.4%
15,166	HARRISON	5,329	2,299	2,998	32	699 D	43.1%	56.3%	43.4%	56.6%
15,402	HART	5,249	2,242	2,996	11	754 D	42.7%	57.1%	42.8%	57.2%
40,849	HENDERSON	13,394	5,197	8,095	102	2,898 D	38.8%	60.4%	39.1%	60.9%
12,740	HENRY	4,871	1,740	3,106	25	1,366 D	35.7%	63.8%	35.9%	64.1%
6,065	HICKMAN	2,430	951	1,475	4	524 D	39.1%	60.7%	39.2%	60.8%
46,174	HOPKINS	14,934	6,907	7,948	79	1,041 D	46.3%	53.2%	46.5%	53.5%
11,996	JACKSON	3,924	3,173	738	13	2,435 R	80.9%	18.8%	81.1%	18.9%
685,004	JEFFERSON	295,130	151,548	142,336	1,246	9,212 R	51.3%	48.2%	51.6%	48.4%
26,146	JESSAMINE	8,985	5,698	3,207	80	2,491 R	63.4%	35.7%	64.0%	36.0%
24,432	JOHNSON	7,223	4,006	3,159	58	847 R	55.5%	43.7%	55.9%	44.1%
137,058	KENTON	45,498	27,017	18,282	199	8,735 R	59.4%	40.2%	59.6%	40.4%
17,940	KNOTT	5,197	1,026	4,146	25	3,120 D	19.7%	79.8%	19.8%	80.2%

KENTUCKY

SENATOR 1984

1980 Census Population	County	Total Vote	Republican	Democratic	Other	Rep.-Dem. Plurality	Total Vote Rep.	Total Vote Dem.	Major Vote Rep.	Major Vote Dem.
30,239	KNOX	8,089	4,754	3,305	30	1,449 R	58.8%	40.9%	59.0%	41.0%
11,922	LARUE	4,166	1,874	2,275	17	401 D	45.0%	54.6%	45.2%	54.8%
38,982	LAUREL	12,188	8,433	3,721	34	4,712 R	69.2%	30.5%	69.4%	30.6%
14,121	LAWRENCE	4,468	1,991	2,456	21	465 D	44.6%	55.0%	44.8%	55.2%
7,754	LEE	2,555	1,555	993	7	562 R	60.9%	38.9%	61.0%	39.0%
14,882	LESLIE	4,001	2,773	1,210	18	1,563 R	69.3%	30.2%	69.6%	30.4%
30,687	LETCHER	7,375	2,828	4,472	75	1,644 D	38.3%	60.6%	38.7%	61.3%
14,545	LEWIS	4,449	2,784	1,645	20	1,139 R	62.6%	37.0%	62.9%	37.1%
19,053	LINCOLN	6,270	3,257	2,995	18	262 R	51.9%	47.8%	52.1%	47.9%
9,219	LIVINGSTON	3,617	1,433	2,149	35	716 D	39.6%	59.4%	40.0%	60.0%
24,138	LOGAN	7,525	3,375	4,079	71	704 D	44.9%	54.2%	45.3%	54.7%
6,490	LYON	2,462	833	1,614	15	781 D	33.8%	65.6%	34.0%	66.0%
61,310	MCCRACKEN	24,056	9,913	13,878	265	3,965 D	41.2%	57.7%	41.7%	58.3%
15,634	MCCREARY	4,517	2,904	1,557	56	1,347 R	64.3%	34.5%	65.1%	34.9%
10,090	MCLEAN	3,710	1,491	2,210	9	719 D	40.2%	59.6%	40.3%	59.7%
53,352	MADISON	16,761	8,851	7,811	99	1,040 R	52.8%	46.6%	53.1%	46.9%
13,515	MAGOFFIN	4,819	1,789	3,010	20	1,221 D	37.1%	62.5%	37.3%	62.7%
17,910	MARION	5,857	1,879	3,950	28	2,071 D	32.1%	67.4%	32.2%	67.8%
25,637	MARSHALL	10,548	4,150	6,379	19	2,229 D	39.3%	60.5%	39.4%	60.6%
13,925	MARTIN	3,741	2,088	1,596	57	492 R	55.8%	42.7%	56.7%	43.3%
17,765	MASON	5,980	2,824	3,135	21	311 D	47.2%	52.4%	47.4%	52.6%
22,854	MEADE	6,130	2,716	3,388	26	672 D	44.3%	55.3%	44.5%	55.5%
5,117	MENIFEE	1,591	551	1,009	31	458 D	34.6%	63.4%	35.3%	64.7%
19,011	MERCER	6,622	3,364	3,182	76	182 R	50.8%	48.1%	51.4%	48.6%
9,484	METCALFE	3,765	1,736	2,015	14	279 D	46.1%	53.5%	46.3%	53.7%
12,353	MONROE	4,940	3,399	1,504	37	1,895 R	68.8%	30.4%	69.3%	30.7%
20,046	MONTGOMERY	5,836	2,842	2,986	8	144 D	48.7%	51.2%	48.8%	51.2%
12,103	MORGAN	3,921	1,124	2,780	17	1,656 D	28.7%	70.9%	28.8%	71.2%
32,238	MUHLENBERG	11,399	4,612	6,722	65	2,110 D	40.5%	59.0%	40.7%	59.3%
27,584	NELSON	9,787	4,069	5,638	80	1,569 D	41.6%	57.6%	41.9%	58.1%
7,157	NICHOLAS	2,353	923	1,407	23	484 D	39.2%	59.8%	39.6%	60.4%
21,765	OHIO	8,117	4,283	3,802	32	481 R	52.8%	46.8%	53.0%	47.0%
27,795	OLDHAM	10,580	6,704	3,847	29	2,857 R	63.4%	36.4%	63.5%	36.5%
8,924	OWEN	3,188	1,009	2,160	19	1,151 D	31.6%	67.8%	31.8%	68.2%
5,709	OWSLEY	1,663	1,138	516	9	622 R	68.4%	31.0%	68.8%	31.2%
10,989	PENDLETON	3,797	1,798	1,970	29	172 D	47.4%	51.9%	47.7%	52.3%
33,763	PERRY	9,326	3,617	5,646	63	2,029 D	38.8%	60.5%	39.0%	61.0%
81,123	PIKE	24,759	8,471	16,088	200	7,617 D	34.2%	65.0%	34.5%	65.5%
11,101	POWELL	3,591	1,508	2,055	28	547 D	42.0%	57.2%	42.3%	57.7%
45,803	PULASKI	17,489	11,897	5,539	53	6,358 R	68.0%	31.7%	68.2%	31.8%
2,265	ROBERTSON	909	333	570	6	237 D	36.6%	62.7%	36.9%	63.1%
13,973	ROCKCASTLE	5,174	3,685	1,475	14	2,210 R	71.2%	28.5%	71.4%	28.6%
19,049	ROWAN	6,015	2,907	3,074	34	167 D	48.3%	51.1%	48.6%	51.4%
13,708	RUSSELL	5,556	3,554	1,989	13	1,565 R	64.0%	35.8%	64.1%	35.9%
21,813	SCOTT	6,540	3,118	3,360	62	242 D	47.7%	51.4%	48.1%	51.9%
23,328	SHELBY	8,154	3,538	4,597	19	1,059 D	43.4%	56.4%	43.5%	56.5%
14,673	SIMPSON	4,708	2,021	2,648	39	627 D	42.9%	56.2%	43.3%	56.7%
5,929	SPENCER	2,295	897	1,387	11	490 D	39.1%	60.4%	39.3%	60.7%
21,178	TAYLOR	8,888	4,348	4,527	13	179 D	48.9%	50.9%	49.0%	51.0%
11,874	TODD	3,224	1,336	1,812	76	476 D	41.4%	56.2%	42.4%	57.6%
9,384	TRIGG	4,049	1,798	2,218	33	420 D	44.4%	54.8%	44.8%	55.2%
6,253	TRIMBLE	2,375	881	1,485	9	604 D	37.1%	62.5%	37.2%	62.8%
17,821	UNION	5,276	1,821	3,412	43	1,591 D	34.5%	64.7%	34.8%	65.2%
71,828	WARREN	23,172	13,085	10,010	77	3,075 R	56.5%	43.2%	56.7%	43.3%
10,764	WASHINGTON	4,362	1,778	2,514	70	736 D	40.8%	57.6%	41.4%	58.6%
17,022	WAYNE	6,396	3,768	2,621	7	1,147 R	58.9%	41.0%	59.0%	41.0%
14,832	WEBSTER	5,285	1,850	3,400	35	1,550 D	35.0%	64.3%	35.2%	64.8%
33,396	WHITLEY	10,045	6,300	3,690	55	2,610 R	62.7%	36.7%	63.1%	36.9%
6,698	WOLFE	2,277	789	1,452	36	663 D	34.7%	63.8%	35.2%	64.8%
17,778	WOODFORD	6,395	3,286	3,029	80	257 R	51.4%	47.4%	52.0%	48.0%
3,660,777	TOTAL	1,292,407	644,990	639,721	7,696	5,269 R	49.9%	49.5%	50.2%	49.8%

KENTUCKY

CONGRESS

CD	Year	Total Vote	Republican Vote	Republican Candidate	Democratic Vote	Democratic Candidate	Other Vote	Rep.-Dem. Plurality	Percentage Total Vote Rep.	Dem.	Major Vote Rep.	Dem.
1	1984	112,180			112,180	HUBBARD, CARROLL		112,180 D		100.0%		100.0%
1	1982	48,356			48,342	HUBBARD, CARROLL	14	48,342 D		100.0%		100.0%
2	1984	149,742	56,700	MORRISON, TIMOTHY A.	93,042	NATCHER, WILLIAM H.		36,342 D	37.9%	62.1%	37.9%	62.1%
2	1982	67,143	17,561	WATSON, MARK T.	49,571	NATCHER, WILLIAM H.	11	32,010 D	26.2%	73.8%	26.2%	73.8%
3	1984	215,138	68,185	WARNER, SUZANNE M.	145,680	MAZZOLI, ROMANO L.	1,273	77,495 D	31.7%	67.7%	31.9%	68.1%
3	1982	142,597	45,900	BROWN, CARL	92,849	MAZZOLI, ROMANO L.	3,848	46,949 D	32.2%	65.1%	33.1%	66.9%
4	1984	202,038	108,398	SNYDER, M. G.	93,640	MULLOY, WILLIAM P.		14,758 R	53.7%	46.3%	53.7%	46.3%
4	1982	136,750	74,109	SNYDER, M. G.	61,937	MANN, TERRY L.	704	12,172 R	54.2%	45.3%	54.5%	45.5%
5	1984	164,947	125,164	ROGERS, HAROLD	39,783	MCINTOSH, SHERMAN W.		85,381 R	75.9%	24.1%	75.9%	24.1%
5	1982	81,217	52,928	ROGERS, HAROLD	28,285	DAVENPORT, DOYE	4	24,643 R	65.2%	34.8%	65.2%	34.8%
6	1984	177,108	126,525	HOPKINS, LARRY J.	49,657	HAMMOND, JERRY	926	76,868 R	71.4%	28.0%	71.8%	28.2%
6	1982	120,360	68,418	HOPKINS, LARRY J.	49,839	MILLS, DON	2,103	18,579 R	56.8%	41.4%	57.9%	42.1%
7	1984	166,569	43,890	RUSSELL, AUBREY	122,679	PERKINS, CARL C.		78,789 D	26.3%	73.7%	26.3%	73.7%
7	1982	103,899	21,436	HAMBY, TOM	82,463	PERKINS, CARL D.		61,027 D	20.6%	79.4%	20.6%	79.4%

KENTUCKY

1983 GENERAL ELECTION

Governor   Other vote was McCubbin (Citizens United).

1984 GENERAL ELECTION

President   Other vote was 3,129 Mason (Socialist Workers); 1,776 LaRouche (Independent); 1,479 Anderson (National Unity); 599 Johnson (Citizens); 428 Dennis (American); 365 Serrette (Independent Alliance); 328 Hall (Communist).

Senator   Other vote was Welters (Socialist Workers).

Congress   Other vote was Kreiner (Socialist Workers) in CD 3; Suruda (Libertarian) in CD 6.

1983 PRIMARIES

MAY 24 REPUBLICAN

Governor   72,808 Jim Bunning; 7,340 Lester Burns; 5,464 Donald C. Wiggins; 5,174 Elizabeth Wickham; 3,578 Thurman J. Hamlin; 3,472 Ben Auxier.

MAY 24 DEMOCRATIC

Governor   223,692 Martha Layne Collins; 219,160 Harvey Sloane; 199,795 Grady Stumbo; 9,445 Ray Adkins; 3,501 Doris S. Binion; 2,861 Fifi Rockefeller.

1984 PRIMARIES

MAY 29 REPUBLICAN

Senator   39,465 Mitch McConnell; 3,798 C. Roger Harker; 3,352 Tommy Klein; 3,202 Thurman J. Hamlin.

Congress   Unopposed in six CD's. Cissy Musselman, the unopposed candidate in CD 3, withdrew after the primary and Suzanne M. Warner was substituted by the local party committee. No candidate in CD 1.

MAY 29 DEMOCRATIC

Senator   Walter Huddleston, unopposed.

Congress   Unopposed in two CD's. Carl D. Perkins, the unopposed candidate in CD 7, died after the primary and his son Carl C. Perkins was substituted by the local party committee. Contested as follows:

CD 1   39,612 Carroll Hubbard; 10,578 Charles K. Hatchett.
CD 2   27,986 William H. Natcher; 11,435 Frank Miller.
CD 3   25,043 Romano L. Mazzoli; 3,460 Jude J. Barton.
CD 4   14,773 William P. Mulloy; 7,171 Maurice McCormick; 3,501 John E. Knipper.
CD 6   11,704 Jerry Hammond; 9,702 Robert K. Landrum; 3,411 Bradley K. Richards; 2,711 Eric Sevdy.

LOUISIANA

GOVERNOR
Edwin W. Edwards (D). Elected October 1983 to a four-year term. Previously elected 1975, 1972.

SENATORS
J. Bennett Johnston (D). Re-elected 1984 to a six-year term. Previously elected 1978, 1972.

Russell B. Long (D). Re-elected 1980 to a six-year term. Previously elected 1974, 1968, 1962, 1956, 1950, and in 1948 to fill out term vacated by the death of Senator John H. Overton.

REPRESENTATIVES
1. Bob Livingston (R)
2. Lindy Boggs (D)
3. W. J. Tauzin (D)
4. Charles Roemer (D)
5. Jerry Huckaby (D)
6. W. Henson Moore (R)
7. John B. Breaux (D)
8. Gillis W. Long (D)

(see page 1)

POSTWAR VOTE FOR GOVERNOR

Year	Total Vote	Republican Vote	Republican Candidate	Democratic Vote	Democratic Candidate	Other Vote	Rep.-Dem. Plurality	Total Vote Rep.	Total Vote Dem.	Major Vote Rep.	Major Vote Dem.
1983*	—	—	—	—	Edwards, Edwin W.	—	—	—	—	—	—
1979	1,371,825	690,691	Treen, David C.	681,134	Lambert, Louis	—	9,557 R	50.3%	49.7%	50.3%	49.7%
1975	430,095	—	—	430,095	Edwards, Edwin W.	—	430,095 D	—	100.0%	—	100.0%
1972	1,121,570	480,424	Treen, David C.	641,146	Edwards, Edwin W.	—	160,722 D	42.8%	57.2%	42.8%	57.2%
1968	372,762	—	—	372,762	McKeithen, John J.	—	372,762 D	—	100.0%	—	100.0%
1964	773,390	297,753	Lyons, C. H.	469,589	McKeithen, John J.	6,048	171,836 D	38.5%	60.7%	38.8%	61.2%
1960	506,562	86,135	Grevemberg, F. C.	407,907	Davis, Jimmie H.	12,520	321,772 D	17.0%	80.5%	17.4%	82.6%
1956	172,291	—	—	172,291	Long, Earl K.	—	172,291 D	—	100.0%	—	100.0%
1952	123,681	4,958	Bagwell, Harrison G.	118,723	Kennon, Robert F.	—	113,765 D	4.0%	96.0%	4.0%	96.0%
1948	76,566	—	—	76,566	Long, Earl K.	—	76,566 D	—	100.0%	—	100.0%

For the 1983 election, see note section; no run-off general election was required.

POSTWAR VOTE FOR SENATOR

Year	Total Vote	Republican Vote	Republican Candidate	Democratic Vote	Democratic Candidate	Other Vote	Rep.-Dem. Plurality	Total Vote Rep.	Total Vote Dem.	Major Vote Rep.	Major Vote Dem.
1984*	—	—	—	—	Johnston, J. Bennett	—	—	—	—	—	—
1980*	—	—	—	—	Long, Russell B.	—	—	—	—	—	—
1978*	—	—	—	—	Johnston, J. Bennett	—	—	—	—	—	—
1974	434,643	—	—	434,643	Long, Russell B.	—	434,643 D	—	100.0%	—	100.0%
1972	1,084,904	206,846	Toledano, Ben C.	598,987	Johnston, J. Bennett	279,071	392,141 D	19.1%	55.2%	25.7%	74.3%
1968	518,586	—	—	518,586	Long, Russell B.	—	518,586 D	—	100.0%	—	100.0%
1966	437,695	—	—	437,695	Ellender, Allen J.	—	437,695 D	—	100.0%	—	100.0%
1962	421,904	103,066	O'Hearn, Taylor W.	318,838	Long, Russell B.	—	215,772 D	24.4%	75.6%	24.4%	75.6%
1960	541,928	109,698	Reese, George W.	432,228	Ellender, Allen J.	2	322,530 D	20.2%	79.8%	20.2%	79.8%
1956	335,564	—	—	335,564	Long, Russell B.	—	335,564 D	—	100.0%	—	100.0%
1954	207,115	—	—	207,115	Ellender, Allen J.	—	207,115 D	—	100.0%	—	100.0%
1950	251,838	30,931	Gerth, Charles S.	220,907	Long, Russell B.	—	189,976 D	12.3%	87.7%	12.3%	87.7%
1948	330,124	—	—	330,115	Ellender, Allen J.	9	330,115 D	—	100.0%	—	100.0%
1948s	408,667	102,331	Clarke, Clem S.	306,336	Long, Russell B.	—	204,005 D	25.0%	75.0%	25.0%	75.0%

One of the 1948 elections was for a short term to fill a vacancy. For the 1978, 1980 and 1984 elections, see note section; no run-off general elections were required.

LOUISIANA

Districts Established December 19, 1983

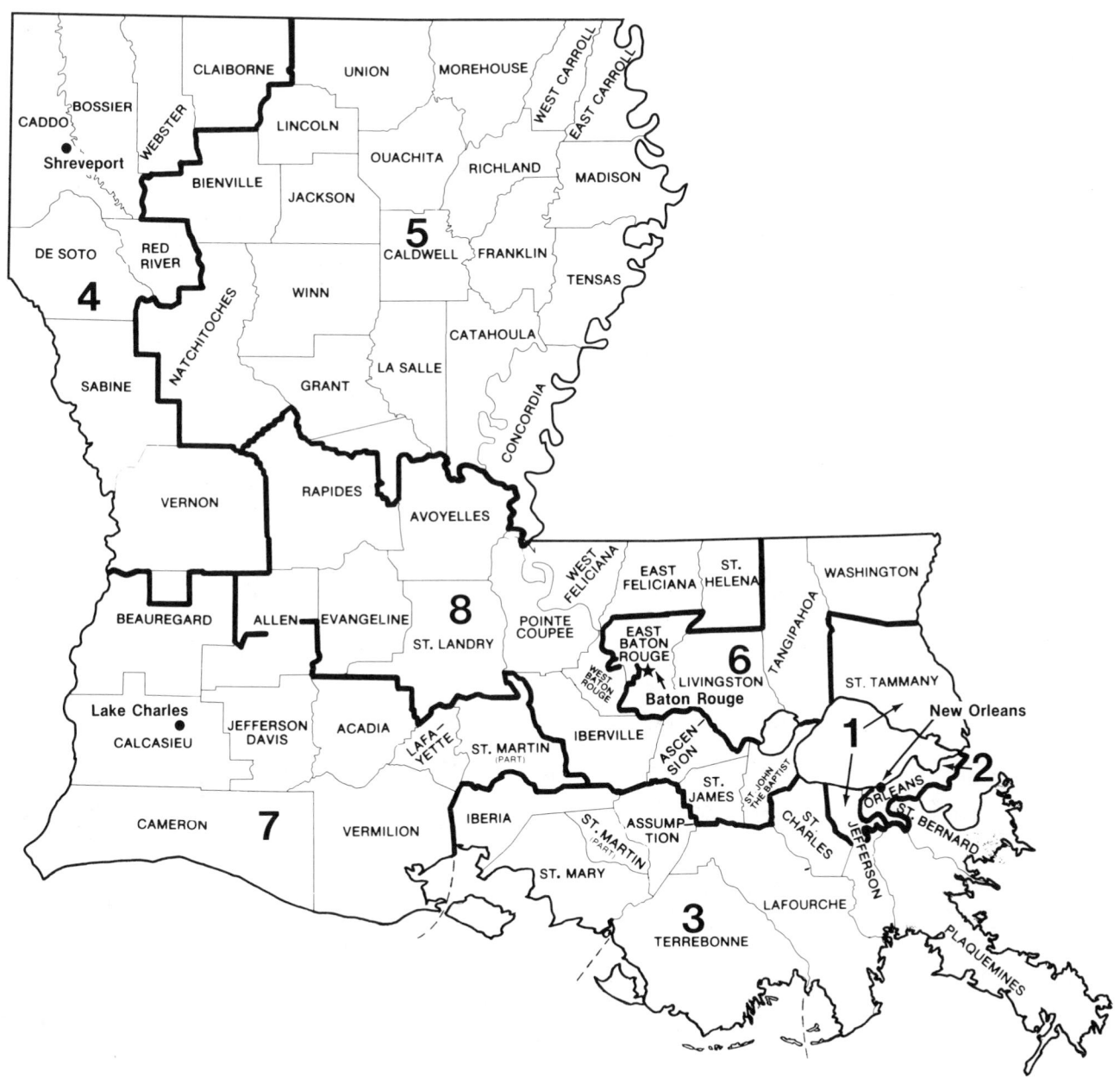

LOUISIANA

PRESIDENT 1984

1980 Census Population	Parish	Total Vote	Republican	Democratic	Other	Rep.-Dem. Plurality	Total Vote Rep.	Total Vote Dem.	Major Vote Rep.	Major Vote Dem.
56,427	ACADIA	24,602	14,906	9,262	434	5,644 R	60.6%	37.6%	61.7%	38.3%
21,390	ALLEN	9,382	4,474	4,842	66	368 D	47.7%	51.6%	48.0%	52.0%
50,068	ASCENSION	23,170	11,945	11,048	177	897 R	51.6%	47.7%	52.0%	48.0%
22,084	ASSUMPTION	10,363	5,433	4,660	270	773 R	52.4%	45.0%	53.8%	46.2%
41,393	AVOYELLES	16,673	9,402	6,808	463	2,594 R	56.4%	40.8%	58.0%	42.0%
29,692	BEAUREGARD	11,648	7,353	4,199	96	3,154 R	63.1%	36.0%	63.7%	36.3%
16,387	BIENVILLE	8,226	4,587	3,530	109	1,057 R	55.8%	42.9%	56.5%	43.5%
80,721	BOSSIER	29,782	22,638	7,006	138	15,632 R	76.0%	23.5%	76.4%	23.6%
252,358	CADDO	99,601	63,429	35,727	445	27,702 R	63.7%	35.9%	64.0%	36.0%
167,223	CALCASIEU	69,210	35,566	33,214	430	2,352 R	51.4%	48.0%	51.7%	48.3%
10,761	CALDWELL	4,819	3,341	1,348	130	1,993 R	69.3%	28.0%	71.3%	28.7%
9,336	CAMERON	3,906	2,265	1,608	33	657 R	58.0%	41.2%	58.5%	41.5%
12,287	CATAHOULA	5,391	3,640	1,649	102	1,991 R	67.5%	30.6%	68.8%	31.2%
17,095	CLAIBORNE	7,214	4,349	2,788	77	1,561 R	60.3%	38.6%	60.9%	39.1%
22,981	CONCORDIA	9,692	6,177	3,332	183	2,845 R	63.7%	34.4%	65.0%	35.0%
25,727	DE SOTO	10,739	5,989	4,642	108	1,347 R	55.8%	43.2%	56.3%	43.7%
366,191	EAST BATON ROUGE	153,268	95,704	56,673	891	39,031 R	62.4%	37.0%	62.8%	37.2%
11,772	EAST CARROLL	4,132	1,974	2,089	69	115 D	47.8%	50.6%	48.6%	51.4%
19,015	EAST FELICIANA	8,401	4,166	4,122	113	44 R	49.6%	49.1%	50.3%	49.7%
33,343	EVANGELINE	15,844	8,680	6,981	183	1,699 R	54.8%	44.1%	55.4%	44.6%
24,141	FRANKLIN	9,894	6,708	2,937	249	3,771 R	67.8%	29.7%	69.5%	30.5%
16,703	GRANT	8,097	5,334	2,588	175	2,746 R	65.9%	32.0%	67.3%	32.7%
63,752	IBERIA	28,526	17,727	10,170	629	7,557 R	62.1%	35.7%	63.5%	36.5%
32,159	IBERVILLE	15,159	6,455	8,587	117	2,132 D	42.6%	56.6%	42.9%	57.1%
17,321	JACKSON	7,761	5,034	2,568	159	2,466 R	64.9%	33.1%	66.2%	33.8%
454,592	JEFFERSON	166,023	123,997	41,183	843	82,814 R	74.7%	24.8%	75.1%	24.9%
32,168	JEFFERSON DAVIS	14,464	8,296	5,962	206	2,334 R	57.4%	41.2%	58.2%	41.8%
150,017	LAFAYETTE	64,458	44,344	19,265	849	25,079 R	68.8%	29.9%	69.7%	30.3%
82,483	LAFOURCHE	32,005	20,930	10,186	889	10,744 R	65.4%	31.8%	67.3%	32.7%
17,004	LA SALLE	6,875	5,404	1,318	153	4,086 R	78.6%	19.2%	80.4%	19.6%
39,763	LINCOLN	14,701	9,087	5,432	182	3,655 R	61.8%	36.9%	62.6%	37.4%
58,806	LIVINGSTON	26,576	17,465	8,913	198	8,552 R	65.7%	33.5%	66.2%	33.8%
15,975	MADISON	5,864	2,849	2,906	109	57 D	48.6%	49.6%	49.5%	50.5%
34,803	MOREHOUSE	13,685	8,585	4,829	271	3,756 R	62.7%	35.3%	64.0%	36.0%
39,863	NATCHITOCHES	14,978	8,836	5,806	336	3,030 R	59.0%	38.8%	60.3%	39.7%
557,515	ORLEANS	206,956	86,316	119,478	1,162	33,162 D	41.7%	57.7%	41.9%	58.1%
139,241	OUACHITA	53,574	37,270	15,525	779	21,745 R	69.6%	29.0%	70.6%	29.4%
26,049	PLAQUEMINES	10,977	7,655	3,261	61	4,394 R	69.7%	29.7%	70.1%	29.9%
24,045	POINTE COUPEE	12,287	5,477	6,732	78	1,255 D	44.6%	54.8%	44.9%	55.1%
135,282	RAPIDES	49,963	32,879	16,121	963	16,758 R	65.8%	32.3%	67.1%	32.9%
10,433	RED RIVER	5,067	3,060	1,958	49	1,102 R	60.4%	38.6%	61.0%	39.0%
22,187	RICHLAND	9,083	5,980	2,918	185	3,062 R	65.8%	32.1%	67.2%	32.8%
25,280	SABINE	9,500	6,295	2,980	225	3,315 R	66.3%	31.4%	67.9%	32.1%
64,097	ST. BERNARD	32,657	24,428	8,076	153	16,352 R	74.8%	24.7%	75.2%	24.8%
37,259	ST. CHARLES	17,082	10,185	6,784	113	3,401 R	59.6%	39.7%	60.0%	40.0%
9,827	ST. HELENA	5,435	2,366	2,956	113	590 D	43.5%	54.4%	44.5%	55.5%
21,495	ST. JAMES	10,735	4,627	5,989	119	1,362 D	43.1%	55.8%	43.6%	56.4%
31,924	ST. JOHN THE BAPTIST	16,851	9,093	7,646	112	1,447 R	54.0%	45.4%	54.3%	45.7%
84,128	ST. LANDRY	37,223	19,055	17,950	218	1,105 R	51.2%	48.2%	51.5%	48.5%
40,214	ST. MARTIN	18,591	9,698	8,589	304	1,109 R	52.2%	46.2%	53.0%	47.0%
64,253	ST. MARY	24,974	15,275	9,411	288	5,864 R	61.2%	37.7%	61.9%	38.1%
110,869	ST. TAMMANY	50,775	38,664	11,719	392	26,945 R	76.1%	23.1%	76.7%	23.3%
80,698	TANGIPAHOA	32,579	19,580	12,799	200	6,781 R	60.1%	39.3%	60.5%	39.5%
8,525	TENSAS	3,655	1,956	1,628	71	328 R	53.5%	44.5%	54.6%	45.4%
94,393	TERREBONNE	34,089	23,696	9,640	753	14,056 R	69.5%	28.3%	71.1%	28.9%
21,167	UNION	9,723	6,585	2,916	222	3,669 R	67.7%	30.0%	69.3%	30.7%
48,458	VERMILION	22,378	12,721	9,033	624	3,688 R	56.8%	40.4%	58.5%	41.5%
53,475	VERNON	13,369	9,035	4,076	258	4,959 R	67.6%	30.5%	68.9%	31.1%
44,207	WASHINGTON	18,988	11,185	7,680	123	3,505 R	58.9%	40.4%	59.3%	40.7%
43,631	WEBSTER	18,677	12,055	6,509	113	5,546 R	64.5%	34.9%	64.9%	35.1%

LOUISIANA

PRESIDENT 1984

1980 Census Population	Parish	Total Vote	Republican	Democratic	Other	Rep.-Dem. Plurality	Percentage			
							Total Vote		Major Vote	
							Rep.	Dem.	Rep.	Dem.
19,086	WEST BATON ROUGE	8,883	4,189	4,631	63	442 D	47.2%	52.1%	47.5%	52.5%
12,922	WEST CARROLL	5,469	3,874	1,474	121	2,400 R	70.8%	27.0%	72.4%	27.6%
12,186	WEST FELICIANA	4,426	2,097	2,296	33	199 D	47.4%	51.9%	47.7%	52.3%
17,253	WINN	7,727	4,934	2,633	160	2,301 R	63.9%	34.1%	65.2%	34.8%
4,205,900	TOTAL	1,706,822	1,037,299	651,586	17,937	385,713 R	60.8%	38.2%	61.4%	38.6%

LOUISIANA

GOVERNOR 1983

(PRIMARY ELECTION)

1980 Census Population	Parish	Total Vote	Treen	Edwards	Other	Treen-Edwards Plurality	Percentage			
							Total Vote		Major Vote	
							Treen	Edwards	Treen	Edwards
56,427	ACADIA	28,117	6,754	21,184	179	14,430 E	24.0%	75.3%	24.2%	75.8%
21,390	ALLEN	10,242	2,499	7,654	89	5,155 E	24.4%	74.7%	24.6%	75.4%
50,068	ASCENSION	22,956	4,850	17,888	218	13,038 E	21.1%	77.9%	21.3%	78.7%
22,084	ASSUMPTION	10,809	2,544	8,027	238	5,483 E	23.5%	74.3%	24.1%	75.9%
41,393	AVOYELLES	18,906	4,522	13,907	477	9,385 E	23.9%	73.6%	24.5%	75.5%
29,692	BEAUREGARD	11,774	4,592	6,984	198	2,392 E	39.0%	59.3%	39.7%	60.3%
16,387	BIENVILLE	8,656	2,449	6,119	88	3,670 E	28.3%	70.7%	28.6%	71.4%
80,721	BOSSIER	24,492	11,543	12,786	163	1,243 E	47.1%	52.2%	47.4%	52.6%
252,358	CADDO	81,772	37,789	43,451	532	5,662 E	46.2%	53.1%	46.5%	53.5%
167,223	CALCASIEU	64,179	23,713	39,812	654	16,099 E	36.9%	62.0%	37.3%	62.7%
10,761	CALDWELL	5,763	1,838	3,801	124	1,963 E	31.9%	66.0%	32.6%	67.4%
9,336	CAMERON	4,890	1,262	3,547	81	2,285 E	25.8%	72.5%	26.2%	73.8%
12,287	CATAHOULA	6,394	1,650	4,568	176	2,918 E	25.8%	71.4%	26.5%	73.5%
17,095	CLAIBORNE	6,953	2,410	4,457	86	2,047 E	34.7%	64.1%	35.1%	64.9%
22,981	CONCORDIA	10,002	3,228	6,549	225	3,321 E	32.3%	65.5%	33.0%	67.0%
25,727	DE SOTO	10,416	3,293	7,052	71	3,759 E	31.6%	67.7%	31.8%	68.2%
366,191	EAST BATON ROUGE	135,131	56,452	77,749	930	21,297 E	41.8%	57.5%	42.1%	57.9%
11,772	EAST CARROLL	4,570	1,124	3,286	160	2,162 E	24.6%	71.9%	25.5%	74.5%
19,015	EAST FELICIANA	7,994	1,646	6,270	78	4,624 E	20.6%	78.4%	20.8%	79.2%
33,343	EVANGELINE	17,772	4,972	12,535	265	7,563 E	28.0%	70.5%	28.4%	71.6%
24,141	FRANKLIN	11,007	3,479	7,210	318	3,731 E	31.6%	65.5%	32.5%	67.5%
16,703	GRANT	8,309	2,629	5,415	265	2,786 E	31.6%	65.2%	32.7%	67.3%
63,752	IBERIA	28,250	10,345	17,481	424	7,136 E	36.6%	61.9%	37.2%	62.8%
32,159	IBERVILLE	16,670	2,951	13,533	186	10,582 E	17.7%	81.2%	17.9%	82.1%
17,321	JACKSON	8,069	2,979	4,889	201	1,910 E	36.9%	60.6%	37.9%	62.1%
454,592	JEFFERSON	143,201	73,763	68,550	888	5,213 T	51.5%	47.9%	51.8%	48.2%
32,168	JEFFERSON DAVIS	14,346	4,533	9,692	121	5,159 E	31.6%	67.6%	31.9%	68.1%
150,017	LAFAYETTE	59,264	24,995	33,134	1,135	8,139 E	42.2%	55.9%	43.0%	57.0%
82,483	LAFOURCHE	34,182	10,066	23,524	592	13,458 E	29.4%	68.8%	30.0%	70.0%
17,004	LA SALLE	7,462	2,716	4,479	267	1,763 E	36.4%	60.0%	37.7%	62.3%
39,763	LINCOLN	13,719	5,969	7,495	255	1,526 E	43.5%	54.6%	44.3%	55.7%
58,806	LIVINGSTON	28,284	7,383	20,610	291	13,227 E	26.1%	72.9%	26.4%	73.6%
15,975	MADISON	6,200	1,515	4,465	220	2,950 E	24.4%	72.0%	25.3%	74.7%
34,803	MOREHOUSE	12,767	5,095	7,353	319	2,258 E	39.9%	57.6%	40.9%	59.1%
39,863	NATCHITOCHES	14,888	4,936	9,619	333	4,683 E	33.2%	64.6%	33.9%	66.1%
557,515	ORLEANS	185,235	65,525	118,289	1,421	52,764 E	35.4%	63.9%	35.6%	64.4%
139,241	OUACHITA	46,327	21,423	24,099	805	2,676 E	46.2%	52.0%	47.1%	52.9%
26,049	PLAQUEMINES	11,034	3,698	7,254	82	3,556 E	33.5%	65.7%	33.8%	66.2%
24,045	POINTE COUPEE	11,815	2,130	9,598	87	7,468 E	18.0%	81.2%	18.2%	81.8%
135,282	RAPIDES	46,643	17,619	28,000	1,024	10,381 E	37.8%	60.0%	38.6%	61.4%
10,433	RED RIVER	5,467	1,369	4,012	86	2,643 E	25.0%	73.4%	25.4%	74.6%
22,187	RICHLAND	9,434	3,460	5,707	267	2,247 E	36.7%	60.5%	37.7%	62.3%
25,280	SABINE	10,055	3,179	6,693	183	3,514 E	31.6%	66.6%	32.2%	67.8%
64,097	ST. BERNARD	32,290	11,507	20,543	240	9,036 E	35.6%	63.6%	35.9%	64.1%
37,259	ST. CHARLES	17,031	5,863	11,030	138	5,167 E	34.4%	64.8%	34.7%	65.3%
9,827	ST. HELENA	6,092	1,062	4,959	71	3,897 E	17.4%	81.4%	17.6%	82.4%
21,495	ST. JAMES	11,040	2,214	8,725	101	6,511 E	20.1%	79.0%	20.2%	79.8%
31,924	ST. JOHN THE BAPTIST	16,787	5,013	11,579	195	6,566 E	29.9%	69.0%	30.2%	69.8%
84,128	ST. LANDRY	37,187	10,174	26,690	323	16,516 E	27.4%	71.8%	27.6%	72.4%
40,214	ST. MARTIN	19,647	4,401	14,476	770	10,075 E	22.4%	73.7%	23.3%	76.7%
64,253	ST. MARY	23,742	7,942	15,075	725	7,133 E	33.5%	63.5%	34.5%	65.5%
110,869	ST. TAMMANY	43,742	22,769	20,681	292	2,088 T	52.1%	47.3%	52.4%	47.6%
80,698	TANGIPAHOA	34,312	10,227	23,770	315	13,543 E	29.8%	69.3%	30.1%	69.9%
8,525	TENSAS	3,970	1,224	2,592	154	1,368 E	30.8%	65.3%	32.1%	67.9%
94,393	TERREBONNE	32,220	11,533	19,917	770	8,384 E	35.8%	61.8%	36.7%	63.3%
21,167	UNION	9,971	3,977	5,736	258	1,759 E	39.9%	57.5%	40.9%	59.1%
48,458	VERMILION	25,039	7,002	17,555	482	10,553 E	28.0%	70.1%	28.5%	71.5%
53,475	VERNON	13,797	3,778	9,680	339	5,902 E	27.4%	70.2%	28.1%	71.9%
44,207	WASHINGTON	19,420	4,987	14,238	195	9,251 E	25.7%	73.3%	25.9%	74.1%
43,631	WEBSTER	17,483	6,288	11,030	165	4,742 E	36.0%	63.1%	36.3%	63.7%

LOUISIANA

GOVERNOR 1983

(PRIMARY ELECTION)

1980 Census Population	Parish	Total Vote	Treen	Edwards	Other	Treen- Edwards Plurality	Percentage			
							Total Vote		Major Vote	
							Treen	Edwards	Treen	Edwards
19,086	WEST BATON ROUGE	9,121	1,818	7,242	61	5,424 E	19.9%	79.4%	20.1%	79.9%
12,922	WEST CARROLL	5,918	2,185	3,586	147	1,401 E	36.9%	60.6%	37.9%	62.1%
12,186	WEST FELICIANA	4,385	880	3,478	27	2,598 E	20.1%	79.3%	20.2%	79.8%
17,253	WINN	8,295	2,777	5,252	266	2,475 E	33.5%	63.3%	34.6%	65.4%
4,205,900	TOTAL	1,615,905	588,508	1,006,561	20,836	418,053 E	36.4%	62.3%	36.9%	63.1%

LOUISIANA

SENATOR 1984

(PRIMARY ELECTION)

1980 Census Population	Parish	Total Vote	Ross	Johnston	Cooper	Plurality	Percentage Ross	Johnston	Cooper
56,427	ACADIA	7,670	580	6,518	572	5,938 J	7.6%	85.0%	7.5%
21,390	ALLEN	5,843	449	5,070	324	4,621 J	7.7%	86.8%	5.5%
50,068	ASCENSION	14,040	992	12,411	637	11,419 J	7.1%	88.4%	4.5%
22,084	ASSUMPTION	8,221	339	7,507	375	7,132 J	4.1%	91.3%	4.6%
41,393	AVOYELLES	11,058	888	9,603	567	8,715 J	8.0%	86.8%	5.1%
29,692	BEAUREGARD	8,740	777	7,462	501	6,685 J	8.9%	85.4%	5.7%
16,387	BIENVILLE	5,389	513	4,419	457	3,906 J	9.5%	82.0%	8.5%
80,721	BOSSIER	17,052	1,898	14,369	785	12,471 J	11.1%	84.3%	4.6%
252,358	CADDO	47,605	5,043	40,173	2,389	35,130 J	10.6%	84.4%	5.0%
167,223	CALCASIEU	51,761	4,290	44,511	2,960	40,221 J	8.3%	86.0%	5.7%
10,761	CALDWELL	1,363	161	1,109	93	948 J	11.8%	81.4%	6.8%
9,336	CAMERON	3,830	209	3,393	228	3,165 J	5.5%	88.6%	6.0%
12,287	CATAHOULA	4,099	366	3,527	206	3,161 J	8.9%	86.0%	5.0%
17,095	CLAIBORNE	4,345	421	3,586	338	3,165 J	9.7%	82.5%	7.8%
22,981	CONCORDIA	5,786	603	4,929	254	4,326 J	10.4%	85.2%	4.4%
25,727	DE SOTO	7,262	590	6,251	421	5,661 J	8.1%	86.1%	5.8%
366,191	EAST BATON ROUGE	114,955	10,184	99,634	5,137	89,450 J	8.9%	86.7%	4.5%
11,772	EAST CARROLL	3,061	257	2,669	135	2,412 J	8.4%	87.2%	4.4%
19,015	EAST FELICIANA	5,448	565	4,560	323	3,995 J	10.4%	83.7%	5.9%
33,343	EVANGELINE	8,442	726	6,978	738	6,240 J	8.6%	82.7%	8.7%
24,141	FRANKLIN	7,414	749	6,255	410	5,506 J	10.1%	84.4%	5.5%
16,703	GRANT	6,470	615	5,561	294	4,946 J	9.5%	86.0%	4.5%
63,752	IBERIA	11,668	1,172	9,927	569	8,755 J	10.0%	85.1%	4.9%
32,159	IBERVILLE	6,857	367	6,049	441	5,608 J	5.4%	88.2%	6.4%
17,321	JACKSON	5,962	729	4,894	339	4,165 J	12.2%	82.1%	5.7%
454,592	JEFFERSON	62,892	7,218	51,832	3,842	44,614 J	11.5%	82.4%	6.1%
32,168	JEFFERSON DAVIS	10,958	790	9,548	620	8,758 J	7.2%	87.1%	5.7%
150,017	LAFAYETTE	12,461	1,076	10,661	724	9,585 J	8.6%	85.6%	5.8%
82,483	LAFOURCHE	4,725	239	4,293	193	4,054 J	5.1%	90.9%	4.1%
17,004	LA SALLE	6,081	641	5,029	411	4,388 J	10.5%	82.7%	6.8%
39,763	LINCOLN	6,201	707	5,161	333	4,454 J	11.4%	83.2%	5.4%
58,806	LIVINGSTON	10,188	946	8,775	467	7,829 J	9.3%	86.1%	4.6%
15,975	MADISON	4,797	364	4,240	193	3,876 J	7.6%	88.4%	4.0%
34,803	MOREHOUSE	10,639	1,114	9,012	513	7,898 J	10.5%	84.7%	4.8%
39,863	NATCHITOCHES	12,381	1,223	10,470	688	9,247 J	9.9%	84.6%	5.6%
557,515	ORLEANS	115,774	7,161	103,118	5,495	95,957 J	6.2%	89.1%	4.7%
139,241	OUACHITA	36,571	4,210	30,615	1,746	26,405 J	11.5%	83.7%	4.8%
26,049	PLAQUEMINES	7,782	500	6,907	375	6,407 J	6.4%	88.8%	4.8%
24,045	POINTE COUPEE	9,135	577	8,080	478	7,503 J	6.3%	88.5%	5.2%
135,282	RAPIDES	34,116	3,275	29,154	1,687	25,879 J	9.6%	85.5%	4.9%
10,433	RED RIVER	3,419	305	2,896	218	2,591 J	8.9%	84.7%	6.4%
22,187	RICHLAND	6,265	612	5,286	367	4,674 J	9.8%	84.4%	5.9%
25,280	SABINE	7,456	709	6,373	374	5,664 J	9.5%	85.5%	5.0%
64,097	ST. BERNARD	27,959	1,881	24,247	1,831	22,366 J	6.7%	86.7%	6.5%
37,259	ST. CHARLES	3,519	286	2,992	241	2,706 J	8.1%	85.0%	6.8%
9,827	ST. HELENA	4,446	401	3,732	313	3,331 J	9.0%	83.9%	7.0%
21,495	ST. JAMES	7,708	401	6,841	466	6,375 J	5.2%	88.8%	6.0%
31,924	ST. JOHN THE BAPTIST	11,808	1,100	9,919	789	8,819 J	9.3%	84.0%	6.7%
84,128	ST. LANDRY	19,573	1,898	16,346	1,329	14,448 J	9.7%	83.5%	6.8%
40,214	ST. MARTIN	11,687	690	10,323	674	9,633 J	5.9%	88.3%	5.8%
64,253	ST. MARY	17,434	1,210	15,436	788	14,226 J	6.9%	88.5%	4.5%
110,869	ST. TAMMANY	29,266	3,772	23,599	1,895	19,827 J	12.9%	80.6%	6.5%
80,698	TANGIPAHOA	18,293	1,539	15,603	1,151	14,064 J	8.4%	85.3%	6.3%
8,525	TENSAS	2,242	182	1,946	114	1,764 J	8.1%	86.8%	5.1%
94,393	TERREBONNE	21,326	1,512	18,564	1,250	17,052 J	7.1%	87.0%	5.9%
21,167	UNION	5,120	614	4,189	317	3,575 J	12.0%	81.8%	6.2%
48,458	VERMILION	9,183	1,567	6,761	855	5,194 J	17.1%	73.6%	9.3%
53,475	VERNON	7,024	522	6,108	394	5,586 J	7.4%	87.0%	5.6%
44,207	WASHINGTON	13,116	921	11,464	731	10,543 J	7.0%	87.4%	5.6%
43,631	WEBSTER	14,489	1,231	12,638	620	11,407 J	8.5%	87.2%	4.3%

LOUISIANA

SENATOR 1984

(PRIMARY ELECTION)

1980 Census Population	Parish	Total Vote	Ross	Johnston	Cooper	Plurality	Percentage		
							Ross	Johnston	Cooper
19,086	WEST BATON ROUGE	4,431	295	3,931	205	3,636 J	6.7%	88.7%	4.6%
12,922	WEST CARROLL	3,990	472	3,356	162	2,884 J	11.8%	84.1%	4.1%
12,186	WEST FELICIANA	2,781	244	2,424	113	2,180 J	8.8%	87.2%	4.1%
17,253	WINN	5,896	658	4,947	291	4,289 J	11.2%	83.9%	4.9%
4,205,900	TOTAL	977,473	86,546	838,181	52,746	751,635 J	8.9%	85.7%	5.4%

LOUISIANA

CONGRESS

		Total Vote	Republican		Democratic		Other Vote	Rep.-Dem. Plurality	Percentage			
CD	Year		Vote	Candidate	Vote	Candidate			Total Vote Rep.	Dem.	Major Vote Rep.	Dem.
1	1984			LIVINGSTON, BOB								
2	1984					BOGGS, LINDY						
3	1984					TAUZIN, W. J.						
4	1984					ROEMER, CHARLES						
4	1982					ROEMER, CHARLES						
5	1984					HUCKABY, JERRY						
5	1982					HUCKABY, JERRY						
6	1984			MOORE, W. HENSON								
6	1982			MOORE, W. HENSON								
7	1984					BREAUX, JOHN B.						
7	1982					BREAUX, JOHN B.						
8	1984					LONG, GILLIS W.						
8	1982					LONG, GILLIS W.						

LOUISIANA

1983 GENERAL ELECTION

Governor   No run-off general election was required. The data carried in the table for Governor 1983 are for the primary contest between the candidates listed in the primary section. A "T" in the plurality column is a David C. Treen plurality and an "E" in that column is an Edwin W. Edwards plurality.

1984 GENERAL ELECTION

President   Other vote was 9,502 Johnson (Citizens); 3,552 LaRouche (Independent); 1,876 Bergland (Libertarian); 1,310 Richards (Populist); 1,164 Mason (Socialist Workers); 533 Serrette (New Alliance).

Senator   No run-off general election was required. The data carried in the table for Senator 1984 are for the primary contest between Ross, Johnston and Cooper. Senator Johnston carried every parish and a "J" in the plurality column represents his plurality.

Congress   See primary note section below. Since candidates who are unopposed in the primary or who receive a majority in the primary are elected unopposed, there were no candidate names on the general election ballot and no votes were canvassed for these candidates.

PRIMARIES

Louisiana holds an open-primary election with candidates from all parties running on the same ballot. Any candidate who receives a majority is elected. If no candidate receives 50 percent, there is a run-off election between the top two finishers.

OCTOBER 22, 1983

Governor   1,006,561 Edwin W. Edwards (D); 588,508 David C. Treen (R); 7,625 Robert M. Ross (R); 4,128 Ken Lewis (D); 2,391 Charles Moore (no party); 2,314 Floyd W. Smith (D); 2,299 Michele A. Smith (no party); 1,048 Joseph T. Robino (no party); 1,031 Michael J. Musmeci (D).

SEPTEMBER 29, 1984

Senator   838,181 J. Bennett Johnston (D); 86,546 Robert M. Ross (R); 52,746 Larry N. Cooper (R). Early uncorrected returns gave the Johnson vote in Union parish as 4,819.

Congress   Unopposed in three CD's. Contested as follows:

CD 1   86,466 Bob Livingston (R); 7,880 John B. Levy (D); 4,257 Kevin Curley (D).
CD 2   76,272 Lindy Boggs (D); 48,976 Israel M. Augustine (D); 626 Derrick Morrison (no party); 526 Bert Lodrig (D); 451 Richard Torregano (D).
CD 6   119,548 W. Henson Moore (R); 33,501 Herb Rothschild (D).
CD 7   98,674 John B. Breaux (D); 15,752 John H. Myers (D).
CD 8   116,141 Gillis W. Long (D); 32,780 Darrell Williamson (R).

MAINE

GOVERNOR
Joseph E. Brennan (D). Re-elected 1982 to a four-year term. Previously elected 1978.

SENATORS
William S. Cohen (R). Re-elected 1984 to a six-year term. Previously elected 1978.

George J. Mitchell (D). Elected 1982 to a six-year term. Appointed to the Senate May 1980 on the resignation of Senator Edmund S. Muskie to become Secretary of State.

REPRESENTATIVES
1. John R. McKernan (R)   2. Olympia J. Snowe (R)

POSTWAR VOTE FOR GOVERNOR

Year	Total Vote	Republican Vote	Candidate	Democratic Vote	Candidate	Other Vote	Rep.-Dem. Plurality	Total Vote Rep.	Total Vote Dem.	Major Vote Rep.	Major Vote Dem.
1982	460,295	172,949	Cragin, Charles L.	281,066	Brennan, Joseph E.	6,280	108,117 D	37.6%	61.1%	38.1%	61.9%
1978	370,258	126,862	Palmer, Linwood E.	176,493	Brennan, Joseph E.	66,903	49,631 D	34.3%	47.7%	41.8%	58.2%
1974*	363,945	84,176	Erwin, James S.	132,219	Mitchell, George J.	147,550	48,043 D	23.1%	36.3%	38.9%	61.1%
1970	325,386	162,248	Erwin, James S.	163,138	Curtis, Kenneth M.	—	890 D	49.9%	50.1%	49.9%	50.1%
1966	323,838	151,802	Reed, John H.	172,036	Curtis, Kenneth M.	—	20,234 D	46.9%	53.1%	46.9%	53.1%
1962	292,725	146,604	Reed, John H.	146,121	Dolloff, Maynard C.	—	483 R	50.1%	49.9%	50.1%	49.9%
1960s	417,315	219,768	Reed, John H.	197,547	Coffin, Frank M.	—	22,221 R	52.7%	47.3%	52.7%	47.3%
1958*	280,295	134,572	Hildreth, Horace A.	145,723	Clauson, Clinton A.	—	11,151 D	48.0%	52.0%	48.0%	52.0%
1956	304,649	124,395	Trafton, Willis A.	180,254	Muskie, Edmund S.	—	55,859 D	40.8%	59.2%	40.8%	59.2%
1954	248,971	113,298	Cross, Burton M.	135,673	Muskie, Edmund S.	—	22,375 D	45.5%	54.5%	45.5%	54.5%
1952	248,441	128,532	Cross, Burton M.	82,538	Oliver, James C.	37,371	45,994 R	51.7%	33.2%	60.9%	39.1%
1950	241,177	145,823	Payne, Frederick G.	94,304	Grant, Earl S.	1,050	51,519 R	60.5%	39.1%	60.7%	39.3%
1948	222,500	145,956	Payne, Frederick G.	76,544	Lausier, Louis B.	—	69,412 R	65.6%	34.4%	65.6%	34.4%
1946	179,951	110,327	Hildreth, Horace A.	69,624	Clark, F. Davis	—	40,703 R	61.3%	38.7%	61.3%	38.7%

The term of office of Maine's Governor was increased from two to four years effective with the 1958 election. The election in 1960 was for a short term to fill a vacancy. In 1974 James B. Longley, an Independent candidate, polled 142,464 votes (39.1% of the total vote) and won the election with a 10,245 plurality.

POSTWAR VOTE FOR SENATOR

Year	Total Vote	Republican Vote	Candidate	Democratic Vote	Candidate	Other Vote	Rep.-Dem. Plurality	Total Vote Rep.	Total Vote Dem.	Major Vote Rep.	Major Vote Dem.
1984	551,406	404,414	Cohen, William S.	142,626	Mitchell, Elizabeth H.	4,366	261,788 R	73.3%	25.9%	73.9%	26.1%
1982	459,715	179,882	Emery, David F.	279,819	Mitchell, George J.	14	99,937 D	39.1%	60.9%	39.1%	60.9%
1978	375,172	212,294	Cohen, William S.	127,327	Hathaway, William D.	35,551	84,967 R	56.6%	33.9%	62.5%	37.5%
1976	486,254	193,489	Monks, Robert A. G.	292,704	Muskie, Edmund S.	61	99,215 D	39.8%	60.2%	39.8%	60.2%
1972	421,310	197,040	Smith, Margaret Chase	224,270	Hathaway, William D.	—	27,230 D	46.8%	53.2%	46.8%	53.2%
1970	323,860	123,906	Bishop, Neil S.	199,954	Muskie, Edmund S.	—	76,048 D	38.3%	61.7%	38.3%	61.7%
1966	319,535	188,291	Smith, Margaret Chase	131,136	Violette, Elmer H.	108	57,155 R	58.9%	41.0%	58.9%	41.1%
1964	380,551	127,040	McIntire, Clifford	253,511	Muskie, Edmund S.	—	126,471 D	33.4%	66.6%	33.4%	66.6%
1960	416,699	256,890	Smith, Margaret Chase	159,809	Cormier, Lucia M.	—	97,081 R	61.6%	38.4%	61.6%	38.4%
1958	284,226	111,522	Payne, Frederick G.	172,704	Muskie, Edmund S.	—	61,182 D	39.2%	60.8%	39.2%	60.8%
1954	246,605	144,530	Smith, Margaret Chase	102,075	Fullam, Paul A.	—	42,455 R	58.6%	41.4%	58.6%	41.4%
1952	237,164	139,205	Payne, Frederick G.	82,665	Dube, Roger P.	15,294	56,540 R	58.7%	34.9%	62.7%	37.3%
1948	223,256	159,182	Smith, Margaret Chase	64,074	Scolten, Adrian H.	—	95,108 R	71.3%	28.7%	71.3%	28.7%
1946	175,014	111,215	Brewster, Owen	63,799	MacDonald, Peter	—	47,416 R	63.5%	36.5%	63.5%	36.5%

MAINE

Districts Established March 28, 1983

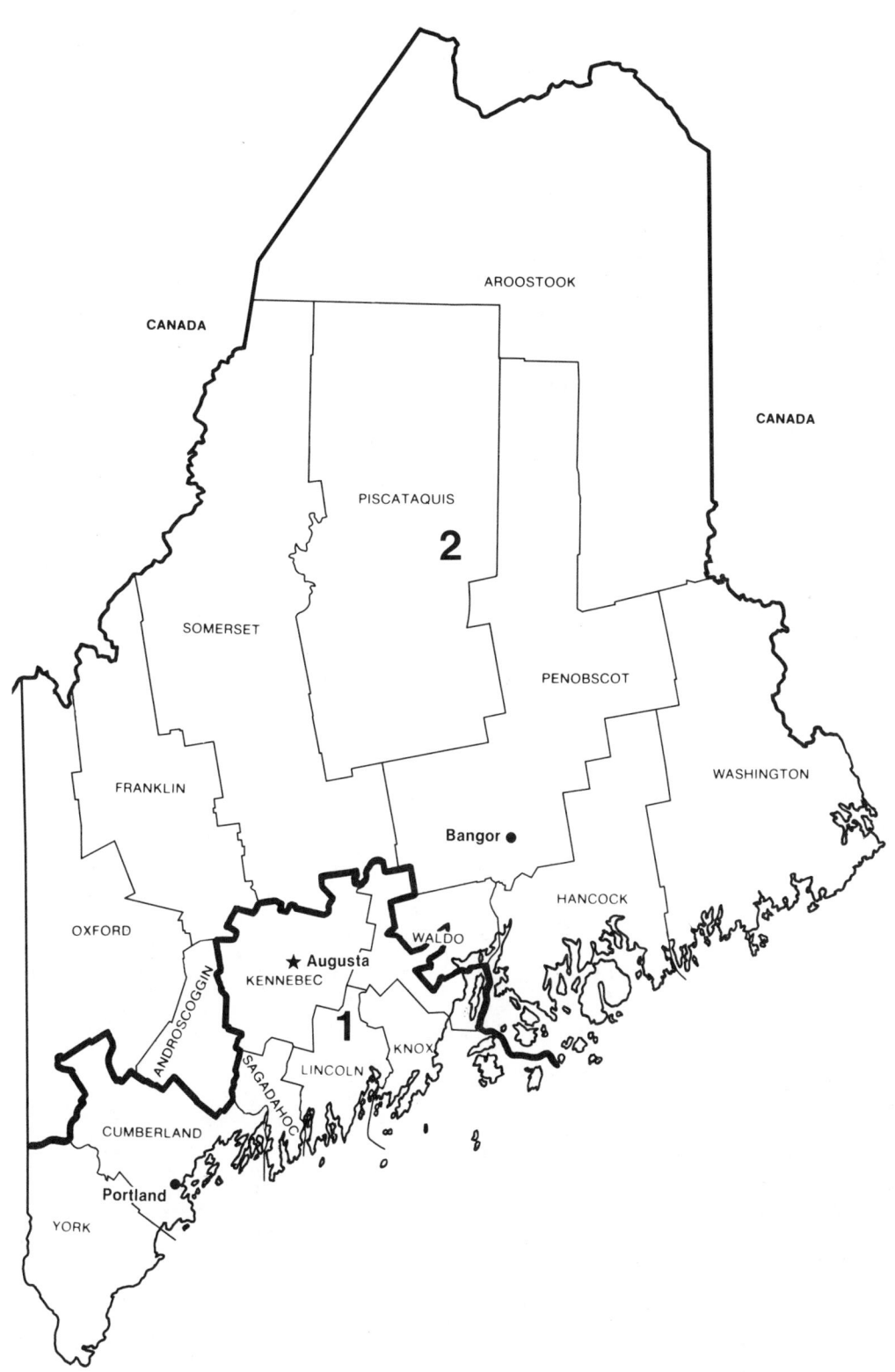

MAINE

PRESIDENT 1984

1980 Census Population	County	Total Vote	Republican	Democratic	Other	Rep.-Dem. Plurality	Percentage			
							Total Vote		Major Vote	
							Rep.	Dem.	Rep.	Dem.
99,657	ANDROSCOGGIN	47,000	26,904	19,885	211	7,019 R	57.2%	42.3%	57.5%	42.5%
91,331	AROOSTOOK	34,338	21,837	12,348	153	9,489 R	63.6%	36.0%	63.9%	36.1%
215,789	CUMBERLAND	116,026	65,842	49,894	290	15,948 R	56.7%	43.0%	56.9%	43.1%
27,098	FRANKLIN	13,349	8,330	4,954	65	3,376 R	62.4%	37.1%	62.7%	37.3%
41,781	HANCOCK	22,511	14,660	7,764	87	6,896 R	65.1%	34.5%	65.4%	34.6%
109,889	KENNEBEC	53,191	31,753	21,183	255	10,570 R	59.7%	39.8%	60.0%	40.0%
32,941	KNOX	17,401	11,311	6,024	66	5,287 R	65.0%	34.6%	65.2%	34.8%
25,691	LINCOLN	15,236	10,312	4,869	55	5,443 R	67.7%	32.0%	67.9%	32.1%
48,968	OXFORD	23,948	15,408	8,430	110	6,978 R	64.3%	35.2%	64.6%	35.4%
137,015	PENOBSCOT	65,054	40,403	24,445	206	15,958 R	62.1%	37.6%	62.3%	37.7%
17,634	PISCATAQUIS	8,482	5,427	3,016	39	2,411 R	64.0%	35.6%	64.3%	35.7%
28,795	SAGADAHOC	14,520	9,222	5,208	90	4,014 R	63.5%	35.9%	63.9%	36.1%
45,028	SOMERSET	20,771	13,010	7,657	104	5,353 R	62.6%	36.9%	63.0%	37.0%
28,414	WALDO	14,166	8,814	5,289	63	3,525 R	62.2%	37.3%	62.5%	37.5%
34,963	WASHINGTON	15,081	9,713	5,308	60	4,405 R	64.4%	35.2%	64.7%	35.3%
139,666	YORK	72,070	43,554	28,241	275	15,313 R	60.4%	39.2%	60.7%	39.3%
1,124,660	TOTAL	553,144	336,500	214,515	2,129	121,985 R	60.8%	38.8%	61.1%	38.9%

MAINE

PRESIDENT 1984

1980 Census Population	City/Town	Total Vote	Republican	Democratic	Other	Rep.-Dem. Plurality	Percentage Total Vote Rep.	Dem.	Major Vote Rep.	Dem.
23,128	AUBURN	11,463	6,994	4,430	39	2,564 R	61.0%	38.6%	61.2%	38.8%
21,819	AUGUSTA	10,515	5,995	4,451	69	1,544 R	57.0%	42.3%	57.4%	42.6%
31,643	BANGOR	14,594	8,389	6,155	50	2,234 R	57.5%	42.2%	57.7%	42.3%
10,246	BATH	4,627	2,899	1,714	14	1,185 R	62.7%	37.0%	62.8%	37.2%
6,243	BELFAST	2,821	1,774	1,037	10	737 R	62.9%	36.8%	63.1%	36.9%
19,638	BIDDEFORD	9,674	4,147	5,489	38	1,342 D	42.9%	56.7%	43.0%	57.0%
9,017	BREWER	4,563	3,093	1,461	9	1,632 R	67.8%	32.0%	67.9%	32.1%
17,366	BRUNSWICK	8,124	4,294	3,818	12	476 R	52.9%	47.0%	52.9%	47.1%
5,775	BUXTON	3,035	1,949	1,071	15	878 R	64.2%	35.3%	64.5%	35.5%
7,838	CAPE ELIZABETH	5,308	3,403	1,901	4	1,502 R	64.1%	35.8%	64.2%	35.8%
9,916	CARIBOU	3,576	2,364	1,187	25	1,177 R	66.1%	33.2%	66.6%	33.4%
5,284	CUMBERLAND TOWN	3,184	2,247	932	5	1,315 R	70.6%	29.3%	70.7%	29.3%
5,179	ELLSWORTH	2,887	2,075	804	8	1,271 R	71.9%	27.8%	72.1%	27.9%
6,113	FAIRFIELD	2,744	1,571	1,163	10	408 R	57.3%	42.4%	57.5%	42.5%
6,853	FALMOUTH	4,647	3,048	1,591	8	1,457 R	65.6%	34.2%	65.7%	34.3%
6,730	FARMINGTON	3,396	2,121	1,270	5	851 R	62.5%	37.4%	62.5%	37.5%
5,863	FREEPORT	3,448	2,043	1,394	11	649 R	59.3%	40.4%	59.4%	40.6%
6,485	GARDINER	3,172	1,942	1,216	14	726 R	61.2%	38.3%	61.5%	38.5%
10,101	GORHAM	5,618	3,548	2,056	14	1,492 R	63.2%	36.6%	63.3%	36.7%
5,250	HAMPDEN	2,882	1,889	992	1	897 R	65.5%	34.4%	65.6%	34.4%
6,766	HOULTON	2,893	2,182	705	6	1,477 R	75.4%	24.4%	75.6%	24.4%
5,080	JAY	2,416	1,275	1,124	17	151 R	52.8%	46.5%	53.1%	46.9%
6,621	KENNEBUNK	4,153	2,923	1,213	17	1,710 R	70.4%	29.2%	70.7%	29.3%
9,314	KITTERY	4,178	2,475	1,697	6	778 R	59.2%	40.6%	59.3%	40.7%
40,481	LEWISTON	19,410	9,480	9,853	77	373 D	48.8%	50.8%	49.0%	51.0%
8,719	LIMESTONE	986	670	314	2	356 R	68.0%	31.8%	68.1%	31.9%
5,066	LINCOLN TOWN	2,231	1,636	593	2	1,043 R	73.3%	26.6%	73.4%	26.6%
8,769	LISBON	3,556	2,345	1,201	10	1,144 R	65.9%	33.8%	66.1%	33.9%
5,282	MADAWASKA	2,010	868	1,134	8	266 D	43.2%	56.4%	43.4%	56.6%
7,567	MILLINOCKET	3,652	2,184	1,459	9	725 R	59.8%	40.0%	60.0%	40.0%
5,162	OAKLAND	2,272	1,402	865	5	537 R	61.7%	38.1%	61.8%	38.2%
6,291	OLD ORCHARD BEACH	3,575	1,910	1,650	15	260 R	53.4%	46.2%	53.7%	46.3%
8,422	OLD TOWN	4,310	2,087	2,217	6	130 D	48.4%	51.4%	48.5%	51.5%
10,578	ORONO	4,636	2,377	2,238	21	139 D	51.3%	48.3%	51.5%	48.5%
61,572	PORTLAND	30,952	13,315	17,543	94	4,228 D	43.0%	56.7%	43.1%	56.9%
11,172	PRESQUE ISLE	4,447	3,032	1,371	44	1,661 R	68.2%	30.8%	68.9%	31.1%
7,919	ROCKLAND	3,237	2,169	1,051	17	1,118 R	67.0%	32.5%	67.4%	32.6%
8,240	RUMFORD	3,712	1,962	1,713	37	249 R	52.9%	46.1%	53.4%	46.6%
12,921	SACO	6,874	3,761	3,094	19	667 R	54.7%	45.0%	54.9%	45.1%
18,020	SANFORD	8,145	4,578	3,517	50	1,061 R	56.2%	43.2%	56.6%	43.4%
11,347	SCARBOROUGH	6,149	4,037	2,103	9	1,934 R	65.7%	34.2%	65.7%	34.3%
8,098	SKOWHEGAN	3,713	2,157	1,535	21	622 R	58.1%	41.3%	58.4%	41.6%
22,712	SOUTH PORTLAND	12,057	6,653	5,377	27	1,276 R	55.2%	44.6%	55.3%	44.7%
5,946	STANDISH	3,009	1,988	1,010	11	978 R	66.1%	33.6%	66.3%	33.7%
6,431	TOPSHAM	3,207	1,980	1,217	10	763 R	61.7%	37.9%	61.9%	38.1%
17,779	WATERVILLE	8,010	3,873	4,075	62	202 D	48.4%	50.9%	48.7%	51.3%
8,211	WELLS	3,395	2,300	1,080	15	1,220 R	67.7%	31.8%	68.0%	32.0%
14,976	WESTBROOK	7,817	4,456	3,345	16	1,111 R	57.0%	42.8%	57.1%	42.9%
11,282	WINDHAM	5,448	3,545	1,883	20	1,662 R	65.1%	34.6%	65.3%	34.7%
8,057	WINSLOW	3,868	2,114	1,734	20	380 R	54.7%	44.8%	54.9%	45.1%
5,889	WINTHROP	2,888	1,892	990	6	902 R	65.5%	34.3%	65.6%	34.4%
6,585	YARMOUTH	3,953	2,505	1,436	12	1,069 R	63.4%	36.3%	63.6%	36.4%
8,465	YORK TOWN	5,065	3,388	1,668	9	1,720 R	66.9%	32.9%	67.0%	33.0%

MAINE

SENATOR 1984

1980 Census Population	County	Total Vote	Republican	Democratic	Other	Rep.-Dem. Plurality	Percentage			
							Total Vote		Major Vote	
							Rep.	Dem.	Rep.	Dem.
99,657	ANDROSCOGGIN	46,761	33,118	13,208	435	19,910 R	70.8%	28.2%	71.5%	28.5%
91,331	AROOSTOOK	34,152	26,536	7,389	227	19,147 R	77.7%	21.6%	78.2%	21.8%
215,789	CUMBERLAND	114,968	81,669	32,846	453	48,823 R	71.0%	28.6%	71.3%	28.7%
27,098	FRANKLIN	13,437	10,237	3,057	143	7,180 R	76.2%	22.8%	77.0%	23.0%
41,781	HANCOCK	22,551	17,546	4,808	197	12,738 R	77.8%	21.3%	78.5%	21.5%
109,889	KENNEBEC	52,956	35,773	16,766	417	19,007 R	67.6%	31.7%	68.1%	31.9%
32,941	KNOX	17,270	13,237	3,934	99	9,303 R	76.6%	22.8%	77.1%	22.9%
25,691	LINCOLN	15,263	11,649	3,505	109	8,144 R	76.3%	23.0%	76.9%	23.1%
48,968	OXFORD	23,880	18,070	5,519	291	12,551 R	75.7%	23.1%	76.6%	23.4%
137,015	PENOBSCOT	65,455	51,342	13,546	567	37,796 R	78.4%	20.7%	79.1%	20.9%
17,634	PISCATAQUIS	8,557	6,652	1,829	76	4,823 R	77.7%	21.4%	78.4%	21.6%
28,795	SAGADAHOC	14,504	10,819	3,569	116	7,250 R	74.6%	24.6%	75.2%	24.8%
45,028	SOMERSET	20,845	15,465	5,089	291	10,376 R	74.2%	24.4%	75.2%	24.8%
28,414	WALDO	14,210	10,210	3,598	402	6,612 R	71.9%	25.3%	73.9%	26.1%
34,963	WASHINGTON	15,054	11,715	3,178	161	8,537 R	77.8%	21.1%	78.7%	21.3%
139,666	YORK	71,543	50,376	20,785	382	29,591 R	70.4%	29.1%	70.8%	29.2%
1,124,660	TOTAL	551,406	404,414	142,626	4,366	261,788 R	73.3%	25.9%	73.9%	26.1%

MAINE

SENATOR 1984

1980 Census Population	City/Town	Total Vote	Republican	Democratic	Other	Rep.-Dem. Plurality	Percentage Total Vote Rep.	Dem.	Major Vote Rep.	Dem.
23,128	AUBURN	11,419	8,525	2,810	84	5,715 R	74.7%	24.6%	75.2%	24.8%
21,819	AUGUSTA	10,374	6,737	3,569	68	3,168 R	64.9%	34.4%	65.4%	34.6%
31,643	BANGOR	14,569	11,220	3,257	92	7,963 R	77.0%	22.4%	77.5%	22.5%
10,246	BATH	4,748	3,670	1,053	25	2,617 R	77.3%	22.2%	77.7%	22.3%
6,243	BELFAST	2,852	2,115	649	88	1,466 R	74.2%	22.8%	76.5%	23.5%
19,638	BIDDEFORD	9,634	5,415	4,176	43	1,239 R	56.2%	43.3%	56.5%	43.5%
9,017	BREWER	4,825	3,970	812	43	3,158 R	82.3%	16.8%	83.0%	17.0%
17,366	BRUNSWICK	8,048	5,361	2,642	45	2,719 R	66.6%	32.8%	67.0%	33.0%
5,775	BUXTON	3,007	2,230	764	13	1,466 R	74.2%	25.4%	74.5%	25.5%
7,838	CAPE ELIZABETH	5,322	4,142	1,165	15	2,977 R	77.8%	21.9%	78.0%	22.0%
9,916	CARIBOU	3,508	2,864	630	14	2,234 R	81.6%	18.0%	82.0%	18.0%
5,284	CUMBERLAND TOWN	3,187	2,613	574		2,039 R	82.0%	18.0%	82.0%	18.0%
5,179	ELLSWORTH	2,841	2,394	419	28	1,975 R	84.3%	14.7%	85.1%	14.9%
6,113	FAIRFIELD	2,791	1,967	787	37	1,180 R	70.5%	28.2%	71.4%	28.6%
6,853	FALMOUTH	4,516	3,533	976	7	2,557 R	78.2%	21.6%	78.4%	21.6%
6,730	FARMINGTON	3,416	2,566	802	48	1,764 R	75.1%	23.5%	76.2%	23.8%
5,863	FREEPORT	3,436	2,420	996	20	1,424 R	70.4%	29.0%	70.8%	29.2%
6,485	GARDINER	3,185	2,206	952	27	1,254 R	69.3%	29.9%	69.9%	30.1%
10,101	GORHAM	5,586	4,295	1,267	24	3,028 R	76.9%	22.7%	77.2%	22.8%
5,250	HAMPDEN	2,895	2,340	533	22	1,807 R	80.8%	18.4%	81.4%	18.6%
6,766	HOULTON	2,895	2,409	465	21	1,944 R	83.2%	16.1%	83.8%	16.2%
5,080	JAY	2,402	1,740	648	14	1,092 R	72.4%	27.0%	72.9%	27.1%
6,621	KENNEBUNK	4,140	3,201	918	21	2,283 R	77.3%	22.2%	77.7%	22.3%
9,314	KITTERY	4,068	2,834	1,194	40	1,640 R	69.7%	29.4%	70.4%	29.6%
40,481	LEWISTON	19,264	12,329	6,765	170	5,564 R	64.0%	35.1%	64.6%	35.4%
8,719	LIMESTONE	986	842	138	6	704 R	85.4%	14.0%	85.9%	14.1%
5,066	LINCOLN TOWN	2,245	1,885	349	11	1,536 R	84.0%	15.5%	84.4%	15.6%
8,769	LISBON	3,570	2,778	758	34	2,020 R	77.8%	21.2%	78.6%	21.4%
5,282	MADAWASKA	1,998	1,265	723	10	542 R	63.3%	36.2%	63.6%	36.4%
7,567	MILLINOCKET	3,659	2,747	886	26	1,861 R	75.1%	24.2%	75.6%	24.4%
5,162	OAKLAND	2,268	1,647	597	24	1,050 R	72.6%	26.3%	73.4%	26.6%
6,291	OLD ORCHARD BEACH	3,541	2,375	1,148	18	1,227 R	67.1%	32.4%	67.4%	32.6%
8,422	OLD TOWN	4,314	3,015	1,256	43	1,759 R	69.9%	29.1%	70.6%	29.4%
10,578	ORONO	4,675	3,324	1,335	16	1,989 R	71.1%	28.6%	71.3%	28.7%
61,572	PORTLAND	30,698	18,595	11,973	130	6,622 R	60.6%	39.0%	60.8%	39.2%
11,172	PRESQUE ISLE	4,420	3,637	759	24	2,878 R	82.3%	17.2%	82.7%	17.3%
7,919	ROCKLAND	3,198	2,481	698	19	1,783 R	77.6%	21.8%	78.0%	22.0%
8,240	RUMFORD	3,692	2,531	1,116	45	1,415 R	68.6%	30.2%	69.4%	30.6%
12,921	SACO	6,925	4,776	2,131	18	2,645 R	69.0%	30.8%	69.1%	30.9%
18,020	SANFORD	8,104	5,344	2,715	45	2,629 R	65.9%	33.5%	66.3%	33.7%
11,347	SCARBOROUGH	6,150	4,802	1,327	21	3,475 R	78.1%	21.6%	78.3%	21.7%
8,098	SKOWHEGAN	3,732	2,684	993	55	1,691 R	71.9%	26.6%	73.0%	27.0%
22,712	SOUTH PORTLAND	11,585	8,085	3,449	51	4,636 R	69.8%	29.8%	70.1%	29.9%
5,946	STANDISH	2,993	2,306	680	7	1,626 R	77.0%	22.7%	77.2%	22.8%
6,431	TOPSHAM	3,188	2,315	824	49	1,491 R	72.6%	25.8%	73.7%	26.3%
17,779	WATERVILLE	7,896	4,820	2,993	83	1,827 R	61.0%	37.9%	61.7%	38.3%
8,211	WELLS	3,377	2,565	794	18	1,771 R	76.0%	23.5%	76.4%	23.6%
14,976	WESTBROOK	7,798	5,578	2,191	29	3,387 R	71.5%	28.1%	71.8%	28.2%
11,282	WINDHAM	5,430	4,237	1,167	26	3,070 R	78.0%	21.5%	78.4%	21.6%
8,057	WINSLOW	3,833	2,481	1,317	35	1,164 R	64.7%	34.4%	65.3%	34.7%
5,889	WINTHROP	2,935	2,184	740	11	1,444 R	74.4%	25.2%	74.7%	25.3%
6,585	YARMOUTH	3,931	3,105	812	14	2,293 R	79.0%	20.7%	79.3%	20.7%
8,465	YORK TOWN	4,995	3,763	1,209	23	2,554 R	75.3%	24.2%	75.7%	24.3%

MAINE

CONGRESS

CD	Year	Total Vote	Republican Vote	Candidate	Democratic Vote	Candidate	Other Vote	Rep.-Dem. Plurality	Percentage Total Vote Rep.	Dem.	Major Vote Rep.	Dem.
1	1984	287,765	182,785	MCKERNAN, JOHN R.	104,972	HOBBINS, BARRY J.	8	77,813 R	63.5%	36.5%	63.5%	36.5%
2	1984	253,773	192,166	SNOWE, OLYMPIA J.	57,347	BULL, CHIPMAN C.	4,260	134,819 R	75.7%	22.6%	77.0%	23.0%

MAINE

1984 GENERAL ELECTION

In addition to the county-by-county figures, data are presented for selected Maine communities. Since not all jurisdictions of the state are listed in this special tabulation, state-wide totals are shown only with the county-by-county statistics.

President   Other vote was 1,292 Hall (Independent); 755 Serrette (Independent); 82 scattered.

Senator   Other vote was 4,338 P. Ann Stoddard (Independent); 28 scattered.

Congress   Other vote was scattered in CD 1; 4,242 Kenneth E. Stoddard (Independent) and 18 scattered in CD 2.

1984 PRIMARIES

JUNE 12 REPUBLICAN

Senator   William S. Cohen, unopposed.

Congress   Unopposed in both CD's.

JUNE 12 DEMOCRATIC

Senator   Elizabeth H. Mitchell, unopposed.

Congress   Unopposed in CD 2. Contested as follows:

CD 1   15,314 Barry J. Hobbins; 9,037 Ralph W. Conant; 2 scattered.

MARYLAND

GOVERNOR
Harry Hughes (D). Re-elected 1982 to a four-year term. Previously elected 1978.

SENATORS
Charles Mathias (R). Re-elected 1980 to a six-year term. Previously elected 1974, 1968.

Paul S. Sarbanes (D). Re-elected 1982 to a six-year term. Previously elected 1976.

REPRESENTATIVES
1. Roy Dyson (D)
2. Helen D. Bentley (R)
3. Barbara A. Mikulski (D)
4. Marjorie S. Holt (R)
5. Steny H. Hoyer (D)
6. Beverly B. Byron (D)
7. Parren J. Mitchell (D)
8. Michael D. Barnes (D)

POSTWAR VOTE FOR GOVERNOR

		Republican		Democratic		Other	Rep.-Dem.	Percentage Total Vote		Major Vote	
Year	Total Vote	Vote	Candidate	Vote	Candidate	Vote	Plurality	Rep.	Dem.	Rep.	Dem.
1982	1,139,149	432,826	Pascal, Robert A.	705,910	Hughes, Harry	413	273,084 D	38.0%	62.0%	38.0%	62.0%
1978	1,011,963	293,635	Beall, J. Glenn, Jr.	718,328	Hughes, Harry	—	424,693 D	29.0%	71.0%	29.0%	71.0%
1974	949,097	346,449	Gore, Louise	602,648	Mandel, Marvin	—	256,199 D	36.5%	63.5%	36.5%	63.5%
1970	973,099	314,336	Blair, C. Stanley	639,579	Mandel, Marvin	19,184	325,243 D	32.3%	65.7%	33.0%	67.0%
1966	918,761	455,318	Agnew, Spiro T.	373,543	Mahoney, George P.	89,900	81,775 R	49.6%	40.7%	54.9%	45.1%
1962	775,101	343,051	Small, Frank	432,045	Tawes, J. Millard	5	88,994 D	44.3%	55.7%	44.3%	55.7%
1958	763,234	278,173	Devereux, James	485,061	Tawes, J. Millard	—	206,888 D	36.4%	63.6%	36.4%	63.6%
1954	700,484	381,451	McKeldin, Theodore	319,033	Byrd, Harry C.	—	62,418 R	54.5%	45.5%	54.5%	45.5%
1950	645,631	369,807	McKeldin, Theodore	275,824	Lane, William P.	—	93,983 R	57.3%	42.7%	57.3%	42.7%
1946	489,836	221,752	McKeldin, Theodore	268,084	Lane, William P.	—	46,332 D	45.3%	54.7%	45.3%	54.7%

POSTWAR VOTE FOR SENATOR

		Republican		Democratic		Other	Rep.-Dem.	Percentage Total Vote		Major Vote	
Year	Total Vote	Vote	Candidate	Vote	Candidate	Vote	Plurality	Rep.	Dem.	Rep.	Dem.
1982	1,114,690	407,334	Hogan, Lawrence J.	707,356	Sarbanes, Paul S.	—	300,022 D	36.5%	63.5%	36.5%	63.5%
1980	1,286,088	850,970	Mathias, Charles	435,118	Conroy, Edward T.	—	415,852 R	66.2%	33.8%	66.2%	33.8%
1976	1,365,568	530,439	Beall, J. Glenn, Jr.	772,101	Sarbanes, Paul S.	63,028	241,662 D	38.8%	56.5%	40.7%	59.3%
1974	877,786	503,223	Mathias, Charles	374,563	Mikulski, Barbara A.	—	128,660 R	57.3%	42.7%	57.3%	42.7%
1970	956,370	484,960	Beall, J. Glenn, Jr.	460,422	Tydings, Joseph D.	10,988	24,538 R	50.7%	48.1%	51.3%	48.7%
1968	1,133,727	541,893	Mathias, Charles	443,367	Brewster, Daniel B.	148,467	98,526 R	47.8%	39.1%	55.0%	45.0%
1964	1,081,049	402,393	Beall, J. Glenn	678,649	Tydings, Joseph D.	7	276,256 D	37.2%	62.8%	37.2%	62.8%
1962	714,248	270,312	Miller, Edward T.	443,935	Brewster, Daniel B.	1	173,623 D	37.8%	62.2%	37.8%	62.2%
1958	749,291	382,021	Beall, J. Glenn	367,270	D'Alesandro, Thomas	—	14,751 R	51.0%	49.0%	51.0%	49.0%
1956	892,167	473,059	Butler, John Marshall	419,108	Mahoney, George P.	—	53,951 R	53.0%	47.0%	53.0%	47.0%
1952	856,193	449,823	Beall, J. Glenn	406,370	Mahoney, George P.	—	43,453 R	52.5%	47.5%	52.5%	47.5%
1950	615,614	326,291	Butler, John Marshall	283,180	Tydings, Millard E.	6,143	43,111 R	53.0%	46.0%	53.5%	46.5%
1946	472,232	235,000	Markey, David John	237,232	O'Conor, Herbert R.	—	2,232 D	49.8%	50.2%	49.8%	50.2%

MARYLAND

Districts Established April 13, 1982

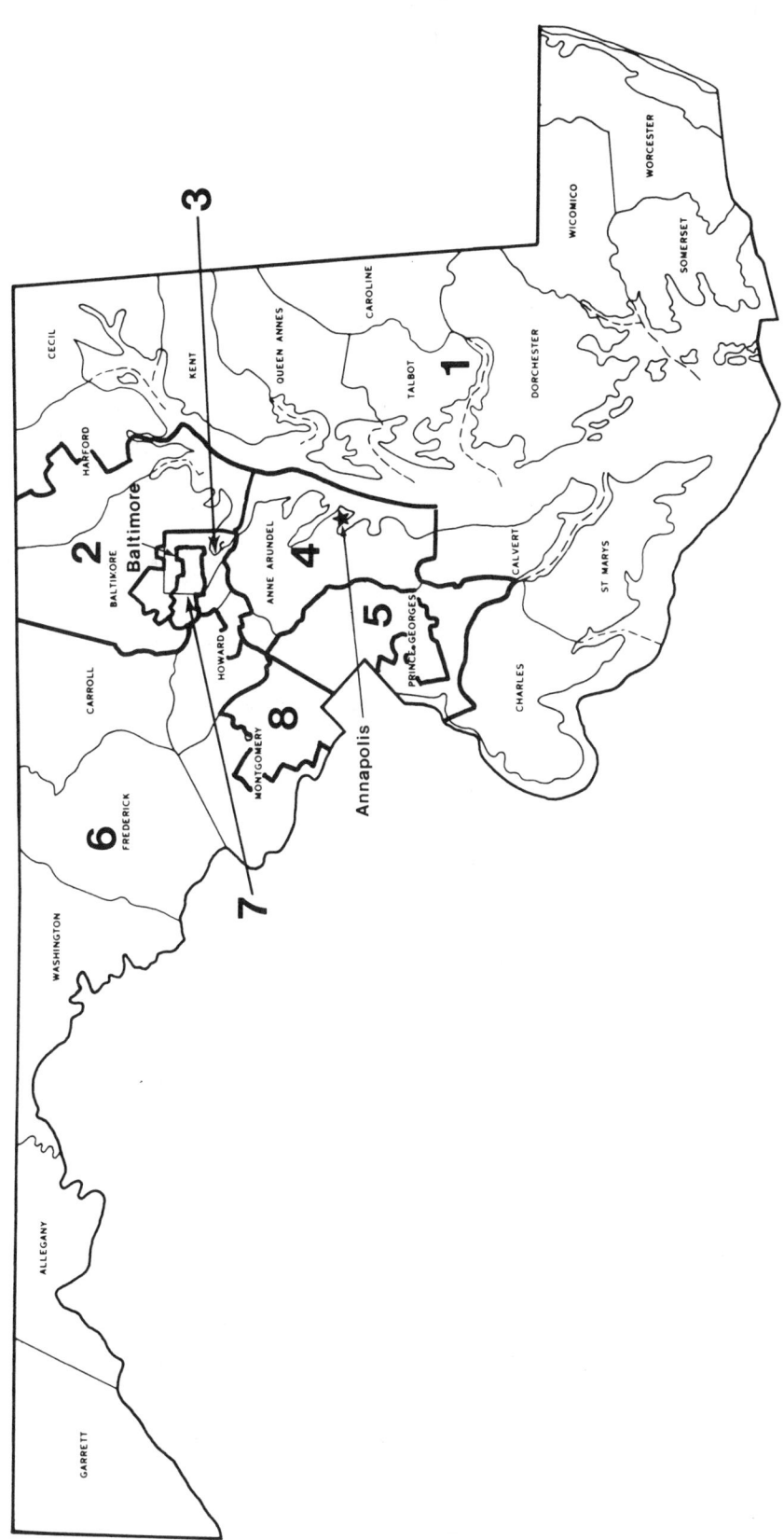

MARYLAND

PRESIDENT 1984

1980 Census Population	County	Total Vote	Republican	Democratic	Other	Rep.-Dem. Plurality	Percentage Total Vote Rep.	Dem.	Major Vote Rep.	Dem.
80,548	ALLEGANY	31,223	19,763	11,143	317	8,620 R	63.3%	35.7%	63.9%	36.1%
370,775	ANNE ARUNDEL	142,591	94,171	47,565	855	46,606 R	66.0%	33.4%	66.4%	33.6%
786,775	BALTIMORE CITY	284,163	80,120	202,277	1,766	122,157 D	28.2%	71.2%	28.4%	71.6%
655,615	BALTIMORE COUNTY	280,428	171,929	106,908	1,591	65,021 R	61.3%	38.1%	61.7%	38.3%
34,638	CALVERT	13,840	8,303	5,455	82	2,848 R	60.0%	39.4%	60.4%	39.6%
23,143	CAROLINE	7,099	4,876	2,198	25	2,678 R	68.7%	31.0%	68.9%	31.1%
96,356	CARROLL	36,199	27,230	8,898	71	18,332 R	75.2%	24.6%	75.4%	24.6%
60,430	CECIL	19,885	13,111	6,681	93	6,430 R	65.9%	33.6%	66.2%	33.8%
72,751	CHARLES	26,460	16,132	10,264	64	5,868 R	61.0%	38.8%	61.1%	38.9%
30,623	DORCHESTER	9,981	6,699	3,160	122	3,539 R	67.1%	31.7%	67.9%	32.1%
114,792	FREDERICK	43,113	29,606	13,411	96	16,195 R	68.7%	31.1%	68.8%	31.2%
26,498	GARRETT	9,477	7,042	2,386	49	4,656 R	74.3%	25.2%	74.7%	25.3%
145,930	HARFORD	54,642	37,382	17,133	127	20,249 R	68.4%	31.4%	68.6%	31.4%
118,572	HOWARD	61,688	35,641	25,713	334	9,928 R	57.8%	41.7%	58.1%	41.9%
16,695	KENT	6,323	3,897	2,390	36	1,507 R	61.6%	37.8%	62.0%	38.0%
579,053	MONTGOMERY	293,870	146,924	146,036	910	888 R	50.0%	49.7%	50.2%	49.8%
665,071	PRINCE GEORGES	232,220	95,121	136,063	1,036	40,942 D	41.0%	58.6%	41.1%	58.9%
25,508	QUEEN ANNES	9,763	6,784	2,938	41	3,846 R	69.5%	30.1%	69.8%	30.2%
59,895	ST. MARYS	17,670	11,201	6,420	49	4,781 R	63.4%	36.3%	63.6%	36.4%
19,188	SOMERSET	6,970	4,508	2,439	23	2,069 R	64.7%	35.0%	64.9%	35.1%
25,604	TALBOT	11,256	8,028	3,198	30	4,830 R	71.3%	28.4%	71.5%	28.5%
113,086	WASHINGTON	40,666	27,118	13,329	219	13,789 R	66.7%	32.8%	67.0%	33.0%
64,540	WICOMICO	24,332	16,124	8,160	48	7,964 R	66.3%	33.5%	66.4%	33.6%
30,889	WORCESTER	12,014	8,208	3,770	36	4,438 R	68.3%	31.4%	68.5%	31.5%
4,216,975	TOTAL	1,675,873	879,918	787,935	8,020	91,983 R	52.5%	47.0%	52.8%	47.2%

MARYLAND

CONGRESS

CD	Year	Total Vote	Republican Vote	Candidate	Democratic Vote	Candidate	Other Vote	Rep.-Dem. Plurality	Percentage Total Vote Rep.	Dem.	Major Vote Rep.	Dem.
1	1984	165,538	68,865	WILLIAMS, HARLAN C.	96,673	DYSON, ROY		27,808 D	41.6%	58.4%	41.6%	58.4%
1	1982	129,159	39,656	HOPKINS, C. A. PORTER	89,503	DYSON, ROY		49,847 D	30.7%	69.3%	30.7%	69.3%
2	1984	217,089	111,517	BENTLEY, HELEN D.	105,571	LONG, CLARENCE D.	1	5,946 R	51.4%	48.6%	51.4%	48.6%
2	1982	158,380	75,062	BENTLEY, HELEN D.	83,318	LONG, CLARENCE D.		8,256 D	47.4%	52.6%	47.4%	52.6%
3	1984	195,261	59,493	PIERPONT, ROSS Z.	133,189	MIKULSKI, BARBARA A.	2,579	73,696 D	30.5%	68.2%	30.9%	69.1%
3	1982	148,301	38,259	SCHERR, H. ROBERT	110,042	MIKULSKI, BARBARA A.		71,783 D	25.8%	74.2%	25.8%	74.2%
4	1984	172,743	114,430	HOLT, MARJORIE S.	58,312	GREENEBAUM, HOWARD	1	56,118 R	66.2%	33.8%	66.2%	33.8%
4	1982	123,564	75,617	HOLT, MARJORIE S.	47,947	AIKEN, PATRICIA O'B.		27,670 R	61.2%	38.8%	61.2%	38.8%
5	1984	161,149	44,839	RITCHIE, JOHN E.	116,310	HOYER, STENY H.		71,471 D	27.8%	72.2%	27.8%	72.2%
5	1982	105,470	21,533	GUTHRIE, WILLIAM P.	83,937	HOYER, STENY H.		62,404 D	20.4%	79.6%	20.4%	79.6%
6	1984	189,442	66,056	FICKER, ROBIN	123,383	BYRON, BEVERLY B.	3	57,327 D	34.9%	65.1%	34.9%	65.1%
6	1982	137,917	35,321	BARTLETT, ROSCOE	102,596	BYRON, BEVERLY B.		67,275 D	25.6%	74.4%	25.6%	74.4%
7	1984	139,489			139,488	MITCHELL, PARREN J.	1	139,488 D		100.0%		100.0%
7	1982	117,699	14,203	JONES, M. LEONORA	103,496	MITCHELL, PARREN J.		89,293 D	12.1%	87.9%	12.1%	87.9%
8	1984	254,569	70,715	CECCONE, ALBERT	181,947	BARNES, MICHAEL D.	1,907	111,232 D	27.8%	71.5%	28.0%	72.0%
8	1982	170,671	48,910	SPENCER, ELIZABETH W.	121,761	BARNES, MICHAEL D.		72,851 D	28.7%	71.3%	28.7%	71.3%

MARYLAND

1984 GENERAL ELECTION

President   Other vote was 5,721 Bergland (Libertarian); 898 Hall (Communist); 745 Holmes (Workers); 656 Serrette (Alliance).

Congress   Other vote was scattered in CD 2; Freeman (Independent) in CD 3; scattered in CD's 4, 6 and 7; 1,903 Grove (Libertarian) and 4 scattered in CD 8.

1984 PRIMARIES

MAY 8 REPUBLICAN

Congress   Unopposed in three CD's. No candidate in CD 7. Contested as follows:

CD 2   8,444 Helen D. Bentley; 7,368 David M. Smick; 507 Joseph A. Arena; 385 Charles G. Grace.
CD 5   4,418 John E. Ritchie; 2,602 Kenneth M. Robinson; 835 John E. Sellner.
CD 6   9,810 Robin Ficker; 1,757 Melvin Perkins.
CD 8   3,785 Albert Ceccone; 3,368 Jayne H. Plank; 2,836 Donald J. Chaney; 1,955 Michael P. D'Aiuto; 1,495 Wallace D. Barlow.

MAY 8 DEMOCRATIC

Congress   Contested as follows:

CD 1   27,574 Roy Dyson; 4,124 Allan B. Canter.
CD 2   44,045 Clarence D. Long; 5,683 Blaine Taylor; 4,666 Charles H. Mott.
CD 3   56,143 Barbara A. Mikulski; 4,345 Debra H. Freeman; 1,713 Monroe Cornish.
CD 4   10,126 Howard Greenebaum; 4,410 Edward Barnum.
CD 5   35,131 Steny H. Hoyer; 2,928 Lawrence E. Keval; 1,780 Craig E. Ransom.
CD 6   26,772 Beverly B. Byron; 6,026 John P. Donoghue; 3,582 William B. McMahon.
CD 7   54,582 Parren J. Mitchell; 3,858 Elizabeth C. Gray; 3,105 Alan R. Ogden.
CD 8   58,501 Michael D. Barnes; 3,709 Thomas A. Torchia.

MASSACHUSETTS

GOVERNOR
Michael S. Dukakis (D). Elected 1982 to a four-year term. Previously elected 1974.

SENATORS
Edward M. Kennedy (D). Re-elected 1982 to a six-year term. Previously elected 1976, 1970, 1964, and in 1962 to fill out term vacated by the resignation of Senator John F. Kennedy.

John F. Kerry (D). Elected 1984 to a six-year term.

REPRESENTATIVES
1. Silvio O. Conte (R)
2. Edward P. Boland (D)
3. Joseph D. Early (D)
4. Barney Frank (D)
5. Chester G. Atkins (D)
6. Nicholas Mavroules (D)
7. Edward J. Markey (D)
8. Thomas P. O'Neill (D)
9. John J. Moakley (D)
10. Gerry E. Studds (D)
11. Brian J. Donnelly (D)

POSTWAR VOTE FOR GOVERNOR

Year	Total Vote	Republican Vote	Candidate	Democratic Vote	Candidate	Other Vote	Rep.-Dem. Plurality	Total Vote Rep.	Total Vote Dem.	Major Vote Rep.	Major Vote Dem.
1982	2,050,254	749,679	Sears, John W.	1,219,109	Dukakis, Michael S.	81,466	469,430 D	36.6%	59.5%	38.1%	61.9%
1978	1,962,251	926,072	Hatch, Francis W.	1,030,294	King, Edward J.	5,885	104,222 D	47.2%	52.5%	47.3%	52.7%
1974	1,854,798	784,353	Sargent, Francis W.	992,284	Dukakis, Michael S.	78,161	207,931 D	42.3%	53.5%	44.1%	55.9%
1970	1,867,906	1,058,623	Sargent, Francis W.	799,269	White, Kevin H.	10,014	259,354 R	56.7%	42.8%	57.0%	43.0%
1966*	2,041,177	1,277,358	Volpe, John A.	752,720	McCormack, Edward J.	11,099	524,638 R	62.6%	36.9%	62.9%	37.1%
1964	2,340,130	1,176,462	Volpe, John A.	1,153,416	Bellotti, Francis X.	10,252	23,046 R	50.3%	49.3%	50.5%	49.5%
1962	2,109,089	1,047,891	Volpe, John A.	1,053,322	Peabody, Endicott	7,876	5,431 D	49.7%	49.9%	49.9%	50.1%
1960	2,417,133	1,269,295	Volpe, John A.	1,130,810	Ward, Joseph D.	17,028	138,485 R	52.5%	46.8%	52.9%	47.1%
1958	1,899,117	818,463	Gibbons, Charles	1,067,020	Furcolo, Foster	13,634	248,557 D	43.1%	56.2%	43.4%	56.6%
1956	2,339,884	1,096,759	Whittier, Sumner G.	1,234,618	Furcolo, Foster	8,507	137,859 D	46.9%	52.8%	47.0%	53.0%
1954	1,903,774	985,339	Herter, Christian A.	910,087	Murphy, Robert F.	8,348	75,252 R	51.8%	47.8%	52.0%	48.0%
1952	2,356,298	1,175,955	Herter, Christian A.	1,161,499	Dever, Paul A.	18,844	14,456 R	49.9%	49.3%	50.3%	49.7%
1950	1,910,180	824,069	Coolidge, Arthur W.	1,074,570	Dever, Paul A.	11,541	250,501 D	43.1%	56.3%	43.4%	56.6%
1948	2,099,250	849,895	Bradford, Robert F.	1,239,247	Dever, Paul A.	10,108	389,352 D	40.5%	59.0%	40.7%	59.3%
1946	1,683,452	911,152	Bradford, Robert F.	762,743	Tobin, Maurice	9,557	148,409 R	54.1%	45.3%	54.4%	45.6%

The term of office of Massachusett's Governor was increased from two to four years effective with the 1966 election.

POSTWAR VOTE FOR SENATOR

Year	Total Vote	Republican Vote	Candidate	Democratic Vote	Candidate	Other Vote	Rep.-Dem. Plurality	Total Vote Rep.	Total Vote Dem.	Major Vote Rep.	Major Vote Dem.
1984	2,530,195	1,136,806	Shamie, Raymond	1,392,981	Kerry, John F.	408	256,175 D	44.9%	55.1%	44.9%	55.1%
1982	2,050,769	784,602	Shamie, Raymond	1,247,084	Kennedy, Edward M.	19,083	462,482 D	38.3%	60.8%	38.6%	61.4%
1978	1,985,700	890,584	Brooke, Edward W.	1,093,283	Tsongas, Paul E.	1,833	202,699 D	44.8%	55.1%	44.9%	55.1%
1976	2,491,255	722,641	Robertson, Michael	1,726,657	Kennedy, Edward M.	41,957	1,004,016 D	29.0%	69.3%	29.5%	70.5%
1972	2,370,676	1,505,932	Brooke, Edward W.	823,278	Droney, John J.	41,466	682,654 R	63.5%	34.7%	64.7%	35.3%
1970	1,935,607	715,978	Spaulding, Josiah A.	1,202,856	Kennedy, Edward M.	16,773	486,878 D	37.0%	62.1%	37.3%	62.7%
1966	1,999,949	1,213,473	Brooke, Edward W.	774,761	Peabody, Endicott	11,715	438,712 R	60.7%	38.7%	61.0%	39.0%
1964	2,312,028	587,663	Whitmore, Howard	1,716,907	Kennedy, Edward M.	7,458	1,129,244 D	25.4%	74.3%	25.5%	74.5%
1962s	2,097,085	877,669	Lodge, George C.	1,162,611	Kennedy, Edward M.	56,805	284,942 D	41.9%	55.4%	43.0%	57.0%
1960	2,417,813	1,358,556	Saltonstall, Leverett	1,050,725	O'Connor, Thomas J.	8,532	307,831 R	56.2%	43.5%	56.4%	43.6%
1958	1,862,041	488,318	Celeste, Vincent J.	1,362,926	Kennedy, John F.	10,797	874,608 D	26.2%	73.2%	26.4%	73.6%
1954	1,892,710	956,605	Saltonstall, Leverett	927,899	Furcolo, Foster	8,206	28,706 R	50.5%	49.0%	50.8%	49.2%
1952	2,360,425	1,141,247	Lodge, Henry Cabot	1,211,984	Kennedy, John F.	7,194	70,737 D	48.3%	51.3%	48.5%	51.5%
1948	2,055,798	1,088,475	Saltonstall, Leverett	954,398	Fitzgerald, John I.	12,925	134,077 R	52.9%	46.4%	53.3%	46.7%
1946	1,662,063	989,736	Lodge, Henry Cabot	660,200	Walsh, David I.	12,127	329,536 R	59.5%	39.7%	60.0%	40.0%

The 1962 election was for a short term to fill a vacancy.

MASSACHUSETTS

Districts Established December 3, 1981

MASSACHUSETTS

PRESIDENT 1984

1980 Census Population	County	Total Vote	Republican	Democratic	Other	Rep.-Dem. Plurality	Percentage			
							Total Vote		Major Vote	
							Rep.	Dem.	Rep.	Dem.
147,925	BARNSTABLE	89,951	51,261	38,369	321	12,892 R	57.0%	42.7%	57.2%	42.8%
145,110	BERKSHIRE	63,785	33,712	29,745	328	3,967 R	52.9%	46.6%	53.1%	46.9%
474,641	BRISTOL	188,039	93,232	94,010	797	778 D	49.6%	50.0%	49.8%	50.2%
8,942	DUKES	6,125	2,788	3,313	24	525 D	45.5%	54.1%	45.7%	54.3%
633,632	ESSEX	295,656	162,152	132,353	1,151	29,799 R	54.8%	44.8%	55.1%	44.9%
64,317	FRANKLIN	31,533	15,883	15,502	148	381 R	50.4%	49.2%	50.6%	49.4%
443,018	HAMPDEN	174,971	89,330	84,985	656	4,345 R	51.1%	48.6%	51.2%	48.8%
138,813	HAMPSHIRE	63,942	28,111	35,597	234	7,486 D	44.0%	55.7%	44.1%	55.9%
1,367,034	MIDDLESEX	646,754	319,604	325,065	2,085	5,461 D	49.4%	50.3%	49.6%	50.4%
5,087	NANTUCKET	3,170	1,697	1,456	17	241 R	53.5%	45.9%	53.8%	46.2%
606,587	NORFOLK	299,319	160,313	138,222	784	22,091 R	53.6%	46.2%	53.7%	46.3%
405,437	PLYMOUTH	174,771	105,230	68,923	618	36,307 R	60.2%	39.4%	60.4%	39.6%
650,142	SUFFOLK	244,997	91,563	152,568	866	61,005 D	37.4%	62.3%	37.5%	62.5%
646,352	WORCESTER	276,440	156,060	119,498	882	36,562 R	56.5%	43.2%	56.6%	43.4%
5,737,037	TOTAL	2,559,453	1,310,936	1,239,606	8,911	71,330 R	51.2%	48.4%	51.4%	48.6%

MASSACHUSETTS

SENATOR 1984

1980 Census Population	County	Total Vote	Republican	Democratic	Other	Rep.-Dem. Plurality	Percentage			
							Total Vote		Major Vote	
							Rep.	Dem.	Rep.	Dem.
147,925	BARNSTABLE	89,452	45,386	44,033	33	1,353 R	50.7%	49.2%	50.8%	49.2%
145,110	BERKSHIRE	62,260	28,720	33,538	2	4,818 D	46.1%	53.9%	46.1%	53.9%
474,641	BRISTOL	185,822	73,260	112,558	4	39,298 D	39.4%	60.6%	39.4%	60.6%
8,942	DUKES	6,025	2,242	3,782	1	1,540 D	37.2%	62.8%	37.2%	62.8%
633,632	ESSEX	293,275	142,594	150,636	45	8,042 D	48.6%	51.4%	48.6%	51.4%
64,317	FRANKLIN	31,068	13,606	17,461	1	3,855 D	43.8%	56.2%	43.8%	56.2%
443,018	HAMPDEN	171,466	78,390	93,070	6	14,680 D	45.7%	54.3%	45.7%	54.3%
138,813	HAMPSHIRE	63,019	24,449	38,559	11	14,110 D	38.8%	61.2%	38.8%	61.2%
1,367,034	MIDDLESEX	640,668	280,523	359,987	158	79,464 D	43.8%	56.2%	43.8%	56.2%
5,087	NANTUCKET	3,119	1,353	1,766		413 D	43.4%	56.6%	43.4%	56.6%
606,587	NORFOLK	297,187	143,445	153,689	53	10,244 D	48.3%	51.7%	48.3%	51.7%
405,437	PLYMOUTH	173,429	90,685	82,733	11	7,952 R	52.3%	47.7%	52.3%	47.7%
650,142	SUFFOLK	239,823	80,335	159,465	23	79,130 D	33.5%	66.5%	33.5%	66.5%
646,352	WORCESTER	273,582	131,818	141,704	60	9,886 D	48.2%	51.8%	48.2%	51.8%
5,737,037	TOTAL	2,530,195	1,136,806	1,392,981	408	256,175 D	44.9%	55.1%	44.9%	55.1%

MASSACHUSETTS

PRESIDENT 1984

1980 Census Population	City/Town	Total Vote	Republican	Democratic	Other	Rep.-Dem. Plurality	Percentage Total Vote Rep.	Dem.	Major Vote Rep.	Dem.
26,271	AGAWAM	10,917	6,347	4,534	36	1,813 R	58.1%	41.5%	58.3%	41.7%
33,229	AMHERST	13,861	3,975	9,844	42	5,869 D	28.7%	71.0%	28.8%	71.2%
26,370	ANDOVER	14,351	8,814	5,479	58	3,335 R	61.4%	38.2%	61.7%	38.3%
48,219	ARLINGTON	26,276	11,254	14,935	87	3,681 D	42.8%	56.8%	43.0%	57.0%
34,196	ATTLEBORO	12,631	8,041	4,524	66	3,517 R	63.7%	35.8%	64.0%	36.0%
30,898	BARNSTABLE TOWN	18,265	10,333	7,856	76	2,477 R	56.6%	43.0%	56.8%	43.2%
26,100	BELMONT	14,909	7,181	7,687	41	506 D	48.2%	51.6%	48.3%	51.7%
37,655	BEVERLY	18,095	10,256	7,791	48	2,465 R	56.7%	43.1%	56.8%	43.2%
36,727	BILLERICA	14,419	8,669	5,692	58	2,977 R	60.1%	39.5%	60.4%	39.6%
562,994	BOSTON	207,799	75,311	131,745	743	56,434 D	36.2%	63.4%	36.4%	63.6%
36,337	BRAINTREE	18,136	10,398	7,734	4	2,664 R	57.3%	42.6%	57.3%	42.7%
95,172	BROCKTON	31,394	17,161	14,130	103	3,031 R	54.7%	45.0%	54.8%	45.2%
55,062	BROOKLINE	27,793	8,524	19,224	45	10,700 D	30.7%	69.2%	30.7%	69.3%
23,486	BURLINGTON	11,477	6,864	4,583	30	2,281 R	59.8%	39.9%	60.0%	40.0%
95,322	CAMBRIDGE	42,771	10,007	32,582	182	22,575 D	23.4%	76.2%	23.5%	76.5%
31,174	CHELMSFORD	15,578	10,279	5,256	43	5,023 R	66.0%	33.7%	66.2%	33.8%
25,431	CHELSEA	9,669	3,809	5,825	35	2,016 D	39.4%	60.2%	39.5%	60.5%
55,112	CHICOPEE	23,444	10,789	12,540	115	1,751 D	46.0%	53.5%	46.2%	53.8%
24,100	DANVERS	11,995	7,486	4,460	49	3,026 R	62.4%	37.2%	62.7%	37.3%
23,966	DARTMOUTH	11,089	5,695	5,355	39	340 R	51.4%	48.3%	51.5%	48.5%
25,298	DEDHAM	12,867	7,040	5,782	45	1,258 R	54.7%	44.9%	54.9%	45.1%
21,249	DRACUT	10,718	6,834	3,840	44	2,994 R	63.8%	35.8%	64.0%	36.0%
37,195	EVERETT	16,410	7,149	9,209	52	2,060 D	43.6%	56.1%	43.7%	56.3%
92,574	FALL RIVER	32,294	11,463	20,722	109	9,259 D	35.5%	64.2%	35.6%	64.4%
23,640	FALMOUTH	13,550	7,100	6,403	47	697 R	52.4%	47.3%	52.6%	47.4%
39,580	FITCHBURG	14,535	7,649	6,832	54	817 R	52.6%	47.0%	52.8%	47.2%
65,113	FRAMINGHAM	29,503	15,074	14,368	61	706 R	51.1%	48.7%	51.2%	48.8%
27,768	GLOUCESTER	12,785	6,978	5,768	39	1,210 R	54.6%	45.1%	54.7%	45.3%
46,865	HAVERHILL	19,638	10,365	9,182	91	1,183 R	52.8%	46.8%	53.0%	47.0%
20,339	HINGHAM	10,841	6,750	4,062	29	2,688 R	62.3%	37.5%	62.4%	37.6%
44,678	HOLYOKE	16,593	7,735	8,803	55	1,068 D	46.6%	53.1%	46.8%	53.2%
63,175	LAWRENCE	20,959	9,877	10,986	96	1,109 D	47.1%	52.4%	47.3%	52.7%
34,508	LEOMINSTER	13,390	7,856	5,507	27	2,349 R	58.7%	41.1%	58.8%	41.2%
29,479	LEXINGTON	17,564	8,118	9,397	49	1,279 D	46.2%	53.5%	46.3%	53.7%
92,418	LOWELL	32,034	16,834	15,042	158	1,792 R	52.6%	47.0%	52.8%	47.2%
78,471	LYNN	31,730	14,445	17,103	182	2,658 D	45.5%	53.9%	45.8%	54.2%
53,386	MALDEN	23,141	9,931	13,142	68	3,211 D	42.9%	56.8%	43.0%	57.0%
20,126	MARBLEHEAD	12,155	7,021	5,122	12	1,899 R	57.8%	42.1%	57.8%	42.2%
30,617	MARLBOROUGH	13,810	8,072	5,690	48	2,382 R	58.5%	41.2%	58.7%	41.3%
20,916	MARSHFIELD	10,116	5,993	4,083	40	1,910 R	59.2%	40.4%	59.5%	40.5%
58,076	MEDFORD	26,485	11,666	14,757	62	3,091 D	44.0%	55.7%	44.2%	55.8%
30,055	MELROSE	15,197	8,189	6,971	37	1,218 R	53.9%	45.9%	54.0%	46.0%
36,701	METHUEN	17,294	9,901	7,323	70	2,578 R	57.3%	42.3%	57.5%	42.5%
23,390	MILFORD	10,243	5,315	4,909	19	406 R	51.9%	47.9%	52.0%	48.0%
25,860	MILTON	14,652	6,689	7,936	27	1,247 D	45.7%	54.2%	45.7%	54.3%
29,461	NATICK	15,810	8,380	7,394	36	986 R	53.0%	46.8%	53.1%	46.9%
27,901	NEEDHAM	16,274	9,115	7,101	58	2,014 R	56.0%	43.6%	56.2%	43.8%
98,478	NEW BEDFORD	35,360	13,147	22,070	143	8,923 D	37.2%	62.4%	37.3%	62.7%
83,622	NEWTON	43,614	16,184	27,343	87	11,159 D	37.1%	62.7%	37.2%	62.8%
29,286	NORTHAMPTON	14,233	5,187	8,994	52	3,807 D	36.4%	63.2%	36.6%	63.4%
20,129	NORTH ANDOVER	10,571	6,334	4,205	32	2,129 R	59.9%	39.8%	60.1%	39.9%
21,095	NORTH ATTLEBORO	8,629	5,851	2,753	25	3,098 R	67.8%	31.9%	68.0%	32.0%
29,711	NORWOOD	14,307	7,618	6,650	39	968 R	53.2%	46.5%	53.4%	46.6%
45,976	PEABODY	21,611	10,894	10,698	19	196 R	50.4%	49.5%	50.5%	49.5%
51,974	PITTSFIELD	22,229	10,963	11,149	117	186 D	49.3%	50.2%	49.6%	50.4%
35,913	PLYMOUTH TOWN	16,496	9,671	6,773	52	2,898 R	58.6%	41.1%	58.8%	41.2%
84,743	QUINCY	39,215	20,123	18,971	121	1,152 R	51.3%	48.4%	51.5%	48.5%
28,218	RANDOLPH	13,377	6,130	7,211	36	1,081 D	45.8%	53.9%	45.9%	54.1%
22,678	READING	12,300	7,206	5,055	39	2,151 R	58.6%	41.1%	58.8%	41.2%
42,423	REVERE	18,121	7,852	10,204	65	2,352 D	43.3%	56.3%	43.5%	56.5%

MASSACHUSETTS

PRESIDENT 1984

1980 Census Population	City/Town	Total Vote	Republican	Democratic	Other	Rep.-Dem. Plurality	Percentage Total Vote Rep.	Dem.	Major Vote Rep.	Dem.
38,220	SALEM	17,008	7,567	9,377	64	1,810 D	44.5%	55.1%	44.7%	55.3%
24,746	SAUGUS	11,879	6,328	5,503	48	825 R	53.3%	46.3%	53.5%	46.5%
22,674	SHREWSBURY	11,541	6,801	4,708	32	2,093 R	58.9%	40.8%	59.1%	40.9%
77,372	SOMERVILLE	32,542	11,318	21,065	159	9,747 D	34.8%	64.7%	35.0%	65.0%
152,319	SPRINGFIELD	50,995	21,431	29,376	188	7,945 D	42.0%	57.6%	42.2%	57.8%
21,424	STONEHAM	10,726	5,648	5,042	36	606 R	52.7%	47.0%	52.8%	47.2%
26,710	STOUGHTON	11,413	6,071	5,319	23	752 R	53.2%	46.6%	53.3%	46.7%
45,001	TAUNTON	15,950	8,337	7,516	97	821 R	52.3%	47.1%	52.6%	47.4%
24,635	TEWKSBURY	10,466	6,462	3,954	50	2,508 R	61.7%	37.8%	62.0%	38.0%
24,895	WAKEFIELD	13,261	7,198	6,020	43	1,178 R	54.3%	45.4%	54.5%	45.5%
58,200	WALTHAM	23,234	11,803	11,372	59	431 R	50.8%	48.9%	50.9%	49.1%
34,384	WATERTOWN	17,000	6,720	10,220	60	3,500 D	39.5%	60.1%	39.7%	60.3%
27,209	WELLESLEY	14,406	8,236	6,128	42	2,108 R	57.2%	42.5%	57.3%	42.7%
27,042	WEST SPRINGFIELD	11,663	6,611	5,003	49	1,608 R	56.7%	42.9%	56.9%	43.1%
36,465	WESTFIELD	14,239	8,010	6,183	46	1,827 R	56.3%	43.4%	56.4%	43.6%
55,601	WEYMOUTH	24,775	13,681	11,008	86	2,673 R	55.2%	44.4%	55.4%	44.6%
20,701	WINCHESTER	11,509	6,347	5,139	23	1,208 R	55.1%	44.7%	55.3%	44.7%
19,294	WINTHROP	9,408	4,591	4,794	23	203 D	48.8%	51.0%	48.9%	51.1%
36,626	WOBURN	17,188	9,021	8,114	53	907 R	52.5%	47.2%	52.6%	47.4%
161,799	WORCESTER CITY	60,053	27,348	32,525	180	5,177 D	45.5%	54.2%	45.7%	54.3%

MASSACHUSETTS

SENATOR 1984

1980 Census Population	City/Town	Total Vote	Republican	Democratic	Other	Rep.-Dem. Plurality	Percentage			
							Total Vote		Major Vote	
							Rep.	Dem.	Rep.	Dem.
26,271	AGAWAM	10,729	5,444	5,285		159 R	50.7%	49.3%	50.7%	49.3%
33,229	AMHERST	13,306	3,180	10,122	4	6,942 D	23.9%	76.1%	23.9%	76.1%
26,370	ANDOVER	14,254	8,081	6,173		1,908 R	56.7%	43.3%	56.7%	43.3%
48,219	ARLINGTON	26,067	10,183	15,852	32	5,669 D	39.1%	60.8%	39.1%	60.9%
34,196	ATTLEBORO	12,469	6,611	5,858		753 R	53.0%	47.0%	53.0%	47.0%
30,898	BARNSTABLE TOWN	18,161	9,115	9,038	8	77 R	50.2%	49.8%	50.2%	49.8%
26,100	BELMONT	14,801	6,681	8,120		1,439 D	45.1%	54.9%	45.1%	54.9%
37,655	BEVERLY	18,000	8,903	9,097		194 D	49.5%	50.5%	49.5%	50.5%
36,727	BILLERICA	14,329	7,510	6,816	3	694 R	52.4%	47.6%	52.4%	47.6%
562,994	BOSTON	203,128	66,605	136,500	23	69,895 D	32.8%	67.2%	32.8%	67.2%
36,337	BRAINTREE	18,041	9,177	8,863	1	314 R	50.9%	49.1%	50.9%	49.1%
95,172	BROCKTON	31,203	14,641	16,562		1,921 D	46.9%	53.1%	46.9%	53.1%
55,062	BROOKLINE	27,411	7,077	20,332	2	13,255 D	25.8%	74.2%	25.8%	74.2%
23,486	BURLINGTON	11,322	5,893	5,428	1	465 R	52.0%	47.9%	52.1%	47.9%
95,322	CAMBRIDGE	42,374	8,722	33,624	28	24,902 D	20.6%	79.4%	20.6%	79.4%
31,174	CHELMSFORD	15,473	9,440	6,025	8	3,415 R	61.0%	38.9%	61.0%	39.0%
25,431	CHELSEA	9,566	2,988	6,578		3,590 D	31.2%	68.8%	31.2%	68.8%
55,112	CHICOPEE	23,434	9,422	14,011	1	4,589 D	40.2%	59.8%	40.2%	59.8%
24,100	DANVERS	11,924	6,687	5,236	1	1,451 R	56.1%	43.9%	56.1%	43.9%
23,966	DARTMOUTH	10,862	4,482	6,380		1,898 D	41.3%	58.7%	41.3%	58.7%
25,298	DEDHAM	12,784	6,621	6,159	4	462 R	51.8%	48.2%	51.8%	48.2%
21,249	DRACUT	10,647	5,993	4,654		1,339 R	56.3%	43.7%	56.3%	43.7%
37,195	EVERETT	16,127	6,282	9,845		3,563 D	39.0%	61.0%	39.0%	61.0%
92,574	FALL RIVER	31,787	7,531	24,256		16,725 D	23.7%	76.3%	23.7%	76.3%
23,640	FALMOUTH	13,431	6,023	7,403	5	1,380 D	44.8%	55.1%	44.9%	55.1%
39,580	FITCHBURG	14,395	6,383	8,012		1,629 D	44.3%	55.7%	44.3%	55.7%
65,113	FRAMINGHAM	29,305	12,850	16,455		3,605 D	43.8%	56.2%	43.8%	56.2%
27,768	GLOUCESTER	12,653	5,991	6,662		671 D	47.3%	52.7%	47.3%	52.7%
46,865	HAVERHILL	19,471	8,795	10,670	6	1,875 D	45.2%	54.8%	45.2%	54.8%
20,339	HINGHAM	10,834	6,111	4,721	2	1,390 R	56.4%	43.6%	56.4%	43.6%
44,678	HOLYOKE	16,027	6,882	9,145		2,263 D	42.9%	57.1%	42.9%	57.1%
63,175	LAWRENCE	20,625	8,824	11,801		2,977 D	42.8%	57.2%	42.8%	57.2%
34,508	LEOMINSTER	13,504	6,675	6,827	2	152 D	49.4%	50.6%	49.4%	50.6%
29,479	LEXINGTON	17,377	7,366	10,006	5	2,640 D	42.4%	57.6%	42.4%	57.6%
92,418	LOWELL	31,790	15,223	16,563	4	1,340 D	47.9%	52.1%	47.9%	52.1%
78,471	LYNN	31,525	12,519	19,003	3	6,484 D	39.7%	60.3%	39.7%	60.3%
53,386	MALDEN	22,860	8,321	14,539		6,218 D	36.4%	63.6%	36.4%	63.6%
20,126	MARBLEHEAD	12,071	6,312	5,757	2	555 R	52.3%	47.7%	52.3%	47.7%
30,617	MARLBOROUGH	13,685	6,693	6,986	6	293 D	48.9%	51.0%	48.9%	51.1%
20,916	MARSHFIELD	10,060	5,177	4,883		294 R	51.5%	48.5%	51.5%	48.5%
58,076	MEDFORD	26,375	10,200	16,175		5,975 D	38.7%	61.3%	38.7%	61.3%
30,055	MELROSE	15,008	7,352	7,656		304 D	49.0%	51.0%	49.0%	51.0%
36,701	METHUEN	17,174	9,021	8,151	2	870 R	52.5%	47.5%	52.5%	47.5%
23,390	MILFORD	10,157	4,509	5,646	2	1,137 D	44.4%	55.6%	44.4%	55.6%
25,860	MILTON	14,531	7,338	7,193		145 R	50.5%	49.5%	50.5%	49.5%
29,461	NATICK	15,550	7,194	8,356		1,162 D	46.3%	53.7%	46.3%	53.7%
27,901	NEEDHAM	16,172	8,305	7,857	10	448 R	51.4%	48.6%	51.4%	48.6%
98,478	NEW BEDFORD	34,973	9,835	25,136	2	15,301 D	28.1%	71.9%	28.1%	71.9%
83,622	NEWTON	43,062	13,490	29,572		16,082 D	31.3%	68.7%	31.3%	68.7%
29,286	NORTHAMPTON	14,101	4,606	9,493	2	4,887 D	32.7%	67.3%	32.7%	67.3%
20,129	NORTH ANDOVER	10,507	5,901	4,606		1,295 R	56.2%	43.8%	56.2%	43.8%
21,095	NORTH ATTLEBORO	8,609	5,099	3,510		1,589 R	59.2%	40.8%	59.2%	40.8%
29,711	NORWOOD	14,219	7,479	6,740		739 R	52.6%	47.4%	52.6%	47.4%
45,976	PEABODY	21,485	8,813	12,664	8	3,851 D	41.0%	58.9%	41.0%	59.0%
51,974	PITTSFIELD	21,496	9,116	12,380		3,264 D	42.4%	57.6%	42.4%	57.6%
35,913	PLYMOUTH TOWN	16,272	7,921	8,351		430 D	48.7%	51.3%	48.7%	51.3%
84,743	QUINCY	38,936	17,920	21,016		3,096 D	46.0%	54.0%	46.0%	54.0%
28,218	RANDOLPH	13,338	4,930	8,408		3,478 D	37.0%	63.0%	37.0%	63.0%
22,678	READING	12,181	6,507	5,674		833 R	53.4%	46.6%	53.4%	46.6%
42,423	REVERE	17,820	6,826	10,994		4,168 D	38.3%	61.7%	38.3%	61.7%

MASSACHUSETTS

SENATOR 1984

1980 Census Population	City/Town	Total Vote	Republican	Democratic	Other	Rep.-Dem. Plurality	Percentage			
							Total Vote		Major Vote	
							Rep.	Dem.	Rep.	Dem.
38,220	SALEM	16,856	6,435	10,419	2	3,984 D	38.2%	61.8%	38.2%	61.8%
24,746	SAUGUS	11,818	5,445	6,373		928 D	46.1%	53.9%	46.1%	53.9%
22,674	SHREWSBURY	11,409	6,000	5,407	2	593 R	52.6%	47.4%	52.6%	47.4%
77,372	SOMERVILLE	32,139	9,711	22,414	14	12,703 D	30.2%	69.7%	30.2%	69.8%
152,319	SPRINGFIELD	48,836	18,735	30,101		11,366 D	38.4%	61.6%	38.4%	61.6%
21,424	STONEHAM	10,657	4,934	5,722	1	788 D	46.3%	53.7%	46.3%	53.7%
26,710	STOUGHTON	11,259	4,949	6,309	1	1,360 D	44.0%	56.0%	44.0%	56.0%
45,001	TAUNTON	15,638	6,878	8,760		1,882 D	44.0%	56.0%	44.0%	56.0%
24,635	TEWKSBURY	10,404	5,655	4,744	5	911 R	54.4%	45.6%	54.4%	45.6%
24,895	WAKEFIELD	13,205	6,269	6,936		667 D	47.5%	52.5%	47.5%	52.5%
58,200	WALTHAM	22,880	10,254	12,626		2,372 D	44.8%	55.2%	44.8%	55.2%
34,384	WATERTOWN	16,957	5,833	11,114	10	5,281 D	34.4%	65.5%	34.4%	65.6%
27,209	WELLESLEY	14,272	7,610	6,653	9	957 R	53.3%	46.6%	53.4%	46.6%
27,042	WEST SPRINGFIELD	11,529	5,879	5,650		229 R	51.0%	49.0%	51.0%	49.0%
36,465	WESTFIELD	14,137	6,771	7,363	3	592 D	47.9%	52.1%	47.9%	52.1%
55,601	WEYMOUTH	24,692	11,864	12,828		964 D	48.0%	52.0%	48.0%	52.0%
20,701	WINCHESTER	11,364	5,925	5,437	2	488 R	52.1%	47.8%	52.1%	47.9%
19,294	WINTHROP	9,309	3,916	5,393		1,477 D	42.1%	57.9%	42.1%	57.9%
36,626	WOBURN	17,030	7,665	9,365		1,700 D	45.0%	55.0%	45.0%	55.0%
161,799	WORCESTER CITY	59,273	23,072	36,201		13,129 D	38.9%	61.1%	38.9%	61.1%

MASSACHUSETTS

CONGRESS

CD	Year	Total Vote	Republican Vote	Republican Candidate	Democratic Vote	Democratic Candidate	Other Vote	Rep.-Dem. Plurality	Rep. Total Vote	Dem. Total Vote	Rep. Major Vote	Dem. Major Vote
1	1984	223,037	162,646	CONTE, SILVIO O.	60,372	WENTWORTH, MARY L.	19	102,274 R	72.9%	27.1%	72.9%	27.1%
1	1982	146,197	145,417	*CONTE, SILVIO O.			780	145,417 R	99.5%		100.0%	
2	1984	193,254	60,463	SWANK, THOMAS P.	132,693	BOLAND, EDWARD P.	98	72,230 D	31.3%	68.7%	31.3%	68.7%
2	1982	162,773	44,544	SWANK, THOMAS P.	118,215	BOLAND, EDWARD P.	14	73,671 D	27.4%	72.6%	27.4%	72.6%
3	1984	220,254	71,765	REDDING, KENNETH J.	148,461	EARLY, JOSEPH D.	28	76,696 D	32.6%	67.4%	32.6%	67.4%
3	1982	142,740			142,611	EARLY, JOSEPH D.	129	142,611 D		99.9%		100.0%
4	1984	233,032	60,121	FORTE, JIM	172,903	FRANK, BARNEY	8	112,782 D	25.8%	74.2%	25.8%	74.2%
4	1982	204,615	82,804	HECKLER, MARGARET M.	121,802	FRANK, BARNEY	9	38,998 D	40.5%	59.5%	40.5%	59.5%
5	1984	224,927	104,912	HYATT, GREGORY S.	120,008	ATKINS, CHESTER G.	7	15,096 D	46.6%	53.4%	46.6%	53.4%
5	1982	165,598			140,177	SHANNON, JAMES M.	25,421	140,177 D		84.6%		100.0%
6	1984	239,649	63,363	LEBER, FREDERICK S.	168,662	MAVROULES, NICHOLAS	7,624	105,299 D	26.4%	70.4%	27.3%	72.7%
6	1982	203,584	85,849	TRIMARCO, THOMAS H.	117,723	MAVROULES, NICHOLAS	12	31,874 D	42.2%	57.8%	42.2%	57.8%
7	1984	234,190	66,930	RALPH, S. LESTER	167,211	MARKEY, EDWARD J.	49	100,281 D	28.6%	71.4%	28.6%	71.4%
7	1982	194,369	43,063	BASILE, DAVID M.	151,305	MARKEY, EDWARD J.	1	108,242 D	22.2%	77.8%	22.2%	77.8%
8	1984	195,603			179,617	O'NEILL, THOMAS P.	15,986	179,617 D		91.8%		100.0%
8	1982	164,672	41,370	MCNAMARA, FRANK L.	123,296	O'NEILL, THOMAS P.	6	81,926 D	25.1%	74.9%	25.1%	74.9%
9	1984	153,252			153,132	MOAKLEY, JOHN J.	120	153,132 D		99.9%		100.0%
9	1982	160,225	55,030	COCHRAN, DEBORAH R.	102,665	MOAKLEY, JOHN J.	2,530	47,635 D	34.3%	64.1%	34.9%	65.1%
10	1984	256,824	113,745	CRAMPTON, LEWIS	143,062	STUDDS, GERRY E.	17	29,317 D	44.3%	55.7%	44.3%	55.7%
10	1982	201,436	63,014	CONWAY, JOHN E.	138,418	STUDDS, GERRY E.	4	75,404 D	31.3%	68.7%	31.3%	68.7%
11	1984	172,025			172,010	DONNELLY, BRIAN J.	15	172,010 D		100.0%		100.0%
11	1982	144,157			144,132	DONNELLY, BRIAN J.	25	144,132 D		100.0%		100.0%

MASSACHUSETTS

1984 GENERAL ELECTION

In addition to the county-by-county figures, data are presented for selected Massachusetts communities. Since not all jurisdictions of the state are listed in this special tabulation, state-wide totals are shown only with the county-by-county statistics.

President   Other vote was 7,998 Serrette (Independent Alliance); 18 Johnson (write-in); 3 Dodge (write-in); 892 scattered.

Senator   Other vote was scattered. Early uncorrected returns gave the Shamie total vote as 1,136,913 and the Kerry total vote as 1,393,150.

Congress   Other vote was scattered in all CD's except 7,615 Batchelder (Rainbow Coalition) and 9 scattered in CD 6; 15,810 Ross (Communist) and 176 scattered in CD 8. Vote listed for CD 1 represents the amended return for that district. An asterisk in the Congressional vote table indicates a candidate received votes as the nominee of an additional party.

1984 PRIMARIES

SEPTEMBER 18 REPUBLICAN

Senator   173,851 Raymond Shamie; 104,761 Elliot L. Richardson; 70 scattered.

Congress   Unopposed in six CD's. No candidate in CD's 8, 9 and 11. Contested as follows:

CD 5   16,148 Gregory S. Hyatt; 11,449 Thomas P. Tierney; 5 scattered.
CD 10   19,890 Lewis Crampton; 12,383 John E. Bennett; 4,475 George Donovan; 127 scattered.

SEPTEMBER 18 DEMOCRATIC

Senator   322,470 John F. Kerry; 297,941 James M. Shannon; 85,910 David M. Bartley; 82,999 Michael J. Connolly; 502 scattered.

Congress   Unopposed in four CD's. Contested as follows:

CD 2   33,771 Edward P. Boland; 14,010 Robert B. Shaffer; 4,416 Robert E. Shaw; 2 scattered.
CD 5   43,538 Chester G. Atkins; 38,737 Philip L. Shea; 21 scattered.
CD 7   55,248 Edward J. Markey; 41,507 Samuel Rotondi; 2,873 Philip E. Doherty; 2,396 Michael J. Barrett; 387 Michael Gelber; 6 scattered.
CD 8   65,041 Thomas P. O'Neill; 10,657 Robert M. Cappucci; 4,355 Debra Gelber; 41 scattered.
CD 9   52,896 John J. Moakley; 7,153 Constance L. Brown; 14 scattered.
CD 10   48,377 Gerry E. Studds; 27,094 Peter Y. Flynn; 3,284 Christopher C. Trundy; 35 scattered.
CD 11   62,480 Brian J. Donnelly; 5,988 John P. Scialdone; 1 scattered.

MICHIGAN

GOVERNOR
James J. Blanchard (D). Elected 1982 to a four-year term.

SENATORS
Carl Levin (D). Re-elected 1984 to a six-year term. Previously elected 1978.

Donald W. Riegle (D). Re-elected 1982 to a six-year term. Previously elected 1976.

REPRESENTATIVES
1. John Conyers (D)
2. Carl D. Pursell (R)
3. Howard Wolpe (D)
4. Mark D. Siljander (R)
5. Paul Henry (R)
6. M. Robert Carr (D)
7. Dale E. Kildee (D)
8. J. Robert Traxler (D)
9. Guy Vander Jagt (R)
10. Bill Schuette (R)
11. Robert W. Davis (R)
12. David E. Bonior (D)
13. George W. Crockett (D)
14. Dennis M. Hertel (D)
15. William D. Ford (D)
16. John D. Dingell, Jr. (D)
17. Sander Levin (D)
18. William S. Broomfield (R)

POSTWAR VOTE FOR GOVERNOR

Year	Total Vote	Republican Vote	Candidate	Democratic Vote	Candidate	Other Vote	Rep.-Dem. Plurality	Total Vote Rep.	Total Vote Dem.	Major Vote Rep.	Major Vote Dem.
1982	3,040,008	1,369,582	Headlee, Richard H.	1,561,291	Blanchard, James J.	109,135	191,709 D	45.1%	51.4%	46.7%	53.3%
1978	2,867,212	1,628,485	Milliken, William G.	1,237,256	Fitzgerald, William	1,471	391,229 R	56.8%	43.2%	56.8%	43.2%
1974	2,657,017	1,356,865	Milliken, William G.	1,242,247	Levin, Sander	57,905	114,618 R	51.1%	46.8%	52.2%	47.8%
1970	2,656,162	1,339,047	Milliken, William G.	1,294,638	Levin, Sander	22,477	44,409 R	50.4%	48.7%	50.8%	49.2%
1966*	2,461,909	1,490,430	Romney, George W.	963,383	Ferency, Zolton A.	8,096	527,047 R	60.5%	39.1%	60.7%	39.3%
1964	3,158,102	1,764,355	Romney, George W.	1,381,442	Staebler, Neil	12,305	382,913 R	55.9%	43.7%	56.1%	43.9%
1962	2,764,839	1,420,086	Romney, George W.	1,339,513	Swainson, John B.	5,240	80,573 R	51.4%	48.4%	51.5%	48.5%
1960	3,255,991	1,602,022	Bagwell, Paul D.	1,643,634	Swainson, John B.	10,335	41,612 D	49.2%	50.5%	49.4%	50.6%
1958	2,312,184	1,078,089	Bagwell, Paul D.	1,225,533	Williams, G. Mennen	8,562	147,444 D	46.6%	53.0%	46.8%	53.2%
1956	3,049,651	1,376,376	Cobo, Albert E.	1,666,689	Williams, G. Mennen	6,586	290,313 D	45.1%	54.7%	45.2%	54.8%
1954	2,187,027	963,300	Leonard, Donald S.	1,216,308	Williams, G. Mennen	7,419	253,008 D	44.0%	55.6%	44.2%	55.8%
1952	2,865,980	1,423,275	Alger, Fred M.	1,431,893	Williams, G. Mennen	10,812	8,618 D	49.7%	50.0%	49.8%	50.2%
1950	1,879,382	933,998	Kelly, Harry F.	935,152	Williams, G. Mennen	10,232	1,154 D	49.7%	49.8%	50.0%	50.0%
1948	2,113,122	964,810	Sigler, Kim	1,128,664	Williams, G. Mennen	19,648	163,854 D	45.7%	53.4%	46.1%	53.9%
1946	1,665,475	1,003,878	Sigler, Kim	644,540	Van Wagoner, Murray	17,057	359,338 R	60.3%	38.7%	60.9%	39.1%

The term of office of Michigan's Governor was increased from two to four years effective with the 1966 election.

POSTWAR VOTE FOR SENATOR

Year	Total Vote	Republican Vote	Candidate	Democratic Vote	Candidate	Other Vote	Rep.-Dem. Plurality	Total Vote Rep.	Total Vote Dem.	Major Vote Rep.	Major Vote Dem.
1984	3,700,938	1,745,302	Lousma, Jack	1,915,831	Levin, Carl	39,805	170,529 D	47.2%	51.8%	47.7%	52.3%
1982	2,994,334	1,223,288	Ruppe, Philip E.	1,728,793	Riegle, Donald W.	42,253	505,505 D	40.9%	57.7%	41.4%	58.6%
1978	2,846,630	1,362,165	Griffin, Robert P.	1,484,193	Levin, Carl	272	122,028 D	47.9%	52.1%	47.9%	52.1%
1976	3,490,664	1,635,087	Esch, Marvin L.	1,831,031	Riegle, Donald W.	24,546	195,944 D	46.8%	52.5%	47.2%	52.8%
1972	3,406,906	1,781,065	Griffin, Robert P.	1,577,178	Kelley, Frank J.	48,663	203,887 R	52.3%	46.3%	53.0%	47.0%
1970	2,610,839	858,470	Romney, Lenore	1,744,716	Hart, Philip A.	7,653	886,246 D	32.9%	66.8%	33.0%	67.0%
1966	2,439,365	1,363,530	Griffin, Robert P.	1,069,484	Williams, G. Mennen	6,351	294,046 R	55.9%	43.8%	56.0%	44.0%
1964	3,101,667	1,096,272	Peterson, Elly M.	1,996,912	Hart, Philip A.	8,483	900,640 D	35.3%	64.4%	35.4%	64.6%
1960	3,226,647	1,548,873	Bentley, Alvin M.	1,669,179	McNamara, Patrick V.	8,595	120,306 D	48.0%	51.7%	48.1%	51.9%
1958	2,271,644	1,046,963	Potter, Charles E.	1,216,966	Hart, Philip A.	7,715	170,003 D	46.1%	53.6%	46.2%	53.8%
1954	2,144,840	1,049,420	Ferguson, Homer	1,088,550	McNamara, Patrick V.	6,870	39,130 D	48.9%	50.8%	49.1%	50.9%
1952	2,821,133	1,428,352	Potter, Charles E.	1,383,416	Moody, Blair	9,365	44,936 R	50.6%	49.0%	50.8%	49.2%
1948	2,062,097	1,045,156	Ferguson, Homer	1,000,329	Hook, Frank E.	16,612	44,827 R	50.7%	48.5%	51.1%	48.9%
1946	1,618,720	1,085,570	Vandenberg, Arthur	517,923	Lee, James H.	15,227	567,647 R	67.1%	32.0%	67.7%	32.3%

MICHIGAN

Districts Established May 24, 1982

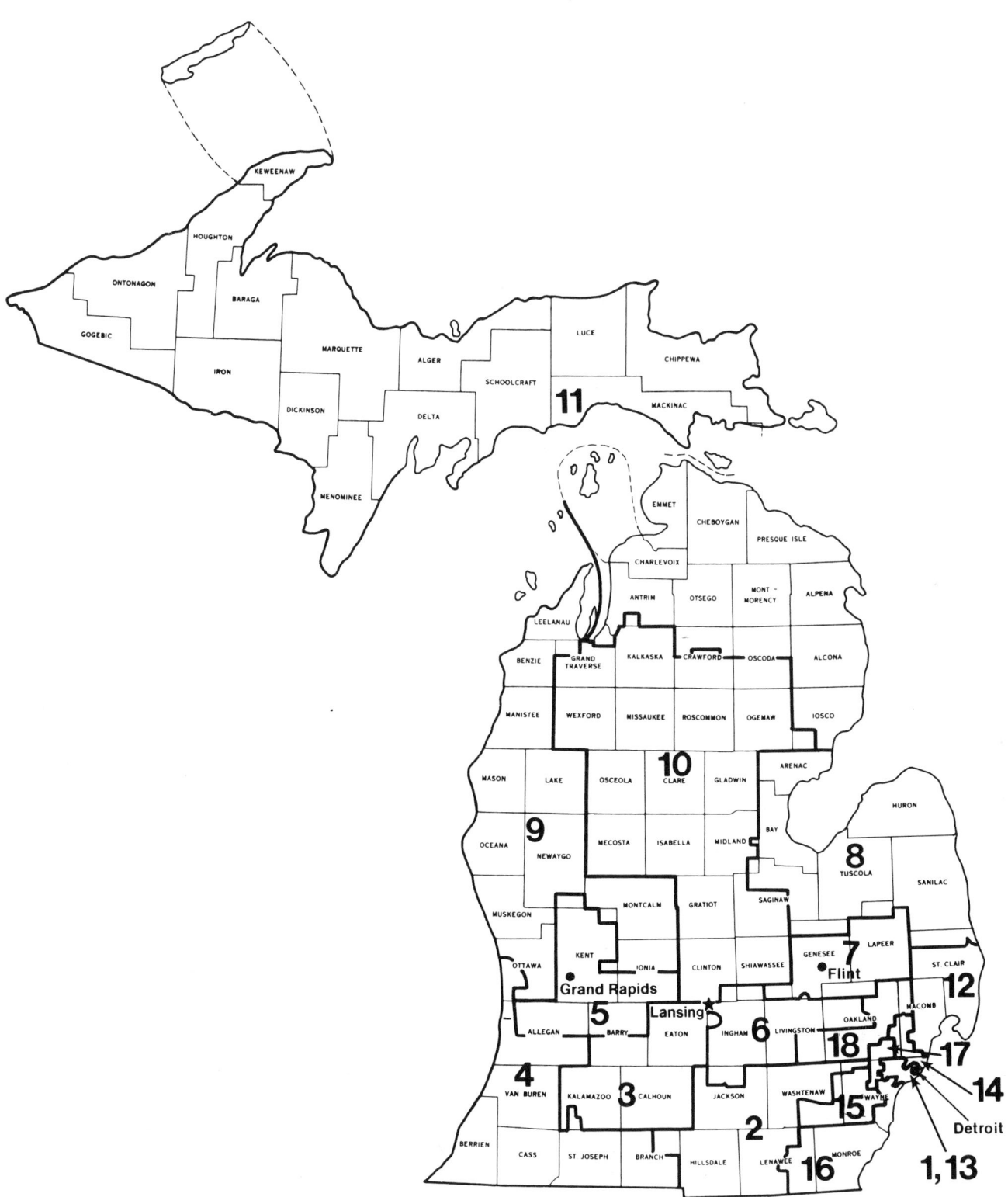

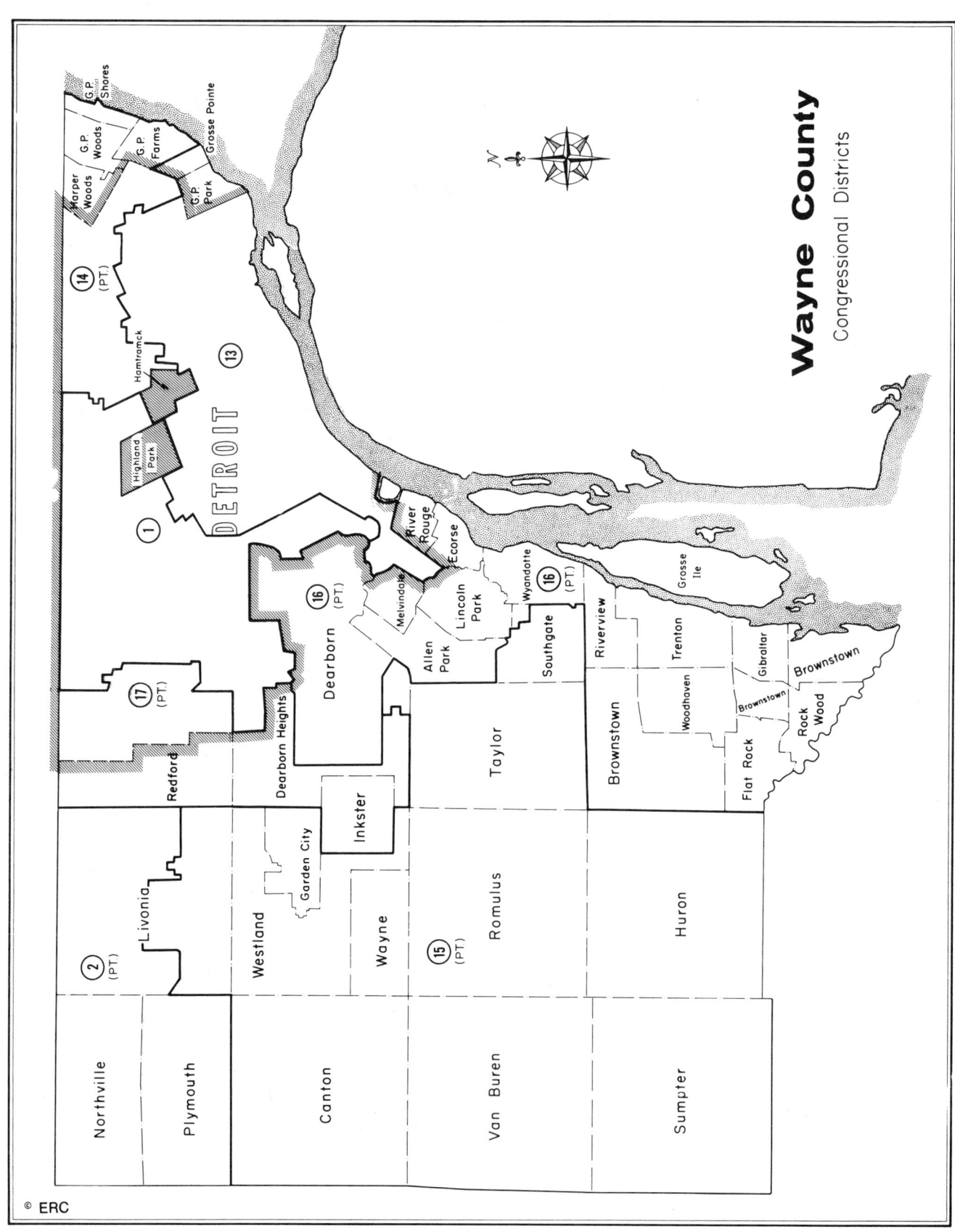

Wayne County
Congressional Districts

© ERC

235

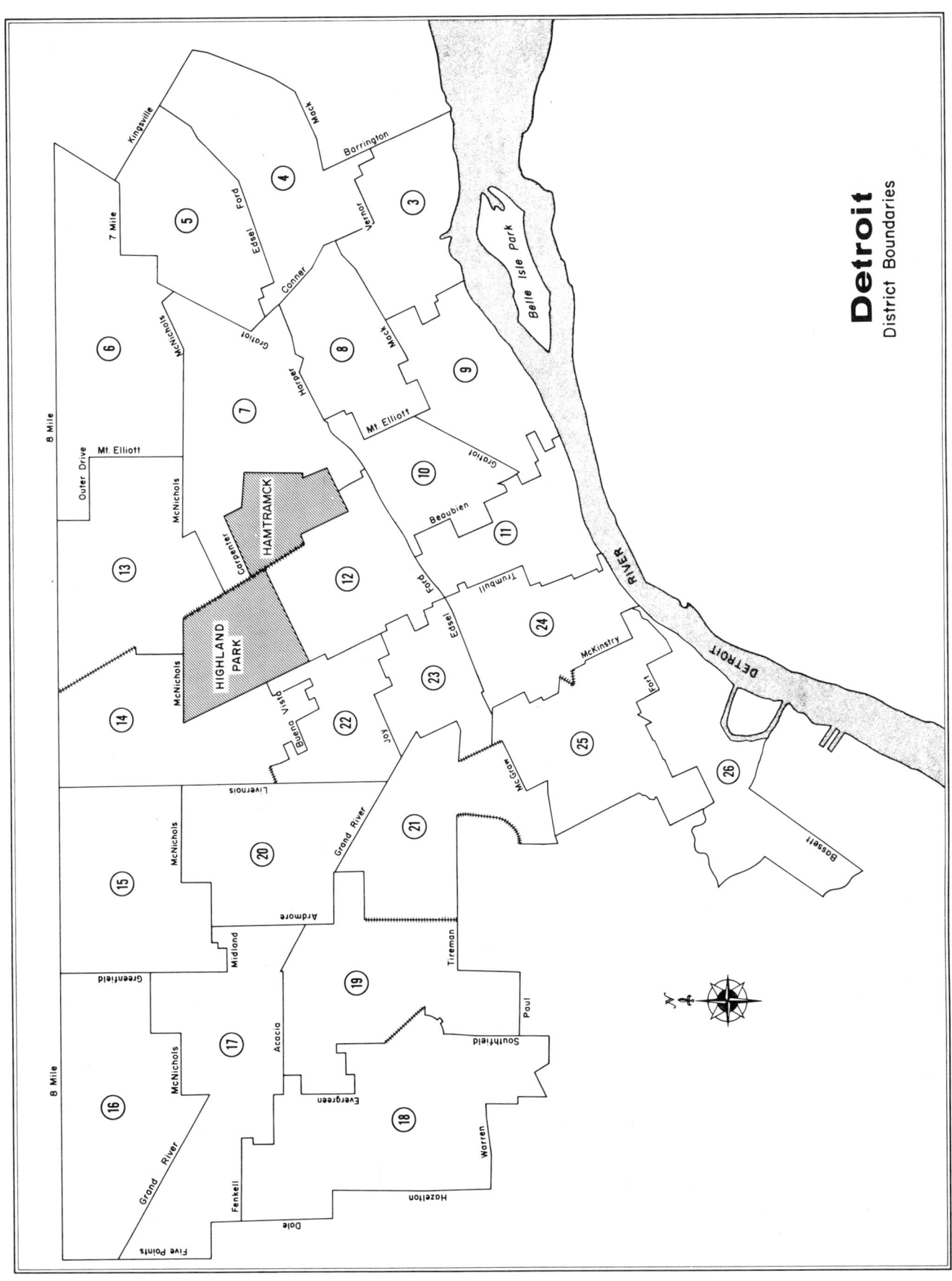

Detroit
District Boundaries

© ERC

MICHIGAN

PRESIDENT 1984

1980 Census Population	County	Total Vote	Republican	Democratic	Other	Rep.-Dem. Plurality	Percentage Total Vote Rep.	Dem.	Major Vote Rep.	Dem.
9,740	ALCONA	4,853	3,223	1,616	14	1,607 R	66.4%	33.3%	66.6%	33.4%
9,225	ALGER	4,208	2,175	2,018	15	157 R	51.7%	48.0%	51.9%	48.1%
81,555	ALLEGAN	32,338	23,762	8,389	187	15,373 R	73.5%	25.9%	73.9%	26.1%
32,315	ALPENA	13,397	8,212	5,136	49	3,076 R	61.3%	38.3%	61.5%	38.5%
16,194	ANTRIM	8,277	5,726	2,507	44	3,219 R	69.2%	30.3%	69.5%	30.5%
14,706	ARENAC	5,941	3,483	2,436	22	1,047 R	58.6%	41.0%	58.8%	41.2%
8,484	BARAGA	3,792	1,965	1,818	9	147 R	51.8%	47.9%	51.9%	48.1%
45,781	BARRY	20,265	14,245	5,898	122	8,347 R	70.3%	29.1%	70.7%	29.3%
119,881	BAY	49,030	26,198	22,597	235	3,601 R	53.4%	46.1%	53.7%	46.3%
11,205	BENZIE	5,502	3,590	1,866	46	1,724 R	65.2%	33.9%	65.8%	34.2%
171,276	BERRIEN	64,824	43,160	21,228	436	21,932 R	66.6%	32.7%	67.0%	33.0%
40,188	BRANCH	14,945	11,004	3,860	81	7,144 R	73.6%	25.8%	74.0%	26.0%
141,557	CALHOUN	55,067	34,470	20,313	284	14,157 R	62.6%	36.9%	62.9%	37.1%
49,499	CASS	18,394	11,647	6,634	113	5,013 R	63.3%	36.1%	63.7%	36.3%
19,907	CHARLEVOIX	9,595	6,355	3,175	65	3,180 R	66.2%	33.1%	66.7%	33.3%
20,649	CHEBOYGAN	9,452	6,053	3,358	41	2,695 R	64.0%	35.5%	64.3%	35.7%
29,029	CHIPPEWA	12,757	8,135	4,575	47	3,560 R	63.8%	35.9%	64.0%	36.0%
23,822	CLARE	10,412	6,587	3,764	61	2,823 R	63.3%	36.2%	63.6%	36.4%
55,893	CLINTON	23,726	17,387	6,226	113	11,161 R	73.3%	26.2%	73.6%	26.4%
9,465	CRAWFORD	4,896	3,303	1,558	35	1,745 R	67.5%	31.8%	67.9%	32.1%
38,947	DELTA	16,942	8,952	7,934	56	1,018 R	52.8%	46.8%	53.0%	47.0%
25,341	DICKINSON	12,530	6,880	5,614	36	1,266 R	54.9%	44.8%	55.1%	44.9%
88,337	EATON	38,199	27,720	10,290	189	17,430 R	72.6%	26.9%	72.9%	27.1%
22,992	EMMET	11,080	7,760	3,254	66	4,506 R	70.0%	29.4%	70.5%	29.5%
450,449	GENESEE	183,387	92,943	89,491	953	3,452 R	50.7%	48.8%	50.9%	49.1%
19,957	GLADWIN	8,844	5,401	3,368	75	2,033 R	61.1%	38.1%	61.6%	38.4%
19,686	GOGEBIC	9,581	4,006	5,554	21	1,548 D	41.8%	58.0%	41.9%	58.1%
54,899	GRAND TRAVERSE	25,464	18,036	7,271	157	10,765 R	70.8%	28.6%	71.3%	28.7%
40,448	GRATIOT	14,506	10,456	4,000	50	6,456 R	72.1%	27.6%	72.3%	27.7%
42,071	HILLSDALE	15,768	12,063	3,616	89	8,447 R	76.5%	22.9%	76.9%	23.1%
37,872	HOUGHTON	15,141	8,652	6,434	55	2,218 R	57.1%	42.5%	57.4%	42.6%
36,459	HURON	15,091	11,073	3,966	52	7,107 R	73.4%	26.3%	73.6%	26.4%
275,520	INGHAM	116,083	68,753	46,411	919	22,342 R	59.2%	40.0%	59.7%	40.3%
51,815	IONIA	20,035	14,162	5,735	138	8,427 R	70.7%	28.6%	71.2%	28.8%
28,349	IOSCO	11,804	7,907	3,850	47	4,057 R	67.0%	32.6%	67.3%	32.7%
13,635	IRON	7,056	3,468	3,559	29	91 D	49.1%	50.4%	49.4%	50.6%
54,110	ISABELLA	18,793	12,215	6,435	143	5,780 R	65.0%	34.2%	65.5%	34.5%
151,495	JACKSON	58,785	40,133	18,340	312	21,793 R	68.3%	31.2%	68.6%	31.4%
212,378	KALAMAZOO	91,388	58,327	32,460	601	25,867 R	63.8%	35.5%	64.2%	35.8%
10,952	KALKASKA	5,239	3,623	1,595	21	2,028 R	69.2%	30.4%	69.4%	30.6%
444,506	KENT	205,020	137,417	66,238	1,365	71,179 R	67.0%	32.3%	67.5%	32.5%
1,963	KEWEENAW	1,227	599	628		29 D	48.8%	51.2%	48.8%	51.2%
7,711	LAKE	4,003	2,125	1,845	33	280 R	53.1%	46.1%	53.5%	46.5%
70,038	LAPEER	27,200	19,222	7,800	178	11,422 R	70.7%	28.7%	71.1%	28.9%
14,007	LEELANAU	7,921	5,356	2,498	67	2,858 R	67.6%	31.5%	68.2%	31.8%
89,948	LENAWEE	33,597	22,409	11,012	176	11,397 R	66.7%	32.8%	67.1%	32.9%
100,289	LIVINGSTON	42,812	31,846	10,720	246	21,126 R	74.4%	25.0%	74.8%	25.2%
6,659	LUCE	2,561	1,715	833	13	882 R	67.0%	32.5%	67.3%	32.7%
10,178	MACKINAC	5,593	3,627	1,949	17	1,678 R	64.8%	34.8%	65.0%	35.0%
694,600	MACOMB	293,525	194,300	97,816	1,409	96,484 R	66.2%	33.3%	66.5%	33.5%
23,019	MANISTEE	10,298	6,328	3,917	53	2,411 R	61.4%	38.0%	61.8%	38.2%
74,101	MARQUETTE	28,402	14,196	14,074	132	122 R	50.0%	49.6%	50.2%	49.8%
26,365	MASON	12,092	8,202	3,803	87	4,399 R	67.8%	31.5%	68.3%	31.7%
36,961	MECOSTA	13,142	9,023	4,048	71	4,975 R	68.7%	30.8%	69.0%	31.0%
26,201	MENOMINEE	11,089	6,618	4,425	46	2,193 R	59.7%	39.9%	59.9%	40.1%
73,578	MIDLAND	32,552	21,521	10,769	262	10,752 R	66.1%	33.1%	66.6%	33.4%
10,009	MISSAUKEE	5,256	3,970	1,256	30	2,714 R	75.5%	23.9%	76.0%	24.0%
134,659	MONROE	49,287	29,419	19,617	251	9,802 R	59.7%	39.8%	60.0%	40.0%
47,555	MONTCALM	18,689	13,109	5,491	89	7,618 R	70.1%	29.4%	70.5%	29.5%
7,492	MONTMORENCY	4,313	2,913	1,387	13	1,526 R	67.5%	32.2%	67.7%	32.3%

MICHIGAN

PRESIDENT 1984

1980 Census Population	County	Total Vote	Republican	Democratic	Other	Rep.-Dem. Plurality	Percentage Total Vote Rep.	Dem.	Major Vote Rep.	Dem.
157,589	MUSKEGON	64,863	39,355	25,247	261	14,108 R	60.7%	38.9%	60.9%	39.1%
34,917	NEWAYGO	15,205	10,636	4,496	73	6,140 R	70.0%	29.6%	70.3%	29.7%
1,011,793	OAKLAND	458,800	306,050	150,286	2,464	155,764 R	66.7%	32.8%	67.1%	32.9%
22,002	OCEANA	9,325	6,405	2,865	55	3,540 R	68.7%	30.7%	69.1%	30.9%
16,436	OGEMAW	8,060	4,901	3,132	27	1,769 R	60.8%	38.9%	61.0%	39.0%
9,861	ONTONAGON	4,836	2,464	2,350	22	114 R	51.0%	48.6%	51.2%	48.8%
18,928	OSCEOLA	8,090	5,923	2,127	40	3,796 R	73.2%	26.3%	73.6%	26.4%
6,858	OSCODA	3,209	2,239	951	19	1,288 R	69.8%	29.6%	70.2%	29.8%
14,993	OTSEGO	6,795	4,639	2,117	39	2,522 R	68.3%	31.2%	68.7%	31.3%
157,174	OTTAWA	75,468	60,142	15,000	326	45,142 R	79.7%	19.9%	80.0%	20.0%
14,267	PRESQUE ISLE	6,724	4,207	2,481	36	1,726 R	62.6%	36.9%	62.9%	37.1%
16,374	ROSCOMMON	9,823	6,419	3,359	45	3,060 R	65.3%	34.2%	65.6%	34.4%
228,059	SAGINAW	90,416	51,495	38,420	501	13,075 R	57.0%	42.5%	57.3%	42.7%
138,802	ST. CLAIR	53,399	36,114	16,998	287	19,116 R	67.6%	31.8%	68.0%	32.0%
56,083	ST. JOSEPH	21,296	15,405	5,795	96	9,610 R	72.3%	27.2%	72.7%	27.3%
40,789	SANILAC	16,810	12,627	4,126	57	8,501 R	75.1%	24.5%	75.4%	24.6%
8,575	SCHOOLCRAFT	4,077	2,139	1,920	18	219 R	52.5%	47.1%	52.7%	47.3%
71,140	SHIAWASSEE	28,431	18,756	9,514	161	9,242 R	66.0%	33.5%	66.3%	33.7%
56,961	TUSCOLA	20,993	14,698	6,212	83	8,486 R	70.0%	29.6%	70.3%	29.7%
66,814	VAN BUREN	25,445	16,426	8,853	166	7,573 R	64.6%	34.8%	65.0%	35.0%
264,748	WASHTENAW	114,569	58,736	55,084	749	3,652 R	51.3%	48.1%	51.6%	48.4%
2,337,891	WAYNE	868,343	367,391	496,632	4,320	129,241 D	42.3%	57.2%	42.5%	57.5%
25,102	WEXFORD	10,715	7,279	3,398	38	3,881 R	67.9%	31.7%	68.2%	31.8%
9,262,078	TOTAL	3,801,658	2,251,571	1,529,638	20,449	721,933 R	59.2%	40.2%	59.5%	40.5%

MICHIGAN

SENATOR 1984

1980 Census Population	County	Total Vote	Republican	Democratic	Other	Rep.-Dem. Plurality	Percentage Total Vote Rep.	Dem.	Major Vote Rep.	Dem.
9,740	ALCONA	4,627	2,358	2,232	37	126 R	51.0%	48.2%	51.4%	48.6%
9,225	ALGER	4,007	1,514	2,471	22	957 D	37.8%	61.7%	38.0%	62.0%
81,555	ALLEGAN	30,854	20,545	9,992	317	10,553 R	66.6%	32.4%	67.3%	32.7%
32,315	ALPENA	12,761	5,729	6,890	142	1,161 D	44.9%	54.0%	45.4%	54.6%
16,194	ANTRIM	7,925	4,649	3,186	90	1,463 R	58.7%	40.2%	59.3%	40.7%
14,706	ARENAC	5,623	2,488	3,091	44	603 D	44.2%	55.0%	44.6%	55.4%
8,484	BARAGA	3,630	1,362	2,241	27	879 D	37.5%	61.7%	37.8%	62.2%
45,781	BARRY	19,263	11,682	7,352	229	4,330 R	60.6%	38.2%	61.4%	38.6%
119,881	BAY	47,272	18,447	28,306	519	9,859 D	39.0%	59.9%	39.5%	60.5%
11,205	BENZIE	5,240	3,069	2,116	55	953 R	58.6%	40.4%	59.2%	40.8%
171,276	BERRIEN	62,154	37,908	23,020	1,226	14,888 R	61.0%	37.0%	62.2%	37.8%
40,188	BRANCH	14,323	8,825	5,301	197	3,524 R	61.6%	37.0%	62.5%	37.5%
141,557	CALHOUN	52,285	24,864	26,887	534	2,023 D	47.6%	51.4%	48.0%	52.0%
49,499	CASS	17,145	9,988	6,869	288	3,119 R	58.3%	40.1%	59.3%	40.7%
19,907	CHARLEVOIX	9,552	5,311	4,107	134	1,204 R	55.6%	43.0%	56.4%	43.6%
20,649	CHEBOYGAN	8,850	4,452	4,309	89	143 R	50.3%	48.7%	50.8%	49.2%
29,029	CHIPPEWA	12,069	5,969	6,001	99	32 D	49.5%	49.7%	49.9%	50.1%
23,822	CLARE	10,301	5,025	5,175	101	150 D	48.8%	50.2%	49.3%	50.7%
55,893	CLINTON	22,946	13,670	9,003	273	4,667 R	59.6%	39.2%	60.3%	39.7%
9,465	CRAWFORD	4,895	2,655	2,191	49	464 R	54.2%	44.8%	54.8%	45.2%
38,947	DELTA	15,975	6,049	9,795	131	3,746 D	37.9%	61.3%	38.2%	61.8%
25,341	DICKINSON	11,280	4,727	6,436	117	1,709 D	41.9%	57.1%	42.3%	57.7%
88,337	EATON	36,417	21,432	14,541	444	6,891 R	58.9%	39.9%	59.6%	40.4%
22,992	EMMET	10,996	6,247	4,637	112	1,610 R	56.8%	42.2%	57.4%	42.6%
450,449	GENESEE	182,301	70,438	109,160	2,703	38,722 D	38.6%	59.9%	39.2%	60.8%
19,957	GLADWIN	8,650	4,033	4,522	95	489 D	46.6%	52.3%	47.1%	52.9%
19,686	GOGEBIC	8,648	2,662	5,933	53	3,271 D	30.8%	68.6%	31.0%	69.0%
54,899	GRAND TRAVERSE	24,445	14,646	9,592	207	5,054 R	59.9%	39.2%	60.4%	39.6%
40,448	GRATIOT	13,880	8,146	5,633	101	2,513 R	58.7%	40.6%	59.1%	40.9%
42,071	HILLSDALE	15,160	9,625	5,327	208	4,298 R	63.5%	35.1%	64.4%	35.6%
37,872	HOUGHTON	14,378	6,208	8,063	107	1,855 D	43.2%	56.1%	43.5%	56.5%
36,459	HURON	13,859	8,321	5,406	132	2,915 R	60.0%	39.0%	60.6%	39.4%
275,520	INGHAM	114,555	53,091	60,081	1,383	6,990 D	46.3%	52.4%	46.9%	53.1%
51,815	IONIA	18,834	11,156	7,449	229	3,707 R	59.2%	39.6%	60.0%	40.0%
28,349	IOSCO	11,467	6,058	5,346	63	712 R	52.8%	46.6%	53.1%	46.9%
13,635	IRON	6,658	2,629	3,992	37	1,363 D	39.5%	60.0%	39.7%	60.3%
54,110	ISABELLA	18,411	9,361	8,820	230	541 R	50.8%	47.9%	51.5%	48.5%
151,495	JACKSON	57,184	32,170	24,365	649	7,805 R	56.3%	42.6%	56.9%	43.1%
212,378	KALAMAZOO	87,626	47,772	39,080	774	8,692 R	54.5%	44.6%	55.0%	45.0%
10,952	KALKASKA	4,997	2,882	2,065	50	817 R	57.7%	41.3%	58.3%	41.7%
444,506	KENT	201,731	114,764	85,056	1,911	29,708 R	56.9%	42.2%	57.4%	42.6%
1,963	KEWEENAW	1,179	418	753	8	335 D	35.5%	63.9%	35.7%	64.3%
7,711	LAKE	3,985	1,711	2,209	65	498 D	42.9%	55.4%	43.6%	56.4%
70,038	LAPEER	27,189	15,388	11,331	470	4,057 R	56.6%	41.7%	57.6%	42.4%
14,007	LEELANAU	7,589	4,465	3,058	66	1,407 R	58.8%	40.3%	59.4%	40.6%
89,948	LENAWEE	31,779	17,575	13,705	499	3,870 R	55.3%	43.1%	56.2%	43.8%
100,289	LIVINGSTON	41,693	25,381	15,811	501	9,570 R	60.9%	37.9%	61.6%	38.4%
6,659	LUCE	2,349	1,184	1,142	23	42 R	50.4%	48.6%	50.9%	49.1%
10,178	MACKINAC	5,294	2,589	2,662	43	73 D	48.9%	50.3%	49.3%	50.7%
694,600	MACOMB	284,757	143,099	138,400	3,258	4,699 R	50.3%	48.6%	50.8%	49.2%
23,019	MANISTEE	9,888	5,221	4,567	100	654 R	52.8%	46.2%	53.3%	46.7%
74,101	MARQUETTE	27,400	9,989	17,198	213	7,209 D	36.5%	62.8%	36.7%	63.3%
26,365	MASON	11,913	6,675	5,039	199	1,636 R	56.0%	42.3%	57.0%	43.0%
36,961	MECOSTA	12,739	7,339	5,268	132	2,071 R	57.6%	41.4%	58.2%	41.8%
26,201	MENOMINEE	9,934	4,667	5,117	150	450 D	47.0%	51.5%	47.7%	52.3%
73,578	MIDLAND	32,244	17,012	14,821	411	2,191 R	52.8%	46.0%	53.4%	46.6%
10,009	MISSAUKEE	5,174	3,359	1,762	53	1,597 R	64.9%	34.1%	65.6%	34.4%
134,659	MONROE	46,765	21,656	24,241	868	2,585 D	46.3%	51.8%	47.2%	52.8%
47,555	MONTCALM	17,642	10,696	6,769	177	3,927 R	60.6%	38.4%	61.2%	38.8%
7,492	MONTMORENCY	4,054	2,158	1,851	45	307 R	53.2%	45.7%	53.8%	46.2%

MICHIGAN

SENATOR 1984

1980 Census Population	County	Total Vote	Republican	Democratic	Other	Rep.-Dem. Plurality	Percentage			
							Total Vote		Major Vote	
							Rep.	Dem.	Rep.	Dem.
157,589	MUSKEGON	63,179	30,106	32,402	671	2,296 D	47.7%	51.3%	48.2%	51.8%
34,917	NEWAYGO	14,518	8,778	5,586	154	3,192 R	60.5%	38.5%	61.1%	38.9%
1,011,793	OAKLAND	448,692	229,499	214,695	4,498	14,804 R	51.1%	47.8%	51.7%	48.3%
22,002	OCEANA	8,857	5,067	3,687	103	1,380 R	57.2%	41.6%	57.9%	42.1%
16,436	OGEMAW	7,654	3,353	4,238	63	885 D	43.8%	55.4%	44.2%	55.8%
9,861	ONTONAGON	4,548	1,745	2,766	37	1,021 D	38.4%	60.8%	38.7%	61.3%
18,928	OSCEOLA	7,588	4,748	2,754	86	1,994 R	62.6%	36.3%	63.3%	36.7%
6,858	OSCODA	3,154	1,763	1,364	27	399 R	55.9%	43.2%	56.4%	43.6%
14,993	OTSEGO	6,495	3,638	2,785	72	853 R	56.0%	42.9%	56.6%	43.4%
157,174	OTTAWA	72,875	52,899	19,466	510	33,433 R	72.6%	26.7%	73.1%	26.9%
14,267	PRESQUE ISLE	6,585	3,063	3,462	60	399 D	46.5%	52.6%	46.9%	53.1%
16,374	ROSCOMMON	9,391	4,713	4,572	106	141 R	50.2%	48.7%	50.8%	49.2%
228,059	SAGINAW	88,530	39,005	48,603	922	9,598 D	44.1%	54.9%	44.5%	55.5%
138,802	ST. CLAIR	51,941	27,832	23,511	598	4,321 R	53.6%	45.3%	54.2%	45.8%
56,083	ST. JOSEPH	19,687	12,524	6,920	243	5,604 R	63.6%	35.2%	64.4%	35.6%
40,789	SANILAC	15,844	10,284	5,439	121	4,845 R	64.9%	34.3%	65.4%	34.6%
8,575	SCHOOLCRAFT	3,813	1,387	2,386	40	999 D	36.4%	62.6%	36.8%	63.2%
71,140	SHIAWASSEE	27,564	14,018	13,030	516	988 R	50.9%	47.3%	51.8%	48.2%
56,961	TUSCOLA	19,665	11,115	8,337	213	2,778 R	56.5%	42.4%	57.1%	42.9%
66,814	VAN BUREN	24,084	13,814	10,022	248	3,792 R	57.4%	41.6%	58.0%	42.0%
264,748	WASHTENAW	112,646	47,238	64,338	1,070	17,100 D	41.9%	57.1%	42.3%	57.7%
2,337,891	WAYNE	856,600	279,709	569,016	7,875	289,307 D	32.7%	66.4%	33.0%	67.0%
25,102	WEXFORD	10,287	5,495	4,709	83	786 R	53.4%	45.8%	53.9%	46.1%
9,262,078	TOTAL	3,700,938	1,745,302	1,915,831	39,805	170,529 D	47.2%	51.8%	47.7%	52.3%

DETROIT

PRESIDENT 1984

1980 Census Population	District	Total Vote	Republican	Democratic	Other	Rep.-Dem. Plurality	Percentage Total Vote Rep.	Dem.	Major Vote Rep.	Dem.
	DISTRICT 3	9,510	579	8,881	50	8,302 D	6.1%	93.4%	6.1%	93.9%
	DISTRICT 4	16,324	5,272	10,942	110	5,670 D	32.3%	67.0%	32.5%	67.5%
	DISTRICT 5	16,093	6,503	9,503	87	3,000 D	40.4%	59.1%	40.6%	59.4%
	DISTRICT 6	16,491	7,992	8,414	85	422 D	48.5%	51.0%	48.7%	51.3%
	DISTRICT 7	12,944	2,235	10,634	75	8,399 D	17.3%	82.2%	17.4%	82.6%
	DISTRICT 8	12,835	311	12,476	48	12,165 D	2.4%	97.2%	2.4%	97.6%
	DISTRICT 9	11,091	1,210	9,818	63	8,608 D	10.9%	88.5%	11.0%	89.0%
	DISTRICT 10	6,200	449	5,705	46	5,256 D	7.2%	92.0%	7.3%	92.7%
	DISTRICT 11	6,318	902	5,366	50	4,464 D	14.3%	84.9%	14.4%	85.6%
	DISTRICT 12	10,107	497	9,574	36	9,077 D	4.9%	94.7%	4.9%	95.1%
	DISTRICT 13	18,193	1,771	16,342	80	14,571 D	9.7%	89.8%	9.8%	90.2%
	DISTRICT 14	16,518	1,556	14,859	103	13,303 D	9.4%	90.0%	9.5%	90.5%
	DISTRICT 15	26,125	999	25,046	80	24,047 D	3.8%	95.9%	3.8%	96.2%
	DISTRICT 16	20,315	3,581	16,659	76	13,078 D	17.6%	82.0%	17.7%	82.3%
	DISTRICT 17	20,931	5,076	15,726	129	10,650 D	24.3%	75.1%	24.4%	75.6%
	DISTRICT 18	17,398	8,042	9,247	109	1,205 D	46.2%	53.1%	46.5%	53.5%
	DISTRICT 19	16,962	2,561	14,341	60	11,780 D	15.1%	84.5%	15.2%	84.8%
	DISTRICT 20	20,049	680	19,300	69	18,620 D	3.4%	96.3%	3.4%	96.6%
	DISTRICT 21	17,691	1,605	16,011	75	14,406 D	9.1%	90.5%	9.1%	90.9%
	DISTRICT 22	14,302	393	13,854	46	13,461 D	2.7%	96.9%	2.8%	97.2%
	DISTRICT 23	11,934	311	11,564	59	11,253 D	2.6%	96.9%	2.6%	97.4%
	DISTRICT 24	6,712	799	5,869	44	5,070 D	11.9%	87.4%	12.0%	88.0%
	DISTRICT 25	9,922	4,049	5,805	59	1,756 D	40.8%	58.5%	41.1%	58.9%
	DISTRICT 26	6,947	1,030	5,883	34	4,853 D	14.8%	84.7%	14.9%	85.1%
	ABSENTEE	58,639	17,888	40,575	176	22,687 D	30.5%	69.2%	30.6%	69.4%
1,203,339	TOTAL	400,551	76,291	322,394	1,849	246,103 D	19.0%	80.5%	19.1%	80.9%

DETROIT

SENATOR 1984

1980 Census Population	District	Total Vote	Republican	Democratic	Other	Rep.-Dem. Plurality	Percentage Total Vote Rep.	Dem.	Major Vote Rep.	Dem.
	DISTRICT 3	9,262	471	8,694	97	8,223 D	5.1%	93.9%	5.1%	94.9%
	DISTRICT 4	16,218	4,087	11,980	151	7,893 D	25.2%	73.9%	25.4%	74.6%
	DISTRICT 5	15,964	4,822	10,978	164	6,156 D	30.2%	68.8%	30.5%	69.5%
	DISTRICT 6	16,337	5,729	10,463	145	4,734 D	35.1%	64.0%	35.4%	64.6%
	DISTRICT 7	12,837	1,631	11,072	134	9,441 D	12.7%	86.3%	12.8%	87.2%
	DISTRICT 8	12,691	236	12,350	105	12,114 D	1.9%	97.3%	1.9%	98.1%
	DISTRICT 9	11,042	896	10,079	67	9,183 D	8.1%	91.3%	8.2%	91.8%
	DISTRICT 10	6,134	345	5,731	58	5,386 D	5.6%	93.4%	5.7%	94.3%
	DISTRICT 11	6,271	662	5,535	74	4,873 D	10.6%	88.3%	10.7%	89.3%
	DISTRICT 12	10,011	375	9,546	90	9,171 D	3.7%	95.4%	3.8%	96.2%
	DISTRICT 13	18,033	1,296	16,578	159	15,282 D	7.2%	91.9%	7.3%	92.7%
	DISTRICT 14	16,409	1,146	15,120	143	13,974 D	7.0%	92.1%	7.0%	93.0%
	DISTRICT 15	26,017	671	25,177	169	24,506 D	2.6%	96.8%	2.6%	97.4%
	DISTRICT 16	20,210	2,700	17,389	121	14,689 D	13.4%	86.0%	13.4%	86.6%
	DISTRICT 17	20,783	3,933	16,651	199	12,718 D	18.9%	80.1%	19.1%	80.9%
	DISTRICT 18	17,286	6,163	10,956	167	4,793 D	35.7%	63.4%	36.0%	64.0%
	DISTRICT 19	16,860	1,893	14,811	156	12,918 D	11.2%	87.8%	11.3%	88.7%
	DISTRICT 20	19,911	449	19,329	133	18,880 D	2.3%	97.1%	2.3%	97.7%
	DISTRICT 21	17,505	1,132	16,248	125	15,116 D	6.5%	92.8%	6.5%	93.5%
	DISTRICT 22	14,194	297	13,815	82	13,518 D	2.1%	97.3%	2.1%	97.9%
	DISTRICT 23	11,801	249	11,473	79	11,224 D	2.1%	97.2%	2.1%	97.9%
	DISTRICT 24	6,640	647	5,930	63	5,283 D	9.7%	89.3%	9.8%	90.2%
	DISTRICT 25	9,844	2,988	6,731	125	3,743 D	30.4%	68.4%	30.7%	69.3%
	DISTRICT 26	6,890	779	6,050	61	5,271 D	11.3%	87.8%	11.4%	88.6%
	ABSENTEE	57,982	12,841	44,792	349	31,951 D	22.1%	77.3%	22.3%	77.7%
1,203,339	TOTAL	397,132	56,438	337,478	3,216	281,040 D	14.2%	85.0%	14.3%	85.7%

MICHIGAN

CONGRESS

CD	Year	Total Vote	Republican Vote	Candidate	Democratic Vote	Candidate	Other Vote	Rep.-Dem. Plurality	Total Vote Rep.	Total Vote Dem.	Major Vote Rep.	Major Vote Dem.
1	1984	170,510	17,393	MACK, EDWARD	152,432	CONYERS, JOHN	685	135,039 D	10.2%	89.4%	10.2%	89.8%
1	1982	129,850			125,517	CONYERS, JOHN	4,333	125,517 D	0.0%	96.7%	0.0%	100.0%
2	1984	205,132	140,688	PURSELL, CARL D.	62,374	MCCAULEY, MIKE	2,070	78,314 R	68.6%	30.4%	69.3%	30.7%
2	1982	163,414	106,960	PURSELL, CARL D.	53,040	SALLADE, GEORGE W.	3,414	53,920 R	65.5%	32.5%	66.9%	33.2%
3	1984	201,224	94,714	MCGREGOR, JACKIE	106,505	WOLPE, HOWARD	5	11,791 D	47.1%	52.9%	47.1%	52.9%
3	1982	171,961	73,315	MILLIMAN, RICHARD L.	96,842	WOLPE, HOWARD	1,804	23,527 D	42.6%	56.3%	43.1%	56.9%
4	1984	191,087	127,907	SILJANDER, MARK D.	63,159	RODEBAUGH, CHARLES	21	64,748 R	66.9%	33.1%	66.9%	33.1%
4	1982	146,605	87,489	SILJANDER, MARK D.	56,877	MASIOKAS, DAVID A.	2,239	30,612 R	59.7%	38.8%	60.6%	39.4%
5	1984	226,678	140,131	HENRY, PAUL	85,232	MCINERNEY, GARY	1,315	54,899 R	61.8%	37.6%	62.2%	37.8%
5	1982	185,881	98,650	SAWYER, HAROLD S.	87,229	MONSMA, STEPHEN V.	2	11,421 R	53.1%	46.9%	53.1%	46.9%
6	1984	203,530	95,113	RITTER, TOM	106,705	CARR, M. ROBERT	1,712	11,592 D	46.7%	52.4%	47.1%	52.9%
6	1982	164,987	78,388	DUNN, JIM	84,778	CARR, M. ROBERT	1,821	6,390 D	47.5%	51.4%	48.0%	52.0%
7	1984	155,748			145,070	KILDEE, DALE E.	10,678	145,070 D	0.0%	93.1%	0.0%	100.0%
7	1982	157,254	36,303	DARRAH, GEORGE R.	118,538	KILDEE, DALE E.	2,413	82,235 D	23.1%	75.4%	23.4%	76.6%
8	1984	195,845	69,683	HEUSSNER, JOHN	126,161	TRAXLER, J. ROBERT	1	56,478 D	35.6%	64.4%	35.6%	64.4%
8	1982	124,737			113,515	TRAXLER, J. ROBERT	11,222	113,515 D	0.0%	91.0%	0.0%	100.0%
9	1984	212,805	150,885	VANDER JAGT, GUY	61,233	SENGER, JOHN	687	89,652 R	70.9%	28.8%	71.1%	28.9%
9	1982	173,439	112,504	VANDER JAGT, GUY	60,932	WARNER, GERALD D.	3	51,572 R	64.9%	35.1%	64.9%	35.1%
10	1984	209,645	104,950	SCHUETTE, BILL	103,636	ALBOSTA, DONALD J.	1,059	1,314 R	50.1%	49.4%	50.3%	49.7%
10	1982	169,687	66,080	REED, LAWRENCE W.	102,048	ALBOSTA, DONALD J.	1,559	35,968 D	38.9%	60.1%	39.3%	60.7%
11	1984	216,634	126,992	DAVIS, ROBERT W.	89,640	STEWART, TOM	2	37,352 R	58.6%	41.4%	58.6%	41.4%
11	1982	175,222	106,039	DAVIS, ROBERT W.	69,181	BOURLAND, KENT	2	36,858 R	60.5%	39.5%	60.5%	39.5%
12	1984	194,984	79,824	TYZA, EUGENE	113,772	BONIOR, DAVID E.	1,388	33,948 D	40.9%	58.3%	41.2%	58.8%
12	1982	157,664	52,312	CONTESTI, RAY	103,851	BONIOR, DAVID E.	1,501	51,539 D	33.2%	65.9%	33.5%	66.5%
13	1984	152,638	20,416	MURPHY, ROBERT	132,222	CROCKETT, GEORGE W.		111,806 D	13.4%	86.6%	13.4%	86.6%
13	1982	123,195	13,732	GUPTA, LETTY	108,351	CROCKETT, GEORGE W.	1,112	94,619 D	11.1%	88.0%	11.2%	88.8%
14	1984	192,142	77,427	LAUVE, JOHN	113,610	HERTEL, DENNIS M.	1,105	36,183 D	40.3%	59.1%	40.5%	59.5%
14	1982	122,613			116,421	HERTEL, DENNIS M.	6,192	116,421 D		94.9%		100.0%
15	1984	165,152	66,172	CARLSON, GERALD	98,973	FORD, WILLIAM D.	7	32,801 D	40.1%	59.9%	40.1%	59.9%
15	1982	130,409	33,904	MORAN, MITCHELL	94,950	FORD, WILLIAM D.	1,555	61,046 D	26.0%	72.8%	26.3%	73.7%
16	1984	190,622	68,116	GRZYWACKI, FRANK	121,463	DINGELL, JOHN D., JR.	1,043	53,347 D	35.7%	63.7%	35.9%	64.1%
16	1982	154,756	39,227	HASKINS, DAVID K.	114,006	DINGELL, JOHN D., JR.	1,523	74,779 D	25.3%	73.7%	25.6%	74.4%
17	1984	133,105			133,064	LEVIN, SANDER	41	133,064 D	0.0%	100.0%	0.0%	100.0%
17	1982	175,480	55,620	ROSEN, GERALD E.	116,901	LEVIN, SANDER	2,959	61,281 D	31.7%	66.6%	32.2%	67.8%
18	1984	234,884	186,505	BROOMFIELD, WILLIAM S.	46,191	SMARGON, VIVIAN	2,188	140,314 R	79.4%	19.7%	80.1%	19.9%
18	1982	181,262	132,902	BROOMFIELD, WILLIAM S.	46,545	SIPHER, ALLEN J.	1,815	86,357 R	73.3%	25.7%	74.1%	25.9%

MICHIGAN

1984 GENERAL ELECTION

President Other vote was 10,055 Bergland (Libertarian); 3,862 LaRouche (Independent); 1,416 Holmes (Workers World); 1,191 Johnson (Independent); 1,049 Mason (Socialist Workers); 1,048 Hall (Communist); 665 Serrette (Independent); 561 Winn (Workers League); 602 scattered.

Senator Other vote was 22,882 Tisch (Tisch Independent Citizens); 7,786 Johnston (Libertarian); 2,686 Meyers (Socialist Workers); 2,279 Roundtree (Workers World); 2,135 Dean (Independent); 1,196 Webb (Communist); 818 Mazelis (Workers League); 23 scattered.

Congress Other vote was Pulley (Socialist Workers) in CD 1; 1,128 Greg Severance (Tish Independent Citizens), 937 Hudler (Libertarian) and 5 scattered in CD 2; scattered in CD's 3 and 4; 1,312 Whitelock (Libertarian) and 3 scattered in CD 5; 936 Russell Severance (Tisch Independent Citizens), 773 Hurrell (Libertarian) and 3 scattered in CD 6; 10,663 Johnson (Independent) and 15 scattered in CD 7; scattered in CD 8; 680 Hamilton (Libertarian) and 7 scattered in CD 9; 1,054 Leef (Libertarian) and 5 scattered in CD 10; scattered in CD 11; Edwards (Libertarian) in CD 12; Cropsey (Libertarian) in CD 14; scattered in CD 15; 1,042 Kostyu (Libertarian) and 1 scattered in CD 16; scattered in CD 17; O'Brien (Libertarian) in CD 18.

DETROIT

Population data is not available for the new 1984 districts.

President Other vote was 502 Bergland (Libertarian); 282 Mason (Socialist Workers); 248 Holmes (Workers World); 232 LaRouche (Independent); 224 Hall (Communist); 141 Johnson (Independent); 124 Winn (Workers League); 96 Serrette (Independent).

Senator Other vote was 987 Tisch (Tisch Independent Citizens); 557 Meyers (Socialist Workers); 548 Roundtree (Workers World); 478 Johnston (Libertarian); 269 Webb (Communist); 193 Dean (Independent); 184 Mazelis (Workers League).

1984 PRIMARIES

AUGUST 7 REPUBLICAN

Senator 328,002 Jack Lousma; 194,657 Jim Dunn; 41 scattered.

Congress Unopposed in nine CD's. No candidate in CD's 7 and 17. Contested as follows:

CD 3 18,867 Jackie McGregor; 8,351 Marvin Lightvoet; 3 scattered.
CD 4 34,128 Mark D. Siljander; 24,978 Tim Horan.
CD 5 33,157 Paul Henry; 14,124 Keary Sawyer; 3,263 Drew Allbritten; 2,038 Greg Doublestein; 10 scattered.
CD 6 16,231 Tom Ritter; 8,328 Douglas Callahan; 2 scattered.
CD 13 2,120 Robert Murphy; 1,223 William Tinsley; 1 scattered.
CD 14 8,342 John Lauve; 4,887 Joan Rashid.
CD 15 5,143 Gerald Carlson; 4,437 Glen Kassel.

MICHIGAN

AUGUST 7 DEMOCRATIC

Senator   Carl Levin, unopposed.

Congress   Unopposed in thirteen CD's. Contested as follows:

CD 2   4,713 Mike McCauley; 4,458 Don Grimes; 1 scattered.
CD 4   3,504 Charles Rodebaugh; 1,769 Jerome Coryell; 1,421 Les Garmire; 1 scattered.
CD 9   9,691 John Senger; 4,847 Paul Vandermus.
CD 11   19,339 Tom Stewart; 9,805 Sven A. Johnson; 8,557 Ted Albert; 7,617 Dennis Mapes; 22 scattered.
CD 13   22,923 George W. Crockett; 3,400 John Barber; 1 scattered.

MINNESOTA

GOVERNOR

Rudy Perpich (D). Elected 1982 to a four-year term. As Lieutenant-Governor, succeeded Governor Wendell R. Anderson on the latter's resignation, after the 1976 election, to accept appointment to the Senate on the resignation of Senator Walter F. Mondale to become Vice-President. Served as Governor December 1976 to January 1979.

SENATORS

Rudy Boschwitz (R). Elected 1984 to a six-year term. Previously elected 1978.

David Durenberger (R). Re-elected 1982 to a six-year term. Previously elected 1978 to fill out the remaining four years of the term vacated by the death of Senator Hubert H. Humphrey.

REPRESENTATIVES

1. Timothy J. Penny (D)
2. Vin Weber (R)
3. Bill Frenzel (R)
4. Bruce F. Vento (D)
5. Martin O. Sabo (D)
6. Gerry Sikorski (D)
7. Arlan Stangeland (R)
8. James L. Oberstar (D)

POSTWAR VOTE FOR GOVERNOR

Year	Total Vote	Republican Vote	Candidate	Democratic Vote	Candidate	Other Vote	Rep.-Dem. Plurality	Total Vote Rep.	Total Vote Dem.	Major Vote Rep.	Major Vote Dem.
1982	1,789,539	715,796	Whitney, Wheelock	1,049,104	Perpich, Rudy	24,639	333,308 D	40.0%	58.6%	40.6%	59.4%
1978	1,585,702	830,019	Quie, Albert H.	718,244	Perpich, Rudy	37,439	111,775 R	52.3%	45.3%	53.6%	46.4%
1974	1,252,898	367,722	Johnson, John W.	786,787	Anderson, Wendell R.	98,389	419,065 D	29.3%	62.8%	31.9%	68.1%
1970	1,365,443	621,780	Head, Douglas M.	737,921	Anderson, Wendell R.	5,742	116,141 D	45.5%	54.0%	45.7%	54.3%
1966	1,295,058	680,593	LeVander, Harold	607,943	Rolvaag, Karl F.	6,522	72,650 R	52.6%	46.9%	52.8%	47.2%
1962*	1,246,904	619,751	Andersen, Elmer L.	619,842	Rolvaag, Karl F.	7,311	91 D	49.7%	49.7%	50.0%	50.0%
1960	1,550,265	783,813	Andersen, Elmer L.	760,934	Freeman, Orville L.	5,518	22,879 R	50.6%	49.1%	50.7%	49.3%
1958	1,159,915	490,731	MacKinnon, George	658,326	Freeman, Orville L.	10,858	167,595 D	42.3%	56.8%	42.7%	57.3%
1956	1,422,161	685,196	Nelsen, Ancher	731,180	Freeman, Orville L.	5,785	45,984 D	48.2%	51.4%	48.4%	51.6%
1954	1,151,417	538,865	Anderson, C. Elmer	607,099	Freeman, Orville L.	5,453	68,234 D	46.8%	52.7%	47.0%	53.0%
1952	1,418,869	785,125	Anderson, C. Elmer	624,480	Freeman, Orville L.	9,264	160,645 R	55.3%	44.0%	55.7%	44.3%
1950	1,046,632	635,800	Youngdahl, Luther	400,637	Peterson, Harry H.	10,195	235,163 R	60.7%	38.3%	61.3%	38.7%
1948	1,210,894	643,572	Youngdahl, Luther	545,766	Halsted, Charles L.	21,556	97,806 R	53.1%	45.1%	54.1%	45.9%
1946	880,348	519,067	Youngdahl, Luther	349,565	Barker, Harold H.	11,716	169,502 R	59.0%	39.7%	59.8%	40.2%

The term of office of Minnesota's Governor was increased from two to four years effective with the 1962 election.

POSTWAR VOTE FOR SENATOR

Year	Total Vote	Republican Vote	Candidate	Democratic Vote	Candidate	Other Vote	Rep.-Dem. Plurality	Total Vote Rep.	Total Vote Dem.	Major Vote Rep.	Major Vote Dem.
1984	2,066,143	1,199,926	Boschwitz, Rudy	852,844	Growe, Joan Anderson	13,373	347,082 R	58.1%	41.3%	58.5%	41.5%
1982	1,804,675	949,207	Durenberger, David	840,401	Dayton, Mark	15,067	108,806 R	52.6%	46.6%	53.0%	47.0%
1978	1,580,778	894,092	Boschwitz, Rudy	638,375	Anderson, Wendell R.	48,311	255,717 R	56.6%	40.4%	58.3%	41.7%
1978s	1,560,724	957,908	Durenberger, David	538,675	Short, Robert E.	64,141	419,233 R	61.4%	34.5%	64.0%	36.0%
1976	1,912,068	478,611	Brekke, Gerald W.	1,290,736	Humphrey, Hubert H.	142,721	812,125 D	25.0%	67.5%	27.1%	72.9%
1972	1,731,653	742,121	Hansen, Philip	981,340	Mondale, Walter F.	8,192	239,219 D	42.9%	56.7%	43.1%	56.9%
1970	1,364,887	568,025	MacGregor, Clark	788,256	Humphrey, Hubert H.	8,606	220,231 D	41.6%	57.8%	41.9%	58.1%
1966	1,271,426	574,868	Forsythe, Robert A.	685,840	Mondale, Walter F.	10,718	110,972 D	45.2%	53.9%	45.6%	54.4%
1964	1,543,590	605,933	Whitney, Wheelock	931,353	McCarthy, Eugene J.	6,304	325,420 D	39.3%	60.3%	39.4%	60.6%
1960	1,536,839	648,586	Peterson, P. K.	884,168	Humphrey, Hubert H.	4,085	235,582 D	42.2%	57.5%	42.3%	57.7%
1958	1,150,883	536,629	Thye, Edward J.	608,847	McCarthy, Eugene J.	5,407	72,218 D	46.6%	52.9%	46.8%	53.2%
1954	1,138,952	479,619	Bjornson, Val	642,193	Humphrey, Hubert H.	17,140	162,574 D	42.1%	56.4%	42.8%	57.2%
1952	1,387,419	785,649	Thye, Edward J.	590,011	Carlson, William E.	11,759	195,638 R	56.6%	42.5%	57.1%	42.9%
1948	1,220,250	485,801	Ball, Joseph H.	729,494	Humphrey, Hubert H.	4,955	243,693 D	39.8%	59.8%	40.0%	60.0%
1946	878,731	517,775	Thye, Edward J.	349,520	Jorgenson, Theodore	11,436	168,255 R	58.9%	39.8%	59.7%	40.3%

One of the 1978 elections was for a short term to fill a vacancy.

246

MINNESOTA

Districts Established March 11, 1982

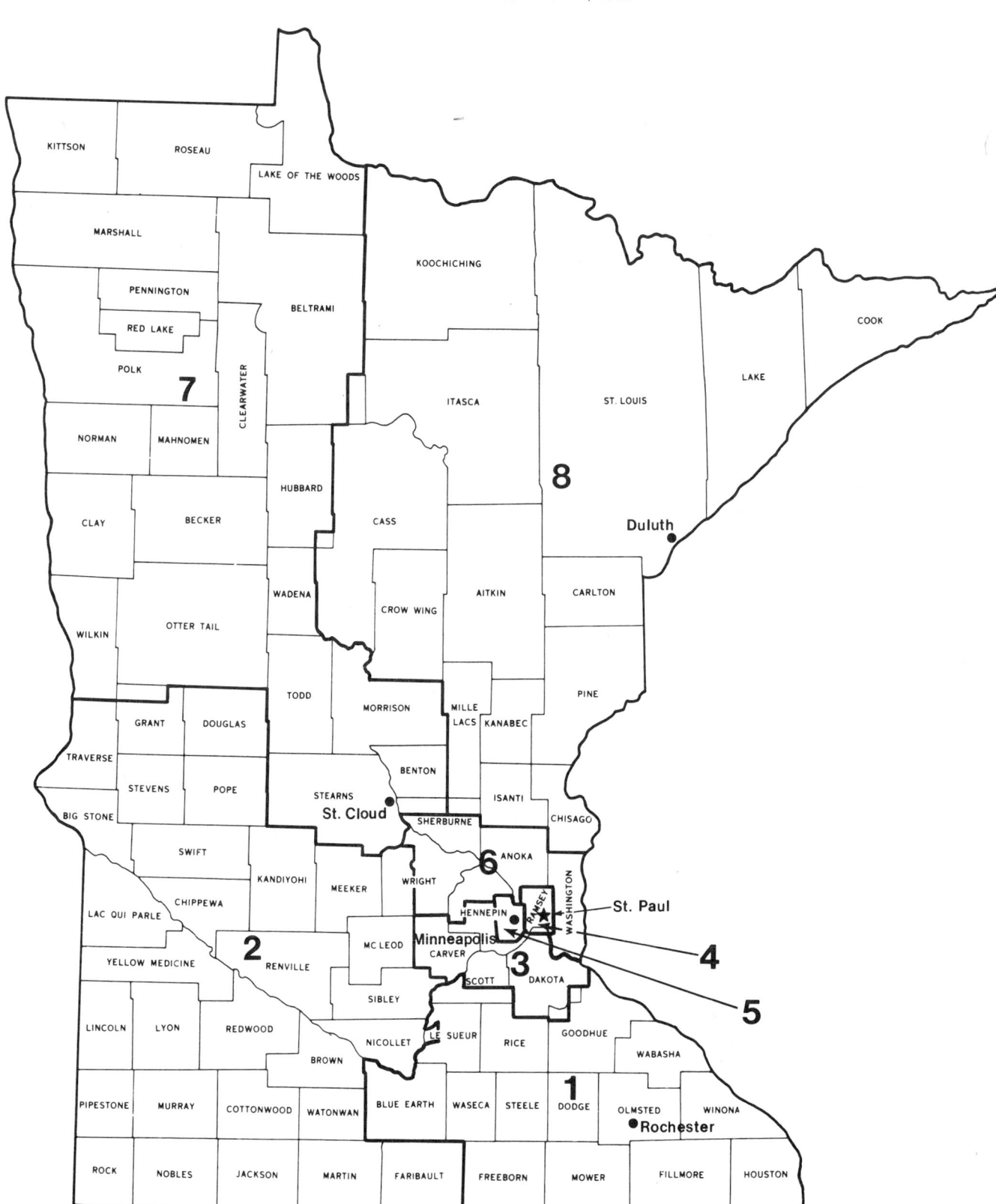

© ERC

MINNESOTA

PRESIDENT 1984

1980 Census Population	County	Total Vote	Republican	Democratic	Other	Rep.-Dem. Plurality		Percentage Total Vote Rep.	Dem.	Major Vote Rep.	Dem.
13,404	AITKIN	7,419	3,422	3,943	54	521	D	46.1%	53.1%	46.5%	53.5%
195,998	ANOKA	97,486	46,578	50,305	603	3,727	D	47.8%	51.6%	48.1%	51.9%
29,336	BECKER	13,107	7,553	5,456	98	2,097	R	57.6%	41.6%	58.1%	41.9%
30,982	BELTRAMI	15,002	7,414	7,481	107	67	D	49.4%	49.9%	49.8%	50.2%
25,187	BENTON	11,886	6,830	4,922	134	1,908	R	57.5%	41.4%	58.1%	41.9%
7,716	BIG STONE	3,847	1,821	1,994	32	173	D	47.3%	51.8%	47.7%	52.3%
52,314	BLUE EARTH	26,353	14,298	11,877	178	2,421	R	54.3%	45.1%	54.6%	45.4%
28,645	BROWN	12,977	8,399	4,469	109	3,930	R	64.7%	34.4%	65.3%	34.7%
29,936	CARLTON	14,206	4,877	9,189	140	4,312	D	34.3%	64.7%	34.7%	65.3%
37,046	CARVER	18,816	11,963	6,725	128	5,238	R	63.6%	35.7%	64.0%	36.0%
21,050	CASS	11,482	6,619	4,773	90	1,846	R	57.6%	41.6%	58.1%	41.9%
14,941	CHIPPEWA	7,085	3,964	3,047	74	917	R	55.9%	43.0%	56.5%	43.5%
25,717	CHISAGO	13,063	6,279	6,683	101	404	D	48.1%	51.2%	48.4%	51.6%
49,327	CLAY	21,978	11,565	10,294	119	1,271	R	52.6%	46.8%	52.9%	47.1%
8,761	CLEARWATER	4,027	2,066	1,917	44	149	R	51.3%	47.6%	51.9%	48.1%
4,092	COOK	2,362	1,219	1,129	14	90	R	51.6%	47.8%	51.9%	48.1%
14,854	COTTONWOOD	7,385	4,275	3,073	37	1,202	R	57.9%	41.6%	58.2%	41.8%
41,722	CROW WING	20,236	11,362	8,719	155	2,643	R	56.1%	43.1%	56.6%	43.4%
194,279	DAKOTA	104,946	55,119	49,125	702	5,994	R	52.5%	46.8%	52.9%	47.1%
14,773	DODGE	7,267	4,428	2,786	53	1,642	R	60.9%	38.3%	61.4%	38.6%
27,839	DOUGLAS	14,546	9,005	5,444	97	3,561	R	61.9%	37.4%	62.3%	37.7%
19,714	FARIBAULT	9,739	5,690	3,993	56	1,697	R	58.4%	41.0%	58.8%	41.2%
21,930	FILLMORE	10,762	6,342	4,351	69	1,991	R	58.9%	40.4%	59.3%	40.7%
36,329	FREEBORN	17,873	8,413	9,338	122	925	D	47.1%	52.2%	47.4%	52.6%
38,749	GOODHUE	19,988	11,171	8,679	138	2,492	R	55.9%	43.4%	56.3%	43.7%
7,171	GRANT	3,999	2,111	1,867	21	244	R	52.8%	46.7%	53.1%	46.9%
941,411	HENNEPIN	529,485	253,921	272,401	3,163	18,480	D	48.0%	51.4%	48.2%	51.8%
18,382	HOUSTON	9,249	5,645	3,512	92	2,133	R	61.0%	38.0%	61.6%	38.4%
14,098	HUBBARD	7,483	4,621	2,806	56	1,815	R	61.8%	37.5%	62.2%	37.8%
23,600	ISANTI	11,120	5,660	5,378	82	282	R	50.9%	48.4%	51.3%	48.7%
43,069	ITASCA	20,958	9,306	11,455	197	2,149	D	44.4%	54.7%	44.8%	55.2%
13,690	JACKSON	6,626	3,131	3,437	58	306	D	47.3%	51.9%	47.7%	52.3%
12,161	KANABEC	5,725	3,027	2,660	38	367	R	52.9%	46.5%	53.2%	46.8%
36,763	KANDIYOHI	18,108	9,539	8,402	167	1,137	R	52.7%	46.4%	53.2%	46.8%
6,672	KITTSON	3,351	1,716	1,610	25	106	R	51.2%	48.0%	51.6%	48.4%
17,571	KOOCHICHING	7,746	3,466	4,238	42	772	D	44.7%	54.7%	45.0%	55.0%
10,592	LAC QUI PARLE	5,497	2,731	2,685	81	46	R	49.7%	48.8%	50.4%	49.6%
13,043	LAKE	6,534	2,003	4,468	63	2,465	D	30.7%	68.4%	31.0%	69.0%
3,764	LAKE OF THE WOODS	1,940	1,094	824	22	270	R	56.4%	42.5%	57.0%	43.0%
23,434	LE SUEUR	11,154	6,033	5,070	51	963	R	54.1%	45.5%	54.3%	45.7%
8,207	LINCOLN	3,815	1,905	1,827	83	78	R	49.9%	47.9%	51.0%	49.0%
25,207	LYON	12,664	7,170	5,389	105	1,781	R	56.6%	42.6%	57.1%	42.9%
29,657	MCLEOD	13,731	8,728	4,864	139	3,864	R	63.6%	35.4%	64.2%	35.8%
5,535	MAHNOMEN	2,597	1,328	1,241	28	87	R	51.1%	47.8%	51.7%	48.3%
13,027	MARSHALL	6,209	3,433	2,705	71	728	R	55.3%	43.6%	55.9%	44.1%
24,687	MARTIN	12,046	7,308	4,673	65	2,635	R	60.7%	38.8%	61.0%	39.0%
20,594	MEEKER	9,726	5,511	4,156	59	1,355	R	56.7%	42.7%	57.0%	43.0%
18,430	MILLE LACS	8,371	4,307	4,011	53	296	R	51.5%	47.9%	51.8%	48.2%
29,311	MORRISON	13,885	7,556	6,225	104	1,331	R	54.4%	44.8%	54.8%	45.2%
40,390	MOWER	20,648	8,054	12,498	96	4,444	D	39.0%	60.5%	39.2%	60.8%
11,507	MURRAY	5,578	2,780	2,741	57	39	R	49.8%	49.1%	50.4%	49.6%
26,929	NICOLLET	13,359	7,472	5,789	98	1,683	R	55.9%	43.3%	56.3%	43.7%
21,840	NOBLES	9,605	4,876	4,619	110	257	R	50.8%	48.1%	51.4%	48.6%
9,379	NORMAN	4,377	2,152	2,202	23	50	D	49.2%	50.3%	49.4%	50.6%
92,006	OLMSTED	44,831	28,129	16,335	367	11,794	R	62.7%	36.4%	63.3%	36.7%
51,937	OTTER TAIL	25,554	15,664	9,714	176	5,950	R	61.3%	38.0%	61.7%	38.3%
15,258	PENNINGTON	6,489	3,536	2,913	40	623	R	54.5%	44.9%	54.8%	45.2%
19,871	PINE	9,780	4,493	5,223	64	730	D	45.9%	53.4%	46.2%	53.8%
11,690	PIPESTONE	5,501	3,043	2,391	67	652	R	55.3%	43.5%	56.0%	44.0%
34,844	POLK	15,789	8,617	7,033	139	1,584	R	54.6%	44.5%	55.1%	44.9%

MINNESOTA

PRESIDENT 1984

1980 Census Population	County	Total Vote	Republican	Democratic	Other	Rep.-Dem. Plurality	Percentage			
							Total Vote Rep.	Dem.	Major Vote Rep.	Dem.
11,657	POPE	5,863	3,064	2,757	42	307 R	52.3%	47.0%	52.6%	47.4%
459,784	RAMSEY	239,511	95,667	141,623	2,221	45,956 D	39.9%	59.1%	40.3%	59.7%
5,471	RED LAKE	2,495	1,184	1,294	17	110 D	47.5%	51.9%	47.8%	52.2%
19,341	REDWOOD	9,061	6,020	2,957	84	3,063 R	66.4%	32.6%	67.1%	32.9%
20,401	RENVILLE	9,632	5,571	3,972	89	1,599 R	57.8%	41.2%	58.4%	41.6%
46,087	RICE	21,537	10,456	10,880	201	424 D	48.5%	50.5%	49.0%	51.0%
10,703	ROCK	5,196	2,971	2,188	37	783 R	57.2%	42.1%	57.6%	42.4%
12,574	ROSEAU	5,811	3,445	2,319	47	1,126 R	59.3%	39.9%	59.8%	40.2%
222,229	ST. LOUIS	112,879	34,162	77,683	1,034	43,521 D	30.3%	68.8%	30.5%	69.5%
43,784	SCOTT	22,133	12,573	9,452	108	3,121 R	56.8%	42.7%	57.1%	42.9%
29,908	SHERBURNE	13,962	7,738	6,140	84	1,598 R	55.4%	44.0%	55.8%	44.2%
15,448	SIBLEY	7,471	4,638	2,761	72	1,877 R	62.1%	37.0%	62.7%	37.3%
108,161	STEARNS	51,663	30,216	20,944	503	9,272 R	58.5%	40.5%	59.1%	40.9%
30,328	STEELE	13,910	8,780	5,060	70	3,720 R	63.1%	36.4%	63.4%	36.6%
11,322	STEVENS	5,752	3,251	2,451	50	800 R	56.5%	42.6%	57.0%	43.0%
12,920	SWIFT	6,488	2,893	3,531	64	638 D	44.6%	54.4%	45.0%	55.0%
24,991	TODD	11,310	6,585	4,657	68	1,928 R	58.2%	41.2%	58.6%	41.4%
5,542	TRAVERSE	2,744	1,399	1,325	20	74 R	51.0%	48.3%	51.4%	48.6%
19,335	WABASHA	9,247	5,299	3,872	76	1,427 R	57.3%	41.9%	57.8%	42.2%
14,192	WADENA	6,794	4,306	2,454	34	1,852 R	63.4%	36.1%	63.7%	36.3%
18,448	WASECA	9,092	5,509	3,527	56	1,982 R	60.6%	38.8%	61.0%	39.0%
113,571	WASHINGTON	57,961	29,046	28,527	388	519 R	50.1%	49.2%	50.5%	49.5%
12,361	WATONWAN	5,978	3,526	2,425	27	1,101 R	59.0%	40.6%	59.3%	40.7%
8,454	WILKIN	3,796	2,367	1,410	19	957 R	62.4%	37.1%	62.7%	37.3%
46,256	WINONA	21,770	11,981	9,577	212	2,404 R	55.0%	44.0%	55.6%	44.4%
58,681	WRIGHT	28,108	15,399	12,486	223	2,913 R	54.8%	44.4%	55.2%	44.8%
13,653	YELLOW MEDICINE	6,917	3,819	3,018	80	801 R	55.2%	43.6%	55.9%	44.1%
4,075,970	TOTAL	2,084,449	1,032,603	1,036,364	15,482	3,761 D	49.5%	49.7%	49.9%	50.1%

MINNESOTA

SENATOR 1984

1980 Census Population	County	Total Vote	Republican	Democratic	Other	Rep.-Dem. Plurality	Percentage Total Vote Rep.	Dem.	Major Vote Rep.	Dem.
13,404	AITKIN	7,424	4,008	3,382	34	626 R	54.0%	45.6%	54.2%	45.8%
195,998	ANOKA	97,445	54,795	42,031	619	12,764 R	56.2%	43.1%	56.6%	43.4%
29,336	BECKER	13,173	8,481	4,588	104	3,893 R	64.4%	34.8%	64.9%	35.1%
30,982	BELTRAMI	15,013	8,203	6,708	102	1,495 R	54.6%	44.7%	55.0%	45.0%
25,187	BENTON	11,828	7,726	4,022	80	3,704 R	65.3%	34.0%	65.8%	34.2%
7,716	BIG STONE	3,854	2,107	1,735	12	372 R	54.7%	45.0%	54.8%	45.2%
52,314	BLUE EARTH	26,449	16,529	9,808	112	6,721 R	62.5%	37.1%	62.8%	37.2%
28,645	BROWN	13,052	9,361	3,633	58	5,728 R	71.7%	27.8%	72.0%	28.0%
29,936	CARLTON	14,520	6,294	8,163	63	1,869 D	43.3%	56.2%	43.5%	56.5%
37,046	CARVER	19,044	13,409	5,547	88	7,862 R	70.4%	29.1%	70.7%	29.3%
21,050	CASS	11,251	6,963	4,244	44	2,719 R	61.9%	37.7%	62.1%	37.9%
14,941	CHIPPEWA	7,147	4,458	2,648	41	1,810 R	62.4%	37.1%	62.7%	37.3%
25,717	CHISAGO	13,075	7,406	5,614	55	1,792 R	56.6%	42.9%	56.9%	43.1%
49,327	CLAY	22,143	13,918	8,110	115	5,808 R	62.9%	36.6%	63.2%	36.8%
8,761	CLEARWATER	4,017	2,279	1,710	28	569 R	56.7%	42.6%	57.1%	42.9%
4,092	COOK	2,357	1,365	983	9	382 R	57.9%	41.7%	58.1%	41.9%
14,854	COTTONWOOD	7,383	4,748	2,611	24	2,137 R	64.3%	35.4%	64.5%	35.5%
41,722	CROW WING	20,478	12,534	7,863	81	4,671 R	61.2%	38.4%	61.5%	38.5%
194,279	DAKOTA	104,078	64,021	39,389	668	24,632 R	61.5%	37.8%	61.9%	38.1%
14,773	DODGE	7,239	5,180	2,025	34	3,155 R	71.6%	28.0%	71.9%	28.1%
27,839	DOUGLAS	14,592	9,661	4,885	46	4,776 R	66.2%	33.5%	66.4%	33.6%
19,714	FARIBAULT	9,752	6,566	3,147	39	3,419 R	67.3%	32.3%	67.6%	32.4%
21,930	FILLMORE	10,735	7,421	3,278	36	4,143 R	69.1%	30.5%	69.4%	30.6%
36,329	FREEBORN	17,303	9,732	7,419	152	2,313 R	56.2%	42.9%	56.7%	43.3%
38,749	GOODHUE	20,026	13,085	6,868	73	6,217 R	65.3%	34.3%	65.6%	34.4%
7,171	GRANT	4,014	2,407	1,593	14	814 R	60.0%	39.7%	60.2%	39.8%
941,411	HENNEPIN	522,098	294,072	224,959	3,067	69,113 R	56.3%	43.1%	56.7%	43.3%
18,382	HOUSTON	9,176	6,717	2,391	68	4,326 R	73.2%	26.1%	73.7%	26.3%
14,098	HUBBARD	7,483	4,932	2,515	36	2,417 R	65.9%	33.6%	66.2%	33.8%
23,600	ISANTI	10,923	6,318	4,548	57	1,770 R	57.8%	41.6%	58.1%	41.9%
43,069	ITASCA	21,278	10,569	10,595	114	26 D	49.7%	49.8%	49.9%	50.1%
13,690	JACKSON	6,607	3,842	2,741	24	1,101 R	58.2%	41.5%	58.4%	41.6%
12,161	KANABEC	5,710	3,191	2,503	16	688 R	55.9%	43.8%	56.0%	44.0%
36,763	KANDIYOHI	17,910	10,333	7,466	111	2,867 R	57.7%	41.7%	58.1%	41.9%
6,672	KITTSON	3,372	1,946	1,412	14	534 R	57.7%	41.9%	58.0%	42.0%
17,571	KOOCHICHING	7,799	4,043	3,723	33	320 R	51.8%	47.7%	52.1%	47.9%
10,592	LAC QUI PARLE	5,495	3,121	2,346	28	775 R	56.8%	42.7%	57.1%	42.9%
13,043	LAKE	6,510	2,699	3,772	39	1,073 D	41.5%	57.9%	41.7%	58.3%
3,764	LAKE OF THE WOODS	1,948	1,210	724	14	486 R	62.1%	37.2%	62.6%	37.4%
23,434	LE SUEUR	11,225	7,116	4,054	55	3,062 R	63.4%	36.1%	63.7%	36.3%
8,207	LINCOLN	3,797	2,248	1,532	17	716 R	59.2%	40.3%	59.5%	40.5%
25,207	LYON	12,660	7,882	4,710	68	3,172 R	62.3%	37.2%	62.6%	37.4%
29,657	MCLEOD	13,543	9,581	3,851	111	5,730 R	70.7%	28.4%	71.3%	28.7%
5,535	MAHNOMEN	2,636	1,510	1,104	22	406 R	57.3%	41.9%	57.8%	42.2%
13,027	MARSHALL	6,284	3,950	2,309	25	1,641 R	62.9%	36.7%	63.1%	36.9%
24,687	MARTIN	12,050	8,221	3,795	34	4,426 R	68.2%	31.5%	68.4%	31.6%
20,594	MEEKER	9,752	6,449	3,255	48	3,194 R	66.1%	33.4%	66.5%	33.5%
18,430	MILLE LACS	8,527	5,123	3,357	47	1,766 R	60.1%	39.4%	60.4%	39.6%
29,311	MORRISON	13,930	8,886	4,950	94	3,936 R	63.8%	35.5%	64.2%	35.8%
40,390	MOWER	20,635	10,141	10,405	89	264 D	49.1%	50.4%	49.4%	50.6%
11,507	MURRAY	5,555	3,440	2,091	24	1,349 R	61.9%	37.6%	62.2%	37.8%
26,929	NICOLLET	13,475	8,551	4,863	61	3,688 R	63.5%	36.1%	63.7%	36.3%
21,840	NOBLES	9,658	5,896	3,707	55	2,189 R	61.0%	38.4%	61.4%	38.6%
9,379	NORMAN	4,426	2,652	1,768	6	884 R	59.9%	39.9%	60.0%	40.0%
92,006	OLMSTED	44,143	31,735	11,933	475	19,802 R	71.9%	27.0%	72.7%	27.3%
51,937	OTTER TAIL	25,363	16,930	8,300	133	8,630 R	66.8%	32.7%	67.1%	32.9%
15,258	PENNINGTON	6,526	4,066	2,423	37	1,643 R	62.3%	37.1%	62.7%	37.3%
19,871	PINE	9,794	5,295	4,456	43	839 R	54.1%	45.5%	54.3%	45.7%
11,690	PIPESTONE	5,489	3,591	1,860	38	1,731 R	65.4%	33.9%	65.9%	34.1%
34,844	POLK	16,060	9,775	6,196	89	3,579 R	60.9%	38.6%	61.2%	38.8%

MINNESOTA

SENATOR 1984

1980 Census Population	County	Total Vote	Republican	Democratic	Other	Rep.-Dem. Plurality	Total Vote Rep.	Total Vote Dem.	Major Vote Rep.	Major Vote Dem.
11,657	POPE	5,885	3,537	2,335	13	1,202 R	60.1%	39.7%	60.2%	39.8%
459,784	RAMSEY	232,317	117,096	112,808	2,413	4,288 R	50.4%	48.6%	50.9%	49.1%
5,471	RED LAKE	2,498	1,471	1,014	13	457 R	58.9%	40.6%	59.2%	40.8%
19,341	REDWOOD	9,035	6,604	2,369	62	4,235 R	73.1%	26.2%	73.6%	26.4%
20,401	RENVILLE	9,657	6,202	3,400	55	2,802 R	64.2%	35.2%	64.6%	35.4%
46,087	RICE	21,336	12,502	8,641	193	3,861 R	58.6%	40.5%	59.1%	40.9%
10,703	ROCK	5,160	3,584	1,551	25	2,033 R	69.5%	30.1%	69.8%	30.2%
12,574	ROSEAU	5,877	3,873	1,977	27	1,896 R	65.9%	33.6%	66.2%	33.8%
222,229	ST. LOUIS	111,112	44,711	65,386	1,015	20,675 D	40.2%	58.8%	40.6%	59.4%
43,784	SCOTT	22,192	14,372	7,724	96	6,648 R	64.8%	34.8%	65.0%	35.0%
29,908	SHERBURNE	13,821	8,561	5,172	88	3,389 R	61.9%	37.4%	62.3%	37.7%
15,448	SIBLEY	7,473	5,296	2,132	45	3,164 R	70.9%	28.5%	71.3%	28.7%
108,161	STEARNS	51,110	34,076	16,635	399	17,441 R	66.7%	32.5%	67.2%	32.8%
30,328	STEELE	13,943	9,978	3,918	47	6,060 R	71.6%	28.1%	71.8%	28.2%
11,322	STEVENS	5,743	3,608	2,118	17	1,490 R	62.8%	36.9%	63.0%	37.0%
12,920	SWIFT	6,495	3,329	3,143	23	186 R	51.3%	48.4%	51.4%	48.6%
24,991	TODD	11,496	7,406	4,042	48	3,364 R	64.4%	35.2%	64.7%	35.3%
5,542	TRAVERSE	2,762	1,671	1,076	15	595 R	60.5%	39.0%	60.8%	39.2%
19,335	WABASHA	9,312	6,286	2,973	53	3,313 R	67.5%	31.9%	67.9%	32.1%
14,192	WADENA	6,784	4,589	2,172	23	2,417 R	67.6%	32.0%	67.9%	32.1%
18,448	WASECA	9,107	6,328	2,743	36	3,585 R	69.5%	30.1%	69.8%	30.2%
113,571	WASHINGTON	57,792	34,154	23,329	309	10,825 R	59.1%	40.4%	59.4%	40.6%
12,361	WATONWAN	5,924	3,985	1,920	19	2,065 R	67.3%	32.4%	67.5%	32.5%
8,454	WILKIN	3,812	2,683	1,113	16	1,570 R	70.4%	29.2%	70.7%	29.3%
46,256	WINONA	21,305	13,759	7,341	205	6,418 R	64.6%	34.5%	65.2%	34.8%
58,681	WRIGHT	28,046	17,355	10,537	154	6,818 R	61.9%	37.6%	62.2%	37.8%
13,653	YELLOW MEDICINE	6,920	4,222	2,657	41	1,565 R	61.0%	38.4%	61.4%	38.6%
4,075,970	TOTAL	2,066,143	1,199,926	852,844	13,373	347,082 R	58.1%	41.3%	58.5%	41.5%

MINNESOTA

CONGRESS

CD	Year	Total Vote	Republican Vote	Republican Candidate	Democratic Vote	Democratic Candidate	Other Vote	Rep.-Dem. Plurality	Total Vote Rep.	Total Vote Dem.	Major Vote Rep.	Major Vote Dem.
1	1984	245,837	105,723	SPICER, KEITH	140,095	PENNY, TIMOTHY J.	19	34,372 D	43.0%	57.0%	43.0%	57.0%
1	1982	213,520	102,298	HAGEDORN, TOM	109,257	PENNY, TIMOTHY J.	1,965	6,959 D	47.9%	51.2%	48.4%	51.6%
2	1984	243,097	153,308	WEBER, VIN	89,770	LUNDQUIST, TODD	19	63,538 R	63.1%	36.9%	63.1%	36.9%
2	1982	226,751	123,508	WEBER, VIN	103,243	NICHOLS, JAMES W.		20,265 R	54.5%	45.5%	54.5%	45.5%
3	1984	283,978	207,819	FRENZEL, BILL	76,132	PETERSON, DAVE	27	131,687 R	73.2%	26.8%	73.2%	26.8%
3	1982	231,311	166,891	FRENZEL, BILL	60,993	SALITERMAN, JOEL A.	3,427	105,898 R	72.2%	26.4%	73.2%	26.8%
4	1984	228,071	57,450	RACHNER, MARY JANE	167,678	VENTO, BRUCE F.	2,943	110,228 D	25.2%	73.5%	25.5%	74.5%
4	1982	209,742	56,248	JAMES, BILL	153,494	VENTO, BRUCE F.		97,246 D	26.8%	73.2%	26.8%	73.2%
5	1984	235,470	62,642	WEIBLEN, RICHARD	165,075	SABO, MARTIN O.	7,753	102,433 D	26.6%	70.1%	27.5%	72.5%
5	1982	208,452	61,184	JOHNSON, KEITH W.	136,634	SABO, MARTIN O.	10,634	75,450 D	29.4%	65.5%	30.9%	69.1%
6	1984	255,692	101,058	TRUEMAN, PATRICK	154,603	SIKORSKI, GERRY	31	53,545 D	39.5%	60.5%	39.5%	60.5%
6	1982	214,980	105,734	ERDAHL, ARLEN	109,246	SIKORSKI, GERRY		3,512 D	49.2%	50.8%	49.2%	50.8%
7	1984	236,839	135,087	STANGELAND, ARLAN	101,720	PETERSON, COLLIN C.	32	33,367 R	57.0%	42.9%	57.0%	43.0%
7	1982	215,316	108,254	STANGELAND, ARLAN	107,062	WENSTROM, GENE		1,192 R	50.3%	49.7%	50.3%	49.7%
8	1984	246,483	79,181	RUED, DAVE	165,727	OBERSTAR, JAMES L.	1,575	86,546 D	32.1%	67.2%	32.3%	67.7%
8	1982	229,859	53,467	LUCE, MARJORY L.	176,392	OBERSTAR, JAMES L.		122,925 D	23.3%	76.7%	23.3%	76.7%

MINNESOTA

1984 GENERAL ELECTION

In Minnesota the Democratic party is known as the Democratic-Farmer-Labor party and the Republican party as the Independent-Republican party; candidates appear on the ballot with these designations.

President   Other vote was 3,865 LaRouche (Independent); 3,180 Mason (Socialist Workers); 2,996 Bergland (Libertarian); 2,377 Richards (American Populist); 1,219 Johnson (Citizens); 630 Hall (Communist); 260 Winn (Workers League); 232 Serrette (National Alliance); 723 scattered.

Senator   Other vote was 5,351 Garcia (Socialist Workers); 4,653 Putman (Libertarian); 3,129 Miller (New Union); 240 scattered.

Congress   Other vote was scattered in CD's 1, 2 and 3; 2,919 Brandli (Socialist Workers) and 24 scattered in CD 4; 7,725 Anderson (Citizens) and 28 scattered in CD 5; scattered in CD's 6 and 7; 1,560 Salner (Socialist Workers) and 15 scattered in CD 8.

1984 PRIMARIES

SEPTEMBER 11 REPUBLICAN

Senator   162,555 Rudy Boschwitz; 3,277 John Barcelona; 2,462 Carlan Lesch.

Congress   Unopposed in four CD's. Contested as follows:

  CD 1   21,387 Keith Spicer; 3,203 E. B. Henderson.
  CD 3   25,986 Bill Frenzel; 3,005 Shelvie Rettmann.
  CD 4   4,382 Mary Jane Rachner; 3,405 Oliver Steinberg; 2,451 Karl Granse.
  CD 5   5,577 Richard Weiblen; 3,570 Ellen Malenke.

SEPTEMBER 11 DEMOCRATIC

Senator   238,190 Joan Anderson Growe; 61,489 Robert W. Mattson; 2,591 Kent S. Herschbach; 2,376 Donald Black; 2,098 Clarence J. Lagermeier; 2,059 William T. Heine; 2,032 Sal Carlone; 1,660 Harris H. Herman; 1,435 Ole Savior.

Congress   Contested as follows:

  CD 1   24,788 Timothy J. Penny; 1,240 Gerald F. Speltz; 929 Wallace Brattrud.
  CD 2   15,358 Todd Lundquist; 9,539 Pat O'Reilly; 1,241 Mel Moench.
  CD 3   9,773 Dave Peterson; 4,147 Joel A. Saliterman; 1,659 Burton C. Kiecker; 1,160 Bruce G. Bulman.
  CD 4   42,089 Bruce F. Vento; 4,236 Daniel Volk.
  CD 5   39,379 Martin O. Sabo; 4,336 William W. Brown.
  CD 6   22,396 Gerry Sikorski; 2,918 James R. Hoss.
  CD 7   23,858 Collin C. Peterson; 3,910 Delaney L. Grinolds.
  CD 8   56,381 James L. Oberstar; 28,743 Thomas E. Dougherty; 852 Dennis C. Schweigart; 618 Noel Maanum.

MISSISSIPPI

GOVERNOR
William A. Allain (D). Elected 1983 to a four-year term.

SENATORS
Thad Cochran (R). Re-elected 1984 to a six-year term. Previously elected 1978.

John Stennis (D). Re-elected 1982 to a six-year term. Previously elected 1976, 1970, 1964, 1958, 1952, and in 1947 to fill out term vacated by the death of Senator Theodore Bilbo.

REPRESENTATIVES
1. Jamie L. Whitten (D)
2. Webb Franklin (R)
3. G. V. Montgomery (D)
4. Wayne Dowdy (D)
5. Trent Lott (R)

POSTWAR VOTE FOR GOVERNOR

									Percentage			
	Total	Republican		Democratic			Other	Rep.-Dem.	Total Vote		Major Vote	
Year	Vote	Vote	Candidate	Vote	Candidate		Vote	Plurality	Rep.	Dem.	Rep.	Dem.
1983	742,737	288,764	Bramlett, Leon	409,209	Allain, William A.		44,764	120,445 D	38.9%	55.1%	41.4%	58.6%
1979	677,322	263,702	Carmichael, Gil	413,620	Winter, William F.		—	149,918 D	38.9%	61.1%	38.9%	61.1%
1975	708,033	319,632	Carmichael, Gil	369,568	Finch, Cliff		18,833	49,936 D	45.1%	52.2%	46.4%	53.6%
1971	780,537	—	—	601,122	Waller, William L.		179,415	601,122 D	—	77.0%	—	100.0%
1967	448,697	133,379	Phillips, Rubel L.	315,318	Williams, John Bell		—	181,939 D	29.7%	70.3%	29.7%	70.3%
1963	363,971	138,515	Phillips, Rubel L.	225,456	Johnson, Paul B.		—	86,941 D	38.1%	61.9%	38.1%	61.9%
1959	57,671	—	—	57,671	Barnett, Ross R.		—	57,671 D	—	100.0%	—	100.0%
1955	40,707	—	—	40,707	Coleman, James P.		—	40,707 D	—	100.0%	—	100.0%
1951	43,422	—	—	43,422	White, Hugh		—	43,422 D	—	100.0%	—	100.0%
1947	166,095	—	—	161,993	Wright, Fielding L.		4,102	161,993 D	—	97.5%	—	100.0%

POSTWAR VOTE FOR SENATOR

									Percentage			
	Total	Republican		Democratic			Other	Rep.-Dem.	Total Vote		Major Vote	
Year	Vote	Vote	Candidate	Vote	Candidate		Vote	Plurality	Rep.	Dem.	Rep.	Dem.
1984	952,240	580,314	Cochran, Thad	371,926	Winter, William F.		—	208,388 R	60.9%	39.1%	60.9%	39.1%
1982	645,026	230,927	Barbour, Haley	414,099	Stennis, John		—	183,172 D	35.8%	64.2%	35.8%	64.2%
1978	583,936	263,089	Cochran, Thad	185,454	Dantin, Maurice		135,393	77,635 R	45.1%	31.8%	58.7%	41.3%
1976	554,433	—	—	554,433	Stennis, John		—	554,433 D	—	100.0%	—	100.0%
1972	645,746	249,779	Carmichael, Gil	375,102	Eastland, James O.		20,865	125,323 D	38.7%	58.1%	40.0%	60.0%
1970	324,215	—	—	286,622	Stennis, John		37,593	286,622 D	—	88.4%	—	100.0%
1966	393,900	105,150	Walker, Prentiss	258,248	Eastland, James O.		30,502	153,098 D	26.7%	65.6%	28.9%	71.1%
1964	343,364	—	—	343,364	Stennis, John		—	343,364 D	—	100.0%	—	100.0%
1960	266,148	21,807	Moore, Joe A.	244,341	Eastland, James O.		—	222,534 D	8.2%	91.8%	8.2%	91.8%
1958	61,039	—	—	61,039	Stennis, John		—	61,039 D	—	100.0%	—	100.0%
1954	105,526	4,678	White, James A.	100,848	Eastland, James O.		—	96,170 D	4.4%	95.6%	4.4%	95.6%
1952	233,919	—	—	233,919	Stennis, John		—	233,919 D	—	100.0%	—	100.0%
1948	151,478	—	—	151,478	Eastland, James O.		—	151,478 D	—	100.0%	—	100.0%
1947s	193,709	[See note below]										
1946	46,747	—	—	46,747	Bilbo, Theodore		—	46,747 D	—	100.0%	—	100.0%

The 1947 election was for a short term to fill a vacancy and was held without party designation or nomination; John Stennis polled 52,068 votes (26.9% of the total vote) and won the election with a 6,343 plurality.

MISSISSIPPI

Districts Established January 6, 1984

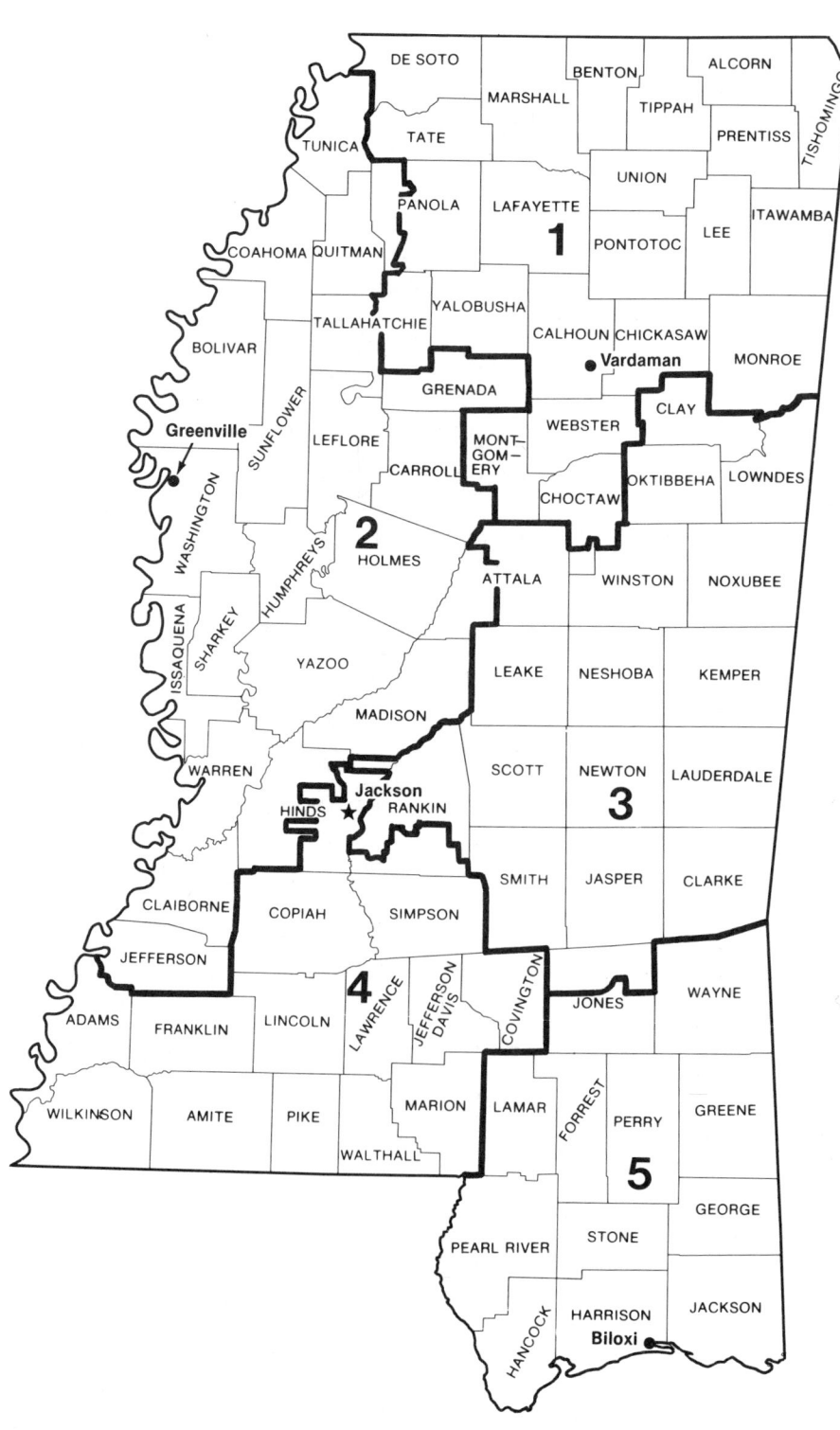

MISSISSIPPI

PRESIDENT 1984

1980 Census Population	County	Total Vote	Republican	Democratic	Other	Rep.-Dem. Plurality	Percentage Total Vote Rep.	Dem.	Major Vote Rep.	Dem.
38,035	ADAMS	17,378	9,440	7,849	89	1,591 R	54.3%	45.2%	54.6%	45.4%
33,036	ALCORN	12,279	7,203	4,862	214	2,341 R	58.7%	39.6%	59.7%	40.3%
13,369	AMITE	6,050	3,463	2,569	18	894 R	57.2%	42.5%	57.4%	42.6%
19,865	ATTALA	8,215	4,870	3,327	18	1,543 R	59.3%	40.5%	59.4%	40.6%
8,153	BENTON	3,466	1,737	1,715	14	22 R	50.1%	49.5%	50.3%	49.7%
45,965	BOLIVAR	15,824	6,939	8,769	116	1,830 D	43.9%	55.4%	44.2%	55.8%
15,664	CALHOUN	5,337	3,579	1,749	9	1,830 R	67.1%	32.8%	67.2%	32.8%
9,776	CARROLL	4,297	2,823	1,462	12	1,361 R	65.7%	34.0%	65.9%	34.1%
17,853	CHICKASAW	5,957	3,605	2,329	23	1,276 R	60.5%	39.1%	60.8%	39.2%
8,996	CHOCTAW	3,663	2,491	1,166	6	1,325 R	68.0%	31.8%	68.1%	31.9%
12,279	CLAIBORNE	4,484	1,294	3,179	11	1,885 D	28.9%	70.9%	28.9%	71.1%
16,945	CLARKE	6,832	4,551	2,262	19	2,289 R	66.6%	33.1%	66.8%	33.2%
21,082	CLAY	8,187	4,112	4,046	29	66 R	50.2%	49.4%	50.4%	49.6%
36,918	COAHOMA	12,810	5,759	6,839	212	1,080 D	45.0%	53.4%	45.7%	54.3%
26,503	COPIAH	10,416	5,806	4,591	19	1,215 R	55.7%	44.1%	55.8%	44.2%
15,927	COVINGTON	6,413	4,165	2,219	29	1,946 R	64.9%	34.6%	65.2%	34.8%
53,930	DE SOTO	17,022	12,576	4,369	77	8,207 R	73.9%	25.7%	74.2%	25.8%
66,018	FORREST	22,576	15,719	6,786	71	8,933 R	69.6%	30.1%	69.8%	30.2%
8,208	FRANKLIN	4,079	2,564	1,494	21	1,070 R	62.9%	36.6%	63.2%	36.8%
15,297	GEORGE	6,028	4,346	1,655	27	2,691 R	72.1%	27.5%	72.4%	27.6%
9,827	GREENE	4,062	2,744	1,297	21	1,447 R	67.6%	31.9%	67.9%	32.1%
21,043	GRENADA	8,521	5,181	3,325	15	1,856 R	60.8%	39.0%	60.9%	39.1%
24,537	HANCOCK	10,344	7,662	2,630	52	5,032 R	74.1%	25.4%	74.4%	25.6%
157,665	HARRISON	46,677	33,995	12,495	187	21,500 R	72.8%	26.8%	73.1%	26.9%
250,998	HINDS	100,468	56,953	42,373	1,142	14,580 R	56.7%	42.2%	57.3%	42.7%
22,970	HOLMES	8,753	3,102	5,641	10	2,539 D	35.4%	64.4%	35.5%	64.5%
13,931	HUMPHREYS	4,914	2,309	2,596	9	287 D	47.0%	52.8%	47.1%	52.9%
2,513	ISSAQUENA	1,034	512	501	21	11 R	49.5%	48.5%	50.5%	49.5%
20,518	ITAWAMBA	7,285	4,587	2,674	24	1,913 R	63.0%	36.7%	63.2%	36.8%
118,015	JACKSON	38,529	29,585	8,821	123	20,764 R	76.8%	22.9%	77.0%	23.0%
17,265	JASPER	6,902	3,727	3,104	71	623 R	54.0%	45.0%	54.6%	45.4%
9,181	JEFFERSON	3,912	856	3,049	7	2,193 D	21.9%	77.9%	21.9%	78.1%
13,846	JEFFERSON DAVIS	5,566	2,884	2,644	38	240 R	51.8%	47.5%	52.2%	47.8%
61,912	JONES	24,954	17,586	7,298	70	10,288 R	70.5%	29.2%	70.7%	29.3%
10,148	KEMPER	4,456	2,354	2,089	13	265 R	52.8%	46.9%	53.0%	47.0%
31,030	LAFAYETTE	9,680	6,006	3,646	28	2,360 R	62.0%	37.7%	62.2%	37.8%
23,821	LAMAR	9,930	7,929	1,964	37	5,965 R	79.8%	19.8%	80.1%	19.9%
77,285	LAUDERDALE	27,267	18,807	7,534	926	11,273 R	69.0%	27.6%	71.4%	28.6%
12,518	LAWRENCE	6,253	3,970	2,274	9	1,696 R	63.5%	36.4%	63.6%	36.4%
18,790	LEAKE	7,516	4,663	2,845	8	1,818 R	62.0%	37.9%	62.1%	37.9%
57,061	LEE	19,730	13,312	6,208	210	7,104 R	67.5%	31.5%	68.2%	31.8%
41,525	LEFLORE	15,212	7,550	7,443	219	107 R	49.6%	48.9%	50.4%	49.6%
30,174	LINCOLN	13,381	8,898	4,458	25	4,440 R	66.5%	33.3%	66.6%	33.4%
57,304	LOWNDES	18,177	12,049	6,078	50	5,971 R	66.3%	33.4%	66.5%	33.5%
41,613	MADISON	17,463	9,298	8,002	163	1,296 R	53.2%	45.8%	53.7%	46.3%
25,708	MARION	11,125	7,355	3,757	13	3,598 R	66.1%	33.8%	66.2%	33.8%
29,296	MARSHALL	10,278	4,389	5,845	44	1,456 D	42.7%	56.9%	42.9%	57.1%
36,404	MONROE	11,860	7,387	4,437	36	2,950 R	62.3%	37.4%	62.5%	37.5%
13,366	MONTGOMERY	4,983	3,093	1,881	9	1,212 R	62.1%	37.7%	62.2%	37.8%
23,789	NESHOBA	9,364	6,715	2,630	19	4,085 R	71.7%	28.1%	71.9%	28.1%
19,944	NEWTON	8,072	5,911	2,127	34	3,784 R	73.2%	26.4%	73.5%	26.5%
13,212	NOXUBEE	5,149	2,123	2,928	98	805 D	41.2%	56.9%	42.0%	58.0%
36,018	OKTIBBEHA	12,697	7,574	5,097	26	2,477 R	59.7%	40.1%	59.8%	40.2%
28,164	PANOLA	11,375	5,850	5,465	60	385 R	51.4%	48.0%	51.7%	48.3%
33,795	PEARL RIVER	13,112	9,978	3,085	49	6,893 R	76.1%	23.5%	76.4%	23.6%
9,864	PERRY	4,744	3,098	1,415	231	1,683 R	65.3%	29.8%	68.6%	31.4%
36,173	PIKE	14,411	8,254	6,137	20	2,117 R	57.3%	42.6%	57.4%	42.6%
20,918	PONTOTOC	7,643	5,182	2,434	27	2,748 R	67.8%	31.8%	68.0%	32.0%
24,025	PRENTISS	7,732	4,821	2,897	14	1,924 R	62.4%	37.5%	62.5%	37.5%
12,636	QUITMAN	4,548	2,198	2,343	7	145 D	48.3%	51.5%	48.4%	51.6%

MISSISSIPPI

PRESIDENT 1984

1980 Census Population	County	Total Vote	Republican	Democratic	Other	Rep.-Dem. Plurality	Percentage Total Vote Rep.	Dem.	Major Vote Rep.	Dem.
69,427	RANKIN	28,308	22,393	5,874	41	16,519 R	79.1%	20.8%	79.2%	20.8%
24,556	SCOTT	9,053	5,763	3,274	16	2,489 R	63.7%	36.2%	63.8%	36.2%
7,964	SHARKEY	3,398	1,487	1,723	188	236 D	43.8%	50.7%	46.3%	53.7%
23,441	SIMPSON	8,924	5,983	2,894	47	3,089 R	67.0%	32.4%	67.4%	32.6%
15,077	SMITH	6,710	5,116	1,573	21	3,543 R	76.2%	23.4%	76.5%	23.5%
9,716	STONE	4,193	2,980	1,185	28	1,795 R	71.1%	28.3%	71.5%	28.5%
34,844	SUNFLOWER	10,111	5,178	4,913	20	265 R	51.2%	48.6%	51.3%	48.7%
17,157	TALLAHATCHIE	5,646	2,901	2,725	20	176 R	51.4%	48.3%	51.6%	48.4%
20,119	TATE	7,557	4,677	2,846	34	1,831 R	61.9%	37.7%	62.2%	37.8%
18,739	TIPPAH	7,301	4,706	2,566	29	2,140 R	64.5%	35.1%	64.7%	35.3%
18,434	TISHOMINGO	6,428	3,527	2,879	22	648 R	54.9%	44.8%	55.1%	44.9%
9,652	TUNICA	2,804	1,109	1,621	74	512 D	39.6%	57.8%	40.6%	59.4%
21,741	UNION	8,617	5,837	2,766	14	3,071 R	67.7%	32.1%	67.8%	32.2%
13,761	WALTHALL	5,541	3,305	2,219	17	1,086 R	59.6%	40.0%	59.8%	40.2%
51,627	WARREN	21,248	12,959	8,054	235	4,905 R	61.0%	37.9%	61.7%	38.3%
72,344	WASHINGTON	23,414	12,454	10,617	343	1,837 R	53.2%	45.3%	54.0%	46.0%
19,135	WAYNE	7,836	5,000	2,818	18	2,182 R	63.8%	36.0%	64.0%	36.0%
10,300	WEBSTER	4,794	3,390	1,397	7	1,993 R	70.7%	29.1%	70.8%	29.2%
10,021	WILKINSON	4,386	1,722	2,627	37	905 D	39.3%	59.9%	39.6%	60.4%
19,474	WINSTON	8,746	5,192	3,543	11	1,649 R	59.4%	40.5%	59.4%	40.6%
13,139	YALOBUSHA	5,285	2,934	2,337	14	597 R	55.5%	44.2%	55.7%	44.3%
27,349	YAZOO	11,412	6,275	5,037	100	1,238 R	55.0%	44.1%	55.5%	44.5%
2,520,638	TOTAL	941,104	582,377	352,192	6,535	230,185 R	61.9%	37.4%	62.3%	37.7%

MISSISSIPPI

GOVERNOR 1983

1980 Census Population	County	Total Vote	Republican	Democratic	Other	Rep.-Dem. Plurality	Percentage Total Vote Rep.	Dem.	Major Vote Rep.	Dem.
38,035	ADAMS	12,636	2,494	9,544	598	7,050 D	19.7%	75.5%	20.7%	79.3%
33,036	ALCORN	10,816	3,090	7,257	469	4,167 D	28.6%	67.1%	29.9%	70.1%
13,369	AMITE	4,777	1,401	3,208	168	1,807 D	29.3%	67.2%	30.4%	69.6%
19,865	ATTALA	6,388	2,375	3,805	208	1,430 D	37.2%	59.6%	38.4%	61.6%
8,153	BENTON	2,856	773	1,959	124	1,186 D	27.1%	68.6%	28.3%	71.7%
45,965	BOLIVAR	13,239	4,837	7,489	913	2,652 D	36.5%	56.6%	39.2%	60.8%
15,664	CALHOUN	4,032	1,403	2,446	183	1,043 D	34.8%	60.7%	36.5%	63.5%
9,776	CARROLL	3,962	1,397	2,376	189	979 D	35.3%	60.0%	37.0%	63.0%
17,853	CHICKASAW	4,180	1,537	2,401	242	864 D	36.8%	57.4%	39.0%	61.0%
8,996	CHOCTAW	3,097	1,274	1,663	160	389 D	41.1%	53.7%	43.4%	56.6%
12,279	CLAIBORNE	4,711	875	2,923	913	2,048 D	18.6%	62.0%	23.0%	77.0%
16,945	CLARKE	5,032	2,027	2,751	254	724 D	40.3%	54.7%	42.4%	57.6%
21,082	CLAY	5,704	2,113	3,297	294	1,184 D	37.0%	57.8%	39.1%	60.9%
36,918	COAHOMA	10,267	4,685	5,227	355	542 D	45.6%	50.9%	47.3%	52.7%
26,503	COPIAH	8,138	2,743	5,128	267	2,385 D	33.7%	63.0%	34.8%	65.2%
15,927	COVINGTON	5,544	2,235	2,956	353	721 D	40.3%	53.3%	43.1%	56.9%
53,930	DE SOTO	12,483	3,931	8,044	508	4,113 D	31.5%	64.4%	32.8%	67.2%
66,018	FORREST	17,835	9,275	7,577	983	1,698 R	52.0%	42.5%	55.0%	45.0%
8,208	FRANKLIN	3,542	741	2,601	200	1,860 D	20.9%	73.4%	22.2%	77.8%
15,297	GEORGE	4,817	2,089	2,513	215	424 D	43.4%	52.2%	45.4%	54.6%
9,827	GREENE	3,444	1,167	2,115	162	948 D	33.9%	61.4%	35.6%	64.4%
21,043	GRENADA	6,661	2,499	3,896	266	1,397 D	37.5%	58.5%	39.1%	60.9%
24,537	HANCOCK	8,074	2,339	5,090	645	2,751 D	29.0%	63.0%	31.5%	68.5%
157,665	HARRISON	35,122	12,979	19,831	2,312	6,852 D	37.0%	56.5%	39.6%	60.4%
250,998	HINDS	75,223	35,994	34,490	4,739	1,504 R	47.8%	45.9%	51.1%	48.9%
22,970	HOLMES	7,810	1,859	5,328	623	3,469 D	23.8%	68.2%	25.9%	74.1%
13,931	HUMPHREYS	5,386	1,543	3,209	634	1,666 D	28.6%	59.6%	32.5%	67.5%
2,513	ISSAQUENA	802	247	510	45	263 D	30.8%	63.6%	32.6%	67.4%
20,518	ITAWAMBA	5,637	1,713	3,686	238	1,973 D	30.4%	65.4%	31.7%	68.3%
118,015	JACKSON	27,964	11,487	14,560	1,917	3,073 D	41.1%	52.1%	44.1%	55.9%
17,265	JASPER	6,334	2,299	3,617	418	1,318 D	36.3%	57.1%	38.9%	61.1%
9,181	JEFFERSON	3,793	333	2,174	1,286	1,841 D	8.8%	57.3%	13.3%	86.7%
13,846	JEFFERSON DAVIS	4,893	1,371	3,249	273	1,878 D	28.0%	66.4%	29.7%	70.3%
61,912	JONES	20,084	9,050	10,015	1,019	965 D	45.1%	49.9%	47.5%	52.5%
10,148	KEMPER	3,895	1,306	2,198	391	892 D	33.5%	56.4%	37.3%	62.7%
31,030	LAFAYETTE	6,797	3,063	3,265	469	202 D	45.1%	48.0%	48.4%	51.6%
23,821	LAMAR	7,822	4,396	3,083	343	1,313 R	56.2%	39.4%	58.8%	41.2%
77,285	LAUDERDALE	19,087	9,431	8,305	1,351	1,126 R	49.4%	43.5%	53.2%	46.8%
12,518	LAWRENCE	5,979	1,666	4,070	243	2,404 D	27.9%	68.1%	29.0%	71.0%
18,790	LEAKE	5,924	1,936	3,789	199	1,853 D	32.7%	64.0%	33.8%	66.2%
57,061	LEE	13,734	6,434	6,038	1,262	396 R	46.8%	44.0%	51.6%	48.4%
41,525	LEFLORE	12,812	5,151	6,709	952	1,558 D	40.2%	52.4%	43.4%	56.6%
30,174	LINCOLN	11,611	4,342	6,801	468	2,459 D	37.4%	58.6%	39.0%	61.0%
57,304	LOWNDES	14,204	7,559	6,036	609	1,523 R	53.2%	42.5%	55.6%	44.4%
41,613	MADISON	13,380	5,157	7,096	1,127	1,939 D	38.5%	53.0%	42.1%	57.9%
25,708	MARION	8,531	3,119	5,093	319	1,974 D	36.6%	59.7%	38.0%	62.0%
29,296	MARSHALL	8,814	2,283	5,660	871	3,377 D	25.9%	64.2%	28.7%	71.3%
36,404	MONROE	8,485	3,307	4,696	482	1,389 D	39.0%	55.3%	41.3%	58.7%
13,366	MONTGOMERY	4,346	1,452	2,753	141	1,301 D	33.4%	63.3%	34.5%	65.5%
23,789	NESHOBA	7,714	2,976	4,423	315	1,447 D	38.6%	57.3%	40.2%	59.8%
19,944	NEWTON	7,113	3,242	3,561	310	319 D	45.6%	50.1%	47.7%	52.3%
13,212	NOXUBEE	4,824	1,582	2,776	466	1,194 D	32.8%	57.5%	36.3%	63.7%
36,018	OKTIBBEHA	9,269	4,449	4,290	530	159 R	48.0%	46.3%	50.9%	49.1%
28,164	PANOLA	8,252	3,041	4,609	602	1,568 D	36.9%	55.9%	39.8%	60.2%
33,795	PEARL RIVER	9,779	3,437	5,781	561	2,344 D	35.1%	59.1%	37.3%	62.7%
9,864	PERRY	3,806	1,339	2,220	247	881 D	35.2%	58.3%	37.6%	62.4%
36,173	PIKE	10,515	3,370	6,834	311	3,464 D	32.0%	65.0%	33.0%	67.0%
20,918	PONTOTOC	5,737	2,089	3,333	315	1,244 D	36.4%	58.1%	38.5%	61.5%
24,025	PRENTISS	7,698	2,452	4,891	355	2,439 D	31.9%	63.5%	33.4%	66.6%
12,636	QUITMAN	4,171	1,412	2,621	138	1,209 D	33.9%	62.8%	35.0%	65.0%

MISSISSIPPI

GOVERNOR 1983

1980 Census Population	County	Total Vote	Republican	Democratic	Other	Rep.-Dem. Plurality	Percentage Total Vote Rep.	Dem.	Major Vote Rep.	Dem.
69,427	RANKIN	23,016	12,182	9,966	868	2,216 R	52.9%	43.3%	55.0%	45.0%
24,556	SCOTT	6,643	2,641	3,731	271	1,090 D	39.8%	56.2%	41.4%	58.6%
7,964	SHARKEY	3,246	877	2,130	239	1,253 D	27.0%	65.6%	29.2%	70.8%
23,441	SIMPSON	8,820	2,804	5,559	457	2,755 D	31.8%	63.0%	33.5%	66.5%
15,077	SMITH	6,115	2,317	3,544	254	1,227 D	37.9%	58.0%	39.5%	60.5%
9,716	STONE	3,656	1,461	1,966	229	505 D	40.0%	53.8%	42.6%	57.4%
34,844	SUNFLOWER	8,291	2,921	4,981	389	2,060 D	35.2%	60.1%	37.0%	63.0%
17,157	TALLAHATCHIE	4,728	1,590	2,844	294	1,254 D	33.6%	60.2%	35.9%	64.1%
20,119	TATE	5,151	1,593	3,173	385	1,580 D	30.9%	61.6%	33.4%	66.6%
18,739	TIPPAH	7,283	2,714	4,253	316	1,539 D	37.3%	58.4%	39.0%	61.0%
18,434	TISHOMINGO	4,409	1,281	2,984	144	1,703 D	29.1%	67.7%	30.0%	70.0%
9,652	TUNICA	2,697	875	1,530	292	655 D	32.4%	56.7%	36.4%	63.6%
21,741	UNION	6,395	2,930	3,224	241	294 D	45.8%	50.4%	47.6%	52.4%
13,761	WALTHALL	4,055	1,176	2,708	171	1,532 D	29.0%	66.8%	30.3%	69.7%
51,627	WARREN	14,849	5,760	8,387	702	2,627 D	38.8%	56.5%	40.7%	59.3%
72,344	WASHINGTON	15,514	5,774	8,798	942	3,024 D	37.2%	56.7%	39.6%	60.4%
19,135	WAYNE	6,630	2,677	3,641	312	964 D	40.4%	54.9%	42.4%	57.6%
10,300	WEBSTER	3,979	1,424	2,417	138	993 D	35.8%	60.7%	37.1%	62.9%
10,021	WILKINSON	4,641	960	2,626	1,055	1,666 D	20.7%	56.6%	26.8%	73.2%
19,474	WINSTON	7,622	3,106	4,119	397	1,013 D	40.8%	54.0%	43.0%	57.0%
13,139	YALOBUSHA	4,386	1,436	2,630	320	1,194 D	32.7%	60.0%	35.3%	64.7%
27,349	YAZOO	11,029	4,099	6,132	798	2,033 D	37.2%	55.6%	40.1%	59.9%
2,520,638	TOTAL	742,737	288,764	409,209	44,764	120,445 D	38.9%	55.1%	41.4%	58.6%

MISSISSIPPI

SENATOR 1984

1980 Census Population	County	Total Vote	Republican	Democratic	Other	Rep.-Dem. Plurality	Percentage Total Vote Rep.	Dem.	Major Vote Rep.	Dem.
38,035	ADAMS	16,764	9,628	7,136		2,492 R	57.4%	42.6%	57.4%	42.6%
33,036	ALCORN	11,652	6,497	5,155		1,342 R	55.8%	44.2%	55.8%	44.2%
13,369	AMITE	6,318	3,539	2,779		760 R	56.0%	44.0%	56.0%	44.0%
19,865	ATTALA	8,312	5,074	3,238		1,836 R	61.0%	39.0%	61.0%	39.0%
8,153	BENTON	3,539	1,770	1,769		1 R	50.0%	50.0%	50.0%	50.0%
45,965	BOLIVAR	14,984	7,311	7,673		362 D	48.8%	51.2%	48.8%	51.2%
15,664	CALHOUN	5,657	3,652	2,005		1,647 R	64.6%	35.4%	64.6%	35.4%
9,776	CARROLL	4,512	2,875	1,637		1,238 R	63.7%	36.3%	63.7%	36.3%
17,853	CHICKASAW	6,153	3,631	2,522		1,109 R	59.0%	41.0%	59.0%	41.0%
8,996	CHOCTAW	3,783	2,641	1,142		1,499 R	69.8%	30.2%	69.8%	30.2%
12,279	CLAIBORNE	4,723	1,395	3,328		1,933 D	29.5%	70.5%	29.5%	70.5%
16,945	CLARKE	6,999	4,719	2,280		2,439 R	67.4%	32.6%	67.4%	32.6%
21,082	CLAY	8,735	4,324	4,411		87 D	49.5%	50.5%	49.5%	50.5%
36,918	COAHOMA	11,850	5,656	6,194		538 D	47.7%	52.3%	47.7%	52.3%
26,503	COPIAH	10,659	5,744	4,915		829 R	53.9%	46.1%	53.9%	46.1%
15,927	COVINGTON	6,784	4,460	2,324		2,136 R	65.7%	34.3%	65.7%	34.3%
53,930	DE SOTO	18,048	11,921	6,127		5,794 R	66.1%	33.9%	66.1%	33.9%
66,018	FORREST	23,206	16,086	7,120		8,966 R	69.3%	30.7%	69.3%	30.7%
8,208	FRANKLIN	4,152	2,704	1,448		1,256 R	65.1%	34.9%	65.1%	34.9%
15,297	GEORGE	6,484	4,231	2,253		1,978 R	65.3%	34.7%	65.3%	34.7%
9,827	GREENE	4,281	2,753	1,528		1,225 R	64.3%	35.7%	64.3%	35.7%
21,043	GRENADA	8,789	5,050	3,739		1,311 R	57.5%	42.5%	57.5%	42.5%
24,537	HANCOCK	10,632	7,014	3,618		3,396 R	66.0%	34.0%	66.0%	34.0%
157,665	HARRISON	48,555	32,946	15,609		17,337 R	67.9%	32.1%	67.9%	32.1%
250,998	HINDS	99,181	57,455	41,726		15,729 R	57.9%	42.1%	57.9%	42.1%
22,970	HOLMES	9,076	3,245	5,831		2,586 D	35.8%	64.2%	35.8%	64.2%
13,931	HUMPHREYS	5,251	2,551	2,700		149 D	48.6%	51.4%	48.6%	51.4%
2,513	ISSAQUENA	983	521	462		59 R	53.0%	47.0%	53.0%	47.0%
20,518	ITAWAMBA	7,639	4,480	3,159		1,321 R	58.6%	41.4%	58.6%	41.4%
118,015	JACKSON	40,763	28,241	12,522		15,719 R	69.3%	30.7%	69.3%	30.7%
17,265	JASPER	7,330	4,106	3,224		882 R	56.0%	44.0%	56.0%	44.0%
9,181	JEFFERSON	4,065	1,045	3,020		1,975 D	25.7%	74.3%	25.7%	74.3%
13,846	JEFFERSON DAVIS	6,206	3,241	2,965		276 R	52.2%	47.8%	52.2%	47.8%
61,912	JONES	25,136	18,164	6,972		11,192 R	72.3%	27.7%	72.3%	27.7%
10,148	KEMPER	4,632	2,436	2,196		240 R	52.6%	47.4%	52.6%	47.4%
31,030	LAFAYETTE	9,797	5,733	4,064		1,669 R	58.5%	41.5%	58.5%	41.5%
23,821	LAMAR	10,383	8,247	2,136		6,111 R	79.4%	20.6%	79.4%	20.6%
77,285	LAUDERDALE	26,440	18,224	8,216		10,008 R	68.9%	31.1%	68.9%	31.1%
12,518	LAWRENCE	6,409	4,105	2,304		1,801 R	64.1%	35.9%	64.1%	35.9%
18,790	LEAKE	7,641	4,748	2,893		1,855 R	62.1%	37.9%	62.1%	37.9%
57,061	LEE	19,148	12,241	6,907		5,334 R	63.9%	36.1%	63.9%	36.1%
41,525	LEFLORE	14,336	7,361	6,975		386 R	51.3%	48.7%	51.3%	48.7%
30,174	LINCOLN	13,719	9,485	4,234		5,251 R	69.1%	30.9%	69.1%	30.9%
57,304	LOWNDES	19,085	11,845	7,240		4,605 R	62.1%	37.9%	62.1%	37.9%
41,613	MADISON	16,541	9,046	7,495		1,551 R	54.7%	45.3%	54.7%	45.3%
25,708	MARION	11,126	7,440	3,686		3,754 R	66.9%	33.1%	66.9%	33.1%
29,296	MARSHALL	10,339	4,757	5,582		825 D	46.0%	54.0%	46.0%	54.0%
36,404	MONROE	12,469	7,181	5,288		1,893 R	57.6%	42.4%	57.6%	42.4%
13,366	MONTGOMERY	5,340	3,197	2,143		1,054 R	59.9%	40.1%	59.9%	40.1%
23,789	NESHOBA	9,562	6,763	2,799		3,964 R	70.7%	29.3%	70.7%	29.3%
19,944	NEWTON	8,383	6,134	2,249		3,885 R	73.2%	26.8%	73.2%	26.8%
13,212	NOXUBEE	5,272	2,271	3,001		730 D	43.1%	56.9%	43.1%	56.9%
36,018	OKTIBBEHA	13,095	7,577	5,518		2,059 R	57.9%	42.1%	57.9%	42.1%
28,164	PANOLA	11,705	5,943	5,762		181 R	50.8%	49.2%	50.8%	49.2%
33,795	PEARL RIVER	12,976	9,027	3,949		5,078 R	69.6%	30.4%	69.6%	30.4%
9,864	PERRY	4,634	3,124	1,510		1,614 R	67.4%	32.6%	67.4%	32.6%
36,173	PIKE	14,634	8,223	6,411		1,812 R	56.2%	43.8%	56.2%	43.8%
20,918	PONTOTOC	7,828	5,026	2,802		2,224 R	64.2%	35.8%	64.2%	35.8%
24,025	PRENTISS	7,869	4,504	3,365		1,139 R	57.2%	42.8%	57.2%	42.8%
12,636	QUITMAN	4,646	2,198	2,448		250 D	47.3%	52.7%	47.3%	52.7%

MISSISSIPPI

SENATOR 1984

1980 Census Population	County	Total Vote	Republican	Democratic	Other	Rep.-Dem. Plurality	Percentage Total Vote Rep.	Dem.	Major Vote Rep.	Dem.
69,427	RANKIN	28,837	22,399	6,438		15,961 R	77.7%	22.3%	77.7%	22.3%
24,556	SCOTT	9,345	5,945	3,400		2,545 R	63.6%	36.4%	63.6%	36.4%
7,964	SHARKEY	3,140	1,438	1,702		264 D	45.8%	54.2%	45.8%	54.2%
23,441	SIMPSON	9,592	6,404	3,188		3,216 R	66.8%	33.2%	66.8%	33.2%
15,077	SMITH	6,938	5,295	1,643		3,652 R	76.3%	23.7%	76.3%	23.7%
9,716	STONE	4,246	2,908	1,338		1,570 R	68.5%	31.5%	68.5%	31.5%
34,844	SUNFLOWER	10,350	5,237	5,113		124 R	50.6%	49.4%	50.6%	49.4%
17,157	TALLAHATCHIE	5,707	2,866	2,841		25 R	50.2%	49.8%	50.2%	49.8%
20,119	TATE	7,650	4,247	3,403		844 R	55.5%	44.5%	55.5%	44.5%
18,739	TIPPAH	7,694	4,597	3,097		1,500 R	59.7%	40.3%	59.7%	40.3%
18,434	TISHOMINGO	6,736	3,428	3,308		120 R	50.9%	49.1%	50.9%	49.1%
9,652	TUNICA	2,827	1,238	1,589		351 D	43.8%	56.2%	43.8%	56.2%
21,741	UNION	8,852	5,611	3,241		2,370 R	63.4%	36.6%	63.4%	36.6%
13,761	WALTHALL	5,678	3,483	2,195		1,288 R	61.3%	38.7%	61.3%	38.7%
51,627	WARREN	20,195	12,729	7,466		5,263 R	63.0%	37.0%	63.0%	37.0%
72,344	WASHINGTON	22,371	11,621	10,750		871 R	51.9%	48.1%	51.9%	48.1%
19,135	WAYNE	7,994	5,271	2,723		2,548 R	65.9%	34.1%	65.9%	34.1%
10,300	WEBSTER	4,843	3,467	1,376		2,091 R	71.6%	28.4%	71.6%	28.4%
10,021	WILKINSON	4,388	1,888	2,500		612 D	43.0%	57.0%	43.0%	57.0%
19,474	WINSTON	9,131	5,375	3,756		1,619 R	58.9%	41.1%	58.9%	41.1%
13,139	YALOBUSHA	5,399	3,025	2,374		651 R	56.0%	44.0%	56.0%	44.0%
27,349	YAZOO	11,117	6,336	4,781		1,555 R	57.0%	43.0%	57.0%	43.0%
2,520,638	TOTAL	952,240	580,314	371,926		208,388 R	60.9%	39.1%	60.9%	39.1%

MISSISSIPPI

CONGRESS

CD	Year	Total Vote	Republican Vote	Candidate	Democratic Vote	Candidate	Other Vote	Rep.-Dem. Plurality	Percentage Total Vote Rep.	Dem.	Major Vote Rep.	Dem.
1	1984	154,521			136,530	WHITTEN, JAMIE L.	17,991	136,530 D		88.4%		100.0%
2	1984	182,420	92,392	FRANKLIN, WEBB	89,154	CLARK, ROBERT G.	874	3,238 R	50.6%	48.9%	50.9%	49.1%
3	1984	158,002			158,002	MONTGOMERY, G. V.		158,002 D		100.0%		100.0%
4	1984	205,432	91,797	ARMSTRONG, DAVID	113,635	DOWDY, WAYNE		21,838 D	44.7%	55.3%	44.7%	55.3%
5	1984	168,477	142,637	LOTT, TRENT	25,840	COATE, ARLON		116,797 R	84.7%	15.3%	84.7%	15.3%

MISSISSIPPI

1983 GENERAL ELECTION

Governor   Other vote was 30,593 Evers (Independent); 7,869 Taylor (Independent); 6,302 Williams (Independent). Mr. Evers ran second in Jefferson and Wilkinson counties.

1984 GENERAL ELECTION

President   Other vote was 2,336 Bergland (Libertarian); 1,169 Holmes (Independent); 1,032 Mason (Independent); 1,001 LaRouche (Independent); 641 Richards (Independent); 356 Serrette (Independent).

Senator

Congress   Other vote was Hargett (Independent) in CD 1; Caraway (Independent) in CD 2.

1983 PRIMARIES

AUGUST 2 REPUBLICAN

Governor   Leon Bramlett, unopposed.

AUGUST 2 DEMOCRATIC

Governor   316,304 Evelyn Gandy; 293,348 William A. Allain; 172,526 Mike P. Sturdivant; 32,861 Lonnie C. Johnson; 13,172 Billy M. Davis.

AUGUST 23 DEMOCRATIC RUN-OFF

Govenor   405,348 William A. Allain; 367,953 Evelyn Gandy.

1984 PRIMARIES

JUNE 5 REPUBLICAN

Senator   Thad Cochran, unopposed.

Congress   Unopposed in three CD's. No candidate in CD's 1 and 3.

JUNE 5 DEMOCRATIC

Senator   88,883 William F. Winter; 15,363 W. W. Easley; 13,843 William L. Gilbert; 9,768 Billy Taylor.

Congress   Unopposed in three CD's. Contested as follows:

CD 1   23,184 Jamie L. Whitten; 3,088 Breezy Weathers.
CD 2   27,534 Robert G. Clark; 9,578 Richard Barrett; 4,118 Robert Gray; 2,927 Evan Doss.

MISSOURI

GOVERNOR
John Ashcroft (R). Elected 1984 to a four-year term.

SENATORS
John C. Danforth (R). Re-elected 1982 to a six-year term. Previously elected 1976.

Thomas F. Eagleton (D). Re-elected 1980 to a six-year term. Previously elected 1974, 1968.

REPRESENTATIVES

1. William Clay (D)
2. Robert A. Young (D)
3. Richard A. Gephardt (D)
4. Ike Skelton (D)
5. Alan Wheat (D)
6. E. Thomas Coleman (R)
7. Gene Taylor (R)
8. Bill Emerson (R)
9. Harold Volkmer (D)

POSTWAR VOTE FOR GOVERNOR

| | | | | | | | | | Percentage | | | |
| | Total | Republican | | Democratic | | Other | Rep.-Dem. | Total Vote | | Major Vote | |
Year	Vote	Vote	Candidate	Vote	Candidate	Vote	Plurality	Rep.	Dem.	Rep.	Dem.
1984	2,108,210	1,194,506	Ashcroft, John	913,700	Rothman, Kenneth J.	4	280,806 R	56.7%	43.3%	56.7%	43.3%
1980	2,088,028	1,098,950	Bond, Christopher	981,884	Teasdale, Joseph P.	7,194	117,066 R	52.6%	47.0%	52.8%	47.2%
1976	1,933,575	958,110	Bond, Christopher	971,184	Teasdale, Joseph P.	4,281	13,074 D	49.6%	50.2%	49.7%	50.3%
1972	1,865,683	1,029,451	Bond, Christopher	832,751	Dowd, Edward L.	3,481	196,700 R	55.2%	44.6%	55.3%	44.7%
1968	1,764,602	691,797	Roos, Lawrence K.	1,072,805	Hearnes, Warren E.	—	381,008 D	39.2%	60.8%	39.2%	60.8%
1964	1,789,600	678,949	Shepley, Ethan	1,110,651	Hearnes, Warren E.	—	431,702 D	37.9%	62.1%	37.9%	62.1%
1960	1,887,331	792,131	Farmer, Edward G.	1,095,200	Dalton, John M.	—	303,069 D	42.0%	58.0%	42.0%	58.0%
1956	1,808,338	866,810	Hocker, Lon	941,528	Blair, James T.	—	74,718 D	47.9%	52.1%	47.9%	52.1%
1952	1,871,095	886,370	Elliott, Howard	983,166	Donnelly, Phil M.	1,559	96,796 D	47.4%	52.5%	47.4%	52.6%
1948	1,567,338	670,064	Thompson, Murray	893,092	Smith, Forrest	4,182	223,028 D	42.8%	57.0%	42.9%	57.1%

POSTWAR VOTE FOR SENATOR

| | | | | | | | | | Percentage | | | |
| | Total | Republican | | Democratic | | Other | Rep.-Dem. | Total Vote | | Major Vote | |
Year	Vote	Vote	Candidate	Vote	Candidate	Vote	Plurality	Rep.	Dem.	Rep.	Dem.
1982	1,543,521	784,876	Danforth, John C.	758,629	Woods, Harriett	16	26,247 R	50.8%	49.1%	50.9%	49.1%
1980	2,066,965	985,399	McNary, Gene	1,074,859	Eagleton, Thomas F.	6,707	89,460 D	47.7%	52.0%	47.8%	52.2%
1976	1,914,777	1,090,067	Danforth, John C.	813,571	Hearnes, Warren E.	11,139	276,496 R	56.9%	42.5%	57.3%	42.7%
1974	1,224,303	480,900	Curtis, Thomas B.	735,433	Eagleton, Thomas F.	7,970	254,533 D	39.3%	60.1%	39.5%	60.5%
1970	1,283,912	617,903	Danforth, John C.	655,431	Symington, Stuart	10,578	37,528 D	48.1%	51.0%	48.5%	51.5%
1968	1,737,958	850,544	Curtis, Thomas B.	887,414	Eagleton, Thomas F.	—	36,870 D	48.9%	51.1%	48.9%	51.1%
1964	1,783,043	596,377	Bradshaw, Jean P.	1,186,666	Symington, Stuart	—	590,289 D	33.4%	66.6%	33.4%	66.6%
1962	1,222,259	555,330	Kemper, Crosby	666,929	Long, Edward V.	—	111,599 D	45.4%	54.6%	45.4%	54.6%
1960s	1,880,232	880,576	Hocker, Lon	999,656	Long, Edward V.	—	119,080 D	46.8%	53.2%	46.8%	53.2%
1958	1,173,903	393,847	Palmer, Hazel	780,056	Symington, Stuart	—	386,209 D	33.6%	66.4%	33.6%	66.4%
1956	1,800,984	785,048	Douglas, Herbert	1,015,936	Hennings, Thomas C.	—	230,888 D	43.6%	56.4%	43.6%	56.4%
1952	1,868,083	858,170	Kem, James P.	1,008,523	Symington, Stuart	1,390	150,353 D	45.9%	54.0%	46.0%	54.0%
1950	1,279,414	592,922	Donnell, Forrest C.	685,732	Hennings, Thomas C.	760	92,810 D	46.3%	53.6%	46.4%	53.6%
1946	1,084,100	572,556	Kem, James P.	511,544	Briggs, Frank P.	—	61,012 R	52.8%	47.2%	52.8%	47.2%

The 1960 election was for a short term to fill a vacancy.

MISSOURI

Districts Established January 7, 1982

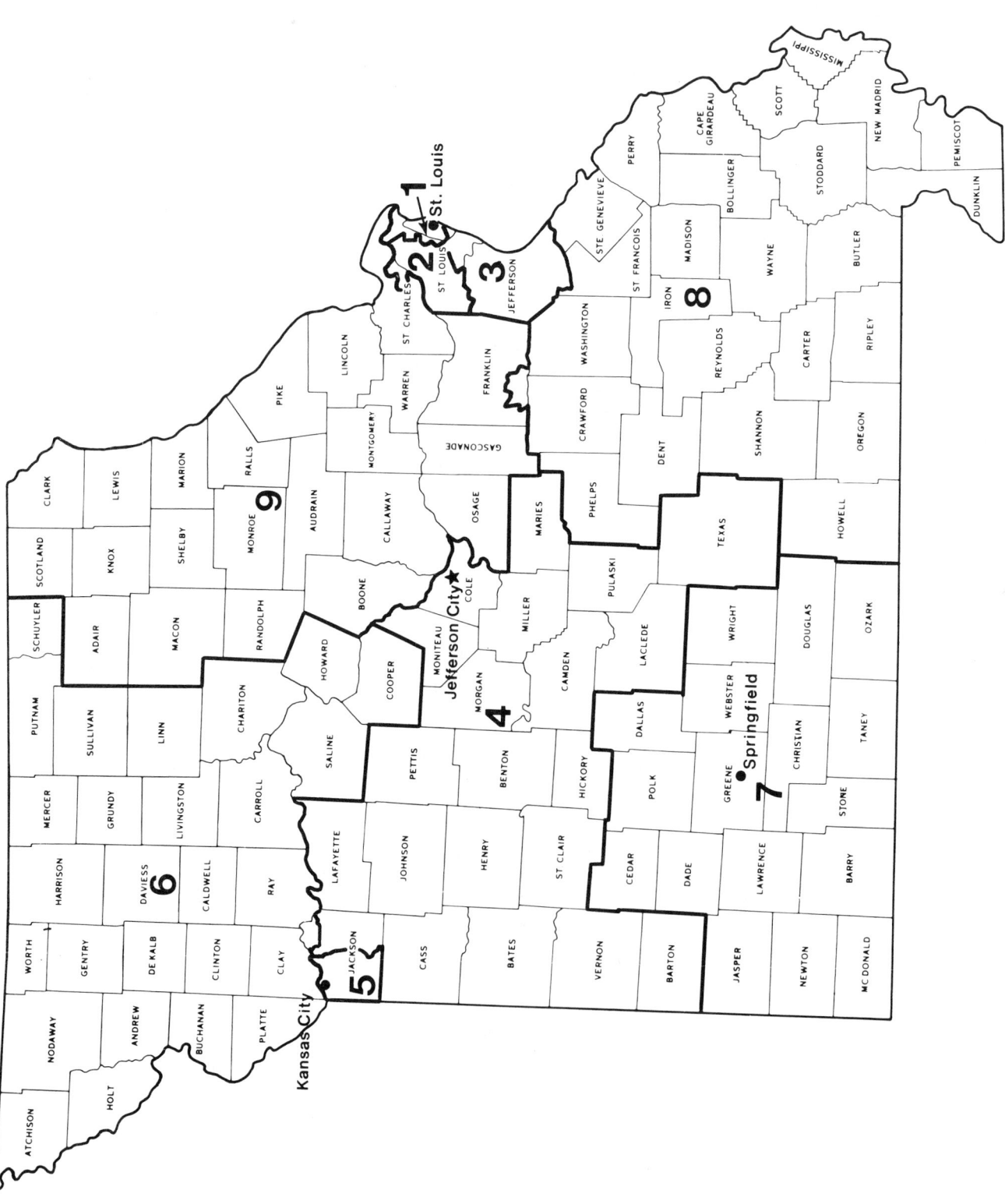

MISSOURI

PRESIDENT 1984

1980 Census Population	County	Total Vote	Republican	Democratic	Other	Rep.-Dem. Plurality	Percentage			
							Total Vote		Major Vote	
							Rep.	Dem.	Rep.	Dem.
24,870	ADAIR	9,549	6,430	3,119		3,311 R	67.3%	32.7%	67.3%	32.7%
13,980	ANDREW	6,709	4,252	2,457		1,795 R	63.4%	36.6%	63.4%	36.6%
8,605	ATCHISON	3,496	2,277	1,219		1,058 R	65.1%	34.9%	65.1%	34.9%
26,458	AUDRAIN	11,923	7,261	4,662		2,599 R	60.9%	39.1%	60.9%	39.1%
24,408	BARRY	11,166	7,683	3,483		4,200 R	68.8%	31.2%	68.8%	31.2%
11,292	BARTON	5,344	3,996	1,348		2,648 R	74.8%	25.2%	74.8%	25.2%
15,873	BATES	7,112	4,223	2,889		1,334 R	59.4%	40.6%	59.4%	40.6%
12,183	BENTON	6,056	3,805	2,251		1,554 R	62.8%	37.2%	62.8%	37.2%
10,301	BOLLINGER	4,701	2,778	1,923		855 R	59.1%	40.9%	59.1%	40.9%
100,376	BOONE	45,964	26,600	19,364		7,236 R	57.9%	42.1%	57.9%	42.1%
87,888	BUCHANAN	35,104	19,735	15,369		4,366 R	56.2%	43.8%	56.2%	43.8%
37,693	BUTLER	13,411	8,712	4,699		4,013 R	65.0%	35.0%	65.0%	35.0%
8,660	CALDWELL	4,060	2,678	1,382		1,296 R	66.0%	34.0%	66.0%	34.0%
32,252	CALLAWAY	12,589	8,262	4,327		3,935 R	65.6%	34.4%	65.6%	34.4%
20,017	CAMDEN	11,145	8,057	3,088		4,969 R	72.3%	27.7%	72.3%	27.7%
58,837	CAPE GIRARDEAU	24,750	17,404	7,346		10,058 R	70.3%	29.7%	70.3%	29.7%
12,131	CARROLL	5,475	3,495	1,980		1,515 R	63.8%	36.2%	63.8%	36.2%
5,428	CARTER	2,318	1,402	916		486 R	60.5%	39.5%	60.5%	39.5%
51,029	CASS	21,973	14,456	7,517		6,939 R	65.8%	34.2%	65.8%	34.2%
11,894	CEDAR	4,979	3,539	1,440		2,099 R	71.1%	28.9%	71.1%	28.9%
10,489	CHARITON	4,988	2,744	2,244		500 R	55.0%	45.0%	55.0%	45.0%
22,402	CHRISTIAN	10,857	7,634	3,223		4,411 R	70.3%	29.7%	70.3%	29.7%
8,493	CLARK	3,695	2,068	1,627		441 R	56.0%	44.0%	56.0%	44.0%
136,488	CLAY	59,116	36,529	22,586	1	13,943 R	61.8%	38.2%	61.8%	38.2%
15,916	CLINTON	7,004	4,226	2,778		1,448 R	60.3%	39.7%	60.3%	39.7%
56,663	COLE	27,068	20,366	6,702		13,664 R	75.2%	24.8%	75.2%	24.8%
14,643	COOPER	6,822	4,603	2,219		2,384 R	67.5%	32.5%	67.5%	32.5%
18,300	CRAWFORD	7,326	4,716	2,610		2,106 R	64.4%	35.6%	64.4%	35.6%
7,383	DADE	3,700	2,600	1,100		1,500 R	70.3%	29.7%	70.3%	29.7%
12,096	DALLAS	5,479	3,577	1,902		1,675 R	65.3%	34.7%	65.3%	34.7%
8,905	DAVIESS	3,940	2,414	1,526		888 R	61.3%	38.7%	61.3%	38.7%
8,222	DE KALB	3,652	2,188	1,464		724 R	59.9%	40.1%	59.9%	40.1%
14,517	DENT	6,034	3,490	2,544		946 R	57.8%	42.2%	57.8%	42.2%
11,594	DOUGLAS	5,199	3,662	1,536	1	2,126 R	70.4%	29.5%	70.5%	29.5%
36,324	DUNKLIN	11,059	6,092	4,967		1,125 R	55.1%	44.9%	55.1%	44.9%
71,233	FRANKLIN	26,988	18,669	8,319		10,350 R	69.2%	30.8%	69.2%	30.8%
13,181	GASCONADE	5,808	4,678	1,130		3,548 R	80.5%	19.5%	80.5%	19.5%
7,887	GENTRY	3,647	2,047	1,600		447 R	56.1%	43.9%	56.1%	43.9%
185,302	GREENE	85,215	57,250	27,965		29,285 R	67.2%	32.8%	67.2%	32.8%
11,959	GRUNDY	5,017	3,156	1,861		1,295 R	62.9%	37.1%	62.9%	37.1%
9,890	HARRISON	4,493	2,844	1,649		1,195 R	63.3%	36.7%	63.3%	36.7%
19,672	HENRY	9,160	5,419	3,741		1,678 R	59.2%	40.8%	59.2%	40.8%
6,367	HICKORY	3,402	2,190	1,212		978 R	64.4%	35.6%	64.4%	35.6%
6,882	HOLT	3,113	2,087	1,026		1,061 R	67.0%	33.0%	67.0%	33.0%
10,008	HOWARD	4,374	2,360	2,014		346 R	54.0%	46.0%	54.0%	46.0%
28,807	HOWELL	11,971	8,204	3,767		4,437 R	68.5%	31.5%	68.5%	31.5%
11,084	IRON	4,339	2,316	2,023		293 R	53.4%	46.6%	53.4%	46.6%
629,266	JACKSON	267,347	132,271	135,067	9	2,796 D	49.5%	50.5%	49.5%	50.5%
86,958	JASPER	32,325	23,066	9,259		13,807 R	71.4%	28.6%	71.4%	28.6%
146,183	JEFFERSON	54,551	34,525	20,026		14,499 R	63.3%	36.7%	63.3%	36.7%
39,059	JOHNSON	12,651	8,413	4,238		4,175 R	66.5%	33.5%	66.5%	33.5%
5,508	KNOX	2,610	1,513	1,097		416 R	58.0%	42.0%	58.0%	42.0%
24,323	LACLEDE	9,071	6,406	2,665		3,741 R	70.6%	29.4%	70.6%	29.4%
29,925	LAFAYETTE	13,429	8,581	4,848		3,733 R	63.9%	36.1%	63.9%	36.1%
28,973	LAWRENCE	12,090	8,370	3,720		4,650 R	69.2%	30.8%	69.2%	30.8%
10,901	LEWIS	4,415	2,438	1,977		461 R	55.2%	44.8%	55.2%	44.8%
22,193	LINCOLN	9,427	6,137	3,290		2,847 R	65.1%	34.9%	65.1%	34.9%
15,495	LINN	6,934	3,822	3,112		710 R	55.1%	44.9%	55.1%	44.9%
15,739	LIVINGSTON	6,789	4,090	2,699		1,391 R	60.2%	39.8%	60.2%	39.8%
14,917	MCDONALD	6,630	4,521	2,109		2,412 R	68.2%	31.8%	68.2%	31.8%

MISSOURI

PRESIDENT 1984

1980 Census Population	County	Total Vote	Republican	Democratic	Other	Rep.-Dem. Plurality	Percentage Total Vote Rep.	Dem.	Major Vote Rep.	Dem.
16,313	MACON	7,579	4,542	3,037		1,505 R	59.9%	40.1%	59.9%	40.1%
10,725	MADISON	4,670	2,808	1,862		946 R	60.1%	39.9%	60.1%	39.9%
7,551	MARIES	3,655	2,267	1,388		879 R	62.0%	38.0%	62.0%	38.0%
28,638	MARION	11,497	6,831	4,666		2,165 R	59.4%	40.6%	59.4%	40.6%
4,685	MERCER	2,104	1,229	875		354 R	58.4%	41.6%	58.4%	41.6%
18,532	MILLER	8,760	6,706	2,054		4,652 R	76.6%	23.4%	76.6%	23.4%
15,726	MISSISSIPPI	5,026	2,502	2,524		22 D	49.8%	50.2%	49.8%	50.2%
12,068	MONITEAU	5,811	4,197	1,614		2,583 R	72.2%	27.8%	72.2%	27.8%
9,716	MONROE	4,155	2,163	1,992		171 R	52.1%	47.9%	52.1%	47.9%
11,537	MONTGOMERY	4,929	3,261	1,668		1,593 R	66.2%	33.8%	66.2%	33.8%
13,807	MORGAN	6,561	4,392	2,169		2,223 R	66.9%	33.1%	66.9%	33.1%
22,945	NEW MADRID	8,099	4,323	3,776		547 R	53.4%	46.6%	53.4%	46.6%
40,555	NEWTON	16,332	11,709	4,623		7,086 R	71.7%	28.3%	71.7%	28.3%
21,996	NODAWAY	9,086	5,471	3,615		1,856 R	60.2%	39.8%	60.2%	39.8%
10,238	OREGON	4,005	1,979	2,026		47 D	49.4%	50.6%	49.4%	50.6%
12,014	OSAGE	5,724	4,381	1,343		3,038 R	76.5%	23.5%	76.5%	23.5%
7,961	OZARK	3,724	2,614	1,110		1,504 R	70.2%	29.8%	70.2%	29.8%
24,987	PEMISCOT	7,026	3,733	3,293		440 R	53.1%	46.9%	53.1%	46.9%
16,784	PERRY	6,330	4,493	1,837		2,656 R	71.0%	29.0%	71.0%	29.0%
36,378	PETTIS	16,404	10,991	5,413		5,578 R	67.0%	33.0%	67.0%	33.0%
33,633	PHELPS	14,086	9,012	5,074		3,938 R	64.0%	36.0%	64.0%	36.0%
17,568	PIKE	7,246	3,933	3,313		620 R	54.3%	45.7%	54.3%	45.7%
46,341	PLATTE	20,527	12,859	7,668		5,191 R	62.6%	37.4%	62.6%	37.4%
18,822	POLK	8,286	5,467	2,819		2,648 R	66.0%	34.0%	66.0%	34.0%
42,011	PULASKI	8,195	5,330	2,865		2,465 R	65.0%	35.0%	65.0%	35.0%
6,092	PUTNAM	2,337	1,540	797		743 R	65.9%	34.1%	65.9%	34.1%
8,911	RALLS	4,078	2,067	2,011		56 R	50.7%	49.3%	50.7%	49.3%
25,460	RANDOLPH	10,206	5,735	4,471		1,264 R	56.2%	43.8%	56.2%	43.8%
21,378	RAY	8,854	4,875	3,979		896 R	55.1%	44.9%	55.1%	44.9%
7,230	REYNOLDS	3,356	1,330	2,026		696 D	39.6%	60.4%	39.6%	60.4%
12,458	RIPLEY	4,810	2,927	1,883		1,044 R	60.9%	39.1%	60.9%	39.1%
144,107	ST. CHARLES	65,401	47,784	17,617		30,167 R	73.1%	26.9%	73.1%	26.9%
8,622	ST. CLAIR	4,322	2,667	1,655		1,012 R	61.7%	38.3%	61.7%	38.3%
42,600	ST. FRANCOIS	16,929	9,792	7,137		2,655 R	57.8%	42.2%	57.8%	42.2%
453,085	ST. LOUIS CITY	173,338	61,020	112,318		51,298 D	35.2%	64.8%	35.2%	64.8%
973,896	ST. LOUIS COUNTY	480,828	307,684	173,144		134,540 R	64.0%	36.0%	64.0%	36.0%
15,180	STE. GENEVIEVE	5,968	3,245	2,723		522 R	54.4%	45.6%	54.4%	45.6%
24,919	SALINE	10,323	6,042	4,281		1,761 R	58.5%	41.5%	58.5%	41.5%
4,979	SCHUYLER	2,391	1,250	1,141		109 R	52.3%	47.7%	52.3%	47.7%
5,415	SCOTLAND	2,560	1,485	1,075		410 R	58.0%	42.0%	58.0%	42.0%
39,647	SCOTT	14,297	8,727	5,569	1	3,158 R	61.0%	39.0%	61.0%	39.0%
7,885	SHANNON	3,359	1,779	1,580		199 R	53.0%	47.0%	53.0%	47.0%
7,826	SHELBY	3,816	2,243	1,573		670 R	58.8%	41.2%	58.8%	41.2%
29,009	STODDARD	10,995	6,701	4,294		2,407 R	60.9%	39.1%	60.9%	39.1%
15,587	STONE	7,825	5,706	2,119		3,587 R	72.9%	27.1%	72.9%	27.1%
7,434	SULLIVAN	4,090	2,306	1,784		522 R	56.4%	43.6%	56.4%	43.6%
20,467	TANEY	9,994	7,082	2,912		4,170 R	70.9%	29.1%	70.9%	29.1%
21,070	TEXAS	9,253	5,591	3,662		1,929 R	60.4%	39.6%	60.4%	39.6%
19,806	VERNON	8,165	5,181	2,984		2,197 R	63.5%	36.5%	63.5%	36.5%
14,900	WARREN	7,114	5,150	1,964		3,186 R	72.4%	27.6%	72.4%	27.6%
17,983	WASHINGTON	6,742	3,755	2,987		768 R	55.7%	44.3%	55.7%	44.3%
11,277	WAYNE	5,230	2,867	2,363		504 R	54.8%	45.2%	54.8%	45.2%
20,414	WEBSTER	8,511	5,529	2,982		2,547 R	65.0%	35.0%	65.0%	35.0%
3,008	WORTH	1,655	921	734		187 R	55.6%	44.4%	55.6%	44.4%
16,188	WRIGHT	6,660	4,687	1,973		2,714 R	70.4%	29.6%	70.4%	29.6%
4,916,686	TOTAL	2,122,783	1,274,188	848,583	12	425,605 R	60.0%	40.0%	60.0%	40.0%

MISSOURI

GOVERNOR 1984

1980 Census Population	County	Total Vote	Republican	Democratic	Other	Rep.-Dem. Plurality	Percentage Total Vote Rep.	Dem.	Major Vote Rep.	Dem.
24,870	ADAIR	9,373	5,924	3,449		2,475 R	63.2%	36.8%	63.2%	36.8%
13,980	ANDREW	6,693	4,173	2,520		1,653 R	62.3%	37.7%	62.3%	37.7%
8,605	ATCHISON	3,395	2,136	1,259		877 R	62.9%	37.1%	62.9%	37.1%
26,458	AUDRAIN	11,906	7,077	4,829		2,248 R	59.4%	40.6%	59.4%	40.6%
24,408	BARRY	11,215	8,129	3,086		5,043 R	72.5%	27.5%	72.5%	27.5%
11,292	BARTON	5,301	3,944	1,357		2,587 R	74.4%	25.6%	74.4%	25.6%
15,873	BATES	7,088	3,932	3,156		776 R	55.5%	44.5%	55.5%	44.5%
12,183	BENTON	6,023	3,777	2,246		1,531 R	62.7%	37.3%	62.7%	37.3%
10,301	BOLLINGER	4,660	2,754	1,906		848 R	59.1%	40.9%	59.1%	40.9%
100,376	BOONE	45,480	25,967	19,513		6,454 R	57.1%	42.9%	57.1%	42.9%
87,888	BUCHANAN	34,987	18,668	16,319		2,349 R	53.4%	46.6%	53.4%	46.6%
37,693	BUTLER	13,198	7,875	5,323		2,552 R	59.7%	40.3%	59.7%	40.3%
8,660	CALDWELL	4,019	2,550	1,469		1,081 R	63.4%	36.6%	63.4%	36.6%
32,252	CALLAWAY	12,924	7,842	5,082		2,760 R	60.7%	39.3%	60.7%	39.3%
20,017	CAMDEN	11,035	7,957	3,078		4,879 R	72.1%	27.9%	72.1%	27.9%
58,837	CAPE GIRARDEAU	24,575	17,299	7,276		10,023 R	70.4%	29.6%	70.4%	29.6%
12,131	CARROLL	5,461	3,522	1,939		1,583 R	64.5%	35.5%	64.5%	35.5%
5,428	CARTER	2,264	1,388	876		512 R	61.3%	38.7%	61.3%	38.7%
51,029	CASS	21,956	13,481	8,475		5,006 R	61.4%	38.6%	61.4%	38.6%
11,894	CEDAR	4,899	3,541	1,358		2,183 R	72.3%	27.7%	72.3%	27.7%
10,489	CHARITON	4,962	2,689	2,273		416 R	54.2%	45.8%	54.2%	45.8%
22,402	CHRISTIAN	10,799	8,266	2,533		5,733 R	76.5%	23.5%	76.5%	23.5%
8,493	CLARK	3,620	1,968	1,652		316 R	54.4%	45.6%	54.4%	45.6%
136,488	CLAY	58,118	34,735	23,383		11,352 R	59.8%	40.2%	59.8%	40.2%
15,916	CLINTON	6,955	3,979	2,976		1,003 R	57.2%	42.8%	57.2%	42.8%
56,663	COLE	26,967	18,185	8,782		9,403 R	67.4%	32.6%	67.4%	32.6%
14,643	COOPER	6,753	4,397	2,356		2,041 R	65.1%	34.9%	65.1%	34.9%
18,300	CRAWFORD	7,242	4,408	2,834		1,574 R	60.9%	39.1%	60.9%	39.1%
7,383	DADE	3,690	2,842	848		1,994 R	77.0%	23.0%	77.0%	23.0%
12,096	DALLAS	5,445	3,857	1,588		2,269 R	70.8%	29.2%	70.8%	29.2%
8,905	DAVIESS	3,975	2,401	1,574		827 R	60.4%	39.6%	60.4%	39.6%
8,222	DE KALB	3,641	2,173	1,468		705 R	59.7%	40.3%	59.7%	40.3%
14,517	DENT	6,009	3,580	2,429		1,151 R	59.6%	40.4%	59.6%	40.4%
11,594	DOUGLAS	5,128	3,846	1,282		2,564 R	75.0%	25.0%	75.0%	25.0%
36,324	DUNKLIN	10,600	5,407	5,193		214 R	51.0%	49.0%	51.0%	49.0%
71,233	FRANKLIN	27,371	16,672	10,699		5,973 R	60.9%	39.1%	60.9%	39.1%
13,181	GASCONADE	5,740	4,341	1,399		2,942 R	75.6%	24.4%	75.6%	24.4%
7,887	GENTRY	3,633	2,061	1,572		489 R	56.7%	43.3%	56.7%	43.3%
185,302	GREENE	84,683	62,646	22,037		40,609 R	74.0%	26.0%	74.0%	26.0%
11,959	GRUNDY	5,003	3,251	1,752		1,499 R	65.0%	35.0%	65.0%	35.0%
9,890	HARRISON	4,431	2,837	1,594		1,243 R	64.0%	36.0%	64.0%	36.0%
19,672	HENRY	9,108	4,975	4,133		842 R	54.6%	45.4%	54.6%	45.4%
6,367	HICKORY	3,381	2,327	1,054		1,273 R	68.8%	31.2%	68.8%	31.2%
6,882	HOLT	3,102	2,055	1,047		1,008 R	66.2%	33.8%	66.2%	33.8%
10,008	HOWARD	4,338	2,281	2,057		224 R	52.6%	47.4%	52.6%	47.4%
28,807	HOWELL	11,955	8,476	3,479		4,997 R	70.9%	29.1%	70.9%	29.1%
11,084	IRON	4,253	2,127	2,126		1 R	50.0%	50.0%	50.0%	50.0%
629,266	JACKSON	264,078	125,538	138,536	4	12,998 D	47.5%	52.5%	47.5%	52.5%
86,958	JASPER	31,820	23,278	8,542		14,736 R	73.2%	26.8%	73.2%	26.8%
146,183	JEFFERSON	54,111	30,058	24,053		6,005 R	55.5%	44.5%	55.5%	44.5%
39,059	JOHNSON	12,587	7,891	4,696		3,195 R	62.7%	37.3%	62.7%	37.3%
5,508	KNOX	2,593	1,441	1,152		289 R	55.6%	44.4%	55.6%	44.4%
24,323	LACLEDE	9,021	6,370	2,651		3,719 R	70.6%	29.4%	70.6%	29.4%
29,925	LAFAYETTE	13,380	7,875	5,505		2,370 R	58.9%	41.1%	58.9%	41.1%
28,973	LAWRENCE	12,069	8,766	3,303		5,463 R	72.6%	27.4%	72.6%	27.4%
10,901	LEWIS	4,312	2,318	1,994		324 R	53.8%	46.2%	53.8%	46.2%
22,193	LINCOLN	9,375	5,165	4,210		955 R	55.1%	44.9%	55.1%	44.9%
15,495	LINN	6,907	3,732	3,175		557 R	54.0%	46.0%	54.0%	46.0%
15,739	LIVINGSTON	6,762	3,834	2,928		906 R	56.7%	43.3%	56.7%	43.3%
14,917	MCDONALD	6,549	4,500	2,049		2,451 R	68.7%	31.3%	68.7%	31.3%

MISSOURI

GOVERNOR 1984

1980 Census Population	County	Total Vote	Republican	Democratic	Other	Rep.-Dem. Plurality	Percentage Total Vote Rep.	Dem.	Major Vote Rep.	Dem.
16,313	MACON	7,552	4,203	3,349		854 R	55.7%	44.3%	55.7%	44.3%
10,725	MADISON	4,659	2,746	1,913		833 R	58.9%	41.1%	58.9%	41.1%
7,551	MARIES	3,693	2,104	1,589		515 R	57.0%	43.0%	57.0%	43.0%
28,638	MARION	11,433	6,039	5,394		645 R	52.8%	47.2%	52.8%	47.2%
4,685	MERCER	2,064	1,279	785		494 R	62.0%	38.0%	62.0%	38.0%
18,532	MILLER	8,731	6,300	2,431		3,869 R	72.2%	27.8%	72.2%	27.8%
15,726	MISSISSIPPI	4,893	2,307	2,586		279 D	47.1%	52.9%	47.1%	52.9%
12,068	MONITEAU	5,803	3,994	1,809		2,185 R	68.8%	31.2%	68.8%	31.2%
9,716	MONROE	4,144	1,930	2,214		284 D	46.6%	53.4%	46.6%	53.4%
11,537	MONTGOMERY	4,863	3,033	1,830		1,203 R	62.4%	37.6%	62.4%	37.6%
13,807	MORGAN	6,534	4,364	2,170		2,194 R	66.8%	33.2%	66.8%	33.2%
22,945	NEW MADRID	7,905	3,979	3,926		53 R	50.3%	49.7%	50.3%	49.7%
40,555	NEWTON	16,020	11,791	4,229		7,562 R	73.6%	26.4%	73.6%	26.4%
21,996	NODAWAY	9,093	5,236	3,857		1,379 R	57.6%	42.4%	57.6%	42.4%
10,238	OREGON	3,943	2,087	1,856		231 R	52.9%	47.1%	52.9%	47.1%
12,014	OSAGE	5,750	3,913	1,837		2,076 R	68.1%	31.9%	68.1%	31.9%
7,961	OZARK	3,660	2,742	918		1,824 R	74.9%	25.1%	74.9%	25.1%
24,987	PEMISCOT	6,741	3,112	3,629		517 D	46.2%	53.8%	46.2%	53.8%
16,784	PERRY	6,318	4,309	2,009		2,300 R	68.2%	31.8%	68.2%	31.8%
36,378	PETTIS	16,271	10,255	6,016		4,239 R	63.0%	37.0%	63.0%	37.0%
33,633	PHELPS	13,928	8,897	5,031		3,866 R	63.9%	36.1%	63.9%	36.1%
17,568	PIKE	7,144	3,573	3,571		2 R	50.0%	50.0%	50.0%	50.0%
46,341	PLATTE	20,398	12,146	8,252		3,894 R	59.5%	40.5%	59.5%	40.5%
18,822	POLK	8,412	5,923	2,489		3,434 R	70.4%	29.6%	70.4%	29.6%
42,011	PULASKI	8,164	5,104	3,060		2,044 R	62.5%	37.5%	62.5%	37.5%
6,092	PUTNAM	2,288	1,521	767		754 R	66.5%	33.5%	66.5%	33.5%
8,911	RALLS	4,034	1,837	2,197		360 D	45.5%	54.5%	45.5%	54.5%
25,460	RANDOLPH	10,178	5,636	4,542		1,094 R	55.4%	44.6%	55.4%	44.6%
21,378	RAY	8,782	4,336	4,446		110 D	49.4%	50.6%	49.4%	50.6%
7,230	REYNOLDS	3,315	1,308	2,007		699 D	39.5%	60.5%	39.5%	60.5%
12,458	RIPLEY	4,683	2,665	2,018		647 R	56.9%	43.1%	56.9%	43.1%
144,107	ST. CHARLES	65,442	41,222	24,220		17,002 R	63.0%	37.0%	63.0%	37.0%
8,622	ST. CLAIR	4,287	2,640	1,647		993 R	61.6%	38.4%	61.6%	38.4%
42,600	ST. FRANCOIS	16,845	8,777	8,068		709 R	52.1%	47.9%	52.1%	47.9%
453,085	ST. LOUIS CITY	172,627	56,169	116,458		60,289 D	32.5%	67.5%	32.5%	67.5%
973,896	ST. LOUIS COUNTY	478,898	269,100	209,798		59,302 R	56.2%	43.8%	56.2%	43.8%
15,180	STE. GENEVIEVE	5,958	3,070	2,888		182 R	51.5%	48.5%	51.5%	48.5%
24,919	SALINE	10,269	5,507	4,762		745 R	53.6%	46.4%	53.6%	46.4%
4,979	SCHUYLER	2,357	1,187	1,170		17 R	50.4%	49.6%	50.4%	49.6%
5,415	SCOTLAND	2,501	1,328	1,173		155 R	53.1%	46.9%	53.1%	46.9%
39,647	SCOTT	14,100	8,446	5,654		2,792 R	59.9%	40.1%	59.9%	40.1%
7,885	SHANNON	3,324	1,821	1,503		318 R	54.8%	45.2%	54.8%	45.2%
7,826	SHELBY	3,773	1,968	1,805		163 R	52.2%	47.8%	52.2%	47.8%
29,009	STODDARD	10,797	6,421	4,376		2,045 R	59.5%	40.5%	59.5%	40.5%
15,587	STONE	7,748	6,051	1,697		4,354 R	78.1%	21.9%	78.1%	21.9%
7,434	SULLIVAN	4,069	2,164	1,905		259 R	53.2%	46.8%	53.2%	46.8%
20,467	TANEY	9,884	7,527	2,357		5,170 R	76.2%	23.8%	76.2%	23.8%
21,070	TEXAS	9,256	5,866	3,390		2,476 R	63.4%	36.6%	63.4%	36.6%
19,806	VERNON	8,088	4,922	3,166		1,756 R	60.9%	39.1%	60.9%	39.1%
14,900	WARREN	6,973	4,313	2,660		1,653 R	61.9%	38.1%	61.9%	38.1%
17,983	WASHINGTON	6,724	3,460	3,264		196 R	51.5%	48.5%	51.5%	48.5%
11,277	WAYNE	5,181	2,787	2,394		393 R	53.8%	46.2%	53.8%	46.2%
20,414	WEBSTER	8,523	5,818	2,705		3,113 R	68.3%	31.7%	68.3%	31.7%
3,008	WORTH	1,639	861	778		83 R	52.5%	47.5%	52.5%	47.5%
16,188	WRIGHT	6,633	4,928	1,705		3,223 R	74.3%	25.7%	74.3%	25.7%
4,916,686	TOTAL	2,108,210	1,194,506	913,700	4	280,806 R	56.7%	43.3%	56.7%	43.3%

MISSOURI

CONGRESS

CD	Year	Total Vote	Republican Vote	Republican Candidate	Democratic Vote	Democratic Candidate	Other Vote	Rep.-Dem. Plurality	Total Vote Rep.	Total Vote Dem.	Major Vote Rep.	Major Vote Dem.
1	1984	215,974	68,538	RATHBONE, ERIC	147,436	CLAY, WILLIAM		78,898 D	31.7%	68.3%	31.7%	68.3%
1	1982	155,255	52,599	WHITE, WILLIAM E.	102,656	CLAY, WILLIAM		50,057 D	33.9%	66.1%	33.9%	66.1%
2	1984	268,616	127,710	BUECHNER, JOHN	139,123	YOUNG, ROBERT A.	1,783	11,413 D	47.5%	51.8%	47.9%	52.1%
2	1982	178,203	77,433	DIELMANN, HAROLD L.	100,770	YOUNG, ROBERT A.		23,337 D	43.5%	56.5%	43.5%	56.5%
3	1984	193,537			193,537	GEPHARDT, RICHARD A.		193,537 D		100.0%		100.0%
3	1982	168,954	37,388	FORISTEL, RICHARD	131,566	GEPHARDT, RICHARD A.		94,178 D	22.1%	77.9%	22.1%	77.9%
4	1984	225,058	74,434	RUSSELL, CARL D.	150,624	SKELTON, IKE		76,190 D	33.1%	66.9%	33.1%	66.9%
4	1982	175,953	79,565	BAILEY, WENDELL	96,388	SKELTON, IKE		16,823 D	45.2%	54.8%	45.2%	54.8%
5	1984	228,230	72,477	KENWORTHY, JIM	150,675	WHEAT, ALAN	5,078	78,198 D	31.8%	66.0%	32.5%	67.5%
5	1982	165,989	66,664	SHARP, JOHN A.	96,059	WHEAT, ALAN	3,266	29,395 D	40.2%	57.9%	41.0%	59.0%
6	1984	232,913	150,996	COLEMAN, E. THOMAS	81,917	HENSLEY, KENNETH C.		69,079 R	64.8%	35.2%	64.8%	35.2%
6	1982	177,046	97,993	COLEMAN, E. THOMAS	79,053	RUSSELL, JIM		18,940 R	55.3%	44.7%	55.3%	44.7%
7	1984	236,453	164,586	TAYLOR, GENE	71,867	YOUNG, KEN		92,719 R	69.6%	30.4%	69.6%	30.4%
7	1982	180,940	91,391	TAYLOR, GENE	89,549	GEISLER, DAVID A.		1,842 R	50.5%	49.5%	50.5%	49.5%
8	1984	205,108	134,186	EMERSON, BILL	70,922	BLUE, BILL		63,264 R	65.4%	34.6%	65.4%	34.6%
8	1982	162,906	86,493	EMERSON, BILL	76,413	FORD, JERRY		10,080 R	53.1%	46.9%	53.1%	46.9%
9	1984	233,688	110,100	FRANCKE, CARRIE	123,588	VOLKMER, HAROLD		13,488 D	47.1%	52.9%	47.1%	52.9%
9	1982	163,170	63,942	MEAD, LARRY E.	99,228	VOLKMER, HAROLD		35,286 D	39.2%	60.8%	39.2%	60.8%

MISSOURI

1984 GENERAL ELECTION

President   Other vote was 8 Mason (write-in); 2 Johnson (write-in); 1 Dennis (write-in); 1 scattered.

Governor   Other vote was scattered.

Congress   Other vote was Colopy (Libertarian) in CD 2; 5,068 Roberts (Libertarian) and 10 scattered in CD 5.

1984 PRIMARIES

AUGUST 7 REPUBLICAN

Governor   245,308 John Ashcroft; 115,516 Gene McNary; 2,814 Paul Binggeli.

Congress   Unopposed in six CD's. No candidate in CD 3. Contested as follows:

CD 1   8,385 Eric Rathbone; 8,272 Hugh V. Murray.
CD 5   8,610 Jim Kenworthy; 8,554 Mike Ethington; 5,295 Jim Olson.

AUGUST 7 DEMOCRATIC

Governor   288,543 Kenneth J. Rothman; 104,368 Mel Carnahan; 97,973 Norman L. Merrell; 10,149 Lavoy Reed; 5,839 Robert L. Buck; 5,141 Roy Smith; 2,832 Don Pine.

Congress   Unopposed in two CD's. Contested as follows:

CD 2   36,942 Robert A. Young; 3,754 Edward P. Roche.
CD 3   54,325 Richard A. Gephardt; 5,773 Anthony Logan.
CD 4   50,343 Ike Skelton; 10,146 Eric D. Hankins.
CD 5   53,141 Alan Wheat; 9,473 Frank Palermo; 2,490 Alan H. Deright.
CD 6   36,306 Kenneth C. Hensley; 20,737 H. N. Sutherland.
CD 7   13,893 Ken Young; 7,722 James W. Roberts.
CD 8   18,454 Bill Blue; 14,474 Shannon Russell; 13,617 Fred DeField; 9,396 Thad Bullock; 4,139 Leonard Bade.

MONTANA

GOVERNOR
Ted Schwinden (D). Re-elected 1984 to a four-year term. Previously elected 1980.

SENATORS
Max S. Baucus (D). Re-elected 1984 to a six-year term. Previously elected 1978.

John Melcher (D). Re-elected 1982 to a six-year term. Previously elected 1976.

REPRESENTATIVES
1. Pat Williams (D)   2. Ron Marlenee (R)

POSTWAR VOTE FOR GOVERNOR

| | | | | | | Other | Rep.-Dem. | Percentage | | | |
| | Total | Republican | | Democratic | | Vote | Plurality | Total Vote | | Major Vote | |
Year	Vote	Vote	Candidate	Vote	Candidate			Rep.	Dem.	Rep.	Dem.
1984	378,970	100,070	Goodover, Pat M.	266,578	Schwinden, Ted	12,322	166,508 D	26.4%	70.3%	27.3%	72.7%
1980	360,466	160,892	Ramirez, Jack	199,574	Schwinden, Ted	—	38,682 D	44.6%	55.4%	44.6%	55.4%
1976	316,720	115,848	Woodahl, Robert	195,420	Judge, Thomas L.	5,452	79,572 D	36.6%	61.7%	37.2%	62.8%
1972	318,754	146,231	Smith, Ed	172,523	Judge, Thomas L.	—	26,292 D	45.9%	54.1%	45.9%	54.1%
1968	278,112	116,432	Babcock, Tim M.	150,481	Anderson, Forrest H.	11,199	34,049 D	41.9%	54.1%	43.6%	56.4%
1964	280,975	144,113	Babcock, Tim M.	136,862	Renne, Roland	—	7,251 R	51.3%	48.7%	51.3%	48.7%
1960	279,881	154,230	Nutter, Donald G.	125,651	Cannon, Paul	—	28,579 R	55.1%	44.9%	55.1%	44.9%
1956	270,366	138,878	Aronson, J. Hugo	131,488	Olsen, Arnold H.	—	7,390 R	51.4%	48.6%	51.4%	48.6%
1952	263,792	134,423	Aronson, J. Hugo	129,369	Bonner, John W.	—	5,054 R	51.0%	49.0%	51.0%	49.0%
1948	222,964	97,792	Ford, Sam C.	124,267	Bonner, John W.	905	26,475 D	43.9%	55.7%	44.0%	56.0%

POSTWAR VOTE FOR SENATOR

| | | | | | | Other | Rep.-Dem. | Percentage | | | |
| | Total | Republican | | Democratic | | Vote | Plurality | Total Vote | | Major Vote | |
Year	Vote	Vote	Candidate	Vote	Candidate			Rep.	Dem.	Rep.	Dem.
1984	379,155	154,308	Cozzens, Chuck	215,704	Baucus, Max S.	9,143	61,396 D	40.7%	56.9%	41.7%	58.3%
1982	321,062	133,789	Williams, Larry	174,861	Melcher, John	12,412	41,072 D	41.7%	54.5%	43.3%	56.7%
1978	287,942	127,589	Williams, Larry	160,353	Baucus, Max S.	—	32,764 D	44.3%	55.7%	44.3%	55.7%
1976	321,445	115,213	Burger, Stanley C.	206,232	Melcher, John	—	91,019 D	35.8%	64.2%	35.8%	64.2%
1972	314,925	151,316	Hibbard, Henry S.	163,609	Metcalf, Lee	—	12,293 D	48.0%	52.0%	48.0%	52.0%
1970	247,869	97,809	Wallace, Harold E.	150,060	Mansfield, Mike	—	52,251 D	39.5%	60.5%	39.5%	60.5%
1966	259,863	121,697	Babcock, Tim M.	138,166	Metcalf, Lee	—	16,469 D	46.8%	53.2%	46.8%	53.2%
1964	280,010	99,367	Blewett, Alex	180,643	Mansfield, Mike	—	81,276 D	35.5%	64.5%	35.5%	64.5%
1960	276,612	136,281	Fjare, Orvin B.	140,331	Metcalf, Lee	—	4,050 D	49.3%	50.7%	49.3%	50.7%
1958	229,483	54,573	Welch. Lou W.	174,910	Mansfield, Mike	—	120,337 D	23.8%	76.2%	23.8%	76.2%
1954	227,454	112,863	D'Ewart, Wesley A.	114,591	Murray, James E.	—	1,728 D	49.6%	50.4%	49.6%	50.4%
1952	262,297	127,360	Ecton, Zales N.	133,109	Mansfield, Mike	1,828	5,749 D	48.6%	50.7%	48.9%	51.1%
1948	221,003	94,458	David, Tom J.	125,193	Murray, James E.	1,352	30,735 D	42.7%	56.6%	43.0%	57.0%
1946	190,566	101,901	Ecton, Zales N.	86,476	Erickson, Leif	2,189	15,425 R	53.5%	45.4%	54.1%	45.9%

MONTANA

Districts Established March 4, 1983

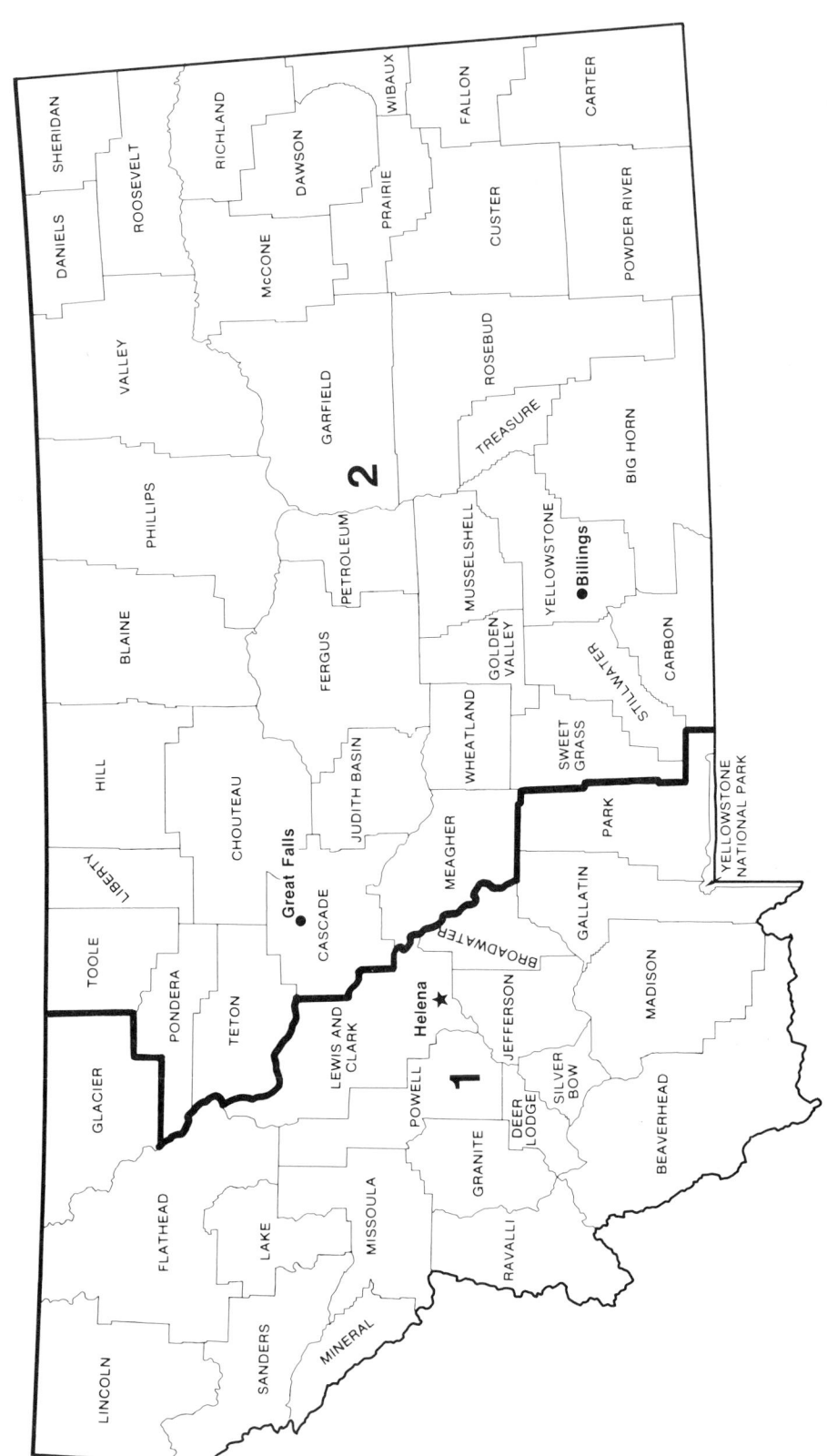

MONTANA

PRESIDENT 1984

1980 Census Population	County	Total Vote	Republican	Democratic	Other	Rep.-Dem. Plurality	Percentage Total Vote Rep.	Dem.	Major Vote Rep.	Dem.
8,186	BEAVERHEAD	4,035	3,044	942	49	2,102 R	75.4%	23.3%	76.4%	23.6%
11,096	BIG HORN	5,110	2,390	2,681	39	291 D	46.8%	52.5%	47.1%	52.9%
6,999	BLAINE	2,997	1,736	1,229	32	507 R	57.9%	41.0%	58.5%	41.5%
3,267	BROADWATER	1,830	1,345	458	27	887 R	73.5%	25.0%	74.6%	25.4%
8,099	CARBON	4,587	2,877	1,657	53	1,220 R	62.7%	36.1%	63.5%	36.5%
1,799	CARTER	1,028	823	194	11	629 R	80.1%	18.9%	80.9%	19.1%
80,696	CASCADE	34,505	19,846	14,252	407	5,594 R	57.5%	41.3%	58.2%	41.8%
6,092	CHOUTEAU	3,360	2,425	896	39	1,529 R	72.2%	26.7%	73.0%	27.0%
13,109	CUSTER	5,919	3,879	1,982	58	1,897 R	65.5%	33.5%	66.2%	33.8%
2,835	DANIELS	1,477	984	473	20	511 R	66.6%	32.0%	67.5%	32.5%
11,805	DAWSON	5,314	3,468	1,776	70	1,692 R	65.3%	33.4%	66.1%	33.9%
12,518	DEER LODGE	5,505	1,901	3,539	65	1,638 D	34.5%	64.3%	34.9%	65.1%
3,763	FALLON	1,829	1,237	569	23	668 R	67.6%	31.1%	68.5%	31.5%
13,076	FERGUS	6,459	4,585	1,804	70	2,781 R	71.0%	27.9%	71.8%	28.2%
51,966	FLATHEAD	25,803	17,012	8,310	481	8,702 R	65.9%	32.2%	67.2%	32.8%
42,865	GALLATIN	24,140	15,643	8,163	334	7,480 R	64.8%	33.8%	65.7%	34.3%
1,656	GARFIELD	911	770	134	7	636 R	84.5%	14.7%	85.2%	14.8%
10,628	GLACIER	4,435	2,228	2,167	40	61 R	50.2%	48.9%	50.7%	49.3%
1,026	GOLDEN VALLEY	600	384	211	5	173 R	64.0%	35.2%	64.5%	35.5%
2,700	GRANITE	1,322	880	417	25	463 R	66.6%	31.5%	67.8%	32.2%
17,985	HILL	8,390	4,635	3,657	98	978 R	55.2%	43.6%	55.9%	44.1%
7,029	JEFFERSON	3,618	2,226	1,324	68	902 R	61.5%	36.6%	62.7%	37.3%
2,646	JUDITH BASIN	1,550	1,050	483	17	567 R	67.7%	31.2%	68.5%	31.5%
19,056	LAKE	9,348	5,754	3,473	121	2,281 R	61.6%	37.2%	62.4%	37.6%
43,039	LEWIS AND CLARK	22,626	13,569	8,768	289	4,801 R	60.0%	38.8%	60.7%	39.3%
2,329	LIBERTY	1,229	895	323	11	572 R	72.8%	26.3%	73.5%	26.5%
17,752	LINCOLN	7,184	4,080	2,959	145	1,121 R	56.8%	41.2%	58.0%	42.0%
2,702	MCCONE	1,497	1,015	459	23	556 R	67.8%	30.7%	68.9%	31.1%
5,448	MADISON	3,069	2,308	708	53	1,600 R	75.2%	23.1%	76.5%	23.5%
2,154	MEAGHER	1,069	771	283	15	488 R	72.1%	26.5%	73.1%	26.9%
3,675	MINERAL	1,704	943	718	43	225 R	55.3%	42.1%	56.8%	43.2%
76,016	MISSOULA	36,937	19,777	16,540	620	3,237 R	53.5%	44.8%	54.5%	45.5%
4,428	MUSSELSHELL	2,359	1,541	781	37	760 R	65.3%	33.1%	66.4%	33.6%
12,660	PARK	6,581	4,115	2,387	79	1,728 R	62.5%	36.3%	63.3%	36.7%
655	PETROLEUM	347	258	86	3	172 R	74.4%	24.8%	75.0%	25.0%
5,367	PHILLIPS	2,749	1,934	787	28	1,147 R	70.4%	28.6%	71.1%	28.9%
6,731	PONDERA	3,316	2,239	1,039	38	1,200 R	67.5%	31.3%	68.3%	31.7%
2,520	POWDER RIVER	1,429	1,066	346	17	720 R	74.6%	24.2%	75.5%	24.5%
6,958	POWELL	3,012	1,877	1,066	69	811 R	62.3%	35.4%	63.8%	36.2%
1,836	PRAIRIE	991	693	289	9	404 R	69.9%	29.2%	70.6%	29.4%
22,493	RAVALLI	12,154	8,161	3,825	168	4,336 R	67.1%	31.5%	68.1%	31.9%
12,243	RICHLAND	5,281	3,847	1,382	52	2,465 R	72.8%	26.2%	73.6%	26.4%
10,467	ROOSEVELT	4,464	2,431	1,962	71	469 R	54.5%	44.0%	55.3%	44.7%
9,899	ROSEBUD	4,402	2,413	1,920	69	493 R	54.8%	43.6%	55.7%	44.3%
8,675	SANDERS	4,204	2,467	1,654	83	813 R	58.7%	39.3%	59.9%	40.1%
5,414	SHERIDAN	2,879	1,774	1,087	18	687 R	61.6%	37.8%	62.0%	38.0%
38,092	SILVER BOW	18,010	6,637	11,095	278	4,458 D	36.9%	61.6%	37.4%	62.6%
5,598	STILLWATER	3,258	2,118	1,100	40	1,018 R	65.0%	33.8%	65.8%	34.2%
3,216	SWEET GRASS	1,803	1,417	378	8	1,039 R	78.6%	21.0%	78.9%	21.1%
6,491	TETON	3,384	2,257	1,102	25	1,155 R	66.7%	32.6%	67.2%	32.8%
5,559	TOOLE	2,768	1,949	789	30	1,160 R	70.4%	28.5%	71.2%	28.8%
981	TREASURE	576	353	209	14	144 R	61.3%	36.3%	62.8%	37.2%
10,250	VALLEY	5,046	3,123	1,849	74	1,274 R	61.9%	36.6%	62.8%	37.2%
2,359	WHEATLAND	1,173	753	407	13	346 R	64.2%	34.7%	64.9%	35.1%
1,476	WIBAUX	651	423	216	12	207 R	65.0%	33.2%	66.2%	33.8%
108,035	YELLOWSTONE	54,153	34,124	19,437	592	14,687 R	63.0%	35.9%	63.7%	36.3%
786,690	TOTAL	384,377	232,450	146,742	5,185	85,708 R	60.5%	38.2%	61.3%	38.7%

MONTANA

GOVERNOR 1984

1980 Census Population	County	Total Vote	Republican	Democratic	Other	Rep.-Dem. Plurality	Percentage			
							Total Vote		Major Vote	
							Rep.	Dem.	Rep.	Dem.
8,186	BEAVERHEAD	4,030	1,680	2,262	88	582 D	41.7%	56.1%	42.6%	57.4%
11,096	BIG HORN	5,005	974	3,932	99	2,958 D	19.5%	78.6%	19.9%	80.1%
6,999	BLAINE	2,998	658	2,259	81	1,601 D	21.9%	75.4%	22.6%	77.4%
3,267	BROADWATER	1,806	501	1,257	48	756 D	27.7%	69.6%	28.5%	71.5%
8,099	CARBON	4,609	1,198	3,328	83	2,130 D	26.0%	72.2%	26.5%	73.5%
1,799	CARTER	985	412	556	17	144 D	41.8%	56.4%	42.6%	57.4%
80,696	CASCADE	33,518	8,622	23,790	1,106	15,168 D	25.7%	71.0%	26.6%	73.4%
6,092	CHOUTEAU	3,346	1,058	2,224	64	1,166 D	31.6%	66.5%	32.2%	67.8%
13,109	CUSTER	5,948	1,464	4,294	190	2,830 D	24.6%	72.2%	25.4%	74.6%
2,835	DANIELS	1,452	518	913	21	395 D	35.7%	62.9%	36.2%	63.8%
11,805	DAWSON	5,338	1,626	3,628	84	2,002 D	30.5%	68.0%	30.9%	69.1%
12,518	DEER LODGE	5,158	831	4,046	281	3,215 D	16.1%	78.4%	17.0%	83.0%
3,763	FALLON	1,773	522	1,208	43	686 D	29.4%	68.1%	30.2%	69.8%
13,076	FERGUS	6,444	2,065	4,230	149	2,165 D	32.0%	65.6%	32.8%	67.2%
51,966	FLATHEAD	25,743	6,916	17,910	917	10,994 D	26.9%	69.6%	27.9%	72.1%
42,865	GALLATIN	23,864	7,212	15,823	829	8,611 D	30.2%	66.3%	31.3%	68.7%
1,656	GARFIELD	895	302	569	24	267 D	33.7%	63.6%	34.7%	65.3%
10,628	GLACIER	4,398	1,136	3,150	112	2,014 D	25.8%	71.6%	26.5%	73.5%
1,026	GOLDEN VALLEY	607	195	402	10	207 D	32.1%	66.2%	32.7%	67.3%
2,700	GRANITE	1,312	420	834	58	414 D	32.0%	63.6%	33.5%	66.5%
17,985	HILL	8,335	1,802	6,367	166	4,565 D	21.6%	76.4%	22.1%	77.9%
7,029	JEFFERSON	3,614	1,015	2,436	163	1,421 D	28.1%	67.4%	29.4%	70.6%
2,646	JUDITH BASIN	1,556	430	1,085	41	655 D	27.6%	69.7%	28.4%	71.6%
19,056	LAKE	9,367	2,554	6,525	288	3,971 D	27.3%	69.7%	28.1%	71.9%
43,039	LEWIS AND CLARK	22,884	5,750	16,253	881	10,503 D	25.1%	71.0%	26.1%	73.9%
2,329	LIBERTY	1,206	410	774	22	364 D	34.0%	64.2%	34.6%	65.4%
17,752	LINCOLN	7,144	1,938	4,909	297	2,971 D	27.1%	68.7%	28.3%	71.7%
2,702	MCCONE	1,509	412	1,069	28	657 D	27.3%	70.8%	27.8%	72.2%
5,448	MADISON	3,019	1,119	1,789	111	670 D	37.1%	59.3%	38.5%	61.5%
2,154	MEAGHER	1,066	291	751	24	460 D	27.3%	70.5%	27.9%	72.1%
3,675	MINERAL	1,696	304	1,308	84	1,004 D	17.9%	77.1%	18.9%	81.1%
76,016	MISSOULA	36,183	8,058	26,422	1,703	18,364 D	22.3%	73.0%	23.4%	76.6%
4,428	MUSSELSHELL	2,328	642	1,636	50	994 D	27.6%	70.3%	28.2%	71.8%
12,660	PARK	6,707	1,757	4,800	150	3,043 D	26.2%	71.6%	26.8%	73.2%
655	PETROLEUM	351	90	254	7	164 D	25.6%	72.4%	26.2%	73.8%
5,367	PHILLIPS	2,746	771	1,909	66	1,138 D	28.1%	69.5%	28.8%	71.2%
6,731	PONDERA	3,280	972	2,239	69	1,267 D	29.6%	68.3%	30.3%	69.7%
2,520	POWDER RIVER	1,385	528	827	30	299 D	38.1%	59.7%	39.0%	61.0%
6,958	POWELL	2,987	981	1,757	249	776 D	32.8%	58.8%	35.8%	64.2%
1,836	PRAIRIE	979	286	675	18	389 D	29.2%	68.9%	29.8%	70.2%
22,493	RAVALLI	12,023	3,715	7,926	382	4,211 D	30.9%	65.9%	31.9%	68.1%
12,243	RICHLAND	5,247	2,516	2,644	87	128 D	48.0%	50.4%	48.8%	51.2%
10,467	ROOSEVELT	4,498	799	3,603	96	2,804 D	17.8%	80.1%	18.2%	81.8%
9,899	ROSEBUD	4,378	930	3,288	160	2,358 D	21.2%	75.1%	22.0%	78.0%
8,675	SANDERS	3,997	957	2,900	140	1,943 D	23.9%	72.6%	24.8%	75.2%
5,414	SHERIDAN	2,813	580	2,202	31	1,622 D	20.6%	78.3%	20.8%	79.2%
38,092	SILVER BOW	17,784	2,934	14,268	582	11,334 D	16.5%	80.2%	17.1%	82.9%
5,598	STILLWATER	3,203	810	2,319	74	1,509 D	25.3%	72.4%	25.9%	74.1%
3,216	SWEET GRASS	1,792	699	1,065	28	366 D	39.0%	59.4%	39.6%	60.4%
6,491	TETON	3,485	1,051	2,358	76	1,307 D	30.2%	67.7%	30.8%	69.2%
5,559	TOOLE	2,739	961	1,702	76	741 D	35.1%	62.1%	36.1%	63.9%
981	TREASURE	568	108	443	17	335 D	19.0%	78.0%	19.6%	80.4%
10,250	VALLEY	4,873	1,198	3,554	121	2,356 D	24.6%	72.9%	25.2%	74.8%
2,359	WHEATLAND	1,179	314	835	30	521 D	26.6%	70.8%	27.3%	72.7%
1,476	WIBAUX	650	174	462	14	288 D	26.8%	71.1%	27.4%	72.6%
108,035	YELLOWSTONE	52,170	13,904	36,609	1,657	22,705 D	26.7%	70.2%	27.5%	72.5%
786,690	TOTAL	378,970	100,070	266,578	12,322	166,508 D	26.4%	70.3%	27.3%	72.7%

MONTANA

SENATOR 1984

1980 Census Population	County	Total Vote	Republican	Democratic	Other	Rep.-Dem. Plurality	Percentage Total Vote Rep.	Dem.	Major Vote Rep.	Dem.
8,186	BEAVERHEAD	4,033	2,328	1,630	75	698 R	57.7%	40.4%	58.8%	41.2%
11,096	BIG HORN	5,174	1,517	3,591	66	2,074 D	29.3%	69.4%	29.7%	70.3%
6,999	BLAINE	3,021	1,122	1,854	45	732 D	37.1%	61.4%	37.7%	62.3%
3,267	BROADWATER	1,827	894	887	46	7 R	48.9%	48.5%	50.2%	49.8%
8,099	CARBON	4,637	1,826	2,707	104	881 D	39.4%	58.4%	40.3%	59.7%
1,799	CARTER	1,009	518	474	17	44 R	51.3%	47.0%	52.2%	47.8%
80,696	CASCADE	30,933	11,396	18,520	1,017	7,124 D	36.8%	59.9%	38.1%	61.9%
6,092	CHOUTEAU	3,387	1,578	1,743	66	165 D	46.6%	51.5%	47.5%	52.5%
13,109	CUSTER	5,928	2,449	3,394	85	945 D	41.3%	57.3%	41.9%	58.1%
2,835	DANIELS	1,455	609	826	20	217 D	41.9%	56.8%	42.4%	57.6%
11,805	DAWSON	5,320	2,370	2,847	103	477 D	44.5%	53.5%	45.4%	54.6%
12,518	DEER LODGE	5,275	1,066	4,082	127	3,016 D	20.2%	77.4%	20.7%	79.3%
3,763	FALLON	1,806	780	1,006	20	226 D	43.2%	55.7%	43.7%	56.3%
13,076	FERGUS	6,425	3,262	3,035	128	227 R	50.8%	47.2%	51.8%	48.2%
51,966	FLATHEAD	25,926	12,116	13,200	610	1,084 D	46.7%	50.9%	47.9%	52.1%
42,865	GALLATIN	24,134	10,497	13,111	526	2,614 D	43.5%	54.3%	44.5%	55.5%
1,656	GARFIELD	911	511	385	15	126 R	56.1%	42.3%	57.0%	43.0%
10,628	GLACIER	4,483	1,612	2,766	105	1,154 D	36.0%	61.7%	36.8%	63.2%
1,026	GOLDEN VALLEY	611	280	319	12	39 D	45.8%	52.2%	46.7%	53.3%
2,700	GRANITE	1,330	630	671	29	41 D	47.4%	50.5%	48.4%	51.6%
17,985	HILL	8,380	2,737	5,545	98	2,808 D	32.7%	66.2%	33.0%	67.0%
7,029	JEFFERSON	3,628	1,485	2,054	89	569 D	40.9%	56.6%	42.0%	58.0%
2,646	JUDITH BASIN	1,562	689	845	28	156 D	44.1%	54.1%	44.9%	55.1%
19,056	LAKE	9,485	4,547	4,690	248	143 D	47.9%	49.4%	49.2%	50.8%
43,039	LEWIS AND CLARK	22,789	8,797	13,459	533	4,662 D	38.6%	59.1%	39.5%	60.5%
2,329	LIBERTY	1,249	665	563	21	102 R	53.2%	45.1%	54.2%	45.8%
17,752	LINCOLN	7,046	2,510	4,329	207	1,819 D	35.6%	61.4%	36.7%	63.3%
2,702	MCCONE	1,520	645	863	12	218 D	42.4%	56.8%	42.8%	57.2%
5,448	MADISON	3,041	1,669	1,303	69	366 R	54.9%	42.8%	56.2%	43.8%
2,154	MEAGHER	1,069	487	557	25	70 D	45.6%	52.1%	46.6%	53.4%
3,675	MINERAL	1,704	593	1,059	52	466 D	34.8%	62.1%	35.9%	64.1%
76,016	MISSOULA	36,820	13,739	21,717	1,364	7,978 D	37.3%	59.0%	38.7%	61.3%
4,428	MUSSELSHELL	2,349	996	1,317	36	321 D	42.4%	56.1%	43.1%	56.9%
12,660	PARK	6,831	2,894	3,830	107	936 D	42.4%	56.1%	43.0%	57.0%
655	PETROLEUM	351	169	174	8	5 D	48.1%	49.6%	49.3%	50.7%
5,367	PHILLIPS	2,778	1,239	1,492	47	253 D	44.6%	53.7%	45.4%	54.6%
6,731	PONDERA	3,322	1,529	1,730	63	201 D	46.0%	52.1%	46.9%	53.1%
2,520	POWDER RIVER	1,410	721	673	16	48 R	51.1%	47.7%	51.7%	48.3%
6,958	POWELL	3,012	1,258	1,624	130	366 D	41.8%	53.9%	43.7%	56.3%
1,836	PRAIRIE	997	454	523	20	69 D	45.5%	52.5%	46.5%	53.5%
22,493	RAVALLI	12,225	6,334	5,614	277	720 R	51.8%	45.9%	53.0%	47.0%
12,243	RICHLAND	5,277	2,710	2,515	52	195 R	51.4%	47.7%	51.9%	48.1%
10,467	ROOSEVELT	4,482	1,313	3,083	86	1,770 D	29.3%	68.8%	29.9%	70.1%
9,899	ROSEBUD	4,398	1,568	2,732	98	1,164 D	35.7%	62.1%	36.5%	63.5%
8,675	SANDERS	4,235	1,722	2,396	117	674 D	40.7%	56.6%	41.8%	58.2%
5,414	SHERIDAN	2,842	915	1,907	20	992 D	32.2%	67.1%	32.4%	67.6%
38,092	SILVER BOW	18,098	3,811	13,862	425	10,051 D	21.1%	76.6%	21.6%	78.4%
5,598	STILLWATER	3,244	1,324	1,873	47	549 D	40.8%	57.7%	41.4%	58.6%
3,216	SWEET GRASS	1,802	1,079	700	23	379 R	59.9%	38.8%	60.7%	39.3%
6,491	TETON	3,483	1,560	1,849	74	289 D	44.8%	53.1%	45.8%	54.2%
5,559	TOOLE	2,764	1,354	1,359	51	5 D	49.0%	49.2%	49.9%	50.1%
981	TREASURE	575	201	361	13	160 D	35.0%	62.8%	35.8%	64.2%
10,250	VALLEY	4,488	1,760	2,630	98	870 D	39.2%	58.6%	40.1%	59.9%
2,359	WHEATLAND	1,193	543	631	19	88 D	45.5%	52.9%	46.3%	53.7%
1,476	WIBAUX	652	307	332	13	25 D	47.1%	50.9%	48.0%	52.0%
108,035	YELLOWSTONE	52,429	22,623	28,465	1,341	5,842 D	43.1%	54.3%	44.3%	55.7%
786,690	TOTAL	379,155	154,308	215,704	9,143	61,396 D	40.7%	56.9%	41.7%	58.3%

MONTANA

CONGRESS

CD	Year	Total Vote	Republican		Democratic		Other Vote	Rep.-Dem. Plurality	Percentage			
			Vote	Candidate	Vote	Candidate			Total Vote		Major Vote	
									Rep.	Dem.	Rep.	Dem.
1	1984	193,452	61,794	CARLSON, GARY K.	126,998	WILLIAMS, PAT	4,660	65,204 D	31.9%	65.6%	32.7%	67.3%
2	1984	177,377	116,932	MARLENEE, RON	60,445	BLAYLOCK, CHET		56,487 R	65.9%	34.1%	65.9%	34.1%

MONTANA

Population total includes 275 persons living in Yellowstone National Park and not under any county jurisdiction.

1984 GENERAL ELECTION

President   Other vote was Bergland (Libertarian).

Governor   Other vote was Dodge (Libertarian).

Senator   Other vote was Halprin (Libertarian).

Congress   Other vote was Warren (Libertarian) in CD 1.

1984 PRIMARIES

JUNE 5 REPUBLICAN

Governor   Pat M. Goodover, unopposed.

Senator   33,661 Chuck Cozzens; 17,900 Ralph Bouma; 14,729 Aubyn Curtiss.

Congress   Unopposed in both CD's.

JUNE 5 DEMOCRATIC

Governor   80,633 Ted Schwinden; 18,423 Robert C. Kelleher.

Senator   80,726 Max S. Baucus; 20,979 Bob Ripley.

Congress   Unopposed in CD 1. Contested as follows:

  CD 2   25,433 Chet Blaylock; 13,781 Frank Hayes.

NEBRASKA

GOVERNOR
Bob Kerrey (D). Elected 1982 to a four-year term.

SENATORS
J. J. Exon (D). Re-elected 1984 to a six-year term. Previously elected 1978.

Edward Zorinsky (D). Re-elected 1982 to a six-year term. Previously elected 1976.

REPRESENTATIVES
1. Douglas K. Bereuter (R)   2. Harold J. Daub (R)   3. Virginia Smith (R)

POSTWAR VOTE FOR GOVERNOR

Year	Total Vote	Republican Vote	Candidate	Democratic Vote	Candidate	Other Vote	Rep.-Dem. Plurality	Total Vote Rep.	Dem.	Major Vote Rep.	Dem.
1982	547,902	270,203	Thone, Charles	277,436	Kerrey, Bob	263	7,233 D	49.3%	50.6%	49.3%	50.7%
1978	492,423	275,473	Thone, Charles	216,754	Whelan, Gerald T.	196	58,719 R	55.9%	44.0%	56.0%	44.0%
1974	451,306	159,780	Marvel, Richard D.	267,012	Exon, J. J.	24,514	107,232 D	35.4%	59.2%	37.4%	62.6%
1970	461,619	201,994	Tiemann, Norbert T.	248,552	Exon, J. J.	11,073	46,558 D	43.8%	53.8%	44.8%	55.2%
1966*	486,396	299,245	Tiemann, Norbert T.	186,985	Sorensen, Philip C.	166	112,260 R	61.5%	38.4%	61.5%	38.5%
1964	578,090	231,029	Burney, Dwight W.	347,026	Morrison, Frank B.	35	115,997 D	40.0%	60.0%	40.0%	60.0%
1962	464,585	221,885	Seaton, Fred A.	242,669	Morrison, Frank B.	31	20,784 D	47.8%	52.2%	47.8%	52.2%
1960	598,971	287,302	Cooper, John R.	311,344	Morrison, Frank B.	325	24,042 D	48.0%	52.0%	48.0%	52.0%
1958	421,067	209,705	Anderson, Victor E.	211,345	Brooks, Ralph G.	17	1,640 D	49.8%	50.2%	49.8%	50.2%
1956	567,933	308,293	Anderson, Victor E.	228,048	Sorrell, Frank	31,592	80,245 R	54.3%	40.2%	57.5%	42.5%
1954	414,841	250,080	Anderson, Victor E.	164,753	Ritchie, William	8	85,327 R	60.3%	39.7%	60.3%	39.7%
1952	595,714	366,009	Crosby, Robert B.	229,700	Raecke, Walter R.	5	136,309 R	61.4%	38.6%	61.4%	38.6%
1950	449,720	247,081	Peterson, Val	202,638	Raecke, Walter R.	1	44,443 R	54.9%	45.1%	54.9%	45.1%
1948	476,352	286,119	Peterson, Val	190,214	Sorrell, Frank	19	95,905 R	60.1%	39.9%	60.1%	39.9%
1946	380,835	249,468	Peterson, Val	131,367	Sorrell, Frank	—	118,101 R	65.5%	34.5%	65.5%	34.5%

The term of office of Nebraska's Governor was increased from two to four years effective with the 1966 election.

POSTWAR VOTE FOR SENATOR

Year	Total Vote	Republican Vote	Candidate	Democratic Vote	Candidate	Other Vote	Rep.-Dem. Plurality	Total Vote Rep.	Dem.	Major Vote Rep.	Dem.
1984	639,668	307,147	Hoch, Nancy	332,217	Exon, J. J.	304	25,070 D	48.0%	51.9%	48.0%	52.0%
1982	545,647	155,760	Keck, Jim	363,350	Zorinsky, Edward	26,537	207,590 D	28.5%	66.6%	30.0%	70.0%
1978	494,368	159,806	Shasteen, Donald	334,276	Exon, J. J.	286	174,470 D	32.3%	67.6%	32.3%	67.7%
1976	598,314	284,284	McCollister, John Y.	313,809	Zorinsky, Edward	221	29,525 D	47.5%	52.4%	47.5%	52.5%
1972	568,580	301,841	Curtis, Carl T.	265,922	Carpenter, Terry	817	35,919 R	53.1%	46.8%	53.2%	46.8%
1970	458,966	240,894	Hruska, Roman L.	217,681	Morrison, Frank B.	391	23,213 R	52.5%	47.4%	52.5%	47.5%
1966	485,101	296,116	Curtis, Carl T.	187,950	Morrison, Frank B.	1,035	108,166 R	61.0%	38.7%	61.2%	38.8%
1964	563,401	345,772	Hruska, Roman L.	217,605	Arndt, Raymond W.	24	128,167 R	61.4%	38.6%	61.4%	38.6%
1960	598,743	352,748	Curtis, Carl T.	245,837	Conrad, Robert	158	106,911 R	58.9%	41.1%	58.9%	41.1%
1958	417,385	232,227	Hruska, Roman L.	185,152	Morrison, Frank B.	6	47,075 R	55.6%	44.4%	55.6%	44.4%
1954	418,691	255,695	Curtis, Carl T.	162,990	Neville, Keith	6	92,705 R	61.1%	38.9%	61.1%	38.9%
1954s	411,225	250,341	Hruska, Roman L.	160,881	Green, James F.	3	89,460 R	60.9%	39.1%	60.9%	39.1%
1952	591,749	408,971	Butler, Hugh	164,660	Long, Stanley D.	18,118	244,311 R	69.1%	27.8%	71.3%	28.7%
1952s	581,750	369,841	Griswold, Dwight	211,898	Ritchie, William	11	157,943 R	63.6%	36.4%	63.6%	36.4%
1948	471,895	267,575	Wherry, Kenneth S.	204,320	Carpenter, Terry	—	63,255 R	56.7%	43.3%	56.7%	43.3%
1946	382,958	271,208	Butler, Hugh	111,750	Mekota, John E.	—	159,458 R	70.8%	29.2%	70.8%	29.2%

One each of the 1954 and 1952 elections was for a short term to fill a vacancy.

NEBRASKA

Districts Established May 28, 1981

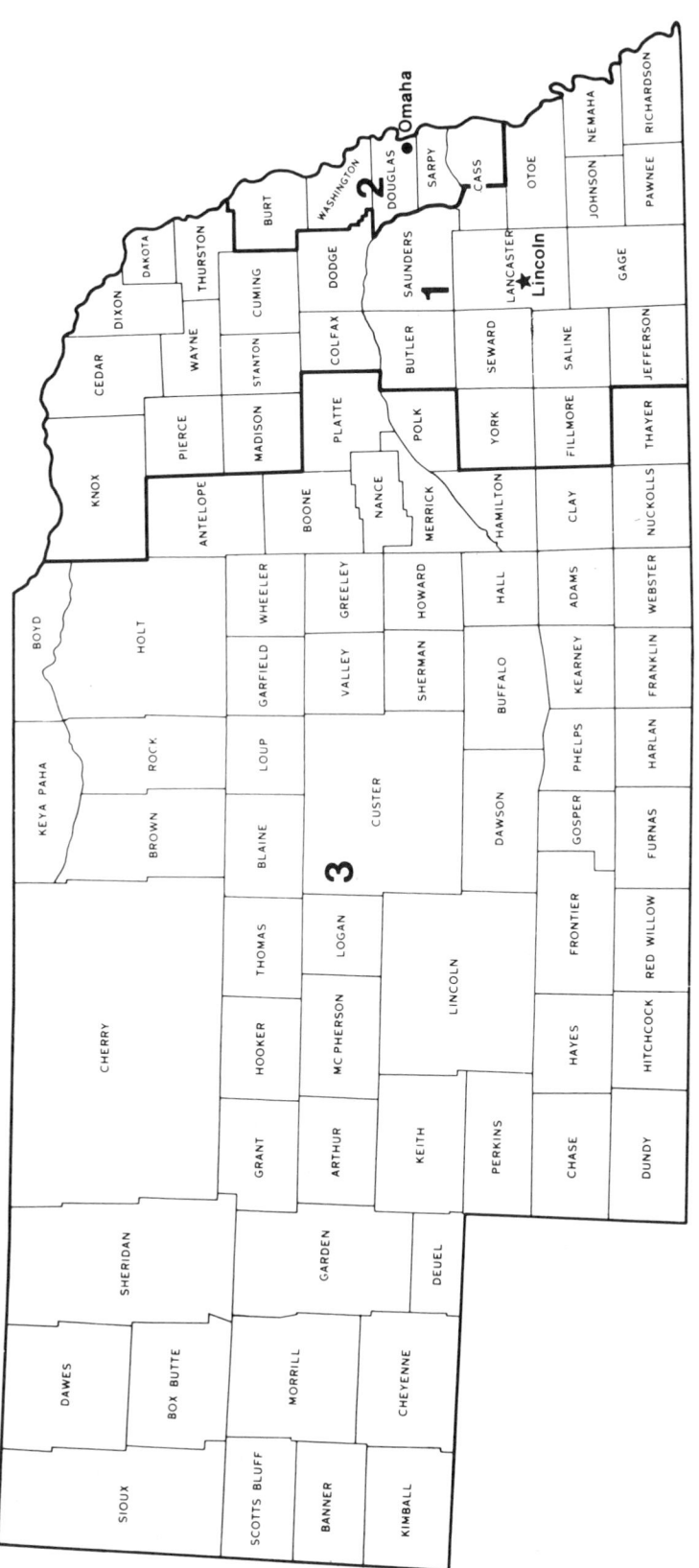

© ERC

NEBRASKA

PRESIDENT 1984

1980 Census Population	County	Total Vote	Republican	Democratic	Other	Rep.-Dem. Plurality	Percentage Total Vote Rep.	Dem.	Major Vote Rep.	Dem.
30,656	ADAMS	12,155	9,127	2,945	83	6,182 R	75.1%	24.2%	75.6%	24.4%
8,675	ANTELOPE	3,939	3,222	697	20	2,525 R	81.8%	17.7%	82.2%	17.8%
513	ARTHUR	281	248	33		215 R	88.3%	11.7%	88.3%	11.7%
918	BANNER	522	457	58	7	399 R	87.5%	11.1%	88.7%	11.3%
867	BLAINE	411	363	48		315 R	88.3%	11.7%	88.3%	11.7%
7,391	BOONE	3,215	2,508	690	17	1,818 R	78.0%	21.5%	78.4%	21.6%
13,696	BOX BUTTE	5,525	4,011	1,471	43	2,540 R	72.6%	26.6%	73.2%	26.8%
3,331	BOYD	1,496	1,175	308	13	867 R	78.5%	20.6%	79.2%	20.8%
4,377	BROWN	1,833	1,514	312	7	1,202 R	82.6%	17.0%	82.9%	17.1%
34,797	BUFFALO	14,550	11,365	3,086	99	8,279 R	78.1%	21.2%	78.6%	21.4%
8,813	BURT	3,721	2,645	1,054	22	1,591 R	71.1%	28.3%	71.5%	28.5%
9,330	BUTLER	3,785	2,557	1,193	35	1,364 R	67.6%	31.5%	68.2%	31.8%
20,297	CASS	8,026	5,461	2,499	66	2,962 R	68.0%	31.1%	68.6%	31.4%
11,375	CEDAR	4,536	3,298	1,201	37	2,097 R	72.7%	26.5%	73.3%	26.7%
4,758	CHASE	2,097	1,697	368	32	1,329 R	80.9%	17.5%	82.2%	17.8%
6,758	CHERRY	3,198	2,720	463	15	2,257 R	85.1%	14.5%	85.5%	14.5%
10,057	CHEYENNE	4,064	3,159	857	48	2,302 R	77.7%	21.1%	78.7%	21.3%
8,106	CLAY	3,756	2,920	811	25	2,109 R	77.7%	21.6%	78.3%	21.7%
9,890	COLFAX	4,016	2,999	981	36	2,018 R	74.7%	24.4%	75.4%	24.6%
11,664	CUMING	4,740	3,931	779	30	3,152 R	82.9%	16.4%	83.5%	16.5%
13,877	CUSTER	5,867	4,749	1,090	28	3,659 R	80.9%	18.6%	81.3%	18.7%
16,573	DAKOTA	6,002	3,467	2,510	25	957 R	57.8%	41.8%	58.0%	42.0%
9,609	DAWES	4,232	3,326	865	41	2,461 R	78.6%	20.4%	79.4%	20.6%
22,304	DAWSON	8,407	6,887	1,487	33	5,400 R	81.9%	17.7%	82.2%	17.8%
2,462	DEUEL	1,167	962	198	7	764 R	82.4%	17.0%	82.9%	17.1%
7,137	DIXON	3,164	2,155	986	23	1,169 R	68.1%	31.2%	68.6%	31.4%
35,847	DODGE	14,541	10,201	4,266	74	5,935 R	70.2%	29.3%	70.5%	29.5%
397,038	DOUGLAS	172,658	112,676	58,979	1,003	53,697 R	65.3%	34.2%	65.6%	34.4%
2,861	DUNDY	1,225	992	225	8	767 R	81.0%	18.4%	81.5%	18.5%
7,920	FILLMORE	3,511	2,474	1,009	28	1,465 R	70.5%	28.7%	71.0%	29.0%
4,377	FRANKLIN	2,127	1,597	522	8	1,075 R	75.1%	24.5%	75.4%	24.6%
3,647	FRONTIER	1,617	1,351	258	8	1,093 R	83.5%	16.0%	84.0%	16.0%
6,486	FURNAS	2,966	2,363	579	24	1,784 R	79.7%	19.5%	80.3%	19.7%
24,456	GAGE	8,892	6,116	2,709	67	3,407 R	68.8%	30.5%	69.3%	30.7%
2,802	GARDEN	1,351	1,158	180	13	978 R	85.7%	13.3%	86.5%	13.5%
2,363	GARFIELD	1,104	899	196	9	703 R	81.4%	17.8%	82.1%	17.9%
2,140	GOSPER	1,011	802	201	8	601 R	79.3%	19.9%	80.0%	20.0%
877	GRANT	459	406	51	2	355 R	88.5%	11.1%	88.8%	11.2%
3,462	GREELEY	1,442	948	485	9	463 R	65.7%	33.6%	66.2%	33.8%
47,690	HALL	17,956	13,193	4,655	108	8,538 R	73.5%	25.9%	73.9%	26.1%
9,301	HAMILTON	4,285	3,418	842	25	2,576 R	79.8%	19.6%	80.2%	19.8%
4,292	HARLAN	2,203	1,692	493	18	1,199 R	76.8%	22.4%	77.4%	22.6%
1,356	HAYES	694	593	101		492 R	85.4%	14.6%	85.4%	14.6%
4,079	HITCHCOCK	1,739	1,391	341	7	1,050 R	80.0%	19.6%	80.3%	19.7%
13,552	HOLT	5,545	4,613	893	39	3,720 R	83.2%	16.1%	83.8%	16.2%
990	HOOKER	493	433	55	5	378 R	87.8%	11.2%	88.7%	11.3%
6,773	HOWARD	2,806	1,899	887	20	1,012 R	67.7%	31.6%	68.2%	31.8%
9,817	JEFFERSON	4,523	3,116	1,367	40	1,749 R	68.9%	30.2%	69.5%	30.5%
5,285	JOHNSON	2,396	1,542	821	33	721 R	64.4%	34.3%	65.3%	34.7%
7,053	KEARNEY	3,262	2,508	726	28	1,782 R	76.9%	22.3%	77.6%	22.4%
9,364	KEITH	4,082	3,433	631	18	2,802 R	84.1%	15.5%	84.5%	15.5%
1,301	KEYA PAHA	635	507	128		379 R	79.8%	20.2%	79.8%	20.2%
4,882	KIMBALL	2,087	1,734	339	14	1,395 R	83.1%	16.2%	83.6%	16.4%
11,457	KNOX	4,560	3,364	1,149	47	2,215 R	73.8%	25.2%	74.5%	25.5%
192,884	LANCASTER	82,245	48,778	32,898	569	15,880 R	59.3%	40.0%	59.7%	40.3%
36,455	LINCOLN	15,307	10,717	4,509	81	6,208 R	70.0%	29.5%	70.4%	29.6%
983	LOGAN	514	446	67	1	379 R	86.8%	13.0%	86.9%	13.1%
859	LOUP	404	323	79	2	244 R	80.0%	19.6%	80.3%	19.7%
593	MCPHERSON	356	295	57	4	238 R	82.9%	16.0%	83.8%	16.2%
31,382	MADISON	11,589	9,790	1,757	42	8,033 R	84.5%	15.2%	84.8%	15.2%

NEBRASKA

PRESIDENT 1984

1980 Census Population	County	Total Vote	Republican	Democratic	Other	Rep.-Dem. Plurality	Percentage Total Vote Rep.	Dem.	Major Vote Rep.	Dem.
8,945	MERRICK	3,546	2,700	818	28	1,882 R	76.1%	23.1%	76.7%	23.3%
6,085	MORRILL	2,366	1,888	464	14	1,424 R	79.8%	19.6%	80.3%	19.7%
4,740	NANCE	1,931	1,393	525	13	868 R	72.1%	27.2%	72.6%	27.4%
8,367	NEMAHA	3,793	2,752	1,004	37	1,748 R	72.6%	26.5%	73.3%	26.7%
6,726	NUCKOLLS	3,098	2,132	947	19	1,185 R	68.8%	30.6%	69.2%	30.8%
15,183	OTOE	6,596	4,679	1,869	48	2,810 R	70.9%	28.3%	71.5%	28.5%
3,937	PAWNEE	1,884	1,306	552	26	754 R	69.3%	29.3%	70.3%	29.7%
3,637	PERKINS	1,736	1,420	307	9	1,113 R	81.8%	17.7%	82.2%	17.8%
9,769	PHELPS	4,501	3,741	740	20	3,001 R	83.1%	16.4%	83.5%	16.5%
8,481	PIERCE	3,589	3,017	545	27	2,472 R	84.1%	15.2%	84.7%	15.3%
28,852	PLATTE	12,222	10,069	2,061	92	8,008 R	82.4%	16.9%	83.0%	17.0%
6,320	POLK	2,776	2,149	610	17	1,539 R	77.4%	22.0%	77.9%	22.1%
12,615	RED WILLOW	5,184	4,131	1,026	27	3,105 R	79.7%	19.8%	80.1%	19.9%
11,315	RICHARDSON	5,098	3,634	1,422	42	2,212 R	71.3%	27.9%	71.9%	28.1%
2,383	ROCK	1,023	873	147	3	726 R	85.3%	14.4%	85.6%	14.4%
13,131	SALINE	5,394	2,942	2,385	67	557 R	54.5%	44.2%	55.2%	44.8%
86,015	SARPY	27,160	20,192	6,838	130	13,354 R	74.3%	25.2%	74.7%	25.3%
18,716	SAUNDERS	7,747	5,217	2,467	63	2,750 R	67.3%	31.8%	67.9%	32.1%
38,344	SCOTTS BLUFF	13,878	10,711	3,074	93	7,637 R	77.2%	22.2%	77.7%	22.3%
15,789	SEWARD	5,937	3,983	1,911	43	2,072 R	67.1%	32.2%	67.6%	32.4%
7,544	SHERIDAN	3,061	2,661	377	23	2,284 R	86.9%	12.3%	87.6%	12.4%
4,226	SHERMAN	1,862	1,144	701	17	443 R	61.4%	37.6%	62.0%	38.0%
1,845	SIOUX	860	732	121	7	611 R	85.1%	14.1%	85.8%	14.2%
6,549	STANTON	2,508	2,082	411	15	1,671 R	83.0%	16.4%	83.5%	16.5%
7,582	THAYER	3,551	2,580	946	25	1,634 R	72.7%	26.6%	73.2%	26.8%
973	THOMAS	374	298	73	3	225 R	79.7%	19.5%	80.3%	19.7%
7,186	THURSTON	2,500	1,410	1,077	13	333 R	56.4%	43.1%	56.7%	43.3%
5,633	VALLEY	2,807	2,055	739	13	1,316 R	73.2%	26.3%	73.6%	26.4%
15,508	WASHINGTON	6,791	5,191	1,565	35	3,626 R	76.4%	23.0%	76.8%	23.2%
9,858	WAYNE	3,936	3,075	833	28	2,242 R	78.1%	21.2%	78.7%	21.3%
4,858	WEBSTER	2,355	1,694	645	16	1,049 R	71.9%	27.4%	72.4%	27.6%
1,060	WHEELER	465	365	97	3	268 R	78.5%	20.9%	79.0%	21.0%
14,798	YORK	6,271	5,147	1,124		4,023 R	82.1%	17.9%	82.1%	17.9%
1,569,825	TOTAL	652,090	460,054	187,866	4,170	272,188 R	70.6%	28.8%	71.0%	29.0%

NEBRASKA

SENATOR 1984

1980 Census Population	County	Total Vote	Republican	Democratic	Other	Rep.-Dem. Plurality	Percentage Total Vote Rep.	Total Vote Dem.	Major Vote Rep.	Major Vote Dem.
30,656	ADAMS	11,375	6,304	5,070	1	1,234 R	55.4%	44.6%	55.4%	44.6%
8,675	ANTELOPE	3,928	2,020	1,908		112 R	51.4%	48.6%	51.4%	48.6%
513	ARTHUR	285	207	78		129 R	72.6%	27.4%	72.6%	27.4%
918	BANNER	528	350	178		172 R	66.3%	33.7%	66.3%	33.7%
867	BLAINE	411	265	146		119 R	64.5%	35.5%	64.5%	35.5%
7,391	BOONE	3,251	1,543	1,708		165 D	47.5%	52.5%	47.5%	52.5%
13,696	BOX BUTTE	5,675	3,078	2,596	1	482 R	54.2%	45.7%	54.2%	45.8%
3,331	BOYD	1,522	717	805		88 D	47.1%	52.9%	47.1%	52.9%
4,377	BROWN	1,843	1,030	813		217 R	55.9%	44.1%	55.9%	44.1%
34,797	BUFFALO	14,532	7,376	7,156		220 R	50.8%	49.2%	50.8%	49.2%
8,813	BURT	3,792	1,933	1,859		74 R	51.0%	49.0%	51.0%	49.0%
9,330	BUTLER	3,909	1,320	2,589		1,269 D	33.8%	66.2%	33.8%	66.2%
20,297	CASS	8,051	3,471	4,574	6	1,103 D	43.1%	56.8%	43.1%	56.9%
11,375	CEDAR	4,501	1,514	2,987		1,473 D	33.6%	66.4%	33.6%	66.4%
4,758	CHASE	2,110	1,150	960		190 R	54.5%	45.5%	54.5%	45.5%
6,758	CHERRY	3,209	1,877	1,332		545 R	58.5%	41.5%	58.5%	41.5%
10,057	CHEYENNE	4,046	2,167	1,879		288 R	53.6%	46.4%	53.6%	46.4%
8,106	CLAY	3,810	1,933	1,876	1	57 R	50.7%	49.2%	50.7%	49.3%
9,890	COLFAX	4,079	1,752	2,326	1	574 D	43.0%	57.0%	43.0%	57.0%
11,664	CUMING	4,808	2,424	2,384		40 R	50.4%	49.6%	50.4%	49.6%
13,877	CUSTER	5,972	2,944	3,028		84 D	49.3%	50.7%	49.3%	50.7%
16,573	DAKOTA	5,992	2,492	3,500		1,008 D	41.6%	58.4%	41.6%	58.4%
9,609	DAWES	4,226	2,400	1,826		574 R	56.8%	43.2%	56.8%	43.2%
22,304	DAWSON	8,635	4,849	3,786		1,063 R	56.2%	43.8%	56.2%	43.8%
2,462	DEUEL	1,165	735	430		305 R	63.1%	36.9%	63.1%	36.9%
7,137	DIXON	3,240	1,421	1,819		398 D	43.9%	56.1%	43.9%	56.1%
35,847	DODGE	14,580	7,086	7,483	11	397 D	48.6%	51.3%	48.6%	51.4%
397,038	DOUGLAS	171,343	78,358	92,755	230	14,397 D	45.7%	54.1%	45.8%	54.2%
2,861	DUNDY	1,181	593	588		5 R	50.2%	49.8%	50.2%	49.8%
7,920	FILLMORE	3,605	1,530	2,075		545 D	42.4%	57.6%	42.4%	57.6%
4,377	FRANKLIN	2,139	1,004	1,135		131 D	46.9%	53.1%	46.9%	53.1%
3,647	FRONTIER	1,620	881	739		142 R	54.4%	45.6%	54.4%	45.6%
6,486	FURNAS	2,997	1,410	1,587		177 D	47.0%	53.0%	47.0%	53.0%
24,456	GAGE	9,429	4,180	5,249		1,069 D	44.3%	55.7%	44.3%	55.7%
2,802	GARDEN	1,371	938	433		505 R	68.4%	31.6%	68.4%	31.6%
2,363	GARFIELD	1,129	601	528		73 R	53.2%	46.8%	53.2%	46.8%
2,140	GOSPER	1,031	515	516		1 D	50.0%	50.0%	50.0%	50.0%
877	GRANT	474	281	193		88 R	59.3%	40.7%	59.3%	40.7%
3,462	GREELEY	1,472	533	939		406 D	36.2%	63.8%	36.2%	63.8%
47,690	HALL	17,670	9,017	8,653		364 R	51.0%	49.0%	51.0%	49.0%
9,301	HAMILTON	4,322	2,199	2,123		76 R	50.9%	49.1%	50.9%	49.1%
4,292	HARLAN	2,234	1,096	1,138		42 D	49.1%	50.9%	49.1%	50.9%
1,356	HAYES	690	355	335		20 R	51.4%	48.6%	51.4%	48.6%
4,079	HITCHCOCK	1,765	815	950		135 D	46.2%	53.8%	46.2%	53.8%
13,552	HOLT	5,407	3,153	2,254		899 R	58.3%	41.7%	58.3%	41.7%
990	HOOKER	507	278	229		49 R	54.8%	45.2%	54.8%	45.2%
6,773	HOWARD	2,848	1,170	1,678		508 D	41.1%	58.9%	41.1%	58.9%
9,817	JEFFERSON	4,575	2,190	2,383	2	193 D	47.9%	52.1%	47.9%	52.1%
5,285	JOHNSON	2,451	1,006	1,445		439 D	41.0%	59.0%	41.0%	59.0%
7,053	KEARNEY	3,286	1,583	1,703		120 D	48.2%	51.8%	48.2%	51.8%
9,364	KEITH	4,080	2,673	1,407		1,266 R	65.5%	34.5%	65.5%	34.5%
1,301	KEYA PAHA	622	348	274		74 R	55.9%	44.1%	55.9%	44.1%
4,882	KIMBALL	2,101	1,237	864		373 R	58.9%	41.1%	58.9%	41.1%
11,457	KNOX	4,543	1,785	2,758		973 D	39.3%	60.7%	39.3%	60.7%
192,884	LANCASTER	68,921	30,747	38,174		7,427 D	44.6%	55.4%	44.6%	55.4%
36,455	LINCOLN	15,340	7,472	7,859	9	387 D	48.7%	51.2%	48.7%	51.3%
983	LOGAN	506	292	214		78 R	57.7%	42.3%	57.7%	42.3%
859	LOUP	411	197	214		17 D	47.9%	52.1%	47.9%	52.1%
593	MCPHERSON	358	211	147		64 R	58.9%	41.1%	58.9%	41.1%
31,382	MADISON	12,128	6,781	5,347		1,434 R	55.9%	44.1%	55.9%	44.1%

NEBRASKA

SENATOR 1984

1980 Census Population	County	Total Vote	Republican	Democratic	Other	Rep.-Dem. Plurality	Percentage Total Vote Rep.	Total Vote Dem.	Major Vote Rep.	Major Vote Dem.
8,945	MERRICK	3,552	1,694	1,858		164 D	47.7%	52.3%	47.7%	52.3%
6,085	MORRILL	2,414	1,517	896	1	621 R	62.8%	37.1%	62.9%	37.1%
4,740	NANCE	1,937	890	1,047		157 D	45.9%	54.1%	45.9%	54.1%
8,367	NEMAHA	3,817	1,799	2,017	1	218 D	47.1%	52.8%	47.1%	52.9%
6,726	NUCKOLLS	3,163	1,517	1,646		129 D	48.0%	52.0%	48.0%	52.0%
15,183	OTOE	6,714	2,835	3,878	1	1,043 D	42.2%	57.8%	42.2%	57.8%
3,937	PAWNEE	1,879	777	1,102		325 D	41.4%	58.6%	41.4%	58.6%
3,637	PERKINS	1,754	965	789		176 R	55.0%	45.0%	55.0%	45.0%
9,769	PHELPS	4,560	2,422	2,138		284 R	53.1%	46.9%	53.1%	46.9%
8,481	PIERCE	3,636	1,746	1,890		144 D	48.0%	52.0%	48.0%	52.0%
28,852	PLATTE	12,235	5,869	6,364	2	495 D	48.0%	52.0%	48.0%	52.0%
6,320	POLK	2,799	1,320	1,479		159 D	47.2%	52.8%	47.2%	52.8%
12,615	RED WILLOW	5,122	2,393	2,728	1	335 D	46.7%	53.3%	46.7%	53.3%
11,315	RICHARDSON	5,136	2,395	2,741		346 D	46.6%	53.4%	46.6%	53.4%
2,383	ROCK	1,044	510	534		24 D	48.9%	51.1%	48.9%	51.1%
13,131	SALINE	5,448	1,714	3,734		2,020 D	31.5%	68.5%	31.5%	68.5%
86,015	SARPY	27,008	14,042	12,939	27	1,103 R	52.0%	47.9%	52.0%	48.0%
18,716	SAUNDERS	8,006	3,389	4,613	4	1,224 D	42.3%	57.6%	42.4%	57.6%
38,344	SCOTTS BLUFF	13,749	8,348	5,401		2,947 R	60.7%	39.3%	60.7%	39.3%
15,789	SEWARD	5,964	2,372	3,589	3	1,217 D	39.8%	60.2%	39.8%	60.2%
7,544	SHERIDAN	3,090	2,089	1,001		1,088 R	67.6%	32.4%	67.6%	32.4%
4,226	SHERMAN	1,893	673	1,220		547 D	35.6%	64.4%	35.6%	64.4%
1,845	SIOUX	859	550	309		241 R	64.0%	36.0%	64.0%	36.0%
6,549	STANTON	2,503	1,262	1,241		21 R	50.4%	49.6%	50.4%	49.6%
7,582	THAYER	3,645	1,614	2,030	1	416 D	44.3%	55.7%	44.3%	55.7%
973	THOMAS	478	275	203		72 R	57.5%	42.5%	57.5%	42.5%
7,186	THURSTON	2,479	947	1,531	1	584 D	38.2%	61.8%	38.2%	61.8%
5,633	VALLEY	2,886	1,250	1,636		386 D	43.3%	56.7%	43.3%	56.7%
15,508	WASHINGTON	6,704	3,353	3,351		2 R	50.0%	50.0%	50.0%	50.0%
9,858	WAYNE	3,996	1,985	2,011		26 D	49.7%	50.3%	49.7%	50.3%
4,858	WEBSTER	2,376	1,148	1,228		80 D	48.3%	51.7%	48.3%	51.7%
1,060	WHEELER	472	206	266		60 D	43.6%	56.4%	43.6%	56.4%
14,798	YORK	6,319	3,494	2,825		669 R	55.3%	44.7%	55.3%	44.7%
1,569,825	TOTAL	639,668	307,147	332,217	304	25,070 D	48.0%	51.9%	48.0%	52.0%

NEBRASKA

CONGRESS

CD	Year	Total Vote	Republican		Democratic		Other Vote	Rep.-Dem. Plurality	Percentage			
			Vote	Candidate	Vote	Candidate			Total Vote Rep.	Dem.	Major Vote Rep.	Dem.
1	1984	214,364	158,836	BEREUTER, DOUGLAS K.	55,508	BAUER, MONICA	20	103,328 R	74.1%	25.9%	74.1%	25.9%
1	1982	183,368	137,675	BEREUTER, DOUGLAS K.	45,676	DONALDSON, CURT	17	91,999 R	75.1%	24.9%	75.1%	24.9%
2	1984	214,883	139,384	DAUB, HAROLD J.	75,210	CAVANAUGH, THOMAS F.	289	64,174 R	64.9%	35.0%	65.0%	35.0%
2	1982	163,349	92,639	DAUB, HAROLD J.	70,431	FELLMAN, RICHARD M.	279	22,208 R	56.7%	43.1%	56.8%	43.2%
3	1984	220,814	183,901	SMITH, VIRGINIA	36,899	VICKERS, TOM	14	147,002 R	83.3%	16.7%	83.3%	16.7%
3	1982	172,364	171,853	SMITH, VIRGINIA			511	171,853 R	99.7%		100.0%	

NEBRASKA

1984 GENERAL ELECTION

President Other vote was 2,079 Bergland (Libertarian); 1,066 Mason (Independent); 1,025 Serrette (Independent). State and county totals include new resident votes reported separately.

Senator Other vote was scattered.

Congress Other vote was scattered in all three CD's.

1984 PRIMARIES

MAY 15 REPUBLICAN

Senator 61,009 Nancy Hoch; 24,730 John W. DeCamp; 23,720 Richard N. Thompson; 21,115 Fred A. Lockwood; 16,123 Ken Cameron; 3,926 George A. Boucher; 178 scattered.

Congress Unopposed in all three CD's.

MAY 15 DEMOCRATIC

Senator J. J. Exon, unopposed.

Congress Unopposed in CD 3. Contested as follows:

CD 1 26,660 Monica Bauer; 8,717 Donald A. Bercey; 5,401 Marlin R. Pals; 36 scattered.
CD 2 26,027 Thomas F. Cavanaugh; 20,606 Walter M. Calinger; 2,358 Daniel K. Powers; 184 scattered.

NEVADA

GOVERNOR
Richard H. Bryan (D). Elected 1982 to a four-year term.

SENATORS
Chic Hecht (R). Elected 1982 to a six-year term.

Paul Laxalt (R). Re-elected 1980 to a six-year term. Previously elected 1974.

REPRESENTATIVES
1. Harry Reid (D)   2. Barbara Vucanovich (R)

POSTWAR VOTE FOR GOVERNOR

| | | | | | | | | | Percentage | | | |
| | Total | Republican | | Democratic | | Other | Rep.-Dem. | | Total Vote | | Major Vote | |
Year	Vote	Vote	Candidate	Vote	Candidate	Vote	Plurality		Rep.	Dem.	Rep.	Dem.
1982	239,751	100,104	List, Robert F.	128,132	Bryan, Richard H.	11,515	28,028	D	41.8%	53.4%	43.9%	56.1%
1978	192,445	108,097	List, Robert F.	76,361	Rose, Robert E.	7,987	31,736	R	56.2%	39.7%	58.6%	41.4%
1974	169,358	28,959	Crumpler, Shirley	114,114	O'Callaghan, Mike	26,285	85,155	D	17.1%	67.4%	20.2%	79.8%
1970	146,991	64,400	Fike, Ed	70,697	O'Callaghan, Mike	11,894	6,297	D	43.8%	48.1%	47.7%	52.3%
1966	137,677	71,807	Laxalt, Paul	65,870	Sawyer, Grant	—	5,937	R	52.2%	47.8%	52.2%	47.8%
1962	96,929	32,145	Gragson, Oran K.	64,784	Sawyer, Grant	—	32,639	D	33.2%	66.8%	33.2%	66.8%
1958	84,889	34,025	Russell, Charles H.	50,864	Sawyer, Grant	—	16,839	D	40.1%	59.9%	40.1%	59.9%
1954	78,462	41,665	Russell, Charles H.	36,797	Pittman, Vail	—	4,868	R	53.1%	46.9%	53.1%	46.9%
1950	61,773	35,609	Russell, Charles H.	26,164	Pittman, Vail	—	9,445	R	57.6%	42.4%	57.6%	42.4%
1946	49,902	21,247	Jepson, Melvin E.	28,655	Pittman, Vail	—	7,408	D	42.6%	57.4%	42.6%	57.4%

POSTWAR VOTE FOR SENATOR

| | | | | | | | | | Percentage | | | |
| | Total | Republican | | Democratic | | Other | Rep.-Dem. | | Total Vote | | Major Vote | |
Year	Vote	Vote	Candidate	Vote	Candidate	Vote	Plurality		Rep.	Dem.	Rep.	Dem.
1982	240,394	120,377	Hecht, Chic	114,720	Cannon, Howard W.	5,297	5,657	R	50.1%	47.7%	51.2%	48.8%
1980	246,436	144,224	Laxalt, Paul	92,129	Gojack, Mary	10,083	52,095	R	58.5%	37.4%	61.0%	39.0%
1976	201,980	63,471	Towell, David	127,295	Cannon, Howard W.	11,214	63,824	D	31.4%	63.0%	33.3%	66.7%
1974	169,473	79,605	Laxalt, Paul	78,981	Reid, Harry	10,887	624	R	47.0%	46.6%	50.2%	49.8%
1970	147,768	60,838	Raggio, William J.	85,187	Cannon, Howard W.	1,743	24,349	D	41.2%	57.6%	41.7%	58.3%
1968	152,690	69,068	Fike, Ed	83,622	Bible, Alan	—	14,554	D	45.2%	54.8%	45.2%	54.8%
1964	134,624	67,288	Laxalt, Paul	67,336	Cannon, Howard W.	—	48	D	50.0%	50.0%	50.0%	50.0%
1962	97,192	33,749	Wright, William B.	63,443	Bible, Alan	—	29,694	D	34.7%	65.3%	34.7%	65.3%
1958	84,492	35,760	Malone, George W.	48,732	Cannon, Howard W.	—	12,972	D	42.3%	57.7%	42.3%	57.7%
1956	96,389	45,712	Young, Clifton	50,677	Bible, Alan	—	4,965	D	47.4%	52.6%	47.4%	52.6%
1954s	77,513	32,470	Brown, Ernest S.	45,043	Bible, Alan	—	12,573	D	41.9%	58.1%	41.9%	58.1%
1952	81,090	41,906	Malone, George W.	39,184	Mechling, Thomas B.	—	2,722	R	51.7%	48.3%	51.7%	48.3%
1950	61,762	25,933	Marshall, George E.	35,829	McCarran, Pat	—	9,896	D	42.0%	58.0%	42.0%	58.0%
1946	50,354	27,801	Malone, George W.	22,553	Bunker, Berkeley	—	5,248	R	55.2%	44.8%	55.2%	44.8%

The 1954 election was for a short term to fill a vacancy.

NEVADA

Districts Established June 4, 1981

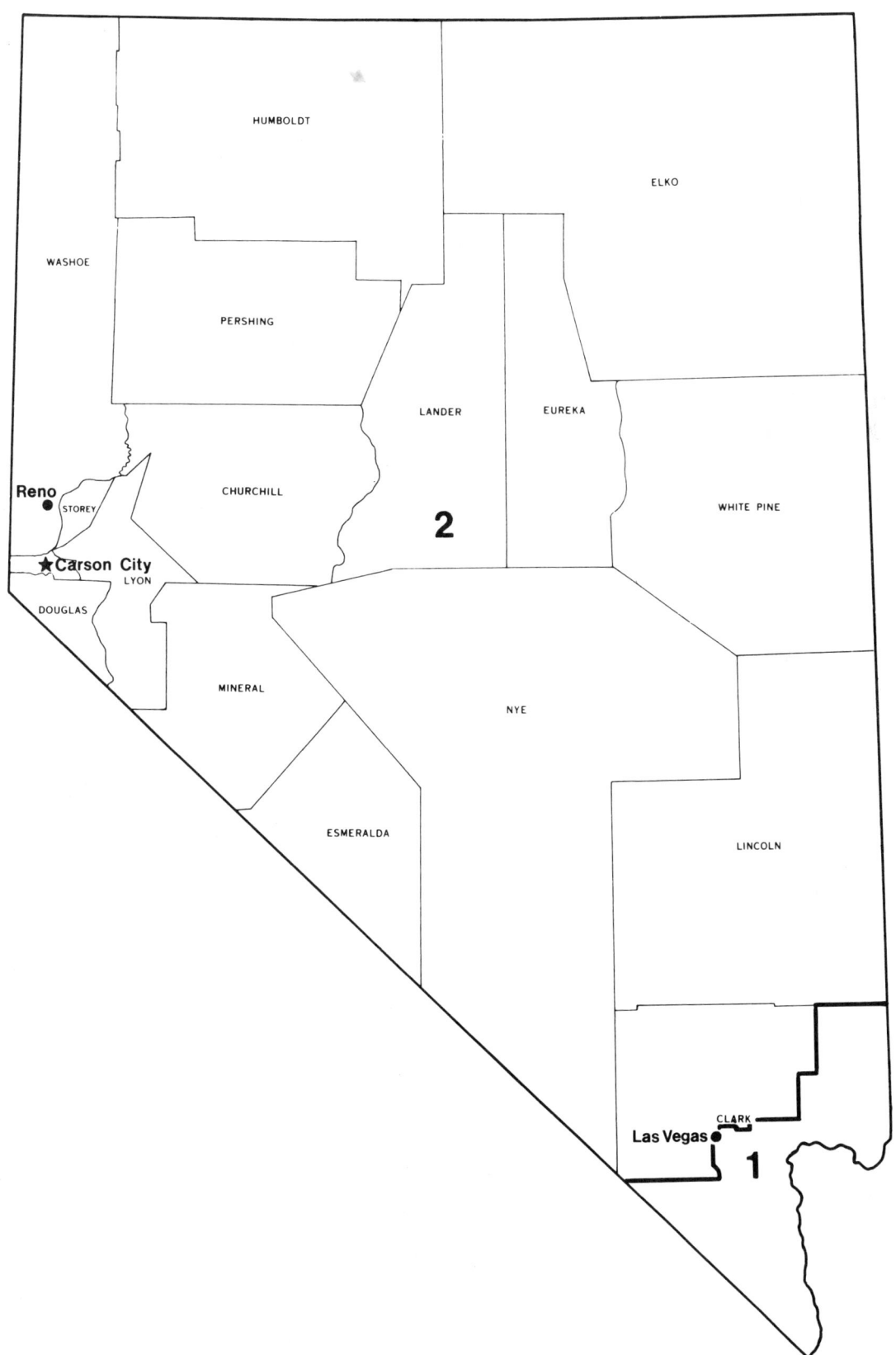

© ERC

NEVADA

PRESIDENT 1984

1980 Census Population	County	Total Vote	Republican	Democratic	Other	Rep.-Dem. Plurality	Percentage			
							Total Vote		Major Vote	
							Rep.	Dem.	Rep.	Dem.
32,022	CARSON CITY	13,536	9,477	3,790	269	5,687 R	70.0%	28.0%	71.4%	28.6%
13,917	CHURCHILL	5,930	4,479	1,304	147	3,175 R	75.5%	22.0%	77.5%	22.5%
463,087	CLARK	150,363	94,133	53,386	2,844	40,747 R	62.6%	35.5%	63.8%	36.2%
19,421	DOUGLAS	8,449	6,385	1,877	187	4,508 R	75.6%	22.2%	77.3%	22.7%
17,269	ELKO	6,861	5,110	1,566	185	3,544 R	74.5%	22.8%	76.5%	23.5%
777	ESMERALDA	647	453	158	36	295 R	70.0%	24.4%	74.1%	25.9%
1,198	EUREKA	578	439	124	15	315 R	76.0%	21.5%	78.0%	22.0%
9,434	HUMBOLDT	3,450	2,498	862	90	1,636 R	72.4%	25.0%	74.3%	25.7%
4,076	LANDER	1,561	1,222	301	38	921 R	78.3%	19.3%	80.2%	19.8%
3,732	LINCOLN	1,616	1,175	397	44	778 R	72.7%	24.6%	74.7%	25.3%
13,594	LYON	6,177	4,320	1,673	184	2,647 R	69.9%	27.1%	72.1%	27.9%
6,217	MINERAL	2,504	1,645	766	93	879 R	65.7%	30.6%	68.2%	31.8%
9,048	NYE	4,989	3,573	1,269	147	2,304 R	71.6%	25.4%	73.8%	26.2%
3,408	PERSHING	1,330	956	333	41	623 R	71.9%	25.0%	74.2%	25.8%
1,503	STOREY	854	570	252	32	318 R	66.7%	29.5%	69.3%	30.7%
193,623	WASHOE	74,511	50,418	22,321	1,772	28,097 R	67.7%	30.0%	69.3%	30.7%
8,167	WHITE PINE	3,311	1,917	1,276	118	641 R	57.9%	38.5%	60.0%	40.0%
800,493	TOTAL	286,667	188,770	91,655	6,242	97,115 R	65.8%	32.0%	67.3%	32.7%

NEVADA

CONGRESS

CD	Year	Total Vote	Republican Vote	Republican Candidate	Democratic Vote	Democratic Candidate	Other Vote	Rep.-Dem. Plurality	Percentage Total Vote Rep.	Total Vote Dem.	Major Vote Rep.	Major Vote Dem.
1	1984	130,518	55,391	CAVNAR, PEGGY	73,242	REID, HARRY	1,885	17,851 D	42.4%	56.1%	43.1%	56.9%
1	1982	107,576	45,675	CAVNAR, PEGGY	61,901	REID, HARRY		16,226 D	42.5%	57.5%	42.5%	57.5%
2	1984	140,106	99,775	VUCANOVICH, BARBARA	36,130	BARBANO, ANDREW	4,201	63,645 R	71.2%	25.8%	73.4%	26.6%
2	1982	126,496	70,188	VUCANOVICH, BARBARA	52,265	GOJACK, MARY	4,043	17,923 R	55.5%	41.3%	57.3%	42.7%

NEVADA

1984 GENERAL ELECTION

President   Other vote was 2,292 Bergland (Libertarian); 3,950 "None of these Candidates."

Congress   Other vote was Morris (Libertarian) in CD 1; Becan (Libertarian) in CD 2.

1984 PRIMARIES

SEPTEMBER 4 REPUBLICAN

Congress   Unopposed in CD 2. Contested as follows:

   CD   1   14,442 Peggy Cavnar; 2,896 Richard Gilster.

SEPTEMBER 4 DEMOCRATIC

Congress   Unopposed in both CD's.

SEPTEMBER 4 LIBERTARIAN

Congress   Unopposed in CD 1. Contested as follows:

   CD   2   67 Dan Becan; 39 Kent Cromwell.

NEW HAMPSHIRE

GOVERNOR
John H. Sununu (R). Re-elected 1984 to a two-year term. Previously elected 1982.

SENATORS
Gordon J. Humphrey (R). Re-elected 1984 to a six-year term. Previously elected 1978.

Warren Rudman (R). Elected 1980 to a six-year term.

REPRESENTATIVES
1. Robert C. Smith (R)   2. Judd Gregg (R)

POSTWAR VOTE FOR GOVERNOR

Year	Total Vote	Republican Vote	Candidate	Democratic Vote	Candidate	Other Vote	Rep.-Dem. Plurality	Total Vote Rep.	Dem.	Major Vote Rep.	Dem.
1984	383,910	256,574	Sununu, John H.	127,156	Spirou, Chris	180	129,418 R	66.8%	33.1%	66.9%	33.1%
1982	282,588	145,389	Sununu, John H.	132,317	Gallen, Hugh J.	4,882	13,072 R	51.4%	46.8%	52.4%	47.6%
1980	384,031	156,178	Thomson, Meldrim	226,436	Gallen, Hugh J.	1,417	70,258 D	40.7%	59.0%	40.8%	59.2%
1978	269,587	122,464	Thomson, Meldrim	133,133	Gallen, Hugh J.	13,990	10,669 D	45.4%	49.4%	47.9%	52.1%
1976	342,669	197,589	Thomson, Meldrim	145,015	Spanos, Harry V.	65	52,574 R	57.7%	42.3%	57.7%	42.3%
1974	226,665	115,933	Thomson, Meldrim	110,591	Leonard, Richard W.	141	5,342 R	51.1%	48.8%	51.2%	48.8%
1972	323,102	133,702	Thomson, Meldrim	126,107	Crowley, Roger J.	63,293	7,595 R	41.4%	39.0%	51.5%	48.5%
1970	222,441	102,298	Peterson, Walter R.	98,098	Crowley, Roger J.	22,045	4,200 R	46.0%	44.1%	51.0%	49.0%
1968	285,342	149,902	Peterson, Walter R.	135,378	Bussiere, Emile R.	62	14,524 R	52.5%	47.4%	52.5%	47.5%
1966	233,642	107,259	Gregg, Hugh	125,882	King, John W.	501	18,623 D	45.9%	53.9%	46.0%	54.0%
.1964	285,863	94,824	Pillsbury, John	190,863	King, John W.	176	96,039 D	33.2%	66.8%	33.2%	66.8%
1962	230,048	94,567	Pillsbury, John	135,481	King, John W.	—	40,914 D	41.1%	58.9%	41.1%	58.9%
1960	290,527	161,123	Powell, Wesley	129,404	Boutin, Bernard L.	—	31,719 R	55.5%	44.5%	55.5%	44.5%
1958	206,745	106,790	Powell, Wesley	99,955	Boutin, Bernard L.	—	6,835 R	51.7%	48.3%	51.7%	48.3%
1956	258,695	141,578	Dwinell, Lane	117,117	Shaw, John	—	24,461 R	54.7%	45.3%	54.7%	45.3%
1954	194,631	107,287	Dwinell, Lane	87,344	Shaw, John	—	19,943 R	55.1%	44.9%	55.1%	44.9%
1952	265,715	167,791	Gregg, Hugh	97,924	Craig, William H.	—	69,867 R	63.1%	36.9%	63.1%	36.9%
1950	191,239	108,907	Adams, Sherman	82,258	Bingham, Robert P.	74	26,649 R	56.9%	43.0%	57.0%	43.0%
1948	222,571	116,212	Adams, Sherman	105,207	Hill, Herbert W.	1,152	11,005 R	52.2%	47.3%	52.5%	47.5%
1946	163,451	103,204	Dale, Charles M.	60,247	Keefe, F. Clyde	—	42,957 R	63.1%	36.9%	63.1%	36.9%

POSTWAR VOTE FOR SENATOR

Year	Total Vote	Republican Vote	Candidate	Democratic Vote	Candidate	Other Vote	Rep.-Dem. Plurality	Total Vote Rep.	Dem.	Major Vote Rep.	Dem.
1984	384,406	225,828	Humphrey, Gordon J.	157,447	D'Amours, Norman E.	1,131	68,381 R	58.7%	41.0%	58.9%	41.1%
1980	375,064	195,563	Rudman, Warren	179,455	Durkin, John A.	46	16,108 R	52.1%	47.8%	52.1%	47.9%
1978	263,779	133,745	Humphrey, Gordon J.	127,945	McIntyre, Thomas J.	2,089	5,800 R	50.7%	48.5%	51.1%	48.9%
1975s	262,682	113,007	Wyman, Louis C.	140,778	Durkin, John A.	8,897	27,771 D	43.0%	53.6%	44.5%	55.5%
1974*	223,363	110,926	Wyman, Louis C.	110,924	Durkin, John A.	1,513	2 R	49.7%	49.7%	50.0%	50.0%
1972	324,354	139,852	Powell, Wesley	184,495	McIntyre, Thomas J.	7	44,643 D	43.1%	56.9%	43.1%	56.9%
1968	286,989	170,163	Cotton, Norris	116,816	King, John W.	10	53,347 R	59.3%	40.7%	59.3%	40.7%
1966	229,305	105,241	Thyng, Harrison R.	123,888	McIntyre, Thomas J.	176	18,647 D	45.9%	54.0%	45.9%	54.1%
1962	224,479	134,035	Cotton, Norris	90,444	Catalfo, Alfred	—	43,591 R	59.7%	40.3%	59.7%	40.3%
1962s	224,811	107,199	Bass, Perkins	117,612	McIntyre, Thomas J.	—	10,413 D	47.7%	52.3%	47.7%	52.3%
1960	287,545	173,521	Bridges, Styles	114,024	Hill, Herbert W.	—	59,497 R	60.3%	39.7%	60.3%	39.7%
1956	251,943	161,424	Cotton, Norris	90,519	Pickett, Laurence M.	—	70,905 R	64.1%	35.9%	64.1%	35.9%
1954	194,536	117,150	Bridges, Styles	77,386	Morin, Gerard L.	—	39,764 R	60.2%	39.8%	60.2%	39.8%
1954s	189,558	114,068	Cotton, Norris	75,490	Bentley, Stanley J.	—	38,578 R	60.2%	39.8%	60.2%	39.8%
1950	190,573	106,142	Tobey, Charles W.	72,473	Kelley, Emmet J.	11,958	33,669 R	55.7%	38.0%	59.4%	40.6%
1948	222,898	129,600	Bridges, Styles	91,760	Fortin, Alfred E.	1,538	37,840 R	58.1%	41.2%	58.5%	41.5%

One each of the 1962 and 1954 elections were for short terms to fill vacancies. Following the 1974 election, neither candidate was seated and the 1975 special election was held for the remaining years of this term.

NEW HAMPSHIRE

Districts Established March 4, 1982

COOS

GRAFTON

2

CARROLL

BELKNAP

1

SULLIVAN

MERRIMACK

STRAFFORD

Concord ★

Manchester ●

CHESHIRE

HILLSBOROUGH

ROCKINGHAM

Nashua ●

© ERC

NEW HAMPSHIRE

PRESIDENT 1984

1980 Census Population	County	Total Vote	Republican	Democratic	Other	Rep.-Dem. Plurality	Percentage Total Vote Rep.	Dem.	Major Vote Rep.	Dem.
42,884	BELKNAP	19,065	14,200	4,743	122	9,457 R	74.5%	24.9%	75.0%	25.0%
27,931	CARROLL	15,764	11,891	3,806	67	8,085 R	75.4%	24.1%	75.8%	24.2%
62,116	CHESHIRE	24,943	15,851	8,990	102	6,861 R	63.5%	36.0%	63.8%	36.2%
35,147	COOS	14,059	10,013	4,004	42	6,009 R	71.2%	28.5%	71.4%	28.6%
65,806	GRAFTON	27,300	18,451	8,757	92	9,694 R	67.6%	32.1%	67.8%	32.2%
276,608	HILLSBOROUGH	115,278	81,462	33,314	502	48,148 R	70.7%	28.9%	71.0%	29.0%
98,302	MERRIMACK	41,591	27,925	13,510	156	14,415 R	67.1%	32.5%	67.4%	32.6%
190,345	ROCKINGHAM	83,439	57,586	25,557	296	32,029 R	69.0%	30.6%	69.3%	30.7%
85,408	STRAFFORD	33,388	20,452	12,752	184	7,700 R	61.3%	38.2%	61.6%	38.4%
36,063	SULLIVAN	14,239	9,220	4,962	57	4,258 R	64.8%	34.8%	65.0%	35.0%
920,610	TOTAL	389,066	267,051	120,395	1,620	146,656 R	68.6%	30.9%	68.9%	31.1%

NEW HAMPSHIRE

PRESIDENT 1984

1980 Census Population	City/Town	Total Vote	Republican	Democratic	Other	Rep.-Dem. Plurality	Percentage Total Vote Rep.	Dem.	Major Vote Rep.	Dem.
8,243	AMHERST	4,147	3,235	899	13	2,336 R	78.0%	21.7%	78.3%	21.7%
9,481	BEDFORD	5,341	4,294	1,034	13	3,260 R	80.4%	19.4%	80.6%	19.4%
13,084	BERLIN	5,147	3,261	1,863	23	1,398 R	63.4%	36.2%	63.6%	36.4%
14,557	CLAREMONT	4,887	2,868	2,006	13	862 R	58.7%	41.0%	58.8%	41.2%
30,400	CONCORD	12,405	7,190	5,172	43	2,018 R	58.0%	41.7%	58.2%	41.8%
7,158	CONWAY	3,236	2,337	881	18	1,456 R	72.2%	27.2%	72.6%	27.4%
18,875	DERRY	7,516	5,501	1,972	43	3,529 R	73.2%	26.2%	73.6%	26.4%
22,377	DOVER	9,267	5,397	3,826	44	1,571 R	58.2%	41.3%	58.5%	41.5%
10,652	DURHAM	3,445	1,628	1,794	23	166 D	47.3%	52.1%	47.6%	52.4%
11,024	EXETER	4,384	2,879	1,498	7	1,381 R	65.7%	34.2%	65.8%	34.2%
7,901	FRANKLIN	2,872	2,056	802	14	1,254 R	71.6%	27.9%	71.9%	28.1%
11,315	GOFFSTOWN	5,028	3,795	1,218	15	2,577 R	75.5%	24.2%	75.7%	24.3%
10,493	HAMPTON	5,389	3,485	1,878	26	1,607 R	64.7%	34.8%	65.0%	35.0%
9,119	HANOVER	3,398	1,501	1,886	11	385 D	44.2%	55.5%	44.3%	55.7%
7,303	HOOKSETT	3,076	2,425	638	13	1,787 R	78.8%	20.7%	79.2%	20.8%
14,022	HUDSON	5,714	4,076	1,617	21	2,459 R	71.3%	28.3%	71.6%	28.4%
21,449	KEENE	8,236	4,975	3,238	23	1,737 R	60.4%	39.3%	60.6%	39.4%
15,575	LACONIA	5,770	4,151	1,552	67	2,599 R	71.9%	26.9%	72.8%	27.2%
11,134	LEBANON	4,389	2,606	1,774	9	832 R	59.4%	40.4%	59.5%	40.5%
5,558	LITTLETON	2,294	1,788	506		1,282 R	77.9%	22.1%	77.9%	22.1%
13,598	LONDONDERRY	5,408	4,154	1,236	18	2,918 R	76.8%	22.9%	77.1%	22.9%
90,936	MANCHESTER	35,182	24,780	10,284	118	14,496 R	70.4%	29.2%	70.7%	29.3%
15,406	MERRIMACK TOWN	6,291	4,736	1,532	23	3,204 R	75.3%	24.4%	75.6%	24.4%
8,684	MILFORD	3,695	2,734	953	8	1,781 R	74.0%	25.8%	74.2%	25.8%
67,865	NASHUA	26,481	16,961	9,305	215	7,656 R	64.0%	35.1%	64.6%	35.4%
6,229	NEWPORT	1,985	1,400	576	9	824 R	70.5%	29.0%	70.9%	29.1%
8,090	PELHAM	3,428	2,532	889	7	1,643 R	73.9%	25.9%	74.0%	26.0%
5,609	PLAISTOW	2,379	1,719	651	9	1,068 R	72.3%	27.4%	72.5%	27.5%
5,094	PLYMOUTH	1,500	1,057	436	7	621 R	70.5%	29.1%	70.8%	29.2%
26,254	PORTSMOUTH	17,192	12,744	4,418	30	8,326 R	74.1%	25.7%	74.3%	25.7%
5,453	RAYMOND	2,329	1,752	574	3	1,178 R	75.2%	24.6%	75.3%	24.7%
21,560	ROCHESTER	8,107	5,457	2,622	28	2,835 R	67.3%	32.3%	67.5%	32.5%
24,124	SALEM	9,642	6,583	3,021	38	3,562 R	68.3%	31.3%	68.5%	31.5%
5,917	SEABROOK	2,592	1,761	812	19	949 R	67.9%	31.3%	68.4%	31.6%
10,350	SOMERSWORTH	3,781	2,135	1,611	35	524 R	56.5%	42.6%	57.0%	43.0%
5,183	SWANZEY	2,044	1,400	639	5	761 R	68.5%	31.3%	68.7%	31.3%
5,664	WINDHAM	3,009	2,220	775	14	1,445 R	73.8%	25.8%	74.1%	25.9%

NEW HAMPSHIRE

GOVERNOR 1984

1980 Census Population	County	Total Vote	Republican	Democratic	Other	Rep.-Dem. Plurality	Percentage			
							Total Vote		Major Vote	
							Rep.	Dem.	Rep.	Dem.
42,884	BELKNAP	18,879	12,994	5,879	6	7,115 R	68.8%	31.1%	68.8%	31.2%
27,931	CARROLL	15,641	12,073	3,565	3	8,508 R	77.2%	22.8%	77.2%	22.8%
62,116	CHESHIRE	24,476	13,560	10,902	14	2,658 R	55.4%	44.5%	55.4%	44.6%
35,147	COOS	14,116	9,601	4,510	5	5,091 R	68.0%	31.9%	68.0%	32.0%
65,806	GRAFTON	26,908	18,655	8,238	15	10,417 R	69.3%	30.6%	69.4%	30.6%
276,608	HILLSBOROUGH	112,035	80,034	31,973	28	48,061 R	71.4%	28.5%	71.5%	28.5%
98,302	MERRIMACK	41,610	25,528	16,045	37	9,483 R	61.4%	38.6%	61.4%	38.6%
190,345	ROCKINGHAM	82,756	55,881	26,835	40	29,046 R	67.5%	32.4%	67.6%	32.4%
85,408	STRAFFORD	33,144	19,299	13,818	27	5,481 R	58.2%	41.7%	58.3%	41.7%
36,063	SULLIVAN	14,345	8,949	5,391	5	3,558 R	62.4%	37.6%	62.4%	37.6%
920,610	TOTAL	383,910	256,574	127,156	180	129,418 R	66.8%	33.1%	66.9%	33.1%

NEW HAMPSHIRE

GOVERNOR 1984

1980 Census Population	City/Town	Total Vote	Republican	Democratic	Other	Rep.-Dem. Plurality	Percentage			
							Total Vote		Major Vote	
							Rep.	Dem.	Rep.	Dem.
8,243	AMHERST	4,069	3,404	665		2,739 R	83.7%	16.3%	83.7%	16.3%
9,481	BEDFORD	5,364	4,477	887		3,590 R	83.5%	16.5%	83.5%	16.5%
13,084	BERLIN	5,214	2,982	2,229	3	753 R	57.2%	42.8%	57.2%	42.8%
14,557	CLAREMONT	4,944	2,793	2,151		642 R	56.5%	43.5%	56.5%	43.5%
30,400	CONCORD	12,226	6,415	5,804	7	611 R	52.5%	47.5%	52.5%	47.5%
7,158	CONWAY	3,214	2,471	743		1,728 R	76.9%	23.1%	76.9%	23.1%
18,875	DERRY	7,399	5,542	1,857		3,685 R	74.9%	25.1%	74.9%	25.1%
22,377	DOVER	9,338	5,426	3,899	13	1,527 R	58.1%	41.8%	58.2%	41.8%
10,652	DURHAM	3,337	1,886	1,433	18	453 R	56.5%	42.9%	56.8%	43.2%
11,024	EXETER	4,238	2,747	1,490	1	1,257 R	64.8%	35.2%	64.8%	35.2%
7,901	FRANKLIN	2,856	1,831	1,025		806 R	64.1%	35.9%	64.1%	35.9%
11,315	GOFFSTOWN	5,171	3,914	1,257		2,657 R	75.7%	24.3%	75.7%	24.3%
10,493	HAMPTON	5,393	3,228	2,158	7	1,070 R	59.9%	40.0%	59.9%	40.1%
9,119	HANOVER	3,254	1,715	1,539		176 R	52.7%	47.3%	52.7%	47.3%
7,303	HOOKSETT	3,106	2,328	776	2	1,552 R	75.0%	25.0%	75.0%	25.0%
14,022	HUDSON	5,789	3,821	1,968		1,853 R	66.0%	34.0%	66.0%	34.0%
21,449	KEENE	8,062	3,987	4,071	4	84 D	49.5%	50.5%	49.5%	50.5%
15,575	LACONIA	5,647	3,683	1,961	3	1,722 R	65.2%	34.7%	65.3%	34.7%
11,134	LEBANON	4,279	2,531	1,742	6	789 R	59.1%	40.7%	59.2%	40.8%
5,558	LITTLETON	2,273	1,747	526		1,221 R	76.9%	23.1%	76.9%	23.1%
13,598	LONDONDERRY	5,329	4,079	1,249	1	2,830 R	76.5%	23.4%	76.6%	23.4%
90,936	MANCHESTER	33,456	23,878	9,568	10	14,310 R	71.4%	28.6%	71.4%	28.6%
15,406	MERRIMACK TOWN	6,367	4,819	1,544	4	3,275 R	75.7%	24.3%	75.7%	24.3%
8,684	MILFORD	3,613	2,756	854	3	1,902 R	76.3%	23.6%	76.3%	23.7%
67,865	NASHUA	25,076	16,042	9,031	3	7,011 R	64.0%	36.0%	64.0%	36.0%
6,229	NEWPORT	2,013	1,330	683		647 R	66.1%	33.9%	66.1%	33.9%
8,090	PELHAM	3,396	2,560	836		1,724 R	75.4%	24.6%	75.4%	24.6%
5,609	PLAISTOW	2,300	1,637	663		974 R	71.2%	28.8%	71.2%	28.8%
5,094	PLYMOUTH	1,514	1,137	372	5	765 R	75.1%	24.6%	75.3%	24.7%
26,254	PORTSMOUTH	8,959	4,443	4,511	5	68 D	49.6%	50.4%	49.6%	50.4%
5,453	RAYMOND	2,332	1,692	636	4	1,056 R	72.6%	27.3%	72.7%	27.3%
21,560	ROCHESTER	7,961	4,896	3,061	4	1,835 R	61.5%	38.4%	61.5%	38.5%
24,124	SALEM	9,742	6,959	2,783		4,176 R	71.4%	28.6%	71.4%	28.6%
5,917	SEABROOK	2,569	1,745	824		921 R	67.9%	32.1%	67.9%	32.1%
10,350	SOMERSWORTH	3,740	1,864	1,873	3	9 D	49.8%	50.1%	49.9%	50.1%
5,183	SWANZEY	2,013	1,063	950		113 R	52.8%	47.2%	52.8%	47.2%
5,664	WINDHAM	2,968	2,262	703	3	1,559 R	76.2%	23.7%	76.3%	23.7%

NEW HAMPSHIRE

SENATOR 1984

1980 Census Population	County	Total Vote	Republican	Democratic	Other	Rep.-Dem. Plurality	Percentage			
							Total Vote		Major Vote	
							Rep.	Dem.	Rep.	Dem.
42,884	BELKNAP	19,015	11,696	7,266	53	4,430 R	61.5%	38.2%	61.7%	38.3%
27,931	CARROLL	15,573	10,495	5,055	23	5,440 R	67.4%	32.5%	67.5%	32.5%
62,116	CHESHIRE	24,856	14,678	10,108	70	4,570 R	59.1%	40.7%	59.2%	40.8%
35,147	COOS	14,027	9,389	4,603	35	4,786 R	66.9%	32.8%	67.1%	32.9%
65,806	GRAFTON	26,957	16,509	10,390	58	6,119 R	61.2%	38.5%	61.4%	38.6%
276,608	HILLSBOROUGH	112,273	66,830	45,014	429	21,816 R	59.5%	40.1%	59.8%	40.2%
98,302	MERRIMACK	41,416	23,804	17,470	142	6,334 R	57.5%	42.2%	57.7%	42.3%
190,345	ROCKINGHAM	82,255	48,260	33,747	248	14,513 R	58.7%	41.0%	58.8%	41.2%
85,408	STRAFFORD	33,590	15,811	17,730	49	1,919 D	47.1%	52.8%	47.1%	52.9%
36,063	SULLIVAN	14,444	8,356	6,064	24	2,292 R	57.9%	42.0%	57.9%	42.1%
920,610	TOTAL	384,406	225,828	157,447	1,131	68,381 R	58.7%	41.0%	58.9%	41.1%

NEW HAMPSHIRE

SENATOR 1984

1980 Census Population	City/Town	Total Vote	Republican	Democratic	Other	Rep.-Dem. Plurality	Percentage			
							Total Vote		Major Vote	
							Rep.	Dem.	Rep.	Dem.
8,243	AMHERST	4,105	3,029	1,030	46	1,999 R	73.8%	25.1%	74.6%	25.4%
9,481	BEDFORD	5,304	3,540	1,756	8	1,784 R	66.7%	33.1%	66.8%	33.2%
13,084	BERLIN	5,446	2,956	2,468	22	488 R	54.3%	45.3%	54.5%	45.5%
14,557	CLAREMONT	4,993	2,561	2,421	11	140 R	51.3%	48.5%	51.4%	48.6%
30,400	CONCORD	11,949	5,730	6,162	57	432 D	48.0%	51.6%	48.2%	51.8%
7,158	CONWAY	3,233	2,181	1,045	7	1,136 R	67.5%	32.3%	67.6%	32.4%
18,875	DERRY	7,311	4,597	2,691	23	1,906 R	62.9%	36.8%	63.1%	36.9%
22,377	DOVER	9,412	4,127	5,270	15	1,143 D	43.8%	56.0%	43.9%	56.1%
10,652	DURHAM	3,361	1,310	2,050	1	740 D	39.0%	61.0%	39.0%	61.0%
11,024	EXETER	4,306	2,256	2,044	6	212 R	52.4%	47.5%	52.5%	47.5%
7,901	FRANKLIN	2,856	1,752	1,095	9	657 R	61.3%	38.3%	61.5%	38.5%
11,315	GOFFSTOWN	5,164	3,036	2,128		908 R	58.8%	41.2%	58.8%	41.2%
10,493	HAMPTON	5,386	2,836	2,536	14	300 R	52.7%	47.1%	52.8%	47.2%
9,119	HANOVER	3,321	1,301	2,007	13	706 D	39.2%	60.4%	39.3%	60.7%
7,303	HOOKSETT	3,103	1,942	1,150	11	792 R	62.6%	37.1%	62.8%	37.2%
14,022	HUDSON	5,763	3,620	2,087	56	1,533 R	62.8%	36.2%	63.4%	36.6%
21,449	KEENE	8,345	4,566	3,761	18	805 R	54.7%	45.1%	54.8%	45.2%
15,575	LACONIA	5,733	3,215	2,500	18	715 R	56.1%	43.6%	56.3%	43.7%
11,134	LEBANON	4,335	2,081	2,248	6	167 D	48.0%	51.9%	48.1%	51.9%
5,558	LITTLETON	2,243	1,645	598		1,047 R	73.3%	26.7%	73.3%	26.7%
13,598	LONDONDERRY	5,213	3,501	1,699	13	1,802 R	67.2%	32.6%	67.3%	32.7%
90,936	MANCHESTER	33,917	17,449	16,388	80	1,061 R	51.4%	48.3%	51.6%	48.4%
15,406	MERRIMACK TOWN	6,272	4,006	2,227	39	1,779 R	63.9%	35.5%	64.3%	35.7%
8,684	MILFORD	3,586	2,545	1,033	8	1,512 R	71.0%	28.8%	71.1%	28.9%
67,865	NASHUA	25,332	14,112	11,109	111	3,003 R	55.7%	43.9%	56.0%	44.0%
6,229	NEWPORT	2,035	1,250	779	6	471 R	61.4%	38.3%	61.6%	38.4%
8,090	PELHAM	3,100	2,091	1,002	7	1,089 R	67.5%	32.3%	67.6%	32.4%
5,609	PLAISTOW	2,308	1,476	829	3	647 R	64.0%	35.9%	64.0%	36.0%
5,094	PLYMOUTH	1,503	942	560	1	382 R	62.7%	37.3%	62.7%	37.3%
26,254	PORTSMOUTH	8,932	3,670	5,246	16	1,576 D	41.1%	58.7%	41.2%	58.8%
5,453	RAYMOND	2,271	1,437	828	6	609 R	63.3%	36.5%	63.4%	36.6%
21,560	ROCHESTER	8,133	4,232	3,892	9	340 R	52.0%	47.9%	52.1%	47.9%
24,124	SALEM	9,733	6,048	3,612	73	2,436 R	62.1%	37.1%	62.6%	37.4%
5,917	SEABROOK	2,494	1,464	1,017	13	447 R	58.7%	40.8%	59.0%	41.0%
10,350	SOMERSWORTH	3,834	1,485	2,344	5	859 D	38.7%	61.1%	38.8%	61.2%
5,183	SWANZEY	2,047	1,309	734	4	575 R	63.9%	35.9%	64.1%	35.9%
5,664	WINDHAM	2,946	2,019	913	14	1,106 R	68.5%	31.0%	68.9%	31.1%

NEW HAMPSHIRE

CONGRESS

CD	Year	Total Vote	Republican Vote	Candidate	Democratic Vote	Candidate	Other Vote	Rep.-Dem. Plurality	Percentage Total Vote Rep.	Dem.	Major Vote Rep.	Dem.
1	1984	190,516	111,627	SMITH, ROBERT C.	76,854	DUDLEY, DUDLEY	2,035	34,773 R	58.6%	40.3%	59.2%	40.8%
1	1982	138,911	61,876	SMITH, ROBERT C.	76,281	D'AMOURS, NORMAN E.	754	14,405 D	44.5%	54.9%	44.8%	55.2%
2	1984	182,444	138,975	GREGG, JUDD	42,257	CONVERSE, LARRY	1,212	96,718 R	76.2%	23.2%	76.7%	23.3%
2	1982	130,007	92,098	GREGG, JUDD	37,906	DUPAY, ROBERT L.	3	54,192 R	70.8%	29.2%	70.8%	29.2%

NEW HAMPSHIRE

1984 GENERAL ELECTION

In addition to the county-by-county figures, data are presented for selected New Hampshire communities. Since not all jurisdictions of the state are listed in this special tabulation, state-wide totals are shown only with the county-by-county statistics.

President Other vote was 735 Bergland (Libertarian); 467 LaRouche (Independent); 305 Serrette (Alliance); 113 scattered. Early uncorrected returns gave the Republican total state vote as 267,050 and the Democratic total state vote as 120,347; vote totals in Hillsborough and Grafton counties were amended.

Governor Other vote was scattered. Early uncorrected returns gave the Republican total state vote as 256,571; vote totals in Strafford county were amended.

Senator Other vote was 1,094 Primack (Libertarian) and 37 scattered.

Congress Other vote was 1,435 Muehlke (Independent), 570 Erickson (Libertarian) and 30 scattered in CD 1; 1,179 Groupe (Libertarian) and 33 scattered in CD 2.

1984 PRIMARIES

SEPTEMBER 11 REPUBLICAN

Governor 52,737 John H. Sununu; 8,994 James F. Fallon; 958 scattered.

Senator Gordon J. Humphrey, unopposed.

Congress Unopposed in CD 2. Contested as follows:

CD 1 14,598 Robert C. Smith; 8,928 Lawrence J. Brady; 5,577 Carleton Eldredge; 4,245 Robert B. Monier; 1,393 Lucille C. Lagasse; 195 scattered.

SEPTEMBER 11 DEMOCRATIC

Governor 22,835 Chris Spirou; 18,460 Paul McEachern; 4,060 Robert L. Dupay; 801 scattered.

Senator Norman E. D'Amours, unopposed.

Congress Contested as follows:

CD 1 14,086 Dudley Dudley; 12,910 James M. Demers; 1,149 Steven J. Grycel; 109 scattered.
CD 2 5,936 Larry Converse; 4,710 Elliot S. Maggin; 3,554 Carmen C. Chimento; 176 scattered.

NEW JERSEY

GOVERNOR
Thomas H. Kean (R). Elected 1981 to a four-year term.

SENATORS
Bill Bradley (D). Re-elected 1984 to a six-year term. Previously elected 1978.

Frank R. Lautenberg (D). Elected 1982 to a six-year term.

REPRESENTATIVES

1. James J. Florio (D)
2. William J. Hughes (D)
3. James J. Howard (D)
4. Christopher H. Smith (R)
5. Margaret S. Roukema (R)
6. Bernard J. Dwyer (D)
7. Matthew J. Rinaldo (R)
8. Robert A. Roe (D)
9. Robert G. Torricelli (D)
10. Peter W. Rodino (D)
11. Dean A. Gallo (R)
12. James A. Courter (R)
13. H. James Saxton (R)
14. Frank J. Guarini (D)

POSTWAR VOTE FOR GOVERNOR

Year	Total Vote	Republican Vote	Candidate	Democratic Vote	Candidate	Other Vote	Rep.-Dem. Plurality	Total Vote Rep.	Total Vote Dem.	Major Vote Rep.	Major Vote Dem.
1981	2,317,239	1,145,999	Kean, Thomas H.	1,144,202	Florio, James J.	27,038	1,797 R	49.5%	49.4%	50.0%	50.0%
1977	2,126,264	888,880	Bateman, Raymond H.	1,184,564	Byrne, Brendan T.	52,820	295,684 D	41.8%	55.7%	42.9%	57.1%
1973	2,122,009	676,235	Sandman, Charles W.	1,414,613	Byrne, Brendan T.	31,161	738,378 D	31.9%	66.7%	32.3%	67.7%
1969	2,366,606	1,411,905	Cahill, William T.	911,003	Meyner, Robert B.	43,698	500,902 R	59.7%	38.5%	60.8%	39.2%
1965	2,229,583	915,996	Dumont, Wayne	1,279,568	Hughes, Richard J.	34,019	363,572 D	41.1%	57.4%	41.7%	58.3%
1961	2,152,662	1,049,274	Mitchell, James P.	1,084,194	Hughes, Richard J.	19,194	34,920 D	48.7%	50.4%	49.2%	50.8%
1957	2,018,488	897,321	Forbes, Malcolm S.	1,101,130	Meyner, Robert B.	20,037	203,809 D	44.5%	54.6%	44.9%	55.1%
1953	1,810,812	809,068	Troast, Paul L.	962,710	Meyner, Robert B.	39,034	153,642 D	44.7%	53.2%	45.7%	54.3%
1949*	1,718,788	885,882	Driscoll, Alfred	810,022	Wene, Elmer H.	22,884	75,860 R	51.5%	47.1%	52.2%	47.8%
1946	1,414,527	807,378	Driscoll, Alfred	585,960	Hansen, Lewis G.	21,189	221,418 R	57.1%	41.4%	57.9%	42.1%

The term of office of New Jersey's Governor was increased from three to four years effective with the 1949 election.

POSTWAR VOTE FOR SENATOR

Year	Total Vote	Republican Vote	Candidate	Democratic Vote	Candidate	Other Vote	Rep.-Dem. Plurality	Total Vote Rep.	Total Vote Dem.	Major Vote Rep.	Major Vote Dem.
1984	3,096,456	1,080,100	Mochary, Mary V.	1,986,644	Bradley, Bill	29,712	906,544 D	34.9%	64.2%	35.2%	64.8%
1982	2,193,945	1,047,626	Fenwick, Millicent	1,117,549	Lautenberg, Frank R.	28,770	69,923 D	47.8%	50.9%	48.4%	51.6%
1978	1,957,515	844,200	Bell, Jeffrey	1,082,960	Bradley, Bill	30,355	238,760 D	43.1%	55.3%	43.8%	56.2%
1976	2,771,390	1,054,508	Norcross, David F.	1,681,140	Williams, Harrison	35,742	626,632 D	38.0%	60.7%	38.5%	61.5%
1972	2,791,907	1,743,854	Case, Clifford P.	963,573	Krebs, Paul J.	84,480	780,281 R	62.5%	34.5%	64.4%	35.6%
1970	2,142,105	903,026	Gross, Nelson G.	1,157,074	Williams, Harrison	82,005	254,048 D	42.2%	54.0%	43.8%	56.2%
1966	2,131,188	1,279,343	Case, Clifford P.	788,021	Wilentz, Warren W.	63,824	491,322 R	60.0%	37.0%	61.9%	38.1%
1964	2,710,441	1,011,610	Shanley, Bernard M.	1,678,051	Williams, Harrison	20,780	666,441 D	37.3%	61.9%	37.6%	62.4%
1960	2,664,556	1,483,832	Case, Clifford P.	1,151,385	Lord, Thorn	29,339	332,447 R	55.7%	43.2%	56.3%	43.7%
1958	1,881,329	882,287	Kean, Robert W.	966,832	Williams, Harrison	32,210	84,545 D	46.9%	51.4%	47.7%	52.3%
1954	1,770,557	861,528	Case, Clifford P.	858,158	Howell, Charles R.	50,871	3,370 R	48.7%	48.5%	50.1%	49.9%
1952	2,318,232	1,286,782	Smith, H. Alexander	1,011,187	Alexander, Archibald	20,263	275,595 R	55.5%	43.6%	56.0%	44.0%
1948	1,869,882	934,720	Hendrickson, Robert	884,414	Alexander, Archibald	50,748	50,306 R	50.0%	47.3%	51.4%	48.6%
1946	1,367,155	799,808	Smith, H. Alexander	548,458	Brunner, George E.	18,889	251,350 R	58.5%	40.1%	59.3%	40.7%

NEW JERSEY

Districts Established February 17, 1984

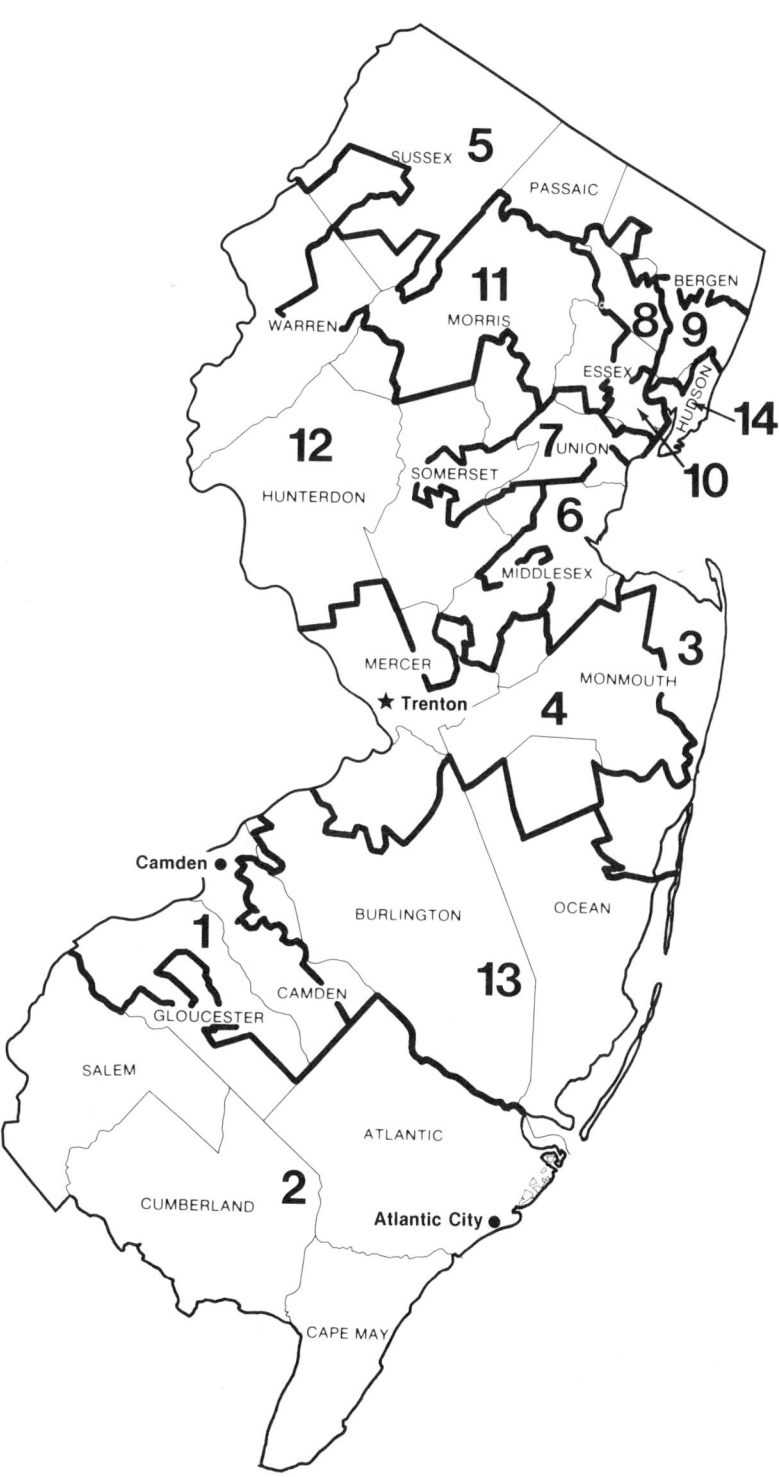

NEW JERSEY

PRESIDENT 1984

1980 Census Population	County	Total Vote	Republican	Democratic	Other	Rep.-Dem. Plurality	Percentage			
							Total Vote		Major Vote	
							Rep.	Dem.	Rep.	Dem.
194,119	ATLANTIC	82,851	49,158	33,240	453	15,918 R	59.3%	40.1%	59.7%	40.3%
845,385	BERGEN	424,718	268,507	155,039	1,172	113,468 R	63.2%	36.5%	63.4%	36.6%
362,542	BURLINGTON	147,659	89,815	57,467	377	32,348 R	60.8%	38.9%	61.0%	39.0%
471,650	CAMDEN	200,886	109,749	90,233	904	19,516 R	54.6%	44.9%	54.9%	45.1%
82,266	CAPE MAY	42,297	28,786	13,378	133	15,408 R	68.1%	31.6%	68.3%	31.7%
132,866	CUMBERLAND	51,155	29,398	21,141	616	8,257 R	57.5%	41.3%	58.2%	41.8%
851,116	ESSEX	314,543	136,798	173,295	4,450	36,497 D	43.5%	55.1%	44.1%	55.9%
199,917	GLOUCESTER	87,050	54,041	32,702	307	21,339 R	62.1%	37.6%	62.3%	37.7%
556,972	HUDSON	208,244	112,834	94,304	1,106	18,530 R	54.2%	45.3%	54.5%	45.5%
87,361	HUNTERDON	41,079	29,737	10,972	370	18,765 R	72.4%	26.7%	73.0%	27.0%
307,863	MERCER	138,121	71,195	66,398	528	4,797 R	51.5%	48.1%	51.7%	48.3%
595,893	MIDDLESEX	267,853	160,221	104,905	2,727	55,316 R	59.8%	39.2%	60.4%	39.6%
503,173	MONMOUTH	232,909	152,595	79,382	932	73,213 R	65.5%	34.1%	65.8%	34.2%
407,630	MORRIS	191,504	137,719	53,201	584	84,518 R	71.9%	27.8%	72.1%	27.9%
346,038	OCEAN	177,113	124,391	51,012	1,710	73,379 R	70.2%	28.8%	70.9%	29.1%
447,585	PASSAIC	174,940	101,951	69,590	3,399	32,361 R	58.3%	39.8%	59.4%	40.6%
64,676	SALEM	26,452	17,368	8,935	149	8,433 R	65.7%	33.8%	66.0%	34.0%
203,129	SOMERSET	99,296	66,303	31,924	1,069	34,379 R	66.8%	32.2%	67.5%	32.5%
116,119	SUSSEX	47,345	35,680	11,502	163	24,178 R	75.4%	24.3%	75.6%	24.4%
504,094	UNION	229,140	135,446	92,056	1,638	43,390 R	59.1%	40.2%	59.5%	40.5%
84,429	WARREN	32,707	21,938	10,647	122	11,291 R	67.1%	32.6%	67.3%	32.7%
7,364,823	TOTAL	3,217,862	1,933,630	1,261,323	22,909	672,307 R	60.1%	39.2%	60.5%	39.5%

NEW JERSEY

SENATOR 1984

1980 Census Population	County	Total Vote	Republican	Democratic	Other	Rep.-Dem. Plurality	Percentage			
							Total Vote		Major Vote	
							Rep.	Dem.	Rep.	Dem.
194,119	ATLANTIC	77,945	29,447	47,478	1,020	18,031 D	37.8%	60.9%	38.3%	61.7%
845,385	BERGEN	412,789	148,080	262,694	2,015	114,614 D	35.9%	63.6%	36.0%	64.0%
362,542	BURLINGTON	140,853	50,653	89,463	737	38,810 D	36.0%	63.5%	36.2%	63.8%
471,650	CAMDEN	193,642	60,581	131,827	1,234	71,246 D	31.3%	68.1%	31.5%	68.5%
82,266	CAPE MAY	40,433	18,365	21,859	209	3,494 D	45.4%	54.1%	45.7%	54.3%
132,866	CUMBERLAND	47,955	17,338	29,520	1,097	12,182 D	36.2%	61.6%	37.0%	63.0%
851,116	ESSEX	299,611	76,179	219,902	3,530	143,723 D	25.4%	73.4%	25.7%	74.3%
199,917	GLOUCESTER	86,589	30,096	56,072	421	25,976 D	34.8%	64.8%	34.9%	65.1%
556,972	HUDSON	200,174	60,844	137,352	1,978	76,508 D	30.4%	68.6%	30.7%	69.3%
87,361	HUNTERDON	39,314	17,839	20,864	611	3,025 D	45.4%	53.1%	46.1%	53.9%
307,863	MERCER	131,563	35,745	94,782	1,036	59,037 D	27.2%	72.0%	27.4%	72.6%
595,893	MIDDLESEX	259,794	83,617	172,478	3,699	88,861 D	32.2%	66.4%	32.7%	67.3%
503,173	MONMOUTH	224,091	80,093	142,084	1,914	61,991 D	35.7%	63.4%	36.0%	64.0%
407,630	MORRIS	185,515	77,683	106,678	1,154	28,995 D	41.9%	57.5%	42.1%	57.9%
346,038	OCEAN	172,032	75,923	94,076	2,033	18,153 D	44.1%	54.7%	44.7%	55.3%
447,585	PASSAIC	163,291	59,468	101,217	2,606	41,749 D	36.4%	62.0%	37.0%	63.0%
64,676	SALEM	26,206	10,099	15,900	207	5,801 D	38.5%	60.7%	38.8%	61.2%
203,129	SOMERSET	96,181	38,862	55,757	1,562	16,895 D	40.4%	58.0%	41.1%	58.9%
116,119	SUSSEX	47,092	21,494	25,334	264	3,840 D	45.6%	53.8%	45.9%	54.1%
504,094	UNION	218,868	74,446	142,320	2,102	67,874 D	34.0%	65.0%	34.3%	65.7%
84,429	WARREN	32,518	13,248	18,987	283	5,739 D	40.7%	58.4%	41.1%	58.9%
7,364,823	TOTAL	3,096,456	1,080,100	1,986,644	29,712	906,544 D	34.9%	64.2%	35.2%	64.8%

NEW JERSEY

CONGRESS

CD	Year	Total Vote	Republican Vote	Republican Candidate	Democratic Vote	Democratic Candidate	Other Vote	Rep.-Dem. Plurality	Total Vote Rep.	Total Vote Dem.	Major Vote Rep.	Major Vote Dem.
1	1984	211,711	58,800	BUSCH, FREDERICK A.	152,125	FLORIO, JAMES J.	786	93,325 D	27.8%	71.9%	27.9%	72.1%
2	1984	210,072	77,231	MASSIE, RAYMOND G.	132,841	HUGHES, WILLIAM J.		55,610 D	36.8%	63.2%	36.8%	63.2%
3	1984	229,422	105,028	KENNEDY, BRIAN T.	122,291	HOWARD, JAMES J.	2,103	17,263 D	45.8%	53.3%	46.2%	53.8%
4	1984	227,203	139,295	SMITH, CHRISTOPHER H.	87,908	HEDDEN, JAMES C.		51,387 R	61.3%	38.7%	61.3%	38.7%
5	1984	241,645	171,979	ROUKEMA, MARGARET S.	69,666	BRUNETTO, ROSE		102,313 R	71.2%	28.8%	71.2%	28.8%
6	1984	212,080	90,862	ADAMS, DENNIS	118,532	DWYER, BERNARD J.	2,686	27,670 D	42.8%	55.9%	43.4%	56.6%
7	1984	223,282	165,685	RINALDO, MATTHEW J.	56,798	FEELEY, JOHN F.	799	108,887 R	74.2%	25.4%	74.5%	25.5%
8	1984	189,395	69,973	PAGE, MARGUERITE A.	118,793	ROE, ROBERT A.	629	48,820 D	36.9%	62.7%	37.1%	62.9%
9	1984	238,659	89,166	ROMANO, NEIL	149,493	TORRICELLI, ROBERT G.		60,327 D	37.4%	62.6%	37.4%	62.6%
10	1984	132,956	21,712	BERKELEY, HOWARD E.	111,244	RODINO, PETER W.		89,532 D	16.3%	83.7%	16.3%	83.7%
11	1984	239,700	133,662	GALLO, DEAN A.	106,038	MINISH, JOSEPH G.		27,624 R	55.8%	44.2%	55.8%	44.2%
12	1984	227,833	148,042	COURTER, JAMES A.	78,167	BEARSE, PETER	1,624	69,875 R	65.0%	34.3%	65.4%	34.6%
13	1984	232,483	141,136	SAXTON, H. JAMES	89,307	SMITH, JAMES B.	2,040	51,829 R	60.7%	38.4%	61.2%	38.8%
14	1984	175,217	58,265	MAGEE, EDWARD T.	115,117	GUARINI, FRANK J.	1,835	56,852 D	33.3%	65.7%	33.6%	66.4%

NEW JERSEY

1984 GENERAL ELECTION

President Other vote was 8,404 Holmes (Workers World); 6,416 Bergland (Libertarian); 2,293 Serrette (New Alliance); 1,721 Winn (Workers League); 1,564 Hall (Communist); 1,264 Mason (Socialist Workers); 1,247 Johnson (Citizens).

Senator Other vote was 10,409 Hagen (Prolife Fiscal Conservative); 7,135 Leiendecker (Libertarian); 6,053 Levin (Socialist Labor); 3,224 Schenk (Socialist Workers); 2,891 Gould (Contempt of Court).

Congress Other vote was Zeldin (Libertarian) in CD 1; 1,196 Krushinski (Christian American) and 907 Erickson (Citizens-Socialist) in CD 3; Friedlander (Libertarian) in CD 6; Nelson (Libertarian) in CD 7; Maiullo (Libertarian) in CD 8; Kerr (Libertarian) in CD 12; 1,516 Smith (Constitutional Freedom) and 524 Doganiero (Socialist Labor) in CD 13; Shaw (Politicians are Crooks) in CD 14.

1984 PRIMARIES

JUNE 5 REPUBLICAN

Senator 111,851 Mary V. Mochary; 70,418 Robert Morris.

Congress Unopposed in twelve CD's. Contested as follows:

CD 8 12,167 Marguerite A. Page; 2,409 William R. Cleveland.
CD 13 16,143 H. James Saxton; 14,955 M. Dean Haines; 5,012 John A. Rocco.

JUNE 5 DEMOCRATIC

Senator 404,301 Bill Bradley; 30,680 Elliot Greenspan.

Congress Unopposed in CD 2. Contested as follows:

CD 1 42,509 James J. Florio; 2,992 Patrick A. Miller.
CD 3 23,278 James J. Howard; 2,315 Dorothy J. Eaton.
CD 4 20,640 James C. Hedden; 15,823 Jeffrey Laurenti; 2,430 Janet C. Sare.
CD 5 18,951 Rose Brunetto; 1,974 John P. Kilroy; 1,755 Mark Rohrlich.
CD 6 27,414 Bernard J. Dwyer; 4,323 Alex Piechocki.
CD 7 14,317 John F. Feeley; 4,911 Dwight Gatling; 3,493 James J. Cleary.
CD 8 30,252 Robert A. Roe; 3,794 Ronald H. Taylor.
CD 9 36,937 Robert G. Torricelli; 2,519 John Graverholz.
CD 10 42,109 Peter W. Rodino; 10,294 Arthur S. Jones; 2,779 Thelma I. Tyree.
CD 11 25,688 Joseph G. Minish; 3,609 Mary Frueholz.
CD 12 10,477 Peter Bearse; 6,951 Norman J. Weinstein; 3,838 Richard P. Forbes; 3,386 Ray Rollinson.
CD 13 15,557 James B. Smith; 5,288 Herbert J. Buehler; 3,637 Eugene Creech; 3,200 Michael Di Marco.
CD 14 58,775 Frank J. Guarini; 19,856 Anthony P. Peduto; 3,398 Edward Malik.

NEW MEXICO

GOVERNOR
Toney Anaya (D). Elected 1982 to a four-year term.

SENATORS
Jeff Bingaman (D). Elected 1982 to a six-year term.

Peter V. Domenici (R). Re-elected 1984 to a six-year term. Previously elected 1978, 1972.

REPRESENTATIVES
1. Manuel Lujan, Jr. (R) 2. Joseph R. Skeen (R) 3. Bill Richardson (D)

POSTWAR VOTE FOR GOVERNOR

Year	Total Vote	Republican Vote	Republican Candidate	Democratic Vote	Democratic Candidate	Other Vote	Rep.-Dem. Plurality	Total Vote Rep.	Total Vote Dem.	Major Vote Rep.	Major Vote Dem.
1982	407,466	191,626	Irick, John B.	215,840	Anaya, Toney	—	24,214 D	47.0%	53.0%	47.0%	53.0%
1978	345,577	170,848	Skeen, Joseph R.	174,631	King, Bruce	98	3,783 D	49.4%	50.5%	49.5%	50.5%
1974	328,742	160,430	Skeen, Joseph R.	164,172	Apodaca, Jerry	4,140	3,742 D	48.8%	49.9%	49.4%	50.6%
1970*	290,375	134,640	Domenici, Peter V.	148,835	King, Bruce	6,900	14,195 D	46.4%	51.3%	47.5%	52.5%
1968	318,975	160,140	Cargo, David F.	157,230	Chavez, Fabian	1,605	2,910 R	50.2%	49.3%	50.5%	49.5%
1966	260,232	134,625	Cargo, David F.	125,587	Lusk, Thomas E.	20	9,038 R	51.7%	48.3%	51.7%	48.3%
1964	318,042	126,540	Tucker, Merle H.	191,497	Campbell, Jack M.	5	64,957 D	39.8%	60.2%	39.8%	60.2%
1962	247,135	116,184	Mechem, Edwin L.	130,933	Campbell, Jack M.	18	14,749 D	47.0%	53.0%	47.0%	53.0%
1960	305,542	153,765	Mechem, Edwin L.	151,777	Burroughs, John	—	1,988 R	50.3%	49.7%	50.3%	49.7%
1958	205,048	101,567	Mechem, Edwin L.	103,481	Burroughs, John	—	1,914 D	49.5%	50.5%	49.5%	50.5%
1956	251,751	131,488	Mechem, Edwin L.	120,263	Simms, John F.	—	11,225 R	52.2%	47.8%	52.2%	47.8%
1954	193,956	83,373	Stockton, Alvin	110,583	Simms, John F.	—	27,210 D	43.0%	57.0%	43.0%	57.0%
1952	240,150	129,116	Mechem, Edwin L.	111,034	Grantham, Everett	—	18,082 R	53.8%	46.2%	53.8%	46.2%
1950	180,205	96,846	Mechem, Edwin L.	83,359	Miles, John E.	—	13,487 R	53.7%	46.3%	53.7%	46.3%
1948	189,992	86,023	Lujan, Manuel	103,969	Mabry, Thomas J.	—	17,946 D	45.3%	54.7%	45.3%	54.7%
1946	132,930	62,875	Safford, Edward L.	70,055	Mabry, Thomas J.	—	7,180 D	47.3%	52.7%	47.3%	52.7%

The term of New Mexico's Governor was increased from two to four years effective with the 1970 election.

POSTWAR VOTE FOR SENATOR

Year	Total Vote	Republican Vote	Republican Candidate	Democratic Vote	Democratic Candidate	Other Vote	Rep.-Dem. Plurality	Total Vote Rep.	Total Vote Dem.	Major Vote Rep.	Major Vote Dem.
1984	502,634	361,371	Domenici, Peter V.	141,253	Pratt, Judith A.	10	220,118 R	71.9%	28.1%	71.9%	28.1%
1982	404,810	187,128	Schmitt, Harrison	217,682	Bingaman, Jeff	—	30,554 D	46.2%	53.8%	46.2%	53.8%
1978	343,554	183,442	Domenici, Peter V.	160,045	Anaya, Toney	67	23,397 R	53.4%	46.6%	53.4%	46.6%
1976	413,141	234,681	Schmitt, Harrison	176,382	Montoya, Joseph M.	2,078	58,299 R	56.8%	42.7%	57.1%	42.9%
1972	378,330	204,253	Domenici, Peter V.	173,815	Daniels, Jack	262	30,438 R	54.0%	45.9%	54.0%	46.0%
1970	289,906	135,004	Carter, Anderson	151,486	Montoya, Joseph M.	3,416	16,482 D	46.6%	52.3%	47.1%	52.9%
1966	258,203	120,988	Carter, Anderson	137,205	Anderson, Clinton P.	10	16,217 D	46.9%	53.1%	46.9%	53.1%
1964	325,774	147,562	Mechem, Edwin L.	178,209	Montoya, Joseph M.	3	30,647 D	45.3%	54.7%	45.3%	54.7%
1960	300,551	109,897	Colwes, William F.	190,654	Anderson, Clinton P.	—	80,757 D	36.6%	63.4%	36.6%	63.4%
1958	203,323	75,827	Atchley, Forrest S.	127,496	Chavez, Dennis	—	51,669 D	37.3%	62.7%	37.3%	62.7%
1954	194,422	83,071	Mechem, Edwin L.	111,351	Anderson, Clinton P.	—	28,280 D	42.7%	57.3%	42.7%	57.3%
1952	239,711	117,168	Hurley, Patrick J.	122,543	Chavez, Dennis	—	5,375 D	48.9%	51.1%	48.9%	51.1%
1948	188,495	80,226	Hurley, Patrick J.	108,269	Anderson, Clinton P.	—	28,043 D	42.6%	57.4%	42.6%	57.4%
1946	133,282	64,632	Hurley, Patrick J.	68,650	Chavez, Dennis	—	4,018 D	48.5%	51.5%	48.5%	51.5%

NEW MEXICO

Districts Established January 19, 1982

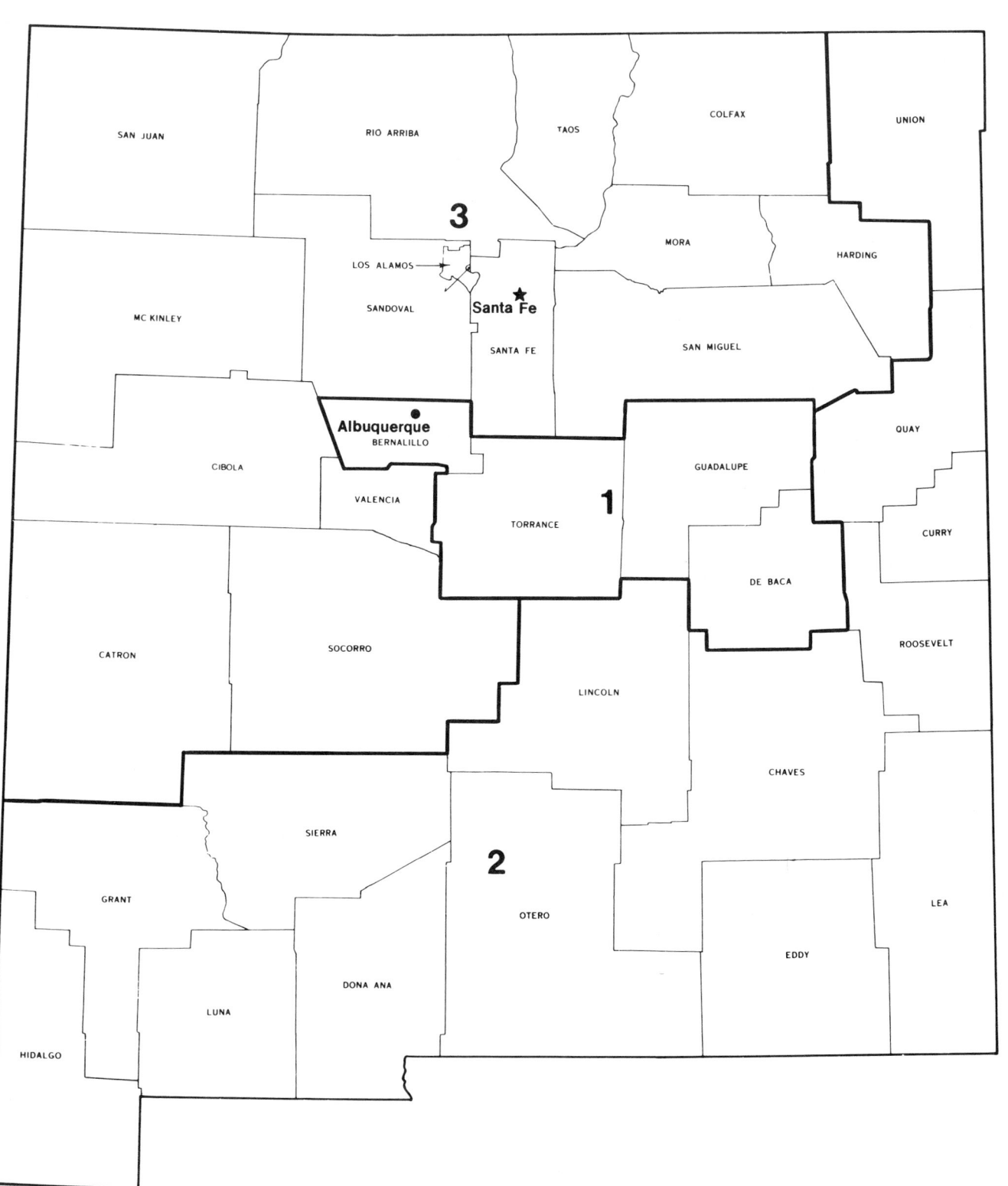

NEW MEXICO

PRESIDENT 1984

1980 Census Population	County	Total Vote	Republican	Democratic	Other	Rep.-Dem. Plurality	Percentage Total Vote Rep.	Dem.	Major Vote Rep.	Dem.
419,700	BERNALILLO	174,262	104,694	67,789	1,779	36,905 R	60.1%	38.9%	60.7%	39.3%
2,720	CATRON	1,415	970	418	27	552 R	68.6%	29.5%	69.9%	30.1%
51,103	CHAVES	20,782	15,248	5,332	202	9,916 R	73.4%	25.7%	74.1%	25.9%
30,364	CIBOLA	6,740	3,578	3,140	22	438 R	53.1%	46.6%	53.3%	46.7%
13,667	COLFAX	5,485	2,994	2,435	56	559 R	54.6%	44.4%	55.1%	44.9%
42,019	CURRY	12,415	9,188	3,108	119	6,080 R	74.0%	25.0%	74.7%	25.3%
2,454	DE BACA	1,159	756	386	17	370 R	65.2%	33.3%	66.2%	33.8%
96,340	DONA ANA	36,393	22,153	13,878	362	8,275 R	60.9%	38.1%	61.5%	38.5%
47,855	EDDY	19,365	11,810	7,364	191	4,446 R	61.0%	38.0%	61.6%	38.4%
26,204	GRANT	10,840	4,979	5,755	106	776 D	45.9%	53.1%	46.4%	53.6%
4,496	GUADALUPE	1,966	990	946	30	44 R	50.4%	48.1%	51.1%	48.9%
1,090	HARDING	631	401	224	6	177 R	63.5%	35.5%	64.2%	35.8%
6,049	HIDALGO	2,161	1,282	860	19	422 R	59.3%	39.8%	59.9%	40.1%
55,993	LEA	19,357	14,569	4,558	230	10,011 R	75.3%	23.5%	76.2%	23.8%
10,997	LINCOLN	5,182	3,992	1,134	56	2,858 R	77.0%	21.9%	77.9%	22.1%
17,599	LOS ALAMOS	9,888	6,882	2,859	147	4,023 R	69.6%	28.9%	70.6%	29.4%
15,585	LUNA	6,776	4,145	2,557	74	1,588 R	61.2%	37.7%	61.8%	38.2%
56,449	MCKINLEY	14,643	6,557	7,915	171	1,358 D	44.8%	54.1%	45.3%	54.7%
4,205	MORA	2,287	1,017	1,235	35	218 D	44.5%	54.0%	45.2%	54.8%
44,665	OTERO	14,087	9,751	4,167	169	5,584 R	69.2%	29.6%	70.1%	29.9%
10,577	QUAY	4,253	2,842	1,368	43	1,474 R	66.8%	32.2%	67.5%	32.5%
29,282	RIO ARRIBA	11,146	4,116	6,938	92	2,822 D	36.9%	62.2%	37.2%	62.8%
15,695	ROOSEVELT	6,363	4,598	1,696	69	2,902 R	72.3%	26.7%	73.1%	26.9%
34,799	SANDOVAL	16,246	9,005	7,080	161	1,925 R	55.4%	43.6%	56.0%	44.0%
81,433	SAN JUAN	27,910	18,690	8,963	257	9,727 R	67.0%	32.1%	67.6%	32.4%
22,751	SAN MIGUEL	8,850	3,485	5,227	138	1,742 D	39.4%	59.1%	40.0%	60.0%
75,360	SANTA FE	34,552	15,886	18,262	404	2,376 D	46.0%	52.9%	46.5%	53.5%
8,454	SIERRA	4,035	2,663	1,335	37	1,328 R	66.0%	33.1%	66.6%	33.4%
12,566	SOCORRO	6,048	3,403	2,541	104	862 R	56.3%	42.0%	57.3%	42.7%
19,456	TAOS	9,432	4,154	5,144	134	990 D	44.0%	54.5%	44.7%	55.3%
7,491	TORRANCE	3,633	2,326	1,274	33	1,052 R	64.0%	35.1%	64.6%	35.4%
4,725	UNION	2,019	1,503	488	28	1,015 R	74.4%	24.2%	75.5%	24.5%
30,751	VALENCIA	14,049	8,474	5,393	182	3,081 R	60.3%	38.4%	61.1%	38.9%
1,302,894	TOTAL	514,370	307,101	201,769	5,500	105,332 R	59.7%	39.2%	60.3%	39.7%

NEW MEXICO

SENATOR 1984

1980 Census Population	County	Total Vote	Republican	Democratic	Other	Rep.-Dem. Plurality	Percentage Total Vote Rep.	Dem.	Major Vote Rep.	Dem.
419,700	BERNALILLO	171,658	124,967	46,689	2	78,278 R	72.8%	27.2%	72.8%	27.2%
2,720	CATRON	1,314	1,030	284		746 R	78.4%	21.6%	78.4%	21.6%
51,103	CHAVES	20,415	16,754	3,661		13,093 R	82.1%	17.9%	82.1%	17.9%
30,364	CIBOLA	6,605	4,429	2,175	1	2,254 R	67.1%	32.9%	67.1%	32.9%
13,667	COLFAX	5,294	3,747	1,547		2,200 R	70.8%	29.2%	70.8%	29.2%
42,019	CURRY	11,975	10,013	1,962		8,051 R	83.6%	16.4%	83.6%	16.4%
2,454	DE BACA	1,104	858	246		612 R	77.7%	22.3%	77.7%	22.3%
96,340	DONA ANA	35,572	26,565	9,007		17,558 R	74.7%	25.3%	74.7%	25.3%
47,855	EDDY	18,988	13,565	5,423		8,142 R	71.4%	28.6%	71.4%	28.6%
26,204	GRANT	10,708	6,266	4,442		1,824 R	58.5%	41.5%	58.5%	41.5%
4,496	GUADALUPE	1,877	1,216	661		555 R	64.8%	35.2%	64.8%	35.2%
1,090	HARDING	614	473	141		332 R	77.0%	23.0%	77.0%	23.0%
6,049	HIDALGO	2,065	1,466	599		867 R	71.0%	29.0%	71.0%	29.0%
55,993	LEA	18,667	15,391	3,276		12,115 R	82.5%	17.5%	82.5%	17.5%
10,997	LINCOLN	5,102	4,354	748		3,606 R	85.3%	14.7%	85.3%	14.7%
17,599	LOS ALAMOS	9,734	8,161	1,573		6,588 R	83.8%	16.2%	83.8%	16.2%
15,585	LUNA	6,541	4,645	1,896		2,749 R	71.0%	29.0%	71.0%	29.0%
56,449	MCKINLEY	13,646	8,192	5,454		2,738 R	60.0%	40.0%	60.0%	40.0%
4,205	MORA	2,210	1,160	1,050		110 R	52.5%	47.5%	52.5%	47.5%
44,665	OTERO	13,726	11,288	2,438		8,850 R	82.2%	17.8%	82.2%	17.8%
10,577	QUAY	4,148	3,174	974		2,200 R	76.5%	23.5%	76.5%	23.5%
29,282	RIO ARRIBA	10,919	5,513	5,406		107 R	50.5%	49.5%	50.5%	49.5%
15,695	ROOSEVELT	6,213	5,092	1,121		3,971 R	82.0%	18.0%	82.0%	18.0%
34,799	SANDOVAL	15,882	10,843	5,039		5,804 R	68.3%	31.7%	68.3%	31.7%
81,433	SAN JUAN	27,219	19,837	7,381	1	12,456 R	72.9%	27.1%	72.9%	27.1%
22,751	SAN MIGUEL	8,507	4,705	3,802		903 R	55.3%	44.7%	55.3%	44.7%
75,360	SANTA FE	33,954	20,595	13,356	3	7,239 R	60.7%	39.3%	60.7%	39.3%
8,454	SIERRA	3,956	2,986	970		2,016 R	75.5%	24.5%	75.5%	24.5%
12,566	SOCORRO	5,690	4,039	1,651		2,388 R	71.0%	29.0%	71.0%	29.0%
19,456	TAOS	9,074	5,652	3,422		2,230 R	62.3%	37.7%	62.3%	37.7%
7,491	TORRANCE	3,584	2,662	921	1	1,741 R	74.3%	25.7%	74.3%	25.7%
4,725	UNION	1,944	1,639	305		1,334 R	84.3%	15.7%	84.3%	15.7%
30,751	VALENCIA	13,729	10,094	3,633	2	6,461 R	73.5%	26.5%	73.5%	26.5%
1,302,894	TOTAL	502,634	361,371	141,253	10	220,118 R	71.9%	28.1%	71.9%	28.1%

NEW MEXICO

CONGRESS

CD	Year	Total Vote	Republican Vote	Republican Candidate	Democratic Vote	Democratic Candidate	Other Vote	Rep.-Dem. Plurality	Total Vote Rep.	Total Vote Dem.	Major Vote Rep.	Major Vote Dem.
1	1984	178,342	115,808	LUJAN, MANUEL, JR.	60,598	ASBURY, CHARLES T.	1,936	55,210 R	64.9%	34.0%	65.6%	34.4%
1	1982	141,993	74,459	LUJAN, MANUEL, JR.	67,534	HARTKE, JAN A.		6,925 R	52.4%	47.6%	52.4%	47.6%
2	1984	156,069	116,006	SKEEN, JOSEPH R.	40,063	YORK, PETER R.		75,943 R	74.3%	25.7%	74.3%	25.7%
2	1982	121,620	71,021	SKEEN, JOSEPH R.	50,599	CHANDLER, CALEB J.		20,422 R	58.4%	41.6%	58.4%	41.6%
3	1984	165,209	62,351	GALLEGOS, LOUIS H.	100,470	RICHARDSON, BILL	2,388	38,119 D	37.7%	60.8%	38.3%	61.7%
3	1982	131,293	46,466	CHAMBERS, MARJORIE B.	84,669	RICHARDSON, BILL	158	38,203 D	35.4%	64.5%	35.4%	64.6%

NEW MEXICO

1984 GENERAL ELECTION

President   Other vote was 4,459 Bergland (Libertarian); 455 Johnson (Citizens); 224 Mason (Socialist Workers); 206 Dodge (Prohibition); 155 Serrette (Alliance); 1 scattered.

Senator   Other vote was Cole (write-in).

Congress   Other vote was Curtis (Libertarian) in CD 1; Jones (Libertarian) in CD 3.

1984 PRIMARIES

JUNE 5 REPUBLICAN

Senator   Peter V. Domenici, unopposed.

Congress   Unopposed in all three CD's.

JUNE 5 DEMOCRATIC

Senator   67,722 Judith A. Pratt; 56,434 Nick Franklin; 24,694 Anselmo A. Chavez.

Congress   Unopposed in CD 2. Contested as follows:

CD   1   24,707 Charles T. Asbury; 17,842 Manny Garcia.
CD   3   51,820 Bill Richardson; 15,341 Edmundo R. Delgado.

NEW YORK

GOVERNOR
Mario M. Cuomo (D). Elected 1982 to a four-year term.

SENATORS
Alfonse M. D'Amato (R). Elected 1980 to a six-year term.

Daniel P. Moynihan (D). Re-elected 1982 to a six-year term. Previously elected 1976.

REPRESENTATIVES
1. William Carney (R)
2. Thomas J. Downey (D)
3. Robert J. Mrazek (D)
4. Norman F. Lent (R)
5. Raymond J. McGrath (R)
6. Joseph P. Addabbo (D)
7. Gary L. Ackerman (D)
8. James H. Scheuer (D)
9. Thomas J. Manton (D)
10. Charles E. Schumer (D)
11. Edolphus Towns (D)
12. Major R. Owens (D)
13. Stephen J. Solarz (D)
14. Guy V. Molinari (R)
15. S. William Green (R)
16. Charles B. Rangel (D)
17. Theodore S. Weiss (D)
18. Robert Garcia (D)
19. Mario Biaggi (D)
20. Joseph J. DioGuardi (R)
21. Hamilton Fish (R)
22. Benjamin A. Gilman (R)
23. Samuel S. Stratton (D)
24. Gerald B. Solomon (R)
25. Sherwood L. Boehlert (R)
26. David O'B. Martin (R)
27. George C. Wortley (R)
28. Matthew F. McHugh (D)
29. Frank J. Horton (R)
30. Fred J. Eckert (R)
31. Jack F. Kemp (R)
32. John J. LaFalce (D)
33. Henry J. Nowak (D)
34. Stanley N. Lundine (D)

POSTWAR VOTE FOR GOVERNOR

Year	Total Vote	Republican Vote	Candidate	Democratic Vote	Candidate	Other Vote	Rep.-Dem. Plurality	Total Vote Rep.	Dem.	Major Vote Rep.	Dem.
1982	5,254,891	2,494,827	Lehrman, Lew	2,675,213	Cuomo, Mario M.	84,851	180,386 D	47.5%	50.9%	48.3%	51.7%
1978	4,768,820	2,156,404	Duryea, Perry B.	2,429,272	Carey, Hugh L.	183,144	272,868 D	45.2%	50.9%	47.0%	53.0%
1974	5,293,176	2,219,667	Wilson, Malcolm	3,028,503	Carey, Hugh L.	45,006	808,836 D	41.9%	57.2%	42.3%	57.7%
1970	6,013,064	3,151,432	Rockefeller, Nelson A.	2,421,426	Goldberg, Arthur	440,206	730,006 R	52.4%	40.3%	56.5%	43.5%
1966	6,031,585	2,690,626	Rockefeller, Nelson A.	2,298,363	O'Connor, Frank D.	1,042,596	392,263 R	44.6%	38.1%	53.9%	46.1%
1962	5,805,631	3,081,587	Rockefeller, Nelson A.	2,552,418	Morgenthau, Robert M.	171,626	529,169 R	53.1%	44.0%	54.7%	45.3%
1958	5,712,665	3,126,929	Rockefeller, Nelson A.	2,553,895	Harriman, Averell	31,841	573,034 R	54.7%	44.7%	55.0%	45.0%
1954	5,161,942	2,549,613	Ives, Irving M.	2,560,738	Harriman, Averell	51,591	11,125 D	49.4%	49.6%	49.9%	50.1%
1950	5,308,889	2,819,523	Dewey, Thomas E.	2,246,855	Lynch, Walter A.	242,511	572,668 R	53.1%	42.3%	55.7%	44.3%
1946	4,964,552	2,825,633	Dewey, Thomas E.	2,138,482	Mead, James M.	437	687,151 R	56.9%	43.1%	56.9%	43.1%

POSTWAR VOTE FOR SENATOR

Year	Total Vote	Republican Vote	Candidate	Democratic Vote	Candidate	Other Vote	Rep.-Dem. Plurality	Total Vote Rep.	Dem.	Major Vote Rep.	Dem.
1982	4,967,729	1,696,766	Sullivan, Florence M.	3,232,146	Moynihan, Daniel P.	38,817	1,535,380 D	34.2%	65.1%	34.4%	65.6%
1980	6,014,914	2,699,652	D'Amato, Alfonse M.	2,618,661	Holtzman, Elizabeth	696,601	80,991 R	44.9%	43.5%	50.8%	49.2%
1976	6,319,755	2,836,633	Buckley, James L.	3,422,594	Moynihan, Daniel P.	60,528	585,961 D	44.9%	54.2%	45.3%	54.7%
1974	5,163,600	2,340,188	Javits, Jacob K.	1,973,781	Clark, Ramsey	849,631	366,407 R	45.3%	38.2%	54.2%	45.8%
1970*	5,904,782	1,434,472	Goodell, Charles	2,171,232	Ottinger, Richard L.	2,299,078	736,760 D	24.3%	36.8%	39.8%	60.2%
1968	6,581,587	3,269,772	Javits, Jacob K.	2,150,695	O'Dwyer, Paul	1,161,120	1,119,077 R	49.7%	32.7%	60.3%	39.7%
1964	7,151,686	3,104,056	Keating, Kenneth B.	3,823,749	Kennedy, Robert F.	223,881	719,693 D	43.4%	53.5%	44.8%	55.2%
1962	5,700,186	3,269,417	Javits, Jacob K.	2,289,341	Donovan, James B.	141,428	980,076 R	57.4%	40.2%	58.8%	41.2%
1958	5,602,088	2,842,942	Keating, Kenneth B.	2,709,950	Hogan, Frank S.	49,196	132,992 R	50.7%	48.4%	51.2%	48.8%
1956	6,991,136	3,723,933	Javits, Jacob K.	3,265,159	Wagner, Robert F.	2,044	458,774 R	53.3%	46.7%	53.3%	46.7%
1952	6,980,259	3,853,934	Ives, Irving M.	2,521,736	Cashmore, John	604,589	1,332,198 R	55.2%	36.1%	60.4%	39.6%
1950	5,228,403	2,367,353	Hanley, Joe R.	2,632,313	Lehman, Herbert H.	228,737	264,960 D	45.3%	50.3%	47.4%	52.6%
1949s	4,966,878	2,384,381	Dulles, John Foster	2,582,438	Lehman, Herbert H.	59	198,057 D	48.0%	52.0%	48.0%	52.0%
1946	4,867,564	2,559,365	Ives, Irving M.	2,308,112	Lehman, Herbert H.	87	251,253 R	52.6%	47.4%	52.6%	47.4%

The 1949 election was for a short term to fill a vacancy. In 1970 James L. Buckley, the Conservative Candidate, polled 2,288,190 votes, (38.8% of the total vote) and won the election with a 116,958 plurality.

NEW YORK

Districts Established September 27, 1983

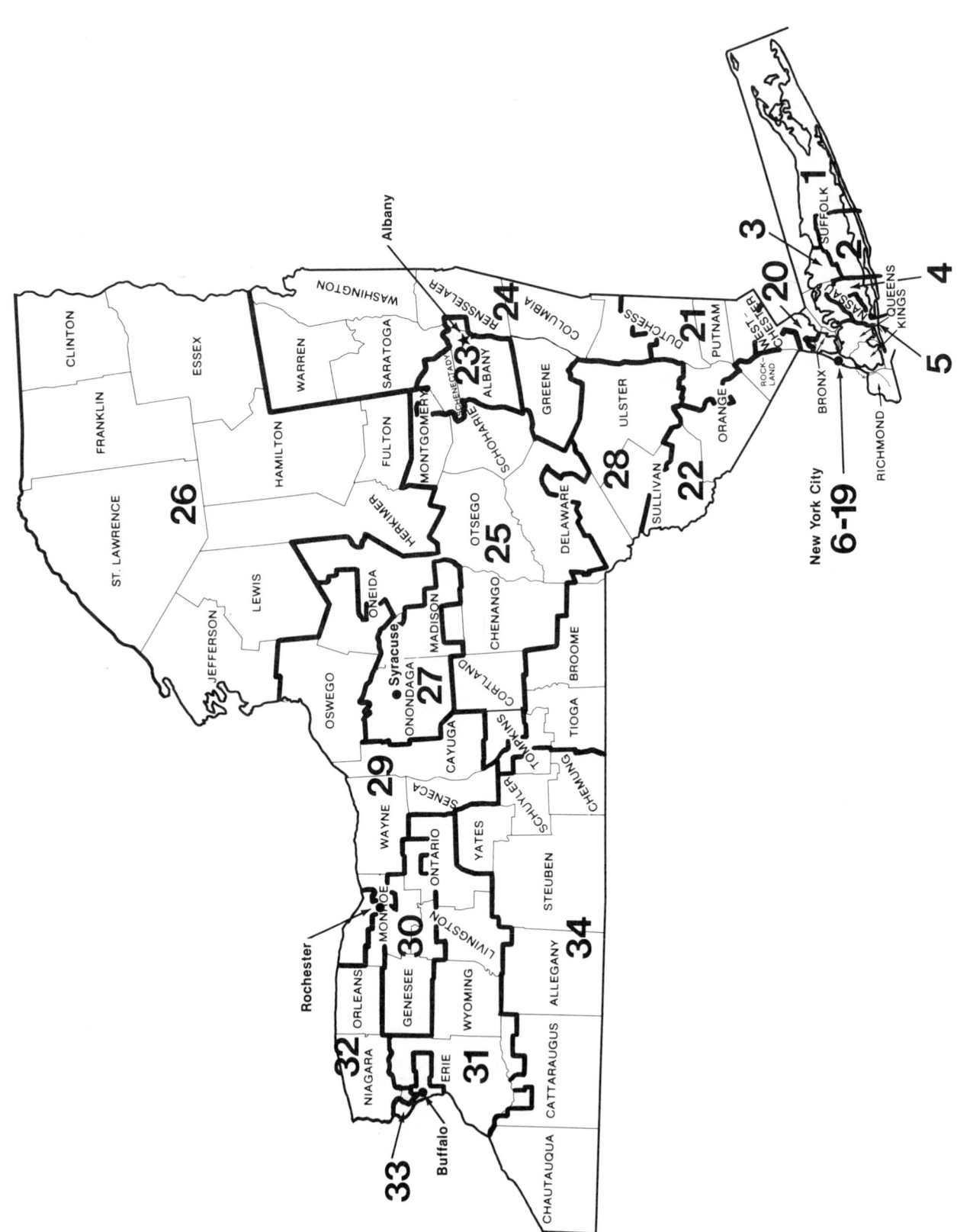

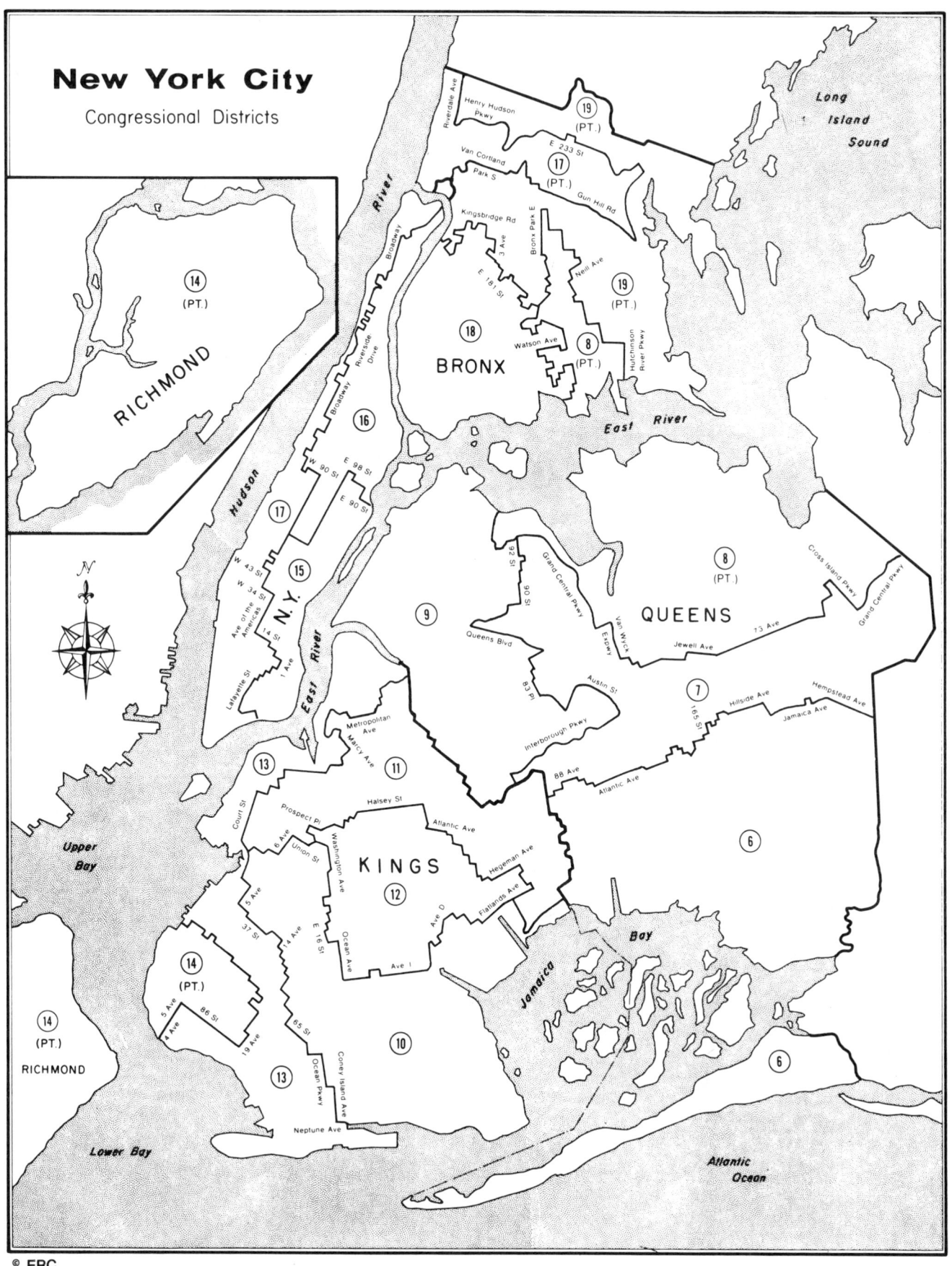

New York City
Congressional Districts

© ERC

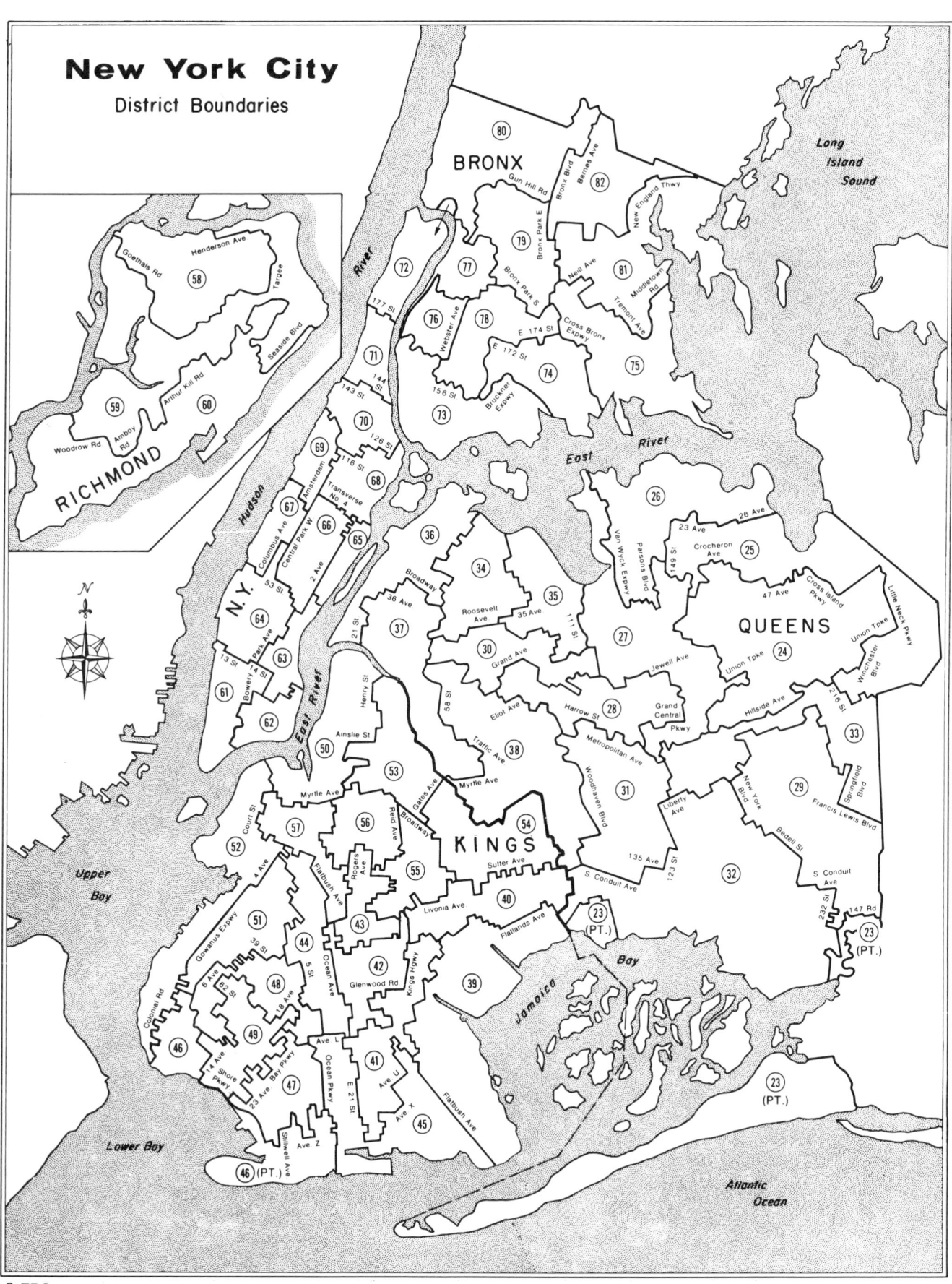

New York City

District Boundaries

BRONX

Long Island Sound

RICHMOND

N.Y.

Hudson River

East River

Upper Bay

QUEENS

KINGS

Jamaica Bay

Lower Bay

Atlantic Ocean

© ERC

NEW YORK

PRESIDENT 1984

1980 Census Population	County	Total Vote	Republican	Democratic	Other	Rep.-Dem. Plurality		Percentage Total Vote Rep.	Dem.	Major Vote Rep.	Dem.
285,909	ALBANY	150,592	74,542	75,447	603	905	D	49.5%	50.1%	49.7%	50.3%
51,742	ALLEGANY	19,304	14,527	4,720	57	9,807	R	75.3%	24.5%	75.5%	24.5%
1,168,972	BRONX	333,683	109,308	223,112	1,263	113,804	D	32.8%	66.9%	32.9%	67.1%
213,648	BROOME	96,089	58,109	37,658	322	20,451	R	60.5%	39.2%	60.7%	39.3%
85,697	CATTARAUGUS	34,468	24,162	10,194	112	13,968	R	70.1%	29.6%	70.3%	29.7%
79,894	CAYUGA	33,779	21,451	12,207	121	9,244	R	63.5%	36.1%	63.7%	36.3%
146,925	CHAUTAUQUA	62,724	39,597	22,986	141	16,611	R	63.1%	36.6%	63.3%	36.7%
97,656	CHEMUNG	39,647	24,909	14,638	100	10,271	R	62.8%	36.9%	63.0%	37.0%
49,344	CHENANGO	20,648	14,254	6,343	51	7,911	R	69.0%	30.7%	69.2%	30.8%
80,750	CLINTON	30,443	19,549	10,804	90	8,745	R	64.2%	35.5%	64.4%	35.6%
59,487	COLUMBIA	27,891	18,814	8,960	117	9,854	R	67.5%	32.1%	67.7%	32.3%
48,820	CORTLAND	20,224	13,691	6,438	95	7,253	R	67.7%	31.8%	68.0%	32.0%
46,824	DELAWARE	19,830	14,002	5,745	83	8,257	R	70.6%	29.0%	70.9%	29.1%
245,055	DUTCHESS	103,580	70,324	32,867	389	37,457	R	67.9%	31.7%	68.1%	31.9%
1,015,472	ERIE	461,671	222,882	237,631	1,158	14,749	D	48.3%	51.5%	48.4%	51.6%
36,176	ESSEX	17,320	12,114	5,119	87	6,995	R	69.9%	29.6%	70.3%	29.7%
44,929	FRANKLIN	17,064	10,617	6,400	47	4,217	R	62.2%	37.5%	62.4%	37.6%
55,153	FULTON	22,618	14,887	7,644	87	7,243	R	65.8%	33.8%	66.1%	33.9%
59,400	GENESEE	25,210	16,582	8,549	79	8,033	R	65.8%	33.9%	66.0%	34.0%
40,861	GREENE	20,070	14,150	5,858	62	8,292	R	70.5%	29.2%	70.7%	29.3%
5,034	HAMILTON	3,382	2,637	737	8	1,900	R	78.0%	21.8%	78.2%	21.8%
66,714	HERKIMER	29,258	18,827	10,346	85	8,481	R	64.3%	35.4%	64.5%	35.5%
88,151	JEFFERSON	34,496	23,445	10,960	91	12,485	R	68.0%	31.8%	68.1%	31.9%
2,230,936	KINGS	600,771	230,064	368,518	2,189	138,454	D	38.3%	61.3%	38.4%	61.6%
25,035	LEWIS	9,860	7,069	2,757	34	4,312	R	71.7%	28.0%	71.9%	28.1%
57,006	LIVINGSTON	23,892	16,389	7,399	104	8,990	R	68.6%	31.0%	68.9%	31.1%
65,150	MADISON	25,963	17,568	8,291	104	9,277	R	67.7%	31.9%	67.9%	32.1%
702,238	MONROE	316,277	182,696	132,109	1,472	50,587	R	57.8%	41.8%	58.0%	42.0%
53,439	MONTGOMERY	23,520	14,398	9,044	78	5,354	R	61.2%	38.5%	61.4%	38.6%
1,321,582	NASSAU	634,063	392,017	240,697	1,349	151,320	R	61.8%	38.0%	62.0%	38.0%
1,428,285	NEW YORK	526,671	144,281	379,521	2,869	235,240	D	27.4%	72.1%	27.5%	72.5%
227,354	NIAGARA	92,858	51,289	41,368	201	9,921	R	55.2%	44.5%	55.4%	44.6%
253,466	ONEIDA	108,269	65,377	42,603	289	22,774	R	60.4%	39.3%	60.5%	39.5%
463,920	ONONDAGA	204,314	121,857	81,777	680	40,080	R	59.6%	40.0%	59.8%	40.2%
88,909	ONTARIO	37,494	24,507	12,844	143	11,663	R	65.4%	34.3%	65.6%	34.4%
259,603	ORANGE	102,413	69,413	32,663	337	36,750	R	67.8%	31.9%	68.0%	32.0%
38,496	ORLEANS	15,024	10,543	4,429	52	6,114	R	70.2%	29.5%	70.4%	29.6%
113,901	OSWEGO	46,034	31,481	14,347	206	17,134	R	68.4%	31.2%	68.7%	31.3%
59,075	OTSEGO	26,511	16,777	9,582	152	7,195	R	63.3%	36.1%	63.6%	36.4%
77,193	PUTNAM	35,277	25,707	9,473	97	16,234	R	72.9%	26.9%	73.1%	26.9%
1,891,325	QUEENS	615,578	285,477	328,379	1,722	42,902	D	46.4%	53.3%	46.5%	53.5%
151,966	RENSSELAER	70,864	43,892	26,755	217	17,137	R	61.9%	37.8%	62.1%	37.9%
352,121	RICHMOND	127,826	83,187	44,345	294	38,842	R	65.1%	34.7%	65.2%	34.8%
259,530	ROCKLAND	115,018	70,020	44,687	311	25,333	R	60.9%	38.9%	61.0%	39.0%
114,254	ST. LAWRENCE	42,149	26,062	15,963	124	10,099	R	61.8%	37.9%	62.0%	38.0%
153,759	SARATOGA	69,788	47,394	22,166	228	25,228	R	67.9%	31.8%	68.1%	31.9%
149,946	SCHENECTADY	73,697	42,808	30,612	277	12,196	R	58.1%	41.5%	58.3%	41.7%
29,710	SCHOHARIE	12,788	8,692	3,996	100	4,696	R	68.0%	31.2%	68.5%	31.5%
17,686	SCHUYLER	7,660	5,207	2,422	31	2,785	R	68.0%	31.6%	68.3%	31.7%
33,733	SENECA	14,307	9,420	4,825	62	4,595	R	65.8%	33.7%	66.1%	33.9%
99,217	STEUBEN	39,417	28,848	10,471	98	18,377	R	73.2%	26.6%	73.4%	26.6%
1,284,231	SUFFOLK	508,056	335,485	171,295	1,276	164,190	R	66.0%	33.7%	66.2%	33.8%
65,155	SULLIVAN	28,590	18,037	10,475	78	7,562	R	63.1%	36.6%	63.3%	36.7%
49,812	TIOGA	20,817	14,856	5,860	101	8,996	R	71.4%	28.2%	71.7%	28.3%
87,085	TOMPKINS	37,777	18,255	19,357	165	1,102	D	48.3%	51.2%	48.5%	51.5%
158,158	ULSTER	74,102	47,372	26,445	285	20,927	R	63.9%	35.7%	64.2%	35.8%
54,854	WARREN	23,568	17,616	5,886	66	11,730	R	74.7%	25.0%	75.0%	25.0%
54,795	WASHINGTON	22,563	16,580	5,909	74	10,671	R	73.5%	26.2%	73.7%	26.3%
84,581	WAYNE	34,051	24,171	9,700	180	14,471	R	71.0%	28.5%	71.4%	28.6%
866,599	WESTCHESTER	390,308	229,005	160,225	1,078	68,780	R	58.7%	41.1%	58.8%	41.2%

NEW YORK

PRESIDENT 1984

1980 Census Population	County	Total Vote	Republican	Democratic	Other	Rep.-Dem. Plurality	Percentage Total Vote Rep.	Dem.	Major Vote Rep.	Dem.
39,895	WYOMING	15,622	11,199	4,381	42	6,818 R	71.7%	28.0%	71.9%	28.1%
21,459	YATES	9,062	6,367	2,670	25	3,697 R	70.3%	29.5%	70.5%	29.5%
17,558,072	TOTAL	6,806,810	3,664,763	3,119,609	22,438	545,154 R	53.8%	45.8%	54.0%	46.0%

NEW YORK CITY

BRONX COUNTY
PRESIDENT 1984

1980 Census Population	Assembly District	Total Vote	Republican	Democratic	Other	Rep.-Dem. Plurality	Percentage			
							Total Vote		Major Vote	
							Rep.	Dem.	Rep.	Dem.
116,902	DISTRICT 73	30,142	5,705	24,253	184	18,548 D	18.9%	80.5%	19.0%	81.0%
116,909	DISTRICT 74	29,590	7,609	21,873	108	14,264 D	25.7%	73.9%	25.8%	74.2%
116,924	DISTRICT 75	39,127	21,297	17,727	103	3,570 R	54.4%	45.3%	54.6%	45.4%
116,909	DISTRICT 76	24,238	3,551	20,541	146	16,990 D	14.7%	84.7%	14.7%	85.3%
116,908	DISTRICT 77	22,466	5,226	17,170	70	11,944 D	23.3%	76.4%	23.3%	76.7%
116,909	DISTRICT 78	30,085	5,471	24,465	149	18,994 D	18.2%	81.3%	18.3%	81.7%
116,909	DISTRICT 79	33,985	13,558	20,300	127	6,742 D	39.9%	59.7%	40.0%	60.0%
116,911	DISTRICT 80	43,082	18,537	24,411	134	5,874 D	43.0%	56.7%	43.2%	56.8%
116,925	DISTRICT 81	46,881	20,348	26,416	117	6,068 D	43.4%	56.3%	43.5%	56.5%
116,909	DISTRICT 82	34,087	8,006	25,956	125	17,950 D	23.5%	76.1%	23.6%	76.4%
1,169,115	TOTAL	333,683	109,308	223,112	1,263	113,804 D	32.8%	66.9%	32.9%	67.1%

NEW YORK CITY

KINGS COUNTY
PRESIDENT 1984

1980 Census Population	Assembly District	Total Vote	Republican	Democratic	Other	Rep.-Dem. Plurality	Percentage			
							Total Vote		Major Vote	
							Rep.	Dem.	Rep.	Dem.
117,424	DISTRICT 39	39,838	19,522	20,206	110	684 D	49.0%	50.7%	49.1%	50.9%
117,423	DISTRICT 40	25,692	2,522	23,080	90	20,558 D	9.8%	89.8%	9.9%	90.1%
117,426	DISTRICT 41	43,717	21,649	21,975	93	326 D	49.5%	50.3%	49.6%	50.4%
117,425	DISTRICT 42	22,525	6,417	16,036	72	9,619 D	28.5%	71.2%	28.6%	71.4%
117,416	DISTRICT 43	22,176	3,409	18,694	73	15,285 D	15.4%	84.3%	15.4%	84.6%
117,435	DISTRICT 44	36,054	13,416	22,477	161	9,061 D	37.2%	62.3%	37.4%	62.6%
117,408	DISTRICT 45	41,424	19,368	21,941	115	2,573 D	46.8%	53.0%	46.9%	53.1%
117,414	DISTRICT 46	39,271	17,296	21,824	151	4,528 D	44.0%	55.6%	44.2%	55.8%
117,402	DISTRICT 47	33,375	17,338	15,941	96	1,397 R	51.9%	47.8%	52.1%	47.9%
117,414	DISTRICT 48	30,955	20,563	10,308	84	10,255 R	66.4%	33.3%	66.6%	33.4%
117,390	DISTRICT 49	30,309	19,103	11,140	66	7,963 R	63.0%	36.8%	63.2%	36.8%
117,418	DISTRICT 50	26,979	12,414	14,461	104	2,047 D	46.0%	53.6%	46.2%	53.8%
117,420	DISTRICT 51	31,032	14,488	16,413	131	1,925 D	46.7%	52.9%	46.9%	53.1%
117,416	DISTRICT 52	43,397	19,900	23,325	172	3,425 D	45.9%	53.7%	46.0%	54.0%
117,421	DISTRICT 53	24,380	7,370	16,905	105	9,535 D	30.2%	69.3%	30.4%	69.6%
117,420	DISTRICT 54	21,805	6,443	15,287	75	8,844 D	29.5%	70.1%	29.7%	70.3%
117,422	DISTRICT 55	26,858	2,220	24,532	106	22,312 D	8.3%	91.3%	8.3%	91.7%
117,420	DISTRICT 56	29,906	2,461	27,297	148	24,836 D	8.2%	91.3%	8.3%	91.7%
117,422	DISTRICT 57	31,078	4,165	26,676	237	22,511 D	13.4%	85.8%	13.5%	86.5%
2,230,936	TOTAL	600,771	230,064	368,518	2,189	138,454 D	38.3%	61.3%	38.4%	61.6%

NEW YORK CITY

NEW YORK COUNTY

PRESIDENT 1984

1980 Census Population	Assembly District	Total Vote	Republican	Democratic	Other	Rep.-Dem. Plurality	Percentage Total Vote Rep.	Dem.	Major Vote Rep.	Dem.
118,950	DISTRICT 61	56,152	12,523	43,307	322	30,784 D	22.3%	77.1%	22.4%	77.6%
118,951	DISTRICT 62	28,793	8,721	19,900	172	11,179 D	30.3%	69.1%	30.5%	69.5%
118,962	DISTRICT 63	52,885	18,859	33,775	251	14,916 D	35.7%	63.9%	35.8%	64.2%
118,973	DISTRICT 64	50,753	14,024	36,419	310	22,395 D	27.6%	71.8%	27.8%	72.2%
119,036	DISTRICT 65	52,689	21,337	31,166	186	9,829 D	40.5%	59.2%	40.6%	59.4%
118,984	DISTRICT 66	51,418	23,601	27,682	135	4,081 D	45.9%	53.8%	46.0%	54.0%
118,949	DISTRICT 67	55,553	13,445	41,856	252	28,411 D	24.2%	75.3%	24.3%	75.7%
118,965	DISTRICT 68	33,790	5,417	28,176	197	22,759 D	16.0%	83.4%	16.1%	83.9%
118,956	DISTRICT 69	48,466	8,065	40,060	341	31,995 D	16.6%	82.7%	16.8%	83.2%
118,963	DISTRICT 70	36,255	2,938	32,972	345	30,034 D	8.1%	90.9%	8.2%	91.8%
118,908	DISTRICT 71	30,428	4,222	25,995	211	21,773 D	13.9%	85.4%	14.0%	86.0%
118,936	DISTRICT 72	29,489	11,129	18,213	147	7,084 D	37.7%	61.8%	37.9%	62.1%
1,427,533	TOTAL	526,671	144,281	379,521	2,869	235,240 D	27.4%	72.1%	27.5%	72.5%

NEW YORK CITY

QUEENS COUNTY

PRESIDENT 1984

1980 Census Population	Assembly District	Total Vote	Republican	Democratic	Other	Rep.-Dem. Plurality	Percentage Total Vote Rep.	Dem.	Major Vote Rep.	Dem.
118,206	DISTRICT 23	37,853	16,906	20,834	113	3,928 D	44.7%	55.0%	44.8%	55.2%
118,191	DISTRICT 24	52,906	24,931	27,860	115	2,929 D	47.1%	52.7%	47.2%	52.8%
118,200	DISTRICT 25	49,718	30,799	18,831	88	11,968 R	61.9%	37.9%	62.1%	37.9%
118,198	DISTRICT 26	42,597	20,487	22,028	82	1,541 D	48.1%	51.7%	48.2%	51.8%
118,201	DISTRICT 27	41,924	19,874	21,938	112	2,064 D	47.4%	52.3%	47.5%	52.5%
118,218	DISTRICT 28	46,621	21,513	25,000	108	3,487 D	46.1%	53.6%	46.3%	53.7%
118,207	DISTRICT 29	41,734	6,355	35,236	143	28,881 D	15.2%	84.4%	15.3%	84.7%
118,215	DISTRICT 30	31,379	16,484	14,806	89	1,678 R	52.5%	47.2%	52.7%	47.3%
118,210	DISTRICT 31	37,456	23,231	14,137	88	9,094 R	62.0%	37.7%	62.2%	37.8%
118,206	DISTRICT 32	40,810	8,954	31,658	198	22,704 D	21.9%	77.6%	22.0%	78.0%
118,203	DISTRICT 33	29,588	7,914	21,535	139	13,621 D	26.7%	72.8%	26.9%	73.1%
118,216	DISTRICT 34	36,007	19,683	16,227	97	3,456 R	54.7%	45.1%	54.8%	45.2%
118,203	DISTRICT 35	23,780	7,912	15,800	68	7,888 D	33.3%	66.4%	33.4%	66.6%
118,217	DISTRICT 36	32,092	15,207	16,771	114	1,564 D	47.4%	52.3%	47.6%	52.4%
118,217	DISTRICT 37	30,674	16,791	13,785	98	3,006 R	54.7%	44.9%	54.9%	45.1%
118,217	DISTRICT 39	40,439	28,436	11,933	70	16,503 R	70.3%	29.5%	70.4%	29.6%
1,891,325	TOTAL	615,578	285,477	328,379	1,722	42,902 D	46.4%	53.3%	46.5%	53.5%

NEW YORK CITY

RICHMOND COUNTY
PRESIDENT 1984

1980 Census Population	Assembly District	Total Vote	Republican	Democratic	Other	Rep.-Dem. Plurality	Percentage Total Vote Rep.	Dem.	Major Vote Rep.	Dem.
117,373	DISTRICT 58	42,116	25,853	16,161	102	9,692 R	61.4%	38.4%	61.5%	38.5%
117,376	DISTRICT 59	38,826	22,965	15,770	91	7,195 R	59.1%	40.6%	59.3%	40.7%
117,372	DISTRICT 60	46,884	34,369	12,414	101	21,955 R	73.3%	26.5%	73.5%	26.5%
352,121	TOTAL	127,826	83,187	44,345	294	38,842 R	65.1%	34.7%	65.2%	34.8%

NEW YORK CITY

PRESIDENT 1984

1980 Census Population	County	Total Vote	Republican	Democratic	Other	Rep.-Dem. Plurality	Percentage Total Vote Rep.	Dem.	Major Vote Rep.	Dem.
1,169,115	BRONX	333,683	109,308	223,112	1,263	113,804 D	32.8%	66.9%	32.9%	67.1%
2,230,936	KINGS	600,771	230,064	368,518	2,189	138,454 D	38.3%	61.3%	38.4%	61.6%
1,427,533	NEW YORK	526,671	144,281	379,521	2,869	235,240 D	27.4%	72.1%	27.5%	72.5%
1,891,325	QUEENS	615,578	285,477	328,379	1,722	42,902 D	46.4%	53.3%	46.5%	53.5%
352,121	RICHMOND	127,826	83,187	44,345	294	38,842 R	65.1%	34.7%	65.2%	34.8%
7,071,030	TOTAL	2,204,529	852,317	1,343,875	8,337	491,558 D	38.7%	61.0%	38.8%	61.2%

NEW YORK

CONGRESS

CD	Year	Total Vote	Republican Vote	Republican Candidate	Democratic Vote	Democratic Candidate	Other Vote	Rep.-Dem. Plurality	Total Vote Rep.	Total Vote Dem.	Major Vote Rep.	Major Vote Dem.
1	1984	201,580	107,029	*CARNEY, WILLIAM	94,551	*HOCHBRUECKNER, GEORGE J.		12,478 R	53.1%	46.9%	53.1%	46.9%
1	1982	138,021	88,234	*CARNEY, WILLIAM	49,787	ELDON, ETHAN C.		38,447 R	63.9%	36.1%	63.9%	36.1%
2	1984	178,503	80,855	*ANIBOLI, PAUL	97,648	*DOWNEY, THOMAS J.		16,793 D	45.3%	54.7%	45.3%	54.7%
2	1982	126,712	42,790	*COSTELLO, PAUL G.	80,951	*DOWNEY, THOMAS J.	2,971	38,161 D	33.8%	63.9%	34.6%	65.4%
3	1984	235,751	112,909	*QUINN, ROBERT P.	120,191	MRAZEK, ROBERT J.	2,651	7,282 D	47.9%	51.0%	48.4%	51.6%
4	1984	224,679	154,875	*LENT, NORMAN F.	65,678	*ENGELHARD, SHELDON	4,126	89,197 R	68.9%	29.2%	70.2%	29.8%
5	1984	222,191	138,560	*MCGRATH, RAYMOND J.	78,429	*D'INNOCENZO, MICHAEL	5,202	60,131 R	62.4%	35.3%	63.9%	36.1%
6	1984	145,138	25,040	*VELTRE, PHILIP J.	120,098	*ADDABBO, JOSEPH P.		95,058 D	17.3%	82.7%	17.3%	82.7%
7	1984	141,044	43,370	*REIFENKUGEL, GUSTAVE A.	97,674	*ACKERMAN, GARY L.		54,304 D	30.7%	69.3%	30.7%	69.3%
8	1984	166,573	62,015	*BRANDOFINO, ROBERT L.	104,558	*SCHEUER, JAMES H.		42,543 D	37.2%	62.8%	37.2%	62.8%
9	1984	135,330	63,910	*MALTESE, SERPHIN R.	71,420	MANTON, THOMAS J.		7,510 D	47.2%	52.8%	47.2%	52.8%
9	1982	102,820	20,352	WEIGANDT, JOHN L.	75,286	FERRARO, GERALDINE A.	7,182	54,934 D	19.8%	73.2%	21.3%	78.7%
10	1984	159,992	42,009	*FOX, JOHN H.	115,867	*SCHUMER, CHARLES E.	2,116	73,858 D	26.3%	72.4%	26.6%	73.4%
11	1984	95,064	12,494	HENDRICKS, NATHANIEL	81,002	*TOWNS, EDOLPHUS	1,568	68,508 D	13.1%	85.2%	13.4%	86.6%
12	1984	90,656	8,609	*CAESAR, JOSEPH N.	82,047	*OWENS, MAJOR R.		73,438 D	9.5%	90.5%	9.5%	90.5%
12	1982	49,259	3,215	KATAN, DAVID	44,586	*OWENS, MAJOR R.	1,458	41,371 D	6.5%	90.5%	6.7%	93.3%
13	1984	125,347	42,737	*LEVIN, LEW Y.	82,610	*SOLARZ, STEPHEN J.		39,873 D	34.1%	65.9%	34.1%	65.9%
14	1984	166,817	117,041	*MOLINARI, GUY V.	49,776	SHEEHY, KEVIN		67,265 R	70.2%	29.8%	70.2%	29.8%
15	1984	192,048	107,644	*GREEN, S. WILLIAM	84,404	*STEIN, ANDREW J.		23,240 R	56.1%	43.9%	56.1%	43.9%
15	1982	123,698	66,262	*GREEN, S. WILLIAM	55,483	*LALL, BETTY G.	1,953	10,779 R	53.6%	44.9%	54.4%	45.6%
16	1984	121,398			117,759	*RANGEL, CHARLES B.	3,639	117,759 D		97.0%		100.0%
16	1982	78,605			76,626	*RANGEL, CHARLES B.	1,979	76,626 D		97.5%		100.0%
17	1984	199,479	33,316	KATZMAN, KENNETH	162,489	*WEISS, THEODORE S.	3,674	129,173 D	16.7%	81.5%	17.0%	83.0%
17	1982	133,100	19,928	*ANTONELLI, LOUIS S.	113,172	*WEISS, THEODORE S.		93,244 D	15.0%	85.0%	15.0%	85.0%
18	1984	96,328	8,970	JOHNSON, CURTIS	85,960	*GARCIA, ROBERT	1,398	76,990 D	9.3%	89.2%	9.4%	90.6%
19	1984	163,539			155,067	*BIAGGI, MARIO	8,472	155,067 D	0.0%	94.8%	0.0%	100.0%
20	1984	213,349	106,958	*DIOGUARDI, JOSEPH J.	102,842	TEICHER, OREN J.	3,549	4,116 R	50.1%	48.2%	51.0%	49.0%
21	1984	204,327	160,053	*FISH, HAMILTON	44,274	GRUNBERGER, LAWRENCE W.		115,779 R	78.3%	21.7%	78.3%	21.7%
21	1982	156,124	117,460	*FISH, HAMILTON	38,664	STRONG, J. MORGAN		78,796 R	75.2%	24.8%	75.2%	24.8%
22	1984	210,486	144,278	GILMAN, BENJAMIN A.	57,934	*LEVINE, BRUCE M.	8,274	86,344 R	68.5%	27.5%	71.3%	28.7%
22	1982	174,286	92,266	GILMAN, BENJAMIN A.	73,124	*PEYSER, PETER A.	8,896	19,142 R	52.9%	42.0%	55.8%	44.2%
23	1984	241,846	53,060	*WICKS, FRANK	188,144	STRATTON, SAMUEL S.	642	135,084 D	21.9%	77.8%	22.0%	78.0%
23	1982	216,083	41,386	*WICKS, FRANK	164,427	STRATTON, SAMUEL S.	10,270	123,041 D	19.2%	76.1%	20.1%	79.9%
24	1984	224,207	164,019	*SOLOMON, GERALD B.	60,188	BLOCH, EDWARD J.		103,831 R	73.2%	26.8%	73.2%	26.8%
24	1982	189,737	140,296	*SOLOMON, GERALD B.	49,441	ESIASON, ROY		90,855 R	73.9%	26.1%	73.9%	26.1%
25	1984	192,690	140,256	BOEHLERT, SHERWOOD L.	52,434	BALL, JAMES J.		87,822 R	72.8%	27.2%	72.8%	27.2%
26	1984	185,920	131,257	*MARTIN, DAVID O'B.	54,663	LAMMERS, BERNARD J.		76,594 R	70.6%	29.4%	70.6%	29.4%
26	1982	152,170	108,962	*MARTIN, DAVID O'B.	43,208	LANDY, DAVID P.		65,754 R	71.6%	28.4%	71.6%	28.4%
27	1984	215,816	122,215	*WORTLEY, GEORGE C.	93,601	*BUCKEL, THOMAS C.		28,614 R	56.6%	43.4%	56.6%	43.4%
28	1984	218,061	90,324	COOK, CONSTANCE E.	123,334	MCHUGH, MATTHEW F.	4,403	33,010 D	41.4%	56.6%	42.3%	57.7%
29	1984	198,662	138,362	*HORTON, FRANK J.	48,301	TOOLE, JAMES R.	11,999	90,061 R	69.6%	24.3%	74.1%	25.9%
30	1984	220,273	119,844	*ECKERT, FRED J.	100,066	CALL, W. DOUGLAS	363	19,778 R	54.4%	45.4%	54.5%	45.5%
30	1982	174,620	119,105	CONABLE, BARBER B.	48,764	BENET, BILL	6,751	70,341 R	68.2%	27.9%	71.0%	29.0%

NEW YORK

CONGRESS

CD	Year	Total Vote	Republican Vote	Republican Candidate	Democratic Vote	Democratic Candidate	Other Vote	Rep.-Dem. Plurality	Total Vote Rep.	Total Vote Dem.	Major Vote Rep.	Major Vote Dem.
31	1984	224,488	168,332	*KEMP, JACK F.	56,156	*MARTINELLI, PETER J.		112,176 R	75.0%	25.0%	75.0%	25.0%
32	1984	201,776	61,797	*MURTY, ANTHONY J.	139,979	*LAFALCE, JOHN J.		78,182 D	30.6%	69.4%	30.6%	69.4%
32	1982	127,383			116,386	*LAFALCE, JOHN J.	10,997	116,386 D		91.4%		100.0%
33	1984	200,078	44,880	*LEWANDOWSKI, DAVID S.	155,198	*NOWAK, HENRY J.		110,318 D	22.4%	77.6%	22.4%	77.6%
33	1982	149,977	19,791	*PILLICH, WALTER J.	126,091	*NOWAK, HENRY J.	4,095	106,300 D	13.2%	84.1%	13.6%	86.4%
34	1984	204,478	91,016	*EMERY, JILL H.	110,902	LUNDINE, STANLEY N.	2,560	19,886 D	44.5%	54.2%	45.1%	54.9%

320

NEW YORK

1984 GENERAL ELECTION

President   The Republican candidate was also the Conservative nominee and 288,244 of his votes were received as the Conservative candidate. The Democratic candidate was also the Liberal nominee and 118,324 of his votes were received as the Liberal candidate. Other vote was 11,949 Bergland (Free Libertarian); 4,226 Hall (Communist); 3,200 Serrette (New Alliance); 2,226 Holmes (Workers World); 837 scattered.

Congress   As asterisk in the Congressional vote table indicates a candidate received votes as the nominee of an additional party/parties. Other vote was Capazzi (Right to Life) in CD 3; Dunkle (Right to Life) in CD 4; 3,572 Callahan (Right to Life) and 1,630 Olchin (Liberal) in CD 5; Donohue (Right to Life) in CD 10; Hamel (Conservative) in CD 11; 2,541 Berns (Conservative) and 1,098 Bailey (Socialist Workers) in CD 16; Steinman (Conservative) in CD 17; John Farrell (Conservative) in CD 18; Alice Farrell (Conservative) in CD 19; O'Grady (Right to Life) in CD 20; DeMaggio (Right to Life) in CD 22; Ariza (Socialist Workers) in CD 23; Masterson (Right to Life) in CD 28; 7,957 Hale (Conservative) and 4,042 Peters (Right to Life) in CD 29; Nero (Workers World) in CD 30; Fisher (Right to Life) in CD 34.

NEW YORK CITY

The city is composed of five counties, each of which for municipal government purposes is known as a borough. Names of counties and boroughs are the same save in the case of New York county (Manhattan borough), Kings county (Brooklyn borough) and Richmond county (Staten Island borough).

President   The Republican vote includes 73,746 votes cast for Reagan as the Conservative candidate. The Democratic vote includes 66,449 votes for Mondale as the Liberal candidate. Other vote was 2,916 Bergland (Free Libertarian); 2,479 Hall (Communist); 1,870 Serrette (New Alliance); 996 Holmes (Workers World); 76 scattered.

1984 PRIMARIES

SEPTEMBER 11 REPUBLICAN

Congress   Unopposed in twenty-nine CD's. Democratic candidate endorsed in CD's 16 and 19. Contested as follows:

CD 1   8,059 William Carney; 7,276 Gregory J. Blass.
CD 9   2,803 Serphin R. Maltese; 1,422 Salvatore J. Calise.
CD 29   8,014 Frank J. Horton; 4,911 E. Kevan Rowlee.

SEPTEMBER 11 DEMOCRATIC

Congress   Unopposed in twenty-two CD's. Contested as follows:

CD 6   33,231 Joseph P. Addabbo; 15,846 Simeon Golar.
CD 9   8,563 Thomas J. Manton; 7,571 Clifford E. Wilson; 6,094 Walter H. Crowley; 6,041 Gloria D'Amico.
CD 11   21,463 Edolphus Towns; 11,782 Rafael Esparra.
CD 12   18,011 Major R. Owens; 5,500 Enoch H. Williams; 3,174 Owen Augustin.
CD 14   7,304 Kevin Sheehy; 4,821 Terence H. Benbow.
CD 15   16,285 Andrew J. Stein; 11,716 Betty G. Lall; 4,143 Robert H. Tembeckjian; 1,685 Arnold Perey.
CD 17   27,654 Theodore S. Weiss; 4,954 Carter R. Perry.
CD 20   9,314 Oren J. Teicher; 7,724 Edward Meyer; 5,865 Peter A. Peyser; 1,433 Bennie O. Batts; 6 scattered.
CD 29   3,591 James R. Toole; 1,428 Kieth R. T. Perez.
CD 31   2,813 Peter J. Martinelli; 1,147 Charles H. Carmen.
CD 32   17,747 John J. LaFalce; 1,025 Stephen R. Kaylor.
CD 33   28,836 Henry J. Nowak; 4,921 Elizabeth Spiro-Carman.

NEW YORK

SEPTEMBER 11 CONSERVATIVE

Congress   Major party candidates endorsed or nominees unopposed in all CD's in which a candidate was named. There was a write-in contest as follows:

CD 27   323 George C. Wortley (the unopposed Republican nominee); 154 John B. Carroll; 1 Thomas Carroll; 1 Edward Bohrer.

SEPTEMBER 11 LIBERAL

Congress   Major party candidates endorsed or nominees unopposed in all CD's in which a candidate was named.

SPETEMBER 11 RIGHT TO LIFE

Congress   Major party candidates endorsed or nominees unopposed in all CD's in which a candidate was named. There were three write-in contests as follows:

CD 27   62 John B. Carroll; 9 George C. Wortley; 2 scattered.
CD 30   9 Fred J. Eckert; 1 Richard Wesley.
CD 34   45 Carol Fisher; 9 scattered.

NORTH CAROLINA

GOVERNOR
James G. Martin (R). Elected 1984 to a four-year term.

SENATORS
John P. East (R). Elected 1980 to a six-year term.

Jesse Helms (R). Re-elected 1984 to a six-year term. Previously elected 1978, 1972.

REPRESENTATIVES
1. Walter B. Jones (D)
2. I. T. Valentine (D)
3. Charles Whitley (D)
4. William Cobey (R)
5. Stephen L. Neal (D)
6. Howard Coble (R)
7. Charles G. Rose (D)
8. W. G. Hefner (D)
9. J. Alex McMillan (R)
10. James T. Broyhill (R)
11. William M. Hendon (R)

POSTWAR VOTE FOR GOVERNOR

Year	Total Vote	Republican Vote	Candidate	Democratic Vote	Candidate	Other Vote	Rep.-Dem. Plurality	Total Vote Rep.	Total Vote Dem.	Major Vote Rep.	Major Vote Dem.
1984	2,226,727	1,208,167	Martin, James G.	1,011,209	Edmisten, Rufus	7,351	196,958 R	54.3%	45.4%	54.4%	45.6%
1980	1,847,432	691,449	Lake, Beverly	1,143,145	Hunt, James B.	12,838	451,696 D	37.4%	61.9%	37.7%	62.3%
1976	1,663,824	564,102	Flaherty, David T.	1,081,293	Hunt, James B.	18,429	517,191 D	33.9%	65.0%	34.3%	65.7%
1972	1,504,785	767,470	Holshouser, James E.	729,104	Bowles, Hargrove	8,211	38,366 R	51.0%	48.5%	51.3%	48.7%
1968	1,558,308	737,075	Gardner, James C.	821,233	Scott, Robert W.	—	84,158 D	47.3%	52.7%	47.3%	52.7%
1964	1,396,508	606,165	Gavin, Robert L.	790,343	Moore, Dan K.	—	184,178 D	43.4%	56.6%	43.4%	56.6%
1960	1,350,360	613,975	Gavin, Robert L.	735,248	Sanford, Terry	1,137	121,273 D	45.5%	54.4%	45.5%	54.5%
1956	1,135,859	375,379	Hayes, Kyle	760,480	Hodges, Luther H.	—	385,101 D	33.0%	67.0%	33.0%	67.0%
1952	1,179,635	383,329	Seawell, H. F.	796,306	Umstead, William B.	—	412,977 D	32.5%	67.5%	32.5%	67.5%
1948	780,525	206,166	Pritchard, George	570,995	Scott, William Kerr	3,364	364,829 D	26.4%	73.2%	26.5%	73.5%

POSTWAR VOTE FOR SENATOR

Year	Total Vote	Republican Vote	Candidate	Democratic Vote	Candidate	Other Vote	Rep.-Dem. Plurality	Total Vote Rep.	Total Vote Dem.	Major Vote Rep.	Major Vote Dem.
1984	2,239,051	1,156,768	Helms, Jesse	1,070,488	Hunt, James B.	11,795	86,280 R	51.7%	47.8%	51.9%	48.1%
1980	1,797,665	898,064	East, John P.	887,653	Morgan, Robert	11,948	10,411 R	50.0%	49.4%	50.3%	49.7%
1978	1,135,814	619,151	Helms, Jesse	516,663	Ingram, John	—	102,488 R	54.5%	45.5%	54.5%	45.5%
1974	1,020,367	377,618	Stevens, William E.	633,775	Morgan, Robert	8,974	256,157 D	37.0%	62.1%	37.3%	62.7%
1972	1,472,541	795,248	Helms, Jesse	677,293	Galifianakis, Nick	—	117,955 R	54.0%	46.0%	54.0%	46.0%
1968	1,437,340	566,934	Somers, Robert V.	870,406	Ervin, Sam J.	—	303,472 D	39.4%	60.6%	39.4%	60.6%
1966	901,978	400,502	Shallcross, John S.	501,440	Jordan, B. Everett	36	100,938 D	44.4%	55.6%	44.4%	55.6%
1962	813,155	321,635	Greene, Claude L.	491,520	Ervin, Sam J.	—	169,885 D	39.6%	60.4%	39.6%	60.4%
1960	1,291,485	497,964	Hayes, Kyle	793,521	Jordan, B. Everett	—	295,557 D	38.6%	61.4%	38.6%	61.4%
1958s	616,469	184,977	Clarke, Richard C.	431,492	Jordan, B. Everett	—	246,515 D	30.0%	70.0%	30.0%	70.0%
1956	1,098,828	367,475	Johnson, Joel A.	731,353	Ervin, Sam J.	—	363,878 D	33.4%	66.6%	33.4%	66.6%
1954	619,634	211,322	West, Paul C.	408,312	Scott, William Kerr	—	196,990 D	34.1%	65.9%	34.1%	65.9%
1954s	410,574	—	—	410,574	Ervin, Sam J.	—	410,574 D	—	100.0%	—	100.0%
1950	548,276	171,804	Leavitt, Halsey B.	376,472	Hoey, Clyde R.	—	204,668 D	31.3%	68.7%	31.3%	68.7%
1950s	544,924	177,753	Gavin, E. L.	364,912	Smith, Willis	2,259	187,159 D	32.6%	67.0%	32.8%	67.2%
1948	764,559	220,307	Wilkinson, John A.	540,762	Broughton, J. M.	3,490	320,455 D	28.8%	70.7%	28.9%	71.1%

The 1958 election and one each of the 1954 and 1950 elections were for short terms to fill vacancies.

NORTH CAROLINA

Districts Established February 11, 1982

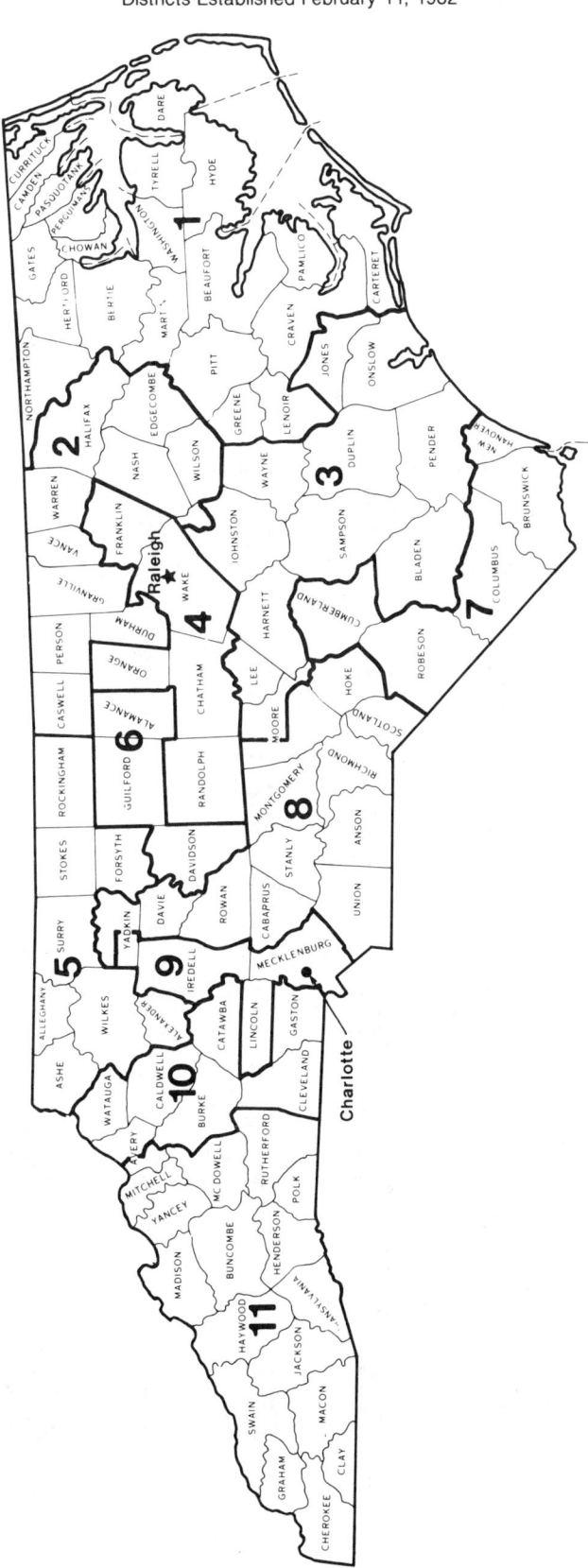

NORTH CAROLINA

PRESIDENT 1984

1980 Census Population	County	Total Vote	Republican	Democratic	Other	Rep.-Dem. Plurality	Percentage Total Vote Rep.	Dem.	Major Vote Rep.	Dem.
99,319	ALAMANCE	37,370	26,063	11,230	77	14,833 R	69.7%	30.1%	69.9%	30.1%
24,999	ALEXANDER	12,107	8,502	3,581	24	4,921 R	70.2%	29.6%	70.4%	29.6%
9,587	ALLEGHANY	4,617	2,589	2,013	15	576 R	56.1%	43.6%	56.3%	43.7%
25,649	ANSON	8,760	3,719	5,015	26	1,296 D	42.5%	57.2%	42.6%	57.4%
22,325	ASHE	10,645	6,611	4,009	25	2,602 R	62.1%	37.7%	62.3%	37.7%
14,409	AVERY	5,886	4,702	1,159	25	3,543 R	79.9%	19.7%	80.2%	19.8%
40,355	BEAUFORT	15,304	9,284	5,987	33	3,297 R	60.7%	39.1%	60.8%	39.2%
21,024	BERTIE	6,870	2,879	3,953	38	1,074 D	41.9%	57.5%	42.1%	57.9%
30,491	BLADEN	9,779	4,701	5,064	14	363 D	48.1%	51.8%	48.1%	51.9%
35,777	BRUNSWICK	16,488	9,673	6,774	41	2,899 R	58.7%	41.1%	58.8%	41.2%
160,934	BUNCOMBE	61,183	37,698	23,337	148	14,361 R	61.6%	38.1%	61.8%	38.2%
72,504	BURKE	29,178	18,766	10,353	59	8,413 R	64.3%	35.5%	64.4%	35.6%
85,895	CABARRUS	31,058	22,528	8,477	53	14,051 R	72.5%	27.3%	72.7%	27.3%
67,746	CALDWELL	24,394	17,024	7,311	59	9,713 R	69.8%	30.0%	70.0%	30.0%
5,829	CAMDEN	2,363	1,282	1,075	6	207 R	54.3%	45.5%	54.4%	45.6%
41,092	CARTERET	17,557	11,637	5,882	38	5,755 R	66.3%	33.5%	66.4%	33.6%
20,705	CASWELL	8,174	3,992	4,157	25	165 D	48.8%	50.9%	49.0%	51.0%
105,208	CATAWBA	43,250	31,476	11,700	74	19,776 R	72.8%	27.1%	72.9%	27.1%
33,415	CHATHAM	16,099	8,595	7,458	46	1,137 R	53.4%	46.3%	53.5%	46.5%
18,933	CHEROKEE	7,679	4,894	2,776	9	2,118 R	63.7%	36.2%	63.8%	36.2%
12,558	CHOWAN	3,918	2,171	1,736	11	435 R	55.4%	44.3%	55.6%	44.4%
6,619	CLAY	3,619	2,259	1,340	20	919 R	62.4%	37.0%	62.8%	37.2%
83,435	CLEVELAND	27,472	17,095	10,288	89	6,807 R	62.2%	37.4%	62.4%	37.6%
51,037	COLUMBUS	17,904	9,150	8,728	26	422 R	51.1%	48.7%	51.2%	48.8%
71,043	CRAVEN	20,134	12,893	7,186	55	5,707 R	64.0%	35.7%	64.2%	35.8%
247,160	CUMBERLAND	54,319	31,602	22,614	103	8,988 R	58.2%	41.6%	58.3%	41.7%
11,089	CURRITUCK	4,562	2,885	1,668	9	1,217 R	63.2%	36.6%	63.4%	36.6%
13,377	DARE	6,596	4,738	1,839	19	2,899 R	71.8%	27.9%	72.0%	28.0%
113,162	DAVIDSON	42,001	30,471	11,469	61	19,002 R	72.5%	27.3%	72.7%	27.3%
24,599	DAVIE	11,125	8,201	2,911	13	5,290 R	73.7%	26.2%	73.8%	26.2%
40,952	DUPLIN	14,555	7,708	6,830	17	878 R	53.0%	46.9%	53.0%	47.0%
152,785	DURHAM	61,584	29,185	32,244	155	3,059 D	47.4%	52.4%	47.5%	52.5%
55,988	EDGECOMBE	20,216	9,635	10,545	36	910 D	47.7%	52.2%	47.7%	52.3%
243,683	FORSYTH	96,211	59,208	36,814	189	22,394 R	61.5%	38.3%	61.7%	38.3%
30,055	FRANKLIN	10,768	5,984	4,766	18	1,218 R	55.6%	44.3%	55.7%	44.3%
162,568	GASTON	53,392	39,167	14,142	83	25,025 R	73.4%	26.5%	73.5%	26.5%
8,875	GATES	3,930	1,694	2,225	11	531 D	43.1%	56.6%	43.2%	56.8%
7,217	GRAHAM	4,014	2,514	1,494	6	1,020 R	62.6%	37.2%	62.7%	37.3%
34,043	GRANVILLE	11,580	6,302	5,217	61	1,085 R	54.4%	45.1%	54.7%	45.3%
16,117	GREENE	5,975	3,195	2,772	8	423 R	53.5%	46.4%	53.5%	46.5%
317,154	GULIFORD	119,336	73,096	46,027	213	27,069 R	61.3%	38.6%	61.4%	38.6%
55,286	HALIFAX	18,153	8,832	9,278	43	446 D	48.7%	51.1%	48.8%	51.2%
59,570	HARNETT	18,323	11,198	7,106	19	4,092 R	61.1%	38.8%	61.2%	38.8%
46,495	HAYWOOD	18,131	10,146	7,958	27	2,188 R	56.0%	43.9%	56.0%	44.0%
58,580	HENDERSON	26,697	19,369	7,222	106	12,147 R	72.6%	27.1%	72.8%	27.2%
23,368	HERTFORD	7,695	3,176	4,498	21	1,322 D	41.3%	58.5%	41.4%	58.6%
20,383	HOKE	5,677	2,449	3,214	14	765 D	43.1%	56.6%	43.2%	56.8%
5,873	HYDE	2,202	1,195	1,004	3	191 R	54.3%	45.6%	54.3%	45.7%
82,538	IREDELL	33,704	23,641	9,999	64	13,642 R	70.1%	29.7%	70.3%	29.7%
25,811	JACKSON	9,974	5,582	4,367	25	1,215 R	56.0%	43.8%	56.1%	43.9%
70,599	JOHNSTON	24,080	16,210	7,833	37	8,377 R	67.3%	32.5%	67.4%	32.6%
9,705	JONES	4,099	2,062	2,025	12	37 R	50.3%	49.4%	50.5%	49.5%
36,718	LEE	12,151	8,198	3,925	28	4,273 R	67.5%	32.3%	67.6%	32.4%
59,819	LENOIR	21,914	13,321	8,556	37	4,765 R	60.8%	39.0%	60.9%	39.1%
42,372	LINCOLN	18,659	12,621	5,996	42	6,625 R	67.6%	32.1%	67.8%	32.2%
35,135	MCDOWELL	11,736	7,639	4,076	21	3,563 R	65.1%	34.7%	65.2%	34.8%
20,178	MACON	10,256	6,661	3,570	25	3,091 R	64.9%	34.8%	65.1%	34.9%
16,827	MADISON	6,689	3,666	2,988	35	678 R	54.8%	44.7%	55.1%	44.9%
25,948	MARTIN	8,153	4,266	3,870	17	396 R	52.3%	47.5%	52.4%	47.6%
404,270	MECKLENBURG	170,337	106,754	63,190	393	43,564 R	62.7%	37.1%	62.8%	37.2%

NORTH CAROLINA

PRESIDENT 1984

1980 Census Population	County	Total Vote	Republican	Democratic	Other	Rep.-Dem. Plurality	Percentage Total Vote Rep.	Dem.	Major Vote Rep.	Dem.
14,428	MITCHELL	6,034	4,737	1,286	11	3,451 R	78.5%	21.3%	78.6%	21.4%
22,469	MONTGOMERY	8,952	5,109	3,831	12	1,278 R	57.1%	42.8%	57.1%	42.9%
50,505	MOORE	21,782	14,681	7,063	38	7,618 R	67.4%	32.4%	67.5%	32.5%
67,153	NASH	25,917	17,295	8,588	34	8,707 R	66.7%	33.1%	66.8%	33.2%
103,471	NEW HANOVER	36,452	23,771	12,591	90	11,180 R	65.2%	34.5%	65.4%	34.6%
22,584	NORTHAMPTON	8,330	3,198	5,094	38	1,896 D	38.4%	61.2%	38.6%	61.4%
112,784	ONSLOW	19,687	13,928	5,713	46	8,215 R	70.7%	29.0%	70.9%	29.1%
77,055	ORANGE	36,277	15,585	20,564	128	4,979 D	43.0%	56.7%	43.1%	56.9%
10,398	PAMLICO	4,717	2,554	2,152	11	402 R	54.1%	45.6%	54.3%	45.7%
28,462	PASQUOTANK	8,513	4,646	3,854	13	792 R	54.6%	45.3%	54.7%	45.3%
22,215	PENDER	9,453	5,079	4,354	20	725 R	53.7%	46.1%	53.8%	46.2%
9,486	PERQUIMANS	3,385	1,939	1,441	5	498 R	57.3%	42.6%	57.4%	42.6%
29,164	PERSON	9,397	5,854	3,528	15	2,326 R	62.3%	37.5%	62.4%	37.6%
90,146	PITT	32,526	18,983	13,481	62	5,502 R	58.4%	41.4%	58.5%	41.5%
12,984	POLK	6,251	4,046	2,169	36	1,877 R	64.7%	34.7%	65.1%	34.9%
91,728	RANDOLPH	33,299	25,759	7,511	29	18,248 R	77.4%	22.6%	77.4%	22.6%
45,481	RICHMOND	14,330	6,807	7,494	29	687 D	47.5%	52.3%	47.6%	52.4%
101,610	ROBESON	28,291	12,947	15,257	87	2,310 D	45.8%	53.9%	45.9%	54.1%
83,426	ROCKINGHAM	28,539	17,895	10,605	39	7,290 R	62.7%	37.2%	62.8%	37.2%
99,186	ROWAN	35,907	25,207	10,643	57	14,564 R	70.2%	29.6%	70.3%	29.7%
53,787	RUTHERFORD	18,268	11,369	6,862	37	4,507 R	62.2%	37.6%	62.4%	37.6%
49,687	SAMPSON	19,796	10,665	9,115	16	1,550 R	53.9%	46.0%	53.9%	46.1%
32,273	SCOTLAND	8,117	4,077	4,028	12	49 R	50.2%	49.6%	50.3%	49.7%
48,517	STANLY	19,289	13,116	6,138	35	6,978 R	68.0%	31.8%	68.1%	31.9%
33,086	STOKES	14,498	9,515	4,950	33	4,565 R	65.6%	34.1%	65.8%	34.2%
59,449	SURRY	20,562	13,340	7,188	34	6,152 R	64.9%	35.0%	65.0%	35.0%
10,283	SWAIN	4,022	2,012	2,000	10	12 R	50.0%	49.7%	50.1%	49.9%
23,417	TRANSYLVANIA	10,717	6,956	3,733	28	3,223 R	64.9%	34.8%	65.1%	34.9%
3,975	TYRRELL	1,583	774	807	2	33 D	48.9%	51.0%	49.0%	51.0%
70,380	UNION	23,968	16,885	7,048	35	9,837 R	70.4%	29.4%	70.6%	29.4%
36,748	VANCE	12,734	6,836	5,880	18	956 R	53.7%	46.2%	53.8%	46.2%
301,327	WAKE	131,871	81,251	50,323	297	30,928 R	61.6%	38.2%	61.8%	38.2%
16,232	WARREN	6,618	2,664	3,946	8	1,282 D	40.3%	59.6%	40.3%	59.7%
14,801	WASHINGTON	5,852	2,731	3,114	7	383 D	46.7%	53.2%	46.7%	53.3%
31,666	WATAUGA	14,579	9,370	5,163	46	4,207 R	64.3%	35.4%	64.5%	35.5%
97,054	WAYNE	28,008	17,961	10,011	36	7,950 R	64.1%	35.7%	64.2%	35.8%
58,657	WILKES	25,564	18,670	6,852	42	11,818 R	73.0%	26.8%	73.2%	26.8%
63,132	WILSON	20,643	12,243	8,343	57	3,900 R	59.3%	40.4%	59.5%	40.5%
28,439	YADKIN	12,070	8,976	3,075	19	5,901 R	74.4%	25.5%	74.5%	25.5%
14,934	YANCEY	7,961	4,296	3,651	14	645 R	54.0%	45.9%	54.1%	45.9%
5,881,766	TOTAL	2,175,361	1,346,481	824,287	4,593	522,194 R	61.9%	37.9%	62.0%	38.0%

NORTH CAROLINA

GOVERNOR 1984

1980 Census Population	County	Total Vote	Republican	Democratic	Other	Rep.-Dem. Plurality	Percentage Total Vote Rep.	Dem.	Major Vote Rep.	Dem.
99,319	ALAMANCE	37,993	23,193	14,568	232	8,625 R	61.0%	38.3%	61.4%	38.6%
24,999	ALEXANDER	11,868	7,260	4,604	4	2,656 R	61.2%	38.8%	61.2%	38.8%
9,587	ALLEGHANY	4,735	2,250	2,479	6	229 D	47.5%	52.4%	47.6%	52.4%
25,649	ANSON	8,684	2,788	5,880	16	3,092 D	32.1%	67.7%	32.2%	67.8%
22,325	ASHE	10,891	5,482	5,393	16	89 R	50.3%	49.5%	50.4%	49.6%
14,409	AVERY	5,958	3,991	1,949	18	2,042 R	67.0%	32.7%	67.2%	32.8%
40,355	BEAUFORT	15,074	7,303	7,753	18	450 D	48.4%	51.4%	48.5%	51.5%
21,024	BERTIE	6,590	1,980	4,532	78	2,552 D	30.0%	68.8%	30.4%	69.6%
30,491	BLADEN	9,678	4,012	5,592	74	1,580 D	41.5%	57.8%	41.8%	58.2%
35,777	BRUNSWICK	16,778	8,528	8,194	56	334 R	50.8%	48.8%	51.0%	49.0%
160,934	BUNCOMBE	64,021	33,673	30,033	315	3,640 R	52.6%	46.9%	52.9%	47.1%
72,504	BURKE	29,104	16,370	12,704	30	3,666 R	56.2%	43.7%	56.3%	43.7%
85,895	CABARRUS	32,975	21,685	11,229	61	10,456 R	65.8%	34.1%	65.9%	34.1%
67,746	CALDWELL	24,437	14,827	9,567	43	5,260 R	60.7%	39.1%	60.8%	39.2%
5,829	CAMDEN	2,352	936	1,412	4	476 D	39.8%	60.0%	39.9%	60.1%
41,092	CARTERET	18,447	9,630	8,781	36	849 R	52.2%	47.6%	52.3%	47.7%
20,705	CASWELL	7,988	2,877	5,097	14	2,220 D	36.0%	63.8%	36.1%	63.9%
105,208	CATAWBA	43,554	28,551	14,928	75	13,623 R	65.6%	34.3%	65.7%	34.3%
33,415	CHATHAM	15,898	7,190	8,667	41	1,477 D	45.2%	54.5%	45.3%	54.7%
18,933	CHEROKEE	7,998	4,707	3,244	47	1,463 R	58.9%	40.6%	59.2%	40.8%
12,558	CHOWAN	3,969	1,740	2,169	60	429 D	43.8%	54.6%	44.5%	55.5%
6,619	CLAY	3,578	2,109	1,463	6	646 R	58.9%	40.9%	59.0%	41.0%
83,435	CLEVELAND	27,904	14,914	12,951	39	1,963 R	53.4%	46.4%	53.5%	46.5%
51,037	COLUMBUS	18,909	7,843	11,009	57	3,166 D	41.5%	58.2%	41.6%	58.4%
71,043	CRAVEN	20,240	9,850	10,282	108	432 D	48.7%	50.8%	48.9%	51.1%
247,160	CUMBERLAND	56,053	26,409	29,497	147	3,088 D	47.1%	52.6%	47.2%	52.8%
11,089	CURRITUCK	4,387	1,935	2,447	5	512 D	44.1%	55.8%	44.2%	55.8%
13,377	DARE	6,740	3,699	3,007	34	692 R	54.9%	44.6%	55.2%	44.8%
113,162	DAVIDSON	44,262	28,171	16,016	75	12,155 R	63.6%	36.2%	63.8%	36.2%
24,599	DAVIE	11,044	7,190	3,848	6	3,342 R	65.1%	34.8%	65.1%	34.9%
40,952	DUPLIN	14,416	6,078	8,331	7	2,253 D	42.2%	57.8%	42.2%	57.8%
152,785	DURHAM	62,361	26,957	34,975	429	8,018 D	43.2%	56.1%	43.5%	56.5%
55,988	EDGECOMBE	20,597	7,884	12,669	44	4,785 D	38.3%	61.5%	38.4%	61.6%
243,683	FORSYTH	99,790	53,242	46,345	203	6,897 R	53.4%	46.4%	53.5%	46.5%
30,055	FRANKLIN	10,811	4,704	6,078	29	1,374 D	43.5%	56.2%	43.6%	56.4%
162,568	GASTON	54,484	35,730	18,628	126	17,102 R	65.6%	34.2%	65.7%	34.3%
8,875	GATES	3,744	991	2,748	5	1,757 D	26.5%	73.4%	26.5%	73.5%
7,217	GRAHAM	4,012	2,207	1,799	6	408 R	55.0%	44.8%	55.1%	44.9%
34,043	GRANVILLE	11,571	4,916	6,638	17	1,722 D	42.5%	57.4%	42.5%	57.5%
16,117	GREENE	5,927	2,078	3,844	5	1,766 D	35.1%	64.9%	35.1%	64.9%
317,154	GULIFORD	123,701	71,336	52,073	292	19,263 R	57.7%	42.1%	57.8%	42.2%
55,286	HALIFAX	18,863	7,825	10,993	45	3,168 D	41.5%	58.3%	41.6%	58.4%
59,570	HARNETT	18,939	9,327	9,569	43	242 D	49.2%	50.5%	49.4%	50.6%
46,495	HAYWOOD	18,763	8,994	9,714	55	720 D	47.9%	51.8%	48.1%	51.9%
58,580	HENDERSON	26,692	17,953	8,675	64	9,278 R	67.3%	32.5%	67.4%	32.6%
23,368	HERTFORD	7,003	2,159	4,739	105	2,580 D	30.8%	67.7%	31.3%	68.7%
20,383	HOKE	5,550	1,800	3,734	16	1,934 D	32.4%	67.3%	32.5%	67.5%
5,873	HYDE	2,174	819	1,352	3	533 D	37.7%	62.2%	37.7%	62.3%
82,538	IREDELL	34,375	22,936	11,379	60	11,557 R	66.7%	33.1%	66.8%	33.2%
25,811	JACKSON	10,563	5,286	5,229	48	57 R	50.0%	49.5%	50.3%	49.7%
70,599	JOHNSTON	24,540	13,769	10,730	41	3,039 R	56.1%	43.7%	56.2%	43.8%
9,705	JONES	4,056	1,542	2,510	4	968 D	38.0%	61.9%	38.1%	61.9%
36,718	LEE	12,913	6,588	6,263	62	325 R	51.0%	48.5%	51.3%	48.7%
59,819	LENOIR	21,787	9,950	11,806	31	1,856 D	45.7%	54.2%	45.7%	54.3%
42,372	LINCOLN	18,946	12,010	6,910	26	5,100 R	63.4%	36.5%	63.5%	36.5%
35,135	MCDOWELL	12,569	6,482	6,060	27	422 R	51.6%	48.2%	51.7%	48.3%
20,178	MACON	10,330	5,623	4,688	19	935 R	54.4%	45.4%	54.5%	45.5%
16,827	MADISON	6,383	2,962	3,388	33	426 D	46.4%	53.1%	46.6%	53.4%
25,948	MARTIN	8,409	2,920	5,422	67	2,502 D	34.7%	64.5%	35.0%	65.0%
404,270	MECKLENBURG	172,091	114,151	57,279	661	56,872 R	66.3%	33.3%	66.6%	33.4%

NORTH CAROLINA

GOVERNOR 1984

1980 Census Population	County	Total Vote	Republican	Democratic	Other	Rep.-Dem. Plurality	Percentage			
							Total Vote		Major Vote	
							Rep.	Dem.	Rep.	Dem.
14,428	MITCHELL	6,480	4,778	1,692	10	3,086 R	73.7%	26.1%	73.8%	26.2%
22,469	MONTGOMERY	8,812	4,356	4,447	9	91 D	49.4%	50.5%	49.5%	50.5%
50,505	MOORE	22,277	13,703	8,529	45	5,174 R	61.5%	38.3%	61.6%	38.4%
67,153	NASH	26,674	15,037	11,585	52	3,452 R	56.4%	43.4%	56.5%	43.5%
103,471	NEW HANOVER	37,028	22,006	14,870	152	7,136 R	59.4%	40.2%	59.7%	40.3%
22,584	NORTHAMPTON	8,768	3,113	5,496	159	2,383 D	35.5%	62.7%	36.2%	63.8%
112,784	ONSLOW	20,342	10,749	9,535	58	1,214 R	52.8%	46.9%	53.0%	47.0%
77,055	ORANGE	35,955	15,083	20,656	216	5,573 D	41.9%	57.4%	42.2%	57.8%
10,398	PAMLICO	4,654	1,836	2,812	6	976 D	39.4%	60.4%	39.5%	60.5%
28,462	PASQUOTANK	8,360	3,924	4,333	103	409 D	46.9%	51.8%	47.5%	52.5%
22,215	PENDER	9,361	4,130	5,227	4	1,097 D	44.1%	55.8%	44.1%	55.9%
9,486	PERQUIMANS	3,299	1,337	1,957	5	620 D	40.5%	59.3%	40.6%	59.4%
29,164	PERSON	9,352	4,752	4,492	108	260 R	50.8%	48.0%	51.4%	48.6%
90,146	PITT	32,744	15,021	17,620	103	2,599 D	45.9%	53.8%	46.0%	54.0%
12,984	POLK	6,755	3,800	2,836	119	964 R	56.3%	42.0%	57.3%	42.7%
91,728	RANDOLPH	35,276	24,341	10,846	89	13,495 R	69.0%	30.7%	69.2%	30.8%
45,481	RICHMOND	14,592	5,942	8,623	27	2,681 D	40.7%	59.1%	40.8%	59.2%
101,610	ROBESON	30,115	10,291	19,630	194	9,339 D	34.2%	65.2%	34.4%	65.6%
83,426	ROCKINGHAM	28,341	15,164	13,090	87	2,074 R	53.5%	46.2%	53.7%	46.3%
99,186	ROWAN	37,091	23,429	13,591	71	9,838 R	63.2%	36.6%	63.3%	36.7%
53,787	RUTHERFORD	19,284	10,409	8,841	34	1,568 R	54.0%	45.8%	54.1%	45.9%
49,687	SAMPSON	20,432	9,846	10,557	29	711 D	48.2%	51.7%	48.3%	51.7%
32,273	SCOTLAND	8,002	3,207	4,753	42	1,546 D	40.1%	59.4%	40.3%	59.7%
48,517	STANLY	20,361	12,893	7,437	31	5,456 R	63.3%	36.5%	63.4%	36.6%
33,086	STOKES	14,619	7,949	6,653	17	1,296 R	54.4%	45.5%	54.4%	45.6%
59,449	SURRY	21,119	11,388	9,661	70	1,727 R	53.9%	45.7%	54.1%	45.9%
10,283	SWAIN	4,432	1,898	2,520	14	622 D	42.8%	56.9%	43.0%	57.0%
23,417	TRANSYLVANIA	10,811	6,151	4,626	34	1,525 R	56.9%	42.8%	57.1%	42.9%
3,975	TYRRELL	1,544	516	1,027	1	511 D	33.4%	66.5%	33.4%	66.6%
70,380	UNION	24,290	15,387	8,856	47	6,531 R	63.3%	36.5%	63.5%	36.5%
36,748	VANCE	13,051	5,472	7,549	30	2,077 D	41.9%	57.8%	42.0%	58.0%
301,327	WAKE	140,319	75,856	63,798	665	12,058 R	54.1%	45.5%	54.3%	45.7%
16,232	WARREN	6,480	2,032	4,442	6	2,410 D	31.4%	68.5%	31.4%	68.6%
14,801	WASHINGTON	5,999	1,842	4,155	2	2,313 D	30.7%	69.3%	30.7%	69.3%
31,666	WATAUGA	14,759	7,070	7,617	72	547 D	47.9%	51.6%	48.1%	51.9%
97,054	WAYNE	28,463	15,288	13,003	172	2,285 R	53.7%	45.7%	54.0%	46.0%
58,657	WILKES	26,785	16,257	10,499	29	5,758 R	60.7%	39.2%	60.8%	39.2%
63,132	WILSON	21,286	10,205	10,942	139	737 D	47.9%	51.4%	48.3%	51.7%
28,439	YADKIN	11,912	7,645	4,263	4	3,382 R	64.2%	35.8%	64.2%	35.8%
14,934	YANCEY	8,034	3,752	4,280	2	528 D	46.7%	53.3%	46.7%	53.3%
5,881,766	TOTAL	2,226,727	1,208,167	1,011,209	7,351	196,958 R	54.3%	45.4%	54.4%	45.6%

NORTH CAROLINA

SENATOR 1984

1980 Census Population	County	Total Vote	Republican	Democratic	Other	Rep.-Dem. Plurality	Total Vote Rep.	Total Vote Dem.	Major Vote Rep.	Major Vote Dem.
99,319	ALAMANCE	38,504	22,657	15,501	346	7,156 R	58.8%	40.3%	59.4%	40.6%
24,999	ALEXANDER	12,039	7,493	4,504	42	2,989 R	62.2%	37.4%	62.5%	37.5%
9,587	ALLEGHANY	4,717	2,335	2,366	16	31 D	49.5%	50.2%	49.7%	50.3%
25,649	ANSON	8,640	3,161	5,451	28	2,290 D	36.6%	63.1%	36.7%	63.3%
22,325	ASHE	10,904	6,069	4,802	33	1,267 R	55.7%	44.0%	55.8%	44.2%
14,409	AVERY	5,891	4,239	1,630	22	2,609 R	72.0%	27.7%	72.2%	27.8%
40,355	BEAUFORT	15,166	7,907	7,203	56	704 R	52.1%	47.5%	52.3%	47.7%
21,024	BERTIE	7,228	2,618	4,544	66	1,926 D	36.2%	62.9%	36.6%	63.4%
30,491	BLADEN	10,019	4,220	5,738	61	1,518 D	42.1%	57.3%	42.4%	57.6%
35,777	BRUNSWICK	16,795	8,403	8,264	128	139 R	50.0%	49.2%	50.4%	49.6%
160,934	BUNCOMBE	64,427	31,338	32,611	478	1,273 D	48.6%	50.6%	49.0%	51.0%
72,504	BURKE	28,842	16,642	12,061	139	4,581 R	57.7%	41.8%	58.0%	42.0%
85,895	CABARRUS	32,935	20,812	11,978	145	8,834 R	63.2%	36.4%	63.5%	36.5%
67,746	CALDWELL	24,267	14,915	9,232	120	5,683 R	61.5%	38.0%	61.8%	38.2%
5,829	CAMDEN	2,322	1,114	1,203	5	89 D	48.0%	51.8%	48.1%	51.9%
41,092	CARTERET	18,426	10,745	7,565	116	3,180 R	58.3%	41.1%	58.7%	41.3%
20,705	CASWELL	8,067	3,414	4,627	26	1,213 D	42.3%	57.4%	42.5%	57.5%
105,208	CATAWBA	43,503	27,914	15,363	226	12,551 R	64.2%	35.3%	64.5%	35.5%
33,415	CHATHAM	15,955	7,108	8,767	80	1,659 D	44.6%	54.9%	44.8%	55.2%
18,933	CHEROKEE	8,252	4,746	3,477	29	1,269 R	57.5%	42.1%	57.7%	42.3%
12,558	CHOWAN	4,282	1,950	2,289	43	339 D	45.5%	53.5%	46.0%	54.0%
6,619	CLAY	3,600	2,079	1,515	6	564 R	57.8%	42.1%	57.8%	42.2%
83,435	CLEVELAND	27,774	15,202	12,461	111	2,741 R	54.7%	44.9%	55.0%	45.0%
51,037	COLUMBUS	19,137	8,549	10,495	93	1,946 D	44.7%	54.8%	44.9%	55.1%
71,043	CRAVEN	21,034	11,355	9,571	108	1,784 R	54.0%	45.5%	54.3%	45.7%
247,160	CUMBERLAND	56,073	25,578	30,214	281	4,636 D	45.6%	53.9%	45.8%	54.2%
11,089	CURRITUCK	4,442	2,275	2,158	9	117 R	51.2%	48.6%	51.3%	48.7%
13,377	DARE	6,770	3,708	3,040	22	668 R	54.8%	44.9%	54.9%	45.1%
113,162	DAVIDSON	44,153	27,533	16,434	186	11,099 R	62.4%	37.2%	62.6%	37.4%
24,599	DAVIE	11,000	7,156	3,785	59	3,371 R	65.1%	34.4%	65.4%	34.6%
40,952	DUPLIN	14,357	6,607	7,718	32	1,111 D	46.0%	53.8%	46.1%	53.9%
152,785	DURHAM	63,479	22,981	40,102	396	17,121 D	36.2%	63.2%	36.4%	63.6%
55,988	EDGECOMBE	20,650	8,738	11,845	67	3,107 D	42.3%	57.4%	42.5%	57.5%
243,683	FORSYTH	99,960	48,575	50,961	424	2,386 D	48.6%	51.0%	48.8%	51.2%
30,055	FRANKLIN	10,832	5,208	5,583	41	375 D	48.1%	51.5%	48.3%	51.7%
162,568	GASTON	54,396	35,010	19,097	289	15,913 R	64.4%	35.1%	64.7%	35.3%
8,875	GATES	3,837	1,364	2,459	14	1,095 D	35.5%	64.1%	35.7%	64.3%
7,217	GRAHAM	4,023	2,273	1,746	4	527 R	56.5%	43.4%	56.6%	43.4%
34,043	GRANVILLE	11,717	5,378	6,318	21	940 D	45.9%	53.9%	46.0%	54.0%
16,117	GREENE	5,907	2,811	3,080	16	269 D	47.6%	52.1%	47.7%	52.3%
317,154	GUILFORD	123,950	61,371	62,021	558	650 D	49.5%	50.0%	49.7%	50.3%
55,286	HALIFAX	18,971	8,412	10,497	62	2,085 D	44.3%	55.3%	44.5%	55.5%
59,570	HARNETT	19,168	10,033	9,064	71	969 R	52.3%	47.3%	52.5%	47.5%
46,495	HAYWOOD	18,740	8,841	9,759	140	918 D	47.2%	52.1%	47.5%	52.5%
58,580	HENDERSON	26,644	16,281	10,202	161	6,079 R	61.1%	38.3%	61.5%	38.5%
23,368	HERTFORD	8,016	2,766	5,195	55	2,429 D	34.5%	64.8%	34.7%	65.3%
20,383	HOKE	5,591	1,913	3,655	23	1,742 D	34.2%	65.4%	34.4%	65.6%
5,873	HYDE	2,155	1,028	1,120	7	92 D	47.7%	52.0%	47.9%	52.1%
82,538	IREDELL	34,199	20,480	13,526	193	6,954 R	59.9%	39.6%	60.2%	39.8%
25,811	JACKSON	10,611	4,864	5,706	41	842 D	45.8%	53.8%	46.0%	54.0%
70,599	JOHNSTON	24,315	14,130	10,089	96	4,041 R	58.1%	41.5%	58.3%	41.7%
9,705	JONES	4,042	1,887	2,147	8	260 D	46.7%	53.1%	46.8%	53.2%
36,718	LEE	13,059	7,030	5,933	96	1,097 R	53.8%	45.4%	54.2%	45.8%
59,819	LENOIR	21,395	11,759	9,576	60	2,183 R	55.0%	44.8%	55.1%	44.9%
42,372	LINCOLN	18,844	11,186	7,554	104	3,632 R	59.4%	40.1%	59.7%	40.3%
35,135	MCDOWELL	12,516	6,953	5,507	56	1,446 R	55.6%	44.0%	55.8%	44.2%
20,178	MACON	10,233	5,664	4,524	45	1,140 R	55.4%	44.2%	55.6%	44.4%
16,827	MADISON	6,434	3,011	3,401	22	390 D	46.8%	52.9%	47.0%	53.0%
25,948	MARTIN	8,654	3,718	4,863	73	1,145 D	43.0%	56.2%	43.3%	56.7%
404,270	MECKLENBURG	172,653	85,013	86,450	1,190	1,437 D	49.2%	50.1%	49.6%	50.4%

NORTH CAROLINA

SENATOR 1984

1980 Census Population	County	Total Vote	Republican	Democratic	Other	Rep.-Dem. Plurality	Percentage Total Vote Rep.	Dem.	Major Vote Rep.	Dem.
14,428	MITCHELL	6,503	4,724	1,743	36	2,981 R	72.6%	26.8%	73.0%	27.0%
22,469	MONTGOMERY	8,774	4,397	4,341	36	56 R	50.1%	49.5%	50.3%	49.7%
50,505	MOORE	22,316	12,836	9,363	117	3,473 R	57.5%	42.0%	57.8%	42.2%
67,153	NASH	26,720	15,800	10,830	90	4,970 R	59.1%	40.5%	59.3%	40.7%
103,471	NEW HANOVER	37,575	19,515	17,829	231	1,686 R	51.9%	47.4%	52.3%	47.7%
22,584	NORTHAMPTON	8,843	3,034	5,759	50	2,725 D	34.3%	65.1%	34.5%	65.5%
112,784	ONSLOW	20,398	12,019	8,260	119	3,759 R	58.9%	40.5%	59.3%	40.7%
77,055	ORANGE	36,130	11,139	24,828	163	13,689 D	30.8%	68.7%	31.0%	69.0%
10,398	PAMLICO	4,636	2,195	2,421	20	226 D	47.3%	52.2%	47.6%	52.4%
28,462	PASQUOTANK	8,935	3,975	4,908	52	933 D	44.5%	54.9%	44.7%	55.3%
22,215	PENDER	9,313	4,373	4,918	22	545 D	47.0%	52.8%	47.1%	52.9%
9,486	PERQUIMANS	3,315	1,581	1,729	5	148 D	47.7%	52.2%	47.8%	52.2%
29,164	PERSON	9,902	5,117	4,668	117	449 R	51.7%	47.1%	52.3%	47.7%
90,146	PITT	32,801	15,699	16,946	156	1,247 D	47.9%	51.7%	48.1%	51.9%
12,984	POLK	6,826	3,657	3,031	138	626 R	53.6%	44.4%	54.7%	45.3%
91,728	RANDOLPH	35,446	23,831	11,478	137	12,353 R	67.2%	32.4%	67.5%	32.5%
45,481	RICHMOND	14,593	5,994	8,521	78	2,527 D	41.1%	58.4%	41.3%	58.7%
101,610	ROBESON	30,390	11,253	18,936	201	7,683 D	37.0%	62.3%	37.3%	62.7%
83,426	ROCKINGHAM	28,415	14,856	13,418	141	1,438 R	52.3%	47.2%	52.5%	47.5%
99,186	ROWAN	37,048	23,162	13,722	164	9,440 R	62.5%	37.0%	62.8%	37.2%
53,787	RUTHERFORD	19,224	10,472	8,618	134	1,854 R	54.5%	44.8%	54.9%	45.1%
49,687	SAMPSON	20,440	9,802	10,583	55	781 D	48.0%	51.8%	48.1%	51.9%
32,273	SCOTLAND	8,286	3,195	5,059	32	1,864 D	38.6%	61.1%	38.7%	61.3%
48,517	STANLY	20,364	12,367	7,927	70	4,440 R	60.7%	38.9%	60.9%	39.1%
33,086	STOKES	14,593	8,350	6,197	46	2,153 R	57.2%	42.5%	57.4%	42.6%
59,449	SURRY	21,807	12,205	9,442	160	2,763 R	56.0%	43.3%	56.4%	43.6%
10,283	SWAIN	4,451	1,967	2,464	20	497 D	44.2%	55.4%	44.4%	55.6%
23,417	TRANSYLVANIA	10,809	5,802	4,926	81	876 R	53.7%	45.6%	54.1%	45.9%
3,975	TYRRELL	1,551	667	883	1	216 D	43.0%	56.9%	43.0%	57.0%
70,380	UNION	24,296	14,684	9,489	123	5,195 R	60.4%	39.1%	60.7%	39.3%
36,748	VANCE	13,122	6,288	6,788	46	500 D	47.9%	51.7%	48.1%	51.9%
301,327	WAKE	141,898	65,062	75,974	862	10,912 D	45.9%	53.5%	46.1%	53.9%
16,232	WARREN	6,654	2,486	4,138	30	1,652 D	37.4%	62.2%	37.5%	62.5%
14,801	WASHINGTON	5,759	2,296	3,448	15	1,152 D	39.9%	59.9%	40.0%	60.0%
31,666	WATAUGA	14,629	7,413	7,093	123	320 R	50.7%	48.5%	51.1%	48.9%
97,054	WAYNE	28,998	16,251	12,536	211	3,715 R	56.0%	43.2%	56.5%	43.5%
58,657	WILKES	26,633	17,247	9,275	111	7,972 R	64.8%	34.8%	65.0%	35.0%
63,132	WILSON	22,189	10,595	11,497	97	902 D	47.7%	51.8%	48.0%	52.0%
28,439	YADKIN	11,971	8,048	3,873	50	4,175 R	67.2%	32.4%	67.5%	32.5%
14,934	YANCEY	7,986	3,894	4,082	10	188 D	48.8%	51.1%	48.8%	51.2%
5,881,766	TOTAL	2,239,051	1,156,768	1,070,488	11,795	86,280 R	51.7%	47.8%	51.9%	48.1%

NORTH CAROLINA

CONGRESS

CD	Year	Total Vote	Republican Vote	Republican Candidate	Democratic Vote	Democratic Candidate	Other Vote	Rep.-Dem. Plurality	Total Vote Rep.	Total Vote Dem.	Major Vote Rep.	Major Vote Dem.
1	1984	182,968	60,153	LEE, HERBERT W.	122,815	JONES, WALTER B.		62,662 D	32.9%	67.1%	32.9%	67.1%
1	1982	98,342	17,478	MCINTYRE, JAMES F.	79,954	JONES, WALTER B.	910	62,476 D	17.8%	81.3%	17.9%	82.1%
2	1984	180,604	58,312	HILL, FRANK H.	122,292	VALENTINE, I. T.		63,980 D	32.3%	67.7%	32.3%	67.7%
2	1982	111,326	34,293	MARIN, JOHN W.	59,617	VALENTINE, I. T.	17,416	25,324 D	30.8%	53.6%	36.5%	63.5%
3	1984	156,281	56,096	MOODY, DANNY G.	100,185	WHITLEY, CHARLES		44,089 D	35.9%	64.1%	35.9%	64.1%
3	1982	108,473	39,046	MCDANIEL, EUGENE	68,936	WHITLEY, CHARLES	491	29,890 D	36.0%	63.6%	36.2%	63.8%
4	1984	231,898	117,436	COBEY, WILLIAM	114,462	ANDREWS, IKE F.		2,974 R	50.6%	49.4%	50.6%	49.4%
4	1982	137,044	64,955	COBEY, WILLIAM	70,369	ANDREWS, IKE F.	1,720	5,414 D	47.4%	51.3%	48.0%	52.0%
5	1984	216,430	106,599	EPPERSON, STUART	109,831	NEAL, STEPHEN L.		3,232 D	49.3%	50.7%	49.3%	50.7%
5	1982	145,707	57,083	BAGNAL, ANNE	87,819	NEAL, STEPHEN L.	805	30,736 D	39.2%	60.3%	39.4%	60.6%
6	1984	203,473	102,925	COBLE, HOWARD	100,263	BRITT, C. ROBIN	285	2,662 R	50.6%	49.3%	50.7%	49.3%
6	1982	127,619	58,244	JOHNSTON, EUGENE	68,696	BRITT, C. ROBIN	679	10,452 D	45.6%	53.8%	45.9%	54.1%
7	1984	155,782	63,625	RHODES, S. THOMAS	92,157	ROSE, CHARLES G.		28,532 D	40.8%	59.2%	40.8%	59.2%
7	1982	96,534	27,015	JOHNSON, EDWARD	68,529	ROSE, CHARLES G.	990	41,514 D	28.0%	71.0%	28.3%	71.7%
8	1984	196,085	96,354	BLAKE, HARRIS D.	99,731	HEFNER, W. G.		3,377 D	49.1%	50.9%	49.1%	50.9%
8	1982	124,938	52,417	BLAKE, HARRIS D.	71,691	HEFNER, W. G.	830	19,274 D	42.0%	57.4%	42.2%	57.8%
9	1984	218,519	109,420	MCMILLAN, J. ALEX	109,099	MARTIN, D. G.		321 R	50.1%	49.9%	50.1%	49.9%
9	1982	112,786	64,297	MARTIN, JAMES G.	47,258	CORNELIUS, PRESTON	1,231	17,039 R	57.0%	41.9%	57.6%	42.4%
10	1984	194,733	142,873	BROYHILL, JAMES T.	51,860	POOVEY, TED A.		91,013 R	73.4%	26.6%	73.4%	26.6%
10	1982	87,264	80,904	BROYHILL, JAMES T.			6,360	80,904 R	92.7%	0.0%	100.0%	0.0%
11	1984	220,882	112,598	HENDON, WILLIAM M.	108,284	CLARKE, JAMES MCC.		4,314 R	51.0%	49.0%	51.0%	49.0%
11	1982	171,047	84,085	HENDON, WILLIAM M.	85,410	CLARKE, JAMES MCC.	1,552	1,325 D	49.2%	49.9%	49.6%	50.4%

NORTH CAROLINA

1984 GENERAL ELECTION

President Other vote was 3,794 Bergland (Libertarian); 799 Mason (Socialist Workers).

Governor Other vote was 4,611 Prochnow (Libertarian); 2,740 McCartan (Socialist Workers).

Senator Other vote was 9,302 Emory (Libertarian); 2,493 Daher (Socialist Workers).

Congress Other vote was Farber (Socialist Workers) in CD 6.

1984 PRIMARIES

MAY 8 REPUBLICAN

Governor 128,714 James G. Martin; 11,640 Ruby T. Hooper.

Senator 134,675 Jesse Helms; 13,899 George Wimbish.

Congress Unopposed in eight CD's. Contested as follows:

   CD 1 3,843 Herbert W. Lee; 2,873 Gene Leggett.
   CD 6 7,764 Howard Coble; 7,600 Walter C. Cockerham.
   CD 9 15,143 J. Alex McMillan; 11,108 Carl Horn.

MAY 8 DEMOCRATIC

Governor 295,051 Rufus Edmisten; 249,286 H. Edward Knox; 153,210 D. M. Faircloth; 82,299 Thomas O. Gilmore; 80,775 James C. Green; 75,248 John Ingram; 9,476 Robert L. Hannon; 5,790 Glenn Miller; 3,148 J. A. Barker; 1,516 J. D. Whaley.

Senator 655,429 James B. Hunt; 126,841 Thomas L. Allred; 63,676 Harrill Jones.

Congress Unopposed in four CD's. Contested as follows:

   CD 1 68,229 Walter B. Jones; 42,728 John Gillam.
   CD 2 65,893 I. T. Valentine; 60,535 Kenneth B. Spaulding.
   CD 4 50,913 Ike F. Andrews; 37,986 Howard N. Lee; 9,129 John Winters.
   CD 5 61,499 Stephen L. Neal; 6,598 Wallace B. Ray.
   CD 7 65,502 Charles G. Rose; 12,402 Tommie Dial.
   CD 8 62,475 W. G. Hefner; 11,993 Leonard T. Tyson.
   CD 9 30,668 Susan Green; 25,846 D. G. Martin; 19,352 Benjamin T. Tison.

JUNE 5 DEMOCRATIC RUN-OFF

Governor 352,351 Rufus Edmisten; 326,278 H. Edward Knox.

Congress

   CD 9 38,307 D. G. Martin; 31,435 Susan Green.

NORTH DAKOTA

GOVERNOR
George Sinner (D). Elected 1984 to a four-year term.

SENATORS
Mark Andrews (R). Elected 1980 to a six-year term.

Quentin N. Burdick (D). Re-elected 1982 to a six-year term. Previously elected 1976, 1970, 1964, and in June 1960 to fill out term vacated by the death of Senator William Langer.

REPRESENTATIVE
At-Large. Byron L. Dorgan (D)

POSTWAR VOTE FOR GOVERNOR

											Percentage			
											Total Vote		Major Vote	
	Total	Republican			Democratic			Other	Rep.-Dem.					
Year	Vote	Vote	Candidate		Vote	Candidate		Vote	Plurality		Rep.	Dem.	Rep.	Dem.
1984	314,382	140,460	Olson, Allen I.		173,922	Sinner, George		—	33,462	D	44.7%	55.3%	44.7%	55.3%
1980	302,621	162,230	Olson, Allen I.		140,391	Link, Arthur A.		—	21,839	R	53.6%	46.4%	53.6%	46.4%
1976	297,249	138,321	Elkin, Richard		153,309	Link, Arthur A.		5,619	14,988	D	46.5%	51.6%	47.4%	52.6%
1972	281,931	138,032	Larsen, Richard		143,899	Link, Arthur A.		—	5,867	D	49.0%	51.0%	49.0%	51.0%
1968	248,000	108,382	McCarney, Robert P.		135,955	Guy, William L.		3,663	27,573	D	43.7%	54.8%	44.4%	55.6%
1964*	262,661	116,247	Halcrow, Donald M.		146,414	Guy, William L.		—	30,167	D	44.3%	55.7%	44.3%	55.7%
1962	228,509	113,251	Andrews, Mark		115,258	Guy, William L.		—	2,007	D	49.6%	50.4%	49.6%	50.4%
1960	275,375	122,486	Dahl, C. P.		136,148	Guy, William L.		16,741	13,662	D	44.5%	49.4%	47.4%	52.6%
1958	210,599	111,836	Davis, John E.		98,763	Lord, John F.		—	13,073	R	53.1%	46.9%	53.1%	46.9%
1956	252,435	147,566	Davis, John E.		104,869	Warner, Wallace E.		—	42,697	R	58.5%	41.5%	58.5%	41.5%
1954	193,501	124,253	Brunsdale, C. Norman		69,248	Bymers, Cornelius		—	55,005	R	64.2%	35.8%	64.2%	35.8%
1952	253,934	199,944	Brunsdale, C. Norman		53,990	Johnson, Ole C.		—	145,954	R	78.7%	21.3%	78.7%	21.3%
1950	183,772	121,822	Brunsdale, C. Norman		61,950	Byerly, Clyde G.		—	59,872	R	66.3%	33.7%	66.3%	33.7%
1948	214,858	131,764	Aandahl, Fred G.		80,555	Henry, Howard		2,539	51,209	R	61.3%	37.5%	62.1%	37.9%
1946	169,391	116,672	Aandahl, Fred G.		52,719	Burdick, Quentin N.		—	63,953	R	68.9%	31.1%	68.9%	31.1%

The term of office of North Dakota's Governor was increased from two to four years effective with the 1964 election.

POSTWAR VOTE FOR SENATOR

											Percentage			
											Total Vote		Major Vote	
	Total	Republican			Democratic			Other	Rep.-Dem.					
Year	Vote	Vote	Candidate		Vote	Candidate		Vote	Plurality		Rep.	Dem.	Rep.	Dem.
1982	262,465	89,304	Knorr, Gene		164,873	Burdick, Quentin N.		8,288	75,569	D	34.0%	62.8%	35.1%	64.9%
1980	299,272	210,347	Andrews, Mark		86,658	Johanneson, Kent		2,267	123,689	R	70.3%	29.0%	70.8%	29.2%
1976	283,062	103,466	Stroup, Richard		175,772	Burdick, Quentin N.		3,824	72,306	D	36.6%	62.1%	37.1%	62.9%
1974	235,661	114,117	Young, Milton R.		113,931	Guy, William L.		7,613	186	R	48.4%	48.3%	50.0%	50.0%
1970	219,560	82,996	Kleppe, Tom		134,519	Burdick, Quentin N.		2,045	51,523	D	37.8%	61.3%	38.2%	61.8%
1968	239,776	154,968	Young, Milton R.		80,815	Lashkowitz, Herschel		3,993	74,153	R	64.6%	33.7%	65.7%	34.3%
1964	258,945	109,681	Kleppe, Tom		149,264	Burdick, Quentin N.		—	39,583	D	42.4%	57.6%	42.4%	57.6%
1962	223,737	135,705	Young, Milton R.		88,032	Lanier, William		—	47,673	R	60.7%	39.3%	60.7%	39.3%
1960s	210,349	103,475	Davis, John E.		104,593	Burdick, Quentin N.		2,281	1,118	D	49.2%	49.7%	49.7%	50.3%
1958	204,635	117,070	Langer, William		84,892	Vendsel, Raymond		2,673	32,178	R	57.2%	41.5%	58.0%	42.0%
1956	244,161	155,305	Young, Milton R.		87,919	Burdick, Quentin N.		937	67,386	R	63.6%	36.0%	63.9%	36.1%
1952	237,995	157,907	Langer, William		55,347	Morrison, Harold A.		24,741	102,560	R	66.3%	23.3%	74.0%	26.0%
1950	186,716	126,209	Young, Milton R.		60,507	O'Brien, Harry		—	65,702	R	67.6%	32.4%	67.6%	32.4%
1946	165,382	88,210	Langer, William		38,368	Larson, Abner B.		38,804	49,842	R	53.3%	23.2%	69.7%	30.3%
1946s	136,852	75,998	Young, Milton R.		37,507	Lanier, William		23,347	38,491	R	55.5%	27.4%	67.0%	33.0%

The 1960 and 1946 special elections were held in June for short terms to fill vacancies.

NORTH DAKOTA

One At Large

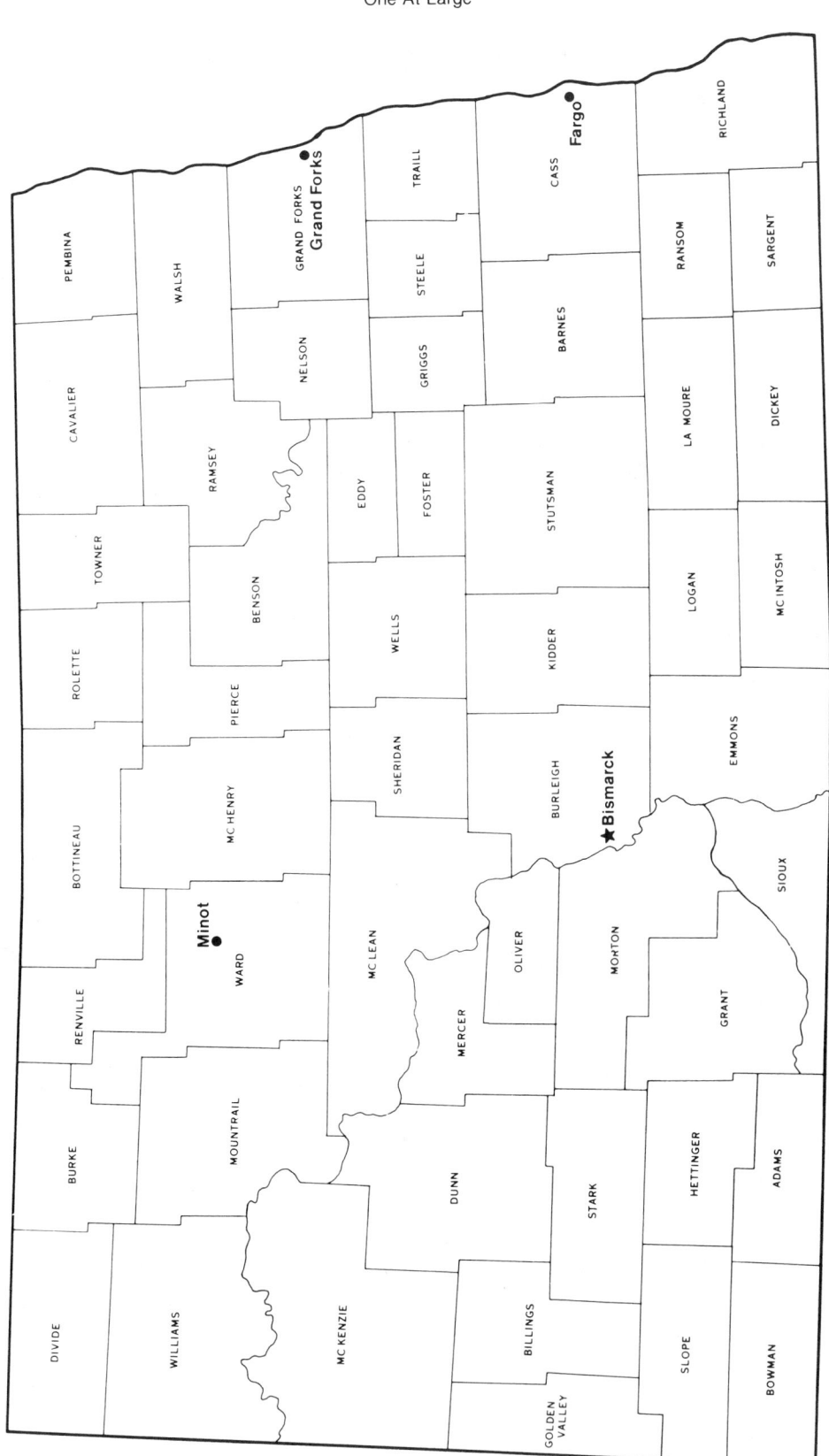

NORTH DAKOTA

PRESIDENT 1984

1980 Census Population	County	Total Vote	Republican	Democratic	Other	Rep.-Dem. Plurality	Percentage Total Vote Rep.	Dem.	Major Vote Rep.	Dem.
3,584	ADAMS	1,900	1,343	530	27	813 R	70.7%	27.9%	71.7%	28.3%
13,960	BARNES	6,925	4,348	2,507	70	1,841 R	62.8%	36.2%	63.4%	36.6%
7,944	BENSON	3,363	1,729	1,599	35	130 R	51.4%	47.5%	52.0%	48.0%
1,138	BILLINGS	653	505	133	15	372 R	77.3%	20.4%	79.2%	20.8%
9,239	BOTTINEAU	4,688	3,356	1,279	53	2,077 R	71.6%	27.3%	72.4%	27.6%
4,229	BOWMAN	2,149	1,559	562	28	997 R	72.5%	26.2%	73.5%	26.5%
3,822	BURKE	1,869	1,298	543	28	755 R	69.4%	29.1%	70.5%	29.5%
54,811	BURLEIGH	29,176	19,913	8,781	482	11,132 R	68.3%	30.1%	69.4%	30.6%
88,247	CASS	47,629	29,221	18,054	354	11,167 R	61.4%	37.9%	61.8%	38.2%
7,636	CAVALIER	3,804	2,661	1,110	33	1,551 R	70.0%	29.2%	70.6%	29.4%
7,207	DICKEY	3,546	2,460	1,051	35	1,409 R	69.4%	29.6%	70.1%	29.9%
3,494	DIVIDE	1,840	1,165	626	49	539 R	63.3%	34.0%	65.0%	35.0%
4,627	DUNN	2,324	1,583	716	25	867 R	68.1%	30.8%	68.9%	31.1%
3,554	EDDY	1,860	1,049	796	15	253 R	56.4%	42.8%	56.9%	43.1%
5,877	EMMONS	2,566	1,885	620	61	1,265 R	73.5%	24.2%	75.2%	24.8%
4,611	FOSTER	2,214	1,422	765	27	657 R	64.2%	34.6%	65.0%	35.0%
2,391	GOLDEN VALLEY	1,319	964	325	30	639 R	73.1%	24.6%	74.8%	25.2%
66,100	GRAND FORKS	26,191	15,898	10,050	243	5,848 R	60.7%	38.4%	61.3%	38.7%
4,274	GRANT	2,145	1,607	507	31	1,100 R	74.9%	23.6%	76.0%	24.0%
3,714	GRIGGS	2,094	1,254	828	12	426 R	59.9%	39.5%	60.2%	39.8%
4,275	HETTINGER	2,202	1,646	524	32	1,122 R	74.8%	23.8%	75.9%	24.1%
3,833	KIDDER	1,807	1,240	506	61	734 R	68.6%	28.0%	71.0%	29.0%
6,473	LA MOURE	3,108	1,978	1,086	44	892 R	63.6%	34.9%	64.6%	35.4%
3,493	LOGAN	1,676	1,222	401	53	821 R	72.9%	23.9%	75.3%	24.7%
7,858	MCHENRY	3,801	2,485	1,283	33	1,202 R	65.4%	33.8%	66.0%	34.0%
4,800	MCINTOSH	2,513	2,047	427	39	1,620 R	81.5%	17.0%	82.7%	17.3%
7,132	MCKENZIE	3,627	2,610	974	43	1,636 R	72.0%	26.9%	72.8%	27.2%
12,383	MCLEAN	5,847	3,673	2,062	112	1,611 R	62.8%	35.3%	64.0%	36.0%
9,404	MERCER	5,510	3,705	1,729	76	1,976 R	67.2%	31.4%	68.2%	31.8%
25,177	MORTON	11,356	7,146	3,996	214	3,150 R	62.9%	35.2%	64.1%	35.9%
7,679	MOUNTRAIL	3,555	1,959	1,565	31	394 R	55.1%	44.0%	55.6%	44.4%
5,233	NELSON	2,513	1,445	1,026	42	419 R	57.5%	40.8%	58.5%	41.5%
2,495	OLIVER	1,357	915	419	23	496 R	67.4%	30.9%	68.6%	31.4%
10,399	PEMBINA	4,387	2,895	1,367	125	1,528 R	66.0%	31.2%	67.9%	32.1%
6,166	PIERCE	2,626	1,883	691	52	1,192 R	71.7%	26.3%	73.2%	26.8%
13,048	RAMSEY	6,553	4,150	2,304	99	1,846 R	63.3%	35.2%	64.3%	35.7%
6,698	RANSOM	2,973	1,706	1,222	45	484 R	57.4%	41.1%	58.3%	41.7%
3,608	RENVILLE	1,774	1,163	592	19	571 R	65.6%	33.4%	66.3%	33.7%
19,207	RICHLAND	9,133	5,980	3,047	106	2,933 R	65.5%	33.4%	66.2%	33.8%
12,177	ROLETTE	3,751	1,479	2,179	93	700 D	39.4%	58.1%	40.4%	59.6%
5,512	SARGENT	2,725	1,385	1,295	45	90 R	50.8%	47.5%	51.7%	48.3%
2,819	SHERIDAN	1,396	1,075	306	15	769 R	77.0%	21.9%	77.8%	22.2%
3,620	SIOUX	1,118	442	655	21	213 D	39.5%	58.6%	40.3%	59.7%
1,157	SLOPE	605	419	174	12	245 R	69.3%	28.8%	70.7%	29.3%
23,697	STARK	10,740	7,641	2,759	340	4,882 R	71.1%	25.7%	73.5%	26.5%
3,106	STEELE	1,740	941	781	18	160 R	54.1%	44.9%	54.6%	45.4%
24,154	STUTSMAN	10,208	6,591	3,495	122	3,096 R	64.6%	34.2%	65.3%	34.7%
4,052	TOWNER	2,065	1,242	789	34	453 R	60.1%	38.2%	61.2%	38.8%
9,624	TRAILL	4,694	3,037	1,580	77	1,457 R	64.7%	33.7%	65.8%	34.2%
15,371	WALSH	6,704	4,347	2,264	93	2,083 R	64.8%	33.8%	65.8%	34.2%
58,392	WARD	23,623	16,077	7,336	210	8,741 R	68.1%	31.1%	68.7%	31.3%
6,979	WELLS	3,506	2,426	1,036	44	1,390 R	69.2%	29.5%	70.1%	29.9%
22,237	WILLIAMS	11,523	8,166	3,177	180	4,989 R	70.9%	27.6%	72.0%	28.0%
652,717	TOTAL	308,971	200,336	104,429	4,206	95,907 R	64.8%	33.8%	65.7%	34.3%

NORTH DAKOTA

GOVERNOR 1984

1980 Census Population	County	Total Vote	Republican	Democratic	Other	Rep.-Dem. Plurality	Percentage Total Vote Rep.	Dem.	Major Vote Rep.	Dem.
3,584	ADAMS	1,940	1,047	893		154 R	54.0%	46.0%	54.0%	46.0%
13,960	BARNES	7,170	3,028	4,142		1,114 D	42.2%	57.8%	42.2%	57.8%
7,944	BENSON	3,492	1,333	2,159		826 D	38.2%	61.8%	38.2%	61.8%
1,138	BILLINGS	656	337	319		18 R	51.4%	48.6%	51.4%	48.6%
9,239	BOTTINEAU	4,789	2,450	2,339		111 R	51.2%	48.8%	51.2%	48.8%
4,229	BOWMAN	2,171	1,233	938		295 R	56.8%	43.2%	56.8%	43.2%
3,822	BURKE	1,912	1,029	883		146 R	53.8%	46.2%	53.8%	46.2%
54,811	BURLEIGH	29,861	12,742	17,119		4,377 D	42.7%	57.3%	42.7%	57.3%
88,247	CASS	47,939	21,404	26,535		5,131 D	44.6%	55.4%	44.6%	55.4%
7,636	CAVALIER	3,930	1,874	2,056		182 D	47.7%	52.3%	47.7%	52.3%
7,207	DICKEY	3,563	2,035	1,528		507 R	57.1%	42.9%	57.1%	42.9%
3,494	DIVIDE	1,894	928	966		38 D	49.0%	51.0%	49.0%	51.0%
4,627	DUNN	2,394	1,032	1,362		330 D	43.1%	56.9%	43.1%	56.9%
3,554	EDDY	1,941	766	1,175		409 D	39.5%	60.5%	39.5%	60.5%
5,877	EMMONS	2,809	1,162	1,647		485 D	41.4%	58.6%	41.4%	58.6%
4,611	FOSTER	2,267	978	1,289		311 D	43.1%	56.9%	43.1%	56.9%
2,391	GOLDEN VALLEY	1,332	627	705		78 D	47.1%	52.9%	47.1%	52.9%
66,100	GRAND FORKS	26,394	10,809	15,585		4,776 D	41.0%	59.0%	41.0%	59.0%
4,274	GRANT	2,247	1,097	1,150		53 D	48.8%	51.2%	48.8%	51.2%
3,714	GRIGGS	2,158	967	1,191		224 D	44.8%	55.2%	44.8%	55.2%
4,275	HETTINGER	2,267	1,150	1,117		33 R	50.7%	49.3%	50.7%	49.3%
3,833	KIDDER	1,908	803	1,105		302 D	42.1%	57.9%	42.1%	57.9%
6,473	LA MOURE	3,169	1,457	1,712		255 D	46.0%	54.0%	46.0%	54.0%
3,493	LOGAN	1,847	895	952		57 D	48.5%	51.5%	48.5%	51.5%
7,858	MCHENRY	3,931	1,732	2,199		467 D	44.1%	55.9%	44.1%	55.9%
4,800	MCINTOSH	2,661	1,629	1,032		597 R	61.2%	38.8%	61.2%	38.8%
7,132	MCKENZIE	3,665	1,890	1,775		115 R	51.6%	48.4%	51.6%	48.4%
12,383	MCLEAN	6,085	2,656	3,429		773 D	43.6%	56.4%	43.6%	56.4%
9,404	MERCER	5,657	2,667	2,990		323 D	47.1%	52.9%	47.1%	52.9%
25,177	MORTON	11,705	4,038	7,667		3,629 D	34.5%	65.5%	34.5%	65.5%
7,679	MOUNTRAIL	3,602	1,344	2,258		914 D	37.3%	62.7%	37.3%	62.7%
5,233	NELSON	2,555	965	1,590		625 D	37.8%	62.2%	37.8%	62.2%
2,495	OLIVER	1,372	584	788		204 D	42.6%	57.4%	42.6%	57.4%
10,399	PEMBINA	4,417	2,061	2,356		295 D	46.7%	53.3%	46.7%	53.3%
6,166	PIERCE	2,790	1,388	1,402		14 D	49.7%	50.3%	49.7%	50.3%
13,048	RAMSEY	6,780	2,799	3,981		1,182 D	41.3%	58.7%	41.3%	58.7%
6,698	RANSOM	3,050	1,278	1,772		494 D	41.9%	58.1%	41.9%	58.1%
3,608	RENVILLE	1,833	913	920		7 D	49.8%	50.2%	49.8%	50.2%
19,207	RICHLAND	9,230	4,291	4,939		648 D	46.5%	53.5%	46.5%	53.5%
12,177	ROLETTE	3,911	1,235	2,676		1,441 D	31.6%	68.4%	31.6%	68.4%
5,512	SARGENT	2,784	1,039	1,745		706 D	37.3%	62.7%	37.3%	62.7%
2,819	SHERIDAN	1,448	834	614		220 R	57.6%	42.4%	57.6%	42.4%
3,620	SIOUX	1,158	375	783		408 D	32.4%	67.6%	32.4%	67.6%
1,157	SLOPE	617	320	297		23 R	51.9%	48.1%	51.9%	48.1%
23,697	STARK	10,125	4,890	5,235		345 D	48.3%	51.7%	48.3%	51.7%
3,106	STEELE	1,793	696	1,097		401 D	38.8%	61.2%	38.8%	61.2%
24,154	STUTSMAN	10,557	4,385	6,172		1,787 D	41.5%	58.5%	41.5%	58.5%
4,052	TOWNER	2,134	918	1,216		298 D	43.0%	57.0%	43.0%	57.0%
9,624	TRAILL	4,875	2,266	2,609		343 D	46.5%	53.5%	46.5%	53.5%
15,371	WALSH	6,828	2,760	4,068		1,308 D	40.4%	59.6%	40.4%	59.6%
58,392	WARD	23,596	11,632	11,964		332 D	49.3%	50.7%	49.3%	50.7%
6,979	WELLS	3,599	1,721	1,878		157 D	47.8%	52.2%	47.8%	52.2%
22,237	WILLIAMS	11,574	5,971	5,603		368 R	51.6%	48.4%	51.6%	48.4%
652,717	TOTAL	314,382	140,460	173,922		33,462 D	44.7%	55.3%	44.7%	55.3%

NORTH DAKOTA

CONGRESS

CD	Year	Total Vote	Republican Vote	Candidate	Democratic Vote	Candidate	Other Vote	Rep.-Dem. Plurality	Percentage Total Vote Rep.	Dem.	Major Vote Rep.	Dem.
AL	1984	308,729	65,761	ALTENBURG, LOIS I.	242,968	DORGAN, BYRON L.		177,207 D	21.3%	78.7%	21.3%	78.7%
AL	1982	260,499	72,241	JONES, KENT	186,534	DORGAN, BYRON L.	1,724	114,293 D	27.7%	71.6%	27.9%	72.1%
AL	1980	293,076	124,707	SMYKOWSKI, JIM	166,437	DORGAN, BYRON L.	1,932	41,730 D	42.6%	56.8%	42.8%	57.2%
AL	1978	220,348	147,746	ANDREWS, MARK	68,016	HAGEN, BRUCE	4,586	79,730 R	67.1%	30.9%	68.5%	31.5%
AL	1976	289,881	181,018	ANDREWS, MARK	104,263	OMDAHL, LLOYD B.	4,600	76,755 R	62.4%	36.0%	63.5%	36.5%
AL	1974	233,688	130,184	ANDREWS, MARK	103,504	DORGAN, BYRON L.		26,680 R	55.7%	44.3%	55.7%	44.3%
AL	1972	268,721	195,360	ANDREWS, MARK	72,850	ISTA, RICHARD	511	122,510 R	72.7%	27.1%	72.8%	27.2%

NORTH DAKOTA

1984 GENERAL ELECTION

President   Other vote was 1,278 LaRouche (Independent); 1,077 Richards (Populist); 703 Bergland (Libertarian); 368 Johnson (Citizens); 239 Mason (Socialist Workers); 220 Dodge (Prohibition); 169 Hall (Communist); 152 Serrette (New Alliance).

Governor

Congress

1984 PRIMARIES

JUNE 12 REPUBLICAN

Governor   Allen I. Olson, unopposed.

Congress   Unopposed at-large.

JUNE 12 DEMOCRATIC

Governor   36,461 George Sinner; 5,180 Anna Belle Bourgois.

Congress   Unopposed at-large.

OHIO

GOVERNOR
Richard F. Celeste (D). Elected 1982 to a four-year term.

SENATORS
John H. Glenn (D). Re-elected 1980 to a six-year term. Previously elected 1974.

Howard Metzenbaum (D). Re-elected 1982 to a six-year term. Previously elected 1976.

REPRESENTATIVES

1. Thomas A. Luken (D)
2. Willis D. Gradison (R)
3. Tony P. Hall (D)
4. Michael G. Oxley (R)
5. Delbert L. Latta (R)
6. Bob McEwen (R)
7. Michael DeWine (R)
8. Thomas N. Kindness (R)
9. Marcy Kaptur (D)
10. Clarence E. Miller (R)
11. Dennis E. Eckart (D)
12. John R. Kasich (R)
13. Donald J. Pease (D)
14. John F. Seiberling (D)
15. Chalmers P. Wylie (R)
16. Ralph S. Regula (R)
17. James A. Traficant (D)
18. Douglas Applegate (D)
19. Edward F. Feighan (D)
20. Mary Rose Oakar (D)
21. Louis Stokes (D)

POSTWAR VOTE FOR GOVERNOR

Year	Total Vote	Republican Vote	Candidate	Democratic Vote	Candidate	Other Vote	Rep.-Dem. Plurality	Total Vote Rep.	Total Vote Dem.	Major Vote Rep.	Major Vote Dem.
1982	3,356,721	1,303,962	Brown, Clarence, Jr.	1,981,882	Celeste, Richard F.	70,877	677,920 D	38.8%	59.0%	39.7%	60.3%
1978	2,843,351	1,402,167	Rhodes, James A.	1,354,631	Celeste, Richard F.	86,553	47,536 R	49.3%	47.6%	50.9%	49.1%
1974	3,072,010	1,493,679	Rhodes, James A.	1,482,191	Gilligan, John J.	96,140	11,488 R	48.6%	48.2%	50.2%	49.8%
1970	3,184,133	1,382,659	Cloud, Roger	1,725,560	Gilligan, John J.	75,914	342,901 D	43.4%	54.2%	44.5%	55.5%
1966	2,887,331	1,795,277	Rhodes, James A.	1,092,054	Reams, Frazier, Jr.	—	703,223 R	62.2%	37.8%	62.2%	37.8%
1962	3,116,711	1,836,190	Rhodes, James A.	1,280,521	DiSalle, Michael V.	—	555,669 R	58.9%	41.1%	58.9%	41.1%
1958*	3,284,134	1,414,874	O'Neill, C. William	1,869,260	DiSalle, Michael V.	—	454,386 D	43.1%	56.9%	43.1%	56.9%
1956	3,542,091	1,984,988	O'Neill, C. William	1,557,103	DiSalle, Michael V.	—	427,885 R	56.0%	44.0%	56.0%	44.0%
1954	2,597,790	1,192,528	Rhodes, James A.	1,405,262	Lausche, Frank J.	—	212,734 D	45.9%	54.1%	45.9%	54.1%
1952	3,605,168	1,590,058	Taft, Charles P.	2,015,110	Lausche, Frank J.	—	425,052 D	44.1%	55.9%	44.1%	55.9%
1950	2,892,819	1,370,570	Ebright, Don H.	1,522,249	Lausche, Frank J.	—	151,679 D	47.4%	52.6%	47.4%	52.6%
1948	3,018,289	1,398,514	Herbert, Thomas J.	1,619,775	Lausche, Frank J.	—	221,261 D	46.3%	53.7%	46.3%	53.7%
1946	2,303,750	1,166,550	Herbert, Thomas J.	1,125,997	Lausche, Frank J.	11,203	40,553 R	50.6%	48.9%	50.9%	49.1%

The term of office of Ohio's Governor was increased from two to four years effective with the 1958 election.

POSTWAR VOTE FOR SENATOR

Year	Total Vote	Republican Vote	Candidate	Democratic Vote	Candidate	Other Vote	Rep.-Dem. Plurality	Total Vote Rep.	Total Vote Dem.	Major Vote Rep.	Major Vote Dem.
1982	3,395,463	1,396,790	Pfeifer, Paul E.	1,923,767	Metzenbaum, Howard	74,906	526,977 D	41.1%	56.7%	42.1%	57.9%
1980	4,027,303	1,137,695	Betts, James E.	2,770,786	Glenn, John H.	118,822	1,633,091 D	28.2%	68.8%	29.1%	70.9%
1976	3,920,613	1,823,774	Taft, Robert A.,Jr.	1,941,113	Metzenbaum, Howard	155,726	117,339 D	46.5%	49.5%	48.4%	51.6%
1974	2,987,951	918,133	Perk, Ralph J.	1,930,670	Glenn, John H.	139,148	1,012,537 D	30.7%	64.6%	32.2%	67.8%
1970	3,151,274	1,565,682	Taft, Robert A.,Jr.	1,495,262	Metzenbaum, Howard	90,330	70,420 R	49.7%	47.4%	51.2%	48.8%
1968	3,743,121	1,928,964	Saxbe, William B.	1,814,152	Gilligan, John J.	5	114,812 R	51.5%	48.5%	51.5%	48.5%
1964	3,830,389	1,906,781	Taft, Robert A.,Jr.	1,923,608	Young, Stephen M.	—	16,827 D	49.8%	50.2%	49.8%	50.2%
1962	2,994,986	1,151,173	Briley, John M.	1,843,813	Lausche, Frank J.	—	692,640 D	38.4%	61.6%	38.4%	61.6%
1958	3,149,410	1,497,199	Bricker, John W.	1,652,211	Young, Stephen M.	—	155,012 D	47.5%	52.5%	47.5%	52.5%
1956	3,525,499	1,660,910	Bender, George H.	1,864,589	Lausche, Frank J.	—	203,679 D	47.1%	52.9%	47.1%	52.9%
1954s	1,257,874		Bender, George H.	1,254,904	Burke, Thomas A.	—	2,970 R	50.1%	49.9%	50.1%	49.9%
1952	3,442,291	1,878,961	Bricker, John W.	1,563,330	DiSalle, Michael V.	—	315,631 R	54.6%	45.4%	54.6%	45.4%
1950	2,860,102	1,645,643	Taft, Robert A.	1,214,459	Ferguson, Joseph T.	—	431,184 R	57.5%	42.5%	57.5%	42.5%
1946	2,237,269	1,275,774	Bricker, John W.	947,610	Huffman, James W.	13,885	328,164 R	57.0%	42.4%	57.4%	42.6%

The 1954 election was for a short term to fill a vacancy.

OHIO

Districts Established March 25, 1982

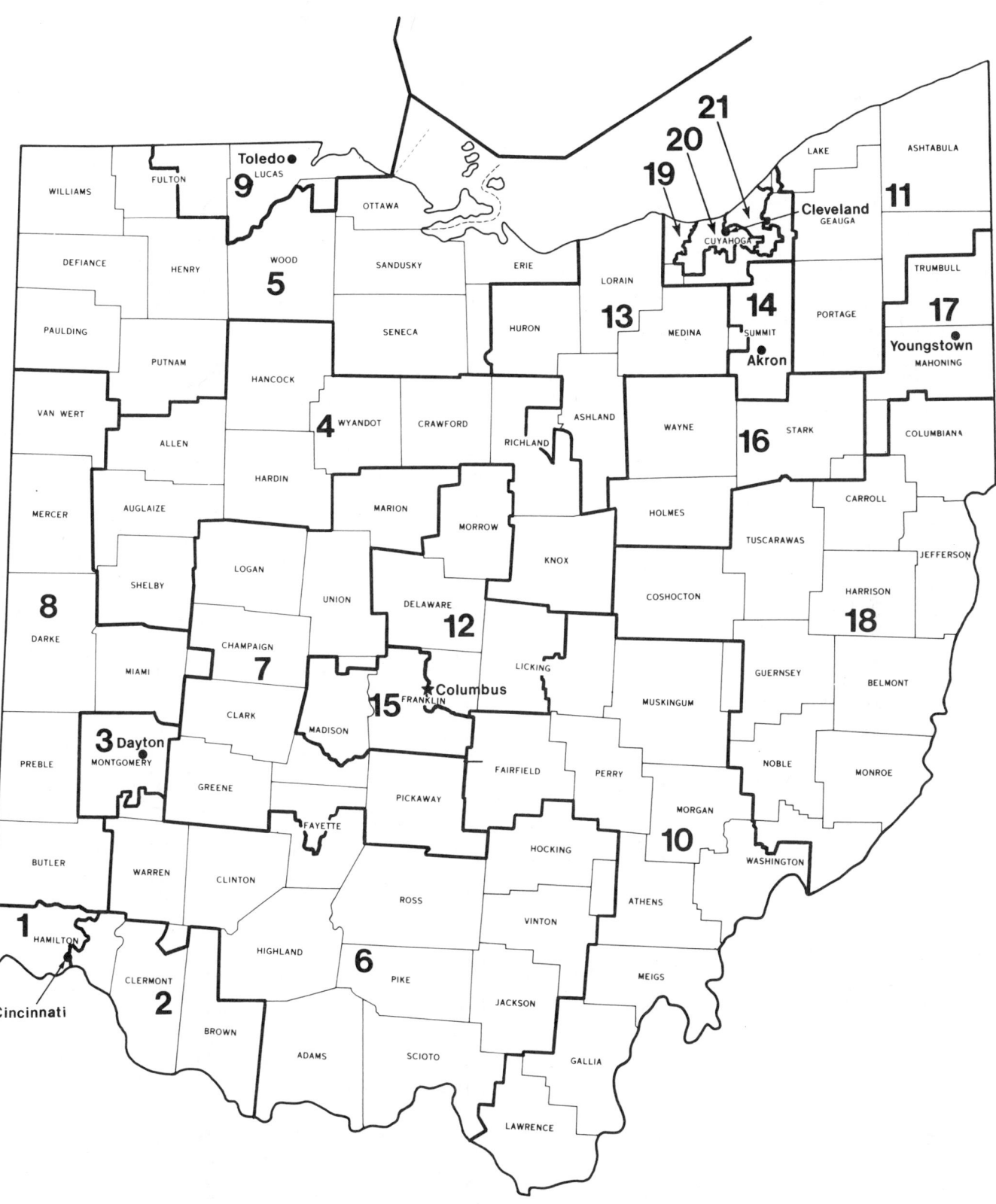

OHIO

PRESIDENT 1984

1980 Census Population	County	Total Vote	Republican	Democratic	Other	Rep.-Dem. Plurality	Percentage Total Vote Rep.	Dem.	Major Vote Rep.	Dem.
24,328	ADAMS	9,729	6,113	3,534	82	2,579 R	62.8%	36.3%	63.4%	36.6%
112,241	ALLEN	45,911	33,506	12,176	229	21,330 R	73.0%	26.5%	73.3%	26.7%
46,178	ASHLAND	19,272	14,339	4,786	147	9,553 R	74.4%	24.8%	75.0%	25.0%
104,215	ASHTABULA	41,397	21,669	19,344	384	2,325 R	52.3%	46.7%	52.8%	47.2%
56,399	ATHENS	21,958	11,548	10,201	209	1,347 R	52.6%	46.5%	53.1%	46.9%
42,554	AUGLAIZE	19,000	14,766	4,102	132	10,664 R	77.7%	21.6%	78.3%	21.7%
82,569	BELMONT	34,856	15,170	19,458	228	4,288 D	43.5%	55.8%	43.8%	56.2%
31,920	BROWN	12,404	8,221	4,067	116	4,154 R	66.3%	32.8%	66.9%	33.1%
258,787	BUTLER	104,514	76,216	27,700	598	48,516 R	72.9%	26.5%	73.3%	26.7%
25,598	CARROLL	10,584	6,703	3,771	110	2,932 R	63.3%	35.6%	64.0%	36.0%
33,649	CHAMPAIGN	13,600	9,935	3,544	121	6,391 R	73.1%	26.1%	73.7%	26.3%
150,236	CLARK	57,744	35,831	21,154	759	14,677 R	62.1%	36.6%	62.9%	37.1%
128,483	CLERMONT	47,319	35,316	11,713	290	23,603 R	74.6%	24.8%	75.1%	24.9%
34,603	CLINTON	13,018	9,603	3,332	83	6,271 R	73.8%	25.6%	74.2%	25.8%
113,572	COLUMBIANA	45,110	24,552	20,155	403	4,397 R	54.4%	44.7%	54.9%	45.1%
36,024	COSHOCTON	14,323	9,842	4,392	89	5,450 R	68.7%	30.7%	69.1%	30.9%
50,075	CRAWFORD	19,820	14,682	4,932	206	9,750 R	74.1%	24.9%	74.9%	25.1%
1,498,400	CUYAHOGA	651,633	284,094	362,626	4,913	78,532 D	43.6%	55.6%	43.9%	56.1%
55,096	DARKE	22,494	16,379	5,904	211	10,475 R	72.8%	26.2%	73.5%	26.5%
39,987	DEFIANCE	16,130	10,951	5,004	175	5,947 R	67.9%	31.0%	68.6%	31.4%
53,840	DELAWARE	24,989	19,050	5,773	166	13,277 R	76.2%	23.1%	76.7%	23.3%
79,655	ERIE	33,154	19,174	13,508	472	5,666 R	57.8%	40.7%	58.7%	41.3%
93,678	FAIRFIELD	41,033	30,843	9,817	373	21,026 R	75.2%	23.9%	75.9%	24.1%
27,467	FAYETTE	9,021	6,838	2,126	57	4,712 R	75.8%	23.6%	76.3%	23.7%
869,132	FRANKLIN	390,474	250,360	131,530	8,584	118,830 R	64.1%	33.7%	65.6%	34.4%
37,751	FULTON	15,730	11,412	4,217	101	7,195 R	72.5%	26.8%	73.0%	27.0%
30,098	GALLIA	12,554	8,194	4,251	109	3,943 R	65.3%	33.9%	65.8%	34.2%
74,474	GEAUGA	32,754	22,369	9,954	431	12,415 R	68.3%	30.4%	69.2%	30.8%
129,769	GREENE	51,711	34,267	17,129	315	17,138 R	66.3%	33.1%	66.7%	33.3%
42,024	GUERNSEY	15,344	10,252	4,967	125	5,285 R	66.8%	32.4%	67.4%	32.6%
873,224	HAMILTON	388,817	246,288	140,350	2,179	105,938 R	63.3%	36.1%	63.7%	36.3%
64,581	HANCOCK	28,295	22,169	5,758	368	16,411 R	78.3%	20.3%	79.4%	20.6%
32,719	HARDIN	12,620	8,722	3,813	85	4,909 R	69.1%	30.2%	69.6%	30.4%
18,152	HARRISON	7,712	4,276	3,370	66	906 R	55.4%	43.7%	55.9%	44.1%
28,383	HENRY	12,173	9,317	2,779	77	6,538 R	76.5%	22.8%	77.0%	23.0%
33,477	HIGHLAND	12,875	9,000	3,784	91	5,216 R	69.9%	29.4%	70.4%	29.6%
24,304	HOCKING	9,463	6,071	3,280	112	2,791 R	64.2%	34.7%	64.9%	35.1%
29,416	HOLMES	6,944	5,146	1,737	61	3,409 R	74.1%	25.0%	74.8%	25.2%
54,608	HURON	21,171	14,388	6,609	174	7,779 R	68.0%	31.2%	68.5%	31.5%
30,592	JACKSON	11,908	7,411	4,369	128	3,042 R	62.2%	36.7%	62.9%	37.1%
91,564	JEFFERSON	40,277	17,105	22,832	340	5,727 D	42.5%	56.7%	42.8%	57.2%
46,304	KNOX	19,901	14,062	5,730	109	8,332 R	70.7%	28.8%	71.0%	29.0%
212,801	LAKE	92,325	54,587	36,711	1,027	17,876 R	59.1%	39.8%	59.8%	40.2%
63,849	LAWRENCE	26,437	14,793	11,431	213	3,362 R	56.0%	43.2%	56.4%	43.6%
120,981	LICKING	51,976	37,560	13,995	421	23,565 R	72.3%	26.9%	72.9%	27.1%
39,155	LOGAN	15,979	12,230	3,645	104	8,585 R	76.5%	22.8%	77.0%	23.0%
274,909	LORAIN	113,021	57,379	52,970	2,672	4,409 R	50.8%	46.9%	52.0%	48.0%
471,741	LUCAS	199,554	100,285	97,293	1,976	2,992 R	50.3%	48.8%	50.8%	49.2%
33,004	MADISON	11,987	8,979	2,928	80	6,051 R	74.9%	24.4%	75.4%	24.6%
289,487	MAHONING	131,438	53,424	76,514	1,500	23,090 D	40.6%	58.2%	41.1%	58.9%
67,974	MARION	26,443	17,392	8,827	224	8,565 R	65.8%	33.4%	66.3%	33.7%
113,150	MEDINA	46,944	30,690	15,897	357	14,793 R	65.4%	33.9%	65.9%	34.1%
23,641	MEIGS	9,929	6,307	3,549	73	2,758 R	63.5%	35.7%	64.0%	36.0%
38,334	MERCER	16,144	11,542	4,422	180	7,120 R	71.5%	27.4%	72.3%	27.7%
90,381	MIAMI	36,315	26,300	9,695	320	16,605 R	72.4%	26.7%	73.1%	26.9%
17,382	MONROE	6,978	3,302	3,611	65	309 D	47.3%	51.7%	47.8%	52.2%
571,697	MONTGOMERY	232,402	137,053	94,016	1,333	43,037 R	59.0%	40.5%	59.3%	40.7%
14,241	MORGAN	5,903	3,994	1,868	41	2,126 R	67.7%	31.6%	68.1%	31.9%
26,480	MORROW	11,042	8,116	2,839	87	5,277 R	73.5%	25.7%	74.1%	25.9%
83,340	MUSKINGUM	32,101	21,821	10,037	243	11,784 R	68.0%	31.3%	68.5%	31.5%

OHIO

PRESIDENT 1984

1980 Census Population	County	Total Vote	Republican	Democratic	Other	Rep.-Dem. Plurality	Percentage			
							Total Vote		Major Vote	
							Rep.	Dem.	Rep.	Dem.
11,310	NOBLE	5,691	3,853	1,777	61	2,076 R	67.7%	31.2%	68.4%	31.6%
40,076	OTTAWA	18,075	10,920	7,053	102	3,867 R	60.4%	39.0%	60.8%	39.2%
21,302	PAULDING	8,439	5,545	2,811	83	2,734 R	65.7%	33.3%	66.4%	33.6%
31,032	PERRY	11,597	7,548	3,961	88	3,587 R	65.1%	34.2%	65.6%	34.4%
43,662	PICKAWAY	16,160	11,942	4,110	108	7,832 R	73.9%	25.4%	74.4%	25.6%
22,802	PIKE	11,302	6,318	4,895	89	1,423 R	55.9%	43.3%	56.3%	43.7%
135,856	PORTAGE	51,687	29,536	21,719	432	7,817 R	57.1%	42.0%	57.6%	42.4%
38,223	PREBLE	15,403	11,065	4,198	140	6,867 R	71.8%	27.3%	72.5%	27.5%
32,991	PUTNAM	15,252	11,937	3,194	121	8,743 R	78.3%	20.9%	78.9%	21.1%
131,205	RICHLAND	51,836	35,299	16,141	396	19,158 R	68.1%	31.1%	68.6%	31.4%
65,004	ROSS	25,548	17,015	8,020	513	8,995 R	66.6%	31.4%	68.0%	32.0%
63,267	SANDUSKY	26,020	17,214	8,564	242	8,650 R	66.2%	32.9%	66.8%	33.2%
84,545	SCIOTO	33,219	18,818	14,120	281	4,698 R	56.6%	42.5%	57.1%	42.9%
61,901	SENECA	24,642	16,520	7,905	217	8,615 R	67.0%	32.1%	67.6%	32.4%
43,089	SHELBY	17,983	13,509	4,315	159	9,194 R	75.1%	24.0%	75.8%	24.2%
378,823	STARK	164,916	98,434	65,157	1,325	33,277 R	59.7%	39.5%	60.2%	39.8%
524,472	SUMMIT	226,780	115,637	109,569	1,574	6,068 R	51.0%	48.3%	51.3%	48.7%
241,863	TRUMBULL	103,259	45,623	56,902	734	11,279 D	44.2%	55.1%	44.5%	55.5%
84,614	TUSCARAWAS	32,754	19,366	13,149	239	6,217 R	59.1%	40.1%	59.6%	40.4%
29,536	UNION	12,001	9,336	2,579	86	6,757 R	77.8%	21.5%	78.4%	21.6%
30,458	VAN WERT	12,988	9,570	3,338	80	6,232 R	73.7%	25.7%	74.1%	25.9%
11,584	VINTON	5,085	3,041	1,990	54	1,051 R	59.8%	39.1%	60.4%	39.6%
99,276	WARREN	39,070	29,848	9,031	191	20,817 R	76.4%	23.1%	76.8%	23.2%
64,266	WASHINGTON	24,993	16,529	7,920	544	8,609 R	66.1%	31.7%	67.6%	32.4%
97,408	WAYNE	36,104	24,475	11,323	306	13,152 R	67.8%	31.4%	68.4%	31.6%
36,369	WILLIAMS	14,577	10,804	3,624	149	7,180 R	74.1%	24.9%	74.9%	25.1%
107,372	WOOD	45,954	29,750	15,907	297	13,843 R	64.7%	34.6%	65.2%	34.8%
22,651	WYANDOT	9,630	7,204	2,342	84	4,862 R	74.8%	24.3%	75.5%	24.5%
10,797,630	TOTAL	4,547,619	2,678,560	1,825,440	43,619	853,120 R	58.9%	40.1%	59.5%	40.5%

OHIO

CONGRESS

CD	Year	Total Vote	Republican Vote	Candidate	Democratic Vote	Candidate	Other Vote	Rep.-Dem. Plurality	Total Vote Rep.	Total Vote Dem.	Major Vote Rep.	Major Vote Dem.
1	1984	220,658	88,859	MURDOCK, NORMAN A.	121,577	LUKEN, THOMAS A.	10,222	32,718 D	40.3%	55.1%	42.2%	57.8%
1	1982	156,187	52,658	HELD, JOHN E.	99,143	LUKEN, THOMAS A.	4,386	46,485 D	33.7%	63.5%	34.7%	65.3%
2	1984	218,453	149,856	GRADISON, WILLIS D.	68,597	PORTER, THOMAS J.		81,259 R	68.6%	31.4%	68.6%	31.4%
2	1982	155,378	97,434	GRADISON, WILLIS D.	53,169	LUTTMER, WILLIAM J.	4,775	44,265 R	62.7%	34.2%	64.7%	35.3%
3	1984	151,398			151,398	HALL, TONY P.		151,398 D		100.0%		100.0%
3	1982	136,754			119,926	HALL, TONY P.	16,828	119,926 D		87.7%		100.0%
4	1984	209,217	162,199	OXLEY, MICHAEL G.	47,018	SUTTON, WILLIAM O.		115,181 R	77.5%	22.5%	77.5%	22.5%
4	1982	162,651	105,087	OXLEY, MICHAEL G.	57,564	MOON, ROBERT W.		47,523 R	64.6%	35.4%	64.6%	35.4%
5	1984	211,391	132,582	LATTA, DELBERT L.	78,809	SHERCK, JAMES R.		53,773 R	62.7%	37.3%	62.7%	37.3%
5	1982	156,570	86,450	LATTA, DELBERT L.	70,120	SHERCK, JAMES R.		16,330 R	55.2%	44.8%	55.2%	44.8%
6	1984	202,828	150,101	MCEWEN, BOB	52,727	SMITH, BOB		97,374 R	74.0%	26.0%	74.0%	26.0%
6	1982	155,570	92,135	MCEWEN, BOB	63,435	GRIMSHAW, LYNN A.		28,700 R	59.2%	40.8%	59.2%	40.8%
7	1984	192,858	147,885	DEWINE, MICHAEL	40,621	SCOTT, DONALD E.	4,352	107,264 R	76.7%	21.1%	78.5%	21.5%
7	1982	156,146	87,842	DEWINE, MICHAEL	65,543	TACKETT, ROGER D.	2,761	22,299 R	56.3%	42.0%	57.3%	42.7%
8	1984	201,873	155,200	KINDNESS, THOMAS N.	46,673	FRANCIS, JOHN T.		108,527 R	76.9%	23.1%	76.9%	23.1%
8	1982	148,404	98,527	KINDNESS, THOMAS N.	49,877	GRIFFIN, JOHN W.		48,650 R	66.4%	33.6%	66.4%	33.6%
9	1984	214,909	93,210	VENNER, FRANK	117,985	KAPTUR, MARCY	3,714	24,775 D	43.4%	54.9%	44.1%	55.9%
9	1982	164,217	64,459	WEBER, ED	95,162	KAPTUR, MARCY	4,596	30,703 D	39.3%	57.9%	40.4%	59.6%
10	1984	204,509	149,337	MILLER, CLARENCE E.	55,172	BUCHANAN, JOHN M.		94,165 R	73.0%	27.0%	73.0%	27.0%
10	1982	158,027	100,044	MILLER, CLARENCE E.	57,983	BUCHANAN, JOHN M.		42,061 R	63.3%	36.7%	63.3%	36.7%
11	1984	199,374	66,278	BEAGLE, DEAN	133,096	ECKART, DENNIS E.		66,818 D	33.2%	66.8%	33.2%	66.8%
11	1982	153,243	56,616	WARNER, GLEN W.	93,302	ECKART, DENNIS E.	3,325	36,686 D	36.9%	60.9%	37.8%	62.2%
12	1984	214,114	148,899	KASICH, JOHN R.	65,215	SLOAN, RICHARD		83,684 R	69.5%	30.5%	69.5%	30.5%
12	1982	175,027	88,335	KASICH, JOHN R.	82,753	SHAMANSKY, BOB	3,939	5,582 R	50.5%	47.3%	51.6%	48.4%
13	1984	198,756	59,610	SCHAFFNER, WILLIAM G.	131,923	PEASE, DONALD J.	7,223	72,313 D	30.0%	66.4%	31.1%	68.9%
13	1982	150,725	53,376	MARTIN, TIMOTHY P.	92,296	PEASE, DONALD J.	5,053	38,920 D	35.4%	61.2%	36.6%	63.4%
14	1984	218,095	62,366	BENDER, JEAN E.	155,729	SEIBERLING, JOHN F.		93,363 D	28.6%	71.4%	28.6%	71.4%
14	1982	164,050	48,421	MANGELS, LOUIS A.	115,629	SEIBERLING, JOHN F.		67,208 D	29.5%	70.5%	29.5%	70.5%
15	1984	207,181	148,311	WYLIE, CHALMERS P.	58,870	JAGER, DUANE		89,441 R	71.6%	28.4%	71.6%	28.4%
15	1982	157,887	104,678	WYLIE, CHALMERS P.	47,070	KOSTELAC, GREG	6,139	57,608 R	66.3%	29.8%	69.0%	31.0%
16	1984	210,447	152,399	REGULA, RALPH S.	58,048	GWIN, JAMES		94,351 R	72.4%	27.6%	72.4%	27.6%
16	1982	167,871	110,485	REGULA, RALPH S.	57,386	ORENSTEIN, JEFFREY R.		53,099 R	65.8%	34.2%	65.8%	34.2%
17	1984	230,661	105,449	WILLIAMS, LYLE	123,014	TRAFICANT, JAMES A.	2,198	17,565 D	45.7%	53.3%	46.2%	53.8%
17	1982	178,851	98,476	WILLIAMS, LYLE	80,375	TABLACK, GEORGE D.		18,101 R	55.1%	44.9%	55.1%	44.9%
18	1984	205,115	49,356	BURT, KENNETH P.	155,759	APPLEGATE, DOUGLAS		106,403 D	24.1%	75.9%	24.1%	75.9%
18	1982	128,670			128,665	APPLEGATE, DOUGLAS	5	128,665 D		100.0%		100.0%
19	1984	252,839	107,957	HATCHADORIAN, MATTHEW J.	139,605	FEIGHAN, EDWARD F.	5,277	31,648 D	42.7%	55.2%	43.6%	56.4%
19	1982	189,942	72,682	ANTER, RICHARD G.	111,760	FEIGHAN, EDWARD F	5,500	39,078 D	38.3%	58.8%	39.4%	60.6%
20	1984	167,155			167,115	OAKAR, MARY ROSE	40	167,115 D		100.0%		100.0%
20	1982	156,052	17,675	LEJEUNE, PARIS T.	133,603	OAKAR, MARY ROSE	4,774	115,928 D	11.3%	85.6%	11.7%	88.3%
21	1984	200,648	29,500	WOODALL, ROBERT L.	165,247	STOKES, LOUIS	5,901	135,747 D	14.7%	82.4%	15.1%	84.9%
21	1982	153,876	21,332	SHATTEEN, ALAN G.	132,544	STOKES, LOUIS		111,212 D	13.9%	86.1%	13.9%	86.1%

OHIO

1984 GENERAL ELECTION

President   Other vote was 12,090 Serrette (Independent); 10,693 LaRouche (Independent); 5,886 Bergland (Independent); 4,438 Hall (Independent); 4,344 Mason (Independent); 3,565 Winn (Independent); 2,565 Holmes (Independent); 4 Dodge (write-in); 34 scattered. Early uncorrected returns gave the Serrette vote as 24,180 and the Winn vote as 7,130.

Congress   Other vote was Denny (Independent) in CD 1; 4,330 Hanna (write-in) and 22 Ogrod (write-in) in CD 7; 2,255 Nun (Independent) and 1,459 Lariscy (Independent) in CD 9; Patton (Independent) in CD 13; Johnjulio (Independent) in CD 17; Gleisser (Independent) in CD 19; Yorko (write-in) in CD 20; 4,363 Norris (Independent) and 1,538 Musa (Independent) in CD 21.

1984 PRIMARIES

MAY 8 REPUBLICAN

Congress   Unopposed in seventeen CD's. No candidate in CD's 3 and 20. Contested as follows:

CD 1   15,087 Norman A. Murdock; 13,824 J. Kenneth Blackwell.
CD 14   13,511 Jean E. Bender; 5,505 John M. Trifero.

MAY 8 DEMOCRATIC

Congress   Unopposed in eight CD's. Contested as follows:

CD 1   36,036 Thomas A. Luken; 5,075 Walter C. Fleissner.
CD 2   22,337 Thomas J. Porter; 9,830 Anthony E. Barkley.
CD 5   35,806 James R. Sherck; 8,186 Larry A. Benschoter.
CD 6   20,345 Bob Smith; 14,789 Philip Holmes; 5,283 David L. Kitz.
CD 7   23,252 Donald E. Scott; 15,075 Dennis J. Geehan.
CD 8   16,119 John T. Francis; 14,415 Peter M. Schuller.
CD 9   57,872 Marcy Kaptur; 4,406 Carol R. Winters.
CD 13   51,010 Donald J. Pease; 8,271 John M. Ryan; 5,850 Caludia J. Cortes.
CD 14   64,741 John F. Seiberling; 10,214 Shelline Dabney.
CD 16   34,449 James Gwin; 15,114 Charles J. Martin; 9,269 William J. Kennick.
CD 17   67,511 James A. Traficant; 35,324 Thomas J. Carney; 10,702 Christopher S. Lardis; 2,988 Michael D. Joseph; 1,605 Samuel R. Savon; 935 Samuel Yiannaki; 895 Allen C. Gillam.
CD 18   80,293 Douglas Applegate; 4,185 Daniel W. Cook; 3,458 Donald K. Dickey.
CD 19   70,539 Edward F. Feighan; 17,991 Margaret I. Scott.

OKLAHOMA

GOVERNOR

George Nigh (D). Re-elected 1982 to a four-year term. Previously elected 1978.

SENATORS

David L. Boren (D). Re-elected 1984 to a six-year term. Previously elected 1978.

Don Nickles (R). Elected 1980 to a six-year term.

REPRESENTATIVES

1. James R. Jones (D)
2. Mike Synar (D)
3. Wes Watkins (D)
4. Dave McCurdy (D)
5. M. H. Edwards (R)
6. Glenn English (D)

POSTWAR VOTE FOR GOVERNOR

Year	Total Vote	Republican Vote	Candidate	Democratic Vote	Candidate	Other Vote	Rep.-Dem. Plurality	Total Vote Rep.	Total Vote Dem.	Major Vote Rep.	Major Vote Dem.
1982	883,130	332,207	Daxon, Tom	548,159	Nigh, George	2,764	215,952 D	37.6%	62.1%	37.7%	62.3%
1978	777,414	367,055	Shotts, Ron	402,240	Nigh, George	8,119	35,185 D	47.2%	51.7%	47.7%	52.3%
1974	804,848	290,459	Inhofe, James M.	514,389	Boren, David L.	—	223,930 D	36.1%	63.9%	36.1%	63.9%
1970	698,790	336,157	Bartlett, Dewey F.	338,338	Hall, David	24,295	2,181 D	48.1%	48.4%	49.8%	50.2%
1966	677,258	377,078	Bartlett, Dewey F.	296,328	Moore, Preston J.	3,852	80,750 R	55.7%	43.8%	56.0%	44.0%
1962	709,763	392,316	Bellmon, Henry	315,357	Atkinson, W. P.	2,090	76,959 R	55.3%	44.4%	55.4%	44.6%
1958	538,839	107,495	Ferguson, Phil	399,504	Edmondson, J. Howard	31,840	292,009 D	19.9%	74.1%	21.2%	78.8%
1954	609,194	251,808	Sparks, Reuben K.	357,386	Gary, Raymond	—	105,578 D	41.3%	58.7%	41.3%	58.7%
1950	644,276	313,205	Ferguson, Jo O.	329,308	Murray, Johnston	1,763	16,103 D	48.6%	51.1%	48.7%	51.3%
1946	494,599	227,426	Flynn, Olney F.	259,491	Turner, Roy J.	7,682	32,065 D	46.0%	52.5%	46.7%	53.3%

POSTWAR VOTE FOR SENATOR

Year	Total Vote	Republican Vote	Candidate	Democratic Vote	Candidate	Other Vote	Rep.-Dem. Plurality	Total Vote Rep.	Total Vote Dem.	Major Vote Rep.	Major Vote Dem.
1984	1,197,937	280,638	Crozier, Will E.	906,131	Boren, David L.	11,168	625,493 D	23.4%	75.6%	23.6%	76.4%
1980	1,098,294	587,252	Nickles, Don	478,283	Coats, Andrew	32,759	108,969 R	53.5%	43.5%	55.1%	44.9%
1978	754,264	247,857	Kamm, Robert B.	493,953	Boren, David L.	12,454	246,096 D	32.9%	65.5%	33.4%	66.6%
1974	791,809	390,997	Bellmon, Henry	387,162	Edmondson, Ed	13,650	3,835 R	49.4%	48.9%	50.2%	49.8%
1972	1,005,148	516,934	Bartlett, Dewey F.	478,212	Edmondson, Ed	10,002	38,722 R	51.4%	47.6%	51.9%	48.1%
1968	909,119	470,120	Bellmon, Henry	419,658	Monroney, A. S. Mike	19,341	50,462 R	51.7%	46.2%	52.8%	47.2%
1966	638,742	295,585	Patterson, Pat J.	343,157	Harris, Fred R.	—	47,572 D	46.3%	53.7%	46.3%	53.7%
1964 s	912,174	445,392	Wilkinson, Bud	466,782	Harris, Fred R.	—	21,390 D	48.8%	51.2%	48.8%	51.2%
1962	664,712	307,966	Crawford, B. Hayden	353,890	Monroney, A. S. Mike	2,856	45,924 D	46.3%	53.2%	46.5%	53.5%
1960	864,475	385,646	Crawford, B. Hayden	474,116	Kerr, Robert S.	4,713	88,470 D	44.6%	54.8%	44.9%	55.1%
1956	831,142	371,146	McKeever, Douglas	459,996	Monroney, A. S. Mike	—	88,850 D	44.7%	55.3%	44.7%	55.3%
1954	600,120	262,013	Mock, Fred M.	335,127	Kerr, Robert S.	2,980	73,114 D	43.7%	55.8%	43.9%	56.1%
1950	631,177	285,224	Alexander, W. H.	345,953	Monroney, A. S. Mike	—	60,729 D	45.2%	54.8%	45.2%	54.8%
1948	708,931	265,169	Rizley, Ross	441,654	Kerr, Robert S.	2,108	176,485 D	37.4%	62.3%	37.5%	62.5%

The 1964 election was for a short term to fill a vacancy.

OKLAHOMA

Districts Established July 22, 1981

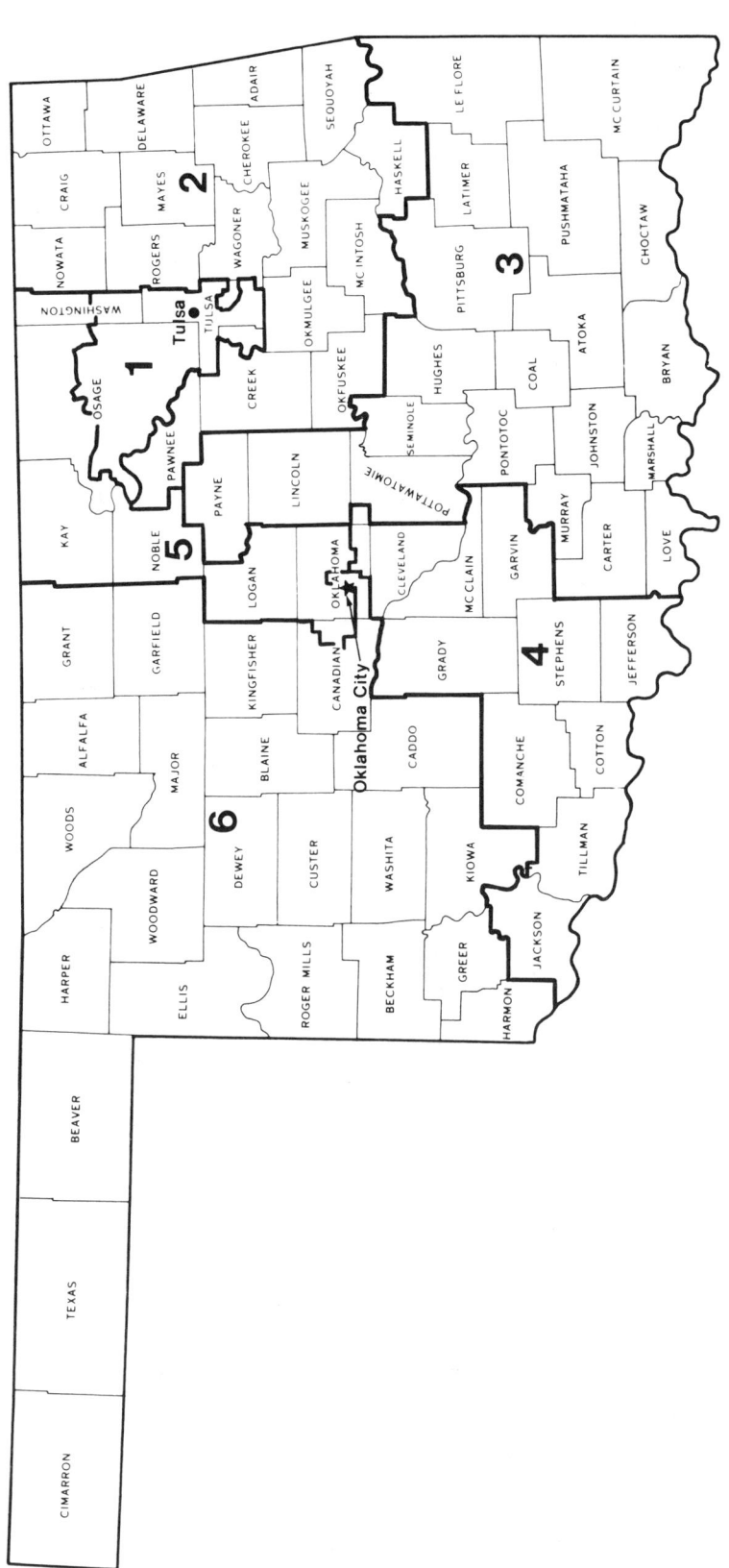

OKLAHOMA

PRESIDENT 1984

1980 Census Population	County	Total Vote	Republican	Democratic	Other	Rep.-Dem. Plurality	Percentage Total Vote Rep.	Dem.	Major Vote Rep.	Dem.
18,575	ADAIR	6,745	4,423	2,266	56	2,157 R	65.6%	33.6%	66.1%	33.9%
7,077	ALFALFA	3,608	2,715	866	27	1,849 R	75.2%	24.0%	75.8%	24.2%
12,748	ATOKA	4,444	2,361	2,047	36	314 R	53.1%	46.1%	53.6%	46.4%
6,806	BEAVER	3,252	2,689	536	27	2,153 R	82.7%	16.5%	83.4%	16.6%
19,243	BECKHAM	7,654	5,005	2,601	48	2,404 R	65.4%	34.0%	65.8%	34.2%
13,443	BLAINE	5,554	4,037	1,484	33	2,553 R	72.7%	26.7%	73.1%	26.9%
30,535	BRYAN	11,769	6,246	5,475	48	771 R	53.1%	46.5%	53.3%	46.7%
30,905	CADDO	11,341	6,811	4,463	67	2,348 R	60.1%	39.4%	60.4%	39.6%
56,452	CANADIAN	26,320	20,929	5,245	146	15,684 R	79.5%	19.9%	80.0%	20.0%
43,610	CARTER	17,822	11,578	6,161	83	5,417 R	65.0%	34.6%	65.3%	34.7%
30,684	CHEROKEE	13,015	7,614	5,307	94	2,307 R	58.5%	40.8%	58.9%	41.1%
17,203	CHOCTAW	5,987	3,155	2,801	31	354 R	52.7%	46.8%	53.0%	47.0%
3,648	CIMARRON	1,794	1,420	359	15	1,061 R	79.2%	20.0%	79.8%	20.2%
133,173	CLEVELAND	59,705	42,806	16,512	387	26,294 R	71.7%	27.7%	72.2%	27.8%
6,041	COAL	2,564	1,259	1,284	21	25 D	49.1%	50.1%	49.5%	50.5%
112,456	COMANCHE	30,394	21,382	8,890	122	12,492 R	70.3%	29.2%	70.6%	29.4%
7,338	COTTON	3,080	1,796	1,264	20	532 R	58.3%	41.0%	58.7%	41.3%
15,014	CRAIG	6,190	3,629	2,515	46	1,114 R	58.6%	40.6%	59.1%	40.9%
59,016	CREEK	22,628	15,011	7,465	152	7,546 R	66.3%	33.0%	66.8%	33.2%
25,995	CUSTER	10,940	8,191	2,700	49	5,491 R	74.9%	24.7%	75.2%	24.8%
23,946	DELAWARE	10,542	6,690	3,789	63	2,901 R	63.5%	35.9%	63.8%	36.2%
5,922	DEWEY	2,777	2,098	664	15	1,434 R	75.5%	23.9%	76.0%	24.0%
5,596	ELLIS	2,460	1,881	562	17	1,319 R	76.5%	22.8%	77.0%	23.0%
62,820	GARFIELD	25,534	19,642	5,730	162	13,912 R	76.9%	22.4%	77.4%	22.6%
27,856	GARVIN	11,811	7,505	4,215	91	3,290 R	63.5%	35.7%	64.0%	36.0%
39,490	GRADY	15,960	11,042	4,846	72	6,196 R	69.2%	30.4%	69.5%	30.5%
6,518	GRANT	3,324	2,470	825	29	1,645 R	74.3%	24.8%	75.0%	25.0%
7,028	GREEN	2,901	1,664	1,220	17	444 R	57.4%	42.1%	57.7%	42.3%
4,519	HARMON	1,805	1,009	785	11	224 R	55.9%	43.5%	56.2%	43.8%
4,715	HARPER	2,146	1,748	373	25	1,375 R	81.5%	17.4%	82.4%	17.6%
11,010	HASKELL	4,981	2,417	2,535	29	118 D	48.5%	50.9%	48.8%	51.2%
14,338	HUGHES	5,598	2,663	2,901	34	238 D	47.6%	51.8%	47.9%	52.1%
30,356	JACKSON	8,795	5,773	2,996	26	2,777 R	65.6%	34.1%	65.8%	34.2%
8,183	JEFFERSON	3,179	1,656	1,496	27	160 R	52.1%	47.1%	52.5%	47.5%
10,356	JOHNSTON	4,038	2,195	1,820	23	375 R	54.4%	45.1%	54.7%	45.3%
49,852	KAY	22,911	16,731	6,044	136	10,687 R	73.0%	26.4%	73.5%	26.5%
14,187	KINGFISHER	6,686	5,528	1,125	33	4,403 R	82.7%	16.8%	83.1%	16.9%
12,711	KIOWA	4,995	2,951	2,016	28	935 R	59.1%	40.4%	59.4%	40.6%
9,840	LATIMER	4,100	2,210	1,858	32	352 R	53.9%	45.3%	54.3%	45.7%
40,698	LE FLORE	14,698	8,604	5,990	104	2,614 R	58.5%	40.8%	59.0%	41.0%
26,601	LINCOLN	11,189	8,088	3,020	81	5,068 R	72.3%	27.0%	72.8%	27.2%
26,881	LOGAN	11,978	8,356	3,551	71	4,805 R	69.8%	29.6%	70.2%	29.8%
7,469	LOVE	3,209	1,833	1,359	17	474 R	57.1%	42.3%	57.4%	42.6%
20,291	MCCLAIN	8,672	6,056	2,549	67	3,507 R	69.8%	29.4%	70.4%	29.6%
36,151	MCCURTAIN	10,416	6,381	3,994	41	2,387 R	61.3%	38.3%	61.5%	38.5%
15,562	MCINTOSH	7,165	3,646	3,479	40	167 R	50.9%	48.6%	51.2%	48.8%
8,772	MAJOR	4,035	3,385	619	31	2,766 R	83.9%	15.3%	84.5%	15.5%
10,550	MARSHALL	4,560	2,488	2,039	33	449 R	54.6%	44.7%	55.0%	45.0%
32,261	MAYES	13,838	8,585	5,154	99	3,431 R	62.0%	37.2%	62.5%	37.5%
12,147	MURRAY	5,347	3,073	2,229	45	844 R	57.5%	41.7%	58.0%	42.0%
66,939	MUSKOGEE	27,183	14,652	12,343	188	2,309 R	53.9%	45.4%	54.3%	45.7%
11,573	NOBLE	5,279	4,018	1,238	23	2,780 R	76.1%	23.5%	76.4%	23.6%
11,486	NOWATA	4,761	3,030	1,687	44	1,343 R	63.6%	35.4%	64.2%	35.8%
11,125	OKFUSKEE	4,145	2,443	1,684	18	759 R	58.9%	40.6%	59.2%	40.8%
568,933	OKLAHOMA	223,261	159,974	60,235	3,052	99,739 R	71.7%	27.0%	72.6%	27.4%
39,169	OKMULGEE	16,189	8,704	7,380	105	1,324 R	53.8%	45.6%	54.1%	45.9%
39,327	OSAGE	16,257	10,083	6,095	79	3,988 R	62.0%	37.5%	62.3%	37.7%
32,870	OTTAWA	13,505	7,666	5,781	58	1,885 R	56.8%	42.8%	57.0%	43.0%
15,310	PAWNEE	6,928	4,699	2,165	64	2,534 R	67.8%	31.3%	68.5%	31.5%
62,435	PAYNE	28,648	20,811	7,653	184	13,158 R	72.6%	26.7%	73.1%	26.9%

OKLAHOMA

PRESIDENT 1984

1980 Census Population	County	Total Vote	Republican	Democratic	Other	Rep.-Dem. Plurality	Percentage			
							Total Vote		Major Vote	
							Rep.	Dem.	Rep.	Dem.
40,524	PITTSBURG	16,760	9,778	6,860	122	2,918 R	58.3%	40.9%	58.8%	41.2%
32,598	PONTOTOC	13,907	8,301	5,526	80	2,775 R	59.7%	39.7%	60.0%	40.0%
55,239	POTTAWATOMIE	23,261	16,143	6,966	152	9,177 R	69.4%	29.9%	69.9%	30.1%
11,773	PUSHMATAHA	4,614	2,499	2,079	36	420 R	54.2%	45.1%	54.6%	45.4%
4,799	ROGER MILLS	2,243	1,550	680	13	870 R	69.1%	30.3%	69.5%	30.5%
46,436	ROGERS	22,288	16,137	6,013	138	10,124 R	72.4%	27.0%	72.9%	27.1%
27,473	SEMINOLE	10,030	6,009	3,957	64	2,052 R	59.9%	39.5%	60.3%	39.7%
30,749	SEQUOYAH	11,300	7,042	4,202	56	2,840 R	62.3%	37.2%	62.6%	37.4%
43,419	STEPHENS	19,333	12,871	6,359	103	6,512 R	66.6%	32.9%	66.9%	33.1%
17,727	TEXAS	7,039	5,968	1,033	38	4,935 R	84.8%	14.7%	85.2%	14.8%
12,398	TILLMAN	4,326	2,637	1,674	15	963 R	61.0%	38.7%	61.2%	38.8%
470,593	TULSA	218,872	159,549	58,274	1,049	101,275 R	72.9%	26.6%	73.2%	26.8%
41,801	WAGONER	17,913	12,534	5,271	108	7,263 R	70.0%	29.4%	70.4%	29.6%
48,113	WASHINGTON	24,667	19,043	5,476	148	13,567 R	77.2%	22.2%	77.7%	22.3%
13,798	WASHITA	5,430	3,847	1,547	36	2,300 R	70.8%	28.5%	71.3%	28.7%
10,923	WOODS	5,018	3,741	1,231	46	2,510 R	74.6%	24.5%	75.2%	24.8%
21,172	WOODWARD	8,063	6,376	1,647	40	4,729 R	79.1%	20.4%	79.5%	20.5%
3,025,290	TOTAL	1,255,676	861,530	385,080	9,066	476,450 R	68.6%	30.7%	69.1%	30.9%

OKLAHOMA

SENATOR 1984

1980 Census Population	County	Total Vote	Republican	Democratic	Other	Rep.-Dem. Plurality	Percentage Total Vote Rep.	Dem.	Major Vote Rep.	Dem.
18,575	ADAIR	6,453	1,769	4,646	38	2,877 D	27.4%	72.0%	27.6%	72.4%
7,077	ALFALFA	3,483	636	2,829	18	2,193 D	18.3%	81.2%	18.4%	81.6%
12,748	ATOKA	4,280	517	3,714	49	3,197 D	12.1%	86.8%	12.2%	87.8%
6,806	BEAVER	3,062	911	2,124	27	1,213 D	29.8%	69.4%	30.0%	70.0%
19,243	BECKHAM	7,282	1,462	5,771	49	4,309 D	20.1%	79.3%	20.2%	79.8%
13,443	BLAINE	5,385	1,185	4,173	27	2,988 D	22.0%	77.5%	22.1%	77.9%
30,535	BRYAN	11,245	1,447	9,720	78	8,273 D	12.9%	86.4%	13.0%	87.0%
30,905	CADDO	11,093	1,749	9,302	42	7,553 D	15.8%	83.9%	15.8%	84.2%
56,452	CANADIAN	25,525	7,470	17,906	149	10,436 D	29.3%	70.2%	29.4%	70.6%
43,610	CARTER	17,077	3,315	13,657	105	10,342 D	19.4%	80.0%	19.5%	80.5%
30,684	CHEROKEE	12,685	2,722	9,866	97	7,144 D	21.5%	77.8%	21.6%	78.4%
17,203	CHOCTAW	5,760	675	5,029	56	4,354 D	11.7%	87.3%	11.8%	88.2%
3,648	CIMARRON	1,642	489	1,130	23	641 D	29.8%	68.8%	30.2%	69.8%
133,173	CLEVELAND	58,983	16,369	41,836	778	25,467 D	27.8%	70.9%	28.1%	71.9%
6,041	COAL	2,448	236	2,187	25	1,951 D	9.6%	89.3%	9.7%	90.3%
112,456	COMANCHE	29,003	7,835	20,983	185	13,148 D	27.0%	72.3%	27.2%	72.8%
7,338	COTTON	2,972	515	2,441	16	1,926 D	17.3%	82.1%	17.4%	82.6%
15,014	CRAIG	5,807	1,110	4,644	53	3,534 D	19.1%	80.0%	19.3%	80.7%
59,016	CREEK	21,511	4,974	16,385	152	11,411 D	23.1%	76.2%	23.3%	76.7%
25,995	CUSTER	10,591	2,139	8,408	44	6,269 D	20.2%	79.4%	20.3%	79.7%
23,946	DELAWARE	10,016	2,489	7,451	76	4,962 D	24.9%	74.4%	25.0%	75.0%
5,922	DEWEY	2,689	411	2,265	13	1,854 D	15.3%	84.2%	15.4%	84.6%
5,596	ELLIS	2,406	493	1,902	11	1,409 D	20.5%	79.1%	20.6%	79.4%
62,820	GARFIELD	24,472	6,755	17,547	170	10,792 D	27.6%	71.7%	27.8%	72.2%
27,856	GARVIN	11,305	1,705	9,520	80	7,815 D	15.1%	84.2%	15.2%	84.8%
39,490	GRADY	15,287	3,144	12,038	105	8,894 D	20.6%	78.7%	20.7%	79.3%
6,518	GRANT	3,221	661	2,541	19	1,880 D	20.5%	78.9%	20.6%	79.4%
7,028	GREEN	2,843	436	2,396	11	1,960 D	15.3%	84.3%	15.4%	84.6%
4,519	HARMON	1,767	167	1,593	7	1,426 D	9.5%	90.2%	9.5%	90.5%
4,715	HARPER	2,079	492	1,570	17	1,078 D	23.7%	75.5%	23.9%	76.1%
11,010	HASKELL	4,813	732	4,045	36	3,313 D	15.2%	84.0%	15.3%	84.7%
14,338	HUGHES	5,478	586	4,861	31	4,275 D	10.7%	88.7%	10.8%	89.2%
30,356	JACKSON	8,537	1,482	7,025	30	5,543 D	17.4%	82.3%	17.4%	82.6%
8,183	JEFFERSON	3,004	432	2,548	24	2,116 D	14.4%	84.8%	14.5%	85.5%
10,356	JOHNSTON	3,912	393	3,478	41	3,085 D	10.0%	88.9%	10.2%	89.8%
49,852	KAY	22,185	5,456	16,583	146	11,127 D	24.6%	74.7%	24.8%	75.2%
14,187	KINGFISHER	6,466	1,359	5,072	35	3,713 D	21.0%	78.4%	21.1%	78.9%
12,711	KIOWA	4,890	612	4,256	22	3,644 D	12.5%	87.0%	12.6%	87.4%
9,840	LATIMER	3,993	662	3,292	39	2,630 D	16.6%	82.4%	16.7%	83.3%
40,698	LE FLORE	14,260	2,377	11,757	126	9,380 D	16.7%	82.4%	16.8%	83.2%
26,601	LINCOLN	11,081	2,385	8,617	79	6,232 D	21.5%	77.8%	21.7%	78.3%
26,881	LOGAN	11,463	2,839	8,513	111	5,674 D	24.8%	74.3%	25.0%	75.0%
7,469	LOVE	3,060	507	2,533	20	2,026 D	16.6%	82.8%	16.7%	83.3%
20,291	MCCLAIN	8,299	1,712	6,515	72	4,803 D	20.6%	78.5%	20.8%	79.2%
36,151	MCCURTAIN	9,786	1,674	7,957	155	6,283 D	17.1%	81.3%	17.4%	82.6%
15,562	MCINTOSH	6,905	1,103	5,760	42	4,657 D	16.0%	83.4%	16.1%	83.9%
8,772	MAJOR	3,875	1,053	2,802	20	1,749 D	27.2%	72.3%	27.3%	72.7%
10,550	MARSHALL	4,440	578	3,827	35	3,249 D	13.0%	86.2%	13.1%	86.9%
32,261	MAYES	13,250	2,764	10,381	105	7,617 D	20.9%	78.3%	21.0%	79.0%
12,147	MURRAY	5,286	666	4,569	51	3,903 D	12.6%	86.4%	12.7%	87.3%
66,939	MUSKOGEE	26,108	4,858	21,067	183	16,209 D	18.6%	80.7%	18.7%	81.3%
11,573	NOBLE	5,083	1,028	4,017	38	2,989 D	20.2%	79.0%	20.4%	79.6%
11,486	NOWATA	4,630	988	3,617	25	2,629 D	21.3%	78.1%	21.5%	78.5%
11,125	OKFUSKEE	4,131	730	3,369	32	2,639 D	17.7%	81.6%	17.8%	82.2%
568,933	OKLAHOMA	200,944	49,484	148,221	3,239	98,737 D	24.6%	73.8%	25.0%	75.0%
39,169	OKMULGEE	15,397	2,427	12,876	94	10,449 D	15.8%	83.6%	15.9%	84.1%
39,327	OSAGE	15,550	3,173	12,280	97	9,107 D	20.4%	79.0%	20.5%	79.5%
32,870	OTTAWA	12,698	2,514	10,084	100	7,570 D	19.8%	79.4%	20.0%	80.0%
15,310	PAWNEE	6,786	1,511	5,235	40	3,724 D	22.3%	77.1%	22.4%	77.6%
62,435	PAYNE	27,853	7,007	20,405	441	13,398 D	25.2%	73.3%	25.6%	74.4%

OKLAHOMA

SENATOR 1984

1980 Census Population	County	Total Vote	Republican	Democratic	Other	Rep.-Dem. Plurality	Percentage			
							Total Vote		Major Vote	
							Rep.	Dem.	Rep.	Dem.
40,524	PITTSBURG	16,401	3,003	13,250	148	10,247 D	18.3%	80.8%	18.5%	81.5%
32,598	PONTOTOC	13,666	1,881	11,687	98	9,806 D	13.8%	85.5%	13.9%	86.1%
55,239	POTTAWATOMIE	22,920	4,734	18,043	143	13,309 D	20.7%	78.7%	20.8%	79.2%
11,773	PUSHMATAHA	4,390	569	3,769	52	3,200 D	13.0%	85.9%	13.1%	86.9%
4,799	ROGER MILLS	2,164	343	1,810	11	1,467 D	15.9%	83.6%	15.9%	84.1%
46,436	ROGERS	21,364	5,673	15,550	141	9,877 D	26.6%	72.8%	26.7%	73.3%
27,473	SEMINOLE	9,939	1,194	8,704	41	7,510 D	12.0%	87.6%	12.1%	87.9%
30,749	SEQUOYAH	10,814	2,493	8,234	87	5,741 D	23.1%	76.1%	23.2%	76.8%
43,419	STEPHENS	18,654	3,846	14,676	132	10,830 D	20.6%	78.7%	20.8%	79.2%
17,727	TEXAS	6,645	2,162	4,423	60	2,261 D	32.5%	66.6%	32.8%	67.2%
12,398	TILLMAN	4,241	652	3,574	15	2,922 D	15.4%	84.3%	15.4%	84.6%
470,593	TULSA	211,653	60,989	148,818	1,846	87,829 D	28.8%	70.3%	29.1%	70.9%
41,801	WAGONER	16,854	4,598	12,129	127	7,531 D	27.3%	72.0%	27.5%	72.5%
48,113	WASHINGTON	23,752	7,407	16,219	126	8,812 D	31.2%	68.3%	31.4%	68.6%
13,798	WASHITA	5,244	923	4,292	29	3,369 D	17.6%	81.8%	17.7%	82.3%
10,923	WOODS	4,881	1,107	3,738	36	2,631 D	22.7%	76.6%	22.8%	77.2%
21,172	WOODWARD	7,820	1,694	6,079	47	4,385 D	21.7%	77.7%	21.8%	78.2%
3,025,290	TOTAL	1,197,937	280,638	906,131	11,168	625,493 D	23.4%	75.6%	23.6%	76.4%

OKLAHOMA

CONGRESS

CD	Year	Total Vote	Republican Vote	Republican Candidate	Democratic Vote	Democratic Candidate	Other Vote	Rep.-Dem. Plurality	Total Vote Rep.	Total Vote Dem.	Major Vote Rep.	Major Vote Dem.
1	1984	218,093	103,098	KEATING, FRANK	113,919	JONES, JAMES R.	1,076	10,821 D	47.3%	52.2%	47.5%	52.5%
1	1982	141,083	64,704	FREEMAN, RICHARD C.	76,379	JONES, JAMES R.		11,675 D	45.9%	54.1%	45.9%	54.1%
2	1984	200,013	51,889	RICE, GARY K.	148,124	SYNAR, MIKE		96,235 D	25.9%	74.1%	25.9%	74.1%
2	1982	154,193	42,298	STRIEGEL, LOU	111,895	SYNAR, MIKE		69,597 D	27.4%	72.6%	27.4%	72.6%
3	1984	177,418	39,454	MILLER, PATRICK K.	137,964	WATKINS, WES		98,510 D	22.2%	77.8%	22.2%	77.8%
3	1982	148,005	26,335	MILLER, PATRICK K.	121,670	WATKINS, WES		95,335 D	17.8%	82.2%	17.8%	82.2%
4	1984	172,039	60,844	SMITH, JERRY	109,447	MCCURDY, DAVE	1,748	48,603 D	35.4%	63.6%	35.7%	64.3%
4	1982	129,504	44,351	RUTLEDGE, HOWARD	84,205	MCCURDY, DAVE	948	39,854 D	34.2%	65.0%	34.5%	65.5%
5	1984	178,726	135,167	EDWARDS, M. H.	39,089	GREESON, ALLEN	4,470	96,078 R	75.6%	21.9%	77.6%	22.4%
5	1982	147,209	98,979	EDWARDS, M. H.	42,453	LANE, DAN	5,777	56,526 R	67.2%	28.8%	70.0%	30.0%
6	1984	164,595	67,601	DODD, CRAIG	96,994	ENGLISH, GLENN		29,393 D	41.1%	58.9%	41.1%	58.9%
6	1982	136,330	33,519	MOORE, ED	102,811	ENGLISH, GLENN		69,292 D	24.6%	75.4%	24.6%	75.4%

OKLAHOMA

1984 GENERAL ELECTION

President   Other vote was Bergland (Libertarian).

Senator   Other vote was Murphy (Libertarian).

Congress   Other vote was Neal (Libertarian) in CD 1; Mobley (Libertarian) in CD 4; Robinson (Libertarian) in CD 5.

1984 PRIMARIES

AUGUST 28 REPUBLICAN

Senator   46,933 George L. Mothershed; 39,581 Will E. Crozier; 32,901 Gar Graham.

Congress   Unopposed in three CD's. Contested as follows:

CD 1   24,682 Frank Keating; 11,589 Tom Cantrell.
CD 2   9,498 Gary K. Rice; 7,971 Vickie L. Cleveland.
CD 5   33,790 M. H. Edwards; 4,236 Elizabeth B. Graham.

AUGUST 28 DEMOCRATIC

Senator   432,534 David L. Boren; 48,761 Marshall Luse.

Congress   Unopposed in five CD's. Contested as follows:

CD 2   87,363 Mike Synar; 11,493 Arlie J. Nixon.

SEPTEMBER 18 REPUBLICAN RUN-OFF

Senator   101,194 Will E. Crozier; 100,995 George L. Mothershed.

OREGON

GOVERNOR
Victor Atiyeh (R). Re-elected 1982 to a four-year term. Previously elected 1978.

SENATORS
Mark Hatfield (R). Re-elected 1984 to a six-year term. Previously elected 1978, 1972, 1966.

Robert W. Packwood (R). Re-elected 1980 to a six-year term. Previously elected 1974, 1968.

REPRESENTATIVES
1. Les AuCoin (D)
2. Robert F. Smith (R)
3. Ron Wyden (D)
4. James Weaver (D)
5. Denny Smith (R)

POSTWAR VOTE FOR GOVERNOR

Year		Total Vote	Republican Vote	Candidate	Democratic Vote	Candidate	Other Vote	Rep.-Dem. Plurality	Total Vote Rep.	Dem.	Major Vote Rep.	Dem.
1982		1,042,009	639,841	Atiyeh, Victor	374,316	Kulongoski, Ted	27,852	265,525 R	61.4%	35.9%	63.1%	36.9%
1978		911,143	498,452	Atiyeh, Victor	409,411	Straub, Robert W.	3,280	89,041 R	54.7%	44.9%	54.9%	45.1%
1974		770,574	324,751	Atiyeh, Victor	444,812	Straub, Robert W.	1,011	120,061 D	42.1%	57.7%	42.2%	57.8%
1970		666,394	369,964	McCall, Tom	293,892	Straub, Robert W.	2,538	76,072 R	55.5%	44.1%	55.7%	44.3%
1966		682,862	377,346	McCall, Tom	305,008	Straub, Robert W.	508	72,338 R	55.3%	44.7%	55.3%	44.7%
1962		637,407	345,497	Hatfield, Mark	265,359	Thornton, Robert Y.	26,551	80,138 R	54.2%	41.6%	56.6%	43.4%
1958		599,994	331,900	Hatfield, Mark	267,934	Holmes, Robert D.	160	63,966 R	55.3%	44.7%	55.3%	44.7%
1956	s	731,279	361,840	Smith, Elmo E.	369,439	Holmes, Robert D.	—	7,599 D	49.5%	50.5%	49.5%	50.5%
1954		566,701	322,522	Patterson, Paul	244,179	Carson, Joseph K.	—	78,343 R	56.9%	43.1%	56.9%	43.1%
1950		505,910	334,160	McKay, Douglas	171,750	Flegel, Austin F.	—	162,410 R	66.1%	33.9%	66.1%	33.9%
1948	s	509,633	271,295	McKay, Douglas	226,958	Wallace, Lew	11,380	44,337 R	53.2%	44.5%	54.4%	45.6%
1946		344,155	237,681	Snell, Earl	106,474	Donaugh, Carl C.	—	131,207 R	69.1%	30.9%	69.1%	30.9%

The 1956 and 1948 elections were for short terms to fill vacancies.

POSTWAR VOTE FOR SENATOR

Year	Total Vote	Republican Vote	Candidate	Democratic Vote	Candidate	Other Vote	Rep.-Dem. Plurality	Total Vote Rep.	Dem.	Major Vote Rep.	Dem.
1984	1,214,735	808,152	Hatfield, Mark	406,122	Hendriksen, Margie	461	402,030 R	66.5%	33.4%	66.6%	33.4%
1980	1,140,494	594,290	Packwood, Robert W.	501,963	Kulongoski, Ted	44,241	92,327 R	52.1%	44.0%	54.2%	45.8%
1978	892,518	550,165	Hatfield, Mark	341,616	Cook, Vernon	737	208,549 R	61.6%	38.3%	61.7%	38.3%
1974	766,414	420,984	Packwood, Robert W.	338,591	Roberts, Betty	6,839	82,393 R	54.9%	44.2%	55.4%	44.6%
1972	920,833	494,671	Hatfield, Mark	425,036	Morse, Wayne L.	1,126	69,635 R	53.7%	46.2%	53.8%	46.2%
1968	814,176	408,646	Packwood, Robert W.	405,353	Morse, Wayne L.	177	3,293 R	50.2%	49.8%	50.2%	49.8%
1966	685,067	354,391	Hatfield, Mark	330,374	Duncan, Robert B.	302	24,017 R	51.7%	48.2%	51.8%	48.2%
1962	636,558	291,587	Unander, Sig	344,716	Morse, Wayne L.	255	53,129 D	45.8%	54.2%	45.8%	54.2%
1960	755,875	343,009	Smith, Elmo E.	412,757	Neuberger, Maurine	109	69,748 D	45.4%	54.6%	45.4%	54.6%
1956	732,254	335,405	McKay, Douglas	396,849	Morse, Wayne L.	—	61,444 D	45.8%	54.2%	45.8%	54.2%
1954	569,088	283,313	Cordon, Guy	285,775	Neuberger, Richard L.	—	2,462 D	49.8%	50.2%	49.8%	50.2%
1950	503,455	376,510	Morse, Wayne L.	116,780	Latourette, Howard	10,165	259,730 R	74.8%	23.2%	76.3%	23.7%
1948	498,570	299,295	Cordon, Guy	199,275	Wilson, Manley J.	—	100,020 R	60.0%	40.0%	60.0%	40.0%

OREGON

Districts Established July 28, 1981

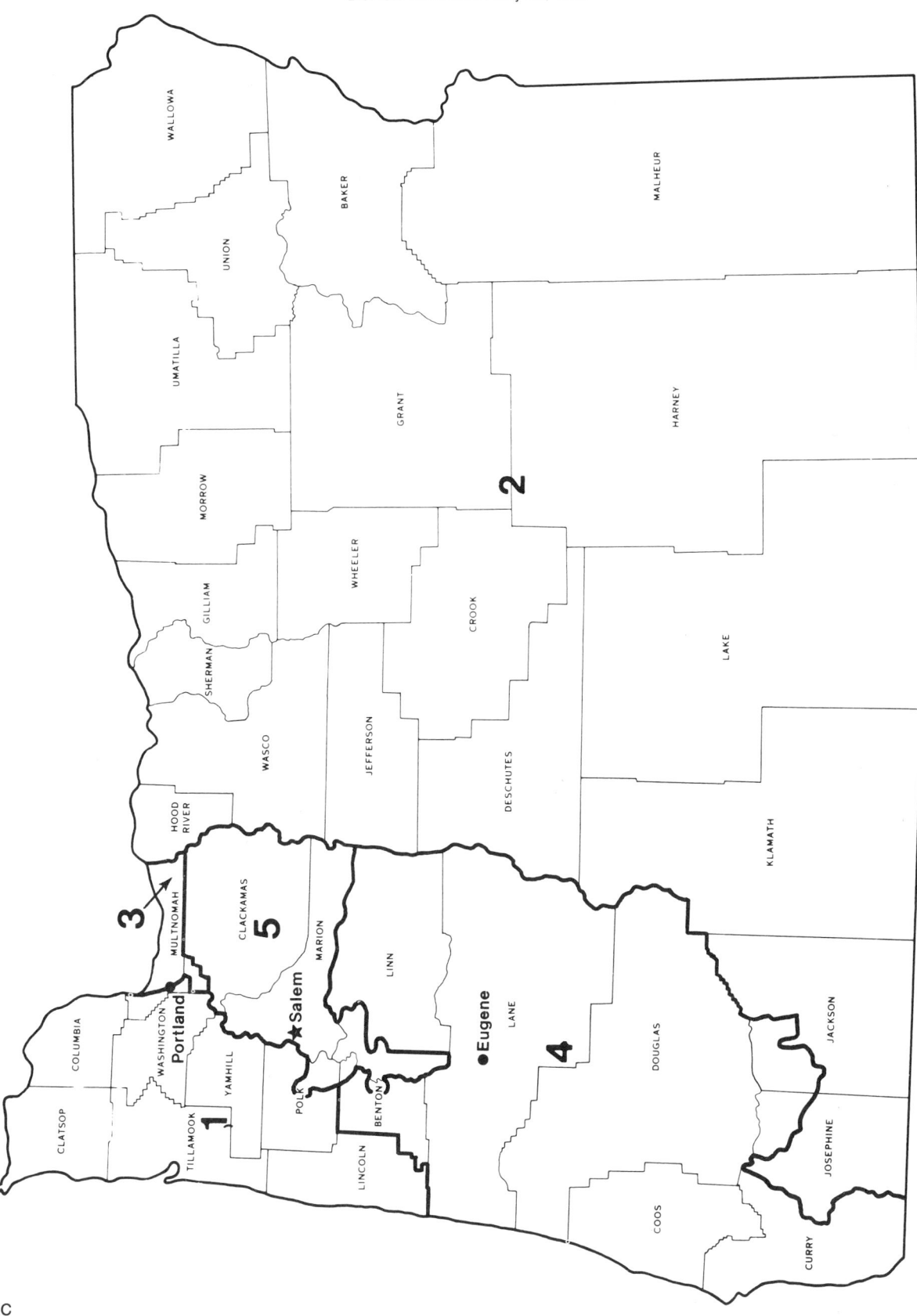

OREGON

PRESIDENT 1984

1980 Census Population	County	Total Vote	Republican	Democratic	Other	Rep.-Dem. Plurality	Percentage Total Vote Rep.	Dem.	Major Vote Rep.	Dem.
16,134	BAKER	7,812	5,204	2,591	17	2,613 R	66.6%	33.2%	66.8%	33.2%
68,211	BENTON	34,062	17,836	16,073	153	1,763 R	52.4%	47.2%	52.6%	47.4%
241,919	CLACKAMAS	116,173	68,630	47,254	289	21,376 R	59.1%	40.7%	59.2%	40.8%
32,489	CLATSOP	15,085	7,522	7,525	38	3 D	49.9%	49.9%	50.0%	50.0%
35,646	COLUMBIA	16,105	7,811	8,219	75	408 D	48.5%	51.0%	48.7%	51.3%
64,047	COOS	27,339	13,637	13,582	120	55 R	49.9%	49.7%	50.1%	49.9%
13,091	CROOK	6,064	3,773	2,268	23	1,505 R	62.2%	37.4%	62.5%	37.5%
16,992	CURRY	8,815	5,363	3,423	29	1,940 R	60.8%	38.8%	61.0%	39.0%
62,142	DESCHUTES	31,066	19,323	11,671	72	7,652 R	62.2%	37.6%	62.3%	37.7%
93,748	DOUGLAS	39,996	25,243	14,609	144	10,634 R	63.1%	36.5%	63.3%	36.7%
2,057	GILLIAM	1,073	700	369	4	331 R	65.2%	34.4%	65.5%	34.5%
8,210	GRANT	4,041	2,695	1,344	2	1,351 R	66.7%	33.3%	66.7%	33.3%
8,314	HARNEY	3,512	2,197	1,290	25	907 R	62.6%	36.7%	63.0%	37.0%
15,835	HOOD RIVER	7,571	4,531	3,022	18	1,509 R	59.8%	39.9%	60.0%	40.0%
132,456	JACKSON	61,359	37,895	23,230	234	14,665 R	61.8%	37.9%	62.0%	38.0%
11,599	JEFFERSON	5,216	3,283	1,920	13	1,363 R	62.9%	36.8%	63.1%	36.9%
58,855	JOSEPHINE	28,062	19,470	8,539	53	10,931 R	69.4%	30.4%	69.5%	30.5%
59,117	KLAMATH	25,335	17,686	7,575	74	10,111 R	69.8%	29.9%	70.0%	30.0%
7,532	LAKE	3,653	2,466	1,184	3	1,282 R	67.5%	32.4%	67.6%	32.4%
275,226	LANE	125,852	61,493	63,999	360	2,506 D	48.9%	50.9%	49.0%	51.0%
35,264	LINCOLN	17,804	9,110	8,637	57	473 R	51.2%	48.5%	51.3%	48.7%
89,495	LINN	39,699	23,463	16,161	75	7,302 R	59.1%	40.7%	59.2%	40.8%
26,896	MALHEUR	11,071	8,441	2,611	19	5,830 R	76.2%	23.6%	76.4%	23.6%
204,692	MARION	91,209	54,535	36,440	234	18,095 R	59.8%	40.0%	59.9%	40.1%
7,519	MORROW	3,397	2,130	1,254	13	876 R	62.7%	36.9%	62.9%	37.1%
562,640	MULTNOMAH	265,539	119,932	144,179	1,428	24,247 D	45.2%	54.3%	45.4%	54.6%
45,203	POLK	21,432	12,678	8,709	45	3,969 R	59.2%	40.6%	59.3%	40.7%
2,172	SHERMAN	1,227	828	398	1	430 R	67.5%	32.4%	67.5%	32.5%
21,164	TILLAMOOK	10,308	5,267	4,988	53	279 R	51.1%	48.4%	51.4%	48.6%
58,861	UMATILLA	22,514	14,211	8,246	57	5,965 R	63.1%	36.6%	63.3%	36.7%
23,921	UNION	10,829	6,645	4,134	50	2,511 R	61.4%	38.2%	61.6%	38.4%
7,273	WALLOWA	3,831	2,619	1,204	8	1,415 R	68.4%	31.4%	68.5%	31.5%
21,732	WASCO	12,472	6,905	5,526	41	1,379 R	55.4%	44.3%	55.5%	44.5%
245,808	WASHINGTON	120,896	75,877	44,602	417	31,275 R	62.8%	36.9%	63.0%	37.0%
1,513	WHEELER	757	504	253		251 R	66.6%	33.4%	66.6%	33.4%
55,332	YAMHILL	25,351	15,797	9,450	104	6,347 R	62.3%	37.3%	62.6%	37.4%
2,633,105	TOTAL	1,226,527	685,700	536,479	4,348	149,221 R	55.9%	43.7%	56.1%	43.9%

OREGON

SENATOR 1984

1980 Census Population	County	Total Vote	Republican	Democratic	Other	Rep.-Dem. Plurality	Percentage Total Vote Rep.	Dem.	Major Vote Rep.	Dem.
16,134	BAKER	7,773	5,279	2,490	4	2,789 R	67.9%	32.0%	67.9%	32.1%
68,211	BENTON	33,350	22,723	10,620	7	12,103 R	68.1%	31.8%	68.1%	31.9%
241,919	CLACKAMAS	116,719	80,006	36,689	24	43,317 R	68.5%	31.4%	68.6%	31.4%
32,489	CLATSOP	14,779	10,221	4,556	2	5,665 R	69.2%	30.8%	69.2%	30.8%
35,646	COLUMBIA	16,115	9,891	6,223	1	3,668 R	61.4%	38.6%	61.4%	38.6%
64,047	COOS	27,338	16,429	10,901	8	5,528 R	60.1%	39.9%	60.1%	39.9%
13,091	CROOK	6,060	3,949	2,110	1	1,839 R	65.2%	34.8%	65.2%	34.8%
16,992	CURRY	8,683	5,646	3,032	5	2,614 R	65.0%	34.9%	65.1%	34.9%
62,142	DESCHUTES	30,731	21,108	9,621	2	11,487 R	68.7%	31.3%	68.7%	31.3%
93,748	DOUGLAS	39,308	25,158	14,143	7	11,015 R	64.0%	36.0%	64.0%	36.0%
2,057	GILLIAM	1,072	775	297		478 R	72.3%	27.7%	72.3%	27.7%
8,210	GRANT	4,018	2,595	1,421	2	1,174 R	64.6%	35.4%	64.6%	35.4%
8,314	HARNEY	3,506	2,288	1,213	5	1,075 R	65.3%	34.6%	65.4%	34.6%
15,835	HOOD RIVER	7,499	5,254	2,245		3,009 R	70.1%	29.9%	70.1%	29.9%
132,456	JACKSON	59,825	41,370	18,432	23	22,938 R	69.2%	30.8%	69.2%	30.8%
11,599	JEFFERSON	5,259	3,473	1,784	2	1,689 R	66.0%	33.9%	66.1%	33.9%
58,855	JOSEPHINE	27,732	19,079	8,647	6	10,432 R	68.8%	31.2%	68.8%	31.2%
59,117	KLAMATH	24,329	14,671	9,641	17	5,030 R	60.3%	39.6%	60.3%	39.7%
7,532	LAKE	3,666	2,353	1,313		1,040 R	64.2%	35.8%	64.2%	35.8%
275,226	LANE	124,096	78,862	45,207	27	33,655 R	63.5%	36.4%	63.6%	36.4%
35,264	LINCOLN	17,747	10,857	6,887	3	3,970 R	61.2%	38.8%	61.2%	38.8%
89,495	LINN	39,177	25,347	13,826	4	11,521 R	64.7%	35.3%	64.7%	35.3%
26,896	MALHEUR	11,051	8,634	2,416	1	6,218 R	78.1%	21.9%	78.1%	21.9%
204,692	MARION	89,472	64,389	25,073	10	39,316 R	72.0%	28.0%	72.0%	28.0%
7,519	MORROW	3,417	2,376	1,040	1	1,336 R	69.5%	30.4%	69.6%	30.4%
562,640	MULTNOMAH	264,323	162,518	101,571	234	60,947 R	61.5%	38.4%	61.5%	38.5%
45,203	POLK	20,737	14,991	5,744	2	9,247 R	72.3%	27.7%	72.3%	27.7%
2,172	SHERMAN	1,242	871	370	1	501 R	70.1%	29.8%	70.2%	29.8%
21,164	TILLAMOOK	10,380	6,607	3,772	1	2,835 R	63.7%	36.3%	63.7%	36.3%
58,861	UMATILLA	21,468	15,109	6,358	1	8,751 R	70.4%	29.6%	70.4%	29.6%
23,921	UNION	10,665	7,629	3,035	1	4,594 R	71.5%	28.5%	71.5%	28.5%
7,273	WALLOWA	3,772	2,620	1,152		1,468 R	69.5%	30.5%	69.5%	30.5%
21,732	WASCO	12,591	8,166	4,419	6	3,747 R	64.9%	35.1%	64.9%	35.1%
245,808	WASHINGTON	120,905	88,595	32,287	23	56,308 R	73.3%	26.7%	73.3%	26.7%
1,513	WHEELER	774	557	217		340 R	72.0%	28.0%	72.0%	28.0%
55,332	YAMHILL	25,156	17,756	7,370	30	10,386 R	70.6%	29.3%	70.7%	29.3%
2,633,105	TOTAL	1,214,735	808,152	406,122	461	402,030 R	66.5%	33.4%	66.6%	33.4%

OREGON

CONGRESS

CD	Year	Total Vote	Republican Vote	Candidate	Democratic Vote	Candidate	Other Vote	Rep.-Dem. Plurality	Percentage Total Vote Rep.	Dem.	Major Vote Rep.	Dem.
1	1984	260,667	122,247	MOSHOFSKY, BILL	138,393	AUCOIN, LES	27	16,146 D	46.9%	53.1%	46.9%	53.1%
1	1982	220,378	101,720	MOSHOFSKY, BILL	118,638	AUCOIN, LES	20	16,918 D	46.2%	53.8%	46.2%	53.8%
2	1984	232,826	132,649	SMITH, ROBERT F.	100,152	WILLIS, LARRYANN	25	32,497 R	57.0%	43.0%	57.0%	43.0%
2	1982	192,427	106,912	SMITH, ROBERT F.	85,495	WILLIS, LARRYANN	20	21,417 R	55.6%	44.4%	55.6%	44.4%
3	1984	239,897	66,394	DAVIS, DREW	173,438	WYDEN, RON	65	107,044 D	27.7%	72.3%	27.7%	72.3%
3	1982	203,662	44,162	PHELAN, THOMAS H.	159,416	WYDEN, RON	84	115,254 D	21.7%	78.3%	21.7%	78.3%
4	1984	230,687	96,487	LONG, BRUCE	134,190	WEAVER, JAMES	10	37,703 D	41.8%	58.2%	41.8%	58.2%
4	1982	195,524	80,054	ANTHONY, ROSS	115,448	WEAVER, JAMES	22	35,394 D	40.9%	59.0%	40.9%	59.1%
5	1984	239,414	130,424	SMITH, DENNY	108,919	MCFARLAND, RUTH	71	21,505 R	54.5%	45.5%	54.5%	45.5%
5	1982	202,901	103,906	SMITH, DENNY	98,952	MCFARLAND, RUTH	43	4,954 R	51.2%	48.8%	51.2%	48.8%

OREGON

1984 GENERAL ELECTION

President   Other vote was scattered.

Senator   Other vote was scattered.

Congress   Other vote was scattered in all CD's.

PRIMARIES

MAY 15 REPUBLICAN

Senator   214,114 Mark Hatfield; 26,848 John T. Schiess; 18,590 Sherry Reynolds; 12,662 Ralph H. Preston; 423 scattered.

Congress   Unopposed in CD 2. Contested as follows:

CD   1   50,541 Bill Moshofsky; 8,913 George R. Vernon; 206 scattered.
CD   3   25,702 Drew Davis; 10,439 Thomas H. Phelan; 1,238 scattered.
CD   4   21,322 Bruce Long; 7,152 James H. Peterson; 6,399 Gene Arvidson; 5,743 John D. Newkirk; 55 scattered.
CD   5   45,785 Denny Smith; 13,392 Josh Reese; 101 scattered.

MAY 15 DEMOCRATIC

Senator   249,152 Margie Hendriksen; 79,317 Sam Kahl; 1,688 scattered.

Congress   Unopposed in four CD's. Contested as follows:

CD   5   28,901 Ruth McFarland; 21,435 Peter C. Courtney; 10,367 Jim Beall; 9,046 Walter F. Brown; 40 scattered.

PENNSYLVANIA

GOVERNOR
Richard L. Thornburgh (R). Re-elected 1982 to a four-year term. Previously elected 1978.

SENATORS
H. John Heinz (R). Re-elected 1982 to a six-year term. Previously elected 1976.

Arlen Specter (R). Elected 1980 to a six-year term.

REPRESENTATIVES
1. Thomas M. Foglietta (D)
2. William H. Gray (D)
3. Robert A. Borski (D)
4. Joseph P. Kolter (D)
5. Richard T. Schulze (R)
6. Gus Yatron (D)
7. Robert W. Edgar (D)
8. Peter H. Kostmayer (D)
9. E. G. Shuster (R)
10. Joseph M. McDade (R)
11. Paul E. Kanjorski (D)
12. John P. Murtha (D)
13. R. Lawrence Coughlin (R)
14. William J. Coyne (D)
15. Donald L. Ritter (R)
16. Robert S. Walker (R)
17. George W. Gekas (R)
18. Douglas Walgren (D)
19. William F. Goodling (R)
20. Joseph M. Gaydos (D)
21. Thomas J. Ridge (R)
22. Austin J. Murphy (D)
23. William F. Clinger (R)

POSTWAR VOTE FOR GOVERNOR

Year	Total Vote	Republican Vote	Republican Candidate	Democratic Vote	Democratic Candidate	Other Vote	Rep.-Dem. Plurality	Total Vote Rep.	Total Vote Dem.	Major Vote Rep.	Major Vote Dem.
1982	3,683,985	1,872,784	Thornburgh, Richard L.	1,772,353	Ertel, Allen E.	38,848	100,431 R	50.8%	48.1%	51.4%	48.6%
1978	3,741,969	1,966,042	Thornburgh, Richard L.	1,737,888	Flaherty, Peter	38,039	228,154 R	52.5%	46.4%	53.1%	46.9%
1974	3,491,234	1,578,917	Lewis, Andrew L.	1,878,252	Shapp, Milton	34,065	299,335 D	45.2%	53.8%	45.7%	54.3%
1970	3,700,060	1,542,854	Broderick, Raymond	2,043,029	Shapp, Milton	114,177	500,175 D	41.7%	55.2%	43.0%	57.0%
1966	4,050,668	2,110,349	Shafer, Raymond P.	1,868,719	Shapp, Milton	71,600	241,630 R	52.1%	46.1%	53.0%	47.0%
1962	4,378,042	2,424,918	Scranton, William W.	1,938,627	Dilworth, Richardson	14,497	486,291 R	55.4%	44.3%	55.6%	44.4%
1958	3,986,918	1,948,769	McGonigle, A. T.	2,024,852	Lawrence, David	13,297	76,083 D	48.9%	50.8%	49.0%	51.0%
1954	3,720,457	1,717,070	Wood, Lloyd H.	1,996,266	Leader, George M.	7,121	279,196 D	46.2%	53.7%	46.2%	53.8%
1950	3,540,059	1,796,119	Fine, John S.	1,710,355	Dilworth, Richardson	33,585	85,764 R	50.7%	48.3%	51.2%	48.8%
1946	3,123,994	1,828,462	Duff, James H.	1,270,947	Rice, John S.	24,585	557,515 R	58.5%	40.7%	59.0%	41.0%

POSTWAR VOTE FOR SENATOR

Year	Total Vote	Republican Vote	Republican Candidate	Democratic Vote	Democratic Candidate	Other Vote	Rep.-Dem. Plurality	Total Vote Rep.	Total Vote Dem.	Major Vote Rep.	Major Vote Dem.
1982	3,604,108	2,136,418	Heinz, H. John	1,412,965	Wecht, Cyril H.	54,725	723,453 R	59.3%	39.2%	60.2%	39.8%
1980	4,418,042	2,230,404	Specter, Arlen	2,122,391	Flaherty, Peter	65,247	108,013 R	50.5%	48.0%	51.2%	48.8%
1976	4,546,353	2,381,891	Heinz, H. John	2,126,977	Green, William J., III	37,485	254,914 R	52.4%	46.8%	52.8%	47.2%
1974	3,477,812	1,843,317	Schweiker, Richard S.	1,596,121	Flaherty, Peter	38,374	247,196 R	53.0%	45.9%	53.6%	46.4%
1970	3,644,305	1,874,106	Scott, Hugh	1,653,774	Sesler, William G.	116,425	220,332 R	51.4%	45.4%	53.1%	46.9%
1968	4,624,218	2,399,762	Schweiker, Richard S.	2,117,662	Clark, Joseph S.	106,794	282,100 R	51.9%	45.8%	53.1%	46.9%
1964	4,803,835	2,429,858	Scott, Hugh	2,359,223	Blatt, Genevieve	14,754	70,635 R	50.6%	49.1%	50.7%	49.3%
1962	4,383,475	2,134,649	Van Zandt, James E.	2,238,383	Clark, Joseph S.	10,443	103,734 D	48.7%	51.1%	48.8%	51.2%
1958	3,988,622	2,042,586	Scott, Hugh	1,929,821	Leader, George M.	16,215	112,765 R	51.2%	48.4%	51.4%	48.6%
1956	4,529,874	2,250,671	Duff, James H.	2,268,641	Clark, Joseph S.	10,562	17,970 D	49.7%	50.1%	49.8%	50.2%
1952	4,519,761	2,331,034	Martin, Edward	2,168,546	Bard, Guy Kurtz	20,181	162,488 R	51.6%	48.0%	51.8%	48.2%
1950	3,548,703	1,820,400	Duff, James H.	1,694,076	Myers, Francis J.	34,227	126,324 R	51.3%	47.7%	51.8%	48.2%
1946	3,127,860	1,853,458	Martin, Edward	1,245,338	Guffey, Joseph F.	29,064	608,120 R	59.3%	39.8%	59.8%	40.2%

PENNSYLVANIA

Districts Established March 3, 1982

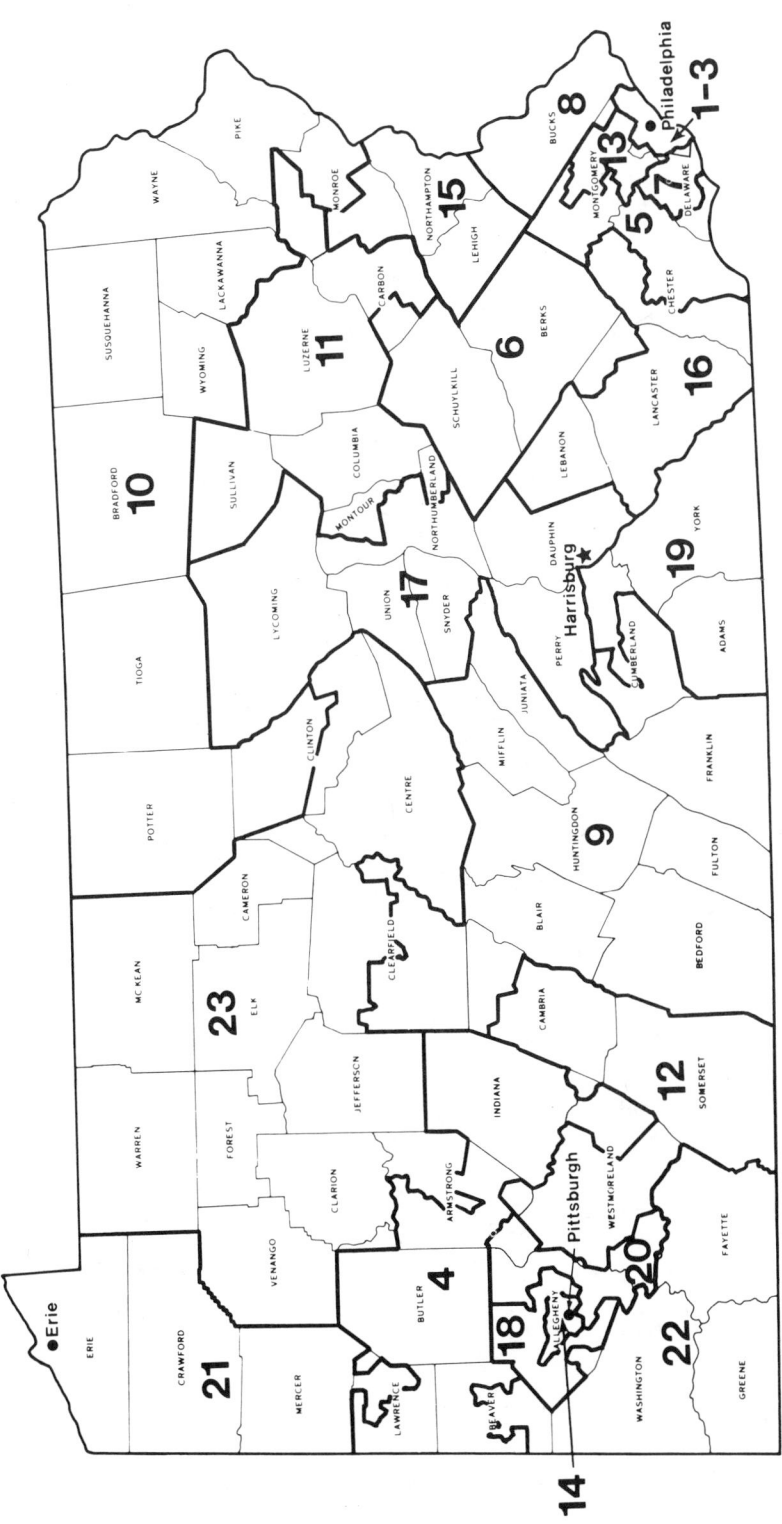

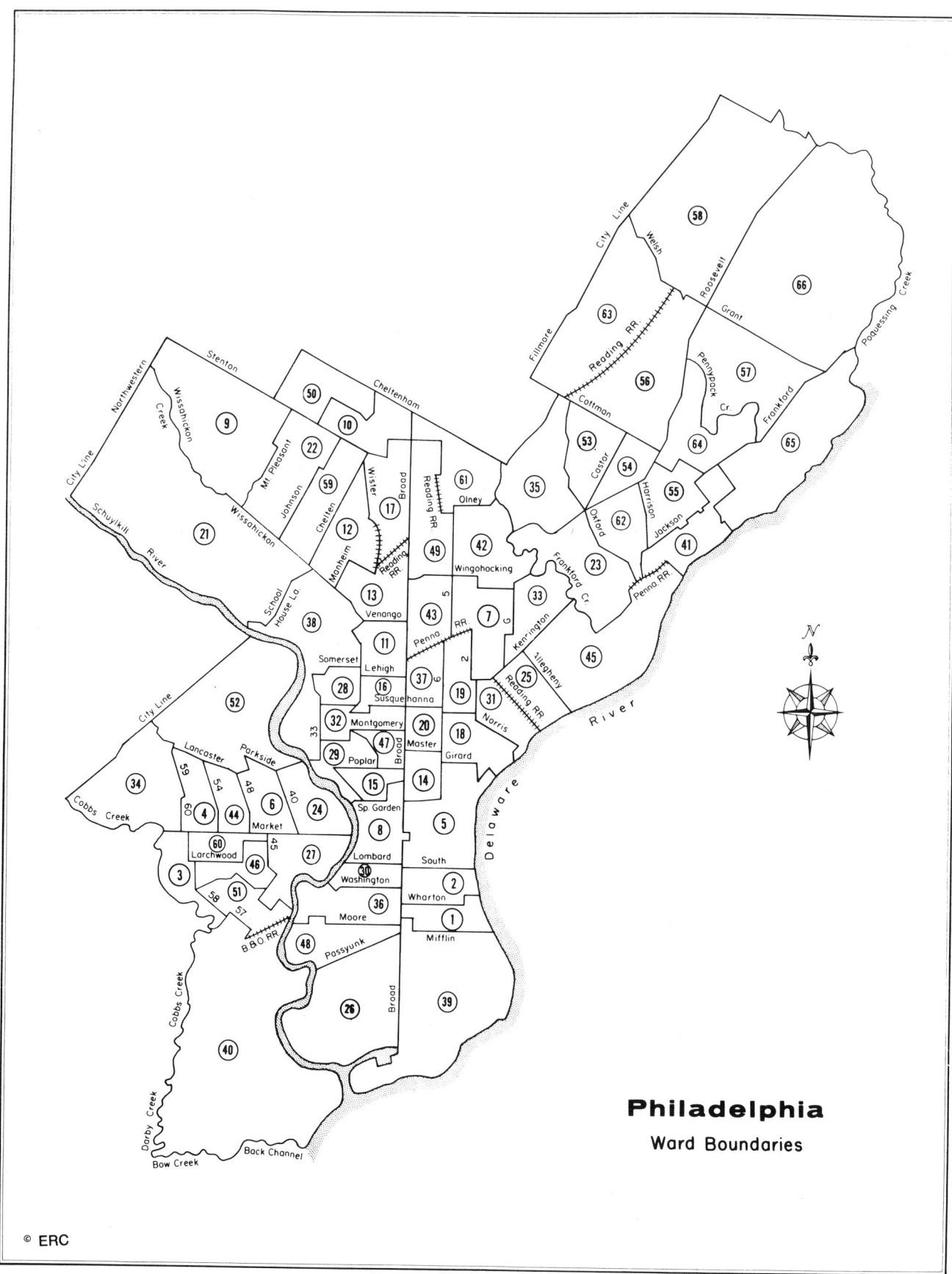

Philadelphia

Ward Boundaries

© ERC

PENNSYLVANIA

PRESIDENT 1984

1980 Census Population	County	Total Vote	Republican	Democratic	Other	Rep.-Dem. Plurality	Percentage Total Vote Rep.	Dem.	Major Vote Rep.	Dem.
68,292	ADAMS	24,174	16,786	7,289	99	9,497 R	69.4%	30.2%	69.7%	30.3%
1,450,085	ALLEGHENY	665,748	284,692	372,576	8,480	87,884 D	42.8%	56.0%	43.3%	56.7%
77,768	ARMSTRONG	28,344	13,709	14,525	110	816 D	48.4%	51.2%	48.6%	51.4%
204,441	BEAVER	87,117	32,052	54,765	300	22,713 D	36.8%	62.9%	36.9%	63.1%
46,784	BEDFORD	18,543	13,085	5,424	34	7,661 R	70.6%	29.3%	70.7%	29.3%
312,509	BERKS	113,145	74,605	37,849	691	36,756 R	65.9%	33.5%	66.3%	33.7%
136,621	BLAIR	45,945	30,104	15,651	190	14,453 R	65.5%	34.1%	65.8%	34.2%
62,919	BRADFORD	20,367	14,808	5,474	85	9,334 R	72.7%	26.9%	73.0%	27.0%
479,211	BUKCS	205,719	130,119	74,568	1,032	55,551 R	63.3%	36.2%	63.6%	36.4%
147,912	BUTLER	56,626	31,676	24,735	215	6,941 R	55.9%	43.7%	56.2%	43.8%
183,263	CAMBRIA	72,296	32,173	39,865	258	7,692 D	44.5%	55.1%	44.7%	55.3%
6,674	CAMERON	3,029	2,031	990	8	1,041 R	67.1%	32.7%	67.2%	32.8%
53,285	CARBON	19,668	10,701	8,836	131	1,865 R	54.4%	44.9%	54.8%	45.2%
112,760	CENTRE	44,236	27,802	16,194	240	11,608 R	62.8%	36.6%	63.2%	36.8%
316,660	CHESTER	131,531	92,221	38,870	440	53,351 R	70.1%	29.6%	70.3%	29.7%
43,362	CLARION	15,304	9,836	5,407	61	4,429 R	64.3%	35.3%	64.5%	35.5%
83,578	CLEARFIELD	30,769	18,653	11,963	153	6,690 R	60.6%	38.9%	60.9%	39.1%
38,971	CLINTON	11,273	6,678	4,525	70	2,153 R	59.2%	40.1%	59.6%	40.4%
61,967	COLUMBIA	22,718	14,402	8,254	62	6,148 R	63.4%	36.3%	63.6%	36.4%
88,869	CRAWFORD	33,195	20,181	12,792	222	7,389 R	60.8%	38.5%	61.2%	38.8%
178,541	CUMBERLAND	71,123	49,282	21,374	467	27,908 R	69.3%	30.1%	69.7%	30.3%
232,317	DAUPHIN	88,658	54,330	33,576	752	20,754 R	61.3%	37.9%	61.8%	38.2%
555,007	DELAWARE	261,782	161,754	98,207	1,821	63,547 R	61.8%	37.5%	62.2%	37.8%
38,338	ELK	14,007	8,470	5,486	51	2,984 R	60.5%	39.2%	60.7%	39.3%
279,780	ERIE	109,266	55,860	52,471	935	3,389 R	51.1%	48.0%	51.6%	48.4%
159,417	FAYETTE	56,547	21,314	35,098	135	13,784 D	37.7%	62.1%	37.8%	62.2%
5,072	FOREST	2,317	1,468	839	10	629 R	63.4%	36.2%	63.6%	36.4%
113,629	FRANKLIN	38,845	27,243	11,480	122	15,763 R	70.1%	29.6%	70.4%	29.6%
12,842	FULTON	4,574	3,254	1,309	11	1,945 R	71.1%	28.6%	71.3%	28.7%
40,476	GREENE	15,784	6,376	9,365	43	2,989 D	40.4%	59.3%	40.5%	59.5%
42,253	HUNTINGDON	14,691	10,220	4,430	41	5,790 R	69.6%	30.2%	69.8%	30.2%
92,281	INDIANA	34,759	18,845	15,791	123	3,054 R	54.2%	45.4%	54.4%	45.6%
48,303	JEFFERSON	17,355	11,334	5,950	71	5,384 R	65.3%	34.3%	65.6%	34.4%
19,188	JUNIATA	7,705	5,059	2,624	22	2,435 R	65.7%	34.1%	65.8%	34.2%
227,908	LACKAWANNA	95,185	48,132	45,851	1,202	2,281 R	50.6%	48.2%	51.2%	48.8%
362,346	LANCASTER	131,016	99,090	31,308	618	67,782 R	75.6%	23.9%	76.0%	24.0%
107,150	LAWRENCE	43,386	19,277	23,981	128	4,704 D	44.4%	55.3%	44.6%	55.4%
108,582	LEBANON	37,716	27,008	10,520	188	16,488 R	71.6%	27.9%	72.0%	28.0%
272,349	LEHIGH	103,537	61,799	41,089	649	20,710 R	59.7%	39.7%	60.1%	39.9%
343,079	LUZERNE	129,291	69,169	58,482	1,640	10,687 R	53.5%	45.2%	54.2%	45.8%
118,416	LYCOMING	41,895	28,498	13,147	250	15,351 R	68.0%	31.4%	68.4%	31.6%
50,635	MCKEAN	15,839	10,963	4,818	58	6,145 R	69.2%	30.4%	69.5%	30.5%
128,299	MERCER	49,303	24,211	24,658	434	447 D	49.1%	50.0%	49.5%	50.5%
46,908	MIFFLIN	14,373	9,106	5,178	89	3,928 R	63.4%	36.0%	63.7%	36.3%
69,409	MONROE	24,474	16,109	8,193	172	7,916 R	65.8%	33.5%	66.3%	33.7%
643,621	MONTGOMERY	282,666	181,426	99,741	1,499	81,685 R	64.2%	35.3%	64.5%	35.5%
16,675	MONTOUR	6,248	4,174	2,055	19	2,119 R	66.8%	32.9%	67.0%	33.0%
225,418	NORTHAMPTON	83,467	44,648	37,979	840	6,669 R	53.5%	45.5%	54.0%	46.0%
100,381	NORTHUMBERLAND	36,165	22,109	13,748	308	8,361 R	61.1%	38.0%	61.7%	38.3%
35,718	PERRY	13,113	9,365	3,692	56	5,673 R	71.4%	28.2%	71.7%	28.3%
1,688,210	PHILADELPHIA	772,102	267,178	501,369	3,555	234,191 D	34.6%	64.9%	34.8%	65.2%
18,271	PIKE	8,913	6,343	2,503	67	3,840 R	71.2%	28.1%	71.7%	28.3%
17,726	POTTER	6,984	5,164	1,789	31	3,375 R	73.9%	25.6%	74.3%	25.7%
160,630	SCHUYLKILL	63,312	37,330	25,758	224	11,572 R	59.0%	40.7%	59.2%	40.8%
33,584	SNYDER	11,391	8,968	2,383	40	6,585 R	78.7%	20.9%	79.0%	21.0%
81,243	SOMERSET	33,491	19,502	13,900	89	5,602 R	58.2%	41.5%	58.4%	41.6%
6,349	SULLIVAN	2,889	1,926	952	11	974 R	66.7%	33.0%	66.9%	33.1%
37,876	SUSQUEHANNA	15,104	10,566	4,471	67	6,095 R	70.0%	29.6%	70.3%	29.7%
40,973	TIOGA	14,644	10,532	4,060	52	6,472 R	71.9%	27.7%	72.2%	27.8%
32,870	UNION	10,579	7,792	2,747	40	5,045 R	73.7%	26.0%	73.9%	26.1%

PENNSYLVANIA

PRESIDENT 1984

1980 Census Population	County	Total Vote	Republican	Democratic	Other	Rep.-Dem. Plurality	Percentage Total Vote Rep.	Dem.	Major Vote Rep.	Dem.
64,444	VENANGO	22,725	13,507	9,114	104	4,393 R	59.4%	40.1%	59.7%	40.3%
47,449	WARREN	17,221	10,838	6,244	139	4,594 R	62.9%	36.3%	63.4%	36.6%
217,074	WASHINGTON	85,937	34,782	50,911	244	16,129 D	40.5%	59.2%	40.6%	59.4%
35,237	WAYNE	13,297	10,061	3,155	81	6,906 R	75.7%	23.7%	76.1%	23.9%
392,294	WESTMORELAND	152,464	71,377	79,906	1,181	8,529 D	46.8%	52.4%	47.2%	52.8%
26,433	WYOMING	9,769	7,230	2,518	21	4,712 R	74.0%	25.8%	74.2%	25.8%
312,963	YORK	109,247	75,020	33,359	868	41,661 R	68.7%	30.5%	69.2%	30.8%
11,863,895	TOTAL	4,844,903	2,584,323	2,228,131	32,449	356,192 R	53.3%	46.0%	53.7%	46.3%

PHILADELPHIA

PRESIDENT 1984

1980 Census Population	Ward	Total Vote	Republican	Democratic	Other	Rep.-Dem. Plurality	Percentage Total Vote Rep.	Dem.	Major Vote Rep.	Dem.
20,177	WARD 1	10,145	5,255	4,867	23	388 R	51.8%	48.0%	51.9%	48.1%
22,751	WARD 2	11,538	4,370	7,078	90	2,708 D	37.9%	61.3%	38.2%	61.8%
24,119	WARD 3	12,034	610	11,391	33	10,781 D	5.1%	94.7%	5.1%	94.9%
22,303	WARD 4	10,955	488	10,418	49	9,930 D	4.5%	95.1%	4.5%	95.5%
21,593	WARD 5	11,208	3,940	7,199	69	3,259 D	35.2%	64.2%	35.4%	64.6%
18,520	WARD 6	7,300	365	6,904	31	6,539 D	5.0%	94.6%	5.0%	95.0%
22,651	WARD 7	7,869	3,729	4,068	72	339 D	47.4%	51.7%	47.8%	52.2%
28,580	WARD 8	15,933	5,286	10,565	82	5,279 D	33.2%	66.3%	33.3%	66.7%
16,994	WARD 9	9,041	3,724	5,276	41	1,552 D	41.2%	58.4%	41.4%	58.6%
29,871	WARD 10	13,832	884	12,908	40	12,024 D	6.4%	93.3%	6.4%	93.6%
18,921	WARD 11	8,225	498	7,653	74	7,155 D	6.1%	93.0%	6.1%	93.9%
25,839	WARD 12	10,836	1,332	9,451	53	8,119 D	12.3%	87.2%	12.4%	87.6%
24,273	WARD 13	10,325	899	9,370	56	8,471 D	8.7%	90.8%	8.8%	91.2%
12,560	WARD 14	4,460	355	4,080	25	3,725 D	8.0%	91.5%	8.0%	92.0%
16,990	WARD 15	8,457	2,833	5,547	77	2,714 D	33.5%	65.6%	33.8%	66.2%
18,656	WARD 16	8,220	281	7,891	48	7,610 D	3.4%	96.0%	3.4%	96.6%
27,667	WARD 17	12,565	912	11,618	35	10,706 D	7.3%	92.5%	7.3%	92.7%
17,121	WARD 18	6,295	2,661	3,578	56	917 D	42.3%	56.8%	42.7%	57.3%
19,150	WARD 19	5,995	1,119	4,598	278	3,479 D	18.7%	76.7%	19.6%	80.4%
11,680	WARD 20	4,215	278	3,878	59	3,600 D	6.6%	92.0%	6.7%	93.3%
48,965	WARD 21	22,348	12,947	9,336	65	3,611 R	57.9%	41.8%	58.1%	41.9%
26,193	WARD 22	13,197	1,413	11,733	51	10,320 D	10.7%	88.9%	10.7%	89.3%
23,829	WARD 23	10,142	5,028	5,042	72	14 D	49.6%	49.7%	49.9%	50.1%
17,473	WARD 24	6,938	818	6,083	37	5,265 D	11.8%	87.7%	11.9%	88.1%
22,200	WARD 25	9,656	5,125	4,493	38	632 R	53.1%	46.5%	53.3%	46.7%
27,679	WARD 26	11,335	6,697	4,619	19	2,078 R	59.1%	40.7%	59.2%	40.8%
25,228	WARD 27	9,727	2,404	7,262	61	4,858 D	24.7%	74.7%	24.9%	75.1%
17,501	WARD 28	8,052	358	7,668	26	7,310 D	4.4%	95.2%	4.5%	95.5%
16,538	WARD 29	6,970	400	6,533	37	6,133 D	5.7%	93.7%	5.8%	94.2%
14,225	WARD 30	6,755	878	5,790	87	4,912 D	13.0%	85.7%	13.2%	86.8%
18,277	WARD 31	7,396	3,988	3,356	52	632 R	53.9%	45.4%	54.3%	45.7%
30,101	WARD 32	12,156	470	11,629	57	11,159 D	3.9%	95.7%	3.9%	96.1%
22,916	WARD 33	10,879	6,226	4,609	44	1,617 R	57.2%	42.4%	57.5%	42.5%
39,985	WARD 34	19,450	5,609	13,781	60	8,172 D	28.8%	70.9%	28.9%	71.1%
32,175	WARD 35	15,794	9,756	5,974	64	3,782 R	61.8%	37.8%	62.0%	38.0%
35,472	WARD 36	17,099	3,044	13,983	72	10,939 D	17.8%	81.8%	17.9%	82.1%
20,306	WARD 37	7,913	586	7,293	34	6,707 D	7.4%	92.2%	7.4%	92.6%
23,399	WARD 38	9,916	2,271	7,592	53	5,321 D	22.9%	76.6%	23.0%	77.0%
47,439	WARD 39	22,841	12,375	10,403	63	1,972 R	54.2%	45.5%	54.3%	45.7%
50,806	WARD 40	21,800	9,715	12,040	45	2,325 D	44.6%	55.2%	44.7%	55.3%
23,528	WARD 41	11,227	6,734	4,429	64	2,305 R	60.0%	39.4%	60.3%	39.7%
29,145	WARD 42	11,301	6,396	4,866	39	1,530 R	56.6%	43.1%	56.8%	43.2%
27,147	WARD 43	9,308	1,695	7,584	29	5,889 D	18.2%	81.5%	18.3%	81.7%
17,276	WARD 44	8,151	471	7,656	24	7,185 D	5.8%	93.9%	5.8%	94.2%
24,576	WARD 45	11,437	6,418	4,885	134	1,533 R	56.1%	42.7%	56.8%	43.2%
24,939	WARD 46	11,101	1,015	10,025	61	9,010 D	9.1%	90.3%	9.2%	90.8%
11,264	WARD 47	4,784	219	4,505	60	4,286 D	4.6%	94.2%	4.6%	95.4%
22,391	WARD 48	10,512	4,857	5,618	37	761 D	46.2%	53.4%	46.4%	53.6%
33,401	WARD 49	11,293	2,071	9,182	40	7,111 D	18.3%	81.3%	18.4%	81.6%
31,271	WARD 50	14,881	1,294	13,551	36	12,257 D	8.7%	91.1%	8.7%	91.3%
28,662	WARD 51	11,769	610	11,108	51	10,498 D	5.2%	94.4%	5.2%	94.8%
28,926	WARD 52	14,802	2,577	12,185	40	9,608 D	17.4%	82.3%	17.5%	82.5%
21,786	WARD 53	12,302	5,776	6,479	47	703 D	47.0%	52.7%	47.1%	52.9%
19,800	WARD 54	11,630	4,559	7,041	30	2,482 D	39.2%	60.5%	39.3%	60.7%
27,590	WARD 55	14,857	9,065	5,753	39	3,312 R	61.0%	38.7%	61.2%	38.8%
35,662	WARD 56	19,874	9,327	10,443	104	1,116 D	46.9%	52.5%	47.2%	52.8%
29,362	WARD 57	14,761	8,567	6,158	36	2,409 R	58.0%	41.7%	58.2%	41.8%
47,404	WARD 58	23,310	13,437	9,829	44	3,608 R	57.6%	42.2%	57.8%	42.2%
24,998	WARD 59	11,271	1,249	9,988	34	8,739 D	11.1%	88.6%	11.1%	88.9%
21,070	WARD 60	10,375	451	9,884	40	9,433 D	4.3%	95.3%	4.4%	95.6%

PHILADELPHIA

PRESIDENT 1984

1980 Census Population	Ward	Total Vote	Republican	Democratic	Other	Rep.-Dem. Plurality	Percentage			
							Total Vote		Major Vote	
							Rep.	Dem.	Rep.	Dem.
27,764	WARD 61	12,556	6,851	5,662	43	1,189 R	54.6%	45.1%	54.8%	45.2%
26,749	WARD 62	12,883	7,607	5,230	46	2,377 R	59.0%	40.6%	59.3%	40.7%
24,050	WARD 63	13,220	8,013	5,173	34	2,840 R	60.6%	39.1%	60.8%	39.2%
16,800	WARD 64	9,332	5,776	3,536	20	2,240 R	61.9%	37.9%	62.0%	38.0%
27,290	WARD 65	11,775	6,658	5,083	34	1,575 R	56.5%	43.2%	56.7%	43.3%
54,236	WARD 66	23,578	15,558	7,959	61	7,599 R	66.0%	33.8%	66.2%	33.8%
1,688,210	TOTAL	772,102	267,178	501,369	3,555	234,191 D	34.6%	64.9%	34.8%	65.2%

PENNSYLVANIA

CONGRESS

CD	Year	Total Vote	Republican Vote	Republican Candidate	Democratic Vote	Democratic Candidate	Other Vote	Rep.-Dem. Plurality	Total Vote Rep.	Total Vote Dem.	Major Vote Rep.	Major Vote Dem.
1	1984	197,682	49,559	DI BIASE, CARMINE	148,123	FOGLIETTA, THOMAS M.		98,564 D	25.1%	74.9%	25.1%	74.9%
1	1982	143,416	38,155	MARINO, MICHAEL	103,626	FOGLIETTA, THOMAS M.	1,635	65,471 D	26.6%	72.3%	26.9%	73.1%
2	1984	220,295	18,224	SHARPER, RONALD J.	200,484	GRAY, WILLIAM H.	1,587	182,260 D	8.3%	91.0%	8.3%	91.7%
2	1982	158,675			120,744	GRAY, WILLIAM H.	37,931	120,744 D		76.1%		100.0%
3	1984	238,786	85,358	BECKER, FLORA L.	152,598	BORSKI, ROBERT A.	830	67,240 D	35.7%	63.9%	35.9%	64.1%
3	1982	193,954	94,497	DOUGHERTY, CHARLES F.	97,161	BORSKI, ROBERT A.	2,296	2,664 D	48.7%	50.1%	49.3%	50.7%
4	1984	200,809	86,769	KUNDER, JAMES	114,040	KOLTER, JOSEPH P.		27,271 D	43.2%	56.8%	43.2%	56.8%
4	1982	167,102	64,539	ATKINSON, EUGENE V.	100,481	KOLTER, JOSEPH P.	2,082	35,942 D	38.6%	60.1%	39.1%	60.9%
5	1984	195,551	141,965	SCHULZE, RICHARD T.	53,586	FANTI, LOUIS J.		88,379 R	72.6%	27.4%	72.6%	27.4%
5	1982	134,818	90,648	SCHULZE, RICHARD T.	44,170	BURGER, BOB		46,478 R	67.2%	32.8%	67.2%	32.8%
6	1984	181,165			181,165	*YATRON, GUS		181,165 D		100.0%		100.0%
6	1982	150,385	42,155	MARTIN, HARRY B.	108,230	YATRON, GUS		66,075 D	28.0%	72.0%	28.0%	72.0%
7	1984	248,504	124,046	WELDON, CURT	124,458	EDGAR, ROBERT W.		412 D	49.9%	50.1%	49.9%	50.1%
7	1982	190,798	85,023	JOACHIM , STEVE	105,775	EDGAR, ROBERT W.		20,752 D	44.6%	55.4%	44.6%	55.4%
8	1984	221,344	108,696	CHRISTIAN, DAVID A.	112,648	KOSTMAYER, PETER H.	3,952 D	49.1%	50.9%	49.1%	50.9%
8	1982	165,535	80,928	COYNE, JAMES K.	83,242	KOSTMAYER, PETER H.	1,365	2,314 D	48.9%	50.3%	49.3%	50.7%
9	1984	177,986	118,437	SHUSTER, E. G.	59,549	KULP, NANCY		58,888 R	66.5%	33.5%	66.5%	33.5%
9	1982	141,905	92,322	SHUSTER, E. G.	49,583	DUNCAN, EUGENE J.		42,739 R	65.1%	34.9%	65.1%	34.9%
10	1984	194,737	150,166	MCDADE, JOSEPH M.	44,571	BASALYGA, GENE		105,595 R	77.1%	22.9%	77.1%	22.9%
10	1982	153,485	103,617	MCDADE, JOSEPH M.	49,868	RAFALKO, ROBERT J.		53,749 R	67.5%	32.5%	67.5%	32.5%
11	1984	185,122	76,692	HUDOCK, ROBERT P.	108,430	KANJORSKI, PAUL E.		31,738 D	41.4%	58.6%	41.4%	58.6%
11	1982	168,856	78,485	NELLIGAN, JAMES L.	90,371	HARRISON, FRANK		11,886 D	46.5%	53.5%	46.5%	53.5%
12	1984	194,494	57,446	FULLARD, THOMAS J.	134,384	MURTHA, JOHN P.	2,664	76,938 D	29.5%	69.1%	29.9%	70.1%
12	1982	157,640	54,212	TUSCANO, WILLIAM N.	96,369	MURTHA, JOHN P.	7,059	42,157 D	34.4%	61.1%	36.0%	64.0%
13	1984	238,704	133,948	COUGHLIN, R. LAWRENCE	104,756	HOEFFEL, JOSEPH M.		29,192 R	56.1%	43.9%	56.1%	43.9%
13	1982	169,824	109,198	COUGHLIN, R. LAWRENCE	59,709	CUNNINGHAM, MARTIN J.	917	49,489 R	64.3%	35.2%	64.6%	35.4%
14	1984	213,797	42,616	CLARK, JOHN R.	163,818	COYNE, WILLIAM J.	7,363	121,202 D	19.9%	76.6%	20.6%	79.4%
14	1982	161,577	32,780	CLARK, JOHN R.	120,980	COYNE, WILLIAM J.	7,817	88,200 D	20.3%	74.9%	21.3%	78.7%
15	1984	189,828	110,338	RITTER, DONALD L.	79,490	WELLS-SCHOOLEY, JANE		30,848 R	58.1%	41.9%	58.1%	41.9%
15	1982	137,457	79,455	RITTER, DONALD L.	58,002	ORLOSKI, RICHARD J.		21,453 R	57.8%	42.2%	57.8%	42.2%
16	1984	177,992	138,477	WALKER, ROBERT S.	39,515	BARD, MARTIN L.		98,962 R	77.8%	22.2%	77.8%	22.2%
16	1982	130,398	93,034	WALKER, ROBERT S.	37,364	MOWERY, JEAN D.		55,670 R	71.3%	28.7%	71.3%	28.7%
17	1984	178,651	129,716	GEKAS, GEORGE W.	48,935	ANDERSON, STEPHEN A.		80,781 R	72.6%	27.4%	72.6%	27.4%
17	1982	146,265	84,291	GEKAS, GEORGE W.	61,974	HOCHENDONER, LARRY J.		22,317 R	57.6%	42.4%	57.6%	42.4%
18	1984	238,489	87,521	MAXWELL, JOHN G.	149,628	WALGREN, DOUGLAS	1,340	62,107 D	36.7%	62.7%	36.9%	63.1%
18	1982	187,683	84,428	JACOB, TED	101,807	WALGREN, DOUGLAS	1,448	17,379 D	45.0%	54.2%	45.3%	54.7%
19	1984	186,742	141,196	GOODLING, WILLIAM F.	44,117	RARIG, JOHN	1,429	97,079 R	75.6%	23.6%	76.2%	23.8%
19	1982	142,950	101,163	GOODLING, WILLIAM F.	41,787	BECKER, LARRY		59,376 R	70.8%	29.2%	70.8%	29.2%
20	1984	208,998	50,247	LLOYD, DANIEL	158,751	GAYDOS, JOSEPH M.		108,504 D	24.0%	76.0%	24.0%	76.0%
20	1982	167,428	38,212	RAY, TERRY T.	127,281	GAYDOS, JOSEPH M.	1,935	89,069 D	22.8%	76.0%	23.1%	76.9%
21	1984	192,109	125,730	RIDGE, THOMAS J.	65,594	YOUNG, JAMES A.	785	60,136 R	65.4%	34.1%	65.7%	34.3%
21	1982	159,631	80,180	RIDGE, THOMAS J.	79,451	ANDREZESKI, ANTHONY		729 R	50.2%	49.8%	50.2%	49.8%
22	1984	194,428	39,752	PRYOR, NANCY S.	153,514	MURPHY, AUSTIN J.	1,162	113,762 D	20.4%	79.0%	20.6%	79.4%
22	1982	157,215	32,176	PATERRA, FRANK J.	123,716	MURPHY, AUSTIN J.	1,323	91,540 D	20.5%	78.7%	20.6%	79.4%
23	1984	183,909	94,952	CLINGER, WILLIAM F.	88,957	WACHOB, BILL		5,995 R	51.6%	48.4%	51.6%	48.4%
23	1982	141,721	92,424	CLINGER, WILLIAM F.	49,297	CALLA, JOSEPH J.		43,127 R	65.2%	34.8%	65.2%	34.8%

PENNSYLVANIA

1984 GENERAL ELECTION

President   Other vote was 21,628 Johnson (Consumer); 6,982 Bergland (Libertarian); 2,059 Winn (Workers League); 1,780 Hall (Communist).

Congress   An asterisk in the Congressional vote table indicates a candidate received votes as the nominee of an additional party. Other vote was Karlin (Socialist Workers) in CD 2; Hughes (Independent) in CD 3; Krill (American Eagle) in CD 12; 6,699 Caligiuri (Libertarian) and 664 Duncan (Socialist Workers) in CD 14; Mulholland (Libertarian) in CD 18; Shoemaker (Libertarian) in CD 19; Hammer (Independent) in CD 21; Fraenzl (Socialist Workers) in CD 22. Early uncorrected returns gave the Anderson (Democratic) vote in CD 17 as 31,770.

PHILADELPHIA

Philadelphia city and county are coterminous.

President   Other vote was 1,795 Johnson (Consumer); 806 Bergland (Libertarian); 560 Hall (Communist); 394 Winn (Workers League).

1984 PRIMARIES

APRIL 10 REPUBLICAN

Congress   Unopposed in fourteen CD's. No candidate in CD 6. Contested as follows:

CD 4   15,350 James Kunder; 6,287 William S. Balint; 4,926 Merle L. Pears; 4,187 Jeff Span; 3,863 John Loth.

CD 5   33,382 Richard T. Schulze; 4,274 P. J. Leonard.

CD 6   No candidate names appeared on the ballot; Gus Yatron, the Democratic nominee, received 3,470 write-in votes and became the nominee.

CD 11   20,365 Robert P. Hudock; 7,540 Samuel W. Daley.

CD 13   32,657 R. Lawrence Coughlin; 3,104 Edward H. Johnson.

CD 16   31,572 Robert S. Walker; 5,800 Dick Brown.

CD 17   38,594 George W. Gekas; 5,841 Max Lampenfeld.

CD 18   13,440 John G. Maxwell; 12,924 Virginia H. Deese; 9,256 Paul F. Hauser.

CD 20   8,670 Daniel Lloyd; 7,582 Steve Andreas.

APRIL 10 DEMOCRATIC

Congress   Unopposed in seven CD's. Contested as follows:

CD 1   56,478 Thomas M. Foglietta; 48,475 James J. Tayoun; 3,392 Bernard Salera.

CD 2   64,754 William H. Gray; 12,112 Susan W. Bowen.

CD 4   54,490 Joseph P. Kolter; 11,793 James D. Kane.

CD 6   40,185 Gus Yatron; 5,604 Paul E. Clark.

CD 7   28,374 Robert W. Edgar; 3,630 Robert E. Moran; 2,166 Steve Douglas.

CD 10   18,749 Gene Basalyga; 10,684 Wanda R. Shirk.

CD 11   33,519 Paul E. Kanjorski; 30,770 Frank Harrison; 4,304 Stephen L. Flood; 2,901 Gene Knox.

CD 13   22,127 Joseph M. Hoeffel; 8,490 Thomas J. Young.

CD 14   71,466 William J. Coyne; 10,386 Robert R. Lansberry; 5,114 Thomas Shepler.

CD 15   23,598 Jane Wells-Schooley; 12,158 Gene Knopf; 4,896 Bernard J. Berg; 4,246 Dick Cusick; 2,724 Charles Buss; 2,563 Jack Smith.

CD 16   9,518 Martin L. Bard; 5,403 James E. McCaffrey.

CD 17   13,822 William R. Minnick; 11,865 Sara M. Phleger. Mr. Minnick withdrew after the primary and Stephen A. Anderson was substituted by the local party committee.

CD 19   15,510 John Rarig; 9,086 Ira R. Seybold.

CD 20   70,681 Joseph M. Gaydos; 15,745 Bob Aber; 10,254 Edward F. McGivern; 5,828 Joseph M. Kapusnik.

CD 21   32,968 James A. Young; 15,095 George R. H. Elder.

CD 22   78,740 Austin J. Murphy; 13,030 Francis J. Cline.

RHODE ISLAND

GOVERNOR
Edward DiPrete (R). Elected 1984 to a two-year term.

SENATORS
John H. Chafee (R). Re-elected 1982 to a six-year term. Previously elected 1976.

Claiborne Pell (D). Re-elected 1984 to a six-year term. Previously elected 1978, 1972, 1966, 1960.

REPRESENTATIVES
1. Fernand St. Germain (D)   2. Claudine Schneider (R)

POSTWAR VOTE FOR GOVERNOR

Year	Total Vote	Republican Vote	Candidate	Democratic Vote	Candidate	Other Vote	Rep.-Dem. Plurality	Total Vote Rep.	Total Vote Dem.	Major Vote Rep.	Major Vote Dem.
1984	408,375	245,059	DiPrete, Edward	163,311	Solomon, Anthony J.	5	81,748 R	60.0%	40.0%	60.0%	40.0%
1982	337,259	79,602	Marzullo, Vincent	247,208	Garrahy, J. Joseph	10,449	167,606 D	23.6%	73.3%	24.4%	75.6%
1980	405,916	106,729	Cianci, Vincent A.	299,174	Garrahy, J. Joseph	13	192,445 D	26.3%	73.7%	26.3%	73.7%
1978	314,363	96,596	Almond, Lincoln	197,386	Garrahy, J. Joseph	20,381	100,790 D	30.7%	62.8%	32.9%	67.1%
1976	398,683	178,254	Taft, James L.	218,561	Garrahy, J. Joseph	1,868	40,307 D	44.7%	54.8%	44.9%	55.1%
1974	321,660	69,224	Nugent, James W.	252,436	Noel, Philip W.	—	183,212 D	21.5%	78.5%	21.5%	78.5%
1972	412,866	194,315	DeSimone, Herbert F.	216,953	Noel, Philip W.	1,598	22,638 D	47.1%	52.5%	47.2%	52.8%
1970	346,342	171,549	DeSimone, Herbert F.	173,420	Licht, Frank	1,373	1,871 D	49.5%	50.1%	49.7%	50.3%
1968	383,725	187,958	Chafee, John H.	195,766	Licht, Frank	1	7,808 D	49.0%	51.0%	49.0%	51.0%
1966	332,064	210,202	Chafee, John H.	121,862	Hobbs, Horace E.	—	88,340 R	63.3%	36.7%	63.3%	36.7%
1964	391,668	239,501	Chafee, John H.	152,165	Gallogly, Edward P.	2	87,336 R	61.1%	38.9%	61.1%	38.9%
1962	327,506	163,952	Chafee, John H.	163,554	Notte, John A.	—	398 R	50.1%	49.9%	50.1%	49.9%
1960	401,362	174,044	Del Sesto, Christopher	227,318	Notte, John A.	—	53,274 D	43.4%	56.6%	43.4%	56.6%
1958	346,780	176,505	Del Sesto, Christopher	170,275	Roberts, Dennis J.	—	6,230 R	50.9%	49.1%	50.9%	49.1%
1956	383,919	191,604	Del Sesto, Christopher	192,315	Roberts, Dennis J.	—	711 D	49.9%	50.1%	49.9%	50.1%
1954	328,670	137,131	Lewis, Dean J.	189,595	Roberts, Dennis J.	1,944	52,464 D	41.7%	57.7%	42.0%	58.0%
1952	409,689	194,102	Archambault, Raoul	215,587	Roberts, Dennis J.	—	21,485 D	47.4%	52.6%	47.4%	52.6%
1950	296,809	120,684	Lachapelle, E. T.	176,125	Roberts, Dennis J.	—	55,441 D	40.7%	59.3%	40.7%	59.3%
1948	323,863	124,441	Ruerat, Albert P.	198,056	Pastore, John O.	1,366	73,615 D	38.4%	61.2%	38.6%	61.4%
1946	275,341	126,456	Murphy, John G.	148,885	Pastore, John O.	—	22,429 D	45.9%	54.1%	45.9%	54.1%

POSTWAR VOTE FOR SENATOR

Year	Total Vote	Republican Vote	Candidate	Democratic Vote	Candidate	Other Vote	Rep.-Dem. Plurality	Total Vote Rep.	Total Vote Dem.	Major Vote Rep.	Major Vote Dem.
1984	395,285	108,492	Leonard, Barbara	286,780	Pell, Claiborne	13	178,288 D	27.4%	72.6%	27.4%	72.6%
1982	342,779	175,495	Chafee, John H.	167,283	Michaelson, Julius C.	1	8,212 R	51.2%	48.8%	51.2%	48.8%
1978	305,618	76,061	Reynolds, James G.	229,557	Pell, Claiborne	—	153,496 D	24.9%	75.1%	24.9%	75.1%
1976	398,906	230,329	Chafee, John H.	167,665	Lorber, Richard P.	912	62,664 R	57.7%	42.0%	57.9%	42.1%
1972	413,432	188,990	Chafee, John H.	221,942	Pell, Claiborne	2,500	32,952 D	45.7%	53.7%	46.0%	54.0%
1970	341,222	107,351	McLaughlin, John	230,469	Pastore, John O.	3,402	123,118 D	31.5%	67.5%	31.8%	68.2%
1966	324,173	104,838	Briggs, Ruth M.	219,331	Pell, Claiborne	4	114,493 D	32.3%	67.7%	32.3%	67.7%
1964	386,322	66,715	Lagueux, Ronald R.	319,607	Pastore, John O.	—	252,892 D	17.3%	82.7%	17.3%	82.7%
1960	399,983	124,408	Archambault, Raoul	275,575	Pell, Claiborne	—	151,167 D	31.1%	68.9%	31.1%	68.9%
1958	344,519	122,353	Ewing, Bayard	222,166	Pastore, John O.	—	99,813 D	35.5%	64.5%	35.5%	64.5%
1954	326,624	132,970	Sundlun, Walter I.	193,654	Green, Theodore F.	—	60,684 D	40.7%	59.3%	40.7%	59.3%
1952	410,978	185,850	Ewing, Bayard	225,128	Pastore, John O.	—	39,278 D	45.2%	54.8%	45.2%	54.8%
1950s	297,909	114,184	Levy, Austin T.	183,725	Pastore, John O.	—	69,541 D	38.3%	61.7%	38.3%	61.7%
1948	320,420	130,262	Hazard, Thomas P.	190,158	Green, Theodore F.	—	59,896 D	40.7%	59.3%	40.7%	59.3%
1946	273,528	122,780	Dyer, W. Gurnee	150,748	McGrath, J. Howard	—	27,968 D	44.9%	55.1%	44.9%	55.1%

The 1950 election was for a short term to fill a vacancy.

RHODE ISLAND

Districts Established April 9, 1982

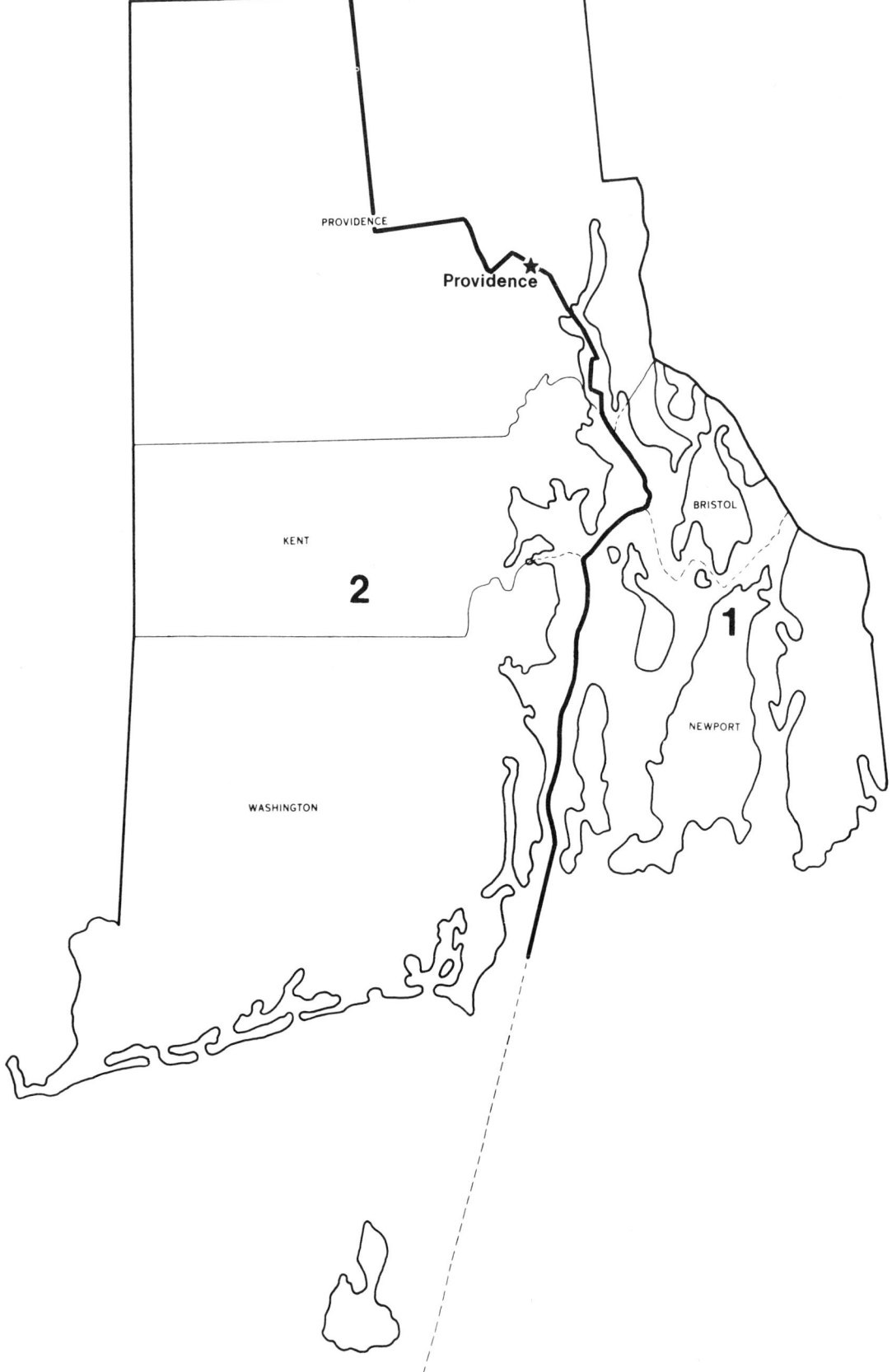

RHODE ISLAND

PRESIDENT 1984

1980 Census Population	County	Total Vote	Republican	Democratic	Other	Rep.-Dem. Plurality	Percentage			
							Total Vote		Major Vote	
							Rep.	Dem.	Rep.	Dem.
46,942	BRISTOL	21,084	11,635	9,386	63	2,249 R	55.2%	44.5%	55.3%	44.7%
154,163	KENT	71,993	40,427	31,352	214	9,075 R	56.2%	43.5%	56.3%	43.7%
81,383	NEWPORT	34,209	19,629	14,466	114	5,163 R	57.4%	42.3%	57.6%	42.4%
571,349	PROVIDENCE	240,898	116,024	124,109	765	8,085 D	48.2%	51.5%	48.3%	51.7%
93,317	WASHINGTON	42,305	24,365	17,793	147	6,572 R	57.6%	42.1%	57.8%	42.2%
947,154	TOTAL	410,492	212,080	197,106	1,306	14,974 R	51.7%	48.0%	51.8%	48.2%

RHODE ISLAND

PRESIDENT 1984

1980 Census Population	City/Town	Total Vote	Republican	Democratic	Other	Rep.-Dem. Plurality	Percentage			
							Total Vote		Major Vote	
							Rep.	Dem.	Rep.	Dem.
16,174	BARRINGTON	8,622	5,179	3,415	28	1,764 R	60.1%	39.6%	60.3%	39.7%
20,128	BRISTOL TOWN	7,879	4,062	3,791	26	271 R	51.6%	48.1%	51.7%	48.3%
13,164	BURRILLVILLE	4,942	2,945	1,988	9	957 R	59.6%	40.2%	59.7%	40.3%
16,995	CENTRAL FALLS	5,489	2,441	3,030	18	589 D	44.5%	55.2%	44.6%	55.4%
4,800	CHARLESTOWN	2,481	1,579	894	8	685 R	63.6%	36.0%	63.8%	36.2%
27,065	COVENTRY	12,247	7,475	4,735	37	2,740 R	61.0%	38.7%	61.2%	38.8%
71,992	CRANSTON	37,351	19,517	17,742	92	1,775 R	52.3%	47.5%	52.4%	47.6%
27,069	CUMBERLAND	13,215	7,854	5,330	31	2,524 R	59.4%	40.3%	59.6%	40.4%
10,211	EAST GREENWICH	5,501	3,588	1,904	9	1,684 R	65.2%	34.6%	65.3%	34.7%
50,980	EAST PROVIDENCE	21,447	10,322	11,064	61	742 D	48.1%	51.6%	48.3%	51.7%
4,453	EXETER	1,846	1,159	681	6	478 R	62.8%	36.9%	63.0%	37.0%
3,370	FOSTER	1,612	967	639	6	328 R	60.0%	39.6%	60.2%	39.8%
7,550	GLOCESTER	3,483	2,121	1,350	12	771 R	60.9%	38.8%	61.1%	38.9%
6,406	HOPKINTON	2,638	1,745	887	6	858 R	66.1%	33.6%	66.3%	33.7%
4,040	JAMESTOWN	2,582	1,398	1,174	10	224 R	54.1%	45.5%	54.4%	45.6%
24,907	JOHNSTON	12,324	6,121	6,164	39	43 D	49.7%	50.0%	49.8%	50.2%
16,949	LINCOLN	9,165	5,527	3,612	26	1,915 R	60.3%	39.4%	60.5%	39.5%
3,085	LITTLE COMPTON	1,775	1,085	674	16	411 R	61.1%	38.0%	61.7%	38.3%
17,216	MIDDLETOWN	6,213	3,841	2,353	19	1,488 R	61.8%	37.9%	62.0%	38.0%
12,088	NARRAGANSETT	5,890	3,098	2,769	23	329 R	52.6%	47.0%	52.8%	47.2%
29,259	NEWPORT CITY	10,729	5,806	4,894	29	912 R	54.1%	45.6%	54.3%	45.7%
620	NEW SHOREHAM	685	346	332	7	14 R	50.5%	48.5%	51.0%	49.0%
21,938	NORTH KINGSTOWN	10,272	6,353	3,882	37	2,471 R	61.8%	37.8%	62.1%	37.9%
29,188	NORTH PROVIDENCE	15,953	7,219	8,692	42	1,473 D	45.3%	54.5%	45.4%	54.6%
9,972	NORTH SMITHFIELD	5,076	3,144	1,920	12	1,224 R	61.9%	37.8%	62.1%	37.9%
71,204	PAWTUCKET	26,665	12,460	14,109	96	1,649 D	46.7%	52.9%	46.9%	53.1%
14,257	PORTSMOUTH	6,786	4,195	2,566	25	1,629 R	61.8%	37.8%	62.0%	38.0%
156,804	PROVIDENCE CITY	55,717	19,748	35,751	218	16,003 D	35.4%	64.2%	35.6%	64.4%
4,018	RICHMOND	1,939	1,126	806	7	320 R	58.1%	41.6%	58.3%	41.7%
8,405	SCITUATE	4,391	2,926	1,444	21	1,482 R	66.6%	32.9%	67.0%	33.0%
16,886	SMITHFIELD	7,647	4,375	3,244	28	1,131 R	57.2%	42.4%	57.4%	42.6%
20,414	SOUTH KINGSTOWN	8,165	4,205	3,923	37	282 R	51.5%	48.0%	51.7%	48.3%
13,526	TIVERTON	6,124	3,304	2,805	15	499 R	54.0%	45.8%	54.1%	45.9%
10,640	WARREN	4,583	2,394	2,180	9	214 R	52.2%	47.6%	52.3%	47.7%
87,123	WARWICK	41,687	22,276	19,278	133	2,998 R	53.4%	46.2%	53.6%	46.4%
18,580	WESTERLY	8,389	4,754	3,619	16	1,135 R	56.7%	43.1%	56.8%	43.2%
2,738	WEST GREENWICH	1,607	1,059	543	5	516 R	65.9%	33.8%	66.1%	33.9%
27,026	WEST WARWICK	10,951	6,029	4,892	30	1,137 R	55.1%	44.7%	55.2%	44.8%
45,914	WOONSOCKET	16,421	8,337	8,030	54	307 R	50.8%	48.9%	50.9%	49.1%
947,154	TOTAL	410,492	212,080	197,106	1,306	14,974 R	51.7%	48.0%	51.8%	48.2%

RHODE ISLAND

GOVERNOR 1984

1980 Census Population	County	Total Vote	Republican	Democratic	Other	Rep.-Dem. Plurality	Percentage Total Vote Rep.	Dem.	Major Vote Rep.	Dem.
46,942	BRISTOL	20,832	13,292	7,540		5,752 R	63.8%	36.2%	63.8%	36.2%
154,163	KENT	71,888	50,200	21,688		28,512 R	69.8%	30.2%	69.8%	30.2%
81,383	NEWPORT	33,715	21,315	12,400		8,915 R	63.2%	36.8%	63.2%	36.8%
571,349	PROVIDENCE	240,230	131,469	108,761		22,708 R	54.7%	45.3%	54.7%	45.3%
93,317	WASHINGTON	41,705	28,783	12,922		15,861 R	69.0%	31.0%	69.0%	31.0%
947,154	TOTAL	408,375	245,059	163,311	5	81,748 R	60.0%	40.0%	60.0%	40.0%

RHODE ISLAND

GOVERNOR 1984

1980 Census Population	City/Town	Total Vote	Republican	Democratic	Other	Rep.-Dem. Plurality	Percentage Total Vote Rep.	Dem.	Major Vote Rep.	Dem.
16,174	BARRINGTON	8,538	6,285	2,253		4,032 R	73.6%	26.4%	73.6%	26.4%
20,128	BRISTOL TOWN	7,740	4,347	3,393		954 R	56.2%	43.8%	56.2%	43.8%
13,164	BURRILLVILLE	4,879	2,889	1,990		899 R	59.2%	40.8%	59.2%	40.8%
16,995	CENTRAL FALLS	5,427	2,079	3,348		1,269 D	38.3%	61.7%	38.3%	61.7%
4,800	CHARLESTOWN	2,453	1,872	581		1,291 R	76.3%	23.7%	76.3%	23.7%
27,065	COVENTRY	12,195	8,381	3,814		4,567 R	68.7%	31.3%	68.7%	31.3%
71,992	CRANSTON	37,753	27,884	9,869		18,015 R	73.9%	26.1%	73.9%	26.1%
27,069	CUMBERLAND	13,113	7,783	5,330		2,453 R	59.4%	40.6%	59.4%	40.6%
10,211	EAST GREENWICH	5,477	4,239	1,238		3,001 R	77.4%	22.6%	77.4%	22.6%
50,980	EAST PROVIDENCE	21,066	11,267	9,799		1,468 R	53.5%	46.5%	53.5%	46.5%
4,453	EXETER	1,841	1,221	620		601 R	66.3%	33.7%	66.3%	33.7%
3,370	FOSTER	1,595	1,133	462		671 R	71.0%	29.0%	71.0%	29.0%
7,550	GLOCESTER	3,465	2,336	1,129		1,207 R	67.4%	32.6%	67.4%	32.6%
6,406	HOPKINTON	2,525	1,750	775		975 R	69.3%	30.7%	69.3%	30.7%
4,040	JAMESTOWN	2,562	1,841	721		1,120 R	71.9%	28.1%	71.9%	28.1%
24,907	JOHNSTON	12,429	6,156	6,273		117 D	49.5%	50.5%	49.5%	50.5%
16,949	LINCOLN	9,192	5,758	3,434		2,324 R	62.6%	37.4%	62.6%	37.4%
3,085	LITTLE COMPTON	1,712	1,163	549		614 R	67.9%	32.1%	67.9%	32.1%
17,216	MIDDLETOWN	6,139	4,030	2,109		1,921 R	65.6%	34.4%	65.6%	34.4%
12,088	NARRAGANSETT	5,811	3,912	1,899		2,013 R	67.3%	32.7%	67.3%	32.7%
29,259	NEWPORT CITY	10,703	6,413	4,290		2,123 R	59.9%	40.1%	59.9%	40.1%
620	NEW SHOREHAM	699	458	241		217 R	65.5%	34.5%	65.5%	34.5%
21,938	NORTH KINGSTOWN	10,168	7,651	2,517		5,134 R	75.2%	24.8%	75.2%	24.8%
29,188	NORTH PROVIDENCE	16,006	7,500	8,506		1,006 D	46.9%	53.1%	46.9%	53.1%
9,972	NORTH SMITHFIELD	5,003	3,144	1,859		1,285 R	62.8%	37.2%	62.8%	37.2%
71,204	PAWTUCKET	26,564	13,034	13,530		496 D	49.1%	50.9%	49.1%	50.9%
14,257	PORTSMOUTH	6,669	4,415	2,254		2,161 R	66.2%	33.8%	66.2%	33.8%
156,804	PROVIDENCE CITY	55,658	24,914	30,744		5,830 D	44.8%	55.2%	44.8%	55.2%
4,018	RICHMOND	1,907	1,353	554		799 R	70.9%	29.1%	70.9%	29.1%
8,405	SCITUATE	4,354	3,294	1,060		2,234 R	75.7%	24.3%	75.7%	24.3%
16,886	SMITHFIELD	7,652	4,732	2,920		1,812 R	61.8%	38.2%	61.8%	38.2%
20,414	SOUTH KINGSTOWN	8,080	5,729	2,351		3,378 R	70.9%	29.1%	70.9%	29.1%
13,526	TIVERTON	5,930	3,453	2,477		976 R	58.2%	41.8%	58.2%	41.8%
10,640	WARREN	4,554	2,660	1,894		766 R	58.4%	41.6%	58.4%	41.6%
87,123	WARWICK	41,749	29,644	12,105		17,539 R	71.0%	29.0%	71.0%	29.0%
18,580	WESTERLY	8,221	4,837	3,384		1,453 R	58.8%	41.2%	58.8%	41.2%
2,738	WEST GREENWICH	1,600	1,085	515		570 R	67.8%	32.2%	67.8%	32.2%
27,026	WEST WARWICK	10,867	6,851	4,016		2,835 R	63.0%	37.0%	63.0%	37.0%
45,914	WOONSOCKET	16,074	7,566	8,508		942 D	47.1%	52.9%	47.1%	52.9%
947,154	TOTAL	408,375	245,059	163,311	5	81,748 R	60.0%	40.0%	60.0%	40.0%

RHODE ISLAND

SENATOR 1984

1980 Census Population	County	Total Vote	Republican	Democratic	Other	Rep.-Dem. Plurality	Percentage Total Vote Rep.	Dem.	Major Vote Rep.	Dem.
46,942	BRISTOL	20,315	6,324	13,991		7,667 D	31.1%	68.9%	31.1%	68.9%
154,163	KENT	70,204	21,082	49,122		28,040 D	30.0%	70.0%	30.0%	70.0%
81,383	NEWPORT	32,886	10,050	22,836		12,786 D	30.6%	69.4%	30.6%	69.4%
571,349	PROVIDENCE	230,837	57,429	173,408		115,979 D	24.9%	75.1%	24.9%	75.1%
93,317	WASHINGTON	41,030	13,607	27,423		13,816 D	33.2%	66.8%	33.2%	66.8%
947,154	TOTAL	395,285	108,492	286,780	13	178,288 D	27.4%	72.6%	27.4%	72.6%

RHODE ISLAND

SENATOR 1984

1980 Census Population	City/Town	Total Vote	Republican	Democratic	Other	Rep.-Dem. Plurality	Percentage Total Vote Rep.	Dem.	Major Vote Rep.	Dem.
16,174	BARRINGTON	8,415	3,021	5,394		2,373 D	35.9%	64.1%	35.9%	64.1%
20,128	BRISTOL TOWN	7,550	1,957	5,593		3,636 D	25.9%	74.1%	25.9%	74.1%
13,164	BURRILLVILLE	4,757	1,583	3,174		1,591 D	33.3%	66.7%	33.3%	66.7%
16,995	CENTRAL FALLS	5,222	1,113	4,109		2,996 D	21.3%	78.7%	21.3%	78.7%
4,800	CHARLESTOWN	2,410	1,011	1,399		388 D	42.0%	58.0%	42.0%	58.0%
27,065	COVENTRY	11,899	3,910	7,989		4,079 D	32.9%	67.1%	32.9%	67.1%
71,992	CRANSTON	35,834	10,624	25,210		14,586 D	29.6%	70.4%	29.6%	70.4%
27,069	CUMBERLAND	12,756	3,627	9,129		5,502 D	28.4%	71.6%	28.4%	71.6%
10,211	EAST GREENWICH	5,380	2,017	3,363		1,346 D	37.5%	62.5%	37.5%	62.5%
50,980	EAST PROVIDENCE	20,618	5,246	15,372		10,126 D	25.4%	74.6%	25.4%	74.6%
4,453	EXETER	1,867	718	1,149		431 D	38.5%	61.5%	38.5%	61.5%
3,370	FOSTER	1,560	563	997		434 D	36.1%	63.9%	36.1%	63.9%
7,550	GLOCESTER	3,425	1,220	2,205		985 D	35.6%	64.4%	35.6%	64.4%
6,406	HOPKINTON	2,528	1,020	1,508		488 D	40.3%	59.7%	40.3%	59.7%
4,040	JAMESTOWN	2,546	828	1,718		890 D	32.5%	67.5%	32.5%	67.5%
24,907	JOHNSTON	11,778	2,830	8,948		6,118 D	24.0%	76.0%	24.0%	76.0%
16,949	LINCOLN	8,902	2,868	6,034		3,166 D	32.2%	67.8%	32.2%	67.8%
3,085	LITTLE COMPTON	1,650	625	1,025		400 D	37.9%	62.1%	37.9%	62.1%
17,216	MIDDLETOWN	6,073	1,979	4,094		2,115 D	32.6%	67.4%	32.6%	67.4%
12,088	NARRAGANSETT	5,641	1,555	4,086		2,531 D	27.6%	72.4%	27.6%	72.4%
29,259	NEWPORT CITY	10,473	2,711	7,762		5,051 D	25.9%	74.1%	25.9%	74.1%
620	NEW SHOREHAM	691	234	457		223 D	33.9%	66.1%	33.9%	66.1%
21,938	NORTH KINGSTOWN	9,986	3,573	6,413		2,840 D	35.8%	64.2%	35.8%	64.2%
29,188	NORTH PROVIDENCE	15,207	3,078	12,129		9,051 D	20.2%	79.8%	20.2%	79.8%
9,972	NORTH SMITHFIELD	4,882	1,510	3,372		1,862 D	30.9%	69.1%	30.9%	69.1%
71,204	PAWTUCKET	25,689	5,810	19,879		14,069 D	22.6%	77.4%	22.6%	77.4%
14,257	PORTSMOUTH	6,480	2,209	4,271		2,062 D	34.1%	65.9%	34.1%	65.9%
156,804	PROVIDENCE CITY	52,895	9,764	43,131		33,367 D	18.5%	81.5%	18.5%	81.5%
4,018	RICHMOND	1,900	626	1,274		648 D	32.9%	67.1%	32.9%	67.1%
8,405	SCITUATE	4,296	1,813	2,483		670 D	42.2%	57.8%	42.2%	57.8%
16,886	SMITHFIELD	7,450	2,206	5,244		3,038 D	29.6%	70.4%	29.6%	70.4%
20,414	SOUTH KINGSTOWN	7,949	2,258	5,691		3,433 D	28.4%	71.6%	28.4%	71.6%
13,526	TIVERTON	5,664	1,698	3,966		2,268 D	30.0%	70.0%	30.0%	70.0%
10,640	WARREN	4,350	1,346	3,004		1,658 D	30.9%	69.1%	30.9%	69.1%
87,123	WARWICK	40,841	11,312	29,529		18,217 D	27.7%	72.3%	27.7%	72.3%
18,580	WESTERLY	8,058	2,612	5,446		2,834 D	32.4%	67.6%	32.4%	67.6%
2,738	WEST GREENWICH	1,561	625	936		311 D	40.0%	60.0%	40.0%	60.0%
27,026	WEST WARWICK	10,523	3,218	7,305		4,087 D	30.6%	69.4%	30.6%	69.4%
45,914	WOONSOCKET	15,566	3,574	11,992		8,418 D	23.0%	77.0%	23.0%	77.0%
947,154	TOTAL	395,285	108,492	286,780	13	178,288 D	27.4%	72.6%	27.4%	72.6%

RHODE ISLAND

CONGRESS

CD	Year	Total Vote	Republican Vote	Candidate	Democratic Vote	Candidate	Other Vote	Rep.-Dem. Plurality	Percentage Total Vote Rep.	Dem.	Major Vote Rep.	Dem.
1	1984	190,511	59,926	REGO, ALFRED	130,585	ST. GERMAIN, FERNAND		70,659 D	31.5%	68.5%	31.5%	68.5%
1	1982	160,131	61,253	STALLWOOD, BURTON	97,254	ST. GERMAIN, FERNAND	1,624	36,001 D	38.3%	60.7%	38.6%	61.4%
2	1984	199,508	135,151	SCHNEIDER, CLAUDINE	64,357	SINAPI, RICHARD		70,794 R	67.7%	32.3%	67.7%	32.3%
2	1982	173,051	96,282	SCHNEIDER, CLAUDINE	76,769	AUKERMAN, JAMES V.		19,513 R	55.6%	44.4%	55.6%	44.4%

RHODE ISLAND

1984 GENERAL ELECTION

In addition to the county-by-county figures, data are presented by cities and towns.

President Other vote was 510 Richards (American Independent); 277 Bergland (Libertarian); 240 Johnson (Citizens); 91 Holmes (Workers World); 75 Hall (Communist); 61 Mason (Socialist Workers); 49 Serrette (Alliance); 3 scattered, not reported by county or city/town.

Governor Other vote was scattered, not reported by county or city/town.

Senator Other vote was scattered, not reported by county or city/town.

Congress

1984 PRIMARIES

SEPTEMBER 11 REPUBLICAN

Governor Edward DiPrete, unopposed.

Senator Barbara Leonard, unopposed.

Congress Unopposed in both districts.

SEPTEMBER 11 DEMOCRATIC

Governor 73,090 Anthony J. Solomon; 53,041 Joseph W. Walsh.

Senator Claiborne Pell, unopposed.

Congress Unopposed in CD 1. Contested as follows:

CD 2 31,736 Richard Sinapi; 7,567 Vincent J. DuBreuil.

SOUTH CAROLINA

GOVERNOR
Richard W. Riley (D). Re-elected 1982 to a four-year term. Previously elected 1978.

SENATORS
Ernest F. Hollings (D). Re-elected 1980 to a six-year term. Previously elected 1974, 1968, and in 1966 to fill out term vacated by the death of Senator Olin D. Johnston.

Strom Thurmond (R). Re-elected 1984 to a six-year term. Previously elected 1978, 1972, 1966, 1960 and in 1956 to fill out term vacated by his own resignation in April 1956; had been elected to this term in 1954 as an Independent Democrat. Changed party affiliation from Democrat to Republican in September 1964.

REPRESENTATIVES
1. Thomas F. Hartnett (R)
2. Floyd Spence (R)
3. Butler Derrick (D)
4. Carroll Campbell (R)
5. John Spratt (D)
6. Robert M. Tallon (D)

POSTWAR VOTE FOR GOVERNOR

Year	Total Vote	Republican Vote	Republican Candidate	Democratic Vote	Democratic Candidate	Other Vote	Rep.-Dem. Plurality	Total Vote Rep.	Total Vote Dem.	Major Vote Rep.	Major Vote Dem.
1982	671,625	202,806	Workman, W. D.	468,819	Riley, Richard W.	—	266,013 D	30.2%	69.8%	30.2%	69.8%
1978	627,182	236,946	Young, Edward L.	384,898	Riley, Richard W.	5,338	147,952 D	37.8%	61.4%	38.1%	61.9%
1974	523,199	266,109	Edwards, James B.	248,938	Dorn, W. J. Bryan	8,152	17,171 R	50.9%	47.6%	51.7%	48.3%
1970	484,857	221,233	Watson, Albert W.	250,551	West, John C.	13,073	29,318 D	45.6%	51.7%	46.9%	53.1%
1966	439,942	184,088	Rogers, Joseph O.	255,854	McNair, Robert E.	—	71,766 D	41.8%	58.2%	41.8%	58.2%
1962	253,721	—	—	253,704	Russell, Donald S.	17	253,704 D	—	100.0%	—	100.0%
1958	77,740	—	—	77,714	Hollings, Ernest F.	26	77,714 D	—	100.0%	—	100.0%
1954	214,212	—	—	214,204	Timmerman, George B.	8	214,204 D	—	100.0%	—	100.0%
1950	50,642	—	—	50,633	Byrnes, James F.	9	50,633 D	—	100.0%	—	100.0%
1946	26,520	—	—	26,520	Thurmond, Strom	—	26,520 D	—	100.0%	—	100.0%

POSTWAR VOTE FOR SENATOR

Year	Total Vote	Republican Vote	Republican Candidate	Democratic Vote	Democratic Candidate	Other Vote	Rep.-Dem. Plurality	Total Vote Rep.	Total Vote Dem.	Major Vote Rep.	Major Vote Dem.
1984	965,130	644,815	Thurmond, Strom	306,982	Purvis, Melvin	13,333	337,833 R	66.8%	31.8%	67.7%	32.3%
1980	870,594	257,946	Mays, Marshall T.	612,554	Hollings, Ernest F.	94	354,608 D	29.6%	70.4%	29.6%	70.4%
1978	632,852	351,733	Thurmond, Strom	281,119	Ravenel, Charles D.	—	70,614 R	55.6%	44.4%	55.6%	44.4%
1974	512,397	146,645	Bush, Gwenyfred	356,126	Hollings, Ernest F.	9,626	209,481 D	28.6%	69.5%	29.2%	70.8%
1972	672,246	426,601	Thurmond, Strom	245,457	Zeigler, Eugene N.	188	181,144 R	63.5%	36.5%	63.5%	36.5%
1968	652,855	248,780	Parker, Marshall	404,060	Hollings, Ernest F.	15	155,280 D	38.1%	61.9%	38.1%	61.9%
1966	436,252	271,297	Thurmond, Strom	164,955	Morrah, Bradley	—	106,342 R	62.2%	37.8%	62.2%	37.8%
1966s	435,822	212,032	Parker, Marshall	223,790	Hollings, Ernest F.	—	11,758 D	48.7%	51.3%	48.7%	51.3%
1962	312,647	133,930	Workman, W. D.	178,712	Johnston, Olin D.	5	44,782 D	42.8%	57.2%	42.8%	57.2%
1960	330,266	—	—	330,164	Thurmond, Strom	102	330,164 D	—	100.0%	—	100.0%
1956	279,845	49,695	Crawford, Leon P.	230,150	Johnston, Olin D.	—	180,455 D	17.8%	82.2%	17.8%	82.2%
1956s	251,907	—	—	251,907	Thurmond, Strom	—	251,907 D	—	100.0%	—	100.0%
1954*	227,232	—	—	83,525	Brown, Edgar A.	143,707	83,525 D	—	36.8%	—	100.0%
1950	50,277	—	—	50,240	Johnston, Olin D.	37	50,240 D	—	99.9%	—	100.0%
1948	141,006	5,008	Gerald, J. Bates	135,998	Maybank, Burnet R.	—	130,990 D	3.6%	96.4%	3.6%	96.4%

One each of the 1966 and 1956 elections was for a short term to fill a vacancy. In 1954, Strom Thurmond polled 143,444 votes as an independent Democratic write-in candidate (63.1% of the total vote) and won the election with a 59,919 plurality.

375

SOUTH CAROLINA

Districts Established April 30, 1982

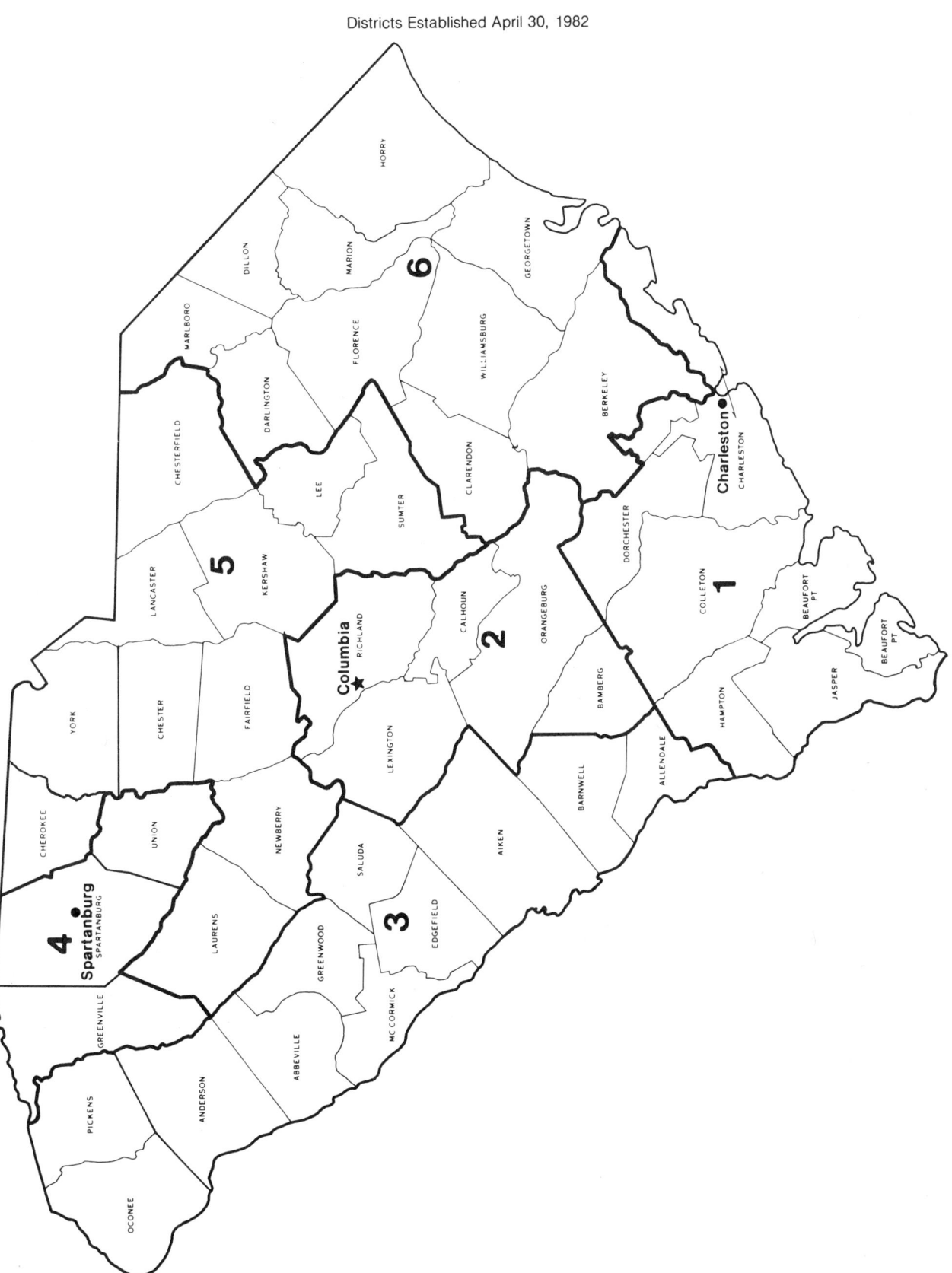

© ERC

SOUTH CAROLINA

PRESIDENT 1984

1980 Census Population	County	Total Vote	Republican	Democratic	Other	Rep.-Dem. Plurality	Percentage Total Vote Rep.	Dem.	Major Vote Rep.	Dem.
22,627	ABBEVILLE	6,875	3,798	3,051	26	747 R	55.2%	44.4%	55.5%	44.5%
105,625	AIKEN	36,133	25,872	9,892	369	15,980 R	71.6%	27.4%	72.3%	27.7%
10,700	ALLENDALE	3,769	1,570	2,170	29	600 D	41.7%	57.6%	42.0%	58.0%
133,235	ANDERSON	34,691	24,123	10,324	244	13,799 R	69.5%	29.8%	70.0%	30.0%
18,118	BAMBERG	5,831	2,908	2,892	31	16 R	49.9%	49.6%	50.1%	49.9%
19,868	BARNWELL	7,189	4,346	2,811	32	1,535 R	60.5%	39.1%	60.7%	39.3%
65,364	BEAUFORT	21,118	13,668	7,347	103	6,321 R	64.7%	34.8%	65.0%	35.0%
94,727	BERKELEY	24,511	16,972	7,380	159	9,592 R	69.2%	30.1%	69.7%	30.3%
12,206	CALHOUN	5,094	2,742	2,315	37	427 R	53.8%	45.4%	54.2%	45.8%
276,974	CHARLESTON	84,249	53,779	29,470	1,000	24,309 R	63.8%	35.0%	64.6%	35.4%
40,983	CHEROKEE	12,809	8,655	4,101	53	4,554 R	67.6%	32.0%	67.9%	32.1%
30,148	CHESTER	8,045	4,441	3,559	45	882 R	55.2%	44.2%	55.5%	44.5%
38,161	CHESTERFIELD	10,067	5,451	4,593	23	858 R	54.1%	45.6%	54.3%	45.7%
27,464	CLARENDON	10,746	5,102	5,591	53	489 D	47.5%	52.0%	47.7%	52.3%
31,776	COLLETON	11,145	6,200	4,910	35	1,290 R	55.6%	44.1%	55.8%	44.2%
62,717	DARLINGTON	18,910	11,100	7,456	354	3,644 R	58.7%	39.4%	59.8%	40.2%
31,083	DILLON	8,050	4,646	3,360	44	1,286 R	57.7%	41.7%	58.0%	42.0%
58,761	DORCHESTER	22,399	15,289	7,037	73	8,252 R	68.3%	31.4%	68.5%	31.5%
17,528	EDGEFIELD	6,478	3,224	3,227	27	3 D	49.8%	49.8%	50.0%	50.0%
20,700	FAIRFIELD	7,287	3,147	4,117	23	970 D	43.2%	56.5%	43.3%	56.7%
110,163	FLORENCE	37,600	22,753	14,639	208	8,114 R	60.5%	38.9%	60.8%	39.2%
42,461	GEORGETOWN	13,830	7,370	6,392	68	978 R	53.3%	46.2%	53.6%	46.4%
287,913	GREENVILLE	91,369	66,766	24,137	466	42,629 R	73.1%	26.4%	73.4%	26.6%
57,847	GREENWOOD	17,307	10,887	6,339	81	4,548 R	62.9%	36.6%	63.2%	36.8%
18,159	HAMPTON	7,228	3,464	3,736	28	272 D	47.9%	51.7%	48.1%	51.9%
101,419	HORRY	29,463	20,396	8,940	127	11,456 R	69.2%	30.3%	69.5%	30.5%
14,504	JASPER	6,879	3,102	3,753	24	651 D	45.1%	54.6%	45.3%	54.7%
39,015	KERSHAW	13,226	8,822	4,323	81	4,499 R	66.7%	32.7%	67.1%	32.9%
53,361	LANCASTER	16,244	10,383	5,804	57	4,579 R	63.9%	35.7%	64.1%	35.9%
52,214	LAURENS	15,086	9,729	5,312	45	4,417 R	64.5%	35.2%	64.7%	35.3%
18,929	LEE	7,500	3,548	3,912	40	364 D	47.3%	52.2%	47.6%	52.4%
140,353	LEXINGTON	47,721	38,628	8,828	265	29,800 R	80.9%	18.5%	81.4%	18.6%
7,797	MCCORMICK	2,726	1,186	1,526	14	340 D	43.5%	56.0%	43.7%	56.3%
34,179	MARION	9,773	4,698	5,043	32	345 D	48.1%	51.6%	48.2%	51.8%
31,634	MARLBORO	8,283	3,951	4,294	38	343 D	47.7%	51.8%	47.9%	52.1%
31,242	NEWBERRY	11,008	7,176	3,790	42	3,386 R	65.2%	34.4%	65.4%	34.6%
48,611	OCONEE	12,044	8,625	3,333	86	5,292 R	71.6%	27.7%	72.1%	27.9%
82,276	ORANGEBURG	29,635	14,286	15,121	228	835 D	48.2%	51.0%	48.6%	51.4%
79,292	PICKENS	19,764	15,155	4,481	128	10,674 R	76.7%	22.7%	77.2%	22.8%
269,735	RICHLAND	81,429	46,773	32,212	2,444	14,561 R	57.4%	39.6%	59.2%	40.8%
16,150	SALUDA	5,501	3,515	1,962	24	1,553 R	63.9%	35.7%	64.2%	35.8%
201,861	SPARTANBURG	62,575	41,553	20,130	892	21,423 R	66.4%	32.2%	67.4%	32.6%
88,243	SUMTER	22,591	12,909	9,566	116	3,343 R	57.1%	42.3%	57.4%	42.6%
30,751	UNION	10,796	6,331	4,424	41	1,907 R	58.6%	41.0%	58.9%	41.1%
38,226	WILLIAMSBURG	14,128	6,492	7,586	50	1,094 D	46.0%	53.7%	46.1%	53.9%
106,720	YORK	29,427	20,008	9,273	146	10,735 R	68.0%	31.5%	68.3%	31.7%
3,121,820	TOTAL	968,529	615,539	344,459	8,531	271,080 R	63.6%	35.6%	64.1%	35.9%

SOUTH CAROLINA

SENATOR 1984

1980 Census Population	County	Total Vote	Republican	Democratic	Other	Rep.-Dem. Plurality	Percentage			
							Total Vote		Major Vote	
							Rep.	Dem.	Rep.	Dem.
22,627	ABBEVILLE	6,558	4,056	2,440	62	1,616 R	61.8%	37.2%	62.4%	37.6%
105,625	AIKEN	37,034	27,529	9,032	473	18,497 R	74.3%	24.4%	75.3%	24.7%
10,700	ALLENDALE	3,447	1,791	1,620	36	171 R	52.0%	47.0%	52.5%	47.5%
133,235	ANDERSON	34,289	23,911	9,939	439	13,972 R	69.7%	29.0%	70.6%	29.4%
18,118	BAMBERG	5,485	3,155	2,288	42	867 R	57.5%	41.7%	58.0%	42.0%
19,868	BARNWELL	6,953	4,590	2,323	40	2,267 R	66.0%	33.4%	66.4%	33.6%
65,364	BEAUFORT	20,348	14,482	5,620	246	8,862 R	71.2%	27.6%	72.0%	28.0%
94,727	BERKELEY	26,860	18,388	8,294	178	10,094 R	68.5%	30.9%	68.9%	31.1%
12,206	CALHOUN	4,443	2,865	1,539	39	1,326 R	64.5%	34.6%	65.1%	34.9%
276,974	CHARLESTON	86,274	56,973	27,339	1,962	29,634 R	66.0%	31.7%	67.6%	32.4%
40,983	CHEROKEE	12,316	8,749	3,457	110	5,292 R	71.0%	28.1%	71.7%	28.3%
30,148	CHESTER	8,207	4,864	3,243	100	1,621 R	59.3%	39.5%	60.0%	40.0%
38,161	CHESTERFIELD	9,764	5,956	3,735	73	2,221 R	61.0%	38.3%	61.5%	38.5%
27,464	CLARENDON	10,371	5,500	4,767	104	733 R	53.0%	46.0%	53.6%	46.4%
31,776	COLLETON	10,972	6,818	4,097	57	2,721 R	62.1%	37.3%	62.5%	37.5%
62,717	DARLINGTON	17,359	10,644	6,351	364	4,293 R	61.3%	36.6%	62.6%	37.4%
31,083	DILLON	7,640	4,716	2,844	80	1,872 R	61.7%	37.2%	62.4%	37.6%
58,761	DORCHESTER	21,847	15,574	6,125	148	9,449 R	71.3%	28.0%	71.8%	28.2%
17,528	EDGEFIELD	6,169	3,438	2,682	49	756 R	55.7%	43.5%	56.2%	43.8%
20,700	FAIRFIELD	7,059	3,487	3,508	64	21 D	49.4%	49.7%	49.8%	50.2%
110,163	FLORENCE	36,291	22,087	13,839	365	8,248 R	60.9%	38.1%	61.5%	38.5%
42,461	GEORGETOWN	13,868	7,716	5,934	218	1,782 R	55.6%	42.8%	56.5%	43.5%
287,913	GREENVILLE	91,664	67,889	22,525	1,250	45,364 R	74.1%	24.6%	75.1%	24.9%
57,847	GREENWOOD	16,670	11,078	5,365	227	5,713 R	66.5%	32.2%	67.4%	32.6%
18,159	HAMPTON	6,917	3,689	3,183	45	506 R	53.3%	46.0%	53.7%	46.3%
101,419	HORRY	32,725	23,943	8,456	326	15,487 R	73.2%	25.8%	73.9%	26.1%
14,504	JASPER	6,462	3,279	3,117	66	162 R	50.7%	48.2%	51.3%	48.7%
39,015	KERSHAW	13,620	9,586	3,831	203	5,755 R	70.4%	28.1%	71.4%	28.6%
53,361	LANCASTER	15,789	10,819	4,838	132	5,981 R	68.5%	30.6%	69.1%	30.9%
52,214	LAURENS	14,517	10,005	4,406	106	5,599 R	68.9%	30.4%	69.4%	30.6%
18,929	LEE	7,278	3,810	3,389	79	421 R	52.3%	46.6%	52.9%	47.1%
140,353	LEXINGTON	49,081	40,907	7,433	741	33,474 R	83.3%	15.1%	84.6%	15.4%
7,797	MCCORMICK	2,580	1,386	1,175	19	211 R	53.7%	45.5%	54.1%	45.9%
34,179	MARION	8,759	4,853	3,865	41	988 R	55.4%	44.1%	55.7%	44.3%
31,634	MARLBORO	7,460	4,324	3,076	60	1,248 R	58.0%	41.2%	58.4%	41.6%
31,242	NEWBERRY	10,843	7,481	3,289	73	4,192 R	69.0%	30.3%	69.5%	30.5%
48,611	OCONEE	12,905	9,380	3,292	233	6,088 R	72.7%	25.5%	74.0%	26.0%
82,276	ORANGEBURG	29,124	14,517	14,476	131	41 R	49.8%	49.7%	50.1%	49.9%
79,292	PICKENS	20,310	15,991	4,018	301	11,973 R	78.7%	19.8%	79.9%	20.1%
269,735	RICHLAND	83,464	51,918	29,867	1,679	22,051 R	62.2%	35.8%	63.5%	36.5%
16,150	SALUDA	5,147	3,628	1,467	52	2,161 R	70.5%	28.5%	71.2%	28.8%
201,861	SPARTANBURG	60,543	41,488	17,423	1,632	24,065 R	68.5%	28.8%	70.4%	29.6%
88,243	SUMTER	22,343	13,218	8,953	172	4,265 R	59.2%	40.1%	59.6%	40.4%
30,751	UNION	10,301	6,770	3,445	86	3,325 R	65.7%	33.4%	66.3%	33.7%
38,226	WILLIAMSBURG	13,165	6,805	6,301	59	504 R	51.7%	47.9%	51.9%	48.1%
106,720	YORK	29,909	20,762	8,776	371	11,986 R	69.4%	29.3%	70.3%	29.7%
3,121,820	TOTAL	965,130	644,815	306,982	13,333	337,833 R	66.8%	31.8%	67.7%	32.3%

SOUTH CAROLINA

CONGRESS

| | | | Republican | | | Democratic | | | | Percentage | | | |
| | | Total | | | | | | Other | Rep.-Dem. | Total Vote | | Major Vote | |
CD	Year	Vote	Vote	Candidate	Vote	Candidate	Vote	Plurality	Rep.	Dem.	Rep.	Dem.
1	1984	167,310	103,288	HARTNETT, THOMAS F.	64,022	PENDARVIS, ED		39,266 R	61.7%	38.3%	61.7%	38.3%
1	1982	117,832	63,945	HARTNETT, THOMAS F.	52,916	MCLEOD, W. MULLINS	971	11,029 R	54.3%	44.9%	54.7%	45.3%
2	1984	174,027	108,085	SPENCE, FLOYD	63,932	MOSELY, KEN	2,010	44,153 R	62.1%	36.7%	62.8%	37.2%
2	1982	122,318	71,569	SPENCE, FLOYD	50,749	MOSELY, KEN		20,820 R	58.5%	41.5%	58.5%	41.5%
3	1984	152,166	61,739	TAYLOR, CLARENCE E.	88,917	DERRICK, BUTLER	1,510	27,178 D	40.6%	58.4%	41.0%	59.0%
3	1982	85,339			77,125	DERRICK, BUTLER	8,214	77,125 D		90.4%		100.0%
4	1984	164,424	105,139	CAMPBELL, CARROLL	57,854	SMITH, JEFF	1,431	47,285 R	63.9%	35.2%	64.5%	35.5%
4	1982	110,196	69,802	CAMPBELL, CARROLL	40,394	TYUS, MARION E.		29,408 R	63.3%	36.7%	63.3%	36.7%
5	1984	107,291			98,513	SPRATT, JOHN	8,778	98,513 D		91.8%		100.0%
5	1982	102,536	33,191	WILKERSON, JOHN S.	69,345	SPRATT, JOHN		36,154 D	32.4%	67.6%	32.4%	67.6%
6	1984	162,384	63,005	EARGLE, LOIS	97,329	TALLON, ROBERT M.	2,050	34,324 D	38.8%	59.9%	39.3%	60.7%
6	1982	119,235	56,653	NAPIER, JOHN L.	62,582	TALLON, ROBERT M.		5,929 D	47.5%	52.5%	47.5%	52.5%

SOUTH CAROLINA

1984 GENERAL ELECTION

President   Other vote was 4,359 Bergland (Libertarian); 3,490 Dennis (American); 682 Serrette (United Citizens). Final published returns may indicate very small adjustments in candidate, county and state vote totals.

Senator   Other vote was Davis (Libertarian). See note above.

Congress   Other vote was Sullivan (Libertarian) in CD 2; Madden (Libertarian) in CD 3; Pike (Libertarian) in CD 4; 4,593 Winchester (American) and 4,185 Blevins (Libertarian) in CD 5; Thompson (Libertarian) in CD 6. Final published returns may indicate single vote adjustments in some district data.

1984 PRIMARIES

JUNE 12 REPUBLICAN

Senator   44,662 Strom Thurmond; 2,693 R. H. Cunningham.

Congress   Unopposed in three CD's. No candidate in CD 5. Contested as follows:

CD 3   3,845 Clarence E. Taylor; 2,096 Garfield Flurett.
CD 6   3,120 Lois Eargle; 1,569 James Maurer.

JUNE 12 DEMOCRATIC

Senator   149,730 Melvin Purvis; 148,586 Cecil J. Williams.

Congress   Unopposed in four CD's. Contested as follows:

CD 2   21,560 Ken Mosely; 19,125 Nancy Stevenson.
CD 6   61,927 Robert M. Tallon; 17,385 Mary Demetrious; 4,053 Luther Lighty.

SOUTH DAKOTA

GOVERNOR
William J. Janklow (R). Re-elected 1982 to a four-year term. Previously elected 1978.

SENATORS
James Abdnor (R). Elected 1980 to a six-year term.

Larry Pressler (R). Re-elected 1984 to a six-year term. Previously elected 1978.

REPRESENTATIVE
At-Large. Thomas A. Daschle (D)

POSTWAR VOTE FOR GOVERNOR

Year	Total Vote	Republican Vote	Candidate	Democratic Vote	Candidate	Other Vote	Rep.-Dem. Plurality	Total Vote Rep.	Total Vote Dem.	Major Vote Rep.	Major Vote Dem.
1982	278,562	197,426	Janklow, William J.	81,136	O'Connor, Michael J.	—	116,290 R	70.9%	29.1%	70.9%	29.1%
1978	259,795	147,116	Janklow, William J.	112,679	McKellips, Roger	—	34,437 R	56.6%	43.4%	56.6%	43.4%
1974*	278,228	129,077	Olson, John E.	149,151	Kneip, Richard F.	—	20,074 D	46.4%	53.6%	46.4%	53.6%
1972	308,177	123,165	Thompson, Carveth	185,012	Kneip, Richard F.	—	61,847 D	40.0%	60.0%	40.0%	60.0%
1970	239,963	108,347	Farrar, Frank	131,616	Kneip, Richard F.	—	23,269 D	45.2%	54.8%	45.2%	54.8%
1968	276,906	159,646	Farrar, Frank	117,260	Chamberlin, Robert	—	42,386 R	57.7%	42.3%	57.7%	42.3%
1966	228,214	131,710	Boe, Nils A.	96,504	Chamberlin, Robert	—	35,206 R	57.7%	42.3%	57.7%	42.3%
1964	290,570	150,151	Boe, Nils A.	140,419	Lindley, John F.	—	9,732 R	51.7%	48.3%	51.7%	48.3%
1962	256,120	143,682	Gubbrud, Archie M.	112,438	Herseth, Ralph	—	31,244 R	56.1%	43.9%	56.1%	43.9%
1960	304,625	154,530	Gubbrud, Archie M.	150,095	Herseth, Ralph	—	4,435 R	50.7%	49.3%	50.7%	49.3%
1958	258,281	125,520	Saunders, Phil	132,761	Herseth, Ralph	—	7,241 D	48.6%	51.4%	48.6%	51.4%
1956	292,017	158,819	Foss, Joe J.	133,198	Herseth, Ralph	—	25,621 R	54.4%	45.6%	54.4%	45.6%
1954	236,255	133,878	Foss, Joe J.	102,377	Martin, Ed C.	—	31,501 R	56.7%	43.3%	56.7%	43.3%
1952	289,515	203,102	Anderson, Sigurd	86,413	Iverson, Sherman A.	—	116,689 R	70.2%	29.8%	70.2%	29.8%
1950	253,316	154,254	Anderson, Sigurd	99,062	Robbie, Joseph	—	55,192 R	60.9%	39.1%	60.9%	39.1%
1948	245,372	149,883	Mickelson, George	95,489	Volz, Harold J.	—	54,394 R	61.1%	38.9%	61.1%	38.9%
1946	162,292	108,998	Mickelson, George	53,294	Haeder, Richard	—	55,704 R	67.2%	32.8%	67.2%	32.8%

The term of office of South Dakota's Governor was increased from two to four years effective with the 1974 election.

POSTWAR VOTE FOR SENATOR

Year	Total Vote	Republican Vote	Candidate	Democratic Vote	Candidate	Other Vote	Rep.-Dem. Plurality	Total Vote Rep.	Total Vote Dem.	Major Vote Rep.	Major Vote Dem.
1984	315,713	235,176	Pressler, Larry	80,537	Cunningham, George V.	—	154,639 R	74.5%	25.5%	74.5%	25.5%
1980	327,478	190,594	Abdnor, James	129,018	McGovern, George S.	7,866	61,576 R	58.2%	39.4%	59.6%	40.4%
1978	255,599	170,832	Pressler, Larry	84,767	Barnett, Don	—	86,065 R	66.8%	33.2%	66.8%	33.2%
1974	278,884	130,955	Thorsness, Leo K.	147,929	McGovern, George S.	—	16,974 D	47.0%	53.0%	47.0%	53.0%
1972	306,386	131,613	Hirsch, Robert W.	174,773	Abourezk, James	—	43,160 D	43.0%	57.0%	43.0%	57.0%
1968	279,912	120,951	Gubbrud, Archie M.	158,961	McGovern, George S.	—	38,010 D	43.2%	56.8%	43.2%	56.8%
1966	227,080	150,517	Mundt, Karl E.	76,563	Wright, Donn H.	—	73,954 R	66.3%	33.7%	66.3%	33.7%
1962	254,319	126,861	Bottum, Joe H.	127,458	McGovern, George S.	—	597 D	49.9%	50.1%	49.9%	50.1%
1960	305,442	160,181	Mundt, Karl E.	145,261	McGovern, George S.	—	14,920 R	52.4%	47.6%	52.4%	47.6%
1956	290,622	147,621	Case, Francis	143,001	Holum, Kenneth	—	4,620 R	50.8%	49.2%	50.8%	49.2%
1954	235,745	135,071	Mundt, Karl E.	100,674	Holum, Kenneth	—	34,397 R	57.3%	42.7%	57.3%	42.7%
1950	251,362	160,670	Case, Francis	90,692	Engel, John A.	—	69,978 R	63.9%	36.1%	63.9%	36.1%
1948	242,833	144,084	Mundt, Karl E.	98,749	Engel, John A.	—	45,335 R	59.3%	40.7%	59.3%	40.7%

SOUTH DAKOTA

One At Large

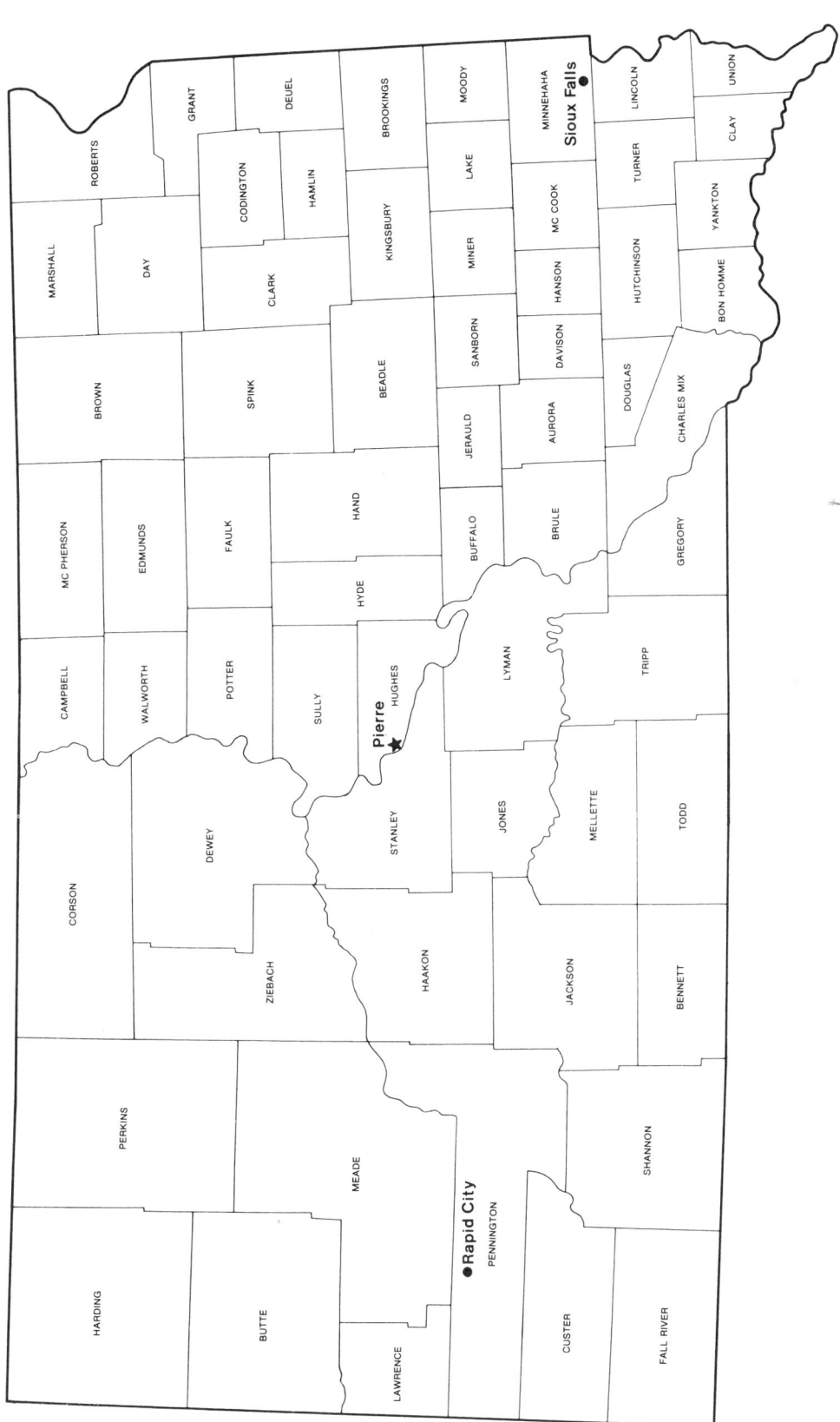

SOUTH DAKOTA

PRESIDENT 1984

1980 Census Population	County	Total Vote	Republican	Democratic	Other	Rep.-Dem. Plurality	Percentage Total Vote Rep.	Dem.	Major Vote Rep.	Dem.
3,628	AURORA	1,883	1,029	840	14	189 R	54.6%	44.6%	55.1%	44.9%
19,195	BEADLE	9,422	5,876	3,523	23	2,353 R	62.4%	37.4%	62.5%	37.5%
3,044	BENNETT	1,316	856	453	7	403 R	65.0%	34.4%	65.4%	34.6%
8,059	BONHOMME	3,906	2,478	1,408	20	1,070 R	63.4%	36.0%	63.8%	36.2%
24,332	BROOKINGS	10,814	6,679	4,089	46	2,590 R	61.8%	37.8%	62.0%	38.0%
36,962	BROWN	17,465	10,541	6,852	72	3,689 R	60.4%	39.2%	60.6%	39.4%
5,245	BRULE	2,556	1,578	961	17	617 R	61.7%	37.6%	62.2%	37.8%
1,795	BUFFALO	494	253	236	5	17 R	51.2%	47.8%	51.7%	48.3%
8,372	BUTTE	3,667	2,865	784	18	2,081 R	78.1%	21.4%	78.5%	21.5%
2,243	CAMPBELL	1,255	1,035	214	6	821 R	82.5%	17.1%	82.9%	17.1%
9,680	CHARLES MIX	4,563	2,660	1,879	24	781 R	58.3%	41.2%	58.6%	41.4%
4,894	CLARK	2,718	1,748	960	10	788 R	64.3%	35.3%	64.5%	35.5%
13,689	CLAY	5,808	3,057	2,711	40	346 R	52.6%	46.7%	53.0%	47.0%
20,885	CODINGTON	9,678	6,108	3,528	42	2,580 R	63.1%	36.5%	63.4%	36.6%
5,196	CORSON	1,753	955	792	6	163 R	54.5%	45.2%	54.7%	45.3%
6,000	CUSTER	3,063	2,183	858	22	1,325 R	71.3%	28.0%	71.8%	28.2%
17,820	DAVISON	8,048	4,783	3,248	17	1,535 R	59.4%	40.4%	59.6%	40.4%
8,133	DAY	4,101	2,150	1,932	19	218 R	52.4%	47.1%	52.7%	47.3%
5,289	DEUEL	2,490	1,537	941	12	596 R	61.7%	37.8%	62.0%	38.0%
5,366	DEWEY	1,727	941	772	14	169 R	54.5%	44.7%	54.9%	45.1%
4,181	DOUGLAS	2,254	1,713	536	5	1,177 R	76.0%	23.8%	76.2%	23.8%
5,159	EDMUNDS	2,570	1,553	1,007	10	546 R	60.4%	39.2%	60.7%	39.3%
8,439	FALL RIVER	3,905	2,748	1,135	22	1,613 R	70.4%	29.1%	70.8%	29.2%
3,327	FAULK	1,706	1,124	579	3	545 R	65.9%	33.9%	66.0%	34.0%
9,013	GRANT	4,360	2,738	1,606	16	1,132 R	62.8%	36.8%	63.0%	37.0%
6,015	GREGORY	2,569	1,777	780	12	997 R	69.2%	30.4%	69.5%	30.5%
2,794	HAAKON	1,410	1,168	237	5	931 R	82.8%	16.8%	83.1%	16.9%
5,261	HAMLIN	2,761	1,782	963	16	819 R	64.5%	34.9%	64.9%	35.1%
4,948	HAND	2,886	2,030	846	10	1,184 R	70.3%	29.3%	70.6%	29.4%
3,415	HANSON	1,530	898	625	7	273 R	58.7%	40.8%	59.0%	41.0%
1,700	HARDING	912	723	186	3	537 R	79.3%	20.4%	79.5%	20.5%
14,220	HUGHES	7,089	4,985	2,072	32	2,913 R	70.3%	29.2%	70.6%	29.4%
9,350	HUTCHINSON	4,624	3,372	1,237	15	2,135 R	72.9%	26.8%	73.2%	26.8%
2,069	HYDE	1,148	797	350	1	447 R	69.4%	30.5%	69.5%	30.5%
3,437	JACKSON	1,275	903	365	7	538 R	70.8%	28.6%	71.2%	28.8%
2,929	JERAULD	1,562	1,012	542	8	470 R	64.8%	34.7%	65.1%	34.9%
1,463	JONES	899	689	206	4	483 R	76.6%	22.9%	77.0%	23.0%
6,679	KINGSBURY	3,383	2,121	1,249	13	872 R	62.7%	36.9%	62.9%	37.1%
10,724	LAKE	5,413	3,027	2,367	19	660 R	55.9%	43.7%	56.1%	43.9%
18,339	LAWRENCE	8,569	5,949	2,565	55	3,384 R	69.4%	29.9%	69.9%	30.1%
13,942	LINCOLN	6,636	3,988	2,626	22	1,362 R	60.1%	39.6%	60.3%	39.7%
3,864	LYMAN	1,605	1,120	478	7	642 R	69.8%	29.8%	70.1%	29.9%
6,444	MCCOOK	3,362	1,902	1,448	12	454 R	56.6%	43.1%	56.8%	43.2%
4,027	MCPHERSON	2,236	1,813	418	5	1,395 R	81.1%	18.7%	81.3%	18.7%
5,404	MARSHALL	2,649	1,529	1,111	9	418 R	57.7%	41.9%	57.9%	42.1%
20,717	MEADE	8,041	5,908	2,093	40	3,815 R	73.5%	26.0%	73.8%	26.2%
2,249	MELLETTE	927	616	303	8	313 R	66.5%	32.7%	67.0%	33.0%
3,739	MINER	1,977	1,004	960	13	44 R	50.8%	48.6%	51.1%	48.9%
109,435	MINNEHAHA	53,171	29,908	23,042	221	6,866 R	56.2%	43.3%	56.5%	43.5%
6,692	MOODY	3,228	1,633	1,586	9	47 R	50.6%	49.1%	50.7%	49.3%
70,361	PENNINGTON	30,389	21,947	8,224	218	13,723 R	72.2%	27.1%	72.7%	27.3%
4,700	PERKINS	2,411	1,686	714	11	972 R	69.9%	29.6%	70.3%	29.8%
3,674	POTTER	2,035	1,551	482	2	1,069 R	76.2%	23.7%	76.3%	23.7%
10,911	ROBERTS	4,840	2,767	2,063	10	704 R	57.2%	42.6%	57.3%	42.7%
3,213	SANBORN	1,695	1,080	611	4	469 R	63.7%	36.0%	63.9%	36.1%
11,323	SHANNON	1,829	324	1,489	16	1,165 D	17.7%	81.4%	17.9%	82.1%
9,201	SPINK	4,324	2,627	1,680	17	947 R	60.8%	38.9%	61.0%	39.0%
2,533	STANLEY	1,299	942	351	6	591 R	72.5%	27.0%	72.9%	27.1%
1,990	SULLY	1,107	836	266	5	570 R	75.5%	24.0%	75.9%	24.1%
7,328	TODD	1,714	679	1,022	13	343 D	39.6%	59.6%	39.9%	60.1%

SOUTH DAKOTA

PRESIDENT 1984

1980 Census Population	County	Total Vote	Republican	Democratic	Other	Rep.-Dem. Plurality	Percentage			
							Total Vote		Major Vote	
							Rep.	Dem.	Rep.	Dem.
7,268	TRIPP	3,440	2,483	935	22	1,548 R	72.2%	27.2%	72.6%	27.4%
9,255	TURNER	4,592	3,086	1,486	20	1,600 R	67.2%	32.4%	67.5%	32.5%
10,938	UNION	4,677	2,431	2,221	25	210 R	52.0%	47.5%	52.3%	47.7%
7,011	WALWORTH	3,194	2,396	779	19	1,617 R	75.0%	24.4%	75.5%	24.5%
18,952	YANKTON	8,145	5,161	2,932	52	2,229 R	63.4%	36.0%	63.8%	36.2%
2,308	ZIEBACH	792	429	359	4	70 R	54.2%	45.3%	54.4%	45.6%
690,768	TOTAL	317,867	200,267	116,113	1,487	84,154 R	63.0%	36.5%	63.3%	36.7%

SOUTH DAKOTA

SENATOR 1984

1980 Census Population	County	Total Vote	Republican	Democratic	Other	Rep.-Dem. Plurality	Percentage Total Vote Rep.	Total Vote Dem.	Major Vote Rep.	Major Vote Dem.
3,628	AURORA	1,888	1,304	584		720 R	69.1%	30.9%	69.1%	30.9%
19,195	BEADLE	9,268	6,523	2,745		3,778 R	70.4%	29.6%	70.4%	29.6%
3,044	BENNETT	1,296	974	322		652 R	75.2%	24.8%	75.2%	24.8%
8,059	BONHOMME	3,924	3,045	879		2,166 R	77.6%	22.4%	77.6%	22.4%
24,332	BROOKINGS	10,743	7,843	2,900		4,943 R	73.0%	27.0%	73.0%	27.0%
36,962	BROWN	17,788	13,069	4,719		8,350 R	73.5%	26.5%	73.5%	26.5%
5,245	BRULE	2,600	1,863	737		1,126 R	71.7%	28.3%	71.7%	28.3%
1,795	BUFFALO	590	346	244		102 R	58.6%	41.4%	58.6%	41.4%
8,372	BUTTE	3,614	3,100	514		2,586 R	85.8%	14.2%	85.8%	14.2%
2,243	CAMPBELL	1,234	1,094	140		954 R	88.7%	11.3%	88.7%	11.3%
9,680	CHARLES MIX	4,541	3,205	1,336		1,869 R	70.6%	29.4%	70.6%	29.4%
4,894	CLARK	2,687	2,096	591		1,505 R	78.0%	22.0%	78.0%	22.0%
13,689	CLAY	5,835	4,029	1,806		2,223 R	69.0%	31.0%	69.0%	31.0%
20,885	CODINGTON	9,868	7,208	2,660		4,548 R	73.0%	27.0%	73.0%	27.0%
5,196	CORSON	1,675	1,178	497		681 R	70.3%	29.7%	70.3%	29.7%
6,000	CUSTER	3,161	2,456	705		1,751 R	77.7%	22.3%	77.7%	22.3%
17,820	DAVISON	8,011	5,698	2,313		3,385 R	71.1%	28.9%	71.1%	28.9%
8,133	DAY	4,064	2,740	1,324		1,416 R	67.4%	32.6%	67.4%	32.6%
5,289	DEUEL	2,461	1,888	573		1,315 R	76.7%	23.3%	76.7%	23.3%
5,366	DEWEY	1,756	1,293	463		830 R	73.6%	26.4%	73.6%	26.4%
4,181	DOUGLAS	2,224	1,866	358		1,508 R	83.9%	16.1%	83.9%	16.1%
5,159	EDMUNDS	2,492	1,859	633		1,226 R	74.6%	25.4%	74.6%	25.4%
8,439	FALL RIVER	3,899	3,114	785		2,329 R	79.9%	20.1%	79.9%	20.1%
3,327	FAULK	1,695	1,275	420		855 R	75.2%	24.8%	75.2%	24.8%
9,013	GRANT	4,337	3,124	1,213		1,911 R	72.0%	28.0%	72.0%	28.0%
6,015	GREGORY	2,611	2,044	567		1,477 R	78.3%	21.7%	78.3%	21.7%
2,794	HAAKON	1,406	1,282	124		1,158 R	91.2%	8.8%	91.2%	8.8%
5,261	HAMLIN	2,743	2,111	632		1,479 R	77.0%	23.0%	77.0%	23.0%
4,948	HAND	2,878	2,228	650		1,578 R	77.4%	22.6%	77.4%	22.6%
3,415	HANSON	1,513	1,102	411		691 R	72.8%	27.2%	72.8%	27.2%
1,700	HARDING	899	793	106		687 R	88.2%	11.8%	88.2%	11.8%
14,220	HUGHES	7,089	5,322	1,767		3,555 R	75.1%	24.9%	75.1%	24.9%
9,350	HUTCHINSON	4,575	3,732	843		2,889 R	81.6%	18.4%	81.6%	18.4%
2,069	HYDE	1,128	874	254		620 R	77.5%	22.5%	77.5%	22.5%
3,437	JACKSON	1,267	1,002	265		737 R	79.1%	20.9%	79.1%	20.9%
2,929	JERAULD	1,552	1,172	380		792 R	75.5%	24.5%	75.5%	24.5%
1,463	JONES	896	765	131		634 R	85.4%	14.6%	85.4%	14.6%
6,679	KINGSBURY	3,383	2,580	803		1,777 R	76.3%	23.7%	76.3%	23.7%
10,724	LAKE	5,471	4,072	1,399		2,673 R	74.4%	25.6%	74.4%	25.6%
18,339	LAWRENCE	8,640	6,933	1,707		5,226 R	80.2%	19.8%	80.2%	19.8%
13,942	LINCOLN	6,636	4,895	1,741		3,154 R	73.8%	26.2%	73.8%	26.2%
3,864	LYMAN	1,630	1,308	322		986 R	80.2%	19.8%	80.2%	19.8%
6,444	MCCOOK	3,363	2,477	886		1,591 R	73.7%	26.3%	73.7%	26.3%
4,027	MCPHERSON	2,176	1,907	269		1,638 R	87.6%	12.4%	87.6%	12.4%
5,404	MARSHALL	2,671	1,808	863		945 R	67.7%	32.3%	67.7%	32.3%
20,717	MEADE	7,951	6,578	1,373		5,205 R	82.7%	17.3%	82.7%	17.3%
2,249	MELLETTE	926	706	220		486 R	76.2%	23.8%	76.2%	23.8%
3,739	MINER	2,024	1,428	596		832 R	70.6%	29.4%	70.6%	29.4%
109,435	MINNEHAHA	51,811	35,309	16,502		18,807 R	68.1%	31.9%	68.1%	31.9%
6,692	MOODY	3,205	2,183	1,022		1,161 R	68.1%	31.9%	68.1%	31.9%
70,361	PENNINGTON	29,645	24,485	5,160		19,325 R	82.6%	17.4%	82.6%	17.4%
4,700	PERKINS	2,321	1,857	464		1,393 R	80.0%	20.0%	80.0%	20.0%
3,674	POTTER	2,028	1,664	364		1,300 R	82.1%	17.9%	82.1%	17.9%
10,911	ROBERTS	4,716	3,133	1,583		1,550 R	66.4%	33.6%	66.4%	33.6%
3,213	SANBORN	1,743	1,324	419		905 R	76.0%	24.0%	76.0%	24.0%
11,323	SHANNON	1,940	887	1,053		166 D	45.7%	54.3%	45.7%	54.3%
9,201	SPINK	4,287	3,239	1,048		2,191 R	75.6%	24.4%	75.6%	24.4%
2,533	STANLEY	1,314	1,003	311		692 R	76.3%	23.7%	76.3%	23.7%
1,990	SULLY	1,107	901	206		695 R	81.4%	18.6%	81.4%	18.6%
7,328	TODD	1,753	1,067	686		381 R	60.9%	39.1%	60.9%	39.1%

SOUTH DAKOTA

SENATOR 1984

1980 Census Population	County	Total Vote	Republican	Democratic	Other	Rep.-Dem. Plurality	Total Vote Rep.	Total Vote Dem.	Major Vote Rep.	Major Vote Dem.
7,268	TRIPP	3,515	2,730	785		1,945 R	77.7%	22.3%	77.7%	22.3%
9,255	TURNER	4,585	3,598	987		2,611 R	78.5%	21.5%	78.5%	21.5%
10,938	UNION	4,642	3,302	1,340		1,962 R	71.1%	28.9%	71.1%	28.9%
7,011	WALWORTH	3,170	2,533	637		1,896 R	79.9%	20.1%	79.9%	20.1%
18,952	YANKTON	8,039	6,077	1,962		4,115 R	75.6%	24.4%	75.6%	24.4%
2,308	ZIEBACH	813	575	238		337 R	70.7%	29.3%	70.7%	29.3%
690,768	TOTAL	315,713	235,176	80,537		154,639 R	74.5%	25.5%	74.5%	25.5%

SOUTH DAKOTA

CONGRESS

CD	Year	Total Vote	Vote	Republican Candidate	Vote	Democratic Candidate	Other Vote	Rep.-Dem. Plurality	Percentage Total Vote Rep.	Dem.	Major Vote Rep.	Dem.
AL	1984	316,222	134,821	BELL, DALE	181,401	DASCHLE, THOMAS A.		46,580 D	42.6%	57.4%	42.6%	57.4%
AL	1982	275,652	133,530	ROBERTS, CLINT	142,122	DASCHLE, THOMAS A.		8,592 D	48.4%	51.6%	48.4%	51.6%

SOUTH DAKOTA

1984 GENERAL ELECTION

President   Other vote was 1,150 Serrette (Independent); 337 Mason (Independent).

Senator

Congress

1984 PRIMARIES

JUNE 5 REPUBLICAN

Senator   Larry Pressler, unopposed.

Congress   Contested as follows:

AL   43,014 Dale Bell; 11,798 Larry Mangels.

JUNE 5 DEMOCRATIC

Senator   31,376 George V. Cunningham; 14,672 Dean L. Sinclair.

Congress   Unopposed at-large.

TENNESSEE

GOVERNOR
Lamar Alexander (R). Re-elected 1982 to a four-year term. Previously elected 1978.

SENATORS
Albert Gore, Jr. (D). Elected 1984 to a six-year term.

James R. Sasser (D). Re-elected 1982 to a six-year term. Previously elected 1976.

REPRESENTATIVES
1. James H. Quillen (R)
2. John J. Duncan (R)
3. Marilyn Lloyd (D)
4. Jim Cooper (D)
5. Bill Boner (D)
6. Bart Gordon (D)
7. Don Sundquist (R)
8. Ed Jones (D)
9. Harold E. Ford (D)

POSTWAR VOTE FOR GOVERNOR

Year	Total Vote	Republican Vote	Candidate	Democratic Vote	Candidate	Other Vote	Rep.-Dem. Plurality	Total Vote Rep.	Total Vote Dem.	Major Vote Rep.	Major Vote Dem.
1982	1,238,927	737,963	Alexander, Lamar	500,937	Tyree, Randy	27	237,026 R	59.6%	40.4%	59.6%	40.4%
1978	1,189,695	661,959	Alexander, Lamar	523,495	Butcher, Jake	4,241	138,464 R	55.6%	44.0%	55.8%	44.2%
1974	1,040,714	455,467	Alexander, Lamar	576,833	Blanton, Ray	8,414	121,366 D	43.8%	55.4%	44.1%	55.9%
1970	1,108,247	575,777	Dunn, Winfield	509,521	Hooker, John J.	22,949	66,256 R	52.0%	46.0%	53.1%	46.9%
1966	656,566	—	—	532,998	Ellington, Buford	123,568	532,998 D	—	81.2%	—	100.0%
1962	621,064	100,190	Patty, Hubert D.	315,648	Clement, Frank G.	205,226	215,458 D	16.1%	50.8%	24.1%	75.9%
1958	432,545	35,938	Wall, Thomas P.	248,874	Ellington, Buford	147,733	212,936 D	8.3%	57.5%	12.6%	87.4%
1954*	322,586	—	—	281,291	Clement, Frank G.	41,295	281,291 D	—	87.2%	—	100.0%
1952	806,771	166,377	Witt, R. Beecher	640,290	Clement, Frank G.	104	473,913 D	20.6%	79.4%	20.6%	79.4%
1950	236,194	—	—	184,437	Browning, Gordon	51,757	184,437 D	—	78.1%	—	100.0%
1948	543,881	179,957	Acuff, Roy	363,903	Browning, Gordon	21	183,946 D	33.1%	66.9%	33.1%	66.9%
1946	229,456	73,222	Lowe, W. O.	149,937	McCord, Jim Nance	6,297	76,715 D	31.9%	65.3%	32.8%	67.2%

The term of office of Tennessee's Governor was increased from two to four years effective with the 1954 election.

POSTWAR VOTE FOR SENATOR

Year	Total Vote	Republican Vote	Candidate	Democratic Vote	Candidate	Other Vote	Rep.-Dem. Plurality	Total Vote Rep.	Total Vote Dem.	Major Vote Rep.	Major Vote Dem.
1984	1,648,064	557,016	Ashe, Victor	1,000,607	Gore, Albert, Jr.	90,441	443,591 D	33.8%	60.7%	35.8%	64.2%
1982	1,259,785	479,642	Beard, Robin L.	780,113	Sasser, James R.	30	300,471 D	38.1%	61.9%	38.1%	61.9%
1978	1,157,094	642,644	Baker, Howard H., Jr.	466,228	Eskind, Jane	48,222	176,416 R	55.5%	40.3%	58.0%	42.0%
1976	1,432,046	673,231	Brock, William E.	751,180	Sasser, James R.	7,635	77,949 D	47.0%	52.5%	47.3%	52.7%
1972	1,164,195	716,539	Baker, Howard H., Jr.	440,599	Blanton, Ray	7,057	275,940 R	61.5%	37.8%	61.9%	38.1%
1970	1,097,041	562,645	Brock, William E.	519,858	Gore, Albert	14,538	42,787 R	51.3%	47.4%	52.0%	48.0%
1966	866,961	483,063	Baker, Howard H., Jr.	383,843	Clement, Frank G.	55	99,220 R	55.7%	44.3%	55.7%	44.3%
1964	1,064,018	493,475	Kuykendall, Daniel H.	570,542	Gore, Albert	1	77,067 D	46.4%	53.6%	46.4%	53.6%
1964s	1,091,093	517,330	Baker, Howard H., Jr.	568,905	Bass, Ross	4,858	51,575 D	47.4%	52.1%	47.6%	52.4%
1960	828,519	234,053	Frazier, A. Bradley	594,460	Kefauver, Estes	6	360,407 D	28.2%	71.7%	28.2%	71.8%
1958	401,666	76,371	Atkins, Hobart F.	317,324	Gore, Albert	7,971	240,953 D	19.0%	79.0%	19.4%	80.6%
1954	356,094	106,971	Wall, Thomas P.	249,121	Kefauver, Estes	2	142,150 D	30.0%	70.0%	30.0%	70.0%
1952	735,219	153,479	Atkins, Hobart F.	545,432	Kefauver, Estes	36,308	391,953 D	20.9%	74.2%	22.0%	78.0%
1948	499,218	166,947	Reece, B. Carroll	326,142	Kefauver, Estes	6,129	159,195 D	33.4%	65.3%	33.9%	66.1%
1946	218,714	57,238	Ladd, William B.	145,654	McKellar, Kenneth	15,822	88,416 D	26.2%	66.6%	28.2%	71.8%

One of the 1964 elections was for a short term to fill a vacancy.

TENNESSEE

Districts Established June 18, 1981

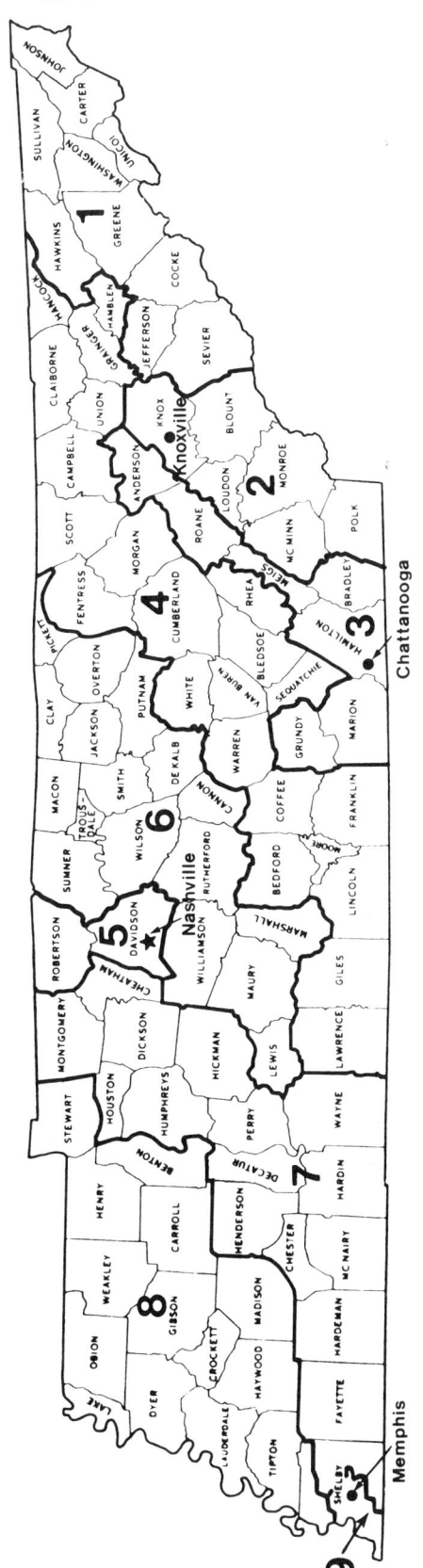

TENNESSEE

PRESIDENT 1984

1980 Census Population	County	Total Vote	Republican	Democratic	Other	Rep.-Dem. Plurality	Percentage Total Vote Rep.	Dem.	Major Vote Rep.	Dem.
67,346	ANDERSON	27,374	16,783	10,415	176	6,368 R	61.3%	38.0%	61.7%	38.3%
27,916	BEDFORD	9,296	4,699	4,499	98	200 R	50.5%	48.4%	51.1%	48.9%
14,901	BENTON	5,897	2,481	3,398	18	917 D	42.1%	57.6%	42.2%	57.8%
9,478	BLEDSOE	3,286	1,950	1,316	20	634 R	59.3%	40.0%	59.7%	40.3%
77,770	BLOUNT	29,859	20,525	9,188	146	11,337 R	68.7%	30.8%	69.1%	30.9%
67,547	BRADLEY	22,502	16,322	6,085	95	10,237 R	72.5%	27.0%	72.8%	27.2%
34,923	CAMPBELL	10,444	5,685	4,692	67	993 R	54.4%	44.9%	54.8%	45.2%
10,234	CANNON	3,560	1,669	1,846	45	177 D	46.9%	51.9%	47.5%	52.5%
28,285	CARROLL	10,662	6,017	4,568	77	1,449 R	56.4%	42.8%	56.8%	43.2%
50,205	CARTER	17,933	13,153	4,642	138	8,511 R	73.3%	25.9%	73.9%	26.1%
21,616	CHEATHAM	7,169	4,109	3,007	53	1,102 R	57.3%	41.9%	57.7%	42.3%
12,727	CHESTER	4,680	2,793	1,854	33	939 R	59.7%	39.6%	60.1%	39.9%
24,595	CLAIBORNE	7,371	4,474	2,870	27	1,604 R	60.7%	38.9%	60.9%	39.1%
7,676	CLAY	2,634	1,338	1,281	15	57 R	50.8%	48.6%	51.1%	48.9%
28,792	COCKE	8,828	6,665	2,068	95	4,597 R	75.5%	23.4%	76.3%	23.7%
38,311	COFFEE	13,468	7,695	5,691	82	2,004 R	57.1%	42.3%	57.5%	42.5%
14,941	CROCKETT	4,429	2,479	1,937	13	542 R	56.0%	43.7%	56.1%	43.9%
28,676	CUMBERLAND	10,756	7,083	3,605	68	3,478 R	65.9%	33.5%	66.3%	33.7%
477,811	DAVIDSON	188,814	98,155	89,498	1,161	8,657 R	52.0%	47.4%	52.3%	47.7%
10,857	DECATUR	4,441	2,390	2,031	20	359 R	53.8%	45.7%	54.1%	45.9%
13,589	DE KALB	5,010	2,337	2,645	28	308 D	46.6%	52.8%	46.9%	53.1%
30,037	DICKSON	11,805	5,846	5,809	150	37 R	49.5%	49.2%	50.2%	49.8%
34,663	DYER	10,642	6,610	3,991	41	2,619 R	62.1%	37.5%	62.4%	37.6%
25,305	FAYETTE	7,401	3,733	3,634	34	99 R	50.4%	49.1%	50.7%	49.3%
14,826	FENTRESS	4,699	2,922	1,755	22	1,167 R	62.2%	37.3%	62.5%	37.5%
31,983	FRANKLIN	11,621	5,705	5,846	70	141 D	49.1%	50.3%	49.4%	50.6%
49,467	GIBSON	17,992	9,484	8,334	174	1,150 R	52.7%	46.3%	53.2%	46.8%
24,625	GILES	7,739	3,875	3,812	52	63 R	50.1%	49.3%	50.4%	49.6%
16,751	GRAINGER	4,814	3,212	1,565	37	1,647 R	66.7%	32.5%	67.2%	32.8%
54,422	GREENE	18,065	13,215	4,763	87	8,452 R	73.2%	26.4%	73.5%	26.5%
13,787	GRUNDY	4,015	1,396	2,596	23	1,200 D	34.8%	64.7%	35.0%	65.0%
49,300	HAMBLEN	16,158	11,144	4,922	92	6,222 R	69.0%	30.5%	69.4%	30.6%
287,740	HAMILTON	111,622	69,626	41,449	547	28,177 R	62.4%	37.1%	62.7%	37.3%
6,887	HANCOCK	2,134	1,491	619	24	872 R	69.9%	29.0%	70.7%	29.3%
23,873	HARDEMAN	7,626	3,712	3,797	117	85 D	48.7%	49.8%	49.4%	50.6%
22,280	HARDIN	7,773	4,632	3,051	90	1,581 R	59.6%	39.3%	60.3%	39.7%
43,751	HAWKINS	14,793	9,863	4,802	128	5,061 R	66.7%	32.5%	67.3%	32.7%
20,318	HAYWOOD	6,166	2,839	3,308	19	469 D	46.0%	53.6%	46.2%	53.8%
21,390	HENDERSON	7,821	5,362	2,426	33	2,936 R	68.6%	31.0%	68.8%	31.2%
28,656	HENRY	10,837	5,376	5,407	54	31 D	49.6%	49.9%	49.9%	50.1%
15,151	HICKMAN	5,334	2,370	2,941	23	571 D	44.4%	55.1%	44.6%	55.4%
6,871	HOUSTON	2,619	882	1,716	21	834 D	33.7%	65.5%	33.9%	66.1%
15,957	HUMPHREYS	5,933	2,249	3,668	16	1,419 D	37.9%	61.8%	38.0%	62.0%
9,398	JACKSON	4,486	1,544	2,894	48	1,350 D	34.4%	64.5%	34.8%	65.2%
31,284	JEFFERSON	10,975	7,721	3,185	69	4,536 R	70.4%	29.0%	70.8%	29.2%
13,745	JOHNSON	4,871	3,853	999	19	2,854 R	79.1%	20.5%	79.4%	20.6%
319,694	KNOX	120,987	76,965	43,448	574	33,517 R	63.6%	35.9%	63.9%	36.1%
7,455	LAKE	2,092	878	1,191	23	313 D	42.0%	56.9%	42.4%	57.6%
24,555	LAUDERDALE	7,099	3,566	3,506	27	60 R	50.2%	49.4%	50.4%	49.6%
34,110	LAWRENCE	11,563	6,034	5,458	71	576 R	52.2%	47.2%	52.5%	47.5%
9,700	LEWIS	3,306	1,733	1,556	17	177 R	52.4%	47.1%	52.7%	47.3%
26,483	LINCOLN	8,114	3,982	4,103	29	121 D	49.1%	50.6%	49.3%	50.7%
28,553	LOUDON	10,405	7,113	3,227	65	3,886 R	68.4%	31.0%	68.8%	31.2%
41,878	MCMINN	14,813	9,604	5,141	68	4,463 R	64.8%	34.7%	65.1%	34.9%
22,525	MCNAIRY	8,631	4,776	3,825	30	951 R	55.3%	44.3%	55.5%	44.5%
15,700	MACON	5,105	3,330	1,747	28	1,583 R	65.2%	34.2%	65.6%	34.4%
74,546	MADISON	29,880	17,819	12,006	55	5,813 R	59.6%	40.2%	59.7%	40.3%
24,416	MARION	8,331	4,337.	3,942	52	395 R	52.1%	47.3%	52.4%	47.6%
19,698	MARSHALL	6,393	3,416	2,935	42	481 R	53.4%	45.9%	53.8%	46.2%
51,095	MAURY	16,033	9,008	6,950	75	2,058 R	56.2%	43.3%	56.4%	43.6%

TENNESSEE

PRESIDENT 1984

1980 Census Population	County	Total Vote	Republican	Democratic	Other	Rep.-Dem. Plurality		Percentage Total Vote Rep.	Dem.	Major Vote Rep.	Dem.
7,431	MEIGS	2,602	1,575	1,012	15	563	R	60.5%	38.9%	60.9%	39.1%
28,700	MONROE	10,947	6,665	4,223	59	2,442	R	60.9%	38.6%	61.2%	38.8%
83,342	MONTGOMERY	23,365	13,228	9,939	198	3,289	R	56.6%	42.5%	57.1%	42.9%
4,510	MOORE	1,680	863	808	9	55	R	51.4%	48.1%	51.6%	48.4%
16,604	MORGAN	5,076	2,903	2,121	52	782	R	57.2%	41.8%	57.8%	42.2%
32,781	OBION	11,252	6,384	4,769	99	1,615	R	56.7%	42.4%	57.2%	42.8%
17,575	OVERTON	4,830	2,054	2,749	27	695	D	42.5%	56.9%	42.8%	57.2%
6,111	PERRY	2,267	948	1,316	3	368	D	41.8%	58.1%	41.9%	58.1%
4,358	PICKETT	1,957	1,246	706	5	540	R	63.7%	36.1%	63.8%	36.2%
13,602	POLK	4,960	2,785	2,112	63	673	R	56.1%	42.6%	56.9%	43.1%
47,690	PUTNAM	16,541	8,999	7,443	99	1,556	R	54.4%	45.0%	54.7%	45.3%
24,235	RHEA	8,587	5,692	2,804	91	2,888	R	66.3%	32.7%	67.0%	33.0%
48,425	ROANE	18,614	11,882	6,623	109	5,259	R	63.8%	35.6%	64.2%	35.8%
37,021	ROBERTSON	11,263	5,445	5,756	62	311	D	48.3%	51.1%	48.6%	51.4%
84,058	RUTHERFORD	31,469	19,503	11,618	348	7,885	R	62.0%	36.9%	62.7%	37.3%
19,259	SCOTT	4,961	3,107	1,810	44	1,297	R	62.6%	36.5%	63.2%	36.8%
8,605	SEQUATCHIE	3,042	1,785	1,238	19	547	R	58.7%	40.7%	59.0%	41.0%
41,418	SEVIER	16,041	12,517	3,384	140	9,133	R	78.0%	21.1%	78.7%	21.3%
777,113	SHELBY	337,302	169,717	165,947	1,638	3,770	R	50.3%	49.2%	50.6%	49.4%
14,935	SMITH	5,691	2,393	3,258	40	865	D	42.0%	57.2%	42.3%	57.7%
8,665	STEWART	3,490	1,285	2,174	31	889	D	36.8%	62.3%	37.1%	62.9%
143,968	SULLIVAN	53,835	36,516	16,925	394	19,591	R	67.8%	31.4%	68.3%	31.7%
85,790	SUMNER	30,186	18,442	11,535	209	6,907	R	61.1%	38.2%	61.5%	38.5%
32,930	TIPTON	9,874	5,945	3,895	34	2,050	R	60.2%	39.4%	60.4%	39.6%
6,137	TROUSDALE	1,935	781	1,142	12	361	D	40.4%	59.0%	40.6%	59.4%
16,362	UNICOI	5,979	4,249	1,696	34	2,553	R	71.1%	28.4%	71.5%	28.5%
11,707	UNION	3,978	2,447	1,495	36	952	R	61.5%	37.6%	62.1%	37.9%
4,728	VAN BUREN	1,535	718	810	7	92	D	46.8%	52.8%	47.0%	53.0%
32,653	WARREN	9,691	4,811	4,813	67	2	D	49.6%	49.7%	50.0%	50.0%
88,755	WASHINGTON	31,368	21,762	9,452	154	12,310	R	69.4%	30.1%	69.7%	30.3%
13,946	WAYNE	4,879	3,332	1,534	13	1,798	R	68.3%	31.4%	68.5%	31.5%
32,896	WEAKLEY	11,287	6,480	4,752	55	1,728	R	57.4%	42.1%	57.7%	42.3%
19,567	WHITE	5,958	2,895	3,033	30	138	D	48.6%	50.9%	48.8%	51.2%
58,108	WILLIAMSON	24,997	17,975	6,929	93	11,046	R	71.9%	27.7%	72.2%	27.8%
56,064	WILSON	21,449	12,858	8,433	158	4,425	R	59.9%	39.3%	60.4%	39.6%
4,591,120	TOTAL	1,711,994	990,212	711,714	10,068	278,498	R	57.8%	41.6%	58.2%	41.8%

TENNESSEE

SENATOR 1984

1980 Census Population	County	Total Vote	Republican	Democratic	Other	Rep.-Dem. Plurality	Percentage Total Vote Rep.	Dem.	Major Vote Rep.	Dem.
67,346	ANDERSON	26,165	9,348	15,971	846	6,623 D	35.7%	61.0%	36.9%	63.1%
27,916	BEDFORD	8,912	1,702	7,075	135	5,373 D	19.1%	79.4%	19.4%	80.6%
14,901	BENTON	5,907	1,214	4,573	120	3,359 D	20.6%	77.4%	21.0%	79.0%
9,478	BLEDSOE	3,412	1,554	1,749	109	195 D	45.5%	51.3%	47.0%	53.0%
77,770	BLOUNT	28,908	13,068	13,431	2,409	363 D	45.2%	46.5%	49.3%	50.7%
67,547	BRADLEY	22,565	12,086	9,444	1,035	2,642 R	53.6%	41.9%	56.1%	43.9%
34,923	CAMPBELL	9,864	3,887	5,827	150	1,940 D	39.4%	59.1%	40.0%	60.0%
10,234	CANNON	3,500	627	2,825	48	2,198 D	17.9%	80.7%	18.2%	81.8%
28,285	CARROLL	10,274	3,504	6,520	250	3,016 D	34.1%	63.5%	35.0%	65.0%
50,205	CARTER	16,255	8,002	6,906	1,347	1,096 R	49.2%	42.5%	53.7%	46.3%
21,616	CHEATHAM	7,053	1,708	5,071	274	3,363 D	24.2%	71.9%	25.2%	74.8%
12,727	CHESTER	4,485	1,605	2,643	237	1,038 D	35.8%	58.9%	37.8%	62.2%
24,595	CLAIBORNE	6,904	3,145	3,662	97	517 D	45.6%	53.0%	46.2%	53.8%
7,676	CLAY	2,581	778	1,795	8	1,017 D	30.1%	69.5%	30.2%	69.8%
28,792	COCKE	8,192	4,848	3,113	231	1,735 R	59.2%	38.0%	60.9%	39.1%
38,311	COFFEE	13,212	3,416	9,522	274	6,106 D	25.9%	72.1%	26.4%	73.6%
14,941	CROCKETT	4,383	1,360	2,772	251	1,412 D	31.0%	63.2%	32.9%	67.1%
28,676	CUMBERLAND	10,635	4,594	5,793	248	1,199 D	43.2%	54.5%	44.2%	55.8%
477,811	DAVIDSON	182,502	43,309	132,696	6,497	89,387 D	23.7%	72.7%	24.6%	75.4%
10,857	DECATUR	4,233	1,243	2,786	204	1,543 D	29.4%	65.8%	30.9%	69.1%
13,589	DE KALB	4,869	909	3,922	38	3,013 D	18.7%	80.6%	18.8%	81.2%
30,037	DICKSON	11,320	2,369	8,668	283	6,299 D	20.9%	76.6%	21.5%	78.5%
34,663	DYER	10,351	3,702	6,166	483	2,464 D	35.8%	59.6%	37.5%	62.5%
25,305	FAYETTE	7,367	2,364	4,577	426	2,213 D	32.1%	62.1%	34.1%	65.9%
14,826	FENTRESS	4,550	1,725	2,791	34	1,066 D	37.9%	61.3%	38.2%	61.8%
31,983	FRANKLIN	11,104	2,419	8,534	151	6,115 D	21.8%	76.9%	22.1%	77.9%
49,467	GIBSON	16,926	4,579	11,729	618	7,150 D	27.1%	69.3%	28.1%	71.9%
24,625	GILES	7,160	1,805	5,240	115	3,435 D	25.2%	73.2%	25.6%	74.4%
16,751	GRAINGER	4,594	2,424	2,010	160	414 R	52.8%	43.8%	54.7%	45.3%
54,422	GREENE	17,507	8,016	7,056	2,435	960 R	45.8%	40.3%	53.2%	46.8%
13,787	GRUNDY	3,839	746	2,993	100	2,247 D	19.4%	78.0%	20.0%	80.0%
49,300	HAMBLEN	15,663	6,628	7,452	1,583	824 D	42.3%	47.6%	47.1%	52.9%
287,740	HAMILTON	110,913	48,548	54,623	7,742	6,075 D	43.8%	49.2%	47.1%	52.9%
6,887	HANCOCK	1,896	1,068	783	45	285 R	56.3%	41.3%	57.7%	42.3%
23,873	HARDEMAN	7,073	1,854	4,494	725	2,640 D	26.2%	63.5%	29.2%	70.8%
22,280	HARDIN	7,402	2,685	4,504	213	1,819 D	36.3%	60.8%	37.3%	62.7%
43,751	HAWKINS	13,980	6,540	6,413	1,027	127 R	46.8%	45.9%	50.5%	49.5%
20,318	HAYWOOD	6,085	1,506	4,005	574	2,499 D	24.7%	65.8%	27.3%	72.7%
21,390	HENDERSON	7,507	2,843	4,423	241	1,580 D	37.9%	58.9%	39.1%	60.9%
28,656	HENRY	10,207	2,563	7,426	218	4,863 D	25.1%	72.8%	25.7%	74.3%
15,151	HICKMAN	5,246	1,161	3,983	102	2,822 D	22.1%	75.9%	22.6%	77.4%
6,871	HOUSTON	2,568	402	2,077	89	1,675 D	15.7%	80.9%	16.2%	83.8%
15,957	HUMPHREYS	5,869	980	4,780	109	3,800 D	16.7%	81.4%	17.0%	83.0%
9,398	JACKSON	4,517	496	3,971	50	3,475 D	11.0%	87.9%	11.1%	88.9%
31,284	JEFFERSON	10,462	5,148	4,733	581	415 R	49.2%	45.2%	52.1%	47.9%
13,745	JOHNSON	4,564	2,900	1,563	101	1,337 R	63.5%	34.2%	65.0%	35.0%
319,694	KNOX	118,992	47,269	65,091	6,632	17,822 D	39.7%	54.7%	42.1%	57.9%
7,455	LAKE	1,812	454	1,312	46	858 D	25.1%	72.4%	25.7%	74.3%
24,555	LAUDERDALE	7,077	1,894	4,893	290	2,999 D	26.8%	69.1%	27.9%	72.1%
34,110	LAWRENCE	11,656	4,126	7,359	171	3,233 D	35.4%	63.1%	35.9%	64.1%
9,700	LEWIS	3,138	665	2,424	49	1,759 D	21.2%	77.2%	21.5%	78.5%
26,483	LINCOLN	7,312	1,505	5,606	201	4,101 D	20.6%	76.7%	21.2%	78.8%
28,553	LOUDON	10,273	4,631	5,190	452	559 D	45.1%	50.5%	47.2%	52.8%
41,878	MCMINN	15,109	7,169	7,478	462	309 D	47.4%	49.5%	48.9%	51.1%
22,525	MCNAIRY	8,357	2,961	5,121	275	2,160 D	35.4%	61.3%	36.6%	63.4%
15,700	MACON	5,098	1,296	3,770	32	2,474 D	25.4%	74.0%	25.6%	74.4%
74,546	MADISON	29,911	8,637	18,791	2,483	10,154 D	28.9%	62.8%	31.5%	68.5%
24,416	MARION	8,574	3,016	5,399	159	2,383 D	35.2%	63.0%	35.8%	64.2%
19,698	MARSHALL	6,208	1,378	4,717	113	3,339 D	22.2%	76.0%	22.6%	77.4%
51,095	MAURY	15,309	4,042	10,990	277	6,948 D	26.4%	71.8%	26.9%	73.1%

TENNESSEE

SENATOR 1984

1980 Census Population	County	Total Vote	Republican	Democratic	Other	Rep.-Dem. Plurality	Percentage			
							Total Vote		Major Vote	
							Rep.	Dem.	Rep.	Dem.
7,431	MEIGS	2,457	1,133	1,270	54	137 D	46.1%	51.7%	47.1%	52.9%
28,700	MONROE	10,776	5,159	5,408	209	249 D	47.9%	50.2%	48.8%	51.2%
83,342	MONTGOMERY	22,171	6,013	14,946	1,212	8,933 D	27.1%	67.4%	28.7%	71.3%
4,510	MOORE	1,639	324	1,294	21	970 D	19.8%	79.0%	20.0%	80.0%
16,604	MORGAN	4,858	1,747	3,001	110	1,254 D	36.0%	61.8%	36.8%	63.2%
32,781	OBION	10,200	3,853	5,903	444	2,050 D	37.8%	57.9%	39.5%	60.5%
17,575	OVERTON	4,999	864	4,089	46	3,225 D	17.3%	81.8%	17.4%	82.6%
6,111	PERRY	2,229	408	1,783	38	1,375 D	18.3%	80.0%	18.6%	81.4%
4,358	PICKETT	1,880	784	1,087	9	303 D	41.7%	57.8%	41.9%	58.1%
13,602	POLK	4,838	2,091	2,678	69	587 D	43.2%	55.4%	43.8%	56.2%
47,690	PUTNAM	16,213	3,638	12,183	392	8,545 D	22.4%	75.1%	23.0%	77.0%
24,235	RHEA	8,245	3,730	3,674	841	56 R	45.2%	44.6%	50.4%	49.6%
48,425	ROANE	17,530	6,897	9,914	719	3,017 D	39.3%	56.6%	41.0%	59.0%
37,021	ROBERTSON	10,872	2,201	8,403	268	6,202 D	20.2%	77.3%	20.8%	79.2%
84,058	RUTHERFORD	29,746	6,852	21,737	1,157	14,885 D	23.0%	73.1%	24.0%	76.0%
19,259	SCOTT	4,523	1,923	2,499	101	576 D	42.5%	55.3%	43.5%	56.5%
8,605	SEQUATCHIE	2,906	1,215	1,616	75	401 D	41.8%	55.6%	42.9%	57.1%
41,418	SEVIER	15,287	8,235	5,652	1,400	2,583 R	53.9%	37.0%	59.3%	40.7%
777,113	SHELBY	315,281	102,831	187,944	24,506	85,113 D	32.6%	59.6%	35.4%	64.6%
14,935	SMITH	5,773	633	5,107	33	4,474 D	11.0%	88.5%	11.0%	89.0%
8,665	STEWART	3,312	666	2,591	55	1,925 D	20.1%	78.2%	20.4%	79.6%
143,968	SULLIVAN	51,684	20,289	25,537	5,858	5,248 D	39.3%	49.4%	44.3%	55.7%
85,790	SUMNER	29,086	6,954	21,292	840	14,338 D	23.9%	73.2%	24.6%	75.4%
32,930	TIPTON	10,027	3,391	6,072	564	2,681 D	33.8%	60.6%	35.8%	64.2%
6,137	TROUSDALE	1,940	215	1,706	19	1,491 D	11.1%	87.9%	11.2%	88.8%
16,362	UNICOI	5,609	2,616	2,460	533	156 R	46.6%	43.9%	51.5%	48.5%
11,707	UNION	3,795	1,758	1,946	91	188 D	46.3%	51.3%	47.5%	52.5%
4,728	VAN BUREN	1,482	311	1,167	4	856 D	21.0%	78.7%	21.0%	79.0%
32,653	WARREN	9,480	1,949	7,272	259	5,323 D	20.6%	76.7%	21.1%	78.9%
88,755	WASHINGTON	30,066	11,859	14,915	3,292	3,056 D	39.4%	49.6%	44.3%	55.7%
13,946	WAYNE	4,438	2,223	2,154	61	69 R	50.1%	48.5%	50.8%	49.2%
32,896	WEAKLEY	11,195	3,444	7,277	474	3,833 D	30.8%	65.0%	32.1%	67.9%
19,567	WHITE	6,081	1,245	4,751	85	3,506 D	20.5%	78.1%	20.8%	79.2%
58,108	WILLIAMSON	24,156	8,442	14,286	1,428	5,844 D	34.9%	59.1%	37.1%	62.9%
56,064	WILSON	20,955	4,702	15,762	491	11,060 D	22.4%	75.2%	23.0%	77.0%
4,591,120	TOTAL	1,648,064	557,016	1,000,607	90,441	443,591 D	33.8%	60.7%	35.8%	64.2%

TENNESSEE

CONGRESS

CD	Year	Total Vote	Republican Vote	Republican Candidate	Democratic Vote	Democratic Candidate	Other Vote	Rep.-Dem. Plurality	Total Vote Rep.	Total Vote Dem.	Major Vote Rep.	Major Vote Dem.
1	1984	113,442	113,407	QUILLEN, JAMES H.			35	113,407 R	100.0%		100.0%	
1	1982	120,858	89,497	QUILLEN, JAMES H.	27,580	CABLE, JESSIE J.	3,781	61,917 R	74.1%	22.8%	76.4%	23.6%
2	1984	171,453	132,604	DUNCAN, JOHN J.	38,846	BOWEN, JOHN F.	3	93,758 R	77.3%	22.7%	77.3%	22.7%
2	1982	109,057	109,045	DUNCAN, JOHN J.			12	109,045 R	100.0%		100.0%	
3	1984	189,683	90,216	DAVIS, JOHN	99,465	LLOYD, MARILYN	2	9,249 D	47.6%	52.4%	47.6%	52.4%
3	1982	137,493	49,885	BYERS, GLEN	84,967	BOUQUARD, MARILYN LLOYD	2,641	35,082 D	36.3%	61.8%	37.0%	63.0%
4	1984	124,863	31,011	SEIGNEUR, JAMES B.	93,848	COOPER, JIM	4	62,837 D	24.8%	75.2%	24.8%	75.2%
4	1982	141,322	47,865	BAKER, CISSY	93,453	COOPER, JIM	4	45,588 D	33.9%	66.1%	33.9%	66.1%
5	1984	138,286			138,233	BONER, BILL	53	138,233 D		100.0%		100.0%
5	1982	136,349	27,061	STEINHICE, LAUREL	109,282	BONER, BILL	6	82,221 D	19.8%	80.1%	19.8%	80.2%
6	1984	165,565	61,559	SIMPKINS, JOE	103,989	GORDON, BART	17	42,430 D	37.2%	62.8%	37.2%	62.8%
6	1982	104,105			104,094	GORE, ALBERT, JR.	11	104,094 D		100.0%		100.0%
7	1984	107,278	107,257	SUNDQUIST, DON			21	107,257 R	100.0%		100.0%	
7	1982	146,197	73,835	SUNDQUIST, DON	72,359	CLEMENT, BOB	3	1,476 R	50.5%	49.5%	50.5%	49.5%
8	1984	118,668			118,653	JONES, ED	15	118,653 D		100.0%		100.0%
8	1982	125,472	31,527	BENSON, BRUCE	93,945	JONES, ED		62,418 D	25.1%	74.9%	25.1%	74.9%
9	1984	186,497	53,064	THOMPSON, WILLIAM B.	133,428	FORD, HAROLD E.	5	80,364 D	28.5%	71.5%	28.5%	71.5%
9	1982	154,830	40,812	CRAWFORD, JOE	112,143	FORD, HAROLD E.	1,875	71,331 D	26.4%	72.4%	26.7%	73.3%

TENNESSEE

1984 GENERAL ELECTION

President   Other vote was 3,072 Bergland (Independent); 1,852 LaRouche (Independent); 1,763 Richards (Independent); 1,036 Hall (Independent); 978 Johnson (Independent); 715 Mason (Independent); 524 Serrette (Independent); 4 Anderson (write-in); 7 Dennis (write-in); 117 scattered.

Senator   Other vote was 87,234 McAteer (Independent); 3,179 Al-Muhaymin (Independent); 28 scattered not reported by county.

Congress   Other vote was scattered in all CD's.

1984 PRIMARIES

AUGUST 2 REPUBLICAN

Senator   145,744 Victor Ashe; 17,970 Jack McNeil; 4,777 Hubert D. Patty; 49 scattered.

Congress   Unopposed in five CD's. No candidate in CD's 5 and 8. Contested as follows:

CD 3   10,147 John Davis; 3,922 Walter Bradley; 1 scattered.
CD 6   10,774 Joe Simpkins; 2,986 Fred Vail; 6 scattered.

AUGUST 2 DEMOCRATIC

Senator   Albert Gore, Jr., unopposed.

Congress   Unopposed in four CD's. No candidate in CD's 1 and 7. Contested as follows:

CD 3   29,304 Marilyn Lloyd; 4,505 Stephen L. Roberts.
CD 6   23,280 Bart Gordon; 18,140 Lincoln Davis; 14,751 Bryant Millsaps; 13,314 Robert N. Moore; 11,986 Martin Sir; 490 Jere R. Young; 1 scattered.
CD 9   34,242 Harold E. Ford; 8,575 Mark F. Flanagan.

TEXAS

GOVERNOR
Mark White (D). Elected 1982 to a four-year term.

SENATORS
Lloyd Bentsen (D). Re-elected 1982 to a six-year term. Previously elected 1976, 1970.

Phil Gramm (R). Elected 1984 to a six-year term.

REPRESENTATIVES
1. Sam B. Hall (D) *(see page 1)*
2. Charles Wilson (D)
3. Steve Bartlett (R)
4. Ralph M. Hall (D)
5. John Bryant (D)
6. Joe L. Barton (R)
7. W. R. Archer (R)
8. Jack Fields (R)
9. Jack B. Brooks (D)
10. Jake Pickle (D)
11. J. Marvin Leath (D)
12. James C. Wright (D)
13. Beau Boulter (R)
14. Mac Sweeney (R)
15. Eligio de la Garza (D)
16. Ronald Coleman (D)
17. Charles W. Stenholm (D)
18. Mickey Leland (D)
19. Larry Combest (R)
20. Henry B. Gonzalez (D)
21. Tom Loeffler (R)
22. Thomas D. DeLay (R)
23. Albert G. Bustamante (D)
24. Martin Frost (D)
25. Mike Andrews (D)
26. Dick Armey (R)
27. Solomon P. Ortiz (D)

POSTWAR VOTE FOR GOVERNOR

Year	Total Vote	Republican Vote	Republican Candidate	Democratic Vote	Democratic Candidate	Other Vote	Rep.-Dem. Plurality	Total Vote Rep.	Total Vote Dem.	Major Vote Rep.	Major Vote Dem.
1982	3,191,091	1,465,937	Clements, William P.	1,697,870	White Mark	27,284	231,933 D	45.9%	53.2%	46.3%	53.7%
1978	2,369,764	1,183,839	Clements, William P.	1,166,979	Hill, John	18,946	16,860 R	50.0%	49.2%	50.4%	49.6%
1974*	1,654,984	514,725	Granberry, Jim	1,016,334	Briscoe, Dolph	123,925	501,609 D	31.1%	61.4%	33.6%	66.4%
1972	3,410,128	1,534,060	Grover, Henry C.	1,633,970	Briscoe, Dolph	242,098	99,910 D	45.0%	47.9%	48.4%	51.6%
1970	2,235,847	1,037,723	Eggers, Paul W.	1,197,726	Smith, Preston	398	160,003 D	46.4%	53.6%	46.4%	53.6%
1968	2,916,509	1,254,333	Eggers, Paul W.	1,662,019	Smith, Preston	157	407,686 D	43.0%	57.0%	43.0%	57.0%
1966	1,425,861	368,025	Kennerly, T. E.	1,037,517	Connally, John B.	20,319	669,492 D	25.8%	72.8%	26.2%	73.8%
1964	2,544,753	661,675	Crichton, Jack	1,877,793	Connally, John B.	5,285	1,216,118 D	26.0%	73.8%	26.1%	73.9%
1962	1,569,181	715,025	Cox, Jack	847,036	Connally, John B.	7,120	132,011 D	45.6%	54.0%	45.8%	54.2%
1960	2,250,718	612,963	Steger, William M.	1,637,755	Daniel, Price	—	1,024,792 D	27.2%	72.8%	27.2%	72.8%
1958	789,133	94,098	Mayer, Edwin S.	695,035	Daniel, Price	—	600,937 D	11.9%	88.1%	11.9%	88.1%
1956	1,828,161	271,088	Bryant, William R.	1,433,051	Daniel, Price	124,022	1,161,963 D	14.8%	78.4%	15.9%	84.1%
1954	636,892	66,154	Adams, Tod R.	569,533	Shivers, Allan	1,205	503,379 D	10.4%	89.4%	10.4%	89.6%
1952	1,881,202	—		1,844,530	Shivers, Allan	36,672	1,844,530 D	—	98.1%	—	100.0%
1950	394,747	39,737	Currie, Ralph W.	355,010	Shivers, Allan		315,273 D	10.1%	89.9%	10.1%	89.9%
1948	1,208,860	177,399	Lane, Alvin H.	1,024,160	Jester, Beauford	7,301	846,761 D	14.7%	84.7%	14.8%	85.2%
1946	378,744	33,231	Nolte, Eugene	345,513	Jester, Beauford	—	312,282 D	8.8%	91.2%	8.8%	91.2%

The term of office of Texas' Governor was increased from two to four years effective with the 1974 election.

POSTWAR VOTE FOR SENATOR

Year	Total Vote	Republican Vote	Republican Candidate	Democratic Vote	Democratic Candidate	Other Vote	Rep.-Dem. Plurality	Total Vote Rep.	Total Vote Dem.	Major Vote Rep.	Major Vote Dem.
1984	5,319,178	3,116,348	Gramm, Phil	2,202,557	Doggett, Lloyd	273	913,791 R	58.6%	41.4%	58.6%	41.4%
1982	3,103,167	1,256,759	Collins, James M.	1,818,223	Bentsen, Lloyd	28,185	561,464 D	40.5%	58.6%	40.9%	59.1%
1978	2,312,540	1,151,376	Tower, John G.	1,139,149	Krueger, Robert	22,015	12,227 R	49.8%	49.3%	50.3%	49.7%
1976	3,874,516	1,636,370	Steelman, Alan	2,199,956	Bentsen, Lloyd	38,190	563,586 D	42.2%	56.8%	42.7%	57.3%
1972	3,413,903	1,822,877	Tower, John G.	1,511,985	Sanders, Barefoot	79,041	310,892 R	53.4%	44.3%	54.7%	45.3%
1970	2,231,671	1,035,794	Bush, George	1,194,069	Bentsen, Lloyd	1,808	158,275 D	46.4%	53.5%	46.5%	53.5%
1966	1,493,182	842,501	Tower, John G.	643,855	Carr, Waggoner	6,826	198,646 R	56.4%	43.1%	56.7%	43.3%
1964	2,603,856	1,134,337	Bush, George	1,463,958	Yarborough, Ralph	5,561	329,621 D	43.6%	56.2%	43.7%	56.3%
1961 s	886,091	448,217	Tower, John G.	437,874	Blakley, William A.	—	10,343 R	50.6%	49.4%	50.6%	49.4%
1960	2,253,784	926,653	Tower, John G.	1,306,625	Johnson, Lyndon B.	20,506	379,972 D	41.1%	58.0%	41.5%	58.5%
1958	787,128	185,926	Whittenburg, Roy	587,030	Yarborough, Ralph	14,172	401,104 D	23.6%	74.6%	24.1%	75.9%
1957 s	957,298		[See note below]								
1954	636,475	94,131	Watson, Carlos G.	539,319	Johnson, Lyndon B.	3,025	445,188 D	14.8%	84.7%	14.9%	85.1%
1952	1,895,192	—		1,895,192	Daniel, Price	—	1,895,192 D	—	100.0%	—	100.0%
1948	1,061,563	349,665	Porter, Jack	702,985	Johnson, Lyndon B.	8,913	353,320 D	32.9%	66.2%	33.2%	66.8%
1946	380,681	43,750	Sells, Murray C.	336,931	Connally, Tom	—	293,181 D	11.5%	88.5%	11.5%	88.5%

The May 1961 and April 1957 elections were for short terms to fill vacancies. Though neither vote was held with official party designations, the 1961 vote above was a run-off contest between unofficial party candidates. In 1957 there was a single ballot without run-off and Ralph Yarborough polled 364,605 votes (38.1% of the total vote) and won the election with a 73,802 plurality.

TEXAS

Districts Established June 19, 1983

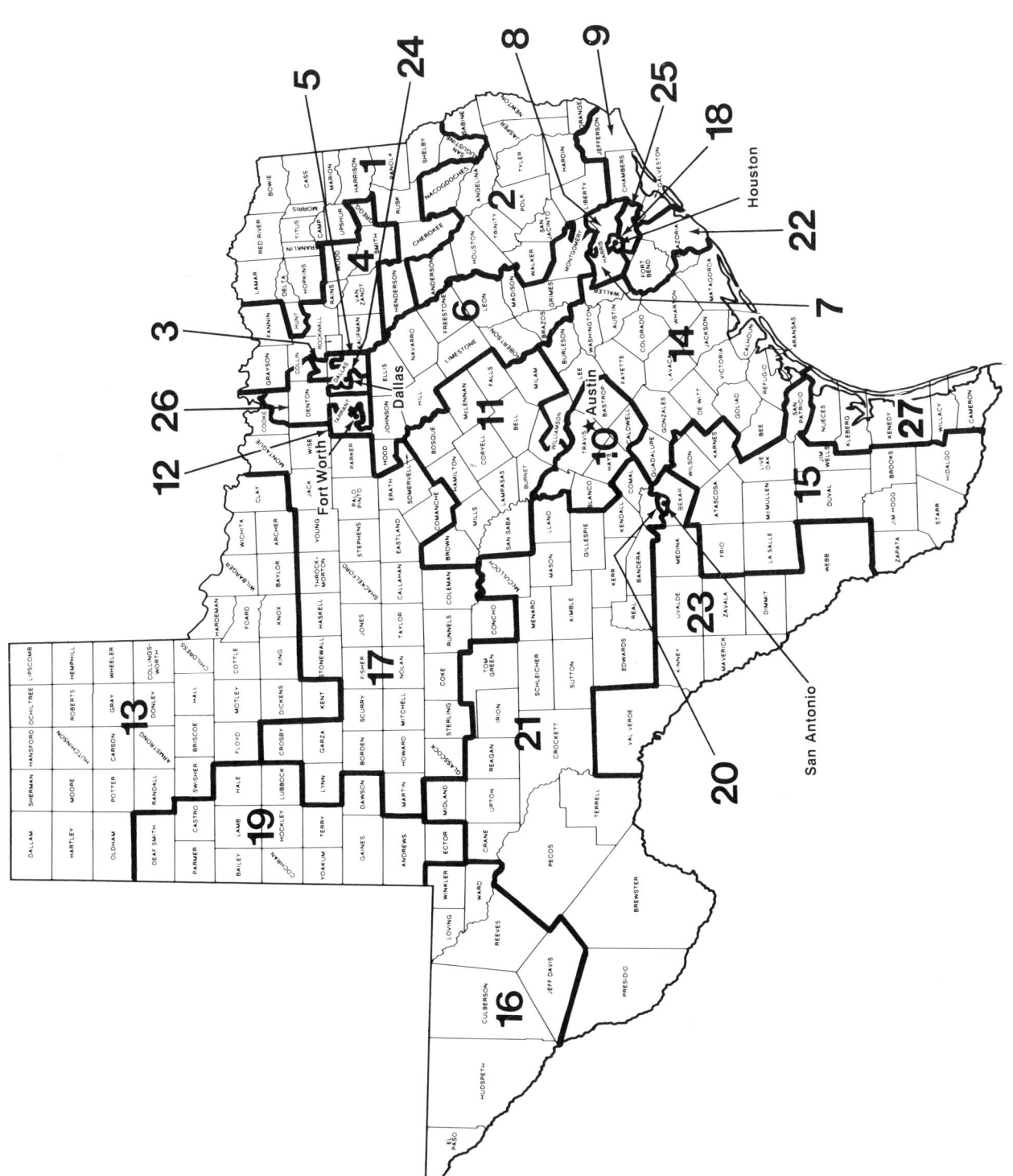

TEXAS

PRESIDENT 1984

1980 Census Population	County	Total Vote	Republican	Democratic	Other	Rep.-Dem. Plurality	Percentage Total Vote Rep.	Dem.	Major Vote Rep.	Dem.
38,381	ANDERSON	13,423	8,634	4,747	42	3,887 R	64.3%	35.4%	64.5%	35.5%
13,323	ANDREWS	4,750	3,918	820	12	3,098 R	82.5%	17.3%	82.7%	17.3%
64,172	ANGELINA	23,831	14,685	9,054	92	5,631 R	61.6%	38.0%	61.9%	38.1%
14,260	ARANSAS	6,067	4,352	1,696	19	2,656 R	71.7%	28.0%	72.0%	28.0%
7,266	ARCHER	3,587	2,487	1,089	11	1,398 R	69.3%	30.4%	69.5%	30.5%
1,994	ARMSTRONG	1,034	791	238	5	553 R	76.5%	23.0%	76.9%	23.1%
25,055	ATASCOSA	8,845	5,279	3,547	19	1,732 R	59.7%	40.1%	59.8%	40.2%
17,726	AUSTIN	6,834	4,872	1,941	21	2,931 R	71.3%	28.4%	71.5%	28.5%
8,168	BAILEY	2,586	1,888	684	14	1,204 R	73.0%	26.5%	73.4%	26.6%
7,084	BANDERA	3,938	3,152	771	15	2,381 R	80.0%	19.6%	80.3%	19.7%
24,726	BASTROP	11,221	6,439	4,744	38	1,695 R	57.4%	42.3%	57.6%	42.4%
4,919	BAYLOR	2,346	1,314	1,019	13	295 R	56.0%	43.4%	56.3%	43.7%
26,030	BEE	9,064	5,377	3,659	28	1,718 R	59.3%	40.4%	59.5%	40.5%
157,889	BELL	44,762	31,117	13,322	323	17,795 R	69.5%	29.8%	70.0%	30.0%
988,800	BEXAR	340,826	203,319	136,947	560	66,372 R	59.7%	40.2%	59.8%	40.2%
4,681	BLANCO	2,665	1,957	700	8	1,257 R	73.4%	26.3%	73.7%	26.3%
859	BORDEN	468	325	140	3	185 R	69.4%	29.9%	69.9%	30.1%
13,401	BOSQUE	5,983	3,923	2,046	14	1,877 R	65.6%	34.2%	65.7%	34.3%
75,301	BOWIE	28,409	18,244	10,077	88	8,167 R	64.2%	35.5%	64.4%	35.6%
169,587	BRAZORIA	58,009	39,166	18,609	234	20,557 R	67.5%	32.1%	67.8%	32.2%
93,588	BRAZOS	47,221	34,733	12,348	140	22,385 R	73.6%	26.1%	73.8%	26.2%
7,573	BREWSTER	3,545	2,066	1,462	17	604 R	58.3%	41.2%	58.6%	41.4%
2,579	BRISCOE	1,017	538	471	8	67 R	52.9%	46.3%	53.3%	46.7%
8,428	BROOKS	3,614	896	2,702	16	1,806 D	24.8%	74.8%	24.9%	75.1%
33,057	BROWN	12,585	8,468	4,070	47	4,398 R	67.3%	32.3%	67.5%	32.5%
12,313	BURLESON	5,666	3,076	2,578	12	498 R	54.3%	45.5%	54.4%	45.6%
17,803	BURNET	8,907	5,895	2,983	29	2,912 R	66.2%	33.5%	66.4%	33.6%
23,637	CALDWELL	7,732	4,315	3,401	16	914 R	55.8%	44.0%	55.9%	44.1%
19,574	CALHOUN	7,039	4,434	2,586	19	1,848 R	63.0%	36.7%	63.2%	36.8%
10,992	CALLAHAN	4,867	3,538	1,305	24	2,233 R	72.7%	26.8%	73.1%	26.9%
209,727	CAMERON	56,126	29,545	26,394	187	3,151 R	52.6%	47.0%	52.8%	47.2%
9,275	CAMP	4,168	2,238	1,917	13	321 R	53.7%	46.0%	53.9%	46.1%
6,672	CARSON	3,254	2,412	826	16	1,586 R	74.1%	25.4%	74.5%	25.5%
29,430	CASS	11,760	6,677	5,053	30	1,624 R	56.8%	43.0%	56.9%	43.1%
10,556	CASTRO	3,056	2,026	1,009	21	1,017 R	66.3%	33.0%	66.8%	33.2%
18,538	CHAMBERS	6,989	4,322	2,632	35	1,690 R	61.8%	37.7%	62.2%	37.8%
38,127	CHEROKEE	12,711	8,187	4,494	30	3,693 R	64.4%	35.4%	64.6%	35.4%
6,950	CHILDRESS	2,481	1,574	900	7	674 R	63.4%	36.3%	63.6%	36.4%
9,582	CLAY	4,426	2,569	1,844	13	725 R	58.0%	41.7%	58.2%	41.8%
4,825	COCHRAN	1,689	1,117	557	15	560 R	66.1%	33.0%	66.7%	33.3%
3,196	COKE	1,600	1,060	532	8	528 R	66.3%	33.3%	66.6%	33.4%
10,439	COLEMAN	4,217	2,790	1,420	7	1,370 R	66.2%	33.7%	66.3%	33.7%
144,576	COLLIN	74,838	61,095	13,604	139	47,491 R	81.6%	18.2%	81.8%	18.2%
4,648	COLLINGSWORTH	2,149	1,396	742	11	654 R	65.0%	34.5%	65.3%	34.7%
18,823	COLORADO	6,971	4,528	2,428	15	2,100 R	65.0%	34.8%	65.1%	34.9%
36,446	COMAL	17,683	13,452	4,179	52	9,273 R	76.1%	23.6%	76.3%	23.7%
12,617	COMANCHE	4,948	2,678	2,248	22	430 R	54.1%	45.4%	54.4%	45.6%
2,915	CONCHO	1,408	821	580	7	241 R	58.3%	41.2%	58.6%	41.4%
27,656	COOKE	11,564	8,260	3,278	26	4,982 R	71.4%	28.3%	71.6%	28.4%
56,767	CORYELL	12,199	9,056	3,113	30	5,943 R	74.2%	25.5%	74.4%	25.6%
2,947	COTTLE	1,150	507	623	20	116 D	44.1%	54.2%	44.9%	55.1%
4,600	CRANE	1,874	1,473	392	9	1,081 R	78.6%	20.9%	79.0%	21.0%
4,608	CROCKETT	1,684	1,094	589	1	505 R	65.0%	35.0%	65.0%	35.0%
8,859	CROSBY	2,599	1,376	1,212	11	164 R	52.9%	46.6%	53.2%	46.8%
3,315	CULBERSON	917	509	407	1	102 R	55.5%	44.4%	55.6%	44.4%
6,531	DALLAM	2,103	1,594	496	13	1,098 R	75.8%	23.6%	76.3%	23.7%
1,556,390	DALLAS	610,496	405,444	203,592	1,460	201,852 R	66.4%	33.3%	66.6%	33.4%
16,184	DAWSON	5,483	3,685	1,781	17	1,904 R	67.2%	32.5%	67.4%	32.6%
21,165	DEAF SMITH	6,283	4,762	1,485	36	3,277 R	75.8%	23.6%	76.2%	23.8%
4,839	DELTA	2,001	1,024	973	4	51 R	51.2%	48.6%	51.3%	48.7%

TEXAS

PRESIDENT 1984

1980 Census Population	County	Total Vote	Republican	Democratic	Other	Rep.-Dem. Plurality	Percentage Total Vote Rep.	Dem.	Major Vote Rep.	Dem.
143,126	DENTON	69,796	52,865	16,772	159	36,093 R	75.7%	24.0%	75.9%	24.1%
18,903	DE WITT	6,292	4,401	1,882	9	2,519 R	69.9%	29.9%	70.0%	30.0%
3,539	DICKENS	1,294	594	692	8	98 D	45.9%	53.5%	46.2%	53.8%
11,367	DIMMIT	3,892	1,338	2,546	8	1,208 D	34.4%	65.4%	34.4%	65.6%
4,075	DONLEY	1,831	1,297	529	5	768 R	70.8%	28.9%	71.0%	29.0%
12,517	DUVAL	4,959	1,201	3,748	10	2,547 D	24.2%	75.6%	24.3%	75.7%
19,480	EASTLAND	7,389	4,841	2,522	26	2,319 R	65.5%	34.1%	65.7%	34.3%
115,374	ECTOR	40,342	31,228	8,913	201	22,315 R	77.4%	22.1%	77.8%	22.2%
2,033	EDWARDS	786	626	159	1	467 R	79.6%	20.2%	79.7%	20.3%
59,743	ELLIS	24,945	16,873	8,029	43	8,844 R	67.6%	32.2%	67.8%	32.2%
479,899	EL PASO	118,459	66,114	51,917	428	14,197 R	55.8%	43.8%	56.0%	44.0%
22,560	ERATH	9,395	6,122	3,234	39	2,888 R	65.2%	34.4%	65.4%	34.6%
17,946	FALLS	5,986	3,133	2,834	19	299 R	52.3%	47.3%	52.5%	47.5%
24,285	FANNIN	9,106	4,692	4,399	15	293 R	51.5%	48.3%	51.6%	48.4%
18,832	FAYETTE	8,112	5,711	2,379	22	3,332 R	70.4%	29.3%	70.6%	29.4%
5,891	FISHER	2,357	965	1,384	8	419 D	40.9%	58.7%	41.1%	58.9%
9,834	FLOYD	3,134	2,092	1,023	19	1,069 R	66.8%	32.6%	67.2%	32.8%
2,158	FOARD	925	472	448	5	24 R	51.0%	48.4%	51.3%	48.7%
130,846	FORT BEND	60,209	41,370	18,729	110	22,641 R	68.7%	31.1%	68.8%	31.2%
6,893	FRANKLIN	2,948	1,836	1,104	8	732 R	62.3%	37.4%	62.4%	37.6%
14,830	FREESTONE	6,122	3,624	2,489	9	1,135 R	59.2%	40.7%	59.3%	40.7%
13,785	FRIO	4,669	2,003	2,656	10	653 D	42.9%	56.9%	43.0%	57.0%
13,150	GAINES	3,533	2,714	797	22	1,917 R	76.8%	22.6%	77.3%	22.7%
195,940	GALVESTON	76,836	40,262	36,092	482	4,170 R	52.4%	47.0%	52.7%	47.3%
5,336	GARZA	1,750	1,219	521	10	698 R	69.7%	29.8%	70.1%	29.9%
13,532	GILLESPIE	6,651	5,496	1,137	18	4,359 R	82.6%	17.1%	82.9%	17.1%
1,304	GLASSCOCK	536	403	128	5	275 R	75.2%	23.9%	75.9%	24.1%
5,193	GOLIAD	2,377	1,540	836	1	704 R	64.8%	35.2%	64.8%	35.2%
16,883	GONZALES	6,172	3,962	2,196	14	1,766 R	64.2%	35.6%	64.3%	35.7%
26,386	GRAY	10,988	8,955	2,003	30	6,952 R	81.5%	18.2%	81.7%	18.3%
89,796	GRAYSON	34,450	22,554	11,803	93	10,751 R	65.5%	34.3%	65.6%	34.4%
99,487	GREGG	40,643	29,697	10,700	246	18,997 R	73.1%	26.3%	73.5%	26.5%
13,580	GRIMES	5,752	3,365	2,370	17	995 R	58.5%	41.2%	58.7%	41.3%
46,708	GUADALUPE	19,488	14,382	5,060	46	9,322 R	73.8%	26.0%	74.0%	26.0%
37,592	HALE	10,891	7,670	3,202	19	4,468 R	70.4%	29.4%	70.5%	29.5%
5,594	HALL	2,045	1,058	984	3	74 R	51.7%	48.1%	51.8%	48.2%
8,297	HAMILTON	3,258	2,118	1,130	10	988 R	65.0%	34.7%	65.2%	34.8%
6,209	HANSFORD	2,476	2,213	259	4	1,954 R	89.4%	10.5%	89.5%	10.5%
6,368	HARDEMAN	2,173	1,238	927	8	311 R	57.0%	42.7%	57.2%	42.8%
40,721	HARDIN	15,206	8,380	6,782	44	1,598 R	55.1%	44.6%	55.3%	44.7%
2,409,547	HARRIS	872,167	536,029	334,135	2,003	201,894 R	61.5%	38.3%	61.6%	38.4%
52,265	HARRISON	20,509	12,618	7,773	118	4,845 R	61.5%	37.9%	61.9%	38.1%
3,987	HARTLEY	1,786	1,419	356	11	1,063 R	79.5%	19.9%	79.9%	20.1%
7,725	HASKELL	3,151	1,701	1,434	16	267 R	54.0%	45.5%	54.3%	45.7%
40,594	HAYS	19,187	12,467	6,663	57	5,804 R	65.0%	34.7%	65.2%	34.8%
5,304	HEMPHILL	2,067	1,650	413	4	1,237 R	79.8%	20.0%	80.0%	20.0%
42,606	HENDERSON	20,076	12,725	7,302	49	5,423 R	63.4%	36.4%	63.5%	36.5%
283,229	HIDALGO	79,432	35,059	44,147	226	9,088 D	44.1%	55.6%	44.3%	55.7%
25,024	HILL	8,790	5,344	3,420	26	1,924 R	60.8%	38.9%	61.0%	39.0%
23,230	HOCKLEY	7,545	5,462	2,044	39	3,418 R	72.4%	27.1%	72.8%	27.2%
17,714	HOOD	9,921	6,817	3,063	41	3,754 R	68.7%	30.9%	69.0%	31.0%
25,247	HOPKINS	9,493	5,772	3,707	14	2,065 R	60.8%	39.0%	60.9%	39.1%
22,299	HOUSTON	7,834	4,542	3,275	17	1,267 R	58.0%	41.8%	58.1%	41.9%
33,142	HOWARD	11,691	7,519	4,115	57	3,404 R	64.3%	35.2%	64.6%	35.4%
2,728	HUDSPETH	923	557	362	4	195 R	60.3%	39.2%	60.6%	39.4%
55,248	HUNT	21,322	14,303	6,971	48	7,332 R	67.1%	32.7%	67.2%	32.8%
26,304	HUTCHINSON	11,171	9,078	2,052	41	7,026 R	81.3%	18.4%	81.6%	18.4%
1,386	IRION	822	619	199	4	420 R	75.3%	24.2%	75.7%	24.3%
7,408	JACK	2,779	1,825	945	9	880 R	65.7%	34.0%	65.9%	34.1%
13,352	JACKSON	5,478	3,661	1,804	13	1,857 R	66.8%	32.9%	67.0%	33.0%

TEXAS

PRESIDENT 1984

1980 Census Population	County	Total Vote	Republican	Democratic	Other	Rep.-Dem. Plurality	Percentage Total Vote Rep.	Dem.	Major Vote Rep.	Dem.
30,781	JASPER	11,779	5,965	5,787	27	178 R	50.6%	49.1%	50.8%	49.2%
1,647	JEFF DAVIS	815	511	299	5	212 R	62.7%	36.7%	63.1%	36.9%
250,938	JEFFERSON	100,215	45,124	54,846	245	9,722 D	45.0%	54.7%	45.1%	54.9%
5,168	JIM HOGG	2,313	608	1,703	2	1,095 D	26.3%	73.6%	26.3%	73.7%
36,498	JIM WELLS	13,715	5,896	7,795	24	1,899 D	43.0%	56.8%	43.1%	56.9%
67,649	JOHNSON	27,474	18,254	9,148	72	9,106 R	66.4%	33.3%	66.6%	33.4%
17,268	JONES	6,383	4,017	2,343	23	1,674 R	62.9%	36.7%	63.2%	36.8%
13,593	KARNES	4,882	3,068	1,802	12	1,266 R	62.8%	36.9%	63.0%	37.0%
39,015	KAUFMAN	14,938	9,343	5,554	41	3,789 R	62.5%	37.2%	62.7%	37.3%
10,635	KENDALL	5,522	4,568	938	16	3,630 R	82.7%	17.0%	83.0%	17.0%
543	KENEDY	207	96	110	1	14 D	46.4%	53.1%	46.6%	53.4%
1,145	KENT	588	332	253	3	79 R	56.5%	43.0%	56.8%	43.2%
28,780	KERR	14,974	11,829	3,102	43	8,727 R	79.0%	20.7%	79.2%	20.8%
4,063	KIMBLE	1,784	1,333	442	9	891 R	74.7%	24.8%	75.1%	24.9%
425	KING	194	141	53		88 R	72.7%	27.3%	72.7%	27.3%
2,279	KINNEY	1,263	774	486	3	288 R	61.3%	38.5%	61.4%	38.6%
33,358	KLEBERG	10,681	5,712	4,924	45	788 R	53.5%	46.1%	53.7%	46.3%
5,329	KNOX	1,952	1,027	921	4	106 R	52.6%	47.2%	52.7%	47.3%
42,156	LAMAR	14,820	9,273	5,504	43	3,769 R	62.6%	37.1%	62.8%	37.2%
18,669	LAMB	5,828	3,892	1,919	17	1,973 R	66.8%	32.9%	67.0%	33.0%
12,005	LAMPASAS	4,653	3,285	1,356	12	1,929 R	70.6%	29.1%	70.8%	29.2%
5,514	LA SALLE	2,514	1,007	1,504	3	497 D	40.1%	59.8%	40.1%	59.9%
19,004	LAVACA	7,532	5,058	2,464	10	2,594 R	67.2%	32.7%	67.2%	32.8%
10,952	LEE	4,632	2,967	1,659	6	1,308 R	64.1%	35.8%	64.1%	35.9%
9,594	LEON	5,038	3,207	1,821	10	1,386 R	63.7%	36.1%	63.8%	36.2%
47,088	LIBERTY	16,866	10,504	6,292	70	4,212 R	62.3%	37.3%	62.5%	37.5%
20,224	LIMESTONE	7,305	4,063	3,228	14	835 R	55.6%	44.2%	55.7%	44.3%
3,766	LIPSCOMB	1,708	1,461	241	6	1,220 R	85.5%	14.1%	85.8%	14.2%
9,606	LIVE OAK	3,759	2,481	1,260	18	1,221 R	66.0%	33.5%	66.3%	33.7%
10,144	LLANO	5,954	4,042	1,894	18	2,148 R	67.9%	31.8%	68.1%	31.9%
91	LOVING	73	57	16		41 R	78.1%	21.9%	78.1%	21.9%
211,651	LUBBOCK	76,219	57,151	18,793	275	38,358 R	75.0%	24.7%	75.3%	24.7%
8,605	LYNN	2,630	1,617	1,009	4	608 R	61.5%	38.4%	61.6%	38.4%
8,735	MCCULLOCH	3,502	2,060	1,433	9	627 R	58.8%	40.9%	59.0%	41.0%
170,755	MCLENNAN	65,578	42,232	23,206	140	19,026 R	64.4%	35.4%	64.5%	35.5%
789	MCMULLEN	398	337	61		276 R	84.7%	15.3%	84.7%	15.3%
10,649	MADISON	3,553	2,158	1,384	11	774 R	60.7%	39.0%	60.9%	39.1%
10,360	MARION	4,463	2,336	2,111	16	225 R	52.3%	47.3%	52.5%	47.5%
4,684	MARTIN	1,740	1,218	512	10	706 R	70.0%	29.4%	70.4%	29.6%
3,683	MASON	1,743	1,168	570	5	598 R	67.0%	32.7%	67.2%	32.8%
37,828	MATAGORDA	13,694	8,452	5,201	41	3,251 R	61.7%	38.0%	61.9%	38.1%
31,398	MAVERICK	4,861	1,783	3,063	15	1,280 D	36.7%	63.0%	36.8%	63.2%
23,164	MEDINA	8,803	5,737	3,053	13	2,684 R	65.2%	34.7%	65.3%	34.7%
2,346	MENARD	1,125	725	394	6	331 R	64.4%	35.0%	64.8%	35.2%
82,636	MIDLAND	41,039	33,706	7,214	119	26,492 R	82.1%	17.6%	82.4%	17.6%
22,732	MILAM	8,140	4,384	3,734	22	650 R	53.9%	45.9%	54.0%	46.0%
4,477	MILLS	1,960	1,262	688	10	574 R	64.4%	35.1%	64.7%	35.3%
9,088	MITCHELL	3,357	2,007	1,332	18	675 R	59.8%	39.7%	60.1%	39.9%
17,410	MONTAGUE	7,030	4,406	2,602	22	1,804 R	62.7%	37.0%	62.9%	37.1%
128,487	MONTGOMERY	54,690	41,230	13,293	167	27,937 R	75.4%	24.3%	75.6%	24.4%
16,575	MOORE	5,796	4,649	1,129	18	3,520 R	80.2%	19.5%	80.5%	19.5%
14,629	MORRIS	5,727	2,778	2,925	24	147 D	48.5%	51.1%	48.7%	51.3%
1,950	MOTLEY	819	533	282	4	251 R	65.1%	34.4%	65.4%	34.6%
46,786	NACOGDOCHES	18,812	13,063	5,694	55	7,369 R	69.4%	30.3%	69.6%	30.4%
35,323	NAVARRO	13,509	7,816	5,672	21	2,144 R	57.9%	42.0%	57.9%	42.1%
13,254	NEWTON	5,439	2,123	3,296	20	1,173 D	39.0%	60.6%	39.2%	60.8%
17,359	NOLAN	6,136	3,608	2,524	4	1,084 R	58.8%	41.1%	58.8%	41.2%
268,215	NUECES	101,213	54,333	46,721	159	7,612 R	53.7%	46.2%	53.8%	46.2%
9,588	OCHILTREE	3,917	3,492	419	6	3,073 R	89.1%	10.7%	89.3%	10.7%
2,283	OLDHAM	990	762	226	2	536 R	77.0%	22.8%	77.1%	22.9%

TEXAS

PRESIDENT 1984

1980 Census Population	County	Total Vote	Republican	Democratic	Other	Rep.-Dem. Plurality	Total Vote Rep.	Total Vote Dem.	Major Vote Rep.	Major Vote Dem.
83,838	ORANGE	32,303	15,386	16,816	101	1,430 D	47.6%	52.1%	47.8%	52.2%
24,062	PALO PINTO	9,077	5,701	3,349	27	2,352 R	62.8%	36.9%	63.0%	37.0%
20,724	PANOLA	8,885	5,676	3,179	30	2,497 R	63.9%	35.8%	64.1%	35.9%
44,609	PARKER	19,759	13,647	6,050	62	7,597 R	69.1%	30.6%	69.3%	30.7%
11,038	PARMER	3,102	2,524	567	11	1,957 R	81.4%	18.3%	81.7%	18.3%
14,618	PECOS	5,080	3,451	1,596	33	1,855 R	67.9%	31.4%	68.4%	31.6%
24,407	POLK	9,918	5,987	3,898	33	2,089 R	60.4%	39.3%	60.6%	39.4%
98,637	POTTER	28,902	20,396	8,365	141	12,031 R	70.6%	28.9%	70.9%	29.1%
5,188	PRESIDIO	1,902	837	992	73	155 D	44.0%	52.2%	45.8%	54.2%
4,839	RAINS	2,591	1,560	1,027	4	533 R	60.2%	39.6%	60.3%	39.7%
75,062	RANDALL	36,409	30,249	6,044	116	24,205 R	83.1%	16.6%	83.3%	16.7%
4,135	REAGAN	1,324	1,079	243	2	836 R	81.5%	18.4%	81.6%	18.4%
2,469	REAL	1,369	1,004	360	5	644 R	73.3%	26.3%	73.6%	26.4%
16,101	RED RIVER	5,512	2,979	2,518	15	461 R	54.0%	45.7%	54.2%	45.8%
15,801	REEVES	4,872	2,461	2,396	15	65 R	50.5%	49.2%	50.7%	49.3%
9,289	REFUGIO	3,988	2,421	1,559	8	862 R	60.7%	39.1%	60.8%	39.2%
1,187	ROBERTS	645	539	106		433 R	83.6%	16.4%	83.6%	16.4%
14,653	ROBERTSON	6,016	2,663	3,339	14	676 D	44.3%	55.5%	44.4%	55.6%
14,528	ROCKWALL	8,349	6,688	1,639	22	5,049 R	80.1%	19.6%	80.3%	19.7%
11,872	RUNNELS	4,177	2,968	1,179	30	1,789 R	71.1%	28.2%	71.6%	28.4%
41,382	RUST	15,741	11,081	4,599	61	6,482 R	70.4%	29.2%	70.7%	29.3%
8,702	SABINE	3,993	2,045	1,940	8	105 R	51.2%	48.6%	51.3%	48.7%
8,785	SAN AUGUSTINE	3,529	1,937	1,583	9	354 R	54.9%	44.9%	55.0%	45.0%
11,434	SAN JACINTO	5,659	3,174	2,466	19	708 R	56.1%	43.6%	56.3%	43.7%
58,013	SAN PATRICIO	19,962	11,074	8,838	50	2,236 R	55.5%	44.3%	55.6%	44.4%
6,204	SAN SABA	2,647	1,566	1,070	11	496 R	59.2%	40.4%	59.4%	40.6%
2,820	SCHLEICHER	1,187	854	326	7	528 R	71.9%	27.5%	72.4%	27.6%
18,192	SCURRY	6,629	5,028	1,564	37	3,464 R	75.8%	23.6%	76.3%	23.7%
3,915	SHACKELFORD	1,604	1,181	415	8	766 R	73.6%	25.9%	74.0%	26.0%
23,084	SHELBY	8,501	4,863	3,610	28	1,253 R	57.2%	42.5%	57.4%	42.6%
3,174	SHERMAN	1,524	1,269	246	9	1,023 R	83.3%	16.1%	83.8%	16.2%
128,366	SMITH	56,119	40,740	15,227	152	25,513 R	72.6%	27.1%	72.8%	27.2%
4,154	SOMERVELL	2,061	1,422	635	4	787 R	69.0%	30.8%	69.1%	30.9%
27,266	STARR	6,713	1,658	5,047	8	3,389 D	24.7%	75.2%	24.7%	75.3%
9,926	STEPHENS	3,955	2,898	1,046	11	1,852 R	73.3%	26.4%	73.5%	26.5%
1,206	STERLING	710	577	129	4	448 R	81.3%	18.2%	81.7%	18.3%
2,406	STONEWALL	1,244	599	643	2	44 D	48.2%	51.7%	48.2%	51.8%
5,130	SUTTON	1,721	1,251	465	5	786 R	72.7%	27.0%	72.9%	27.1%
9,723	SWISHER	3,261	1,611	1,642	8	31 D	49.4%	50.4%	49.5%	50.5%
860,880	TARRANT	368,862	248,050	120,147	665	127,903 R	67.2%	32.6%	67.4%	32.6%
110,932	TAYLOR	44,202	34,444	9,628	130	24,816 R	77.9%	21.8%	78.2%	21.8%
1,595	TERRELL	698	407	289	2	118 R	58.3%	41.4%	58.5%	41.5%
14,581	TERRY	4,724	3,181	1,535	8	1,646 R	67.3%	32.5%	67.5%	32.5%
2,053	THROCKMORTON	979	586	388	5	198 R	59.9%	39.6%	60.2%	39.8%
21,442	TITUS	8,727	5,069	3,631	27	1,438 R	58.1%	41.6%	58.3%	41.7%
84,784	TOM GREEN	32,910	23,847	8,981	82	14,866 R	72.5%	27.3%	72.6%	27.4%
419,573	TRAVIS	219,813	124,944	94,124	745	30,820 R	56.8%	42.8%	57.0%	43.0%
9,450	TRINITY	4,735	2,599	2,115	21	484 R	54.9%	44.7%	55.1%	44.9%
16,223	TYLER	6,785	3,638	3,119	28	519 R	53.6%	46.0%	53.8%	46.2%
28,595	UPSHUR	11,976	7,325	4,614	37	2,711 R	61.2%	38.5%	61.4%	38.6%
4,619	UPTON	1,994	1,603	380	11	1,223 R	80.4%	19.1%	80.8%	19.2%
22,441	UVALDE	7,287	4,790	2,482	15	2,308 R	65.7%	34.1%	65.9%	34.1%
35,910	VAL VERDE	9,787	5,909	3,857	21	2,052 R	60.4%	39.4%	60.5%	39.5%
31,426	VAN ZANDT	13,003	8,474	4,506	23	3,968 R	65.2%	34.7%	65.3%	34.7%
68,807	VICTORIA	25,945	18,787	7,037	121	11,750 R	72.4%	27.1%	72.8%	27.2%
41,789	WALKER	13,100	8,809	4,263	28	4,546 R	67.2%	32.5%	67.4%	32.6%
19,798	WALLER	7,963	4,116	3,828	19	288 R	51.7%	48.1%	51.8%	48.2%
13,976	WARD	4,693	3,474	1,188	31	2,286 R	74.0%	25.3%	74.5%	25.5%
21,998	WASHINGTON	8,996	6,506	2,483	7	4,023 R	72.3%	27.6%	72.4%	27.6%
99,258	WEBB	20,936	8,582	12,308	46	3,726 D	41.0%	58.8%	41.1%	58.9%

TEXAS

PRESIDENT 1984

| 1980 Census Population | County | Total Vote | Republican | Democratic | Other | Rep.-Dem. Plurality | | Percentage | | | |
| | | | | | | | | Total Vote | | Major Vote | |
								Rep.	Dem.	Rep.	Dem.
40,242	WHARTON	13,584	8,495	5,072	17	3,423	R	62.5%	37.3%	62.6%	37.4%
7,137	WHEELER	3,062	2,251	805	6	1,446	R	73.5%	26.3%	73.7%	26.3%
121,082	WICHITA	45,080	28,932	16,009	139	12,923	R	64.2%	35.5%	64.4%	35.6%
15,931	WILBARGER	5,673	3,644	2,011	18	1,633	R	64.2%	35.4%	64.4%	35.6%
17,495	WILLACY	5,391	2,340	3,037	14	697	D	43.4%	56.3%	43.5%	56.5%
76,521	WILLIAMSON	35,784	25,774	9,911	99	15,863	R	72.0%	27.7%	72.2%	27.8%
16,756	WILSON	7,434	4,588	2,829	17	1,759	R	61.7%	38.1%	61.9%	38.1%
9,944	WINKLER	2,974	2,213	752	9	1,461	R	74.4%	25.3%	74.6%	25.4%
26,575	WISE	10,853	6,958	3,856	39	3,102	R	64.1%	35.5%	64.3%	35.7%
24,697	WOOD	10,612	7,144	3,449	19	3,695	R	67.3%	32.5%	67.4%	32.6%
8,299	YOAKUM	2,668	2,204	456	8	1,748	R	82.6%	17.1%	82.9%	17.1%
19,083	YOUNG	7,503	5,282	2,203	18	3,079	R	70.4%	29.4%	70.6%	29.4%
6,628	ZAPATA	2,801	1,214	1,577	10	363	D	43.3%	56.3%	43.5%	56.5%
11,666	ZAVALA	3,868	924	2,937	7	2,013	D	23.9%	75.9%	23.9%	76.1%
14,229,191	TOTAL	5,397,571	3,433,428	1,949,276	14,867	1,484,152	R	63.6%	36.1%	63.8%	36.2%

TEXAS

SENATOR 1984

1980 Census Population	County	Total Vote	Republican	Democratic	Other	Rep.-Dem. Plurality	Percentage Total Vote Rep.	Total Vote Dem.	Major Vote Rep.	Major Vote Dem.
38,381	ANDERSON	13,317	7,747	5,570		2,177 R	58.2%	41.8%	58.2%	41.8%
13,323	ANDREWS	4,718	3,660	1,058		2,602 R	77.6%	22.4%	77.6%	22.4%
64,172	ANGELINA	23,843	13,462	10,381		3,081 R	56.5%	43.5%	56.5%	43.5%
14,260	ARANSAS	5,956	4,008	1,948		2,060 R	67.3%	32.7%	67.3%	32.7%
7,266	ARCHER	3,544	2,173	1,371		802 R	61.3%	38.7%	61.3%	38.7%
1,994	ARMSTRONG	1,024	725	299		426 R	70.8%	29.2%	70.8%	29.2%
25,055	ATASCOSA	8,691	4,710	3,981		729 R	54.2%	45.8%	54.2%	45.8%
17,726	AUSTIN	6,714	4,467	2,247		2,220 R	66.5%	33.5%	66.5%	33.5%
8,168	BAILEY	2,400	1,562	838		724 R	65.1%	34.9%	65.1%	34.9%
7,084	BANDERA	3,885	2,866	1,019		1,847 R	73.8%	26.2%	73.8%	26.2%
24,726	BASTROP	11,081	5,547	5,534		13 R	50.1%	49.9%	50.1%	49.9%
4,919	BAYLOR	2,300	1,158	1,142		16 R	50.3%	49.7%	50.3%	49.7%
26,030	BEE	8,854	4,899	3,955		944 R	55.3%	44.7%	55.3%	44.7%
157,889	BELL	43,665	27,911	15,754		12,157 R	63.9%	36.1%	63.9%	36.1%
988,800	BEXAR	330,493	178,958	151,535		27,423 R	54.1%	45.9%	54.1%	45.9%
4,681	BLANCO	2,631	1,706	921	4	785 R	64.8%	35.0%	64.9%	35.1%
859	BORDEN	458	310	148		162 R	67.7%	32.3%	67.7%	32.3%
13,401	BOSQUE	5,978	3,583	2,395		1,188 R	59.9%	40.1%	59.9%	40.1%
75,301	BOWIE	28,448	16,350	12,098		4,252 R	57.5%	42.5%	57.5%	42.5%
169,587	BRAZORIA	58,832	36,487	22,343	2	14,144 R	62.0%	38.0%	62.0%	38.0%
93,588	BRAZOS	47,382	33,786	13,595	1	20,191 R	71.3%	28.7%	71.3%	28.7%
7,573	BREWSTER	3,424	1,835	1,587	2	248 R	53.6%	46.3%	53.6%	46.4%
2,579	BRISCOE	1,019	477	542		65 D	46.8%	53.2%	46.8%	53.2%
8,428	BROOKS	3,444	684	2,760		2,076 D	19.9%	80.1%	19.9%	80.1%
33,057	BROWN	12,493	8,031	4,461	1	3,570 R	64.3%	35.7%	64.3%	35.7%
12,313	BURLESON	5,615	2,786	2,829		43 D	49.6%	50.4%	49.6%	50.4%
17,803	BURNET	8,375	4,817	3,558		1,259 R	57.5%	42.5%	57.5%	42.5%
23,637	CALDWELL	7,642	3,741	3,901		160 D	49.0%	51.0%	49.0%	51.0%
19,574	CALHOUN	7,000	3,884	3,116		768 R	55.5%	44.5%	55.5%	44.5%
10,992	CALLAHAN	4,831	3,275	1,554	2	1,721 R	67.8%	32.2%	67.8%	32.2%
209,727	CAMERON	53,791	26,010	27,781		1,771 D	48.4%	51.6%	48.4%	51.6%
9,275	CAMP	4,100	2,006	2,094		88 D	48.9%	51.1%	48.9%	51.1%
6,672	CARSON	3,227	2,229	998		1,231 R	69.1%	30.9%	69.1%	30.9%
29,430	CASS	11,340	5,938	5,402		536 R	52.4%	47.6%	52.4%	47.6%
10,556	CASTRO	2,977	1,824	1,153		671 R	61.3%	38.7%	61.3%	38.7%
18,538	CHAMBERS	7,168	4,000	3,168		832 R	55.8%	44.2%	55.8%	44.2%
38,127	CHEROKEE	12,308	7,165	5,143		2,022 R	58.2%	41.8%	58.2%	41.8%
6,950	CHILDRESS	2,446	1,449	997		452 R	59.2%	40.8%	59.2%	40.8%
9,582	CLAY	4,387	2,281	2,106		175 R	52.0%	48.0%	52.0%	48.0%
4,825	COCHRAN	1,605	957	648		309 R	59.6%	40.4%	59.6%	40.4%
3,196	COKE	1,576	965	611		354 R	61.2%	38.8%	61.2%	38.8%
10,439	COLEMAN	4,168	2,509	1,659		850 R	60.2%	39.8%	60.2%	39.8%
144,576	COLLIN	74,022	56,349	17,673		38,676 R	76.1%	23.9%	76.1%	23.9%
4,648	COLLINGSWORTH	2,029	1,219	810		409 R	60.1%	39.9%	60.1%	39.9%
18,823	COLORADO	6,605	3,966	2,639		1,327 R	60.0%	40.0%	60.0%	40.0%
36,446	COMAL	17,629	12,478	5,146	5	7,332 R	70.8%	29.2%	70.8%	29.2%
12,617	COMANCHE	4,934	2,504	2,430		74 R	50.7%	49.3%	50.7%	49.3%
2,915	CONCHO	1,382	702	679	1	23 R	50.8%	49.1%	50.8%	49.2%
27,656	COOKE	11,388	7,592	3,794	2	3,798 R	66.7%	33.3%	66.7%	33.3%
56,767	CORYELL	12,050	7,920	4,130		3,790 R	65.7%	34.3%	65.7%	34.3%
2,947	COTTLE	1,127	466	661		195 D	41.3%	58.7%	41.3%	58.7%
4,600	CRANE	1,839	1,338	501		837 R	72.8%	27.2%	72.8%	27.2%
4,608	CROCKETT	1,617	1,051	566		485 R	65.0%	35.0%	65.0%	35.0%
8,859	CROSBY	2,561	1,242	1,319		77 D	48.5%	51.5%	48.5%	51.5%
3,315	CULBERSON	857	457	400		57 R	53.3%	46.7%	53.3%	46.7%
6,531	DALLAM	2,051	1,455	596		859 R	70.9%	29.1%	70.9%	29.1%
1,556,390	DALLAS	600,788	371,128	229,649	11	141,479 R	61.8%	38.2%	61.8%	38.2%
16,184	DAWSON	5,320	3,465	1,855		1,610 R	65.1%	34.9%	65.1%	34.9%
21,165	DEAF SMITH	6,130	4,379	1,751		2,628 R	71.4%	28.6%	71.4%	28.6%
4,839	DELTA	1,958	888	1,070		182 D	45.4%	54.6%	45.4%	54.6%

TEXAS

SENATOR 1984

1980 Census Population	County	Total Vote	Republican	Democratic	Other	Rep.-Dem. Plurality	Percentage Total Vote Rep.	Dem.	Major Vote Rep.	Dem.
143,126	DENTON	69,241	48,325	20,915	1	27,410 R	69.8%	30.2%	69.8%	30.2%
18,903	DE WITT	6,156	4,063	2,093		1,970 R	66.0%	34.0%	66.0%	34.0%
3,539	DICKENS	1,257	508	749		241 D	40.4%	59.6%	40.4%	59.6%
11,367	DIMMIT	3,769	1,171	2,598		1,427 D	31.1%	68.9%	31.1%	68.9%
4,075	DONLEY	1,787	1,179	608		571 R	66.0%	34.0%	66.0%	34.0%
12,517	DUVAL	4,793	1,037	3,756		2,719 D	21.6%	78.4%	21.6%	78.4%
19,480	EASTLAND	7,326	4,518	2,808		1,710 R	61.7%	38.3%	61.7%	38.3%
115,374	ECTOR	39,996	29,352	10,644		18,708 R	73.4%	26.6%	73.4%	26.6%
2,033	EDWARDS	756	545	209	2	336 R	72.1%	27.6%	72.3%	27.7%
59,743	ELLIS	24,815	15,832	8,983		6,849 R	63.8%	36.2%	63.8%	36.2%
479,899	EL PASO	117,462	57,696	59,741	25	2,045 D	49.1%	50.9%	49.1%	50.9%
22,560	ERATH	9,359	5,574	3,785		1,789 R	59.6%	40.4%	59.6%	40.4%
17,946	FALLS	5,850	2,733	3,117		384 D	46.7%	53.3%	46.7%	53.3%
24,285	FANNIN	9,025	4,130	4,895		765 D	45.8%	54.2%	45.8%	54.2%
18,832	FAYETTE	7,840	4,934	2,906		2,028 R	62.9%	37.1%	62.9%	37.1%
5,891	FISHER	2,330	903	1,427		524 D	38.8%	61.2%	38.8%	61.2%
9,834	FLOYD	3,080	1,922	1,158		764 R	62.4%	37.6%	62.4%	37.6%
2,158	FOARD	890	398	492		94 D	44.7%	55.3%	44.7%	55.3%
130,846	FORT BEND	59,162	37,425	21,702	35	15,723 R	63.3%	36.7%	63.3%	36.7%
6,893	FRANKLIN	2,910	1,703	1,207		496 R	58.5%	41.5%	58.5%	41.5%
14,830	FREESTONE	6,104	3,407	2,697		710 R	55.8%	44.2%	55.8%	44.2%
13,785	FRIO	4,473	1,800	2,673		873 D	40.2%	59.8%	40.2%	59.8%
13,150	GAINES	3,500	2,453	1,047		1,406 R	70.1%	29.9%	70.1%	29.9%
195,940	GALVESTON	74,792	36,266	38,525	1	2,259 D	48.5%	51.5%	48.5%	51.5%
5,336	GARZA	1,694	1,097	597		500 R	64.8%	35.2%	64.8%	35.2%
13,532	GILLESPIE	6,696	5,239	1,457		3,782 R	78.2%	21.8%	78.2%	21.8%
1,304	GLASSCOCK	525	372	153		219 R	70.9%	29.1%	70.9%	29.1%
5,193	GOLIAD	2,293	1,402	891		511 R	61.1%	38.9%	61.1%	38.9%
16,883	GONZALES	5,961	3,541	2,420		1,121 R	59.4%	40.6%	59.4%	40.6%
26,386	GRAY	10,864	8,408	2,454	2	5,954 R	77.4%	22.6%	77.4%	22.6%
89,796	GRAYSON	34,213	20,327	13,886		6,441 R	59.4%	40.6%	59.4%	40.6%
99,487	GREGG	39,350	27,004	12,346		14,658 R	68.6%	31.4%	68.6%	31.4%
13,580	GRIMES	5,650	3,148	2,502		646 R	55.7%	44.3%	55.7%	44.3%
46,708	GUADALUPE	19,155	12,961	6,191	3	6,770 R	67.7%	32.3%	67.7%	32.3%
37,592	HALE	10,442	7,150	3,292		3,858 R	68.5%	31.5%	68.5%	31.5%
5,594	HALL	1,938	894	1,044		150 D	46.1%	53.9%	46.1%	53.9%
8,297	HAMILTON	3,236	1,882	1,354		528 R	58.2%	41.8%	58.2%	41.8%
6,209	HANSFORD	2,438	2,073	365		1,708 R	85.0%	15.0%	85.0%	15.0%
6,368	HARDEMAN	1,994	1,034	960		74 R	51.9%	48.1%	51.9%	48.1%
40,721	HARDIN	15,159	7,706	7,453		253 R	50.8%	49.2%	50.8%	49.2%
2,409,547	HARRIS	860,959	493,618	367,293	48	126,325 R	57.3%	42.7%	57.3%	42.7%
52,265	HARRISON	19,727	11,566	8,161		3,405 R	58.6%	41.4%	58.6%	41.4%
3,987	HARTLEY	1,765	1,341	424		917 R	76.0%	24.0%	76.0%	24.0%
7,725	HASKELL	3,068	1,540	1,528		12 R	50.2%	49.8%	50.2%	49.8%
40,594	HAYS	19,119	10,435	8,684		1,751 R	54.6%	45.4%	54.6%	45.4%
5,304	HEMPHILL	1,995	1,498	496	1	1,002 R	75.1%	24.9%	75.1%	24.9%
42,606	HENDERSON	19,872	11,380	8,492		2,888 R	57.3%	42.7%	57.3%	42.7%
283,229	HIDALGO	76,494	31,792	44,702		12,910 D	41.6%	58.4%	41.6%	58.4%
25,024	HILL	8,785	5,095	3,690		1,405 R	58.0%	42.0%	58.0%	42.0%
23,230	HOCKLEY	7,515	4,980	2,535		2,445 R	66.3%	33.7%	66.3%	33.7%
17,714	HOOD	9,887	6,398	3,489		2,909 R	64.7%	35.3%	64.7%	35.3%
25,247	HOPKINS	9,391	5,416	3,975		1,441 R	57.7%	42.3%	57.7%	42.3%
22,299	HOUSTON	7,658	4,065	3,593		472 R	53.1%	46.9%	53.1%	46.9%
33,142	HOWARD	11,620	6,944	4,676		2,268 R	59.8%	40.2%	59.8%	40.2%
2,728	HUDSPETH	829	439	387	3	52 R	53.0%	46.7%	53.1%	46.9%
55,248	HUNT	21,088	12,795	8,293		4,502 R	60.7%	39.3%	60.7%	39.3%
26,304	HUTCHINSON	11,033	8,400	2,633		5,767 R	76.1%	23.9%	76.1%	23.9%
1,386	IRION	810	544	266		278 R	67.2%	32.8%	67.2%	32.8%
7,408	JACK	2,750	1,653	1,097		556 R	60.1%	39.9%	60.1%	39.9%
13,352	JACKSON	5,315	3,230	2,085		1,145 R	60.8%	39.2%	60.8%	39.2%

TEXAS

SENATOR 1984

1980 Census Population	County	Total Vote	Republican	Democratic	Other	Rep.-Dem. Plurality	Percentage Total Vote Rep.	Dem.	Major Vote Rep.	Dem.
30,781	JASPER	11,591	5,228	6,363		1,135 D	45.1%	54.9%	45.1%	54.9%
1,647	JEFF DAVIS	715	409	306		103 R	57.2%	42.8%	57.2%	42.8%
250,938	JEFFERSON	100,225	41,322	58,903		17,581 D	41.2%	58.8%	41.2%	58.8%
5,168	JIM HOGG	2,233	442	1,791		1,349 D	19.8%	80.2%	19.8%	80.2%
36,498	JIM WELLS	13,359	5,233	8,124	2	2,891 D	39.2%	60.8%	39.2%	60.8%
67,649	JOHNSON	27,510	17,174	10,335	1	6,839 R	62.4%	37.6%	62.4%	37.6%
17,268	JONES	6,323	3,687	2,636		1,051 R	58.3%	41.7%	58.3%	41.7%
13,593	KARNES	4,731	2,771	1,960		811 R	58.6%	41.4%	58.6%	41.4%
39,015	KAUFMAN	14,785	8,329	6,456		1,873 R	56.3%	43.7%	56.3%	43.7%
10,635	KENDALL	5,563	4,367	1,196		3,171 R	78.5%	21.5%	78.5%	21.5%
543	KENEDY	193	83	110		27 D	43.0%	57.0%	43.0%	57.0%
1,145	KENT	583	309	273	1	36 R	53.0%	46.8%	53.1%	46.9%
28,780	KERR	14,599	10,897	3,701	1	7,196 R	74.6%	25.4%	74.6%	25.4%
4,063	KIMBLE	1,745	1,271	474		797 R	72.8%	27.2%	72.8%	27.2%
425	KING	193	124	69		55 R	64.2%	35.8%	64.2%	35.8%
2,279	KINNEY	1,186	616	569	1	47 R	51.9%	48.0%	52.0%	48.0%
33,358	KLEBERG	10,232	5,218	5,014		204 R	51.0%	49.0%	51.0%	49.0%
5,329	KNOX	1,930	875	1,055		180 D	45.3%	54.7%	45.3%	54.7%
42,156	LAMAR	14,629	7,979	6,650		1,329 R	54.5%	45.5%	54.5%	45.5%
18,669	LAMB	5,696	3,533	2,163		1,370 R	62.0%	38.0%	62.0%	38.0%
12,005	LAMPASAS	4,618	2,994	1,624		1,370 R	64.8%	35.2%	64.8%	35.2%
5,514	LA SALLE	2,353	827	1,526		699 D	35.1%	64.9%	35.1%	64.9%
19,004	LAVACA	7,379	4,488	2,891		1,597 R	60.8%	39.2%	60.8%	39.2%
10,952	LEE	4,586	2,582	2,004		578 R	56.3%	43.7%	56.3%	43.7%
9,594	LEON	4,949	2,957	1,992		965 R	59.7%	40.3%	59.7%	40.3%
47,088	LIBERTY	16,562	9,490	7,071	1	2,419 R	57.3%	42.7%	57.3%	42.7%
20,224	LIMESTONE	7,257	3,861	3,393	3	468 R	53.2%	46.8%	53.2%	46.8%
3,766	LIPSCOMB	1,667	1,321	346		975 R	79.2%	20.8%	79.2%	20.8%
9,606	LIVE OAK	3,684	2,280	1,404		876 R	61.9%	38.1%	61.9%	38.1%
10,144	LLANO	5,899	3,628	2,270	1	1,358 R	61.5%	38.5%	61.5%	38.5%
91	LOVING	70	55	15		40 R	78.6%	21.4%	78.6%	21.4%
211,651	LUBBOCK	76,394	53,612	22,779	3	30,833 R	70.2%	29.8%	70.2%	29.8%
8,605	LYNN	2,613	1,446	1,167		279 R	55.3%	44.7%	55.3%	44.7%
8,735	MCCULLOCH	3,478	1,959	1,519		440 R	56.3%	43.7%	56.3%	43.7%
170,755	MCLENNAN	65,356	39,067	26,289		12,778 R	59.8%	40.2%	59.8%	40.2%
789	MCMULLEN	392	325	67		258 R	82.9%	17.1%	82.9%	17.1%
10,649	MADISON	3,486	1,954	1,532		422 R	56.1%	43.9%	56.1%	43.9%
10,360	MARION	4,314	2,066	2,248		182 D	47.9%	52.1%	47.9%	52.1%
4,684	MARTIN	1,711	1,142	569		573 R	66.7%	33.3%	66.7%	33.3%
3,683	MASON	1,724	1,097	627		470 R	63.6%	36.4%	63.6%	36.4%
37,828	MATAGORDA	13,544	7,752	5,792		1,960 R	57.2%	42.8%	57.2%	42.8%
31,398	MAVERICK	4,612	1,495	3,117		1,622 D	32.4%	67.6%	32.4%	67.6%
23,164	MEDINA	8,639	5,223	3,416		1,807 R	60.5%	39.5%	60.5%	39.5%
2,346	MENARD	958	504	454		50 R	52.6%	47.4%	52.6%	47.4%
82,636	MIDLAND	40,360	32,078	8,281	1	23,797 R	79.5%	20.5%	79.5%	20.5%
22,732	MILAM	8,049	3,798	4,251		453 D	47.2%	52.8%	47.2%	52.8%
4,477	MILLS	1,746	1,016	730		286 R	58.2%	41.8%	58.2%	41.8%
9,088	MITCHELL	3,294	1,788	1,506		282 R	54.3%	45.7%	54.3%	45.7%
17,410	MONTAGUE	6,972	4,117	2,855		1,262 R	59.1%	40.9%	59.1%	40.9%
128,487	MONTGOMERY	53,896	38,188	15,704	4	22,484 R	70.9%	29.1%	70.9%	29.1%
16,575	MOORE	5,722	4,303	1,419		2,884 R	75.2%	24.8%	75.2%	24.8%
14,629	MORRIS	5,631	2,545	3,086		541 D	45.2%	54.8%	45.2%	54.8%
1,950	MOTLEY	799	475	324		151 R	59.4%	40.6%	59.4%	40.6%
46,786	NACOGDOCHES	18,784	12,079	6,705		5,374 R	64.3%	35.7%	64.3%	35.7%
35,323	NAVARRO	13,408	7,231	6,177		1,054 R	53.9%	46.1%	53.9%	46.1%
13,254	NEWTON	5,329	1,791	3,538		1,747 D	33.6%	66.4%	33.6%	66.4%
17,359	NOLAN	5,983	3,319	2,664		655 R	55.5%	44.5%	55.5%	44.5%
268,215	NUECES	99,016	49,784	49,232		552 R	50.3%	49.7%	50.3%	49.7%
9,588	OCHILTREE	3,862	3,304	558		2,746 R	85.6%	14.4%	85.6%	14.4%
2,283	OLDHAM	957	662	295		367 R	69.2%	30.8%	69.2%	30.8%

TEXAS

SENATOR 1984

1980 Census Population	County	Total Vote	Republican	Democratic	Other	Rep.-Dem. Plurality	Percentage Total Vote Rep.	Dem.	Major Vote Rep.	Dem.
83,838	ORANGE	31,814	13,647	18,156	11	4,509 D	42.9%	57.1%	42.9%	57.1%
24,062	PALO PINTO	9,026	5,161	3,865		1,296 R	57.2%	42.8%	57.2%	42.8%
20,724	PANOLA	8,684	4,995	3,689		1,306 R	57.5%	42.5%	57.5%	42.5%
44,609	PARKER	19,583	12,309	7,274		5,035 R	62.9%	37.1%	62.9%	37.1%
11,038	PARMER	3,063	2,340	723		1,617 R	76.4%	23.6%	76.4%	23.6%
14,618	PECOS	4,985	3,034	1,934	17	1,100 R	60.9%	38.8%	61.1%	38.9%
24,407	POLK	9,873	5,416	4,457		959 R	54.9%	45.1%	54.9%	45.1%
98,637	POTTER	29,097	19,273	9,824		9,449 R	66.2%	33.8%	66.2%	33.8%
5,188	PRESIDIO	1,700	737	963		226 D	43.4%	56.6%	43.4%	56.6%
4,839	RAINS	2,551	1,316	1,235		81 R	51.6%	48.4%	51.6%	48.4%
75,062	RANDALL	36,352	28,578	7,774		20,804 R	78.6%	21.4%	78.6%	21.4%
4,135	REAGAN	1,311	989	322		667 R	75.4%	24.6%	75.4%	24.6%
2,469	REAL	1,309	847	462		385 R	64.7%	35.3%	64.7%	35.3%
16,101	RED RIVER	5,315	2,559	2,756		197 D	48.1%	51.9%	48.1%	51.9%
15,801	REEVES	4,732	2,228	2,504		276 D	47.1%	52.9%	47.1%	52.9%
9,289	REFUGIO	3,885	2,147	1,738		409 R	55.3%	44.7%	55.3%	44.7%
1,187	ROBERTS	636	498	138		360 R	78.3%	21.7%	78.3%	21.7%
14,653	ROBERTSON	5,959	2,489	3,470		981 D	41.8%	58.2%	41.8%	58.2%
14,528	ROCKWALL	8,262	6,172	2,090		4,082 R	74.7%	25.3%	74.7%	25.3%
11,872	RUNNELS	4,117	2,653	1,464		1,189 R	64.4%	35.6%	64.4%	35.6%
41,382	RUST	15,523	10,042	5,481		4,561 R	64.7%	35.3%	64.7%	35.3%
8,702	SABINE	3,922	1,816	2,106		290 D	46.3%	53.7%	46.3%	53.7%
8,785	SAN AUGUSTINE	3,431	1,667	1,764		97 D	48.6%	51.4%	48.6%	51.4%
11,434	SAN JACINTO	5,457	2,852	2,605		247 R	52.3%	47.7%	52.3%	47.7%
58,013	SAN PATRICIO	19,487	10,327	9,160		1,167 R	53.0%	47.0%	53.0%	47.0%
6,204	SAN SABA	2,602	1,406	1,195	1	211 R	54.0%	45.9%	54.1%	45.9%
2,820	SCHLEICHER	1,165	771	394		377 R	66.2%	33.8%	66.2%	33.8%
18,192	SCURRY	6,582	4,829	1,753		3,076 R	73.4%	26.6%	73.4%	26.6%
3,915	SHACKELFORD	1,583	1,087	496		591 R	68.7%	31.3%	68.7%	31.3%
23,084	SHELBY	8,308	4,278	4,023	7	255 R	51.5%	48.4%	51.5%	48.5%
3,174	SHERMAN	1,481	1,148	333		815 R	77.5%	22.5%	77.5%	22.5%
128,366	SMITH	55,877	37,613	18,261	3	19,352 R	67.3%	32.7%	67.3%	32.7%
4,154	SOMERVELL	1,989	1,159	826	4	333 R	58.3%	41.5%	58.4%	41.6%
27,266	STARR	6,484	1,290	5,194		3,904 D	19.9%	80.1%	19.9%	80.1%
9,926	STEPHENS	3,916	2,750	1,164	2	1,586 R	70.2%	29.7%	70.3%	29.7%
1,206	STERLING	673	488	185		303 R	72.5%	27.5%	72.5%	27.5%
2,406	STONEWALL	1,214	519	695		176 D	42.8%	57.2%	42.8%	57.2%
5,130	SUTTON	1,698	1,195	503		692 R	70.4%	29.6%	70.4%	29.6%
9,723	SWISHER	3,187	1,370	1,817		447 D	43.0%	57.0%	43.0%	57.0%
860,880	TARRANT	363,659	228,117	135,541	1	92,576 R	62.7%	37.3%	62.7%	37.3%
110,932	TAYLOR	44,069	32,290	11,771	8	20,519 R	73.3%	26.7%	73.3%	26.7%
1,595	TERRELL	672	357	315		42 R	53.1%	46.9%	53.1%	46.9%
14,581	TERRY	4,609	3,056	1,551	2	1,505 R	66.3%	33.7%	66.3%	33.7%
2,053	THROCKMORTON	978	557	421		136 R	57.0%	43.0%	57.0%	43.0%
21,442	TITUS	8,609	4,466	4,143		323 R	51.9%	48.1%	51.9%	48.1%
84,784	TOM GREEN	32,953	21,840	11,111	2	10,729 R	66.3%	33.7%	66.3%	33.7%
419,573	TRAVIS	218,891	101,337	117,518	36	16,181 D	46.3%	53.7%	46.3%	53.7%
9,450	TRINITY	4,618	2,238	2,380		142 D	48.5%	51.5%	48.5%	51.5%
16,223	TYLER	6,684	3,286	3,398		112 D	49.2%	50.8%	49.2%	50.8%
28,595	UPSHUR	11,788	6,473	5,315		1,158 R	54.9%	45.1%	54.9%	45.1%
4,619	UPTON	1,885	1,361	522	2	839 R	72.2%	27.7%	72.3%	27.7%
22,441	UVALDE	7,087	4,309	2,778		1,531 R	60.8%	39.2%	60.8%	39.2%
35,910	VAL VERDE	9,470	5,065	4,405		660 R	53.5%	46.5%	53.5%	46.5%
31,426	VAN ZANDT	12,871	7,564	5,307		2,257 R	58.8%	41.2%	58.8%	41.2%
68,807	VICTORIA	24,821	17,241	7,579	1	9,662 R	69.5%	30.5%	69.5%	30.5%
41,789	WALKER	12,962	7,998	4,964		3,034 R	61.7%	38.3%	61.7%	38.3%
19,798	WALLER	7,976	3,843	4,133		290 D	48.2%	51.8%	48.2%	51.8%
13,976	WARD	4,739	3,257	1,478		1,779 R	68.7%	31.2%	68.8%	31.2%
21,998	WASHINGTON	8,934	5,964	2,970	4	2,994 R	66.8%	33.2%	66.8%	33.2%
99,258	WEBB	21,402	6,370	15,032		8,662 D	29.8%	70.2%	29.8%	70.2%

TEXAS

SENATOR 1984

1980 Census Population	County	Total Vote	Republican	Democratic	Other	Rep.-Dem. Plurality	Percentage Total Vote Rep.	Dem.	Major Vote Rep.	Dem.
40,242	WHARTON	13,506	7,630	5,876		1,754 R	56.5%	43.5%	56.5%	43.5%
7,137	WHEELER	2,978	2,024	954		1,070 R	68.0%	32.0%	68.0%	32.0%
121,082	WICHITA	44,842	25,856	18,986		6,870 R	57.7%	42.3%	57.7%	42.3%
15,931	WILBARGER	5,551	3,264	2,287		977 R	58.8%	41.2%	58.8%	41.2%
17,495	WILLACY	5,205	2,077	3,128		1,051 D	39.9%	60.1%	39.9%	60.1%
76,521	WILLIAMSON	35,365	21,931	13,434		8,497 R	62.0%	38.0%	62.0%	38.0%
16,756	WILSON	7,194	4,044	3,150		894 R	56.2%	43.8%	56.2%	43.8%
9,944	WINKLER	2,943	2,083	860		1,223 R	70.8%	29.2%	70.8%	29.2%
26,575	WISE	10,783	6,260	4,523		1,737 R	58.1%	41.9%	58.1%	41.9%
24,697	WOOD	10,480	6,454	4,026		2,428 R	61.6%	38.4%	61.6%	38.4%
8,299	YOAKUM	2,652	1,996	656		1,340 R	75.3%	24.7%	75.3%	24.7%
19,083	YOUNG	7,450	4,823	2,627		2,196 R	64.7%	35.3%	64.7%	35.3%
6,628	ZAPATA	2,685	962	1,723		761 D	35.8%	64.2%	35.8%	64.2%
11,666	ZAVALA	3,562	712	2,849	1	2,137 D	20.0%	80.0%	20.0%	80.0%
14,229,191	TOTAL	5,319,178	3,116,348	2,202,557	273	913,791 R	58.6%	41.4%	58.6%	41.4%

TEXAS

CONGRESS

CD	Year	Total Vote	Republican Vote	Republican Candidate	Democratic Vote	Democratic Candidate	Other Vote	Rep.-Dem. Plurality	Total Vote Rep.	Total Vote Dem.	Major Vote Rep.	Major Vote Dem.
1	1984	139,829			139,829	HALL, SAM B.		139,829 D		100.0%		100.0%
1	1982	103,283			100,685	HALL, SAM B.	2,598	100,685 D		97.5%		100.0%
2	1984	191,067	77,842	DUGAS, LOUIS	113,225	WILSON, CHARLES		35,383 D	40.7%	59.3%	40.7%	59.3%
2	1982	97,346			91,762	WILSON, CHARLES	5,584	91,762 D		94.3%		100.0%
3	1984	275,709	228,819	BARTLETT, STEVE	46,890	WESTBROOK, JIM		181,929 R	83.0%	17.0%	83.0%	17.0%
4	1984	208,341	87,553	BLOW, THOMAS	120,749	HALL, RALPH M.	39	33,196 D	42.0%	58.0%	42.0%	58.0%
4	1982	127,496	32,221	COLLUMB, PETER J.	94,134	HALL, RALPH M.	1,141	61,913 D	25.3%	73.8%	25.5%	74.5%
5	1984	94,391			94,391	BRYANT, JOHN		94,391 D		100.0%		100.0%
5	1982	80,530	27,121	DEVANY, JOE	52,214	BRYANT, JOHN	1,195	25,093 D	33.7%	64.8%	34.2%	65.8%
6	1984	232,281	131,482	BARTON, JOE L.	100,799	KUBIAK, DAN		30,683 R	56.6%	43.4%	56.6%	43.4%
7	1984	246,315	213,480	ARCHER, W. R.	32,835	WILLIBEY, BILLY		180,645 R	86.7%	13.3%	86.7%	13.3%
7	1982	127,922	108,718	ARCHER, W. R.	17,866	SCOGGINS, DENNIS G.	1,338	90,852 R	85.0%	14.0%	85.9%	14.1%
8	1984	175,103	113,031	FIELDS, JACK	62,072	BUFORD, DON		50,959 R	64.6%	35.4%	64.6%	35.4%
8	1982	89,218	50,630	FIELDS, JACK	38,041	ALLEE, HENRY E.	547	12,589 R	56.7%	42.6%	57.1%	42.9%
9	1984	204,865	84,306	MAHAN, JIM	120,559	BROOKS, JACK B.		36,253 D	41.2%	58.8%	41.2%	58.8%
9	1982	116,897	35,422	LEWIS, JOHN W.	78,965	BROOKS, JACK B.	2,510	43,543 D	30.3%	67.6%	31.0%	69.0%
10	1984	186,785			186,447	PICKLE, JAKE	338	186,447 D		99.8%		100.0%
10	1982	134,276			121,030	PICKLE, JAKE	13,246	121,030 D		90.1%		100.0%
11	1984	112,940			112,940	LEATH, J. MARVIN		112,940 D		100.0%		100.0%
11	1982	86,395			83,236	LEATH, J. MARVIN	3,159	83,236 D		96.3%		100.0%
12	1984	106,302			106,299	WRIGHT, JAMES C.	3	106,299 D		100.0%		100.0%
13	1984	202,967	107,600	BOULTER, BEAU	95,367	HIGHTOWER, JOHN		12,233 R	53.0%	47.0%	53.0%	47.0%
13	1982	135,820	47,877	SLOVER, RON	86,376	HIGHTOWER, JOHN	1,567	38,499 D	35.3%	63.6%	35.7%	64.3%
14	1984	203,066	104,181	SWEENEY, MAC	98,885	PATMAN, WILLIAM N.		5,296 R	51.3%	48.7%	51.3%	48.7%
14	1982	126,712	48,942	WYATT, JOE	76,851	PATMAN, WILLIAM N.	919	27,909 D	38.6%	60.7%	38.9%	61.1%
15	1984	104,863			104,863	DE LA GARZA, ELIGIO		104,863 D		100.0%		100.0%
15	1982	80,002			76,544	DE LA GARZA, ELIGIO	3,458	76,544 D		95.7%		100.0%
16	1984	132,964	56,589	HAMMOND, JACK	76,375	COLEMAN, RONALD		19,786 D	42.6%	57.4%	42.6%	57.4%
16	1982	81,671	36,064	HAGGERTY, PAT	44,024	COLEMAN, RONALD	1,583	7,960 D	44.2%	53.9%	45.0%	55.0%
17	1984	143,012			143,012	STENHOLM, CHARLES W.		143,012 D		100.0%		100.0%
17	1982	112,630			109,359	STENHOLM, CHARLES W.	3,271	109,359 D		97.1%		100.0%
18	1984	139,110	26,400	BEAMAN, GLEN E.	109,626	LELAND, MICKEY	3,084	83,226 D	19.0%	78.8%	19.4%	80.6%
18	1982	82,335	12,104	PICKETT, C. LEON	68,014	LELAND, MICKEY	2,217	55,910 D	14.7%	82.6%	15.1%	84.9%
19	1984	176,849	102,805	COMBEST, LARRY	74,044	RICHARDS, DON R.		28,761 R	58.1%	41.9%	58.1%	41.9%
19	1982	109,970	19,062	HICKS, E. L.	89,702	HANCE, KENT	1,206	70,640 D	17.3%	81.6%	17.5%	82.5%
20	1984	100,443			100,443	GONZALEZ, HENRY B.		100,443 D		100.0%		100.0%
21	1984	247,980	199,909	LOEFFLER, TOM	48,039	SULLIVAN, JOE	32	151,870 R	80.6%	19.4%	80.6%	19.4%
22	1984	191,751	125,225	DELAY, THOMAS D.	66,495	WILLIAMS, DOUG	31	58,730 R	65.3%	34.7%	65.3%	34.7%
22	1982	67,479	66,536	PAUL, RON			943	66,536 R	98.6%		100.0%	
23	1984	95,721			95,721	BUSTAMANTE, ALBERT G.		95,721 D		100.0%		100.0%
24	1984	176,918	71,703	BURK, BOB	105,210	FROST, MARTIN	5	33,507 D	40.5%	59.5%	40.5%	59.5%
25	1984	177,920	63,974	PATTERSON, JERRY	113,946	ANDREWS, MIKE		49,972 D	36.0%	64.0%	36.0%	64.0%
25	1982	105,914	40,112	FAUBION, MIKE	63,974	ANDREWS, MIKE	1,828	23,862 D	37.9%	60.4%	38.5%	61.5%
26	1984	247,094	126,641	ARMEY, DICK	120,451	VANDERGRIFF, TOM	2	6,190 R	51.3%	48.7%	51.3%	48.7%
27	1984	165,799	60,283	MOORE, RICHARD	105,516	ORTIZ, SOLOMON P.		45,233 D	36.4%	63.6%	36.4%	63.6%
27	1982	104,044	35,209	LUBY, JASON	66,604	ORTIZ, SOLOMON P.	2,231	31,395 D	33.8%	64.0%	34.6%	65.4%

TEXAS

1984 GENERAL ELECTION

President   Other vote was 14,613 LaRouche (Independent); 126 Hall (write-in); 87 Johnson (write-in); 41 Serrette (write-in).

Senator   Other vote was 170 Davis (write-in); 103 Gambrel (write-in). The state and Coryell county returns have been adjusted to reflect an under-report of 5,000 Republican votes in the original state canvass.

Congress   Other vote was Becker (write-in) in CD 4; Wilson (write-in) in CD 10; Taliaferro (write-in) in CD 12; 3,064 Alvarado (Independent) and 20 Cashin (write-in) in CD 18; 26 Campbell (write-in) and 6 Swilling (write-in) in CD 21; Edwards (write-in) in CD 22; Iverson (write-in) in CD 24; Kendall (write-in) in CD 26.

1984 PRIMARIES

MAY 5 REPUBLICAN

Senator   246,716 Phil Gramm; 55,431 Ron Paul; 26,279 Rob Mosbacher; 8,388 Henry C. Grover.

Congress   Unopposed in twelve CD's. No candidate in CD's 1, 5, 10, 11, 12, 15, 17, 20, 23. Contested as follows:

CD   6   7,563 Joe L. Barton; 5,590 Max Hoyt; 2,857 Bob Harris; 2,014 Patsy H. Friedrichs.
CD   9   4,227 Jim Mahan; 3,675 Lisa Duperier.
CD 14   4,455 Mac Sweeney; 3,346 Chris Mealy; 1,167 Wayne Pryor.
CD 19   5,562 Larry Combest; 3,881 Ron Fleming; 1,624 Tom Schaefer; 421 Richard Wilder.
CD 22   11,580 Thomas D. DeLay; 5,711 J. C. Helms; 2,135 Ellen Heath; 1,006 Gary Engebretson; 1,029 Don L. Richardson; 279 Joe Agris.
CD 24   5,570 Bob Burk; 3,598 Jack Bower.

MAY 5 DEMOCRATIC

Senator   456,446 Kent Hance; 456,173 Lloyd Doggett; 454,886 Robert Krueger; 47,062 David L. Young; 34,733 Robert S. Sullivan; 14,149 Harley Schlanger.

Congress   Unopposed in fifteen CD's. Contested as follows:

CD   2   61,684 Charles Wilson; 32,438 Jerry K. Johnson; 9,045 Lloyd T. Dickens; 4,373 William B. Duncan; 4,245 Mitch Hickman.
CD   3   6,889 Jim Westbrook; 4,928 Jim McNees.
CD   6   38,143 Dan Kubiak; 26,770 Hugh Parmer; 5,279 J. M. Van Winkle.
CD   8   11,083 Don Buford; 10,621 Marc Hill.
CD 17   81,312 Charles W. Stenholm; 10,867 Noel S. Cowling.
CD 18   33,072 Mickey Leland; 3,421 Franklin D. Saulsberry.
CD 19   18,411 Don R. Richards; 17,481 Thomas M. Richards; 10,808 John Selby; 7,987 Delwin Jones; 4,779 Gary D. Condra.
CD 21   24,431 Joe Sullivan; 18,582 Bobby Locke.
CD 22   10,256 Doug Williams; 6,507 Jim Mooney; 4,873 Nick Benton.
CD 23   40,855 Albert G. Bustamante; 25,588 Abraham Kazen; 3,286 Stanley C. Green.
CD 24   25,248 Martin Frost; 2,185 Dan Leach.
CD 25   28,513 Mike Andrews; 1,737 Bruce Director.

TEXAS

JUNE 2 REPUBLICAN RUN-OFF

Congress

    CD 6   4,632 Joe L. Barton; 4,622 Max Hoyt.
    CD 14   2,887 Mac Sweeney; 1,944 Chris Mealy.
    CD 19   4,255 Larry Combest; 3,143 Ron Fleming.

JUNE 2 DEMOCRATIC RUN-OFF

Senator   491,251 Lloyd Doggett; 489,906 Kent Hance. Vote given here is for the re-count.

Congress

    CD 19   29,144 Don R. Richards; 28,429 Thomas M. Richards.
    CD 22   8,717 Doug Williams; 5,398 Jim Mooney.

UTAH

GOVERNOR
Norman H. Bangerter (R). Elected 1984 to a four-year term.

SENATORS
E. J. Garn (R). Re-elected 1980 to a six-year term. Previously elected 1974.

Orrin G. Hatch (R). Re-elected 1982 to a six-year term. Previously elected 1976.

REPRESENTATIVES
1. James V. Hansen (R)   2. David S. Monson (R)   3. Howard C. Nielson (R)

POSTWAR VOTE FOR GOVERNOR

| | Total | Republican | | Democratic | | Other | Rep.-Dem. | Percentage | | | |
| | | | | | | | | Total Vote | | Major Vote | |
Year	Vote	Vote	Candidate	Vote	Candidate	Vote	Plurality	Rep.	Dem.	Rep.	Dem.
1984	629,619	351,792	Bangerter, Norman H.	275,669	Owens, Wayne	2,158	76,123 R	55.9%	43.8%	56.1%	43.9%
1980	600,019	266,578	Wright, Bob	330,974	Matheson, Scott M.	2,467	64,396 D	44.4%	55.2%	44.6%	55.4%
1976	539,649	248,027	Romney, Vernon B.	280,706	Matheson, Scott M.	10,916	32,679 D	46.0%	52.0%	46.9%	53.1%
1972	476,447	144,449	Strike, Nicholas L.	331,998	Rampton, Calvin L.	—	187,549 D	30.3%	69.7%	30.3%	69.7%
1968	421,012	131,729	Buehner, Carl W.	289,283	Rampton, Calvin L.	—	157,554 D	31.3%	68.7%	31.3%	68.7%
1964	398,256	171,300	Melich, Mitchell	226,956	Rampton, Calvin L.	—	55,656 D	43.0%	57.0%	43.0%	57.0%
1960	371,489	195,634	Clyde, George D.	175,855	Barlocker, W. A.	—	19,779 R	52.7%	47.3%	52.7%	47.3%
1956	332,889	127,164	Clyde, George D.	111,297	Romney, L. C.	94,428	15,867 R	38.2%	33.4%	53.3%	46.7%
1952	327,704	180,516	Lee, J. Bracken	147,188	Glade, Earl J.	—	33,328 R	55.1%	44.9%	55.1%	44.9%
1948	275,067	151,253	Lee, J. Bracken	123,814	Maw, Herbert B.	—	27,439 R	55.0%	45.0%	55.0%	45.0%

POSTWAR VOTE FOR SENATOR

| | Total | Republican | | Democratic | | Other | Rep.-Dem. | Percentage | | | |
| | | | | | | | | Total Vote | | Major Vote | |
Year	Vote	Vote	Candidate	Vote	Candidate	Vote	Plurality	Rep.	Dem.	Rep.	Dem.
1982	530,802	309,332	Hatch, Orrin G.	219,482	Wilson, Ted	1,988	89,850 R	58.3%	41.3%	58.5%	41.5%
1980	594,298	437,675	Garn, E. J.	151,454	Berman, Dan	5,169	286,221 R	73.6%	25.5%	74.3%	25.7%
1976	540,108	290,221	Hatch, Orrin G.	241,948	Moss, Frank E.	7,939	48,273 R	53.7%	44.8%	54.5%	45.5%
1974	420,642	210,299	Garn, E. J.	185,377	Owens, Wayne	24,966	24,922 R	50.0%	44.1%	53.1%	46.9%
1970	374,303	159,004	Burton, Laurence J.	210,207	Moss, Frank E.	5,092	51,203 D	42.5%	56.2%	43.1%	56.9%
1968	419,262	225,075	Bennett, Wallace F.	192,168	Weilenmann, Milton	2,019	32,907 R	53.7%	45.8%	53.9%	46.1%
1964	397,384	169,562	Wilkinson, Ernest L.	227,822	Moss, Frank E.	—	58,260 D	42.7%	57.3%	42.7%	57.3%
1962	318,411	166,755	Bennett, Wallace F.	151,656	King, David S.	—	15,099 R	52.4%	47.6%	52.4%	47.6%
1958	291,311	101,471	Watkins, Arthur V.	112,827	Moss, Frank E.	77,013	11,356 D	34.8%	38.7%	47.4%	52.6%
1956	330,381	178,261	Bennett, Wallace F.	152,120	Hopkin, Alonzo F.	—	26,141 R	54.0%	46.0%	54.0%	46.0%
1952	327,033	177,435	Watkins, Arthur V.	149,598	Granger, Walter K.	—	27,837 R	54.3%	45.7%	54.3%	45.7%
1950	264,440	142,427	Bennett, Wallace F.	121,198	Thomas, Elbert D.	815	21,229 R	53.9%	45.8%	54.0%	46.0%
1946	197,399	101,142	Watkins, Arthur V.	96,257	Murdock, Abe	—	4,885 R	51.2%	48.8%	51.2%	48.8%

UTAH

Districts Established January 1, 1982

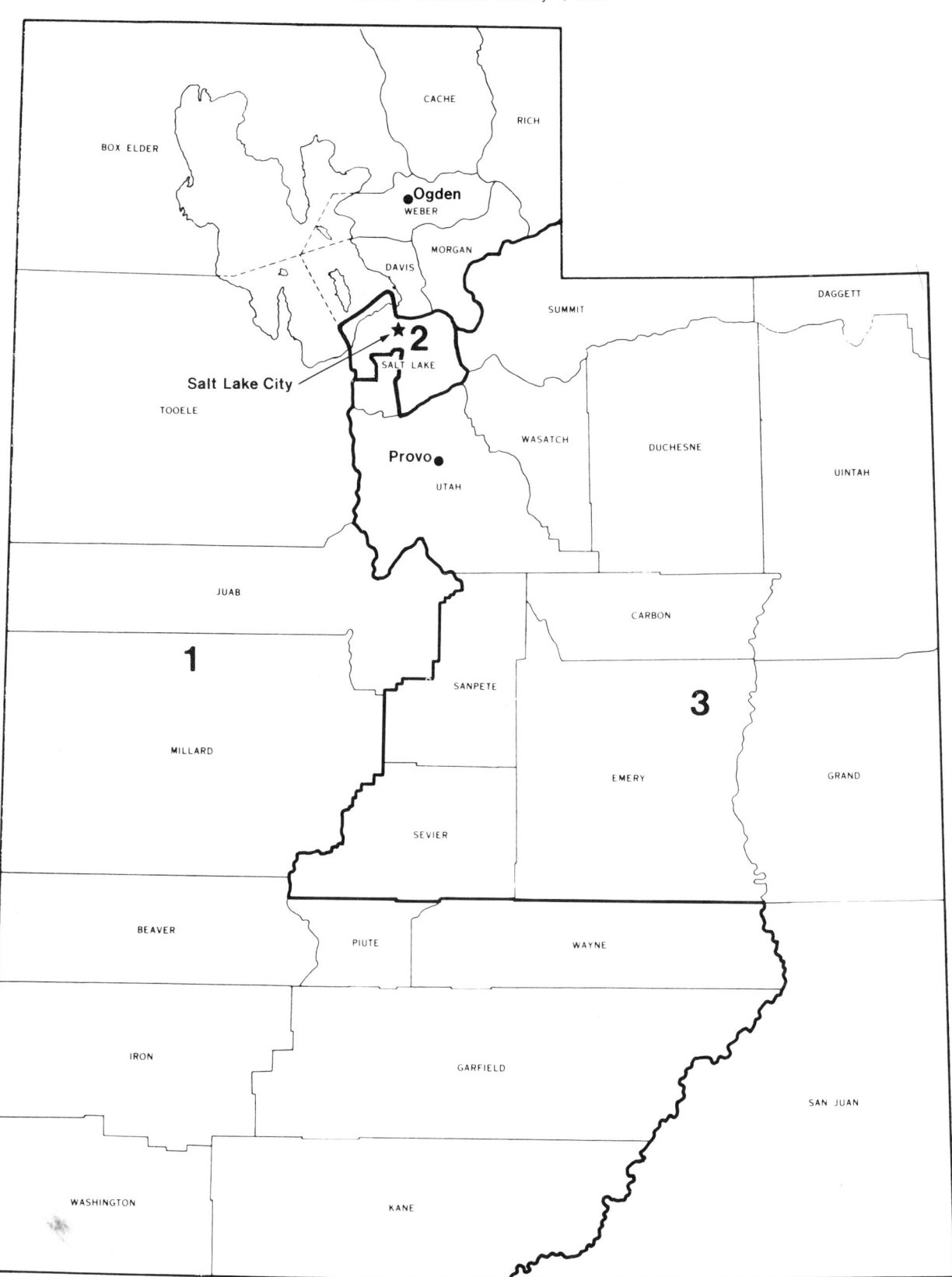

UTAH

PRESIDENT 1984

1980 Census Population	County	Total Vote	Republican	Democratic	Other	Rep.-Dem. Plurality	Percentage Total Vote Rep.	Dem.	Major Vote Rep.	Dem.
4,378	BEAVER	2,231	1,516	708	7	808 R	68.0%	31.7%	68.2%	31.8%
33,222	BOX ELDER	15,283	13,243	1,983	57	11,260 R	86.7%	13.0%	87.0%	13.0%
57,176	CACHE	26,442	22,127	4,123	192	18,004 R	83.7%	15.6%	84.3%	15.7%
22,179	CARBON	8,818	4,393	4,357	68	36 R	49.8%	49.4%	50.2%	49.8%
769	DAGGETT	525	296	227	2	69 R	56.4%	43.2%	56.6%	43.4%
146,540	DAVIS	62,102	49,863	11,727	512	38,136 R	80.3%	18.9%	81.0%	19.0%
12,565	DUCHESNE	5,210	4,437	746	27	3,691 R	85.2%	14.3%	85.6%	14.4%
11,451	EMERY	4,439	3,081	1,326	32	1,755 R	69.4%	29.9%	69.9%	30.1%
3,673	GARFIELD	1,935	1,609	315	11	1,294 R	83.2%	16.3%	83.6%	16.4%
8,241	GRAND	3,367	2,463	876	28	1,587 R	73.2%	26.0%	73.8%	26.2%
17,349	IRON	8,251	6,856	1,342	53	5,514 R	83.1%	16.3%	83.6%	16.4%
5,530	JUAB	2,829	1,902	917	10	985 R	67.2%	32.4%	67.5%	32.5%
4,024	KANE	2,009	1,710	294	5	1,416 R	85.1%	14.6%	85.3%	14.7%
8,970	MILLARD	5,563	4,345	1,192	26	3,153 R	78.1%	21.4%	78.5%	21.5%
4,917	MORGAN	2,430	1,934	481	15	1,453 R	79.6%	19.8%	80.1%	19.9%
1,329	PIUTE	757	606	151		455 R	80.1%	19.9%	80.1%	19.9%
2,100	RICH	931	797	131	3	666 R	85.6%	14.1%	85.9%	14.1%
619,066	SALT LAKE	264,926	183,536	78,488	2,902	105,048 R	69.3%	29.6%	70.0%	30.0%
12,253	SAN JUAN	3,758	2,598	1,145	15	1,453 R	69.1%	30.5%	69.4%	30.6%
14,620	SANPETE	6,777	5,507	1,227	43	4,280 R	81.3%	18.1%	81.8%	18.2%
14,727	SEVIER	6,870	5,736	1,072	62	4,664 R	83.5%	15.6%	84.3%	15.7%
10,198	SUMMIT	5,701	4,093	1,539	69	2,554 R	71.8%	27.0%	72.7%	27.3%
26,033	TOOELE	10,130	6,478	3,584	68	2,894 R	63.9%	35.4%	64.4%	35.6%
20,506	UINTAH	8,574	7,337	1,186	51	6,151 R	85.6%	13.8%	86.1%	13.9%
218,106	UTAH	87,504	72,284	14,801	419	57,483 R	82.6%	16.9%	83.0%	17.0%
8,523	WASATCH	3,824	2,789	1,015	20	1,774 R	72.9%	26.5%	73.3%	26.7%
26,065	WASHINGTON	13,977	12,049	1,846	82	10,203 R	86.2%	13.2%	86.7%	13.3%
1,911	WAYNE	1,159	930	224	5	706 R	80.2%	19.3%	80.6%	19.4%
144,616	WEBER	63,334	44,590	18,346	398	26,244 R	70.4%	29.0%	70.8%	29.2%
1,461,037	TOTAL	629,656	469,105	155,369	5,182	313,736 R	74.5%	24.7%	75.1%	24.9%

UTAH

GOVERNOR 1984

1980 Census Population	County	Total Vote	Republican	Democratic	Other	Rep.-Dem. Plurality		Percentage			
								Total Vote		Major Vote	
								Rep.	Dem.	Rep.	Dem.
4,378	BEAVER	2,220	1,085	1,135		50	D	48.9%	51.1%	48.9%	51.1%
33,222	BOX ELDER	15,197	10,061	5,114	22	4,947	R	66.2%	33.7%	66.3%	33.7%
57,176	CACHE	26,494	16,508	9,910	76	6,598	R	62.3%	37.4%	62.5%	37.5%
22,179	CARBON	8,877	2,817	6,046	14	3,229	D	31.7%	68.1%	31.8%	68.2%
769	DAGGETT	418	249	169		80	R	59.6%	40.4%	59.6%	40.4%
146,540	DAVIS	62,273	37,648	24,362	263	13,286	R	60.5%	39.1%	60.7%	39.3%
12,565	DUCHESNE	5,180	3,518	1,648	14	1,870	R	67.9%	31.8%	68.1%	31.9%
11,451	EMERY	4,459	2,214	2,238	7	24	D	49.7%	50.2%	49.7%	50.3%
3,673	GARFIELD	1,941	987	950	4	37	R	50.9%	48.9%	51.0%	49.0%
8,241	GRAND	3,342	2,191	1,144	7	1,047	R	65.6%	34.2%	65.7%	34.3%
17,349	IRON	8,172	4,826	3,329	17	1,497	R	59.1%	40.7%	59.2%	40.8%
5,530	JUAB	2,828	1,487	1,340	1	147	R	52.6%	47.4%	52.6%	47.4%
4,024	KANE	1,998	1,419	579		840	R	71.0%	29.0%	71.0%	29.0%
8,970	MILLARD	5,459	3,260	2,185	14	1,075	R	59.7%	40.0%	59.9%	40.1%
4,917	MORGAN	2,418	1,415	1,002	1	413	R	58.5%	41.4%	58.5%	41.5%
1,329	PIUTE	755	390	360	5	30	R	51.7%	47.7%	52.0%	48.0%
2,100	RICH	930	611	316	3	295	R	65.7%	34.0%	65.9%	34.1%
619,066	SALT LAKE	266,223	136,119	128,995	1,109	7,124	R	51.1%	48.5%	51.3%	48.7%
12,253	SAN JUAN	3,669	2,255	1,407	7	848	R	61.5%	38.3%	61.6%	38.4%
14,620	SANPETE	6,739	4,243	2,469	27	1,774	R	63.0%	36.6%	63.2%	36.8%
14,727	SEVIER	6,844	4,257	2,480	107	1,777	R	62.2%	36.2%	63.2%	36.8%
10,198	SUMMIT	5,616	2,783	2,818	15	35	D	49.6%	50.2%	49.7%	50.3%
26,033	TOOELE	10,105	4,755	5,330	20	575	D	47.1%	52.7%	47.1%	52.9%
20,506	UINTAH	8,467	5,797	2,642	28	3,155	R	68.5%	31.2%	68.7%	31.3%
218,106	UTAH	87,045	56,069	30,861	115	25,208	R	64.4%	35.5%	64.5%	35.5%
8,523	WASATCH	3,794	2,205	1,582	7	623	R	58.1%	41.7%	58.2%	41.8%
26,065	WASHINGTON	13,878	9,580	4,239	59	5,341	R	69.0%	30.5%	69.3%	30.7%
1,911	WAYNE	1,153	750	388	15	362	R	65.0%	33.7%	65.9%	34.1%
144,616	WEBER	63,125	32,293	30,631	201	1,662	R	51.2%	48.5%	51.3%	48.7%
1,461,037	TOTAL	629,619	351,792	275,669	2,158	76,123	R	55.9%	43.8%	56.1%	43.9%

ɔ

UTAH

CONGRESS

CD	Year	Total Vote	Republican Vote	Candidate	Democratic Vote	Candidate	Other Vote	Rep.-Dem. Plurality	Total Vote Rep.	Total Vote Dem.	Major Vote Rep.	Major Vote Dem.
1	1984	200,717	142,952	HANSEN, JAMES V.	56,619	ABRAMS, MILTON C.	1,146	86,333 R	71.2%	28.2%	71.6%	28.4%
1	1982	177,422	111,416	HANSEN, JAMES V.	66,006	DIRKS, A. STEPHEN		45,410 R	62.8%	37.2%	62.8%	37.2%
2	1984	213,793	105,540	MONSON, DAVID S.	105,044	FARLEY, FRANCES	3,209	496 R	49.4%	49.1%	50.1%	49.9%
2	1982	171,090	92,109	MARRIOTT, DAN	78,981	FARLEY, FRANCES		13,128 R	53.8%	46.2%	53.8%	46.2%
3	1984	186,572	138,918	NIELSON, HOWARD C.	46,560	BAIRD, BRUCE R.	1,094	92,358 R	74.5%	25.0%	74.9%	25.1%
3	1982	141,139	108,478	NIELSON, HOWARD C.			32,661	108,478 R	76.9%		100.0%	

UTAH

1984 GENERAL ELECTION

President   Other vote was 2,447 Bergland (Libertarian); 1,345 Dennis (American); 844 Johnson (Citizens); 220 Serrette (Independent Alliance); 184 Hall (Communist); 142 Mason (Socialist Workers).

Governor   Other vote was Brown (American).

Congress   Other vote was Marshall (Libertarian) in CD 1; 1,456 Butler (Libertarian), 962 Waters (Independent) and 791 Gardner (American) in CD 2; Crosby (Libertarian) in CD 3.

1984 PRIMARIES

AUGUST 21 REPUBLICAN

Governor   94,347 Norman H. Bangerter; 72,940 Dan Marriott.

Congress   Candidates nominated by convention in CD's 1 and 3. Contested as follows:

  CD   2   32,031 David S. Monson; 15,809 Alice Shearer.

AUGUST 21 DEMOCRATIC

Governor   51,302 Wayne Owens; 31,421 Kem C. Gardner.

Congress   Candidates nominated by convention in all three CD's.

VERMONT

GOVERNOR
Madeleine M. Kunin (D). Elected 1984 to a two-year term.

SENATORS
Patrick J. Leahy (D). Re-elected 1980 to a six-year term. Previously elected 1974.

Robert T. Stafford (R). Re-elected 1982 to a six-year term. Previously elected 1976 and in January 1972 to fill out term vacated by the death of Senator Winston L. Prouty; had been appointed September 1971 to fill this same vacancy.

REPRESENTATIVE
At-Large. James M. Jeffords (R)

POSTWAR VOTE FOR GOVERNOR

Year	Total Vote	Republican Vote	Candidate	Democratic Vote	Candidate	Other Vote	Rep.-Dem. Plurality	Total Vote Rep.	Total Vote Dem.	Major Vote Rep.	Major Vote Dem.
1984	233,753	113,264	Easton, John J.	116,938	Kunin, Madeleine M.	3,551	3,674 D	48.5%	50.0%	49.2%	50.8%
1982	169,251	93,111	Snelling, Richard A.	74,394	Kunin, Madeleine M.	1,746	18,717 R	55.0%	44.0%	55.6%	44.4%
1980	210,381	123,229	Snelling, Richard A.	77,363	Diamond, J. Jerome	9,789	45,866 R	58.6%	36.8%	61.4%	38.6%
1978	124,482	78,181	Snelling, Richard A.	42,482	Granai, Edwin C.	3,819	35,699 R	62.8%	34.1%	64.8%	35.2%
1976	185,929	99,268	Snelling, Richard A.	75,262	Hackel, Stella B.	11,399	24,006 R	53.4%	40.5%	56.9%	43.1%
1974	141,156	53,672	Kennedy, Walter L.	79,842	Salmon, Thomas P.	7,642	26,170 D	38.0%	56.6%	40.2%	59.8%
1972	189,237	82,491	Hackett, Luther F.	104,533	Salmon, Thomas P.	2,213	22,042 D	43.6%	55.2%	44.1%	55.9%
1970	153,528	87,458	Davis, Deane C.	66,028	O'Brien, Leo	42	21,430 R	57.0%	43.0%	57.0%	43.0%
1968	161,089	89,387	Davis, Deane C.	71,656	Daley, John J.	46	17,731 R	55.5%	44.5%	55.5%	44.5%
1966	136,262	57,577	Snelling, Richard A.	78,669	Hoff, Philip H.	16	21,092 D	42.3%	57.7%	42.3%	57.7%
1964	164,199	57,576	Foote, Ralph A.	106,611	Hoff, Philip H.	12	49,035 D	35.1%	64.9%	35.1%	64.9%
1962	121,422	60,035	Keyser, F. Ray	61,383	Hoff, Philip H.	4	1,348 D	49.4%	50.6%	49.4%	50.6%
1960	164,632	92,861	Keyser, F. Ray	71,755	Niquette, Russell F.	16	21,106 R	56.4%	43.6%	56.4%	43.6%
1958	123,728	62,222	Stafford, Robert T.	61,503	Leddy, Bernard J.	3	719 R	50.3%	49.7%	50.3%	49.7%
1956	153,809	88,379	Johnson, Joseph B.	65,420	Branon, E. Frank	10	22,959 R	57.5%	42.5%	57.5%	42.5%
1954	114,360	59,778	Johnson, Joseph B.	54,554	Branon, E. Frank	28	5,224 R	52.3%	47.7%	52.3%	47.7%
1952	150,862	78,338	Emerson, Lee E.	60,051	Larrow, Robert W.	12,473	18,287 R	51.9%	39.8%	56.6%	43.4%
1950	87,155	64,915	Emerson, Lee E.	22,227	Moran, J. Edward	13	42,688 R	74.5%	25.5%	74.5%	25.5%
1948	120,183	86,394	Gibson, Ernest W., Jr.	33,588	Ryan, Charles F.	201	52,806 R	71.9%	27.9%	72.0%	28.0%
1946	72,044	57,849	Gibson, Ernest W., Jr.	14,096	Coburn, Berthold	99	43,753 R	80.3%	19.6%	80.4%	19.6%

POSTWAR VOTE FOR SENATOR

Year	Total Vote	Republican Vote	Candidate	Democratic Vote	Candidate	Other Vote	Rep.-Dem. Plurality	Total Vote Rep.	Total Vote Dem.	Major Vote Rep.	Major Vote Dem.
1982	168,003	84,450	Stafford, Robert T.	79,340	Guest, James A.	4,213	5,110 R	50.3%	47.2%	51.6%	48.4%
1980	209,124	101,421	Ledbetter, Stewart M.	104,176	Leahy, Patrick J.	3,527	2,755 D	48.5%	49.8%	49.3%	50.7%
1976	189,060	94,481	Stafford, Robert T.	85,682	Salmon, Thomas P.	8,897	8,799 R	50.0%	45.3%	52.4%	47.6%
1974	142,772	66,223	Mallary, Richard W.	70,629	Leahy, Patrick J.	5,920	4,406 D	46.4%	49.5%	48.4%	51.6%
1972s	71,348	45,888	Stafford, Robert T.	23,842	Major, Randolph T.	1,618	22,046 R	64.3%	33.4%	65.8%	34.2%
1970	154,899	91,198	Prouty, Winston L.	62,271	Hoff, Philip H.	1,430	28,927 R	58.9%	40.2%	59.4%	40.6%
1968*	157,375	157,154	Aiken, George D.	—	—	221	157,154 R	99.9%	—	100.0%	—
1964	164,350	87,879	Prouty, Winston L.	76,457	Fayette, Frederick J.	14	11,422 R	53.5%	46.5%	53.5%	46.5%
1962	121,571	81,241	Aiken, George D.	40,134	Johnson, W. Robert	196	41,107 R	66.8%	33.0%	66.9%	33.1%
1958	124,442	64,900	Prouty, Winston L.	59,536	Fayette, Frederick J.	6	5,364 R	52.2%	47.8%	52.2%	47.8%
1956	155,289	103,101	Aiken, George D.	52,184	O'Shea, Bernard G.	4	50,917 R	66.4%	33.6%	66.4%	33.6%
1952	154,052	111,406	Flanders, Ralph E.	42,630	Johnston, Allan R.	16	68,776 R	72.3%	27.7%	72.3%	27.7%
1950	89,171	69,543	Aiken, George D.	19,608	Bigelow, James E.	20	49,935 R	78.0%	22.0%	78.0%	22.0%
1946	73,340	54,729	Flanders, Ralph E.	18,594	McDevitt, Charles P.	17	36,135 R	74.6%	25.4%	74.6%	25.4%

In 1968 the Republican candidate won both major party Nominations. The January 1972 election was for a short term to fill a vacancy.

418

VERMONT

One At Large

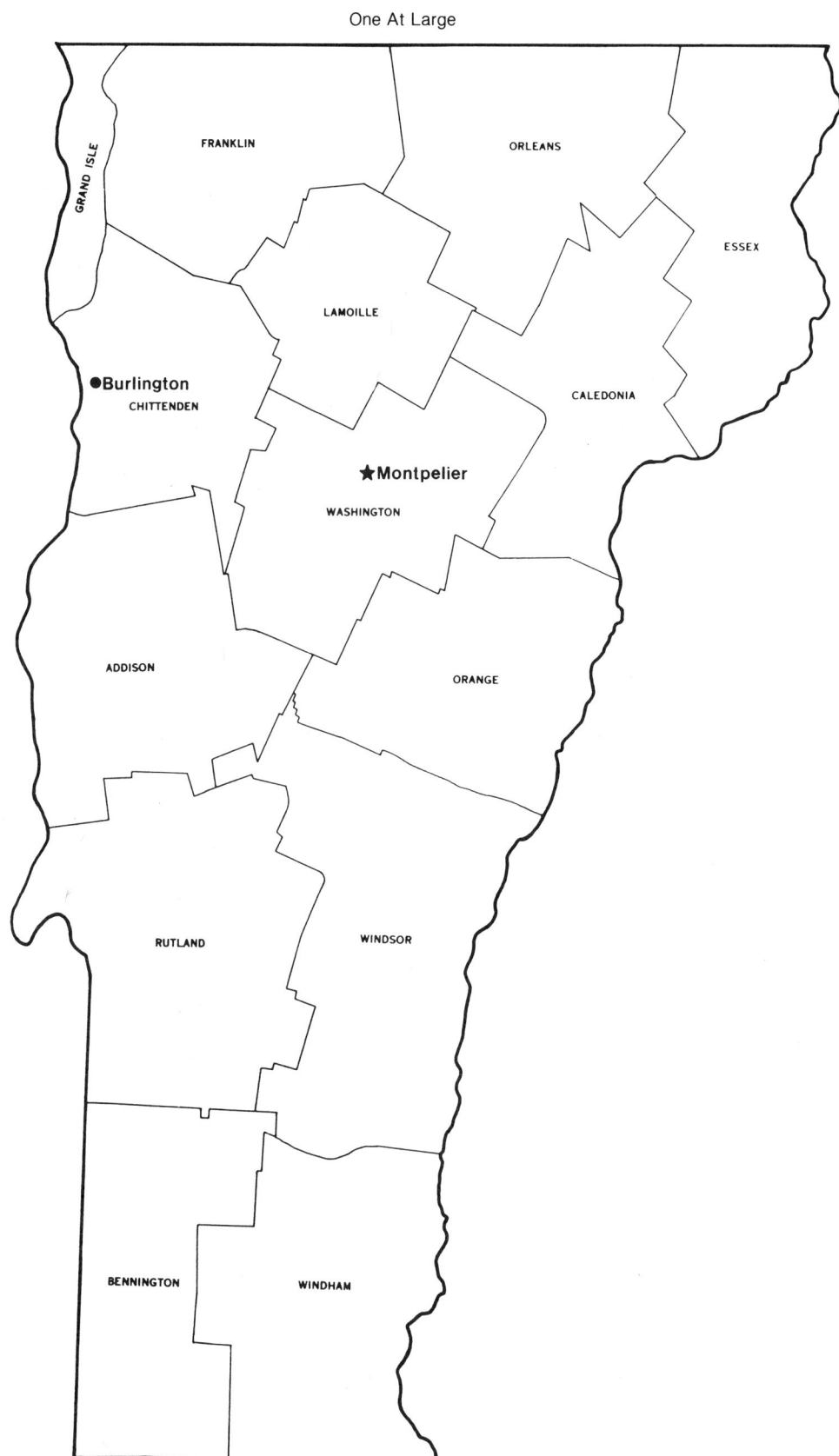

VERMONT

PRESIDENT 1984

1980 Census Population	County	Total Vote	Republican	Democratic	Other	Rep.-Dem. Plurality	Percentage			
							Total Vote		Major Vote	
							Rep.	Dem.	Rep.	Dem.
29,406	ADDISON	13,030	7,589	5,299	142	2,290 R	58.2%	40.7%	58.9%	41.1%
33,345	BENNINGTON	15,304	9,035	6,039	230	2,996 R	59.0%	39.5%	59.9%	40.1%
25,808	CALEDONIA	10,614	7,249	3,223	142	4,026 R	68.3%	30.4%	69.2%	30.8%
115,534	CHITTENDEN	55,869	30,217	24,830	822	5,387 R	54.1%	44.4%	54.9%	45.1%
6,313	ESSEX	2,349	1,632	693	24	939 R	69.5%	29.5%	70.2%	29.8%
34,788	FRANKLIN	14,574	8,683	5,755	136	2,928 R	59.6%	39.5%	60.1%	39.9%
4,613	GRAND ISLE	2,551	1,537	980	34	557 R	60.3%	38.4%	61.1%	38.9%
16,767	LAMOILLE	7,528	4,674	2,746	108	1,928 R	62.1%	36.5%	63.0%	37.0%
22,739	ORANGE	10,645	6,407	4,088	150	2,319 R	60.2%	38.4%	61.0%	39.0%
23,440	ORLEANS	9,395	5,966	3,294	135	2,672 R	63.5%	35.1%	64.4%	35.6%
58,347	RUTLAND	24,991	15,236	9,545	210	5,691 R	61.0%	38.2%	61.5%	38.5%
52,393	WASHINGTON	25,168	13,706	11,163	299	2,543 R	54.5%	44.4%	55.1%	44.9%
36,933	WINDHAM	18,283	9,880	8,206	197	1,674 R	54.0%	44.9%	54.6%	45.4%
51,030	WINDSOR	24,260	14,054	9,869	337	4,185 R	57.9%	40.7%	58.7%	41.3%
511,456	TOTAL	234,561	135,865	95,730	2,966	40,135 R	57.9%	40.8%	58.7%	41.3%

VERMONT

PRESIDENT 1984

1980 Census Population	City/Town	Total Vote	Republican	Democratic	Other	Rep.-Dem. Plurality	Percentage			
							Total Vote		Major Vote	
							Rep.	Dem.	Rep.	Dem.
9,824	BARRE CITY	4,152	2,195	1,903	54	292 R	52.9%	45.8%	53.6%	46.4%
7,090	BARRE TOWN	3,368	2,090	1,257	21	833 R	62.1%	37.3%	62.4%	37.6%
15,815	BENNINGTON TOWN	6,248	3,237	2,879	132	358 R	51.8%	46.1%	52.9%	47.1%
11,886	BRATTLEBORO	5,440	2,645	2,741	54	96 D	48.6%	50.4%	49.1%	50.9%
37,712	BURLINGTON	18,219	7,857	10,080	282	2,223 D	43.1%	55.3%	43.8%	56.2%
12,629	COLCHESTER	5,009	3,075	1,838	96	1,237 R	61.4%	36.7%	62.6%	37.4%
14,392	ESSEX TOWN	6,583	4,320	2,189	74	2,131 R	65.6%	33.3%	66.4%	33.6%
7,963	HARTFORD	3,329	1,978	1,290	61	688 R	59.4%	38.8%	60.5%	39.5%
7,574	MIDDLEBURY	3,117	1,581	1,502	34	79 R	50.7%	48.2%	51.3%	48.7%
6,829	MILTON	2,791	1,861	914	16	947 R	66.7%	32.7%	67.1%	32.9%
8,241	MONTPELIER	4,437	2,257	2,120	60	137 R	50.9%	47.8%	51.6%	48.4%
5,435	NORTHFIELD	2,256	1,437	785	34	652 R	63.7%	34.8%	64.7%	35.3%
5,538	ROCKINGHAM	2,214	1,115	1,076	23	39 R	50.4%	48.6%	50.9%	49.1%
18,436	RUTLAND CITY	7,328	3,970	3,298	60	672 R	54.2%	45.0%	54.6%	45.4%
7,308	ST. ALBANS CITY	3,130	1,748	1,346	36	402 R	55.8%	43.0%	56.5%	43.5%
7,938	ST. JOHNSBURY	3,102	2,152	915	35	1,237 R	69.4%	29.5%	70.2%	29.8%
5,000	SHELBURNE	2,995	1,742	1,216	37	526 R	58.2%	40.6%	58.9%	41.1%
10,679	SOUTH BURLINGTON	6,274	3,443	2,728	103	715 R	54.9%	43.5%	55.8%	44.2%
10,190	SPRINGFIELD	4,407	2,638	1,719	50	919 R	59.9%	39.0%	60.5%	39.5%
5,141	SWANTON	1,835	1,088	741	6	347 R	59.3%	40.4%	59.5%	40.5%
6,318	WINOOSKI	2,705	1,264	1,361	80	97 D	46.7%	50.3%	48.2%	51.8%

VERMONT

GOVERNOR 1984

1980 Census Population	County	Total Vote	Republican	Democratic	Other	Rep.-Dem. Plurality	Percentage			
							Total Vote		Major Vote	
							Rep.	Dem.	Rep.	Dem.
29,406	ADDISON	12,956	6,344	6,437	175	93 D	49.0%	49.7%	49.6%	50.4%
33,345	BENNINGTON	14,955	7,387	7,235	333	152 R	49.4%	48.4%	50.5%	49.5%
25,808	CALEDONIA	10,580	5,878	4,484	218	1,394 R	55.6%	42.4%	56.7%	43.3%
115,534	CHITTENDEN	55,790	24,749	30,023	1,018	5,274 D	44.4%	53.8%	45.2%	54.8%
6,313	ESSEX	2,318	1,303	975	40	328 R	56.2%	42.1%	57.2%	42.8%
34,788	FRANKLIN	14,568	6,985	7,431	152	446 D	47.9%	51.0%	48.5%	51.5%
4,613	GRAND ISLE	2,549	1,287	1,224	38	63 R	50.5%	48.0%	51.3%	48.7%
16,767	LAMOILLE	7,497	4,135	3,265	97	870 R	55.2%	43.6%	55.9%	44.1%
22,739	ORANGE	10,580	5,422	5,013	145	409 R	51.2%	47.4%	52.0%	48.0%
23,440	ORLEANS	9,386	4,847	4,426	113	421 R	51.6%	47.2%	52.3%	47.7%
58,347	RUTLAND	25,109	13,291	11,557	261	1,734 R	52.9%	46.0%	53.5%	46.5%
52,393	WASHINGTON	25,178	11,292	13,512	374	2,220 D	44.8%	53.7%	45.5%	54.5%
36,933	WINDHAM	18,064	8,517	9,232	315	715 D	47.1%	51.1%	48.0%	52.0%
51,030	WINDSOR	24,223	11,827	12,124	272	297 D	48.8%	50.1%	49.4%	50.6%
511,456	TOTAL	233,753	113,264	116,938	3,551	3,674 D	48.5%	50.0%	49.2%	50.8%

VERMONT

GOVERNOR 1984

1980 Census Population	City/Town	Total Vote	Republican	Democratic	Other	Rep.-Dem. Plurality	Percentage			
							Total Vote		Major Vote	
							Rep.	Dem.	Rep.	Dem.
9,824	BARRE CITY	4,192	1,719	2,423	50	704 D	41.0%	57.8%	41.5%	58.5%
7,090	BARRE TOWN	3,367	1,576	1,758	33	182 D	46.8%	52.2%	47.3%	52.7%
15,815	BENNINGTON TOWN	6,020	2,399	3,378	243	979 D	39.9%	56.1%	41.5%	58.5%
11,886	BRATTLEBORO	5,383	2,265	3,045	73	780 D	42.1%	56.6%	42.7%	57.3%
37,712	BURLINGTON	18,180	6,925	10,989	266	4,064 D	38.1%	60.4%	38.7%	61.3%
12,629	COLCHESTER	4,996	2,333	2,528	135	195 D	46.7%	50.6%	48.0%	52.0%
14,392	ESSEX TOWN	6,593	3,369	3,083	141	286 R	51.1%	46.8%	52.2%	47.8%
7,963	HARTFORD	3,338	1,663	1,639	36	24 R	49.8%	49.1%	50.4%	49.6%
7,574	MIDDLEBURY	3,079	1,383	1,661	35	278 D	44.9%	53.9%	45.4%	54.6%
6,829	MILTON	2,785	1,379	1,369	37	10 R	49.5%	49.2%	50.2%	49.8%
8,241	MONTPELIER	4,435	1,833	2,468	134	635 D	41.3%	55.6%	42.6%	57.4%
5,435	NORTHFIELD	2,236	1,166	1,058	12	108 R	52.1%	47.3%	52.4%	47.6%
5,538	ROCKINGHAM	2,197	938	1,237	22	299 D	42.7%	56.3%	43.1%	56.9%
18,436	RUTLAND CITY	7,360	3,593	3,676	91	83 D	48.8%	49.9%	49.4%	50.6%
7,308	ST. ALBANS CITY	3,132	1,449	1,650	33	201 D	46.3%	52.7%	46.8%	53.2%
7,938	ST. JOHNSBURY	3,098	1,753	1,300	45	453 R	56.6%	42.0%	57.4%	42.6%
5,000	SHELBURNE	2,994	1,491	1,460	43	31 R	49.8%	48.8%	50.5%	49.5%
10,679	SOUTH BURLINGTON	6,277	2,851	3,304	122	453 D	45.4%	52.6%	46.3%	53.7%
10,190	SPRINGFIELD	4,441	2,091	2,309	41	218 D	47.1%	52.0%	47.5%	52.5%
5,141	SWANTON	1,834	876	950	8	74 D	47.8%	51.8%	48.0%	52.0%
6,318	WINOOSKI	2,675	943	1,647	85	704 D	35.3%	61.6%	36.4%	63.6%

VERMONT

CONGRESS

CD	Year	Total Vote	Republican Vote	Republican Candidate	Democratic Vote	Democratic Candidate	Other Vote	Rep.-Dem. Plurality	Total Vote Rep.	Total Vote Dem.	Major Vote Rep.	Major Vote Dem.
AL	1984	226,297	148,025	JEFFORDS, JAMES M.	60,360	POLLINA, ANTHONY	17,912	87,665 R	65.4%	26.7%	71.0%	29.0%
AL	1982	164,951	114,191	JEFFORDS, JAMES M.	38,296	KAPLAN, MARK A.	12,464	75,895 R	69.2%	23.2%	74.9%	25.1%
AL	1980	194,697	154,274	JEFFORDS, JAMES M.			40,423	154,274 R	79.2%		100.0%	
AL	1978	120,502	90,688	JEFFORDS, JAMES M.	23,228	DIETZ, S. MARIE	6,586	67,460 R	75.3%	19.3%	79.6%	20.4%
AL	1976	184,783	124,458	JEFFORDS, JAMES M.	60,202	*BURGESS, JOHN A.	123	64,256 R	67.4%	32.6%	67.4%	32.6%
AL	1974	140,899	74,561	JEFFORDS, JAMES M.	56,342	*CAIN, FRANCIS J.	9,996	18,219 R	52.9%	40.0%	57.0%	43.0%
AL	1972	186,028	120,924	MALLARY, RICHARD W.	65,062	MEYER, WILLIAM H.	42	55,862 R	65.0%	35.0%	65.0%	35.0%
AL	1970	152,557	103,806	STAFFORD, ROBERT T.	44,415	O'SHEA, BERNARD G.	4,336	59,391 R	68.0%	29.1%	70.0%	30.0%
AL	1968	157,133	156,956	*STAFFORD, ROBERT T.			177	156,956 R	99.9%		100.0%	
AL	1966	135,748	89,097	STAFFORD, ROBERT T.	46,643	RYAN, WILLIAM J.	8	42,454 R	65.6%	34.4%	65.6%	34.4%
AL	1964	163,452	92,252	STAFFORD, ROBERT T.	71,193	O'SHEA, BERNARD G.	7	21,059 R	56.4%	43.6%	56.4%	43.6%
AL	1962	121,381	68,822	STAFFORD, ROBERT T.	52,535	RAYNOLDS, HAROLD	24	16,287 R	56.7%	43.3%	56.7%	43.3%
AL	1960	166,035	94,905	STAFFORD, ROBERT T.	71,111	MEYER, WILLIAM H.	19	23,794 R	57.2%	42.8%	57.2%	42.8%
AL	1958	122,702	59,536	ARTHUR, HAROLD J.	63,131	MEYER, WILLIAM H.	35	3,595 D	48.5%	51.5%	48.5%	51.5%
AL	1956	154,536	103,736	PROUTY, WINSTON L.	50,797	ST. AMOUR, CAMILLE	3	52,939 R	67.1%	32.9%	67.1%	32.9%
AL	1954	114,289	70,143	PROUTY, WINSTON L.	44,141	BOYLAN, JOHN J.	5	26,002 R	61.4%	38.6%	61.4%	38.6%
AL	1952	153,060	109,871	PROUTY, WINSTON L.	43,187	COMINGS, HERBERT B.	2	66,684 R	71.8%	28.2%	71.8%	28.2%
AL	1950	88,851	65,248	PROUTY, WINSTON L.	22,709	COMINGS, HERBERT B.	894	42,539 R	73.4%	25.6%	74.2%	25.8%
AL	1948	121,968	74,076	PLUMLEY, CHARLES A.	47,767	READY, ROBERT W.	125	26,309 R	60.7%	39.2%	60.8%	39.2%
AL	1946	73,066	46,985	PLUMLEY, CHARLES A.	26,056	CALDBECK, MATTHEW J.	25	20,929 R	64.3%	35.7%	64.3%	35.7%

VERMONT

1984 GENERAL ELECTION

In addition to the county-by-county figures, data are presented for selected Vermont communities. Since not all jurisdictions of the state are listed in this tabulation, state-wide totals are shown only with the county-by-county statistics.

President   Other vote was 1,002 Bergland (Libertarian); 423 LaRouche (Independent); 323 Serrette (Liberty Union); 264 Johnson (Citizens); 127 Mason (Socialist Workers); 115 Hall (Communist); 712 scattered.

Governor   Other vote was 1,904 Wicker (Libertarian); 730 Wagner (Citizens); 695 Gottlieb (Liberty Union); 222 scattered.

Congress   Other vote was 9,359 Hedbor (Libertarian); 4,858 Diamondstone (Liberty Union); 3,313 Earle (Independent); 382 scattered. An asterisk in the Congressional vote table indicates a candidate received votes from another party endorsing his/her candidacy.

1984 PRIMARIES

SEPTEMBER 11 REPUBLICAN

Governor   30,436 John J. Easton; 19,170 Hilton Wick; 379 scattered.

Congress   Contested as follows:

AL   35,038 James M. Jeffords; 13,455 Mike Jacobs; 166 scattered.

SEPTEMBER 11 DEMOCRATIC

Governor   Madeleine M. Kunin, unopposed.

Congress   Contested as follows:

AL   6,520 Anthony Pollina; 4,022 John F. Tatro; 3,624 Paul Forlenza; 699 scattered.

SEPTEMBER 11 LIBERTY UNION

Governor   Richard F. Gottlieb, unopposed.

Congress   Unopposed at-large.

VIRGINIA

GOVERNOR
Charles S. Robb (D). Elected 1981 to a four-year term.

SENATORS
Paul Trible (R). Elected 1982 to a six-year term.

John Warner (R). Re-elected 1984 to a six-year term. Previously elected 1978.

REPRESENTATIVES
1. Herbet H. Bateman (R)
2. G. W. Whitehurst (R)
3. Thomas J. Bliley (R)
4. Norman Sisisky (D)
5. W. C. Daniel (D)
6. James R. Olin (D)
7. D. French Slaughter (R)
8. Stanford E. Parris (R)
9. Frederick C. Boucher (D)
10. Frank R. Wolf (R)

POSTWAR VOTE FOR GOVERNOR

Year	Total Vote	Republican Vote	Candidate	Democratic Vote	Candidate	Other Vote	Rep.-Dem. Plurality	Total Vote Rep.	Total Vote Dem.	Major Vote Rep.	Major Vote Dem.
1981	1,420,611	659,398	Coleman, J. Marshall	760,357	Robb, Charles S.	856	100,959 D	46.4%	53.5%	46.4%	53.6%
1977	1,250,940	699,302	Dalton, John	541,319	Howell, Henry	10,319	157,983 R	55.9%	43.3%	56.4%	43.6%
1973*	1,035,495	525,075	Godwin, Mills E.	—	—	510,420	525,075 R	50.7%	—	100.0%	—
1969	915,764	480,869	Holton, Linwood	415,695	Battle, William C.	19,200	65,174 R	52.5%	45.4%	53.6%	46.4%
1965	562,789	212,207	Holton, Linwood	269,526	Godwin, Mills E.	81,056	57,319 D	37.7%	47.9%	44.1%	55.9%
1961	394,490	142,567	Pearson, H. Clyde	251,861	Harrison, Albertis	62	109,294 D	36.1%	63.8%	36.1%	63.9%
1957	517,655	188,628	Dalton, Ted	326,921	Almond, J. Lindsay	2,106	138,293 D	36.4%	63.2%	36.6%	63.4%
1953	414,025	183,328	Dalton, Ted	226,998	Stanley, Thomas B.	3,699	43,670 D	44.3%	54.8%	44.7%	55.3%
1949	262,350	71,991	Johnson, Walter	184,772	Battle, John S.	5,587	112,781 D	27.4%	70.4%	28.0%	72.0%
1945	168,783	52,386	Landreth, S. Floyd	112,355	Tuck, William M.	4,042	59,969 D	31.0%	66.6%	31.8%	68.2%

In 1973, other vote was 510,103 Henry Howell (Independent) and 317 scattered.

POSTWAR VOTE FOR SENATOR

Year	Total Vote	Republican Vote	Candidate	Democratic Vote	Candidate	Other Vote	Rep.-Dem. Plurality	Total Vote Rep.	Total Vote Dem.	Major Vote Rep.	Major Vote Dem.
1984	2,007,487	1,406,194	Warner, John	601,142	Harrison, Edythe C.	151	805,052 R	70.0%	29.9%	70.1%	29.9%
1982	1,415,622	724,571	Trible, Paul	690,839	Davis, Richard	212	33,732 R	51.2%	48.8%	51.2%	48.8%
1978	1,222,256	613,232	Warner, John	608,511	Miller, Andrew P.	513	4,721 R	50.2%	49.8%	50.2%	49.8%
1976*	1,557,500	—	—	596,009	Zumwalt, Elmo R.	961,491	596,009 D	—	38.3%	—	100.0%
1972	1,396,268	718,337	Scott, William L.	643,963	Spong, William B.	33,968	74,374 R	51.4%	46.1%	52.7%	47.3%
1970*	946,751	145,031	Garland, Ray	295,057	Rawlings, George C.	506,663	150,026 D	15.3%	31.2%	33.0%	67.0%
1966	733,879	245,681	Ould, James P.	429,855	Spong, William B.	58,343	184,174 D	33.5%	58.6%	36.4%	63.6%
1966s	729,839	272,804	Traylor, Lawrence M.	389,028	Byrd, Harry Flood, Jr.	68,007	116,224 D	37.4%	53.3%	41.2%	58.8%
1964	928,363	176,624	May, Richard A.	592,260	Byrd, Harry Flood	159,479	415,636 D	19.0%	63.8%	23.0%	77.0%
1960	622,820	—	—	506,169	Robertson, A. Willis	116,651	506,169 D	—	81.3%	—	100.0%
1958	457,640	—	—	317,221	Byrd, Harry Flood	140,419	317,221 D	—	69.3%	—	100.0%
1954	306,510	—	—	244,844	Robertson, A. Willis	61,666	244,844 D	—	79.9%	—	100.0%
1952	543,516	—	—	398,677	Byrd, Harry Flood	144,839	398,677 D	—	73.4%	—	100.0%
1948	386,178	118,546	Woods, Robert	253,865	Robertson, A. Willis	13,767	135,319 D	30.7%	65.7%	31.8%	68.2%
1946	252,863	77,005	Parsons, Lester S.	163,960	Byrd, Harry Flood	11,898	86,955 D	30.5%	64.8%	32.0%	68.0%
1946s	248,962	72,253	Woods, Robert	169,680	Robertson, A. Willis	7,029	97,427 D	29.0%	68.2%	29.9%	70.1%

One each of the 1966 and 1946 elections was for a short term to fill a vacancy. In 1970 Harry Flood Byrd, Jr., the Independent candidate, polled 506,633 votes (53.5% of the total vote) and won the election with a 211,576 plurality. In 1976 Harry Flood Byrd, Jr., polled 890,778 votes as an Independent candidate (57.2% of the total vote) and won the election with a 294,769 plurality.

424

VIRGINIA

Districts Established June 12, 1981

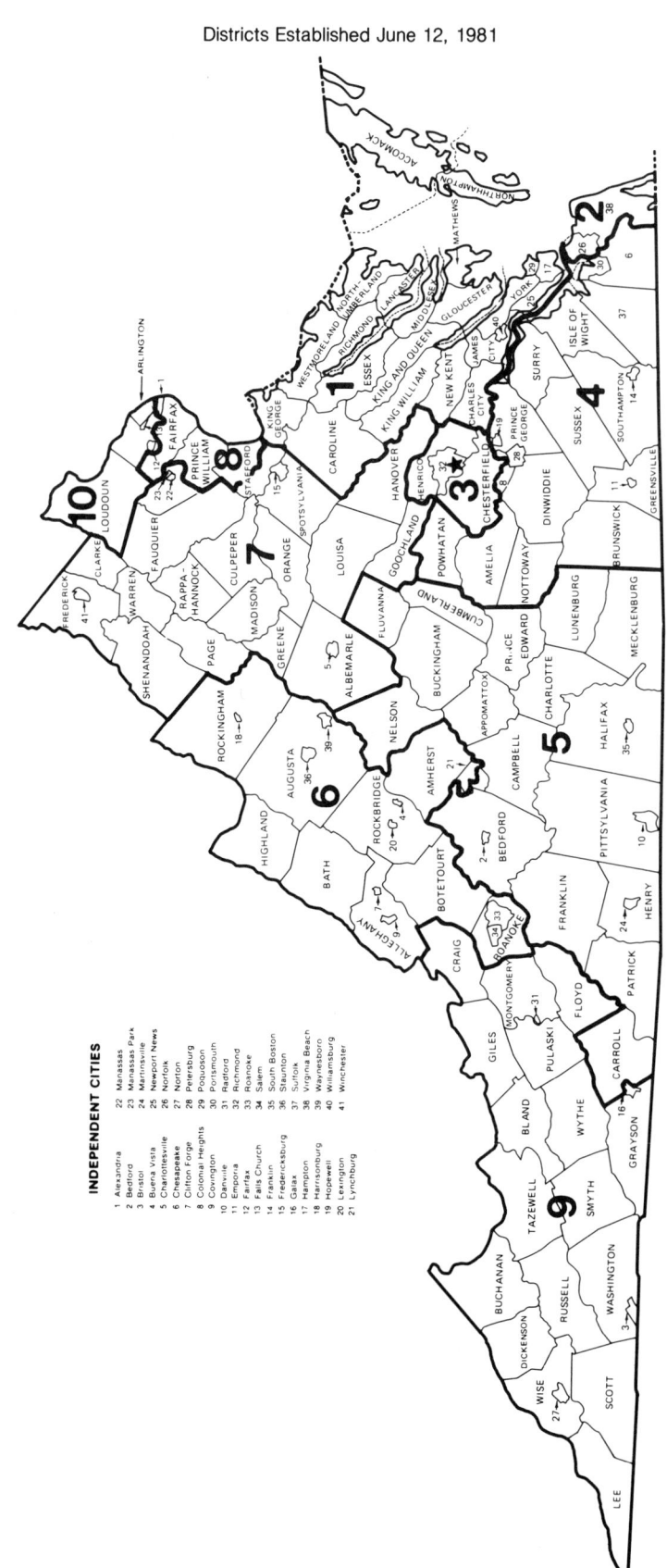

© ERC

VIRGINIA

PRESIDENT 1984

1980 Census Population	County	Total Vote	Republican	Democratic	Other	Rep.-Dem. Plurality	Percentage Total Vote Rep.	Dem.	Major Vote Rep.	Dem.
31,268	ACCOMACK	12,466	8,047	4,355	64	3,692 R	64.6%	34.9%	64.9%	35.1%
55,783	ALBEMARLE	22,530	14,455	7,982	93	6,473 R	64.2%	35.4%	64.4%	35.6%
14,333	ALLEGHANY	5,037	3,067	1,932	38	1,135 R	60.9%	38.4%	61.4%	38.6%
8,405	AMELIA	3,804	2,336	1,432	36	904 R	61.4%	37.6%	62.0%	38.0%
29,122	AMHERST	10,530	7,004	3,409	117	3,595 R	66.5%	32.4%	67.3%	32.7%
11,971	APPOMATTOX	4,932	3,386	1,498	48	1,888 R	68.7%	30.4%	69.3%	30.7%
152,599	ARLINGTON	72,242	34,848	37,031	363	2,183 D	48.2%	51.3%	48.5%	51.5%
53,732	AUGUSTA	19,323	15,308	3,899	116	11,409 R	79.2%	20.2%	79.7%	20.3%
5,860	BATH	2,175	1,434	727	14	707 R	65.9%	33.4%	66.4%	33.6%
34,927	BEDFORD COUNTY	15,217	10,371	4,754	92	5,617 R	68.2%	31.2%	68.6%	31.4%
6,349	BLAND	2,693	1,812	867	14	945 R	67.3%	32.2%	67.6%	32.4%
23,270	BOTETOURT	9,289	5,959	3,243	87	2,716 R	64.2%	34.9%	64.8%	35.2%
15,632	BRUNSWICK	6,073	2,950	3,040	83	90 D	48.6%	50.1%	49.2%	50.8%
37,989	BUCHANAN	13,053	5,053	7,828	172	2,775 D	38.7%	60.0%	39.2%	60.8%
11,751	BUCKINGHAM	4,580	2,627	1,879	74	748 R	57.4%	41.0%	58.3%	41.7%
45,424	CAMPBELL	17,924	13,388	4,380	156	9,008 R	74.7%	24.4%	75.3%	24.7%
17,904	CAROLINE	6,138	2,949	3,111	78	162 D	48.0%	50.7%	48.7%	51.3%
27,270	CARROLL	10,042	7,056	2,914	72	4,142 R	70.3%	29.0%	70.8%	29.2%
6,692	CHARLES CITY	2,584	776	1,776	32	1,000 D	30.0%	68.7%	30.4%	69.6%
12,266	CHARLOTTE	4,856	2,999	1,811	46	1,188 R	61.8%	37.3%	62.3%	37.7%
141,372	CHESTERFIELD	68,811	54,896	13,739	176	41,157 R	79.8%	20.0%	80.0%	20.0%
9,965	CLARKE	3,763	2,529	1,215	19	1,314 R	67.2%	32.3%	67.5%	32.5%
3,948	CRAIG	2,033	1,173	845	15	328 R	57.7%	41.6%	58.1%	41.9%
22,620	CULPEPER	7,926	5,596	2,255	75	3,341 R	70.6%	28.5%	71.3%	28.7%
7,881	CUMBERLAND	3,329	2,027	1,237	65	790 R	60.9%	37.2%	62.1%	37.9%
19,806	DICKENSON	8,844	3,921	4,848	75	927 D	44.3%	54.8%	44.7%	55.3%
22,602	DINWIDDIE	8,114	4,547	3,485	82	1,062 R	56.0%	43.0%	56.6%	43.4%
8,864	ESSEX	3,440	2,120	1,300	20	820 R	61.6%	37.8%	62.0%	38.0%
596,901	FAIRFAX COUNTY	291,298	183,181	107,295	822	75,886 R	62.9%	36.8%	63.1%	36.9%
35,889	FAUQUIER	14,451	10,319	4,056	76	6,263 R	71.4%	28.1%	71.8%	28.2%
11,563	FLOYD	5,069	3,431	1,599	39	1,832 R	67.7%	31.5%	68.2%	31.8%
10,244	FLUVANNA	3,612	2,247	1,332	33	915 R	62.2%	36.9%	62.8%	37.2%
35,740	FRANKLIN COUNTY	12,762	7,684	4,903	175	2,781 R	60.2%	38.4%	61.0%	39.0%
34,150	FREDERICK	12,267	9,542	2,671	54	6,871 R	77.8%	21.8%	78.1%	21.9%
17,810	GILES	7,460	4,340	3,047	73	1,293 R	58.2%	40.8%	58.8%	41.2%
20,107	GLOUCESTER	10,025	7,109	2,830	86	4,279 R	70.9%	28.2%	71.5%	28.5%
11,761	GOOCHLAND	5,617	3,404	2,178	35	1,226 R	60.6%	38.8%	61.0%	39.0%
16,579	GRAYSON	6,890	4,508	2,319	63	2,189 R	65.4%	33.7%	66.0%	34.0%
7,625	GREENE	3,000	2,216	760	24	1,456 R	73.9%	25.3%	74.5%	25.5%
10,903	GREENSVILLE	4,772	2,304	2,352	116	48 D	48.3%	49.3%	49.5%	50.5%
30,599	HALIFAX	11,103	6,726	4,231	146	2,495 R	60.6%	38.1%	61.4%	38.6%
50,398	HANOVER	23,718	18,800	4,831	87	13,969 R	79.3%	20.4%	79.6%	20.4%
180,735	HENRICO	85,448	63,864	21,336	248	42,528 R	74.7%	25.0%	75.0%	25.0%
57,654	HENRY	19,906	12,693	6,976	237	5,717 R	63.8%	35.0%	64.5%	35.5%
2,937	HIGHLAND	1,406	997	398	11	599 R	70.9%	28.3%	71.5%	28.5%
21,603	ISLE OF WIGHT	9,412	5,664	3,650	98	2,014 R	60.2%	38.8%	60.8%	39.2%
22,763	JAMES CITY	10,677	7,104	3,486	87	3,618 R	66.5%	32.6%	67.1%	32.9%
5,968	KING AND QUEEN	2,664	1,449	1,201	14	248 R	54.4%	45.1%	54.7%	45.3%
10,543	KING GEORGE	3,841	2,356	1,450	35	906 R	61.3%	37.8%	61.9%	38.1%
9,334	KING WILLIAM	4,284	2,803	1,448	33	1,355 R	65.4%	33.8%	65.9%	34.1%
10,129	LANCASTER	5,044	3,416	1,559	69	1,857 R	67.7%	30.9%	68.7%	31.3%
25,956	LEE	10,554	5,365	5,085	104	280 R	50.8%	48.2%	51.3%	48.7%
57,427	LOUDOUN	26,128	17,765	8,227	136	9,538 R	68.0%	31.5%	68.3%	31.7%
17,825	LOUISA	6,543	3,789	2,703	51	1,086 R	57.9%	41.3%	58.4%	41.6%
12,124	LUNENBURG	4,526	2,713	1,754	59	959 R	59.9%	38.8%	60.7%	39.3%
10,232	MADISON	4,055	2,723	1,302	30	1,421 R	67.2%	32.1%	67.7%	32.3%
7,995	MATHEWS	4,005	2,868	1,106	31	1,762 R	71.6%	27.6%	72.2%	27.8%
29,444	MECKLENBURG	10,316	6,777	3,438	101	3,339 R	65.7%	33.3%	66.3%	33.7%
7,719	MIDDLESEX	3,885	2,612	1,206	67	1,406 R	67.2%	31.0%	68.4%	31.6%
63,516	MONTGOMERY	19,765	12,428	7,202	135	5,226 R	62.9%	36.4%	63.3%	36.7%

VIRGINIA

PRESIDENT 1984

1980 Census Population	County	Total Vote	Republican	Democratic	Other	Rep.-Dem. Plurality	Percentage Total Vote Rep.	Dem.	Major Vote Rep.	Dem.
12,204	NELSON	4,853	2,777	2,021	55	756 R	57.2%	41.6%	57.9%	42.1%
8,781	NEW KENT	3,899	2,679	1,204	16	1,475 R	68.7%	30.9%	69.0%	31.0%
14,625	NORTHAMPTON	5,207	2,906	2,226	75	680 R	55.8%	42.8%	56.6%	43.4%
9,828	NORTHUMBERLAND	4,628	3,166	1,407	55	1,759 R	68.4%	30.4%	69.2%	30.8%
14,666	NOTTOWAY	5,793	3,418	2,296	79	1,122 R	59.0%	39.6%	59.8%	40.2%
18,063	ORANGE	6,821	4,483	2,285	53	2,198 R	65.7%	33.5%	66.2%	33.8%
19,401	PAGE	7,519	5,021	2,437	61	2,584 R	66.8%	32.4%	67.3%	32.7%
17,647	PATRICK	6,674	4,703	1,908	63	2,795 R	70.5%	28.6%	71.1%	28.9%
66,147	PITTSYLVANIA	23,824	15,743	7,791	290	7,952 R	66.1%	32.7%	66.9%	33.1%
13,062	POWHATAN	5,327	3,921	1,381	25	2,540 R	73.6%	25.9%	74.0%	26.0%
16,456	PRINCE EDWARD	6,156	3,454	2,589	113	865 R	56.1%	42.1%	57.2%	42.8%
25,733	PRINCE GEORGE	7,178	4,999	2,136	43	2,863 R	69.6%	29.8%	70.1%	29.9%
144,703	PRINCE WILLIAM	50,803	34,992	15,631	180	19,361 R	68.9%	30.8%	69.1%	30.9%
35,229	PULASKI	12,699	8,242	4,364	93	3,878 R	64.9%	34.4%	65.4%	34.6%
6,093	RAPPAHANNOCK	2,707	1,696	999	12	697 R	62.7%	36.9%	62.9%	37.1%
6,952	RICHMOND COUNTY	2,730	1,869	830	31	1,039 R	68.5%	30.4%	69.2%	30.8%
72,945	ROANOKE COUNTY	34,054	23,348	10,569	137	12,779 R	68.6%	31.0%	68.8%	31.2%
17,911	ROCKBRIDGE	6,194	4,067	2,098	29	1,969 R	65.7%	33.9%	66.0%	34.0%
57,038	ROCKINGHAM	17,807	13,480	4,220	107	9,260 R	75.7%	23.7%	76.2%	23.8%
31,761	RUSSELL	12,599	5,738	6,760	101	1,022 D	45.5%	53.7%	45.9%	54.1%
25,068	SCOTT	9,821	5,804	3,904	113	1,900 R	59.1%	39.8%	59.8%	40.2%
27,559	SHENANDOAH	11,900	9,048	2,771	81	6,277 R	76.0%	23.3%	76.6%	23.4%
33,366	SMYTH	12,811	8,593	4,102	116	4,491 R	67.1%	32.0%	67.7%	32.3%
18,731	SOUTHAMPTON	8,051	4,669	3,300	82	1,369 R	58.0%	41.0%	58.6%	41.4%
34,435	SPOTSYLVANIA	12,297	8,207	4,012	78	4,195 R	66.7%	32.6%	67.2%	32.8%
40,470	STAFFORD	14,782	10,293	4,429	60	5,864 R	69.6%	30.0%	69.9%	30.1%
6,046	SURRY	3,370	1,462	1,875	33	413 D	43.4%	55.6%	43.8%	56.2%
10,874	SUSSEX	4,731	2,183	2,408	140	225 D	46.1%	50.9%	47.5%	52.5%
50,511	TAZEWELL	17,896	9,645	8,014	237	1,631 R	53.9%	44.8%	54.6%	45.4%
21,200	WARREN	7,631	5,016	2,551	64	2,465 R	65.7%	33.4%	66.3%	33.7%
46,487	WASHINGTON	17,826	12,132	5,573	121	6,559 R	68.1%	31.3%	68.5%	31.5%
14,041	WESTMORELAND	5,663	3,219	2,363	81	856 R	56.8%	41.7%	57.7%	42.3%
43,863	WISE	15,399	7,909	7,303	187	606 R	51.4%	47.4%	52.0%	48.0%
25,522	WYTHE	9,866	6,773	2,996	97	3,777 R	68.6%	30.4%	69.3%	30.7%
35,463	YORK	14,337	10,214	4,063	60	6,151 R	71.2%	28.3%	71.5%	28.5%

City

1980 Census Population	City	Total Vote	Republican	Democratic	Other	Rep.-Dem. Plurality	Rep.	Dem.	Rep.	Dem.
103,217	ALEXANDRIA	45,253	21,166	23,552	535	2,386 D	46.8%	52.0%	47.3%	52.7%
5,991	BEDFORD CITY	2,573	1,553	997	23	556 R	60.4%	38.7%	60.9%	39.1%
19,042	BRISTOL	7,468	5,012	2,429	27	2,583 R	67.1%	32.5%	67.4%	32.6%
6,717	BUENA VISTA	2,073	1,335	724	14	611 R	64.4%	34.9%	64.8%	35.2%
39,916	CHARLOTTESVILLE	14,306	6,947	7,317	42	370 D	48.6%	51.1%	48.7%	51.3%
114,486	CHESAPEAKE	44,684	27,542	16,740	402	10,802 R	61.6%	37.5%	62.2%	37.8%
5,046	CLIFTON FORGE	1,876	965	896	15	69 R	51.4%	47.8%	51.9%	48.1%
16,509	COLONIAL HEIGHTS	7,630	6,387	1,218	25	5,169 R	83.7%	16.0%	84.0%	16.0%
9,063	COVINGTON	3,162	1,722	1,391	49	331 R	54.5%	44.0%	55.3%	44.7%
45,642	DANVILLE	18,161	12,141	5,846	174	6,295 R	66.9%	32.2%	67.5%	32.5%
4,840	EMPORIA	2,078	1,252	807	19	445 R	60.3%	38.8%	60.8%	39.2%
19,390	FAIRFAX CITY	9,538	6,234	3,263	41	2,971 R	65.4%	34.2%	65.6%	34.4%
9,515	FALLS CHURCH	5,101	2,684	2,398	19	286 R	52.6%	47.0%	52.8%	47.2%
7,308	FRANKLIN CITY	3,130	1,561	1,537	32	24 R	49.9%	49.1%	50.4%	49.6%
15,322	FREDERICKSBURG	5,973	3,500	2,439	34	1,061 R	58.6%	40.8%	58.9%	41.1%
6,524	GALAX	2,375	1,548	814	13	734 R	65.2%	34.3%	65.5%	34.5%
122,617	HAMPTON	44,068	25,537	18,180	351	7,357 R	57.9%	41.3%	58.4%	41.6%
19,671	HARRISONBURG	7,661	5,221	2,384	56	2,837 R	68.2%	31.1%	68.7%	31.3%
23,397	HOPEWELL	8,292	5,661	2,564	67	3,097 R	68.3%	30.9%	68.8%	31.2%
7,292	LEXINGTON	2,163	1,197	946	20	251 R	55.3%	43.7%	55.9%	44.1%
66,743	LYNCHBURG	26,772	18,047	8,542	183	9,505 R	67.4%	31.9%	67.9%	32.1%
15,438	MANASSAS	6,466	4,613	1,824	29	2,789 R	71.3%	28.2%	71.7%	28.3%
6,524	MANASSAS PARK	1,355	975	375	5	600 R	72.0%	27.7%	72.2%	27.8%
18,149	MARTINSVILLE	7,254	4,234	2,942	78	1,292 R	58.4%	40.6%	59.0%	41.0%
144,903	NEWPORT NEWS	55,698	33,614	21,834	250	11,780 R	60.4%	39.2%	60.6%	39.4%

VIRGINIA

PRESIDENT 1984

1980 Census Population	City	Total Vote	Republican	Democratic	Other	Rep.-Dem. Plurality	Percentage Total Vote Rep.	Dem.	Major Vote Rep.	Dem.
266,979	NORFOLK	75,516	36,360	38,913	243	2,553 D	48.1%	51.5%	48.3%	51.7%
4,757	NORTON	1,668	806	842	20	36 D	48.3%	50.5%	48.9%	51.1%
41,055	PETERSBURG	15,074	5,753	9,248	73	3,495 D	38.2%	61.4%	38.4%	61.6%
8,726	POQUOSON	4,328	3,667	647	14	3,020 R	84.7%	14.9%	85.0%	15.0%
104,577	PORTSMOUTH	40,801	18,940	21,623	238	2,683 D	46.4%	53.0%	46.7%	53.3%
13,225	RADFORD	4,669	2,855	1,781	33	1,074 R	61.1%	38.1%	61.6%	38.4%
219,214	RICHMOND CITY	88,628	38,754	49,408	466	10,654 D	43.7%	55.7%	44.0%	56.0%
100,220	ROANOKE CITY	36,492	19,008	17,300	184	1,708 R	52.1%	47.4%	52.4%	47.6%
23,958	SALEM	9,810	6,419	3,347	44	3,072 R	65.4%	34.1%	65.7%	34.3%
7,093	SOUTH BOSTON	2,893	1,899	974	20	925 R	65.6%	33.7%	66.1%	33.9%
21,857	STAUNTON	8,196	6,137	2,012	47	4,125 R	74.9%	24.5%	75.3%	24.7%
47,621	SUFFOLK	19,119	10,128	8,842	149	1,286 R	53.0%	46.2%	53.4%	46.6%
262,199	VIRGINIA BEACH	97,594	72,571	24,703	320	47,868 R	74.4%	25.3%	74.6%	25.4%
15,329	WAYNESBORO	6,079	4,465	1,579	35	2,886 R	73.4%	26.0%	73.9%	26.1%
9,870	WILLIAMSBURG	3,402	1,913	1,469	20	444 R	56.2%	43.2%	56.6%	43.4%
20,217	WINCHESTER	7,152	5,055	2,064	33	2,991 R	70.7%	28.9%	71.0%	29.0%
5,346,818	TOTAL	2,146,635	1,337,078	796,250	13,307	540,828 R	62.3%	37.1%	62.7%	37.3%

VIRGINIA

SENATOR 1984

1980 Census Population	County	Total Vote	Republican	Democratic	Other	Rep.-Dem. Plurality	Percentage Total Vote Rep.	Dem.	Major Vote Rep.	Dem.
31,268	ACCOMACK	11,398	8,466	2,932		5,534 R	74.3%	25.7%	74.3%	25.7%
55,783	ALBEMARLE	21,424	15,606	5,818		9,788 R	72.8%	27.2%	72.8%	27.2%
14,333	ALLEGHANY	4,748	3,297	1,451		1,846 R	69.4%	30.6%	69.4%	30.6%
8,405	AMELIA	3,454	2,472	982		1,490 R	71.6%	28.4%	71.6%	28.4%
29,122	AMHERST	9,686	7,407	2,279		5,128 R	76.5%	23.5%	76.5%	23.5%
11,971	APPOMATTOX	4,504	3,450	1,053	1	2,397 R	76.6%	23.4%	76.6%	23.4%
152,599	ARLINGTON	69,999	39,174	30,819	6	8,355 R	56.0%	44.0%	56.0%	44.0%
53,732	AUGUSTA	18,296	15,597	2,698	1	12,899 R	85.2%	14.7%	85.3%	14.7%
5,860	BATH	2,085	1,595	490		1,105 R	76.5%	23.5%	76.5%	23.5%
34,927	BEDFORD COUNTY	14,426	10,978	3,446	2	7,532 R	76.1%	23.9%	76.1%	23.9%
6,349	BLAND	2,497	1,850	647		1,203 R	74.1%	25.9%	74.1%	25.9%
23,270	BOTETOURT	8,723	6,217	2,506		3,711 R	71.3%	28.7%	71.3%	28.7%
15,632	BRUNSWICK	5,294	3,337	1,957		1,380 R	63.0%	37.0%	63.0%	37.0%
37,989	BUCHANAN	11,974	5,293	6,681		1,388 D	44.2%	55.8%	44.2%	55.8%
11,751	BUCKINGHAM	4,040	2,970	1,070		1,900 R	73.5%	26.5%	73.5%	26.5%
45,424	CAMPBELL	16,800	13,509	3,290	1	10,219 R	80.4%	19.6%	80.4%	19.6%
17,904	CAROLINE	5,515	3,340	2,174	1	1,166 R	60.6%	39.4%	60.6%	39.4%
27,270	CARROLL	9,209	7,022	2,187		4,835 R	76.3%	23.7%	76.3%	23.7%
6,692	CHARLES CITY	2,330	956	1,374		418 D	41.0%	59.0%	41.0%	59.0%
12,266	CHARLOTTE	4,369	3,239	1,130		2,109 R	74.1%	25.9%	74.1%	25.9%
141,372	CHESTERFIELD	66,873	56,025	10,840	8	45,185 R	83.8%	16.2%	83.8%	16.2%
9,965	CLARKE	3,512	2,796	716		2,080 R	79.6%	20.4%	79.6%	20.4%
3,948	CRAIG	1,946	1,251	695		556 R	64.3%	35.7%	64.3%	35.7%
22,620	CULPEPER	7,199	5,756	1,443		4,313 R	80.0%	20.0%	80.0%	20.0%
7,881	CUMBERLAND	3,045	2,045	1,000		1,045 R	67.2%	32.8%	67.2%	32.8%
19,806	DICKENSON	7,794	4,332	3,462		870 R	55.6%	44.4%	55.6%	44.4%
22,602	DINWIDDIE	7,402	4,996	2,406		2,590 R	67.5%	32.5%	67.5%	32.5%
8,864	ESSEX	3,090	2,245	845		1,400 R	72.7%	27.3%	72.7%	27.3%
596,901	FAIRFAX COUNTY	278,011	195,186	82,799	26	112,387 R	70.2%	29.8%	70.2%	29.8%
35,889	FAUQUIER	13,564	10,753	2,810	1	7,943 R	79.3%	20.7%	79.3%	20.7%
11,563	FLOYD	4,714	3,430	1,284		2,146 R	72.8%	27.2%	72.8%	27.2%
10,244	FLUVANNA	3,347	2,527	820		1,707 R	75.5%	24.5%	75.5%	24.5%
35,740	FRANKLIN COUNTY	11,289	8,334	2,955		5,379 R	73.8%	26.2%	73.8%	26.2%
34,150	FREDERICK	11,660	9,896	1,763	1	8,133 R	84.9%	15.1%	84.9%	15.1%
17,810	GILES	6,496	4,369	2,127		2,242 R	67.3%	32.7%	67.3%	32.7%
20,107	GLOUCESTER	9,326	7,086	2,240		4,846 R	76.0%	24.0%	76.0%	24.0%
11,761	GOOCHLAND	5,204	3,442	1,762		1,680 R	66.1%	33.9%	66.1%	33.9%
16,579	GRAYSON	6,340	4,484	1,856		2,628 R	70.7%	29.3%	70.7%	29.3%
7,625	GREENE	2,743	2,190	553		1,637 R	79.8%	20.2%	79.8%	20.2%
10,903	GREENSVILLE	4,063	2,523	1,540		983 R	62.1%	37.9%	62.1%	37.9%
30,599	HALIFAX	9,441	6,828	2,613		4,215 R	72.3%	27.7%	72.3%	27.7%
50,398	HANOVER	22,495	18,765	3,723	7	15,042 R	83.4%	16.6%	83.4%	16.6%
180,735	HENRICO	82,805	65,830	16,967	8	48,863 R	79.5%	20.5%	79.5%	20.5%
57,654	HENRY	17,915	12,762	5,153		7,609 R	71.2%	28.8%	71.2%	28.8%
2,937	HIGHLAND	1,359	991	368		623 R	72.9%	27.1%	72.9%	27.1%
21,603	ISLE OF WIGHT	8,707	6,203	2,504		3,699 R	71.2%	28.8%	71.2%	28.8%
22,763	JAMES CITY	10,055	7,182	2,873		4,309 R	71.4%	28.6%	71.4%	28.6%
5,968	KING AND QUEEN	2,418	1,623	795		828 R	67.1%	32.9%	67.1%	32.9%
10,543	KING GEORGE	3,588	2,725	863		1,862 R	75.9%	24.1%	75.9%	24.1%
9,334	KING WILLIAM	3,897	2,990	907		2,083 R	76.7%	23.3%	76.7%	23.3%
10,129	LANCASTER	4,662	3,452	1,210		2,242 R	74.0%	26.0%	74.0%	26.0%
25,956	LEE	9,324	5,703	3,621		2,082 R	61.2%	38.8%	61.2%	38.8%
57,427	LOUDOUN	24,665	18,680	5,985		12,695 R	75.7%	24.3%	75.7%	24.3%
17,825	LOUISA	5,828	4,096	1,731	1	2,365 R	70.3%	29.7%	70.3%	29.7%
12,124	LUNENBURG	3,903	2,808	1,095		1,713 R	71.9%	28.1%	71.9%	28.1%
10,232	MADISON	3,775	2,809	962	4	1,847 R	74.4%	25.5%	74.5%	25.5%
7,995	MATHEWS	3,625	2,846	779		2,067 R	78.5%	21.5%	78.5%	21.5%
29,444	MECKLENBURG	9,087	6,788	2,298	1	4,490 R	74.7%	25.3%	74.7%	25.3%
7,719	MIDDLESEX	3,546	2,638	907	1	1,731 R	74.4%	25.6%	74.4%	25.6%
63,516	MONTGOMERY	18,589	13,054	5,535		7,519 R	70.2%	29.8%	70.2%	29.8%

VIRGINIA

SENATOR 1984

1980 Census Population	County	Total Vote	Republican	Democratic	Other	Rep.-Dem. Plurality	Percentage Total Vote Rep.	Dem.	Major Vote Rep.	Dem.
12,204	NELSON	4,566	3,192	1,373	1	1,819 R	69.9%	30.1%	69.9%	30.1%
8,781	NEW KENT	3,748	2,799	948	1	1,851 R	74.7%	25.3%	74.7%	25.3%
14,625	NORTHAMPTON	4,741	2,954	1,787		1,167 R	62.3%	37.7%	62.3%	37.7%
9,828	NORTHUMBERLAND	4,245	3,212	1,033		2,179 R	75.7%	24.3%	75.7%	24.3%
14,666	NOTTOWAY	5,184	3,657	1,527		2,130 R	70.5%	29.5%	70.5%	29.5%
18,063	ORANGE	6,321	4,673	1,648		3,025 R	73.9%	26.1%	73.9%	26.1%
19,401	PAGE	6,864	5,307	1,557		3,750 R	77.3%	22.7%	77.3%	22.7%
17,647	PATRICK	5,470	4,218	1,252		2,966 R	77.1%	22.9%	77.1%	22.9%
66,147	PITTSYLVANIA	21,319	15,553	5,765	1	9,788 R	73.0%	27.0%	73.0%	27.0%
13,062	POWHATAN	4,833	3,778	1,055		2,723 R	78.2%	21.8%	78.2%	21.8%
16,456	PRINCE EDWARD	5,651	3,695	1,956		1,739 R	65.4%	34.6%	65.4%	34.6%
25,733	PRINCE GEORGE	6,765	5,229	1,534	2	3,695 R	77.3%	22.7%	77.3%	22.7%
144,703	PRINCE WILLIAM	47,725	36,337	11,386	2	24,951 R	76.1%	23.9%	76.1%	23.9%
35,229	PULASKI	11,920	8,293	3,627		4,666 R	69.6%	30.4%	69.6%	30.4%
6,093	RAPPAHANNOCK	2,632	1,849	781	2	1,068 R	70.3%	29.7%	70.3%	29.7%
6,952	RICHMOND COUNTY	2,487	1,993	494		1,499 R	80.1%	19.9%	80.1%	19.9%
72,945	ROANOKE COUNTY	32,257	25,239	7,017	1	18,222 R	78.2%	21.8%	78.2%	21.8%
17,911	ROCKBRIDGE	5,766	4,300	1,466		2,834 R	74.6%	25.4%	74.6%	25.4%
57,038	ROCKINGHAM	16,798	13,846	2,952		10,894 R	82.4%	17.6%	82.4%	17.6%
31,761	RUSSELL	11,696	6,064	5,632		432 R	51.8%	48.2%	51.8%	48.2%
25,068	SCOTT	8,652	5,779	2,873		2,906 R	66.8%	33.2%	66.8%	33.2%
27,559	SHENANDOAH	11,175	9,440	1,734	1	7,706 R	84.5%	15.5%	84.5%	15.5%
33,366	SMYTH	11,703	8,567	3,136		5,431 R	73.2%	26.8%	73.2%	26.8%
18,731	SOUTHAMPTON	6,913	5,002	1,911		3,091 R	72.4%	27.6%	72.4%	27.6%
34,435	SPOTSYLVANIA	11,439	8,917	2,522		6,395 R	78.0%	22.0%	78.0%	22.0%
40,470	STAFFORD	14,038	11,306	2,732		8,574 R	80.5%	19.5%	80.5%	19.5%
6,046	SURRY	2,996	1,654	1,342		312 R	55.2%	44.8%	55.2%	44.8%
10,874	SUSSEX	4,038	2,416	1,622		794 R	59.8%	40.2%	59.8%	40.2%
50,511	TAZEWELL	15,968	9,632	6,336		3,296 R	60.3%	39.7%	60.3%	39.7%
21,200	WARREN	7,157	5,329	1,828		3,501 R	74.5%	25.5%	74.5%	25.5%
46,487	WASHINGTON	16,170	12,199	3,971		8,228 R	75.4%	24.6%	75.4%	24.6%
14,041	WESTMORELAND	5,189	3,442	1,747		1,695 R	66.3%	33.7%	66.3%	33.7%
43,863	WISE	14,466	8,059	6,407		1,652 R	55.7%	44.3%	55.7%	44.3%
25,522	WYTHE	9,115	6,738	2,377		4,361 R	73.9%	26.1%	73.9%	26.1%
35,463	YORK	13,566	10,529	3,037		7,492 R	77.6%	22.4%	77.6%	22.4%
	City									
103,217	ALEXANDRIA	41,894	23,452	18,435	7	5,017 R	56.0%	44.0%	56.0%	44.0%
5,991	BEDFORD CITY	2,333	1,636	697		939 R	70.1%	29.9%	70.1%	29.9%
19,042	BRISTOL	6,546	5,267	1,279		3,988 R	80.5%	19.5%	80.5%	19.5%
6,717	BUENA VISTA	1,884	1,363	521		842 R	72.3%	27.7%	72.3%	27.7%
39,916	CHARLOTTESVILLE	13,714	8,163	5,545	6	2,618 R	59.5%	40.4%	59.5%	40.5%
114,486	CHESAPEAKE	42,123	27,699	14,423	1	13,276 R	65.8%	34.2%	65.8%	34.2%
5,046	CLIFTON FORGE	1,668	1,057	611		446 R	63.4%	36.6%	63.4%	36.6%
16,509	COLONIAL HEIGHTS	7,376	6,460	915	1	5,545 R	87.6%	12.4%	87.6%	12.4%
9,063	COVINGTON	2,844	1,799	1,044	1	755 R	63.3%	36.7%	63.3%	36.7%
45,642	DANVILLE	16,012	12,372	3,639	1	8,733 R	77.3%	22.7%	77.3%	22.7%
4,840	EMPORIA	1,869	1,363	506		857 R	72.9%	27.1%	72.9%	27.1%
19,390	FAIRFAX CITY	9,128	6,651	2,476	1	4,175 R	72.9%	27.1%	72.9%	27.1%
9,515	FALLS CHURCH	4,836	3,117	1,719		1,398 R	64.5%	35.5%	64.5%	35.5%
7,308	FRANKLIN CITY	2,600	1,791	809		982 R	68.9%	31.1%	68.9%	31.1%
15,322	FREDERICKSBURG	5,555	3,994	1,559	2	2,435 R	71.9%	28.1%	71.9%	28.1%
6,524	GALAX	2,190	1,572	618		954 R	71.8%	28.2%	71.8%	28.2%
122,617	HAMPTON	40,779	25,802	14,972	5	10,830 R	63.3%	36.7%	63.3%	36.7%
19,671	HARRISONBURG	7,295	5,599	1,694	2	3,905 R	76.8%	23.2%	76.8%	23.2%
23,397	HOPEWELL	7,524	5,784	1,740		4,044 R	76.9%	23.1%	76.9%	23.1%
7,292	LEXINGTON	2,032	1,341	691		650 R	66.0%	34.0%	66.0%	34.0%
66,743	LYNCHBURG	25,309	18,297	7,011	1	11,286 R	72.3%	27.7%	72.3%	27.7%
15,438	MANASSAS	6,176	4,790	1,385	1	3,405 R	77.6%	22.4%	77.6%	22.4%
6,524	MANASSAS PARK	1,283	982	301		681 R	76.5%	23.5%	76.5%	23.5%
18,149	MARTINSVILLE	6,520	4,306	2,212	2	2,094 R	66.0%	33.9%	66.1%	33.9%
144,903	NEWPORT NEWS	51,231	34,754	16,477		18,277 R	67.8%	32.2%	67.8%	32.2%

VIRGINIA

SENATOR 1984

1980 Census Population	City	Total Vote	Republican	Democratic	Other	Rep.-Dem. Plurality	Percentage Total Vote Rep.	Dem.	Major Vote Rep.	Dem.
266,979	NORFOLK	72,720	38,676	34,029	15	4,647 R	53.2%	46.8%	53.2%	46.8%
4,757	NORTON	1,538	847	691		156 R	55.1%	44.9%	55.1%	44.9%
41,055	PETERSBURG	13,695	6,906	6,788	1	118 R	50.4%	49.6%	50.4%	49.6%
8,726	POQUOSON	4,184	3,645	539		3,106 R	87.1%	12.9%	87.1%	12.9%
104,577	PORTSMOUTH	37,790	21,324	16,466		4,858 R	56.4%	43.6%	56.4%	43.6%
13,225	RADFORD	4,241	3,013	1,228		1,785 R	71.0%	29.0%	71.0%	29.0%
219,214	RICHMOND CITY	80,300	46,638	33,657	5	12,981 R	58.1%	41.9%	58.1%	41.9%
100,220	ROANOKE CITY	33,132	21,253	11,879		9,374 R	64.1%	35.9%	64.1%	35.9%
23,958	SALEM	9,063	6,811	2,252		4,559 R	75.2%	24.8%	75.2%	24.8%
7,093	SOUTH BOSTON	2,531	2,014	517		1,497 R	79.6%	20.4%	79.6%	20.4%
21,857	STAUNTON	7,678	6,306	1,372		4,934 R	82.1%	17.9%	82.1%	17.9%
47,621	SUFFOLK	17,255	10,841	6,414		4,427 R	62.8%	37.2%	62.8%	37.2%
262,199	VIRGINIA BEACH	95,328	72,981	22,330	17	50,651 R	76.6%	23.4%	76.6%	23.4%
15,329	WAYNESBORO	5,758	4,681	1,077		3,604 R	81.3%	18.7%	81.3%	18.7%
9,870	WILLIAMSBURG	3,220	2,037	1,183		854 R	63.3%	36.7%	63.3%	36.7%
20,217	WINCHESTER	6,687	5,399	1,287	1	4,112 R	80.7%	19.2%	80.8%	19.2%
5,346,818	TOTAL	2,007,487	1,406,194	601,142	151	805,052 R	70.0%	29.9%	70.1%	29.9%

VIRGINIA

CONGRESS

CD	Year	Total Vote	Republican Vote	Republican Candidate	Democratic Vote	Democratic Candidate	Other Vote	Rep.-Dem. Plurality	Total Vote Rep.	Total Vote Dem.	Major Vote Rep.	Major Vote Dem.
1	1984	199,822	118,085	BATEMAN, HERBERT H.	79,577	MCGLENNON, JOHN J.	2,160	38,508 R	59.1%	39.8%	59.7%	40.3%
1	1982	142,802	76,926	BATEMAN, HERBERT H.	62,379	MCGLENNON, JOHN J.	3,497	14,547 R	53.9%	43.7%	55.2%	44.8%
2	1984	136,888	136,632	WHITEHURST, G. W.			256	136,632 R	99.8%		100.0%	
2	1982	78,205	78,108	WHITEHURST, G. W.			97	78,108 R	99.9%		100.0%	
3	1984	198,567	169,987	BLILEY, THOMAS J.			28,580	169,987 R	85.6%		100.0%	
3	1982	156,891	92,928	BLILEY, THOMAS J.	63,946	WALDROP, JOHN A.	17	28,982 R	59.2%	40.8%	59.2%	40.8%
4	1984	120,162			120,093	SISISKY, NORMAN	69	120,093 D		99.9%		100.0%
4	1982	148,406	67,708	DANIEL, ROBERT W.	80,695	SISISKY, NORMAN	3	12,987 D	45.6%	54.4%	45.6%	54.4%
5	1984	117,778			117,738	DANIEL, W. C.	40	117,738 D		100.0%		100.0%
5	1982	88,324			88,293	DANIEL, W. C.	31	88,293 D		100.0%		100.0%
6	1984	196,560	91,344	GARLAND, RAY L	105,207	OLIN, JAMES R.	9	13,863 D	46.5%	53.5%	46.5%	53.5%
6	1982	137,140	66,537	MILLER, KEVIN G.	68,192	OLIN, JAMES R.	2,411	1,655 D	48.5%	49.7%	49.4%	50.6%
7	1984	193,156	109,110	SLAUGHTER, D. FRENCH	77,624	COSTELLO, LEWIS M.	6,422	31,486 R	56.5%	40.2%	58.4%	41.6%
7	1982	128,224	76,752	ROBINSON, J. KENNETH	46,514	DORRIER, LINDSAY G.	4,958	30,238 R	59.9%	36.3%	62.3%	37.7%
8	1984	224,091	125,015	PARRIS, STANFORD E.	97,250	SASLAW, RICHARD L.	1,826	27,765 R	55.8%	43.4%	56.2%	43.8%
8	1982	140,070	69,620	PARRIS, STANFORD E.	68,071	HARRIS, HERBERT E.	2,379	1,549 R	49.7%	48.6%	50.6%	49.4%
9	1984	196,956	94,510	STAFFORD, C. JEFFERSON	102,446	BOUCHER, FREDERICK C.		7,936 D	48.0%	52.0%	48.0%	52.0%
9	1982	151,289	75,082	WAMPLER, WILLIAM C.	76,205	BOUCHER, FREDERICK C.	2	1,123 D	49.6%	50.4%	49.6%	50.4%
10	1984	253,625	158,528	WOLF, FRANK R.	95,074	FLANNERY, JOHN P.	23	63,454 R	62.5%	37.5%	62.5%	37.5%
10	1982	164,035	86,506	WOLF, FRANK R.	75,361	LECHNER, IRA M.	2,168	11,145 R	52.7%	45.9%	53.4%	46.6%
10	1980	216,744	110,840	WOLF, FRANK R.	105,883	FISHER, JOSEPH L.	21	4,957 R	51.1%	48.9%	51.1%	48.9%
10	1978	132,882	61,981	WOLF, FRANK R.	70,892	FISHER, JOSEPH L.	9	8,911 D	46.6%	53.3%	46.6%	53.4%
10	1976	189,489	73,616	CALLAHAN, VINCENT F.	103,689	FISHER, JOSEPH L.	12,184	30,073 D	38.8%	54.7%	41.5%	58.5%
10	1974	125,304	56,649	BROYHILL, JOEL T.	67,184	FISHER, JOSEPH L.	1,471	10,535 D	45.2%	53.6%	45.7%	54.3%
10	1972	179,778	101,138	BROYHILL, JOEL T.	78,638	MILLER, HAROLD O.	2	22,500 R	56.3%	43.7%	56.3%	43.7%

VIRGINIA

Under Virginia's local government system a number of urban areas — 41 since 1977 — are organized as cities independent of county authority. The number of these cities is subject to change and their boundaries alter from year to year.

1984 GENERAL ELECTION

President   Other vote was LaRouche (Independent).

Senator   Other vote was scattered.

Congress   Other vote was 2,154 Green (Independent) and 6 scattered in CD 1; scattered in CD 2; 28,556 Coffey (Independent) and 24 scattered in CD 3; scattered in CD's 4, 5, and 6; 6,397 Frazier (Independent) and 25 scattered in CD 7; 1,814 Carpenter (Independent) and 12 scattered in CD 8; scattered in CD 10.

1984 PRIMARIES

JUNE 12 REPUBLICAN

Senator   None. Edythe C. Harrison, nominated by convention.

Congress   None. Candidates nominated by convention in all CD's except CD's 4 and 5 where there were no candidates.

JUNE 12 DEMOCRATIC

Senator   None. John Warner, nominated by convention.

Congress   Candidates nominated by convention in CD's 1, 4 , 5, 6, 7 and 9. No candidate in CD's 2 and 3. Contested as follows:

CD 8   8,066 Richard L. Saslaw; 1,929 Craig G. Coverdale; 411 David S. Holland.
CD 10   7,481 John P. Flannery; 6,043 Harris N. Miller.

WASHINGTON

GOVERNOR
Booth Gardner (D). Elected 1984 to a four-year term.

SENATORS
Daniel J. Evans (R). Elected November 1983 to fill out term vacated by the death of Senator Henry M. Jackson; had been appointed September 1983 to fill this vacancy.

Slade Gorton (R). Elected 1980 to a six-year term.

REPRESENTATIVES
1. John R. Miller (R)
2. Al Swift (D)
3. Don Bonker (D)
4. Sid Morrison (R)
5. Thomas S. Foley (D)
6. Norman D. Dicks (D)
7. Mike Lowry (D)
8. Rod Chandler (R)

POSTWAR VOTE FOR GOVERNOR

| | Total | Republican | | Democratic | | Other | Rep.-Dem. | Percentage Total Vote | | Major Vote | |
| | Vote | Vote | Candidate | Vote | Candidate | Vote | Plurality | Rep. | Dem. | Rep. | Dem. |
Year											
1984	1,888,987	881,994	Spellman, John D.	1,006,993	Gardner, Booth	—	124,999 D	46.7%	53.3%	46.7%	53.3%
1980	1,730,896	981,083	Spellman, John D.	749,813	McDermott, James A.	—	231,270 R	56.7%	43.3%	56.7%	43.3%
1976	1,546,382	687,039	Spellman, John D.	821,797	Ray, Dixy Lee	37,546	134,758 D	44.4%	53.1%	45.5%	54.5%
1972	1,472,542	747,825	Evans, Daniel J.	630,613	Rosellini, Albert D.	94,104	117,212 R	50.8%	42.8%	54.3%	45.7%
1968	1,265,355	692,378	Evans, Daniel J.	560,262	O'Connell, John J.	12,715	132,116 R	54.7%	44.3%	55.3%	44.7%
1964	1,250,274	697,256	Evans, Daniel J.	548,692	Rosellini, Albert D.	4,326	148,564 R	55.8%	43.9%	56.0%	44.0%
1960	1,215,748	594,122	Andrews, Lloyd J.	611,987	Rosellini, Albert D.	9,639	17,865 D	48.9%	50.3%	49.3%	50.7%
1956	1,128,977	508,041	Anderson, Emmett T.	616,773	Rosellini, Albert D.	4,163	108,732 D	45.0%	54.6%	45.2%	54.8%
1952	1,078,497	567,822	Langlie, Arthur B.	510,675	Mitchell, Hugh B.	—	57,147 R	52.6%	47.4%	52.6%	47.4%
1948	883,141	445,958	Langlie, Arthur B.	417,035	Wallgren, Mon C.	20,148	28,923 R	50.5%	47.2%	51.7%	48.3%

POSTWAR VOTE FOR SENATOR

| | Total | Republican | | Democratic | | Other | Rep.-Dem. | Percentage Total Vote | | Major Vote | |
| | Vote | Vote | Candidate | Vote | Candidate | Vote | Plurality | Rep. | Dem. | Rep. | Dem. |
Year											
1983s	1,213,307	672,326	Evans, Daniel J.	540,981	Lowry, Mike	—	131,345 R	55.4%	44.6%	55.4%	44.6%
1982	1,368,476	332,273	Jewett, Doug	943,655	Jackson, Henry M.	92,548	611,382 D	24.3%	69.0%	26.0%	74.0%
1980	1,728,369	936,317	Gorton, Slade	792,052	Magnuson, Warren G.	—	144,265 R	54.2%	45.8%	54.2%	45.8%
1976	1,491,111	361,546	Brown, George M.	1,071,219	Jackson, Henry M.	58,346	709,673 D	24.2%	71.8%	25.2%	74.8%
1974	1,007,847	363,626	Metcalf, Jack	611,811	Magnuson, Warren G.	32,410	248,185 D	36.1%	60.7%	37.3%	62.7%
1970	1,066,807	170,790	Elicker, Charles W.	879,385	Jackson, Henry M.	16,632	708,595 D	16.0%	82.4%	16.3%	83.7%
1968	1,236,063	435,894	Metcalf, Jack	796,183	Magnuson, Warren G.	3,986	360,289 D	35.3%	64.4%	35.4%	64.6%
1964	1,213,088	337,138	Andrews, Lloyd J.	875,950	Jackson, Henry M.	—	538,812 D	27.8%	72.2%	27.8%	72.2%
1962	943,229	446,204	Christensen, Richard G.	491,365	Magnuson, Warren G.	5,660	45,161 D	47.3%	52.1%	47.6%	52.4%
1958	886,822	278,271	Bantz, William B.	597,040	Jackson, Henry M.	11,511	318,769 D	31.4%	67.3%	31.8%	68.2%
1956	1,122,217	436,652	Langlie, Arthur B.	685,565	Magnuson, Warren G.	—	248,913 D	38.9%	61.1%	38.9%	61.1%
1952	1,058,735	460,884	Cain, Harry P.	595,288	Jackson, Henry M.	2,563	134,404 D	43.5%	56.2%	43.6%	56.4%
1950	744,783	342,464	Williams, Walter	397,719	Magnuson, Warren G.	4,600	55,255 D	46.0%	53.4%	46.3%	53.7%
1946	660,342	358,847	Cain, Harry P.	298,683	Mitchell, Hugh B.	2,812	60,164 R	54.3%	45.2%	54.6%	45.4%

The 1983 election was for a short term to fill a vacancy.

434

WASHINGTON

Districts Established March 29, 1983

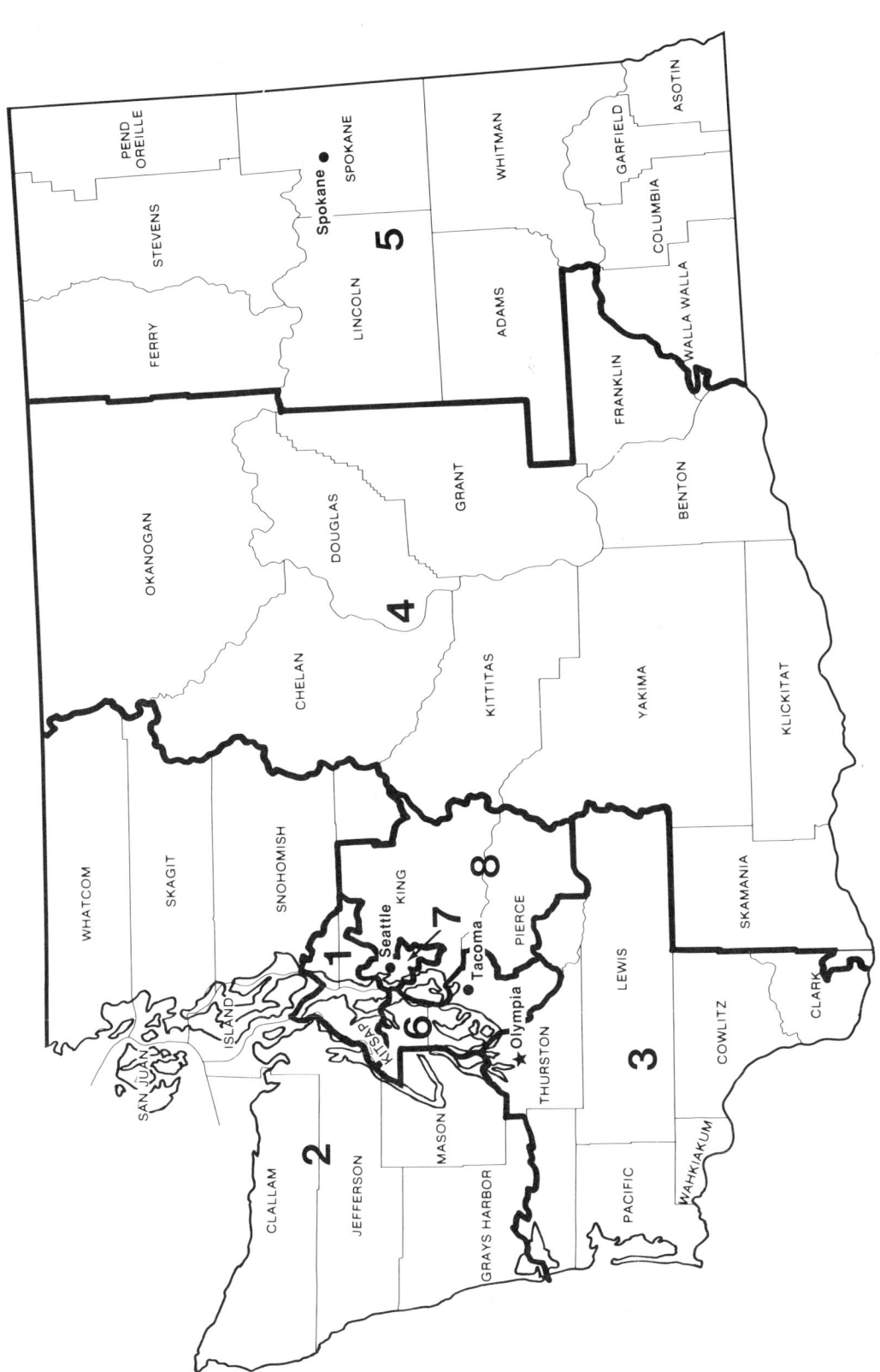

WASHINGTON

PRESIDENT 1984

1980 Census Population	County	Total Vote	Republican	Democratic	Other	Rep.-Dem. Plurality	Percentage Total Vote Rep.	Dem.	Major Vote Rep.	Dem.
13,267	ADAMS	4,809	3,449	1,311	49	2,138 R	71.7%	27.3%	72.5%	27.5%
16,823	ASOTIN	7,021	3,876	3,042	103	834 R	55.2%	43.3%	56.0%	44.0%
109,444	BENTON	46,631	32,307	13,784	540	18,523 R	69.3%	29.6%	70.1%	29.9%
45,061	CHELAN	20,994	13,667	6,978	349	6,689 R	65.1%	33.2%	66.2%	33.8%
51,648	CLALLAM	23,735	13,605	9,701	429	3,904 R	57.3%	40.9%	58.4%	41.6%
192,227	CLARK	76,957	40,681	35,248	1,028	5,433 R	52.9%	45.8%	53.6%	46.4%
4,057	COLUMBIA	2,095	1,404	673	18	731 R	67.0%	32.1%	67.6%	32.4%
79,548	COWLITZ	30,968	14,858	15,361	749	503 D	48.0%	49.6%	49.2%	50.8%
22,144	DOUGLAS	9,698	6,443	3,127	128	3,316 R	66.4%	32.2%	67.3%	32.7%
5,811	FERRY	2,210	1,232	935	43	297 R	55.7%	42.3%	56.9%	43.1%
35,025	FRANKLIN	12,268	7,724	4,328	216	3,396 R	63.0%	35.3%	64.1%	35.9%
2,468	GARFIELD	1,428	913	493	22	420 R	63.9%	34.5%	64.9%	35.1%
48,522	GRANT	19,584	12,888	6,298	398	6,590 R	65.8%	32.2%	67.2%	32.8%
66,314	GRAYS HARBOR	25,671	11,286	14,050	335	2,764 D	44.0%	54.7%	44.5%	55.5%
44,048	ISLAND	20,616	13,548	6,850	218	6,698 R	65.7%	33.2%	66.4%	33.6%
15,965	JEFFERSON	9,334	4,543	4,602	189	59 D	48.7%	49.3%	49.7%	50.3%
1,269,749	KING	639,261	332,987	298,620	7,654	34,367 R	52.1%	46.7%	52.7%	47.3%
147,152	KITSAP	66,713	36,101	29,681	931	6,420 R	54.1%	44.5%	54.9%	45.1%
24,877	KITTITAS	11,531	6,580	4,830	121	1,750 R	57.1%	41.9%	57.7%	42.3%
15,822	KLICKITAT	6,757	3,910	2,712	135	1,198 R	57.9%	40.1%	59.0%	41.0%
56,025	LEWIS	23,931	15,846	7,634	451	8,212 R	66.2%	31.9%	67.5%	32.5%
9,604	LINCOLN	5,193	3,474	1,671	48	1,803 R	66.9%	32.2%	67.5%	32.5%
31,184	MASON	15,650	8,410	7,007	233	1,403 R	53.7%	44.8%	54.6%	45.4%
30,639	OKANOGAN	13,059	7,476	5,330	253	2,146 R	57.2%	40.8%	58.4%	41.6%
17,237	PACIFIC	8,421	3,613	4,679	129	1,066 D	42.9%	55.6%	43.6%	56.4%
8,580	PEND OREILLE	4,075	2,374	1,655	46	719 R	58.3%	40.6%	58.9%	41.1%
485,643	PIERCE	195,108	112,877	79,498	2,733	33,379 R	57.9%	40.7%	58.7%	41.3%
7,838	SAN JUAN	5,526	2,900	2,514	112	386 R	52.5%	45.5%	53.6%	46.4%
64,138	SKAGIT	33,326	18,840	13,947	539	4,893 R	56.5%	41.9%	57.5%	42.5%
7,919	SKAMANIA	3,339	1,736	1,552	51	184 R	52.0%	46.5%	52.8%	47.2%
337,720	SNOHOMISH	158,995	90,362	66,728	1,905	23,634 R	56.8%	42.0%	57.5%	42.5%
341,835	SPOKANE	149,336	88,043	59,620	1,673	28,423 R	59.0%	39.9%	59.6%	40.4%
28,979	STEVENS	12,771	8,211	4,304	256	3,907 R	64.3%	33.7%	65.6%	34.4%
124,264	THURSTON	62,045	34,442	26,840	763	7,602 R	55.5%	43.3%	56.2%	43.8%
3,832	WAHKIAKUM	1,739	776	930	33	154 D	44.6%	53.5%	45.5%	54.5%
47,435	WALLA WALLA	19,398	12,361	6,804	233	5,557 R	63.7%	35.1%	64.5%	35.5%
106,701	WHATCOM	50,686	27,228	22,670	788	4,558 R	53.7%	44.7%	54.6%	45.4%
40,103	WHITMAN	16,849	10,021	6,621	207	3,400 R	59.5%	39.3%	60.2%	39.8%
172,508	YAKIMA	66,182	40,678	24,724	780	15,954 R	61.5%	37.4%	62.2%	37.8%
4,132,156	TOTAL	1,883,910	1,051,670	807,352	24,888	244,318 R	55.8%	42.9%	56.6%	43.4%

WASHINGTON

GOVERNOR 1984

1980 Census Population	County	Total Vote	Republican	Democratic	Other	Rep.-Dem. Plurality	Percentage Total Vote Rep.	Dem.	Major Vote Rep.	Dem.
13,267	ADAMS	4,879	2,809	2,070		739 R	57.6%	42.4%	57.6%	42.4%
16,823	ASOTIN	7,141	3,308	3,833		525 D	46.3%	53.7%	46.3%	53.7%
109,444	BENTON	47,218	26,236	20,982		5,254 R	55.6%	44.4%	55.6%	44.4%
45,061	CHELAN	20,803	11,960	8,843		3,117 R	57.5%	42.5%	57.5%	42.5%
51,648	CLALLAM	23,976	11,820	12,156		336 D	49.3%	50.7%	49.3%	50.7%
192,227	CLARK	77,773	31,629	46,144		14,515 D	40.7%	59.3%	40.7%	59.3%
4,057	COLUMBIA	2,092	1,157	935		222 R	55.3%	44.7%	55.3%	44.7%
79,548	COWLITZ	30,323	11,553	18,770		7,217 D	38.1%	61.9%	38.1%	61.9%
22,144	DOUGLAS	9,759	5,361	4,398		963 R	54.9%	45.1%	54.9%	45.1%
5,811	FERRY	2,129	935	1,194		259 D	43.9%	56.1%	43.9%	56.1%
35,025	FRANKLIN	12,011	6,250	5,761		489 R	52.0%	48.0%	52.0%	48.0%
2,468	GARFIELD	1,421	736	685		51 R	51.8%	48.2%	51.8%	48.2%
48,522	GRANT	19,155	10,238	8,917		1,321 R	53.4%	46.6%	53.4%	46.6%
66,314	GRAYS HARBOR	26,513	7,761	18,752		10,991 D	29.3%	70.7%	29.3%	70.7%
44,048	ISLAND	20,824	11,664	9,160		2,504 R	56.0%	44.0%	56.0%	44.0%
15,965	JEFFERSON	9,128	4,224	4,904		680 D	46.3%	53.7%	46.3%	53.7%
1,269,749	KING	643,483	306,605	336,878		30,273 D	47.6%	52.4%	47.6%	52.4%
147,152	KITSAP	67,295	29,835	37,460		7,625 D	44.3%	55.7%	44.3%	55.7%
24,877	KITTITAS	11,081	4,504	6,577		2,073 D	40.6%	59.4%	40.6%	59.4%
15,822	KLICKITAT	6,707	2,910	3,797		887 D	43.4%	56.6%	43.4%	56.6%
56,025	LEWIS	23,780	9,969	13,811		3,842 D	41.9%	58.1%	41.9%	58.1%
9,604	LINCOLN	5,233	2,888	2,345		543 R	55.2%	44.8%	55.2%	44.8%
31,184	MASON	15,844	6,528	9,316		2,788 D	41.2%	58.8%	41.2%	58.8%
30,639	OKANOGAN	13,159	6,802	6,357		445 R	51.7%	48.3%	51.7%	48.3%
17,237	PACIFIC	8,428	2,955	5,473		2,518 D	35.1%	64.9%	35.1%	64.9%
8,580	PEND OREILLE	4,064	1,766	2,298		532 D	43.5%	56.5%	43.5%	56.5%
485,643	PIERCE	192,042	79,246	112,796		33,550 D	41.3%	58.7%	41.3%	58.7%
7,838	SAN JUAN	5,433	2,799	2,634		165 R	51.5%	48.5%	51.5%	48.5%
64,138	SKAGIT	33,587	15,130	18,457		3,327 D	45.0%	55.0%	45.0%	55.0%
7,919	SKAMANIA	3,310	1,376	1,934		558 D	41.6%	58.4%	41.6%	58.4%
337,720	SNOHOMISH	160,151	75,823	84,328		8,505 D	47.3%	52.7%	47.3%	52.7%
341,835	SPOKANE	150,746	76,502	74,244		2,258 R	50.7%	49.3%	50.7%	49.3%
28,979	STEVENS	12,861	6,428	6,433		5 D	50.0%	50.0%	50.0%	50.0%
124,264	THURSTON	62,451	26,950	35,501		8,551 D	43.2%	56.8%	43.2%	56.8%
3,832	WAHKIAKUM	1,697	619	1,078		459 D	36.5%	63.5%	36.5%	63.5%
47,435	WALLA WALLA	19,579	11,106	8,473		2,633 R	56.7%	43.3%	56.7%	43.3%
106,701	WHATCOM	50,780	20,255	30,525		10,270 D	39.9%	60.1%	39.9%	60.1%
40,103	WHITMAN	16,758	9,246	7,512		1,734 R	55.2%	44.8%	55.2%	44.8%
172,508	YAKIMA	65,373	34,111	31,262		2,849 R	52.2%	47.8%	52.2%	47.8%
4,132,156	TOTAL	1,888,987	881,994	1,006,993		124,999 D	46.7%	53.3%	46.7%	53.3%

WASHINGTON

SENATOR 1983

1980 Census Population	County	Total Vote	Republican	Democratic	Other	Rep.-Dem. Plurality	Percentage Total Vote Rep.	Dem.	Major Vote Rep.	Dem.
13,267	ADAMS	3,259	2,118	1,141		977 R	65.0%	35.0%	65.0%	35.0%
16,823	ASOTIN	4,258	2,486	1,772		714 R	58.4%	41.6%	58.4%	41.6%
109,444	BENTON	25,906	17,477	8,429		9,048 R	67.5%	32.5%	67.5%	32.5%
45,061	CHELAN	13,646	8,757	4,889		3,868 R	64.2%	35.8%	64.2%	35.8%
51,648	CLALLAM	16,462	8,849	7,613		1,236 R	53.8%	46.2%	53.8%	46.2%
192,227	CLARK	39,655	19,924	19,731		193 R	50.2%	49.8%	50.2%	49.8%
4,057	COLUMBIA	1,524	879	645		234 R	57.7%	42.3%	57.7%	42.3%
79,548	COWLITZ	18,364	9,012	9,352		340 D	49.1%	50.9%	49.1%	50.9%
22,144	DOUGLAS	6,218	3,926	2,292		1,634 R	63.1%	36.9%	63.1%	36.9%
5,811	FERRY	1,518	697	821		124 D	45.9%	54.1%	45.9%	54.1%
35,025	FRANKLIN	7,289	4,107	3,182		925 R	56.3%	43.7%	56.3%	43.7%
2,468	GARFIELD	1,112	649	463		186 R	58.4%	41.6%	58.4%	41.6%
48,522	GRANT	12,311	7,539	4,772		2,767 R	61.2%	38.8%	61.2%	38.8%
66,314	GRAYS HARBOR	18,768	7,977	10,791		2,814 D	42.5%	57.5%	42.5%	57.5%
44,048	ISLAND	13,886	8,862	5,024		3,838 R	63.8%	36.2%	63.8%	36.2%
15,965	JEFFERSON	6,863	3,393	3,470		77 D	49.4%	50.6%	49.4%	50.6%
1,269,749	KING	436,409	244,145	192,264		51,881 R	55.9%	44.1%	55.9%	44.1%
147,152	KITSAP	43,229	23,375	19,854		3,521 R	54.1%	45.9%	54.1%	45.9%
24,877	KITTITAS	7,981	4,193	3,788		405 R	52.5%	47.5%	52.5%	47.5%
15,822	KLICKITAT	3,528	1,880	1,648		232 R	53.3%	46.7%	53.3%	46.7%
56,025	LEWIS	16,294	8,681	7,613		1,068 R	53.3%	46.7%	53.3%	46.7%
9,604	LINCOLN	4,051	2,428	1,623		805 R	59.9%	40.1%	59.9%	40.1%
31,184	MASON	11,087	5,661	5,426		235 R	51.1%	48.9%	51.1%	48.9%
30,639	OKANOGAN	8,361	4,480	3,881		599 R	53.6%	46.4%	53.6%	46.4%
17,237	PACIFIC	6,082	2,601	3,481		880 D	42.8%	57.2%	42.8%	57.2%
8,580	PEND OREILLE	2,545	1,287	1,258		29 R	50.6%	49.4%	50.6%	49.4%
485,643	PIERCE	118,738	63,447	55,291		8,156 R	53.4%	46.6%	53.4%	46.6%
7,838	SAN JUAN	3,937	2,188	1,749		439 R	55.6%	44.4%	55.6%	44.4%
64,138	SKAGIT	22,731	11,815	10,916		899 R	52.0%	48.0%	52.0%	48.0%
7,919	SKAMANIA	1,903	950	953		3 D	49.9%	50.1%	49.9%	50.1%
337,720	SNOHOMISH	99,539	55,515	44,024		11,491 R	55.8%	44.2%	55.8%	44.2%
341,835	SPOKANE	89,837	49,893	39,944		9,949 R	55.5%	44.5%	55.5%	44.5%
28,979	STEVENS	7,825	4,499	3,326		1,173 R	57.5%	42.5%	57.5%	42.5%
124,264	THURSTON	42,498	24,752	17,746		7,006 R	58.2%	41.8%	58.2%	41.8%
3,832	WAHKIAKUM	1,225	535	690		155 D	43.7%	56.3%	43.7%	56.3%
47,435	WALLA WALLA	11,831	6,898	4,933		1,965 R	58.3%	41.7%	58.3%	41.7%
106,701	WHATCOM	34,208	17,932	16,276		1,656 R	52.4%	47.6%	52.4%	47.6%
40,103	WHITMAN	9,898	6,184	3,714		2,470 R	62.5%	37.5%	62.5%	37.5%
172,508	YAKIMA	38,531	22,335	16,196		6,139 R	58.0%	42.0%	58.0%	42.0%
4,132,156	TOTAL	1,213,307	672,326	540,981		131,345 R	55.4%	44.6%	55.4%	44.6%

WASHINGTON

CONGRESS

CD	Year	Total Vote	Republican Vote	Candidate	Democratic Vote	Candidate	Other Vote	Rep.-Dem. Plurality	Percentage Total Vote Rep.	Dem.	Major Vote Rep.	Dem.
1	1984	262,927	147,926	MILLER, JOHN R.	115,001	EVANS, BROCK		32,925 R	56.3%	43.7%	56.3%	43.7%
2	1984	242,392	93,472	KLAUDER, JIM	142,065	SWIFT, AL	6,855	48,593 D	38.6%	58.6%	39.7%	60.3%
3	1984	211,651	61,219	ELDER, HERB	150,432	BONKER, DON		89,213 D	28.9%	71.1%	28.9%	71.1%
4	1984	197,480	150,322	MORRISON, SID	47,158	EPPERSON, MARK		103,164 R	76.1%	23.9%	76.1%	23.9%
5	1984	222,426	67,438	HEBNER, JACK	154,988	FOLEY, THOMAS S.		87,550 D	30.3%	69.7%	30.3%	69.7%
6	1984	188,041	60,721	LONERGAN, MIKE	124,367	DICKS, NORMAN D.	2,953	63,646 D	32.3%	66.1%	32.8%	67.2%
7	1984	247,846	71,576	DORSE, BOB	174,560	LOWRY, MIKE	1,710	102,984 D	28.9%	70.4%	29.1%	70.9%
8	1984	235,270	146,891	CHANDLER, ROD	88,379	LAMSON, BOB		58,512 R	62.4%	37.6%	62.4%	37.6%

WASHINGTON

1983 SPECIAL GENERAL ELECTION

Senator

1984 GENERAL ELECTION

President   Other vote was 8,844 Bergland (Libertarian); 5,724 Richards (Populist); 4,712 LaRouche (Independent); 1,891 Johnson (Citizens); 1,654 Serrette (New Alliance); 814 Hall (Communist); 641 Holmes (Workers World); 608 Mason (Socialist Workers). The Mondale (Democratic) vote in King county and the total state Democratic vote have been adjusted to correct a 9,000 vote undercount in that county.

Governor

Congress   Other vote was Franco (Populist) in CD 2; Blachly (Libertarian) in CD 6; Manning (Socialist Workers) in CD 7.

PRIMARIES

Washington's primaries are completely open, with all candidates for an office carried on the ballot together; thus a voter may vote for a Republican for Governor, a Democrat for Senator, and so on. Actual nominations go to the highest Republican and the highest Democrat, as determined in this so-called "jungle primary." Independents and minor parties gain a place on the General Election ballot by obtaining one percent of the total vote cast in the primary.

1983 PRIMARIES

OCTOBER 11 REPUBLICAN

Senator   250,046 Daniel J. Evans; 133,799 Lloyd E. Cooney; 1,642 Larry Penberthy; 730 Andrew B. Higgins; 701 Ted P. Fix; 574 Dave Peterson; 382 J. Gunnar Thompson; 324 Howard Landon; 269 Chalres H. Hetrick; 211 John Patric; 188 Glenn L. Blubaugh; 162 C. E. Stites; 105 Stan Maine.

OCTOBER 11 DEMOCRATIC

Senator   179,509 Mike Lowry; 103,304 Charles Royer; 1,206 James Curdy; 1,032 Mike Olmer; 964 Eunice I. McKinney; 763 Jo Anne M. Yohey; 743 Cheryl Schilling; 620 Kenneth J. Staloch; 495 Leonard W. Fuller; 473 James E. Chappelle; 428 Timothy J. Blair; 362 Omari T. Garrett; 341 Victor A. Gee; 341 Wendell D. Maze; 339 Gary S. Siebel; 312 Duke Stockton; 266 Don Pilson; 240 Arthur Bauder; 223 Clarice L. R. Privette.

OCTOBER 11 MINOR PARTIES/INDEPENDENTS

Senator   596 Dean Peoples (Socialist Workers); did not qualify for the November ballot.

WASHINGTON

1984 PRIMARIES

SEPTEMBER 18 REPUBLICAN

Governor   239,463 John D. Spellman; 11,193 Ted P. Fix.

Congress

CD 1   23,802 John R. Miller; 20,057 Sue Gould; 11,508 Jim Galbraith; 8,499 John Rabel; 8,081 Alan Bluechel; 6,103 Bob Eberle; 1,103 John Graham; 814 John B. Still; 673 Alison M. Barden.
CD 2   31,381 Jim Klauder (only Republican candidate).
CD 3   26,889 Herb Elder (only Republican candidate).
CD 4   68,810 Sid Morrison (only Republican candidate).
CD 5   26,909 Jack Hebner (only Republican candidate).
CD 6   16,236 Mike Lonergan; 9,493 Jim Huff.
CD 7   29,213 Bob Dorse (only Republican candidate).
CD 8   56,456 Rod Chandler (only Republican candidate).

SEPTEMBER 18 DEMOCRATIC

Governor   421,087 Booth Gardner; 209,435 James A. McDermott; 23,699 John Jovanovich.

Congress

CD 1   31,552 Brock Evans; 4,300 Tom Bice; 3,683 Brian Long; 1,088 Charles M. Cosby.
CD 2   77,916 Al Swift; 11,916 Jim McKinney; 2,063 Gene T. Bahlman.
CD 3   72,811 Don Bonker (only Democratic candidate).
CD 4   13,341 Mark Epperson; 10,598 Robert C. Dupuy.
CD 5   68,197 Thomas S. Foley (only Democratic candidate).
CD 6   65,238 Norman D. Dicks; 5,070 Jim Klaproth.
CD 7   80,773 Mike Lowry; 6,652 Don Pilson.
CD 8   31,116 Bob Lamson; 7,953 Dorrie Wolfe.

SEPTEMBER 18 MINOR PARTIES/INDEPENDENTS

Governor   3,601 Bob LeRoy (Populist); 2,851 Mark Calney (Independent); 2,672 Cheryll Hidalgo (Socialist Workers). None of these candidates qualified for the November ballot.

Congress

CD 2   2,442 Gary Franco (Populist).
CD 6   2,100 Dan Blachly (Libertarian).
CD 7   1,194 Mark Manning (Socialist Workers).

WEST VIRGINIA

GOVERNOR
Arch A. Moore (R). Elected 1984 to a four-year term. Previously elected 1972, 1968.

SENATORS
Robert C. Byrd (D). Re-elected 1982 to a six-year term. Previously elected 1976, 1970, 1964, 1958.

John D. Rockefeller (D). Elected 1984 to a six-year term.

REPRESENTATIVES
1. Alan B. Mollohan (D)
2. Harley O. Staggers, Jr. (D)
3. Robert E. Wise (D)
4. Nick J. Rahall (D)

POSTWAR VOTE FOR GOVERNOR

Year	Total Vote	Republican Vote	Candidate	Democratic Vote	Candidate	Other Vote	Rep.-Dem. Plurality	Total Vote Rep.	Total Vote Dem.	Major Vote Rep.	Major Vote Dem.
1984	741,502	394,937	Moore, Arch A.	346,565	See, Clyde M.	—	48,372 R	53.3%	46.7%	53.3%	46.7%
1980	742,150	337,240	Moore, Arch A.	401,863	Rockefeller, John D.	3,047	64,623 D	45.4%	54.1%	45.6%	54.4%
1976	749,270	253,420	Underwood, Cecil H.	495,661	Rockefeller, John D.	189	242,241 D	33.8%	66.2%	33.8%	66.2%
1972	774,279	423,817	Moore, Arch A.	350,462	Rockefeller, John D.	—	73,355 R	54.7%	45.3%	54.7%	45.3%
1968	743,845	378,315	Moore, Arch A.	365,530	Sprouse, James M.	—	12,785 R	50.9%	49.1%	50.9%	49.1%
1964	788,582	355,559	Underwood, Cecil H.	433,023	Smith, Hulett C.	—	77,464 D	45.1%	54.9%	45.1%	54.9%
1960	827,420	380,665	Neely, Harold E.	446,755	Barron, W. W.	—	66,090 D	46.0%	54.0%	46.0%	54.0%
1956	817,623	440,502	Underwood, Cecil H.	377,121	Mollohan, Robert H.	—	63,381 R	53.9%	46.1%	53.9%	46.1%
1952	882,527	427,629	Holt, Rush D.	454,898	Marland, William C.	—	27,269 D	48.5%	51.5%	48.5%	51.5%
1948	768,061	329,309	Boreman, Herbert	438,752	Patteson, Okey L.	—	109,443 D	42.9%	57.1%	42.9%	57.1%

POSTWAR VOTE FOR SENATOR

Year	Total Vote	Republican Vote	Candidate	Democratic Vote	Candidate	Other Vote	Rep.-Dem. Plurality	Total Vote Rep.	Total Vote Dem.	Major Vote Rep.	Major Vote Dem.
1984	722,212	344,680	Raese, John R.	374,233	Rockefeller, John D.	3,299	29,553 D	47.7%	51.8%	47.9%	52.1%
1982	565,314	173,910	Benedict, Cleveland K.	387,170	Byrd, Robert C.	4,234	213,260 D	30.8%	68.5%	31.0%	69.0%
1978	493,351	244,317	Moore, Arch A.	249,034	Randolph, Jennings	—	4,717 D	49.5%	50.5%	49.5%	50.5%
1976	566,790	—	—	566,423	Byrd, Robert C.	367	566,423 D	—	99.9%	—	100.0%
1972	731,841	245,531	Leonard, Louise	486,310	Randolph, Jennings	—	240,779 D	33.5%	66.5%	33.5%	66.5%
1970	445,623	99,658	Dodson, Elmer H.	345,965	Byrd, Robert C.	—	246,307 D	22.4%	77.6%	22.4%	77.6%
1966	491,216	198,891	Love, Francis J.	292,325	Randolph, Jennings	—	93,434 D	40.5%	59.5%	40.5%	59.5%
1964	761,087	246,072	Benedict, Cooper P.	515,015	Byrd, Robert C.	—	268,943 D	32.3%	67.7%	32.3%	67.7%
1960	828,292	369,935	Underwood, Cecil H.	458,355	Randolph, Jennings	2	88,420 D	44.7%	55.3%	44.7%	55.3%
1958	644,917	263,172	Revercomb, Chapman	381,745	Byrd, Robert C.	—	118,573 D	40.8%	59.2%	40.8%	59.2%
1958s	630,677	256,510	Hoblitzell, John D.	374,167	Randolph, Jennings	—	117,657 D	40.7%	59.3%	40.7%	59.3%
1956s	805,174	432,123	Revercomb, Chapman	373,051	Marland, William C.	—	59,072 R	53.7%	46.3%	53.7%	46.3%
1954	593,329	268,066	Sweeney, Tom	325,263	Neely, Matthew M.	—	57,197 D	45.2%	54.8%	45.2%	54.8%
1952	876,573	406,554	Revercomb, Chapman	470,019	Kilgore, Harley M.	—	63,465 D	46.4%	53.6%	46.4%	53.6%
1948	763,888	328,534	Revercomb, Chapman	435,354	Neely, Matthew M.	—	106,820 D	43.0%	57.0%	43.0%	57.0%
1946	542,768	269,617	Sweeney, Tom	273,151	Kilgore, Harley M.	—	3,534 D	49.7%	50.3%	49.7%	50.3%

One of the 1958 elections and the 1956 election were for short terms to fill vacancies.

WEST VIRGINIA

Districts Established February 8, 1982

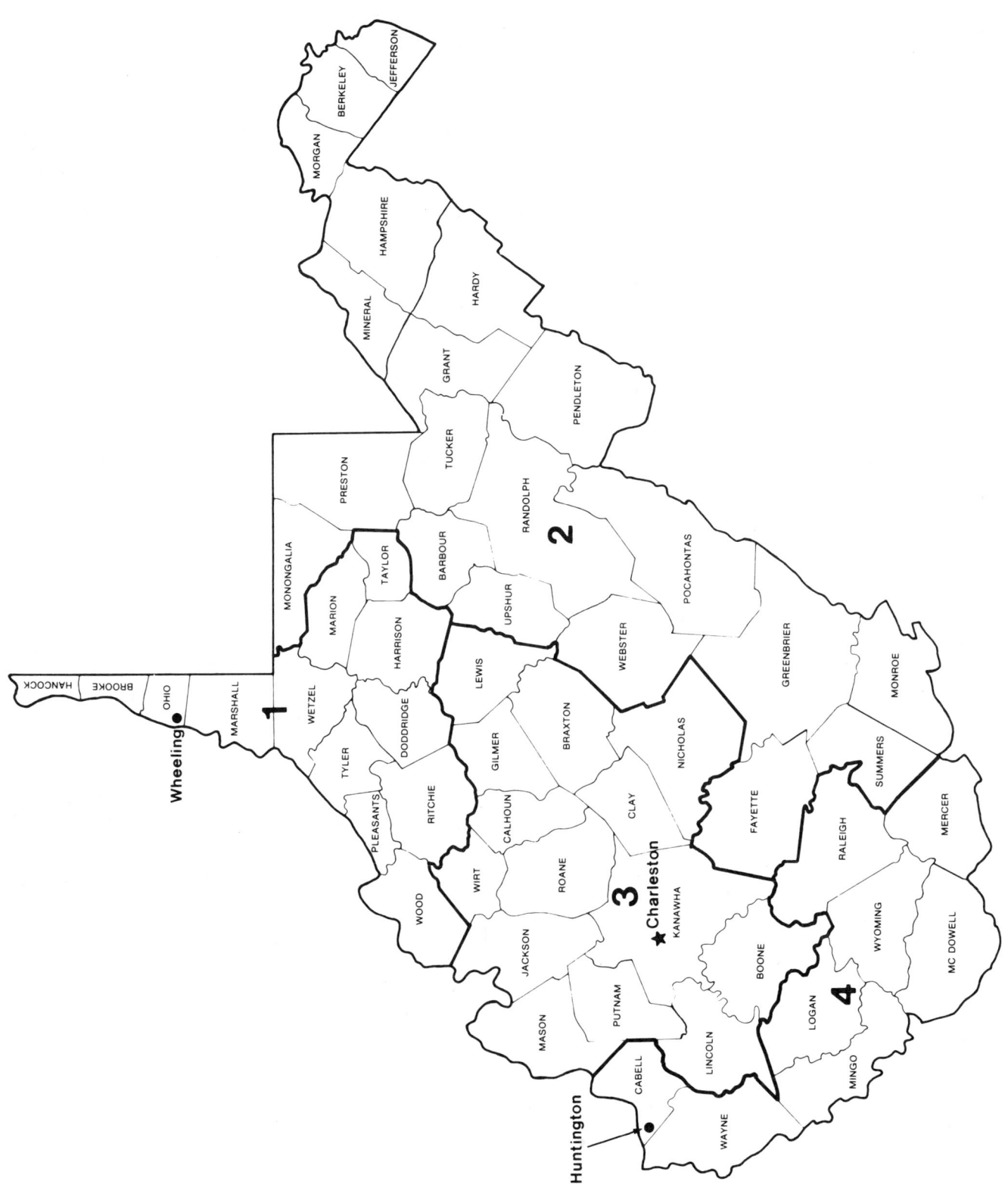

WEST VIRGINIA

PRESIDENT 1984

1980 Census Population	County	Total Vote	Republican	Democratic	Other	Rep.-Dem. Plurality	Percentage Total Vote Rep.	Dem.	Major Vote Rep.	Dem.
16,639	BARBOUR	6,995	3,877	3,108	10	769 R	55.4%	44.4%	55.5%	44.5%
46,775	BERKELEY	19,092	12,887	6,181	24	6,706 R	67.5%	32.4%	67.6%	32.4%
30,447	BOONE	11,821	4,656	7,121	44	2,465 D	39.4%	60.2%	39.5%	60.5%
13,894	BRAXTON	6,265	2,902	3,350	13	448 D	46.3%	53.5%	46.4%	53.6%
31,117	BROOKE	11,498	4,819	6,636	43	1,817 D	41.9%	57.7%	42.1%	57.9%
106,835	CABELL	37,445	21,815	15,513	117	6,302 R	58.3%	41.4%	58.4%	41.6%
8,250	CALHOUN	3,276	1,765	1,473	38	292 R	53.9%	45.0%	54.5%	45.5%
11,265	CLAY	3,796	1,667	2,117	12	450 D	43.9%	55.8%	44.1%	55.9%
7,433	DODDRIDGE	3,195	2,343	836	16	1,507 R	73.3%	26.2%	73.7%	26.3%
57,863	FAYETTE	19,086	7,360	11,650	76	4,290 D	38.6%	61.0%	38.7%	61.3%
8,334	GILMER	3,452	1,953	1,494	5	459 R	56.6%	43.3%	56.7%	43.3%
10,210	GRANT	4,554	3,715	828	11	2,887 R	81.6%	18.2%	81.8%	18.2%
37,665	GREENBRIER	12,974	7,337	5,599	38	1,738 R	56.6%	43.2%	56.7%	43.3%
14,867	HAMPSHIRE	6,187	4,065	2,102	20	1,963 R	65.7%	34.0%	65.9%	34.1%
40,418	HANCOCK	16,124	7,326	8,708	90	1,382 D	45.4%	54.0%	45.7%	54.3%
10,030	HARDY	4,587	2,938	1,641	8	1,297 R	64.1%	35.8%	64.2%	35.8%
77,710	HARRISON	34,437	19,400	14,969	68	4,431 R	56.3%	43.5%	56.4%	43.6%
25,794	JACKSON	11,310	7,117	4,147	46	2,970 R	62.9%	36.7%	63.2%	36.8%
30,302	JEFFERSON	10,134	5,884	4,216	34	1,668 R	58.1%	41.6%	58.3%	41.7%
231,414	KANAWHA	89,542	51,499	37,832	211	13,667 R	57.5%	42.3%	57.6%	42.4%
18,813	LEWIS	8,031	5,297	2,693	41	2,604 R	66.0%	33.5%	66.3%	33.7%
23,675	LINCOLN	9,902	4,405	5,467	30	1,062 D	44.5%	55.2%	44.6%	55.4%
50,679	LOGAN	17,382	6,425	10,892	65	4,467 D	37.0%	62.7%	37.1%	62.9%
49,899	MCDOWELL	12,883	4,284	8,546	53	4,262 D	33.3%	66.3%	33.4%	66.6%
65,789	MARION	27,020	13,106	13,833	81	727 D	48.5%	51.2%	48.7%	51.3%
41,608	MARSHALL	16,616	8,615	7,947	54	668 R	51.8%	47.8%	52.0%	48.0%
27,045	MASON	12,393	6,648	5,701	44	947 R	53.6%	46.0%	53.8%	46.2%
73,942	MERCER	23,155	13,910	9,164	81	4,746 R	60.1%	39.6%	60.3%	39.7%
27,234	MINERAL	11,138	7,291	3,832	15	3,459 R	65.5%	34.4%	65.5%	34.5%
37,336	MINGO	12,726	4,275	8,434	17	4,159 D	33.6%	66.3%	33.6%	66.4%
75,024	MONONGALIA	28,274	14,972	13,236	66	1,736 R	53.0%	46.8%	53.1%	46.9%
12,873	MONROE	5,954	3,612	2,333	9	1,279 R	60.7%	39.2%	60.8%	39.2%
10,711	MORGAN	4,932	3,469	1,457	6	2,012 R	70.3%	29.5%	70.4%	29.6%
28,126	NICHOLAS	9,273	4,656	4,588	29	68 R	50.2%	49.5%	50.4%	49.6%
61,389	OHIO	23,662	13,447	10,163	52	3,284 R	56.8%	43.0%	57.0%	43.0%
7,910	PENDLETON	3,518	2,047	1,464	7	583 R	58.2%	41.6%	58.3%	41.7%
8,236	PLEASANTS	3,725	2,255	1,458	12	797 R	60.5%	39.1%	60.7%	39.3%
9,919	POCAHONTAS	4,386	2,479	1,903	4	576 R	56.5%	43.4%	56.6%	43.4%
30,460	PRESTON	11,031	6,955	4,054	22	2,901 R	63.0%	36.8%	63.2%	36.8%
38,181	PUTNAM	14,492	9,238	5,208	46	4,030 R	63.7%	35.9%	63.9%	36.1%
86,821	RALEIGH	29,122	14,571	14,442	109	129 R	50.0%	49.6%	50.2%	49.8%
28,734	RANDOLPH	10,964	6,100	4,839	25	1,261 R	55.6%	44.1%	55.8%	44.2%
11,442	RITCHIE	4,609	3,355	1,231	23	2,124 R	72.8%	26.7%	73.2%	26.8%
15,952	ROANE	6,240	3,751	2,468	21	1,283 R	60.1%	39.6%	60.3%	39.7%
15,875	SUMMERS	5,659	2,975	2,670	14	305 R	52.6%	47.2%	52.7%	47.3%
16,584	TAYLOR	6,765	4,007	2,754	4	1,253 R	59.2%	40.7%	59.3%	40.7%
8,675	TUCKER	4,014	2,240	1,766	8	474 R	55.8%	44.0%	55.9%	44.1%
11,320	TYLER	4,575	3,170	1,395	10	1,775 R	69.3%	30.5%	69.4%	30.6%
23,427	UPSHUR	8,466	5,951	2,468	47	3,483 R	70.3%	29.2%	70.7%	29.3%
46,021	WAYNE	17,236	8,811	8,378	47	433 R	51.1%	48.6%	51.3%	48.7%
12,245	WEBSTER	3,926	1,565	2,355	6	790 D	39.9%	60.0%	39.9%	60.1%
21,874	WETZEL	8,207	4,626	3,549	32	1,077 R	56.4%	43.2%	56.6%	43.4%
4,922	WIRT	2,322	1,450	868	4	582 R	62.4%	37.4%	62.6%	37.4%
93,648	WOOD	36,279	24,821	11,357	101	13,464 R	68.4%	31.3%	68.6%	31.4%
35,993	WYOMING	11,095	5,379	5,691	25	312 D	48.5%	51.3%	48.6%	51.4%
1,949,644	TOTAL	735,742	405,483	328,125	2,134	77,358 R	55.1%	44.6%	55.3%	44.7%

WEST VIRGINIA

GOVERNOR 1984

1980 Census Population	County	Total Vote	Republican	Democratic	Other	Rep.-Dem. Plurality	Percentage Total Vote Rep.	Dem.	Major Vote Rep.	Dem.
16,639	BARBOUR	7,069	4,032	3,037		995 R	57.0%	43.0%	57.0%	43.0%
46,775	BERKELEY	18,862	11,793	7,069		4,724 R	62.5%	37.5%	62.5%	37.5%
30,447	BOONE	12,159	5,210	6,949		1,739 D	42.8%	57.2%	42.8%	57.2%
13,894	BRAXTON	6,307	3,008	3,299		291 D	47.7%	52.3%	47.7%	52.3%
31,117	BROOKE	11,533	5,035	6,498		1,463 D	43.7%	56.3%	43.7%	56.3%
106,835	CABELL	38,120	20,429	17,691		2,738 R	53.6%	46.4%	53.6%	46.4%
8,250	CALHOUN	3,315	1,786	1,529		257 R	53.9%	46.1%	53.9%	46.1%
11,265	CLAY	3,838	1,692	2,146		454 D	44.1%	55.9%	44.1%	55.9%
7,433	DODDRIDGE	3,227	2,278	949		1,329 R	70.6%	29.4%	70.6%	29.4%
57,863	FAYETTE	19,433	7,452	11,981		4,529 D	38.3%	61.7%	38.3%	61.7%
8,334	GILMER	3,496	1,962	1,534		428 R	56.1%	43.9%	56.1%	43.9%
10,210	GRANT	4,610	3,292	1,318		1,974 R	71.4%	28.6%	71.4%	28.6%
37,665	GREENBRIER	13,244	6,948	6,296		652 R	52.5%	47.5%	52.5%	47.5%
14,867	HAMPSHIRE	6,214	3,112	3,102		10 R	50.1%	49.9%	50.1%	49.9%
40,418	HANCOCK	15,329	6,467	8,862		2,395 D	42.2%	57.8%	42.2%	57.8%
10,030	HARDY	4,670	1,579	3,091		1,512 D	33.8%	66.2%	33.8%	66.2%
77,710	HARRISON	34,373	19,444	14,929		4,515 R	56.6%	43.4%	56.6%	43.4%
25,794	JACKSON	11,546	7,056	4,490		2,566 R	61.1%	38.9%	61.1%	38.9%
30,302	JEFFERSON	10,073	5,451	4,622		829 R	54.1%	45.9%	54.1%	45.9%
231,414	KANAWHA	90,882	49,215	41,667		7,548 R	54.2%	45.8%	54.2%	45.8%
18,813	LEWIS	8,107	4,865	3,242		1,623 R	60.0%	40.0%	60.0%	40.0%
23,675	LINCOLN	10,111	4,510	5,601		1,091 D	44.6%	55.4%	44.6%	55.4%
50,679	LOGAN	17,648	7,287	10,361		3,074 D	41.3%	58.7%	41.3%	58.7%
49,899	MCDOWELL	12,706	4,776	7,930		3,154 D	37.6%	62.4%	37.6%	62.4%
65,789	MARION	26,976	15,269	11,707		3,562 R	56.6%	43.4%	56.6%	43.4%
41,608	MARSHALL	16,906	11,262	5,644		5,618 R	66.6%	33.4%	66.6%	33.4%
27,045	MASON	12,606	6,536	6,070		466 R	51.8%	48.2%	51.8%	48.2%
73,942	MERCER	23,329	13,580	9,749		3,831 R	58.2%	41.8%	58.2%	41.8%
27,234	MINERAL	11,028	5,979	5,049		930 R	54.2%	45.8%	54.2%	45.8%
37,336	MINGO	12,984	4,301	8,683		4,382 D	33.1%	66.9%	33.1%	66.9%
75,024	MONONGALIA	28,022	15,870	12,152		3,718 R	56.6%	43.4%	56.6%	43.4%
12,873	MONROE	6,038	3,252	2,786		466 R	53.9%	46.1%	53.9%	46.1%
10,711	MORGAN	4,915	2,895	2,020		875 R	58.9%	41.1%	58.9%	41.1%
28,126	NICHOLAS	9,440	4,384	5,056		672 D	46.4%	53.6%	46.4%	53.6%
61,389	OHIO	24,138	14,858	9,280		5,578 R	61.6%	38.4%	61.6%	38.4%
7,910	PENDLETON	3,552	1,667	1,885		218 D	46.9%	53.1%	46.9%	53.1%
8,236	PLEASANTS	3,727	2,072	1,655		417 R	55.6%	44.4%	55.6%	44.4%
9,919	POCAHONTAS	4,428	2,341	2,087		254 R	52.9%	47.1%	52.9%	47.1%
30,460	PRESTON	11,026	7,341	3,685		3,656 R	66.6%	33.4%	66.6%	33.4%
38,181	PUTNAM	14,800	8,237	6,563		1,674 R	55.7%	44.3%	55.7%	44.3%
86,821	RALEIGH	28,700	11,401	17,299		5,898 D	39.7%	60.3%	39.7%	60.3%
28,734	RANDOLPH	11,136	6,029	5,107		922 R	54.1%	45.9%	54.1%	45.9%
11,442	RITCHIE	4,669	3,254	1,415		1,839 R	69.7%	30.3%	69.7%	30.3%
15,952	ROANE	6,419	3,921	2,498		1,423 R	61.1%	38.9%	61.1%	38.9%
15,875	SUMMERS	5,822	2,885	2,937		52 D	49.6%	50.4%	49.6%	50.4%
16,584	TAYLOR	6,795	4,282	2,513		1,769 R	63.0%	37.0%	63.0%	37.0%
8,675	TUCKER	4,081	2,420	1,661		759 R	59.3%	40.7%	59.3%	40.7%
11,320	TYLER	4,613	3,157	1,456		1,701 R	68.4%	31.6%	68.4%	31.6%
23,427	UPSHUR	8,660	5,663	2,997		2,666 R	65.4%	34.6%	65.4%	34.6%
46,021	WAYNE	17,353	8,529	8,824		295 D	49.2%	50.8%	49.2%	50.8%
12,245	WEBSTER	3,918	1,526	2,392		866 D	38.9%	61.1%	38.9%	61.1%
21,874	WETZEL	8,484	4,555	3,929		626 R	53.7%	46.3%	53.7%	46.3%
4,922	WIRT	2,361	1,339	1,022		317 R	56.7%	43.3%	56.7%	43.3%
93,648	WOOD	36,485	22,003	14,482		7,521 R	60.3%	39.7%	60.3%	39.7%
35,993	WYOMING	11,219	5,450	5,769		319 D	48.6%	51.4%	48.6%	51.4%
1,949,644	TOTAL	741,502	394,937	346,565		48,372 R	53.3%	46.7%	53.3%	46.7%

WEST VIRGINIA

SENATOR 1984

1980 Census Population	County	Total Vote	Republican	Democratic	Other	Rep.-Dem. Plurality	Percentage Total Vote Rep.	Dem.	Major Vote Rep.	Dem.
16,639	BARBOUR	6,859	3,873	2,969	17	904 R	56.5%	43.3%	56.6%	43.4%
46,775	BERKELEY	18,199	9,765	8,415	19	1,350 R	53.7%	46.2%	53.7%	46.3%
30,447	BOONE	11,821	4,295	7,483	43	3,188 D	36.3%	63.3%	36.5%	63.5%
13,894	BRAXTON	6,130	2,723	3,385	22	662 D	44.4%	55.2%	44.6%	55.4%
31,117	BROOKE	11,160	3,192	7,874	94	4,682 D	28.6%	70.6%	28.8%	71.2%
106,835	CABELL	36,492	18,075	18,213	204	138 D	49.5%	49.9%	49.8%	50.2%
8,250	CALHOUN	3,180	1,722	1,443	15	279 R	54.2%	45.4%	54.4%	45.6%
11,265	CLAY	3,747	1,544	2,192	11	648 D	41.2%	58.5%	41.3%	58.7%
7,433	DODDRIDGE	3,108	2,216	880	12	1,336 R	71.3%	28.3%	71.6%	28.4%
57,863	FAYETTE	19,111	6,605	12,417	89	5,812 D	34.6%	65.0%	34.7%	65.3%
8,334	GILMER	3,361	1,911	1,436	14	475 R	56.9%	42.7%	57.1%	42.9%
10,210	GRANT	4,367	3,183	1,173	11	2,010 R	72.9%	26.9%	73.1%	26.9%
37,665	GREENBRIER	12,839	6,339	6,400	100	61 R	49.4%	49.8%	49.8%	50.2%
14,867	HAMPSHIRE	5,859	2,961	2,882	16	79 R	50.5%	49.2%	50.7%	49.3%
40,418	HANCOCK	15,228	4,432	10,688	108	6,256 D	29.1%	70.2%	29.3%	70.7%
10,030	HARDY	4,329	2,071	2,243	15	172 D	47.8%	51.8%	48.0%	52.0%
77,710	HARRISON	33,809	16,951	16,782	76	169 R	50.1%	49.6%	50.3%	49.7%
25,794	JACKSON	11,334	6,700	4,579	55	2,121 R	59.1%	40.4%	59.4%	40.6%
30,302	JEFFERSON	9,723	3,778	5,838	107	2,060 D	38.9%	60.0%	39.3%	60.7%
231,414	KANAWHA	86,903	44,267	42,226	410	2,041 R	50.9%	48.6%	51.2%	48.8%
18,813	LEWIS	7,742	4,852	2,856	34	1,996 R	62.7%	36.9%	62.9%	37.1%
23,675	LINCOLN	9,875	4,312	5,538	25	1,226 D	43.7%	56.1%	43.8%	56.2%
50,679	LOGAN	17,344	5,746	11,543	55	5,797 D	33.1%	66.6%	33.2%	66.8%
49,899	MCDOWELL	12,514	3,964	8,493	57	4,529 D	31.7%	67.9%	31.8%	68.2%
65,789	MARION	26,510	11,565	14,860	85	3,295 D	43.6%	56.1%	43.8%	56.2%
41,608	MARSHALL	16,474	7,611	8,718	145	1,107 D	46.2%	52.9%	46.6%	53.4%
27,045	MASON	12,405	6,053	6,330	22	277 D	48.8%	51.0%	48.9%	51.1%
73,942	MERCER	23,056	12,295	10,669	92	1,626 R	53.3%	46.3%	53.5%	46.5%
27,234	MINERAL	10,850	5,508	5,320	22	188 R	50.8%	49.0%	50.9%	49.1%
37,336	MINGO	12,827	3,195	9,604	28	6,409 D	24.9%	74.9%	25.0%	75.0%
75,024	MONONGALIA	27,659	11,583	15,946	130	4,363 D	41.9%	57.7%	42.1%	57.9%
12,873	MONROE	5,826	3,075	2,746	5	329 R	52.8%	47.1%	52.8%	47.2%
10,711	MORGAN	4,716	2,614	2,098	4	516 R	55.4%	44.5%	55.5%	44.5%
28,126	NICHOLAS	9,098	3,920	5,144	34	1,224 D	43.1%	56.5%	43.2%	56.8%
61,389	OHIO	23,608	9,458	13,922	228	4,464 D	40.1%	59.0%	40.5%	59.5%
7,910	PENDLETON	3,376	1,735	1,619	22	116 R	51.4%	48.0%	51.7%	48.3%
8,236	PLEASANTS	3,629	1,937	1,681	11	256 R	53.4%	46.3%	53.5%	46.5%
9,919	POCAHONTAS	4,284	2,147	2,127	10	20 R	50.1%	49.6%	50.2%	49.8%
30,460	PRESTON	10,733	6,559	4,152	22	2,407 R	61.1%	38.7%	61.2%	38.8%
38,181	PUTNAM	14,631	8,286	6,267	78	2,019 R	56.6%	42.8%	56.9%	43.1%
86,821	RALEIGH	28,996	11,866	16,979	151	5,113 D	40.9%	58.6%	41.1%	58.9%
28,734	RANDOLPH	10,867	5,684	5,092	91	592 R	52.3%	46.9%	52.7%	47.3%
11,442	RITCHIE	4,509	3,206	1,280	23	1,926 R	71.1%	28.4%	71.5%	28.5%
15,952	ROANE	6,199	3,943	2,206	50	1,737 R	63.6%	35.6%	64.1%	35.9%
15,875	SUMMERS	5,585	2,808	2,738	39	70 R	50.3%	49.0%	50.6%	49.4%
16,584	TAYLOR	6,532	3,898	2,634		1,264 R	59.7%	40.3%	59.7%	40.3%
8,675	TUCKER	3,828	2,306	1,516	6	790 R	60.2%	39.6%	60.3%	39.7%
11,320	TYLER	4,445	2,838	1,591	16	1,247 R	63.8%	35.8%	64.1%	35.9%
23,427	UPSHUR	8,352	5,441	2,838	73	2,603 R	65.1%	34.0%	65.7%	34.3%
46,021	WAYNE	16,979	7,855	9,089	35	1,234 D	46.3%	53.5%	46.4%	53.6%
12,245	WEBSTER	3,766	1,446	2,312	8	866 D	38.4%	61.4%	38.5%	61.5%
21,874	WETZEL	8,137	3,596	4,499	42	903 D	44.2%	55.3%	44.4%	55.6%
4,922	WIRT	2,296	1,356	938	2	418 R	59.1%	40.9%	59.1%	40.9%
93,648	WOOD	36,014	20,513	15,285	216	5,228 R	57.0%	42.4%	57.3%	42.7%
35,993	WYOMING	10,991	4,906	6,085		1,179 D	44.6%	55.4%	44.6%	55.4%
1,949,644	TOTAL	722,212	344,680	374,233	3,299	29,553 D	47.7%	51.8%	47.9%	52.1%

WEST VIRGINIA

CONGRESS

CD	Year	Total Vote	Republican Vote	Candidate	Democratic Vote	Candidate	Other Vote	Rep.-Dem. Plurality	Percentage Total Vote Rep.	Dem.	Major Vote Rep.	Dem.
1	1984	192,261	87,622	ALTMEYER, JAMES	104,639	MOLLOHAN, ALAN B.		17,017 D	45.6%	54.4%	45.6%	54.4%
1	1982	149,598	70,069	MCCUSKEY, JOHN F.	79,529	MOLLOHAN, ALAN B.		9,460 D	46.8%	53.2%	46.8%	53.2%
2	1984	179,281	78,936	BENEDICT, CLEVELAND K.	100,345	STAGGERS, HARLEY O., JR.		21,409 D	44.0%	56.0%	44.0%	56.0%
2	1982	137,317	49,413	HINKLE, J. D.	87,904	STAGGERS, HARLEY O., JR.		38,491 D	36.0%	64.0%	36.0%	64.0%
3	1984	184,434	59,128	MILLER, MARGARET P.	125,306	WISE, ROBERT E.		66,178 D	32.1%	67.9%	32.1%	67.9%
3	1982	146,250	60,844	STATON, DAVID M.	84,619	WISE, ROBERT E.	787	23,775 D	41.6%	57.9%	41.8%	58.2%
4	1984	148,393	49,474	SHUMATE, JESS T.	98,919	RAHALL, NICK J.		49,445 D	33.3%	66.7%	33.3%	66.7%
4	1982	113,238	22,054	HARRIS, HOMER L.	91,184	RAHALL, NICK J.		69,130 D	19.5%	80.5%	19.5%	80.5%
4	1980	153,615	36,020	COVEY, WINTON G.	117,595	RAHALL, NICK J.		81,575 D	23.4%	76.6%	23.4%	76.6%
4	1978	70,035			70,035	RAHALL, NICK J.		70,035 D		100.0%		100.0%
4	1976	161,520	28,825	GOODMAN, E. S.	73,626	RAHALL, NICK J.	59,069	44,801 D	17.8%	45.6%	28.1%	71.9%
4	1974	66,420			66,420	HECHLER, KEN		66,420 D		100.0%		100.0%
4	1972	164,842	64,242	NEAL, JOE	100,600	HECHLER, KEN		36,358 D	39.0%	61.0%	39.0%	61.0%

WEST VIRGINIA

1984 GENERAL ELECTION

President Other vote was 996 Richards (Populist); 645 Mason (Socialist Workers); 493 Serrette (Alliance). Early uncorrected returns gave the Mondale (Democratic) vote in Jackson county as 4,179.

Governor

Senator Other vote was Radin (Socialist Workers).

Congress

1984 PRIMARIES

JUNE 5 REPUBLICAN

Governor Arch A. Moore, unopposed.

Senator 61,389 John R. Raese; 44,820 Samuel N. Kusic; 13,707 J. Frank Deem; 5,308 Frederick A. Weiland; 3,113 Henry C. Vigilianco.

Congress Unopposed in all four CD's.

JUNE 5 DEMOCRATIC

Governor 148,049 Clyde M. See; 104,138 Warren R. McGraw; 101,712 Chauncey H. Browning; 7,581 Dusty Rhodes; 5,234 Glenn W. Mullett; 2,935 Powell Lane; 1,960 E. E. Cumptan.

Senator 240,559 John D. Rockefeller; 51,591 Lacy Wright; 41,408 Ken Auvil; 29,138 Homer L. Harris.

Congress Unopposed in two CD's. Contested as follows:

CD 2 71,443 Harley O. Staggers, Jr.; 16,356 E. H. Warfield.
CD 3 80,972 Robert E. Wise; 7,763 Nick Ciccarello.

WISCONSIN

GOVERNOR
Anthony S. Earl (D). Elected 1982 to a four-year term.

SENATORS
Robert W. Kasten (R). Elected 1980 to a six-year term.

William Proxmire (D). Re-elected 1982 to a six-year term. Previously elected 1976, 1970, 1964, 1958, and in August 1957 to fill out term vacated by the death of Senator Joseph R. McCarthy.

REPRESENTATIVES
1. Les Aspin (D)
2. Robert Kastenmeier (D)
3. Steven Gunderson (R)
4. Gerald D. Kleczka (D)
5. Jim Moody (D)
6. Thomas E. Petri (R)
7. David R. Obey (D)
8. Toby Roth (R)
9. F. James Sensenbrenner (R)

POSTWAR VOTE FOR GOVERNOR

Year	Total Vote	Republican Vote	Candidate	Democratic Vote	Candidate	Other Vote	Rep.-Dem. Plurality	Total Vote Rep.	Total Vote Dem.	Major Vote Rep.	Major Vote Dem.
1982	1,580,344	662,838	Kohler, Terry J.	896,812	Earl, Anthony S.	20,694	233,974 D	41.9%	56.7%	42.5%	57.5%
1978	1,500,996	816,056	Dreyfus, Lee S.	673,813	Schreiber, Martin J.	11,127	142,243 R	54.4%	44.9%	54.8%	45.2%
1974	1,181,976	497,195	Dyke, William D.	628,639	Lucey, Patrick J.	56,142	131,444 D	42.1%	53.2%	44.2%	55.8%
1970*	1,343,160	602,617	Olson, Jack B.	728,403	Lucey, Patrick J.	12,140	125,786 D	44.9%	54.2%	45.3%	54.7%
1968	1,689,738	893,463	Knowles, Warren P.	791,100	LaFollette, Bronson C.	5,175	102,363 R	52.9%	46.8%	53.0%	47.0%
1966	1,170,173	626,041	Knowles, Warren P.	539,258	Lucey, Patrick J.	4,874	86,783 R	53.5%	46.1%	53.7%	46.3%
1964	1,694,887	856,779	Knowles, Warren P.	837,901	Reynolds, John W.	207	18,878 R	50.6%	49.4%	50.6%	49.4%
1962	1,265,900	625,536	Kuehn, Philip G.	637,491	Reynolds, John W.	2,873	11,955 D	49.4%	50.4%	49.5%	50.5%
1960	1,728,009	837,123	Kuehn, Philip G.	890,868	Nelson, Gaylord A.	18	53,745 D	48.4%	51.6%	48.4%	51.6%
1958	1,202,219	556,391	Thomson, Vernon W.	644,296	Nelson, Gaylord A.	1,532	87,905 D	46.3%	53.6%	46.3%	53.7%
1956	1,557,788	808,273	Thomson, Vernon W.	749,421	Proxmire, William	94	58,852 R	51.9%	48.1%	51.9%	48.1%
1954	1,158,666	596,158	Kohler, Walter J.	560,747	Proxmire, William	1,761	35,411 R	51.5%	48.4%	51.5%	48.5%
1952	1,615,214	1,009,171	Kohler, Walter J.	601,844	Proxmire, William	4,199	407,327 R	62.5%	37.3%	62.6%	37.4%
1950	1,138,148	605,649	Kohler, Walter J.	525,319	Thompson, Carl W.	7,180	80,330 R	53.2%	46.2%	53.6%	46.4%
1948	1,266,139	684,839	Rennebohm, Oscar	558,497	Thompson, Carl W.	22,803	126,342 R	54.1%	44.1%	55.1%	44.9%
1946	1,040,444	621,970	Goodland, Walter	406,499	Hoan, Daniel W.	11,975	215,471 R	59.8%	39.1%	60.5%	39.5%

The term of office of Wisconsin's Governor was increased from two to four years effective with the 1970 election.

POSTWAR VOTE FOR SENATOR

Year	Total Vote	Republican Vote	Candidate	Democratic Vote	Candidate	Other Vote	Rep.-Dem. Plurality	Total Vote Rep.	Total Vote Dem.	Major Vote Rep.	Major Vote Dem.
1982	1,544,981	527,355	McCallum, Scott	983,311	Proxmire, William	34,315	455,956 D	34.1%	63.6%	34.9%	65.1%
1980	2,204,202	1,106,311	Kasten, Robert W.	1,065,487	Nelson, Gaylord A.	32,404	40,824 R	50.2%	48.3%	50.9%	49.1%
1976	1,935,183	521,902	York, Stanley	1,396,970	Proxmire, William	16,311	875,068 D	27.0%	72.2%	27.2%	72.8%
1974	1,199,495	429,327	Petri, Thomas E.	740,700	Nelson, Gaylord A.	29,468	311,373 D	35.8%	61.8%	36.7%	63.3%
1970	1,338,967	381,297	Erickson, John E.	948,445	Proxmire, William	9,225	567,148 D	28.5%	70.8%	28.7%	71.3%
1968	1,654,861	633,910	Leonard, Jerris	1,020,931	Nelson, Gaylord A.	20	387,021 D	38.3%	61.7%	38.3%	61.7%
1964	1,673,776	780,116	Renk, Wilbur N.	892,013	Proxmire, William	1,647	111,897 D	46.6%	53.3%	46.7%	53.3%
1962	1,260,168	594,846	Wiley, Alexander	662,342	Nelson, Gaylord A.	2,980	67,496 D	47.2%	52.6%	47.3%	52.7%
1958	1,194,678	510,398	Steinle, Roland J.	682,440	Proxmire, William	1,840	172,042 D	42.7%	57.1%	42.8%	57.2%
1957s	772,620	312,911	Kohler, Walter J.	435,985	Proxmire, William	23,704	123,054 D	40.5%	56.4%	41.8%	58.2%
1956	1,523,356	892,473	Wiley, Alexander	627,903	Maier, Henry W.	2,980	264,570 R	58.6%	41.2%	58.7%	41.3%
1952	1,605,228	870,444	McCarthy, Joseph R.	731,402	Fairchild, Thomas E.	3,382	139,042 R	54.2%	45.6%	54.3%	45.7%
1950	1,116,135	595,283	Wiley, Alexander	515,539	Fairchild, Thomas E.	5,313	79,744 R	53.3%	46.2%	53.6%	46.4%
1946	1,014,594	620,430	McCarthy, Joseph R.	378,772	McMurray, Howard J.	15,392	241,658 R	61.2%	37.3%	62.1%	37.9%

The 1957 election was held in August for a short term to fill a vacancy.

WISCONSIN

Districts Established March 31, 1982

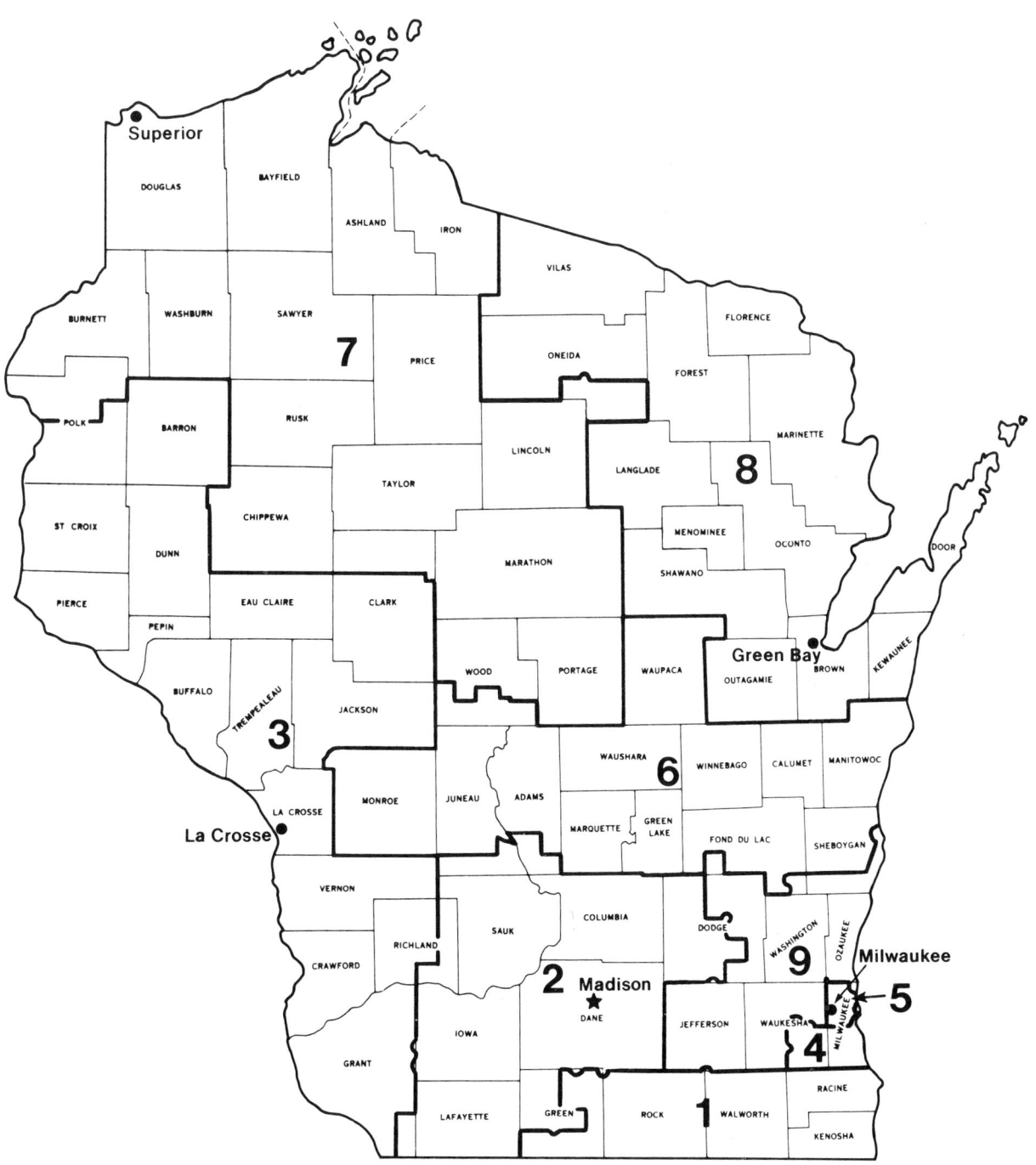

© ERC

WISCONSIN

PRESIDENT 1984

1980 Census Population	County	Total Vote	Republican	Democratic	Other	Rep.-Dem. Plurality	Percentage			
							Total Vote		Major Vote	
							Rep.	Dem.	Rep.	Dem.
13,457	ADAMS	6,413	3,644	2,713	56	931 R	56.8%	42.3%	57.3%	42.7%
16,783	ASHLAND	8,271	3,517	4,680	74	1,163 D	42.5%	56.6%	42.9%	57.1%
38,730	BARRON	17,784	9,587	8,060	137	1,527 R	53.9%	45.3%	54.3%	45.7%
13,822	BAYFIELD	7,567	3,474	4,034	59	560 D	45.9%	53.3%	46.3%	53.7%
175,280	BROWN	81,976	51,186	30,208	582	20,978 R	62.4%	36.8%	62.9%	37.1%
14,309	BUFFALO	6,308	3,325	2,921	62	404 R	52.7%	46.3%	53.2%	46.8%
12,340	BURNETT	6,918	3,528	3,328	62	200 R	51.0%	48.1%	51.5%	48.5%
30,867	CALUMET	13,898	8,969	4,735	194	4,234 R	64.5%	34.1%	65.4%	34.6%
52,127	CHIPPEWA	21,350	10,983	10,200	167	783 R	51.4%	47.8%	51.8%	48.2%
32,910	CLARK	13,918	8,098	5,647	173	2,451 R	58.2%	40.6%	58.9%	41.1%
43,222	COLUMBIA	19,941	11,658	8,124	159	3,534 R	58.5%	40.7%	58.9%	41.1%
16,556	CRAWFORD	7,906	4,411	3,435	60	976 R	55.8%	43.4%	56.2%	43.8%
323,545	DANE	169,978	74,009	94,638	1,331	20,629 D	43.5%	55.7%	43.9%	56.1%
75,064	DODGE	31,758	20,455	11,052	251	9,403 R	64.4%	34.8%	64.9%	35.1%
25,029	DOOR	12,270	8,264	3,915	91	4,349 R	67.4%	31.9%	67.9%	32.1%
44,421	DOUGLAS	21,467	7,066	14,290	111	7,224 D	32.9%	66.6%	33.1%	66.9%
34,314	DUNN	16,364	8,472	7,709	183	763 R	51.8%	47.1%	52.4%	47.6%
78,805	EAU CLAIRE	39,931	20,394	19,344	193	1,050 R	51.1%	48.4%	51.3%	48.7%
4,172	FLORENCE	2,115	1,227	870	18	357 R	58.0%	41.1%	58.5%	41.5%
88,964	FOND DU LAC	40,361	26,067	13,982	312	12,085 R	64.6%	34.6%	65.1%	34.9%
9,044	FOREST	4,546	2,296	2,213	37	83 R	50.5%	48.7%	50.9%	49.1%
51,736	GRANT	21,471	13,427	7,890	154	5,537 R	62.5%	36.7%	63.0%	37.0%
30,012	GREEN	12,299	7,826	4,367	106	3,459 R	63.6%	35.5%	64.2%	35.8%
18,370	GREEN LAKE	8,721	6,198	2,441	82	3,757 R	71.1%	28.0%	71.7%	28.3%
19,802	IOWA	8,902	4,982	3,842	78	1,140 R	56.0%	43.2%	56.5%	43.5%
6,730	IRON	3,653	1,667	1,967	19	300 D	45.6%	53.8%	45.9%	54.1%
16,831	JACKSON	7,856	4,383	3,427	46	956 R	55.8%	43.6%	56.1%	43.9%
66,152	JEFFERSON	28,783	17,779	10,788	216	6,991 R	61.8%	37.5%	62.2%	37.8%
21,039	JUNEAU	8,855	5,627	3,151	77	2,476 R	63.5%	35.6%	64.1%	35.9%
123,137	KENOSHA	55,697	26,112	29,233	352	3,121 D	46.9%	52.5%	47.2%	52.8%
19,539	KEWAUNEE	9,213	5,705	3,444	64	2,261 R	61.9%	37.4%	62.4%	37.6%
91,056	LA CROSSE	43,765	25,717	17,787	261	7,930 R	58.8%	40.6%	59.1%	40.9%
17,412	LAFAYETTE	7,592	4,582	2,959	51	1,623 R	60.4%	39.0%	60.8%	39.2%
19,978	LANGLADE	9,582	5,828	3,675	79	2,153 R	60.8%	38.4%	61.3%	38.7%
26,555	LINCOLN	12,134	6,681	5,352	101	1,329 R	55.1%	44.1%	55.5%	44.5%
82,918	MANITOWOC	37,390	19,635	17,249	506	2,386 R	52.5%	46.1%	53.2%	46.8%
111,270	MARATHON	48,672	27,077	20,126	1,469	6,951 R	55.6%	41.4%	57.4%	42.6%
39,314	MARINETTE	18,365	11,439	6,798	128	4,641 R	62.3%	37.0%	62.7%	37.3%
11,672	MARQUETTE	5,512	3,404	2,031	77	1,373 R	61.8%	36.8%	62.6%	37.4%
3,373	MENOMINEE	1,231	392	832	7	440 D	31.8%	67.6%	32.0%	68.0%
964,988	MILWAUKEE	458,042	196,259	259,134	2,649	62,875 D	42.8%	56.6%	43.1%	56.9%
35,074	MONROE	13,884	8,225	5,564	95	2,661 R	59.2%	40.1%	59.6%	40.4%
28,947	OCONTO	14,140	8,713	5,288	139	3,425 R	61.6%	37.4%	62.2%	37.8%
31,216	ONEIDA	16,384	9,782	6,416	186	3,366 R	59.7%	39.2%	60.4%	39.6%
128,799	OUTAGAMIE	56,971	36,765	19,789	417	16,976 R	64.5%	34.7%	65.0%	35.0%
66,981	OZAUKEE	34,892	23,896	10,763	233	13,133 R	68.5%	30.8%	68.9%	31.1%
7,477	PEPIN	3,203	1,555	1,629	19	74 D	48.5%	50.9%	48.8%	51.2%
31,149	PIERCE	15,022	7,611	7,285	126	326 R	50.7%	48.5%	51.1%	48.9%
32,351	POLK	16,263	8,101	8,033	129	68 R	49.8%	49.4%	50.2%	49.8%
57,420	PORTAGE	28,192	13,603	14,399	190	796 D	48.3%	51.1%	48.6%	51.4%
15,788	PRICE	7,856	4,286	3,479	91	807 R	54.6%	44.3%	55.2%	44.8%
173,132	RACINE	79,654	42,085	36,953	616	5,132 R	52.8%	46.4%	53.2%	46.8%
17,476	RICHLAND	7,760	4,857	2,844	59	2,013 R	62.6%	36.6%	63.1%	36.9%
139,420	ROCK	59,329	32,483	26,430	416	6,053 R	54.8%	44.5%	55.1%	44.9%
15,589	RUSK	7,985	4,061	3,843	81	218 R	50.9%	48.1%	51.4%	48.6%
43,262	ST. CROIX	21,644	11,365	10,126	153	1,239 R	52.5%	46.8%	52.9%	47.1%
43,469	SAUK	18,310	11,067	7,157	86	3,910 R	60.4%	39.1%	60.7%	39.3%
12,843	SAWYER	6,971	3,911	2,981	79	930 R	56.1%	42.8%	56.7%	43.3%
35,928	SHAWANO	16,235	10,635	5,469	131	5,166 R	65.5%	33.7%	66.0%	34.0%
100,935	SHEBOYGAN	47,876	26,343	21,111	422	5,232 R	55.0%	44.1%	55.5%	44.5%

WISCONSIN

PRESIDENT 1984

1980 Census Population	County	Total Vote	Republican	Democratic	Other	Rep.-Dem. Plurality	Percentage			
							Total Vote		Major Vote	
							Rep.	Dem.	Rep.	Dem.
18,817	TAYLOR	8,276	4,918	3,271	87	1,647 R	59.4%	39.5%	60.1%	39.9%
26,158	TREMPEALEAU	11,522	6,007	5,405	110	602 R	52.1%	46.9%	52.6%	47.4%
25,642	VERNON	11,608	6,468	5,051	89	1,417 R	55.7%	43.5%	56.2%	43.8%
16,535	VILAS	9,024	5,963	2,940	121	3,023 R	66.1%	32.6%	67.0%	33.0%
71,507	WALWORTH	30,715	20,590	9,876	249	10,714 R	67.0%	32.2%	67.6%	32.4%
13,174	WASHBURN	7,078	3,847	3,188	43	659 R	54.4%	45.0%	54.7%	45.3%
84,848	WASHINGTON	38,572	25,278	12,966	328	12,312 R	65.5%	33.6%	66.1%	33.9%
280,326	WAUKESHA	140,663	92,415	47,308	940	45,107 R	65.7%	33.6%	66.1%	33.9%
42,831	WAUPACA	19,184	13,097	5,894	193	7,203 R	68.3%	30.7%	69.0%	31.0%
18,526	WAUSHARA	8,636	5,768	2,782	86	2,986 R	66.8%	32.2%	67.5%	32.5%
131,703	WINNEBAGO	62,183	39,014	22,791	378	16,223 R	62.7%	36.7%	63.1%	36.9%
72,799	WOOD	32,882	20,525	12,118	239	8,407 R	62.4%	36.9%	62.9%	37.1%
4,705,767	TOTAL	2,211,689	1,198,584	995,740	17,365	202,844 R	54.2%	45.0%	54.6%	45.4%

WISCONSIN

CONGRESS

CD	Year	Total Vote	Republican Vote	Candidate	Democratic Vote	Candidate	Other Vote	Rep.-Dem. Plurality	Total Vote Rep.	Total Vote Dem.	Major Vote Rep.	Major Vote Dem.
1	1984	226,264	99,080	JANSSON, PETER N.	127,184	ASPIN, LES		28,104 D	43.8%	56.2%	43.8%	56.2%
1	1982	155,804	59,309	JANSSON, PETER N.	95,055	ASPIN, LES	1,440	35,746 D	38.1%	61.0%	38.4%	61.6%
2	1984	251,357	91,345	WILEY, ALBERT E.	159,987	KASTENMEIER, ROBERT	25	68,642 D	36.3%	63.6%	36.3%	63.7%
2	1982	186,045	71,989	JOHNSON, JIM	112,677	KASTENMEIER, ROBERT	1,379	40,688 D	38.7%	60.6%	39.0%	61.0%
3	1984	234,695	160,437	GUNDERSON, STEVEN	74,253	DAHL, CHARLES F.	5	86,184 R	68.4%	31.6%	68.4%	31.6%
3	1982	175,465	99,304	GUNDERSON, STEVEN	75,132	OFFNER, PAUL	1,029	24,172 R	56.6%	42.8%	56.9%	43.1%
4	1984	238,222	78,056	NOLAN, ROBERT V.	158,722	KLECZKA, GERALD D.	1,444	80,666 D	32.8%	66.6%	33.0%	67.0%
4	1982	137,024			129,557	ZABLOCKI, CLEMENT J.	7,467	129,557 D		94.6%		100.0%
5	1984	178,819			175,243	MOODY, JIM	3,576	175,243 D		98.0%		100.0%
5	1982	156,921	54,826	JOHNSTON, ROD K.	99,713	MOODY, JIM	2,382	44,887 D	34.9%	63.5%	35.5%	64.5%
6	1984	224,546	170,271	PETRI, THOMAS E.	54,266	IAQUINTA, DAVID L.	9	116,005 R	75.8%	24.2%	75.8%	24.2%
6	1982	171,283	111,348	PETRI, THOMAS E.	59,922	LOEHR, GORDON E.	13	51,426 R	65.0%	35.0%	65.0%	35.0%
7	1984	238,652	92,507	MICHAELSEN, MARK G.	146,131	OBEY, DAVID R.	14	53,624 D	38.8%	61.2%	38.8%	61.2%
7	1982	179,668	57,535	ZIMMERMANN, BERNARD A.	122,124	OBEY, DAVID R.	9	64,589 D	32.0%	68.0%	32.0%	68.0%
8	1984	237,107	161,005	ROTH, TOBY	73,090	WILLEMS, PAUL	3,012	87,915 R	67.9%	30.8%	68.8%	31.2%
8	1982	177,152	101,379	ROTH, TOBY	74,436	CLUSEN, RUTH C.	1,337	26,943 R	57.2%	42.0%	57.7%	42.3%
9	1984	245,716	180,247	SENSENBRENNER, F. JAMES	64,157	KRAUSE, JOHN	1,312	116,090 R	73.4%	26.1%	73.7%	26.3%
9	1982	111,570	111,503	SENSENBRENNER, F. JAMES			67	111,503 R	99.9%		100.0%	

WISCONSIN

1984 GENERAL ELECTION

President   Other vote was 4,883 Bergland (Libertarian); 3,864 Richards (Constitution); 3,791 La Rouche (Independent); 1,456 Johnson (Citizens); 1,006 Serrette (Independent Alliance); 619 Holmes (Workers World); 596 Hall (Communist); 444 Mason (Socialist Workers); 706 scattered.

Congress   Other vote was scattered in CD's 2 and 3; 1,427 Kissell (Labor and Farm) and 17 scattered in CD 4; 3,364 Breihan (Independent) and 212 scattered in CD 5; scattered in CD's 6 and 7; 2,005 Barnes (Libertarian), 1,006 Van Handel (Labor and Farm) and 1 scattered in CD 8; 1,306 Hauser (Constitution) and 6 scattered in CD 9.

1984 PRIMARIES

SEPTEMBER 11 REPUBLICAN

Congress   Unopposed in seven CD's. No candidate in CD 5. Contested as follows:

  CD 7   11,074 Mark G. Michaelsen; 4,440 Lee B. Hall; 23 scattered.

SEPTEMBER 11 DEMOCRATIC

Congress   Unopposed in six CD's. Contested as follows:

  CD 2   27,967 Robert Kastenmeier; 6,007 Eileen C. Courtney; 2 scattered.
  CD 3   11,399 Charles F. Dahl; 6,855 Patricia E. Kirk; 3,613 John M. Hardin; 1 scattered.
  CD 9   7,583 John Krause; 2,507 Howard J. Ver duin.

SEPTEMBER 11 LIBERTARIAN

Congress   Unopposed in CD 8; no other candidates.

SEPTEMBER 11 CONSTITUTION

Congress   Unopposed in CD 9; no other candidates.

SEPTEMBER 11 LABOR AND FARM

Congress   Unopposed in CD's 4 and 8; no other candidates.

WYOMING

GOVERNOR
Ed Herschler (D). Re-elected 1982 to a four-year term. Previously elected 1978, 1974.

SENATORS
Alan K. Simpson (R). Re-elected 1984 to a six-year term. Previously elected 1978.

Malcolm Wallop (R). Re-elected 1982 to a six-year term. Previously elected 1976.

REPRESENTATIVE
At-Large. Richard Cheney (R)

POSTWAR VOTE FOR GOVERNOR

Year	Total Vote	Republican Vote	Candidate	Democratic Vote	Candidate	Other Vote	Rep.-Dem. Plurality	Total Vote Rep.	Total Vote Dem.	Major Vote Rep.	Major Vote Dem.
1982	168,555	62,128	Morton, Warren A.	106,427	Herschler, Ed	—	44,299 D	36.9%	63.1%	36.9%	63.1%
1978	137,567	67,595	Ostlund, John C.	69,972	Herschler, Ed	—	2,377 D	49.1%	50.9%	49.1%	50.9%
1974	128,386	56,645	Jones, Dick	71,741	Herschler, Ed	—	15,096 D	44.1%	55.9%	44.1%	55.9%
1970	118,257	74,249	Hathaway, Stan	44,008	Rooney, John J.	—	30,241 R	62.8%	37.2%	62.8%	37.2%
1966	120,873	65,624	Hathaway, Stan	55,249	Wilkerson, Ernest	—	10,375 R	54.3%	45.7%	54.3%	45.7%
1962	119,268	64,970	Hansen, Clifford P.	54,298	Gage, Jack R.	—	10,672 R	54.5%	45.5%	54.5%	45.5%
1958	112,537	52,488	Simpson, Milward L.	55,070	Hickey, J. J.	4,979	2,582 D	46.6%	48.9%	48.8%	51.2%
1954	111,438	56,275	Simpson, Milward L.	55,163	Jack, William	—	1,112 R	50.5%	49.5%	50.5%	49.5%
1950	96,959	54,441	Barrett, Frank A.	42,518	McIntyre, John J.	—	11,923 R	56.1%	43.9%	56.1%	43.9%
1946	81,353	38,333	Wright, Earl	43,020	Hunt, Lester C.	—	4,687 D	47.1%	52.9%	47.1%	52.9%

POSTWAR VOTE FOR SENATOR

Year	Total Vote	Republican Vote	Candidate	Democratic Vote	Candidate	Other Vote	Rep.-Dem. Plurality	Total Vote Rep.	Total Vote Dem.	Major Vote Rep.	Major Vote Dem.
1984	186,898	146,373	Simpson, Alan K.	40,525	Ryan, Victor A.	—	105,848 R	78.3%	21.7%	78.3%	21.7%
1982	167,191	94,725	Wallop, Malcolm	72,466	McDaniel, Rodger	—	22,259 R	56.7%	43.3%	56.7%	43.3%
1978	133,364	82,908	Simpson, Alan K.	50,456	Whitaker, Raymond B.	—	32,452 R	62.2%	37.8%	62.2%	37.8%
1976	155,368	84,810	Wallop, Malcolm	70,558	McGee, Gale	—	14,252 R	54.6%	45.4%	54.6%	45.4%
1972	142,067	101,314	Hansen, Clifford P.	40,753	Vinich, Mike	—	60,561 R	71.3%	28.7%	71.3%	28.7%
1970	120,486	53,279	Wold, John S.	67,207	McGee, Gale	—	13,928 D	44.2%	55.8%	44.2%	55.8%
1966	122,689	63,548	Hansen, Clifford P.	59,141	Roncalio, Teno	—	4,407 R	51.8%	48.2%	51.8%	48.2%
1964	141,670	65,185	Wold, John S.	76,485	McGee, Gale	—	11,300 D	46.0%	54.0%	46.0%	54.0%
1962s	119,372	69,043	Simpson, Milward L.	50,329	Hickey, J. J.	—	18,714 R	57.8%	42.2%	57.8%	42.2%
1960	138,550	78,103	Thomson, E. Keith	60,447	Whitaker, Ray	—	17,656 R	56.4%	43.6%	56.4%	43.6%
1958	114,157	56,122	Barrett, Frank A.	58,035	McGee, Gale	—	1,913 D	49.2%	50.8%	49.2%	50.8%
1954	112,252	54,407	Harrison, William H.	57,845	O'Mahoney, Joseph C.	—	3,438 D	48.5%	51.5%	48.5%	51.5%
1952	130,097	67,176	Barrett, Frank A.	62,921	O'Mahoney, Joseph C.	—	4,255 R	51.6%	48.4%	51.6%	48.4%
1948	101,480	43,527	Robertson, Edward V.	57,953	Hunt, Lester C.	—	14,426 D	42.9%	57.1%	42.9%	57.1%
1946	81,557	35,714	Henderson, Harry B.	45,843	O'Mahoney, Joseph C.	—	10,129 D	43.8%	56.2%	43.8%	56.2%

The 1962 election was for a short term to fill a vacancy.

WYOMING

One At Large

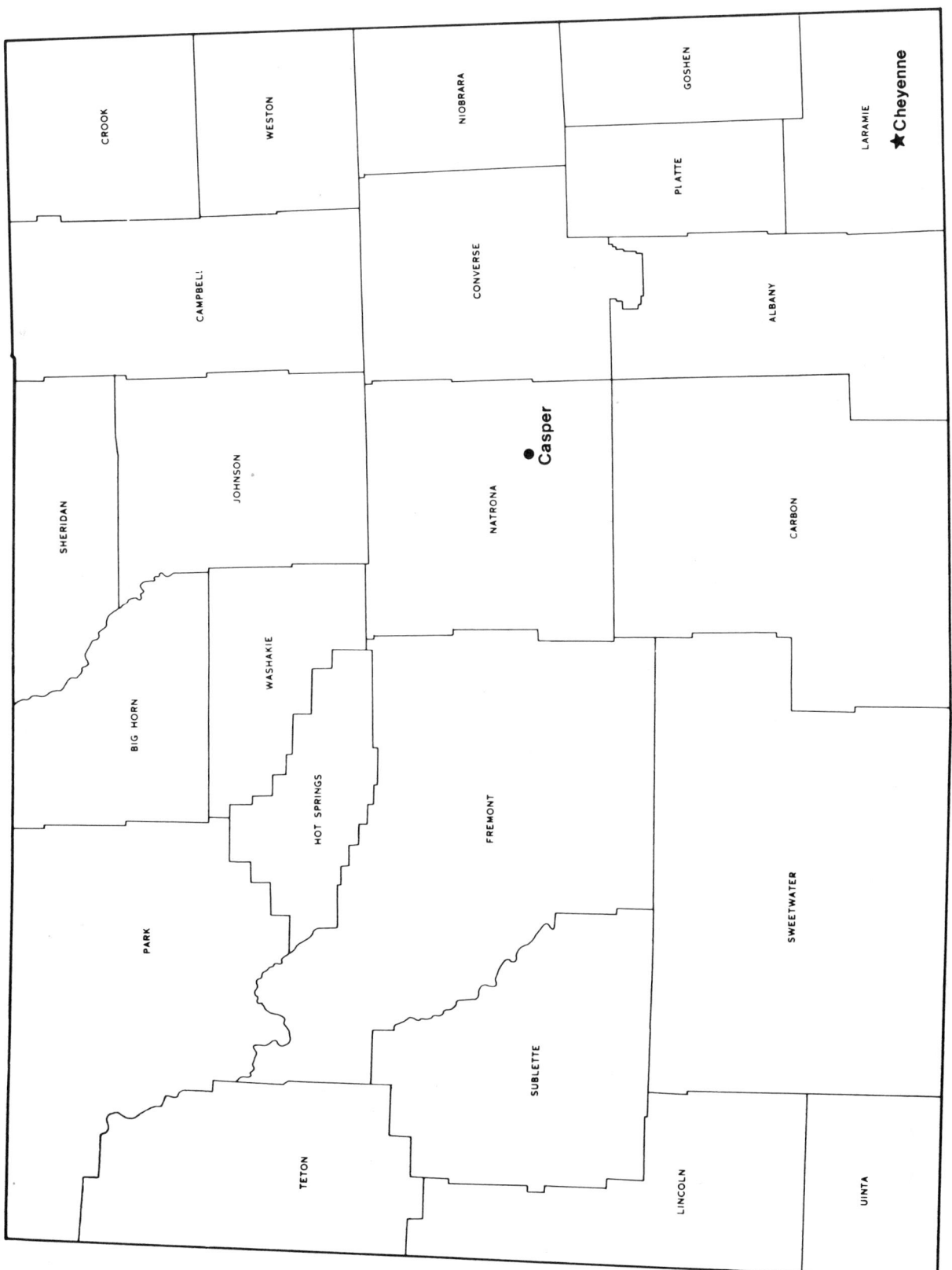

WYOMING

PRESIDENT 1984

1980 Census Population	County	Total Vote	Republican	Democratic	Other	Rep.-Dem. Plurality	Percentage Total Vote Rep.	Dem.	Major Vote Rep.	Dem.
29,062	ALBANY	12,346	7,452	4,708	186	2,744 R	60.4%	38.1%	61.3%	38.7%
11,896	BIG HORN	5,253	4,019	1,175	59	2,844 R	76.5%	22.4%	77.4%	22.6%
24,367	CAMPBELL	9,995	8,387	1,525	83	6,862 R	83.9%	15.3%	84.6%	15.4%
21,896	CARBON	6,952	4,557	2,295	100	2,262 R	65.5%	33.0%	66.5%	33.5%
14,069	CONVERSE	4,523	3,542	929	52	2,613 R	78.3%	20.5%	79.2%	20.8%
5,308	CROOK	2,754	2,286	450	18	1,836 R	83.0%	16.3%	83.6%	16.4%
38,992	FREMONT	13,999	9,885	3,969	145	5,916 R	70.6%	28.4%	71.4%	28.6%
12,040	GOSHEN	5,184	3,776	1,364	44	2,412 R	72.8%	26.3%	73.5%	26.5%
5,710	HOT SPRINGS	2,646	1,943	672	31	1,271 R	73.4%	25.4%	74.3%	25.7%
6,700	JOHNSON	3,241	2,634	558	49	2,076 R	81.3%	17.2%	82.5%	17.5%
68,649	LARAMIE	29,799	19,348	10,110	341	9,238 R	64.9%	33.9%	65.7%	34.3%
12,177	LINCOLN	4,921	3,854	1,021	46	2,833 R	78.3%	20.7%	79.1%	20.9%
71,856	NATRONA	26,464	18,488	7,598	378	10,890 R	69.9%	28.7%	70.9%	29.1%
2,924	NIOBRARA	1,359	1,098	239	22	859 R	80.8%	17.6%	82.1%	17.9%
21,639	PARK	10,095	7,994	1,965	136	6,029 R	79.2%	19.5%	80.3%	19.7%
11,975	PLATTE	4,120	2,813	1,232	75	1,581 R	68.3%	29.9%	69.5%	30.5%
25,048	SHERIDAN	11,279	7,460	3,648	171	3,812 R	66.1%	32.3%	67.2%	32.8%
4,548	SUBLETTE	2,396	1,976	389	31	1,587 R	82.5%	16.2%	83.6%	16.4%
41,723	SWEETWATER	13,712	8,308	5,230	174	3,078 R	60.6%	38.1%	61.4%	38.6%
9,355	TETON	5,139	3,487	1,565	87	1,922 R	67.9%	30.5%	69.0%	31.0%
13,021	UINTA	5,411	4,075	1,276	60	2,799 R	75.3%	23.6%	76.2%	23.8%
9,496	WASHAKIE	4,253	3,245	970	38	2,275 R	76.3%	22.8%	77.0%	23.0%
7,106	WESTON	3,127	2,614	482	31	2,132 R	83.6%	15.4%	84.4%	15.6%
469,557	TOTAL	188,968	133,241	53,370	2,357	79,871 R	70.5%	28.2%	71.4%	28.6%

WYOMING

SENATOR 1984

1980 Census Population	County	Total Vote	Republican	Democratic	Other	Rep.-Dem. Plurality	Percentage Total Vote Rep.	Dem.	Major Vote Rep.	Dem.
29,062	ALBANY	11,986	8,795	3,191		5,604 R	73.4%	26.6%	73.4%	26.6%
11,896	BIG HORN	5,048	4,300	748		3,552 R	85.2%	14.8%	85.2%	14.8%
24,367	CAMPBELL	9,991	8,765	1,226		7,539 R	87.7%	12.3%	87.7%	12.3%
21,896	CARBON	7,230	5,209	2,021		3,188 R	72.0%	28.0%	72.0%	28.0%
14,069	CONVERSE	4,566	3,817	749		3,068 R	83.6%	16.4%	83.6%	16.4%
5,308	CROOK	2,785	2,443	342		2,101 R	87.7%	12.3%	87.7%	12.3%
38,992	FREMONT	12,968	10,423	2,545		7,878 R	80.4%	19.6%	80.4%	19.6%
12,040	GOSHEN	5,299	4,131	1,168		2,963 R	78.0%	22.0%	78.0%	22.0%
5,710	HOT SPRINGS	2,336	1,987	349		1,638 R	85.1%	14.9%	85.1%	14.9%
6,700	JOHNSON	2,964	2,628	336		2,292 R	88.7%	11.3%	88.7%	11.3%
68,649	LARAMIE	30,032	21,211	8,821		12,390 R	70.6%	29.4%	70.6%	29.4%
12,177	LINCOLN	5,152	4,035	1,117		2,918 R	78.3%	21.7%	78.3%	21.7%
71,856	NATRONA	27,048	21,241	5,807		15,434 R	78.5%	21.5%	78.5%	21.5%
2,924	NIOBRARA	1,381	1,200	181		1,019 R	86.9%	13.1%	86.9%	13.1%
21,639	PARK	10,297	8,980	1,317		7,663 R	87.2%	12.8%	87.2%	12.8%
11,975	PLATTE	4,180	3,206	974		2,232 R	76.7%	23.3%	76.7%	23.3%
25,048	SHERIDAN	11,228	8,767	2,461		6,306 R	78.1%	21.9%	78.1%	21.9%
4,548	SUBLETTE	2,439	2,116	323		1,793 R	86.8%	13.2%	86.8%	13.2%
41,723	SWEETWATER	12,013	8,253	3,760		4,493 R	68.7%	31.3%	68.7%	31.3%
9,355	TETON	5,106	4,213	893		3,320 R	82.5%	17.5%	82.5%	17.5%
13,021	UINTA	5,509	4,315	1,194		3,121 R	78.3%	21.7%	78.3%	21.7%
9,496	WASHAKIE	4,158	3,549	609		2,940 R	85.4%	14.6%	85.4%	14.6%
7,106	WESTON	3,182	2,789	393		2,396 R	87.6%	12.4%	87.6%	12.4%
469,557	TOTAL	186,898	146,373	40,525		105,848 R	78.3%	21.7%	78.3%	21.7%

WYOMING

CONGRESS

CD	Year	Total Vote	Republican Vote	Republican Candidate	Democratic Vote	Democratic Candidate	Other Vote	Rep.-Dem. Plurality	Total Vote Rep.	Total Vote Dem.	Major Vote Rep.	Major Vote Dem.
AL	1984	187,904	138,234	CHENEY, RICHARD	45,857	MCFADDEN, HUGH B.	3,813	92,377 R	73.6%	24.4%	75.1%	24.9%
AL	1982	159,277	113,236	CHENEY, RICHARD	46,041	HOMMEL, THEODORE H.		67,195 R	71.1%	28.9%	71.1%	28.9%
AL	1980	169,699	116,361	CHENEY, RICHARD	53,338	ROGERS, JIM		63,023 R	68.6%	31.4%	68.6%	31.4%
AL	1978	129,377	75,855	CHENEY, RICHARD	53,522	BAGLEY, BILL		22,333 R	58.6%	41.4%	58.6%	41.4%
AL	1976	151,868	66,147	HART, LARRY	85,721	RONCALIO, TENO		19,574 D	43.6%	56.4%	43.6%	56.4%
AL	1974	126,933	57,499	STROOCK, TOM	69,434	RONCALIO, TENO		11,935 D	45.3%	54.7%	45.3%	54.7%
AL	1972	146,299	70,667	KIDD, WILLIAM	75,632	RONCALIO, TENO		4,965 D	48.3%	51.7%	48.3%	51.7%
AL	1970	116,304	57,848	ROBERTS, HARRY	58,456	RONCALIO, TENO		608 D	49.7%	50.3%	49.7%	50.3%
AL	1968	123,313	77,363	WOLD, JOHN S.	45,950	LINFORD, VELMA		31,413 R	62.7%	37.3%	62.7%	37.3%
AL	1966	119,426	62,984	HARRISON, WILLIAM H.	56,442	CHRISTIAN, AL		6,542 R	52.7%	47.3%	52.7%	47.3%
AL	1964	139,175	68,482	HARRISON, WILLIAM H.	70,693	RONCALIO, TENO		2,211 D	49.2%	50.8%	49.2%	50.8%
AL	1962	116,474	71,489	HARRISON, WILLIAM H.	44,985	MANKUS, LOUIS A.		26,504 R	61.4%	38.6%	61.4%	38.6%
AL	1960	134,331	70,241	HARRISON, WILLIAM H.	64,090	ARMSTRONG, H. T		6,151 R	52.3%	47.7%	52.3%	47.7%
AL	1958	111,780	59,894	THOMSON, E. KEITH	51,886	WHITAKER, RAY		8,008 R	53.6%	46.4%	53.6%	46.4%
AL	1956	120,128	69,903	THOMSON, E. KEITH	50,225	O'CALLAGHAN, JERRY		19,678 R	58.2%	41.8%	58.2%	41.8%
AL	1954	108,771	61,111	THOMSON, E. KEITH	47,660	TULLY, SAM		13,451 R	56.2%	43.8%	56.2%	43.8%
AL	1952	126,720	76,161	HARRISON, WILLIAM H.	50,559	ROSE, ROBERT R		25,602 R	60.1%	39.9%	60.1%	39.9%
AL	1950	93,348	50,865	HARRISON, WILLIAM H.	42,483	CLARK, JOHN B.		8,382 R	54.5%	45.5%	54.5%	45.5%
AL	1948	97,464	50,218	BARRETT, FRANK A.	47,246	FLANNERY, L. G.		2,972 R	51.5%	48.5%	51.5%	48.5%
AL	1946	79,438	44,482	BARRETT, FRANK A.	34,956	MCINTYRE, JOHN J.		9,526 R	56.0%	44.0%	56.0%	44.0%

458

WYOMING

1984 GENERAL ELECTION

President   Other vote was Bergland (Libertarian).

Senator

Congress   Other vote at-large was McCune (Libertarian).

1984 PRIMARIES

SEPTEMBER 11 REPUBLICAN

Senator   66,178 Alan K. Simpson; 9,137 Stephen Tarver.

Congress   Unopposed at-large.

SEPTEMBER 11 DEMOCRATIC

Senator   17,608 Victor A. Ryan; 12,088 Al Hamburg; 9,187 Michael J. Dee.

Congress   Contested as follows:

AL   29,361 Hugh B. McFadden; 10,742 Keith B. Goodenough.

DISTRICT OF COLUMBIA

GOVERNMENT
The District of Columbia is governed by a Mayor and a City Council of thirteen.

MAYOR
Marion Barry (D). Re-elected 1982 to a four-year term. Previously elected 1978.

DELEGATE
Walter E. Fauntroy (D)

POSTWAR VOTE FOR MAYOR

| | | | | | | Other | Rep.-Dem. | Percentage | | | |
| | Total | Republican | | Democratic | | | | Total Vote | | Major Vote | |
Year	Vote	Vote	Candidate	Vote	Candidate	Vote	Plurality	Rep.	Dem.	Rep.	Dem.
1982	117,623	16,501	Lee, E. Brooke	95,007	Barry, Marion	6,115	78,506 D	14.0%	80.8%	14.8%	85.2%
1978	100,861	28,032	Fletcher, Arthur	69,888	Barry, Marion	2,941	41,856 D	27.8%	69.3%	28.6%	71.4%
1974	105,183	3,703	Champion, Jackson R.	84,676	Washington, Walter E.	16,804	80,973 D	3.5%	80.5%	4.2%	95.8%

POSTWAR VOTE FOR DELEGATE

| | | | | | | Other | Rep.-Dem. | Percentage | | | |
| | Total | Republican | | Democratic | | | | Total Vote | | Major Vote | |
Year	Vote	Vote	Candidate	Vote	Candidate	Vote	Plurality	Rep.	Dem.	Rep.	Dem.
1984*	161,771	—	—	154,583	Fauntroy, Walter E.	7,188	154,583 D	—	95.6%	—	100.0%
1982	112,543	17,242	West, John	93,422	Fauntroy, Walter E.	1,879	76,180 D	15.3%	83.0%	15.6%	84.4%
1980	151,046	21,245	Roehr, Robert J.	112,339	Fauntroy, Walter E.	17,462	91,094 D	14.1%	74.4%	15.9%	84.1%
1978	96,306	11,677	Champion, Jackson R.	76,557	Fauntroy, Walter E.	8,072	64,880 D	12.1%	79.5%	13.2%	86.8%
1976	159,790	21,699	Hall, Daniel L.	123,464	Fauntroy, Walter E.	14,627	101,765 D	13.6%	77.3%	14.9%	85.1%
1974	104,014	9,166	Phillips, William R.	66,337	Fauntroy, Walter E.	28,511	57,171 D	8.8%	63.8%	12.1%	87.9%
1972	159,612	39,487	Chin-Lee, William	95,300	Fauntroy, Walter E.	24,825	55,813 D	24.7%	59.7%	29.3%	70.7%
1971s	116,635	29,249	Nevius, John A.	68,166	Fauntroy, Walter E.	19,220	38,917 D	25.1%	58.4%	30.0%	70.0%

The 1971 election was held in March for a short term to the end of the 92nd Congress. In 1984, the Democratic candidate was also the nominee of the Republican and Statehood parties.

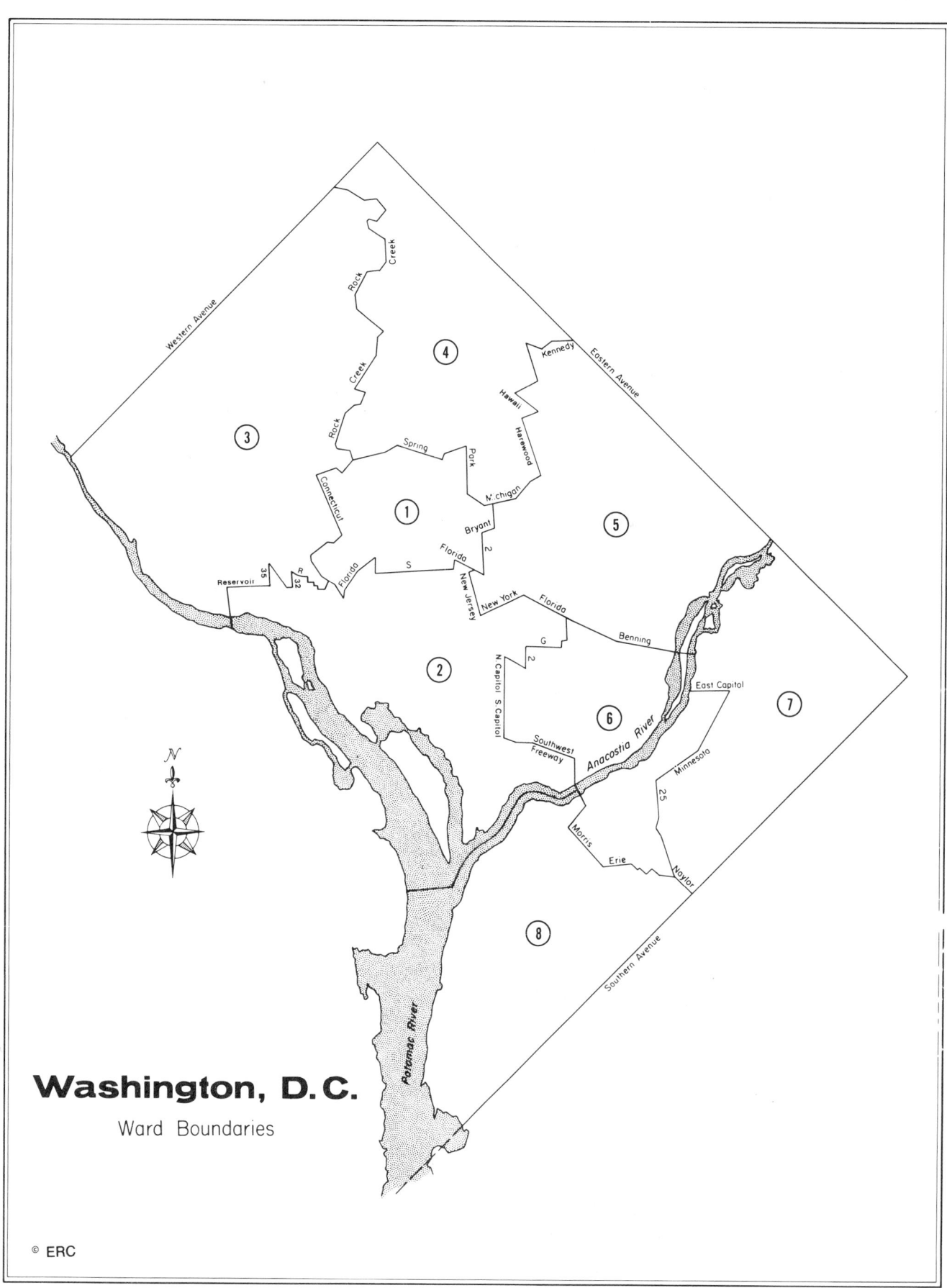

Washington, D.C.

Ward Boundaries

DISTRICT OF COLUMBIA

PRESIDENT 1984

1980 Census Population	Ward	Total Vote	Republican	Democratic	Other	Rep.-Dem. Plurality	Percentage			
							Total Vote		Major Vote	
							Rep.	Dem.	Rep.	Dem.
78,700	WARD 1	23,501	2,550	20,638	313	18,088 D	10.9%	87.8%	11.0%	89.0%
81,400	WARD 2	25,393	5,435	19,677	281	14,242 D	21.4%	77.5%	21.6%	78.4%
77,800	WARD 3	35,047	12,496	22,234	317	9,738 D	35.7%	63.4%	36.0%	64.0%
81,900	WARD 4	32,084	2,264	29,551	269	27,287 D	7.1%	92.1%	7.1%	92.9%
82,600	WARD 5	28,112	1,523	26,394	195	24,871 D	5.4%	93.9%	5.5%	94.5%
75,700	WARD 6	25,239	2,589	22,415	235	19,826 D	10.3%	88.8%	10.4%	89.6%
82,400	WARD 7	25,195	1,303	23,734	158	22,431 D	5.2%	94.2%	5.2%	94.8%
77,900	WARD 8	16,101	628	15,377	96	14,749 D	3.9%	95.5%	3.9%	96.1%
	FEDERAL BALLOTS	616	221	388	7	167 D	35.9%	63.0%	36.3%	63.7%
638,400	TOTAL	211,288	29,009	180,408	1,871	151,399 D	13.7%	85.4%	13.9%	86.1%

DISTRICT OF COLUMBIA

DELEGATE 1984

1980 Census Population	Ward	Total Vote	Republican	Democratic	Other	Rep.-Dem. Plurality	Percentage			
							Total Vote		Major Vote	
							Rep.	Dem.	Rep.	Dem.
78,700	WARD 1	18,222		17,303	919	17,303 D		95.0%		100.0%
81,400	WARD 2	18,039		16,896	1,143	16,896 D		93.7%		100.0%
77,800	WARD 3	20,564		18,500	2,064	18,500 D		90.0%		100.0%
81,900	WARD 4	26,609		25,861	748	25,861 D		97.2%		100.0%
82,600	WARD 5	23,470		22,916	554	22,916 D		97.6%		100.0%
75,700	WARD 6	19,925		18,982	943	18,982 D		95.3%		100.0%
82,400	WARD 7	21,001		20,477	524	20,477 D		97.5%		100.0%
77,900	WARD 8	13,608		13,331	277	13,331 D		98.0%		100.0%
	FEDERAL BALLOTS	333		317	16	317 D		95.2%		100.0%
638,400	TOTAL	161,771		154,583	7,188	154,583 D		95.6%		100.0%

DISTRICT OF COLUMBIA

Population data for wards are from the Office of Planning and Development of the District of Columbia and represent rounded-off figures.

1984 GENERAL ELECTION

President Other vote was 279 Bergland (Libertarian); 257 Hall (Communist); 165 Serrette (Independent); 127 LaRouche (Independent); 127 Mason (Socialist Workers); 107 Holmes (Workers World); 809 scattered.

Delegate Other vote was scattered.

1984 PRIMARIES

MAY 1 REPUBLICAN

Delegate No candidate names appeared on the ballot; Walter E. Fauntroy, the unopposed Democratic candidate, was declared the nominee on write-in votes.

MAY 1 DEMOCRATIC

Delegate Walter E. Fauntroy, unopposed.

MAY 1 STATEHOOD

Delegate No candidate names appeared on the ballot; Walter E. Fountroy, the unopposed Democratic candidate, was declared the nominee on write-in votes.